SO-BOC-587

FLORIDA STATE
UNIVERSITY LIBRARIES

APR 2 7 2010

TALLAHASSEE, FLORIDA

SOMETHING ABOUT THE AUTHOR®

Something about
the Author *was named
an "**Outstanding
Reference Source,**"
the highest honor given
by the American
Library Association
Reference and Adult
Services Division.*

ISSN 0276-816X

SOMETHING ABOUT THE AUTHOR®

Facts and Pictures about Authors and Illustrators of Books for Young People

volume 207

GALE
CENGAGE Learning™

Detroit • New York • San Francisco • New Haven, Conn • Waterville, Maine • London

LSL
PN
451
.S6
V.207

GALE
CENGAGE Learning

Something about the Author, Volume 207

Project Editor: Lisa Kumar

Editorial: Laura Avery, Pamela Bow, Jim Craddock, Amy Fuller, Andrea Henderson, Margaret Mazurkiewicz, Tracie Moy, Jeff Muhr, Kathy Nemeh, Mary Ruby, Mike Tyrkus

Permissions: Dean Dauphinais, Jacqueline Flowers, Jhanay Williams

Imaging and Multimedia: Dean Dauphinais, John Watkins

Composition and Electronic Capture: Amy Darga

Manufacturing: Drew Kalasky

Product Manager: Janet Witalec

© 2010 Gale, Cengage Learning

ALL RIGHTS RESERVED. No part of this work covered by the copyright herein may be reproduced, transmitted, stored, or used in any form or by any means graphic, electronic, or mechanical, including but not limited to photocopying, recording, scanning, digitizing, taping, Web distribution, information networks, or information storage and retrieval systems, except as permitted under Section 107 or 108 of the 1976 United States Copyright Act, without the prior written permission of the publisher.

This publication is a creative work fully protected by all applicable copyright laws, as well as by misappropriation, trade secret, unfair competition, and other applicable laws. The authors and editors of this work have added value to the underlying factual material herein through one or more of the following: unique and original selection, coordination, expression, arrangement, and classification of the information.

For product information and technology assistance, contact us at **Gale Customer Support, 1-800-877-4253.** For permission to use material from this text or product, submit all requests online at **www.cengage.com/permissions.** Further permissions questions can be emailed to **permissionrequest@cengage.com**

Since this page cannot legibly accommodate all copyright notices, the acknowledgments constitute an extension of the copyright notice.

While every effort has been made to ensure the reliability of the information presented in this publication, Gale, a part of Cengage Learning, does not guarantee the accuracy of the data contained herein. Gale accepts no payment for listing; and inclusion in the publication of any organization, agency, institution, publication, service, or individual does not imply endorsement of the editors or publisher. Errors brought to the attention of the publisher and verified to the satisfaction of the publisher will be corrected in future editions.

EDITORIAL DATA PRIVACY POLICY: Does this publication contain information about you as an individual? If so, for more information about our editorial data privacy policies, please see our Privacy Statement at www.gale.cengage.com.

Gale
27500 Drake Rd.
Farmington Hills, MI, 48331-3535

LIBRARY OF CONGRESS CATALOG CARD NUMBER 62-52046

ISBN-13: 978-1-4144-4220-4
ISBN-10: 1-4144-4220-3

ISSN 0276-816X

This title is also available as an e-book.
ISBN-13: 978-1-4144-6439-8
ISBN-10: 1-4144-6439-8
Contact your Gale, Cengage Learning sales representative for ordering information.

Printed in the United States of America
1 2 3 4 5 6 7 14 13 12 11 10

Contents

Authors in Forthcoming Volumes vii

Introduction ix

SATA Product Advisory Board xi

Illustrations Index 197

Author Index 231

A

Alcorn, Stephen 1958- 1

Arnold, Ann 1953(?)- 5

Arsenault, Isabelle 1978- 6

Ashland, Monk 1972- 7

B

Baker, Sharon Reiss 1962- 9

Barrett, Tracy 1955- 9

Bingham, Kelly 1967- 13

Bleck, Linda 14

Bunge, Daniela 1973- 15

Burningham, Robin Yoko
   See Racoma, Robin Yoko 138

Butler, Dori Hillestad 1965- 16

C

Campbell, Sarah C. 1966- 20

Chan, Peter 1980(?)- 21

Chesworth, Michael 1961- 22

Cook, Sally 26

Cumpiano, Ina 27

D

Dawson, Arthur L. 29

de Lint, Charles 1951- 30

Dob, Bob 37

duPont, Lindsay 38

duPont, Lindsay Harper
   See duPont, Lindsay 38

E

Endle, Kate 40

Eriksson, Eva 1949- 41

F

Farooqi, Musharraf Ali 1968- 45

Fisher, Suzanne
   See Staples, Suzanne Fisher 154

Frankland, David 46

Frederick, Heather Vogel 48

Friesner, Esther 1951- 51

Friesner, Esther M.
   See Friesner, Esther 51

G

Gerber, Carole 1947- 56

Geus, Mireille 1964- 58

Goldman, Arthur Steven
   See Goldman, Steven . . . .

Goldman, Steven 1964- 59

H

Hall, August 60

Haworth, Danette 60

Hayes, Geoffrey 1947- 62

Hayes, Karel 1949- 64

Henkes, Kevin 1960- 66

Hurley, Tonya 73

J

Jinks, Catherine 1963- 76

K

Kalis, Jennifer 81

Key, Samuel M.
   See de Lint, Charles 30

Keyes, Diane 82

Klass, David 1960- 83

Kohara, Kazuno 88

Konigsberg, Bill 1970- 88

L

Landman, Tanya 91

Laugesen, Malene 93

Laugesen, Malene Reynolds
   See Laugesen, Malene 93

Lendroth, Susan 93

Leonard, Tom 1955- 94

Lindgren, Barbro 1937- 96

Lyon, George Ella 1949- 101

M

Martin, C.K. Kelly 108

Meade, Holly 1956- 109

Menzel, Peter 1948- 112

Miranda, Inaki 1983(?)- 115

Morais, Flavio 115

Morris, Gerald 1963- 116

Morris, Gerald Paul
   See Morris, Gerald 116

Musgrove, Marianne 120

N

Ness, Patrick 1971- 122

O

Ofer, Avi 1975- 123

P

Palatini, Margie 124

Patricelli, Leslie 129

Pearle, Ida 130

Pfister, Marcus 130

R

Racoma, Robin Yoko 1953- 138

Raschka, Chris 1959- 139

Raschka, Christopher
   See Raschka, Chris 139

Rettstatt, Chris
   See Ashland, Monk 7

S

Schmitz, Tamara 146

Skeers, Linda 1958- 148

Slonim, David 1966- 149

Smith, Andy J. 1975- 151

Sogabe, Aki 152

Staples, Suzanne Fisher 1945- 154

Stevenson, Emma 158

Sydor, Colleen 1960- 159

T

Tusa, Tricia 1960- 162

V

Vance, Cynthia 165

Vance-Abrams, Cynthia
   See Vance, Cynthia 165

Van Draanen, Wendelin 166

Vila, Laura 171

Vohwinkel, Astrid 1969- 173

W

Wasserman, Robin 1978- 174

Wells, Rosemary 1943- 176

Wilcox, Leah 1975(?)- 187

Williams, Suzanne
   See Williams, Suzanne Morgan 188

Williams, Suzanne M.
   See Williams, Suzanne Morgan 188

Williams, Suzanne Morgan 1949- 188

Wingerter, Linda S. 1973(?)- 189

Woo, Howie 1974- 192

Y

Young, Judy 1956- 192

Z

Zecca, Katherine 194

Authors in Forthcoming Volumes

Below are some of the authors and illustrators that will be featured in upcoming volumes of *SATA*. These include new entries on the swiftly rising stars of the field, as well as completely revised and updated entries (indicated with *) on some of the most notable and best-loved creators of books for children.

Ari Berk ▮ An award-winning writer and scholar of literature, iconography, and comparative myth, Berk is also a folklorist, poet, and visual artist. In *The Runes of Elfland,* which is illustrated by fantasy artist Brian Froud, Berk treats readers to an explanation of each rune, as well as the symbol's history and other related facts of interest. In his collaboration with Native-American poet and writer Carolyn Dunn on *Coyote Speaks* he focuses on myths and legends, drawing on the diverse culture of the Americas.

Jenna Bush ▮ Bush, the daughter of former U.S. President George W. Bush, shares the passion of her mother, former First Lady and teacher Laura Bush, for education and literacy. While interning for UNICEF in Latin America, Bush met a Panamanian woman whose triumph over adversity and a diagnosis of HIV/AIDS inspired Bush's book *Anna's Story.* In addition to her work as a teacher, Bush has also collaborated with her mother on the pro-literacy picture book *Read All about It.*

Willow Dawson ▮ Raised in a creative family, Canadian artist and illustrator Dawson is a sequential artist who works in India ink and soft-toned acrylics on recycled cardboard. Beginning her publishing career while still in college, she teamed up with Susan Hughes to illustrate *No Girls Allowed: Tales of Daring Women Dressed as Men for Love, Freedom, and Adventure.* Praised for Dawson's bold art, Hughes' graphic novel draws from history in inspiring the independence of modern young women.

*Bill Harley ▮ A full-time performer since 1980, Harley has made a career of entertaining young audiences with his delightfully humorous and universally recognizable vignettes about growing up. Many of his performance pieces have been produced as award-winning recordings as well as adapted as picture books, including *Carna and the Boots of Seven Strides* and *Dirty Joe, the Pirate.* In addition, Harley has channeled his humor into the quirkily titled chapter books *The Amazing Flight of Darius Frobisher* and *Night of the Spadefoot Toads.*

*Beth Krommes ▮ Known for her wood engravings, Krommes is a Caldecott Medal-winning illustrator who lives and works in New Hampshire. Since the early 1990s, she has illustrated children's books with her detailed scratchboard-and-watercolor images. Krommes's artwork is a feature of *Grandmother Winter* by Phyllis Root, the folklore collection *The Hidden Folk* by Lise Lunge-Larsen, and the award-winning *The House in the Night* by Susan Marie Swanson.

*Hilary McKay ▮ Writing stories that she herself would like to read, British author McKay has charmed young readers with books that include *The Exiles, Dog Friday,* the "Charlie" books, and the popular young-adult novels in the "Casson Family" series, which include *Saffy's Angel* and *Caddy Ever After.* Noted for their realistic plots, likable characters, and humorous highlights, McKay's stories have won her numerous fans in both her native England and the United States.

*William Sleator ▮ A popular and prolific writer of fiction for children and young adults, Sleator incorporates current scientific theories, suspense, and the supernatural in stories that challenge readers to take active roles in their lives. In novels that include *House of Stairs, Interstellar Pig,* and *The Green Future of Tycho,* Sleator takes young-adult characters from their everyday lives into confrontations with unusual, even unnerving situations that can involve everything from alien beings and ESP to black holes and time travel into the past and the future.

April Stevens ▮ New England author Stevens charmed critics with her first novel, *Angel Angel,* which focuses on two boys growing up in an eccentric and somewhat troubled family. Demonstrating her versatility, she also attracts a younger readership with her picture book *Waking up Wendell,* a clever and original counting story illustrated by Tad Hills.

Tim Tingle ▮ Tingle is a professional storyteller and musician who has appeared at conferences and festivals throughout the United States and abroad. A member of the Choctaw Nation of Oklahoma, he tells stories that reflect his Native-American heritage, combining personal tales with historical events and traditional lore. Tingle's books for children include *Walking the Choctaw Road,* the award-winning *Crossing Bok Chitto,* and *Spirits Dark and Light: Supernatural Tales from the Five Civilized Tribes.*

Kelly Yates ▮ Beginning his career creating licensed images ranging from comic-book superheroes to Sesame Street characters, Yates has also illustrated the "Doctor Who" comic-book series and made his children's-book debut illustrating Christopher Krovatin's young-adult novel *Venomous.* Continuing his career in comics, the North Carolina-based Yates is also the creator of the "Amber Atoms" series published by Image Comics.

Introduction

Something about the Author (SATA) is an ongoing reference series that examines the lives and works of authors and illustrators of books for children. SATA includes not only well-known writers and artists but also less prominent individuals whose works are just coming to be recognized. This series is often the only readily available information source on emerging authors and illustrators. You'll find SATA informative and entertaining, whether you are a student, a librarian, an English teacher, a parent, or simply an adult who enjoys children's literature.

What's Inside SATA

SATA provides detailed information about authors and illustrators who span the full time range of children's literature, from early figures like John Newbery and L. Frank Baum to contemporary figures like Judy Blume and Richard Peck. Authors in the series represent primarily English-speaking countries, particularly the United States, Canada, and the United Kingdom. Also included, however, are authors from around the world whose works are available in English translation. The writings represented in SATA include those created intentionally for children and young adults as well as those written for a general audience and known to interest younger readers. These writings cover the entire spectrum of children's literature, including picture books, humor, folk and fairy tales, animal stories, mystery and adventure, science fiction and fantasy, historical fiction, poetry and nonsense verse, drama, biography, and nonfiction. Obituaries are also included in SATA and are intended not only as death notices but also as concise overviews of people's lives and work. Additionally, each edition features newly revised and updated entries for a selection of SATA listees who remain of interest to today's readers and who have been active enough to require extensive revisions of their earlier biographies.

Autobiography Feature

Beginning with Volume 103, many volumes of SATA feature one or more specially commissioned autobiographical essays. These unique essays, averaging about ten thousand words in length and illustrated with an abundance of personal photos, present an entertaining and informative first-person perspective on the lives and careers of prominent authors and illustrators profiled in SATA.

Two Convenient Indexes

In response to suggestions from librarians, SATA indexes no longer appear in every volume but are included in alternate (odd-numbered) volumes of the series, beginning with Volume 57.

SATA continues to include two indexes that cumulate with each alternate volume: the Illustrations Index, arranged by the name of the illustrator, gives the number of the volume and page where the illustrator's work appears in the current volume as well as all preceding volumes in the series; the Author Index gives the number of the volume in which a person's biographical sketch, autobiographical essay, or obituary appears in the current volume as well as all preceding volumes in the series.

These indexes also include references to authors and illustrators who appear in Gale's Yesterday's Authors of Books for Children, Children's Literature Review, and Something about the Author Autobiography Series.

Easy-to-Use Entry Format

Whether you're already familiar with the SATA series or just getting acquainted, you will want to be aware of the kind of information that an entry provides. In every SATA entry the editors attempt to give as complete a picture of the person's life and work as possible. A typical entry in SATA includes the following clearly labeled information sections:

PERSONAL: date and place of birth and death, parents' names and occupations, name of spouse, date of marriage, names of children, educational institutions attended, degrees received, religious and political affiliations, hobbies and other interests.

ADDRESSES: complete home, office, electronic mail, and agent addresses, whenever available.

CAREER: name of employer, position, and dates for each career post; art exhibitions; military service; memberships and offices held in professional and civic organizations.

MEMBER: professional, civic, and other association memberships and any official posts held.

AWARDS, HONORS: literary and professional awards received.

WRITINGS: title-by-title chronological bibliography of books written and/or illustrated, listed by genre when known; lists of other notable publications, such as plays, screenplays, and periodical contributions.

ADAPTATIONS: a list of films, television programs, plays, CD-ROMs, recordings, and other media presentations that have been adapted from the author's work.

WORK IN PROGRESS: description of projects in progress.

SIDELIGHTS: a biographical portrait of the author or illustrator's development, either directly from the biographee—and often written specifically for the *SATA* entry—or gathered from diaries, letters, interviews, or other published sources.

BIOGRAPHICAL AND CRITICAL SOURCES: cites sources quoted in "Sidelights" along with references for further reading.

EXTENSIVE ILLUSTRATIONS: photographs, movie stills, book illustrations, and other interesting visual materials supplement the text.

How a *SATA* Entry Is Compiled

SATA editors examine a wide variety of published sources to gather information for an entry. Biographical and bibliographic sources are consulted, as are book reviews, feature articles, published interviews, and material sometimes obtained from the biographee's family, publishers, agent, or other associates. Whenever possible, the author or illustrator is sent a copy of the entry to check for accuracy and completeness.

Entries that have not been verified by the biographees or their representatives are marked with an asterisk (*).

Contact the Editor

We encourage our readers to examine the entire *SATA* series. Please write and tell us if we can make *SATA* even more helpful to you. Give your comments and suggestions to the editor:

Editor
Something about the Author
Gale, Cengage Learning
27500 Drake Rd.
Farmington Hills MI 48331-3535

Toll-free: 800-877-GALE
Fax: 248-699-8070

Something about the Author Product Advisory Board

The editors of *Something about the Author* are dedicated to maintaining a high standard of excellence by publishing comprehensive, accurate, and highly readable entries on a wide array of writers for children and young adults. In addition to the quality of the content, the editors take pride in the graphic design of the series, which is intended to be orderly yet inviting, allowing readers to utilize the pages of *SATA* easily and with efficiency. Despite the longevity of the *SATA* print series, and the success of its format, we are mindful that the vitality of a literary reference product is dependent on its ability to serve its users over time. As literature, and attitudes about literature, constantly evolve, so do the reference needs of students, teachers, scholars, journalists, researchers, and book club members. To be certain that we continue to keep pace with the expectations of our customers, the editors of *SATA* listen carefully to their comments regarding the value, utility, and quality of the series. Librarians, who have firsthand knowledge of the needs of library users, are a valuable resource for us. The *Something about the Author* Product Advisory Board, made up of school, public, and academic librarians, is a forum to promote focused feedback about *SATA* on a regular basis. The nine-member advisory board includes the following individuals, whom the editors wish to thank for sharing their expertise:

Eva M. Davis
Director,
Canton Public Library,
Canton, Michigan

Joan B. Eisenberg
Lower School Librarian,
Milton Academy,
Milton, Massachusetts

Francisca Goldsmith
Teen Services Librarian,
Berkeley Public Library,
Berkeley, California

Susan Dove Lempke
Children's Services Supervisor,
Niles Public Library District,
Niles, Illinois

Robyn Lupa
Head of Children's Services,
Jefferson County Public Library,
Lakewood, Colorado

Victor L. Schill
Assistant Branch Librarian/Children's Librarian,
Harris County Public Library/Fairbanks Branch,
Houston, Texas

Caryn Sipos
Community Librarian,
Three Creeks Community Library,
Vancouver, Washington

Steven Weiner
Director,
Maynard Public Library,
Maynard, Massachusetts

SOMETHING ABOUT THE AUTHOR

ALCORN, Stephen 1958-

Personal

Born 1958, in New York, NY; son of John Alcorn (an artist); married Sabina Fascione (a botanical artist and textile designer), 1981; children: Lucrezia, Ludovica. *Education:* Attended Istituto Statale d'Arte (Florence, Italy), 1971-77, and Cooper Union for the Advancement of the Arts and Sciences, 1977; Purchase College of the State University of New York, B.F.A. (with honors), 1980.

Addresses

Office—Alcorn Studio & Gallery, 112 W. Main St., Cambridge, NY 12816. *E-mail*—stephen.alcorn@veri zon.net.

Career

Painter, printmaker, and illustrator, 1975—; founder and director of Alcorn Studio and Gallery, Cambridge, NY, 1993—. Istituto Statale d'Arte, Florence, Italy, visiting professor, 1984-86; Waldorf School, Saratoga Springs, NY, instructor, 1990; University of Connecticut, Storrs, visiting professor, 2005; Salem Art Works, Salem, NY, instructor, 2005; Skidmore College, Saratoga Springs, visiting lecturer, 2008. Co-founder of musical ensemble

Stephen Alcorn (Photograph by Luca Martelli. Reproduced by permission.)

ADESSO. *Exhibitions:* Work has been exhibited in various cities, including Siena, Italy; New York, NY; and Bennington, VT. Inclusion in Original Art show, Society of Illustrators, 1998, 2000. Work included in permanent collections at Library of Congress, New York Public Library, Random House, Southwestern Bell Foundation, Gutenberg Museum, Southern Poverty Law Center, and Trinity College (Hartford, CT), and in private collections in the United States and in Europe.

Awards, Honors

Parents' Choice Honor Award, Parents' Choice Foundation, for *Frederick Douglass;* New York Book Show Award for best nonfiction book jacket of the year, and Carter G. Woodson Book Award, National Council for the Social Studies, both 1998, both for *Langston Hughes;* Best Books for Young Adults designation, American Library Association, and Best of the Best designation, Chicago Public Library, both 1998, and Best 100 Titles for Reading and Sharing inclusion, New York Public Library, all for *I, Too, Sing America;* Carter G. Woodson Book Award, 2000, and Coretta Scott King Award Honor Book designation, both for *Let It Shine;* One Hundred Titles for Reading and Sharing inclusion, New York Public Library, for *My America.*

Writings

SELF-ILLUSTRATED

A Gift of Days: The Greatest Words to Live By, Atheneum Books for Young Readers (New York, NY), 2008.
Odetta, the Queen of Folk, Scholastic Press (New York, NY), 2010.

ILLUSTRATOR

Stephen Vincent Benét, *John Brown's Body,* Franklin Mint (New York, NY), 1985.
David Mamet and Lindsay Krouse, *The Owl: A Story for Children,* Kipling Press (New York, NY), 1987.
Johnny Alcorn, *Rembrandt's Beret; or, The Painter's Crown,* Tambourine Books (New York, NY), 1991.
Helen and Dick Witty, *Feed the Birds,* Workman (New York, NY), 1991.
Milton Meltzer, editor, *Lincoln: In His Own Words,* Harcourt Brace (New York, NY), 1993, Sandpiper (New York, NY), 2008
Milton Meltzer, editor, *Frederick Douglass: In His Own Words,* Harcourt Brace (San Diego, CA), 1995.
Milton Meltzer, editor, *Langston Hughes,* Millbrook Press (Brookfield, CT), 1997.
Catherine Clinton, editor, *I, Too, Sing America: Three Centuries of African-American Poetry,* Houghton Mifflin (Boston, MA), 1998.
Paul LaFarge, *The Artist of the Missing,* Farrar, Straus (New York, NY), 1999.

Andrea Davis Pinckney, *Let It Shine: Stories of Black Women Freedom Fighters,* Harcourt (San Diego, CA), 2000.
Lee Bennett Hopkins, editor, *My America: A Poetry Atlas of the United States,* Simon & Schuster (New York, NY), 2000.
Ted Gottfried, *Nazi Germany: The Face of Tyranny,* Twenty-first Century Books (Brookfield, CT), 2000.
Doreen Rappaport, *The Year of the Paper Menorahs,* Hyperion (New York, NY), 2000.
Ted Gottfried, *Children of the Slaughter: Young People of the Holocaust,* Twenty-first Century Books (Brookfield, CT), 2001.
Ted Gottfried, *Deniers of the Holocaust: Who They Are, What They Do, Why They Do It,* Twenty-first Century Books (Brookfield, CT), 2001.
Ted Gottfried, *Displaced Persons: The Liberation and Abuse of Holocaust Survivors,* Twenty-first Century Books (Brookfield, CT), 2001
Ted Gottfried, *Heroes of the Holocaust,* Twenty-first Century Books (Brookfield, CT), 2001.
Verla Kay, *Broken Feather,* Putnam (New York, NY), 2002.
Lee Bennett Hopkins, editor, *Home to Me: Poems across America,* Orchard Books (New York, NY), 2002.
Lee Bennett Hopkins, editor, *Hoofbeats, Claws, and Rippled Fins: Creature Poems,* HarperCollins (New York, NY), 2002.
Catherine Clinton, editor, *A Poem of Her Own: Voices of American Women Yesterday and Today,* Abrams (New York, NY), 2003.
Kathleen Krull, *The Book of Rock Stars: Twenty-four Musical Icons That Shine through History,* Hyperion Books (New York, NY), 2003.
Tanya Denckla, *The Gardener's A-Z Guide to Growing Organic Food,* Storey Books (North Adams, MA), 2003.
Lee Bennett Hopkins, editor, *Days to Celebrate: A Full Year of Poetry, People, Holidays, History, Fascinating Facts, and More,* Greenwillow Books (New York, NY), 2005.
John le Carré, *The Spy Who Came in from the Cold,* Oak Tree Press (London, England), 2007.
Lee Bennett Hopkins, editor, *America at War: Poems,* Margaret K. McElderry Books (New York, NY), 2008.
Philip Dray, *Yours for Justice, Ida B. Wells: The Daring Life of a Crusading Journalist,* Peachtree Publishers (Atlanta, GA), 2008.
Deborah Hopkinson, *Keep On!: The Story of Matthew Henson, Co-Discoverer of the North Pole,* Peachtree Publishers (Atlanta, GA), 2009.

Also illustrator of *Il Naso* by Nicholaj Gogol. Contributor to *Graphis, Print,* and *Linea Grafica.*

Sidelights

Although he is first and foremost a fine artist with his own print workshop and gallery, Stephen Alcorn also creates illustrations for a wide range of books. Among Alcorn's works for children are such award-winning titles as *Langston Hughes, Let It Shine: Stories of Black Women Freedom Fighters,* and *My America: A Poetry*

Atlas of the United States. "I've always thought of art as being the perfect marriage of things seen and things dreamed," Alcorn remarked to Carol Stevens in *Print* magazine. "It's that marriage of the way we see things in our imagination and the way we perceive them physically in nature that creates tension and dynamic."

Alcorn, the son of an artist, moved to Italy with his family when he was a teenager. He studied art at the Istituto Statale d'Arte in Florence, where he met his future wife. At age sixteen Alcorn illustrated his first manuscript, *Il Naso,* an Italian edition of a story by Nikolai Gogol. In 1977 he moved back to the United States, and graduated in 1980 with a fine arts degree from Purchase College of the State University of New York.

Alcorn began his career as a printmaker and soon gained serious critical and commercial acclaim. After 1981, he settled in Florence with his wife, artist Sabina Fascione. His growing portfolio of relief-block prints attracted the attention of such firms as Arnoldo Mondadori Editore, one of Italy's largest publishers, which hired the artist to create interpretive portraits of literary figures for a series of classic titles by notable twentieth-century authors. In 1982, Random House in New York City contracted Alcorn to create the same type of dust-jacket illustration for their famed "Modern Library" series.

Alcorn and his family returned to the United States in 1986. The following year, he illustrated his first book for children, *The Owl,* a story written by playwright David Mamet and Mamet's then-wife Lindsay Krouse. He then collaborated with his brother, Johnny Alcorn, and published *Rembrandt's Beret; or, The Painter's Crown,* in 1991. The story begins with an artist attempting to paint a portrait of his energetic young granddaughter. In order to capture her attention, he recounts, aloud, an enthralling story about his long-ago visit to the famed Uffizi Gallery in Florence when he was a boy. When a storm comes he finds himself locked in a special gallery that is usually closed to the public. Here paintings of the Old Masters speak to him—literally. The famed artists all cavort with the boy in this secret hall, and Rembrandt himself paints the boy's portrait and gives him his signature beret as a parting gift. Later, the little boy's mother refuses to believe his tale, but still, she buys him a set of art supplies the next day. *Rembrandt's Beret* won praise for the quality of its imagery. "The illustrations are painterly . . . modernistic compositions that echo the 17th-century masters," remarked Shirley Wilton in *School Library Journal.*

Alcorn has also illustrated a number of award-winning titles for young-adult readers about heroes of the U.S. civil rights movement. Two biographies edited by Milton Meltzer—1993's *Lincoln: In His Own Words* and *Frederick Douglass: In His Own Words,* published two years later—include Alcorn's linoleum-block prints depicting events and personages from the lives of these leaders. The Lincoln book features the president's speeches alongside explanatory text, and draws upon primary source material, such as the briefs he wrote early on as an Illinois lawyer. Later excerpts concentrate on his impassioned writings on slavery. Janice Del Negro, writing in *Booklist,* declared that "Alcorn's powerful black and white linocuts have impact and majesty," while a *Publishers Weekly* contributor asserted: "the artist's haunting visions of slavery are a highlight of the book."

Frederick Douglass chronicles the life and times of the man considered to be the most significant African-American leader of his century. Born a slave in 1818, Douglass learned to read and write against great odds and later escaped from bondage to become a famed orator for the abolitionist cause. Alcorn's images accompany excerpts from Douglass's speeches and writings. Mary M. Burns, critiquing *Frederick Douglass* in *Horn Book,* gave the work enthusiastic praise, both for Meltzer's scholarship and for Alcorn's illustrations, which she termed "strong, dramatic statements . . . memorable in their intensity, haunting in their effect—fitting accompaniments to a remarkable work." *School Library Journal* reviewer Joanne Kelleher remarked that "the

Alcorn creates inspiring paintings to capture the spirit of Catherine Clinton's patriotic picture book I, Too, Sing America. (Houghton Mifflin Company, 1998. Illustrations copyright © 1998 by Stephen Alcorn. Reprinted by permission of Houghton Mifflin Harcourt Publishing Company. All rights reserved.)

emotional impact of the text is given form and substance" by Alcorn's linocuts, calling the illustrations "pictures of stark majesty sharply defined by unquestioned skill."

Alcorn also collaborated with Meltzer on *Langston Hughes,* his revised edition of the biography of the noted African-American poet that was written for teenagers and first published in 1968. For the new edition, Alcorn created black-and-white illustrations tinted in tones of sepia and blue. These images "combine elements of folk art, social realism, and abstract imagery," noted *Booklist* critic Hazel Rochman, while Marilyn Fairbanks declared in her *School Library Journal* review that Alcorn's images "pique excitement and interest and invite repeated viewings."

Let It Shine: Stories of Black Women Freedom Fighters, a work by Andrea Davis Pinckney, offers profiles of Sojourner Truth, Harriet Tubman, and Rosa Parks, as well as other significant historical figures. "Alcorn's extraordinary bold tableaux, framed like stage pieces, consistently declare their own individuality as well as that of their subjects," as *Horn Book* reviewer Susan P. Bloom stated. Marie Orlando, writing in *School Library Journal,* also praised the "vibrant, inspired oil paintings," remarking that "line, color, and canvas texture give the pictures depth and dynamism, vastly enriching the reading experience." Philip Dray's *Yours for Justice, Ida B. Wells: The Daring Life of a Crusading Journalist,* a picture-book biography, looks at the accomplishments of a famed anti-lynching advocate. "Alcorn's outstanding illustrations give readers a sense of the woman," Lucinda Snyder Whitehurst commented in *School Library Journal,* and a reviewer in *Publishers Weekly* similarly noted that the "stylized illustrations, soaring vignettes in muted hues that portray a statuesque and self-assured Wells."

Alcorn created the artwork for the anthology *I, Too, Sing America: Three Centuries of African-American Poetry,* published in 1998. The work, selected and annotated by Catherine Clinton, features works by authors ranging from Phyllis Wheatley, who lived in colonial America, to twentieth-century radical Amiri Baraka. With high praise for Alcorn's collaborative artwork, a critic for *Publishers Weekly* described "each illustration [as] . . . a complex response to the poem, inviting readers to both study the artwork and muse over the text." Alcorn and Clinton also join forces on *A Poem of Her Own: Voices of American Women Yesterday and Today,* a collection of twenty-five works that includes Emma Lazarus's "The New Colossus" and Julia Ward Howe's "The Battle Hymn of the Republic." According to *Booklist* critic Ilene Cooper, "the intelligent selection is matched by the fresh, open design, highlighted by Alcorn's exciting paintings, executed in light-fast casein paint," and a *Kirkus Reviews* contributor noted that the artist's "occasionally surreal casein paintings clearly use the poems as jumping-off places, sometimes they go to a slightly different place than the poetry does."

Alcorn has also enjoyed a successful collaboration with prolific anthologist Lee Bennett Hopkins. *My America* contains more than fifty works by such writers as Carl Sandburg, Nikki Giovanni, and X.J. Kennedy. "Alcorn's paintings reflect the emotional range of the poems through a variety of styles and images," remarked *School Library Journal* reviewer Barbara Chatton, and Rochman wrote that the illustrations "capture the sweep of the land and the rhythm of the words." In *Home to Me: Poems across America* Hopkins presents selections from fifteen poets who examine the diversity of the American landscape. According to a *Kirkus Reviews* critic, "Alcorn's softly colored, stylized illustrations interpret the text in imagery that is both literal and figurative."

Hoofbeats, Claws, and Rippled Fins: Creature Poems, a collection of fourteen verses edited by Hopkins, was inspired by Alcorn's woodblock prints. The artwork "stands alone," Gillian Engberg stated in *Booklist,* "inviting readers to find their own stories within the handsome images." Selections from Robert Frost, Langston Hughes, and Richard Wilbur highlight *Days to Celebrate: A Full Year of Poetry, People, Holidays, History, Fascinating Facts, and More,* another volume by Hopkins. Here "Alcorn's large, vibrant, whimsical artwork perfectly enhances the prose and verse," as Lynda Ritterman commented in *School Library Journal.* In *America at War: Poems* editor Hopkins focuses on military engagements from the American Revolution to the war in Iraq. Alcorn's watercolor illustrations "often set the accompanying words in a specific time," Nancy Palmer maintained in her review of the book for *School Library Journal.* "Their dramatic compositions with their recurring and creatively arranged iconography of war further dramatize and expand the poets' words."

Daniele Baroni, in an article in *Linea Grafica,* discussed Alcorn's career, declaring: "Not since the Belgian master Frans Masereel . . . has an artist reached such elevated heights in the art of printmaking." John A. Glusman, in a statement on Alcorn's home page, observed that "there's no question that Stephen Alcorn is one of our most technically sophisticated and inspired of artists. The sheer craftsmanship is breathtaking, revealing a kind of artistry that hasn't existed for half a century." Alcorn and his wife, Sabina Fascione, a botanical artist, enjoy combining their artwork for exhibitions. In 1993 they opened a gallery and printmaking workshop in an eighteenth-century farmhouse in Cambridge, New York, where they continue to live and work.

Biographical and Critical Sources

PERIODICALS

Booklist, September 1, 1993, Janice Del Negro, review of *Lincoln: In His Own Words,* p. 48; August, 1997, Hazel Rochman, review of *Langston Hughes,* p. 1890;

November 15, 2000, Hazel Rochman, review of *My America: A Poetry Atlas of the United States*, p. 637; May 15, 2001, Hazel Rochman, review of *Children of the Slaughter: Young People of the Holocaust*, p. 1741; May 1, 2002, Gillian Engberg, review of *Hoofbeats, Claws, and Rippled Fins: Creature Poems*, p. 1520; November 1, 2002, Susan Dove Lempke, review of *Broken Feather*, p. 500; April 1, 2003, Ilene Cooper, review of *A Poem of Her Own: Voices of American Women Yesterday and Today*, p. 1405; October 15, 2003, John Peters, review of *The Book of Rock Stars: Twenty-four Musical Icons That Shine through History*, p. 407; January 1, 2005, Gillian Engberg, review of *Days to Celebrate: A Full Year of Poetry, People, Holidays, History, Fascinating Facts, and More*, p. 848; March 1, 2008, Carolyn Phelan, review of *America at War: Poems*, p. 66; February 15, 2009, Carolyn Phelan, review of *Keep On! The Story of Matthew Henson, Co-Discoverer of the North Pole*, p. 77.

Horn Book, July-August, 1995, Mary M. Burns, review of *Frederick Douglass: In His Own Words*, pp. 480-481; November, 2000, Susan P. Bloom, review of *Let It Shine: Stories of Black Women Freedom Fighters*, p. 770; March-April, 2002, Susan P. Bloom, review of *Hoofbeats, Claws, and Rippled Fins*, p. 222.

Kirkus Reviews, August 1, 2002, review of *Home to Me: Poems across America*, p. 1132; March 15, 2003, review of *A Poem of Her Own*, p. 462; January 15, 2009, review of *Keep On!*

Linea Grafica, number 296 (1995), Daniele Baroni, "The Illustration of Stephen Alcorn," pp. 10-19.

Print, January-February, 1994, Carol Stevens, "Choice Cuts: Stephen Alcorn Exploits the Linocut to Brilliant Effect," pp. 32-41.

Publishers Weekly, July 19, 1993, review of *Lincoln*, p. 256; November 9, 1998, review of *I, Too, Sing America: Three Centuries of African-American Poetry*, p. 74; December 22, 2003, review of *The Book of Rock Stars*, p. 62; February 11, 2008, review of *Yours for Justice, Ida B. Wells: The Daring Life of a Crusading Journalist*, p. 69; March 17, 2008, review of *America at War*, p. 71.

School Library Journal, June, 1991, Wilton, Shirley, review of *Rembrandt's Beret, or, The Painter's Crown*, p. 100; February, 1995, Joanne Kelleher, review of *Frederick Douglass*, pp. 121-122; November, 1997, Marilyn Fairbanks, review of *Langston Hughes*, p. 132; September, 2000, Barbara Chatton, review of *My America*, p. 248; October, 2000, Marie Orlando, review of *Let It Shine*, p. 190; June, 2001, Jack Forman, review of *Children of the Slaughter*, p. 172; October, 2002, Shawn Brommer, review of *Home to Me*, p. 146; November, 2002, S.K. Joiner, review of *Broken Feather*, p. 145; January, 2005, Lynda Ritterman, review of *Days to Celebrate*, p. 110; March, 2008, Nancy Palmer, review of *America at War*, p. 220; April, 2008, Lucinda Snyder Whitehurst, review of *Yours for Justice, Ida B. Wells*, p. 130.

ONLINE

Stephen Alcorn Home Page, http://www.alcorngallery.com (November 1, 2009).

Simon & Schuster Web site, http://www.simonandschuster.com/ (November 1, 2009), "Stephen Alcorn: Author Revealed."*

*   *   *

ARNOLD, Ann 1953(?)-

Personal

Born c. 1953, in CA. *Education:* Attended Silvermine Guild School of the Arts; University of California at Santa Cruz, degree.

Addresses

Home—Berkeley, CA.

Career

Author, illustrator, and figurative artist. *Exhibitions:* Works exhibited at galleries in United States and in London, England, including North Point Gallery, San Francisco, CA.

Awards, Honors

Children's Book Award Notable Book designation, International Reading Association, for *The Adventurous Chef*.

Writings

SELF-ILLUSTRATED

(Self-illustrated) *The Adventurous Chef: Alexis Soyer*, Francis Foster Books (New York, NY), 2002.

Sea Cows, Shamans, and Scurvy: Alaska's First Naturalist: Georg Wilhelm Steller, Farrar, Straus & Giroux (New York, NY), 2008.

ILLUSTRATOR

Brian Patten, selector, *Clare's Countryside*, Heinemann (London, England), 1981.

Alice Waters with Bob Carrau and Patricia Curtan, *Fanny at Chez Panisse*, HarperCollins (New York, NY), 1992.

Ian Jackson, *Ranjitsinhji's 9,000 Elephants Visit Serendipity Books*, privately published (CA), 1997.

Sara London, *Firehorse Max*, HarperCollins (New York, NY), 1997.

Biographical and Critical Sources

PERIODICALS

American Artist, August, 1995, Karen Haber, "Meditation on Form and Color," p. 24.

Booklist, February 1, 1993, Janice Del Negro, review of *Fanny at Chez Panisse,* p. 980; October 1, 1997, review of *Firehorse Max,* p. 336; October, 2002, Lauralyn Persson, review of *The Adventurous Chef: Alexix Soyer,* p. 136; December 1, 2008, Carolyn Phelan, review of *Sea Cows, Shamans, and Scurvy: Alaska's First Naturalist: Georg Wilhelm Steller,* p. 60; December, 2002, review of *The Adventurous Chef,* p. 142.

Bulletin of the Center for Children's Books, December, 1997, review of *Firehorse Max,* p. 75.

Horn Book, January-February, 1998, Hanna B. Zeiger, review of *Firehorse Max,* p. 65; November-December, 2002, Mary M. Burns, review of *The Adventurous Chef,* p. 772; January-February, 2009, Betty Carter, review of *Sea Cows, Shamans, and Scurvy,* p. 108.

Kirkus Reviews, August 15, 2002, review of *The Adventurous Chef,* p. 1214; October 15, 2008, review of *Sea Cows, Shamans, and Scurvy.*

Kliatt, September, 2008, Janet Julian, review of *Sea Cows, Shamans, and Scurvy,* p. 36.

New Yorker, November 23, 1992, review of *Fanny at Chez Panisse,* p. 81.

Publishers Weekly, September 28, 1992, review of *Fanny at Chez Panisse,* p. 74; September 15, 1997, review of *Firehorse Max,* p. 75; July 8, 2002, review of *The Adventurous Chef,* p. 49.

School Library Journal, February, 2009, Sue Sherif, review of *Sea Cows, Shamans, and Scurvy,* p. 114.

ONLINE

Pippin Properties Web site, http://www.pippinproperties. com/ (November 15, 2009), "Ann Arnold."*

* * *

ARSENAULT, Isabelle 1978-

Personal

Born 1978, in Sept-Iles, Québec, Canada. *Education:* Degree (graphic design).

Addresses

Home—Montréal, Québec, Canada. *E-mail*—isabelle arsenault@videotron.ca.

Career

Illustrator.

Awards, Honors

Communication Arts award; National Magazine Awards of Canada; Governor General's Literary Award for Illustration, 2005, for *Le coeur de monsieur Gauguin* by Marie-Danielle Croteau; Governor General's Literary Award finalist, and International Reading Association Children's Choice listee, both 2008, and Best Children's Books of the Year designation, Bank Street College of Education Children Book Committee 2009, all for *My Letter to the World, and Other Poems.*

Illustrator

Marie-Danielle Croteau, *Le coeur de monsieur Gauguin,* Diffusion le Seuil (Montréal, Québec, Canada), 2004, translated by Susan Ouriou as *Mr. Gauguin's Heart,* Tundra Books (Toronto, Ontario, Canada), 2007.

Raymond Plante, *Pas sérieux,* Les 400 Coups (Montréal, Québec, Canada), 2006.

Gilles Tibo, *Rêves d'enfance* (poems), Dominique et Cie. (Saint-Lambert, Québec, Canada), 2007.

Emily Dickinson, *My Letter to the World, and Other Poems,* new edition, Kids Can Press (Toronto, Ontario, Canada), 2008.

Contributor to *L'appareil,* Éditions de la Pastèque; contributor to periodicals.

Sidelights

Isabelle Arsenault is an award-winning illustrator based in Montréal, Québec, Canada. Although her original training was in graphic design, Arsenault's love of children's books has inspired her to expand her work into book illustration. In addition to illustrating the picture book *Mr. Gauguin's Heart,* a story by Marie-Danielle Croteau that was originally published in French as *Le coeur de monsieur Gauguin,* she has created artwork for several collections of verse. Her work for *My Letter to the World, and Other Poems* contains the writing of noted nineteenth-century American poet Emily Dickinson.

Winner of the Governor General's Literary Award for Illustration, *Mr. Gauguin's Heart* describes the future painter's emotional turmoil following the untimely death of his father during a family voyage to South America. While noting that Croteau takes some "poetic license" in telling her romantic story about the inspiration of artistic vision, a *Publishers Weekly* critic wrote that Arsenault's watercolor pictures, with their "subdued grays and blues," feature "bright spots that speak to Paul's innocence and resilience." In *Resource Links* Linda Ludke dubbed the book "exquisite"; in both text and illustration "the restorative powers of the imagination and creativity are eloquently presented," Ludke added.

Part of Kids Can Press's "Visions in Poetry" series, *My Letter to the World, and Other Poems* pairs Dickinson's spare, melancholy verses about loss and death with Arsenault's mixed-media pictures. The artist's "angular and shadowy" style utilizes only a minimal amount of color, observed Donna Cardon in *School Library Journal,* and in *Booklist* Hazel Rochman wrote that Arsenault's "surreal" images for *My Letter to the World, and Other Poems* are "as spare, intense, and mysterious as the [poet's] words." Calling the work "an elegant introduction to the work of th[e] . . . mysterious belle of Amherst," *New York Times Book Review* critic Sara London also had special praise for the book's art. The illustrator's "delicate color-washed drawings of a ghostlike Emily . . . depict a dreamlike 19th-century otherworld," London noted. "Yet for all the muted tones . . . Arsenault avoids the dreary. Amid the shadows there's lightness and humor to be found."

Isabelle Arsenault's highly praised artwork conveys the sensitivity of the verses of Emily Dickinson that are collected in **My Letter to the World, and Other Poems.** (KCP Poetry, 2008. Illustrations © 2008 Isabelle Arsenault. All rights reserved. Reproduced by Kids Can Press Ltd.)

Biographical and Critical Sources

PERIODICALS

Booklist, September 1, 2008, Hazel Rochman, review of *My Letter to the World, and Other Poems,* p. 86.

Canadian Review of Materials, October 10, 2008, Gregory Bryan, review of *My Letter to the World, and Other Poems.*

New York Times Book Review, November 9, 2008, Sara London, review of *My Letter to the World, and Other Poems,* p. 24.

Publishers Weekly, September 17, 2007, review of *Mr. Gauguin's Heart,* p. 53.

Quill & Quire, July, 2007, Laurie McNeill, review of *Mr. Gauguin's Heart.*

Resource Links, June, 2007, Linda Ludke, review of *Mr. Gauguin's Heart,* p. 2.

School Library Journal, November, 2008, Donna Cardon, review of *My Letter to the World, and Other Poems,* p. 142.

ONLINE

Isabelle Arsenault Home Page, http://www.isabelle arsenault.com (November 3, 2009).*

ASHLAND, Monk 1972-
(Chris Rettstatt)

Personal

Born 1972, in AR; married; children: Zoe, Echo (twin daughters). *Education:* University of Illinois Chicago, B.A. (English). *Hobbies and other interests:* Travel, languages, playing with his daughters.

Addresses

Home—Chicago, IL; and Chongquing, China. *E-mail*—rettstatt@gmail.com.

Career

Author, transmedia storyteller, and youth media consultant. Star Farm Productions (entertainment company), Chicago, IL, former director of story development; Story Monk Studios (IP development studio), Chongquing, China, director.

Awards, Honors

CYBILS Award, nomination, 2008, for *The Sky Village.*

Writings

"KAIMIRA" FANTASY SERIES

(With Nigel Ashland) *The Sky Village,* illustrated by Jeff Nentrup, Candlewick Press (Cambridge, MA), 2008.
The Terrible Everything, illustrated by Jeff Nentrup, Candlewick Press (Cambridge, MA), 2010.

Contributor to books, including *Settlers of the New Virtual Worlds.*

Sidelights

Monk Ashland is the pen name of Chris Rettstatt, the coauthor of the dystopian fantasy *The Sky Village.* The first novel in the proposed five-book "Kaimira" series, *The Sky Village* takes place in the future, following the Trinary Wars and the devastation they have wrought. Now men must battle wild creatures and intelligent robots called meks in order to survive. Twelve-year-old Mei Long has been sent from China to live in the floating network of hot-air-balloons known as Sky Village since her mother was captured by meks. Through the pages of the Tree Book, Mei is able to communicate with a slightly older boy named Rom. Rom lives in the wilds of Las Vegas, and his younger sister is in the clutches of mek-beast hybrid creatures. As Mei and Rom both learn, they each have the Kaimira gene, which endows them with powers they hope to use to rescue their family members.

The Sky Village combines the text of the pseudonymous Ashland brothers (Rettstatt's coauthor Nigel Ashland also writes using a pen name) with links to online activities referencing the "Kaimira" world. Although Michael Cart wrote in *Booklist* that *The Sky Village* is "short on characterization," he predicted that young readers will nonetheless "be tantalized." "In *Voice of Youth Advocates,* Lynne Farrell Stover found more to like in the novel, cited the story's "strong characters . . . , terrifyingly unpredictable villains, frightening futuristic settings, and wonderfully written action sequences." Stover predicted that the "Kaimira" books will find ready fans among readers who enjoy "adventure, science fiction, and fantasy."

Discussing the growing interest in post-apocalyptic fiction with a *YPulse.com* interviewer, Rettstatt noted: "Post-apocalyptic fiction has been going strong for as long as I can remember. Just look at how many times Tokyo has been obliterated on TV and film. And in this Golden Age of YA literature, it makes sense that a few of us are going to . . . create a fresh start and a new sandbox for our imaginary characters.

"That said, when a community experiences a traumatic reminder of its mortality and its vulnerability to destruction, I do think the resulting surge of anxiety tends to erupt in a renewed interest in post-apocalyptic stories. And if there is something in the YA lit *zeitgeist* giving a leg up to that sort of fiction, it would be convenient to connect it to modern fears of terrorist attack.

"But my gut feeling is that many of today's post-apocalyptic stories have roots that are older than that. I think these more modern fears will be played out in the stories our children write. It scares me to imagine what forms their fictional disasters will take, oozing from primal fears caused by our generation's mistakes."

Biographical and Critical Sources

PERIODICALS

Booklist, July 1, 2008, Michael Cart, review of *The Sky Village,* p. 68.
Kirkus Reviews, June 15, 2008, review of *The Sky Village.*
Tribune Books (Chicago, IL), July 5, 2008, Mary Harris Russell, review of *The Sky Village,* p. 7.
Voice of Youth Advocates, October 14, 2008, Lynne Farrell Stover, review of *The Sky Village.*

ONLINE

Chris Rettstatt Home Page, http://rettstatt.com (November 3, 2009).
Chris Rettstatt Professional Page, http://storymonk.com (December 1, 2009).
Kaimira Web site, http://www.kaimiracode.com/ (November 3, 2009).
YPulse.com, http://www.ypulse.com/ (August 27, 2008), interview with Rettstatt.

B

BAKER, Sharon Reiss 1962-

Personal
Born December 29, 1962; married; has children. *Education:* Harvard University, B.A.; graduate study at Lesley University and University of Miami (education). *Religion:* Jewish. *Hobbies and other interests:* Travel.

Addresses
Home—W. Hartford, CT. *E-mail*—info@sharonreiss baker.com.

Career
Educator and author. Elementary and middle-school teacher in FL, MD, MA, and PR. Conducts writing workshops.

Member
Society of Children's Book Writers and Illustrators.

Awards, Honors
Association of Jewish Libraries Notable Book for Younger Readers designation, 2007, for *A Nickel, a Trolley, a Treasure House.*

Writings

A Nickel, a Trolley, a Treasure House, illustrated by Beth Peck, Viking (New York, NY), 2007.

Biographical and Critical Sources

PERIODICALS

Booklinks, September-October, 2007, Lizabeth Deskins and Christina Dorr, review of *A Nickel, a Trolley, a Treasure House,* p. 55.

Kirkus Reviews, January 15, 2007, review of *A Nickel, a Trolley, a Treasure House,* p. 69.
School Library Journal, March, 2007, Barbara Auerbach, review of *A Nickel, a Trolley, a Treasure House,* p. 151.

ONLINE

Sharon Reiss Baker Home Page, http://www.sharonreiss baker.com (April 10, 2008).*

*   *   *

BARRETT, Tracy 1955-

Personal
Born March 1, 1955, in Cleveland, OH; daughter of Richard Sears (a psychologist) and Shirley Irene (a teacher and literacy volunteer) Barrett; married Gregory Giles (a telephone interconnect owner), November, 1983; children: Laura, Patrick. *Education:* Attended Intercollegiate Center for Classical Studies (Rome, Italy), 1974-75; Brown University, A.B. (classics; magna cum laude; with honors), 1976; University of California, Berkeley, M.A. (Italian), 1979, Ph.D. (medieval Italian), 1988. *Politics:* Democrat. *Hobbies and other interests:* Knitting, traveling to Italy with her family.

Addresses
Home—P.O. Box 120061, Nashville, TN 37212. *E-mail*—tracytbarrett@yahoo.com.

Career
Vanderbilt University, Nashville, TN, senior lecturer in Italian and director of Italian language program, 1984—, affiliated with women's studies, humanities, and comparative literature programs. Presenter at numerous conferences.

Tracy Barrett (Photograph by Jenny Mandeville/Vanderbilt University. Reproduced by permission.)

Member

Society of Children's Book Writers and Illustrators (regional advisor to Mid-South region, 1999-2009), Authors Guild.

Awards, Honors

National Endowment for the Humanities summer study grant; American Library Association Best Book for Young Adults designation, National Council for the Social Studies Notable Trade Book designation, and Arizona State University English Education Honor List designation, all 2000, all for *Anna of Byzantium;* New York Public Library Best Book for the Teen Age designation, and Bank Street College Children's Book Committee's Best Children's Books of the Year listee, both 2004, both for *Cold in Summer;* William Allen White Award master list inclusion, and Mark Twain Award nomination, both 2008, both for *On Etruscan Time;* Great Stone Face Book Award nominee, Children's Librarians of New Hampshire, Volunteer State Book Award nomination, and Young Hoosier Book Award nominee, all 2010, all for *The Hundred-Year-Old Secret.*

Writings

JUVENILE NONFICTION

Nat Turner and the Slave Revolt, Millbrook Press (Brookfield, CT), 1993.
Harpers Ferry: The Story of John Brown's Raid, Millbrook Press (Brookfield, CT), 1993.
Growing up in Colonial America, Millbrook Press (Brookfield, CT), 1995.
Virginia, Marshall Cavendish,1997, 2nd edition, Benchmark Books (New York, NY), 2004.
Tennessee, Marshall Cavendish, 1997, 2nd edition, Benchmark Books (New York, NY), 2006.
Kidding around Nashville: What to Do, Where to Go, and How to Have Fun in Nashville, John Muir Publications, 1998.
Kentucky, Benchmark Books (New York, NY), 1999, 2nd edition, 2008.
The Trail of Tears: An American Tragedy, Perfection Learning (Logan, IA), 2000.
(With Jennifer T. Roberts) *The Ancient Greek World,* Oxford University Press (New York, NY), 2004.
(With Terry Kleeman) *The Ancient Chinese World,* Oxford University Press (New York, NY), 2005.

JUVENILE FICTION

Anna of Byzantium, Delacorte (New York, NY), 1999.
Cold in Summer, Henry Holt (New York, NY), 2003.
On Etruscan Time, Henry Holt (New York, NY), 2005.
King of Ithaka, Henry Holt (New York, NY), 2010.

"SHERLOCK FILES" SERIES; JUVENILE FICTION

The Hundred-Year-Old Secret, Henry Holt (New York, NY), 2008.
The Beast of Blackslope, Henry Holt (New York, NY), 2009.
The Case That Time Forgot, Henry Holt (New York, NY), 2010.

Contributor to "Reading Works" educational series, 1975. Contributor to periodicals, including *Appleseeds.*

Author's work has been translated into Dutch, Japanese, French, Turkish, Korean, and Italian.

OTHER

(Translator and author of introduction) *Cecco, as I Am and Was: The Poems of Cecco Angiolieri,* International Pocket Library, 1994.

Editorial assistant, *Romance Philology,* 1978-79, and *Kidney International,* 1984.

Sidelights

A senior lecturer in Italian literature and civilization at Nashville's Vanderbilt University, Tracy Barrett has balanced her academic writing with a mix of fact and fic-

tion geared for younger readers. Beginning her second career as a children's book author by penning nonfiction based on American history, Barrett expanded into fiction with *Anna of Byzantium.* That novel, which was highly praised by critics, has inspired her to write further fiction, although Barrett has also continued to dedicate much of her writing to sharing her interest and enthusiasm for history with children. Reviewing *The Ancient Greek World,* a book Barrett coauthored with Jennifer T. Roberts, *School Library Journal* reviewer Cynthia M. Sturgis praised the text as "lively" and added that the coauthors' "infusion of humor" makes the book "a palatable, solid resource" for middle-grade students.

"I grew up in a town where many authors lived," Barrett once recalled to *SATA,* "and thought of writers as just ordinary neighbors. The wonderful Jean Fritz was one of these authors. She gave me an original illustration from her book that is still my favorite, *The Cabin Faced West.* And since I liked writing I thought it might be a good job to have someday.

"But when I grew older I got discouraged about writing, because every time I read a wonderful book I would think, 'Oh, I could never write that. Why even try?' And I was right. I could never write *Charlotte's Web* or *Mrs. Mike,* two of my favorite books. It took until I was grown up to realize that this was okay—I didn't need to write those books. Someone else had already done it! But there were other books that no one but I could write. So I started writing again. My first book wasn't published until I was almost forty, and I regret that I wasted all that time being discouraged."

Barrett's first book, *Nat Turner and the Slave Revolt,* was released as part of the "Gateway Civil Rights" series. The book tells the story of the African-American slave and preacher who came to believe that God wanted him to free the slaves. Based on his visions, Turner led a group of his fellow slaves in a bloody revolt that ultimately took the lives of over 260 people. Beginning with Turner's court conviction in 1831, Barrett then goes back in time and traces her subject's upbringing and education, and concludes with the famous revolt. In a review for *Booklist,* Janice Del Negro praised Barrett's objectivity, stating that she "attempts to place the event in its historical context in a concise, noninflammatory text."

Harpers Ferry: The Story of John Brown's Raid, published as part of the "Spotlight on American History" series, profiles another revolt inspired by slavery. John Brown, an abolitionist whose extreme religious zeal motivated him to organize a small civilian force and make war on the United States in the hopes of ending slavery, took weapons during a raid on the U.S. arsenal at Harpers Ferry, West Virginia, in 1859. Reviewing *Harpers Ferry* and several other books in the series for *School Library Journal,* George Gleason noted that the volumes "cover their subjects well and occasionally include unusual tidbits of information."

Barrett contributed to Benchmark Press's "Celebrate the States" series with *Virginia, Tennessee,* and *Kentucky,* each of which features information on the geography, history, economy, and culture of the state under examination. Of special interest, according to Denise E. Agosto in *School Library Journal,* is a section called "state survey," in which famous people and popular tourist sites are discussed. Describing the books as "well-written," Agosto concluded that they "will be useful for reports."

In *Growing up in Colonial America* Barrett describes the lives of the youngest European settlers in the American colonies, differentiating them from both Native-American children and the children of slaves. In the first part of the book, she describes the food, clothing, chores, education, and recreation experienced by children in the Plymouth and Chesapeake settlements. In the second part, common child-rearing practices of the day are recounted. Elaine Fort Weischedel, writing in *School Library Journal,* observed that similar books on colonial life do not address the care of infants as Barrett does. The section containing chapters on housing,

Cover of Barrett's young-adult novel **Anna of Byzantium,** *featuring artwork by David Bowers.* (Delacorte Press, 1999. Jacket illustration © 1999 by David Bowers. Used by permission of Delacorte Press, an imprint of Random House Children's Books, a division of Random House, Inc.)

attire, and recreation will be "of keenest interest to modern readers," added Susan Dove Lempke in *Booklist,* the critic recommending *Growing up in Colonial America* as "a good choice for reports or pleasure reading."

Turning to fiction, Barrett's first novel, *Anna of Byzantium,* centers on real-life twelfth-century princess Anna Commena. In a first-person narrative, Barrett details the claustrophobic circumstances experienced by seventeen-year-old Anna after she is exiled to a convent for plotting to overthrow her brother. From there, Barrett uses flashbacks to detail Anna's childhood as the chosen successor of her father the king, her education and upbringing, and her cruel fall from favor following the birth of a brother. Over time, Anna is transformed from beloved child to a pawn in her grandmother's power schemes, and thence to an outcast and eventual scholar. "Barrett uses an effective first-person narrative to draw readers into Anna's story," remarked Ilene Cooper in *Booklist,* the critic going on to praise Barrett's use of detail in making Anna's world real to modern readers. Although Barrett's treatment of Anna's brother in particular contradicts the historical record, *Anna of Byzantium* succeeds as "a plausible character study of a brilliant and tempestuous young woman," concluded Shirley Wilton in a *School Library Journal* review.

Barrett's contemporary novel *Cold in Summer* takes place in a small town in Tennessee. Seventh grader Ariadne hates the fact that she has left her friends and school in Florida to move to a new town, the move caused by her mother's job teaching at a local college. Soon she meets May, who becomes her new confidante despite the fact that May's behavior, clothing, and startling comings and goings cause Ariadne some concern. During a social studies class, Adriadne learns about a local girl named May Butler who disappeared a century earlier, and now her time is taken up with solving the mystery of her reclusive new friend. Praising Barrett's portrayal of the "mutual concern" between the two girls, *School Library Journal* reviewer Alison Ching dubbed *Cold in Summer* a "light, easy read," while a *Kirkus Reviews* critic described Barrett's novel as a "genuine ghost story . . . that will draw readers eerily in."

Barrett mixes history and modern life in *On Etruscan Time,* as preteen Hector works alongside his archaeologist mother at a dig in Florence, Italy, during summer vacation. When Hector unearths a strangely shaped artifact, his dreams become haunted by an Etruscan named Arath, who seems to be in danger. The artifact allows Hector to travel back to Arath's time, where he quickly realizes that the boy is soon to be given up in sacrifice by a callous relative. The fact that Hector is invisible to everyone but Arath helps him rescue his new friend. The "vivid details" about Etruscan life and the work of modern-day archeologists "will capture readers interested in ancient civilizations," wrote *Booklist* contributor Gillian Engberg, and *School Library Journal* contributor Anna M. Nelson claimed that Barrett's "well researched and interesting" setting adds interest to a plot full of "excitement and suspense."

In *The Hundred-Year-Old Secret* Barrett begins her "Sherlock Files" series. When Xena and Xander Holmes move from Florida to England, they learn that they are direct descendants of famous Scotland Yard detective Sherlock Holmes. Curious and adventurous, they decide to tackle the mysteries their great-great-great grandfather left unsolved at his death. Reviewing his casebook, they set about the business of discovering the whereabouts of a painting that has now been missing for several generations. The siblings take a logical, well-thought-out approach, interviewing survivors, tracking down leads, and piecing together facts from the past. The young sleuths' adventures continue in *The Beast of Blackslope,* as they get to the bottom of persistent rumors about a creature said to be haunting the forests around a rural village, and *The Case That Time Forgot.* Describing Xena and Xander as "observant, bright, and gifted with powers of deduction," Kathryn Kosiorek called *The Hundred-Year-Old Secret* "a well-paced beginning to a new series" in her *School Library Journal* review. A *Kirkus Reviews* writer praised the book's "great characters" and "believable mystery," and in *Booklist* Carolyn Phelan dubbed *The Hundred-Year-Old Secret* "a fastpaced, entertaining mystery."

"Perhaps because of my academic background, I am more drawn to nonfiction than to fiction when writing for children," Barrett once explained to *SATA.* "I enjoy researching complicated and sometimes confusing events and organizing them into coherent and exciting narratives." She also shared her thoughts on writing nonfiction for children, noting that authors "must pay scrupulous attention to accuracy and must present a balanced view. Children are interested in the truth and are willing to think about quite 'adult' issues if they are presented in a way accessible to them. This does not mean talking down to children; it means keeping in mind their more limited exposure to ideas and helping them learn how to formulate their own ideas and opinions."

Biographical and Critical Sources

PERIODICALS

Booklist, August, 1993, Janice Del Negro, review of *Nat Turner and the Slave Revolt,* pp. 2051-2052; December 15, 1995, Susan Dove Lempke, review of *Growing up in Colonial America,* p. 700; April 1, 1999, Ilene Cooper, review of *Anna of Byzantium,* p. 1425; April 1, 2003, Carolyn Phelan, review of *Cold in Summer,* p. 1395; June 1, 2005, Gillian Engberg, review of *On Etruscan Time,* p. 1805; May 1, 2008, Carolyn Phelan, review of *The Hundred-Year-Old Secret,* p. 50.

Bulletin of the Center for Children's Books, April, 1993, Betsy Hearne, review of *Nat Turner and the Slave Revolt,* p. 240.

Horn Book, May-June, 2003, Betty Carter, review of *Cold in Summer,* p. 338.

Kirkus Reviews, May 1, 2003, review of *Cold in Summer,* p. 674; June 1, 2004, review of *The Ancient Greek World,* p. 540; April 15, 2005, review of *On Etruscan Time,* p. 468; April 1, 2008, review of *The Hundred-Year-Old Secret.*

Kliatt, May, 2003, Michele Winship, review of *Cold in Summer,* p. 6.

Publishers Weekly, June 28, 1999, review of *Anna of Byzantium,* p. 80; May 5, 2003, review of *Cold in Summer,* p. 221.

School Library Journal, January, 1994, George Gleason, review of *Harpers Ferry: The Story of John Brown's Raid,* p. 118; December, 1995, Elaine Fort Weischedel, review of *Growing up in Colonial America,* p. 112; June, 1997, Denise E. Agosto, review of *Virginia,* p. 130; July, 1999, Shirley Wilton, review of *Anna of Byzantium,* p. 92; July, 2003, Alison Ching, review of *Cold in Summer,* p. 123; August, 2004, Cynthia M. Sturgis, review of *The Ancient Greek World,* p. 142; July, 2005, Anna M. Nelson, review of *On Etruscan Time,* p. 95; June, 2005, Patricia D. Lothrop, review of *The Ancient Chinese World,* p. 179; June, 2008, Kathryn Kosiorek, review of *The Hundred-Year-Old Secret,* p. 134.

ONLINE

Tracy Barrett Web site, http://www.tracybarrett.com (November 5, 2009).

*   *   *

BINGHAM, Kelly 1967-

Personal

Born 1967; married; children: five. *Education:* Vermont College, M.F.A.

Addresses

Home—Ellijay, GA.

Career

Author and illustrator. Worked as a story artist and director for Walt Disney Feature Animation, Burbank, CA, for twelve years.

Member

Society of Children's Book Writers and Illustrators.

Awards, Honors

Best Books for Young Adults citation, American Library Association, for *Shark Girl.*

Writings

Shark Girl, Candlewick Press (Cambridge, MA), 2007.

Sidelights

Kelly Bingham is the author of *Shark Girl,* a critically acclaimed young-adult novel about a teenage artist recovering from a horrifying shark attack. The work "is for anyone who likes stories about uncontrollable, life-changing events, and how a person deals with that," Bingham stated in an interview on the *Class of 2K7* Web site. "It's about losing something you think you can't live without, then discovering . . . maybe you can. It's also about fitting in and not fitting in, the importance (and non-importance) of looking 'normal,' the way kids treat each other in high school, the fallout of a disabling injury in a teen's life as well as that of her family, and the capacity we all have to love and to overcome and move on."

An avid reader, Bingham notes that literature has had a tremendous impact on her life. "The act of reading was something that fed my soul, and I read quite a bit growing up," she remarked in her *Class of 2K7* interview. "I loved the 'Little House' books by Laura Ingalls Wilder, and must have reread each one a hundred times. In short, I was always reading, and good or bad, I would lose myself in the story entirely." A former story artist at Walt Disney Feature Animation, she worked on such popular films as *Hercules* and *The Hunchback of Notre Dame* while pursuing a literary career. "I spent over ten years trying to 'learn' how to write for children," she related to Cynthia Leitich Smith on the *Cynsations* Web site. "I took classes and workshops, had a critique group, and wrote a lot. After a long time, I realized my level of writing had plateaued . . . and it wasn't that good." Bingham later attended Vermont College, earning a master's degree in writing for children and young adults. "I learned more there in the first semester than I had in the previous ten years of self-teaching," she recalled to Smith. "And I began working in earnest on the story I had brought with me to my first workshop . . . the manuscript that would become *Shark Girl.*"

In *Shark Girl* Bingham introduces fifteen-year-old Californian Jane Arrowood, a promising artist who loses her right arm in a near-fatal shark attack. As she recovers, Jane struggles to re-master simple tasks such as opening cans and buttoning her pants. she also mourns the loss of her ability to draw. Bingham tells her protagonist's story through a series of prose poems, newspaper clippings, and letters; according to *School Library Journal* critic Janet S. Thompson, Jane's "voice is authentic and believable as both a teenager and victim."

Shark Girl received strong reviews. "Powerful without being maudlin or preachy, the book explores hurdles that are bound to follow a physical disfigurement," observed a contributor to *Publishers Weekly,* and Frances

Bradburn, writing in *Booklist,* stated that Bingham's novel "offers a strong view of a teenager struggling to survive and learn to live again."

Bingham has a number of writing projects planned for the future. As she told Smith, "I love it when a character begins to take shape in my writing and in my mind, and even begins to 'speak' to me and tell me her own story; what has happened, how she feels, where she's going, what she wants to do. That's very exciting."

Biographical and Critical Sources

PERIODICALS

Booklist, May 1, 2007, Frances Bradburn, review of *Shark Girl,* p. 81.

Horn Book, May-June, 2007, Lauren Adams, review of *Shark Girl,* p. 278.

Kirkus Reviews, April 1, 2007, review of *Shark Girl.*

Kliatt, May, 2007, Claire Rosser, review of *Shark Girl,* p. 6.

Publishers Weekly, April 16, 2007, review of *Shark Girl,* p. 52.

School Library Journal, June, 2007, Janet S. Thompson, review of *Shark Girl,* p. 140.

ONLINE

Class of 2K7 Web site, http://classof2k7.com/ (March 1, 2008), "Kelly Bingham."

Cynsations Web site, http://cynthialeitichsmith.blogspot. com/ (April 25, 2007), Cynthia Leitich Smith, interview with Bingham.

Kelly Bingham Home Page, http://www.kellybingham.net (March 1, 2008).*

*   *   *

BLECK, Linda

Personal

Born in IL; father an architect, mother an artist; married; children: David, Sara. *Education:* University of Illinois, B.A. (graphic design).

Addresses

Home—Mequon, WI. *Agent*—Lori Nowicki, Painted-Words, loripainted-words.com. *E-mail*—linda@linda bleck.com.

Career

Illustrator and author.

Awards, Honors

National Parenting Publication Award, 2006, for *Pepper Goes to School;* Mom's Choice Award, 2009, for *The Moon Shines Down.*

Writings

SELF-ILLUSTRATED; POP-UP BOOKS

Pepper Goes to School, Little Simon (New York, NY), 2006.

Pepper's Snowy Day, Little Simon (New York, NY), 2006.

Pepper's Valentine Surprise, Little Simon (New York, NY), 2007.

Pepper Picks a Pumpkin, Little Simon (New York, NY), 2007.

ILLUSTRATOR

Wendy Pfeffer, *The Shortest Day: Celebrating the Winter Solstice,* Dutton (New York, NY), 2003.

A Children's Treasury of Prayers, Sterling Pub. (New York, NY), 2006.

A Children's Treasury of Songs, Sterling Pub. (New York, NY), 2006.

A Children's Treasury of Nursery Rhymes, Sterling Pub. (New York, NY), 2006.

A Children's Treasury of Lullabies, Sterling Pub. (New York, NY), 2006.

Wendy Pfeffer, *We Gather Together: Celebrating the Harvest Season,* Dutton (New York, NY), 2006.

Margaret Wise Brown, *The Moon Shines Down,* adapted by Laura Minchew, Thomas Nelson (Nashville, TN), 2008.

Wendy Pfeffer, *A New Beginning: Celebrating the Spring Equinox,* Dutton (New York, NY), 2008.

Deb Pilutti, *The City Kid and the Suburb Kid,* Sterling Pub. (New York, NY), 2008.

A Children's Treasury of Mother Goose, Sterling Pub. (New York, NY), 2009.

Contributor to books, including *Wonderful You: Self-Awareness: Accepting and Knowing Myself, Let's Share!: Friendship: Sharing and Taking Turns,* and *My Feelings and Me: Feelings: Experiencing Feelings,* all published by Family Skills (New York, NY), 1985. Contributor to periodicals, including *New Yorker, New York Times, Parenting, Child,* and *Time.*

Sidelights

Linda Bleck was inspired by her parents—her father was an architect and her mother created artwork for greeting cards—with a love of drawing and design. "My mother always stressed how important it was to make your artwork move and have feeling," Bleck explained on her *Pepper the Dog* Web site. The picture-book series that inspired that Web site is based on a novelty-book character Bleck developed while raising her own two children. The first volume in the "Pepper the Dog" series, *Pepper Goes to School,* introduces readers to Bleck's round-nosed, floppy-eared puppy, and the book has earned its author/illustrator a National Parenting Publication award.

In 2007 Bleck was hired to illustrate an unpublished and recently discovered manuscript by Margaret Wise Brown, author of the childhood classic *Goodnight Moon.*

Although she had not sought out the project, an art director at Nashville publisher Thomas Nelson selected Bleck because of the similarity between her style and that of *Goodnight Moon's* illustrator Clement Hurd. Based on a prayer and adapted by Laura Minchew, *The Moon Shines Down* describes how the moon shines its light on children all around the world, its rhyming text carrying children through many lands. "Bleck's paintings are a literal bright spot," asserted a *Publishers Weekly* reviewer, and invoke a "peaceful mood" that lifts the book's "unexceptional verses."

Bleck's illustration work has also been paired with texts by other writers, and her paintings have been a feature of child-centered anthologies such as *A Children's Treasury of Poems* and *A Children's Treasury of Lullabies.* Her brightly colored and "cheerful cartoon illustrations are well matched" to Wendy Pfeffer's text for *A New Beginning: Celebrating the Spring Equinox,* in the opinion of *School Library Journal* contributor Gloria Koster. Marge Loch-Wouters, appraising Bleck's gouache paintings for Deb Pilutti's *The City Kid and the Suburb Kid* in the same periodical, concluded that the artist's "slightly flattened, retro cartoon illustrations . . . perfectly capture" the spirit of Pilutti's story.

Bleck worked for several years as a commercial illustrator and graphic artist before turning her attention to children's publishing. "I didn't just wake up one day and say I think I'll publish a book and then the next day I got a letter saying we like your idea," she explained to *OnMilwaukee* online interviewer Bobby Tanzillo. "I had worked as an editorial illustrator for fifteen years. I illustrated package designs, display posters, zoo signage, and many articles on business, science, health, etc. Making the transition was hard work and sheer determination."

"I enjoyed my previous accomplishments as an editorial illustrator, but [I am now] onto the next phase of this career," Bleck explained in discussing her transition from editorial to book illustration. "It's wonderful to have something that stays on a shelf longer than a month or day. As in any creative field you never know what project and path your career will take. You can guide it, but the winds push it along."

Biographical and Critical Sources

PERIODICALS

Booklist, October 1, 2006, Ilene Cooper, review of *A Children's Treasury of Prayers,* p. 62; December 1, 2007, Krista Hutley, review of *A New Beginning: Celebrating the Spring Equinox,* p. 46.
Kirkus Reviews, January 1, 2008, review of *A New Beginning;* April 15, 2008, review of *The City Kid and the Suburb Kid.*
Publishers Weekly, June 12, 2006, review of *Pepper Goes to School,* p. 54; November 10, 2008, review of *The Moon Shines Down,* p. 49.

School Library Journal, November, 2006, Grace Oliff, review of *We Gather Together: Celebrating the Harvest Season,* p. 122; March, 2008, Gloria Koster, review of *A New Beginning,* p. 187; May, 2008, Marge Loch-Wouters, review of *The City Kid and the Suburb Kid,* p. 106; January, 2009, Sally R. Dow, review of *A Children's Treasury of Poems,* p. 88.

ONLINE

Linda Bleck Home Page, http://www.lindableck.com (November 5, 2009).
Linda Bleck Web log, http://lindableck.blogspot.com (November 5, 2009).
OnMilwaukee Online, http://www.onmilwaukee.com/ (March 8, 2009), Bobby Tanzillo, interview with Bleck.
Pepper the Dog Web site, http://pepperthedog.com (November 5, 2009).*

*   *   *

BUNGE, Daniela 1973-

Personal

Born 1973, in Zweisel, Bavaria, Germany. *Education:* University of Regensburg, B.A. (fine arts); Academy of Applied Arts and Design (Münster, Germany), degree (illustration), 2005.

Addresses

Home—Berlin, Germany.

Career

Author and illustrator of books for children.

Writings

SELF-ILLUSTRATED

Bist du mein Schatz?, Residenz Verlag (Pölten, Austria), 2006.
Schneetreiben, Minedition (Bargteheide, Germany), translated by Kathryn Bishop as *The Scarves,* Minedition (New York, NY), 2006.
Kirschenzeit mit Rubinella, Minedition (Bargteheide, Germany), translated by Kathryn Bishop as *Cherry Time,* Minedition (New York, NY), 2007.

ILLUSTRATOR

Geraldine Elschner, *Frisch und Frech,* Minedition (Bargteheide, Germany), translated by Kathryn Bishop as *Fritz's Fish,* Minedition (New York, NY), 2005.

Sidelights

Daniela Bunge, a German children's book author and illustrator, made what a *Publishers Weekly* contributor characterized as a "remarkable debut" in *Fritz's Fish,* a story written by Géraldine Elschner and featuring Bunge's art. First published in German as *Frisch und Frech, Fritz's Fish* focuses on a city boy who rescues a fish that has been washed from its river home during a flood. Although the boy loves his new pet, Fresh, he soon realizes that the fish is not happy swimming in the boy's bathtub. Fritz learns an important lesson about the meaning of love in a story that features what *Booklist* Shelle Rosenfeld described as "whimsical, . . . naive-style" images that feature "playful perspectives and European cityscapes." Bunge "brings a fresh beauty and grace to a familiar story," stated a *Publishers Weekly* contributor, the critic calling the art in *Fritz's Fish* "reminiscent of old-fashioned fairy tale illustrations."

In addition to her illustration work, Bunge has created original self-illustrated picture books that have been translated into English. Featuring watercolor-and-ink images that feature the author/illustrator's characteristically playful perspectives, *Cherry Time* finds a shy little boy gaining a special new friend after his new pet dog inspires him with self-confidence. The "lovely, highly stylized paintings" in *Cherry Time* balance Bunge's "simple story" of transformation, noted Erika Qualls in a *School Library Journal* review of the book, while a *Kirkus Reviews* writer dubbed *Cherry Time* a "quiet story of reaching out to touch someone."

The Scarves, another self-illustrated story, also focuses on the importance of relationships, but in this case the child at the center of the story is not the lonely one. When a little girl is told that her grandparents have decided to live away from each other, she quickly realizes that the reasons Grandma and Grandpa give to show that they are happier apart are only masks for their new loneliness. The girl's efforts to reunite the couple are brought to life in "angular ink-and-watercolor" images that "artfully convey feelings of emptiness," according to *School Library Journal* critic Linda Ludke. In telling a familiar story, Bunge "evinces a far greater sense of complexity," wrote a *Publishers Weekly* critic, the reviewer adding that the young narrator in *The Scarves* exhibits "powers of observation and insight" that are "utterly authentic."

Biographical and Critical Sources

PERIODICALS

Booklist, January 1, 2006, Shelle Rosenfeld, review of *Fritz's Fish,* p. 111.
Kirkus Reviews, May 15, 2007, review of *Cherry Time.*
Publishers Weekly, December 12, 2005, review of *Fritz's Fish,* p. 65; September 11, 2006, review of *The Scarves,* p. 54.

School Library Journal, January, 2006, Blair Christolon, review of *Fritz's Fish,* p. 96; January, 2007, Linda Ludke, review of *The Scarves,* p. 90; July, 2007, Erika Qualls, review of *Cherry Time,* p. 73.

ONLINE

Residenz Verlag Web site, http://www.residenzverlag.at/ (November 15, 2009), "Daniella Bunge."*

* * *

BURNINGHAM, Robin Yoko
See RACOMA, Robin Yoko

* * *

BUTLER, Dori Hillestad 1965-

Personal

Born August 25, 1965, in Fairmont, MN; daughter of John (a pharmacist) and Donna (a nurse) Hillestad; married Bob Butler (a software engineer); children: Ben, Andy. *Education:* Attended Bemidji State University, 1983-85, University of Minnesota, 1985-86, and Hamline University, 1986-87. *Hobbies and other interests:* Reading, hiking, playing the piano, Scrabble, biking, learning to juggle.

Addresses

Home—Coralville, IA. *E-mail*—dhbutler@kidswriter.com.

Career

Freelance writer. Friends of the Coralville Public Library, teen writing-group facilitator; sponsor of teen Web site *The Leaky Pen;* active with local youth theatre. Reader for Iowa Children's Choice Award and Iowa Teen Award.

Member

Society of Children's Book Writers and Illustrators (Iowa regional advisor, 1998-2000).

Awards, Honors

Bulletin of the Center for Children's Books Best Books designation, 2003, and Sequoyah Children's Book Award nominee, Sunshine State Award nominee, and Volunteer State Book Award nominee, all 2005-06, all for *Trading Places with Tank Talbott;* Pennsylvania School Library Association Young-Adult Top Forty inclusion, 2003, Honor Book designation, Society of School Librarians International, 2004, and Nebraska Golden Sower Award nomination, Young Hoosier Book Award nomination, Mark Twain Award listee, and Penn-

sylvania Young Readers Choice Award nominee, all 2005-06, and Volunteer State Award nominee, 2006-07, all for *Sliding into Home.*

Writings

The Great Tooth Fairy Rip-Off, illustrated by Jack Lindstrom, Fairview Press (Minneapolis, MN), 1997.

M Is for Minnesota, illustrated by Janice Lee Porter, University of Minnesota Press (Minneapolis, MN), 1998.

W Is for Wisconsin, illustrated by Eileen Potts Dawson, Trails Media Group (Madison, WI), 1998.

ABC's of Wisconsin, illustrated by Alison Relyea, Trails Media Group (Madison, WI), 2000.

H Is for Hoosier, illustrated by Eileen Potts Dawson, Trails Media Group (Black Earth, WI), 2001.

Sliding into Home, Peachtree (Atlanta, GA), 2003.

Trading Places with Tank Talbott, Albert Whitman (Morton Grove, IL), 2003.

Whodunnit: How the Police Solve Crimes, Perfection Learning, 2004.

My Mom's Having a Baby!, illustrated by Carol Thompson, Albert Whitman (Morton Grove, IL), 2005.

Do You Know the Monkey Man?, Peachtree (Atlanta, GA), 2005.

Alexandra Hopewell, Labor Coach, Albert Whitman (Morton Grove, IL), 2005.

Tank Talbott's Guide to Girls, Albert Whitman (Morton Grove, IL), 2006.

Zoe's Potty: A Learn-to-Go Book, illustrated by Penny Dann, Running Press (Philadelphia, PA), 2006.

Zack's Potty A Learn-to-Go Book, illustrated by Penny Dann, Running Press (Philadelphia, PA), 2006.

Christmas: Season of Peace and Joy, Capstone Press (Mankato, MN), 2007.

F Is for Firefighting, illustrated by Joan C. Waites, Pelican Publishing (Gretna, LA), 2007.

My Grandpa Had a Stroke, illustrated by Nicole Wong, Magination Press (Washington, DC), 2007.

The Truth about Truman School, Albert Whiman (Morton Grove, IL), 2008.

Yes, I Know the Monkey Man, Peachtree (Atlanta, GA), 2009.

P Is for Police, illustrated by Joan C. Waites, Pelican Publishing (Gretna, LA), 2009.

The Buddy Files: The Case of the Lost Boy, Albert Whitman (Morton Grove, LA), 2010.

The Buddy Files: The Case of the Mixed-up Mutts, illustrated by Jeremy Tugeau, Albert Whitman (Morton Grove, LA), 2010.

Contributor of short fiction to periodicals, including *Child Life, Children's Digest, Cricket, Spider, Highlights for Children, Guidepost for Teens,* and various parenting and Sunday-school publications. Ghostwriter for "Sweet Valley Twins" and "Boxcar Children" novel series; author of scripts for classroom plays published by Benchmark Education; author of reading curricula.

Sidelights

Beginning her authorial career writing picture-book texts such as *ABC's of Wisconsin* and *F Is for Firefighting,* Dori Hillestad Butler also addresses older readers in chapter books and middle-grade novels such as *Trading Places with Tank Talbot, Sliding into Home, Do You Know the Monkey Man?,* as well as in her humorous "Buddy Files" novels. In addition, the author has also ventured into nonfiction with *Whodunit? How the Police Solve Crimes.*

Geared for preteen boys, *Trading Places with Tank Talbott* finds Jason Pfeiffer in a quandary. While busy translating his annoyance over his sister into an amazing horror-film script, Jason's parents drag him away from his desk and into the local recreation center to take swimming lessons. As if the pool's cold water is not bad enough, when Jason sees school bully Tank Talbott there too, things quickly go from bad to worse. Embarrassed by the fact that his parents have forced him into taking dancing lessons, Tank is less threatening than normal, and ultimately the two boys find that they can help each other out of an uncomfortable situation. In *School Library Journal* Sharon R. Pearce praised *Trading Places with Tank Talbott* as "well-written" and "laced with humor and a good sense of adolescent growing pains."

Tank looks forward to a dismal summer in *Tank Talbott's Guide to Girls.* In addition to attending summer school in order to pass fifth grade, the preteen will have to endure a house with no bathroom when his three stepsisters return home during school vacation. When Tank's friend Jason completes a movie script and asks Tank to market it, the almost-sixth-grader has a brainstorm: he will also make money by writing, using the strange behavior of his three teenaged stepsisters as the subject. Calling *Tank Talbott's Guide to Girls* "a satisfying, often humorous read," *Booklist* critic Shelle Rosenfeld predicted that young readers "will like Tank and . . . understand his hope to demystify the opposite sex." Praising Tank as an "irrepressible" character, Quinby Frank added in *School Library Journal* that Butler's "painfully honest portrayal of growing up" in *Tank Talbott's Guide to Girls* is shown "from a believable [preteen] . . . boy's perspective."

Teenage girls feature in several of Butler's novels, including *Sliding into Home, Do You Know the Monkey Man?,* and *Yes, I Know the Monkey Man.* In *Sliding into Home* thirteen-year-old Joelle Cunningham lives and breathes baseball, but when she moves to a new state and a new school she learns that baseball is only for boys; girls are restricted to softball only. Suddenly, Joelle has a crusade on her hands, and she draws on her determination and her love of the game to inspire change. Praising *Sliding into Home,* a *Kirkus Reviews* critic dubbed the novel "breezy and fast-paced, with a feminist slant," while *Booklist* contributor Roger Leslie praised Joelle's "passionate commitment and . . . broadening vision."

Do You Know the Monkey Man? finds thirteen-year-old Samantha haunted by the tragic death of her twin sister, T.J., ten years ago and the disappearance of her father shortly after that tragedy. Now that her mother is getting remarried, Samantha decides that it is time to uncover the truth, but in her search for her father she uncovers a new threat to her family. In a sequel, *Yes, I Know the Monkey Man,* Butler focuses on the other twin, as T.J. comes to terms with her father's deception and attempts to start a relationship with the mother and twin sister she hardly knows. Noting the emotional complexity of Butler's novel, Carol A. Edwards observed that *Do You Know the Monkey Man?* features "a simplicity of narrative voice that makes the story" accessible to its intended middle-grade audience. For *Kliatt* critic Claire Rosser, "the intelligence" of the novel's young narrators are the story's "strength," and *Booklist* contributor Cindy Dobrez predicted that *Do You Know the Monkey Man?* will prompt readers "to think about the concepts of identity and family" that factor into Butler's tale. Equally thought provoking, *Yes, I Know*

the Monkey Man was acknowledged as a strong sequel, Faith Brautigam writing in *School Library Journal* that Butler's "highly readable" novel features "enough action and tension" to appeal to "reluctant readers."

Zebby Bower quits her post as editor of her middle-school newspaper when she detects administration censorship in *The Truth about Truman School.* Instead, she joins with friend Amr to start a Web site where students can read and reveal the truth. Unfortunately, the site is eventually co-opted by an anonymous contributor who uses the student-monitored forum to verbally attack a popular girl named Lilly, and when Lilly becomes upset and then goes missing Zebby feels responsible. *The Truth about Truman School* "moves at a good pace," according to Bethany A. Lafferty, the *School Library Journal* contributor adding that Butler's decision to address cyber-bullying makes the novel "relevant to readers." In *Kirkus Reviews* another critic had a similar assessment, noting that with its focus on "bullying, cliques, and peer pressure," *The Truth about Truman School* provides "an exercise in ethics and morality."

Cover of Butler's picture book My Mom's Having a Baby!, *featuring artwork by Carol Thompson.* (Albert Whitman & Company, 2005. Illustrations copyright © 2005 by Carol Thompson. Reproduced by permission.)

Butler once told *SATA:* "I've always wanted to be a writer. It was my childhood dream. When I finished college, I considered going to graduate school to study child psychology, but my husband told me I should try writing. He said graduate school would still be there in a year or two, but if I didn't give my writing a chance, I'd always wonder whether I could've done it. He was right. So I took a year to concentrate on being a writer. I sold two short stories to magazines in that year and took that as a sign that I should keep at it. I've never looked back.

"I write for two reasons. One: To connect with other people; and Two: To get kids interested in reading. Sometimes people ask me if I'm ever going to write anything for adults—as though somehow writing for adults is more important or more serious than writing for kids. I have written a few parenting articles for adults, but for the most part I prefer writing for kids. There is no more important audience. If I can grab them while they're young and turn them into readers, someone else can keep them reading as adults.

"Though I live the first thirty years of my life in Minnesota, I had to move to Iowa in order to write *M Is for Minnesota.* Shortly after I moved here, I met an author who'd written a book called *I Is for Iowa.* She said she was a native Iowan and wasn't interested in writing an ABC book on Minnesota. I wrote *Alexandra Hopewell, Labor Coach* because when I was pregnant with my second child, my four year old really wanted to come to the hospital with us to see the baby be born.

"Judy Blume and Paula Danzinger are the writers who most influenced my work. They were my favorite authors when I was growing up. I trusted them to tell me the truth about everything I wanted to know, but was afraid to ask.

"My advice to aspiring writers: Read and write every day!"

Biographical and Critical Sources

PERIODICALS

Booklist, January 1, 1999, Kathleen Squires, review of *M Is for Minnesota,* p. 862; May 1, 2003, Roger Leslie, review of *Sliding into Home,* p. 1591; April 1, 2005, Stephanie Zvirin, review of *My Mom's Having a Baby!,* p. 1358; April 15, 2005, Jennifer Locke, review of *Alexandra Hopewell, Labor Coach,* p. 1456; May 1, 2005, Cindy Dobrez, review of *Do You Know the Monkey Man?,* p. 1542; April 15, 2006, Shelle Rosenfeld, review of *Tank Talbott's Guide to Girls,* p. 47; July 1, 2007, Ilene Cooper, review of *My Grandpa Had a Stroke,* p. 63; March 15, 2008, Suzanne Harold, review of *The Truth about Truman School,* p. 54.

Kirkus Reviews, May 15, 2003, review of *Sliding into Home,* p. 747; March 1, 2005, review of *My Mom's Having a Baby!,* p. 284; February 15, 2007, review of *F Is for Firefighting;* April 1, 2008, review of *The Truth about Truman School.*

Cover of Butler's middle-grade novel **The Truth about Truman School,** *in which two young journalists learn that freedom of speech sometimes has unpleasant consequences.* (Albert Whitman & Company, 2008. Cover photography © Getty Images. Reproduced by permission.)

Kliatt, July, 2005, Claire Rosser, review of *Do You Know the Monkey Man?,* p. 152.

School Library Journal, March, 1999, Kathy Piehl, review of *M Is for Minnesota,* p. 190; June, 2003, Sharon R. Pearce, review of *Trading Places with Tank Talbott,* p. 137; May, 2005, Martha Topol, review of *My Mom's Having a Baby!,* p. 106, and Caitlin Augusta, review of *Alexandra Hopewell, Labor Coach,* p. 125; May, 2006, Quinby Frank, review of *Tank Talbott's Guide to Girls,* p. 120; June, 2007, Gloria Koster, review of *F Is for Firefighting,* p. 92; July, 2007, Maryann H. Owen, review of *My Grandpa Had a Stroke,* p. 88; May, 2008, Bethany A. Lafferty, review of *The Truth about Truman School,* p. 120; July, 2009, Faith Brautigam, review of *Yes, I Know the Monkey Man,* p. 80.

Voice of Youth Advocates, February, 2006, Francesca Goldsmith, review of *Do You Know the Monkey Man?,* p. 482.

ONLINE

Dori Hillestad Butler Home Page, http://www.dorihillestad butler.com (November 5, 2009).*

C

CAMPBELL, Sarah C. 1966-

Personal
Born 1966, in IL; married Richard P. Campbell (an executive); children: three sons. *Education:* Northwestern University, bachelor's degree (journalism), M.A. (journalism); attended Oxford University.

Addresses
Home—Jackson, MS.

Career
Writer and photographer. Milsaps College, Jackson, MS, instructor in journalism. Artist-in-residence at Davis Magnet IB World School, Jackson; teacher at camps and workshops.

Awards, Honors
Theodor Seuss Geisel Honor Book designation, and Cooperative Children's Book Center Choices listee, both 2009, both for *Wolfsnail.*

Writings

(And photographer with husband, Richard P. Campbell)
  Wolfsnail: A Backyard Predator, Boyds Mills Press (Honesdale, PA), 2008.
Growing Patterns: Fibonacci Numbers in Nature, 2010.

Contributor to periodicals, including *New York Times, Highlights for Children,* and *Highlights' High Five.*

Sidelights
Sarah C. Campbell is a teacher and photographer whose background in journalism and interest in science and nature have inspired her work as a children's book author. Her first book-length work, *Wolfsnail: A Backyard Predator,* earned a Theodor Seuss Geisel Honor-Book designation.

Although she was born in Illinois, Campbell grew up in rural Mississippi, and she learned the skill of photography while covering high-school sports for her local newspaper. Attending Northwestern University, she earned a master's degree in journalism and went on to teach that subject on the college level. Campbell started writing stories for young people when her youngest son was a toddler, and she published *Wolfsnail* in 2008.

Wolfsnail came about after Campbell noticed that an interesting creature had made its home in her backyard.

Sarah C. Campbell joins husband and photographer Richard P. Campbell to create the nonfiction picture book Wolfsnail: A Backyard Predator. (Photographs copyright © 2008 by Sarah C. Campbell and Richard P. Campbell. All rights reserved. Reproduced by permission of Boyds Mills Press.)

Although it lives among succulent green leaves, the wolfsnail is actually a carnivore that hunts smaller insects, such as herbivore snails and the much-maligned garden slug. In her book, Campbell pairs the colorful close-up photographs taken with her husband, Richard P. Campbell, with her factual text and an appendix full of detailed information on the unusual creature. According to *Horn Book* contributor Danielle J. Ford, *Wolfsnail* demonstrates the "deliberate and single-minded focus on food" that characterizes all living creatures in the natural world, while in *Booklist* Hazel Rochman described the book as "a survival story that will help youngsters . . . understand the role of predators in the natural cycle." A *Kirkus Reviews* critic predicted that Campbell's book will inspire budding naturalists "to explore their own backyards for similarly wondrous creatures."

Biographical and Critical Sources

PERIODICALS

Booklist, April 1, 2008, Hazel Rochman, review of *Wolfsnail: A Backyard Predator,* p. 53.
Horn Book, July-August, 2008, review of *Wolfsnail,* p. 463.
Kirkus Reviews, April 1, 2008, review of *Wolfsnail.*
School Library Journal, May, 2008, Patricia Manning, review of *Wolfsnail,* p. 112.
Science News, April 5, 2008, review of *Wolfsnail,* p. 223.

ONLINE

Sarah C. Campbell Home Page, http://www.sarahccampbell.com (November 5, 2009).*

*   *   *

CHAN, Peter 1980(?)-

Personal

Born c. 1980. *Education:* Rhode Island Center for the Arts, B.F.A (furniture design), 2004; Art Center College of Design, (industrial design), 2007; also attended Interlochen Center for the Arts. *Hobbies and other interests:* Basketball, golf, movies, pool.

Addresses

Home—Los Angeles, CA. *E-mail*—nahcretep@hotmail.com.

Career

Illustrator and concept designer. Concept artist at Design Studio Press, 2006, and Pandemic Studios; Sony Pictures Animation, visual development, 2009—.

Illustrator

(With Courtney Booker) Henry Selick, *Moongirl* (based on an animated film), Candlewick Press (Boston, MA), 2006, published as *Moongirl: The Collector's Edition* (with DVD), 2006.
Paul Feig, *Ignatius MacFarland: Frequenaut!,* Little, Brown (New York, NY), 2008.

Sidelights

A concept designer working in the film industry, Peter Chan has designed and storyboarded several Hollywood films, including two that are based on popular children's books: Lemony Snicket's *A Series of Unfortunate Events* and J.K Rowling's *Harry Potter and the Philosopher's Stone.* Chan's work in film has also inspired his book-illustration projects. The book *Moongirl,* which is based on an animated film directed by Henry Selick, features artwork by Chan and fellow artist/animator Courtney Booker. The second book con-

Peter Chan's graphic-style illustrations are featured in Paul Feig's middle-grade novel **Ignatius MacFarland, Infrequenaut!** (Little, Brown and Company, 2008. Copyright © 2008. By permission of Little, Brown and Company. All rights reserved.)

taining Chan's illustrations, the middle-grade novel *Ignatius MacFarland: Frequenaut!,* also has its roots in the film industry: its author, Paul Feig, is the creator of the television program *Freeks and Geeks.*

In *Moongirl* a boy named Leon is fishing one night with his pet squirrel when suddenly the light of the moon is extinguished. Casting his line as far as he can in the dark, Leon is hooked to a fish that drags both boy and squirrel up to the moon. There he meets Moongirl, who lives with a white cat. By helping Moongirl defeat the gargaloon, a creature that has stolen the moon's light, Leon earns a spot on the moon as Moonboy. Calling *Moongirl* a "whimsical tale," *Booklist* contributor Janice Del Negro added that Chan and Booker's dusky-toned images possess "a flowing romanticism" that "will hold [the attention of] youngsters." The artists' "cartoon illustrations carry the exciting plot," wrote *School Library Journal* contributor Julie Roach, the critic adding that the oversized pictures in *Moongirl* add "energy and a fantastical mood" to Selick's text.

Biographical and Critical Sources

PERIODICALS

Booklist, November 1, 2006, Janice Del Negro, review of *Moongirl,* p. 62; October 15, 2008, Ian Chipman, review of *Ignatius MacFarland: Frequenaut!,* p. 39.

Kirkus Reviews, October 1, 2006, review of *Moongirl,* p. 1024.

School Library Journal, December, 2006, Julie Roach, review of *Moongirl,* p. 116; December, 2008, Necia Blundy, review of *Ignatius MacFarland,* p. 122.

ONLINE

Peter Chan Home Page, http://www.drawpeterdraw.com (November 5, 2009).

Peter Chan Web log, http://drawpeterdraw.blogspot.com (November 5, 2009).*

*   *   *

CHESWORTH, Michael 1961-

Personal

Born 1961. *Education:* Parsons School of Design, B.F.A. (illustration).

Addresses

Office—10 Morrow La., Amherst, MA 01002. *E-mail*—mc@crashbangboom.com.

Career

Author and illustrator.

Writings

SELF-ILLUSTRATED

Rainy Day Dream, Farrar, Straus & Giroux (New York, NY), 1992.

Archibald Frisby, Farrar, Straus & Giroux (New York, NY), 1994.

Monsters on the Loose, WhistleStop Press (Mahwah, NJ), 1996.

Alphaboat, Farrar, Straus & Giroux (New York, NY), 2002.

ILLUSTRATOR

Dwight L. Holden, *Gran-gran's Best Trick,* Magination Press (New York, NY), 1989.

Roberta Chaplan, *Tell Me a Story, Paint Me the Sun: When a Girl Feels Ignored by Her Father,* Magination Press (New York, NY), 1991.

Saxby Pridemore, *Julia, Mungo, and the Earthquake: A Story for Young People about Epilepsy,* Magination Press (New York, NY), 1991.

Patricia O. Quinn, *Putting on the Brakes: Young People's Guide to Understanding Attention Deficit Hyperactivity Disorder (ADHD),* Magination Press (New York, NY), 1991.

William Harry Harding, *Alvin's Famous No-Horse,* Henry Holt (New York, NY), 1992.

Joyce C. Mills, *Little Tree: A Story for Children with Serious Medical Problems,* Magination Press (New York, NY), 1992.

Dian Curtis Regan, *The Curse of the Trouble Dolls,* Henry Holt (New York, NY), 1992.

Burton Marks, *Duck's Truck,* Reader's Digest Association (Pleasantville, NY), 1993.

Burton Marks, *Pig's Car,* Reader's Digest Association (Pleasantville, NY), 1993.

Joyce C. Mills, *Gentle Willow: A Story for Children about Dying,* Magination Press (New York, NY), 1993.

Susan Beth Pfeffer, *The Riddle Streak,* Henry Holt (New York, NY), 1993.

Jonathan H. Weiss, *Breath Easy: Young People's Guide to Asthma,* Magination Press (New York, NY), 1994.

Steve Charney, *Six Thick Thumbs: A Tongue-twisting Tale,* Troll Associates (Mahwah, NJ), 1994.

Justine Korman, *The Monster in Room 202,* Troll Associates (Mahwah, NJ), 1994.

Steven Kroll, *Doctor on an Elephant,* Henry Holt (New York, NY), 1994.

John M. Lexau, *Trouble Will Find You,* Houghton Mifflin (Boston, MA), 1994.

Joyce C. Mills, *Gentle Willow: A Story for Children about Dying,* Gareth Stevens (Milwaukee, WI), 1994.

B.G. Hennessy, *Olympics!,* Viking (New York, NY), 1996.

Astrid Lindgren, *Pippi Longstocking's After-Christmas Party,* Viking (New York, NY), 1996.

W. Carter Merbreier, *Television: What's behind What You See,* Farrar, Straus & Giroux (New York, NY), 1996.

Louis Phillips, *Keep 'em Laughing: Jokes to Amuse and Annoy Your Friends,* Viking (New York, NY), 1996.

Judith M. Stern, *Many Ways to Learn: Young People's Guide to Learning Disabilities,* Magination Press (New York, NY), 1996.

Astrid Lindgren, *The Adventures of Pippi Longstocking,* Viking (New York, NY), 1997.

Bonnie S. Mark-Goldstein, *I'll Know What to Do: A Kid's Guide to Natural Disasters,* Magination Press (Washington, DC), 1997.

Bill Martin, *Swish!,* Henry Holt (New York, NY), 1997.

Mordecai Richler, *Jacob Two-Two's First Spy Case,* Farrar, Straus & Giroux (New York, NY), 1997.

Astrid Lindgren, *Pippi Goes to School,* Viking (New York, NY), 1998.

Sara Swan Miller, *Better than TV,* Bantam Doubleday Dell (New York, NY), 1998.

Maggie Lewis, *Morgy Makes His Move,* Houghton Mifflin (Boston, MA), 1999.

Astrid Lindgren, *Pippi Goes to the Circus,* Viking (New York, NY), 1999.

Astrid Lindgren, *Pippi's Extraordinary Ordinary Day,* Viking (New York, NY), 1999.

Nancy Matson, *The Boy Trap,* Front Street/Cricket Books (Chicago, IL), 1999.

Mary Quattlebaum, *Aunt CeeCee, Aunt Belle, and Mama's Surprise,* Doubleday Book for Young Readers (New York, NY), 1999.

Astrid Lindgren, *Pippi to the Rescue,* Viking (New York, NY), 2000.

Pat McKissack, *Miami Gets It Straight,* Golden Books (New York, NY), 2000.

Peggy Wethered, *Touchdwon Mars!: An ABC Adventure,* Putnam (New York, NY), 2000.

Bill Martin, *Little Granny Quarterback,* Boyds Mills Press (Honesdale, PA), 2001.

Pat McKissack, *Miami Makes the Play,* Golden Books (New York, NY), 2001.

Pat McKissack, *Miami Sees It Through,* Golden Books (New York, NY), 2002.

Laurence P. Pringle, *Come to the Ocean's Edge: A Nature Cycle Book,* Boyds Mills Press (Honesdale, PA), 2003.

Jonathan H. Weiss, *Breathe Easy: Young People's Guide to Asthma,* Magination Press (Washington, DC), 2003.

Patricia Newman, *Jingle the Brass,* Farrar, Straus & Giroux (New York, NY), 2004.

Teresa Bateman, *Fluffy, Scourge of the Sea,* Charlesbridge (Watertown, MA), 2005.

Maggie Lewis, *Morgy Coast to Coast,* Houghton Mifflin (Boston, MA), 2005.

Harold P. Gershenson, *America the Musical 1776-1899: A Nation's History through Music,* Kindermusik International (Greensboro, NC), 2005.

Kathleen T. Pelley, *Inventor McGregor,* Farrar, Straus & Giroux (New York, NY), 2006.

Nancy Edwards, *Mom for Mayor,* Cricket Books (Chicago, IL), 2006.

Harold P. Gershenson, *America the Musical 1900-2000: A Nation's History through Music,* Kindermusik International (Greensboro, NC), 2007.

Ellen Dee Davidson, *Princess Justina Albertina: A Cautionary Tale,* Charlesbridge (Watertown, MA), 2007.

Maggie Lewis, *Morgy's Musical Summer,* Houghton Mifflin (Boston, MA), 2008.

Michael Chesworth contributes his cartoon art to numerous books, among them Jacob Two-Two's First Spy Case *by Mordecai Richler.* (Frances Foster Books, 1997. Copyright © 1995 by Mordecai Richler. Illustrations copyright © 1997 by Michael Chesworth. All rights reserved. Reproduced by permission of Frances Foster Books, a division of Farrar, Straus and Giroux, LLC.)

Heather Lynn Miller, *This Is Your Life Cycle,* Clarion Books (New York, NY), 2008.

Linda Ashman, *Creaky Old House,* Sterling (New York, NY), 2009.

M.D. Usher, *Diogenes,* Farrar, Straus & Giroux (New York, NY), 2009.

Sidelights

Children's author and illustrator Michael Chesworth has animated the pages of numerous books, among them stories by Bill Martin, Astrid Lindgren, and Pat McKissack, just to name a few. While titles such as *Jingle the Brass, Fluffy, Scourge of the Sea,* and *Inventor McGregor* feature Chesworth's engaging artwork, books *Rainy Day Dream* and *Alphaboat* also include the illustrator's original text. Writing in *California Kids,* Patricia Newman praised Chesworth's "unique cartoon-style illustrations," which portray "his characters' full range of emotion and movement in a light-hearted way with instant kid-appeal."

Full of word play, *Alphaboat* engages readers in both a playful and educational tale that follows Mellow D's quest to find a hidden treasure chest on the I-land with

the help of all the letters of the alphabet, both upper and lower case. Each letter is personified in a colorful illustration that distinguishes its unique characteristics. In addition, Chesworth utilizes a rhyme scheme to keep kids entertained and the story enjoyable. "The light-hearted play will make you giggle as you read this tale to your children," commented *Childhood Education* reviewer Lisa Bilansky. A *Publishers Weekly* contributor also enjoyed the work, dubbing *Alphaboat* "witty" and noting that Chesworth's "brain-teasing voyage . . . should tickle the newly literate and old salts as well."

Chesworth has also contributed illustrations to dozens of books by other authors. In Newman's *Jingle the Brass,* a veteran engineer takes a youngster for a ride aboard a steam-powered freight train. According to *Horn Book* critic Peter D. Sieruta, Chesworth's watercolor pictures for this book "have an inviting, kid-friendly

quality—especially in the action sequences." *Fluffy, Scourge of the Sea,* a work by Teresa Bateman, concerns an elegant poodle that battles a scurvy band of canine pirates to regain control of his yacht. "The bouncing rhyming text is perfectly matched by [Chesworth's] . . . watercolor art," Marge Loch-Wouters commented in *School Library Journal,* and Carolyn Phelan, writing in *Booklist,* praised the artist for contributing "well-composed, energetic, entertaining scenes that meld the drama with plenty of comedy."

Chesworth teams up with Maggie Lewis on a series of chapter books about a youngster dealing with the ups-and-downs of daily life. In *Morgy Makes His Move* Lewis introduces her protagonist, young Morgy MacDougal-MacDuff, as he moves with his family from California to a small New England town. According to *Booklist* reviewer GraceAnne A. DeCandido, "Ches-

Twenty-six letters gain a nautical flair in Chesworth's self-illustrated **Alphaboat.** (Farrar, Straus and Giroux, 2002. Copyright © 2002 by Michael Chesworth. Reproduced by permission of Farrar, Straus and Giroux, a division of Farrar, Straus and Giroux, LLC.)

worth's illustrations are funny and exaggerated." A sequel, *Morgy Coast to Coast,* continues the misadventures of the misplaced grade-schooler, who cares for an anxious greyhound and tries his hand at hockey, among other things. The pictures "add some much-needed focus," wrote Carol L. MacKay in *School Library Journal.* Morgy heads to camp to develop his budding trumpeting skills in *Morgy's Musical Summer.* "Chesworth's action-packed black-and-white illustrations complement the breezy text," remarked a *Kirkus Reviews* contributor.

Inventor McGregor, a picture book by Kathleen T. Pelley, centers on a clever fellow whose love of creating new contraptions turns sour when he takes a job in a dreary laboratory. Grace Oliff, writing in *School Library Journal,* remarked that "Chesworth's exuberant cartoons capture Hector's joyful family life as well as his forlorn isolation." A youngster tries to save his favorite local park in *Mom for Mayor,* a chapter book by Nancy Edwards. Phelan noted that "Chesworth's full-page, black-and-white illustrations depict the characters with expression as well as humor."

In Ellen Dee Davidson's *Princess Justina Albertina: A Cautionary Tale,* another story featuring art by Chesworth, a sassy young royal meets her match when her nanny brings home a ferocious pet. Here "humorous details pack the cartoon illustrations, which are done with a mix of watercolor, colored pencil, and gouache," Suzanne Myers Harold wrote in *School Library Journal.* A dragonfly nymph finds itself in the spotlight in Heather Lynn Miller's *This Is Your Life Cycle,* a picture book that spoofs a classic 1950s television show. A critic in *Kirkus Reviews* praised this story, citing "Chesworth's comical cartoon pictures and Miller's riotous take on nature in action."

Biographical and Critical Sources

PERIODICALS

Booklist, April 1, 1994, Hazel Rochman, review of *Archibald Frisby,* p. 1458; April 1, 1994, Carolyn Phelan, review of *Trouble Will Find You,* p. 1448; November 15, 1994, Carolyn Phelan, review of *Doctor on an Elephant,* p. 607; October 15, 1999, Kay Weisman, review of *Pippi's Extraordinary Ordinary Day,* p. 446; December 15, 1999, GraceAnne A. DeCandido, review of *Morgy Makes His Move,* p. 784; October 1, 2000, Lauren Peterson, review of *Pippi to the Rescue,* p. 340; October 15, 2002, Julie Cummins, review of *Alphaboat,* p. 410; January 1, 2005, Carolyn Phelan, review of *Fluffy: The Scourge of the Sea,* p. 867; June 1, 2005, Carolyn Phelan, review of *Morgy Coast to Coast,* p. 1811; February 15, 2006, Hazel Rochman, review of *Inventor McGregor,* p. 104; March 15, 2006, Carolyn Phelan, review of *Mom for Mayor,* p. 49.

Chesworth's cartoon illustrations capture the foibles of childhood retold in Susan Beth Pfeffer's story **The Riddle Streak.** (Henry Holt 1995. Text copyright © 2008 by Susan Beth Pfeffer. Illustrations copyright © 1993 by Michael Chesworth. All rights reserved. Reprinted by permission of Henry Holt and Company, LLC.)

California Kids, July, 2007, Patricia Newman, "Who Wrote That?: Featuring Michael Chesworth."

Childhood Education, spring, 2003, Lisa Bilansky, review of *Alphaboat,* p. 178.

Children's Playmate, July-August, 1995, Christine De la Croix, review of *Archibald Frisby,* p. 31.

Horn Book, September-October, 2004, Peter D. Sieruta, review of *Jingle the Brass,* p. 573.

Kirkus Reviews, August 1, 2002, review of *Alphaboat,* p. 1124; August 1, 2004, review of *Jingle the Brass,* p. 746; April 1, 2006, review of *Inventor McGregor,* p. 354; April 1, 2008, review of *Morgy's Musical Summer;* June 1, 2008, review of *This Is Your Life Cycle.*

Publishers Weekly, November 9, 1992, review of *Rainy Day Dream,* p. 82; April 4, 1994, review of *Archibald Frisby,* p. 78; July 21, 1997, review of *Swish!,* p. 200; August 12, 2002, review of *Alphaboat,* p. 299.

School Library Journal, October, 2000, Carolyn Stacey, review of *Touchdown Mars!: An ABC Adventure,* p. 154; September, 2002, Marge Loch-Wouters, review of *Alphaboat,* p. 182; June, 2004, Steven Engelfried, review of *Alphaboat,* p. 56; March, 2005, Marge Loch-Wouters, review of *Fluffy,* p. 166; May, 2005, Carol L. MacKay, review of *Morgy Coast to Coast,* p. 88; March, 2006, Debbie Whitbeck, review of *Mom for Mayor,* p. 186; April, 2006, Grace Oliff, review of *Inventor McGregor,* p. 115; March, 2007, Suzanne Myers Harold, review of *Princess Justina Albertina: A Cautionary Tale,* p. 157; May, 2008, Sharon R. Pearce, review of *Morgy's Musical Summer,* p. 102.

ONLINE

Michael Chesworth Home Page, http://www.crashbang boom.com (November 1, 2009).

*   *   *

COOK, Sally

Personal

Born in Bryn Mawr, PA; married, husband's name, Bob; children: Liz, Alex. *Education:* Graduated from college.

Addresses

Home—New York, NY. *E-mail*—swcook@rcn.com.

Career

Author. Previously worked as a reporter for the Associated Press.

Member

Authors Guild.

Awards, Honors

Oppenheim Toy Portfolio Gold Seal Award, 2007, for *Hey Batta Batta, Swing!: The Wild Old Days of Baseball.*

Writings

(With Gene Stallings) *Another Season: A Coach's Story of Raising an Exceptional Son,* Little, Brown (Boston, MA), 1997.
Good Night Pillow Fight, illustrated by Laura Cornell, Joanna Cotler Books (New York, NY) 2004.
(With James Charlton) *Hey Batta Batta, Swing!: The Wild Old Days of Baseball,* illustrated by Ross MacDonald, Margaret K. McElderry Books (New York, NY) 2007.

Also author of reviews and articles for the *New York Times, Family Circle, Family Life, McCall's, Stagebill,* and *Parenting.*

Sidelights

Sally Cook has written books for children that span a wide range of topics, from the memoir of a father with a special-needs child to a history of baseball. Cook has been inspired to write stories since she was very young. On her home page, she talked about the beginning of this desire: "One day I revealed my secret ambition to be a children's book writer to Mrs. Smith, my second grade teacher. She said, 'How would you like to write creative stories during cursive writing period?' I never looked back and miraculously my handwriting didn't suffer too much either!"

The variety of her book themes may be due to the fact that Cook was once a reporter, and she has interviewed many people. The life stories that stuck in her mind the most, however, were from children's book illustrators. On her home page, she noted: "These artists inspired me and I couldn't wait to start writing for children."

It was another interview, however, that paved the way for her to write her very first book for children. Gene Stallings, former coach of the football team at the University of Alabama, told her the story of his son, Johnny, who was born with Down's syndrome in 1962. At that time, the prognosis for these children was not good, and doctors generally advised parents to put them into institutions. In addition, Johnny had a heart problem. The Stallings family refused to give up on their son, however, and raised him at home. Along the way, they became advocates for parents dealing with Down's syndrome and launched a successful campaign to improve an educational center for these children.

Cook was so touched by the Stallings' story that she teamed with Gene Stallings to write *Another Season: A Coach's Story of Raising an Exceptional Son.* She recalled in a *Redbook* interview with Kathleen Jacobs that her motivation for this book was more than just a professional one. "I think that as a writer you have a lot of power to change things," Cook explained. "I want to make it easier for families with disabled children." Because of her personal experience dealing with special-needs children, Cook understands that it may be a great challenge for the family. However, as she told Jacobs, "Sometimes what seems like the worst thing in your life can actually turn out to be the best."

A *Publishers Weekly* reviewer wrote that *Another Season* provides a balanced portrayal of the family's challenge, stating that the work "has many moving moments that should give heart to others raising a child with Down's syndrome." Steve Gietschier, writing in the *Sporting News,* praised the book for its sensitive look at the family's courage and dedication to their son. "This blessed book is an inspiration," Gietschier observed.

In *Good Night Pillow Fight* Cook tells a humorous children's story about parents trying to get their children to sleep. Gillian Engberg commented in *Booklist* that this work is a "sly, exuberant view of a fundamental struggle that parents and children everywhere know." Shelley B. Sutherland, writing in the *School Library Journal,* remarked that *Good Night Pillow Fight* "is a book that children and parents will want to enjoy together again and again."

In *Hey Batta Batta, Swing!: The Wild Old Days of Baseball,* coauthored with James Charlton, Cook provides a detailed look at the history of baseball. Geared toward young adults, the book combines facts about the sport, including information about its rules, equipment, and scandals. Cook also explains the history of certain

phrases that have become baseball tradition, such as the term 'frozen rope,' used to describe a line drive. Although a *Kirkus Reviews* critic indicated that "it will take a die-hard baseball aficionado to appreciate this effort," other reviewers gave *Hey Batta Batta, Swing!* a more positive assessment, Marilyn Taniguchi stating in *School Library Journal* that Cook's "text is highly readable." A *Publishers Weekly* reviewer predicted that "baseball buffs will find this a diverting—and occasionally wild—outing," and Vicky Smith concluded in *Horn Book* that "baseball's days of yore receive a sunny treatment in this beguiling tribute to the national pastime."

Biographical and Critical Sources

PERIODICALS

Booklist, April 15, 2004, Gillian Engberg, review of *Good Night Pillow Fight,* p. 1440; January 1, 2007, Grace Anne A. DeCandido, review of *Hey Batta Batta, Swing!: The Wild Old Days of Baseball,* p. 84.
Horn Book, March-April, 2007, Vicky Smith, review of *Hey Batta Batta, Swing!,* p. 213.
Kirkus Reviews, April 15, 2004, review of *Good Night Pillow Fight,* p. 392; January 15, 2007, review of *Hey Batta Batta, Swing!,* p. 71.
Publishers Weekly, July 21, 1997, review of *Another Season: A Coach's Story of Raising an Exceptional Son,* p. 195; April 26, 2004, review of *Good Night Pillow Fight,* p. 64; January 8, 2007, review of *Hey Batta Batta, Swing!,* p. 50.
Redbook, June, 1998, Kathleen Jacobs, "What I Learned from a Less-than-Perfect Child," p. G4.
San Francisco Chronicle, March 25, 2007, Regan McMahon, "Get in the Swing—It's Baseball Season," p. M3.
School Library Journal, July, 2004, Shelley B. Sutherland, review of *Good Night Pillow Fight,,* p. 68; March, 2007, Marilyn Taniguchi, review of *Hey Batta Batta, Swing!,* p. 225.
Sporting News, October 27, 1997, Steve Gietschier, review of *Another Season,* p. 7.

ONLINE

HarperCollins Web site, http://www.harpercollinschildrens.com/ (February 1, 2008), "Sally Cook."
Pippin Properties Web site, http://www.pippinproperties.com/ (February 1, 2008), "Sally Cook."
Sally Cook Home Page, http://members.authorsguild.net/sallycook (January 10, 2010).*

*   *   *

CUMPIANO, Ina

Personal

Born in PR; married; children. *Education:* University of Northern Colorado, degree; Johns Hopkins University,

M.A.; University of California, Santa Cruz, Ph.D., 1996; attended University of Iowa Writers Workshop.

Addresses

Home—San Francisco, CA. *Office*—Children's Book Press, 965 Mission St., Ste. 425, San Francisco, CA 94103.

Career

Poet, translator, and editor. Curriculum designer, beginning 1996; Children's Book Press, San Francisco, CA, editorial director, 2001—.

Awards, Honors

Jaime Suárez/Editores Salvadoreños Poetry Award; *New Millennium Review* Poetry Competition award, 1999; second place, El Andar Prize for Literary Excellence.

Writings

Quinito's Neighborhood/El vecindario de Quinito, illustrated by José Ramirez, Children's Book Press (San Francisco, CA), 2005.
Quinito, Day and Night/Quinito, día y noche, illustrated by José Ramirez, Children's Book Press (San Francisco, CA), 2008.

Ina Cumpiano teams with artist Jose Ramirez to create the bilingual picture book Quinito's Neighborhood/El vecindario de Quinito. (Children's Book Press, 2005. Illustrations copyright © 2005 by Jose Ramirez. Reproduced by permission of Children's Book Press.)

Also author of educational books, including *Weather Watch, What a Week!,* and *Homes Are for Living.* Contributor to periodicals, including *Iowa, Black Warrior, Seneca, Five Fingers,* and *Americas Reviews.*

Sidelights

Born in Puerto Rico, poet and translator Ina Cumpiano is also the editorial director of Children's Book Press, a nonprofit publisher that specializes in culturally enriching, bilingual books for children. As director, she helps the award-winning publisher to acquire and publish literature geared toward the many ethnic cultures that make up the diverse United States: African American, Asian American, Hispanic, and Native American.

As an author, Cumpiano draws from her own Latina culture in her stories featuring an engaging young boy. Readers meet young Quinito in *Quinito's Neighborhood/El vecindario de Quinito* and *Quinito, Day and Night/Quinito, día y noche,* both of which feature a bilingual Spanish/English text enlivened by José Ramirez' colorful art. In *Quinito's Neighborhood/El vecindario de Quinito* Quinito introduces readers to his lively community, beginning with his family—his mother is a carpenter, his father is a nurse—and extending outward to include teachers, shop owners, and the other people he interacts with every day. As a *Kirkus Reviews* writer noted, Cumpiano is careful to avoid "subscrib[ing] . . . to traditional gender roles" in her story, while *School Arts* contributor Rebecca Martin praised the "luscious" folkstyle paintings by educator and artist Ramirez. Reviewing *Quinito's Neighborhood/El vecindario de Quinito* in *School Library Journal,* Ann Welton cited the book's "child appeal, lovely message, and potential inspiration" to young children eager to feel a sense of acceptance.

Cumpiano combines a multicultural story with a simple concept—identifying opposites—in *Quinito, Day and Night/Quinito, día y noche.* Again teaming with Ramirez, she uses the activities within Quinito's busy home to show youngsters that opposites are all around them. Older siblings move fast, while babies move slow; Papi keeps his room tidy, while Quinito's brother Juan lives in typical kid-style disorder. The story is brought to life in heavily outlined art that *School Library Journal* critic Madeline Walton-Hadlock characterized as "expressionistic . . . and vividly colored," while Cumpiano's use of verbs makes *Quinito, Day and Night/Quinito, día y noche* "a great read-aloud." "Full of images and words that will engage preschoolers," the book "works on multiple levels," concluded *Horn Book* contributor Nina Lindsay, while in *Booklist* Hazel Rochman dubbed *Quinito, Day and Night/Quinito, día y noche* "a celebration of differences."

Biographical and Critical Sources

PERIODICALS

Booklist, July 1, 2008, Hazel Rochman, review of *Quinito, Day and Night/Quinito, día y noche,* p. 73.
Horn Book, January-February, 2009, Nina Lindsay, review of *Quinito, Day and Night/Quinito, día y noche,* p. 76.
Kirkus Reviews, August 1, 2005, review of *Quinito's Neighborhood/El vecindario de Quinito,* p. 846; June 15, 2008, review of *Quinito, Day and Night/Quinito, día y noche.*
School Arts, May-June, 2006, Rebecca Martin, review of *Quinito's Neighborhood/El vecindario de Quinito,* p. 60.
School Library Journal, October, 2005, Ann Welton, review of *Quintito's Neighborhood/El vecindario de Quinito,* p. 148; September, 2008, Madeline Walton-Hadlock, review of *Quinito, Day and Night/Quinito, día y noche,* p. 144.

ONLINE

McGraw-Hill Higher Education Web site, http://www.mhhe.com/ (November 15, 2009), "Ina Cumpiano."*

D

DAWSON, Arthur L.

Personal

Born in Wakulla County, FL. *Education:* Tallahassee Community College, forensic art certification, 1990. *Hobbies and other interests:* The arts, sports, reading, cooking, film, music, comics, videogames, photography, music.

Addresses

Office—Doc & AJ Comics, P.O. Box 681177, Orlando, FL 32868. *E-mail*—art@arthurldawson.com.

Career

Fine artist, illustrator, and entrepreneur. Lake County Sheriff's Office, Tavares, FL, forensic investigator and artist, 1988-90; Ethnic Visions (art publishing distribution company), founder, 1991—; Doc & AJ Comics (publishing company), Orlando, FL, owner, 2002—. Artist coordinator for Zora Neale Hurston Festival of the Arts and Humanities, 2003-06; creator of Youth Art Program and Younique Art Parables (nonprofit art programs), 2006—.

Member

Society of Children's Book Writers and Illustrators.

Awards, Honors

Storytelling World Resource Award, *Smithsonian* magazine Notable Children's Books designation, and Reading Circle Recommended Title selection, Missouri State Teachers Association, all 2008, all for *Howard Thurman's Great Hope;* national awards for artwork.

Writings

ILLUSTRATOR

Kai Jackson Issa, *Howard Thurman's Great Hope,* Lee & Low Books (New York, NY), 2008.

Arthur L. Dawson (Courtesy of Arthur L. Dawson.)

OTHER

Author and illustrator of "Tobacco Avengers" comic-book series.

Sidelights

A former forensic artist, Arthur L. Dawson has provided the illustrations for *Howard Thurman's Great Hope,* Kai Jackson Issa's award-winning picture-book biography about one the forerunners of the civil rights movement in the United States. Dawson, a self-taught artist who once worked for the Lake County Sheriff's Office in Florida, is also the creator of the "Tobacco

Avengers" comic-book series, and he founded Doc & AJ Comics, a nonprofit publishing company that is devoted to educating youth about health, fitness, and the dangers of tobacco.

In *Howard Thurman's Great Hope* Issa examines the early life of Thurman, who was born in Daytona, Florida, in 1900 and raised by his grandmother while his widowed mother worked. An excellent student, Thurman had almost no hope of furthering his education beyond elementary school; at that time, the only public school for African Americans in his town ended at seventh grade. With the help of a strong-willed principal and a stranger who financially subsidized his studies, Thurman earned a scholarship to a high school in Jacksonville, graduated first in his class, and eventually earned a degree from Morehouse College. He later served as dean at Howard University, and his teachings inspired James Farmer, founder of the Congress of Racial Equality, as well as Martin Luther King, Jr.

Dawson's illustrations for *Howard Thurman's Great Hope* drew critical praise. Linda Perkins, writing in *Booklist,* remarked that the artist's "realistic oil paintings capture the fatigue, hope, and dignity of Thurman and his hard-working family," and a contributor in *Kirkus Reviews* noted that the characters "stand in dignity with downcast or averted eyes as if posing for statues or formal portraits."

Biographical and Critical Sources

PERIODICALS

Booklist, November 15, 2008, Linda Perkins, review of *Howard Thurman's Great Hope,* p. 42.
Kirkus Reviews, August 1, 2008, review of *Howard Thurman's Great Hope.*
School Library Journal, September, 2008, Barbara Auerback, review of *Howard Thurman's Great Hope,* p. 164.

ONLINE

Arthur L. Dawson Home Page, http://www.arthurldawson.com (November 1, 2009).
Doc & AJ Comics Web site, http://www.docandajcomicsandtoons.com/ (November 1, 2009).

*   *   *

de LINT, Charles 1951-
(Samuel M. Key)

Personal

Born December 22, 1951, in Bussum, Netherlands; immigrated to Canada, 1952, naturalized citizen, 1961; son of Frederick Charles (a navigator and survey project manager) Hoefsmit and Gerardina Margaretha (a high-school teacher) Hoefsmit-de Lint; married MaryAnn Harris (an artist and musician), 1980. *Hobbies and other interests:* Music, fine arts.

Addresses

Home and office—P.O. Box 9480, Ottawa, Ontario K1G 3V2, Canada. *Agent*—Russell Galen, Scovil Chichak Galen Literary Agency, Inc., 381 Park Ave. S., Ste. 1020, New York, NY 10016. *E-mail*—cdl@charlesdelint.com.

Career

Writer. Worked variously as clerical and construction positions, 1967-71; retail clerk and manager of record stores, 1971-83; writer in Ottawa, Ontario, Canada, 1983—. Owner and editor of Triskell Press. Juror for William L. Crawford Award, Canadian SF/Fantasy Award, World Fantasy Award, Theodore Sturgeon Memorial Short-Fiction Award, Horror Writers of America Award, and Nebula Short Fiction Award. Member of Wickentree (traditional Celtic folk music band), Ottawa, 1972-85, and Jump at the Sun (Celtic/Americana folk band).

Member

Science Fiction Writers of America, SF Canada.

Awards, Honors

William L. Crawford Award for Best New Fantasy Author, International Association for the Fantastic in the Arts, 1984; Canadian SF/Fantasy Award ("Casper") nominations, 1986, for *Mulengro,* and 1987, for *Yarrow;* Casper Award for best work in English, 1988, for *Jack the Giant-Killer;* Readercon Small Press Award for Best Short Work, 1989, for short story, "The Drowned Man's Reel"; Reality I Commendations, Best Fantasy Author Award, 1991; Best Books for the Teen Age listee, New York Public Library, and CompuServe Science Fiction and Fantasy Forum Homer Award for Best Fantasy Novel, both 1992, both for *The Little Country;* Prix Ozone for Best Foreign Fantasy Short Story, 1997, for "Timeskip"; Best Books for Young Adults selection, YALSA/American Library Association, 1998, for *Trader,* 2003, for *Seven Wild Sisters* and *Jack of Kinrowan,* and 2007, for *The Blue Girl;* World Fantasy Awards for Best Collection, 2000, for *Moonlight and Vines,* 2003, for *Waifs and Strays,* for best novel, 2002, for *The Onion Girl,* for best novella, 2003, for *Seven Wild Sisters,* for short fiction, 2003, for *A Circle of Cats;* Nebula Award finalist, and Mythopoeic Fantasy Award finalist, both 2001, both for *Forests of the Heart;* White Pine Award, Ontario Library Association, 2006, and August Derleth Fantasy Award finalist, and Great Lakes Great Book s Award, both 2007, all for *The Blue Girl;* Book for the Teen Age citation, 2008, New York Public Library, for *Little (Grrl) Lost.*

Writings

FICTION

De Grijze Roos (title means "The Grey Rose"; short stories), Een Exa Uitgave (Belgium), 1983.

The Riddle of the Wren, Ace Books (New York, NY), 1984.

Moonheart: A Romance, Ace Books (New York, NY), 1984.

The Harp of the Grey Rose, Starblaze, 1985, published as *The Harp of the Grey Rose: The Legend of Cerin Songweaver,* Firebird (New York, NY), 2004.

Mulengro: A Romany Tale, Ace Books (New York, NY), 1985.

Yarrow: An Autumn Tale, Ace Books (New York, NY), 1986.

Ascian in Rose (novella), Axolotl Press (Eugene, OR), 1987.

Jack the Giant-Killer: A Novel of Urban Faerie, Armadillo-Ace (New York, NY), 1987.

Greenmantle, Ace Books (New York, NY), 1988.

Wolf Moon, New American Library (New York, NY), 1988, reprinted, Firebird (New York, NY), 2004.

Westlin Wind (novella), Axolotl Press (Eugene, OR), 1988.

(With others) *Philip Jose Farmer's The Dungeon: Book Three* (shared series), Byron Preiss/Bantam (New York, NY), 1988.

(With others) *Philip Jose Farmer's The Dungeon: Book Five* (shared series), Byron Preiss/Bantam (New York, NY), 1988.

Svaha, Ace Books (New York, NY), 1989.

Berlin (novella), Fourth Avenue Press, 1989, published in *Life on the Border,* Tor (New York, NY), 1991.

The Fair in Emain Macha, Tor (New York, NY), 1990.

Drink down the Moon: A Novel of Urban Faerie, Ace Books (New York, NY), 1990.

The Dreaming Place, illustrated by Brian Froud, Atheneum (New York, NY), 1990.

Ghostwood, illustration by Donna Gordon, Axolotl Press (Eugene, OR), 1990.

Paperjack (novella), illustrated by Judy J. King, Cheap Street (New Castle, VA), 1991.

Ghosts of Wind and Shadow (novella), Axolotl Press (Eugene, OR), 1991.

The Little Country, Morrow (New York, NY), 1991.

Spiritwalk, Tor (New York, NY), 1992.

Into the Green, Tor (New York, NY), 1993.

Dreams Underfoot: The Newford Collection, Tor (New York, NY), 1993.

The Wild Wood, Bantam Books (New York, NY), 1994, reprinted, Orb (New York, NY), 2004.

Memory and Dream, Tor (New York, NY), 1994.

The Ivory and the Horn, Tor (New York, NY), 1995.

Jack of Kinrowan, Tor (New York, NY), 1995.

Trader, Tor (New York, NY), 1997.

Someplace to Be Flying, Tor (New York, NY), 1998.

Moonlight and Vines, Tor (New York, NY), 1999.

The Newford Stories, SF Book Club, 1999.

Triskell Tales, Subterranean Press (Burton, MI), 2000.

Forests of the Heart, Tor (New York, NY), 2000.

The Road to Lisdoonvarnia, Subterranean Press (Burton, MI), 2001.

Seven Wild Sisters, illustrated by Charles Vess, Subterranean Press (Burton, MI), 2001.

The Onion Girl, Tor (New York, NY), 2001.

Tapping the Dream Tree (stories), Tor (New York, NY), 2002.

A Handful of Coppers; Collected Early Stories, Volume One: *Heroic Fantasy,* Subterranean Press (Burton, MI), 2003.

Waifs and Strays (stories), Viking (New York, NY), 2003.

A Circle of Cats, illustrated by Charles Vess, Viking (New York, NY), 2003.

Spirits in the Wind, Tor (New York, NY), 2003.

The Blue Girl (young-adult novel), Viking (New York, NY), 2004.

Medicine Road, illustrated by Charles Vess, Subterranean Press (Burton, MI), 2004.

Widdershins, Tor (New York, NY), 2006.

Little (Grrl) Lost, Viking (New York, NY), 2007.

Promises to Keep, Subterranean Press (Burton, MI), 2007.

Dingo, Firebird (New York, NY), 2008.

The Mystery of Grace, Tor (New York, NY), 2009.

Author of "The Fane of the Grey Rose" (novelette), published in *Swords against Darkness IV,* edited by Andrew J. Offutt, Zebra, 1979; and *Stick* (novella), published in *Borderland,* edited by Terri Windling and Mark Arnold, Signet (New York, NY), 1986; and coauthor of *Death Leaves an Echo* (novella), published in *Café Purgatorium,* Tor Horror (New York, NY), 1991. Work represented in anthologies, including *The Year's Best Fantasy Stories: 8,* edited by Arthur W. Saha, DAW, 1982; *Dragons and Dreams* and *Spaceships and Spells,* both edited by Jane Yolen, Martin H. Greenberg, and Charles G. Waugh, Harper, 1986 and 1987; and *The Annual Review of Fantasy and Science Fiction,* Meckler Publishing, 1988. Author of columns in horror and science-fiction magazines, including *Magazine of Fantasy and Science Fiction, Short Form, Horrorstruck, OtherRealms, Mystery Scene,* and *Pulphouse.* Contributor to periodicals, including *Isaac Asimov's Science Fiction Magazine.*

FICTION; UNDER PSEUDONYM SAMUEL M. KEY

Angel of Darkness, Jove (New York, NY), 1990.

From a Whisper to a Scream, Berkley (New York, NY), 1992.

I'll Be Watching You, Jove (New York, NY), 1994.

Sidelights

Considered one of the preeminent fantasy writers of his generation, Canadian author Charles de Lint melds the world of faerie with modern urban life in dozens of novels and works of short fiction. Beginning with his 1979 novelette "The Fane of the Grey Rose," de Lint has proven himself to be a versatile and prolific author whose work is informed by both folk tales and myths. His works often include themes of music—de Lint is also a musician—and he uses artists and other creative characters as bridges to deeper insight into the world.

"If . . . de Lint didn't create the contemporary fantasy," announced Tanya Huff in *Quill & Quire,* "he certainly defined it. . . . Unlike most fantasy writers who deal with battles between ultimate good and evil, de Lint concentrates on smaller, very personal conflicts." This may be the reason why his writings appeal to all types of readers. As Donna Scanlon noted in Toronto's *Globe & Mail,* "De Lint's gift for capturing the essence of the 'other,' his thoughtful explorations of identity and his strong characterizations all have powerful appeal for teenagers. That he often includes teenaged characters and writes about them respectfully certainly adds to that appeal."

Born in Bussum, Netherlands, in 1951, de Lint immigrated with his family to Canada when he was four months old. His father worked with a surveying company, a job that took the family from Ontario to Western Canada to Quebec and on to Turkey and Lebanon until they finally settled near Ottawa. During these years of uprootedness, de Lint found stability in books, reading widely in myth and folklore and books by E.B. White, Tolkien, H.P. Lovecraft, William Morris, and Mervyn Peake. He never thought of becoming a writer, however; for the young de Lint, it was music that beckoned, and growing up he formed a love for Celtic music long before it became popular. Leaving high school two credits short of graduation, de Lint took a variety of jobs to support his music, including working as a clerk at a record store.

De Lint's writing started out as a hobby, creating fantasy short stories that a friend illustrated. A recommendation to submit his work for publication was successful; as de Lint wrote on his home page, "Here was something that I loved to do and people would actually pay me to do it." Over the next few years, de Lint continued to perform music on the weekend and produce stories for magazines during the week. His first published novella, "The Fane of the Grey Rose," appeared in an anthology and was later expanded into the novel *The Harp of the Grey Rose.* When he lost his job at the record shop in 1983, de Lint's wife encouraged him to write full time.

As a full-time writer, de Lint sold three manuscripts during his first year, one of which, *Riddle of the Wren,* earned the author critical attention With his novel *Moonheart* de Lint made his move to the urban setting that has characterized much of his work, also developed his peculiar blending of Canadian mythologies: the traditions found in Native-Indian shamanism and in Welsh Druidism. The novel blends suspense, horror, and romance in the tale of an Ottawa mansion that proves to be linked to an old battle between good and evil. Tamson House is actually a gate between the earthbound world and a magical realm. De Lint's cast of characters ranges from a mage's apprentice, a reformed biker, and an inspector for the Canadian Mounted Police to a race of magical little people called manitous along with legendary figures drawn from Welsh and Celtic myth. Writ-

ing in *Voice of Youth Advocates,* David Snider called *Moonheart: A Romance* "a fascinating and enthralling work that should be in every YA collection," while *Booklist* critic Roland Green dubbed the book "very good and distinctly unconventional."

De Lint turns to Romany culture as inspiration for *Mulengro: A Romany Tale,* a hybrid of the horror and fantasy genres. Set among Canada's modern-day gypsy communities, the novel tells the story of a series of bizarre murders that have police baffled. The gypsies know they are dealing with the mythic Mulengro, "He Who Walks with Ghosts," and it is up to a reclusive gypsy man and a young woman to locate and eliminate this mythic threat. Gary Farber commented in *S.F. Chronicle* that *Mulengro* is "suspenseful, original, and extremely well written," and Green concluded that de Lint "deserves high marks for his research, storytelling," and well-drawn characters.

Other early books considered notable in the development of de Lint's mythic fiction include *Yarrow: An Autumn Tale* and *Jack the Giant-Killer: A Novel of Urban Faerie. Yarrow* deals with a young fantasy writer

Cover of de Lint's middle-grade fantasy Yarrow, *featuring artwork by John Howe.* (Orb Paperbacks, Tom Doherty Associates, Inc., 1997. Reproduced by permission of St. Martin's Press.)

named Cat whose stories comes from her nightly dream-scape; when her dreams are increasingly being stolen by a telepathic vampire-type creature, she loses the ability to create. Nancy Choice, writing in *Voice of Youth Advocates,* called the novel "filled with suspense and tension from beginning to end," and described Cat as a "just plain nice person [who] you would like to have living next door." Part of a series of modern retellings of fairy tales, *Jack the Giant-Killer* centers on Jacky Rowan, a boy who develops magical powers through the use of a red cap that reveals to its wearer the giant in the city park and the elves in the oaks. Jacky learns that the good elves are dwindling in number while the bad ones prosper. The only way to stop this process is to set the princess free and recapture the Horn for the forces of good. Identifying with the elves as part of the Kinrowan clan, Jacky takes on the task with a little help from her friends, in a "very satisfying" tale, according to Tom Easton of *Analog Science Fiction/Science Fact.* De Lint reprises Jacky in *Drink down the Moon: A Novel of Urban Faerie,* another blend of fairy-tale motifs and modern settings; both books are included in the omnibus *Jack of Kinrowan.*

De Lint crafts his characteristic mix of Native-American mythology and Celtic story in *The Dreaming Place,* a novel illustrated by Brian Froud. Featuring teenaged cousins Nina and Ashley, and emphasizing realism, this book "might . . . encourage some realistic fiction fans to give . . . fantasy a try," according to Kathryn Pierson in a review for the *Bulletin of the Center for Children's Books.*

One of de Lint's most popular novels, *The Little Country,* is a story within a story and stands as a loving exposition of de Lint's own affection for folk music. Set in modern Cornwall, the novel tells the story of Janey Little, a successful musician who comes back to the village of Mousehole in England. Apart from her music, a major influence on Janey's life is the writings of Billy Dunthorn, and she soon discovers an unpublished Dunthorn manuscript in the family attic. This manuscript tells the story of Jodi and her friend Denzil, who lives in the fictional village of Bodbury. As Janey gets further into the story, parallels develop between real life and that of the Dunthorn's tale. Outside forces conspire in the form of John Madden, a member of the Order of the Grey Dove who desires the manuscript because it can provide the possessor with ultimate power. As Peter Crowther noted in the *St. James Guide to Fantasy Writers, The Little Country* is filled with "charm, excitement, and above all, complete believability." According to Crowther, "it is [de Lint's] unerring knack of concentrating on his characters and filling them out, making them so real, that places his work at the forefront of the field."

"Much of what I write about requires a root in the real world," de Lint once noted in an interview with Lawrence Schimel for *Marion Zimmer Bradley's Fantasy Magazine.* First developed as the unnamed urban

Cover of de Lint's novel **Jack of Kinrowan,** *which includes the author's retelling of the story of Jack the Giant Killer.* (Orb Books, Tom Doherty Associates, LLC, 1999. Reproduced by permission of St. Martin's Press.)

setting for a story he was writing for a fantasy anthology, the city of Newford has served as the locale for a number of de Lint's books. Containing stories that were published in magazines over a period of several years, *Dreams Underfoot: The Newford Collection* introduces the ensemble cast of characters that flow in and out of all the "Newford" stories. There is Jilly, the artist; Lorio, part gypsy and part punk; Lesli, who sets free the faerie with her music; and a rich assortment of other urban types. One of the outstanding stories in the collection, "Timeskip," won France's Prix Ozone. Elizabeth Hand, writing in the *Washington Post Book World,* called this tale "a genuinely chilling ghost story as poignant as it is creepy." Further additions to the "Newford" saga include *The Ivory and the Horn,* a "fanciful and moving collection," according to a *Publishers Weekly* critic, and *Moonlight and Vines,* a collection of stories that demonstrates de Lint to be, according to Green, "the most literate and ingenious purveyor of urban fantasy." In 2000, de Lint received the World Fantasy Award for *Moonlight and Vines.*

De Lint has also used the fictional town of Newford as the setting for several novels, among them *Memory and Dream, Trader, Someplace to Be Flying, Forests of the Heart,* and *Widdershins.* In *Memory and Dreams* an artist named Isabelle learns to paint amazing creatures that unleash ancient spirits into the modern world. "It is hard to imagine urban fantasy done better than it is by de Lint at his best," remarked Green in reviewing the novel for *Booklist.* Jodi L. Israel, writing in *Kliatt,* commented that "de Lint is a master of contemporary fantasy," and the "literate and flowing style" he exhibits in *Memory and Dreams* "makes his words a pleasure to read."

In *Trader* a man named Trader awakes to discover that he has traded bodies with a reprobate named Johnny Devlin. Trying to reclaim his own life, Trader becomes involved in the lives of all those whom Devlin has injured. Along the way, readers are re-introduced to stock characters out of Newford, including Jilly Coppercorn and street musician Geordie Riddell, as well as the shaman, Bones. "Readers familiar with de Lint's work know that he is a master of imagery and trenchant detail," wrote Donna Scanlon in a *Voice of Youth Advo-*

De Lint weaves a Celtic fantasy in **Moonheart,** *featuring artwork by David Bergen.* (Orb Books, Tom Doherty Associates, Inc., 1994. Reproduced by permission.)

cates review of *Trader.* "He continues to demonstrate his remarkable ability here," Scanlon concluded, "never los[ing] control of his myriad plot threads or deftly drawn characters."

One of the most popular "Newford" novels—and one of de Lint's personal favorites—is *Someplace to Be Flying,* a story featuring freelance photographer Lily Carson and gypsy cab driver Hank Walker. Once again, de Lint draws the reader into a parallel otherworld—a city beneath the city in the Tombs—and into the realm of the shape-shifting animal people who originally inhabited the earth. These animal people, as de Lint has it, ultimately evolve into the separate animals and people we know today, and in *Someplace to Be Flying* the focus is on corvids: crows and ravens. *Library Journal* contributor Jackie Cassada praised de Lint's "elegant prose and effective storytelling" in the novel, and Brian Jacomb concluded his laudatory *Washington Post Book World* review by calling *Someplace to Be Flying* "a solid thriller" that is "full of suspense and peppered with villains of various talents and their adversaries, the decent folk who constantly try to thwart their evil intentions."

In *Forests of the Heart* de Lint "weaves a complex story of intrigue and suspense while exploring the power of spirituality and friendship," observed a contributor in *Resource Links.* Set in and around Newford, the work concerns four individuals—a sculptor with psychic powers, a music-store owner, a New Mexican healer, and a musician—who join together to combat the Gentry, a force of ancient, amoral spirits who traveled to the New World with early Irish immigrants and who seek to displace the native spirits, the manitou. According to Cassada, de Lint convincingly portrays "the relationship between artistic creation and the magical energies that permeate the world these characters inhabit," and a *Publishers Weekly* reviewer called *Forests of the Heart* "a leisurely, intriguing expedition into the spirit world, studded with Spanish and Gaelic words and an impressive depth of imagination."

Artist Jilly Coppercorn, a recurring character in the "Newford" tales, is the protagonist of *The Onion Girl.* Hospitalized after a devastating hit-and-run accident, Jilly visits manido-aki, a spirit world she enters through her dreams and in which she must face her personal demons in order to heal her physical self. Jilly's recovery is complicated by the sudden appearance of a troubled figure from her past: her sister Raylene. Jilly also appears in *Promises to Me* and *Widdershins,* In *Widdershins* it is Celtic fiddler Lizzy Mahone, rather than Jilly, who takes center stage when an automotive mishap leads her to discover the region's magical inhabitants. While attempting to mediate a host of age-old antagonism among the fairy residents, Lizzie runs afoul of the dwarflike bogans and ultimately discovers that she and Jilly share the ability to shift shapes. *Promises to Me* finds a younger Jilly transported to a space between the worlds of the living and the dead while on the way to a

De Lint turns to science fiction in his young-adult novel Trader, *featuring artwork by John Howe.* (Tor, 1997. Copyright © 1997 by Charles de Lint. Reproduced by permission of St. Martin's Press.)

friend's concert on All Hallows' Eve. At first Jilly does not realize that this serene, peaceful place is actually inhabited by unhappy souls of those who have perished. When she learns the truth, the young woman must decide between remaining in a stress-free world or returning to accept the responsibilities of life.

"De Lint's novels are driven not so much by destinations as by journeys, and *The Onion Girl* is no exception," observed *Booklist* contributor Regina Schroeder, and a *Kirkus Reviews* critic called the work an "absorbing tale, as believable and insightful as they come." A *Publishers Weekly* reviewer noted of *The Onion Girl* that de Lint's "crazy-quilt fantasy moves from the outer to the inner world with amazing ease," while Frieda Murray concluded her *Booklist* review of *Widdershins* by noting that the "Newford" books "weave . . . individual characters' stories into a tight-knit whole, accompanied by music, love, pugnacity, frustration, and healing." In *Kirkus Reviews* a critic described *Widdershins* as a "sentimental, wildly imaginative" follow-up to *The Onion Girl,* while Murray praised *Promises to*

Keep for allowing readers a more-intimate view of a favorite de Lint character through the author's "characteristic powerful yet intimate style."

Spirits in the Wires draws readers into "a magical otherworld, where spirits of faerie and folklore occupy modern technology and cyberspace is a fantasy realm in which imagination fuels artificial intelligence," according to a *Publishers Weekly* critic. In the novel, a popular research Web site known as Wordwood is disrupted by a virus, causing everyone visiting the site to disappear and prompting a group of Newford residents to journey to the technological otherworld, hoping to rescue their missing friends. According to Cassada, writing in *Library Journal, Spirits in the Wires* "combines world mythologies with cyber-culture to produce a new vision of interwoven realities."

Also set in Newford, *The Blue Girl* features a story geared specifically for teen readers. In the story, feisty Imogene Yeck wants to put aside her wild image when she moves with her family to Newford. A friendship with shy, bookish student Maxine Chancy proves helpful to both girls as they provide each other with encouragement. At Reading High the girls unite against local bullies, while also fighting the soul-stealing anathimim. To save their own souls, the girls must obtain help from family, friends, and also the lonely ghost of a deceased student named Adrian Dumbrell. A "lively novel," according to *School Library Journal* critic Sarah Couri, *The Blue Girl* "thoughtfully examines friendships that cross magical boundaries and explores how love can strengthen and save us." In *Quill & Quire* Scanlon noted of *The Blue Girl* that de Lint's "storytelling is superb, taut with suspense, leavened with humour and packed with [a] fresh, frank" teen narrative.

De Lint focuses on younger readers in his collaborations with award-winning illustrator Charles Vess on the fantasy novels *Seven Wild Sisters, Medicine Road,* and *A Circle of Cats.* The rambunctious, red-haired Dillard sisters are introduced in *Seven Wild Sisters,* "a gentle and at times humorous enchantment," in the words of a *Publishers Weekly* reviewer. In *Medicine Road* twins Laurel and Bess Dillard encounter a pair of restless spirits that seek human soul mates. *Medicine Road* is "well-laced with humor, romance, and Native American mythology," observed Sally Estes in a *Booklist* review. Geared for even younger readers, *A Circle of Cats* concerns a young girl's transformation from a human into a kitten. Here "de Lint's sonorous, ingenuous language is complemented beautifully by Vess's full-color line-and-watercolor illustrations," noted a contributor in *Kirkus Reviews.*

Geared for teen readers, *Dingo* "ingeniously incorporates Aboriginal mythology into an intriguing story," according to *School Library Journal* contributor Quinby Frank. In the story, seventeen-year-old Miguel and Miguel's dad live near the ocean and make their living selling comic books and vintage LP's. When he realizes

Cover of de Lint's young-adult novel Waifs and Strays, *featuring artwork by Jude Palencar.* (Viking, 2002. Cover copyright © 2002 by John Jude Palencar. Reproduced by permission of Viking Children's Books, a division of Penguin Putnam Books for Young Readers.)

that his new friend, Lainey, is a shape-shifter who is being hunted by the spirit of an ancient Australian dingo called Warrigal, Miguel works to save her, teaming up with a town tough in the process. "A rich vein of Australian lore wraps around this story," observed a *Kirkus Reviews* writer in reviewing *Dingo,* and a *Publishers Weekly* contributor predicted that the novel "will . . . attract readers to de Lint's more powerful work for older teens and adults."

Dubbed "a quirky fantasy" by *Kliatt* contributor Claire Rosser, *Little (Grrl) Lost* is a fantasy that draws on *The Borrowers* in its story about a young teen who learns that a tiny family lives in the walls of her bedroom. When shy T.J. meets a tiny teenaged runaway with attitude to spare, her new friend helps T.J. make new friends while also taking a few risks. Noting that *Little (Grrl) Lost* is a departure for de Lint, Rhona Campbell wrote in *School Library Journal* that its "emphasis" is on "the differences in the girls and their personal growth" rather than the story's fantasy element. In *Publishers Weekly* a critic concluded that in *Little (Grrl) Lost* the author "adeptly braids the fantastic and the everyday."

De Lint has described his writing style as "organic." In an interview with Mike Timonin for *Wordsworth,* the author stated, "I write a lot of material to get the character's voice right, sometimes hundreds of pages, but not all of that goes into the novel." He added, "I guess I lose a lot of time that way, unlike someone who uses an outline, but it's what works for me." "It's strange, when I started writing, I thought it would get easier as I went on, but it doesn't," De Lint concluded. "It actually gets harder, each novel I write. I have to find something new to say, and because I don't want to repeat what I've said before, I have to go deeper, further."

Biographical and Critical Sources

BOOKS

Clute, John, and Peter Nicholls, editors, *The Encyclopedia of Science Fiction,* St. Martin's Press (New York, NY), 1993.
St. James Guide to Fantasy Writers, St. James Press (Detroit, MI), 1996.
St. James Guide to Young-Adult Writers, 2nd edition, St. James Press (Detroit, MI), 1999.
Science Fiction and Fantasy Literature, 1975-1991, Gale (Detroit, MI), 1992.
Twentieth-Century Science-Fiction Writers, 3rd edition, St. James Press (Detroit, MI), 1991, pp. 196-198.

PERIODICALS

Booklist, December 15, 1984, Roland Green, review of *Moonheart: A Romance,* p. 558; November 15, 1985, Roland Green, review of *Mulengro: A Romany Tale,* p. 468; October 1, 1994, Roland Green, review of *Memory and Dreams,* p. 246; December 1, 1998, Roland Green, review of *Moonlight and Vines,* p. 655; May 1, 2000, Patricia Monaghan, review of *Forests of the Heart,* p. 1655; November 15, 2000, Roland Green review of *Triskell Tales: Twenty-two Years of Chapbooks,* p. 625; October 1, 2001, Regina Schroeder, review of *The Onion Girl,* p. 304; October 1, 2002, Sally Estes, review of *Waifs and Strays,* p. 312; November 15, 2002, Roland Green, review of *Tapping the Dream Tree,* p. 584; February 1, 2003, review of *A Handful of Coppers; Collected Early Stories,* pp. 978-979; August, 2003, Frieda Murray, review of *Spirits in the Wires,* p. 1967; April 15, 2004, Sally Estes, review of *Medicine Road,* p. 1431; March 15, 2006, Frieda Murray, review of *Widershins,* p. 35; May 15, 2007, Frieda Murray, review of *Promises to Keep,* p. 34; March 15, 2009, Frieda Murray, review of *The Mystery of Grace,* p. 33.
Bulletin of the Center for Children's Books, January, 1991, Kathryn Pierson, review of *The Dreaming Place,* p. 114.
Globe & Mail (Toronto, Ontario, Canada), December 11, 2004, Donna Scanlon, "Fresh, Frank, and Fanciful," p. D26.

Kirkus Reviews, September 1, 2001, review of *The Onion Girl,* p. 1252; August 15, 2002, review of *Waifs and Strays,* p. 1221; September 15, 2002, review of *Tapping the Dream Tree,* pp. 1357-1358; June 1, 2003, review of *A Circle of Cats,* p. 802; October 1, 2004, review of *The Blue Girl,* p. 959; March 15, 2006, review of *Widdershins,* p. 266; March 15, 2008, review of *Dingo.*

Kliatt, January, 1996, Jodi L. Israel, review of *Memory and Dreams,* p. 14; November, 2002, Deirdre B. Root, review of *The Onion Girl,* p. 24; January, 2004, review of *Tapping the Dream Tree,* p. 22; November, 2004, Janis Flint-Ferguson, review of *The Blue Girl,* p. 6; September, 2007, Claire Rosser, review of *Little (Grrl) Lost,* p. 10.

Library Journal, January, 1998, Jackie Cassada, review of *Someplace to Be Flying,* p. 148; February 15, 1999, Jackie Cassada, review of *Moonlight and Vines,* p. 188; May 15, 2000, Jackie Cassada, review of *Forests of the Heart,* p. 128; November 15, 2002, Jackie Cassada, review of *Tapping the Dream Tree,* p. 106; August, 2003, Jackie Cassada, review of *Spirits in the Wires,* p. 140; August 1, 2007, Jackie Cassada, review of *Promises to Keep,* p. 76; February 15, 2009, Jackie Cassada, review of *The Mystery of Grace,* p. 98.

Locus, June, 2003, Richard B. Brignall, "Charles de Lint: Mythic Fiction," p. 6.

Cover of Dingo, *a young-adult fantasy featuring artwork by Scott Fischer.* (Firebird, 2008. Jacket illustration copyright © Scott Fischer. Reproduced by permission of Firebird, a division of Penguin Putnam Books for Young Readers.)

Los Angeles Times Book Review, February 3, 1991, Gary Westfahl, "Orange County Apple and Other Aberrations," p. 11.

Marion Zimmer Bradley's Fantasy Magazine, summer, 1996, Lawrence Schimel, interview with de Lint.

Publishers Weekly, December 7, 1990, review of *The Little Country,* p. 74; March 27, 1995, review of *The Ivory and Horn,* p. 77; December 21, 1998, review of *Moonlight and Vines,* p. 60; May 1, 2000, review of *Forests of the Heart,* p. 54; April 30, 2001, review of *The Road to Lisdoonvarna,* p. 59; October 22, 2001, M.M. Hall, interview with de Lint, and review of *The Onion Girl,* p. 53; February 18, 2002, review of *Seven Wild Sisters,* p. 81; October, 28, 2002, review of *Tapping the Dream Tree,* p. 56; January 27, 2003, review of *A Handful of Coppers,* p. 241; July 7, 2003, review of *Spirits in the Wires,* p. 57; March 29, 2004, review of *Medicine Road,* p. 43; July 16, 2007, review of *Promises to Keep,* p. 150; August 13, 2007, review of *Little (Grrl) Lost,* p. 68; February 18, 2008, review of *Dingo,* p. 156; January 12, 2009, review of *The Mystery of Grace,* p. 33.

Quill & Quire, July, 1992, Michelle Sagara, review of *Spiritwalk,* pp. 37-38; May, 1993, Tanya Huff, "Rising Stars in Fantasy Worlds," p. 26.

Resource Links, October, 2000, review of *Forests of the Heart,* pp. 48-49; October, 2002, Gail de Vos, reviews of *Seven Wild Sisters* and *The Onion Girl,* pp. 55-56.

School Library Journal, November, 2002, Vicki Reutter, review of *Waifs and Strays,* pp. 160-161; October, 2003, Teri Markson and Stephen S. Wise, review of *A Circle of Cats,* p. 116; November, 2004, Sarah Couri, review of *The Blue Girl,* p. 141; November, 2007, Rhona Campbell, review of *Little (Grrl) Lost,* p. 118; August, 2008, Quinby Frank, review of *Dingo,* p. 118.

Science Fiction Chronicle, July, 1986, Gary Farber, review of *Mulengro,* p. 41.

Toronto Star, April 8, 2009, "Fantasy Author Melds Now with Then," p. E2.

Voice of Youth Advocates, February, 1985, David Snider, review of *Moonheart,* pp. 335-336; February, 1987, Nancy Choice, review of *Yarrow: An Autumn Tale,* p. 291; August, 1997, Donna Scanlon, review of *Trader,* p. 192.

Washington Post Book World, May 30, 1993, Elizabeth Hand, review of *Dreams Underfoot: The Newford Collection,* p. 9; March 15, 1998, Brian Jacomb, review of *Someplace to Be Flying,* p. 9.

Wordsworth, January, 1998, Mike Timonin, interview with de Lint.

ONLINE

Charles de Lint Home Page, http://www.sfsite.com/charlesdelint (November 5, 2009).*

*   *   *

DOB, Bob

Personal

Born in Hermosa Beach, CA; married; children: one son, twins. *Education:* Otis College of Art and Design, B.F.A., 2001. *Hobbies and other interests:* Film noir.

Addresses

Home—San Francisco, CA. *Agent*—Jennifer Vaughn Artist Agent, 1927 Grant Ave., San Francisco, CA 94133. *E-mail*—jen@jenvaughnart.com.

Career

Painter, graphic artist, and illustrator. Otis College of Art and Design, lecturer. Creator of "Luey" vinyl toy figure; founder of Imp Clothing (children's clothing line). Performed in Lunacy (punk band), for ten years. *Exhibitions:* Works exhibited at galleries in Los Angeles, CA, including La Luz de Jesus Gallery, 2004, and throughout the United States and Europe.

Illustrator

Dale E. Basye, *Heck: Where the Bad Kids Go,* Random House (New York, NY), 2008.

Dale E. Basye, *Rapacia: The Second Circle of Heck,* Random House (New York, NY), 2009.

Dale E. Basye, *Blimpo: The Third Circle of Heck,* Random House (New York, NY), 2010.

Biographical and Critical Sources

PERIODICALS

Publishers Weekly, June 30, 2008, review of *Heck: Where the Bad Kids Go,* p. 184.

School Library Journal, September, 2008, Elaine E. Knight, review of *Heck,* p. 173.

ONLINE

Bob Dob Home Page, http://www.bobdob.com (November 5, 2009).

Format Online, http://www.formatmag.com/ (November 4, 2007), Kemp Illups, interview with Dob.*

*   *   *

DuPONT, Lindsay Harper
See DuPONT, Lindsay

*   *   *

DuPONT, Lindsay
(Lindsay Harper duPont)

Personal

Married Frank duPont (a documentary filmmaker); children: three children. *Education:* Rhode Island School of Design, degree.

Addresses

Home—Hastings-on-Hudson, NY. *E-mail*—lhdp@veri zon.net.

Career

Illustrator.

Illustrator

Jessica Harper, *I'm Not Going to Chase the Cat Today,* HarperCollins (New York, NY), 2000.

(Under name Lindsay Harper duPont) Jessica Harper, *Nora's Room,* HarperCollins (New York, NY), 2001.

Jessica Harper, *Lizzy's Do's and Don'ts,* HarperCollins (New York, NY), 2002.

Jessica Harper, *Lizzy's Ups and Downs: Not an Ordinary School Day,* HarperCollins (New York, NY), 2004.

Jim Copp, *Jim Copp, Will You Tell Me a Story?: Three Uncommonly Clever Tales,* Harcourt (Orlando, FL), 2008.

Sidelights

Lindsay duPont did not consider creating illustrations for children's books until she was introduced to James Howe, the author of the popular "Bunnicula" stories. Howe saw duPont's work at a local art show, where she was showing a series of images illustrating a song written by her sister, actress Jessica Harper. At Howe's suggestion, the sisters packaged the song lyrics and art and sent them to a publisher, resulting in the publication of *I'm Not Going to Chase the Cat Today.* A cumulative story that starts when a family dog decides that it is not in the mood to start barking at its feline housemate, *I'm Not Going to Chase the Cat Today* captures "a delightful air of ennui," according to *Booklist* contributor Ilene Cooper. The critic went on to praise duPont's "colorful New Wave art" and Harper's "insouciant text," adding that the toe-tapping tale will inspire readers "to dance around." In *Publishers Weekly* a contributor made special note of duPont's watercolor-and-ink images, writing that they "benefit from long, lean lines and a crisp palette," while in *School Library Journal* Linda Ludke wrote that her "colorful, stylized" art helps advance the story's themes of "peace and friendship."

Published in 2000, *I'm Not Going to Chase the Cat Today* has inspired further sibling collaborations. In *Nora's Room* the sisters craft what *School Library Journal* contributor Debbie Stewart dubbed "a playful, rollicking romp." As Mom and siblings listen outside a closed door, pumpkins fall to the ground, rhinos frolic, and a host of other heavy-footed animals dance in the bedroom of an imaginative (and noisy) girl, creating an energetic picture-book adaptation of another of Harper's songs. DuPont's upbeat images "depict a thoroughly contemporary household," wrote *Booklist* critic Connie Fletcher, and in *Publishers Weekly* a reviewer dubbed *Nora's Room* "a jaunty" tale that gains energy from its "cheery slightly stylized artwork."

DuPont also joins her sister in creating the "Lizzie" books, which include *Lizzy's Do's and Don'ts* and *Lizzy's Ups and Downs: Not an Ordinary School Day.* Both Mom and daughter adopt a negative view in *Lizzy's*

Lindsay Harper duPont's artwork captures the adventures of the young heroine in sister Jessica Harper's picture book **Lizzy's Do's and Don'ts.** (HarperCollins, 2002. Illustrations copyright © 2002 by Lindsay Harper DuPont. Reproduced by permission of illustrator.)

Do's and Don'ts, that is until they both realize that "Do" is a much more pleasant way to deal with life than "Don't". The story's "rhyming text is . . . linked to fresh, comical cartoon-style art," wrote Susan Zvirin in *Booklist,* and *School Library Journal* contributor Laurie von Mehren maintained that duPont's "engaging pictures . . . match the fun-loving mood of the story." A *Kirkus Reviews* writer characterized Harper's text as containing "keen insight and a comic touch," adding that her sister's "bold illustrations perfectly capture the [story's] energy."

The sadness left behind when a best friend moves away is the focus of *Lizzy's Ups and Downs,* and here duPont's use of "bright hues" draw in readers while "her ever-expressive drawings of Lizzy artfully convey [the girl's] . . . spunk and charm." "Show with short pigtails and an expressive . . . faced, the child is adorable," asserted Linda L. Walkins in a review of *Lizzy's Ups and Downs* for *School Library Journal.*

Biographical and Critical Sources

PERIODICALS

Booklist, April 15, 2000, Ilene Cooper, review of *I'm Not Going to Chase the Cat Today,* p. 1550; July, 2001, Connie Fletcher, review of *Nora's Room,* p. 2019; March 15, 2002, Stephanie Zvirin, review of *Lizzy's Do's and Don'ts,* p. 1262.

Kirkus Reviews, March 1, 2002, review of *Lizzy's Do's and Don'ts,* p. 335; May 15, 2004, review of *Lizzy's Ups and Downs: Not an Ordinary School Day,* p. 492.

New York Times Book Review, August 12, 2001, review of *Nora's Room,* p. 24; November 23, 2008, Iris Hiskey Arno, "Ilustrator Breathes New Life into an Eccentric's Tales," p. WE10.

Publishers Weekly, May 29, 2000, review of *I'm Not Going to Chase the Cat Today,* p. 82; July 2, 2001, review of *Nora's Room,* p. 74; March 25, 2002, review of *Lizzy's Do's and Don'ts,* p. 64.

School Library Journal, May, 2000, Linda Ludke, review of *I'm Not Going to Chase the Cat Today,* p. 142; July, 2001, Debbie Stewart, review of *Nora's Room,* p. 82; July, 2002, Laurie Von Mehren, review of *Lizzy's Do's and Don'ts,* p. 92; June, 2004, Linda L. Walkins, review of *Lizzy's Ups and Downs,* p. 110.

ONLINE

Lindsay duPont Home Page, http://www.lindsaydupont. com (November 5, 2009).*

E-F

ENDLE, Kate

Personal
Born in OH. *Education:* Columbus College of Art and Design, B.F.A., 1993. *Hobbies and other interests:* Folk art, Inuit art, primitive art, collecting kokeshi dolls, traveling.

Addresses
Home—Seattle, WA. *E-mail*—kateendle@earthlink.net.

Career
Illustrator. Kate Endle Illustration and Collage, Seattle, WA, founder and owner, 1994—. Also worked at Seattle Art Supply for ten years. *Exhibitions:* Works have been shown at galleries in Seattle, WA, and Portland, OR.

Member
Society of Children's Book Writers and Illustrators.

Illustrator
Kate Davis, *What Do You Want to Be?,* Innovative KIDS (Norwalk, CT), 2000.

Andrew Larsen, *Bella and the Bunny,* Kids Can Press (Toronto, Ontario, Canada), 2007.

April Pulley Sayre, *Trout Are Made of Trees,* Charlesbridge (Watertown, MA), 2008.

Sidelights
Kate Endle, a Seattle-based illustrator who specializes in collage, has provided the artwork for children's books such as *Bella and the Bunny* by Andrew Larsen and *Trout Are Made of Trees* by April Pulley Sayre. "I've always loved collage—Eric Carle and Leo Lionni have been big favorites of mine since I was a kid," Endle remarked in an *Etsy Stalker* online interview. "I just love the mix of textures, color, and pattern."

In *Bella and the Bunny* a preschooler leaves her soft, furry, white sweater—a gift from her Nonna—at school. When Bella returns the next day, she learns that both her sweater and the class pet, a friendly rabbit, are missing. According to *Resource Links* reviewer Ken Kilback, "the beautiful collage illustrations by Endle are simple and playful as well as rich and warm," and Susan E. Murray noted in *School Library Journal* that "the textured paper in the collages adds to the depth of the art."

Sayre offers an ecological tale in *Trout Are Made of Trees,* an "unique introduction to how changes in nature create the food web," according to Christine Markley in *School Library Journal.* The work follows a pair of youngsters learning about the life cycle of a trout while camping with their father. *Horn Book* critic Danielle J. Ford remarked that Endle's "mixed-media collage illustrations are filled with the golds, browns, and greens of fall in the woods," and Stephanie Zvirin commented in *Booklist* that the illustrator's "minimalist figures . . . are juxtaposed very effectively against crisp yet intricate, layered backgrounds of painted-and-patterned cut-papers."

Biographical and Critical Sources

PERIODICALS

Booklist, February 15, 2008, Stephanie Zvirin, review of *Trout Are Made of Trees,* p. 94.

Horn Book, July-August, 2008, Danielle J. Ford, review of *Trout Are Made of Trees,* p. 472.

Kirkus Reviews, January 15, 2008, review of *Trout Are Made of Trees.*

Publishers Weekly, February 18, 2008, review of *Trout Are Made of Trees,* p. 153.

Resource Links, June, 2007, Ken Kilback, review of *Bella and the Bunny,* p. 4.

***Kate Endle takes young children on an unusual nature walk in her artwork for April Pulley Sayre's* Trout Are Made of Trees.** (Text copyright © 2008 by April Pulley Sayre. Illustrations copyright © 2008 by Kate Endle. All rights reserved, including the right of reproduction in whole or in part of any form. Charlesbridge and colophon are registered trademarks of Charlesbridge Publishing, Inc. Reproduced by permission.)

School Library Journal, May, 2007, Susan E. Murray, review of *Bella and the Bunny,* p. 102; April, 2008, Christine Markley, review of *Trout Are Made of Trees,* p. 136.

ONLINE

Etsy Stalker Web log, http://etsystalker.com/ (July 19, 2009), interview with Endle.
Kate Endle Home Page, http://www.kateendle.com (November 1, 2009).

Seven Impossible Things before Breakfast Web log, http://blaine.org/sevenimpossiblethings/ (February 3, 2009), "Random Illustrator Feature: Kate Endle."*

*　　*　　*

ERIKSSON, Eva 1949-

Personal

Born 1949, in Halmstad, Sweden.

Addresses

Home—Sweden.

Career

Illustrator beginning 1977. Worked variously as a mental hospital staff member and sign designer.

Awards, Honors

Litteraturfrëmjandets stipendium, 1980; Premio Europeo di Letteratura Giovanile Provincia di Trento, 1980; Elsa Beskow medal, 1981, for *Mamman och den vilda bebin* by Barbro Lindgren; *Expressen* Heffaklump award, 1981; Gold medal, biennale Bratislava, 1981; BMF medal, 1984, 1999, for *Malla handlar;* Rabén & Sjögrens tecknarstipendium, 1986; Wettergrens Barnbokollon, 1986; Konstnärligt stipendium, Albert Bonniers, 1990; Kulturstipendium, Grafiska fackförbundet, 1990; Augustnominerad, 1997, for *Andrejs längtan* by Lindgren; Astrid Lindgren prize, 2001; Hans Christian Andersen Award nomination, 2004, 2008; Ottilia Adelborg prize, 2006.

Writings

SELF-ILLUSTRATED

Om en liten vecka eller när Bella äntigen träffade Gustav, Rabén & Sjögren (Stockholm, Sweden), 1978, translated by Barbro Eriksson Roehrdanz as *Victor and Rosalie in One Short Week,* Carolrhoda Books (Minneapolis, MN), 1985.

Hokus pokus eller när Gustav inte ville gå och lägga sig, Rabén & Sjögren (Stockholm, Sweden), 1978, translated by Barbro Eriksson Roehrdanz as *Victor and Rosalie in Hocus-Pocus,* Carolrhoda Books (Minneapolis, MN), 1985.

Svartsjuka eller Kan man vara tre i en sandlåda, Rabén & Sjögren (Stockholm, Sweden), 1979, translated by Barbro Eriksson Roehrdanz as *Victor and Rosalie in Jealousy,* Carolrhoda Books (Minneapolis, MN), 1985.

Tandresan eller när Bella tappade en tand, Rabén & Sjögren (Stockholm, Sweden), 1979, translated by Barbro Eriksson Roehrdanz as *Victor and Rosalie in The Tooth Trip,* Carolrhoda Books (Minneapolis, MN), 1985.

Stures nya jacka Rabén & Sjögren (Stockholm, Sweden), 1987.

Lådbilen Rabén & Sjögren (Stockholm, Sweden), 1987.

Elsas hemlighet Rabén & Sjögren (Stockholm, Sweden), 1990.

Malla Handlar, Erisson & Lindgren (Stockholm, Sweden), 1998, translated as *Molly Goes Shopping,* R & S Books (New York, NY), 2003.

Lådbilen, Rabén & Sjögren (Stockholm, Sweden), 1999.

Min egen bok, Rabén & Sjögren (Stockholm, Sweden), 2000.

Boken om Bella och Gustav, Rabén & Sjögren (Stockholm, Sweden), 2003.

Malla cyclar, Rabén & Sjögren (Stockholm, Sweden), 2003, translated as *A Crash Course for Molly,* R & S Books (London, England), 2005.

ILLUSTRATOR

Björn Nordström and Jonas Sima, *Blåsjöbarna i Vilda Västern,* Rabén & Sjögren (Stockholm, Sweden), 1977.

Viveca Lärn, *Monstret i skåpet,* Rabén & Sjögren (Stockholm, Sweden), 1979, reprinted, 2005.

Barbro Lindgren, *Sagan om den lill farbrom,* Rabén & Sjögren (Stockholm, Sweden), 1979, translated by Steven T. Murray as *The Story of the Little Old Man,* R & S Books (New York, NY), 1992.

Barbro Lindgren, *Mamman och den vilda bebin,* Rabén & Sjögren (Stockholm, Sweden), 1980, translated by Jack Prelutsky as *The Wild Baby,* Greenwillow Books (New York, NY), 1981.

Barbro Lindgren, *Max bil,* Rabén & Sjögren (Stockholm, Sweden), 1981, translated as *Sam's Car,* William Morrow (New York, NY), 1982.

Barbro Lindgren, *Max kaka,* Rabén & Sjögren (Stockholm, Sweden), 1981, translated as *Sam's Cookie,* William Morrow (New York, NY), 1982, published as *Sam's Biscuit,* Methuen (London, England), 1984.

Barbro Lindgren, *Max nalle,* Rabén & Sjögren (Stockholm, Sweden), 1981, translated as *Sam's Teddy Bear,* William Morrow (New York, NY), 1982, published as *Sam's Teddy,* Methuen (London, England), 1984.

Ulf Nilsson, *Älskade lilla gris,* Bonniers Junior (Stockholm, Sweden), 1982.

Barbro Lindgren, *Max boll,* Rabén & Sjögren (Stockholm, Sweden), 1982, translated as *Sam's Ball,* William Morrow (New York, NY), 1983.

Barbro Lindgren, *Max balja,* Rabén & Sjögren (Stockholm, Sweden), 1982, translated as *Sam's Bath,* William Morrow (New York, NY), 1983, translated by Julia Marshall as *Max's Bath,* Gecko Press (Wellington, New Zealand), 2008.

Barbro Lindgren, *Max lampa,* Rabén & Sjögren (Stockholm, Sweden), 1982, translated as *Sam's Lamp,* William Morrow (New York, NY), 1983, published as *Bad Sam!,* Methuen (London, England), 1983.

Barbro Lindgren, *De vilda bebiresan,* Rabén & Sjögren (Stockholm, Sweden), 1982, reprinted, 2007, translated by Jack Prelutsky as *The Wild Baby Goes to Sea,* Greenwillow Books (New York, NY), 1983, translated by Alison Winn as *The Wild Baby's Boat Trip,* Hodder & Stoughton (London, England), 1983.

Ulf Nilsson, *Lilla syster kanin,* Bonniers Junior (Stockholm, Sweden), 1983, translated as *Little Sister Rabbit,* Atlantic Monthly Press (Boston, MA), 1983.

Barbro Lindgren, *Vilda bebin får en hund,* Rabén & Sjögren (Stockholm, Sweden), 1985, translated by Alison Winn as *The Wild Baby's Dog,* Hodder & Stoughton (London, England), 1986, translated by Jack Prelutsky as *The Wild Baby Gets a Puppy,* Greenwillow Books (New York, NY), 1988.

Ulf Nilsson, *Om ni inte hade mig,* Bonniers Junior (Stockholm, Sweden), 1985 translated by Lone Thygesen

Blecher and George Blecher as *If You Didn't Have Me,* Margaret K. McElderry Books (New York, NY), 1987.

Ulf Nilsson, *Den fräcka kråkan,* Bonniers Junior (Stockholm, Sweden), 1985.

Barbro Lindgren, *Max potta,* Rabén & Sjögren (Stockholm, Sweden), 1986, translated as *Sam's Potty,* William Morrow (New York, NY), 1986.

Rose and Samuel Langercrantz, *Brave Little Pete of Geranium Street,* translated by Jack Prelutsky, Greenwillow Books (New York, NY), 1986.

Barbro Lindgren, *Max dockvagn,* Rabén & Sjögren (Stockholm, Sweden), 1986, translated as *Sam's Wagon,* William Morrow (New York, NY), 1986, published as *Sam's Cart,* Methuen (London, England), 1986, translated by Julia Marshall as *Max's Wagon,* Gecko Press (Wellington, New Zealand), 2008.

Ulf Nilsson, *När lilla syster Kanin gick alldeles vilse,* Bonnier Carlsen (Stockholm, Sweden), 1987, translated as *Little Bunny Gets Lost,* Chronicle Books (San Francisco, CA), 1987.

Barbro Lindgren, *Vems lilla mössa flyger,* Rabén & Sjögren (Stockholm, Sweden), 1987.

Ulf Nilsson, *Lilla syster kanin oc alla hennes vänner,* Bonnier Carlsen (Stockholm, Sweden), 1987, translated as *Little Bunny and Her Friends,* Chronicle Books (San Francisco, CA), 1988.

Ulf Nilsson, *När lilla syster Kanin blev jagad av en räv,* 1987, translated as *Little Bunny and the Hungry Fox,* Chronicle Books (San Francisco, CA), 1989.

Ulf Nilsson, *När lilla syster Kanin anin badade i det stora havet,* Bonnier Carlsen (Stockholm, Sweden), 1987, translated as *Little Bunny at the Beach,* Chronicle Books (San Francisco, CA), 1989.

Ulf Nilsson, *Fem feta cirkusgrisar,* Bonniers Junior (Stockholm, Sweden), 1989.

Viveca Lärn, *Mimmi får en farfar,* Rabén & Sjögren (Stockholm, Sweden), 1989, translated by Richard E. Fisher as *Mimi Gets a Grandpa,* R & S Books (New York, NY), 1990.

Barbro Lindgren, *Titta Max grav!,* Rabén & Sjögren (Stockholm, Sweden), 1991.

Kicki Stridh, *Hemska spokhuset,* Gidlunds (Stockholm, Sweden), 1992, translated as *The Horrible Spookhouse,* Carolrhoda (Minneapolis, MN), 1994.

Barbro Lindgren, *Stora syster lilla bror,* Eriksson & Lindgren (Stockholm, Sweden), 1992.

Ulf Nilsson, *Se upp för spader knekt,* Bonniers Junior (Stockholm, Sweden), 1992.

Barbro Lindgren, *Max blöja,* Rabén & Sjögren (Stockholm, Sweden), 1994.

Barbro Lindgren, *Max napp,* Rabén & Sjögren (Stockholm, Sweden), 1994.

Ulf Nilsson, *En dag med müssens brandkår,* Bonnier Carlsen (Stockholm, Sweden), 1995.

Rose and Samuel Langercrantz, *Mettebofgs samlade öden oc äventyr i ettan tvåan oc trean,* Rabén & Sjögren (Stockholm, Sweden), 1995.

Barbro Lindgren, *Lilla lokomotivet Rosa,* illustrated by Eva Eriksson, Eriksson & Lindgren (Stockholm, Sweden), 1995 translated as *Rosa: Perpetual Motion Machine,* Publishers Group West, 1996.

Barbro Lindgren, *Rosa flytta till stan,* illustrated by Eva Eriksson, Eriksson & Lindgren (Stockholm, Sweden), 1996, translated by Jennifer Hawkins as *Rosa Moves to Town,* Groundwood Books (New York, NY), 1997.

Barbro Lindgren, *Andrejs läntan,* Rabén & Sjögren (Stockholm, Sweden), 1997, translated by Elisabeth Kallick Dyssegaard as *Andrei's Search,* R & S Books (New York, NY), 2000.

Barbro Lindgren, *Per och Pompe,* Eriksson & Lindgren (Stockholm, Sweden), 1998.

Barbro Lindgren, *Rosa på dagis,* Eriksson & Lindgren (Stockholm, Sweden), 1999, translated as *Rosa Goes to Daycare,* Groundwood Books (New York, NY), 2000.

Barbro Lindgren, *Prinsessen Rosa,* Rabén & Sjögren (Stockholm, Sweden), 1999.

Rose Langercrantz, *Metteborg och Little Ben,* Rabén & Sjögren (Stockholm, Sweden), 1999.

Rose Langercrantz, *Modge Metteborg—även kallad Erik,* Rabén & Sjögren (Stockholm, Sweden), 1999.

Pelle Plutt, Rabén & Sjögren (Stockholm, Sweden), 1999.

Lennart Hellsing, *Lappricka pappricka,* Rabén & Sjögren (Stockholm, Sweden), 1999.

Rose Langercrantz, *Metteborgs loppis,* Rabén & Sjögren (Stockholm, Sweden), 2000.

Barbro Lindgren, *Här är det lilla huset,* Rabén & Sjögren (Stockholm, Sweden), 2000.

Barbro Lindgren, *Vi leker att du är en humla,* Rabén & Sjögren (Stockholm, Sweden), 2000.

Nisse Hilldén, *Catzy Lindell får valpar,* Rabén & Sjögren (Stockholm, Sweden), 2000.

Viveca Lärn, *Eddie och Johanna,* Rabén & Sjögren (Stockholm, Sweden), 2001.

Gunilla Linn Persson, *Lilla Moffes stora dag,* Rabén & Sjögren (Stockholm, Sweden), 2001.

Viveca Lärn, *En barkbåt till Eddie,* Rabén & Sjögren (Stockholm, Sweden), 2001.

Barbro Lindgren, *Julia vill ha ett djur,* Rabén & Sjögren (Stockholm, Sweden), 2002, translated by Elisabeth Kallick Dyssengaard as *Julia Wants a Pet,* R & S Books (New York, NY), 2003.

Bo R. Holmberg, *En dag med Johnny,* Alfabeta (Stockholm, Sweden), 2002.

Johanna Nilsson, *Alva och familjen Låtsas,* Rabén & Sjögren (Stockholm, Sweden), 2003.

Bo R. Holmberg, *Linnea och snomannen,* Rabén & Sjögren (Stockholm, Sweden), 2004.

Barbro Lindgren, *Rosas sånger,* Rabén & Sjögren (Stockholm, Sweden), 2004.

Margareta Strömstedt, *Boken om Majken,* Rabén & Sjögren (Stockholm, Sweden), 2004.

Viveca Lärn, *En ettas dagbok,* Rabén & Sjögren (Stockholm, Sweden), 2005.

Barbro Lindgren, *Dollans dagis,* Rabén & Sjögren (Stockholm, Sweden), 2005.

Ulf Nilsson, *Alla döda små djur,* Bonnier Carlsen (Stockholm, Sweden), 2006, translated as *All the Dear Little Animals,* Gecko Press (Wellington, New Zealand), 2006.

Barbro Lindgren, *VLMF: vad lever man för?,* Rabén & Sjögren (Stockholm, Sweden), 2006.

Viveca Lärn, *Roberta Karlsson och kungen,* Rabén & Sjögren (Stockholm, Sweden), 2006.

Barbro Lindgren, *Korken flyger,* Rabén & Sjögren (Stockholm, Sweden), 2006.

Christina Björk, *Astrids äventyr,* Rabén & Sjögren (Stockholm, Sweden), 2007.

Bo R. Holmberg, *A Day with Dad,* Candlewick Press (Cambridge, MA), 2008.

Barbro Lindgren, *Max: babypussel,* Rabén & Sjögren (Stockholm, Sweden), 2009.

Ulf Nilsson, *When We Were Alone in the World,* Gecko Press (Wellington, New Zealand), 2009.

Sidelights

Eva Eriksson is an award-winning Swedish artist and illustrator whose work has been featured in children's books since the 1970s. In addition to creating original, self-illustrated books such as her "Bella and Gustav" series—translated for English-language readers as *Victor and Rosalie in One Short Week, Victor and Rosalie in Hocus-Pocus,* and *Victor and Rosalie in Jealousy*—Eriksson has contributed her engaging, soft-edged watercolor and colored-pencil illustrations to books by Barbro Lindgren, Ulf Nilsson, and Bo. R. Holmberg, three of Sweden's most popular writers for young children. Praising the humorous *A Crash Course for Molly* in *Booklist,* Carolyn Phelan predicted that Eriksson's original story about a spunky young piglet is a rarity: a "picture book that will have both children and their parents laughing out loud." In 2001 Eriksson was honored

with the prestigious Astrid Lindgren prize, an award named in honor of one of the most beloved children's authors of all time.

Eriksson made her illustration debut in 1977, creating artwork for Björn Nordström and Jonas Sima's *Blåsjöbarna i vilda västern.* Beginning with her second book, *Om en liten vecka eller när Bella träffade Gustav*—translated as *Victor and Rosalie in One Short Week*—she proved her talent as an author and illustrator, and during the years since she has alternated between writing her own stories and illustrating books by others.

One of Eriksson's most frequent collaborators has been Lindgren, whose picture books for the young include gentle stories that cast pigs, dogs, and other animals in childlike roles. A spunky puppy is the star of *Rosa: Perpetual Motion Machine, Rosa Moves to Town,* and *Rosa Goes to Daycare,* which follow the frisky pet as she learns to control her desire to play, chew, and explore unfettered. The artist treats the humorous story in *Rosa: Perpetual Motion Machine* "with comic flair," according to *Booklist* contributor Susan Dove Lempke, by working "many funny details" into the art for each page. Reviewing *Rosa Goes to Daycare,* John Peters predicted in *Booklist* that Eriksson's "appealingly drawn" doggy heroine provides children with a "fresh, lightly disguised alternative" to human-centered stories about parent-child separation.

Lindgren and Eriksson also create stories featuring human characters. Praising the "expressive and tender" images of children that Eriksson contributes to Lindgren's *Andrei's Search,* Margaret A. Chang wrote in *School Library Journal* that "they provide a realistic counterpoint" to the author's "dreamlike" story about a boy searching for his mother. According to Lempke, writing for *Horn Book,* Lindgren's *Julia Wants a Pet* captures an oft-held child's dream and benefits from drawings that depict the "energy and purpose" of Lindgren's seven-year-old heroine "with remarkable economy of line." Calling Julia "a force of nature in a tutu," a *Publishers Weekly* contributor added that Eriksson's warm-hued and textured pencil drawings "ground the heroine in the real world" while also capturing the story's "playful tones."

One of the many collaborations between Holmberg and Eriksson, *A Day with Dad* describes the experiences of Tim as he prepares to take the train by himself to visit his divorced dad. The images the artist contributes to this subdued story "convey strong emotions," wrote *Booklist* critic Abby Nolan, and in *Horn Book* Kitty Flynn wrote that Eriksson's "unfussy" pencil drawings feature the "expressive body language and facial expressions" capture the varied emotions in Holmberg's "gentle, poignant" tale.

Eva Eriksson's soft-edged pencil artwork captures the gentle nature of Bo R. Holmberg's A Day with Dad. *(Candlewick Press, 2008. Illustrations copyright © 2008 by Eva Eriksson. Text copyright © 2008 by Bo R. Holmberg. Reproduced by permission of the publisher, Candlewick Press, Inc., Somerville, MA.)*

Biographical and Critical Sources

PERIODICALS

Booklist, March 15, 2000, John Peters, review of *Andrei's Search,* p. 1388; April 15, 2003, Hazel Rochman, review of *Molly Goes Shopping,* p. 1477; April 1, 2005, Carolyn Phelan, review of *A Crash Course for Molly,* p. 1365; April 15, 2008, Abby Nolan, review of *A Day with Dad,* p. 49.
Horn Book, May-June, 2003, Christine M. Hepperman, review of *Molly Goes Shopping,* p. 327; September-October, 2003, Susan Dove Lempke, review of *Julia Wants a Pet,* p. 599; May-June, 2005, Jennifer M. Brabander, review of *A Crash Course for Molly,* p. 307; May-June, 2008, Kitty Flynn, review of *A Day with Dad,* p. 295.
Kirkus Reviews, May 1, 2005, review of *A Crash Course for Molly,* p. 538.
Publishers Weekly, September 29, 2003, review of *Julia Wants a Pet,* p. 65.
School Library Journal, July, 2000, Margaret A. Chang, review of *Andrei's Search,* p. 82; April, 2003, Andrea Tarr, review of *Molly Goes Shopping,* p. 118; June, 2005, Martha Topol, review of *A Crash Course for Molly,* p. 109; August, 2008, Ieva Bates, review of *A Day with Dad,* p. 94.

ONLINE

Rabén & Sjögren Web site, http://www.rabensjogren.se/ (November 15, 2009), "Eva Eriksson."*

* * *

FAROOQI, Musharraf Ali 1968-

Personal

Born 1968, in Hyderabad, Pakistan; immigrated to Canada, 1994; married; wife's name Michelle (an illustrator and artist). *Education:* Attended NED University of Engineering and Technology (Karachi, Pakistan).

Addresses

Home—Toronto, Ontario, Canada. *E-mail*—musharraf. ali.farooqi@gmail.com.

Career

Author, translator, and publisher. Urdu Project (publisher), founder and publisher; Oxford University Press Pakistan, Urdu publisher, 2009—.

Awards, Honors

IMPAC Dublin Literary Award finalist, 2010, for *The Story of a Widow.*

Writings

Passion in the Time of Termites, HarperCollins (New Delhi, India), 2001.

(Translator) Ghalib Lakhnavi and Abdullah Bilgrami, *The Adventures of Amir Hamza: Lord of the Auspicious Planetary Conjunction,* Modern Library (New York, NY), 2007.
The Cobbler's Holiday; or, Why Ants Don't Wear Shoes, illustrated by Eugene Yelchin, Roaring Brook Press (New York, NY), 2008.
The Story of a Widow (novel), Alfred A. Knopf (Canada), 2008.
(Translator) Muhammad Husain Jah and Ahmed Husain Qamar, *The Land and the Tilism* (volume one of "Hoshruba" series; based on *Tilism-e Hoshruba*), Urdu Project (Toronto, Ontario, Canada), 2009.
(Translator) Afzal Ahmed Syed, *Rococo and Other Worlds,* Wesleyan University Press (Middletown, CT), 2010.
(Translator) Syed Muhammad Ashraf, *The Beast,* Tranquebar Press/Westland Books (New Delhi, India), 2010.
The Amazing Moustaches of Moochhander the Iron Man, illustrated by Michelle Farooqi, Puffin Books (New Delhi, India), 2010.

Contributor of essays to *Annual of Urdu Studies.*

Sidelights

Although he originally planned to become an engineer, Musharraf Ali Farooqi realized part way through his studies that his real love was literature and language. Born in Pakistan and educated in Canada, Farooqi is now a Toronto-based writer and translator who has been highly praised for his translation of classical works written in Persian and Urdu. The author's versatility can be demonstrated by noting his creative range, from the novel *The Story of a Widow* to the children's picture book *The Cobbler's Holiday; or, Why Ants Don't Wear Shoes.* In addition, Farooqi's enthusiasm for his work seems tireless: as the founder and publisher of the Urdu Project, he has undertaken the translation, printing, and marketing of the "Hoshruba," a twenty-four-volume fantasy that was first written in Urdu.

In *The Cobbler's Holiday* Farooqi weaves an amusing story around a whimsical premise: that tiny ants used to wear clothes and shoes much as humans now do. With many feet to shoe, the cobbler ant worked overtime, for every ant wanted many pairs of shoes to choose from, and they wore out these shoes doing a special ant dance. Finally, the cobbler ant retires, leaving the ant community worried about their shoe supply until Red Ant arrives and proves that one can be shoeless and a graceful dancer to boot. A *Kirkus Reviews* writer cited illustrator Eugen Yelchin's contribution of "stylish, sophisticated" art, adding that "math exercises, as well as some conclusions about human nature, can be extrapolated from [Farooqi's] . . . wry tale." The author creates "scenarios ripe with comedy," wrote a *Publishers Weekly* contributor, and he adds to the comedy through the words of his "deadpan narrator." In *School Library Journal* Mary Jean Smith praised Yelchin's depiction of "ants with large heads and eyes," dubbing *The Cobbler's Holiday* a "droll fable" that will prove useful to parents hoping to "spark a discussion about wants and needs."

Musharraf Ali Farooqi tells an original folk-type tale in his colorful picture book The Cobbler's Holiday; or, Why Ants Don't Wear Shoes, *featuring illustrations by Eugene Yelchin.* (Roaring Book Press, 2008. Illustrations copyright © 2008 by Eugene Yelchin. All rights reserved. Reprinted by permission of Henry Holt and Company, LLC.)

While Farooqi's fiction has received consistent praise, he has become best known for his work translating books such as Ghalib Lakhnavi and Abdullah Bilgrami's *The Adventures of Amir Hamza: Lord of the Auspicious Planetary Conjunction.* Describing this book's origins, the Indo-Islamic "Hamzanama," as "the 'Iliad' and 'Odyssey' of medieval Persia," William Dalrymple added in the *New York Times Book Review* that in *The Adventures of Amir Hamza* Farooqi creates a "remarkable translation" of what the critic characterized as "great miscellany of fireside yarns and shaggy-dog stories that over time had gathered around the travels of its protagonist, the historical uncle of the Prophet Muhammad." "At this perilous moment in history," Dalrymple concluded, *The Adventures of Amir Hamza . . .* is a reminder of an Islamic world the West seems to have forgotten: one that is imaginative and heterodox." In her review for the *Magazine of Fantasy and Science Fiction,* Elizabeth Hand viewed the same work as an "exotic, populous, Eastern variant" on *Le Morte d'Arthur* or *Orlando Furioso* that she compared to works by Isak Dinesen, Robert E. Howard, Clark Ashton Smith, and J.K. Rowling. According to Hand, Farooqi's "piquant new translation" of this eleventh-century work allows English-language readers to "sit, transfixed, as this most enthralling and ancient tale unfolds."

An Urdu epic written in the late nineteenth century by Muhammad Husain Jah and Ahmed Husain Qamar, the "Hoshruba" is also introduced to English-language readers by Farooqi, who had plans to complete all two-dozen volumes methodically over a span of years. Beginning in *The Land and the Tilism,* the epic tells the story of a sorcerer emperor who takes under his protection a giant and goes to war against that giant's enemies. Responding to a question by *Open* online interviewer regarding his motives for tackling such a daunting translation project, Farooqi explained: "My effort is aimed at readers worldwide who are unaware of this awesome, fantastic story. I want to get the book into their hands. And they will know what to do with it."

Biographical and Critical Sources

PERIODICALS

Kirkus Reviews, August 15, 2008, review of *The Cobbler's Holiday; or, Why Ants Don't Wear Shoes.*
Library Journal, October 15, 2007, Amanda Sprochi, review of *The Adventures of Amir Hamza: Lord of the Auspicious Planetary Conjunction,* p. 67.
Magazine of Fantasy and Science Fiction, February, 2008, Elizabeth Hand, review of *The Adventures of Amir Hamza,* p. 32.
New York Times Book Review, January 6, 2008, William Dalrymple, review of *The Adventures of Amir Hamza,* p. 11.
Publishers Weekly, September 15, 2008, review of *The Cobbler's Holiday,* p. 66.
Quill & Quire, May 5, 2009, Eric Emin Wood, "New Publishing Venture Debuts with 24-Volume Fantasy Saga."
School Library Journal, September, 2008, Mary Jean Smith, review of *The Cobbler's Holiday,* p. 145.

ONLINE

Musharraf Ali Farooqi Home Page, http://www.mafarooqi.com (November 5, 2009).
Open Online, http://www.openthemagazine.com/ (July 11, 2009), Saaz Aggarwal, "Adventures of Musharraf Ali Farooqi."
Urdu Project Web site, http://urduproject.wordpress.com/ (November 5, 2009).

*   *   *

FISHER, Suzanne
See STAPLES, Suzanne Fisher

*   *   *

FRANKLAND, David

Personal

Born in England.

Addresses

Home—Sussex, England. *Agent*—Bernstein & Andriulli, 58 W. 40th St., New York, NY 10018.

Career

Illustrator and commercial artist. Formerly worked in advertising as an art director, London, England.

Illustrator

Carolyn Bear, *The Last Loneliest Dodo,* Schlesinger (London, England), 1974.

Carolyn Bear, *No Time for Dinosaurs,* Schlesinger (London, England), 1975.

Robin Chambers, *The Ice Warrior, and Other Stories,* Kestrell (Harmondsworth, England), 1976.

Jenny Taylor and Terry Ingleby, *Can You Do This?,* two volumes, Longman (London, England), 1978.

(With Meg Rutherford) Robert Mathias, *Aesop's Fables,* Silver Burdett (Morristown, NJ), 1983.

Susan Dickinson, reteller, *Brer Rabbit and the Peanut Patch,* Collins (London, England), 1985, Forest House Publishing (Lake Forest, IL), 1990.

(With Julius Lester) Leila Berg, *Mr Wolf and His Tail; and, The Knee-high Man,* BBC Books (London, England), 1990.

Joyce Faraday, reteller, *Treasure Island* (based on the book by Robert Louis Stevenson), Ladybird (Loughborough, England), 1994, Dutton Children's Books (New York, NY), 1996.

Joan Collins, reteller, *Alice in Wonderland* (based on the story by Lewis Carroll), Ladybird (Loughborough, England), 1994, Dutton Children's Books (New York, NY), 1996.

Robert Westall, *Blitz,* Collins (London, England), 1995.

Ronne Randall, reteller, *Aesop's Fables,* Ladybird (Loughborough, England), 1995.

S.H. Burton, *Eight Ghost Stories,* new edition, Longman (Harlow, England), 1997.

Louise Cooper, *Storm Ghost,* Puffin (London, England), 1998.

Helen Paiba, compiler, *Scary Stories for Nine Year Olds,* Macmillan (London, England), 1999.

Helen Paiba, compiler, *Animal Stories for Nine Year Olds,* Macmillan (London, England), 1999.

Clare West, reteller, *Cold Comfort Farm,* second edition (based on the novel by Stella Gibbons), Oxford University Press (Oxford, England), 2000.

Helen Paiba, compiler, *Animal Stories for Ten Year Olds,* Macmillan (London, England), 2000.

Helen Paiba, compiler, *Scary Stories for Ten Year Olds,* Macmillan (London, England), 2000.

Ann Kramer, *Black Peoples of America,* Franklin Watts (London, England), 2002.

Simon Adams, *Cavalier and Roundheads,* Franklin Watts (London, England), 2002.

John Escott, reteller, *White Fang* (based on the novel by Jack London), Oxford University Press (Oxford, England), 2002.

Dick King-Smith, *Just Binnie,* Puffin (London, England), 2004.

Anthony Read, *The Baker Street Boys: The Case of the Ranjipur Ruby,* Walker (London, England), 2006.

Anthony Read, *The Baker Street Boys: The Case of the Limehouse Laundry,* Walker (London, England), 2007.

Anthony Read, *The Baker Street Boys: The Case of the Stolen Sparklers,* Walker (London, England), 2008.

Jeanne Birdsall, *The Penderwicks on Gardam Street,* Alfred A. Knopf (New York, NY), 2008.

Janet Taylor Lisle, *Highway Cats,* Philomel (New York, NY), 2008.

Anthony Read, *The Baker Street Boys: The Case of the Haunted Horrors,* Walker (London, England), 2009.

Sidelights

David Frankland is an English illustrator who is known for the nostalgic, high-contrast silhouette art he has contributed to books such as Robert Westall's *Blitz,* Jeanne Birdsall's *The Penderwicks on Gardam Street,* and Janet Taylor Lisle's *Highway Cats.* Citing Arthur Rackham as among those artists who have inspired his unique style, Frankland also explained on a Walker Books online interview that his training was in design rather than illustration. His move from pen and ink to brush "made my work bolder and more atmospheric," the artist noted. "I became less interested in close-up features and facial expressions of characters and more interested in the mood, drama and action of a drawing and in what the characters were doing and why and where they were doing it."

In *Highway Cats* Lisle takes inspiration from Robert Lawson's classic *Rabbit Hill* in her story about a community of wild cats that is threatened by the encroachments of man. Living in the woods bordering an interstate highway, the feral cats Murray the Claw, Shredder, and Kahlia Koo sense that something has changed when a trio of abandoned kittens joins them in their hardscrabble life. When earthmoving equipment rumbles in, signaling the construction of a new highway, the cats find their natural cynicism giving way to resilience as the kittens share their own optimism about the changes the future will bring. Frankland's "dramatic" spot art for *Highway Cats* reflects Lisle's story, with its "slightly wry . . . humor," wrote *School Library Journal* critic Eva Mitnick, and Joanna Rudge Long noted in *Horn Book* that the "lively silhouettes" created by Frankland "nicely reflect . . . the story's mood." In *Booklist* Kathleen Isaacs cited the "deftly written and attractively illustrated" story as "a treat" for upper-elementary-grade readers.

Biographical and Critical Sources

PERIODICALS

Booklist, July 1, 2008, Kathleen Isaacs, review of *Highway Cats,* p. 64.

Horn Book, September-October, 2008, Joanna Rudge Long, review of *Highway Cats,* p. 59.

Kirkus Reviews, July 15, 2008, review of *Highway Cats.*
School Library Journal, November, 2008, Eva Mitnick, review of *Highway Cats,* p. 92.

ONLINE

Artist Partners Ltd. Web site, http://www.artistpartners. com/ (November 15, 2009), "David Frankland."
Walker Books Web site, http://www.walker.co.uk/ (November 15, 2009), "David Frankland."*

* * *

FREDERICK, Heather Vogel

Personal

Born in Peterborough, NH; father an elementary teacher and principal; married; children: two sons. *Education:* Principia College, B.A. (English literature and German); attended University of Cologne on a Fulbright grant.

Addresses

Home—Portland, OR.

Career

Journalist and author. Christian Science Monitor, Boston, MA, staff writer and editor, then children's book review editor. Freelance writer; presenter at schools.

Awards, Honors

Books for the Teen Age designation, New York Public Library, Amelia Bloomer Project inclusion, American Library Association, and Oregon Book Award for Young Adults, all 2003, Sequoyah Book Award finalist, Oklahoma Library Association, and Lamplighter Award finalist, both 2004, Beacon of Freedom Award finalist, 2005, Connecticut Nutmeg Children's Book Award finalist, 2006, and Arizona Young Readers Award finalist, 2007, all for *The Voyage of Patience Goodspeed;* Amelia Bloomer Project inclusion, 2005, for *The Education of Patience Goodspeed;* 100 Titles for Reading and Sharing listee, New York Public Library, 2005, and Oregon Book Award finalist, 2006, both for *For Your Paws Only;* West Sussex, England, Children's Book Award shortlist, 2007, Garden State Book Award finalist, 2008, and Hawai'i Nene Award nominee, 2010, all for *The Black Paw;* Massachusetts Children's Book Award nomination, 2009, for *Goldwhiskers.*

Writings

FOR CHILDREN

The Voyage of Patience Goodspeed (novel), Simon & Schuster Books for Young Readers (New York, NY), 2002.

Heather Vogel Frederick (Photograph by Steve Frederick. Reproduced by permission.)

The Education of Patience Goodspeed (novel), Simon & Schuster Books for Young Readers (New York, NY), 2004
Babyberry Pie (picture book), illustrated by Amy Schwartz, Harcourt (New York, NY), 2010.
Hide-and-Squeak (picture book), illustrated by C.F. Payne, Simon & Schuster Books for Young Readers (New York, NY), 2011.

Contributor to periodicals, including *Child, Family Life,* and *New York Times;* former contributing editor, *Publishers Weekly.*

"SPY MICE" SERIES

The Black Paw, illustrated by Sally Wern Comport, Simon & Schuster Books for Young Readers (New York, NY), 2005.
For Your Paws Only, illustrated by Sally Wern Comport, Simon & Schuster Books for Young Readers (New York, NY), 2005.
Goldwhiskers, illustrated by Sally Wern Comport, Simon & Schuster Books for Young Readers (New York, NY), 2007.

"MOTHER-DAUGHTER BOOK CLUB" NOVEL SERIES

The Mother-Daughter Book Club, Simon & Schuster Books for Young Readers (New York, NY), 2007.
Much Ado about Anne, Simon & Schuster Books for Young Readers (New York, NY), 2008.
Dear Pen Pal, Simon & Schuster Books for Young Readers (New York, NY), 2009.

Sidelights

Although Heather Vogel Frederick has fulfilled her childhood dream of making writing her life, she worked as a journalist for many years and only turned to children's books while raising her own two children. Beloved by the young fans of her fanciful "Spy Mice" series, Frederick is also the author of the award-winning middle-grade historical novel *The Voyage of Patience Goodspeed.* Her popular "Mother-Daughter Book Club" novels, which include *The Mother-Daughter Book Club, Much Ado about Anne,* and *Dear Pen Pal,* have inspired modern 'tweens with an appreciation for the role good books can play in shaping one's own life.

While growing up in New England, Frederick followed in her family's tradition: she loved books and loved telling stories. "My mother used to say that if Heather had her nose in a book, the house would have to burn down around her before she'd sit up and take notice!," the author recalled on her home page. "Those are the best books, though, aren't they? The ones that take your imagination by storm and spirit you off into a different world?" After attending college and marrying, Frederick became a journalist and worked for several years on the staff of the highly respected *Christian Science Monitor* newspaper.

Frederick published her first book, the historical novel *The Voyage of Patience Goodspeed,* in 2002. Set on Nantucket island, off the coast of Massachusetts, in 1835, the story follows twelve-year-old Patience Goodspeed as she joins her younger brother Thaddeus and her father, Captain Goodspeed, on a prolonged whaling voyage. Aboard the *Morning Star* Patience misses the studious home life she had enjoyed, and the countless chores allow her few opportunities to channel her intellectual curiosity. However, the girl's math skills soon qualify her to assist the ship's navigator, and when the crew mutinies, stranding the family on a barren island, she uses her newfound skills to aid in their survival. Describing the many dangers faced by New England whalers during the nineteenth century, Frederick effectively captures "the personalities and activities on board," making *The Voyage of Patience Goodspeed* "a voyage readers will be glad to make," according to *Booklist* contributor Diane Foote. Comparing Frederick's novel to Avi's award-winning novel *The Adventures of Charlotte Doyle* a *Kirkus Reviews* writer praised the story's "feisty heroine" and "rich" details, while a *Publishers Weekly* critic wrote that the well-researched novel is further buoyed by "atmospheric details" and an "eclectic cast and crew."

The adventures of Frederick's young heroine continue in *The Education of Patience Goodspeed,* as Patience and Thaddeus find themselves boarding with a missionary family on the Hawaiian island of Maui while the *Morning Star* takes on provisions in Lahaina. While Patience bucks heads with Reverend Wiggins over his constraining views of "a woman's place," a troublesome neighbor from Nantucket arrives and tries to ingratiate herself with the widowed Captain Goodspeed.

According to a *Kirkus Reviews* writer, the "tart narration" of the now-thirteen-year-old Patience "is . . . smart and funny," as well as "deftly done." Calling *The Education of Patience Goodspeed* "action-packed," Ginny Gustin added in *School Library Journal* that Frederick "skillfully portrays Patience's emotional development and growing maturity."

In *The Mother-Daughter Book Club* Frederick introduces four typical middle graders: book-loving Emma, shopaholic Megan, sports-loving Cassidy, and country girl Jess. Together with their moms, the girls join a local book club that meets once a month. With their mothers' encouragement, the girls grudgingly tackle Louisa May Alcott's *Little Women,* and they are surprised to find that the century-old novel with its beloved characters Jo, Beth, Amy, Meg, and Marmee, has much to teach today's tech-savvy sixth grader. Told in alternating chapters by each of the girls, *The Mother-Daughter Book Club* features "plenty of detail," according to *Booklist* critic Heather Booth. Teens "will be easily pulled along" by Frederick's story, predicted Booth, and a *Publishers Weekly* critic suggested that "the club's success . . . may well inspire readers to start one of their own."

Cover of Frederick's young-adult novel **The Mother-Daughter Book Club,** *which inspired a number of real-life reading groups.* (Aladdin Paperbacks, 2007. Reproduced by permission.)

Frederick focuses on a diminutive super spy in her middle-grade novel Spy Mice: For Your Paws Only, *featuring artwork by Sally Wern Comport.* (G.P. Putnam's, 2007. Illustrations copyright © 2007 by Sally Wern Comport. Reproduced by permission of Penguin Young Readers Group.)

The cast of *The Mother-Daughter Book Club* return in several other novels for preteen readers. In *Much Ado about Anne* the girls are in seventh grade and *Anne of Green Gables* is on the reading list. The plot of L.M. Montgomery's classic novel seems more than timely to Jess; she has just learned that her family may have to sell off their farm. Although the girls worry when their moms invite stuck-up Becca Chadwick and her mother to join the club, the new members prove their worth in a busy year full of camping trips, school challenges, and efforts to help each other fulfill their dreams. The club membership may change in *Dear Pen Pal* as Jess is offered a full scholarship to a well-known boarding school. Meanwhile, each of the other girls encounters changes in her own life, and reading Jean Webster's novel *Daddy-Long-Legs* speaks to each of the girls while it also captures Jess's dilemma. Although Maria B. Salvadore found the grown-up characters "cliched," she described the teen girls as "gutsy problem-solvers" in her *School Library Journal* review of *Much Ado about Anne.* "The pace is fast, the concerns and emotions real," the critic added of Frederick's "satisfying" series installment.

Geared for readers in the upper elementary grades, Frederick's whimsical "Spy Mice" books include *The Black Paw, For Your Paws Only,* and *Goldwhiskers.* The books focus on a boy named Ozymandias "Oz" Levinson. When his father moves the family from Seattle to Washington, DC, in order to take a job at the International Spy Museum café, Oz meets some tiny mouse spies and quickly becomes involved in a city-wide battle between the mice and the rats. In *The Black Paw* Oz joins a field-mouse secret agent named Morning Glory Goldenleaf in her effort to battle the nefarious work of rat kingpin Roquefort Dupont. Dupont is intent on taking control of the entire rodent world and he sets the stage for this revolution by uniting all the rats of Europe in *For Your Paws Only.* Now it is up to Oz and his bewhiskered secret-agent friends at the Spy Mice Agency to travel to the Big Apple and stop this global rodent threat. Kidnapping (or rather, mousenapping) figures in the plot of *Goldwhiskers,* as Oz and company travel to London on a holiday, only to find themselves in the center of a mystery involving the crown jewels and a group of mouse orphans. In *Publishers Weekly,* a reviewer called *The Black Paw* "a lighthearted, clever combination of fast-moving adventure and talking-animal fantasy," while *School Library Journal* critic Elizabeth Bird praised *For Your Paws Only* as "fast-paced without becoming too predictable." Citing the amusing cartoon art by Sally Wern Comport, another critic for *Publishers Weekly* enjoyed the "engaging banter" in *The Black Paw,* predicting that Frederick's "tale of tails will especially tickle aspiring sleuths."

Biographical and Critical Sources

PERIODICALS

Booklist, June 1, 2002, Diane Foote, review of *The Voyage of Patience Goodspeed,* p. 1722; July, 2005, Todd Morning, review of *The Black Paw,* p. 1924; June 1, 2007, Heather Booth, review of *The Mother-Daughter Book Club,* p. 75.

Kirkus Reviews, June 15, 2002, review of *The Voyage of Patience Goodspeed,* p. 880; August 1, 2004, review of *The Education of Patience Goodspeed,* p. 741; September 15, 2005, review of *For Your Paws Only,* p. 1025.

Publishers Weekly, June 17, 2002, review of *The Voyage of Patience Goodspeed,* p. 65; July 18, 2005, review of *The Black Paw,* p. 206; April 2, 2007, review of *The Mother-Daughter Book Club,* p. 57.

School Library Journal, October, 2004, Ginny Gustin, review of *The Education of Patience Goodspeed,* p. 163; October, 2005, Elizabeth Bird, review of *The Black Paw,* p. 160; December, 2005, Elizabeth Bird, review of *For Your Paws Only,* p. 147; August, 2007, Susan Moorhead, review of *The Mother-Daughter Book Club,* p. 116; November, 2008, Maria B. Salvadore, review of *Much Ado about Anne,* p. 120.

ONLINE

Heather Vogel Frederick Home Page, http://www.heather vogelfrederick.com (November 15, 2009).

Heather Vogel Frederick Web log, http://heathervogel
frederick/wordpress.com/ (November 15, 2009).

* * *

FRIESNER, Esther 1951-
(Esther M. Friesner)

Personal

Born July 16, 1951, in New York, NY; daughter of
David R. (a teacher) and Beatrice (a teacher) Friesner;
married Walter Stutzman (a software engineer), December 22, 1974; children: Michael Jacob, Anne Elizabeth.
Education: Vassar College, B.A. (cum laude; Spanish
and drama), 1972; Yale University, M.A. (Spanish),
1975, Ph.D. (Spanish), 1977.

Addresses

Home—Madison, CT. *E-mail*—efriesner@cshore.com.

Career

Writer. Yale University, New Haven, CT, instructor in
Spanish, 1977-79, 1983.

Member

Science Fiction Writers of America.

Awards, Honors

Named Outstanding New Fantasy Writer, *Romantic
Times,* 1986; Best Science Fiction/Fantasy Titles cita-
tion, *Voice of Youth Advocates,* 1988, for *New York by
Knight;* Skylark Award, 1994; Nebula Award finalist for
Best Novelette, 1995, for *Jesus at the Bat*; Nebula
Award for Best Short Story, 1995, for "Death and the
Librarian"; Hugo Award finalist, and Nebula Award for
Best Short Story, both 1996, both for "A Birthday."

Writings

FANTASY NOVELS

(As Esther M. Friesner) *Harlot's Ruse,* Popular Library
  (New York, NY), 1986.
(As Esther M. Friesner) *The Silver Mountain,* Popular Li-
  brary (New York, NY), 1986.
(As Esther M. Friesner) *Druid's Blood,* New American Li-
  brary (New York, NY), 1988.
(As Esther M. Friesner) *Yesterday We Saw Mermaids,* Tor
  (New York, NY), 1992.
Wishing Season (young-adult novel), Atheneum (New
  York, NY), 1993.
(With Laurence Watt-Evans; as Esther M. Friesner) *Split
  Heirs,* Tor (New York, NY), 1993.

(As Esther M. Friesner) *The Psalms of Herod,* White Wolf,
  1995.
The Sherwood Game, Pocket Books (New York, NY),
  1995.
Child of the Eagle: A Myth of Rome, Baen (Riverdale,
  NY), 1996.
The Sword of Mary, White Wolf Publishing, 1996.
(With Robert Asprin) *E. Godz,* Baen (Riverdale, NY),
  2003.
Temping Fate, Dutton (New York, NY), 2006.
Sphinx's Princess, Random House (New York, NY), 2009.

*"CHRONICLES OF THE TWELVE KINGDOMS" FANTASY
SERIES; AS ESTHER M. FRIESNER*

Mustapha and His Wise Dog, Avon (New York, NY), 1985.
Spells of Mortal Weaving, Avon (New York, NY), 1986.
The Witchwood Cradle, Avon (New York, NY), 1987.
The Water King's Laughter, Avon (New York, NY), 1989.

"DEMONS" SERIES; FANTASY NOVELS

Here Be Demons, Ace (New York, NY), 1988.
Demon Blues, Ace (New York, NY), 1989.
Hooray for Hellywood, Ace (New York, NY), 1990.

*"NEW YORK BY KNIGHT" FANTASY SERIES; AS ESTHER M.
FRIESNER*

New York by Knight, New American Library (New York,
  NY), 1986.
Elf Defense, New American Library (New York, NY),
  1988.
Sphynxes Wild, New American Library (New York, NY),
  1989.

"GNOME MAN'S LAND" FANTASY SERIES

Gnome Man's Land (first volume in trilogy), Ace (New
  York, NY), 1991.
Harpy High (second volume in trilogy), Ace (New York,
  NY), 1991.
Unicorn U (third volume in trilogy), Ace (New York, NY),
  1992.

"MAJYK" FANTASY SERIES

Majyk by Accident, Ace (New York, NY), 1993.
Majyk by Hook or Crook, Ace (New York, NY), 1994.
Majyk by Design, Ace (New York, NY), 1994.

"NOBODY" SERIES

Nobody's Princess, Random House (New York, NY), 2007.
Nobody's Prize, Random House (New York, NY), 2008.

*"CHICKS IN CHAINMAIL" SERIES; EDITOR AND
CONTRIBUTOR*

Chicks in Chainmail, Baen (Riverdale, NY), 1995.
Did You Say "Chicks"?!, Baen (Riverdale, NY), 1998.
Chicks 'n' Chained Males, Baen (Riverdale, NY), 1999.

The Chick Is in the Mail, Baen (Riverdale, NY), 2000.
Turn the Other Chick, Baen (Riverdale, NY), 2004.

SCIENCE FICTION

Warchild ("Star Trek: Deep Space Nine" series), Pocket Books (New York, NY), 1994.
To Storm Heaven ("Star Trek: The Next Generation" series) Pocket Books (New York, NY), 1997.

OTHER

(Editor, with Martin H. Greenberg; as Esther M. Friesner) *Alien Pregnant by Elvis,* DAW (New York, NY), 1994.
(Editor, with Martin H. Greenberg; as Esther M. Friesner) *Blood Muse: Timeless Tales of Vampires in the Arts,* Donald I. Fine (New York, NY), 1995.
(As Esther M. Friesner) *Men in Black II* (based on the screenplay by Robert Gordon and Barry Fanaro), Del Rey (New York, NY), 2002.
Death and the Librarian and Other Stories (anthology), Five Star (Waterville, ME), 2002.
(Editor) *Witch Way to the Mall,* Baen (Riverdale, NY), 2009.
(Editor) *Strip Mauled,* Baen (Riverdale, NY), 2009.

Fiction published in anthologies, sometimes under name Esther M. Friesner, including *Elsewhere III,* Ace, 1984; *Afterwar,* Baen Books, 1985; *Werewolves,* Harper & Row, 1988; *Arabesques II,* Avon, 1989; *Carmen Miranda's Ghost Is Haunting Space Station Three,* Baen Books, 1990; *Cthluthu 2000,* edited by Jim Turner; Arkham House, 1995; *Newer York,* ROC, 1991; *The Ultimate Frankenstein,* Dell, 1991; *What Might Have Been,* Bantam, 1992; *Snow White, Blood Red,* Morrow, 1993; *Alternate Warriors,* Tor, 1993; *Bet You Can't Read Just One,* edited by Alan Dean Foster, Ace, 1993; *Weird Shakespeare,* edited by Kitt Kerr, DAW Books, 1994; *Excalibur,* edited by Richard Gilliam, Ed Kramer, and Martin H. Greenberg, Warner Books, 1995; *Fantastic Alice,* edited by Margaret Weis, Ace, 1995; *Gothic Ghosts,* edited by Charles Grant and Wendy Webb, Tor Books, 1997; *The Mammoth Book of Comic Fantasy,* edited by Mike Ashley, Carroll & Graf, 1998; *Black Cats and Broken Mirrors,* edited by Greenberg and John Helfers, DAW Books, 1998; *Streets of Blood: Vampire Stories from New York City,* edited by Lawrence Schimel and Greenberg, Cumberland House, 1998; *Merlin,* edited by Greenberg, DAW Books, 1999; *Black Heart, Ivory Bones,* edited by Ellen Datlow and Terri Windling, Avon, 2000; *Single White Vampire Seeks Same,* edited by Brittany A. Koren, DAW Books, 2001; *Knight Fantastic,* edited by Greenberg and John Helfers, DAW Books, 2002; *Murder by Magic,* edited by Rosemary Edghill, Warner Aspect, 2004; *You Bet Your Planet,* edited by Greenberg and Koren, DAW Books, 2005; *My Big Fat Supernatural Wedding,* edited by P.N. Elrod, St. Martin's Griffin, 2006; *Heroes in Training,* edited by Jim Hines, DAW Books, 2007; and *Something Magic This Way Comes,* edited by Greenberg and

Sarah Hoyt, DAW Books, 2008. Contributor of short fiction and poetry, sometimes under name Esther M. Friesner, to periodicals, including *Isaac Asimov's Science-Fiction Magazine, Fantasy and Science Fiction, Marion Zimmer Bradley's Fantasy Magazine, Amazing Stories, Fantasy Book, H.P. Lovecraft's Magazine of Horror,* and *Pulphouse.*

Sidelights

Esther Friesner "is undeniably a very funny lady and the Queen of Comedy in contemporary fantasy," observed *Intergalatic Medicine Show* contributor Darrell Schweitzer. Called by Fred Lerner in *Voice of Youth Advocates* "one of the most prolific writers of fantasy fiction, and one of the funniest," Friesner overturns many of the conventions of the fantasy genre in works that include her "New York by Knight" novel series, in which a dragon and his armored pursuer bring their ages-old battle to the streets of modern-day New York, and the "Gnome Man's Land" trilogy, which finds high schooler Tim Desmond forced to cope not only with

Cover of **Split Heirs,** *a fantasy coauthored by Friesner and Lawrence Watt-Evans and featuring cover art by Walter Velez.* (Copyright © 1993 by Lawrence Watt-Evans and Esther M. Friesner. Reproduced by permission of St. Martin's Press.)

adolescence, but also with everything from a plague of "little people" to exotic monsters and gods. According to Lerner, Friesner "has made a specialty of ferreting out obscure creatures from the mythologies and demonologies of the world and turning them loose on unsuspecting places like Brooklyn, New Haven, and Hollywood."

In addition to her many novels and award-winning short stories, Friesner has also flaunted fantasy tradition by editing the multi-volume "Chicks in Chainmail" series of penned-by-invitation short stories in which amazons co-opt the hero role reserved for macho men in traditional fantasy. "I can't say that there's one particular sort of writing I prefer over another," Friesner remarked to Lazette Gifford in an interview in *Vision: A Resource for Writers.* "Funny, serious, what-you-will, as long as I'm deriving satisfaction from the work at hand, it's good for me."

Born and raised in Brooklyn, New York, Friesner took an early interest in the wonders of literature. As she once recalled to *SATA:* "My mother told me long stories when we were going on car trips—stories from the works of Washington Irving, for instance. She'd tell me 'The Legend of Sleepy Hollow,' and I kept saying, 'I want another story, I want another story.' Finally she said, 'Look, learn to read and you can have all the stories you want.' So I thought 'That sounds like a good idea,' and I learned to read. Instead of bedtime stories, my father would sit down and read me collections of the 'Pogo' comic strip by Walt Kelly. That was wonderful. It totally warped my sense of humor in just the right way."

Friesner attended Vassar College, studying Spanish and drama, and Yale University, where she earned her master's and doctoral degrees in classical Spanish literature, specializing in the works of playwright Lope de Vega. While attending Yale, Friesner got to know Shariann Lewitt, a published science-fiction author who was then at work on a fantasy novel. "We saw her building a whole world," Friesner once recalled to *SATA,* "working out all the details on a big legal pad she had. This was quite different from writing a short story. I thought, 'Oh, building a world. I get to be God! How nice. I'm going to try that.' And that was how I got started on fantasy novels." Friesner's first world-building book became *Spells of Mortal Weaving,* in her "Chronicles of the Twelve Kingdoms" series.

Spells of Mortal Weaving is actually the second book in Friesner's "Chronicles of the Twelve Kingdoms"; the series begins with the Arabian Nights-styled adventure novel *Mustapha and His Wise Dog,* which is "enlivened by an exotic and evocative fantasy setting, and a pair of captivating characters," according to Don D'Ammassa in *Twentieth-Century Science-Fiction Writers.* The series, which also includes *The Witchwood Cradle* and *The Water King's Laughter,* follows the struggles of various mortals through several generations as they at-

Cover of Nobody's Princess, *a novel by Friesner that features artwork by Larry Rostant.* (Random House Children's Books, 2007. Jacket art copyright © 2007 by Larry Rostant. All rights reserved. Used by permission of Random House Children's Books, a division of Random House, Inc.)

tempt to overthrow Morgeld, an evil demigod. "Although Friesner followed traditional forms for the most part in this series," D'Ammassa concluded, "her wry humor and gift for characterization marked her early as someone to watch."

Friesner's original short fiction, which has won several awards, is collected in the anthology *Death and the Librarian and Other Stories.* The dozen tales include the Nebula-winning title story as well as a haunting response to 9/11 titled "Ilion," the poignant "All Vows," and the humorous stories "True Believer" and "Jesus at the Bat." Praising the title story as "darkly humorous," Jackie Cassada noted in *Library Journal* that the collection as a whole "illustrate[s] the author's acutely sensitive vision of wonder in the everyday world," while *Booklist* critic Paula Luedtke wrote that Friesner's short stories "fearlessly explore the depths and breadths of feeling and experience exquisitely well." Noting the range of emotions that the author skillfully calls forth with her tales, Luedtke added that Friesner "writes boldly, and her wit is sharp, funny, and often wry."

Temping Fate a humorous work for teens, centers on Ilana Newhouse, a sardonic, unconventional young

woman who desperately hopes to find a summer job. With help from the Divine Relief Temp Agency, Ilana is sent to work at Tabby Fabricant Textiles, where she soon discovers herself attending to a most unusual task: typing death receipts for the Fates: Clotho, Lachesis, and Atropos. "Teens familiar with Greek mythology will have the most fun with this book," Ginny Gustin noted in *School Library Journal,* and Gillian Engberg, writing in *Booklist,* maintained that "the clever, brash concept will easily draw teens."

Friesner's novel *Nobody's Princess* offers a unique take on the life of Helen of Troy. "I've always been interested in the 'untold stories' of fictional characters, especially those whose roles in their stories are one-dimensional," Friesner remarked in her *Weekly Reader* interview, adding: "In the myths, Helen was always The Beautiful One. She was seldom given the chance to act as a person. Things were done to her more than *by* her." Friesner concluded, "I thought it was about time some-

Cover of Friesner's edited story collection Witch Way to the Mall, *featuring artwork by Tom Kid.* (Baen Publishing Enterprises, 2009. Reproduced by permission of Baen Publishing Enterprises.)

thing was written in which Helen could do things for herself and to show that she was more than just The Beautiful One." Not content to live the life of a princess, Helen trains to be a warrior with her brothers, learning how to yield weapons, hunt and kill game, and ride a horse. Cheri Dobbs, writing in *School Library Journal,* stated that fans of books on mythology "will enjoy this lively tale," and Claire Rosser, writing in *Kliatt,* claimed "this story will please readers interested in ancient Greek legends." A sequel, *Nobody's Prize,* was released the following year. In the work, Helen, disguised as a male, follows Jason and the Argonauts in their quest to find the Golden Fleece. Rosser observed that the author "clearly is gifted at weaving myth, history, and adventure into an exciting YA novel." In a review for *School Library Journal,* Beth L. Meister recognized that the "characters are given depth and flaws" and noted that "details about food and customs of the time are woven into the story."

Aside from her fantasy series, Friesner is also the author of several stand-alone works, including novels, anthologies, and collections of short stories. In her novel *Split Heirs,* which was coauthored with Laurence Watt-Evans, Friesner tells the tale of Gorgonan marauders who take over the city of Hydrangea. The leader of the marauders, Gudge, crowns himself king and forcibly marries the princess of Hydrangea, Artemesia. The couple has triplets, yet the siblings are raised separately, with only one remaining in the palace. Thus, according to a *Publishers Weekly* contributor, the plot is peppered with "mistaken identities," resulting in "a lighthearted fantasy." She teamed up with fellow writer Robert Asprin on *E. Godz,* which follows a successful business woman's efforts to make her children worthy of inheriting her business empire. Edwina Godz is CEO of E.GODZ, which supports the nonprofit efforts of magic-related organizations. Because the Godz offspring, Peez and Dov, are more concerned with battling each other than advancing the family business, Edwina feigns a fatal illness and devises a contest through which the siblings learn to deal with each other. Reviewing the novel, *Kliatt* contributor Sherry Hoy dubbed Friesner's work "light fun with a touch of Carlos Castaneda."

Friesner views humor as an important ingredient in her works, but not necessarily the defining one. As she mentioned in an *Intergalactic Medicine Show* interview with Darrell Schweitzer, "My reputation seems to still be very much about the comedy. And yet I have almost a shadow-reputation of being able to write very dark things, or certainly serious, if not dark things. Both of my Nebula Award stories were dark stories, especially 'A Birthday.'" Friesner's refusal to pigeonhole her writing is a key to her success, as she told Gifford. "I'm not a funny writer or a serious writer or a fantasy writer or a poet or a playwright. I'm a writer. Either I write in the vein that a particular story demands or I wind up writing a less than satisfactory (for me) story."

Ideas for Friesner's fiction can come from overheard conversations, family vacations, newspaper accounts,

favorite comics such as Walt Kelly's "Pogo"—just about anywhere, in fact. "Finding ideas for stories has never been a problem for me," she remarked to *Suite101* online interviewer Lynne Jamneck. "They're everywhere! Finding the time to get them all down on paper . . . that's the problem. But it's so satisfying when I get the initial inspiration and am—finally—able to tame it to the point where I'm successfully communicating it to readers."

"When I write," Friesner once explained to a *SATA* interviewer, "I try to make the story so interesting that I wouldn't mind rereading it myself. . . . It's important to interest your readers because if you don't you won't have readers anymore. But if you don't interest yourself in what you're writing. . . . Well, the process of going from the first draft to the published book takes an awfully long time. You will have to look at that story and those characters a lot—you'll have to do another draft, perhaps even a third, then the editor will go over it, then the copy editor. Every time you're going to be reading the same words. If they aren't good words, you're going to get the feeling of being trapped at a party with people you don't like."

Biographical and Critical Sources

BOOKS

Twentieth-Century Science-Fiction Writers, 3rd edition, St. James Press (Detroit, MI), 1991.

PERIODICALS

Booklist, December 1, 1995, Roland Green, review of *Blood Muse: Timeless Tales of Vampires in the Arts,* p. 609; December 1, 2002, Paula Luedtke, review of *Death and the Librarian and Other Stories,* p. 651; November 1, 2004, Roland Green, review of *Turn the Other Chick,* p. 472; May 15, 2006, Gillian Engberg, review of *Temping Fate,* p. 53; March 15, 2007, Frances Bradburn, review of *Nobody's Princess,* p. 42; February 1, 2008, Frances Bradburn, review of *Nobody's Prize,* p. 42.

Intergalactic Medicine Show, July, 2008, Darrell Schweitzer, interview with Friesner.

Journal of Adolescent & Adult Literacy, March, 2007, Jennifer Michalicek, review of *Nobody's Princess,* p. 512.

Kliatt, September, 2005, Sherry Hoy, review of *E. Godz,* p. 23; May, 2007, Claire Rosser, review of *Nobody's Princess,* p. 10; March, 2008, Claire Rosser, review of *Nobody's Prize,* p. 12.

Library Journal, December, 2002, Jackie Cassada, review of *Death and the Librarian and Other Stories,* p. 185.

Publishers Weekly, June 21, 1993, review of *Split Heirs,* p. 90; November 1, 1993, review of *Wishing Season,* p. 81; October 9, 1995, review of *Blood Muse,* p. 77; April 30, 2007, review of *Nobody's Princess,* p. 161.

School Library Journal, September, 2002, Pam Johnson, review of *Men in Black II,* p. 256; August, 2006, Ginny Gustin, review of *Temping Fate,* p. 120; July 1, 2007, Cheri Dobbs, review of *Nobody's Princess,* p. 101; June, 2008, Beth L. Meister, review of *Nobody's Prize,* p. 140.

Voice of Youth Advocates, December, 1991, Fred Lerner, "The Newcomer," p. 294.

ONLINE

Baen Books Web site, http://www.baen.com/ (November 1, 2009), interview with Friesner.

Esther Friesner Home Page, http://www.sff.net/people/e.friesner (November 1, 2009).

Vision: A Resource for Writers Web site, http://www.lazette.net/vision/ (January 1, 2002), Lazette Gifford, interview with Friesner.

Suite101.com, http://scififantasyfiction.suite101.com/ (August 25, 2009), Lynne Jamneck, interview with Friesner.

Suvudu Web site, http://www.suvudu.com/ (October 20, 2009), Shawn Speakman, interview with Friesner.

Weekly Reader Online, http://www.weeklyreader.com/readandwriting/ (September 10, 2009), interview with Friesner.*

*   *   *

FRIESNER, Esther M.
See FRIESNER, Esther

G

GERBER, Carole 1947-

Personal
Born 1947; married; husband's name Mark; children: Jess, Paige. *Education:* Ohio State University, B.S. (English), M.A. (journalism). *Hobbies and other interests:* Gardening, reading, travel, yoga.

Addresses
Home—Powell, OH. *E-mail*—carolegerber@gmail.com.

Career
Author, educator, and poet. High school and middle-school English teacher; Ohio State University, former adjunct professor of journalism; worked variously as a marketing director, in-house magazine editor, and in advertising.

Member
Society of Children's Book Writers and Illustrators.

Awards, Honors
Parent Council Award of Excellence, 1997, for *Hush!*; Great Lakes Booksellers' Association Pick of the List inclusion, 1999, for *Arctic Dreams;* Ohioana and Oklahoma Book Award finalist, both 2000, both for *Firefly Night;* Cooperative Children's Book Center Recommended Book designation, 2001, for *Blizzard;* National Science Teachers Association (NSTA) Recommended designation, 2004, for *Leaf Jumpers*; John Burroughs List of Nature Books for Young Readers inclusion, 2008, and NSTA/Children's Book Council Outstanding Trade Books designation, 2009, both for *Winter Trees.*

Writings

FOR CHILDREN

The Golden Christmas Tree, illustrated by Unada, Worthington Press (St. Petersburg, FL), 1994.

Carole Gerber (Courtesy of Carole Gerber.)

A Christmas Eve Alphabet, illustrated by Susan Scarpitti, Sparrow Books (Columbus, OH), 1995.

Hush! A Gaelic Lullaby, illustrated by Marty Husted, Whispering Coyote Press (Danvers, MA), 1997.

Arctic Dreams, illustrated by Marty Husted, Whispering Coyote Press (Dallas, TX), 1999.

Firefly Night, illustrated by Marty Husted, Whispering Coyote (Watertown, MA), 2000.

Blizzard, illustrated by Marty Husted, Whispering Coyote (Watertown, MA), 2001.

Tundra Food Chains, Lake Street Publishers (Minneapolis, MN), 2003.

Leaf Jumpers, illustrated by Leslie Evans, Charlesbridge (Watertown, MA), 2004.

Jessica McBean, Tap Dance Queen, illustrated by Patrice Barton, Blooming Tree Press (Austin, TX), 2006.

Winter Trees, illustrated by Leslie Evans, Charlesbridge (Watertown, MA), 2008.

Little Red Bat, illustrated by Christina Wald, Sylvan Dell (Mt. Pleasant, SC), 2010.

Also author of *Tales of Old Columbus,* Columbus Historical Society. Contributor to educational publications.

Sidelights

Carole Gerber is an Ohio-based poet and author who came to writing after working as an English teacher, journalism instructor, and editor of a variety of publications. Her award-winning books for young children focus predominately on nature and include *Arctic Dreams, Firefly Night, Leaf Jumpers,* and *Winter Trees.* In presentations to school children, Gerber mixes an informative talk on how books are made with a "poetry jam," an original verse collaboration that draws from the creativity of each young participant.

Several of Gerber's books focus on the winter season. In *Blizzard* her brief rhymes capture a young boy's comparison of the winter seen outside his window with the cozy comforts of his own home. While the boy is covered by a thick quilt, nature is blanketed by a covering of snow, and when the snowfall ends he bundles up to join the wintery scene. Readers take a walk through a snow-covered forest in *Winter Trees,* identifying the shapes of different trees and also learning about how wildlife survives the coldest months of the year. Gerber's "short, rhyming phrases . . . create familiar, concrete images," wrote *Booklist* critic Carolyn Phelan in a review of *Blizzard,* and in *School Library Journal* Lauralyn Persson praised *Winter Trees* for its pairing of Leslie Evans' "intriguing" mixed-media-enhanced block print and Gerber's "simple poetic" text describing "the subtle charms of trees in winter." A *Kirkus Reviews* writer dubbed *Winter Trees* a "visually striking, cozy winter read," and Hazel Rochman concluded in *Booklist* that the book stands as a "beautiful" mix of "play, science, poetry, and art."

In *Firefly Night* Gerber focuses on a Chippewa girl who asks the firefly to guide her home through a dusky forest. On her way, the girl is joined by several forest creatures that guide her path in the dark. The forest in autumn is the focus of *Leaf Jumpers,* and here the author uses poetic language to capture the myriad colors and shapes that can be found amid fall leaves. In her *Booklist* review of *Firefly Night,* Shelle Rosenfeld praised Gerber's "lyrical" prose as "rhythmic and soothing" and added that the book serves as "a gentle, reassuring lead-in to . . . sweet dreams." Noting the influence of Henry Wadsworth Longfellow's classic poem

"The Song of Hiawatha," *School Library Journal* critic Nina Lindsay described the text of *Firefly Night* as "lullabylike." In contrast, "the crisp excitement that fall brings sparkles on each page of *Leaf Jumpers,* according to Lynda Ritterman in her review for the same periodical. *Leaf Jumpers* serves young children as an "attractive . . . introduction to eight common leaf varieties," according to Perssons, the critic giving special praise to the "vibrant, hand-colored linoleum prints" Evans creates to bring Gerber's text to life.

Biographical and Critical Sources

PERIODICALS

Booklist, November 1, 2000, Shelle Rosenfeld, review of *Firefly Night,* p. 548; September 15, 2001, Carolyn Phelan, review of *Blizzard,* p. 231; September 1, 2004, Lauren Peterson, review of *Leaf Jumpers,* p. 127; July 1, 2008, Hazel Rochman, review of *Winter Trees,* p. 69.

Gerber captures the beauty of the changing seasons in **Leaf Jumpers,** *a picture book featuring illustrations by Leslie Evans.* (Charlesbridge, 2006. Illustrations copyright © 2004 by Leslie Evans. Reproduced by permission of Charlesbridge Publishing.)

Kirkus Reviews, June 15, 2008, review of *Winter Trees.*
School Library Journal, January, 1998, Helen Gregory, review of *Hush! A Gaelic Lullaby,* p. 99; January, 2001, Nina Lindsay, review of *Firefly Night,* p. 100; October, 2001, Melinda Piehler, review of *Blizzard,* p. 118; August, 2004, Lynda Ritterman, review of *Leaf Jumpers,* p. 107; October, 2008, Lauralyn Persson, review of *Winter Trees,* p. 131.

ONLINE

Carole Gerber Home Page, http://www.carolegerber.com (November 5, 2009).

*   *   *

GEUS, Mireille 1964-

Personal

Born 1964, in Amsterdam, Netherlands; married; children: one son, one daughter.

Addresses

Home—Haarlem, Netherlands.

Career

Author and writing coach.

Awards, Honors

Vlag en Wimpel award, 2004, for *Virenzo en ik,* and 2008, for *Naar Wolf;* Golden Pen award, 2006, for *Big.*

Writings

Virenzo en ik, Lemniscaat (Rotterdam, Netherlands), 2003.
Big, illustrated by Mies van Hout, Lemniscaat (Rotterdam, Netherlands), 2005, translated by Nancy Forest-Flier as *Piggy,* Front Street Books (Asheville, NC), 2008.
Naar Wolf, Lemniscaat (Rotterdam, Netherlands), 2007.

Sidelights

Dutch author Mireille Geus focuses her writing on young teens, mixing spare, compelling prose with stories that reflect the concerns of modern-day middle graders. Her first three books—*Virenzo en ik, Big,* and *Naar Wolf*—were honored with major awards in Geus's native Netherlands, and *Big* was also translated for English-language audiences as *Piggy.*

In *Piggy* readers meet twelve-year-old "Dizzy" Lizzy Bekell and, through her deliberately paced narration, see the world through her eyes. Lizzy is considered an outsider by the other children in her neighborhood, who call her retarded. Because of her autism, Lizzy goes to a different school and knows few of her neighbors, so when another lonely girl welcomes her efforts at friend-

ship, Lizzy is elated. Unfortunately, Margaret (whose nickname is "Piggy") views the relationship differently. An aggressive girl, she manipulates the emotionally needy Lizzy and ultimately involves the naïve and autistic girl in her plan to exact retribution on some local bullies while risking a tragic outcome. The "slightly confused" narration allows readers to experience Lizzy's mistreatment at the hands of her new 'friend,'" wrote *School Library Journal* critic Wendy Smith-D'Arezzo, the critic praising *Piggy* as "a strong story with believable characters." "Geus creates suspense" by threading Lizzy's narrative with her subsequent interrogation by the police, and introduces "standout" adults that support the girl, wrote a *Kirkus Reviews* writer. In *Horn Book,* Sarah Ellis praised *Piggy* as a "short, powerful novel" that is "structured like a detective novel, and told with the spare tautness of a mystery."

Biographical and Critical Sources

PERIODICALS

Horn Book, January-February, 2009, Sarah Ellis, review of *Piggy,* p. 91.
Kirkus Reviews, September 1, 2008, review of *Piggy.*

Copy of Mireille Geus's dramatic young-adult novel Piggy, *featuring cover art by Mies van Hout.* (Front Street, 2008. Jacket art © 2008 by Mies van Hout. Reproduced by permission of Boyds Mills Press.)

School Library Journal, January, 2009, Wendy Smith-D'
Arezzo, review of *Piggy,* p. 100.

ONLINE

Lemniscaat Web site, http://lemniscaat.nl/ (November 15,
2009), "Mireille Geus."
Mireille Geus Home Page, http://www.mireillegeus.nl (November 15, 2009).*

* * *

GOLDMAN, Arthur Steven
See GOLDMAN, Steven

* * *

GOLDMAN, Steven 1964-
(Arthur Steven Goldman)

Personal

Born 1964, in Winston-Salem, NC; married; children:
two sons. *Education:* Haverford College, B.A. (classics,
religion), 1986; Columbia University Teachers College,
M.A; Emerson College, M.F.A. *Religion:* Jewish.

Addresses

Home—Boston, MA. *E-mail*—steven@stevengoldman
books.com.

Career

Author. Formerly taught middle school.

Awards, Honors

Rainbow Project Outstanding Book selection, American
Library Association Gay, Lesbian, Bisexual and Trans-
gendered Round Table/ Social Responsibilities Round
Table, 2008, for *Two Parties, One Tux, and a Very Short
Film about "The Grapes of Wrath."*

Writings

*Two Parties, One Tux, and a Very Short Film about "The
Grapes of Wrath",* Bloomsbury Children's Books
(New York, NY), 2008.

Contributor, under name Arthur Goldman, to journals
and magazines, including *Ascent, Educational Digest,
Gettysburg Review, In the Family, Nimrod, Phi Delta
Kappan,* and *Teachers and Writers.*

Sidelights

In *Two Parties, One Tux, and a Very Short Film about
"The Grapes of Wrath"* Steven Goldman tells the story
of what it is like to be a teen and be different. A former

middle-school teacher, the author became interested in
writing for young adults while working toward his
M.F.A. at Emerson College. As Goldman told *Boston
Globe* contributor Ellen Steinbaum, his novel "is about
how groups accept and reject people. My interest is in
how that happens. I like to inhabit a character and see it
from that perspective."

Eleventh grader Mitchell, the protagonist of *Two Parties, One Tux, and a Very Short Film about "The Grapes
of Wrath",* is a gawky, socially inept teen with little experience of either life or love. Fortunately, Mitchell is
saved from social limbo by his best friend, David. But
what to do when David confides that he is gay? Meanwhile, Mitchell's social life gets a lift when he decides
to make a problematic claymation film in lieu of submitting the required book report, and soon he finds
himself with two potential dates for the junior prom.

In his first novel, Goldman serves up "a side-splitting
slice of male adolescence," according to *School Library
Journal* contributor Rhona Campbell in a review of
*Two Parties, One Tux, and a Very Short Film about
"The Grapes of Wrath".* While Campbell maintained
that the novel's storyline—flush with talk of parties,
beer-drinking, and the potential for sex—"takes a back-
seat to gems of dialogue," she concluded that it is "so
funny and yet so realistic." Noting the "dry wit" running through the novel, a *Kirkus Reviews* contributor
noted Goldman's ability to capture the "angst and . . .
absurdities of high-school politics" in Mitchell's
"strangely flat" and humorous narration and concluded
that he "clearly understands how teen boys think and
speak." *Two Parties, One Tux, and a Very Short Film
about "The Grapes of Wrath"* "speaks to the importance of friendship regardless of one's sexual orientation," asserted Dan Waxman, addressing the story's underlying theme in a review for *Gay and Lesbian Review
Worldwide.*

Biographical and Critical Sources

PERIODICALS

Boston Globe, March 22, 2009, Ellen Steinbaum, inter-
view with Goldman.
Gay and Lesbian Review Worldwide, March-April, 2009,
Dan Waxman, review of *Two Parties, One Tux, and a
Very Short Film about "The Grapes of Wrath",* p. 43.
Kirkus Reviews, August 15, 2008, review of *Two Parties,
One Tux, and a Very Short Film about "The Grapes
of Wrath."*
School Library Journal, October, 2008, Rhona Campbell,
review of *Two Parties, One Tux, and a Very Short
Film about "The Grapes of Wrath",* p. 146.

ONLINE

Steven Goldman Home Page, http://www.stevengoldman
books.com (November 5, 2009).*

H

HALL, August

Personal
Born in Albuquerque, NM.

Addresses
Home—CA. *Agent*—Alan Spiegel Fine Arts, 221 Lobos Ave., Pacific Grove, CA 93950.

Career
Illustrator and concept artist. Has worked on animation projects for Pixar, Industrial Light and Magic, and Dreamworks.

Writings

SELF-ILLUSTRATED

Song and Juniper, Big Kid Books, 2005.

ILLUSTRATOR

Odo Hirsch, *Antonio S. and the Mystery of Theodore Guzman,* Hyperion (New York, NY), 2001.
Deborah Noyes, *When I Met the Wolf Girls,* Houghton Mifflin (Boston, MA), 2007.

Also illustrator of comic-book covers for DC's Vertigo imprint.

Biographical and Critical Sources

PERIODICALS

Booklist, March 15, 2007, Hazel Rochman, review of *When I Met the Wolf Girls,* p. 47.

Horn Book, May-June, 2007, Elissa Gershowitz, review of *When I Met the Wolf Girls,* p. 270.
Kirkus Reviews, April 15, 2007, review of *When I Met the Wolf Girls.*
School Library Journal, June, 2007, Marianne Saccardi, review of *When I Met the Wolf Girls,* p. 156.

ONLINE

Alan Spiegel Fine Arts Web site, http://www.asfa.biz/ (April 15, 2008), "August Hall."*

* * *

HAWORTH, Danette

Personal
Born in Battle Creek, MI; daughter of an Air Force recruiter; married Steve Haworth; children: three. *Education:* Earned bachelor's degree (English).

Addresses
Home—Orlando, FL. *E-mail*—dhaworthbooks@yahoo.com.

Career
Author. Worked as a technical writer, a travel writer for an automobile club, and as a freelance writer and editor.

Member
Society of Children's Book Writers and Illustrators.

Writings

Violet Raines Almost Got Struck by Lightning (novel), Walker & Company (New York, NY), 2008.

Danette Haworth (Courtesy of Danette Haworth.)

The Summer of Moonlight Secrets (novel), Walker & Company (New York, NY), 2010.

Me and Jack (novel), Walker & Company (New York, NY), 2011.

Also contributor of short stories to periodicals and online publications.

Sidelights

A former technical writer and travel writer, Danette Haworth is the author of *Violet Raines Almost Got Struck by Lightning,* a sensitive coming-of-age tale for middle-grade readers. "When I got a hold of Violet, she was so complete, so real, I could have dropped her into any situation and I would have known exactly how she would react," Haworth remarked to *Writers Inspired* online interviewer Mary Jo Campbell. "Boy, was she feisty! I wanted to come up with a story that would be a match for her."

Haworth knew from a young age that she wanted to be a writer. "My sister and I used to sit in my grandma's basement and write volumes of poetry," she told Courtney Summers in an online interview. "I created all sorts of comic books featuring Peter Pan; they make me laugh when I look at them now, but they did actually contain conflict and resolution (and a cliffhanger with Captain Hook raising his sword shouting, 'I'll get you, Pan!')." Haworth attempted her first novel while in seventh grade, took creative writing courses throughout high school, and graduated from college with a degree in English. As she related to Summers, "My first professional job was as a technical writer and though that might sound a bit dry, I found it very interesting. It was also weird that I could edit these huge reports discussing DIS and ET without knowing the engineering behind it." She later found work as a travel writer with an automobile club. "In this new job," she told Summers, "I worked with ten or eleven other editors. Oh! It was wonderful. We could use our big words with each other. Lunchtime conversations were most erudite and quite lofty. I loved it!"

Haworth also began writing short stories and submitting them to periodicals. "When I had a piece published in a national magazine," she recalled to *Writing for Children and Teens* online contributor Cynthea Liu, "I finally felt like a 'real writer.' Even that wasn't enough. I wanted to write a book. I started reading books on the craft of writing, researching writing Web sites, and connecting to other writers." The inspiration for Haworth's debut novel came from her mother's childhood experiences. "I thought I was going to write an adult book, a kind of mother/daughter thing with issues," she related to Sandy Nawrot in an online interview. "Then Violet walked in one day and took over! She came to me as a complete character, her attitude, her looks, her accent; she even brought her friends with her!"

Set in the small, backwoods town of Mitchell Hammock, Florida, *Violet Raines Almost Got Struck by Lightning* centers on a spunky eleven year old who still enjoys playing with dolls and exploring the riverbank near her home. When Melissa Gold arrives in town, Violet finds that her best friend, Lottie, has taken an interest in the mature, tough-talking newcomer, and this brings dramatic changes to Violet and Lottie's relationship. "Violet passes through the last doors of childhood

Cover of Haworth's middle-grade novel Violet Raines Almost Got Struck by Lightning. (Jacket photograph © Getty Images/Joos Mind. Reproduced by permission.)

and into the uncertain entryway of junior high with acute sensitivity," D. Maria LaRocco commented in *School Library Journal,* and a contributor in *Kirkus Reviews* observed that readers will appreciated Haworth's "competent management of such crucial tween issues as best friends, fidelity and impending maturity" in *Violet Raines Almost Got Struck by Lightning.*

Biographical and Critical Sources

PERIODICALS

Bulletin of the Center for Children's Books, October, 2008, Deborah Stevenson, review of *Violet Raines Almost Got Struck by Lightning,* p. 73.

Kirkus Reviews, August 15, 2008, review of *Violet Raines Almost Got Struck by Lightning.*

School Library Journal, October, 2008, D. Maria LaRocco, review of *Violet Raines Almost Got Struck by Lightning,* p. 148.

ONLINE

Courtney Summers Web log, http://courtneysummers.ca/blog/ (October 19, 2007), interview with Haworth.

Danette Haworth Home Page, http://www.danettehaworth.com (November 1, 2009).

Danette Haworth Web log, http://summerfriend.blogspot.com/ (November 1, 2009).

Jillian Clemmons Web site, http://jillianclemmons.com/ (May 15, 2009), interview with Haworth.

Sandy Nawrot Web log, http://sandynawrot.blogspot.com/ (March 18, 2009), interview with Haworth.

Writers Inspired Web log, http://writerinspired.wordpress.com/ (May 26, 2009), Mary Jo Campbell, interview with Haworth.

Writing for Children and Teens Web site, http://www.writingforchildrenandteens.com/ (June 19, 2008), Cynthea Liu, interview with Haworth.

*   *   *

HAYES, Geoffrey 1947-

Personal

Born December 3, 1947, in Pasadena, CA; son of Philip Dutton (a waiter) and Juliette (a secretary) Hayes. *Education:* Attended John O'Connell Institute, San Francisco Academy of Art, New York School of Visual Arts, and Hunter College.

Addresses

Home—New York, NY. *Agent*—Edite Kroll, 12 Grayhurst Park, Portland, ME 04102.

Career

Author and artist of books for children. Marling, Marx & Seidman (advertising agency), New York, NY, worked in art department, 1972-73; Kajima International, New York, NY, interior designer, 1973-75; Harper & Row Publishers, New York, NY, artist and designer, 1975-84; writer and illustrator, 1984—; Vanguard Public Foundation, San Francisco, CA, grants associate, beginning 1994.

Awards, Honors

Ten Best Illustrated Books inclusion, *New York Times,* 1977, for *When the Wind Blew* by Margaret Wise Brown.

Writings

FOR CHILDREN; SELF-ILLUSTRATED

Bear by Himself, Harper (New York, NY), 1976, reprinted, Random House (New York, NY), 1998.

The Alligator and His Uncle Tooth: A Novel of the Sea, Harper (New York, NY), 1977.

Patrick Comes to Puttyville and Other Stories, Harper (New York, NY), 1978.

The Secret Inside, Harper (New York, NY), 1980.

Elroy and the Witch's Child, Harper (New York, NY), 1982.

Patrick and Ted, Four Winds Press (New York, NY), 1984.

Patrick Buys a Coat, Knopf (New York, NY), 1985.

Patrick Eats His Dinner, Knopf (New York, NY), 1985.

Patrick Takes a Bath, Knopf (New York, NY), 1985.

Patrick Goes to Bed, Knopf (New York, NY), 1985.

The Mystery of the Pirate Ghost: An Otto and Uncle Tooth Adventure, Random House (New York, NY), 1985.

Christmas in Puttyville, Random House (New York, NY), 1985.

Patrick and His Grandpa, Random House (New York, NY), 1986.

The Lantern Keeper's Bedtime Book, Random House (New York, NY), 1986.

Patrick and Ted at the Beach, Random House (New York, NY), 1987.

Patrick and Ted Ride the Train, Random House (New York, NY), 1988.

The Secret of Foghorn Island, Random House (New York, NY), 1988, reprinted, 2003.

The Treasure of the Lost Lagoon, Random House (New York, NY), 1991.

The Curse of the Cobweb Queen, Random House (New York, NY), 1994.

The Night of the Circus Monsters, Random House (New York, NY), 1996.

Swamp of the Hideous Zombies, Random House (New York, NY), 1996.

House of the Horrible Ghosts, Random House (New York, NY), 1997.

Patrick's Christmas Tree, Random House (New York, NY), 1999.

Patrick and the Big Bully, Hyperion Books for Children (New York, NY), 2001.

Patrick at the Circus, Hyperion Books for Children (New York, NY), 2002.

Patrick Perks Up, Hyperion Books for Children (New York, NY), 2003.

Patrick and the Get-well Day, Hyperion Books for Children (New York, NY), 2003.

The Mystery of the Pirate Ghost, Random House (New York, NY), 2003.

A Night-light for Bunny, HarperCollins (New York, NY), 2004.

A Very Merry Christmas, HarperFestival (New York, NY), 2007.

A Very Special Valentine, HarperFestvial (New York, NY), 2007.

A Very Spooky Halloween, HarperFestival (New York, NY), 2008.

Benny and Penny in Just Pretend, RAW Junior (New York, NY), 2008.

Benny and Penny in The Big No-No!, RAW Junior (New York, NY), 2009.

ILLUSTRATOR

Margaret Wise Brown, *When the Wind Blew,* Harper (New York, NY), 1977.

Joan Lowery Nixon, *Muffie Mouse and the Busy Birthday,* Seabury Press (New York, NY), 1978.

Fran Manushkin, *Moon Dragon,* Macmillan (New York, NY), 1980.

Fran Manushkin, *Hocus and Pocus at the Circus,* Harper (New York, NY), 1981.

Janice May Udry, *Thump and Plunk,* HarperCollins (New York, NY), 2000.

Ken Baker, *Brave Little Monster,* HarperCollins (New York, NY), 2001.

Sidelights

In addition to creating artwork for other writers, author and illustrator Geoffrey Hayes has written dozens of self-illustrated books for beginning readers that feature animal duos such as the young bears Patrick and Ted, the young mouse siblings Benny and Penny, and the amateur alligator sleuths Otto and crusty Uncle Tooth. In his whimsical watercolor illustrations, which several critics have noted for their nostalgic feel, Hayes both entertains and educates young readers with tales geared both to reluctant readers and those seeking more sophisticated material. He has also moved into sequential art, combining his love of comics with his desire to tell a simple story in his "Benny and Penny" books, published by Art Spiegelman and Françoise Mouly's innovative Toon Books.

Readers are first introduced to Patrick in *Patrick Comes to Puttyville and Other Stories* In this collection, the young bear moves with his family to a new house in a small town, where Patrick makes new friends—including Ted—and has several real-life adventures with which young children can identify. In *Patrick and Ted Ride the Train,* the two take a day trip on the Skitter & Scoo Railway to visit an elderly relative; fortunately armed with squirt guns, they make short work of a gang of annoying weasels.

Geoffrey Hayes melds comic-book art with a toddler-friendly story in his self-illustrated **Benny and Penny in Just Pretend.** (RAW Junior, LLC/ Toon Books. © 2008 by Geoffrey Hayes. Reproduced by permission.)

Patrick stars in several more "Adventures of Patrick Brown" stories, a series that includes *Patrick at the Circus* and *Patrick and the Big Bully.* In *Patrick at the Circus* the young bear learns about his father's long-ago job working as a circus clown, and when the older bear performs as a clown for the circus that is then in town, Patrick finds an opportunity to earn a few cheers of his own under the big top. A trip to a favorite bakery puts the little bear in the path of the town tough but ultimately has a pleasant outcome thanks to the cub's quick thinking in *Patrick and the Big Bully.* In *School Library Journal* Laurie Edwards wrote that *Patrick at the Circus* features an "intriguing" page design and Hayes' "detailed cartoons . . . are reminiscent of comic-book art." In addition to a "comforting" story, *Patrick and the Big Bully* treats readers to "a crazy quilt of cheery visual elements," according to a *Publishers Weekly* contributor, and in *School Library Journal* Blair Christolon credited the "myriad action-packed details" for giving Hayes' story its brisk pace.

In *The Alligator and His Uncle Tooth: A Novel of the Sea* Hayes introduces readers to an entirely different community of animal characters: one that includes young Corduroy Alligator, Captain Poopdeck, the rov-

ing adventurer Uncle Tooth, and woebegone Ducky Doodle. Uncle Tooth is joined by young Otto in mystery stories that include *The Treasure of the Lost Lagoon, Swamp of the Hideous Zombies,* and *The Curse of the Cobweb Queen.* Whether encountering treasure ships, mermaids, suspicious fortune tellers, a gang of dastardly rats, or a sinister, pearl-snatching witch, the long-jawed duo manages to save the day in the town of Boogle Bay.

In *Elroy and the Witch's Child* an orphaned kitten seeking its fortune encounters a witch and a little girl with whom it travels after sorting out several misunderstandings and confused introductions. "Hayes's new romp, cause for rejoicing, sparkles with his recital of nonsense and the gaudy hues in the cartoons," noted a *Publishers Weekly* reviewer in appraising *Elroy and the Witch's Child.* Other original pictures books by Hayes include *A Night-Light for Bunny* and *A Very Merry Christmas.*

Hayes introduces an engaging mouse family in *Benny and Penny in Just Pretend* and *Benny and Penny in The Big No-No!,* "successfully combining a comic-book format with effective easy-reader elements," according to Joy Fleishhacker in *School Library Journal.* As readers meet him in the cartoon-styled panels of *Benny and Penny in Just Pretend,* Benny wants to be a pirate, but his game ceases to be fun when little sister Penny wants to play princess aboard his make-believe pirate ship. After the older mouse becomes frustrated by his tag-along sibling, tempers flare, until Penny proves to be as helpful as the bravest pirate captain ever. In *Booklist* Kat Kan praised the "sweet, delicately colored" pencil art created by Hayes, noting that the "timeless quality" that the images conjure up is reflected by the author/ illustrator's repetitive text. *Benny and Penny in Just Pretend* is "a charmer that will invite repeated readings," concluded Kan, while in *Publishers Weekly* a contributor described Hayes' "skillful drawings" as engaging enough to "lever beginning readers right into the story.

Hayes' mouse siblings return in *Benny and Penny in The Big No-No!,* as the arrival of new neighbors and the disappearance of Benny's favorite pail lead to a problematic confrontation. In search of the lost pail, Benny and Penny follow a set of strange footprints that leads to the next yard. There they find a young hedgehog named Melina playing in a sandbox. The pail Melina is using must certainly be Benny's, but when the mouse claims it the hedgehog gets angry and a fight ensues. When Benny's pail is then discovered to be right where he had left it—in his own sandbox—the mice return to Melina's yard to make their apologies and win a new friend. Praising the author/illustrator's invention of "charming" animal characters, Kan predicted that the "great dialogue, easy-to-follow panels, and fun" onomatopoeic text will win *Benny and Penny in The Big No-No!* a loyal readership.

"Writing and drawing have always come naturally to me," Hayes once told *SATA.* "My brother and I, being only two years apart, channeled our creative energies into stories and books which we gave to one another. All the writing I do now is an extension and development of those early works. Many authors relive their past in their fiction, but while some (such as Marcel Proust) do so in autobiographical novels, I find fantasy not only the best form for expressing my feelings, but as viable as any literary genre."

Biographical and Critical Sources

PERIODICALS

Booklist, September 1, 1976, review of *Bear by Himself,* p. 38; March 15, 2008, Kat Kan, review of *Benny and Penny in Just Pretend,* p. 66; March 1, 2009, Kat Kan, review of *Benny and Penny in The Big No-No!,* p. 66.

Horn Book, July-August, 2008, Martha V. Parravano, review of *Benny and Penny in Just Pretend,* p. 447.

Kirkus Reviews, June 15, 1976, review of *Bear by Himself,* p. 680; August 1, 2001, review of *Brave Little Monster,* p. 1116; May 1, 2002, review of *Patrick at the Circus,* p. 656; March 15, 2008, review of *Benny and Penny in Just Pretend.*

New York Times Book Review, November 14, 1976, review of *Bear by Himself,* p. 26.

Publishers Weekly, September 10, 1982, review of *Elroy and the Witch's Child,* p. 76; October 1, 2001, review of *Patrick and the Big Bully,* p. 61; March 17, 2008, review of *Benny and Penny in Just Pretend,* p. 68.

School Library Journal, October, 1976, review of *Bear by Himself,* p. 98; April, 1992, review of *The Treasure of the Lost Lagoon,* p. 92; September, 2001, Be Astengo, review of *Brave Little Monster,* p. 182; January 2002, Blair Christolon, review of *Patrick and the Big Bully,* p. 101; July, 2002, Laurie Edwards, review of *Patrick at the Circus,* p. 92; February, 2004, Andrea Tarr, review of *A Night-Light for Bunny,* p. 113; October, 2007, Eva Mitnick, review of *A Very Merry Christmas,* p. 99; May, 2008, Joy Fleishhacker, review of *Benny and Penny in Just Pretend,* p. 154.

ONLINE

HarperCollins Web site, http://www.harpercollins.com/ (November 15, 2009), "Geoffrey Hayes."

Toon Books Web site, http://www.toon-books.com/ (November 15, 2009), Bill Kartalopoulos, interview with Hayes.*

*   *   *

HAYES, Karel 1949-

Personal

Born 1949; married; husband's name Brent; children: John.

Addresses

Home—Center Harbor, NH. *E-mail*—karel@karelhayes. com.

Career

Author, illustrator, and artist. Leader of watercolor-painting workshops.

Awards, Honors

Bronze Medal for Children's Picture Books, Independent Book Publishers, and Time of Wonder Award, Maine Discovery Museum, both 2007, and Maine Literary Award honorable mention, 2008, all for *The Winter Visitor.*

Writings

SELF-ILLUSTRATED

The Winter Visitors, Down East Books (Camden, ME), 2007.

The Amazing Journey of Lucky the Lobster Buoy, Down East Books (Camden, ME), 2009.

ILLUSTRATOR

Mary Train, *Time for the Fair,* Down East Books (Camden, ME), 2005.
(Illustrator) Fran Hodgkins, *Who's Been Here?: A Tale in Tracks,* Down East Books (Camden, ME), 2008.

Also illustrator of other works, including children's reading books, textbooks, and periodicals.

Sidelights

In addition to illustrating picture books for other authors, New Hampshire-based artist Karel Hayes has created several of her own works, including *The Winter Visitors.* Published in 2007, *The Winter Visitors* offers a new twist on the traditional story of the Three Little Bears by focusing on a family closing up a lakefront cottage for the winter. As the family readies to depart, the young son accidentally leaves the front door unlocked, allowing a family of bears to take occupancy a short time later. Enjoying the humans' absence in the

Karel Hayes adds realistic details to her illustrations for Fran Hodgkins' picture book **Who's Been Here?: A Tale in Tracks.** (Down East Books, 2008.
Illustrations copyright © 2008 by Karel Hayes. All rights reserved. Reproduced by Down East Books.)

off-season, the bears make themselves at home and even host a party on New Year's Eve for all of the other forest creatures. After a short hibernation, the bears clean and straighten the house, leaving everything ready for the unsuspecting humans when they return. "Readers will enjoy the many fun and clever details as the story unfolds," predicted *School Library Journal* critic Amanda Moss in an appraisal of *The Winter Visitors,* while a *Publishers Weekly* critic applauded Hayes' intricate artwork by noting that, "the more closely readers look, the more they'll find to like."

Working as illustrator, Hayes teams up with author Fran Hodgkins to produce *Who's Been Here?: A Tale in Tracks.* Geared for younger children, the nature-themed picture book follows three siblings who are chasing their dog through the snow. Using clues provided in the text, together with Hayes' illustrations of animal tracks, readers are encouraged to figure out which animal will be depicted on the next page. Reviewers offered positive comments about Hayes' contributions to *Who's Been Here?,* Kathleen Kelly MacMillan writing in *School Library Journal* that her "watercolors evoke the frosty air of a winter wood." A *Kirkus Reviews* contributor reached a similar conclusion, remarking that the artist's "subdued palette of blues and grays nicely suits the wintry setting" of Hodgkins' story.

Biographical and Critical Sources

PERIODICALS

Kirkus Reviews, September 1, 2008, review of *Who's Been Here?: A Tale in Tracks.*
Publishers Weekly, September 24, 2007, review of *The Winter Visitors,* p. 70.
School Library Journal, December, 2005, Mary Hazelton, review of *Time for the Fair,* p. 122; November, 2007, Amanda Moss, review of *The Winter Visitors,* p. 93; December, 2008, Kathleen Kelly MacMillan, review of *Who's Been Here?,* p. 90.

ONLINE

Karel Hayes Home Page, http://karelhayes.com (November 6, 2009).

*   *   *

HENKES, Kevin 1960-

Personal

Born November, 1960, in Racine, WI; married Laura Dronzek (an author); children: two. *Education:* University of Wisconsin—Madison, degree.

Addresses

Home—Madison, WI.

Kevin Henkes (Photograph by Tom Beckley. Reproduced by permission of Kevin Henkes.)

Career

Writer and illustrator. May Arbuthnot lecturer, 2007.

Awards, Honors

Cooperative Children's Book Center (CCBC) Choice designation, 1982, for *Clean Enough,* 1985, for *Bailey Goes Camping,* 1986, for *Grandpa and Bo* and *A Weekend with Wendell,* 1987, for *Once around the Block* and *Sheila Rae, the Brave,* 1988, for *Chester's Way,* 1989, for *Shhhh,* 1990, for *Julius, the Baby of the World,* 1995, for *The Biggest Boy* and *Good-Bye Curtis,* 1998, for *Circle Dogs,* and 2000, for *Oh!;* Children's Choice Book selection, Children's Book Council/International Reading Association (IRA), 1986, both for *A Weekend with Wendell;* Library of Congress Best Books of the Year citation, 1988, for *Once around the Block;* Notable Book citation, American Library Association (ALA), 1988, and Keystone to Reading Award, Keystone State Reading Association, 1990, both for *Chester's Way;* Best Books citation, *School Library Journal,* 1989, for *Jessica;* ALA Notable Book citation, 1990, for *Julius, the Baby of the World;* Library of Congress Best Books citation, *School Library Journal* Best Books citation, and ALA Notable Book citation, all 1991, and Outstanding Achievement award, Wisconsin Library Association, 1992, all for *Chrysanthemum; School Li-*

brary *Journal* Best Books citation, 1992, and Elizabeth Burr Award, Wisconsin Library Association, 1993, both for *Words of Stone; School Library Journal* Best Books citation, and ALA Notable Children's Book citation, both 1993, *Boston Globe/Horn Book* Award Honor designation, Elizabeth Burr Award, Archer/Ekblad Children's Picture Book Award, Council for Wisconsin Writers, and Caldecott Honor Book designation, all 1994, all for *Owen; Booklist* Top of the List Picture-Book Award, 1996, and American Booksellers Book of the Year (ABBY) Award, 1997, all for *Lilly's Purple Plastic Purse; School Library Journal* Best Books citation, 1997, and ALA Notable Book citation, 1998, both for *Sun and Spoon;* Charlotte Zolotow Award Highly Commended designation, 1999, for *Circle Dogs;* ALA Notable Children's Book citation, 2000, and *School Library Journal* Best Children's Books citation, both 2001, both for *Wemberly Worried;* ALA Notable Children's Book citation, 2001, for *Sheila Rae's Peppermint Stick;* Jo Osborne Award for Humor in Children's Literature, 2002; Newbery Honor Book designation, 2004, for *Olive's Ocean;* Caldecott Medal, and Charlotte Zolotow Award, CCBC, both 2005, both for *Kitten's First Full Moon;* Sterling North Legacy Award, 2006, for excellence in children's literature.

Writings

SELF-ILLUSTRATED PICTURE BOOKS

All Alone, Greenwillow (New York, NY), 1981.
Clean Enough, Greenwillow (New York, NY), 1982.
Margaret and Taylor, Greenwillow (New York, NY), 1983.
Bailey Goes Camping, Greenwillow (New York, NY), 1985.
Grandpa and Bo, Greenwillow (New York, NY), 1986.
Sheila Rae, the Brave, Greenwillow (New York, NY), 1987.
A Weekend with Wendell, Greenwillow (New York, NY), 1987.
Chester's Way, Greenwillow (New York, NY), 1988.
Jessica, Greenwillow (New York, NY), 1989.
Shhhh, Greenwillow (New York, NY), 1989.
Julius, the Baby of the World, Greenwillow (New York, NY), 1990.
Chrysanthemum, Greenwillow (New York, NY), 1991, reprinted, 2007.
Owen, Greenwillow (New York, NY), 1993.
Lilly's Purple Plastic Purse, Greenwillow (New York, NY), 1996.
Wemberly Worried, Greenwillow (New York, NY), 2000.
Sheila Rae's Peppermint Stick, Greenwillow (New York, NY), 2002.
Owen's Marshmallow Chick, Greenwillow (New York, NY), 2002.
Julius's Candy Corn, HarperFestival (New York, NY), 2003.
Wemberly's Ice-Cream Star, HarperFestival (New York, NY), 2003.

Lilly's Chocolate Heart, Greenwillow (New York, NY), 2004.
Kitten's First Full Moon, Greenwillow (New York, NY), 2004.
A Box of Treats: Five Little Picture Books, Greenwillow (New York, NY), 2004.
Lilly's Big Day, Greenwillow (New York, NY), 2006.
A Good Day, Greenwillow (New York, NY), 2007.
Old Bear, Greenwillow (New York, NY), 2008.
My Garden, Greenwillow (New York, NY), 2010.

JUVENILE FICTION

(Self-illustrated) *Return to Sender,* Greenwillow (New York, NY), 1984.
(Self-illustrated) *Two under Par,* Greenwillow (New York, NY), 1987.
The Zebra Wall, Greenwillow (New York, NY), 1988.
Words of Stone, Greenwillow (New York, NY), 1992.
Protecting Marie, Greenwillow (New York, NY), 1995.
Sun and Spoon, Greenwillow (New York, NY), 1997.
The Birthday Room, Greenwillow (New York, NY), 1999.
Olive's Ocean, Greenwillow (New York, NY), 2003.
Bird Lake Moon, Greenwillow (New York, NY), 2008.

OTHER

Once around the Block, illustrated by Victoria Chess, Greenwillow (New York, NY), 1987.
Good-bye, Curtis, illustrated by Marisabina Russo, Greenwillow (New York, NY), 1995.
The Biggest Boy, illustrated by Nancy Tafuri, Greenwillow (New York, NY), 1995.
Circle Dogs, illustrated by Dan Yaccarino, Greenwillow (New York, NY), 1998.
Oh!, illustrated by wife, Laura Dronzek, Greenwillow (New York, NY), 1999.
So Happy!, illustrated by Anita Lobel, Greenwillow (New York, NY), 2005.
Birds, illustrated by Laura Dronzek, Greenwillow Books (New York, NY), 2009.

Author of introduction to *Bonjour, Babar!: The Six Unabridged Classics by the Creator of Babar,* by Jean de Brunhoff.

Adaptations

A Weekend with Wendell was adapted as a filmstrip and cassette, Weston Woods, 1988; Recorded Books recorded audiocassettes of *Words of Stone,* 1993, *Two under Par,* 1997, and *The Zebra Wall,* 1997; Listening Library recorded an audiocassette of *Sun and Spoon,* 1998. Weston Woods made videocassette adaptations of *A Weekend with Wendell, Owen,* and *Chrysanthemum.* Broderbund Software created a "Living Books" CD-ROM game based on *Sheila Rae, the Brave.*

Sidelights

Kevin Henkes is consistently praised for the funny and realistic way he portrays the childlike characters in his picture books. Many of his award-winning stories fea-

ture unforgettable mouse characters such as Lilly, Sheila Rae, Chester, Julius, Wemberly, and Owen, while his novels for young readers vividly capture the ups and downs of growing up. *Bulletin of the Center for Children's Books* reviewer Betsy Hearne observed that Henkes's writing "sounds as if the author has been eavesdropping on children at play," while Chicago's *Tribune Books* critic Mary Harris Veeder wrote that his young characters "are full of the imperfections and emotions which mark real life." As Martha Vaughan Parravano similarly noted in *Children's Books and Their Creators:* "Henkes is the creator of true picture books—in which text and illustrations work together to make a seamless whole—that exhibit an innate understanding of children and always contain a strong element of security and comfort."

Books played an important part in Henkes's Wisconsin childhood. On regular family visits to the local public library, he checking out his own books and carried them home himself. Illustrations by Crockett Johnson and Garth Williams were particular favorites of the future author/illustrator, and they inspired his own artistic efforts. In high school, Henkes was encouraged by a teacher to develop his writing skills as well, thus inspiring his future career. "I wondered about authors and illustrators when I was growing up," Henkes wrote on his home page. He continued, "I never imagined that one day I would be one myself."

Henkes attended the University of Wisconsin, where he majored in art. Prior to the start of his junior year, he traveled to New York City with the intent to find a publisher interested in his work. "I picked the week I would go to New York, made a list of my ten favorite publishers, and set up appointments," he told Nathalie Op de Beeck in *Publishers Weekly.* "I went thinking, 'I'll come back with a book contract.'" Henkes did his homework and included among his interviews one with an editor whom he had heard lecture on tape. "Magically enough," Henkes wrote on his home page, "Susan Hirschman at Greenwillow Books made my dream come true." When he returned to school, the nineteen year old had a contract for his first book in hand. In 1981, he published his first picture book, *All Alone,* which he had first drafted while still in high school.

"I love rhythm in picture books," Henkes explained in an interview with *School Library Journal* contributor Kathleen T. Horning. "I love repetition. And when I'm writing a picture book I read it aloud again and again and again and again. The right rhythm just seems to find itself. . . . What sometimes happens is, after I've written it and I think it's exactly right, I will cut up the words and put it into book form. . . . The words and the page turning have to be perfect, or else you break the rhythm, you break the magic. Sometimes when I think it's perfect on a piece of paper, it needs to be reworked to make it fit into book form. I do all of that before I begin working on pictures. For me, it's the only way to work, because I want to get those words absolutely right first."

Both *All Alone* and its follow-up, *Clean Enough,* are gentle stories that capture the ordinary, everyday activities of children. While critics found the text to be undistinguished, they praised Henkes's artwork. Reviewing *All Alone,* in which a little boy uses his imagination while playing outside, a *Publishers Weekly* reviewer stated that "muted colors [and] delicate lines reflect the sensitivity in the text." A *Kirkus Reviews* writer likewise observed that "Henkes paints with a delicate palette . . . and the illustrations have a degree of feeling." Bathtime is the focus of *Clean Enough,* as a little boy considers how to mix water that is just the right temperature while remembering previous bathtub adventures. In *School Library Journal* Joan W. Blos deemed *Clean Enough* "highly successful" because of the text's "nuances of humor" and Henkes's "affectionate drawings."

After publishing *Margaret and Taylor,* which relates the travails of a boy trying to overcome the nasty tricks played on him by his older sister, and *Return to Sender,* in which a postal worker responds to a boy's letter to a favorite superhero, Henkes introduces his first animal characters. In *Bailey Goes Camping* young rabbit Bailey is disappointed at being left behind while his older siblings go on a Bunny Scouts camping trip, until his understanding mother finds ways to enjoy camping activities while at home. A loving spirit also infuses *Grandpa and Bo,* about a shared summer between a boy and his grandfather. With its "wit and warmth," *Bailey Goes Camping* "truly captures the world of the small child," Anne Devereaux Jordan Crouse remarked in *Children's Book Review Service,* and in *Booklist* Denise M. Wilms described it as "a cozy, comfortable book that will leave youngsters smiling." *Grandpa and Bo* "is a welcome addition to [Henkes's] growing list of accomplishments," a *Kirkus Reviews* critic stated, explaining that the artist's "soft pencil drawings accurately convey the story's mood of quiet simplicity."

Many of Henkes's books cast mice in the child's role. "I found I could get much more humor out of animals, and besides it freed me from having to sketch from a human model," the artist revealed to Cooper. "I tried rabbits for a while, but I found mice to be the most fun." In the first of these mouse-based works, *A Weekend with Wendell,* the mouse's parents have gone out of town, leaving Wendell to stay with Sophie's family for the weekend. The young rodent proves to be a difficult house guest, however: When the two play house, for example, Wendell is the father, mother, and children, leaving Sophie to be the dog; when they play hospital, Wendell makes himself the doctor, the patient, and the nurse, making Sophie the desk clerk; and while playing bakery, Wendell is the baker while Sophie is a sweet roll. Although Wendell ultimately gets his comeuppance, the two mice become close friends. *A Weekend with Wendell* is "divertingly recounted . . . with good hu-

Cover of Kevin Henkes' middle-grade novel Sun and Spoon, *featuring artwork by Laura Dronzek.* (Puffin Books, 1998. Reproduced by permission of Puffin Books, a division of Penguin Putnam Books for Young Readers.)

mor and charm," a *Publishers Weekly* critic stated, adding that "the postures of [the book's] . . . mice children speak volumes."

In *Sheila Rae, the Brave* boastful elder sister Sheila Rae impresses her meek younger sister Louise with her ability to combat dogs, bullies, and monsters in the closet. When Sheila Rae's imagination gets the best of her while taking a new route home from school, however, it is Louise who comes to the rescue. "Everything that happens here is completely credible," a *Publishers Weekly* writer commented in reviewing *Sheila Rae, the Brave,* and *School Library Journal* contributor David Gale praised Henkes's "bouncy watercolors" and his characters' "highly expressive faces" while predicting that children will enjoy the book's humor and realism.

Chester's Way introduces one of the author's most popular characters: the imaginative and impish Lilly. When Lilly moves into the neighborhood, best friends Chester and Wilson both have some adjusting to do before the newly founded trio becomes good friends. "Henkes's vision of friendship captures the essence of the childlike," a *Publishers Weekly* critic noted of the book, add-

ing that "every sentence is either downright funny or dense with playful, deadpan humor." Calling *Chester's Way* an "amusing, believable story" starring "delightful little mice," Ann A. Flowers added in *Horn Book* that the work demonstrates Henkes's "strong empathy with the feelings of children."

In *Julius, the Baby of the World* readers reunite with spunky young Lilly as she is now about to become a big sister, much to her displeasure. Before the baby is born, Lilly is sure she is up to the task: as she watches her parents buy toys for the new arrival and talk to her mother's swollen belly. When little Julius is born, however, the girl is disgusted by the attention he commands, attention that was, until recently, reserved for her alone. Now Lilly wishes Julius away, pinches his tender flesh, and tries to teach him a mixed-up alphabet to undo the lessons of her parents. However, when a visiting cousin criticizes the little boy/mouse, big sister Lilly quickly comes to Julius's defense. "There is much to admire, giggle over and learn from *Julius, the Baby of the World,*" Ann Pleshette Murphy wrote in the *New York Times Book Review.* "No matter how vitriolic a big sister may become, she really does love her little brother after all."

Lilly returns in *Lilly's Purple Plastic Purse* and by now the spunky little girl/mouse is attending school. Lilly loves everything about school, especially her teacher, Mr. Slinger. However, when her excitement over sharing her musical purse with him leads to a reprimand, Lilly's ardent devotion turns into anger. In portraying Lilly's journey from remorse to reconciliation, Henkes "once again demonstrates his direct line to the rollercoaster emotions of small children," a *Kirkus Reviews* writer stated. Reviewers highlighted the artist's use of humor as well as his ability to express feelings in his drawings; as *School Library Journal* contributor Marianne Saccardi observed, "with a few deft strokes, Henkes changes Lilly's facial expressions and body language to reveal a full range of emotions." M.P. Dunleavey reviewed *Lilly's Purple Plastic Purse* for the *New York Times Book Review,* calling it "a book so delightful, so exuberant, honest and evocative of the passionate life that children live as we look on, that one considers nailing a proclamation to the door of the local bookseller or wearing a copy around one's neck to advertise it."

In *Wemberly Worried* Henkes introduces readers to a white mouse with a dark spot around her left eye who worries about absolutely everything. When she has to face going to school, her worries become even bigger than normal. Luckily for Wemberly and her constant companion, a small rabbit doll, she meets another girl mouse, Jewel, who is also nervous about the first day of school. As the two become friends, Wemberly finds her worries diminish. "Henkes adroitly juggles the main narrative, hand-lettered asides and watercolor-and-ink imagery," wrote a critic in *Publishers Weekly,* and *School Library Journal* reviewer Joy Fleishhacker

praised *Wemberly Worried* as a book "filled with perfectly chosen details." Cooper called Wemberly a "winsome worrywart," and a *Horn Book* reviewer noted that "Henkes's picture books make finding your way in the world a little less daunting."

Other everyday concerns are explored in books such as *Chrysanthemum*, in which a young mouse discovers that being different can mean being special, and *Owen*, which earned Henkes a Caldecott Honor citation. Because Owen is about to start school, his nosy neighbor Mrs. Tweezers suggests that the young mouse must relinquish his cherished blanket, Fuzzy. The resourceful Owen thwarts every trick his parents use to acquire Fuzzy, until his mother finds the perfect solution: turn Fuzzy into a series of handkerchiefs small enough to fit in Owen's pocket. "Owen is a great addition to Kevin Henkes's many endearing characters," Hanna B. Zeiger wrote in *Horn Book*, while Hazel Rochman explained in *Booklist* that the author/illustrator can convey emotion "with a few simple lines."

Lilly, Owen, Wemberly, and Henkes's other mouse characters also appear in board books for the very young. Lilly searches for a place to hide her last piece of Valentine's candy in *Lilly's Chocolate Heart*, while Sheila Rae convinces her sister Louise to do the impossible before sharing her own candy in *Sheila Rae's Peppermint Stick*. Wemberly waits too long to eat her ice cream and ends up with ice-cream soup in *Wemberly's Ice-Cream Star*, which Melinda Piehler considered in *School Library Journal* to be "another winning story." In what *School Library Journal* critic Ann Cook described as "a sweet friendship story," Owen becomes attached to one of his Easter candies in *Owen's Marshmallow Chick*, and Julius is not allowed to eat Halloween cupcakes, but instead counts the candy corn decorating them, in *Julius's Candy Corn*. A *Horn Book* reviewer wrote that "Henkes's expressive illustrations work perfectly with the short-and-sweet text" of *Sheila Rae's Peppermint Stick* and in *Booklist* Kathy Broderick deemed the same story "beautifully told." Commenting on the series as a whole, a critic for *Kirkus Reviews* proclaimed that "Henkes has mastered the art of transferring his mouse children to the simplicity required for a board book."

Although he has earned critical and popular acclaim for his mouse-centered stories, Henkes has also branched out from that successful formula. In *Jessica* he tells the story of Ruthie and the imaginary playmate who "becomes real" when Ruthie meets a similarly named new student at school. "Not one extraneous element in text or pictures mars the [story's] lyrical, joyous tone," Mary M. Burns declared in *Horn Book*, while *Bulletin of the Center for Children's Books* writer Roger Sutton hailed *Jessica* for its "witty use of white space and . . . imaginative variety of type and line placement." Henkes creates broad-stroked acrylic paintings for *Shhhh*, a gentle portrayal of a child awake in the quiet early morning. The artwork for this book was deemed perfect in con-

veying "the hushed world of a child's first waking moments" by a *Publishers Weekly* critic.

Henkes experiments with black-and-white illustrations in his Caldecott Medal-winning picture book *Kitten's First Full Moon*, the story of a kitten who thinks the moon is a big bowl of milk in the sky. Kitten tries and tries to capture the big bowl of milk for herself, but after a night of failure she returns home to find her own small bowl of milk waiting for her. In *Booklist* Gillian Engberg wrote that Henkes "creates a loveable, expressive character in the determined kitten," and a *Kirkus Reviews* critic cited the book's "retro look" and "simply charming" story. According to a reviewer for *Publishers Weekly*, the "determined" kitten and her "comical quest will win over" young readers. Christine M. Heppermann, writing in *Horn Book*, called *Kitten's First Full Moon* a "sweet story," and *School Library Journal* contributor Wendy Lukehart dubbed it "an irresistible offering from the multifaceted Henkes." In *Booklist* Carolyn Phelan concluded that the "precise, unaffected, and easy . . . to understand" rhyming story is matched by "clearly defined" watercolor-and-line art, while Marianne Saccard deemed *A Good Day* a "gentle" tale that "affords an opportunity to introduce the very young to ways of dealing with life's small disappointments."

A Good Day and *Old Bear* also feature Henkes's engaging mix of story and art. Featuring the heavy-edged, brightly colored illustrations that prompted Lempke to describe it as "a picture book of grace and simplicity," *A Good Day* begins as four little animals—a yellow bird, a white dog, a brown squirrel, and an orange fox—learn how to transform a run of bad luck into something positive. Also brought to life in Henkes's child-friendly art, a fuzzy brown bear spends his hibernating time dreaming of the fun he had exploring the wide world as a cub in *Old Bear*. Characterizing *A Good Day* as a "a soothing story about turning lemons into lemonade," a *Publishers Weekly* critic commented on the "skillful circularity" of Henkes's tale, and Lempke deemed the book a "rare example of near-perfection in a picture book." "Every word, line, color choice, and composition element . . . fits beautifully" within the pages of *Old Bear*, wrote Engberg, the reviewer hailing the work as "a picture-book celebration of simple, pure joy." A *Publishers Weekly* critic also deemed *Old Bear* "masterful," adding that Henkes's story "lyrically describ[es] . . . the young-at-heart."

During the 1980s, Henkes published the first of his novels for older children. *Two under Par* is the story of a boy named Wedge who tries to adapt to his new stepfather and stepbrother. When his mother becomes pregnant, Wedge feels more isolated than ever. A *Publishers Weekly* reviewer applauded *Two under Par*, noting in particular the "complicated process of learning acceptance and being accepted" which the author "explores with confidence and care." "Henkes's handling of Wedge's problems is masterful and shows a keen understanding of childhood," Robert Unsworth similarly re-

marked in *School Library Journal.* A new baby also arrives in *The Zebra Wall,* prompting a visit by the eccentric and slightly annoying Aunt Irene. Adine, the young girl who must share her room with Aunt Irene during her stay, is none too pleased—about either new arrival. "This is not [just] another new baby story," claimed a reviewer for *Publishers Weekly,* adding that "Henkes knows that every worry in a child's life has many layers." Elizabeth S. Watson likewise concluded in *Horn Book* that *The Zebra Wall* "embodies genuine understanding of a ten-year-old's fears," making for a "beguiling story peopled with true characters."

In *Sun and Spoon* Henkes "offers another meticulously crafted, quietly engaging epiphany," according to a *Kirkus Reviews* writer. In this novel, ten-year-old Spoon is having difficulty adjusting to his first summer without his beloved grandmother, especially since his grandfather now finds it too painful to continue their once-frequent card games. Fearing he will lose his precious memories of his grandmother, Spoon takes her favorite deck of cards as a memento, triggering a family crisis. The resolution provides the boy with new insights about himself and his family, and the book as a whole "glitters with small, memorable moments that seem true to life, yet fresh and unexpected," As Elizabeth Spires remarked in the *New York Times Book Review. School Library Journal* contributor Marilyn Payne Phillips praised how the author "captures young angst with respect and honesty," while a *Publishers Weekly* reviewer hailed the use of "both sensitively planted metaphors and realistic experiences to explore different phases of the healing process." Comparing *Sun and Spoon* with Henkes's books for younger children, a *Kirkus Reviews* critic concluded that "it is infused with the same good humor, wisdom, and respect for children's hearts and minds that characterize all his works."

Ben is given his own studio for painting in *The Birthday Room,* another novel for elementary-grade readers. Instead of feeling grateful for his parents' support, however, Ben finds that the room makes him feel pressured to succeed with his art work. His second gift, however, is a much-requested plane ticket to go see his uncle Ian, also an artist. Ben's mother, who accompanies her son on the trip, still holds her brother Ian responsible for an accident in which Ben lost a finger years before; though Ben's mother does not get along with her brother, she immediately becomes friends with his wife, who is pregnant. Meanwhile, with the help of the neighboring children, Ben begins to learn more about his family, and comes up with a solution to the problem of the "birthday room." "Henkes creates a world that appeals to the five senses even when he is using words as his paintbrush," praised Jennifer M. Brown in her *Publishers Weekly* review of *The Birthday Room.* In *Horn Book* a critic dubbed the novel "a story that helps us see our own chances for benefiting from mutual tolerance, creative conflict resolution, and other forms of good will," while a *Publishers Weekly* contributor wrote that Henkes's book "explores family relationships with breathtaking tenderness."

Olive's Ocean introduces readers to Martha, a twelve year old whose classmate, Olive, died in a car accident. Though they hardly knew each other, Olive had written in her diary that the next year in school, she hoped to become Martha's friend, because Martha was "the nicest person in my whole entire class." Olive's mother gives Martha an extract from Olive's diary, and Martha begins to feel closer to the deceased girl, discovering that Olive had hoped to become an author and that she had always wanted to see the ocean. Martha's summer visit to her grandmother's house on the shoreline becomes a visit for Olive as well, when Martha finds a way to take Olive to the ocean with her. Noting that *Olive's Ocean* contains "all the elements of a traditional summer novel"—including Martha's summer crush, which goes badly—Sarah Ellis noted in *Horn Book* that, while "in other hands this might be too much material, . . . Henkes has a jeweler's touch, strong and delicate." *Olives's Ocean* "isn't big and splashy," *Booklist* reviewer Michael Cart asserted, and "its quiet art and intelligence will stick with readers." Maria B. Salvadore wrote in *School Library Journal* that, "though Martha remains the focus, others around her become equally realized, including Olive." As a critic for *Kirkus Reviews* commented, "characters and setting are painted in with the deft strokes of an experienced artist," and Claire Rosser proclaimed in *Kliatt* that the novel's protagonist "is one of the most memorable 12-year-old girls of fiction, smart, confused, compassionate."

Two boys build a friendship that also rekindles a past tragedy in *Bird Lake Moon.* For twelve-year-old Mitch Sinclair, a summer spent at his grandparents' house at Bird Lake allows him the chance to deal with the anger his father's abandonment has sparked inside. Then Spencer Stone and his family arrive at the cottage next door, returning after many years to the place where Spencer's brother Matty drowned. Although Mitch first plays on Spencer's feelings, by convincing the boy that Matty's ghost still haunts the lake, his ruse soon feels like a betrayal when the boys establish a close friendship. In *Booklist* Cooper praised Henkes for his subtle storytelling, writing that the boys' overlapping narratives create a text "as evocative as it is precise." For *School Library Journal* contributor Lee Bock, Henkes's "superbly crafted plot moves smoothly and unhurriedly," and his mix of humor, "complex" characters, and a "believable resolution" come together to make *Bird Lake Moon* "a significant and highly readable book."

At no loss for story ideas, Henkes has authored several picture books illustrated by other artists. In the first such collaboration, *Once around the Block,* Henkes and illustrator Victoria Chess portray a little girl who turns the boredom of waiting for her father into a fun journey around the neighborhood. The conclusion—in which the girl comes home to find her bored father waiting for

her return—is "a masterstroke of child appeal on the part of the author," as Betsy Hearne observed in the *Bulletin of the Center for Children's Books.* "As in his other books," a *Kirkus Reviews* writer remarked, "Henkes creates a comfortable story with understated, believable characters and events" in *Once around the Block.*

The Biggest Boy, illustrated by Nancy Tafuri, similarly exhibits Henkes's sensitivity toward young children's concerns by depicting how a little boy imagines himself to be big and powerful. *New York Times Book Review* contributor Meg Wolitzer praised how, in Henkes's text for *The Biggest Boy,* "the parents encourage the child's fantasies of power and separation and take great pleasure in his responses." Another picture-book collaboration, this one with Anita Lobel, resulted in *So Happy!* This book takes readers to the Southwest, where a little boy, a lost rabbit, a book, and a magic seed each play a part in a circular story that shows the interrelationships that exist in nature. In *So Happy!* Henkes presents what *School Library Journal* critic Wendy Lukehart described as a "satisfying look at the interplay of nature, time, and love," while Lempke made special note of Lobel's "lush, impressionistic, and dramatic" paintings.

Oh!, a story illustrated by Henkes's wife Laura Dronzek, introduces an even-younger set of readers to the author's fans. In the story, everyone from squirrels to rabbits to children encounters the first snow of the season. Another collaboration between Henkes and Dronzek, *Birds* "bridges the space between concept book and longer narrative," according to *Booklist* contributor Thom Barthelmess. In *Birds* the sound of a bird song draws a young narrator to investigate the many characteristics of the melodious creature and how it interplays with the world at large. In *The Biggest Boy* "Henkes keeps his prose succinct and unadorned," noted a *Publishers Weekly* reviewer, while *Booklist* contributor Cooper added: "As soft as snow, this book's simple, playful premise will make readers sigh, 'Oh!'"

Henkes takes his time with his work. "I write very, very slowly," he explained to Cooper in an interview for *Booklist.* "Sometimes it will take me a week to write a paragraph. Then I'll go over it for a couple of days. I'll take things out and put things back in. I do very few drafts; I usually write one draft exceedingly slowly." Also, by varying his projects from children's books for the very young to picture books to novels, Henkes prevents his writing from becoming routine. Sharing his enjoyment of art and writing with his readers remains one of his most important goals, as he wrote in *Children's Books and Their Creators:* "I hope that there is something about my books that connects with children, and something that connects with the adult readers. Even if something traumatic happens to one of my characters, I like to have my stories end on a hopeful note. That's my gift to the reader."

Biographical and Critical Sources

BOOKS

Children's Literature Review, Volume 23, Gale (Detroit, MI), 1991, pp. 124-131.
Silvey, Anita, *Children's Books and Their Creators,* Houghton (Boston, MA), 1995.

PERIODICALS

Booklist, September 15, 1985, Denise M. Wilms, review of *Bailey Goes Camping,* p. 134; August, 1993, Hazel Rochman, review of *Owen,* p. 2060; March 15, 1995, Hazel Rochman, review of *Protecting Marie,* p. 1330; October 15, 1995, Carolyn Phelan, review of *Goodbye, Curtis,* p. 411; August, 1996, Ilene Cooper, review of *Lilly's Purple Plastic Purse,* p. 1904; January, 1997, Ilene Cooper, interview with Henkes, p. 868; July, 1999, Ilene Cooper, review of *The Birthday Room,* p. 1946; October 1, 1999, Ilene Cooper, review of *Oh!,* p. 354; September, 2000, Ilene Cooper, review of *Wemberly Worried,* p. 2146; August, 2001, Kathy Broderick, review of *Sheila Rae's Peppermint Stick,* p. 2130; January 1, 2002, Ilene Cooper, review of *Owen's Marshmallow Chick,* p. 864; September 1, 2003, Michael Cart, review of *Olive's Ocean,* p. 122; September 15, 2003, Ilene Cooper, review of *Wemberly's Ice Cream Star* and *Julius's Candy Corn,* p. 245; January 1, 2004, Ilene Cooper, interview with Henkes, p. 853; February 15, 2004, Gillian Engberg, review of *Kitten's First Full Moon,* p. 1056; December 15, 2006, Carolyn Phelan, review of *A Good Day,* p. 47; March 15, 2008, Ilene Cooper, review of *Bird Lake Moon,* p. 52; June 1, 2008, Gillian Engberg, review of *Old Bear,* p. 79; January 1, 2009, Thom Barthelmess, review of *Birds,* p. 76.
Bulletin of the Center for Children's Books, October, 1986, Betsy Hearne, review of *A Weekend with Wendell,* pp. 27-28; March, 1987, Betsy Hearne, review of *Once around the Block,* p. 126; February, 1989, Roger Sutton, review of *Jessica,* p. 148.
Children's Book Review Service, November, 1985, Anne Deveraux Jordan Crouse, review of *Bailey Goes Camping,* p. 25.
Horn Book, May-June, 1988, Elizabeth S. Watson, review of *The Zebra Wall,* p. 352; September-October, 1988, Ann A. Flowers, review of *Chester's Way,* p. 616; May-June, 1989, Mary M. Burns, review of *Jessica,* p. 357; November-December, 1993, Hanna B. Zeiger, review of *Owen,* pp. 733-734; September, 1999, review of *The Birthday Room,* p. 611; September, 2000, review of *Wemberly Worried,* p. 550; September, 2001, review of *Sheila Rae's Peppermint Stick,* p. 574; November-December, 2003, Sarah Ellis, review of *Olive's Ocean,* p. 745; May-June, 2004, Christine M. Heppermann, review of *Kitten's First Full Moon,* p. 314; March-April, 2005, Susan Dove Lempke, review of *So Happy!,* p. 188; March-April, 2006, Susan Dove Lempke, review of *Lilly's Big Day,* p. 171; March-April, 2007, Susan Dove Lempke, review of *A Good Day,* p. 184.

Kirkus Reviews, December 15, 1981, review of *All Alone,* p. 1517; February 15, 1986, review of *Grandpa and Bo,* p. 303; April 15, 1987, review of *Once around the Block,* p. 638; April 1, 1995, review of *Protecting Marie,* p. 469; June 15, 1996, review of *Lilly's Purple Plastic Purse,* p. 899; June 1, 1997, review of *Sun and Spoon,* p. 873; July 15, 1998, review of *Circle Dogs,* p. 1035; March 1, 2003, review of *Wemberly's Ice Cream Star,* p. 386; July 1, 2003, review of *Olive's Ocean,* p. 911; February 15, 2004, review of *Kitten's First Full Moon,* p. 179.

Kliatt, July, 2003, Claire Rosser, review of *Olive's Ocean,* p. 13.

New York Times Book Review, April 28, 1991, Ann Pleshette Murphy, review of *Julius, the Baby of the World,* p. 22; September 24, 1995, Meg Wolitzer, review of *The Biggest Boy,* p. 29; November 10, 1996, M.P. Dunleavey, "The Mouse That Boogied," p. 41; November 16, 1997, Elizabeth Spires, "The Last Flip," p. 47; May 15, 2004, Karla Kuskin, review of *Kitten's First Full Moon,* p. 18; June 18, 2006, review of *Lilly's Big Day,* p. 15; May 13, 2007, Bruce Handy, review of *A Good Day,* p. 15; December 21, 2008, Sarah Ellis, review of *A Bear's Life,* p. 13; May 10, 2009, Lisa Von Drasek, review of *Birds,* p. 17.

Publishers Weekly, December 18, 1981, review of *All Alone,* p. 70; July 25, 1986, review of *A Weekend with Wendell,* p. 187; March 13, 1987, review of *Two under Par,* pp. 84-85; June 26, 1987, review of *Sheila Rae, the Brave,* p. 71; March 11, 1988, review of *The Zebra Wall,* pp. 104-105; July 8, 1988, review of *Chester's Way,* p. 53; June 9, 1989, review of *Shhhh,* p. 65; September 20, 1993, review of *Owen,* p. 71; August 12, 1996, Nathalie Op de Beeck, interview with Henkes, p. 26; June 16, 1997, review of *Sun and Spoon,* p. 60; July 6, 1998, review of *Circle Dogs,* p. 59; July 5, 1999, review of *The Birthday Room,* p. 72; October 11, 1999, review of *Oh!,* p. 74; November 22, 1999, Jennifer M. Brown, review of *The Birthday Room,* p. 21; July 3, 2000, review of *Wemberly Worried,* p. 70; August 18, 2003, review of *Olive's Ocean,* p. 80; February 16, 2004, review of *Kitten's First Full Moon,* p. 171; February 21, 2005, review of *So Happy!,* p. 173; December 18, 2006, review of *A Good Day,* p. 61; June 7, 2008, review of *Old Bear,* p. 57; December 15, 2008, review of *Birds,* p. 52.

Quill & Quire, June, 1995, Joanne Schott, review of *Protecting Marie,* p. 60; November 10, 2003, review of *Olive's Ocean,* p. 37.

School Library Journal, October, 1982, Joan W. Blos, review of *Clean Enough,* p. 141; June, 1987, Robert Unsworth, review of *Two under Par,* p. 96; September, 1987, David Gale, review of *Sheila Rae, the Brave,* p. 164; August, 1996, Marianne Saccardi, review of *Lilly's Purple Plastic Purse,* p. 122; July, 1997, Marilyn Payne Phillips, review of *Sun and Spoon,* p. 94; October, 1999, Alicia Eames, review of *Oh!,* p. 115, Corinne Camarata, review of *The Birthday Room,* p. 152; August, 2000, Joy Fleishhacker, review of *Wemberly Worried,* p. 156; December, 2001, Roxanne Burg, review of *Sheila Rae's Peppermint Stick,* p. 104; February, 2002, Ann Cook, review of *Owen's Marshmallow Chick,* p. 107; May, 2003, Melinda Piehler, review of *Wemberly's Ice Cream Star,* p. 120; August, 2003, Maria B. Salvadore, review of *Olive's Ocean,* p. 160; August, 2003, Olga R. Kuharets, review of *Julius's Candy Corn,* p. 129; April, 2004, Wendy Lukehart, review of *Kitten's First Full Moon,* p. 114; October, 2004, Kathleen T. Horning, interview with Henkes, p. 50; March, 2005, Wendy Lukehart, review of *So Happy!,* p. 172; April, 2006, Marianne Saccardi, review of *Lilly's Big Day,* p. 108; March, 2007, Marianne Saccardi, review of *A Good Day,* p. 173; March, 2008, Lee Bock, review of *Bird Lake Boon,* p. 200.

Tribune Books (Chicago, IL), May 14, 1989, Mary Harris Veeder, review of *Jessica,* p. 5; August 12, 1990, Mary Harris Veeder, review of *Julius, the Baby of the World,* p. 5.

ONLINE

Kevin Henkes Home Page, http://www.kevinhenkes.com (November 15, 2009).*

*   *   *

HURLEY, Tonya

Personal

Born in Uniontown, PA; married Michael Pagnotta; children: Isabelle Rose. *Education:* University of Pittsburgh, B.A. (writing).

Addresses

Home—New York, NY. *E-mail*—info@tonyahurley productions.com.

Career

Author, screenwriter, and filmmaker. Director of animated and live-action short films, including *Kiss My Brain, The Biblical Real World, Solo-Me, Baptism of Solitude: A Tribute to Paul Bowles,* and *best friEND.* Television series work includes: (co-producer and a co-writer) *In Action!,* 2000-01; and (co-creator and co-producer) *So Little Time,* ABC. Director of television commercials; content provider for Web sites; creator of video games, board games, and dolls. Formerly worked as a publicist in New York, NY.

Member

Writers Guild of America.

Awards, Honors

Rockefeller Foundation Award in film nomination, 2001; Canadian International Film Festival second-place award in animated short category, for *Kiss My Brain;* Webby Award nominations, 2006, 2007, both for ghostgirl.com; numerous official selections for film festivals.

Writings

Ghostgirl, Little, Brown (Boston, MA), 2008.

Ghostgirl: Homecoming, Little, Brown (New York, NY), 2009.

Author of scripts for short films, including *Kiss My Brain,* 1997, *The Biblical Real World,* 1998, *Solo-Me-O,* 1999, *Baptism of Solitude: A Tribute to Paul Bowles,* 2000, and *best friEND,* 2001. Scriptwriter for television, including *In Action!* (animated series), ABC, 2000-01; and *Big, Big World,* PBS.

Adaptations

Ghostgirl, narrated by Parker Posey, was adapted as an audiobook, Recorded Books.

Cover of Tonya Hurley's amusingly macabre middle-grade novel Ghost-girl, featuring artwork by Craig Phillips. (Little, Brown and Company, 2008. Silhouette interiors copyright © 2008 by Craig Phillips. Reproduced by permission of Hatchette Book Group USA.)

Sidelights

An independent filmmaker and writer, Tonya Hurley took the first step toward her sideline career as a children's writer when she was developing her unique Web site ghostgirl.com. Full of strong graphic images, opportunities for creative expression, and a wry take on teen enui, ghostgirl.com struck a chord with many teens, and Hurley captures the same theme in her novels *Ghostgirl* and *Ghostgirl: Homecoming.*

When readers first meet her, drab, unstylish, and listless high-school misfit Charlotte Usher is barely a blip on her school's social scene. Her scheme to change her status at Hawthorne High is tragically derailed, however, when the teen chokes on a gummy bear and dies on the first day of physics class. Charlotte's lust for popularity is enough to keep her spirit in limbo, however, and in *Ghostgirl* Hurley follows Charlotte's humorous efforts to win over her still-living high-school crush and get her first kiss as his date at the Fall Ball. Calling *Ghostgirl* "a prime exemplar of . . . a growing subgenre of satire about teens who will not or cannot die," a *Publishers Weekly* critic cited Hurley for her "consistent wit" and "polished dark and deadpan humor." Threading her story with morbid song lyrics and her own stylishly inky Goth art, Hurley creates "pitch-perfect dialogue and clever names . . . [to] keep readers laughing," according to *School Library Journal* critic Shelley Huntington. *Ghostgirl* also boasts what a *Kirkus Reviews* writer described as "a kooky slew of offbeat minor characters," all of whom help energize a story that is "goofy, ghastly, intelligent, [and] electrifying."

As Hurley told Deidre Futon in an online interview posted on the novelist's home page, "Teen years are the most formative in anyone's life, socially. I think we're all stuck there to some extent, insofar as our insecurities are born there, our personalities are cultivated there. It's the best of times and, for a lot of us, the worst. It can be cruel but it's really where you learn to survive. It's the time when you find out who you are, who you want to be, and who you don't. It's the most fertile territory imaginable for a writer. It fascinates me."

Biographical and Critical Sources

PERIODICALS

Bulletin of the Center for Children's Books, September, 2008, April Spisak, review of *Ghostgirl,* p. 22.

Kirkus Reviews, July 1, 2008, review of *Ghostgirl.*

Publishers Weekly, July 14, 2008, review of *Ghostgirl* p. 66.

School Library Journal, August, 2008, Shelley Huntington, review of *Ghostgirl,* p. 124; August, 2009, Emily Garrett Cassidy, review of *Ghostgirl: Homecoming,* p. 104.

Voice of Youth Advocates, August, 2008, Lauri Vaughan and Denzil Sikka, review of *Ghostgirl,* p. 261.

ONLINE

Ghostgirl.com, http://www.ghostgirl.com/ (November 5, 2009).

Tonya Hurley Home Page, http://www.tonyahurley.com (November 5, 2009).*

J

JINKS, Catherine 1963-

Personal
Born November 17, 1963, in Brisbane, Queensland, Australia; daughter of Brian and Rhonda Jinks; married Peter Dockrill (a journalist), November 22, 1992; children: Hannah. *Education:* University of Sydney, B.A. (medieval history; with honors), 1986. *Politics:* "Left." *Hobbies and other interests:* Gardening, history, films, television.

Addresses
Home—Leura, New South Wales, Australia. *Agent*—Margaret Connolly, 16 Winton St., Warrawee, Sydney, New South Wales 2074, Australia.

Career
Author and illustrator. Westpac Banking Corp., Sydney, New South Wales, Australia, journalist, 1986-93; full-time writer. Lecturer, workshop presenter, and writer-in-residence at Australian schools.

Awards, Honors
Literature Board of the Australia Council grant; Australian Children's Book of the Year Award shortlist, Children's Book Council of Australia (CBCA), 1993, for *Pagan's Crusade,* 1997, for *Pagan's Scribe,* and 2001 for *You'll Wake the Baby!;* Victoria Premier's Award shortlist, 1993, for *Pagan's Crusade;* Adelaide Festival Award shortlist, 1996, for *Pagan's Vows;* Australian Children's Book of the Year Award in older-readers category, 1996, for *Pagan's Vows,* and 1998, for *Eye to Eye;* Victoria Premier's Award, 1997, for *Pagan's Scribe;* Fantasy, Sci-Fi, Horror Award in young-adult division, 1997, and CROW Award shortlist, 1998, both for *Eye to Eye;* New South Wales State Literary Award shortlist, 1999, for *Eye to Eye,* and 2000, for *The Stinking Great Lie;* Family Award for Children's Book in picture-book category, 2001, Young Australian Best

Catherine Jinks (Photograph by Peter Dockrill. Reproduced by permission of Peter Dockrill.)

Book Award shortlist, and Kids Own Australian Literature Award shortlist, both 2002, all for *You'll Wake the Baby!;* Aurealis Award for fantasy shortlist, 2002, and CBCA Notable Book designation, both for *Eglantine;* Aurealis Award shortlist for long fiction, 2003, for *Eustace;* CBCA Notable Book designation, both for *Elysium;* special commendation, Sisters in Crime Davitt Award, 2005, for *Road;* Davitt Young-Adult Award, Sisters in Crime, 2006, for *Evil Genius,* 2009, for *Genius Squad.*

Writings

This Way Out, Omnibus (Sydney, New South Wales, Australia), 1991.

The Future Trap, Omnibus (Sydney, New South Wales, Australia), 1993, new edition, Puffin (Ringwood, Victoria, Australia), 1999.

Witch Bank, Puffin (Ringwood, Victoria, Australia), 1995.

An Evening with the Messiah (adult novel), Penguin (Camberwell, Victoria, Australia), 1996.

Eye to Eye, Puffin (Ringwood, Victoria, Australia), 1997.

Little White Secrets (adult novel), Penguin (Ringwood, Victoria, Australia), 1997.

(And illustrator) *The Bone Quest Saga,* Volume I: *The Secret of Hermitage Isle* (comic book), ABC Books (Sydney, New South Wales, Australia), 1997.

Piggy in the Middle, Penguin (Ringwood, Victoria, Australia), 1998.

(And illustrator) *The Horrible Holiday,* Puffin (Ringwood, Victoria, Australia), 1998.

The Inquisitor, Pan Macmillan (Sydney, New South Wales, Australia), 1999, St. Martin's Minotaur (New York, NY), 2002.

The Stinking Great Lie, Puffin (Ringwood, Victoria, Australia), 1999.

The Notary (adult mystery), Pan Macmillan (Sydney, New South Wales, Australia), 2000.

You'll Wake the Baby! (picture book), illustrated by Andrew Mclean, Viking (Ringwood, Victoria, Australia), 2000.

What's Hector McKerrow Doing These Days?, Pan Macmillan (Sydney, New South Wales, Australia), 2000.

Bella Vista (adult story collection), Putnam (New York, NY), 2001.

The Rapture, Pan Macmillan (Sydney, New South Wales, Australia), 2001.

The Gentleman's Garden, Allen & Unwin (Crows Nest, New South Wales, Australia), 2002.

(And illustrator) *Daryl's Dinner,* Puffin (Camberwell, Victoria, Australia), 2002.

Spinning Around (adult novel), Allen & Unwin (Crows Nest, New South Wales, Australia), 2004.

The Road, Allen & Unwin (Crows Nest, New South Wales, Australia), 2004.

Evil Genius, Allen & Unwin (Crows Nest, New South Wales, Australia), 2005.

The Secret Familiar: Confessions of an Inquisitor's Spy, Allen & Unwin (Crows Nest, New South Wales, Australia), 2006.

Living Hell, Allen & Unwin (Crows Nest, New South Wales, Australia), 2007, Houghton Mifflin Harcourt (Boston, MA), 2010.

Katie and Cleo Move In, illustrated by Andrew McLean, Penguin Australia (Camberwell, Victoria, Australia), 2007.

The Dark Mountain, Allen & Unwin (Crows Nest, New South Wales, Australia), 2008.

Babylonne, Candlewick Press (Cambridge, MA), 2008.

The Reformed Vampire Support Group, Houghton Mifflin Harcourt (Boston, MA), 2009.

Author's works have been translated into German, French, and Spanish, among other languages.

"PAGAN'S CHRONICLES" NOVEL SERIES

Pagan's Crusade, Oxford University Press (Melbourne, Victoria, Australia), 1992, Candlewick Press (Cambridge, MA), 2003.

Pagan in Exile, Omnibus (Sydney, New South Wales, Australia), 1994, Candlewick Press (Cambridge, MA), 2004.

Pagan's Vows, Omnibus (Sydney, New South Wales, Australia), 1995, Candlewick Press (Cambridge, MA), 2004.

Pagan's Scribe, Omnibus (Sydney, New South Wales, Australia), 1996, Candlewick Press (Cambridge, MA), 2005.

Pagan's Daughter, Allen & Unwin (Crows Nest, New South Wales, Australia), 2006.

"ALLIE'S GHOST HUNTERS" SERIES

Eglantine: A Ghost Story, Allen & Unwin (Crows Nest, New South Wales, Australia), 2002, published as *Eglantine: A Paranormal Adventure,* 2007.

Eustace: A Ghost Story, Allen & Unwin (Crows Nest, New South Wales, Australia), 2003, published as *Eustace: A Paranormal Adventure,* 2007.

Eloise: A Ghost Story, Allen & Unwin (Crows Nest, New South Wales, Australia), 2003, published as *Eloise: A Paranormal Adventure,* 2007.

Elysium: A Ghost Story, Allen & Unwin (Crows Nest, New South Wales, Australia), 2004, published as *Elysium: A Paranormal Adventure,* 2007.

"GENIUS" NOVEL SERIES

Evil Genius, Allen & Unwin (Crows Nest, New South Wales, Australia), 2005, Harcourt (Orlando, FL), 2007.

Genius Squad, Harcourt (Orlando, FL), 2008.

The Genius Wars, Allen & Unwin (Crows Nest, New South Wales, Australia), 2009.

Sidelights

Australian author Catherine Jinks is best known for her "Pagan's Chronicles" series, which draws readers into the medieval world. The series, which includes the books *Pagan's Crusade* and *Pagan's Scribe,* grew out of Jinks's interest in medieval history and focuses on sixteen-year-old Christian Arab Pagan Kidrouk, who works as a squire for Templar Knight Lord Roland Roucy de Bram during the Crusades. The "Pagan Chronciles" combine Jinks's wide-ranging knowledge of the medieval period with her engaging writing style and quirky sense of humor. Other books that draw readers into the medieval past include *Babylonne* and the murder mystery *The Inquisitor,* while Jinks returns to the present for several picture books and young-adult works, including the titles comprising her popular "Allie's Ghost Hunters" and "Genius" series.

Jinks was born in Australia in 1963 and grew up amid a book-loving family in Papua New Guinea. An avid writer since childhood, she once recalled to an Allen & Unwin online interviewer, "My first 'book' was a picture book called *I Want to Be a Jungle Girl.* I sent my first 'novel' to a publisher when I was twelve (it was turned down, needless to say)." After moving to Australia and graduating from the University of Sydney with a degree in medieval history, she married and relocated with her Canadian husband to Nova Scotia from 1993 to 1994, before returning to Australia with her family.

Cover of Jinks's young-adult novel **Pagan's Crusade,** *featuring artwork by Peter de Seve.* (Candlewick Press, 1992. Jacket illustrations copyright © 2003 Peter de Seve. Reproduced by permission of the publisher Candlewick Press, Inc., Cambridge, MA.)

Jinks's first book for young adults, *This Way Out,* was published in 1991, after its author had spent several years working as a journalist. The contemporary story focuses on a fifteen-year-old girl's dissatisfaction with her life and her search for a job that will pay for the photographs she hopes will begin her modeling career. "*This Way Out* reveals the author's awareness of some of the frustrations and longings of youth," remarked Cathryn Crowe in *Magpies.*

For her second book, *Pagan's Crusade,* Jinks introduces her twelfth-century ragamuffin character, Pagan, as he attempts to rise above a childhood on the streets of Jerusalem by finding a place with the Knights Templar. The novel, which takes place in 1187, focuses on the relationship between the streetwise Pagan and Templar Knight Lord Roland, who as a member of the order charged with protecting travelers, is the epitome of upper-class strength and valor. Touring the Middle East to advance the cause of Christianity, the pair are forced to enter battle to defend the city of Jerusalem and the Christian pilgrims visiting the Holy City from the Muslim warlord Saladin, who is attempting to recapture the

city for Islam. "The aristocratic Templar and his scruffy squire make an unlikely partnership and it is a measure of the success of Ms. Jinks' story that we accept the mutual respect that grows up between the partners under the stress of violent action," noted Marcus Crouch in his *Junior Bookshelf* review of *Pagan's Crusade.*

Critics have noted the author's unusual choice of modern vernacular speech for her medieval characters, a choice that, in *Pagan's Crusade,* yields "a style which is elliptical and abrupt and, at times, wildly funny," according to a reviewer for *Magpies.* Praising Jinks' characters as "lively and engaging," *Horn Book* contributor Anita L. Burkam added that the irreverent squire's "sarcastic first-person narration, while faithful to the details of medieval life, contains more than a touch of irony." Comparing Jinks's humor to that of British comedy troupe Monty Python, a *Publishers Weekly* reviewer wrote that the "alternately hilarious, often poignant novel . . . turns medieval history into fodder for both high comedy and allegory." Also praising *Pagan's Crusade,* a *Kirkus Reviews* critic maintained that the book's "orphan's-eye view" helps readers visualize "the overripe streets of 12th-century Jerusalem" and also "introduces a character as lovable, stubbornly loyal, and smart-mouthed as any Disney film sidekick."

In *Pagan in Exile,* the first sequel to *Pagan's Crusade,* Lord Roland takes Pagan back to his estate in Languedoc, France, where the knight becomes involved in the domestic wars among the twelfth-century landed aristocracy while also trying to summon others to help the Order retake Jerusalem. Like Jinks's first volume, *Pagan in Exile* was praised for its young protagonist's humorous first-person narration, although its plot contains a darker focus due to its depiction of the brutality and squalor of medieval life. Noting that the author successfully brings to life an epoch "that was particularly dark and dirty," *Booklist* contributor Ilene Cooper added that followers of the "Pagan" series will likely "find other books set in the Middle Ages pallid" by comparison.

Other books in the "Pagan Chronicles" series include *Pagan's Vows* and *Pagan's Scribe. Pagan's Vows* finds Pagan and Lord Roland serving as novices at the Abbey of Saint Martin as a way of avoiding the brutality of medieval French society. While Roland quickly accepts the way of life at the Benedictine monastery, Pagan sees the dishonesty and hypocrisy running rampant in this house of God. Rejecting the blind obedience demanded of him, as well as the discomfort, he is determined to unveil the corruption in the monastic hierarchy, even if it angers Lord Roland. "The historical details in this fast-moving, humorous tale are precise and fascinating," Anita L. Burkam noted in her *Booklist* review of *Pagan's Vows.*

Jinks concludes her series with *Pagan's Scribe,* in which Isadore recounts Pagan's rise to become an archdeacon of the Roman Catholic Church in France. Burkam remarked that the "emotionally satisfying epic

brings the Middle Ages to life," and Paula Rohrlick, writing in *Kliatt,* described the novel as a "moving ending to a vivid, gritty historical fiction series." *Pagan's Vows* won the Australian Children's Book of the Year Award in the older-readers category from the Children's Book Council of Australia, one of several awards accorded the series. In her acceptance speech, published in *Reading Time,* Jinks noted: "In a funny sort of way I see the award as more of a tribute to Pagan than to me." Describing her popular fictional character, she added, "He's been through a lot, yet he's kept his humour and his courage and his loving heart."

Like the "Pagan" books, *The Inquisitor* is another novel by Jinks that has found its way into the hands of U.S. readers. Taking place in fourteenth-century France during the Inquisition, the novel focuses on the efforts of Inquisitor Father Bernard Peyre to track down the person who murdered and dismembered the corpse of the father's supervisor, Father Augustin. As his search uncovers corruption in the church hierarchy, Bernard finds his reputation sullied—and his life threatened—by charges of heresy in what *Booklist* reviewer Carrie Bissey dubbed a "smart page-turner that paints a convinc-

ing portrait of the struggle to live in the shadow of a . . . [corrupt] institution." Citing Bernard as a "sympathetic and engaging narrator," a *Publishers Weekly* reviewer also praised Jinks for her creation of a "gripping escape sequence" to crown the novel's plot.

Babylonne, another work set in medieval France, centers on the title character, a rebellious teenager who flees from an arranged marriage to an elderly man. Disguised as a boy, Babylonne must place her trust in her traveling companion, Father Isadore, a Catholic priest who knew her father, Pagan Kidrouk. According to *Kliatt* reviewer Aimee Cole, "Issues of faith and truth are presented seamlessly within the story for readers to question," and Burkam observed that Jinks's "characters will touch readers' sympathies even as the faultless scholarship steeps them in the deeds and customs of the era."

Jinks embarks on a second series with *Eglantine: A Paranormal Adventure.* As the first of the "Allie's Ghost Hunters" books, *Eglantine* introduces Allie Gebhardt, junior ghost hunter. In this book, as well as its sequels *Eustace: A Paranormal Adventure, Eloise: A Paranormal Adventure,* and *Elysium: A Paranormal Adventure,* Allie gradually gains the tools of the ghost-hunting trade—séances, dealing with emanations, and how to put a spirit to rest—as various unearthly spectres cross her path. The works "feature well-drawn settings," Elaine E. Knight commented in *School Library Journal.*

Jinks introduces child prodigy Cadel Piggott in *Evil Genius,* "an engrossingly complex tale," according to a critic in *Kirkus Reviews.* After his adoptive parents can no longer cope with his destructive behaviors, the mischievous Cadel is placed in the Axis Institute by his longtime psychologist, Dr. Thaddeus Roth. Cadel soon realizes, however, that he is being groomed to take the place of his biological father, Phineas Darkkon, an imprisoned criminal mastermind. "Jinks sets up a compelling world of lies, deceit, and betrayal," Dylan Thomarie observed in *School Library Journal,* and a *Publishers Weekly* contributor wrote that, "as the complex deceptions that have shaped Cadel's life come to light, his emotional unraveling and awakening will likely engross readers." In *Genius Squad,* a sequel, Cadel joins forces with an elite group of computer experts who are investigating a criminal empire. "Jinks writes hacker lingo accessible to nontechies, imparting the edgy thrill of computer espionage," Burkam noted, and a *Publishers Weekly* contributor remarked that the cast of characters "help populate this story with fresh twists and eyebrow-raising, technologically over-the-top antics."

A group of rundown, whiny bloodsuckers is involved in a murder mystery in *The Reformed Vampire Support Group,* a "droll vampire send-up," according to *Booklist* critic Ian Chipman. After one of its members gets himself staked, a band of weary vampires, whose members suffer from anemia and find immortality stifling, must

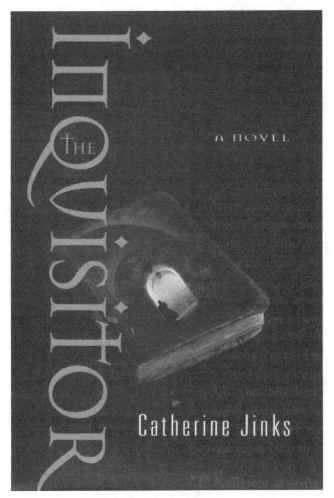

Cover of Jinks's young-adult mystery **The Inquisitor,** *which is set in the middle ages.* (St. Martin's Minotaur, 2002. Reprinted by permission of St. Martin's Press.)

Cover of The Road, *one of many award-winning novels by Jinks.* (Allen & Unwin, 2004. Reproduced by permission.)

track down the killer before he strikes again. "Jinks's signature facility with plot and character development is intact," a *Publishers Weekly* reviewer commented, and *Horn Book* critic Lauren Adams stated of *The Reformed Vampire Support Group* that "this alternative vampire story is for outsiders of all kinds, underground or otherwise."

Biographical and Critical Sources

PERIODICALS

Booklist, October 1, 2002, Carrie Bissey, review of *The Inquisitor,* p. 304; January 1, 2004, Ilene Cooper, review of *Pagan in Exile,* p. 844; May 15, 2007, Jennifer Mattson, review of *Evil Genius,* p. 46; January 1, 2009, Ian Chipman, review of *The Reformed Vampire Support Group,* p. 71.

Horn Book, July, 1993, Karen Jameyson, review of *Pagan's Crusade,* p. 498; September-October, 2003, Anita L. Burkam, review of *Pagan's Crusade,* p. 611; May-June, 2004, Anita L. Burkam, review of *Pagan in Exile,* p. 328; September-October, 2004, Anita L. Burkam, review of *Pagan's Vows,* p. 587; March-April, 2005, Anita L. Burkam, review of *Pagan's Scribe,* p. 203; July-August, 2008, Anita L. Burkam, review of *Genius Squad,* p. 449; January-February, 2009, Anita L. Burkam, review of *Babylonne,* p. 94; May-June, 2009, Lauren Adams, review of *The Reformed Vampire Support Group,* p. 298.

Junior Bookshelf, December, 1993, Marcus Crouch, review of *Pagan's Crusade,* pp. 246-247.

Kirkus Reviews, September 15, 2002, review of *The Inquisitor,* p. 1355; October 14, 2003, review of *Pagan's Crusade,* p. 1272; December 15, 2003, review of *Pagan in Exile,* p. 1450; April 1, 2007, review of *Evil Genius.*

Kliatt, January, 2004, Paula Rohrlick, reviews of *Pagan's Crusade* and *Pagan in Exile,* p. 8; March, 2005, Paula Rohrlick, review of *Pagan's Scribe,* p. 13; November, 2008, Aimee Cole, review of *Babylonne,* p. 12.

Magpies, November, 1992, review of *Pagan's Crusade,* p. 14; March, 1993, Cathryn Crowe, review of *This Way Out,* p. 32; May, 1993, Joan Zahnleiter, review of *Pagan's Crusade,* p. 24; July, 1995, review of *Pagan in Exile,* p. 24.

Publishers Weekly, September 30, 2002, review of *The Inquisitor,* p. 53; November 10, 2003, review of *Pagan's Crusade,* p. 63; April 2, 2007, review of *Evil Genius,* p. 57; March 31, 2008, review of *Genius Squad,* p. 62; January 26, 2009, review of *The Reformed Vampire Support Group,* p. 120.

Reading Time, November, 1996, Catherine Jinks, acceptance speech for Australian Children's Book of the Year Award, pp. 7-8.

School Library Journal, December, 2003, Douglas P. Davey, review of *Pagan's Crusade,* p. 153; September, 2004, Kirsten Oravec, review of *Pagan's Vows,* p. 209; July, 2007, Dylan Thomarie, review of *Evil Genius,* p. 104; November, 2007, Elaine E. reviews of *Eglantine: A Paranormal Adventure* and *Eustace: A Paranormal Adventure,* p. 126; June, 2008, Steven Engelfried, review of *Genius Squad,* p. 144; December, 2008, Wendy Scalfaro, review of *Babylonne,* p. 128.

ONLINE

Allen & Unwin Web site, http://www.allenandunwin.com/ (November 15, 2009), "Catherine Jinks."

Candlewick Press Web site, http://www.candlewick.com/ (November 15, 2009), "Catherine Jinks."

Catherine Jinks Home Page, http://www.catherinejinks.com (November 15, 2009).

Lateral Learning Speakers' Agency Web site, http://www.laterallearning.com/ (November 15, 2009), "Catherine Jinks."*

K

KALIS, Jennifer

Personal

Married; children: two. *Education:* Maryland Institute College of Art, B.F.A., 1999.

Addresses

Home—Columbus, OH. *E-mail*—jen@kalisillustration. com.

Career

Illustrator.

Illustrator

Madalyn Aslan, *What's Your Sign?: A Cosmic Guide for Young Astrologers,* Grosset & Dunlap (New York, NY), 2002.

Dr. Harvey Karp, *The Happiest Baby on the Block,* Bantam (New York, NY), 2002.

Jane O'Connor, *Mary Cassatt: Family Pictures,* Grosset & Dunlap (New York, NY), 2003

Every Kid Needs a Marshmallow Launcher, Gibbs Smith (Layton, UT), 2005.

Melanie Marks, *The Tooth Fairy Rules,* Innovative Kids, 2006.

Bart King, *The Big Book of Girl Stuff,* Gibbs Smith (Layton, UT), 2006, selections published as *Pocket Guide to Girl Stuff,* 2009.

The Lull-a-Baby Sleep Plan, Wiley, 2006.

Carol Lynch Williams, *Twenty-four Games You Can Play on a Checkerboard,* Gibbs Smith (Layton, UT), 2007.

Alan Katz, *Stinky Thinking Number 2: Another Big Book of Gross Games and Brainteasers,* Simon & Schuster (New York, NY), 2007.

Made with Love for Dad, Innovative Kids, 2008.

Made with Love for Mom, Innovative Kids, 2008.

Monica Shah, Mariam McGregor, and Alison Hill, *Amaze!: The Twists and Turns of Getting Along,* Girl Scouts of the USA (New York, NY), 2008.

Laura Tuchman, *Welcome to the Daisy Flower Garden,* Girl Scouts of the USA (New York, NY), 2008.

Laurie Friedman, *Campfire Mallory,* Carolrhoda (Minneapolis, MN), 2008.

Laurie Friedman, *Step Fourth, Mallory!,* Carolrhoda (Minneapolis, MN), 2008.

Laurie Friedman, *Red, White, and True Blue Mallory,* Carolrhoda (Minneapolis, MN), 2009.

Laurie Friedman, *Happy New Year, Mallory!,* Carolrhoda (Minneapolis, MN), 2009.

Laurie Friedman, *Mallory Goes Green,* Carolrhoda (Minneapolis, MN), 2010.

Pocket Doodles for Girls, Gibbs Smith (Layton, UT), 2010.

Paul on the Farm, Hermanhesse (Korea), 2010.

Also illustrator of concept books. Contributor to periodicals, including *American Baby, Woman's Day, Parents, New York Times, Girl's Life, Time,* and *American Girl.*

Sidelights

Jennifer Kalis is an Ohio-based illustrator whose whimsical gouache and collage art is featured in novelty books as well as in the pages of children's books and magazines. Her "funky cartoon illustrations" for Madalyn Aslan's *What's Your Sign?: A Cosmic Guide for Young Astrologers* were cited by *School Library Journal* critic Ann G. Brouse as "add[ing] to the book's attractiveness," and Augusta R. Malvagnao wrote in the same publication that Kalis's "great color graphics" contribute to the "hours of endless fun" provided in the pages of Carol Lynch Williams' *Twenty-four Games You Can Play on a Checkerboard.*

Although Kalis's concept-book and standalone illustrations are perhaps her best-known work, upper-elementary-grade readers are most familiar with her collaborations with writer Laurie Friedman for the ongoing "Mallory" novel series. In *Campfire Mallory,* the ninth volume of the series, readers follow the spunky nine year old who stars in the series as she attends sum-

Jennifer Kalis brings to life the adventures of a spunky heroine in her artwork for Laurie Friedman's amusing middle-grade novel Campfire Mallory. (Carolhoda Books, 2008. Illustrations copyright © 2008 by Lerner Publishing Group, Inc. All rights reserved. Reproduced by Carolhoda Books, a division of Lerner Publishing Group.)

mer camp and chronicles her many adventures. Written in a diary format, Friedman's text is accompanied by Kalis's black-and-white drawings in the series installments *Step Fourth, Mallory!, Red, White, and True Blue Mallory, Happy New Year, Mallory!,* and *Mallory Goes Green.* Reviewing *Red, White, and True Blue Mallory* for *Booklist,* Carolyn Phelan wrote that Kalis's "pencil drawings . . . illustrate the journal effectively," and her "fresh, childlike drawings" highlight Mallory's chronicle of entering fourth grade in *Step Fourth, Mallory!*

Biographical and Critical Sources

PERIODICALS

Booklist, October 15, 2008, Carolyn Phelan, review of *Step Fourth, Mallory!,* p. 36; April 1, 2009, Carolyn Phelan, review of *Red, White, and True Blue Mallory,* p. 32.
School Library Journal, September, 2002, Ann G. Brouse, review of *What's Your Sign?: A Cosmic Guide for Young Astrologers,* p. 238; January, 2007, Elaine Baran Black, review of *The Big Book of Girl Stuff,* p. 151; March, 2008, Esther Moberg, review of *Campfire Mallory,* p. 162, and Augusta R. Malvagno, review of *Twenty-four Games You Can Play on a Checkerboard,* p. 225.

ONLINE

Jennifer Kalis Home Page, http://www.kalisillustration. com (November 5, 2009).*

*   *   *

KEY, Samuel M.
See DE LINT, Charles

*   *   *

KEYES, Diane

Personal

Married; has children. *Education:* University of Minnesota—Twin Cities, B.A. (1968). *Hobbies and other interests:* Decorating, gardening, painting, hiking, traveling, floral design, entertaining, spending time with her grandson.

Addresses

Home—Minneapolis, MN. *E-mail*—dkeyes@ifbhomesale.com.

Career

Home stager, entrepreneur, and writer. In Full Bloom, former co-owner, 1980-85; IFB Home Staging Consultants, Minneapolis, MN, and Ann Arbor, MI, founder, 1986—. Speaker, retreat director, lay minister, and grief counselor.

Awards, Honors

Midwest Independent Publishers Association Book Awards for best business and best how-to book, both for *This Sold House.*

Writings

This Sold House: Home Staging for a Quick Sale and High Profits, Expert Pub. Inc. (Andover, MN), 2007.
Spirit of the Snowpeople, illustrated by Helen Stevens, Down East Books (Camden, ME), 2008.

Adaptations

Spirit of the Snowpeople was adapted for the state by the Open Book Players, Gardiner, ME.

Sidelights

Diane Keyes' picture book *Spirit of the Snowpeople* tells a gentle story about a town where the winters were long and dreary. To buoy their spirits during the snowy months, the townspeople created statues of snow that were so beautiful that visitors came from miles around to enjoy them. With the coming of spring, however, the snow statues began to melt, upsetting some but also signifying that change is a central part of life. Praising the "magical illustrations" by artist Helen Stevens that bring Keyes' story to life, a *Kirkus Reviews* writer added that *Spirit of the Snowpeople* illustrates for children the "message of the connectedness of the seasons."

In addition to her writing for children, Keyes works as a professional home stager as well as a lay minister and grief counselor. One of the first to pursue home staging (decorating a home to facilitate its sale), she also wrote a book about her work, titled *This Sold House: Home Staging for a Quick Sale and High Profits*, as a way to help homeowners more easily sell their homes in a competitive real-estate market. According to Keyes, her goal for *Spirit of the Snowpeople* is "to get it into the hands of as many sick children as possible," as she noted on her home page. "Although young readers love its magical illustrations and uplifting story, it is also resonating with children and adults who identify with its deeper message of hope in the midst of loss and proving to be a comfort to them."

Diane Keyes' debut picture book **Spirit of the Snowpeople** *features a wintertime fable that is captured in Helen Stevens' gentle art.* (Down East Books, 2008. Illustrations © by Helen Stevens. All rights reserved. Reproduced by permission of Down East Books.)

Biographical and Critical Sources

PERIODICALS

Kirkus Reviews, August 15, 2008, review of *Spirit of the Snowpeople.*
School Library Journal, January, 2009, Martha Simpson, review of *Spirit of the Snowpeople,* p. 78.

ONLINE

Diane Keyes Professional Web page, http://www.ifbhomesale.com (November 5, 2009).*

*   *   *

KLASS, David 1960-

Personal

Born March 8, 1960, in VT; son of Morton (an anthropology professor) and Sheila (a writer and English professor) Klass; married Giselle Benatar; children: two. *Education:* Yale University, B.A., 1982; University of Southern California School of Cinema and Television, M.A., 1989.

Addresses

Home—New York, NY. *Agent*—Aaron M. Priest Literary Agency, 708 3rd Ave., 23rd Fl., New York, NY 10017.

Career

Novelist and screenwriter. Director of film *Shelter in the Storm,* 1987. Formerly worked as an English teacher.

Member

Writers Guild of America West.

Awards, Honors

Outstanding Works of Fiction for Young Adults Award, Southern California Council, and One Hundred Best of the Best inclusion, American Library Association (ALA), both 1990, both for *Wrestling with Honor;* Notable Children's Trade Book in the Field of Social Studies designation, Children's Book Council/National Council for the Social Studies, Best Book for Young Adults selection, ALA, and Bank Street College Annual Children's Book Award runner up, all 1994, all for *California Blue;* Best Book for Young Adults selection, ALA, 1995, for *Danger Zone;* Young Adults' Choices designation, International Reading Association (IRA), Books for the Teen Age designation, New York Public Library, and Best Book for Young Adults selection, ALA, 2002, all for *You Don't Know Me;* Young Adults'

David Klass (Reproduced by permission.)

Choices designation, IRA, and Books for the Teen Age designation, New York Public Library, both 2002, both for *Home of the Braves;* Quick Picks for Reluctant Young Adult Readers selection, ALA, Best Children's Book of the Year selection, Bank Street College of Education, and Books for the Teen Age designation, New York Public Library, all 2005, all for *Dark Angel.*

Writings

FOR YOUNG ADULTS

The Atami Dragons, Scribner (New York, NY), 1984.
Breakaway Run, Dutton (New York, NY), 1986.
A Different Season, Dutton (New York, NY), 1988.
Wrestling with Honor, Dutton (New York, NY), 1989.
California Blue, Scholastic (New York, NY), 1994.
Danger Zone, Scholastic (New York, NY), 1995.
Screen Test, Scholastic, (New York, NY), 1997.
You Don't Know Me, Frances Foster Books (New York, NY), 2001.
Home of the Braves, Farrar, Straus (New York, NY), 2002.
Dark Angel, Farrar, Straus (New York, NY), 2005.
Stuck on Earth, Farrar, Straus (New York, NY), 2010.

"CARETAKER" TRILOGY

Firestorm, Farrar, Straus (New York, NY), 2006.
Whirlwind, Farrar, Straus (New York, NY), 2008.
Timelock, Farrar, Straus (New York, NY), 2009.

OTHER

Night of the Tyger (adult novel), St. Martin's Press (New York, NY), 1990.
Samuri, Inc. (adult novel), Fawcett (New York, NY), 1992.

Also contributor of short stories to anthologies.

SCREENPLAYS

Kiss the Girls, Paramount Pictures, 1997.
Desperate Measures, Columbia TriStar, 1998.
Runaway Virus, American Broadcasting Company, 2000.
(With sister, Judy Klass) *In the Time of Butterflies* (based on the novel of the same name by Julia Alvarez), Showtime, 2001.
Walking Tall, Metro-Goldwyn-Meyer, 2004.

Adaptations

Desperate Measures was adapted into a novel by Robert Tine, Berkley Boulevard Books (New York, NY), 1998.

Sidelights

David Klass, an award-winning novelist and screenwriter, is the author of such highly regarded young-adult novels as *Wrestling with Honor, Home of the Braves,* and *Dark Angel.* Klass's characters find themselves confronting issues ranging from feminism to environmentalism, in contexts that are very familiar to many young adults—the playing field or competitive arena. While critics have lauded Klass's attention to detail and the evocative narratives in his sports scenes, many have also noted his complex presentation of social issues and his ability to avoid sentimentality in discussing personal traumas like divorce, child abuse, or the loss of a parent. Perhaps the key to Klass's success has been the philosophy he once declared in an essay on the Scholastic Web site: "If I write truthfully about the characters, the issues will come alive."

The son of Morton Klass, an anthropology professor, and Shelia Solomon Klass, a prominent young-adult writer, Klass grew up in a Leonia, New Jersey, home surrounded by a strong love for literature. An avid athlete in high school, he attended Yale University, but quickly realized that professional athletics would not be a realistic goal. Instead he increased his efforts at Yale, winning an award for best creative writing as an undergraduate. After graduation, Klass decided to try his hand in the world of law, interning at a law office for one year, but soon realized that he wanted more from life. Opting for adventure, he took a job as a teacher in Japan, instructing students in conversational English. He realized that if he was going to write a book, this would be the place.

The inspiration for Klass's first young-adult novel came from his immersion in a new culture, experiencing all the sights and sounds of a provincial Japanese town.

The Atami Dragons, features a young male protagonist who leaves trouble at home when he goes to Japan. Jerry Sanders has just lost his mother, and he decides to accompany his father and sister on a business trip to Japan for the summer. As he sacrifices the opportunity to play baseball in the United States when he leaves for Japan, Jerry jumps at the chance to play baseball in Japan. He makes new friends, experiences baseball in another culture, and begins to come to terms with his mother's death. As *Booklist* critic Stephanie Zvirin noted, Klass brings "equal shares of humor, sports, and sentiment" to this story of loss and recovery.

Breakaway Run, Klass's next novel, was written with the insight he gained as an English teacher working in a Japanese high school. It begins when Tony Ross leaves his quarreling parents to study for five months in Atami, Japan, the same town Klass taught in. Tony initially finds adjusting to the ways of his host family and Japanese culture difficult; he is frustrated by his inability to communicate with others and disturbed by the way he is treated as an outsider. Gradually, however, Tony's personal qualities and his athletic abilities (especially in soccer) earn him the respect and affection of his host family and schoolmates. He even manages to cope with and adjust to the news that his parents are divorcing. According to Zvirin, Klass includes details about the sports Tony plays, and his "portrayal of Japanese culture and customs" demonstrates "obvious respect and knowledge."

While writing *Breakaway Run,* Klass received some exciting news. His first novel had been optioned for film and a Hollywood producer came to Atami to visit Klass and view the possible location. Although Klass had been toying with the idea of going to law school once he was back in the United States, the producer convinced him that his real future lay in Hollywood as a screenwriter. Giving this plan a try for seven years, Klass lived close to the bone economically, working at various odd jobs while doing treatments for producers that earned him a meager living. He also studied for a master's degree at the University of Southern California, putting himself through college by working as a teacher's assistant in English composition sections.

During his time in Hollywood, Klass published three more young-adult novels: *A Different Season, Wrestling with Honor,* and *California Blue.* According to a *Kirkus Reviews* critic, Klass presents "another thoughtful, expertly crafted story" with *A Different Season.* In this novel, the protagonist does not enjoy baseball in another culture, but he does experience cultural pressure to transform his favorite sport. Jim Roark, known to everyone as "Streak," is a talented pitcher who finds himself attracted to Jennifer Douglas, another outstanding athlete. When Jennifer attempts to join the baseball team, however, Jim insists that girls and women have no business playing baseball, and the teens' relationship suffers.

As critics have noted, Klass uses the disagreement between Jim and Jennifer, and the public debate that ensues, to present arguments for and against the integration of sports teams. Jennifer is finally allowed to join the team, and although their team loses the final game, Jennifer and Jim learn to respect their differences of opinion. "Klass writes with precision and grace about baseball," asserted Hazel Rochman in *Booklist.* A *Publishers Weekly* critic appreciated Klass's decision not to "resolve the book's central conflict," instead letting readers "draw their own conclusions."

Wrestling with Honor takes up the issue of drug testing. Ron Woods, an honor student, Eagle Scout, and captain of the wrestling team, never expected that the mandatory drug test he had to take would demonstrate positive for marijuana use. Although Ron is not a drug user and realizes that the test results must be a mistake, he refuses to take another test to clear his name because he believes that the tests violate his right to privacy. Ron is subsequently banned from his team, and his relationships with his teammates, family, and girlfriend deteriorate. Before the novel ends, however, he explores his feelings about the death of his father in the Vietnam

Cover of David Klass's young-adult novel Danger Zone, *featuring cover art by Mike Benny.* (Scholastic Inc., 1996. Jacket painting copyright © 1996 by Mike Benny. Reproduced by permission of Scholastic Inc.)

War, discovers why his drug test was positive, and confronts his fiercest wrestling competitor. Readers "will be cheering all the way through [the novel's] exciting—if manipulated—final scene," concluded a critic in *Publishers Weekly.*

Klass focuses on environmentalism in *California Blue,* a novel that follows the conflict between a teenage boy who discovers a rare butterfly in the forest surrounding his home and the boy's father, a mill worker. The conflict between John and his father is intensified by the fact that each has always disagreed with the other about the relative merits of athleticism and intellectualism. Adding to the strained relationship is the fact that John's father may be dying from leukemia. A *Publishers Weekly* critic stated that in *California Blue,* Klass has written a "beautifully rendered novel" in which he "handles complex situations with grace and subtlety."

As critics began to favorably notice the works of Klass, the author's screenwriting career also began taking off, with successes such as *Kiss the Girls,* a thriller starring Morgan Freeman and Ashley Judd, and *Desperate Measures,* featuring Michael Keaton and Andy Garcia. Klass was able to leave Hollywood for the East Coast, settling in Manhattan, where he could write for the movies at a distance and continue with his YA novels.

Klass's novels *Danger Zone* and *Screen Test* were written in an energetic three-month period following his move from Hollywood. With *Danger Zone,* Klass turns to basketball and a high school "Teen Dream Team" which competes in Europe in an international tournament. Jimmy Doyle, a star guard from Minnesota, finds that he is distrusted by much of the rest of the team, largely made up of inner-city African-American players. Doyle must win their respect, battling against rivalry and racism to do so. Once in Europe, however, a new form of racism appears. German skinheads threaten the team, and in the final game, Jimmy takes a terrorist bullet just as he sinks the winning shot. A *Kirkus Reviews* contributor wrote that Klass embroiders his plot with "frank, thoughtful observations about fathers and sons, city versus small-town values, race, friendship, and courage," while Tom S. Hurlburt noted in *School Library Journal* that "the racial tension throughout the book rings true, and readers seeking lots of hoop action will be thoroughly satisfied." Nancy Zachary, writing in *Voice of Youth Advocates,* called *Danger Zone* a "fast-paced adventure that deals realistically with pressure, racism, and terrorism."

Screen Test is Klass's take on Hollywood; it involves sixteen-year-old Liz, who is discovered by a big-shot Hollywood producer when she takes part in a student film. Offered a starring role in a feature film, Liz leaves her New Jersey home for a summer in Hollywood and a possible film career. However, Liz discovers painful truths about "Tinsel Town" and her seductive male co-star; she eventually learns to value her parents and the East Coast more than the flaky values of Hollywood. Writing in *Booklist,* Ilene Cooper found that Klass offers "some good lessons here on finding your own way."

Reviewing Klass's novel *You Don't Know Me, School Library Journal* reviewer Joel Schumaker remarked that the author "blazes past his previous efforts stylistically." Faced with abuse from his mother's violent live-in boyfriend, pressure from his teachers at school, and confusion over the girl of his dreams, fourteen-year-old John creates a detailed conversation in his head, the only place where he can escape the absurdity of the world he lives in. As readers discover the thoughts in the young protagonist's head, they come to understand John's desperation as he feels no one understands him. After a near-fatal beating at the hands of his soon-to-be stepfather, John's world opens up, and he learns how well regarded he is by not only his teachers and classmates but also, and perhaps most importantly, by his mother. According to a *Publishers Weekly* contributor, John's "underlying sense of isolation and thread of hope will strike a chord with nearly every adolescent." Describing the book as "vivid and original" with "a strange, hopeful ending," *Horn Book* critic Anita L. Burkam dubbed John "a genuinely sympathetic character whose pathos may dip into self-pity but never into self-indulgence." *Journal of Adolescent and Adult Literacy* reviewer Tshegofatso Mmolawa offered high marks for Klass's richly-woven novel. "*You Don't Know Me* is multilayered," observed Mmolawa, "but presents the complex life of an understandably angst-ridden adolescent in an enlightening and humorous way."

Klass returns to an athletic-themed book in *Home of the Braves,* a story about high-school senior Joe Brickman. A star soccer player, Joe expects to be the popular boy in school and finally find the courage to ask his long-time crush out on a date. However, when a Brazilian transfer student, nicknamed "Phenom," pushes the young narrator out of his top-dog status, he also upsets Joe's plans for the school year. Soon, more important problems arise when conflicts between students from different parts of town turn violent and Joe must stand up to the ringleader of the tension, a football player whose gang pummels Joe's best friend. *School Library Journal* reviewer Joanne K. Cecere wrote that Klass's "multilayered" story offers young-adult readers "characters [that] are, for the most part, believable teens searching for answers to complex societal and individual issues." The author's "strong doses of realism and grittiness" enhances the book's setting, claimed *Booklist* contributor Todd Morning, the critic going on to call *Home of the Braves* "a winning novel with many elements that will ring true for older readers."

A high school student questions the nature of evil in *Dark Angel,* "an absorbing and disturbing tale," according to Paula Rohrlick in *Kliatt.* After his older brother, Troy, is sentenced to life in prison for murder, seventeen-year-old Jeff moves with his family to a small New Jersey town, where no one knows their terrible se-

cret. When Troy is released from prison on a technical-ity, an unforgiving Jeff finds it difficult to welcome his brother back home as easily as his devoutly religious parents do. Jeff's suspicions about his brother's sinister intentions are further aroused when one of his class-mates, with whom he recently fought, mysteriously dis-appears. "Klass tackles large issues here with varying degrees of subtlety, thoroughness, and success," Holly Koelling noted in *Booklist,* and Melanie Toledo, writing in the *Journal of Adolescent and Adult Literacy,* stated that "Jeff's pondering of good versus evil is thought provoking. Are humans born innately good or are they born evil?"

Klass again tackles environmental issues in his "Care-taker" trilogy of science-fiction thrillers. *Firestorm,* the opening work, introduces Jack Danielson, a high-school student who discovers that his seemingly normal life is a mirage. After his football exploits appear on the evening news, Jack finds himself hunted by members of the Dark Army, and he must go on the run, aided by Gisco, a telepathic canine, and Eko, a female ninja war-rior. During his odyssey, the teen also learns the truth about his secretive upbringing: he is actually from the future and possesses incredible powers that can save the planet from ecological devastation. "The sobering events and tone are leavened with engaging humor," observed Melissa Moore in *School Library Journal,* and Rohrlick commented that "Jack's thrilling adventures and the creepy villainy of the bad guys will keep read-ers turning the pages."

Whirlwind, which takes place six months after the events in *Firestorm,* centers on Jack's mission to the Amazon jungle, where he must locate Kidah, a time-traveling wizard, and battle the Dark Lord, who has kidnapped Jack's girlfriend and threatens to destroy the rainforest. "The fast-paced, gripping plot is an excellent vehicle for presenting a significant environmental mes-sage," Ginny Gustin remarked in *School Library Jour-nal.* Rohrlick also praised *Whirlwind,* stating that read-ers "will enjoy the nonstop action, the fantasy and horror elements, and the heartfelt ecological message."

In *Timelock,* the conclusion to the "Caretaker" trilogy, Jack, now a college student in New York City, is trans-ported to a future Earth where the Arctic region faces ruin. Jack now joins forces with his mother, a warrior queen, to rescue his father from the clutches of the Dark Lord. Cindy Welch in *Booklist* described *Timelock* as a "pulse-pounding, rapid-fire race against time," and Gustin commented that the work "will keep readers ab-sorbed while presenting them with a valuable warning about the need for environmental awareness."

Klass believes that his books fill an important space on young-adult shelves. As he remarked to Don Gallo in a *Writing!* online interview, "The most enjoyable thing for me is creating something real and true that has the power to touch a reader. Books can help people, cheer them up, teach them valuable lessons about life, excite

them, and help them get through dark days. When I get a letter from a young reader telling me that one of my books has made a difference in his or her life, it's truly a wonderful feeling."

Biographical and Critical Sources

BOOKS

St. James Guide to Young Adult Writers, 2nd edition, St. James Press (Detroit, MI), 1999.

PERIODICALS

Booklist, December 1, 1984, Stephanie Zvirin, review of *The Atami Dragons,* p. 518; August, 1987, Stephanie Zvirin, review of *Breakaway Run,* pp. 1737-1738; January 1, 1988, Hazel Rochman, review of *A Differ-ent Season,* p. 775; December 1, 1997, Ilene Cooper, review of *Screen Test,* p. 615; September 1, 2002, Todd Morning, review of *Home of the Braves,* p. 127; September 15, 2005, Holly Koelling, review of *Dark Angel,* p. 58; September 15, 2006, Krista Hurley, re-view of *Firestorm,* p. 55; August 1, 2009, Cindy Welch, review of *Timelock,* p. 60.

Horn Book, July, 2001, Anita L. Burkam, review of *You Don't Know Me,* p. 455.

Journal of Adolescent and Adult Literacy, October, 2001, Tshegofatso Mmolawa, review of *You Don't Know Me,* p. 172; November, 2005, Melanie Toledo, review of *Dark Angel,* p. 249.

Kirkus Reviews, November 1, 1987, review of *A Different Season,* p. 1576; February 15, 1994, review of *Cali-fornia Blue;* November 15, 1995, review of *Danger Zone;* July 15, 1997, review of *Screen Test;* Septem-ber 15, 2005, review of *Dark Angel,* p. 1029.

Kliatt, September, 2005, Paula Rohrlick, review of *Dark Angel,* p. 9; September, 2006, Paula Rohrlick, review of *Firestorm,* p. 14; March, 2008, Paula Rohrlick, re-view of *Whirlwind,* p. 16.

Publishers Weekly, November 27, 1987, review of *A Dif-ferent Season,* p. 86; September 30, 1988, review of *Wrestling with Honor,* p. 71; February 14, 1994, re-view of *California Blue,* p. 90; March 12, 2001, re-view of *You Don't Know Me,* p. 92.

School Library Journal, March, 1996, Tom S. Hurlburt, review of *Danger Zone,* p. 218; March, 2001, Joel Shoemaker, review of *You Don't Know Me,* p. 252; September, 2002, Joanne K. Cecere, review of *Home of the Braves,* p. 226; September, 2006, Melissa Moore, review of *Firestorm,* p. 209; March, 2008, Ginny Gustin, review of *Whirlwind,* p. 202; August, 2009, Ginny Gustin, review of *Timelock,* p. 106.

Voice of Youth Advocates, April, 1996, Nancy Zachary, re-view of *Danger Zone,* p. 27.

Writing!, November-December, 2003, Don Gallo, "'Just Trusting My Instincts': A Conversation with David Klass," p. 21.

ONLINE

Embracing the Child Web site, http://www.embracing thechild.org/ (December, 2005), interview with Klass.
Macmillan Web site, http://us.macmillan.com/ (November 15, 2009), "David Klass."
Scholastic Web site, http://www2.scholastic.com/ (November 15, 2009), "David Klass."*

*   *   *

KOHARA, Kazuno

Personal

Born in Japan. *Education:* B.F.A; pursuing M.A. (printmaking).

Addresses

Home—Cambridge, England.

Career

Author, illustrator, and printmaker.

Awards, Honors

New York Times Best Illustrated Book designation, CCBC Choice designation, and American Library Association Notable Children's Book designation, all 2009, all for *Ghosts in the House!*

Writings

(Self-illustrated) *Ghosts in the House!,* Roaring Brook Press (New York, NY), 2008.
Here Comes Jack Frost, Roaring Brook Press (New York, NY), 2009.

Sidelights

Born in Japan, Kazuno Kohara now makes her home in London, where she is pursuing a career in printmaking. She completed her first published picture book, *Ghosts in the House!,* while she was still in school, and the book's minimally colored linoleum-block illustrations earned the young artist widespread recognition. Reviewing Kohara's picture-book debut for *School Library Journal,* Catherine Threadgill dubbed *Ghosts in the House!* "visually arresting" and "a surprisingly powerful masterpiece of design."

In *Ghosts in the House!* Kohara uses black, white, and pumpkin orange to give her mildly scary story a Halloween flair. In the story, a young witch lives in a haunted house where the resident ghosts are becoming a bit of a problem. Demonstrating pragmatism rather than fear, the witch traps the pesky spirits, scrubs them clean in the washing machine, and hangs them on a clothesline in her sunny backyard. Soon the ghosts find themselves utilized as slip covers, curtains, bedspreads, and tablecloths to freshen up the home's tatty furniture. In *Booklist* Ilene Cooper had praise for *Ghosts in the House!,* citing Kohara's "wonderfully distinctive art" and recommending the book as "a must have for Halloween." Kitty Flynn also praised the author/illustrator's "attention-holding" artwork, writing in *Horn Book* that these "child-friendly pictures help set the tone" in a story full of "old-fashioned charm." For a *Kirkus Reviews* writer, the book's major triumph is its "simplicity of color and line," and a *New York Times Book Review* writer dubbed *Ghosts in the House!* "sweet and beautiful."

Kohara turns from fall to winter in *Here Comes Jack Frost,* and this time her "gorgeous prints illuminate an unusual friendship," in the opinion of a *Kirkus Reviews* writer. Her simple story focuses on a young boy who sees no friends in sight as he looks out on a wintry, snow-covered world. Then the elf-like Jack Frost appears, frosting the windows of the boy's home and enlivening outside play all winter long. Comparing Kohara's black, white, and blue illustrations to "old Japanese woodblock prints," a *Publishers Weekly* writer described *Here Comes Jack Frost* as "a sparkling winter treat."

Biographical and Critical Sources

PERIODICALS

Booklist, September 1, 2008, Ilene Cooper, review of *Ghosts in the House!,* p. 96.
Bulletin of the Center for Children's Books, September, 2008, Deborah Stevenson, review of *Ghosts in the House!,* p. 28.
Horn Book, September-October, 2008, Kitty Flynn, review of *Ghosts in the House!,* p. 569.
Kirkus Reviews, July 15, 2008, review of *Ghosts in the House!;* October 15, 2009, review of *Here Comes Jack Frost.*
Publishers Weekly, October 12, 2009, review of *Here Comes Jack Frost,* p. 47.
New York Times Book Review, October 12, 2008, review of *Ghosts in the House!,* p. 25.
School Library Journal, October, 2008, Catherine Threadgill, review of *Ghosts in the House!,* p. 114.*

*   *   *

KONIGSBERG, Bill 1970-

Personal

Born 1970; partner of Chuck Cahoy. *Education:* Columbia University, B.A., 1994; Arizona State University, M.F.A., 2005.

Addresses

Home—Billings, MT. *E-mail*—bkonigsberg@gmail.com.

Career

Sports journalist and young-adult author. Worked for newspapers, magazines, online publications, and wire services; *ESPN.com,* assistant editor, c. 2001; Associated Press, writer and editor, 2005-08.

Awards, Honors

GLAAD Media Award, Gay and Lesbian Alliance Against Discrimination, 2002, for article "Sports World Still a Struggle for Gays"; Lambda Literary Award for Children/Young Adults, 2009, for *Out of the Pocket.*

Writings

Out of the Pocket, Dutton (New York, NY), 2008.
Openly Straight, Dutton (New York, NY), 2010.

Contributor to periodicals, including *Out, Denver Post, Miami Herald, New York Daily News, New York Times, San Francisco Chronicle,* and *North Jersey Herald and News,* and to Outsports.com and ESPN.com. Author of weekly syndicated column about fantasy baseball.

Sidelights

Beginning his career in journalism in the mid-1990s, Bill Konigsberg has covered the sporting world for a variety of news outlets, including the Associated Press, the *Denver Post,* the *Arizona Republic,* and ESPN.com. Konigsberg first became known to sports fans when he used a computer program to calculate the theoretical outcome of Major League Baseball's 1994 season after that season was shortened by a player's strike. In 2001 Konigsberg once again earned attention as the result of an article he wrote as assistant editor at ESPN.com. After publicly announcing his homosexuality, he discussed the absence of openly gay figures in professional athletics, a void Konigsberg had begun to notice as a teen. As he shared on his home page, "When I started to realize I was gay I thought it meant that I wasn't supposed to be an athlete, because I didn't know of a single role model who played sports and was gay." After learning of the suicide attempt of a former college football player who had been troubled by his inability to express himself as a homosexual in a rigidly defined heterosexual sports environment, Konigsberg channeled his concern into a young-adult novel.

Published in 2008, *Out of the Pocket* follows the experiences of Bobby Framingham, a senior quarterback who hopes to transition from his California high school football team to a career in college and perhaps even in the National Football League. While an outstanding athlete, the teen soon becomes known not for his success on the gridiron but for his sexual status after a friend reveals to others that Bobby is gay. For his admission, the teen receives overwhelming attention, ranging from gossipy fellow students to national media coverage. Bobby discovers how quickly his world has changed when some fellow teammates stop speaking to him, his coach initially refuses to acknowledge his orientation, and opposing players make him a target for particularly vicious hits. Compounding his troubles at school, Bobby must also witness his father's health slowly decline as the elder Framingham battles cancer.

For his first novel, Konigsberg earned widespread praise from reviewers who cited his ability to bring to life a teen-aged boy facing the challenge of being openly gay in the hyper-masculine world of football. Calling *Out of the Pocket* to be "a thoughtful, powerful novel," *Booklist* critic Todd Morning added that the author creates a narrator with an "authentic first-person voice." In *School Library Journal* Megan Honig described Bobby as "a likable narrator" and considered the book "a thought-provoking, funny, and ultimately uplifting story of self-actualization." A *Kirkus Reviews* contributor noted that

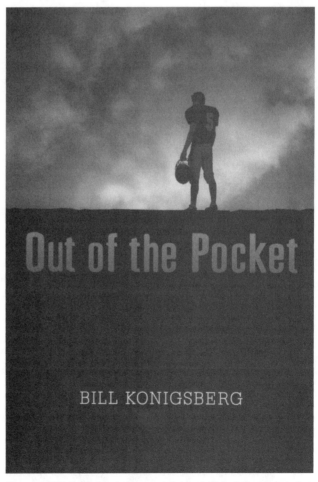

Cover of Bill Konigsberg's young-adult novel Out of the Pocket, *featuring artwork by Tony Sahara.* (Dutton Books, 2008. Jacket art © 2008 and design by Tony Sahara. Reproduced by permission of Dutton Books, a division of Penguin Putnam Books for Young Readers.)

Konigsberg's message of "being who you are" comes through strongly in an "unusual hybrid that juxtaposes hard-hitting, play-by-play football action with scenes of psychological soul-searching." In addition to finding *Out of the Pocket* "an amazing first novel," *Journal of Adolescent and Adult Literacy* writer James Blasingame maintained that Konigsberg does not compromise on either the sports-action elements of the book nor the complex emotions Bobby encounters during his journey as an openly gay athlete. "The author's knowledge of sports is impeccable," Blasingame wrote, "and his understanding of the social interaction of teenagers weaves the story together to make it funny, heartbreaking, and heartwarming." *Out of the Pocket* won a Lambda literary award in 2009.

Konigsberg's second novel, *Openly Straight*, deals with a well-adjusted, openly gay high school senior whose problem is not acceptance, but confining labels. One of the first YA novels to deal with a gay protagonist while not focusing on homophobia, the novel focuses on seventeen-year-old Rafe Goldberg, who trades in his comfortable high-school existence in Boulder, Colorado, for a label-free existence at an all-boys' boarding school in Natick, Massachusetts.

Biographical and Critical Sources

PERIODICALS

Booklist, September 1, 2008, Todd Morning, review of *Out of the Pocket,* p. 110.

Journal of Adolescent and Adult Literacy, October, 2008, James Blasingame, review of *Out of the Pocket,* p. 170.

Kirkus Reviews, August 15, 2008, review of *Out of the Pocket.*

School Library Journal, September, 2008, Megan Honig, review of *Out of the Pocket,* p. 188.

ONLINE

Bill Konigsberg Web Log, http://billkonigsberg.blogspot.com (November 10, 2009).

Bill Konigsberg Home Page, http://www.billkonigsberg.com (November 10, 2009).

L

LANDMAN, Tanya

Personal

Born in Gravesend, Kent, England; partner of Rod Burnett (a puppeteer); children: Isaac, Jack. *Education:* University degree (English literature).

Addresses

Home—Bideford, Devon, England. *E-mail*—tanyalandman@tantraweb.co.uk.

Career

Writer and actor. Storybox Theatre, Bristol, Devon, England, administrator, beginning 1992; freelance writer, 1992—. Presenter at schools.

Awards, Honors

British Booktrust Teenage Prize shortlist, and Carnegie Medal shortlist, both 2008, both for *Apache;* Phoenix Book Award shortlist, 2009, for *Mondays Are Murder;* Carnegie Medal longlist, 2009, for *The Goldsmith's Daughter.*

Writings

PICTURE BOOKS

One Hundred Percent Pig, illustrated by Judy Brown, A. & C. Black (London, England), 2005.
The Little Egg, illustrated by Shoo Rayner, Collins (London, England), 2006.
The World's Bellybutton, illustrated by Ross Collins, Walker (London, England), 2007.
The Kranken Snores (sequel to *The World's Bellybutton*), illustrated by Ross Collins, Walker (London, England), 2008.
Mary's Penny, illustrated by Richard Holland, Candlewick Press (Somerville, MA), 2010.

Geronimo, Barrington Stoke (Edinburgh, Scotland), 2010.

Contributor to anthologies, including *Winter Magic.*

"MERLIN" SERIES

Merlin's Apprentice, illustrated by Thomas Taylor, Walker (London, England), 2006.
Waking Merlin, illustrated by Thomas Taylor, Walker (London, England), 2006.

"FLOTSAM AND JETSAM" SERIES

Flotsam and Jetsam, illustrated by Ruth Rivers, Walker (London, England), 2006.
Flotsam and Jetsam and the Stormy Surprise, illustrated by Ruth Rivers, Walker (London, England), 2007.
Flotsam and Jetsam and the Grooof, illustrated by Ruth Rivers, Walker (London, England), 2008.

"POPPY FIELDS MYSTERIES" SERIES

Mondays Are Murder, Walker (London, England), 2009.
Dead Funny, Walker (London, England), 2009.
Dying to Be Famous, Walker (London, England), 2009.
The Head Is Dead, Walker (London, England), 2009.
The Scent of Blood, Walker (London, England), 2010.
Certain Death, Walker (London, England), 2010.

YOUNG-ADULT NOVELS

Useless, illustrated by Julia Page, Barrington Stoke (Edinburgh, Scotland), 2007.
Apache, Walker (London, England), 2007, published as *I Am Apache,* Candlewick Press (Cambridge, MA), 2008.
Two Words, illustrated by Julia Page, Barrington Stoke (Edinburgh, Scotland), 2008.
The Goldsmith's Daughter, Walker (London, England), 2008, Candlewick Press (Somerville, MA), 2009.

Sidelights

Tanya Landman is a British writer whose books include the middle-grade novels *Waking Merlin* and *The World's Bellybutton* as well as beginning readers featuring the characters Flotsam and Jetsam. Turning to older readers, Landman has also produced several critically praised teen novels, both contemporary fiction such as *Useless* and *Two Words* and the historical novels *I Am Apache* and *The Goldsmith's Daughter*. In addition to her work as a writer, Landman helps run Storybox Theatre, a touring puppet theatre for children that was founded by her husband, Rod Burnett.

First published in England as *Apache, I Am Apache* draws readers into a family tragedy set in what is now Arizona: after a four-year-old boy is horribly killed when Mexican soldiers overrun his village, his fourteen-year-old sister Siki resolves to avenge his death. Orphaned, she has only vengeance to live for, and she now trains to master the skills that will make her a warrior. In her training, Siki is aided by Golahka, an elder of the (fictional) Black Mountain Apache tribe who is also suffering the loss of family. As Siki becomes skilled

Cover of Tanya Landman's middle-grade historical novel **I Am Apache,** *which was inspired by the story of Pocahontas.* (Candlewick Press, 2008. Jacket photographs copyright © 2008 by Trinette Reed/Blend Images/Corbis (woman): George Burba/iStockphoto (background). Reproduced by permission.)

as a fighter, her once-proud people are slowly becoming dispirited at the increasing migration of white settlers into their tribal lands, and a truth about the girl's parentage ultimately affects both her path and that of her people. Noting that the scenes between Siki and Golahka are "riveting and unusual," *Kliatt* critic Claire Rosser praised *I Am Apache* as "a dramatic story" that is based on the true story of an Apache woman named Lozez, who fought with Geronimo. Although Riva Pollard maintained in *School Library Journal* that the story's "historical accuracy is questionable," she asserted that, as fiction, *I Am Apache* draws readers into "a complex adventure full of jealousy, romance, . . . bloody battles, [and] daring rescues." Landman's story "ring[s] with authenticity," Francisca Goldsmith stated in *Booklist,* the critic adding that the author's "artistic" prose benefits from "an eloquent voice and [a] dignified pace." In *Publishers Weekly* a contributor also cited Landman's "deliberately exotic" narrative voice, and added that Siki's "fiery spirit" will register with many teens.

Although Landman is British, her decision to focus on Native Americans in *I Am Apache* was sparked by the grave of Pocahontas, which is located in her home town of Gravesend, England. "There's this beautiful statue of her by the Thames silhouetted against this cold, grey expanse of the river," Landman explained to British Booktrust online interviewer Madelyn Travis. "I used to find it very moving, and when I learned more about the story of what had happened to her and how she'd died before she'd made it home I found it terribly sad. That image of her must have sunk somewhere into my subconscious." In 2008 *I Am Apache* was shortlisted for the prestigious Carnegie medal.

Biographical and Critical Sources

PERIODICALS

Booklist, October 1, 2008, Francisca Goldsmith, review of *I Am Apache,* p. 38.
Kirkus Reviews, July 1, 2008, review of *I Am Apache.*
Kliatt, July, 2008, Claire Rosser, review of *I Am Apache,* p. 17.
Publishers Weekly, July 14, 2008, review of *I Am Apache,* p. 67.
School Library Journal, August, 2008, Riva Pollard, review of *I Am Apache,* p. 126.

ONLINE

British Book Trust Web site, http://www.booktrust childrensbooks.org.uk/ (November 1, 2009), Madelyn Travis, interview with Landman.
Storybox Theater Web site, http://www.storyboxtheatre.co. uk/ (November 11, 2009).
Tanya Landman Home Page, http://www.tanyalandman. com (November 15, 2009).*

LAUGESEN, Malene
(Malene Reynolds Laugesen)

Personal

Born in Denmark. *Education:* Attended Danish School of Design; studied with Svend Wiig Hansen.

Addresses

Home—Copenhagen, Denmark. *Office*—Pinligt Selskab, Struenseegade 15, 4.tv., 2200 Copenhagen N, Denmark. *Agent*—Shannon Associates, 630 9th Ave., Ste. 707, New York, NY 10036. *E-mail*—malenelaugesen@hotmail.com.

Career

Illustrator and animator. Assistant animator for films, including *Der kleene Punker,* 1992, *Jungledyret,* 1993, *Asterix in America,* 1994, *All Dogs Go to Heaven 2,* 1996, *Jungledyret 2,* 1996, *Quest for Camelot,* 1998, and *Hjaelp, jeg er en fisk,* 2000; art director for *The Fairytaler* (animated film), 2004. Freelance illustrator, 1998—.

Illustrator

My First Treasury (based on stories by Hans Christian Andersen), Funtastic Publishing (Rowville, Victoria, Australia), 2003, stories published separately as *The Shepherdess and the Chimney Sweep, The Tin Soldier and Clod Hans, The Flying Trunk, The Swineherd; and, The Little Match Girl, The Ugly Duckling, The Tinderbox, The Nightingale,* and *The Princess and the Pea; and, The Emperor's New Clothes,* all 2005.

Kathleen Karr, *Mama Went to Jail for the Vote,* Hyperion Books for Children (New York, NY), 2005.

Linda Leopold Strauss, *The Princess Gown,* Houghton Mifflin (Boston, MA), 2008.

Also illustrator of books published in Denmark.

Biographical and Critical Sources

PERIODICALS

Booklist, May 1, 2005, Ilene Cooper, review of *Mama Went to Jail for the Vote,* p. 1561.

Kirkus Reviews, March 14, 2005, review of *Mama Went to Jail for the Vote,* p. 354.

New York Times Book Review, November 13, 2005, Gail Collins, review of *Getting It All,* p. 27.

School Library Journal, May, 2005, Wendy Lukehart, review of *Mama Went to Jail for the Vote,* p. 86; November, 2008, Miriam Lang Budin, review of *The Princess Gown,* p. 102.

ONLINE

Malene Laugesen Home Page, http://www.malenelaug esen.com (November 10, 2009).*

LAUGESEN, Malene Reynolds
See LAUGESEN, Malene

*   *   *

LENDROTH, Susan

Personal

Children: one daughter. *Education:* Utah State University, degree. *Hobbies and other interests:* Beach combing, book shops, British films, journals, journeys, libraries, new places, old letters.

Addresses

Home—Pasadena, CA.

Career

Writer and journalist. Planetary Society, Pasadena, CA, events and communications manager, beginning 1988.

Member

Society of Children's Book Writers and Illustrators.

Susan Lendroth (Courtesy of Susan Lendroth.)

Lendroth tells the story of an adventurous young girl in Ocean Wide, Ocean Deep, *a novel featuring artwork by Raul Allen.* (Tricycle Press, 2008. Illustrations copyright © 2008 by Raul Allen. All rights reserved. Used by permission of Tricycle Press, an imprint of the Crown Publishing Group, a division of Random House, Inc.)

Writings

Why Explore?, illustrated by Enrique S. Moreiro, Tricycle Press (Berkeley, CA), 2005.

Ocean Wide, Ocean Deep, illustrated by Raul Allen, Tricycle Press (Berkeley, CA), 2007.

Calico Dorsey: Mail Dog of the Mining Camps, Tricycle Press (Berkeley, CA), 2010.

Maneki Neko: The Tale of the Beckoning Cat, Shen Books, 2010.

Contributor of articles and essays to periodicals, including *Los Angeles Times, Newsweek, San Francisco Chronicle,* and *Sunset.*

Sidelights

In her picture books for children, as well as through her work as an independent journalist, Susan Lendroth is able to pursue her lifelong interest in history. Based in southern California, Lendroth balances her work as a writer with her job as communications manager for the Planetary Society, a nonprofit organization cofounded by the late astronomer and writer Carl Sagan to promote space exploration and further the search for extraterrestrial life.

Featuring richly hued oil paintings by Enrique Moreino, Lendroth's first picture book, *Why Explore?*, captures the human drive to question, learn, and explore. In a

rhyming text, the author ranges in time from prehistoric times up through the centuries to the present, using a question-and-answer format to introduce the many disciplines that have translated man's curiosity into scientific advances along the way. From ship's captain to biologist to astronaut, the many avenues of exploration are also covered by Lendroth in the book's appendix. Although Julie Roach found the rhythm of the text to be distracting, she nonetheless wrote in *Horn Book* that *Why Explore?* benefits from a "thought-provoking topic and serious art." In *Kirkus Reviews* a critic recommended *Why Explore?* as "a good choice" for young children when "a broad focus is the goal."

A young girl living in Cape Cod, Massachusetts, during the 1800s is the focus of *Ocean Wide, Ocean Deep.* Baby brother masters the art of walking and the seasons change as the girl counts the many days, weeks, and months that pass while she waits for her father to return from his lengthy voyage to China and back. In the book's "quiet" text, a "family's love shines through," wrote Kathleen Whalin in *School Library Journal,* and a *Kirkus Reviews* writer cited Lendroth's "gently rocking rhymed text." Raul Allen's "gorgeous" paintings "convey the characters' emotions," Whalin noted, the critic adding that the illustrations for *Ocean Wide, Ocean Deep* reflect the blue-grey tones of sea and sky. According to a *Publishers Weekly* critic, "The comfort of [Lendroth's] . . . melodic language and happy ending" will be appreciated by young readers worried about a family member not at home.

"My favorite quote (at the moment) is by Emily Dickinson: 'Dwell in possibility,'" Lendroth told *SATA.* "Who would want to dwell anywhere else?"

Biographical and Critical Sources

PERIODICALS

Kirkus Reviews, August 15, 2005, review of *Why Explore?,* p. 918; July 1, 2008, review of *Ocean Wide, Ocean Deep.*

Publishers Weekly, August 11, 2008, review of *Ocean Wide, Ocean Deep,* p. 45.

School Library Journal, January, 2006, Julie Roach, review of *Why Explore?,* p. 106; October, 2008, Kathleen Whalin, review of *Ocean Wide, Ocean Deep,* p. 115.

ONLINE

Planetary Society Web site, http://www.planetary.org/ (November 15, 2009), "Susan Lendroth."

*   *   *

LEONARD, Tom 1955-

Personal

Born 1955. *Education:* Philadelphia College of Art (now University of the Arts), degree.

Addresses

Home—Philadelphia, PA. *E-mail*—tleon@prodigy.net.

Career

Illustrator. Philadelphia University of the arts, instructor in illustration. Presenter at schools.

Awards, Honors

Charlotte Award finalist, New York State Reading Association, and Tennessee Volunteer State Book Award finalist, 1994, both for *All Eyes on the Pond*

Illustrator

Isaac Asimov, Martin Harry Greenberg, and Charles Waugh, editors, *Travels through Time*, Raintree Publishers (Milwaukee, WI), 1981.

M.V. Carey, *The Three Investigators in: The Case of the Savage Statue* (based on characters created by Robert Arthur), Random House (New York, NY), 1987.

Margaret Wise Brown, *Under the Sun and the Moon, and Other Poems*, Hyperion Books for Children (New York, NY), 1993.

Michael J. Rosen, *All Eyes on the Pond*, Hyperion Books for Children (New York, NY), 1994.

Melvin Berger, *Discovering Jupiter: The Amazing Collision in Space*, Scholastic (New York, NY), 1995.

Madeleine Dunphy, *Here Is the Coral Reef*, Hyperion Books for Children (New York, NY), 1998.

Madeleine Dunphy, *Here Is the African Savanna*, Hyperion Books for Children (New York, NY), 1999.

Catherine Daly, *Whiskers*, Golden Books (New York, NY), 2000.

Emily Neye, *Honeybees*, Golden Books (New York, NY), 2002.

Barbara Brenner, *One Small Place in a Tree*, HarperCollins (New York, NY), 2003.

Barbara Brenner, *One Small Place by the Sea*, HarperCollins (New York, NY), 2003.

Madeleine Dunphy, *Here Is Antarctica*, Web of Life Children's Books (Berkeley, CA), 2008.

Contributor to periodicals, including *Philadelphia Bulletin, PC Magazine, Psychology Today, Science Digest, U.S. Air Magazine*, and *Readers' Digest*.

Sidelights

Tom Leonard, a freelance illustrator, worked for magazines and in advertising for over two decades before beginning his work in children's books. A graduate of the Philadelphia College of Art (now the University of the Arts), Leonard continues to make his home in the Philadelphia area. In his picture-book projects, which include creating artwork for Margaret Wise Brown's *Under the Sun and the Moon, and Other Poems* and Barbara Brenner's *One Small Place in a Tree*, as well as a series of geography-based books by Madeleine Dunphy, Leonard focuses his acrylic paintings on the world of nature. In reviewing the artist's work for *All Eyes on the Pond* by Michael J. Rosen, *Booklist* contributor Stephanie Zvirin wrote that "Leonard's striking illustrations" contribute to a book crafted "with considerable cleverness and great visual flair."

Praising the illustrations in *One Small Place in a Tree*, a *Kirkus Reviews* writer maintained that Leonard's "bright" acrylic paintings "match the text well" and

Tom Leonard captures a frigid world in his artwork for **Here Is Antarctica**, *a picture book with a text by Madeleine Dunphy.* (Web of Life, 2008. Illustrations © 2008 by Tom Leonard. All rights reserved. Reproduced by permission of Web of Life Children's Books.)

contribute "a good sense of movement and life" to Brenner's ecological overview. Pairing that volume with its companion volume, *One Small Place by the Sea,* Jenna Miller recommended Brennan and Leonard's nature-based collaborations as "excellent choices to share with young naturalists." Dunphy's series, which includes *Here Is the African Savanna, Here Is the Coral Reef,* and *Here Is Antarctica,* also gains from Leonard's well-studied images. According to *Booklist* contributor Hazel Rochman, "each new picture" in *Here Is the African Savanna* "takes a surprising leap" and reveals "a hint of what's to come." As Carolyn Phelan predicted in the same periodical, Leonard's "large, brightly colored" paintings for *Here Is the Coral Reef* "will appeal to children."

Biographical and Critical Sources

PERIODICALS

Booklist, May 1, 1994, Stephanie Zvirin, review of *All Eyes on the Pond,* p. 1604; April, 1998, Carolyn Phelan, review of *Here Is the Coral Reef,* p. 1323; May 15, 1999, Hazel Rochman, review of *Here Is the African Savanna,* p. 1699; December 1, 2000, Gillian Engberg, review of *Whiskers,* p. 725; March 1, 2004, Lauren Peterson, review of *One Small Place by the Sea,* p. 1190.
Kirkus Reviews, February 15, 2004, review of *One Small Place in a Tree,* p. 174.
New York Times Book Review, May 15, 2004, Maud Lavin, review of *One Small Place in a Tree,* p. 22.
Publishers Weekly, May 30, 1994, review of *All Eyes on the Pond,* p. 56.
School Library Journal, May, 2002, Edith Ching, review of *Honeybees,* p. 142; April, 2004, Jenna Miller, review of *One Small Place by the Sea,* p. 128.

ONLINE

Tom Leonard Home Page, http://www.tomleonard.com (November 5, 2009).*

*   *   *

LINDGREN, Barbro 1937-

Personal

Born March 18, 1937, in Stockholm, Sweden; daughter of George (a civil engineer) and Maja (an artist) Enskog; children: Andreas, Mathias. *Education:* Attended Konstfackskolan art school, 1954-58, and Konstakademin academy of arts, 1959.

Addresses

Home—Glömminge, Öland, Sweden. *Office*—Eriksson & Lindgren Books, Box 22108, 10422 Stockholm, Sweden.

Career

Author, artist, and designer.

Awards, Honors

Swedish Foundation of Authors Labor scholarship, 1967; Literary Promotion scholarship, 1967, 1971; Swedish Foundation of Authors scholarship, 1968-69; Gramophone-70 Award, 1970, for children's song lyrics; Marsta municipal culture prize, 1970; Swedish Foundation of Authors Five-Year labor scholarship, 1971-75; *Expressen* Heffaklump award (Sweden), 1971, for *Jättehemligt;* Astrid Lindgren Award, 1973, for honorable authorship; Nils Holgersson-Plaketten, Swedish Library Association, 1977, for *Lilla Sparvel;* Premio Europeo Citta di Caorle in picture-book category, 1980, for *Sagan om den lilla farbrorn; School Library Journal* Best Books designation, 1981, for *The Wild Baby,* 1983, for *The Wild Baby Goes to Sea*; Hans Christian Andersen Award nomination, International Board on Books for Young People, 1988, 2004, 2006, 2008; Lista d'Onore Narrativa del Premio Europeo di Letteratura Giovanile, 1989, for *Vems lilla mössa flyger*; Stockholms Stads Hederspris, and Litteraturframjandets Stora prize, both 1991; numerous other book awards in Sweden.

Writings

FOR CHILDREN

Mattias sommar, illustrated by Stan Tusan, Rabén & Sjögren (Stockholm, Sweden), 1965, reprinted, 1980, translated by Annabelle MacMillan as *Hilding's Summer,* Macmillan (New York, NY), 1967.
Mera om Mattias (title means "More about Mattias"), Rabén & Sjögren (Stockholm, Sweden), 1966.
Hej, hej Mattias (title means "Hi, Hi, Mattias"), Rabén & Sjögren (Stockholm, Sweden), 1967.
I Vaestan grind (title means "Westwind Gate"), illustrated by Monica Schultz, Rabén & Sjögren (Stockholm, Sweden), 1968.
Loranga, Masarin och Dartanjang, (title means "Loranga, Masarin, and Dartanjang"), Rabén & Sjögren (Stockholm, Sweden), 1969.
Loranga Loranga, Rabén & Sjögren (Stockholm, Sweden), 1970.
Nu har Kalle fätt en liten syster (title means "Kalle Now Has a New Little Sister"), Rabén & Sjögren (Stockholm, Sweden), 1970.
Jättehemligt (title means "Giant Secret"), illustrated by Olof Landstrom, Rabén & Sjögren (Stockholm, Sweden), 1971.
Goda goda (poems; title means "Good, Good"), Rabén & Sjögren (Stockholm, Sweden), 1971, new edition, 1976.
Nu år vi gorillor laassas vi, Rabén & Sjögren (Stockholm, Sweden), 1971, translated by Suzanne Carlson as *Let's Be Gorillas!,* illustrated by Susan Acker, Clamshell Press, 1976.

Världshemligt (title means "World Secret"), Rabén & Sjögren (Stockholm, Sweden), 1972, 4th edition, 1979.

Alban: Popmuffa för små hunder (title means "Alban: A Muff Hat for Small Dogs"), Rabén & Sjögren (Stockholm, Sweden), 1972, translated by Joan Tate as *Alban*, A. & C. Black (London, England), 1974.

Gröngoelingen aer på vaeg: Dikter för barn och andra (title means "The Green Woodpecker Is on His Way: Poems for Children and Others"), illustrated by Katarina Olausson, Rabén & Sjögren (Stockholm, Sweden), 1974.

Babros pjaeser för barn och andra (title means "Barbro's Plays for Kids and Others"), Rabén & Sjögren (Stockholm, Sweden), 1975, new edition, 1978.

Lilla Sparvel (title means "Little Sparrow"), illustrated by Andreas Lindgren and Mathias Lindgren, Rabén & Sjögren (Stockholm, Sweden), 1976.

Vad tycker du? (title means "What Do You Think?"), Liber, 1976.

Stora Sparvel (title means "Big Sparrow"), Rabén & Sjögren (Stockholm, Sweden), 1977.

(With L. Westman) *Hemliga lådans hemligheter* (title means "The Secret Box's Secrets"), Liber, 1978.

(With L. Westman) *Jag har en tam myra* (title means "I Have a Tame Aunt"), Liber, 1978.

(With L. Westman) *Kom ner från traedet* (title means "Come Down from the Tree"), Liber, 1978.

(With L. Westman) *Var är mina byxor?* (title means "Where Are My Pants?"), Liber, 1978.

(With L. Westman) *Vaerldens laengsta korv* (title means "The World's Longest Hot Dog"), Liber, 1978.

(With L. Westman) *Laesa med varandra* (title means "Reading with Each Other"), Liber, 1978.

Garderobsbio (title means "The Movie Closet"), Rabén & Sjögren (Stockholm, Sweden), 1978.

Bara Sparvel (title means "Only the Sparrow"), Rabén & Sjögren (Stockholm, Sweden), 1979.

Sagan om den lilla farbrorn, illustrated by Eva Eriksson, Rabén & Sjögren (Stockholm, Sweden), 1979, translated by Steven T. Murray as *The Story of the Little Old Man*, R & S Books (New York, NY), 1992.

Nils Pantaloni Penell, Rabén & Sjögren (Stockholm, Sweden), 1980.

Fotograf Jag (title means "Me, the Photographer"), Liber, 1980.

Mamman och den vilda bebin, illustrated by Eva Eriksson, Rabén & Sjögren (Stockholm, Sweden), 1980, translated by Jack Prelutsky as *The Wild Baby*, Greenwillow (New York, NY), 1981.

Max nalle, illustrated by Eva Eriksson, Rabén & Sjögren (Stockholm, Sweden), 1981, translated as *Sam's Teddy Bear*, Morrow (New York, NY), 1982, published as *Sam's Teddy*, Methuen (London, England), 1984.

Max bil, illustrated by Eva Eriksson, Rabén & Sjögren (Stockholm, Sweden), 1981, translated as *Sam's Car*, Morrow (New York, NY), 1982.

Max kaka, illustrated by Eva Eriksson, Rabén & Sjögren (Stockholm, Sweden), 1981, translated as *Sam's Cookie*, Morrow (New York, NY), 1982, published as *Sam's Biscuit*, Methuen (London, England), 1984.

Den vilda bebiresan, illustrated by Eva Eriksson, Rabén & Sjögren (Stockholm, Sweden), 1982, translated by Jack Prelutsky as *The Wild Baby Goes to Sea*, Greenwillow (New York, NY), 1983, translated by Alison Winn as *The Wild Baby's Boat Trip*, Hodder & Stoughton (London, England), 1983.

Max boll, illustrated by Eva Eriksson, Rabén & Sjögren (Stockholm, Sweden), 1982, translated as *Sam's Ball*, Morrow (New York, NY), 1983.

Max lampa, illustrated by Eva Eriksson, Rabén & Sjögren (Stockholm, Sweden), 1982, translated as *Sam's Lamp*, Morrow (New York, NY), 1983, published as *Bad Sam!*, Methuen (London, England), 1983.

Max balja, illustrated by Eva Eriksson, Rabén & Sjögren (Stockholm, Sweden), 1982, translated as *Sam's Bath*, Morrow (New York, NY), 1983.

OBS! Viktigt! (title means "Please Note! Important"), illustrated by Dan Jonsson, Liber, 1983.

Sagan om Karlknut, illustrated by Cecilla Torudd, Rabén & Sjögren (Stockholm, Sweden), 1985, translated as *A Worm's Tale*, Farrar, Straus (New York, NY), 1988.

Vilda bebin får en hund, illustrated by Eva Eriksson, Rabén & Sjögren (Stockholm, Sweden), 1985, translated by Alison Winn as *The Wild Baby's Dog*, Hodder & Stoughton (London, England), 1986, translated by Jack Prelutsky as *The Wild Baby Gets a Puppy*, Greenwillow (New York, NY), 1988.

Max potta, illustrated by Eva Eriksson, Rabén & Sjögren (Stockholm, Sweden), 1986, translated as *Sam's Potty*, Morrow (New York, NY), 1986.

Max dockvagn, illustrated by Eva Eriksson, Rabén & Sjögren (Stockholm, Sweden), 1986, translated as *Sam's Wagon*, Morrow (New York, NY), 1986, published as *Sam's Cart*, Methuen (London, England), 1986, translated by Julia Marshall as *Max's Wagon*, Gecko Press (Wellington, New Zealand), 2008.

Vems lilla mössa flyger, illustrated by Eva Eriksson, Rabén & Sjögren (Stockholm, Sweden), 1987.

Pellerell, illustrated by Johannes Schneider, Rabén & Sjögren (Stockholm, Sweden), 1987.

Sunkan flyger, illustrated by Olof Landstrom, Rabén & Sjögren (Stockholm, Sweden), 1989, translated by Richard Fisher as *Shorty Takes Off*, R & S Books (New York, NY), 1990.

Korken flyger, illustrated by Eva Eriksson, Rabén & Sjögren (Stockholm, Sweden), 1990.

Stackars Alan, illustrated by Sven Nordqvist, Eriksson & Lindgren (Stockholm, Sweden), 1990.

Pojken och stjarnan, illustrated by Anna-Clara Tidholm, Eriksson & Lindgren (Stockholm, Sweden), 1991.

Titta Max grav!, illustrated by Eva Eriksson, Eriksson & Lindgren (Stockholm, Sweden), 1991.

Jam Jam Ib-Ib, illustrated by Madeleine Pyk, Eriksson & Lindgren (Stockholm, Sweden), 1992.

Stora syster lilla bror, illustrated by Eva Eriksson, Eriksson & Lindgren (Stockholm, Sweden), 1992.

Bra Borje, illustrated by Pija Lindenbaum, Rabén & Sjögren (Stockholm, Sweden), published as *Louie*, R & S Books (New York, NY), 1994.

Gomorron Gud, illustrated by Madeleine Pyk, Eriksson & Lindgren (Stockholm, Sweden), 1994.

Här är det lilla huset, illustrated by Eva Eriksson, Eriksson & Lindgren (Stockholm, Sweden), 1994.

Max napp, illustrated by Eva Eriksson, Rabén & Sjögren (Stockholm, Sweden), 1994.

Max blöja, illustrated by Eva Eriksson, Rabén & Sjögren (Stockholm, Sweden), 1994.

Svempa vill ha manga nappar, illustrated by Fibben Hald, Eriksson & Lindgren (Stockholm, Sweden), 1995.

Kungsholmens Ros, Alfabeta, 1995.

Lilla lokomotivet Rosa, illustrated by Eva Eriksson, Eriksson & Lindgren, 1996, translated as *Rosa: Perpetual Motion Machine,* Publishers Group West, 1996.

Rosa flytta till stan, illustrated by Eva Eriksson, Eriksson & Lindgren (Stockholm, Sweden), 1996, translated by Jennifer Hawkins as *Rosa Moves to Town,* Groundwood Books (New York, NY), 1997.

Rosa på bal, Alfabeta, 1997.

Mössan och korken flyger, illustrated by Eva Eriksson, Rabén & Sjögren (Stockholm, Sweden), 1997.

Nu är vi gorillor, illustrated by Anna Hoglund, Eriksson & Lindgren (Stockholm, Sweden), 1997.

Nu är vi jobbarkaniner, illustrated by Anna Hoglund, Eriksson & Lindgren (Stockholm, Sweden), 1997.

Andrejs langtan, illustrated by Eva Eriksson, Rabén & Sjögren (Stockholm, Sweden), 1997, translated as *Andrei's Search,* R & S Books (New York, NY), 2000.

Nämen Benny, illustrated by Olof Landstrom, Rabén & Sjögren (Stockholm, Sweden), 1998, translated as *Benny's Had Enough!,* R & S Books (New York, NY), 1999.

Per och Pompe, illustrated by Eva Eriksson, Eriksson & Lindgren (Stockholm, Sweden), 1998.

Rosa på dagis, illustrated by Eva Eriksson, Eriksson & Lindgren (Stockholm, Sweden), 1999, translated as *Rosa Goes to Daycare,* Groundwood Books (New York, NY), 2000.

Prinsessen Rosa, illustrated by Eva Eriksson, Rabén & Sjögren (Stockholm, Sweden), 1999.

Angeln Gunnar dimper ner, illustrated by Charlotte Ramel, Eriksson & Lindgren (Stockholm, Sweden), 2000.

Vi leker att du är en humla, illustrated by Eva Eriksson, Rabén & Sjögren (Stockholm, Sweden), 2000.

Jamen Benny, illustrated by Olof Landstrom, Rabén & Sjögren (Stockholm, Sweden), 2001, translated by Elisabeth Kallick Dyssegaard as *Benny and the Binky,* R & S (New York, NY), 2002.

Julia vill ha ett djur, illustrated by Eva Eriksson, Rabén & Sjögren (Stockholm, Sweden), 2002, translated by Elisabeth Kallick Dyssengaard as *Julia Wants a Pet,* R & S Books (New York, NY), 2003.

Rosas sånger, illustrated by Eva Eriksson, Rabén & Sjögren (Stockholm, Sweden), 2004.

Boken om Benny, illustrated by Olof Landstrom, Rabén & Sjögren (Stockholm, Sweden), 2004.

Dollans dagis, illustrated by Eva Eriksson, Rabén & Sjögren (Stockholm, Sweden), 2005.

Korken flyger, illustrated by Eva Eriksson, Rabén & Sjögren (Stockholm, Sweden), 2006.

Nöff nöff Benny, illustrated by Olof Landstrom, Rabén & Sjögren (Stockholm, Sweden), 2007, translated by Elizabeth Kallick Dyssegaard as *Oink, Oink, Benny,* R & S Books (New York, NY), 2008.

Max: babypussel, illustrated by Eva Eriksson, Rabén & Sjögren (Stockholm, Sweden), 2009.

OTHER

Genom ventilerna (title means "Through the Ventilators"), Bonnier (Stockholm, Sweden), 1967.

Felipe, Bonnier (Stockholm, Sweden), 1970.

Eldvin (title means "Winefire"), Bonnier, 1972.

Bladen brinner (title means "Burning Pages"), Rabén & Sjögren (Stockholm, Sweden), 1973, new edition, 1978.

Molnens bröder (title means "The Celestial Brothers"), Bonnier (Stockholm, Sweden), 1975.

Rapporter från marken (poems; title means "Reports from the Land"), Rabén & Sjögren (Stockholm, Sweden), 1976.

Det riktiga havet (title means "The Real Ocean"), Bonnier (Stockholm, Sweden), 1979.

En liten cyklist (title means "The Little Cyclist"), Rabén & Sjögren (Stockholm, Sweden), 1982.

Elegi över en död råtta (poems; title means "Elegy over a Dead Rat"), Rabén & Sjögren (Stockholm, Sweden), 1983.

Hunden med rocken: prosadikter (title means "The Dog with the Overcoat"), Rabén & Sjögren (Stockholm, Sweden), 1985.

Vitkind. I ett barns hjärta, hösten (novel), Rabén & Sjögren (Stockholm, Sweden), 1986.

Nu ä du mitt barn, illustrated by Katarina Olausson Saell, Rabén & Sjögren (Stockholm, Sweden), 1988.

Jag sajer bara Elitchoklad, Rabén & Sjögren (Stockholm, Sweden), 1993.

Om sorgen och den lilla glädjen, Karneval (Stockholm, Sweden), 2009.

Contributor to *Loranga, Masarin och Dartanjang* (CD-ROM), music by Mathias Lindgren and Andreas Lindgren, Rabénforlagen, 1997. Composer of lyrics for operas, including *Goda Goda,* music by Jojje Wadenius; *Nu sjunger naktergalen,* music by Georg Riedel; and *Lilla ungen min,* music by Riedel.

Adaptations

The Wild Baby was adapted by Random House into a filmstrip. Several of Lindgren's books have been adapted as musicals and produced on the Swedish stage, among them *Mamman och den vilda bebin* and *VLMF.*

Sidelights

One of the most beloved authors for young children in her native Sweden, Barbro Lindgren is a prolific writer whose works have also been translated for children around the world. In addition to receiving the Astrid Lindgren prize and the Nils Holgersson plaque, Lindgren has represented her country several times in competition for the prestigious Hans Christian Andersen Medal awarded every two years by the International Board on Books for Young People. The author of books for teens and adults as well as for children, she draws stories from life experiences that mesh challenges with understanding, sensitivity, love, and humor. Lindgren has a clear recollection of her childhood, and in particu-

lar "the sounds, the scents, the feeling of security when you squeezed somebody's hand, the fear of dark corners," as she revealed to Lena Rydin in *Vi foräldrar.*

"You have to experience sorrow and passion to be able to write well," Lindgren once claimed in an interview with Marit Andersson for *Femina.* Admitting to countless childhood fears, she was also a curious child with an excitement for learning. Unfortunately, the structured environment school provided did little to inspire her.

Lindgren's writings began in her childhood diaries. "I wanted to be famous at any price—to be a child genius on the front page of newspapers was my grandest dream," she told Rydin. "I submitted fairy tales to newspapers and publishers, but my work was rejected. One day when I was thirteen years old, however, *Daily News* printed one of my stories on the children's page. A great moment."

Although Lindgren published a few more stories, she eventually turned from writing to drawing and painting. She met her future husband while attending art school, and after graduation she worked briefly in advertising. "I tried writing again," she later recalled, "but was again unsuccessful and stopped altogether. My writing was superficial. It was not until I realized that I must write about things with which I am familiar, drawing from my own experiences, that my writing took shape."

Taking the counsel of other writers, such as Astrid Lindgren (no relation), Lindgren honed her skills, incorporating minimal characters, slowly culminating action, and brief texts into her stories. Her first published book for children, *Mattias sommar,* was published in 1964 and drew on the events of her own childhood. Lindgren mined her childhood in several other books published in early in her career, among them *Lilla Sparvel, Stora Sparvel, Bara Sparvel, Jättehmligt, Världshemligt,* and *Bladen brinner.*

Lindgren's whimsical sense of humor is highlighted in her picture book *Shorty Takes Off,* in which a little boy is so resentful of his short stature that he wishes he could grow wings and fly high above his world. When he wakes up one day to find his wish has come true, the boy promptly flies away for the day, locating a runaway cat and a lost soccer ball before returning home, exhausted, in time for dinner. Shorty's wings disappear as he grows up, and he eventually becomes a rock star. In *Publishers Weekly* a critic called *Shorty Takes Off* a story in which Lindberg treats readers to her "offbeat humor and some decidedly unconventional twists."

Lindgren's childhood experiences of loneliness and her belief that children adapt within a world that is not idyllic are at the heart of her picture book *The Story of the Little Old Man.* Here, she tells the story of an old man who has no friends in the town until one day a dog befriends him, and he is finally happy. When the dog makes friends with a little girl, the old man's heart breaks, until he realizes that all three of them can be friends together. *The Story of the Little Old Man* was described as "an offbeat story" that exhibits the author's "droll humor," according to Carolyn Phelan in *Booklist,* while *School Library Journal* contributor Rita Soltan called the book "a simple yet profound story about an old man's search for companionship."

The Story of the Little Old Man marked the first collaboration between Lindgren and Swedish illustrator Eva Eriksson, and this partnership had yielded dozens of successful children's books, including a board-book series about a little boy named Sam. Another series created by Lindgren and Eriksson starts in *Rosa: Perpetual Motion Machine,* which tells the story of a puppy's young life as she chews on everything in sight, digs holes, and runs away when she is taken for a walk. Whether or not readers will find Rosa's antics humorous depends on their relationship with dogs, contended Susan Dove Lempke in *Booklist,* although the critic stated that "Lindgren captures the puppy stage with zesty humor." As Joanne Schott remarked, "anyone who has ever brought home a new puppy will know the nonstop Rosa is barely exaggerated." Readers learn more about the black-and-white puppy in *Rosa Moves to Town, Rosa Goes to Daycare,* and several other books. *Rosa Moves to Town* focuses on the rambunctious pup's adventures while eating everything in sight, and "Lindgren renders the entire piece from a dog's view," according to a *Kirkus Reviews* critic. A trip to doggy daycare finds the spunky puppy making new friends of Tuffy the cocker spaniel and several others in *Rosa Goes to Daycare,* "a story with charm and appeal," according to *School Library Journal* contributor Jane Marino.

In her long career, Lindgren has established a working relationships with Olof Landstrom, another award-winning illustrator. The "Benny" books, which feature Landstrom's art, focus on a young pig named Benny, who finds himself in a variety of situations that human children can relate to. In *Benny and the Binky,* for example, the piglet becomes jealous when his new baby brother gets to use a colorful pacifier while Benny is told that he is too old to be allowed one. Benny is caught digging a hole in his neighbor's yard in *Benny's Had Enough* while a clandestine trip to the local mud hole gets the young pig into trouble in *Oink, Oink Benny* Noting that "preschooler pig Benny isn't big on impulse control," Christine M. Heppermann praised Lindgren for "comically" capturing toddler behavior in *Oink, Oink Benny,* while a *Kirkus Reviews* writer observed of *Benny and the Binky* that the author "speaks unpretentiously" to young children in her characteristic "simple, straightforward language." *Benny's Had Enough!* serves up a "fanciful yet on-target look into the thinking of preschoolers, according to *Booklist* critic Ilene Cooper, and Lauren Adams wrote in *Horn Book* of the same book that Lindstrom's "strangely successful mix of the absurd and the everyday" generates "first-rate entertainment with a heart."

Touching on a more serious topic—children's worries about being separated from a parent—*Andrei's Search* also features Eriksson's soft-toned pencil-and-watercolor art. In Lindgren's story, Andrei and his friend Vova are looking for Andrei's mother in the city of St. Petersburg. In fact, Andrei is an orphan and his search for his mother gains resonance as he recalls his early life, before he was taken to an orphanage. As they search, the boys meet several helpful adults and also are joined by a stray dog. Andrei's search ends in a joyous reunion, although readers are left to wonder whether the story chronicles reality or a lonely boy's imaginings. In *School Library Journal* Margaret A. Chang described Lindgren's tale as a "dreamlike narrative" that is "seemingly untethered to objective reality," while Ericsson's "expressive and tender" images ground the story in reality. "Despite some odd twists," wrote *Booklist* critic John Peters, *Andrei's Search* "will carry children along on its emotional currents."

Julia Wants a Pet also captures a common childhood dream: the desire for a pet of one's very own. In Julia's case, determination in the face of being told "No" results in several near-thefts of other people's pets until the seven-year-old girl decides that her toddler brother will do as a suitable pet substitute. Lindgren's story captures "Julia's playtime with complete understanding of the child's hilariously egocentric point of view," according to *Horn Book* contributor Susan Dove Lempke, while a *Publishers Weekly* critic dubbed the story's stubborn young heroine "a force of nature in a tutu, boots, and pigtails." In *School Library Journal* Linda L. Walkins described *Julia Wants a Pet* as a "delightful Swedish import," adding that Eriksson's charcoal and pastel illustrations "contribute . . . energy and movement" to Lindgren's inspirational tale.

"I have a longing to write and work with language," Lindgren told Ann Rudberg in discussing her vocation for *Vi mänskor.* "If children experience some relief in reading my books, it makes me happy. I pull together things that are burdensome and thorny and I peel away idyll, because that doesn't interest me. . . . I like to describe the best relationships between people, warm and friendly, but deep." Her work as a writer "captures everything for me," Lindgren admitted to *Författarportratt* interviewer Helena Ridelberg, while also noting her passion for music and art. "What I may wish to paint, I instead translate into words. I can express myself more subtly with words, although nothing moves me as deeply as music. Mozart, Mahler, Pettersson. But I can always *listen* to music. I don't have to play it myself."

"I have to feel completely free when I start writing a book," Lindgren told Rudberg. "I have a starting point after which I don't know where it will lead. Suddenly there will be twists and turns I had never thought of before. That is fun and adventure." While writing is an adventure, it is also, for Lindgren, a search for elemental truth. "Towards the origin, towards the 'seed' is what we all strive for," she told Birgitta Fransson in *Opsis Kalopsis.* "This is not easy, because we are not always honest with ourselves. Then we must start all over, like rolling yarn into a ball. It is too easy to be influenced by trends. At least I think that was the case when I was younger. Now it's easier for me to be truthful and as such I always have to be obstinate. I need tranquility and reflection. . . . I find tranquility in nature."

Biographical and Critical Sources

PERIODICALS

Booklist, December 1, 1992, Carolyn Phelan, review of *The Story of the Little Old Man,* p. 680; June 1, 1996, Susan Dove Lempke, review of *Rosa: Perpetual Motion Machine,* pp. 1734-1735; October 15, 1999, Ilene Cooper, review of *Benny's Had Enough!,* p. 456; March 15, 2000, John Peters, review of *Andrei's Search,* p. 1388; July, 2000, John Peters, review of *Rosa Goes to Daycare,* p. 2041; April 1, 2008, Hazel Rochman, review of *Oink, Oink Benny,* p. 58.

Femina, September, 1981, Marit Andersson, "Barbro Lindgren: Man måste ha upplevt sorg och passion för att skriva bra."

Författarportratt, March, 1986, Helena Ridelberg, "Barbro Lindgren: Jag är en typisk bakvägsmänniska."

Horn Book, November, 1999, Lauren Adams, review of *Benny's Had Enough!,* p. 729; September-October, 2003, Susan Dove Lempke, review of *Julia Wants a Pet,* p. 599; May-June, 2008, Christine M. Heppermann, review of *Oink, Oink Benny,* p. 296.

Kirkus Reviews, March 1, 1997, review of *Rosa Moves to Town,* p. 384; February 15, 2002, review of *Benny and the Binky,* p. 261.

Opsis Kalopsis, February, 1988, Birgitta Fransson, "Barbro Lindgren: Också en cyklist."

Publishers Weekly, October 12, 1990, review of *Shorty Takes Off,* p. 63; November 15, 1999, review of *Benny's Had Enough!,* 64; September 29, 2003, review of *Julia Wants a Pet,* p. 65.

Quill & Quire, March, 1996, Joanne Schott, review of *Rosa,* p. 76.

School Library Journal, February, 1993, Rita Soltan, review of *The Story of the Little Old Man,* pp. 75-76; July, 1996, Kathy Piehl, review of *Rosa,* p. 68; July, 2000, Margaret A. Chang, review of *Andrei's Search,* p. 82; August, 2000, Jane Marino, review of *Rosa Goes to Daycare,* p. 158; April, 2002, Martha Topol, review of *Benny and the Binky,* p. 116; November, 2003, Linda L. Walkins, review of *Julia Wants a Pet,* p. 106; May, 2008, Donna Cardon, review of *Oink, Oink Benny,* p. 102.

Vår bostad, 1986, Annika Rosell, "Barbro Lindgren: Bakom idyllen lurar."

Vi föräldrar, 1977, Lena Rydin, "Minns du din barndom?"

Vi mänskor, 1982, Ann Rudberg, "Barbro Lindgren, Nu gör jag bara det jag vill!"

ONLINE

Swedish Performing Rights Society Web site, http://www. stim.se/ (March 1, 2007), Mattian Franzén, "Barbro Lindgren: It's Great Knowing Best!"*

*   *   *

LYON, George Ella 1949-

Personal

Born April 25, 1949, in Harlan, KY; daughter of Robert Vernon, Jr. (a dry cleaner and later savings and loan vice president) and Gladys (a chamber of commerce executive director) Hoskins; married Stephen C. Lyon (a musician and composer), June 3, 1972; children: Benjamin Gerard, Joseph Fowler. *Education:* Centre College of Kentucky, B.A. (English), 1971; University of Arkansas, M.A. (English), 1972; Indiana University—Bloomington, Ph.D. (English and creative writing), 1978. *Politics:* Democrat. *Religion:* "Seeker." *Hobbies and other interests:* Singing, playing guitar, traveling, watching movies, hiking, yoga, peace work, reading, listening to music.

Addresses

Home and office—Lexington, KY. *Agent*—Kendra Marcus, Bookstop Literary Agency, 67 Meadow View Rd., Orinda, CA 94563. *E-mail*—allwrite@georgeellalyon. com.

Career

Writer and educator. University of Kentucky, Lexington, instructor in English and creative writing, beginning 1977, member of executive committee of Women Writers Conference, 1979-84, visiting assistant professor, 1991-92. Centre College of Kentucky, visiting assistant professor, 1979-80, writer-in-residence, 1985, 1995; Transylvania University, lecturer in humanities and creative writing, 1984-86; Sayre School, Lexington, writer-in-residence, 1986; Radford University, member of visiting faculty, 1986; Shepherdstown College, writer-in-residence, 2001. Executive director of Appalachian Poetry Project, 1980; Kentucky Arts Council, Frankfort, coordinator of writers' residency program, 1982-84; creator and host of writing program *Everyday Voices,* Kennedy Educational Television, 2001; member of Public Outcry (musical group); speaker at schools.

Member

Modern Language Association of America, Virginia Woolf Society, Society of Children's Book Writers and Illustrators, Appalachian Writers Association, War Resisters League, Central Kentucky Council for Peace and Justice, Phi Beta Kappa.

Awards, Honors

Lamont Hall Award, Andrew Mountain Press, 1983, for *Mountain;* One Hundred Titles for Reading and Sharing inclusion, New York Public Library, and Golden Kite

George Ella Lyon (Photograph by Ann W. Olson. Reproduced by permission.)

Award, Society of Children's Book Writers and Illustrators, both for *Borrowed Children;* Kentucky Bluegrass Award, for *Basket* and *One Lucky Girl;* Jesse Stuart Media Award for body of work, Kentucky School Media Association; Book of the Year award, Appalachian Studies Association, 1993, for *Catalpa;* Best Books for the Teen Age selection, New York Public Library, for *Where I'm From;* Parents' Choice Silver Honor, 2002, for *Mother to Tigers;* Children's Choices selection, Cooperative Children's Book Council, Best of the Best designation, Chicago Public Library, and Best Books for the Teen Age selection, New York Public Library, all 2004, all for *Sonny's House of Spies;* Marion Vannett Ridgway Award, 2004, for *Weaving the Rainbow.*

Writings

PICTURE BOOKS

Father Time and the Day Boxes, illustrated by Robert Andrew Parker, Bradbury (Scarsdale, NY), 1985.
A Regular Rolling Noah, illustrated by Stephen Gammell, Bradbury (Scarsdale, NY), 1986.
ABCedar: An Alphabet of Trees, Orchard Books (New York, NY), 1989.
Together, illustrated by Vera Rosenberry, Orchard Books (New York, NY), 1989.

Come a Tide, Orchard Books (New York, NY), 1990.

Basket, illustrated by Mary Szilagyi, Orchard Books (New York, NY), 1990.

Cecil's Story, illustrated by Peter Catalanotto, Orchard Books (New York, NY), 1991.

The Outside Inn, illustrated by Vera Rosenberry, Orchard Books (New York, NY), 1991.

Who Came down That Road?, illustrated by Peter Catalanotto, Orchard Books (New York, NY), 1992.

Dreamplace, illustrated by Peter Catalanotto, Orchard Books (New York, NY), 1993.

Mama Is a Miner, illustrated by Peter Catalanotto, Orchard Books (New York, NY), 1994.

Five Live Bongos, illustrated by Jacqueline Rogers, Scholastic (New York, NY), 1994.

A Day at Damp Camp, illustrated by Peter Catalanotto, Orchard Books (New York, NY), 1996.

Ada's Pal, illustrated by Marguerite Casparian, Orchard Books (New York, NY), 1996.

A Wordful Child, photographs by Ann W. Olson, Richard C. Owen (Katonah, NY), 1996.

A Sign, illustrated by Chris K. Soentpiet, Orchard Books (New York, NY), 1998.

Counting on the Woods: A Poem, photographs by Ann W. Olson, DK Publishing (New York, NY), 1998.

A Traveling Cat, illustrated by Paul Brett Johnson, Orchard Books (New York, NY), 1998.

BOOK, illustrated by Peter Catalanotto, DK Ink (New York, NY), 1999.

One Lucky Girl, illustrated by Irene Trivas, DK Publishing (New York, NY), 2000.

Mother to Tigers (biography), illustrated by Peter Catalanotto, Atheneum Books for Young Readers (New York, NY), 2002.

Weaving the Rainbow, illustrated by Stephanie Anderson, Atheneum Books for Young Readers (New York, NY), 2004.

When You Get Little and I Get Big, illustrated by Peter Catalanotto, Atheneum Books for Young Readers (New York, NY), 2006.

No Dessert Forever!, illustrated by Peter Catalanotto, Atheneum Books for Young Readers (New York, NY), 2006.

Trucks Roll!, illustrated by Craig Frazier, Atheneum Books for Young Readers (New York, NY), 2007.

My Friend, the Starfinder, illustrated by Stephen Gammell, Atheneum Books for Young Readers (New York, NY), 2008.

You and Me and Home Sweet Home, illustrated by Stephanie Anderson, Atheneum Books for Young Readers (New York, NY), 2009.

Sleepsong, illustrated by Peter Catalanotto, Atheneum Books for Young Readers (New York, NY), 2009.

YOUNG-ADULT NOVELS

Borrowed Children, Orchard Books (New York, NY), 1988.

Red Rover, Red Rover, Orchard Books (New York, NY), 1989, published as *The Stranger I Left Behind,* Troll (New York, NY), 1997.

Here and Then, Orchard Books (New York, NY), 1994.

Gina.Jamie.Father.Bear, Atheneum Books for Young Readers (New York, NY), 2002.

Sonny's House of Spies, Atheneum Books for Young Readers (New York, NY), 2004.

POETRY; FOR ADULTS

Mountain (chapbook), Andrew Mountain Press (Hartford, CT), 1983.

Growing Light, Mill Springs Press, 1987.

Catalpa, Wind Publications (Lexington, KY), 1993, 2nd edition, 2007.

OTHER

Braids (two-act play), produced in Lexington, KY, 1985.

Choices: Stories for Adult New Readers, University Press of Kentucky (Lexington, KY), 1989.

(Editor, with Jim Wayne Miller and Gurney Norman) *A Gathering at the Forks: Fifteen Years of the Hindman Settlement School Appalachian Writers Workshop,* Vision Books (Wise, VA), 1993.

(Editor, with Bob Henry Baber and Gurney Norman, and author of introduction) *Old Wounds, New Words: Poems from the Appalachian Poetry Project,* preface by Jim Wayne Miller, Jesse Stuart Foundation (Ashland, KY), 1994.

With a Hammer for My Heart (novel), DK Ink (New York, NY), 1997.

Where I'm From: Where Poems Come From, photographs by Robert Hoskins, Absey & Co. (Spring, TX), 1999.

(Editor, with Leatha Kendrick) *Crossing Troublesome: Twenty-five Years of the Appalachian Writers Workshop,* Wind Publications (Lexington, KY), 2002.

(Editor) *A Kentucky Christmas,* University Press of Kentucky (Lexington, KY), 2003.

Don't You Remember? (memoir), Motes Books (Lexington, KY), 2007.

Also author of play *Looking Back for Words.* Contributor to books, including *Virginia Woolf: Centennial Essays,* Whitston Press, 1984; *Strings: A Gathering of Family Poems,* edited by Paul Janeczko, Bradbury, 1984; *A Gift of Tongues: Critical Challenges in American Poetry,* University of Georgia Press, 1987; *Looking for Your Name,* edited by Janeczko, Orchard Books, 1993; and *The United States of Poetry,* Abrams, 1996. Contributor to periodicals, including *Indiana Writes, American Voice, Appalachian Journal, California Quarterly, Prairie Schooner,* and *Kentucky Review.*

Adaptations

Lyon's work was featured in the PBS television series *The United States of Poetry,* 1996. *With a Hammer for My Heart* was adapted as a play by Ed Smith and produced at Georgetown College, 1998.

Sidelights

A native of Kentucky, George Ella Lyon is a prolific author whose works include picture books and novels as well as poetry and plays. Praised for using what

School Library Journal contributor Ellen Fader called a "spare and elegant text" that "creates a poetic yet child-like mood," Lyon has penned highly regarded titles for the story-circle set, including *Who Came down That Road?*, *My Friend, the Starfinder*, and *Sleepsong*. "I don't write from ideas so much as from feelings," Lyon noted on her home page. "When something touches me deeply, I write to capture or explore or understand it."

In addition to picture books, Lyon has written novels for young adults, such as *Borrowed Children* and *Son-*

ny's House of Spies, that reflect her own upbringing in a close-knit Southern family. "I think much of Appalachian literature springs from the richness and originality of mountain speech," Lyon told *AppLit* online interviewer Tracy L. Roberts. "My ears and heart were tuned to these voices, and I listen for their energy, emotion, and wisdom and I write."

Born in eastern Kentucky in 1949, Lyon grew up outside a small coal-mining town in the Appalachian mountains. Her parents were both "mountain folk," she once

Lyon's picture book **Who Came down That Road?** *features expressive paintings by Peter Catalanotto.* (Orchard Books, 1992. Text © 1992 by George Ella Lyon. Illustrations © 1992 by Peter Catalanotto. Reproduced by permission of Orchard Books, an imprint of Scholastic Inc.)

told *SATA,* and all four of her grandparents lived nearby. "Family loomed large as the mountains for me, both secure and confining," she commented. Suffering from poor vision as a young child, Lyon compensated by developing a "good ear for a culture rich in stories," she once recalled to *SATA.* Her early fantasies took her away from her mountain home, and she dreamed of becoming everything from a neon sign maker to a tightrope walker. Her later aspirations to be a veterinarian, a folk singer, a midwife, or a simultaneous translator at the United Nations were much more down to earth, however. As an adult, Lyon stated, "I try to do all these things: keep a tricky balance, heal, find music in words, and translate or bring to birth the lives that are inside us."

Lyon spent her childhood in the house her grandfather built, which included a room over the garage dedicated solely to books. "Before I could read myself, I was listening to stories and building cities and mazes out of books," she explained to *SATA.* "The thing that interested me most as listener and maker was poetry, which made sense (using all the senses) to me whether I understood [the literal meaning] or not." Encouraged by her teachers, Lyon began writing poems in the third grade. After graduating from high school, she attended Centre College of Kentucky, graduating in 1971 with a bachelor's degree in English. A year later, she got married and started a family of her own. At the same time she began submitting her poems for publication. While she worked a succession of part-time jobs to help make ends meet, Lyon recalled that she was "always wary of giving myself to any career other than writing."

Over a decade later, her first book, the poetry collection *Mountain,* was published by a small press in Hartford, Connecticut. The following year her career began to move more quickly, when poetry anthologist Paul Janeczko passed a letter of hers on to his editor, Dick Jackson, who asked if she wrote for children. "'No,' I said, 'but hold on.'" Jackson's interest was the impetus for *Father Time and the Day Boxes* and *Borrowed Children.* both books for young readers.

Since the success of *Father Time and the Day Boxes,* Lyon has created many other picture books, each exploring an interesting and compelling theme. In *Who Came down That Road?,* for instance, she depicts a curious young boy questioning his mother about the past during a walk along an old country road. Lyon spins a poetic chronology of time that stretches from the boy's own parents and great-grandparents all the way back through farmers clearing the land, U.S. Civil War soldiers, Native Americans, grizzly bears, and even a time when mastodons walked North America. While *Booklist* contributor Stephanie Zvirin noted that the "majestic leap from concrete to abstract" might require some further explanation, Lyon's text is "brief and plainly spoken, and it is filled with an unmistakable sense of joyful respect." A *Kirkus Reviews* writer called *Who Came*

down That Road? a "beautifully crafted book that makes an unusually effective response to a prototypical question."

The past serves as the focus for several picture books by Lyon, among them *Cecil's Story,* set during the U.S. Civil War, and *Dreamplace,* which focuses on the culture of the Anasazi. In *Cecil's Story* a young boy waits with neighbors while his mother goes to fetch his father, who has been wounded in battle. Published during the Gulf War in 1991, the book was praised by *School Library Journal* reviewer Lee Bock for addressing "separation fears" about parents going to war "honestly and feelingly, with a believable and reassuring conclusion," reminding children that life still goes on, despite dramatic change. Also highly praised by critics, *Dreamplace* introduces an imaginative girl who, while touring the 800-year-old Anasazi ruins, envisions what it would be like to live among the ancient tribe as drought forces its members to abandon their homes. Featuring lush illustrations by Peter Catalanotto, *Dreamplace* was praised by *Booklist* contributor Ilene Cooper as "rich with atmosphere, delicate with sensitivity, and dreamlike in its evocation of dual realities."

Lyon has collaborated with Catalanotto on several other critically acclaimed picture books, including *No Dessert Forever!* and *Sleepsong.* In the former, a young girl accidentally breaks a lamp after she is startled by her pesky brother, but their mother—who did not witness the incident—directs her anger solely at her daughter. During a timeout, the youngster unleashes her own frustrations by delivering stern warnings to her favorite doll about keeping a tidy room and finishing meals. The girl's resentment turns to forgiveness, however, after her mother spies her son creating more mischief and realizes her mistake. Cooper praised the combination of Lyon's narrative and Catalanotto's illustrations, stating that the pictures bring "a warm glow to the goings-on, which many children—and adults—will find utterly familiar." *Sleepsong* looks at another universal childhood experience. As night falls, a preschooler prepares for bed by taking a bath, playing hide-and-seek with her parents, and listening to a story. Writing in *Booklist,* Julie Cummins noted that "the loving family bond is warmheartedly expressed, especially the dad's participation." Interestingly, Lyon wrote music to accompany her lyrical text, and the tune is available for listening through her Web site.

Like the catastrophe of war in *Cecil's Story,* weather can sometimes make a dramatic impression on children. In *One Lucky Girl,* Lyon tells her story through a young boy nicknamed Hawkeye, an energetic narrator who lives with his family in a trailer camp. When his home is literally ripped from its foundation during a ferocious tornado, Hawkeye's little sister, Becky, becomes lost. Lyon's ability to pace her story to sustain interest "is a masterful roller coaster of roiling emotion," claimed Elizabeth Bush in her review for the *Bulletin of the Center for Children's Books.* Noting that the book's

ending brings "a delightful flurry of shivers, followed by the comforting relief of a family unharmed and inseparable," Bush called *One Lucky Girl* "the action picture book at its best."

Also praised for its pacing and plot, *Come a Tide* focuses on water rather than wind in depicting the frenzy of activity caused by flooding in the Kentucky mountains after many days of heavy rains. In weaving her tale about a small, closely knit community that rallies together during a time of disaster, Lyon "wastes not a word" in "depict[ing] two complete worlds—those of an Appalachian community and of a small child's hopes and fears," in the opinion of *New York Times Book Review* contributor Kathleen Krull.

As with her picture books, Lyon's young-adult novels are frequently set in poor southern communities. *Borrowed Children,* for instance, takes place during the Great Depression of the early twentieth century. Twelve-year-old Amanda Perritt is spending a holiday in Tennessee with her grandparents, away from the hardships of her home in Goose Rock, Kentucky, where she has to take care of her family because her mother is ill. Anna has come to resent taking care of her sisters and baby brother, but when she meets her mother's sister, Laura, she gains a new appreciation for her siblings and understanding for her mother.

The relationship between children and their parents is also examined in *Sonny's House of Spies,* a work that examines racism and homophobia. Set during the early 1950s, the novel concerns Sonny Bradshaw, a thirteen year old who uncovers a family secret while investigating his father's abrupt departure from their Alabama home years earlier. "This lively novel crackles with wit . . . as it sensitively explores Sonny's world," Barbara Scotto noted in *Horn Book,* and a *Publishers Weekly* contributor described *Sonny's House of Spies* as an "exceptionally well-crafted coming-of-age story."

Unlike her other, more realistic young-adult novels, *Gina.Jamie.Father.Bear* is a fantasy about a high-school student named Gina, who lives in modern-day Cleveland, and a boy named Jamie, who inhabits a magical world of the past. The two are brought together through their mutual concern for their fathers. After losing her mother, Gina is puzzled by her dad's behavior when he begins visiting a psychic in secret; Jamie's father has suffered a similar loss, but his strange behavior involves turning into a bear. When Gina tracks down Esther the psychic after one of her father's disappearances, the medium becomes her spiritual guide on a journey that causes Gina and Jamie's worlds to intertwine. Gina's adventure in helping Jamie escape from the forbidden woods of his world has a reverberating effect on her own life in Ohio, as the two teens become connected through their mutual love for their parents and by a magical gold ring.

While some reviewers of *Gina.Jamie.Father.Bear* felt that the ambiguous, recondite mysticism in the story might "frustrate some readers," according to *School Library Journal* reviewer Beth Wright, it will "appeal to others." Christine M. Heppermann, writing in *Horn Book,* similarly felt that "the narrative gets analogy-heavy at times," but added that Lyon's story should "keep readers entranced while they try to sort through what it all means." Several critics particularly noted the appropriately mystical writing style in *Gina.Jamie.Father.Bear,* a style characterized by what Wright called Lyon's "skillful, poetic use of language." A similar observation was made by a *Publishers Weekly* critic, who called Lyon's fantasy "a lyrical, memorable tale."

In *Weaving the Rainbow,* winner of the Marion Vannett Ridgway Award, Lyon centers on a textile artist who raises and shears her own sheep, spinning the wool to create her yarn that is dyed by hand. According to Jennifer Mattson in *Booklist,* readers "will be fascinated by Lyon's lyrical yet concrete descriptions of the multi-step process," and Liza Graybill, writing in *School Library Journal,* noted that the author's "writing is lyrical, and the gentle pacing is calming." A tribute to the power of imagination, *My Friend, the Starfinder* centers on a man's recollections of his elderly neighbor, an accomplished storyteller. "Though poetic, Lyon's words are spare, never florid, for an elegantly powerful effect with silence built in," wrote *Horn Book* contributor Susan Dove Lempke.

Lyon's entire life has been influenced by writing. "I remember being fascinated by words early on," she remarked in an interview with Sarah Malouf on the Shepherd University Web site. "I began writing because I loved poems—the fact that words could cast an emotional spell—and wanted to make some. As I made the transition from being an outgoing child to a fairly shy adolescent, writing offered an important way of expressing myself. It brought me delight and insight, comfort and hope. It still does, I write because it's my way of understanding and loving the world, of participating in the ongoing work of creation."

To Lyon, one of the fascinating things about a literary career is that "it frees you from the confines of having only one life," as she once noted in an autobiographical essay for *SATA.* "I get to imagine reaching into a parallel universe as Gina does in *Gina.Jamie.Father.Bear,* or growing up in Alabama in the fifties like Sonny in *Sonny's House of Spies.* I can be a lion cub rescued by Helen Martini in *Mother to Tigers* or raise sheep and weave their wool into art in *Weaving the Rainbow.* Writing leads and teaches me—and not only when I'm at my desk. The truth is that books are written inside the writer, too, in thought and feeling, blood and bone, cell and soul. Taking part in Creation in turn creates me, and I feel blessed every day I get to do it."

Biographical and Critical Sources

BOOKS

Something about the Author, Volume 148, Gale (Detroit, MI), 2004.

PERIODICALS

Appleseeds, November, 1999, Sharron A. Crowson, review of *Dreamplace,* p. 32.

Booklist, January 1, 1991, Denise Perry Donovan, review of *Come a Tide,* p. 811; March 15, 1991, Bill Ott, review of *Come a Tide,* p. 1483; July, 1991, Denise Wilms, review of *The Outside Inn,* p. 2051; September 1, 1992, Stephanie Zvirin, review of *Who Came down That Road?,* p. 67; March 14, 1993, Ilene Cooper, review of *Dreamplace,* p. 1321; June 1, 1994, Hazel Rochman, review of *Mama Is a Miner,* p. 1810; October 1, 1994, Janice Del Negro, review of *Here and Then,* p. 319; October 15, 1994, Hazel Rochman, review of *Five Live Bongos,* p. 437; May 1, 1996, Susan Dove Lempke, review of *A Day at Damp Camp,* p. 1512; September 1, 1996, Carolyn Phelan, review of *A Wordful Child,* p. 121; September 15, 1996, review of *Ada's Pal,* p. 248; September 1, 1997, GraceAnne A. DeCandido, review of *With a Hammer for My Heart,* p. 61; February 15, 1998, Ilene Cooper, review of *A Sign,* p. 1014; March 1, 1998, Helen Rosenberg, review of *Counting on the Woods: A Poem,* p. 1130; November 15, 1998, Carolyn Phelan, review of *A Traveling Cat,* p. 591; May 15, 1999, Susan Dove Dempke, review of *BOOK,* p. 1693; September 1, 1999, review of *Where I'm From: Where Poems Come From,* p. 121; March 1, 2000, Hazel Rochman, review of *One Lucky Girl,* p. 1250; December 15, 2002, Gillian Engberg, review of *Gina.Jamie.Father.Bear,* p. 754; March 1, 2003, Kay Weisman, review of *Mother to Tigers,* p. 1208; February 15, 2004, Jennifer Mattson, review of *Weaving the Rainbow,* p. 1063; May 15, 2004, Hazel Rochman, review of *Sonny's House of Spies,* p. 1628; November 1, 2006, Ilene Cooper, review of *No Dessert Forever!,* p. 60; January 1, 2008, Ilene Cooper, review of *My Friend, the Starfinder,* p. 92; December 1, 2008, Julie Cummins, review of *Sleepsong,* p. 58.

Bulletin of the Center for Children's Books, September, 1994, Roger Sutton, review of *Mama Is a Miner,* p. 18; May, 1996, review of *A Day at Damp Camp,* p. 306; April, 1998, review of *A Sign,* p. 287; March, 2000, Elizabeth Bush, review of *One Lucky Girl.*

Children's Book Review Service, January, 1997, Lois K. Nichols, review of *Ada's Pal,* pp. 51-52.

Five Owls, May-June, 1995, Susan Stan, review of *Come a Tide,* p. 95.

Horn Book, September-October, 1989; January-February, 1991; May-June, 1991, Mary M. Burns, review of *Cecil's Story,* p. 317; January-June, 1993, review of *Dreamplace,* p. 267; March-April, 1993, Ellen Fader, review of *Dreamplace,* p. 199; July-December, 1994, review of *Five Live Bongos,* p. 45; March-April, 1995, Nancy Vasilakis, review of *Here and Then,* p. 193; September-October, 1996, Nancy Vasilakis, review of *A Wordful Child,* p. 613; November, 1998, Mary M. Burns, review of *A Traveling Cat,* p. 716; May, 2000, review of *One Lucky Girl,* p. 297; September-October, 2002, Christine M. Heppermann, review of *Gina.Jamie.Father.Bear,* p. 576; May-June, 2003, Betty Carter, review of *Mother to Tigers,* p. 369; September-October, 2004, Barbara Scotto, review of *Sonny's*

House of Spies, p. 590; July-August, 2007, Joanna Rudge Long, review of *Trucks Roll!,* p. 382; March-April, 2008, Susan Dove Lempke, review of *My Friend, the Starfinder,* p. 207.

Journal of Appalachian Studies Association, fall, 1996, Roberta T. Herrin, "Gloria Houston and the Burden of the 'Old Culture'," pp. 30-42.

Kirkus Reviews, July 1, 1992, review of *Who Came down That Road?,* p. 851; January 1, 1993, review of *Dreamplace,* p. 64; August 15, 1994, review of *Mama Is a Miner,* p. 1133; October 15, 1994, review of *Five Live Bongos,* p. 1411; January 15, 1996, review of *A Day at Damp Camp,* p. 138; July 1, 1996, review of *Ada's Pal,* p. 971; January 15, 1998, review of *Counting on the Woods,* p. 115; February 1, 1998, review of *A Sign,* p. 198; February 1, 2003, review of *Mother to Tigers;* February 1, 2004, review of *Weaving the Rainbow,* p. 136.

New York Times Book Review, October 14, 1990, Kathleen Krull, review of *Come a Tide,* p. 33.

Publishers Weekly, January 12, 1990, review of *Come a Tide,* p. 60; March 15, 1991, review of *Cecil's Story,* pp. 15, 193; August 2, 1991, review of *The Outside Inn,* p. 71; June 29, 1992, review of *Who Came down That Road?,* p. 62; January, 25, 1993, review of *Dreamplace,* p. 86; July 11, 1994, review of *Mama Is a Miner,* p. 78; September 26, 1994, review of *Here and Then,* p. 71; February 12, 1996, review of *A Day at Damp Camp,* p. 78; September 1, 1997, review of *With a Hammer for My Heart,* p. 97; February 2, 1998, review of *A Sign,* p. 90; February 23, 1998, review of *Counting on the Woods,* p. 75; July 27, 1998, review of *A Traveling Cat,* p. 76; March 15, 1999, review of *BOOK,* p. 57; October 11, 1999, review of *Borrowed Children,* p. 78; October 18, 1999, review of *Where I'm From,* p. 85; March 13, 2000, review of *One Lucky Girl,* p. 84; September 9, 2002, review of *Gina. Jamie.Father.Bear,* p. 69; December 23, 2002, review of *Mother to Tigers,* p. 71; February 16, 2004, review of *Weaving the Rainbow,* p. 170; November 6, 2006, review of *Sonny's House of Spies,* p. 61; January 28, 2008, review of *My Friend, the Starfinder,* p. 67.

Reading Teacher, February, 1991, Barbara Kiefer, review of *Come a Tide,* p. 408.

School Library Journal, December, 1990, review of *Come a Tide,* p. 23; April, 1991, Lee Bock, review of *Cecil's Story,* p. 98; September, 1991, Jody McCoy, review of *The Outside Inn;* p. 236; October, 1992, Ellen Fader, review of *Who Came down That Road?,* p. 92; September, 1994, reviews of *Here and Then,* p. 71, and *Mama Is a Miner,* p. 189; October, 1994, Amy Kellman, review of *Here and Then,* p. 124; April, 1996, Ruth Semrau, review of *A Day at Damp Camp,* p. 114; September, 1996, Carolyn Nash, review of *Ada's Pal,* p. 184; January, 1997, Anne Parker, review of *A Wordful Child,* p. 102; October, 1997, Molly Connally, review of *With a Hammer for My Heart,* p. 160; March, 1998, Ruth Semrau, review of *A Sign,* p. 198; April, 1998, Angela J. Reynolds, review of *Counting on the Woods,* p. 120; September, 1998, Julie Cummins, review of *A Traveling Cat,* p. 176; June, 1999, review of *BOOK,* p. 119; March, 2000, Joy Fleishhacker, review of *One Lucky Girl,* p. 210; August, 2002, Beth Wright, review of *Gina.Jamie.Father.Bear,*

p. 194; March, 2003, Margaret Bush, review of *Mother to Tigers,* p. 220; February, 2004, Liza Graybill, review of *Weaving the Rainbow,* p. 118; September, 2007, Lynn K. Vanca, review of *Trucks Roll!,* p. 170; January, 2009, Martha Simpson, review of *Sleepsong,* p. 80.

Southern Living, October, 1997, Valerie Fraser, review of *With a Hammer for My Heart,* p. 76.

Voice of Youth Advocates, June, 1998, Cindy Lombardo, review of *With a Hammer for My Heart,* pp. 122-123.

ONLINE

AppLit Web site, http://www.ferrum.edu/applit/ (spring, 2001), Tracy L. Roberts, interview with Lyon.

George Ella Lyon Web site, http://www.georgeellalyon. com (November 15, 2009).

Shepherd University Web site, http://www.shepherd.edu/ (July 18, 2001), Sarah Alouf, "George Ella Lyon— Writer-in-Residence 2001."*

M

MARTIN, C.K. Kelly

Personal

Born in Canada; married. *Education:* York University (Toronto, Ontario, Canada), B.A. (film studies; with honors).

Addresses

Home—Toronto, Ontario, Canada. *E-mail*—ckkellymartin@hotmail.com.

Career

Writer.

Writings

FOR YOUNG ADULTS

I Know It's Over, Random House (New York, NY), 2008.
One Lonely Degree, Random House (New York, NY), 2009.
The Lighter Side of Life and Death, Random House (New York, NY), 2010.

Sidelights

After earning a university degree in Toronto, Canadian author C.K. Kelly Martin moved to Ireland, "spen[ding] the majority of the nineties there in forgettable jobs meeting unforgettable people," as she explained on her home page. During her stay in Ireland, Martin also began working seriously on her writing after discovering her interest in literature for teen readers. As she told *Cynsations* online interviewer Cynthia Leitich Smith, "It wasn't until 1999, after several years of living in Ireland, that I discovered I specifically wanted to write YA. I hadn't read any young adult literature in years." Once she became aware of her desire to write for the young-adult audience, "I started snatching up all the teen books I could get my hands on. The process of becoming a writer was largely an unconscious one—just doing what felt right at the time, learning things by osmosis from reading."

Martin's work resulted in the publication of *I Know It's Over,* a novel about a teenaged couple facing an unplanned pregnancy. Told from the perspective of sixteen-year-old Nick, *I Know It's Over* traces the development of Nick's relationship with Sasha, from their initial infatuation with each other, to their first awkward attempts at intimacy, to their eventual break up. Martin earned much attention from reviewers for her ability to develop a convincing character in a book dealing with teen pregnancy. According to *School Library Journal* reviewer Lynn Rashid, *I Know It's Over* rises above other books about the same topic due to "the authentic voice and emotion of the protagonist." A *Kirkus Reviews* critic offered similar comments, writing that "rich characters and honest interactions set Martin's debut novel apart." Martin also earned favorable remarks from a *Publishers Weekly* contributor who suggested that she "displays uncanny insight" in *I Know It's Over,* crafting "an emotionally complex and disarmingly frank coming-of-age tale."

Biographical and Critical Sources

PERIODICALS

Booklist, November 15, 2008, Ilene Cooper, review of *I Know It's Over,* p. 54.
Kirkus Reviews, August 1, 2008, review of *I Know It's Over;* April 1, 2009, review of *One Lonely Degree.*
Kliatt, September, 2008, Claire Rosser, review of *I Know It's Over,* p. 16.
Publishers Weekly, August 18, 2008, review of *I Know It's Over,* p. 63.
School Library Journal, November, 2008, Lynn Rashid, review of *I Know It's Over,* p. 130.

Cover of C.K. Kelly Martin's teen novel I Know It's Over, *which focuses on a unmarried couple dealing with an unwanted pregnancy.* (Random House, 2008. Cover photograph copyright © PhotoAlto Photograph/Veer. All rights reserved. Used by permission of Random House Children's Books, a division of Random House, Inc.)

ONLINE

C.K. Kelly Martin Home Page, http://www.ckkellymartin. com (November 8, 2009).

C.K. Kelly Martin Web Log, http://ckkellymartin.blogspot. com (November 7, 2009).

Cynsations, http://cynthialeitichsmith.blogspot.com/ (December 4, 2008), Cynthia Leitich Smith, interview with Martin.

*   *   *

MEADE, Holly 1956-

Personal

Born 1956. *Education:* Rhode Island School of Design, B.F.A.

Addresses

Home—Sedgwick, ME. *Office*—Reach Road Gallery, 62 Reach Rd., Sedgwick, ME 04676. *E-mail*—holly meade@prexar.com.

Career

Artist; children's book writer and illustrator, 1992—. *Exhibitions:* Woodblock prints have been exhibited at art galleries, including Elan Fine Arts, Rockport, ME; Center for Maine Contemporary Art, Rockport; Firehouse Center for the Arts, Newburyport, MA; Capitol Show, Augusta, ME; George-Marshall Store Gallery, York, ME; Court House Gallery, Ellsworth, ME; and Handworks Gallery, Blue Hill, ME. Book illustrations have been exhibited at galleries and museums, including DeCordova Museum and Sculpture Park, Lincoln, MA; Art Institute of Chicago, Chicago, IL; Wenham Museum, Wenham, MA, and at Original Art Show, Society of Illustrators, New York, NY.

Awards, Honors

Charlotte Zolotow Award Honor Book designation, Cooperative Children's Book Center, 1999, for *John Willy and Freddy McGee;* Caldecott Medal Honor Book selection, American Library Association, 1997, for *Hush!: A Thai Lullaby.*

Writings

SELF-ILLUSTRATED CHILDREN'S BOOKS

John Willy and Freddy McGee, Marshall Cavendish (New York, NY), 1998.

A Place to Sleep, Marshall Cavendish (New York, NY), 2001.

Inside, Inside, Inside, Marshall Cavendish (New York, NY), 2005.

ILLUSTRATOR

Nancy Van Laan, *This Is the Hat: A Story in Rhyme,* Joy Street Books (Boston, MA), 1992.

Phillis Gershator, *Rata-Pata-Scata-Fata: A Caribbean Story,* Joy Street Books (Boston, MA), 1993.

Libba Moore Gray, *Small Green Snake,* Orchard Books (New York, NY), 1994.

Nancy Van Laan, *Sleep, Sleep, Sleep: A Lullaby for Little Ones around the World,* Little, Brown (Boston, MA), 1995.

Betty G. Birney, *Pie's in the Oven,* Houghton (Boston, MA), 1996.

Minfong Ho, *Hush!: A Thai Lullaby,* Orchard Books (New York, NY), 1996.

Diane Karter Appelbaum, *Cocoa Ice,* Orchard Books (New York, NY), 1997.

Laurie M. Carlson, *Boss of the Plains: The Hat That Won the West,* DK Ink/DK Publishing (New York, NY), 1998.

Judith Heide Gilliland, *Steamboat: The Story of Captain Blanche Leathers,* DK Publishing (New York, NY), 2000.

Melinda Long, *When Papa Snores,* Simon & Schuster Books for Young Readers (New York, NY), 2000.

(And reteller) Brothers Grimm, *The Rabbit's Bride,* Marshall Cavendish (New York, NY), 2001.

Ann-Jeanette Campbell, *Queenie Farmer Had Fifteen Daughters,* Silver Whistle/Harcourt (San Diego, CA), 2002.

Reeve Lindbergh, *On Morning Wings,* Candlewick Press (Cambridge, MA), 2002.

Cari Best, *Goose's Story,* Melanie Kroupa Books/Farrar, Straus (New York, NY), 2002.

Florence Parry Heide and Sylvia Van Clief, *That's What Friends Are For,* Candlewick Press (Cambridge, MA), 2003.

Phyllis Root, *Quack!,* Candlewick Press (Cambridge, MA), 2004.

C.M. Millen, *Blue Bowl Down: An Appalachian Rhyme,* Candlewick Press (Cambridge, MA), 2004.

Mingfong Ho, *Peek!: A Thai Hide-and-Seek Story,* Candlewick Press (Cambridge, MA), 2004.

Phillis Gershator, *Sky Sweeper,* Farrar, Straus (New York, NY), 2007.

Dori Chaconas, *Virginnie's Hat,* Candlewick Press (Cambridge, MA), 2007.

David Elliott, *On the Farm,* Candlewick Press (Cambridge, MA), 2008.

OTHER

Hop!, illustrated by Petra Mathers, Candlewick Press (Cambridge, MA), 2004.

Adaptations

John Willy and Freddy McGee was adapted as an audio book.

Sidelights

Holly Meade is a renowned children's book illustrator who has gone on to pen her own children's stories. Meade often works in mixed-media collage; she begins each piece with a sketch, adds torn or cut colored paper, then finishes the collage with ink, paint, or pencil. "I find it difficult, but more like serious play than serious work," she remarked on the Houghton Mifflin Web site.

Meade's first illustrated work, *This Is the Hat: A Story in Rhyme,* was written by Nancy Van Laan and tells the story of a man who loses his hat while walking during a storm. The hat is then occupied, in turn, by various creatures, including a crow. A *Publishers Weekly* contributor commented that, "in Meade's illustrative debut, torn paper collages in happy blues, greens and magentas perfectly partner the text." Jim Jaske, writing in *Booklist,* noted that Meade's illustrations "add a friendly air to the story."

In *Rata-Pata-Scata-Fata: A Caribbean Story,* Meade's illustrations help tell Phillis Gershator's story of a daydreaming youth named Junjun who believes himself capable of making magic wishes come true. *Booklist* contributor Julie Corsaro observed that Meade's collages

"rhythmically echo" the story, while in *Horn Book,* Ellen Fader felt that Meade's illustrations "evoke the essence of a Caribbean landscape [and] invite readers into young Junjun's tropical world."

Another of Meade's illustration projects, *Small Green Snake* by Libba Moore Gray, tells the story of a defiant young garter snake who ignores his mother's warning and roams away from home, only to be captured and held in a glass jar. When the snake escapes after the jar is broken, his adventure inspires his siblings to also venture forth in a story a *Publishers Weekly* contributor commended for its "bold, graphic artwork." In her second book with Nancy Van Laan, *Sleep, Sleep, Sleep: A Lullaby for Little Ones around the World,* Meade illustrates the story of both human and animal mothers soothing their offspring to sleep. Leone McDermott wrote in *Booklist* that Meade's collages possess "a tender quality."

Meade's collaboration with writer Minfong Ho on *Hush!: A Thai Lullaby* was described by *Booklist* contributor Janice del Negro as "visually arresting" because "the comforting earth tones suit the quiet nature of the story." Told in verse, the work centers on a mother's efforts to quiet the animals of the forest, including lizards, elephants, and ducks, as she tries to put her baby to sleep. According to a *Publishers Weekly* reviewer, "Meade uses cut paper and ink to produce intriguing textures, layers and shapes," and *School Library Journal* critic John Philbrook noted that Meade's collages generate a "somnolent atmosphere." In 1997, *Hush!* was selected as a Caldecott Medal honor book.

Meade has also illustrated *Peek!: A Thai Hide-and-Seek Story,* another work written by Ho. Set in rural Thailand, *Peek!* centers on a father and daughter's game of peek-a-boo. As the youngster makes her way through their home and garden, her father playfully questions a dragonfly, rooster, and puppy as to her whereabouts. "Meade's watercolor and cut-paper collages are drenched in tropical colors: chartreuse, apricot, bright blue," observed a critic in *Kirkus Reviews,* and Diane Foote, critiquing the work in *Booklist,* similarly noted that her "textured collage illustrations evoke a tropical setting and showcase animals indigenous to Thailand." According to *School Library Journal* reviewer Wendy Lukehart, Meade's "exuberant illustrations convey the energy of the high jinks and the girl's satisfaction at being found."

Meade's artwork brings to life Betty G. Birney's *Pie's in the Oven,* a story about a young boy who is waiting to eat his grandmother's pie. *Booklist* contributor Ilene Cooper noted that Meade's collages for this book "look like thick oil paintings" and are "deftly rendered, full of life, and demanding a second look." *Cocoa Ice,* by Diana Karter Appelbaum, tells the story of an unusual tie between a Caribbean girl and an American girl living in New England: their businessmen fathers trade cocoa for ice. Writing in *School Library Journal,* Luann Toth

commented that "Meade's vibrant cut-paper and gouache illustrations capture the action, industry, and natural beauty of each locale."

In *Boss of the Plains: The Hat That Won the West,* Meade's illustrations help tell author Laurie M. Carlson's story of John Baterson Stetson, who created the famous brand of western Stetson hats. *New York Times Book Review* contributor Anne Scott MacLeod noted that Meade's "exuberant illustrations, in slightly muted colors, show 19th-century people going about their daily lives, earning their daily bread."

Meade's collaboration with Judith Heide Gilliland resulted in *Steamboat: The Story of Captain Blanche Leathers,* which tells the true story Blanche Douglas, the first woman steamboat captain on the Mississippi River. A *Publishers Weekly* contributor praised Meade's work, citing in particular "two climactic collages in midnight blue and black tones [that] detail Blanche's triumphant test run on a moonless night." As the illustrator for Melinda Long's *When Papa Snores,* Meade was praised by *Booklist* contributor Kathy Broderick for creating illustrations that "capture the energy of the story and the personalities of the characters." A *Horn Book* contributor noted that "Meade's lively line keeps the simple story moving and gives expressive charm not only to the little girl but also to the overactive household objects."

Discussing her work for Reeve Lindberg's *On Morning Wings* which was adapted from Psalm 139, Carolyn Phelan noted in *Booklist* that "the simplicity, clarity, and grace of both the words and the illustrations make this a lovely and potentially moving picture book." Meade has also illustrated the 2003 republication of the 1968 book about friendship titled *That's What Friends Are For,* by Florence Parry Heide and Sylvia Van Clief. *School Library Journal* contributor Lauralyn Persson called the illustrations for this reissue "fresh and lively."

In C.M. Millen's *Blue Bowl Down: An Appalachian Rhyme,* a toddler helps his mother with an evening ritual: making bread dough. In her work for Miller's tale, Meade "composes her watercolor and collage pictures from simple shapes and soft, earthy hues," remarked a critic in *Publishers Weekly.* In a review in Chicago's *Tribune Books,* Mary Harris Russell dubbed Meade's illustrations "luminous and comforting." Inspired by the artistry of Japanese gardens, Gershator's *Sky Sweeper* centers on Takeboki, the flower keeper for the temple monks. "Meade's richly textured, luminous collage illustrations are as simple and graceful as Gershator's narrative," a *Publishers Weekly* contributor observed in reviewing *Sky Sweeper.* According to Joanna Rudge Long in *Horn Book,* Meade's pictures "intimately depict Takeboki's dedication to a simple-seeming task that is, in truth, an art." In *Virginnie's Hat,* a rhyming tale by Dori Chaconas, a spunky bayou gal searches for her hat in the swamp. "Meade's watercolor-and-collage paintings are as light and breezy as Virginnie's mood," Martha Simpson commented in *School Library Journal.*

After several years of focusing on her career as an illustrator, Meade wrote her first children' book, *John Willy and Freddy McGee.* The story focuses on two curious guinea pigs who forsake the safety of their cage and wander off to freedom. They soon hop onto a billiards table and scurry through the tunnels circulating beneath the tabletop. Their fun is disrupted, however, when an inquisitive cat begins flicking billiard balls into the pockets. As the balls roll through the tunnels, the guinea pigs must dodge them and also get past the cat to make it back safely to their cage. Writing in *Booklist,* John Peters noted that Meade's text "has a roll and bounce to it that effectively capture the pace and excitement" of the guinea pigs' escapade. *School Library Journal* contributor Joy Fleishhacker deemed *John Willy and Freddy McGee* "a fine tale" and noted that Meade's "colorful, cut-paper collages work in harmony with the text, adding details and extending the action of the story."

In *A Place to Sleep,* which Meade both wrote and illustrated, the author uses a riddle format to get readers to think about where various animals sleep. The text also shares information about how animals sleep, such as the fact that elephants sleep standing up and fish sleep with their eyes open. A *Kirkus Reviews* contributor commented that the "alliterative text is rich in wordplay," while a *Publishers Weekly* contributor called the book's design "innovative" and commended Meade for writing "a soothing bedtime read for young animal lovers." Writing in *School Library Journal,* Cathie Reed commented that, "with its oversized format, stunning art, and lyrical text, [*A Place to Sleep*] . . . is a great choice for story hours as well as bedtime reading."

A pair of siblings invent their own game in another self-illustrated work, *Inside, Inside, Inside.* After Jenny discovers her brother Noah's peewee marble, he drops the toy into an empty salt shaker, which is then placed into a small cereal box, which in turn is set into a recipe box. The children continue to hide their objects inside a series of larger and larger containers, finally relying on their drawing skills to extend the game beyond their home. "Meade cheerfully mixes cut-paper collage and watercolor," noted Margaret Bush in her *School Library Journal* review of *Inside, Inside, Inside,* and Cooper stated that "the idea is interesting enough, and the richly colored artwork is terrific."

Meade has also applied her artistic and authorial talents to the classic Brothers Grimm fairytale *The Rabbit's Bride.* The story focuses on a young girl who is supposed to chase a white rabbit from a cabbage patch but ends up being charmed by the rabbit. After becoming betrothed to the animal, she finds that the rabbit is not as nice as he seems. Tina Hudak, writing in *Library Journal,* questioned Meade's decision to give the story a happier ending but added: "The artwork, done in vibrant watercolors, effectively illustrates the rabbit's changing personality from harmless to demonic, but the effect may be too scary for young readers." *Booklist* contributor Ilene Cooper called the book "an interesting version of a little-told tale."

Biographical and Critical Sources

PERIODICALS

Booklist, November 15, 1992, Jim Laske, review of *This Is the Hat: A Story in Rhyme,* p. 611; April 15, 1994, Julie Corsaro, review of *Rata-Pata-Scata-Fata: A Caribbean Story,* p. 1541; September 15, 1994, Hazel Rochman, review of *Small Green Snake,* p. 132; December 15, 1995, Leone McDermott, review of *Sleep, Sleep, Sleep: A Lullaby for Little Ones around the World,* p. 715; April 15, 1996, Janice del Negro, review of *Hush!: A Thai Lullaby,* p. 1443; July, 1996, Ilene Cooper, review of *Pie's in the Oven,* p. 1828; November 1, 1997, Lauren Peterson, review of *Cocoa Ice,* p. 466; September 1, 1998, John Peters, review of *John Willy and Freddy McGee,* p. 127; February 1, 2000, Kathy Broderick, review of *When Papa Snores,* p. 1056; May 15, 2001, Ilene Cooper, review of *The Rabbit's Bride,* p. 1754; September 1, 2001, Lauren Peterson, review of *A Place to Sleep,* p. 117; March 1, 2002, Denise Wilms, review of *Queenie Farmer Had Fifteen Daughters,* p. 1148; March 1, 2002, Ilene Cooper, review of *Steamboat: The Story of Captain Blanche Leathers,* p. 1147; September 15, 2002, Carolyn Phelan, review of *On Morning Wings,* p. 233; May 1, 2004, Jennifer Mattson, review of *Blue Bowl Down: An Appalachian Rhyme,* p. 1557; October 1, 2004, Diane Foote, review of *Peek! A Thai Hide-and-Seek,* p. 334; April 15, 2005, Ilene Cooper, review of *Inside, Inside, Inside,* p. 1461; March 15, 2007, Gillian Engberg, review of *Sky Sweeper,* p. 53; June 1, 2007, Kristen McKulski, review of *Virginnie's Hat,* p. 86.

Horn Book, September-October, 1994, Ellen Fader, review of *Rata-Pata-Scata-Fata,* p. 574; March-April, 1995, Ellen Fader, review of *Small Green Snake,* p. 183; November-December, 1995, Hanna B. Zeiger, review of *Sleep, Sleep, Sleep,* p. 739; May-June, 1998, Martha V. Parravano, review of *Boss of the Plains: The Hat That Won the West,* p. 356; March, 2000, review of *Steamboat,* p. 211; September, 2000, review of *When Papa Snores,* p. 552; May 1, 2002, Hazel Rochman, review of *Goose's Story,* p. 1520; November-December, 2004, Jennifer M. Brabander, review of *Peek!,* p. 697; May-June, 2007, Joanna Rudge Long, review of *Sky Sweeper,* p. 264.

Kirkus Reviews, August 1, 2001, review of *A Place to Sleep,* p. 1129; April 1, 2002, review of *Queenie Farmer Had Fifteen Daughters,* p. 488; April 15, 2002, review of *Goose's Story,* p. 562; June 15, 2002, review of *On Morning Wings,* p. 884; April 15, 2003, review of *That's What Friends Are For,* p. 608; May 1, 2004, review of *Blue Bowl Down,* p. 445; September 1, 2004, review of *Peek!,* p. 867; March 15, 2005, review of *Inside, Inside, Inside,* p. 355; March 1, 2007, review of *Sky Sweeper,* p. 221.

New York Times Book Review, May 17, 1998, Anne Scott MacLeod, review of *Boss of the Plains,* p. 23.

Publishers Weekly, October 26, 1992, review of *This Is the Hat,* p. 69; April 4, 1994, review of *Rata-Pata-Scata-Fata,* p. 79; September 5, 1994, review of *Small Green Snake,* p. 108; March 25, 1996, review of *Hush!,* p. 82; May 4, 1998, review of *Boss of the Plains,* p. 213; August, 17, 1998, review of *John Willy and Freddy McGee,* p. 71; April 3, 2000, review of *Steamboat,* p. 80; February 12, 2001, review of *The Rabbit's Bride,* p. 211; October 1, 2001, review of *A Place to Sleep,* p. 60; April 1, 2002, review of *Queenie Farmer Had Fifteen Daughters,* p. 82; May 5, 2003, review of *That's What Friends Are For,* p. 223; May 31, 2004, review of *Blue Bowl Down,* p. 73; May 14, 2007, review of *Sky Sweeper,* p. 53.

School Library Journal, October, 1992, Alexandra Marris, review of *This Is the Hat,* p. 98; September, 1994, Jody McCoy, review of *Small Green Snake,* p. 184; January, 1996, Ruth K. MacDonald, review of *Sleep, Sleep, Sleep,* p. 97; March, 1996, John Philbrook, review of *Hush!,* pp. 175-176; September, 1996, Kathy Piehl, review of *Pie's in the Oven,* p. 170; January, 1998, Luann Toth, review of *Cocoa Ice,* p. 80; September, 1998, Joy Fleishhacker, review of *John Willy and Freddy McGee,* p. 177; March, 2000, Susan Hepler, review of *Steamboat,* p. 224; May, 2001, Tina Hudak, review of *The Rabbit's Bride,* p. 142; September, 2001, Cathie Reed, review of *A Place to Sleep,* p. 199; August, 2002, Jeanne Clancy Watkins, review of *Goose's Story,* p. 148; August, 2002, Jeanne Clancy Watkins, review of *Queenie Farmer Had Fifteen Daughters,* p. 148; December, 2002, Marian Drabkin, review of *On Morning Wings,* p. 126; May, 2003, Lauralyn Persson, review of *That's What Friends Are For,* p. 120; September, 2004, Kathleen Whalin, review of *Blue Bowl Down,* p. 174; October, 2004, Wendy Lukehart, review of *Peek!,* p. 115; March, 2005, Kathleen T. Isaacs, review of *The Stone Goddess,* p. 69; May, 2005, Margaret Bush, review of *Inside, Inside, Inside,* p. 92; April, 2007, Margaret Bush, review of *Sky Sweeper,* p. 106; May, 2007, Martha Simpson, review of *Virginnie's Hat,* p. 86.

Tribune Books (Chicago, IL), June 6, 2004, Mary Harris Russell, review of *Blue Bowl Down,* p. 2.

ONLINE

Houghton Mifflin Web site, http://www.eduplace.com/ (January 1, 2010), "Holly Meade."

Reach Road Gallery Web site, http://www.reachroadgallery. com/ (April 1, 2008).*

*   *   *

MENZEL, Peter 1948-

Personal

Born 1948, in Farmington, CT; married Faith D'Alusio (a writer); children: Josh, Jack, Adam, Evan. *Education:* Boston University, B.S.

Addresses

Office—Material World Books, 199 Kreuzer Ln., Napa, CA 94559. *E-mail*—peter@menzelphoto.com.

Career

Photojournalist. *Exhibitions:* Work exhibited at United Nations, New York, NY; Museum of Science and Industry, Chicago, IL; National Museum of Natural History, Washington, DC; and other venues in the United States and Europe.

Awards, Honors

Harry Chapin Media Award, 1994, for *Material World* by Charles C. Mann; Books for the Teen Age selection, New York Public Library, 1996, for *Women in the Material World;* James Beard Foundation Award, 1999, for *Man Eating Bugs;* Best Science Portfolio Award, World Press Photo, and Independent Publisher Book Award in Science Category, both 2000, both for *Robo Sapiens;* Book of the Year selection, Harry Chapin World Hunger Media Foundation, 2005, and James Beard Foundation Award, 2006, both for *Hungry Planet;* has also received World Press Awards for photography.

Writings

AND PHOTOGRAPHER

(With wife, Faith D'Aluisio) *Women in the Material World,* Sierra Club Books (San Francisco, CA), 1996.

(With Faith D'Aluisio) *Man Eating Bugs: The Art and Science of Eating Insects,* Ten Speed Press (Berkeley, CA), 1998.

(With Faith D'Aluisio) *Robo Sapiens: Evolution of a New Species,* MIT Press (Cambridge, MA), 2000.

(With Faith D'Aluisio) *Hungry Planet: What the World Eats,* Ten Speed Press (Berkeley, CA), 2005, children's edition, Tricycle Press (Berkeley, CA), 2008.

(With Faith D'Aluisio) *What the World Eats: Around the World in Eighty Diets,* Random House (New York, NY), 2010.

PHOTOGRAPHER

David Weber, *Oakland, Hub of the West,* Continental Heritage Press (Tulsa, OK), 1981.

Charles C. Mann, *Material World: A Global Family Portrait,* introduction by Paul Kennedy, Sierra Club Books (San Francisco, CA), 1994.

Julieta Ramos-Elorduy, *Creepy Crawly Cuisine: The Gourmet Guide to Edible Insects,* translated by Nancy Esteban, Park Street Press (Rochester, VT), 1998.

Contributor to periodicals, including *GEO, Stern, Figaro, Der Spiegel, Paris Match, Focus, Muy Interesante, El País, Life, National Geographic, Smithsonian, New York Times Magazine, Newsweek,* and *Time.*

Adaptations

Women in the Material World was adapted as an audiobook, Sierra Club Audio Library, 1998.

Sidelights

Photojournalist Peter Menzel and his wife, Faith D'Aluisio, have collaborated on nonfiction books that include *Hungry Planet: What the World Eats,* winner of the James Beard Foundation Award. The duo has traveled the globe in search of interesting stories; their works have introduced readers to a restaurant that serves live scorpions, the development of anthropomorphic robots, and the daily activities of a Mongolian family. Menzel told *Photo.net* interviewer Philip Greenspun that "having a partner who is your wife traveling with you can be great. We each have our roles in the work and then can help each other out on the emotional front when things get stressful, which they are. Most of the time when you try to get a lot done in an efficient and timely manner it's stressful. I would recommend trying it for other husband-wife teams. If you don't get divorced or kill each other after the first few months, you might learn to like it."

Menzel and D'Aluisio's first book, *Women in the Material World,* offers portraits of twenty women, their homes ranging from China, Mali, and Jordan to Italy and Haiti. The work, which is illustrated with full-color photographs taken by a host of female photojournalists, includes interviews with these women in which they discuss their day-to-day lives and reflect on the social, cultural, and political issues in their native lands. A contributor in *Publishers Weekly* called the work a "beautiful and moving photo-essay," and Leon Wagner, writing in *Booklist* described *Women in the Material World* as a "great book for a wide range of readers and thinkers."

In *Man Eating Bugs: The Art and Science of Eating Insects,* Menzel and D'Aluisio present a global study of entomophagy: the practice of devouring bugs. While entomophagy is common in many parts of the world, including Asia and Africa, many Westerners frown upon it, Menzel notes. As he told Jonathan Dyson in the London *Independent,* "I remember . . . thinking it was just inconceivable that people could eat something so lowly and disgusting. But then I came across this piece in the *Wall Street Journal* about the *Food Insect Newsletter,* and it had some recipes and talked about the strange people who subscribed to the newsletter, and I just became fascinated with it. I made a point of looking for insect-eating whenever I went abroad on assignment." A reviewer in *Whole Earth* called *Man Eating Bugs* "by far the most informative, fun, and mind/stomach-bending book ever on insect eating." The critic added that D'Aluisio and Menzel's narrative "chronicles their journeys with lovely anecdotes of each day's new events."

Menzel and D'Aluisio profile the creation of synthetic beings in *Robo Sapiens: Evolution of a New Species.* The volume includes interviews with scientists who research and design robots, and it examines the different types of machines they construct, such as those with industrial and military applications and others that mimic

Peter Menzel's photographs team with a text by his wife, Faith D'Aluisio, in nonfiction books such as **What the World Eats.** (Tricycle Press, 2008. Photograph copyright © 2005 by Peter Menzel./menzelphoto.com Reproduced by permission.)

human skills. Reviewing *Robo Sapiens* in *Publishers Weekly,* a critic deemed the work "an informative—and handsome—view of some current work in robotics, from out-there A[rtificial] I[ntelligence] research to practical (and profitable) surgical technology."

In *Hungry Planet* the husband-and-wife team describes the food consumption of families from more than twenty nations. Each entry opens with a photograph of family members standing with a week's worth of food purchases, along with a list of the items and their prices in both local and U.S. currency. The work also includes narratives about the family members' lifestyles and the food traditions of their native lands. "We found it shocking that a lot of people don't know what they're eating," Menzel remarked to *USA Today* interviewer Shawn Sell, "and by that I mean not just what's in food, in terms of preservatives and additives, but many people don't know where their food comes from or how it's processed."

Hungry Planet, which was released in two versions—one for adults and another for younger readers—earned strong reviews. Gillian Engberg, writing in *Booklist,* called the book "a fascinating, sobering, and instructive look at daily life around the world," while a *Publishers Weekly* critic described it as a "beautiful, quietly provocative volume." In the words of *Geographical* critic Jo Sargent, by examining "how our spending patterns reflect cultural traditions and how globalisation is affecting our diet, *Hungry Planet* offers plenty of food for thought."

Biographical and Critical Sources

PERIODICALS

Booklist, September 15, 1996, Leon Wagner, review of *Women in the Material World,* p. 186; March 15, 2000, review of *Man Eating Bugs: The Art and Science of Eating Insects,* p. 1360; July 1, 2008, Gillian Engberg, review of *Hungry Planet: What the World Eats,* p. 65.

Environment, October, 2006, Robert W. Kates, review of *Hungry Planet,* p. 40.

Geographical, February, 2006, Jo Sargent, review of *Hungry Planet,* p. 90.

Independent (London, England), February 13, 1999, Jonathan Dyson, "Eating Insects," p. 28.

New York Times Book Review, November 9, 2008, Regina Marler, review of *Hungry Planet,* p. 42.

PhotoMedia, August 1, 2007, Eric Rudolph, "Peter Menzel: Food for Thought," pp. 34-40.

Publishers Weekly, July 29, 1996, review of *Women in the Material World,* p. 77; July 3, 2000, review of *Robo Sapiens: Evolution of a New Species,* p. 55; August 22, 2005, review of *Hungry Planet,* p. 47; September 1, 2008, review of *Hungry Planet,* p. 55.

School Library Journal, April, 2006, Eva Elisabeth VonAncken, review of *Hungry Planet,* p. 68; July, 2008, Joyce Adams Burner, review of *Hungry Planet,* p. 111.

Technology Review, September, 2000, Wade Roush, review of *Robo Sapiens,* p. 127.

UN Chronicle, June, 1995, Elsa B. Endrst, review of *Material World: A Global Family Portrait,* p. 64.

USA Today, December 15, 2005, Shawn Sell, interview with D'Aluisio and Menzel.

U.S. News & World Report, December 26, 2005, Diane Cole, review of *Hungry Planet,* p. 87.

Whole Earth, spring, 1999, review of *Man Eating Bugs,* p. 73.

ONLINE

Light Connection Web site, http://www.lightconnection.us/ (November, 2008), Jennifer Joe, interview with D'Aluisio and Menzel.

Peter Menzel and Faith D'Aluisio Home Page, http://www.menzelphoto.com (September 1, 2009).

Photo.net, http://photo.net/ (April, 2007), Philip Greenspun, interview with D'Aluisio and Menzel.

*   *   *

MIRANDA, Inaki 1983(?)-

Personal

Born c. 1983, in Argentina. *Education:* Complutense University, B.F.A.

Addresses

Home—Madrid, Spain. *E-mail*—inaki-eva@inakieva.com.

Career

Illustrator and comic artist. Also worked in animation and video-game illustration.

Illustrator

Rebecca Donner *Burnout* (graphic novel), Minx (New York, NY), 2008.

Michael Geszel, *Tribes: The Dog Years,* IDW Publishing, 2010.

Illustrator of comic books, including *Judge Dredd, The Lexian Chronicles,* and *The Chase,* for 2000AD; *Fables,* for Vertigo; and *Tribes* and *Vines* for Soulcraft Comics.

Biographical and Critical Sources

PERIODICALS

School Library Journal, July, 2009, Andrea Lipinski, review of *Burnout,* p. 119.

ONLINE

Inaki Miranda Home Page, http://www.inakieva.com (November 5, 2009).

Inaki Miranda Web log, http://inakimiranda.blogsot.com/ (November 5, 2009).*

*   *   *

MORAIS, Flavio

Personal

Born in Brazil; immigrated to Spain. *Education:* Chelsea School of Art, degree.

Addresses

Home—Barcelona, Spain. *E-mail*—fdemorais@yahoo.es.

Career

Illustrator, animator, and muralist. *Exhibitions:* Works exhibited at galleries in Spain, France, Belgium, and Brazil.

Illustrator

Lori Marie Carlson, editor, *Voices in First Person: Reflections on Latino Identity,* photographs by Manuel Rivera-Ortiz, Atheneum Books for Young Readers (New York, NY), 2008.

Contributor to periodicals, including *El Mundo, Editora Abril, Avui, Camper, LV,* and *New Republic.*

Biographical and Critical Sources

PERIODICALS

Booklist, October 1, 2008, Hazel Rochman, review of *Voices in First Person: Reflections on Latino Identity,* p. 39.

Horn Book, July-August, 2008, Jonathan Hunt, review of *Voices in First Person,* p. 464.

ONLINE

Flavio Morais Home Page, http://www.flaviomorais.net (November 5, 2009).*

*   *   *

MORRIS, Gerald 1963-
(Gerald Paul Morris)

Personal

Born October 29, 1963, in Riverside, WI; son of Russell A. (a missionary) and Lena May (a missionary) Morris; married Rebecca Hughes (a registered nurse), August 2, 1986; children: William, Ethan, Grace. *Education:* Oklahoma Baptist University, B.A., 1985; Southern Baptist Theological Seminary, M.Div., 1989, Ph.D., 1994. *Politics:* Democrat. *Religion:* Baptist.

Addresses

Home—Wassau, WI. *Office*—P.O. Box 2014, Wausau, WI 54401-2014.

Career

Southern Baptist Theological Seminary, Louisville, KY, adjunct professor of Hebrew and biblical interpretation, 1994-95; Ouachita Baptist University, Arkadelphia, AR, assistant professor of biblical studies, 1995-96; teacher at Christian school in Arkadelphia, 1997; HortCo Landscaping, Norman, OK, contract laborer, 1997-98; First Baptist Church, Wausau, WI, pastor, beginning 1998.

Member

Society of Biblical Literature, American Academy of Religion, Society of Children's Book Writers and Illustrators, Minnesota-Wisconsin Baptist Convention.

Awards, Honors

Best Books for Young Adults designation, Young Adult Library Services Association/American Library Association, 2000, for *The Squire, His Knight, and His Lady,* 2001, for *The Savage Damsel and the Dwarf.*

Writings

"SQUIRE'S TALES" NOVEL SERIES

The Squire's Tale, Houghton Mifflin (Boston, MA), 1998.
The Squire, His Knight, and His Lady, Houghton Mifflin (Boston, MA), 1999.

Gerald Morris (Photograph by Greg Behrendt. Courtesy of Gerald Morris.)

The Savage Damsel and the Dwarf, Houghton Mifflin (Boston, MA), 2000.
Parsifal's Page, Houghton Mifflin (Boston, MA), 2001.
The Ballad of Sir Dinadan, Houghton Mifflin (Boston, MA), 2003.
The Princess, the Crone, and the Dung-Cart Knight, Houghton Mifflin (Boston, MA), 2004.
The Lioness and Her Knight, Houghton Mifflin (Boston, MA), 2005.
The Quest of the Fair Unknown, Houghton Mifflin (Boston, MA), 2006.
The Squire's Quest, Houghton Mifflin Harcourt (Boston, MA), 2009.

"KNIGHTS' TALES" SERIES; CHAPTER BOOKS

The Adventures of Sir Lancelot the Great, illustrated by Aaron Renier, Houghton Mifflin (Boston, MA), 2008.
The Adventures of Sir Givret the Short, illustrated by Aaron Renier, Houghton Mifflin (Boston, MA), 2008.

OTHER

(As Gerald Paul Morris) *Prophecy, Poetry, and Hosea,* Sheffield Academic Press, 1996.
(Old Testament editor) *Life and Times Historical Reference Bible,* Thomas Nelson (Nashville, TN), 1998.

Sidelights

Gerald Morris is the author of a series of rollicking novels based on the Arthurian legends as told by Sir Thomas Mallory and other writers. Older sources seek

seriousness of purpose and embroil their tales in allegory, but in Morris's versions—which include *The Squire's Tale, The Savage Damsel and the Dwarf,* and *The Quest of the Fair Unknown*—concentrate on the humanity of secondary characters and the way in which great quests sometimes boil down to small moments of self-discovery. In addition to his work for older readers, Morris's "Knights' Tales" books are illustrated adaptations of his "Squire's Tales" novels. In *Booklist* Sally Estes noted that, in all his works, Morris puts "a humorous spin on Camelot and its denizens while still providing plenty of adventure, dimensional characters, and fresh, modern dialogue."

In his first book for children, *The Squire's Tale,* Morris uses Arthurian legend as inspiration for his story about a young lad who serves as a squire for Sir Gawain. Uncertain of his parentage, fourteen-year-old Terence decides to leave the wizard who raised him and join Sir Gawain on his quest to become The Maiden's Knight. As he follows the adventures of the future knight of the Round Table, Terence not only discovers who his real parents are, but also what his destiny will be. *The Squire's Tale* offers a different view of Sir Gawain as he is seen through the boy's eyes, a perspective that *School Library Journal* reviewer Helen Gregory claimed is "both original and true to the legend of Gawain." Gregory went on to suggest that "readers who savor swashbuckling tales of knighthood will enjoy this adventure." *Horn Book* critic Ann A. Flowers also praised Morris's characters, writing that "both Sir Gawain and Terence are remarkably engaging figures, holding our attention and affection." Shelle Rosenfeld noted in a *Booklist* review that, in addition to being a "well-written, fast read," *The Squire's Tale* also offers "well-drawn characters, excellent, snappy dialogue, detailed descriptions of medieval life, and a dry wit."

Terence and Gawain continue their adventures in *The Squire, His Knight, and His Lady,* a sequel that a *Kirkus Reviews* critic dubbed "an ideal follow-up to the first book and just as full of characters who are brave, loyal, and admirably human." In this story, Sir Gawain accepts a challenge in King Arthur's stead to meet the knight of the Green Chapel, and sets out to find him with the assistance of his squire, Terence. The two are joined in their quest by Lady Eileen, whom they rescue from her evil uncle. Together, the trio encounters a cannibal hag, a sea monster, the treacherous marquis of Alva, and the Green Knight in disguise at an enchanted castle. "Laced with magic, humor, and chivalry," according to *Horn Book* reviewer Anne St. John, "this reworking of 'Sir Gawain and the Green Knight' . . . provides an engaging introduction to the original tale." A *Publishers Weekly* commentator asserted that "Morris retells various medieval legends with plenty of action, tongue-in-cheek humor and moments of keen perception."

Another episode from Mallory's *Le Morte d'Arthur* forms the basis for *The Savage Damsel and the Dwarf.*

Here sixteen-year-old Lady Lynet travels to Camelot in the company of a wise dwarf in search of a knight willing to come to the aid of her besieged home. Lynet finds little sympathy at King Arthur's court beyond a ragged kitchen servant named Beaumains. Beaumains is actually a brash knight in disguise, however, and if Lynet can keep him from picking quarrels with every other knight he meets on the way, he might actually be the hero she needs to defeat the story's villain. Beth Wright, reviewing the novel for *School Library Journal,* described *The Savage Damsel and the Dwarf* as "great fun and [a book that] will be enjoyed by fans of the genre."

Parsifal's Page offers a new spin on another Arthurian hero, again from the point of view of his servant. The son of a blacksmith, Piers longs to live a noble life and he thinks he has found his chance when he becomes page to the ignorant and backward Parsifal. When Piers' attempts to educate Parsifal backfire and cause the boy to be fired, he joins forces with Sir Gawain and Ter-

Cover of Morris's novel **The Squire's Tale,** *a fantasy novel featuring artwork by Lou Beach.* (Dell-Laurel Leaf, 2000. Used by permission of Laurel-Leaf, an imprint of Random House Children's Books, a division of Random House, Inc.)

Morris's "Squire's Tale" series continues with **Parsifal's Page,** *a book featuring cover art by Lou Beach.* (Houghton Mifflin Company, 2001. Jacket art © 2001 by Lou Beach. Reprinted by permission of Houghton Mifflin Harcourt Publishing Company. All rights reserved.)

ence. Together they try to locate Parsifal, who is now missing and presumed to be in danger. In her *Horn Book* review of the work, Anne St. John noted that while readers already familiar with Morris's series will enjoy re-encountering familiar characters, *Parsifal's Page* "also stands on its own." St. John added that the legendary but believable figures in the tale "provide a perfect backdrop for Piers's growing understanding of his role in the world."

The titular hero of *The Ballad of Sir Dinadan* was described by several reviewers as one of Morris's most engaging characters. With a quick wit and the ability to see humor in every situation, Sir Dinadan is an artist at heart—specifically, a musician. His martial-minded father has other ideas, however, and Dinadan is knighted against his will and sent off to make his way as a soldier. Among his varied tasks, Dinadan helps his cloddish brother Tristram deal with a decidedly unlikable Iseult, as well as aiding the efforts of a deposed king to win back his throne. Throughout, young Dinadan continues to mature while still maintaining his individuality as an artist and a thinker. In *Booklist* Carolyn Phelan

described *The Ballad of Sir Dinadan* as "a witty tale of adventure and reflection," and Steven Engelfried praised the book in *School Library Journal,* citing Morris's "skilled storytelling" for providing "a lighthearted introduction to the period."

In *The Princess, the Crone, and the Dung-Cart Knight* a teenaged princess named Sarah is determined to track down the knight responsible for having her mother burned at the stake. During her search, Sarah watches, undetected, as a group of men abducts both Sir Kay and Queen Guinevere. With the help of Terence and the valiant Sir Gawain, she tracks the kidnappers and attempts a daring rescue, befriended along the way by an odd assortment of people that includes a faery, a monk, a princess, and an unnamed knight hiding in a dung cart. In *Booklist* Carolyn Phelan noted the inspiration of Crétien de Troyes' "Lancelot, the Knight of the Cart" and added that Morris "infuses" the traditional Arthurian stories "with humor and fantasy" to produce "a highly readable story." In *Kliatt* Claire Rosser expressed approval at having the opportunity to once again enter the author's "wonderfully realized world of King Arthur," while in a *School Library Journal* review of *The Princess, the Crone, and the Dung-Cart Knight* Cheri Dobbs praised the author's "grand storytelling style" and recommended the book to "readers looking for page-turning adventure, a strong heroine, and some fun."

Based on a poem from the middle ages, *The Lioness and Her Knight* introduces Luneta, the sixteen-year-old teen daughter of a knight of King Arthur's round table. Lured by the adventure at court, she requests to become companion to her widowed cousin, Lady Laudine, in order to join her cousin Sir Ywain on his entry into court. During their trip to court, Luneta and Ywain meet up with the foolish Sir Rhience, and both the engaging knight and a lioness join the young people when they decide to go in search of a magical artifact know as the Storm Stone. "Filled with wry comments and dramatic encounters," *The Lioness and Her Knight* "represents the best kind of minstrel's tale," according to Rosser, and in *Booklist* Phelan dubbed it "a fine romance" with "magical as well as heroic elements." In *School Library Journal* Kristen Oravec described *The Lioness and Her Knight* "a gem" gaining its sparkle from "characters reminiscent of a Monty Python sketch and a knight with a Don Quixote complex."

A seventeen year old raised in a distant forest is the focus of the search at the center of *The Quest of the Fair Unknown.* For Beaufils, a promise to his dying mother propels him to leave home and go in search of the long-lost knight who is his father. An innocent abroad, the naive Beaufils amuses the traveling companions he meets along the way, which include Sir Galahad, Sir Gawain, and Lady Ellyn. In *Horn Book* Claire E. Gross wrote that in *The Quest of the Fair Unknown* Morris sustains the "comfortable balance of epic adventure, earnest idealism, and gentle humor" that readers of his series have come to expect. In praise of the novel's

"immensely likable" hero, a *Kirkus Reviews* writer added that the novel "will leave readers ruminating on . . . surface beauty, marrow-minded religious views, [and] misconceptions about the nature of honor."

Although humor is a major feature of his novels for teens, Morris adopts an even lighter tone in his "Knights' Tales" chapter books, which are humorously illustrated with black-and-white spot art by Aaron Renier. In *The Adventures of Sir Lancelot the Great* the author takes the jewel of King Arthur's crown of valiant knights and shows him to exhibit some foibles as well, while in *The Adventures of Sir Givret the Short* readers meet a young knight whose native intelligence more than compensates for his diminutive size. While cautioning readers that *The Adventures of Sir Lancelot the Great* is "not for the Arthurian purist," Dobbs maintained in *School Library Journal* that the story's "brevity and humor" recommend it to reluctant readers. Despite the subtle satire, wrote a *Kirkus Reviews* writer, Lancelot is still portrayed as a hero to admire; Morris's message in the novel is "that true heroes are good in

Morris adapts his "Squire's Tale" stories for younger readers in books such as The Adventures of Sir Lancelot, *featuring artwork by Aaron Renier.* (Houghton Mifflin Company, 2008. Illustrations copyright © 2008 by Aaron Renier. Reproduced by permission of Houghton Mifflin Harcourt Publishing Company. All rights reserved.)

fights, but equally capable of solving problems" without use of a sword. In *The Adventures of Sir Givret the Short* Morris serves up "an entertaining tale . . . sure to please young readers enamored with medieval derring-do," asserted Maryann H. Owen in *School Library Journal,* and in *Booklist* Ian Chipman cited the book's focus on "cleverness over heroism."

Moris once told *SATA:* "I began my first novel when I was in the eighth grade. It was a perfectly dreadful western in which sharp-eyed gunslingers squinted into the sun and tough-as-boot-leather old-timers called people 'young 'un' and spat into the dust. The early chapters were, providentially, lost.

"I returned to writing novels when I went to graduate school. Writing fiction was an antidote to the gaseous prose I was churning out for my professors. Maybe because I wrote as a sort of simplifying exercise, I chose to write for children and adolescents. A child's world is no simpler than an adult's, but children often see their world with clearer eyes. These first attempts at children's novels received some very fine, preprinted rejection cards in a variety of pretty colors. Pastels were big in the late 1980s. Then my first child, William, was born, to be followed two years later by Ethan, then Grace. Life was busier then, so I put the novels aside.

"Then, for a while, I was an academic. I finished my doctorate and became a professor of Hebrew and biblical interpretation for a couple of years. When my last academic contract ended, I was rather at loose ends, and so I decided to rework some of those old novels. This time, one was accepted: *The Squire's Tale.* Encouraged, I kept writing. Meanwhile, I tutored Greek, taught middle schoolers, taught English as a second language, did some substitute teaching, and worked for a landscaper. At the end of that time, I became the pastor of the First Baptist Church of Wausau, Wisconsin. So now, I suppose, I write children's novels as an antidote to my own sermons."

Biographical and Critical Sources

PERIODICALS

Booklist, April 15, 1998, Shelle Rosenfeld, review of *The Squire's Tale,* pp. 1436-1437; May 1, 1999, Shelle Rosenfeld, review of *The Squire, His Knight, and His Lady,* p. 1587; March 1, 2000, GraceAnne A. DeCandido, review of *The Savage Damsel and the Dwarf,* p. 1244; April 15, 2000, Sally Estes, "The Denizens of Camelot Series," p. 1544; April 15, 2001, Carolyn Phelan, review of *Parsifal's Page,* p. 1558; May 1, 2003, Carolyn Phelan, review of *The Ballad of Sir Dinadan,* p. 1589; April 15, 2004, Carolyn Phelan, review of *The Princess, the Crone, and the Dung-Cart Knight,* p. 1450; September 15, 2005, review of *The Lioness and Her Knight,* p. 77; June 1, 2008, Carolyn

Phelan, review of *The Adventures of Sir Lancelot the Great*, p. 69; February 1, 2009, Ian Chipman, review of *The Adventures of Sir Givret the Short*, p. 44.

Horn Book, July-August, 1998, Ann A. Flowers, review of *The Squire's Tale*, p. 492; March-April, 1999, Anne St. John, review of *The Squire, His Knight, and His Lady*, p. 210; May, 2000, review of *The Savage Damsel and the Dwarf*, p. 317; May, 2001, Anne St. John, review of *Parsifal's Page*, p. 333; May-June, 2003, Peter D. Sieruta, review of *The Ballad of Sir Dinadan*, p. 353; November-December, 2006, Claire E. Gross, review of *The Quest of the Fair Unknown*, p. 720.

Kirkus Reviews, April 1, 1999, review of *The Squire, His Knight, and His Lady*, p. 536; October 15, 2006, review of *The Quest of the Fair Unknown*, p. 1075; April 1, 2008, review of *The Adventures of Sir Lancelot the Great.*

Kliatt, March, 2004, Claire Rosser, review of *The Princess, the Crone, and the Dung-Cart Knight*, p. 15; September, 2005, Claire Rosser, review of *The Lioness and Her Knight*, p. 11; September, 2006, Claire Rosser, review of *The Quest of the Fair Unknown*, p. 16.

Publishers Weekly, March 15, 1999, review of *The Squire, His Knight, and His Lady*, p. 60.

School Library Journal, July, 1998, Helen Gregory, review of *The Squire's Tale*, p. 97; May, 2000, Beth Wright, review of *The Savage Damsel and the Dwarf*, p. 174; April, 2001, Cheri Estes, review of *Parsifal's Page*, p. 146; April, 2003, Steven Engelfried, review of *The Ballad of Sir Dinadan*, p. 166; May, 2004, Cheri Dobbs, review of *The Princess, the Crone, and the Dung-Cart Knight*, p. 154; September, 2005, Kristen Oravec, review of *The Lioness and Her Knight*, p. 208; June, 2008, Cheri Dobbs, review of *The Adventures of Sir Lancelot the Great*, p. 112; January, 2009, Maryann H. Owen, review of *The Adventures of Sir Givret the Short*, p. 81.

ONLINE

Bulletin of the Center for Children's Books Online, http://bccb.lis.illinois.edu/ (February 1, 2005), Kristin Hungerford, "Gerald Morris."*

*   *   *

MORRIS, Gerald Paul
See MORRIS, Gerald

*   *   *

MUSGROVE, Marianne

Personal

Born in Sydney, New South Wales, Australia. *Education:* University of Adelaide, B.A. (jurisprudence); Flinders University, B.S.W. *Hobbies and other interests:* Reading, visiting the beach, spending time with friends and family.

Marianne Musgrove (Photograph by Impressions Photography Studio. Courtesy of Marianne Musgrove.)

Addresses

Home—South Australia, Australia. *E-mail*—marianne@mariannemusgrove.com.au.

Career

Author. Former social worker; worked as a museum guide and for Australian *Daily Mirror.*

Member

Society of Children's Book Writers and Illustrators (Australian chapter), Australian Society of Authors.

Awards, Honors

National Children's Peace Literature Award shortlist, 2007, and Queensland Premier's Literary Award shortlist, and South Australia Festival Award for Children's Literature shortlist, both 2008, and Australian Family Therapists' Award for Children' Literature, 2008, all for *The Worry Tree;* Speech Pathology Australia Children's Book of the Year shortlist, and Victorian Premiers' Reading Challenge selection, both 2009, both for *Lucy the Good.*

Writings

The Worry Tree, Random House Australia (Sydney, New South Wales, Australia), 2007, Henry Holt (New York, NY), 2008.

Lucy the Good, illustrated by Cheryl Orsini, Random House Australia (Sydney, New South Wales, Australia), 2009.

Don't Breathe a Word, Random House Australia (Sydney, New South Wales, Australia), 2009.

Lucy the Lie Detector, Random House Australia (Sydney, New South Wales, Australia), 2010.

Author's work has been published in Germany and Indonesia.

Adaptations

Musgrove's books have been adapted for audiobook by Bolinda Books Audio.

Sidelights

Australian author Marianne Musgrove always enjoyed writing, which is not surprising given that she is a descendent of the librarian of England's King Henry VIII. It was a lucky brush with her past that prompted her to begin what became her first published novel. "I come from a family of storytellers," Musgrove explained on her home page. "My grandma used to give dramatic public poetry recitals and make the audience cry. I also had a string of excellent teachers who inspired me to write and write and write. In my late twenties, I spent an afternoon reading back over my old diaries. I came across an entry I'd written when I was sixteen: 'I think I'd like to write a book,' it said. Not long after I read this, the opening chapter of *The Worry Tree* came to me."

In *The Worry Tree* readers meet a preteen who worries way too much. In her busy family, Juliet Jennifer Jones finds a lot to worry about, from her annoying little sister to her beloved Nana's health to her friendships with Gemma and Lindsay. After a move to a new bedroom—more worries!—Juliet discovers a painting of a tree hidden under layers of wallpaper. Nana explains that the room was once hers and that the painting can help take care of her worries. Juliet's challenge comes when a family tumult puts Nana's claim to the test in a chapter book that a *Kirkus Reviews* writer cited for portraying a "delightfully normal and realistically flawed family." In *Booklist* Connie Rockman reviewed the audiobook version of Musgrove's award-winning story, dubbing it "insightful" and "reassuring."

Other books by Musgrove include the middle-grade novel *Don't Breathe a Word,* as well as two humorous books for younger readers that focus on a girl named Lucy van Loon. In *Lucy the Good* a feisty young girl spends a great portion of her day sitting in the Time Out chair until an unusual present from a traveling relative threatens even worse reprisals.

Biographical and Critical Sources

PERIODICALS

Booklist, May 1, 2009, Connie Rockman, review of *The Worry Tree,* p. 94.

Kirkus Reviews, July 15, 2008, review of *The Worry Tree.*

School Library Journal, March, 2009. Elaine Morgan, review of *The Worry Tree,* p. 124.

ONLINE

Marianne Musgrove Home Page, http://www.marianne musgrove.com.au (November 10, 2009).

N-P

NESS, Patrick 1971-

Personal
Born 1971, in Alexandria, VA. *Education:* University of Southern California, B.A. (English literature).

Addresses
Home—London, England.

Career
Writer. Former corporate writer in CA; freelance writer, beginning c. 1997. Oxford University, Oxford, England, instructor in creative writing.

Awards, Honors
London *Guardian* Children's Fiction Prize, and Booktrust Teenage Prize, both 2008, both for *The Knife of Never Letting Go.*

Writings

"CHAOS WALKING" TRILOGY; FOR YOUNG ADULTS

The Knife of Never Letting Go, Walker Books (London, England), 2008, Candlewick Press (Cambridge, MA), 2009.
The Ask and the Answer, Candlewick Press (Somerville, MA), 2009.
Monsters of Men, Candlewick Press (Somerville, MA), 2010.

OTHER

The Crash of Hennington (adult novel), Flamingo (London, England), 2003.
Topics about Which I Know Nothing (short fiction), Flamingo (London, England), 2004.

Contributor to periodicals, including *Genre.*

Sidelights
Patrick Ness combines fantasy with science fiction in his award-winning novel *The Knife of Never Letting Go.* Born in the United States but living in London, England, Ness began working as a fiction writer in the late 1990s and produced his first novel, *The Crash of Hennington,* in 2003. *Topics about Which I Know Nothing,* a book of short fiction, followed before Ness turned his attention to teen readers.

The first book in Ness's "Chaos Walking" trilogy, *The Knife of Never Letting Go* takes readers to Prentisstown, a rural community on a newly colonized planet in which no women can be found. Prentisstown has another odd characteristic: every thought of every resident—human and animal—can be heard by all, resulting in the total lack of privacy and the unceasing, overbearing mental cacophony called Noise. At twelve years of age, Todd Hewitt is the youngest resident of Prentisstown. It is almost time for Todd to undergo initiation when he discovers a place where he is immune from the Noise. This discovery prompts Todd's adoptive parents to help him escape from town. Pursued by the army of Mayor Prentiss, the preteen discovers the wreckage of a space ship in a local swamp and finds a young girl named Viola hiding in the woods nearby. Todd had assumed all the women had been killed by the Noise; however, he now realizes, the actual history of Prentisstown is far more horrific and far more deadly.

In *Kliatt* Paula Rohrlick called *The Knife of Never Letting Go* a "haunting page-turner" featuring "edge-of-your-seat chase scenes" and "moments of both anguish and triumph." Although a *Kirkus Reviews* critic found the novel's pacing to be "uneven" and the premise "unbelievable," its "emotional physical, and intellectual drama is well-crafted and relentless," wrote *School Library Journal* contributor Megan Honig. In *Horn Book* Claire E. Gross cited Ness's "subtle world-building" and his ability to create relationships between charac-

ters that are "nuanced" and feature "considerable emotional depth." Calling *The Knife of Never Letting Go* a "troubling, unforgettable [series] opener," *Booklist* critic Ian Chipman concluded of the novel that Ness's "cliffhanger ending is as effective as a shot to the gut."

Ness's "Chaos Walking" trilogy continues with *The Ask and the Answer* and *Monsters of Men.* Pursued by the army of Prentisstown in *The Ask and the Answer,* Todd and Viola arrive at the city of Haven only to become separated when they are captured by the maniacal Mayor Prentiss. With his freedom gone, Todd must now cooperate with Prentiss's scheme to create the perfect society, even as that plan begins to drive the teen mad. Meanwhile, Viola is sent to a female compound where she joins a loosely formed resistance group that selectively bombs area targets. In *Publishers Weekly* a contributor praised *The Ask and the Answer* as a "grim and beautifully written sequel" that prompts readers to question "the nature of evil and humanity." The "Chaos Walking" trilogy "continues to develop a fascinating world," wrote *Horn Book* critic Claire E. Gross, "and its fully formed characters and conflicts draw attention to difficult issues with a rare, unblinking candor." In *The Ask and the Answer* "Ness delivers a leaner, meaner narrative," concluded a *Kirkus Reviews* writer, and in *Booklist* Chipman wrote that, while the novel is slightly "less exhilarating" than *The Knife of Never Letting Go,* it is "far weightier and no less stunning to read."

Biographical and Critical Sources

PERIODICALS

Booklist, September 1, 2008, Ian Chipman, review of *The Knife of Never Letting Go,* p. 97; August 1, 2009, Ian Chipman, review of *The Ask and the Answer,* p. 66.

Financial Times, April 26, 2008, James Lovegrove, review of *The Knife of Never Letting Go,* p. 19.

Horn Book, November-December, 2008, Claire E. Gross, review of *The Knife of Never Letting Go,* p. 712; September-October, 2998, Claire E. Gross, review of *The Ask and the Answer,* p. 570.

Kirkus Reviews, August 15, 2008, review of *The Knife of Never Letting Go;* August 15, 2009, review of *The Ask and the Answer.*

Kliatt, September, 2008, Paula Rohrlick, review of *The Knife of Never Letting Go,* p. 18.

Publishers Weekly, August 31, 2009, review of *The Ask and the Answer,* p. 59.

School Library Journal, November, 2008, Megan Honig, review of *The Knife of Never Letting Go,* p. 133.

ONLINE

Patrick Ness Home Page, http://www.patrickness.com (November 10, 2009).

OFER, Avi 1975-

Personal

Born July 31, 1975, in Israel. *Education:* Attended Camera Obscura School of Arts (Tel-Aviv, Israel), 1996-97; attended Kalisher School of Arts (Tel-Aviv), 1997-98; attended Bezalel Academy (Jerusalem, Israel), 1998-99; studied with Eldad Rafaeli and Eyal Landsman, 2007-08. *Religion:* Jewish.

Addresses

Home—Tel Aviv, Israel. *E-mail*—aviofer@gmail.com.

Career

Illustrator, animator, photographer, and designer. Animator for Hot Kids TV, 2001-02, and in short films, including "Autofoto," 2001, "Escapism," 2002, "Mermaid S.O.S.," 2004, "Sandbox," 2006, "Tulik," 2007, "Dream Child," 2007, "Get the Picture," 2009, and "Ella Takes World Cup," 2009. Freelance illustrator, c. 2000. *Exhibitions:* Work exhibited at galleries in Tel-Aviv, Israel, including Beit Haomanim, Museum Ashdot, Yaakov, Limbos Gallery, Tzadik Gallery, and Tel-Aviv Station Gallery. *Military service:* Israeli Army Engineering Corps, animator and graphic designer for Multimedia and Filming Unit, 1994-97.

Awards, Honors

Numerous awards for short films.

Illustrator

Christopher Lincoln, *Billy Bones: Tales from the Secrets Closet,* Little, Brown (New York, NY), 2008.

Contributor of illustrations to Israeli periodicals, including *Maariv* and *Haaretz.*

Biographical and Critical Sources

PERIODICALS

Bulletin of the Center for Children's Books, October, 2008, April Spisak, review of *Billy Bones: Tales from the Secrets Closet,* p. 31.

School Library Journal, October, 2008, Jennifer D. Montgomery, review of *Billy Bones,* p. 152.

Voice of Youth Advocates, December, 2008, Courtney Wika, review of *Billy Bones,* p. 454.

ONLINE

Avi Ofer Home Page, http://www.aviofer.com (November 10, 2009).

Animation World Network Web site, http://www.awn.com/ (April 17, 2003), Jon Hofferman, review of "Autofoto"; (September 24, 2003) Greg Singer, review of "Escapism"; (November 26, 2008) Andrew Farago, review of "Sandbox."

San Francisco Jewish Film Festival Web site, http://fest. sjff.org/ (September 30, 2009), Shira Zucker, interview with Ofer.*

* * *

PALATINI, Margie

Personal

Born in Edison, NJ; married; children: Jamie (son). *Education:* Moore College of Art and Design, B.F.A.

Addresses

Home—Plainfield, NJ 07060. *E-mail*—margiepalatini@ netscape.net.

Career

Children's author and illustrator. Co-owner of interior design business.

Awards, Honors

Notable Book designation, American Library Association (ALA), Notable Trade Book in Language Arts designation, National Council of Teachers of English (NCTE), Pennsylvania Keystone State Reading Award, Kentucky Bluegrass Children's Book Award, Vermont Red Clover Award, Bill Martin, Jr., Picture-Book Award, Kansas Reading Association, Florida Reading Association Award Honor designation, Nebraska Golden Sower Award Honor designation, California Young Readers' Medal nomination, Ohio Buckeye Award nomination, and Georgia Children's Book Award nomination, all c. 1995, all for *Piggie Pie!;* Indiana Young Hoosier Award nomination, 1995, for *Piggie Pie!,* 2002, for *Bedhead,* and 2003, for both *The Web Files* and *Earthquack!;* Children's Choice designation, International Reading Association, 1997, for *Moosetache,* 1998, for *Zak's Lunch,* 2000, for *Good as Goldie,* 2004, for both *Stinky Smelly Feet* and *The Perfect Pet,* and 2006, for both *Oink?* and *Bad Boys Get Cookie!;* Irma S. and James H. Black Award, Bank Street College, 1998, for *Zak's Lunch;* Tennessee Volunteer State Book Award nominee and Wyoming Buckaroo Award nominee, both 2000-01, both for *Zoom Broom;* Pennsylvania Keystone State Reading Award, 2002, Golden Sower Award, 2003, and North Dakota Flicker Tale Award nominee and M. Jerry Weiss Book Award nominee, both 2004, all for *Bedhead;* ALA Notable Book designation, 2002, Keystone State Reading Award, Maryland Black-eyed Susan Award, Colorado Children's Book Award nominee, North Carolina Children's Book Award nominee, Pennsylvania Young Readers Award nominee, Golden Sower Award nominee, and South Dakota Prairie Bud Award nominee, all, 2003, and Michigan Great Lakes Great Books Award honor designation, 2004, all for *The Web Files;* New Hampshire Ladybug Picture Book Award nominee, 2004, for *Tub-Boo-Boo;* Georgia Picture Storybook Award nominee, Volunteer State Book Award nominee, and Pennsylvania Young Readers Award nominee, all 2004, and Oregon Patricia Gallaher Picture Book Award nominee, 2005, all for *Earthquack!;* Children's Literature Choice designation, Missouri Show Me Book Award, Black-eyed Susan Award nominee, and Kentucky Bluegrass Award nomination, all 2004, North Carolina Children's Book Award, 2005, and Pennsylvania Young Readers Award nominee and Volunteer State Book Award, both 2006, all for *Bad Boys;* Buckaroo Award nominee, Flicker Tale Award nominee, and New Hampshire Ladybug Picture Book Award nominee, all 2005, all for *Moo Who?;* Chicago Public Library Best of the Best designation, 2005, and Oppenheim Toy Portfolio Platinum Award, and CCBC Choice designation, both 2006, all for *Three French Hens;* Mississippi Mockingbird Award, 2006, for *Oink?;* Florida Reading Association Award nominee and North Carolina Children's Book Award nominee, both 2006, and Bill Martin, Jr., Picture Book Award nominee, 2007, all for *The Three Silly Billies;* Bill Martin, Jr., Picture Book Award nominee, Washington State Picture Book Award nominee, Illinois Picture Book Monarch Award nominee, and Arizona Grand Canyon Book Award nominee, all 2007, all for *The Cheese.*

Writings

Piggy Pie!, illustrated by Howard Fine, Clarion Books (New York, NY), 1995.

The Wonder Worm Wars, Hyperion Books for Children (New York, NY), 1997.

Moosetache, illustrated by Henry Cole, Hyperion Books for Children (New York, NY), 1997.

Zak's Lunch, illustrated by Howard Fine, Clarion Books (New York, NY), 1998.

Elf Help, illustrated by Mike Reed, Hyperion Books for Children (New York, NY), 1998.

Zoom Broom, illustrated by Howard Fine, Hyperion Books for Children (New York, NY), 1998.

Ding Dong Ding Dong, illustrated by Howard Fine, Hyperion Books for Children (New York, NY), 1999.

Lab Coat Girl in Cool Fuel, Hyperion Books for Children (New York, NY), 1999.

Lab Coat Girl and the Amazing Benjamin Bone, Hyperion Books for Children (New York, NY), 1999.

Mooseltoe, illustrated by Henry Cole, Hyperion Books for Children (New York, NY), 2000.

Lab Coat Girl in My Triple-Decker Hero, Hyperion Books for Children (New York, NY), 2000.

Bedhead, illustrated by Jack E. Davis, Simon & Schuster Books for Young Readers (New York, NY), 2000.

(And illustrator) *Good as Goldie,* Hyperion Books for Young Readers (New York, NY), 2000.

The Web Files, illustrated by Richard Egielski, Hyperion Books for Children (New York, NY), 2001.

Tub-Boo-Boo, illustrated by Glin Dibley, Simon & Schuster Books for Young Readers (New York, NY), 2001.

(And illustrator) *Goldie Is Mad,* Hyperion Books for Children (New York, NY), 2001.

Earthquack!, Simon & Schuster Books for Young Readers (New York, NY), 2002.

The Perfect Pet, illustrated by Bruce Whatley, HarperCollins Publishers (New York, NY), 2003.

Broom Mates, illustrated by Howard Fine, Hyperion Books for Children (New York, NY), 2003.

Bad Boys, illustrated by Henry Cole, Harpercollins Children's Books (New York, NY), 2003.

Mary Had a Little Ham, illustrated by Guy Francis, Hyperion Books for Children (New York, NY), 2003.

Moosekitos: A Moose Family Reunion, Hyperion Books for Children (New York, NY), 2004.

Stinky Smelly Feet: A Love Story, illustrated by Ethan Long, Dutton Children's Books (New York, NY), 2004.

Moo Who?, illustrated by Keith Graves, Katherine Tegen Books (New York, NY), 2004.

The Sweet Tooth, illustrated by Jack E. Davis, Simon & Schuster Books for Young Readers (New York, NY), 2004.

The Three Silly Billies, illustrated by Barry Moser, Simon & Schuster Books for Young Readers (New York, NY), 2005.

Three French Hens, illustrated by Richard Egielski, Hyperion Books for Children (New York, NY), 2005.

Oink?, illustrated by Henry Cole, Simon & Schuster Books for Young Readers (New York, NY), 2006.

Shelly, illustrated by Guy Francis, Dutton Children's Books (New York, NY), 2006.

Bad Boys Get Cookie!, illustrated by Henry Cole, Katherine Tegen Books (New York, NY), 2006.

The Cheese, illustrated by Steve Johnson and Lou Fancher, Katherine Tegen Books (New York, NY), 2007.

No Biting, Louise!, illustrated by Matthew Reinhart, Katherine Tegen Books (New York, NY), 2007.

Gone with the Wand, illustrated by Brian Ahjar, Orchard Books (New York, NY), 2008.

(And illustrator) *Geek Chic: The Zoey Zone,* Katherine Tegen Books (New York, NY), 2008.

Gorgonzola: A Very Stinkysaurus, illustrated by Tim Bowers, Katherine Tegen Books (New York, NY), 2008.

Bad Boys Get Henpecked!, illustrated by Henry Cole, Katherine Tegen Books (New York, NY), 2009.

Boo-hoo Moo, illustrated by Keith Graves, Katherine Tegen Books (New York, NY), 2009.

Lousy Rotten Stinkin' Grapes, illustrated by Barry Moser, Simon & Schuster Books for Young Readers (New York, NY), 2009.

Goldie and the Three Hares, illustrated by Jack E. Davis, Katherine Tegen Books (New York, NY), 2010.

Adaptations

Several of Palatini's stories have been adapted for audio, including *Bad Boys* and *Bad Boys Get Cookie!,* narrated by Jim Brownold, Spoken Arts, 2007.

Sidelights

Margie Palatini is a highly regarded author of humorous picture books for young readers. A review of her work, which includes *Bad Boys, The Three Silly Billies,*

Bedhead, and *Lousy, Rotten, Stinkin' Grapes,* has prompted critics to cite Palatini's use of offbeat humor, rhyme, and allusion; her "lively wordplay—in the form of puns, allusions, and wink-wink-nudge-nudge humor—ensures that, whatever the story, the reader or listener can be assured of a giggle-inducing ride," remarked Loretta M. Gaffney in the *Bulletin of the Center for Children's Books.* "Palatini also propels sentence-level (and often, phrase-level) frolicking into satisfying arcs," Gaffney added, "giving old stories fresh twists and familiar characters new life, splicing genres together to create a whole that is more than the sum of its punny parts."

The Web Files, which is classic Palatini, parodies the 1960s television show *Dragnet* as two "ducktectives" try to "quack" cases that involve robberies on a farm. Fairytale characters abound; Little Boy Blue has an alibi that eliminates him as a potential suspect in a crime where the pilfered objects include, among other things, a peck of pickled peppers. Beloved by readers, *The Web Files* was named a notable book by the American Library Association and earned several state book awards.

In *Earthquack!* Palatini treats readers to a takeoff on the Henny Penny warning that "the sky is falling"—except that, in this case, it is the ground that is rumbling. A beloved nursery song, "The Farmer in the Dell" undergoes a slight skewering when the author plays it back

Margie Palatini's humorous picture book The Web Files *features cartoon art by Richard Egielski.* (Hyperion Books for Children, 2001. Copyright © 2001 by Margie Palatini. Reprinted by permission of Disney-Hyperion, an imprint of Disney Book Group LLC. All rights reserved.)

Palatini teams up with artist Brian Ahjar to create the whimsical picture book **Gone with the Wand.** (Orchard Books, 2009. Illustrations copyright © 2009 by Brian Ajhar. All rights reserved. Reproduced by permission of Scholastic Inc.)

in reverse order in *The Cheese,* as first the rat, then a cat, dog, child, mother, and farmer, all decide that the cheese is too tasty to stand alone. In *Earthquack!* "Palatini's text is funny, with contemporary dialogue, puns, and a fast-paced narrative rich in rhythm and alliteration (but not overwhelmingly so)," noted *School Library Journal* contributor Carol L. MacKay. As *Booklist* critic Gillian Engberg noted, the author's "raucous twist" in a well-known song benefits from the "high-energy, mixed media" illustrations created by Steve Johnson and Lou Fancher. By including the lyrics to the original song throughout the pages of *The Cheese,* Palatini produces a book that "will no doubt be the feature star in a number of sing-alongs," according to *School Library Journal* contributor Susan Moorhead.

Another time-honored story gets the Palatini treatment in *The Three Silly Billies.* Here a surly troll demands a fee from anyone wishing to cross the wooden bridge he guards. Billy Bob, Billy Bo, and Just Plain Billy do not have the necessary funds, so they convince other travelers—including the Three Bears, Little Red Riding Hood, and Jack the beanstalk climber—to pool their resources. "The sounds of the words and the puns . . . are as much fun as the quarrels," remarked *Booklist* critic Hazel Rochman.

Palatini uses both "The Three Little Pigs" and "Little Red Riding Hood" as the starting point for *Bad Boys.* Willy and Wally Wolf have a bad track record: by now they have escaped from three very angry pigs as well as

from a testy Red Riding Hood. Going undercover, they disguise themselves by wearing "sheep's clothing." Because the "sheep" in question are wearing dresses, the wily wolves rename themselves Willimina and Wallanda and infiltrate the flock in drag. All goes well until the shearer relieves them of their furry coats, leaving the two wolves knitting to cover their nakedness. According to a reviewer for *Publishers Weekly,* Palatini's author's "flair for puns and arch repartee shines through every exchange."

Willy and Wally return in *Bad Boys Get Cookie!* and *Bad Boys Get Henpecked!,* both of which feature Henry Cole's engaging art. In *Bad Boys Get Cookie!* Palatini draws on the childhood classics "Hanzel and Gretel" and "The Gingerbread Man," as the two wolves decide to track down a tasty treat that proves smarter than they are, while "The Little Red Hen" plays into the plot of *Bad Boys Get Henpecked!* In *School Library Journal* Peper L. Nyman dubbed *Bad Boys Get Cookie!* a "pun-filled adventure replete with tomfoolery, fairy-tale references, and attempted cookie thievery," while a *Kirkus Reviews* writer praised the book's "merry, slapstick art."

In Palatini's slightly askew fairy tale *Mary Had a Little Ham* a little pig named Stanley begins a career on Broadway with the encouragement of his friend, Mary. With a nod to adult storytellers, *Mary Had a Little Ham* contains sly theatrical references, as when Stanley appears in a production of *Pork Chop on a Hot Tin Roof.* With another nod to classic productions, *Gone with the Wand* finds a fairy godmother looking for a new line of work after her magic wand goes on the fritz. A *Kirkus Reviews* contributor wrote that in *Mary Had a Little Ham* Palatini "keeps the puns and jokes coming thick and fast, even as she keeps narrative tongue firmly in cheek." With its "delightful, droll spin on familiar fairy-tale characters," *Gone with the Wand* features what *Booklist* critic Shelle Rosenfeld dubbed an "entertaining tale of friendship, magic, and overcoming challenges."

In the fanciful *Broom Mates* Gritch the witch—who also appears in Palatini's debut book *Piggie Pie!,* as well as in *Zoom Broom*—is busy throwing a "howliday" party. When her sister, Mag the Hag, shows up early, sibling rivalry ensues, sparking a witches' competition for the affection of their "mummy." *Booklist* writer Jennifer Mattson noted that Gritch and Mag favor fashion accessories that look like they may have come from country singer Dolly Parton's wardrobe and concluded that, "throughout, [the author's inclusion of] puns and witchy bons mots will carry children along on a comic tidal wave."

Described by *School Library Journal* reviewer Kara Schaff Dean as a "hilarious story about an awkward subject," *Gorgonzola: A Very Stinkysaurus* finds an orphaned triceratops in the dark about why he has no friends. Finally a brave bird sheds light on Gorgonzola's quandary by explaining that dinos need to bathe, brush their teeth, and blow their noses in order to gain

social acceptance. Dean recommended the book as useful for parents of those who need to be "wrestle[d] into the bathtub or dentist's chair," and a *Kirkus Reviews* writer described *Gorgonzola* as "redolent with high-spirited humor and capped by a magnificent pun."

Wily animals are the focus of many of Palatini's farmyard tales. A pair of slovenly pigs turns the tables on their barnyard neighbors in *Oink?* as, try as they might, they are unable to competently master the fine arts of house painting, harvesting, or shoveling, and end up being waited on by the other animals. *Shelly* concerns a young duckling who refuses to come out of his shell, despite the protestations of his three older sisters. Each sister attempts to coax Shelly outside by exhibiting her unique talent, but it is not until the siblings leave that the little fellow emerges, ready to engage in the quiet activities he loves. According to *School Library Journal* reviewer Robin L. Gibson, *Shelly* "is a story for all children who march to a different drummer." Birds of another feather are the subject of *Three French Hens,* a "clever and original tale," in the words of a *Kirkus Reviews* writer. When Poulette, Colette, and Fifi get lost in the mail during the holidays, they wind up at the home of Phil Fox, a bushy-tailed, down-on-his-luck fellow from the Bronx who perks up with the thought that he has scored a free meal. As *Horn Book* reviewer Claire E. Gross stated, "this feel-good farce will leave readers speaking in French accents."

Palatini chooses an unlikely picture-book hero in her stories *Moosetache, Mooseltoe,* and *Moosekitos: A Moose Family Reunion:* a moose with an enormous moosetache. In *Moosekitos* Moose summons his relatives from Moosechusetts and Moossissippi for a family reunion. Poor Moose cannot get them all to stay in one place long enough to take a family picture, however,

because busy family members set out in all different directions from the lodge to hike, swim, and bike. "The puns are fun for confident readers, and work well when read aloud," noted Jane Barrer in a *School Library Journal.*

Featuring anthropomorphosized bovine Hilda Mae Heifer, *Moo Who?* and *Boo-Hoo Moo* shift the attention from moose to cows. *Moo Who?* finds Hilda Mae Heifer hit by a flying cow pie and knocked unconscious, only to wake up unable to recall what sound she is supposed to make. Other animals help her by giving Hilda hints, and it is the cat that finally returns the befuddled cow to normal, leaving the other animals running for earplugs. Hilda's farm friends come to her aid again in *Boo-Hoo Moo* as the hefty heifer feels sad and listless and the conclusion is that a contest for the saddest song is in order. In *Moo Who?* "Palatini maintains a simultaneously arch and familiar tone throughout, narrating like a daffy relative," wrote a contributor for *Publishers Weekly,* while *School Library Journal* contributor Susan Weitz dubbed *Boo-Hoo Moo* a clever satire of television's *American Idol* in which illustrator Keith Graves "escalates the sophisticated silliness."

Palatini's *Stinky Smelly Feet: A Love Story* finds duck sweethearts Dolores and Douglas in love. Unfortunately, poor Dolores—as well as everyone else who comes in contact with her true love—keels over in the vicinity of Douglas and his feet. Their love survives, however, in spite of the smell. A *Kirkus Reviews* critic noted that Palatini "delivers her story with her usual sly, understated humor." The author's "characteristic exaggeration and outrageousness are in full swing in this goofy tale," wrote *School Library Journal* reviewer Marge Loch-Wouters, adding that the story will be especially enjoyed by kids "who delight in subversive humor."

A young girl tries every trick imaginable to convince her parents to buy her a furry friend in *The Perfect Pet.* Despite Elizabeth's best efforts, her parents resist the girl's suggestions to trade in her prickly cactus for something more cuddly, such as a dog, a horse, or even a rat. Then the youngster comes up with the ideal solution: adopting a bug that fits perfectly with the family on their living room couch. "Palatini is once again exercising her masterful grip on picture-book humor," noted a critic for *Kirkus Reviews.*

In *Geek Chic: The Zoey Zone* Palatini turns her attention to older readers, writing and illustrating a story that has the quality of a graphic novel. Fifth grader Zoey realizes that her favorite fun-time activities—catching bullfrogs and memorizing facts about the U.S. presidents—will not win her any points on the Cool scale at school. However, her ranking rises when her clever use of an old fedora to hide her slept-upon hair at school wins her some surprising attention from professional arbiters of cool: reps from a popular magazine. Zoey's "brisk, hilarious commentary and confessions" will attract preteen readers, predicted Rochman, the critic adding that *Geek Chic* has "a real story that builds to a sur-

A common search leads to a surprising ending in Palatini's **The Perfect Pet,** *a picture book featuring artwork by Bruce Whatley.* (HarperCollins Publishers, 2003. Illustrations copyright © 2003 by Bruce Whatley. Used by permission of HarperCollins Children's Books, a division of HarperCollins Publishers.)

prising climax." Noting the book's graphic format, which incorporates "wrinkled-looking notes, varied typefaces, [and] wacky line drawings," Tina Zubak added in *School Library Journal* that Palatini's tale will likely appeal to tweens "who cultivate offbeat interests with as much enthusiasm and zaniness as Zoey."

As her list of publications continues to grow, Palatini's works remain consistently popular with readers and critics alike. The reason is simple; as Gaffney explained: The popular author's "snort-worthy way with words puts puns, rhymes, and refrains to work in the service of narrative, using familiar hooks to snare readers in a refreshingly original whole."

Biographical and Critical Sources

PERIODICALS

Booklist, April 15, 1997, Lauren Peterson, review of *Moosetache,* p. 1436; October 1, 1998, Stephanie Zvirin, review of *Zoom Broom,* p. 336; September 1, 2000, Ilene Cooper, review of *Mooseltoe,* p. 134; May 1, 2001, Ilene Cooper, review of *The Web Files,* p. 1690; September 1, 2001, Kathy Broderick, review of *Tub-Boo-Boo,* p. 117; July, 2002, Hazel Rochman, review of *Earthquack!,* p. 1860; July, 2003, Helen Rosenberg, review of *The Perfect Pet,* p. 1898; November 1, 2003, Jennifer Mattson, review of *Broom Mates,* p. 505; November 15, 2003, GraceAnne A. DeCandido, review of *Bad Boys,* p. 602; December 15, 2003, Jennifer Mattson, review of *Mary Had a Little Ham,* p. 754; August 1, 2004, GraceAnne A. DeCandido, review of *Moosekitos: A Moose Family Reunion,* p. 1944; September 1, 2004, Terry Glover, review of *Moo Who?,* p. 135; October 1, 2004, Todd Morning, review of *The Sweet Tooth,* p. 335; March 1, 2005, Hazel Rochman, review of *The Three Silly Billies,* p. 1205; November 1, 2005, Ilene Cooper, review of *Three French Hens,* p. 41; February 1, 2006, Gillian Engberg, review of *Shelly,* p. 56; March 15, 2006, Kathleen Odean, review of *Oink?,* p. 53; May 15, 2007, Gillian Engberg, review of *The Cheese,* p. 50; October 15, 2008, Hazel Rochman, review of *Geek Chic: The Zoey Zone,* p. 39; May 15, 2009, Shelle Rosenfeld, review of *Gone with the Wand,* p. 45.

Horn Book, March-April, 1996, Ann A. Flowers, review of *Piggie Pie,* p. 189; May, 2000, review of *The Web Files,* p. 314; November-December, 2005, Claire E. Gross, review of *Three French Hens,* p. 695.

Kirkus Reviews, May 1, 2002, review of *Earthquack!,* p. 664; March 15, 2003, review of *The Perfect Pet,* p. 475; June 15, 2003, review of *Broom Mates,* p. 862; August 1, 2003, review of *Bad Boys,* p. 1021; September 15, 2003, review of *Mary Had a Little Ham,* p. 1180; May 1, 2004, review of *Stinky Smelly Feet: A Love Story,* p. 446; May 15, 2004, review of *Moo Who?,* p. 496; June 1, 2004, review of *Moosekitos,* p. 539; August 1, 2004, review of *The Sweet Tooth,* p. 748; June 1, 2005, review of *The Three Silly Billies,*

p. 642; November 1, 2005, review of *Three French Hens,* p. 1195; December 15, 2005, review of *Shelly,* p. 1326; August 15, 2006, review of *Bad Boys Get Cookie!,* p. 849; August 1, 2007, review of *No Biting, Louise;* April 1, 2008, review of *Gorgonzola.*

Publishers Weekly, March 3, 1997, review of *Moosetache,* p. 74; April 27, 1998, review of *Zak's Lunch,* p. 66; November 9, 1998, review of *Zoom Broom,* p. 76; September 13, 1999, review of *Ding Dong Ding Dong,* p. 83; May 14, 2001, review of *The Web Files,* p. 81; July 2, 2001, review of *Goldie Is Mad,* p. 78; August 20, 2001, review of *Tub-Boo-Boo,* p. 79; March 15, 2002, review of *The Perfect Pet,* p. 475; May 6, 2002, review of *Earthquack!,* p. 57; August 4, 2003, review of *Broom Mates,* p. 77; October 6, 2003, review of *Bad Boys,* p. 83, review of *Mary Had a Little Ham,* p. 84; April 26, 2004, review of *Stinky Smelly Feet,* p. 65; June 14, 2004, review of *Moo Who?,* p. 62; November 1, 2004, review of *Sweet Tooth,* p. 60; September 26, 2005, review of *Three French Hens,* p. 86; February 13, 2006, review of *Shelly,* p. 89; April 2, 1007, review of *The Cheese,* p. 55; September 3, 2007, review of *No Biting, Louise,* p. 57.

School Library Journal, May, 2000, Shawn Brommer, review of *Good as Goldie,* p. 151; October, 2000, review of *Mooseltoe,* p. 62; April, 2001, Elaine Lesh Morgan, review of *Lab Coat Girl in My Triple-Decker Hero,* p. 148; July, 2001, Laura Scott, review of *Goldie Is Mad,* p. 86; October, 2001, Linda M. Kenton, review of *Tub-Boo-Boo,* p. 128; November, 2001, John Peters, review of *The Web Files,* p. 132; June, 2002, Carol L. MacKay, review of *Earthquack!,* p. 106; May, 2003, Marlene Gawron, review of *The Perfect Pet,* p. 128; September, 2003, Maryann H. Owen, review of *Broom Mates,* p. 186; November, 2003, Helen Foster Jones, review of *Bad Boys,* p. 112, Ellen A. Greever, review of *Mary Had a Little Ham,* p. 112; June, 2004, Marge Loch-Wouters, review of *Stinky Smelly Feet,* p. 116; July, 2004, Steven Engelfried, review of *Moo Who?,* p. 84, and Jane Barrer, review of *Moosekitos,* p. 84; November, 2004, James K. Irwin, review of *Sweet Tooth,* p. 114; June, 2005, Steven Engelfried, review of *The Web Files,* p. 56; August, 2005, Susan Hepler, review of *The Three Silly Billies,* p. 103; February, 2006, Robin L. Gibson, review of *Shelly,* p. 108; March, 2006, Maryann H. Owen, review of *Oink?,* p. 200; October, 2006, Piper L. Nyman, review of *Bad Boys Get Cookie!,* p. 122; June, 2007, Susan Moorhead, review of *The Cheese,* p. 119; September, 2007, Donna Atmur, review of *No Biting, Louise,* p. 173; May, 2008, Kara Schaff Dean, review of *Gorgonzola,* p. 105; December, 2008, Tina Zubak, review of *Geek Chic,* p. 134; February, 2009, Susan Weitz, review of *Boo-Hoo Moo,* p. 82.

ONLINE

Bulletin of the Center for Children's Books Online, http://bbcb.lis.uiuc.edu/ (July 1, 2006), Loretta M. Gaffney, "Rising Star—Margie Palatini."

Margie Palatini Home Page, http://www.margiepalatini.com (November 5, 2009).*

PATRICELLI, Leslie

Personal

Born in WA; married; husband's name Jason (a musician); children: Beck, Tia, Tatum. *Education:* University of Washington, bachelor's degree (communications); attended School of Visual Concepts (Seattle, WA).

Addresses

Home—Ketcham, ID.

Career

Writer and illustrator. Worked variously as a ski instructor in Italy, and a nanny, advertising copywriter, and animator.

Awards, Honors

Child magazine Best of the Year selection, 2003, for *Yummy YUCKY, Quiet LOUD,* and *BIG Little,* 2005, for *Binky* and *Blankie;* Best Books for Children designation, Chicago Public Library, 2007, for *The Birthday Box;* Scripps-Howard Best Children's Book of the Year designation, 2008, for *Baby HAPPY Baby SAD* and *No NO Yes YES;* Boston Globe/Horn Book Honor Book designation, 2009, for *Higher! Higher!*

Writings

SELF-ILLUSTRATED BOARD BOOKS

BIG Little, Candlewick Press (Cambridge, MA), 2003.
Quiet LOUD, Candlewick Press (Cambridge, MA), 2003.
Yummy YUCKY, Candlewick Press (Cambridge, MA), 2003.
Binky, Candlewick Press (Cambridge, MA), 2005.
Blankie, Candlewick Press (Cambridge, MA), 2005.
Baby HAPPY Baby SAD, Candlewick Press (Cambridge, MA), 2008.
No NO Yes YES, Candlewick Press (Cambridge, MA), 2008.

OTHER; SELF-ILLUSTRATED

(With Michelle Gruening) *Espresso Served Here! Featuring Linda Latte: The Official Espresso Humor Book,* Gooddog Press (Seattle, WA), 1993.
The Birthday Box (picture book), Candlewick Press (Cambridge, MA), 2007.
Higher! Higher! (picture book), Candlewick Press (Somerville, MA), 2009.
The Patterson Puppies and the Rainy Day (picture book), Candlewick Press (Somerville, MA), 2009.

Sidelights

Board books featuring toddler-friendly cartoon images are the specialty of Utah author/illustrator Leslie Patricelli. With titles such as *Yummy YUCKY, Quiet LOUD, Blankie,* and *Baby HAPPY Baby SAD,* she brings delight to young children eager to put names to the things in the world around them. Expanding into large-format picture books, Patricelli has also created *Higher! Higher!,* an award-winning story about a young girl's exhilarating ride on a swing that *Booklist* critic Carolyn Phelan dubbed "a wonderfully simple book that's simply wonderful for reading aloud." In each of her books, the author/illustrator features her characteristic acrylic images, which are heavily outlined and often feature smiling, diaper-clad toddlers. In a review of *Blankie* for *Booklist,* Ilene Cooper wrote that the simply drawn, "pleasing figures" contribute to Patricelli's "warm, comforting view of a toddler's daily world," and in *School Library Journal* Richelle Roth praised the "delightful and amusing acrylic illustrations" in *Baby HAPPY Baby SAD.*

Every parent learns that, to a young child, the container is often a better toy than what it contains, and Patricelli taps into this toddler truism in *The Birthday Box.* In her story, a smiling toddler pulls the festive wrapping paper from a large cardboard box, and suddenly his play options include a sailing ship, an airplane, a toboggan, and a cozy den in which to take a nap. "Patricelli's simple, first-person narration is refreshing," wrote Martha Topol, reviewing *The Birthday Box* in *School Library Journal,* and her simple illustrations are "expressive and endearing." According to *New York Times Book*

Leslie Patricelli's engaging cartoon art captures the rambunctious toddler spirit in her picture book No NO Yes YES. *(Candlewick Press, 2008.*
Copyright © 2008 by Leslie Patricelli. All rights reserved. Reproduced by permission of the publisher Candlewick Press, Inc., Somerville, MA.)

Review contributor Joanna Rudge Long, "babies will relate to the bright colors, clear drawings, and toddler-proven activities" in *The Birthday Box.*

Biographical and Critical Sources

PERIODICALS

Booklist, April 1, 2005, Gillian Engberg, review of *Blankie,* p. 1369; February 19, 2009, Carolyn Phelan, review of *Higher! Higher!,* p. 80.
Horn Book, March-April, 2009, Martha V. Parravano, review of *Higher! Higher!,* p. 183.
Kirkus Reviews, March 1, 2007, review of *The Birthday Box,* p. 229; July 1, 2008, review of *No NO Yes YES;* February 1, 2009, review of *Higher! Higher!*
New York Times Book Review, April 15, 2007, Joanna Rudge Long, review of *The Birthday Box,* p. 19.
School Library Journal, July, 2005, Sheilah Kosco, reviews of *Binky* and *Blanky,* p. 80; May, 2007, Martha Topol, review of *The Birthday Box,* p. 106; April, 2008, Richelle Roth, review of *Baby HAPPY Baby SAD,* p. 118; February, 2009, Gay Lynn Van Vleck, review of *Higher! Higher!,* p. 82.

ONLINE

Leslie Patricelli Home Page, http://www.lesliepatricelli. com (November 10, 2009).
Random House Web site, http://www.randomhouse.com/ (November 10, 2009), "Leslie Patricelli."*

*　　*　　*

PEARLE, Ida

Personal

Born in New York, NY. *Education:* The Cooper Union for the Advancement of Science and Art, B.F.A.

Addresses

Home—New York, NY. *E-mail*—ida@idapearle.com.

Career

Author, musician, and collage artist. Violinist, performing and recording with numerous musical groups.

Writings

(Self-illustrated) *A Child's Day: An Alphabet of Play,* Harcourt (Orlando, FL), 2008.

Sidelights

Born and raised in New York City, Ida Pearle shares her creativity with others through musical performance—she is a talented violinist—as well as through her unique cut-paper collages. In her studies at The Cooper Union, one of the most selective art schools in the United States, Pearle was encouraged to follow a personalized curriculum that allowed her to master her medium of choice and expand its creative expression.

Featuring intricately detailed, nostalgic images of childhood that call to mind Japanese woodcuts, *A Child's Day: An Alphabet of Play* marks Pearle's first foray into picture-book illustration. Featuring a poem by Robert Louis Stevenson, the book brings to life an alphabet full of action words, from "act" to "zoom", each accompanied by what *Booklist* critic Patricia Austin described as a "bold, crisp" image featuring "colorfully patterned papers and [a] great use of line." In *Kirkus Reviews* a critic noted Pearle's inclusion of children of many ethnicities and observed that her "word choices and illustrations vary from straightforward . . . to unusual." *A Child's Day* serves as "a colorful ode to the world of young children," maintained Becca Zerkin, the critic adding in her *New York Times Book Review* appraisal that "loving details lie in the children's silhouettes, head tilts and gestures."

On her home page, Pearle described the techniques used in the carefully constructed cut-paper collage art that appears in both *A Child's Day* and the artist's other graphic work. "Each collage . . . is primarily composed of Color-aid, a silk-screened artist's paper," she explained. "Other specialty papers . . . are used to add accents of pattern and texture to the collages. For example, Origami paper is used for clothing and other forms which require patterns. Other papers used, include construction paper, craft paper, wrapping paper, tissue paper, wallpaper, and decorative paper. Materials like string, ribbon, and cloth lend the pieces even greater dimension and texture."

Biographical and Critical Sources

PERIODICALS

Booklist, November 1, 2008, Patricia Austin, review of *A Child's Day: An Alphabet of Play,* p. 45.
Kirkus Reviews, July 15, 2008, review of *A Child's Day.*
New York Times Book Review, November 9, 2008, Becca Zerkin, review of *A Child's Day,* p. 22.
School Library Journal, October, 2008, Sally R. Dow, review of *A Child's Day,* p. 135.

ONLINE

Ida Pearle Home Page, http://www.idapearle.com (November 5, 2009).*

*　　*　　*

PFISTER, Marcus

Personal

Born in Berne, Switzerland; married; wife's name, Kathrin; children: four. *Education:* Attended art school

Marcus Pfister (Used with permission of North-South Books, Inc., New York.)

(Berne, Switzerland). *Hobbies and other interests:* Travel, fine arts, reading novels, mysteries, and travel stories.

Addresses
Home—Berne, Switzerland.

Career
Author, graphic artist, and illustrator of children's books. Freelance writer, 1986—. Has worked at advertising agencies in Berne and Zurich, Switzerland; graphic designer, photographer, sculptor, and fine-art painter.

Awards, Honors
Critici in Erba Prize, Bologna Children's Book Fair, and Christopher Award, both 1993, American Booksellers Book of the Year for Children's Book, 1995, and Children's Choice Book, International Reading Association (IRA)/Children's Book Council, all for *The Rainbow Fish;* Children's Choices selection, IRA, 1996, for *Rainbow Fish to the Rescue!*

Writings

SELF-ILLUSTRATED

The Sleepy Owl, translated by J.J. Curle, North-South Books (New York, NY), 1986.

Where Is My Friend?, North-South Books (New York, NY), 1986.

Sun and Moon, translated by R. Lanning, North-South Books (New York, NY), 1990.

Shaggy, translated by Lenny Hort, North-South Books (New York, NY), 1990.

(Editor) *I See the Moon: Good-Night Poems and Lullabies,* North-South Books (New York, NY), 1991.

The Christmas Star, translated by J. Alison James, North-South Books (New York, NY), 1993.

Chris and Croc, North-South Books (New York, NY), 1994.

Dazzle the Dinosaur, translated by J. Alison James, North-South Books (New York, NY), 1994.

Wake up, Santa Claus!, translated by J. Alison James, North-South Books (New York, NY), 1996.

Milo and the Magical Stones, translated by Marianne Martens, North-South Books (New York, NY), 1997.

How Leo Learned to Be King, translated by J. Alison James, North-South Books (New York, NY), 1997.

Make a Wish, Honey Bear!, translated by Sibylle Kazeroid, North-South Books (New York, NY), 1999.

The Happy Hedgehog, translated by J. Alison James, North-South Books (New York, NY), 2000.

Milo and the Mysterious Island, translated by Marianne Martens, North-South Books (New York, NY), 2001.

Just the Way You Are, translated by Marianne Martens, North-South Books (New York, NY), 2002.

The Magic Book, translated by Marianne Martens, North-South Books (New York, NY), 2003.

Aaron's Secret Message, translated by Marianne Martens, North-South Books (New York, NY), 2005.

Holey Moley, translated by J. Alison James, North-South Books (New York, NY), 2006.

Charlie at the Zoo, translated by J. Alison James, North-South Books (New York, NY), 2007.

Henri, Egg Artiste, translated by J. Alison James, North-South Books (New York, NY), 2007.

The Friendly Monsters, North-South Books (New York, NY), 2008.

"PENGUIN PETE" SERIES

Penguin Pete, translated by Anthea Bell, North-South Books (New York, NY), 1987.

Penguin Pete's New Friends, translated by Anthea Bell, North-South Books (New York, NY), 1988.

Penguin Pete and Pat, translated by Anthea Bell, North-South Books (New York, NY), 1989.

Penguin Pete, Ahoy!, translated by Rosemary Lanning, North-South Books (New York, NY), 1993.

Penguin Pete and Little Tim, translated by Rosemary Lanning, North-South Books (New York, NY), 1994.

"HOPPER" SERIES

Hopper, North-South Books (New York, NY), 1991.

Hopper Hunts for Spring, translated by Rosemary Lanning, North-South Books (New York, NY), 1992.

(With wife, Kathrin Siegenthaler) *Hopper's Easter Surprise,* translated by Rosemary Lanning, North-South Books (New York, NY), 1993.

Hang on, Hopper!, North-South Books (New York, NY), 1995.

Hopper's Treetop Adventure, translated by Rosemary Lanning, North-South Books (New York, NY), 1997.

"RAINBOW FISH" SERIES

The Rainbow Fish, translated by J. Alison James, North-South Books (New York, NY), 1992.

Rainbow Fish to the Rescue!, translated by J. Alison James, North-South Books (New York, NY), 1997.

The Rainbow Fish Treasury (contains *The Rainbow Fish* and *Rainbow Fish to the Rescue!*), translated by J. Alison James, North-South Books (New York, NY), 1997.

Rainbow Fish and the Big Blue Whale, translated by J. Alison James, North-South Books (New York, NY), 1998.

Rainbow Fish and the Sea Monster's Cave, North-South Books (New York, NY), 2001.

Rainbow Fish 1, 2, 3, North-South Books (New York, NY), 2002.

Rainbow Fish A, B, C, North-South Books (New York, NY), 2002.

Playtime with Rainbow Fish, Night Sky Books (New York, NY), 2003.

The Rainbow Fish Floor Puzzle Book, North-South Books (New York, NY), 2003.

Rainbow Fish Sea of Riddles, North-South Books (New York, NY), 2003.

Rainbow Fish Hide-and-Seek, North-South Books (New York, NY), 2003.

Rainbow Fish Counting (board book), North-South Books (New York, NY), 2004.

Rainbow Fish Opposites (board book), North-South Books (New York, NY), 2005.

Rainbow Fish Finds His Way, North-South Books (New York, NY), 2006.

The Rainbow Fish has been translated into thirty languages, including Spanish, German, French, Dutch, Greek, Korean, Thai, Croatian, Khmer, Tagalog and Faroese. Some of *The Rainbow Fish* books are available in bilingual, Spanish-language editions.

"BERTIE" SERIES

Bertie at Bedtime, North-South Books (New York, NY), 2008.

Bertie: Just like Daddy, North-South Books (New York, NY), 2009.

ILLUSTRATOR

Gerda Marie Scheidl, *Four Candles for Simon: A Christmas Story,* translated by Anthea Bell, North-South Books (New York, NY), 1987.

Kathrin Siegenthaler, *Santa Claus and the Woodcutter,* translated by Elizabeth Crawford, North-South Books (New York, NY), 1988.

Gerda Marie Scheidl, *Miriam's Gift: A Christmas Story,* translated by Rosemary Lanning, North-South Books (New York, NY), 1989.

Adaptations

The Rainbow Fish inspired products such as puppets and a mobile; its character was also used in stories by others and in videos produced by Sony Entertainment. *The Rainbow Fish* was also adapted as a stage musical.

Sidelights

A Swiss author and illustrator, Marcus Pfister is the popular and prolific creator of warm, gentle works that are credited for their sensitive depictions of emotion and for their distinctive, eye-catching illustrations. Pfister's books—written in German and translated into English—feature animal protagonists with human characteristics and explore friendship, courage, sharing, and other themes that resonate with young readers. He is best known as the artist behind Rainbow Fish, a sweet-faced aquatic creature with beautiful iridescent, holographic scales that has shimmered through dozens of books since making its U.S. debut in 1992. Pfister cites such revered authors as Eric Carle and Leo Lionni among his influences. "They all have a simplicity in their work that I like very much," he told Ingram Library Services online interviewer Kristen Switzer. "The most important thing is to be able to 'translate' (with words and pictures) even complex and complicated themes in an easy, child-like language."

Pfister is also the creator of other well-received series, including "Penguin Pete," about a small Antarctic penguin and his family, and "Hopper," featuring a childlike

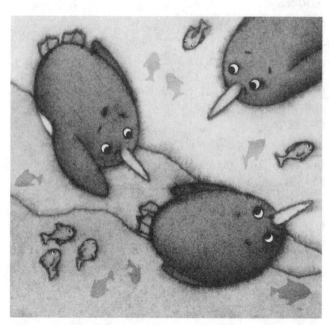

Pfister's self-illustrated picture books include **Penguin Pete,** *which combines a simple story with Pfister's cartoon art.* (North-South Books, 1987. Copyright © 1987 by NordSüd Verlag AG, CH-8005 Zurich/Switzerland. Used by permission of North-South Books Books Inc., New York.)

white hare. In addition, Pfister has written and illustrated a number of books about shared friendships between animals, such as *Milo and the Magical Stones, Holey Moley,* and *Charlie at the Zoo.*

Often considered a moralist who creates parables in picture-book form, Pfister underscores his works with themes about sharing, trust, cooperation, consideration, courage, and acting responsibly. Written in simple but fluid texts, his stories are generally illustrated with pen drawings and watercolors in pastel colors. A distinctive feature of many of Pfister's books is their foil technique: the artist uses holographic foil stamping to create pictures that have a shimmering, reflective effect when placed in the light. This technique has made Rainbow Fish an enduring icon of modern children's literature and has added visual excitement to other Pfister titles as well.

Born in Berne, Switzerland, Pfister was the third of five children. He attended art school in Berne while working at an advertising agency. In 1981 he moved to Zurich to work as a graphic designer at another agency. He has also done photography, sculpting, and painting. Two years after moving to Zurich, he took a leave of absence and traveled around the United States for six months with his wife Kathrin, a teacher, and his three children, Yannik, Miro, and Nina. It was during his family's trip to America that Pfister decided to devote more time to his own artistic pursuits. After returning to Switzerland, he began working part time at the advertising agency while writing and illustrating his first book, *The Sleepy Owl.*

Published in 1986, *The Sleepy Owl* is a picture book about Little Owl and her human friend, Tom. The two friends realize that they cannot play together because of the difference in their sleeping patterns and agree to somehow keep their friendship fresh anyway. At the end of the story, Tom paints an owl face on his kite to let Little Owl know that he still remembers her. Pfister illustrated *The Sleepy Owl* with rich, dark-hued watercolors that are textured by sponge applications of color. Susan Scheps predicted in *School Library Journal:* "The appeal of the illustrations will ensure the popularity of this . . . pleasant story."

In Pfister's board book *Where Is My Friend?,* a lonely porcupine searches for a companion and encounters a cactus, a brush, a seed, and a pod before finding a real fellow porcupine. Writing in *Horn Book,* Anita Silvey called *Where Is My Friend?* "refreshing because it delves into the realm of emotion for the very young." Louise M. Zuckerman, also reviewing the book, noted in *School Library Journal* that Pfister's porcupine "has a certain amount of appeal and is drawn with some humor."

Penguin Pete appeared in 1987. In this book the smallest penguin in his colony learns to walk, fly, and swim; he also finds a friend who is even smaller than he is.

Pfister illustrates Pete's adventures in pictures that combine cartoonlike caricatures of the penguins with soft, muted watercolors. In *School Library Journal,* Jane Gardner Connor noted that the illustrations "are humorous and appealing." In the second volume of the series, *Penguin Pete's New Friends,* Pete goes fishing by himself when he is shunned by the other penguins for being too small. After falling asleep on top of a whale, he is whisked away to visit with an Eskimo boy and plays with him as well as some sea lions before returning home. Kathryn Weisman, writing in *School Library Journal,* commented that the "soft, child-like illustrations will appeal to very young listeners as will the simple plot line."

As readers rejoin Penguin Pete in other volumes of the series, he gets married to Pat, a blue-beaked penguin, and has a son Tim; explores an abandoned ship and saves the ship's mouse from drowning; and takes little Tim out for winter fun, only to be separated from him and finally reunited. In her review of *Penguin Pete and Little Tim,* Lauren Peterson predicted in *Booklist* that Pfister's "endearing father-and-son team will warm a child's heart on the coldest winter day." The first two volumes of the series, *Penguin Pete* and *Penguin Pete's New Friends,* have also been published as board books.

The first volume of another Pfister series, *Hopper,* is a quiet picture book with illustrations in large pastel watercolors. The story describes how the title character, a small white hare with blue-tipped ears, is reassured by its mother that spring will come after the long winter. Joan McGrath noted in *School Library Journal* that *Hopper* conveys the same sense of security and warmth as "that classic of the nursery by Margaret Wise Brown, *The Runaway Bunny.*" In *Hopper Hunts for Spring* Hopper bounds away from home to look for spring, which it thinks is another animal. The bunny meets a mole and a bear before coming home to be set straight by its mother. In *Hang on, Hopper!* the bunny gets into trouble when it tries to swim across a stream in order to get home more quickly after visiting a friend. Hopper drifts downstream to a beaver's dam, where it makes friends with the beaver and learns that water is dangerous for non-swimmers. Judith Constantinides, writing in *School Library Journal,* praised the book's "lovely pastel watercolors somewhat in the style of Garth Williams's work," and called *Hang on, Hopper!* "a simple story that gently preaches water safety while entertaining readers."

Pfister's best-known book, *The Rainbow Fish,* was first published in English in 1992. An oversize picture book illustrated in fluid watercolors and shimmering holographs, the story revolves around a beautiful but conceited fish that possesses sparkling blue, green, purple, and silver shimmering scales. When Rainbow Fish refuses to share its scales with the plainer fish in its school, it is ostracized. Rainbow Fish becomes lonely and asks a wise octopus for advice. When it gives away its scales, the fish is told, it will discover true happi-

ness. Rainbow Fish does as the octopus suggests and learns that the more one gives away, the happier one feels. Writing in *School Library Journal,* Ellen Fader wrote that *The Rainbow Fish* "is certainly a story written to convey a message, but . . . what three-year-old doesn't need reinforcement about sharing?"

In her *Magpies* review of *The Rainbow Fish,* Anne Freier noted that young readers received the book "with wide-eyed wonder, and parents and teachers welcomed this parable-like tale which reinforced the value of sharing and seeing past possessions in the search for true happiness. It was a storyteller's dream." Although not widely reviewed on its first publication, the book drew fans largely by word of mouth. It became an international bestseller and has since become one of the best-selling picture books of all time, with a variety of spin-off products from games and videos to puppets, postcards, mobiles, and many more books. Such is the popularity of Rainbow Fish that Pfister went on to write new titles himself, while other authors also created stories about the character.

In *Rainbow Fish to the Rescue!,* Rainbow Fish and its friends are playing "flash tag" when a little tiger fish wants to join in. The other fish ignore the tiger fish because it is not equipped with a shiny scale in order to

Pfister treats readers to an undersea adventure in his aquatic-themed picture book The Rainbow Fish. (North-South Books, 1992. Copyright © 1992 by Nord-Süd Verlag AG, Gossau Zurich, Switzerland. Used by permission of North-South Books, Inc., New York.)

play the game. Rainbow Fish disagrees with their decision but is afraid to lose its friends if it speaks up. When a shark appears and puts the tiger fish in danger, it is Rainbow Fish—remembering what it feels like to be an outsider—who organizes the rescue. It has the other fish swim straight for the shark to confuse it, and then it leads the tiger fish to safety. The next time that the fish play the game, it is modified so that the tiger fish can join in. Carolyn Phelan, writing in *Booklist,* predicted that parents and teachers will find *Rainbow Fish to the Rescue!* "a good vehicle for discussing courage in the face of peer pressure."

A gentle whale loves to watch Rainbow Fish and its friends in *Rainbow Fish and the Big Blue Whale.* However, when the whale gets too close, the smaller fish assume that it is going to eat them. The hurt and angry whale pretends to do just that. It is up to Rainbow Fish to restore peace. He makes the fish apologize to the whale, and then they all become friends. A *Kirkus Reviews* critic commented that "some children will never get enough of Rainbow Fish, who has now been promoted to ambassador of peace of the pelagic domain."

Pfister begins each of his holographic works by stretching watercolor paper over a wooden board in order to keep the paper from warping when wet. He then copies his rough sketches onto the paper using pencil. In order to create his backgrounds and blended contours, Pfister uses wet paint on wet paper to get a soft effect; for sharper details, he paints the final picture layer by layer on dry paper. When the illustration is finished, he cuts the paper from the wooden board. He creates his signature holographic foil stamping by taping a piece of transparent film over the picture and then indicating where the foil stamping should go. The foil stamping is applied after the pages are printed.

Pfister has used his holographic illustrations technique in several other picture books. Among these is *Dazzle the Dinosaur,* in which a young dinosaur with a set of glittering spines on his back sets off with his friend Maia to find the vicious Dragonosaurus, who has taken away their ancestral site, a lush valley. After Dazzle and Maia scare away the Dragonosaurus by using Dazzle's spines, they take their families and friends to the peaceful valley. In her *Booklist* review of the work, Lauren Peterson declared that Pfister's "plot is fast paced and imaginative, and the shimmering artwork is integral to the goings-on, not merely decorative."

Other Pfister works include *Make a Wish, Honey Bear!, The Happy Hedgehog,* and *Just the Way You Are.* Each of these titles uses humanlike animals to make points about values and ideals. In *Make a Wish, Honey Bear!* Honey Bear's family members are overly eager to help the little bear come up with a birthday wish. Most of the wishes suggested to Honey Bear are self-serving, however, and in the end he wisely decides just to wish for more happy birthdays. The title character of *The Happy Hedgehog* is happy because he enjoys life's

Pfister chooses an interesting animal character to star in his original story The Happy Hedgehog. (North-South Books, Inc., 2000. Used with permission of North-South Books, Inc., New York.)

simple pleasures. Prodded by his grandfather to be more ambitious, the hedgehog visits other animals that are busier but also certainly not as happy. In *School Library Journal* Holly Belli cited *The Happy Hedgehog* as a book about "the value of dreamers in society." *Just the Way You Are* celebrates diversity as a group of animals, planning a party together, long for each other's attributes until they realize that they each have unique qualities of their own. Martha Link, writing in *School Library Journal,* called the book "a gentle, predictable tale" of special value to teachers "looking for titles on self-esteem and self-acceptance."

Two of Pfister's most highly regarded works are *Milo and the Magical Stones,* an interactive picture book published in tall format in 1997, and its sequel, *Milo and the Mysterious Island.* In *Milo and the Magical Stone,* Milo, a hardworking mouse, lives on an idyllic island. Forced into a cave by the cold of winter, he finds a glowing stone that turns out to be a chunk of gold. When the other mice see Milo's gold—which Pfister represents with reflective gold paper—they want the stones as well. At a pivotal point, the pages split into two horizontal sections that offer young readers the opportunity to choose a "happy" or a "sad" ending. The happy ending finds Milo and the other mice heeding the advice of Balthazar, a wise elder who says that if you take something from the island you should give something in return. The mice then carve stones that add fortification and beauty to the island to show their gratitude. In the alternative ending, the mice are consumed with greed. They squabble, taking so much from the is-

land that they cause it to collapse. A *Publishers Weekly* reviewer liked the way Pfister's watercolors provide "an effective counterpoint to the bright gold of the shiny stones." The critic added: "Pfister fans will definitely want to add this one to their collection."

A similar plot unfolds in *Milo and the Mysterious Island.* This time Milo leads a voyage of discovery to a new island, inhabited by strange, striped mice. Once again the reader can choose between endings—in one, the island mice and the visitors cooperate and share their treasures, learning about each other and enjoying their time together. In the other, distrust and greed cause misunderstanding and hard feelings. In her *School Library Journal* review, Carolyn Jenks felt that the "well-written" story would spark "discussion about . . . encountering people who are different."

A pair of quarrelsome siblings learns the value of cooperation in *Holey Moley.* Tim and Matt, two young mole brothers, cannot agree whether they should dig a hole or build a hill, and after a brief squabble they go their separate ways. After they complete their solo projects, they discover—much to their chagrin—that they have achieved the exact same results. A *Publishers Weekly* critic observed that "the ending arises authentically out of the comedy inherent in a familiar domestic rivalry." DeAnn Okamura in *School Library Journal* complimented the artwork, remarking that Pfister's "warm, earth-toned illustrations with touches of bright flora and fauna have child appeal." A curious duckling goes exploring in *Charlie at the Zoo,* a work that incorporates die-cut pages for visual effect. After waddling away from his pond, Charlie finds himself at a nearby zoo where he encounters hippos, orangutans, chameleons, among other creatures. As the duckling greets each animal, Pfister provides factual data about its diet, appearance, and habitat. "The artwork is detailed and softly realistic," Catherine Callegari wrote in *School Library Journal.*

An ambitious rabbit who wishes to broaden his creative horizons is the focus of *Henri, Egg Artiste.* Tired of painting Easter eggs in traditional fashion, Henri decides to brighten their appearance by copy the styles of the world's most celebrated artists, including Rembrandt and Salvador Dali. Instead of hiding his creations on Easter morning, as expected, Henri proudly displays them on pedestals, creating quite a stir. In *Booklist,* Randall Enos noted that "Pfister's sturdy, broadly appealing illustrations provide an interesting contrast to the styles of the masters," and *School Library Journal* reviewer Carol Schene wrote that the "large illustrations are bright and expressive with perspectives that invite readers into the action."

Pfister introduces an energetic young hippopotamus in *Bertie at Bedtime,* a picture book for beginning readers. Though he needs to be fed and bathed before going to sleep, Bertie convinces his father to chase him around the house, play a game of hide-and-seek, and read a trio

A hippo enjoys a quiet moment at the end of its busy day in Pfister's picture-book import **Bertie at Bedtime.** (NorthSouth Books, 2008. Copyright © 2008 by NordSud Verlag AG, CH-8005 Zurich/Switzerland. Used with permission of North-South Books, Inc., New York.)

of stories. As the evening progresses, the lively hippo manages to outlast his exhausted parent. "Pfister's hippos are an irresistible pair, full of sweetness and life," Abby Nolan stated in *Booklist.* Susan Weitz wrote in *School Library Journal* that Pfister's illustrations employ a variety of floral patterns and are "sweet, funny, and colorful," while a *Kirkus Reviews* writer dubbed them "gentle, sweet and endearing." In a sequel, *Bertie: Just like Daddy,* Bertie and his father spend a day enjoying each other's company. According to *School Library Journal* critic Linda M. Kenton, this work "joins a class of father-and-son books sure to be popular with the youngest children."

Pfister has earned accolades for both his writing and illustrating. Asked what part of the creative process he most enjoys, Pfister told a North-South Books online interviewer: "The most interesting part of my work is inventing new stories, new characters and new concepts. Of course, I do also like to illustrate, but then the really creative part of my work is already done."

Biographical and Critical Sources

BOOKS

Children's Literature Review, Volume 42, Gale (Detroit, MI), 1997.

PERIODICALS

Booklist, January 1, 1993, Carolyn Phelan, review of *The Rainbow Fish,* p. 811; December 15, 1994, Lauren Peterson, review of *Penguin Pete and Little Tim,* p. 760; February 1, 1995, Lauren Peterson, review of *Dazzle the Dinosaur,* p. 1011; September 15, 1995, Carolyn Phelan, review of *Rainbow Fish to the Rescue!,* p. 176; March 15, 1996, Carolyn Phelan, review of *The Rainbow Fish Board Book,* p. 1269; April 1, 1997, April Judge, review of *Hopper's Treetop Adventure,* p. 1338; October 1, 1997, Ilene Cooper, review of *Milo and the Magical Stones,* p. 338; March 1, 1998, Ilene Cooper, review of *How Leo Learned to Be King,* p. 1141; September 15, 1998, Ilene Cooper, review of *Rainbow Fish and the Big Blue Whale,* p. 239; November 1, 1999, Shelley Townsend-Hudson, review of *Make a Wish, Honey Bear!,* p. 540; July, 2002, Lauren Peterson, review of *Just the Way You Are,* p. 1860; November 15, 2007, Krista Hutley, review of *Charlie at the Zoo,* p. 47; December 15, 2007, Randall Enos, review of *Henri, Egg Artiste,* p. 49; April 15, 2008, Abby Nolan, review of *Bertie at Bedtime,* p. 48.

Horn Book, September-October, 1986, Anita Silvey, review of *Where Is My Friend?,* pp. 583-584.

Kirkus Reviews, July 1, 1998, review of *Rainbow Fish and the Big Blue Whale,* p. 976; May 1, 2002, review of *Just the Way You Are,* p. 664; April 1, 2008, review of *Bertie at Bedtime;* September 1, 2008, review of *The Friendly Monsters.*

Magpies, November, 1995, Anne Freier, review of *The Rainbow Fish,* p. 12.

Publishers Weekly, April 14, 1989, review of *Penguin Pete and Pat,* p. 68; October 3, 1994, review of *Dazzle the Dinosaur,* p. 69; September 30, 1996, review of *Wake up, Santa Claus!,* p. 91; June 2, 1997, review of *Milo and the Magical Stone,* p. 71; March 16, 1998, review of *How Leo Learned to Be King,* p. 63; February 14, 2000, review of *The Happy Hedgehog,* p. 197; September 26, 2005, review of *Aaron's Secret Message,* p. 88; March 20, 2006, review of *Holey Moley,* p. 54; August 13, 2007, review of *Charlie at the Zoo,* p. 66.

School Library Journal, October, 1986, Louise M. Zuckerman, review of *Where Is My Friend?,* p. 156; February, 1987, Susan Scheps, review of *The Sleepy Owl,* p. 73; June-July, 1987, Carol McMichael, review of *Camomile Heads for Home,* p. 86; March, 1988, Jane Gardner Connor, review of *Penguin Pete,* p. 174; August, 1988, Kathryn Weisman, review of *Penguin Pete's New Friends,* p. 84; October, 1988, Susan Hepler, review of *Santa Claus and the Woodcutter,* pp. 37-38; July, 1990, Regina Pauly, review of *Sun and Moon,* p. 63; March, 1991, Dorothy Houlihan, review of *Shaggy,* p. 177; September, 1991, Joan McGrath, review of *Hopper,* p. 239; February, 1992, Ronald Jobe, review of *I See the Moon: Good-night Poems and Lullabies,* p. 83; July, 1992, Anne Conor, review of *Hopper Hunts for Spring,* pp. 62-63; November, 1992, Ellen Fader, review of *The Rainbow Fish,* pp. 75-76; January, 1994, Bambi L. Williams, review of *Penguin Pete, Ahoy!,* p. 97; January, 1995, Alexandra Marris, review of *Dazzle the Dinosaur,* pp. 91-92; February,

1995, Lynn Cockett, review of *Penguin Pete and Little Tim,* p. 79; June, 1995, Judy Constantinides, review of *Hang on, Hopper!,* p. 94; October, 1996, Jane Marino, review of *Wake up, Santa Claus!,* p. 39; March, 1997, Sally R. Dow, review of *Hopper's Treetop Adventure,* p. 163; September, 1997, Martha Topol, review of *Milo and the Magical Stones,* p. 190; June, 1998, Mollie Bynum, review of *How Leo Learned to Be King,* p. 116; September, 1998, Jackie Hechtkopf, review of *Rainbow Fish and the Big Blue Whale,* pp. 178-179; November, 1999, Carolyn Jenks, review of *Make a Wish, Honey Bear!,* p. 127; July, 2000, Holly Belli, review of *The Happy Hedgehog,* p. 85; March, 2001, Carolyn Jenks, review of *Milo and the Mysterious Island,* p. 218; September, 2002, Martha Link, review of *Just the Way You Are,* p. 204; February, 2003, Roxanne Burg, review of *Rainbow Fish A, B, C,* p. 119; June, 2006, DeAnn Okamura, review of *Holey Moley,* p. 124; September, 2006, Sandra Welzenbach, review of *Rainbow Fish Finds His Way,* p. 182; October, 2007, Catherine Callegari, review of *Charlie at the Zoo,* p. 125; March, 2008, Carol Schene, review of *Henri, Egg Artiste,* p. 174; May, 2008, Susan Weitz, review of *Bertie at Bedtime,* p. 106; March, 2009, Linda M. Kenton, review of *Just like Daddy,* p. 124.

ONLINE

Children's Literature Comprehensive Database Online, http://www.childrenslit.com/ (January 1, 2009), Sharon Salluzzo and Marilyn Courtot, "Marcus Pfister."

Ingram Library Services Web site, http://www.ingram library.com/ (fall, 2006), Kristen Switzer, interview with Pfister.

North-South Books Web site, http://www.northsouth.com/ (November 15, 2009), "Marcus Pfister."*

R-S

RACOMA, Robin Yoko 1953-
(Robin Yoko Burningham)

Personal

Born 1953; daughter of David Lorch (a band director) and Allie Forbes; married; children: four.

Addresses

Home—Waipahu, HI. *E-mail*—info@robinyokoracoma. com.

Career

Illustrator, fine artist, and graphic designer. Kamehameha Schools (private school for children of Hawaiian ancestry), Honolulu, HI, graphic designer and illustrator of curriculum, beginning 1975. *Exhibitions:* Work exhibited at Honolulu Academy of Arts, 1994.

Awards, Honors

Ka Palapala Po'okela Award for Excellence honorable mention, Hawai'i Book Publisher Association, 1997, for *The Illustrated Hawaiian Dictionary* by Kahikahealani Wight, 2006, for *Princess Pauahi* by Julie Stewart Williams, and 2009, for *Lauka'ie'ie.*

Writings

SELF-ILLUSTRATED

Lauka'ie'ie, Kamehameha Schools Press (Honolulu, HI), 2008.
'O Lauka'ie'ie, Kamehameha Schools Press (Honolulu, HI), 2008.

ILLUSTRATOR

(As Robin Yoko Burningham) Robert Lokomaika'iokalani Snakenberg, *Hawaiian Word Book,* Bess Press (Honolulu, HI), 1983.

(As Robin Yoko Burningham) Mary Kawena Pukui, *Tales of the Menuhune,* Kamehameha Schools Press (Honolulu, HI), 1985.
(As Robin Yoko Burningham) Julie Stewart Williams, *And the Birds Appeared,* University of Hawaii Press (Honolulu, HI), 1988.
(As Robin Yoko Burningham) Suelyn Ching Tune, *How Maui Slowed the Sun,* University of Hawaii Press (Honolulu, HI), 1988.
(As Robin Yoko Burningham) Robert Lokomaika'iokalani Snackenberg, *The Hawaiian Sentence Book,* Bess Press (Honolulu, HI), 1988.
(As Robin Yoko Burningham) Suelyn Ching Tune, *Ma'aui Goes Fishing,* University of Hawaii Press (Honolulu, HI), 1991.
(As Robin Yoko Burningham) Suelyn Ching Tune, *Ma'aui and the Secret of Fire,* University of Hawaii Press (Honolulu, HI), 1991.
(As Robin Yoko Burningham) Ruby Hasegawa Lowe, *Lili' uokalani,* Kamehameha Schools/Bernice Pauahi Bishop Estate (Honolulu, HI), 1993.
(As Robin Yoko Burningham) Peter Galuteria, *Lunalilo,* Kamehameha Schools/Bernice Pauahi Bishop Estate (Honolulu, HI), 1993.
(As Robin Yoko Burningham) Jean Iwata Cachola, *Kamehameha III: Kauikeaouli,* Kamehameha Schools Press (Honolulu, HI), 1995.
Naomi N.Y. Chun, *Hawaiian Canoe-building Traditions,* Kamehameha Schools Press (Honolulu, HI), 1995.
(As Robin Yoko Burningham) Rosalin Uphus Comeau, *Kamehameha V: Lot Kapua'iwa,* Kamehameha Schools Press (Honolulu, HI), 1996.
Julie Stewart Williams, *From the Mountains to the Sea: A Hawaiian Lifestyle,* Kamehameha Schools Press (Honolulu, HI), 1997.
Kahika'healani Wight, *Illustrated Hawaiian Dictionary,* Bess Press (Honolulu, HI), 1997, pocket edition, 2005.
Ruby Hasegawa Lowe, *Kamehameha IV, Alexander Liholiho,* Kamehameha Schools Press (Honolulu, HI), 1997.
Ruby Hasegawa Lowe, *David Kala'kaua,* Kamehameha Schools Press (Honolulu, HI), 1999.

Peter Galuteria, *Heart of a Hero: Charles Reed Bishop,* P. Galuteria (Honolulu, HI), 1999.

Julie Stewart Williams and Suelyn Ching Tune, *Kamehameha II: Liholiho and the Impact of Change,* Kamehameha Schools Press (Honolulu, HI), 2001.

Julie Stewart Williams, *Prince Pauahi,* Kamehameha Schools Press (Honolulu, HI), 2005.

Nancy Alpert Mower, *Tutu's Stories,* Kamehameha Schools Press (Honolulu, HI), 2006.

Corinne Matsumoto and Kenda Kauwe, *Children Are Special,* Kamehameha Schools Press (Honolulu, HI), 2006.

Also illustrator of school curricula, including "Where I Live" series by Julie Stewart Williams.

Biographical and Critical Sources

ONLINE

Kamehameha Schools Web site, http://www.ksbe.edu/ (November 10, 2009), "Robin Yoko Racoma."

Robin Yoko Racoma Home Page, http://robinyokoracoma.com (November 10, 2009).

*   *   *

RASCHKA, Chris 1959-
(Christopher Raschka)

Personal

Born March 6, 1959, in Huntingdon, PA; son of Donald F. (an historian) and Hedwig T. (a translator) Durnbaugh; married Lydie Olson (a teacher), August 4, 1984. *Education:* St. Olaf College, B.A., 1981. *Hobbies and other interests:* Yoga, walking, playing solitaire, playing viola and concertina, knitting.

Addresses

Office—310 Riverside Dr., No. 418, New York, NY 10025.

Career

Writer, artist, and musician. Art teacher in St. Croix, Virgin Islands, 1985-86; freelance artist, cartoonist, and editorial illustrator, Ann Arbor, MI, 1987-89; freelance artist and children's book writer and illustrator, New York, NY, 1989—. Intern in an orthopedic clinic in Germany, 1981-82; respite care worker in Ypsilanti, MI, 1982-84. Member, New York City School Volunteers Program; member, Ann Arbor Symphony Orchestra, 1982-84, 1986-89, and Flint Symphony Orchestra, Flint, MI, 1983-84. *Exhibitions:* Artwork included in exhibitions, including Library of Congress, Washington, DC, 1998; Bolzano, Padua, Rome, and Venice, Italy, 1998-

2000; Grand Valley State University, Allendale, MI, 1999; Katonah Museum of Art, Katonah, NY, 2001; Thurber Center Gallery, Columbus, OH, 2003; and Padiglione Esprit Nouveau, Bologna, Italy, 2005.

Member

Authors Guild, Authors League of America, Society of Children's Book Writers and Illustrators, Municipal Art Society, New York-New Jersey Trail Conference.

Awards, Honors

Best Books of the Year citation, *Publishers Weekly,* Notable Children's Book citation, American Library Association (ALA), and Pick of the Lists citation, American Booksellers Association, all 1992, all for *Charlie Parker Played Be Bop; New York Times* Best Illustrated Book of the Year inclusion, Caldecott Honor Book award, ALA, and U.S. winner of UNICEF-Ezra Jack Keats Award, all 1994, all for *Yo! Yes?;* Caldecott Medal, 2006, for *The Hello, Goodbye Window* by Norton Juster.

Writings

FOR CHILDREN; SELF-ILLUSTRATED, UNLESS OTHERWISE NOTED

(Under name Christopher Raschka) *R and : A Story about Two Alphabets,* Brethren Press, 1990.

Charlie Parker Played Be Bop, Orchard (New York, NY), 1992.

Yo! Yes?, Orchard (New York, NY), 1993.

Elizabeth Imagined an Iceberg, Orchard (New York, NY), 1994.

Can't Sleep, Orchard (New York, NY), 1995.

The Blushful Hippopotamus, Orchard (New York, NY), 1995.

Mysterious Thelonious, Orchard (New York, NY), 1997.

Arlene Sardine, Orchard (New York, NY), 1998.

Like Likes Like, DK (New York, NY), 1999.

Moosey Moose, Hyperion (New York, NY), 2000.

Doggy Dog, Hyperion (New York, NY), 2000.

Goosey Goose, Hyperion (New York, NY), 2000.

Lamby Lamb, Hyperion (New York, NY), 2000.

Ring! Yo?, DK (New York, NY), 2000.

Sluggy Slug, Hyperion (New York, NY), 2000.

Snaily Snail, Hyperion (New York, NY), 2000.

Whaley Whale, Hyperion (New York, NY), 2000.

Wormy Worm, Hyperion (New York, NY), 2000.

Waffle, Atheneum (New York, NY), 2001.

Little Tree, based on a poem by e. e. cummings, Hyperion (New York, NY), 2001.

(With Vladimir Radunsky) *Table Manners: The Edifying Story of Two Friends Whose Discovery of Good Manners Promises Them a Glorious Future,* Candlewick Press (Cambridge, MA), 2001.

John Coltrane's Giant Steps, Atheneum (New York, NY), 2002.

Talk to Me about the Alphabet, Holt (New York, NY), 2003.

(With Vladimir Radunsky) *Boy Meets Girl; Girl Meets Boy,* Seuil Chronicle (San Francisco, CA), 2004.

New York Is English, Chattanooga Is Creek, Atheneum (New York, NY), 2005.

Five for a Little One, Atheneum (New York, NY), 2006.

The Purple Balloon, Schwartz & Wade Books (New York, NY), 2007.

Jimmy Grasshopper versus the Ants, Candlewick Press (Cambridge, MA), 2008.

(Reteller) *Peter and the Wolf,* Atheneum Books for Young Readers (New York, NY), 2008.

Hip Hop Dog, illustrated by Vladimir Radunsky, Harper-Collins (New York, NY), 2009.

ILLUSTRATOR

James H. Lehman, *The Saga of Shakespeare Pintlewood and the Great Silver Fountain Pen,* Brotherstone (Elgin, IL), 1990.

James H. Lehman, *Owl and the Tuba,* Brotherstone (Elgin, IL), 1991.

Phyllis Vos Wezeman and Colleen Aalsburg Wiessner, *Benjamin Brody's Backyard Bag,* Brethren Press (Elgin, IL), 1991.

George Dolnikowski, *This I Remember,* Brethren Press (Elgin, IL), 1994.

Nikki Giovanni, *The Genie in the Jar,* Holt (New York, NY), 1996.

Simple Gifts: A Shaker Hymn, Holt (New York, NY), 1998.

Margaret Wise Brown, *Another Important Book,* Harper-Collins (New York, NY), 1999.

bell hooks, *Happy to Be Nappy,* Hyperion (New York, NY), 1999.

Sharon Creech, *Fishing in the Air,* HarperCollins (New York, NY), 2000.

Paul Janeczko, editor, *A Poke in the I,* Candlewick Press (Cambridge, MA), 2001.

bell hooks, *Be Boy Buzz,* Hyperion (New York, NY), 2002.

Claude Nougaro, *Armstrong,* Didier Jeunesse (Paris, France), 2002.

Francis Bellamy, *I Pledge Allegiance: The Pledge of Allegiance,* with commentary by Bill Martin, Jr., and Michael Sampson, Candlewick Press (Cambridge, MA), 2002.

Dylan Thomas, *A Child's Christmas in Wales,* Candlewick Press (Cambridge, MA), 2004.

bell hooks, *Skin Again,* Hyperion (New York, NY), 2004.

Agnès Grunelius-Hollard, *Petite fille et le loup,* Didier Jeunesse (Paris, France), 2004.

Paul B. Janeczko, editor, *A Kick in the Head: An Everyday Guide to Poetic Forms,* Candlewick Press (Cambridge, MA), 2005.

Norton Juster, *The Hello, Good-bye Window,* Hyperion (New York, NY), 2005.

Avi and Carolyn Shute, selectors, *Best Shorts: Favorite Short Stories for Sharing,* afterword by Katherine Paterson, Houghton Mifflin (Boston, MA), 2006.

Jack Prelutsky, *Good Sports: Rhymes about Running, Jumping, Throwing, and More,* Alfred A. Knopf (New York, NY), 2007.

bell hooks, *Grump Groan Growl,* Hyperion (New York, NY), 2008.

Nikki Giovanni, *The Grasshopper's Song: An Aesop's Fable Revisited,* Candlewick Press (Cambridge, MA), 2008.

Norton Juster, *Sourpus and Sweetie Pie,* Scholastic (New York, NY), 2008.

Paul Janeczko, editor, *A Foot in the Mouth: Poems to Speak, Sing, and Shout,* Candlewick Press (Cambridge, MA), 2009.

A. Bitterman, *Fortune Cookie,* Atheneum Books for Young Readers (New York, NY), 2009.

Soyna Sones and Bennett Tramer, *Violet and Winston,* Dial Books for Young Readers (New York, NY), 2009.

Contributor to anthologies, including *Why Did the Chicken Cross the Road?,* Dial (New York, NY), 2006, and *Knock, Knock!,* Dial, 2007.

Sidelights

Caldecott Medal-winning author and illustrator Chris Raschka likes to take chances. Employing only thirty-four well-chosen words in his book *Yo! Yes?,* and artwork that a *Publishers Weekly* contributor dubbed "brash, witty, and offbeat," Raschka conveys volumes about not only the process of making friends, but also about race relations and the subtle nuances of emotion. His *Charlie Parker Played Be Bop,* which is constructed like a jazz piece with its text forming the rhythm and

***Chris Raschka creates the sunwashed artwork for bell hooks' upbeat picture book* Happy to Be Nappy.** (Hyperion Books for Children, 1999. Text copyright © 1999 by Bell Hooks. Illustration copyright © 1999 by Chris Raschka. All rights reserved. Reprinted by permission of Disney Hyperion, an imprint of Disney Book Group LLC.)

cadence of be bop, "stretched the definition of picture book," according to another *Publishers Weekly* reviewer. In addition to his original stories, Raschka has also created art for books by an impressive list of other writers that includes Nikki Giovanni, Paul Janeczko, Norton Juster, bell hooks, and Margaret Wise Brown. His collaboration with Juster on *The Hello, Goodbye Window* secured Raschka the 2006 Caldecott Medal.

Born in Pennsylvania, Raschka was raised by parents who met while both were doing refugee work in Europe after World War II: his father is an American from Detroit, and his mother is from Vienna, Austria. Growing up speaking both German and English, Raschka attended first grade in Marburg, Germany, where his father, a seminary professor of church history, was on sabbatical. When the family returned to the United States the following year, they moved to suburban Chicago, where the young Raschka "played in the storm sewers and ditches," as he once recalled to *SATA*. "They were the one interesting place in the whole bleak environment."

The European picture books that informed Raschka's earliest imaginings would eventually influence his work as an author and illustrator. "I loved books such as *Die kleine Hexe* (*The Little Witch*) by [Otfried] Preussler," he once explained to *SATA*. "Another all-time favorite is the illustrator Winnie Gebhardt Gayler and Wilhelm Busch with his 'Max and Moritz' stories. I even liked *Struwelpeter* when I was growing up. I know they are all pretty frightening, with horrific things happening to children who disobey their parents, but I think that kids are so used to seeing dangers all around them that they can deal with it. I was disturbed by some of the cruelty of the old German stories, but I loved the drawings and still do." Only as an adult did Raschka "catch up" on the great illustrators known to British and American audiences.

Raschka was involved in art and music from an early age. As a child, he loved to draw, and also started studying the piano at age six. From the piano he went on to the recorder and then the violin. Eventually moving to viola, he went on to play in both high school and college orchestras. "But all the while I planned to be a biologist," he later recalled. "I just loved animals of all types, especially crocodiles and turtles. I also loved drawing and music, but never thought I could make a living at those." At college Raschka majored in biology, and then took a position as an intern in a children's orthopedic clinic in Germany. "I learned so much from those kids," he later said, "and I loved the work. It was after that experience that I decided to go to medical school." After studying for and passing the entrance tests, Raschka was ultimately admitted to medical school, but a visit to St. Croix, Virgin Islands, with his new wife led to a change in those plans.

"I had a lot of luck in St. Croix," Raschka recalled. "My wife and I both decided to try our art—we had met in an art class—and we had shows there. My work was in galleries and I began to get freelance work as an illustrator. It was there that I first realized I might be able to make it as an artist." But the time Raschka and his wife returned to the United States and the University of Michigan, he had decided not to go to school. Instead, he opted to work as an illustrator for regional newspapers and magazines, doing everything from political cartoons to illustrations for legal texts. Meanwhile, Raschka's wife trained as a Montessori teacher. "After a couple of years illustrating, I thought I would try a children's book," Raschka said. "That's how *R and* came about."

According to its author, *R and : A Story about Two Alphabets* "is a story that contrasts the English and Russian alphabets and the two letters are the main characters. It's a Russian-American friendship book and the text is both in English and Russian." With this first book, Raschka demonstrated the care and attention to detail that have become characteristic of his work. "My goal is to create a book where the entire book—text, pictures, shape of book—work together to create the theme," he explained to *SATA*. "The placement of images and text on the page is crucial for me."

After *R and* , Raschka entered what he views as his "apprenticeship period," working on several illustration projects for other writers. "It taught me the amount of work involved in creating a picture book and how to put books together. And most of all this work taught me to see the book as a whole work and not just one illustration after another."

Meanwhile, Raschka was still pursuing his second love, music, and in considering a career as a viola player New York City began to beckon. In 1989, with no job prospects, Raschka and his wife decided to make the move, realizing it was time to make a commitment to either art or music. All that summer Raschka practiced his viola, hoping to audition for a major orchestra in the fall. However, while experimenting with a new fingering position, he developed tendonitis. "I simply couldn't play anymore," he explained. "My decision was made for me."

Raschka's love of music eventually won him his first big break in children's books. Guided by his own love of jazz music, he wanted to inspire young people with a love of the music of jazz greats such as Charlie Parker. The very first sentence of his book, "Charlie Parker played be bop," also became the book's title. "I realized these words could fit one of the great be bop tunes of the time, 'Night in Tunisia,' by Dizzy Gillespie," Raschka once recounted for *SATA*. "After these first words I put away the notion of a regular biography and decided to convey just two facts: that Parker played the saxophone and played be bop. The rest was like a be bop tune itself, based on a repeating stanza or motif, with pure nonsense stanzas in between—a simple line that gets modified over and over again." Raschka blended this text with original art done in charcoal and watercolors, angular and skewed and humorous.

Doubts as to whether the public would understand what Raschka was trying to do with *Charlie Parker Played Be Bop* were quickly dispelled by reviews. "Rather than attempting to teach his young audience about Parker's music," *Booklist* contributor Bill Ott noted, "Raschka allows them to hear it—not with sounds but with words and pictures." Raschka's text sticks in the head like a persistent ditty; in addition, his artwork gives his figures "extraordinary energy; creating jaunty, fantastical creatures to move with the beat," explained a *Kirkus Reviews* critic. Writing that "even the typeface joins in the fun as italics and boldface strut and swing across the pages," a *Publishers Weekly* critic also cited the inside jokes Raschka plays, such as the birds which are used as decorative motifs on some pages (Parker's nickname was "Bird"). Raschka "has created a memorable tribute" to Parker, wrote Elizabeth S. Watson in *Horn Book,* calling the work "one of the most innovative picture books of recent times." Jazz great Dizzy Gillespie himself praised the book in *Entertainment Weekly.* Comparing the text to scat singing, Gillespie enjoyed the "drawings of Bird, too; they're funny. So was he. I think this book would make him laugh a lot. It will surely make kids laugh."

Like *Charlie Parker Played Be Bop,* Raschka's *Mysterious Thelonious* is a tribute to a famous figure in jazz history; composer Thelonious Monk. Also like *Charlie Parker Played Be Bop,* the text of *Mysterious Thelonious* mimics the music created by its subject. Critics compared the text of the earlier book to the improvisational be-bop music it celebrates; in *Mysterious Thelonious* the author/illustrator associates the placement and color of each page's illustration with placement of a note on the musical scale, allowing the book to be "played" to the tune of the composer's famous "Mysterioso." Watson, in another *Horn Book* review, remarked of *Mysterious Thelonious* that while not all readers will be able to access this aspect of Raschka's tribute, those who can will find that the book "fresh, inventive use of color, rhythm, and melody will sing."

Returning to jazz with *John Coltrane's Giant Steps,* Raschka adapts one of Coltrane's songs to the printed page by representing each instrument with a "performer": a kitten representing the saxophone, snowflakes taking the part of the piano, raindrops serving as drums, and boxes representing the bass. The characters depicting the instruments all refer to Coltrane's jazz interpretation of the popular song "My Favorite Things." Raschka explained his goal with *John Coltrane's Giant Steps* to a writer for *Children's Literature Web site:* "The thing that I hoped to get across with this book was mostly a feeling of the potential for complexity that comes from a very simple layering of abstract things. Which is the case in Coltrane's music. It's more a visual experimentation to see what happens if you follow principles that are developed in music and try to translate them into graphic materials." While some reviewers noted that *John Coltrane's Giant Steps* would be best accompanied by a recording of Coltrane playing

"Giant Steps," most applauded its visual representation. "Raschka's transparent watercolors layer colors and shapes the way a musician would notes and harmonies," reported a *Publishers Weekly* critic, and Wendy Lukehart noted in *School Library Journal* that "the sequential design and layering of the organic forms are a creative, joyful, and energetic match" for the original music.

The positive reception earned by *Charlie Parker Played Be Bop* encouraged Raschka to push ahead with another project that had been germinating for some time. "I was walking to the post office one day," he recalled, "and was suddenly struck with how rich the street scene was. I've got a real interest in language and how words such as 'Yo' come into use. And so I began thinking about how language and culture and race all seem so big, but are actually small. They shouldn't really stand between people and keep us apart." With this germ of an idea— the interplay of language and race—Raschka started playing with story ideas. He wanted to talk about friendship, about the process of making friends. And he wanted to keep it simple and direct. "When I was a kid, my dad would play this little one-word game with us. We used to carry on whole dialogues with just one word back and forth." From these elements, *Yo! Yes?* was born.

With just thirty-four words Raschka portrays a potential racial stand-off that turns into friendship. On the left-hand page, an African-American boy, coolly outfitted in baggy shorts and unlaced sneakers, calls "Yo!" across the book to a shy white boy who seems to be inching off the right-hand page. From this beginning, the picture book progresses through one-word exchanges that show the white kid to be lonely for lack of friends, and culminates in the more-outgoing black kid offering friendship. The offer is accepted in an ecstatic high-five as the two join together on the final page and shout "Yow!" with joy. "Raschka exhibits an appreciation of the rhythms of both language and human exchange in his deceptively simple story," Maeve Visser Knoth wrote in *Horn Book.* "The succinct, rhythmic text and the strong cartoon-like watercolor-and-charcoal illustrations are perfect complements," Judy Constantinides similarly commented in *School Library Journal.* Raschka's artwork and layout are "bold, spare and expressive," summarized a *Bulletin of the Center for Children's Books* reviewer, who concluded that "the language has the strength of a playground chant; the story is a ritual played out worldwide."

Named a Caldecott honor book, *Yo! Yes?* marked another step in Raschka's innovation of the picture book: his placement of illustrations on the very bottom edge of the page is as important as the hand-lettered text. The structure of the book itself also adds to the story, as the two boys seem to be looking across, and eventually bridge, the actual seam between the book's left and right pages. The book is also a distillation of the artist's impression of some of the kids Raschka plays basket-

Raschka's original picture book The Blushful Hippopotamus *focuses on an unusual friendship.* (Orchard Books, 1996. Copyright © 1996 by Chris Raschka. Reproduced by permission of the publisher, Orchard Books, an imprint of Scholastic Inc.)

ball with in New York and of himself as the shy new white kid on the block. "Beneath it all," Raschka told *SATA,* "the black kid is shy too. It's a risk for him to offer friendship. I hope it's always a risk worth taking."

In *The Blushful Hippopotamus* Raschka offers up his signature combination of expressionistic characters and unusual, rhythmic text. Like *Yo! Yes?,* he tells much of the story visually, rendering confident characters as large and timid characters as small. Roosevelt Hippopotamus is so overpowered by his sister's teasing that he practically slinks off the right-hand page while his sister looms so large that only part of her face and body can fit on the left-hand page. As Roosevelt's bird friend Lombard boosts his confidence, however, the hippo grows in stature, while his sister shrinks correspondingly, and the book ends with a grateful embrace by the two friends. "Ah, the sweet balm of friendship," beamed a reviewer for *Publishers Weekly,* continuing that the book's "magic works as admirably on these pages as it does in real life."

Raschka's *Like Likes Like* contains another celebration of friendship, its story playing out mainly in the author/illustrator's expressive drawings. This book "features Raschka at his most amenable," contended Julie Corsaro in *Booklist.* Reviewers likewise praised the evident sympathy for the uncomfortable feelings of children that the author/artist demonstrates in *Can't Sleep,* by depicting a small dog as he goes to bed and lies awake listening to the sounds of the rest of his family preparing for sleep. In *Horn Book* Mary M. Burns described Raschka's illustrations for this book as containing "a minimum of detail but supercharged with emotion" and singled out for praise the author's "brilliantly imaginative and completely childlike conclusion."

Known for being an innovator, Raschka sparked a measure of controversy with *Arlene Sardine.* In this book, he chronicles the two-year life of Arlene, from her birth in a fjord among thousands of her kind, to her death on the deck of a fishing boat and, beyond death, to her processing in a sardine factory. Writing in *Booklist,* Ilene Cooper summed up much of the critical reaction, observing that the sardine's short life and subsequent death "seems a dubious topic upon which to write a book for preschoolers." *School Library Journal* reviewer Carol Ann Wilson expressed a similar viewpoint while praising the touches of whimsy that are injected into the fact-based account of Arlene's life through the poetic rhythms and use of repetition in the text. "Arlene's saga, like sardines, is an acquired taste," Wilson concluded. While Betsy Hearne, in the *Bulletin of the Center for Children's Books,* questioned the appropriateness of the book for its intended audience, she nonetheless praised *Arlene Sardine* by writing that "it's refreshing to have a visual storyteller trying innovative things." "One thing for sure," Hearne continued: "Raschka's work always surprises, challenges, and intrigues us one way or another."

Raschka also deals with death in *The Purple Balloon,* a picture book created for terminally ill children and those dealing with death. He depicts family, friends, and caregivers as soft-edged balloons, an image suggested by art therapists as the means used by many children to depict the fragility and tenuousness of life. The balloons that bear human faces are colored—green for someone elderly and red for a child—and as death comes the balloon's face assumes a peaceful expression and its hue resolves to purple. In addition to helping children make sense of their own terminal illness, the book also aids those who are attempting to comfort others in hospitals or hospice situations. Noting Raschka's "sensitive" approach to a difficult topic, *Booklist* critic Randall Enos described *The Purple Balloon* as "a useful tool for the right child with the right adult at the right time."

Raschka's more mainstream picture books include animal-centered stories such as *Snaily Snail, Sluggy Slug,* and *Wormy Worm.* A young bunny is the focus of *Five for a Little One,* which inspires readers to be conscious of everything they can see, smell, touch, hear, and taste, while the story of a bird who cannot summon the courage it takes to fly is the focus of *Waffle.* In *Five for a Little One* "graceful, Zen-like spreads" capture the bunny's experiences of nature, the art reflecting "Raschka's focus on simplicity and natural materials," according to a *Publishers Weekly* critic. The author/artist's "rhyming verses and ebullient artwork convey a child's curiosity and enthusiasm," maintained *School Library*

Journal critic Joy Fleishhacker, the critic adding that Raschka's highly textured ink brush and potato-print art is "irresistible." "Conceptually, and visually, the book is ingenious," praised Martha V. Parravano in a *Horn Book* review of *Waffle*, and Michael Cart commented in *Booklist* that the author/illustrator's "spare, alliterative text will be great fun to read aloud." According to a *Publishers Weekly* critic, in *Waffle* Raschka "captures the essence of a mood with the merest hint of text and the briefest of brush strokes."

Raschka's innovative approach to picture-book art continues in *New York Is English, Chattanooga Is Creek,* which illustrates the source of America's place names by depicting cities as representatives of the many countries and cultures that founded them. New York, for example, is portrayed as the British duke of York, complete with powdered wig and buckled shoes, while San Francisco is dressed in somber monk's robes and other cities reflect similarly unique origins. Noting the author's focus on cultures coming together rather than breaking apart, a *Publishers Weekly* reviewer wrote that the "lilting approximate rhyme, and . . . piquant watercolors . . . make [*New York Is English, Chattanooga Is Creek*] an aural and visual pleasure." For Kate McClelland, writing in *School Library Journal*, Raschka's "farcical flight-of-fancy" is "at once carefully intentional and casually random," with whimsy captured in its "loose, impressionistic" watercolor-and-ink art.

In searching for new ways to use the picture-book format, Raschka has occasionally worked with other writ-

Norton Juster and Raschka collaborated on Sourpuss and Sweetie Pie, *a follow-up to their award-winning* The Hello, Goodbye Window. (Michael Di Capua Books, 2008. Pictures copyright © 2008 by Chris Raschka. Reproduced by permission of Scholastic Inc.)

ers and artists. His most frequent collaborator is fellow artist Vladimir Radunsky, a good friend with whom he has created the books *Table Manners: The Edifying Story of Two Friends Whose Discovery of Good Manners Promises Them a Glorious Future, Boy Meets Girl; Girl Meets Boy,* and *Hip Hop Dog.* In *Table Manners* Chester and Dudunya ask questions about appropriate manners and give examples of good restaurant conduct, as well as teaching readers to say "please" and "thank you" in six different languages. Commenting on the "free-spirited" illustration style, a *Publishers Weekly* reviewer found that, "together, these two [artists] are anything but uptight." Kathleen Whalin, writing in *School Library Journal,* called the collaboration "a funny, artistic creation on the subject of living well." In *Girl Meets Boy; Boy Meets Girl,* the words of the story are the same from right to left and from left to right, and are occasionally sprawled across the page upside-down. The experimental format "busts linear narrative to smithereens," according to a *Kirkus Reviews* contributor, while a *Publishers Weekly* reviewer likened the story to "a Mobius strip that never stops."

Working as an illustrator, Raschka has contributed art to a number of stories by other writers. His collaboration with Sharon Creech on *Granny Torrelli Makes Soup* was considered by Maria B. Salvadore in *School Library Journal* to be "a meal that should not be missed," and his paintings for Nikki Giovanni's *The Grasshopper's Song: An Aesop's Fable Revisited* ground the book "solidly in the realm of fable," according to Joan Kindig in the same periodical. Norton Juster's gentle, multigenerational story about a playful girl's visits with her doting grandparents inspired the artist's Caldecott Medal-winning illustrations for *The Hello, Goodbye Window* and also for its sequel, *Sourpuss and Sweetie Pie.* In *The Hello, Goodbye Window* an "endearing" story comes to life in "lush paintings" of brilliant hue, observed a *Publishers Weekly* critic, while a *Kirkus Reviews* writer noted that Raschka captures the happiness of the book's multicultural family in "loose and energetic" paintings rendered "in jewel tones and extravagant swirls." While its "simple lines and squiggles . . . suggest a child's own drawings," *The Hello, Goodbye Window* contains "the art of a masterful hand," concluded *School Library Journal* critic Angela J. Reynolds.

When Raschka illustrated poet bell hooks's picture book *Happy to Be Nappy,* he faced controversy as a white illustrator of black-themed books. "My own perspective is that bell hooks asked me to illustrate her lovely text and I said 'sure,' and that's the level on which I view it," he explained to a writer for *ChildrensLit.com.* Reviewing his illustrations for hooks's *Be Boy Buzz,* a *Publishers Weekly* contributor cited "Raschka's trademark visual haiku," while *Booklist* contributor Hazel Rochman concluded of *Skin Again,* another Raschka-hooks collaboration, that the book's images "vividly celebrate . . . history and the realism, fun, and fantasy inside each one of us." In her appraisal of *Grump Groan*

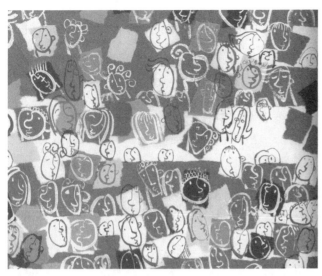

Raschka teams with writers Bill Martin, Jr., and Michael Sampson to create the patriotic picture book **I Pledge Allegiance.** (Candlewick Press, 2002. Text copyright ©2002 by Bill Martin Jr., & Michael Sampson. Illustrations © 2002 by Chris Raschka. Reproduced by permission of the publisher Candlewick Press, Inc., Somerville, MA.)

Growl, hooks's story about controlling one's moods, Heidi Estrin asserted in *School Library Journal* that the artist's "thick, almost tactile lines of paint are slathered onto the pages with gusto, capturing a feeling of movement and strong emotion."

Raschka's illustrations have also adorned a number of poetry collections, among them *A Poke in the I, A Kick in the Head: An Everyday Guide to Poetic Forms,* and *A Foot in the Mouth: Poems to Speak, Sing, and Shout,* all of which are edited by Paul B. Janeczko. Raschka "works in tandem with each poem's design," noted a *Publishers Weekly* critic in a review of *A Poke in the I,* while a *Horn Book* critic noted that "Raschka decorates rather than interprets, but he does so with strong, vertical lines and bold colors that add energy to the collection without overwhelming it." The artist's "high-spirited, spare torn-paper-and-paint collages" expand on the "wide-ranging emotional tones" of Janeczko's verses in *A Kick in the Head,* wrote Engberg, and in *Publishers Weekly* a critic cited Raschka's "spirited Asian-inspired images" in the same book for "add[ing] oomph to this joyful poetry lesson."

Raschka often has several projects going at once. "I may be finishing up one book while another one is in the early stages of artwork and still another one is just a few words scribbled onto a bit of scrap paper and left to ripen for a time," he once explained to *SATA.* "With my illustrations, I am working very close to the surface. Most of the information is right up front without great detail in the background. That's why I like to position them on the bottom of the page. To make them almost come out of the frame, to jump off the page. I work for young kids who want things close up and are immediate and tactile." As for content and theme, Raschka writes out of personal experience and necessity: "My books are my own thoughts about things that are important to me," he noted. "I work through how I feel about such things as language, art, music, and friendship with these loose, colorful and slightly wild drawings."

Biographical and Critical Sources

PERIODICALS

Booklist, September 1, 1988, Ilene Cooper, review of *Arlene Sardine,* p. 126; June 15, 1992, Bill Ott, review of *Charlie Parker Played Be Bop,* p. 1843; April 1, 1999, Julie Corsaro, review of *Like Likes Like,* p. 1409; May 15, 2001, Michael Cart, review of *Waffle,* p. 1760; November 1, 2002, review of *Be Boy Buzz,* p. 508; April 1, 2003, Gillian Engberg, review of *John Coltrane's Giant Steps,* p. 1414; May 1, 2003, GraceAnne A. DeCandido, review of *Talk to Me about the Alphabet,* p. 1606; September 15, 2004, Hazel Rochman, review of *Skin Again,* p. 250; March 15, 2005, Ilene Cooper, review of *The Hello, Goodbye Window,* p. 1286, and Gillian Engberg, review of *A Kick in the Head: An Everyday Guide to Poetic Forms,* p. 1291; August 22, 2005, review of *New York Is English, Chattanooga Is Creek,* p. 63; March 1, 2007, Jennifer Mattson, review of *Good Sports: Rhymes about Running, Jumping, Throwing, and More,* p. 85; April 1, 2007, Randall Enos, review of *The Purple Balloon,* p. 60; February 15, 2009, Thom Barthlemess, review of *Violet and Winston,* p. 88.

Bulletin of the Center for Children's Books, April, 1993, review of *Yo! Yes?,* pp. 262-263; September, 1998, Betsy Hearne, review of *Arlene Sardine,* pp. 3-4.

Entertainment Weekly, October 9, 1992, Dizzy Gillespie, "What about Bop?," p. 70.

Horn Book, November-December, 1992, Elizabeth S. Watson, review of *Charlie Parker Played Be Bop,* pp. 718-719; May-June, 1993, Maeve Visser Knoth, review of *Yo! Yes?,* p. 323; March-April, 1996, Mary M. Burns, review of *Can't Sleep,* p. 191; January-February, 1998, Elizabeth S. Watson, review of *Mysterious Thelonious,* p. 68; May, 2001, Martha V. Parravano, review of *Waffle,* p. 315; July, 2001, review of *A Poke in the I,* p. 466; November-December, 2004, Susan Dove Lempke, review of *Skin Again,* p. 498.

Kirkus Reviews, July 1, 1992, review of *Charlie Parker Played Be Bop,* p. 853; August 15, 2001, review of *Little Tree,* p. 1210; October 1, 2001, review of *Table Manners,* p. 1431; July 1, 2003, review of *Granny Torrelli Makes Soup,* p. 908; August 1, 2004, review of *Boy Meets Girl; Girl Meets Boy,* p. 748; March 1, 2005, review of *The Hello, Goodbye Window,* p. 289; March 15, 2008, review of *Grump Groan Growl;* September 15, 2008, review of *Peter and the Wolf.*

New York Times Book Review, November 14, 2004, Marigny Dupuy, review of *A Child's Christmas in Wales,* p. 28; May 13, 2007, John Green, review of *The Purple Balloon,* p. 21.

Publishers Weekly, October, 1992, review of *Charlie Parker Played Be Bop,* p. 108; February 15, 1993, review of *Yo! Yes?,* p. 236; December 13, 1993, review

of *Elizabeth Imagined an Iceberg,* p. 69; August 5, 1996, review of *The Blushful Hippopotamus,* p. 441; April 16, 2001, review of *Waffle,* p. 64; September 24, 2001, review of *Little Tree,* p. 49; October 29, 2001, review of *Table Manners,* p. 62; June 25, 2002, review of *John Coltrane's Giant Steps,* p. 55; August 26, 2002, review of *I Pledge Allegiance,* p. 68; September 30, 2002, review of *Be Boy Buzz,* p. 71; February 3, 2003, review of *Talk to Me about the Alphabet,* p. 74; December 22, 2003, review of *Charlie Parker Played Be Bop,* p. 63; August 30, 2004, review of *Boy Meets Girl,* p. 53; February 21, 2005, review of *The Hello, Goodbye Window,* p. 173; March 14, 2005, review of *A Kick in the Head,* p. 67; August 22, 2005, review of *New York Is English, Chattanooga Is Creek,* p. 63; July 17, 2006, review of *Five for a Little One,* p. 155; April 16, 2007, review of *The Purple Balloon,* p. 49; May 15, 2008, Jennifer Mattson, review of *The Grasshopper's Song,* p. 42; September 15, 2008, review of *Sourpuss and Sweetie Pie,* p. 65; January 5, 2009, review of *A Foot in the Mouth,* p. 50.

School Library Journal, May, 1993, Judy Constantinides, review of *Yo! Yes?,* p. 90; April, 1994, Kate McClelland, review of *Elizabeth Imagined an Iceberg,* p. 112; September, 1996, Barbara Kiefer, review of *The Blushful Hippopotamus,* pp. 117-118; September, 1998, Carol Ann Wilson, review of *Arlene Sardine,* p. 179; October, 2001, review of *Little Tree,* p. 63; November, 2001, Kathleen Whalin, review of *Table Manners,* p. 134; July, 2002, Wendy Lukehart, review of *John Coltrane's Giant Steps,* p. 97; December, 2002, Anna DeWind Walls, review of *Be Boy Buzz,* p. 97, and Krista Tokarz, review of *I Pledge Allegiance,* p. 127; February, 2003, Lee Bock, review of *Yo! Yes?,* p. 97; June, 2003, Marian Creamer, review of *Talk to Me about the Alphabet,* p. 113; August, 2003, Maria B. Salvadore, review of *Granny Torrelli Makes Soup,* p. 158; September, 2004, Grace Oliff, review of *Skin Again,* p. 162; November, 2004, Marie Orlando, review of *Boy Meets Girl,* p. 116; March, 2005, Angela J. Reynolds, review of *The Hello, Goodbye Window,* p. 174; October, 2005, Kate McClelland, review of *New York Is English, Chattanooga Is Creek,* p. 125; July, 2006, Joy Fleishhacker, review of *Five for a Little One,* p. 85; February, 2007, Teresa Pfeifer, review of *Good Sports,* p. 111; March, 2008, Heidi Estrin, review of *Grump Groan Growl,* p. 168; June, 2008, Joan Kindig, review of *The Grasshopper's Song: An Aesop's Fable Revisited,* p. 102; October, 2008, Joan Kindig, review of *Sourpuss and Sweetie Pie,* p. 112, and Wendy Lukehart, review of *Peter and the Wolf,* p. 120; February, 2009, Kathleen Finn, review of *Violet and Winston,* p. 86; March, 2009, Julie Roach, review of *A Foot in the Mouth,* p. 164.

ONLINE

BookPage.com, http://www.bookpage.com/ (September, 1998), Etta Wilson, interview with Raschka.

ChildrensLit.com, http://www.childrenslit.com/ (November 15, 2009), "Chris Raschka."

Storyopolis Art Gallery Online, http://www.storyopolis.com/ (November 15, 2009).*

* * *

RASCHKA, Christopher
See RASCHKA, Chris

* * *

RETTSTATT, Chris
See ASHLAND, Monk

* * *

SCHMITZ, Tamara

Personal

Born in Carey, OH; daughter of Earl and Alma Schmitz; married (divorced, 2001); married; second husband's name Paul; children: Olivia, Addison, Ian (stepson). *Education:* Columbus College of Art and Design, degree. *Hobbies and other interests:* Taekwondo.

Addresses

Home—Cincinnati, OH. *E-mail*—schmitztamara@mac.com.

Career

Author and illustrator. Former art director for an advertising agency; teacher of art.

Member

Society of Children's Book Writers and Illustrators.

Awards, Honors

New York Book Festival honorable mention, 2009, for *Standing on My Own Two Feet.*

Writings

SELF-ILLUSTRATED

Standing on My Own Two Feet: A Child's Affirmation of Love in the Midst of Divorce, Price Stern Sloan (New York, NY), 2008.

Contributor to periodicals, including *ParentGuide.*

ILLUSTRATOR

Christine Harder Tangvald, *Playtime Devotions: Sharing Bible Moments with Your Baby or Toddler,* Standard Pub. (Cincinnati, OH), 2002.

Tamara Schmitz (Photograph by Sharon Kinder-Geiger. Reproduced by permission.)

Laurie Friedman, *Mallory on the Move,* Carolrhoda Books (Minneapolis, MN), 2004.

Laurie Friedman, *Back to School, Mallory,* Carolrhoda Books (Minneapolis, MN), 2004.

Laurie Friedman, *Mallory vs. Max,* Carolrhoda Books (Minneapolis, MN), 2005.

Laurie Friedman, *Happy Birthday, Mallory!,* Carolrhoda Books (Minneapolis, MN), 2005.

Sidelights

As an illustrator, Tamara Schmitz is well known to the many elementary-grade fans of Laurie Friedman's "Mallory" chapter books. Through Schmitz's lighthearted black-and-white cartoons, readers come to know the popular star of the series, which includes *Mallory on the Move, Back to School, Mallory, Mallory vs. Max,* and *Happy Birthday, Mallory!* In her *Booklist* review of *Mallory on the Move*, Shelle Rosenfeld described Friedman's eight-year-old heroine as "a lively, appealing character with a penchant for jokes," and Tina Zubak wrote in *School Library Journal* that Schmitz's "cartoonlike drawings . . . make the story [in *Happy Birthday, Mallory!*] accessible to early chapter-book readers." The artist's "fun, accessible illustrations" capture

the girl's story by bringing to life "easily identifiable emotions and situations," according to Tracey Karbel, reviewing *Back to School, Mallory* for *School Library Journal.*

Schmitz addresses a topic close to her own heart in her original self-illustrated picture book *Standing on My Own Two Feet: A Child's Affirmation of Love in the Midst of Divorce.* Illustrated with what a *Kirkus Reviews* writer described as "brightly colored, realistic illustrations," *Standing on My Own Two Feet* focuses on a little boy named Addison as he remains confident in the love of each of his parents as his family breaks apart through a divorce. The *Kirkus Reviews* critic also cited Schmitz's "simple, clearly worded" story as full of toddler appeal, while in *School Library Journal* Catherine Callegari praised *Standing on My Own Two Feet* for its "positive feel, [and] easy-to-understand message," delivered in the author/illustrator's "simple, straightforward" prose.

"Every year in the United States, over one million children are affected by divorce," Schmitz asserted on her home page. In addition to writing *Standing on My Own Two Feet* she has also created a Web site dedicated to providing adults resources to help children adjust to this reality. "Children will do best if they know that their mother and father will still be their parents even though the marriage has ended," Schmitz explained. "They need to know it is not their fault, and, that their Mom and Dad's love is unconditional."

A toddler's cautious move toward independence is captured in Schmitz's self-illustrated picture book **Standing on My Own Two Feet.** (Price Stern Sloan, 2008. Text and illustrations copyright © 2008 by Tamara Schmitz. All rights reserved. Reproduced by permission of Price Stern Sloan, a division of Penguin Putnam Books for Young Readers.)

Biographical and Critical Sources

PERIODICALS

Booklist, April 15, 2004, Shelle Rosenfeld, review of *Mallory on the Move,* p. 1442.

Kirkus Reviews, February 15, 2005, review of *Mallory vs. Max,* p. 228; April 15, 2008, reveiw of *Standing on My Own Two Feet: A Child's Affirmation of Love in the Midst of Divorce.*

School Library Journal, April, 2004, Debbie Stewart Hoskins, review of *Mallory on the Move,* p. 110; August, 2004, Tracy Karbel, review of *Back to School, Mallory,* p. 86; April, 2005, Sharon R. Pearce, review of *Mallory vs. Max,* p. 97; September, 2005, Tina Zubak, review of *Happy Birthday, Mallory!,* p. 170; July, 2008, Catherine Callegari, review of *Standing on My Own Two Feet,* p. 81.

ONLINE

Tamara Schmitz Home Page, http://www.tamaraschmitz. com (November 10, 2009).

*   *   *

SKEERS, Linda 1958-

Personal

Born 1958; married. *Education:* Nursing degree; attended Institute of Children's Literature.

Addresses

Home—Cedar Rapids, IA.

Career

Author. Formerly worked as a licensed practical nurse. Instructor at Institute of Children's Literature; presenter at schools and writing conferences.

Member

Society of Children's Book Writers and Illustrators (listserve moderator for Iowa chapter).

Awards, Honors

Award of Outstanding Merit, Mississippi Valley Writer's Conference.

Writings

History Makers: Toy Makers, Lucent Books (San Diego, CA), 2004.

The Impossible Patriotism Project, illustrated by Ard Hoyt, Dial Books for Young Readers (New York, NY), 2007.

Tutus Aren't My Style, illustrated by Anne Wilsdorf, Dial Books for Young Readers (New York, NY), 2010.

Contributor to periodicals, including *Humpty Dumpty's* and *Turtle.*

Sidelights

Linda Skeers, an author for children and an instructor at the Institute of Children's Literature, wrote *The Impossible Patriotism Project* to honor the many people who dedicate years of their life to serve their country in the U.S. military. Featuring artwork by Ard Hoyt, the picture book focuses on a boy named Caleb, whose father, a soldier, is currently serving overseas. Caleb misses his dad, and he also senses that his mom feels the same. When Caleb's teacher asks each member of the class to construct something that captures the meaning of patriotism for a display on Parents' Night, the boy is unsure what his contribution should be; besides, his dad will not be there to see his project anyway. Thoughts about his dad eventually lead Caleb to ponder the reasons the man has made such sacrifices for his country, and ultimately he finds a way to share his feelings in a tangible way that also honors his absent father. Praising Hoyt for "sensitively captur[ing] the commingled pain and pride" felt by Caleb in lively cartoon images, Jennifer Mattson added in *Booklist* that *The Impossible Patriotism Project* works well as "a discussion starter . . . with special relevance for children affected by deployment." In *School Library Journal* Mary Hazelton

Ard Hoyt creates the cartoon art for Linda Skeers' humorous **The Impossible Patriotism Project.** (Puffin Books, 2007. Pictures copyright © Ard Hoyt, 2007. All rights reserved. Reproduced by permission of Puffin Books, a division of Penguin Putnam Books for Young Readers.)

praised Skeers' story as "heartwarming," and predicted that it will be enjoyed "by proud families and friends of soldiers who are engaged in battle."

In addition to *The Impossible Patriotism Project,* Skeers is also the author of the nonfiction *History Makers: Toy Makers* and the humorous picture book *Tutus Aren't My Style.* Featuring art by Anne Wilsdorf, *Tutus Aren't My Style* introduces a young tomboy named Emma, who counts chasing bugs and pretending to be a pirate among her favorite pastimes. When a gift from Uncle Leo arrives that turns out to be a ballet outfit, Emma makes a try at making ballet-dancer moves. However, her twirls and spins soon take on an original flair, as Emma devises her own brand of dancing.

Biographical and Critical Sources

PERIODICALS

Booklist, May 1, 2007, Jennifer Mattson, review of *The Impossible Patriotism Project,* p. 100.
Kirkus Reviews, May 15, 2007, review of *The Impossible Patriotism Project.*
School Library Journal, August, 2007, Mary Hazelton, review of *The Impossible Patriotism Project,* p. 93.

ONLINE

Institute of Children's Literature Web site, http://www. institutechildrenslit.com/ (November 15, 2009), "Linda Skeers."
Linda Skeers Home Page, http://www.linda-skeers.com (November 15, 2009).

*   *   *

SLONIM, David 1966-

Personal

Born May 6, 1966; married; wife's name Bonnie; children: four. *Education:* Rhode Island School of Design, B.F.A., 1988.

Addresses

Home—IN. *E-mail*—david@davidslonim.com.

Career

Artist, writer, illustrator, and graphic designer. Corporate clients include IBM, UPS, Disney Press, HarperCollins, and T.G.I. Fridays. *Exhibitions:* Slonim's fine art has been included in numerous group exhibitions, including at Society of Illustrators Original Art exhibitions, and in solo exhibitions in Arizona and Indiana. Work included in permanent collections of Minnetrista Cultural Center, Muncie, IN; Richmond Art Museum, Richmond, IN; and Mazza Museum, Findlay, OH.

Awards, Honors

Gold Medal, National Jewish Book Award, Gold Award, Oppenheim Toy Portfolio, and Top-Ten Picture Books of the Year selection, *New York Times,* all 2000, all for *Moishe's Miracle.*

Writings

SELF-ILLUSTRATED

Oh, Ducky!: A Chocolate Calamity, Chronicle Books (San Francisco, CA), 2003.
He Came with the Couch, Chronicle Books (New York, NY), 2005.

ILLUSTRATOR

Bill Wallace, *Watchdog and the Coyotes,* Pocket Books (New York, NY), 1995.
Bill Wallace, *The Backward Bird Song,* Pocket Books (New York, NY), 1997.
Bill Wallace, *Upchuck and the Rotten Willy,* Pocket Books (New York, NY), 1998.
C. Anne Scott, *Old Jake's Skirts,* Northland Publishing (Flagstaff, AZ), 1998.
Laura Krauss Melmed, *Moishe's Miracle: A Hanukkah Story,* HarperCollins (New York, NY), 2000.
Jan Ormerod, *Emily and Albert,* Chronicle Books (San Francisco, CA), 2004.
Susan Pearson, *Squeal and Squawk: Barnyard Talk,* Marshall Cavendish (New York, NY), 2004.
Susan Pearson, *Who Swallowed Harold? and Other Poems about Pets,* Marshall Cavendish (New York, NY), 2005.
Sheri Bell-Rehwoldt, *You Think It's Easy Being the Tooth Fairy?,* Chronicle Books (San Francisco, CA), 2007.
Susan Goldman Rubin, *Haym Salomon: American Patriot,* Abrams Books for Young Readers (New York, NY), 2007.
Alice Schertle, *Look out, Jeremy Bean!,* Chronicle Books (San Francisco, CA), 2009.
Eileen Spinelli, *Silly Tilly,* Marshall Cavendish (New York, NY), 2009.

Sidelights

Writer and illustrator David Slonim fell in love with picture books as a young boy when his father and mother read to him from such childhood classics as *Mike Mulligan and the Steam Shovel, Harry the Dirty Dog,* and *Madeline and the Bad Hat.* Creating his own stories and illustrations since childhood, he went on to experiment with animated films, stained glass, and puppetry, influenced by artists and writers such as C.S. Lewis, Kenneth Graham, Chris Van Allsburg, Charles Schultz, Quentin Blake, William Steig, and Chuck Jones. Slonim has developed a flexible illustration style that ranges from cartoon to fine art. As he noted on his

home page, "I always try to match the style of art to the tone of the story." In his self-illustrated picture book *Oh, Ducky!: A Chocolate Calamity* he draws in a cartoon-like style reminiscent of *Looney Tunes* to represent the zany quality of the story, while *Moishe's Miracle: A Hanukkah Story,* by Laura Krauss Melmed, features art rendered in a style much like Russian art. As Slonim explained on his home page, "My goal [as an illustrator] is to find the simplest, most fun, and memorable way to express the ideas and emotions in the story."

Slonim began his career in art as a graphic artist, but by 1998 he had turned to fine art and illustration. Early work included his illustrations on Bill Wallace's books of animal adventures, such as *Upchuck and the Rotten Willy* and *Watchdog and the Coyotes.* With *Old Jake's Skirts,* by C. Anne Scott, Slonim provides simple sketches as well as full-color illustrations to bring to life the story about an old man and a trunk full of calico skirts that prove helpful in a variety of ways around his farm. *Booklist* contributor Linda Perkins noted that the illustrations "burst with color, as the skirts change [the old man's] life," while a *Publishers Weekly* reviewer observed that Slonim's "thickly textured oil paintings, . . . folksy in feeling and essentially realistic in their renderings, reward readers with quietly comic flourishes."

Moishe's Miracle won Slonim numerous awards and cemented his reputation as a children's book illustrator. Here he adds artwork to a folksy Hanukkah story in which a kind milkman helps to feed his hungry neighbors. A *Horn Book* reviewer noted of the book that "Slonim's art . . . portrays a soul reborn." Stephanie Zvirin, writing in *Booklist,* applauded the artist's pictures, stating that "their rich golds and browns evoke the bubbling goodness of the holiday's fried pancakes," while *Publishers Weekly* critic Elizabeth Devereaux commented that the artwork "has a satirical edge, and mischief abounds in the incidental details." The artist's "wonderfully expressive, deeply toned oil paintings evoke" both the starkness of winter and the warmth of the holiday, concluded a *School Library Journal* contributor.

Slonim has teamed with other authors, including Susan Pearson and Jan Ormerod. His illustrations for Pearson's *Squeal and Squawk: Barnyard Talk,* according to *School Library Journal* critic Lee Bock as "add energy and vitality to the rhymes." Working with Ormerod on *Emily and Albert,* Slonim provided "cartoon drawings [that] add just the right amount of enthusiasm and personality," in the words of Erlene Bishop Killeen in *School Library Journal.* Slonim also supplied the artwork for Sheri Bell-Rehwoldt's *You Think it's Easy Being the Tooth Fairy?* This work drew positive remarks from a *Kirkus Reviews* critic, who commented that the artist's "energetic paintings are humorous and showcase the tooth fairy's vim and vigor in saturated colors and clever perspectives."

Additionally, Slonim has created his own picture books. His debut as a writer/illustrator came with *Oh, Ducky!,* a zany tale about a rubber duck that gets stuck in a chocolate-making machine. "Connoisseurs of the madcap can only hope for more in this vein from Slonim in the future," wrote a critic for *Kirkus Reviews.* Likewise, *School Library Journal* reviewer Judith Constantinides commented that"this wildly nonsensical story should appeal to the younger set." A *Publishers Weekly* reviewer added to the positive critical reception of *Oh, Ducky!,* noting that Slonim's "first solo book venture is a lighthearted caper with a kid-pleasing setting: a candy factory."

Slonim's second self-illustrated work, *He Came with the Couch,* finds Rosie and her family buying a couch that unexpectedly comes with a resident "couch potato." In *School Library Journal* Maura Bresnahan stated that "Slonim's very funny picture book will appeal to children with a taste for the zany," and a *Publishers Weekly* reviewer commented that the book's "multimedia paintings are both silly and clever in their depiction of a boisterous, take-charge clan."

Biographical and Critical Sources

PERIODICALS

Booklist, December 15, 1995, Ellen Mandel, review of *Watchdog and the Coyotes,* p. 706; June 1, 1998, Linda Perkins, review of *Old Jake's Skirts,* p. 1784; September 1, 2000, Stephanie Zvirin, review of *Moishe's Miracle: A Hanukkah Story,* p. 134.

Horn Book, September-October, 2000, review of *Moishe's Miracle,* p. 588.

Kirkus Reviews, February 15, 2003, review of *Oh, Ducky!: A Chocolate Calamity,* p. 316; August 15, 2005, review of *He Came with the Couch,* p. 922; March 15, 2007, review of *Haym Salomon: American Patriot;* September 1, 2007, review of *You Think It's Easy Being the Tooth Fairy?*

New York Times Book Review, December 3, 2000, Richard Michelson, review of *Moishe's Miracle.*

Publishers Weekly, December 22, 1997, review of *Upchuck and the Rotten Willy,* p. 60; April 27, 1998, review of *Old Jake's Skirts,* p. 66; September 25, 2000, Elizabeth Devereaux, review of *Moishe's Miracle,* p. 66; December 23, 2002, review of *O Ducky!,* p. 70; March 8, 2004, review of *Squeal and Squawk: Barnyard Talk,* p. 74; October 3, 2005, review of *He Came with the Couch,* p. 68; March 26, 2007, review of *Haym Salomon,* p. 73.

School Library Journal, October, 2000, review of *Moishe's Miracle,* p. 65; April, 2003, Judith Constantinides, review of *O Ducky!,* p. 138; June, 2004, Lee Bock, review of *Squeal and Squawk,* p. 131; July, 2004, Erlene Bishop Killeen, review of *Emily and Albert,* p. 83; April, 2005, Linda Staskus, review of *Who Swallowed Harold? and Other Poems about Pets,* p. 124;

November, 2005, Maura Bresnahan, review of _He Came with the Couch,_ p. 107; May, 2007, Heidi Estrin, review of _Haym Salomon,_ p. 124; December, 2007, Maryann H. Owen, review of _You Think It's Easy Being the Tooth Fairy?,_ p. 86.

ONLINE

Chronicle Books Web site, http://www.chroniclebooks. com/ (March 28, 2008), "A Conversation with David Slonim," and "A Conversation with Author Sheri Bell-Rehwoldt and Illustrator David Slonim."

David Slonim Home Page, http://www.davidslonim.com (January 1, 2010).

Kavanaugh Gallery Web site, http://www.kavanaugh gallery.com/ (March 28, 2008), "David Slonim."

Official David Slonim Fine Art Web site, http://www.david slonimfineart.com (January 1, 2010).

Scholastic Web site, http://www2.scholastic.com/ (March 28, 2008), "David Slonim."*

*   *   *

SMITH, Andy J. 1975-

Personal

Born 1975; married; children: one daughter.

Addresses

Home—Newburyport, MA. _Agent_—Deborah Warren, East-West Literary Agency, ewmdwarren@aol.com. _E-mail_—andy@andyjsmithillustration.com.

Career

Illustrator. Formerly worked as an animator for television programming in New York, NY; former high-school and college art teacher.

Member

Society of Children's Book Writers and Illustrators (New England chapter), Picture Book Artists Association.

Writings

SELF-ILLUSTRATED

Jeremy Kreep: Fang Fairy (graphic novel), Stone Arch Books (Minneapolis, MN), 2008.

ILLUSTRATOR

Scott Nickel, _Backyard Bug Battle: A Buzz Beaker Brainstorm_ (graphic novel), Stone Arch Books (Minneapolis, MN), 2007.

Scott Nickel, _Billions of Bats: A Buzz Beaker Brainstorm_ (graphic novel), Stone Arch Books (Mankato, MN), 2007.

Scott Nickel, _Robot Rampage: A Buzz Beaker Brainstorm_ (graphic novel), Stone Arch Books (Minneapolis, MN), 2007.

Scott Nickel, _Attack of the Mutant Lunch Lady: A Buzz Beaker Brainstorm_ (graphic novel), Stone Arch Books (Minneapolis, MN), 2008.

**Bill Myers' adaptations of Bible stories are brought to life in Andy J. Smith's cartoon art n books that include** **Stink Bug Saves the Day!** (Zonderkidz, 2008. Illustrations © 2008 by Bill Myers. Used by permission of Zondervan.)

Bill Myers, *Stink Bug Saves the Day!: The Parable of the Good Samaritan* ("Bug Parable" series), Zonderkidz (Grand Rapids, MI), 2008.

Bill Myers, *The House That Went Ker-splat!: The Parable of the Wise and Foolish Builders* ("Bug Parable" series), Zonderkidz (Grand Rapids, MI), 2008.

Scott Nickel, *Buzz Beaker vs. Dracula* (graphic novel), Stone Arch Books (Minneapolis, MN), 2009.

Bill Myers, *Freddie's Fast-Cash Getaway: The Parable of the Prodigal Son* ("Bug Parable" series), Zonderkidz (Grand Rapids, MI), 2009.

Bill Myers, *Nervous Norman Hot on the Trail: The Parable of the Lost Sheep* ("Bug Parable" series), Zonderkidz (Grand Rapids, MI), 2009.

Scott Nickel, *Wind Power Whiz Kid: A Buzz Beaker Brainstorm* (graphic novel), Stone Arch Books (Minneapolis, MN), 2009.

Contributor to periodicals, including *Highlights for Children* and *Your Big Backyard.*

Sidelights

After working for several years as an animator, during which time he created cartoon characters for television programs such as *Courage the Cowardly Dog* and *Sheep in the Big City,* Andy J. Smith moved north to Massachusetts and started a new career as a children's book illustrator. His illustration projects, which include artwork for Bill Myers' "Bug Parables" books and Scott Nickel's "Buzz Beaker Brainstorm" graphic novels, draw on Smith's career background by capturing action-filled stories in sequential cartoon images. In *Jeremy Kreep: Fang Fairy* Smith also takes a turn as author/illustrator, creating a humorous graphic novel about a tooth fairy-gone-bad that *School Library Journal* contributor Nancy Kunz cited for its kid-power story and "kid-friendly cartoon drawings."

Myers' "Bug Parables" books retell well-known biblical stories in a way young children will find engaging and cast insects in the role of the traditional human characters. "Children will be entertained by the many details in Smith's comical cartoon-style artwork," maintained *School Library Journal* contributor Lynn K. Vanca in a review of *The House That Went KerSplat!: The Parable of the Wise and Foolish Builders,* and a *Kirkus Reviews* critic deemed *Stink Bug Saves the Day!: The Parable of the Good Samaritan* "anything but staid" on the strength of Myers' "punchy" text and the "witty details" included in Smith's multi-paneled images. In his collaboration with Nickel, Smith continues to tap a humorous vein; his work for *Billions of Bats: A Buzz Beaker Brainstorm* features a Smith specialty: "engaging characters with exaggerated, off-center features," according to *School Library Journal* critic Mary Elam.

Biographical and Critical Sources

PERIODICALS

Kirkus Reviews, August 15, 2008, review of *Stink Bug Saves the Day!: The Parable of the Good Samaritan.*

School Library Journal, January, 2007, Benjamin Russell, review of *Backyard Bug Battle: A Buzz Beaker Brainstorm,* p. 160; September, 2007, Mary Elam, review of *Billions of Bats: A Buzz Beaker Brainstorm,* p. 224; January, 2007, Nancy Kunz, review of *Jeremy Kreep, Fang Fairy,* p. 153; January, 2009, Lynn K. Vanca, reviews of *The House That Went KerSplat!: The Parable of the Wise and Foolish Builders* and *Stink Bug Saves the Day!,* both p. 82.

ONLINE

Andy J. Smith Home Page, http://www.andyjsmithillustration.com (November 10, 2009).

Andy J. Smith Web log, http://sillydrawings.blogspot.com/ (November 10, 2009).

*   *   *

SOGABE, Aki

Personal

Born in Shizuoka prefecture, Japan; immigrated to United States, 1978; naturalized U.S. citizen, 1997; married; husband's name Bill; children: one son, one daughter. *Education:* Graduated from Japan Art Institute.

Addresses

Home—Bellevue, WA. *E-mail*—akiart@comcast.net.

Career

Artist and children's-book illustrator. *Exhibitions:* Public art is installed in the Pike Place Market, Seattle Center, Nikkei Manor, and Uwajimaya Village in Seattle, WA. Work is also included in Washington State Arts Commission Art in Public Places Program; Oregon's State Art Collection; Mitsubishi International Corporation of Tokyo, Japan, and Seattle, WA; University of Oregon, Eugene; Fort Lewis Army Reservation, WA; Autrey Art Museum, Los Angeles, CA; and at more than thirty public schools in Washington State.

Member

Society of Children's Book Writers and Illustrators, National Collage Society, Guild of American Paper Cutters.

Awards, Honors

Marion Vannetta Ridgway Memorial Award, and Certificate of Merit, Society of Illustrators, both for *Cinnamon, Mint, and Mothballs;* Golden Kite Honor Book Award in Illustration, and Certificate of Merit, Society of Illustrators, both for *The Loyal Cat;* One Hundred Titles for Reading and Sharing selection, New York Public Library, for *Aesop's Fox;* One Hundred Titles

for Reading and Sharing selection, New York Public Library, and Society of Illustrators Original Show selection, both for *Kogi's Mysterious Journey.*

Writings

(Reteller and illustrator) *Aesop's Fox,* Browndeer Press (San Diego, CA), 1999.

ILLUSTRATOR

Ruth Tiller, *Cinnamon, Mint, and Mothballs: A Visit to Grandmother's House,* Browndeer Press (San Diego, CA), 1993.

Lensey Namioka, reteller, *The Loyal Cat,* Harcourt Brace (San Diego, CA), 1995.

Lensey Namioka, *The Hungriest Boy in the World,* Holiday House (New York, NY), 2001.

Elizabeth Partridge, *Oranges on Golden Mountain,* Dutton Children's Books (New York, NY), 2001.

Margaret Hodges, adapter, *The Boy Who Drew Cats,* Holiday House (New York, NY), 2002.

Elizabeth Partridge, adapter, *Kogi's Mysterious Journey,* Dutton Children's Books (New York, NY), 2003.

Nathaniel Lachenmeyer, *The Origami Master,* Albert Whitman (Morton Grove, IL), 2008.

Sidelights

Aki Sogabe has served as the illustrator for a number of award-winning children's books, including Ruth Tiller's *Cinnamon, Mint, and Mothballs: A Visit to Grandmother's House* and Elizabeth Partridge's *Kogi's Mysterious Journey.* Sogabe is especially well known as a practitioner of *kiri-e,* the Japanese art of paper cutting. *School Library Journal* critic Margaret A. Chang, describing the illustrator's contributions to *The Boy Who Drew Cats,* remarked that "Sogabe's cut-paper, watercolor, and airbrush illustrations resonate with the spirit of Japanese woodcuts, and are distinguished by striking composition and harmonious, muted colors."

Born in Japan, Sogabe developed an interest in kiri-e as a student. As she told Elisa Oreglia in a *PaperTigers. org* interview, "One day when I was in middle school I saw Chinese papercut illustrations in a newspaper, and I really liked them, so I copied them. I used origami paper and then cut it with scissors. I used to cut out little pictures and give them to my friends as birthday presents." After moving to the United States with her family, she joined an artist's group and began displaying

Aki Sogabe's delicate cut-paper art includes the illustration "Spring Nap." (Illustration courtesy of Aki Sogabe.)

her work at festivals and galleries in the Pacific Northwest. During one exhibition Sogabe's work was spotted by a children's book editor, leading to her first illustration contract. "I really feel like luck and destiny and chance all worked for me," the artist remarked to Oreglia.

Cinnamon, Mint, and Mothballs, Sogabe's picture-book debut, describes a little girl's visit to her grandmother's house in the country. "The exquisite cut-paper illustrations mix bright and muted hues with subtle texture," a *Publishers Weekly* contributor noted. Based on a folktale, Lensey Namioka's *The Loyal Cat* tells of a kindly priest who rescues a kitten that has magical powers. *Horn Book* reviewer Maria B. Salvadore complimented Sogabe's illustrations for this "hansomely designed" book, stating that "each framed picture augments the mood of the tale and creates a strong sense of place." Namioka and Sogabe have also collaborated on *The Hungriest Boy in the World,* a humorous story about Jiro, a Japanese youngster whose habit of placing things in his mouth leads to trouble. "The tale's comic drama is apparent in the close-up views of characters' tragic expressions," Jennifer M. Brabander observed in *Horn Book,* and a *Publishers Weekly* contributor remarked that Sogabe's "airy compositions underscore the folktale aura, while the impossibly fat-cheeked Jiro steals every scene."

Set in the nineteenth century, *Oranges on Golden Mountain,* a work by Partridge, centers on a Chinese boy who leaves his drought-stricken home to live with his uncle in a California fishing village. A strength of the work, remarked a *Publishers Weekly* critic, is "Sogabe's eye-catching art. Her bold, confident lines and sophisticated shades combine the vigor of woodcuts with the delicacy of watercolor." In *Kogi's Mysterious Journey,* a painter who longs to capture nature's beauty on paper finds himself transformed into a golden carp. "Dignified and handsome, Sogabe's carefully composed cut-paper art employs muted colors to bring Kogi's inner and outer worlds to life," Margaret A. Chang wrote in a review of the story for the *School Library Journal.*

The Boy Who Drew Cats, a work adapted by Margaret Hodges, concerns a young artist whose magical illustrations spring to life to battle a murderous goblin. "Sogabe's . . . crisp paper cutouts" for this story, "often lined in black, stand out starkly against misty, dramatic landscapes," a *Publishers Weekly* reviewer maintained. The artist's work also appears in Nathaniel Lachenmeyer's *The Origami Master,* in which an expert craftsman reacts with anger and jealousy after a songbird proves itself to be his equal. Sogabe's "cut paper and watercolor illustrations have the feel of woodcuts," *Booklist* critic Linda Perkins remarked in a review of Lachenmeyer's evocative picture book.

Biographical and Critical Sources

PERIODICALS

Booklist, September 15, 1995, Susan Dove Lempke, review of *The Loyal Cat,* p. 175; January 1, 2001, Gillian Engberg, review of *Oranges on Golden Mountain,* p. 970; April 1, 2001, Gillian Engberg, review of *The Hungriest Boy in the World,* p. 1479; June 1, 2002, Gillian Engberg, review of *The Boy Who Drew Cats,* p. 1726; October 1, 2008, Linda Perkins, review of *The Origami Master,* p. 48.

Horn Book, January-February, 1996, Maria B. Salvadore, review of *The Loyal Cat,* p. 68; May, 2001, Jennifer M. Brabander, review of *The Hungriest Boy in the World,* p. 313; May-June, 2002, Joanna Rudge Long, review of *The Boy Who Drew Cats,* p. 339.

International Examiner, October 24, 2005, Judith Van Praag, "Aki Sogabe: A Celebrated Creator of Kiri-e (Paper Cut)."

Kirkus Reviews, February 1, 2002, review of *The Boy Who Drew Cats,* p. 182; October 1, 2003, review of *Kogi's Mysterious Journey,* p. 1228; August 1, 2008, review of *The Origami Master.*

New York Times Book Review, October 21, 2001, Laurence Downes, review of *Oranges on Golden Mountain,* p. 31.

Northwest Asian Weekly, October 4-10, 2008, Yoon S. Park, "Creative: Aki Sogabe."

Publishers Weekly, September 13, 1993, review of *Cinnamon, Mint, and Mothballs: A Visit to Grandmother's House,* p. 128; September 4, 1995, review of *The Loyal Cat,* p. 69; August 16, 1999, review of *Aesop's Fox,* p. 84; December 11, 2000, review of *Oranges on Golden Mountain,* p. 84; February 5, 2001, review of *The Hungriest Boy in the World,* p. 88; January 28, 2002, review of *The Boy Who Drew Cats,* p. 290; December 15, 2003, review of *Kogi's Mysterious Journey,* p. 72.

School Library Journal, March, 2001, Margaret A. Chang, review of *Oranges on Golden Mountain,* p. 218; April, 2001, Grace Oliff, review of *The Hungriest Boy in the World,* p. 119; March, 2002, Margaret A. Chang, review of *The Boy Who Drew Cats,* p. 214; November, 2002, Margaret A. Chang, review of *Kogi's Mysterious Journey,* p. 128; October, 2008, Susan Scheps, review of *The Origami Master,* p. 114.

ONLINE

Aki Sogabe Home Page, http://akipapercut.com (November 1, 2009).

PaperTigers.org, http://www.papertigers.org/ (March, 2003), Elia Oreglia, interview with Elizabeth Partridge and Sogabe.

*   *   *

STAPLES, Suzanne Fisher 1945-
(Suzanne Fisher)

Personal

Born August 27, 1945, in Philadelphia, PA; daughter of Robert Charles (an engineer) and Helen Brittain (a manager) Fisher; married Nicholas Green, September 2, 1967 (divorced, August, 1976); married Eugene Staples

Suzanne Fisher Staples (Reproduced by permission of Suzanne Fisher Staples.)

(a teacher and writer), January 25, 1980 (divorced, 1992); married Wayne Harley. *Education:* Cedar Crest College, B.A., 1967. *Politics:* "Independent." *Religion:* Episcopalian. *Hobbies and other interests:* Running, tennis, music, theater.

Addresses

Home—PA.

Career

Novelist. Business International Corp., Asian marketing director, 1974-76; United Press International, Washington, DC, news editor and correspondent in New York, NY, Washington, DC, Hong Kong, and India, 1975-83; *Washington Post,* part-time editor for foreign desk, 1983-85; U.S. Agency for International Development, consultant, 1986-87; freelance writer, 1988—. Lecturer on the status of women in the Islamic Republic of Pakistan. Citizens for a Better Eastern Shore, member of board.

Member

Asia Society, Authors Guild, Authors League of America.

Awards, Honors

Newbery Honor book selection, 1990, Best Books for Young Adults citation, and Notable Books for Children citation, all American Library Association (ALA), Children's Book of the Year selection, Library of Congress, Notable Book of the Year selection, *New York Times,* Notable Children's Trade Book in the Field of Social Studies, National Council for the Social Studies/Children's Book Council, and International Board on Books for Young People Honor List selection, 1992, all for *Shabanu;* Best Books for Young Adults citation, ALA, Notable Books for a Global Society, International Reading Association, Notable Children's Books in the Language Arts, National Council of Teachers of English, Books for the Teen Age designation, New York Public Library, and Best Children's Book of the Year selection, Bank Street College of Education, all for *Dangerous Skies;* Children's Crown Collection, National Christian Schools Association, for *The Green Dog;* Notable Children's Books selection, ALA, for *Under the Persimmon Tree;* Best Children's Book of the Year selection, Bank Street College of Education, and International Book Award Honor Book, Society of School Librarians, both for *The House of Djinn.*

Writings

Shabanu: Daughter of the Wind, Knopf (New York, NY), 1989.
Haveli, Knopf (New York, NY), 1993.
Dangerous Skies, Farrar, Straus (New York, NY), 1996, published as *Storm,* Julia MacRae (London, England), 1998.
Shiva's Fire, Farrar, Straus (New York, NY), 2000.
The Green Dog: A Mostly True Story, Farrar, Straus (New York, NY), 2003.
Under the Permission Tree, Farrar, Straus (New York, NY), 2005.
The House of Djinn, Farrar, Straus (New York, NY), 2008.

Contributor to *Shattered: Stories of Children and War,* Knopf (New York, NY), 2002; contributor, sometimes under name Suzanne Fisher, to periodicals, including *Smithsonian.*

Adaptations

Dangerous Skies was adapted as an audiobook by Bantam Doubleday, 1997; *Shiva's Fire* was adapted as an audiobook by Recorded Books, 2000.

Sidelights

A former international reporter stationed in South Asia, Suzanne Fisher Staples is known for creating compelling coming-of-age stories for young adults that sensitively portray other cultures, including the novels *Shabanu: Daughter of the Wind* and *Under the Persimmon Tree.* Her stories about adolescent girls from around the

world have been well received, in part because of their nuanced portrayals of unfamiliar locales such as those of Pakistan, India, and Afghanistan. Staples' works have also garnered praise for their intense subject matter, wealth of detail, and realistic characters. Her "literary protagonists wrestle with developing themselves, while yielding to the culture which imbues them with the whisper of their inevitability," Jinx Stapleton Watson explained in *ALAN Review.*

Staples's own experiences, including her years spent working as a journalist, fuel her works. As she told *Publishers Weekly* interviewer Lynda Brill, "My books are made up of real stories about real people." A graduate of Cedar Crest College, Staples began her journalism career at a small newspaper in Evergreen, Colorado. In 1974 she decided to see the world, and moved to Hong Kong to work as a marketing director for the Business International Corporation. She later found a job with the United Press International's New Delhi Bureau as head of the South Asia edition. In 1983 she returned to the United States and took a part-time editor's job on the foreign desk of the *Washington Post.* However, Staples' wanderlust returned, and just two years later she returned to Pakistan as a consultant for the United States Agency for International Development (USAID) project in the Cholistan Desert of the Punjab province. Her focus there was on improving the health, nutrition, and housing of poor women and their families in rural areas. Upon her return to the United States in 1987, Staples began writing about what she had seen and heard in Pakistan. The resulting novel, *Shabanu,* was an auspicious literary debut.

Shabanu, which was published in 1989, earned critical praise and was named a 1990 Newbery Honor book. In the novel, Staples tells the story of a spirited young nomadic girl who lives in the Cholistan desert in Pakistan. Although she is perfectly happy to tend to her beloved band of camels, twelve-year-old Shabanu soon finds herself unwillingly betrothed to an older man of her parents' choosing. A series of unfortunate occurrences presents her with the opportunity to choose between this arranged marriage to a wealthy landowner—who already has three wives and her independence. Echoing the praises of numerous reviewers, *Horn Book* reviewer Hanna B. Zeiger claimed of *Shabanu* that the "vivid portrayal of life and death in this desert world is stunning in its honesty."

Shabanu provides vivid pictures of everyday life in a nomadic community, in addition to descriptions of the region's more-colorful marriage preparations and rituals. Maurya Simon, writing in the *New York Times Book Review,* noted that "some of the most affecting and lyrical passages of the book detail the austere beauty of the Cholistan, as seen through the young narrator's eyes." "It is a pleasure to read a book that explores a way of life so profoundly different from our own," the critic added, "and that does so with such sensitivity, admiration, and verisimilitude." *Voice of Youth Advocates* re-

viewer Marijo Grimes also praised Staples' story, writing that "more multi-cultural [young adult] novels of this caliber are needed in today's market."

Staples continues Shabanu's story in *Haveli,* a novel that takes its name from the home where Shabanu finds shelter during her tumultuous life. Picking up Shabanu's story six years after the earlier book ended, Staples explores the intrigues among the four wives of the aging Rahim. The youngest, the most beautiful, and the least-cultured of the wives, Shabanu falls prey to the scheming of the elder wives and must use all her wits to protect herself and her young daughter, Mumtaz. Ever the idealist, Shabanu also seeks to protect her best friend from an arranged marriage to her husband's mentally-deficient son. As the intricate plot unwinds, Shabanu loses both her husband and her friend to violent deaths, and falls in love with Omar, a relative of her husband who has returned from the United States.

"While the intricate cast and unfamiliar terms will send readers scuttling to the list of characters and glossary from time to time," *Bulletin of the Center for Children's Books* reviewer Betsy Hearne added of *Haveli* that "the dramatic plot will bring them breathlessly back to the story." Although there is sex and violence, the critic added that "it's never sensationalized and yet will draw YA readers like a magnet." As with *Shabanu,* reviewers praised Staples' vivid characterization and her power at communicating the essence of an unfamiliar culture. Ellen Fader observed in *Horn Book* that in *Haveli* "Staples shows considerable talent in crafting a taut, suspenseful narrative with strong female characters and a terrific sense of place."

Staples returns to the world of Shabanu in *The House of Djinn,* "a thoroughly absorbing read," according to *Horn Book* contributor Deirdre F. Baker. Set ten years after the events of *Haveli,* the novel focuses on Shabanu's fifteen-year-old daughter, Mumtaz, who has been raised by abusive relatives since her father's murder and her mother's subsequent disappearance. When Mumtaz's grandfather, a tribal leader, passes away, her beloved American cousin, Jameel, is named as his successor. Mumtaz is shocked to learn, however, that her grandfather's will also decrees that she must marry Jameel, and her life is further thrown into disarray when she learns that Shabanu has finally emerged from hiding. "Readers will ponder the questions about responsibility and freedom Staples raises in the intriguing marriage drama," Rochman observed, and a *Kirkus Reviews* critic praised the "fascinating tale of the conflict between tribal tradition and modernization in contemporary Pakistan." In the words of a *Publishers Weekly* reviewer, Staples "transports readers to an intriguing corner of the universe to provide an insightful look at modern Middle Eastern culture."

In *Dangerous Skies* Staples turned her attention to the racism that continues to pervade a small town on the shore of Virginia's Chesapeake Bay. Two twelve-year-

old friends, Buck (who is white) and Tunes (who is black), find the body of their older friend Jorge Rodrigues floating in a creek. The friends suspect Jumbo Rawlins, a respected white landowner, but when Jumbo implicates Tunes in the murder, the friends are brought face-to-face with the different worlds they inhabit. Fearing that her word will not be trusted against the word of a white man, Tunes flees, and Buck begins to question whom he should trust, his longtime friend or the family who advises him to stay clear of Tunes. "Buck's loss of innocence is played out with anguished energy," noted *Horn Book* reviewer Nancy Vasilakis, and though Tunes is not convicted, she leaves the town forever, her reputation ruined. While some critics thought that some plot elements and characters in *Dangerous Skies* are not up to the standards of *Shabanu* and *Haveli,* many applauded Staples's nuanced treatment of the perils of racism. Several made comparisons between *Dangerous Skies* and Harper Lee's classic *To Kill a Mockingbird.* A *Publishers Weekly* reviewer, for instance, called *Dangerous Skies* a "masterfully crafted story" that "boldly conveys uncomfortable truths about society while expressing the innocence of children."

Shiva's Fire focuses on the life of a Hindu Indian girl from South Asia. From the time she is born, it is clear that Parvati is different from other girls. The circumstances of her birth are unusual: she is born in the middle of the tremendous cyclone that kills her father and destroys much of her village. The other babies in the village die, but magically, Parvati lives. The maharajah, for who Parvati's father had been an elephant keeper, also has a seemingly magical child that day—a son, with whom, many years later, Parvati falls in love. An excellent dancer, Parvati receives an offer from a renowned guru to study to become a *devadasi,* one who serves the gods through sacred dances. Parvati thinks that it is her *dharma,* her sacred duty, to be a dancer, but when she returns home and meets the maharajah's son, she begins to question if that really is her destiny. Like Parvati, Rama, the maharaja's son, has been living a lonely life, shunned by others for his otherworldly talents yet trying to serve the gods by fulfilling his own dharma. Now the two both wonder if it would be better to continue in their current paths or give in to their growing love. "

Many reviewers noted that, just as Staples faithfully recreated Pakistani culture in *Shabanu,* she evokes the beauty of India in *Shiva's Fire.* She "is a magnificent storyteller who beautifully recreates the colors, sounds, and smells of India," Debra Mitts Smith wrote in *Kliatt.* The injection of a romance in the final quarter of the book might not have worked in less-capable hands," commented *Booklist* critic Ilene Cooper, "but Staples makes the element seem like a natural evolution." Beyond that, Brill commented in *Publishers Weekly,* "Staples gives an 'insider's' view of Asian culture without imposing judgment or injecting American values."

The Green Dog: A Mostly True Story is a departure from Staples's previous books and offers a fictionalized account of a summer from her childhood when a dog adopted her family. The work centers on a soon-to-be fifth-grader named Suzanne, whose dreams of owning a pet come true when a scruffy canine she spotted on the highway miraculously appears at her family's door. Despite his misgivings, Suzanne's father allows her to keep the dog, which she names Jeff. "What follows is a perfectly riotous summer with Jeff getting into laugh-aloud trouble at every turn," wrote *School Library Journal* contributor Barbara Scotto. Eventually, Suzanne's father sends the dog away to live on a farm, and this bittersweet ending caused other reviewers to have a much different reaction to the book. *Horn Book* contributor Susan Dove Lempke maintained that "the tone is anxious and sad," and Staples writes about her memories of "loneliness and pain with visceral intensity." A *Kirkus Reviews* contributor offered a more positive assessment of the work, writing that the "story is written with style, humor, and empathy."

Set in northern Afghanistan just months after the events of 9/11, *Under the Permission Tree* focuses on the unlikely relationship between two individuals from vastly different backgrounds. After her father and brother are kidnapped by Taliban forces, and her mother and infant brother are killed in an air raid, twelve-year-old Najmah disguises herself as a boy and flees her homeland. Arriving at a refugee camp in Pakistan, the youngster meets Nusrat, a former New Yorker who now teaches at the camp while awaiting word from her husband, an Afghani doctor. A reviewer in *Publishers Weekly* commented that the author "powerfully and honestly expresses the plight of a civilization caught between terrorists and American bombs," and Claire Rosser, writing in *Kliatt,* described *Under the Permission Tree* as "a powerful story that helps us understand the complexities of life in that part of the world." Although Staples offers some background information about the political and military conflict in Afghanistan, Hazel Rochman noted in *Booklist,* "it's the personal story, not the history, that compels as it takes readers beyond the modern stereotypes of Muslims as fundamentalist fanatics."

Staples continues to find inspiration for her novels through her travels to the Middle East and Asia. She remarked in an essay on the Macmillan Web site that "that the world is wondrous and wide, and I hope I will never cease to be moved by places and people who give rise to ideas for stories. Because stories are the most important thing in the world. They teach us how to live, how to love, and, most important, how to find magic wherever we are."

Biographical and Critical Sources

BOOKS

Children's Literature Review, Gale (Detroit, MI), Volume 60, 2000, Volume 137, 2008.

St. James Guide to Young Adult Writers, 2nd edition, St. James Press (Detroit, MI), 1999.

Sutherland, Zena, editor, *Children's Books and Their Creators,* Houghton Mifflin (Boston, MA), 1995.

PERIODICALS

ALAN Review, fall, 1999, Jinx Stapleton Watson, "Individual Choice and Family Loyalty: Suzanne Fisher Staples' Protagonists Come of Age," pp. 25-28.

Booklist, June 1-15, 1993, Ilene Cooper, review of *Haveli,* p. 1813; March 15, 2000, Ilene Cooper, review of *Shiva's Fire,* p. 1375; June 1, 2000, Stephanie Zvirin, review of *Shabanu: Daughter of the Wind,* p. 1874; May 15, 2001, Lolly Gepson, review of *Shiva's Fire,* p. 1764; October 1, 2003, Gillian Engberg, review of *The Green Dog: A Mostly True Story,* p. 322; July, 2005, Hazel Rochman, review of *Under the Persimmon Tree,* p. 1923; February 15, 2008, Hazel Rochman, review of *The House of Djinn,* p. 75.

Bulletin of the Center for Children's Books, November, 1993, Betsy Hearne, review of *Haveli,* pp. 73-74.

Guardian (London, England), April 14, 1998, Philip Pullman, review of *Storm,* p. 5.

Horn Book, January-February, 1990, Hanna B. Zeiger, review of *Shabanu,* p. 72; January-February, 1994, Ellen Fader, review of *Haveli,* pp. 75-76; January-February, 1997, Nancy Vasilakis, review of *Dangerous Skies,* pp. 67-68; May, 2000, review of *Shiva's Fire,* p. 321; January, 2001, Kristi Beavin, review of *Shiva's Fire,* p. 125; September-October, 2003, Susan Dove Lempke, review of *The Green Dog,* p. 620; May-June, 2008, Deirdre F. Baker, review of *The House of Djinn,* p. 328.

Journal of Adolescent and Adult Literacy, May, 2000, Jo-Ann Thom, review of *Dangerous Skies,* pp. 779-780.

Kirkus Reviews, August 1, 2003, review of *The Green Dog,* p. 1024; July 1, 2005, review of *Under the Persimmon Tree;* April 1, 2008, review of *The House of Djinn.*

Kliatt, January, 2002, Debra Mitts Smith, review of *Shiva's Fire,* pp. 13-14; September, 2005, Claire Rosser, review of *Under the Persimmon Tree,* p. 15; March, 2008, Claire Rosser, review of *The House of Djinn,* p. 20.

New York Times Book Review, November 12, 1989, Maurya Simon, review of *Shabanu,* p. 32; November 14, 1993, Daniyal Mueenuddin, review of *Haveli,* p. 59; July 16, 2000, Laura Shapiro, review of *Shiva's Fire,* p. 26.

Publishers Weekly, July 1, 1996, review of *Dangerous Skies,* p. 61; January 31, 2000, review of *Shiva's Fire,* p. 108; February 14, 2000, Lynda Brill, interview with Staples, p. 168; July 28, 2003, review of *The Green Dog,* p. 95; June 20, 2005, review of *Under the Persimmon Tree,* p. 78; February 11, 2008, review of *The House of Djinn,* p. 70.

San Francisco Chronicle, December 1, 1996, Evelyn C. White, review of *Dangerous Skies,* p. 8.

School Library Journal, October, 1996, Cindy Darling Codell, review of *Dangerous Skies,* pp. 149-150; January, 2001, JoAnn Carhart, review of *Shiva's Fire,* p. 75; September, 2003, Barbara Scotto, review of *The Green Dog,* pp. 221-222; July, 2005, Kathleen Isaacs, review of *Under the Persimmon Tree,* p. 109; April, 2008, Joyce Adams Burner, review of *The House of Djinn,* p. 150.

Times Educational Supplement, June 8, 1990, Ashok Bery, review of *Daughter of the Wind,* p. B13; September 9, 1994, Imogen Forster, review of *Haveli,* p. A20.

Voice of Youth Advocates, April, 1990, Marijo Grimes, review of *Shabanu,* pp. 34-35.

ONLINE

BookPage.com, http://www.bookpage.com/ (November 15, 2009), Alice Cary, "Stories Gleaned from the Suffering in Afghanistan."

Macmillan Web site, http://us.macmillan.com/ (November 15, 2009), "Suzanne Fisher Staples."

Random House Web site, http://www.randomhouse.com/ (November 15, 2009), "Suzanne Fisher Staples."

Suzanne Fisher Staples Home Page, http://www.suzanne fisherstaples.com (November 15, 2009).*

* * *

STEVENSON, Emma

Personal

Born in Birmingham, England. *Education:* University College Falmouth, degree (illustration), 2006.

Addresses

Home—Birmingham, England. *Agent*—Herman Agency, 350 Central Park W., New York, NY 10025. *E-mail*—elstevenson76@hotmail.co.uk.

Career

Illustrator, specializing in natural history, beginning 2006.

Awards, Honors

Cybils Nonfiction Picture Book Award nomination, 2008, and AAAS/Subaru SB&F Prize for Excellence in Science Books finalist, Best of the Best designation, Chicago Public Library, and Outstanding Science Trade Book designation, National Science Teacher's Association, all 2009, all for *Eggs* by Marilyn Singer.

Illustrator

Marilyn Singer, *Eggs,* Holiday House (New York, NY), 2008.

Nicholas Nigrotis, *Killer Ants,* Holiday House (New York, NY), 2009.

Katherine Kirkpatrick and Jennifer Kirkpatrick, *Faces of the Ancient One,* Holiday House (New York, NY), 2010.

Biographical and Critical Sources

PERIODICALS

Booklist, April 1, 2008, Carolyn Phelan, review of *Eggs,* p. 52.

Horn Book, May-June, 2008, Danielle J. Ford, review of *Eggs,* p. 341.

Kirkus Reviews, February 15, 2008, review of *Eggs.*

School Library Journal, April, 2008, Margaret Bush, review of *Eggs,* p. 137.

ONLINE

Emma Stevenson Web log, http://emmastevensonillustra tion.blogspot.com/ (November 10, 2009).

Herman Agency Web site, http://www.hermanagencyinc. com/ (November 10, 2009), "Emma Stevenson."*

SYDOR, Colleen 1960-

Personal
Born 1960, in Winnipeg, Manitoba, Canada. *Education:* University of Manitoba, B.A.

Addresses
Home—Winnipeg, Canada. *E-mail*—sydor123@mts.net.

Career
Author and floral designer.

Writings

Ooo-cha!, illustrated by Ruth Ohi, Annick Press (New York, NY), 1999.

Colleen Sydor's picture book **Camilla Chameleon** *comes to life in Pascale Constantin's quirky cartoon art.* (Kids Can Press, 2005. Illustrations © 2005 Pascale Constantin. Used by permission of Kids Can Press Ltd., Toronto.)

Smarty Pants, illustrated by Suzane Langlois, Lobster Press (Montréal, Québec, Canada), 1999.

Fashion Fandango, illustrated by Lenka Vernex, Lobster Press (Montréal, Québec, Canada), 2000.

Maxwell's Metamorphosis, illustrated by Lenka Vernex, Lobster Press (Montréal, Québec, Canada), 2000.

Camilla Chameleon, illustrated by Pascale Constantin, Kids Can Press (Toronto, Ontario, Canada), 2005.

Raising a Little Stink, Kids Can Press (Toronto, Ontario, Canada), 2006.

My Mother Is a French Fry and Further Proof of My Fuzzed-up Life, Kids Can Press (Toronto, Ontario, Canada), 2008.

Timmerman Was Here, illustrated by Nicolas Debron, Tundra Books (Toronto, Ontario, Canada), 2009.

Sidelights

A native of Manitoba, Canadian author Colleen Sydor has written a variety of works for children, ranging from picture books to elementary-school chapter books to young-adult novels. After the appearance of *Ooocha!* in 1999, Sydor penned three novels featuring a preteen girl named Norah. In the first installment, *Smarty Pants,* Norah stays with her namesake great aunt. While the two enjoy their time together, the younger Norah does not always believe all of her great aunt's superstitious stories, particularly the one which warns that bad things will happen if she does not shake out her clothes in the evening. Disaster hits later when a forgotten pair of the previous day's underwear slips out from Nora's pant leg while she is at school. While embarrassed by her exposed undergarment, the girl decides to take a lighthearted approach to the situation and turn her misfortune into a funny scene by claiming she has invented a new hat, with built-in holes for pig tails. The girl's unusual antics continue in *Fashion Fandango,* where Norah hopes to be selected as a peer mediator at school, and *Maxwell's Metamorphosis,* which follows Norah as she deals with a classroom bully. Reviewing *Smarty Pants* in *Resource Links,* a reviewer applauded the "well-developed but not stereotypical characters," while another critic in the same periodical called *Fashion Fandango* an "engaging story" by Sydor that is "sure to be a hit."

Animal characters figure in several of Sydor's picture books, such as *Camilla Chameleon* and *Raising a Little Stink.* Illustrated by Pascale Constantin, *Camilla Chameleon* begins with a mother-to-be who has a craving for cream of chameleon soup. The daughter she bears consequently ends up with an unusual talent for camouflaging herself, particularly when it comes to activities she dislikes. A teacher, however, turns Camilla's disappearing act to good use when she recruits the girl to help actors remember their lines for the school play. A stinkbug also puts his unique skill to action in *Raising a Little Stink.* The insect, a mouse, a lion, and his tamer all leave the circus and settle in a small, abandoned home. Unfortunately, the other three leave all of the work to the stinkbug, forcing him to take care of the

Cover of Sydor's novel middle-grade novel **My Mother Is a French Fry and Further Proof of My Fuzzed-up Life.** (KCP Fiction, 2008. Used by permission of Kids Can Press Ltd., Toronto.)

cooking and cleaning. Tiring of being taken advantage of, the insect resorts to releasing a powerful odor to drive out his freeloading friends. In her *School Library Journal* review, JoAnn Jonas described *Camilla Chameleon* as "a fresh story about an unusual child who gets into some bizarre situations." Discussing the same work in *Quill & Quire,* Carol L. MacKay commented favorably on the author's narrative, finding it full of "plenty of playful word choices and a penchant for descriptive silliness." *Raising a Little Stink* also found a favorable audience with *Resource Links* reviewer Linda Ludke who predicted that Sydor's "funny fable will be a story-time hit."

In her first young-adult work, *My Mother Is a French Fry and Further Proof of My Fuzzed-up Life,* Sydor follows the coming-of-age angst of a teenager who is embarrassed by her overfriendly mother. The woman loves her job at a fast-food restaurant, part of which involves dressing in a French fry costume. Mortified by her mother's behavior, fifteen-year-old Eli believes that Mom behaves this way only to torment her, particularly when the woman announces that she is going to have another baby. This unexpected event proves to be a

turning point in the relationship between mother and daughter, however, when it is revealed that much of Eli's resentment about her mom stems from the guilt she feels over the sudden death of a sibling years earlier. Several reviewers thought that Sydor captures the character of a self-centered adolescent exceptionally well, *Canadian Review of Materials* contributor Gregory Bryan writing that "the 15-year-old protagonist's irreverent, sarcastic, goo-eyed and love-struck voice is perfect." *School Library Journal* reviewer Lindsay Cesari also concluded of *My Mother Is a French Fry and Further Proof of My Fuzzed-up Life* that "readers will relate to Eli's conflicted feelings about her mother." Describing the characters as "wonderfully original," a *Publishers Weekly* critic praised Sydor's novel as "a funny and tender story" and Eli a "touching heroine."

Biographical and Critical Sources

PERIODICALS

Canadian Review of Materials, November 21, 2008, Gregory Bryan, review of *My Mother Is a French Fry and Further Proof of My Fuzzed-up Life.*

Kirkus Reviews, September 15, 2005, review of *Camilla Chameleon,* p. 1035; August 1, 2008, review of *My Mother Is a French Fry and Further Proof of My Fuzzed-up Life.*

Kliatt, September, 2008, Myrna Marler, review of *My Mother Is a French Fry and Further Proof of My Fuzzed-up Life,* p. 22.

Publishers Weekly, July 14, 2008, review of *My Mother Is a French Fry and Further Proof of My Fuzzed-up Life,* p. 67.

Quill & Quire, August, 2005, Carol L. MacKay, review of *Camilla Chameleon;* March, 2006, Gwyneth Evans, review of *Raising a Little Stink.*

Resource Links, February, 2000, reviews of *Ooo-cha!,* pp. 5-6, and *Smarty Pants,* p. 6; December, 2000, review of *Fashion Fandango,* p. 12; February, 2001, review of *Maxwell's Metamorphosis,* p. 20; February, 2006, Zoe Johnstone, review of *Camilla Chameleon,* p. 13; April, 2006, Linda Ludke, review of *Raising a Little Stink,* p. 12.

School Library Journal, March, 2000, Amy Lilien-Harper, review of *Ooo-cha!,* p. 214; June, 2006, JoAnn Jonas, review of *Camilla Chameleon,* p. 128; November, 2008, Lindsay Cesari, review of *My Mother Is a French Fry and Further Proof of My Fuzzed-up Life,* p. 138.*

T-V

TUSA, Tricia 1960-

Personal
Surname is pronounced "*too*-sa"; born July 19, 1960, in Houston, TX; daughter of Theodore S., Jr., and Francese Tusa; married; children: one daughter. *Education:* Attended University of California, Santa Cruz, 1978; studied art in Paris, 1981; University of Texas at Austin, B.F.A. (painting and sculpture), 1982; New York University, M.A. (art therapy), 1989. *Hobbies and other interests:* Horseback riding, oil painting, reading.

Addresses
Home—Santa Fe, NM.

Career
Author and illustrator of children's books. Art therapist with learning-disabled and emotionally disturbed children, Acquired Immune Deficiency Syndrome (AIDS) patients, and psychiatric-care patients at various institutions, including Mount Sinai Hospital, New York, NY, 1988, Kingsboro Hospital, Brooklyn, NY, 1988, and Reece School, New York, NY, 1989. Art instructor at numerous institutions, including Houston Retarded Center, Houston, TX, 1980, Children's Museum, Houston, 1984, and Post Oak Montessori School, Houston, 1989-90. Designer and illustrator for Estee Lauder, 1982, DC Comics, 1983, and Cooper Hewitt Museum. Head chef at soup kitchen in Santa Fe, NM.

Member
American Art Therapy Association, Southwest Writers.

Awards, Honors
Children's Choice designation, International Reading Association/Children's Book Council, 1986, for *Miranda;* Pick of the List selection, American Booksellers, 1987, for *Maebelle's Suitcase*

Writings

SELF-ILLUSTRATED

Libby's New Glasses, Holiday House (New York, NY), 1984.
Miranda, Macmillan (New York, NY), 1985.
Chicken, Macmillan (New York, NY), 1986.
Maebelle's Suitcase, Macmillan (New York, NY), 1987.
Stay Away from the Junkyard!, Macmillan (New York, NY), 1988.
Sherman and Pearl, Macmillan (New York, NY), 1989.
Camilla's New Hairdo, Farrar, Straus (New York, NY), 1991.
The Family Reunion, Farrar, Straus (New York, NY), 1993.
Sisters, Crown (New York, NY), 1995.
Bunnies in My Head, afterword by Barbara Bush, University of Texas (Austin, TX), 1998.

ILLUSTRATOR

Steven Kroll, *Loose Tooth,* Holiday House (New York, NY), 1984.
Angela Shelf Medaris, *We Eat Dinner in the Bathtub,* State House Press (Austin, TX), 1990.
William H. Hooks, *Lo-Jack and the Pirates,* Bantam (New York, NY), 1991.
Stuart J. Murphy, *Lemonade for Sale,* HarperCollins (New York, NY), 1998.
Susan Bartlett Weber, *Seal Island School,* Viking (New York, NY), 1999.
Edith Pattou, *Mrs. Spitzer's Garden,* Harcourt (San Diego, CA), 2001.
Alison Jackson, *The Ballad of Valentine,* Dutton Children's Books (New York, NY), 2002.
Mem Fox, *The Magic Hat,* Harcourt (San Diego, CA), 2002.
Susan Bartlett, *The Seal Island Seven,* Viking (New York, NY), 2002.
Katherine Ayres, *A Long Way,* Candlewick Press (Cambridge, MA), 2003.

Linda Ashman, *How to Make a Night,* HarperCollins (New York, NY), 2004.

Jacquelyn Mitchard, *Starring Prima!: The Mouse of the Ballet Jolie,* HarperCollins (New York, NY), 2004.

Avi, *The End of the Beginning: Being the Adventures of a Small Snail (and an Even Smaller Ant),* Harcourt (Orlando, FL), 2004.

Stuart J. Murphy, *Treasure Map,* HarperCollins (New York, NY), 2004.

Janice Earl, *Jan Has a Doll,* Harcourt (Orlando, FL), 2005.

Paul B. Janeczko and J. Patrick Lewis, *Wing Nuts: Screwy Haiku,* Little, Brown (New York, NY), 2006.

Nancy Coffelt, *Fred Stays with Me!,* Little, Brown (New York, NY), 2007.

Avi, *A Beginning, a Muddle, and an End: The Right Way to Write Writing,* Harcourt (Orlando, FL), 2008.

Jim Averbeck, *In a Blue Room,* Harcourt (Orlando, FL), 2008.

Kate Feiffer, *The Problem with the Puddles,* Simon & Schuster Books for Young Readers (New York, NY), 2009.

Sarah Sullivan, *Once upon a Baby Brother,* Farrar, Straus & Giroux (New York, NY), 2010.

Kelly DiPucchio, *The Sandwich Swap, by Her Majesty Queen Rania,* Hyperion (New York, NY), 2010.

Contributor of illustrations to children's magazines.

Sidelights

Picture-book author and illustrator Tricia Tusa brings an off-beat, humorous slant to the stories she enlivens with her colorful artwork. In addition to illustrating texts by authors such as Steven Kroll and Stuart J. Murphy, Tusa has also authored several books of her own, which she fills with her unique illustrations. Describing the watercolor work she features in her original picture book *Sisters, School Library Journal* contributor Tana Elias noted that Tusa's "sly illustrations perfectly capture small details, such as expressions of shock and annoyance on the faces of the characters," resulting in a book that youngsters would "delight in." Other titles both written and illustrated by Tusa include *The Family Reunion, Bunnies in My Head,* and the award-winning *Miranda.*

Born in 1960, Tusa attended the University of California, continued her art training in Paris, and then earned a master's degree in art therapy at New York University in 1989. Her early illustration projects, published during the early 1980s, included creating art for Stephen Kroll's *Loose Tooth* and producing the original, self-illustrated picture book *Libby's New Glasses. Libby's New Glasses* expresses the discomfort children often feel upon donning their first pair of eyeglasses. While a *Bulletin of the Center for Children's Books* reviewer characterized the book's text as weak, praise was given to Tusa's artwork, which exhibits "vigor, humor, and scrabbly details." In the story, a young girl with new glasses meets a beautiful ostrich, only to discover that the bird buries its head in the sand because it sports a

hated pair of eyeglasses. In *Publishers Weekly,* a contributor called *Libby's New Glasses* "a fanciful tale that will hearten children as much as it amuses them."

Tusa finds the inspiration for her artwork in everyday life. "I study people's faces down the aisles at the grocery store, at the Laundromat," she once admitted to *SATA.* "I eavesdrop at the hardware store. An unusual face or an innocuous comment from a stranger can sometimes spark or complete an idea." Indeed, several of Tusa's books depict very unusual faces, and these are usually attached to rather eccentric characters. In *Maebelle's Suitcase,* for example, an elderly woman who loves birds makes her own home in a tree so that she can look out for her feathered friends while she plies her trade as a hat-maker. The woman's creativity helps to solve a problem for Binkle the bird, whose plans to fly south for the winter have been stalled until he can find a way to transport his belongings. Maebelle works Binkle's tiny possessions—small rocks, dirt, some flowers, leaves, and a lovely forked branch—into a hat that is put on permanent display in town over the winter, allowing Binkle to take flight unencumbered, knowing that his things will be under lock and key. In *Booklist* Denise M. Wilms praised Tusa's use of charcoal and watercolor, noting that the artwork creates "a feeling of spaciousness that suits the story's mood and concept."

Tricia Tusa creates whimsical illustrations that brings to life her original story in **Maebelle's Suitcase.** (Simon & Schuster for Young Readers, 1987. Reproduced by permission of Simon & Schuster for Young Readers, an imprint of Simon & Schuster Macmillan.)

Tusa's engaging illustrations capture the sometimes poignant story in Nancy Coffelt's story for **Fred Stays with Me!** (Text copyright © 2007 by Nancy Coffelt. Illustrations copyright © 1997 by Tricia Tusa. By permission of Little Brown and Company. All rights reserved.)

Writing in *School Library Journal,* Helen E. Williams concluded of *Maebelle's Suitcase* that "text and illustrations are harmonious and wonderfully complementary in [Tusa's] . . . quiet but humorous book."

Eccentric characters are also the focal point of *The Family Reunion,* as the Beneada family converges on a quiet house in the suburbs, food and drink in hand, only to discover that two of the people assembled are strangers to everyone present. At first, the Beneadas try to place Esther and Fester, who arrive on time but seem strangely uncomfortable amid the genial gathering. Finally it is discovered that it is the Beneada family that has met at the wrong house: Esther and Fester are the home's owners, and the scheduled family party is accidentally taking place across the street. "The dazzling visual humor will have young readers rolling on the floor while acknowledging the common problem of not remembering who someone is," maintained *Booklist* contributor Deborah Abbott, while a critic for *Kirkus Reviews* called *The Family Reunion* "pure comedy— especially Tusa's wonderfully pointed cartoon caricatures of family types in full, over ebullient swing."

In contrast to her engaging cast of humorous eccentrics, Tusa has also created a number of young characters who discover their own creativity, whether it be through drawing or some other talent. In *Miranda,* a young pianist has been fed a daily dose of Mozart, Bartok, and Hayden by her supportive parents and her piano teacher.

When she hears a street musician playing boogie-woogie music, Miranda realizes that her piano is capable of creating a variety of different sounds. While trying to conjure these new musical moods on the piano keyboard, the girl is met with so much resistance by well-meaning adults that she boycotts the instrument altogether, until her parents and teacher relent. Tusa creates a "spirited story" enhanced by what Clarissa Erwin characterized in *School Library Journal* as "scratchy comical drawings . . . that capture a wild Miranda who just has to cut loose."

In *Bunnies in My Head,* a young artist is struck with an equally powerful muse, filling every part of her life with artwork. In addition to reflecting the exuberance of a creative child, the book has a special significance for Tusa: it is filled with miniature versions of drawings done by young patients at Houston's M.D. Anderson Cancer Center where Tusa has worked as an art therapist. Noting that Tusa's framing illustrations successfully enhance the children's art, *School Library Journal* contributor Christine A. Moesch added that "some of the pictures . . . are charming preschool efforts, while others . . . are astounding in their maturity and beauty." Former First Lady Barbara Bush contributed an afterword to *Bunnies in My Head,* which was published in 1998.

Since that late 1990s Tusa has primarily worked as an illustrator, and her engaging drawings are a feature of *How to Make a Night* by Linda Ashman, *A Long Way* by Katherine Ayres, Nancy Coffelt's *Fred Stays with Me!,* and Jim Averbeck's *In a Blue Room.* In Ashman's story, the wreckage of a busy day in a bustling family spills across the beginning pages, until a young girl sets to work cleaning things up and then pulling down and pocketing the sun for safekeeping until the following morning. Calling *How to Make a Night* "a beautifully executed bounce of a bedtime tale," Susan Weitz added in *School Library Journal* that Tusa incorporates "playful touches" into her "cheerful watercolor-and-ink designs." Another nighttime tale, *In a Blue Room,* finds a young girl lulled to sleep by sweetly scented flowers, a warm cup of tea, and a snugly quilt, all of which fade to blue when Mama shuts off the light. "Adrift in sleepy hues," wrote a *Kirkus Reviews* writer, Tusa's "engaging watercolor-and-ink illustrations are the perfect touch" for Averbeck's "inventive" story. "Prose and pictures partner each other effortlessly, all the way to the last page," concluded a *Publishers Weekly* contributor of *In a Blue Room.*

Coffelt's picture book provides Tusa with yet another opportunity to show that humor and poignancy can stem from the same source. In *Fred Stays with Me!* a little girl lives at her mother's house on some days, and at her father's house on others. Although the rules at each home are different, Fred the dog provides the girl with the thread of consistency she needs to feel at home in a family fractured by divorce; despite the objections of both parents to the dog's visit, the girl explains clearly

that Fred goes where she goes. Calling Coffelt's story "a gem," a *Kirkus Reviews* writer added that "Tusa's . . . soft-edged . . . watercolor illustrations perfectly complement the quiet story, infusing humor" into Coffelt's "understated text."

Tusa's work illustrating Avi's *The End of the Beginning; Being the Adventures of a Small Snail (and an Even Smaller Ant)* ranks as a significant contribution to "a charming modern fable," according to *School Library Journal* contributor Connie Tyrrell Burns. In Avi's chapter book, Avon the ant and Edward the ant set out in search of adventure. While their travels never take the duo further than the tip of the tree branch where they live, they see the world with fresh eyes and learn some important lessons. Tusa's "whimsical pen-and-ink sketches add much to this wise little book," concluded Burns, and in *Kirkus Reviews* a critic wrote that the "simple line drawings" that mirror Avi's story "bestow a droll sincerity" on the tale's diminutive insect adventurers.

"I think I do what I do because I am endlessly fascinated by children—how they think and feel, what delights them, what scares them, how they wonder about things," Tusa once told *SATA*. "I often wonder if children aren't here as complex gifts for us to learn from. I admire their uncanny ability to cut to the truth. They can often be the most honest reflection you may have around of yourself.

"I am also aware of and am concerned about children's vulnerability. There are so many outside influences interfering with the child doing what comes so very naturally—discovering and developing into and becoming who they are. Quite unconsciously, my books seem to repeatedly reflect this idea of becoming who you are—and that it's okay to be different. Also, my books are embarrassingly autobiographical. Again, quite unconsciously, they inevitably reflect whatever feelings, issues, struggles I am dealing with at the time. And, strangely enough, they are usually the same issues I wondered about as a child—yet, now with older eyes and ears."

Biographical and Critical Sources

PERIODICALS

Booklist, April 1, 1987, Denise M. Wilms, review of *Maebelle's Suitcase,* pp. 1210-1211; January 15, 1994, Deborah Abbott, review of *The Family Reunion,* p. 941; April 15, 2002, Ilene Cooper, review of *The Magic Hat,* p. 1408; July, 2004, Carolyn Phelan, review of *Starring Prima!: The Mouse of the Ballet Jolie,* p. 1844; September 1, 2004, Lauren Peterson, review of *Treasure Map,* p. 127; March 15, 2006, Ilene Cooper, review of *Wing Nuts: Screwy Haiku,* p. 48; February 15, 2009, Carolyn Phelan, review of *The Problem with the Puddles,* p. 83.

Bulletin of the Center for Children's Books, November, 1984, review of *Libby's New Glasses,* p. 57.
Kirkus Reviews, November 15, 1993, review of *The Family Reunion,* p. 1469; June 15, 2002, review of *The Seal Island Seven,* p. 876; August, 2004, review of *Treasure Map,* p. 746; May 15, 2007, review of *Fred Stays with Me!;* March 15, 2008, review of *In a Blue Room;* April 1, 2008, *A Beginning, a Muddle, and an End: The Right Way to Write Writing.*
Publishers Weekly, July 20, 1984, review of *Libby's New Glasses,* p. 82; March 26, 2001, review of *Mrs. Spitzer's Garden,* p. 92; December 2, 2002, review of *The Ballad of Valentine,* p. 52; March 17, 2003, review of *A Long Way,* p. 75; June 7, 2004, review of *Starring Prima!,* p. 51; October 25, 2004, review of *The End of the Beginning: Being the Adventures of a Small Snail (and an Even Smaller Ant),* p. 48; December 13, 2004, review of *How to Make a Night,* p. 68; March 31, 2008, review of *In a Blue Room,* p. 62; March 15, 2009, review of *The Problem of the Puddles,* p. 62.
School Library Journal, September, 1985, Clarissa Erwin, review of *Miranda,* p. 127; June-July, 1987, Helen E. Williams, review of *Maebelle's Suitcase,* p. 91; January, 1996, Tana Elias, review of *Sisters,* p. 97; February, 1999, Christine A. Moesch, review of *Bunnies in My Head,* p. 90; April, 2001, Margaret Bush, review of *Mrs. Spitzer's Garden,* p. 120; April, 2002, Wendy Lukehart, review of *The Magic Hat,* p. 110; October, 2002, Jean Lowery, review of *The Seal Island Seven,* p. 98; December, 2002, Shawn Brommer, review of *The Battle of Valentine,* p. 98; May, 2003, Dona Ratterree, review of *A Long Way,* p. 108; October, 2004, Connie Tyrrell Burns, review of *The End of the Beginning,* p. 154; November, 2004, Susan Weitz, review of *How to Make a Night,* p. 90; May, 2006, Teresa Pfeifer, review of *Wing Nuts,* p. 112; June, 2007, Marua Bresnahan, review of *Fred Stays with Me,* p. 96; May, 2008, Robyn Gioia, review of *A Beginning, a Muddle, and an End,* p. 119.

ONLINE

Seven Impossible Things before Breakfast Web sit, http://blaine.org/sevenimpossiblethings/ (June 11, 2008), interview with Tusa.*

*   *   *

VANCE, Cynthia
(Cynthia Vance-Abrams)

Personal

Married Robert E. Abrams (a publisher); children: one son. *Education:* Rollins College, B.A., 1983; Southern Methodist University, M.F.A.

Addresses

Home—New York, NY. *Office*—Abbeville Press, 137 Varick St., New York, NY 10013. *E-mail*—cynthia@cynthiavance.com.

Cynthia Vance (Photo by Leslie Hassler. Courtesy of Cynthia Vance.)

Career

Actor, publisher, and author. Abbeville Press, New York, NY, head of Abbeville Kids division, beginning 2007. Stage work includes off-Broadway productions at Signature Theatre Co. and Playwright's Horizons. Television work includes roles on *Guiding Light, All My Children, One Life to Live, Law & Order, Spin City,* and *Law & Order: S.V.U.* Film work includes roles in *Knots* and *Animal Behavior.* Actor in commercials and voice overs.

Member

Screen Actors Guild, American Federation of Television and Radio Artists, Actors' Equity Association.

Writings

Red, Yellow, Blue, and You, illustrated by Candace Whitman, Abbebille Kids (New York, NY), 2008.

Biographical and Critical Sources

PERIODICALS

Kirkus Reviews, July 1, 2008, review of *Red, Yellow, Blue, and You.*

ONLINE

Abbeville Press Web site, http://www.abbeville.com (November 10, 2009), "Cynthia Vance."
Cynthia Vance Home Page, http://www.cynthiavance.com (November 10, 2009).

*   *   *

VANCE-ABRAMS, Cynthia
See VANCE, Cynthia

*   *   *

Van DRAANEN, Wendelin

Personal

Born January 6, in Chicago, IL; married; children: two sons. *Hobbies and other interests:* Reading, running, playing in a rock band.

Addresses

Home—CA.

Career

Writer and former educator. Former teacher of high-school math and computer science; worked variously as a forklift driver, a sports coach, and a musician.

Awards, Honors

Edgar Allan Poe Award for Best Children's Mystery, Mystery Writers of America, and Best Book for Young Adults selection, American Library Association, both 1999, for *Sammy Keyes and the Hotel Thief;* Judy Lopez Memorial Award, 2001, for *Flipped;* Edgar Allan Poe Award nomination for best juvenile novel, 2001, for *Sammy Keyes and the Curse of Moustache Mary,* 2003, for *Sammy Keyes and the Search for Snake Eyes,* 2004, for *Sammy Keyes and the Art of Deception.*

Writings

MIDDLE-GRADE NOVELS

How I Survived Being a Girl, HarperCollins (New York, NY), 1997.
Flipped, Knopf (New York, NY), 2001.
Swear to Howdy, Knopf (New York, NY), 2003.
Runaway, Knopf (New York, NY), 2006.
Confessions of a Serial Kisser, Knopf (New York, NY), 2008.

"SAMMY KEYES" NOVEL SERIES

Sammy Keyes and the Hotel Thief, illustrated by Dan Yaccarino, Knopf (New York, NY), 1998.

Wendelin Van Draanan (Reproduced by permission.)

Sammy Keyes and the Skeleton Man, illustrated by Dan Yaccarino, Knopf (New York, NY), 1998.

Sammy Keyes and the Sisters of Mercy, illustrated by Dan Yaccarino, Knopf (New York, NY), 1999.

Sammy Keyes and the Runaway Elf, illustrated by Dan Yaccarino, Knopf (New York, NY), 1999.

Sammy Keyes and the Curse of Moustache Mary, illustrated by Dan Yaccarino, Knopf (New York, NY), 2000.

Sammy Keyes and the Hollywood Mummy, illustrated by Dan Yaccarino, Knopf (New York, NY), 2001.

Sammy Keyes and the Search for Snake Eyes, illustrated by Dan Yaccarino, Knopf (New York, NY), 2002.

Sammy Keyes and the Art of Deception, illustrated by Dan Yaccarino, Knopf (New York, NY), 2003.

Sammy Keyes and the Psycho Kitty Queen, illustrated by Dan Yaccarino, Knopf (New York, NY), 2004.

Sammy Keyes and the Dead Giveaway, illustrated by Dan Yaccarino, Knopf (New York, NY), 2005.

Sammy Keyes and the Wild Things, illustrated by Dan Yaccarino, Knopf (New York, NY), 2007.

Sammy Keyes and the Cold Hard Cash, illustrated by Dan Yaccarino, Knopf (New York, NY), 2008.

"SHREDDERMAN" NOVEL SERIES

Secret Identity, illustrated by Brian Biggs, Knopf (New York, NY), 2004.

Attack of the Tagger, illustrated by Brian Biggs, Knopf (New York, NY), 2004.

Meet the Gecko, illustrated by Brian Biggs, Knopf (New York, NY), 2005.

Enemy Spy, illustrated by Brian Biggs, Knopf (New York, NY), 2005.

"GECKO AND STICKY" CHAPTER-BOOK SERIES

The Greatest Power, illustrated by Stephen Gilpin, Knopf (New York, NY), 2009.

Villain's Lair, illustrated by Stephen Gilpin, Knopf (New York, NY), 2009.

Sinister Substitute, illustrated by Stephen Gilpin, Knopf (New York, NY), 2010.

Sidelights

While she has also written the highly praised middle-grade novels *Swear to Howdy* and *Runaway,* Wendelin Van Draanen is best known as the author of the popular "Sammy Keyes," "Shredderman," and "Gecko and Sticky" series. Her "Sammy Keyes" mysteries feature a tomboy with a penchant for finding trouble, while the "Shredderman" books focus on a geeky preteen who uses a cyber-hero to right the wrongs in his middle school. Salted with Aztec magic, the "Gecko and Sticky" chapter-book series follows a boy and his talking gecko as they undo the deviltry caused by the dastardly Damian Black while also entertaining readers with their humorous banter. As Van Draanen once explained, she writes for "the kid who's coming to a place where they have to make decisions on their own. I try to shed a little light on the merits of being good, heroic, and honest. I hope that kids come away from reading my work with a little more strength and belief in themselves and the sense that they *can* shape their own destiny."

Van Draanen grew up sandwiched by brothers, and her childhood experiences provide much of the inspiration for the intrepid young people that she features in her books. Although the future author described her childhood self as tentative and shy, she also had a daring streak when backed up by her siblings. Van Draanen found the greatest comfort in the world of books, such as the "Nancy Drew," "Hardy Boys," and "Encyclopedia Brown" teen sleuth series, having learned to read at an early age, thanks to one of her siblings. "I began to read by watching my older brother learn to read," she once recalled. "I'd hang over his shoulder while he got help from my mother, and that's how I picked it up. My mother worked with all of us, teaching us reading and mathematics at a very early age. One of my favorite pictures of me as a young girl was taken at the age of about eighteen months—I'm sitting on the toilet, feet dangling, engrossed in a book that's in my lap."

When Van Draanen was in college, a catastrophe in her family inadvertently opened up a new door for her: the family business was destroyed by arson and she took time off from school to help out in the aftermath. For a time, the family endured financial difficulties and Van

Draanen experienced feelings of anger and helplessness. When she began to have problems sleeping, she turned to writing as a way to help alleviate some of the stress. Writing was not only cathartic but enjoyable, she discovered, and in her stories she could create happy endings and allow her characters survive and thrive despite personal difficulties. Although she eventually found her vocation as a teacher of high-school computer sciences, she also produced ten finished novels by the mid-1990s. By then she also was married, living in California, and raising children of her own.

Van Draanen's first published book, 1997's *How I Survived Being a Girl,* was inspired by a gift from her husband: a copy of Ray Bradbury's *Dandelion Wine.* Carolyn, the story's preteen narrator, is a tomboy who feels like an outsider compared to the girls in her neighborhood; she prefers tagging along with her brothers and their friends, especially the neighbor boy Charlie. Carolyn spends the summer spying on neighbors, digging foxholes with Charlie, stealing a book, and helping her brother with his paper route. In the fall, however, she finds her attitudes changing: she sees Charlie in a new way, starts to speak out, and becomes more politically active.

Cover of Van Draanan's Sammy Keyes and the Sister of Mercy, *a middle-grade novel featuring artwork by Dan Yaccarino.* (Knopf, 1999. Cover art © 1999 by Dan Yaccarino. Used by permission of Alfred A. Knopf, an imprint of Random House Children's Books, a division of Random House, Inc.)

A *Publishers Weekly* review called *How I Survived Being a Girl* an "energetic first novel" and "a sunny, funny look at a girl with a smart mouth and scabby knees." Writing in *Kirkus Reviews,* a critic praised Van Draanen's style and the narrative voice of her young heroine. Carolyn's "irreverent narration is engaging," stated the reviewer, "and she's refreshingly astute about family and neighborhood dynamics."

Estranged from her musician dad since her parents' separation, sixteen-year-old Evangeline becomes caught up in the lure of romantic love in *Confessions of a Serial Kisser,* another novel by Van Draanen. Her grades begin to slide as the high schooler starts to obsess over the passion and undying love she finds in the pages of her mother's romance novels. As Van Draanen shows, Evangeline acts out these longings by searching for the single kiss that will kindle that sort of passion in her own heart. The teen's confusion of romantic passion with a deep-seated longing for an intact family becomes the crux of a novel that a *Publishers Weekly* critic described as "tender and convincing" and *School Library Journal* critic Amy S. Pattee dubbed "compulsively readable." While *Kliatt* critic Myrna Marler characterized the story's humorous plot twist as somewhat "silly," she added that *Confessions of a Serial Kisser* deals with "themes of forgiveness and the best way to heal" in a way that is "strangely thought provoking."

Other novels for middle-grader readers include *Runaway* and *Swear to Howdy,* the latter described by a *Publishers Weekly* critic as a "trenchant tale" of two best friends. In *Swear to Howdy* middle-graders Rusty and Joey become inseparable almost immediately after Rusty moves next door, and their summer is filled with building forts, making pacts, and sharing their favorite things. Gradually, problems from the boys' respective families intrude on their play, however, and their friendship is tested by a tragic accident. In *Publishers Weekly* a reviewer praised Van Draanen for creating "sympathetic protagonists" and bringing Rusty and Joey to life in "convincing colloquial dialogue."

Van Draanen turns to a more serious theme in *Runaway.* Telling her own story through journal entries and poetry, twelve-year-old Holly Janquell recounts her experiences as a homeless runaway escaping from overly strict and suspicious foster parents. In *Publishers Weekly* a reviewer praised the combination of poetry and prose in *Runaway* as "gravely realistic" and compelling, while *Booklist* critic GraceAnne A. DeCandido wrote that "the ending of this taut, powerful story seems possible and deeply hopeful." Teens "won't look at [the] homeless . . . in quite the same way after meeting Holly," asserted Faith Brautigam in a *School Library Journal* review of *Runaway.*

Setting a far lighter tone than her standalone novels, Van Draanen's first "Sammy Keyes" book, *Sammy Keyes and the Hotel Thief,* won an Edgar Allen Poe award for best children's mystery in 1999. Feisty, intelligent tomboy Samantha lives with her grandmother in

Cover of Van Draanan's entertaining middle-grade novel Confessions of a Serial Kisser. (Alfred A. Knopf, 2008. Jacket art copyright © 2008 by Alfred A. Knopf.Used by permission of Alfred A. Knopf, an imprint of Random House Children's Books, a division of Random House, Inc.)

a fifth-floor apartment in a seniors-only apartment building. Because children are not allowed, Sammy is forced to sneak around just to get to school, a fact that severely curtails her social life. As readers soon learn, Sammy lives with her grandmother because her mother has moved to Hollywood. To keep amused, she watches the goings-on outside with a pair of binoculars, and is particularly fascinated by the seedy Heavenly Hotel across the street. One afternoon she observes some suspicious activity through a fourth-floor window, and suspects that she may have witnessed a crime. Although the police fail to take her seriously at first, Sammy's cleverness uncovers the plot in time. Van Draanen's ending "will likely come as a surprise, and the sleuth delights from start to finish," asserted a *Publishers Weekly* review in a review of *Sammy Keyes and the Hotel Thief.* In *Horn Book* Martha V. Parravano described Sammy as "one tough, smart, resourceful seventh grader," and compared the novel's lighthearted style to the books of popular mystery writer Sue Grafton.

Sammy Keyes and the Skeleton Man opens near Halloween, and Sammy plans to trick or treat in a Marsh Monster costume. When she and her friends bravely approach the Bush House, a crumbling mansion with wildly overgrown shrubbery, the girl is almost knocked down by a man wearing a skeleton costume and carrying a pillowcase. Entering the house, the children discover a fire, which Sammy puts out. When they learn that a burglary has also occurred, Sammy wants to solve it. Her sleuthing uncovers a feud between the mansion's owners, two brothers, and her cleverness helps her solve the crime and patch up family problems into the bargain. Reviewing *Sammy Keyes and the Skeleton Man*, Parravano praised it as a "highly readable mystery [that] hits the ground running," and Lynda Short predicted in *School Library Journal* that Van Draanen's "readers will enjoy the mystery, hijinks, plotting, and adult comeuppance."

Walking her characteristic fine line between intellectual brilliance and juvenile delinquency, Sammy is sentenced to twenty hours of detention in *Sammy Keyes and the Sisters of Mercy.* She fulfills this obligation by helping out at the local Roman Catholic Church, and while cleaning the windows of St. Mary's she sees a girl who then seems to vanish. Shortly afterward, Sammy realizes that Father Mayhew is upset; he has just discovered that his valuable ivory cross is missing. While Sammy is the first suspect in the theft, other possible culprits surface as well, and in order to clear her own name, she resolves to solve the mystery. She also solves the mystery of the vanishing girl, and learns an important lesson about compassion into the bargain.

"As always, quirky characters are Van Draanen's strength," remarked Kay Weisman in a *Booklist* review of *Sammy Keyes and the Sisters of Mercy.* In *School Library Journal* Jennifer Ralston novel's storyline and noted that Van Draanen's plot adds "depth and interest to an already engrossing mystery while capturing the angst of junior high school." Beth E. Anderson, reviewing the book in *Voice of Youth Advocates,* had praise for Sammy, who she described as "genuine, funny, devoted to her friends and blessed with a strength of character that lets her reach for a peaceful solution."

Set during the Christmas season, *Sammy Keyes and the Runaway Elf* finds Sammy still in seventh grade and involved in her community's holiday parade. She is assigned to the Canine Calendar Float and charged with babysitting Marique, a famous Pomeranian. It all goes to the dogs when several individuals disguised as the Three Kings throw cats onto the dogs-only float. When the prized Pom vanishes and a ransom is demanded, its wealthy owner manipulates Sammy into thwarting the dognappers and finding Marique. As always, Sammy must eliminate several suspects, even as comical plot twists play out. Remarking upon Sammy's ability to befriend people of many ages, *School Library Journal* reviewer Linda Bindner noted that "Van Draanen handles the[se] relationships with style and sensitivity."

Other "Sammy Keyes" novels include *Sammy Keyes and the Hollywood Mummy, Sammy Keyes and the Psycho Kitty Queen, Sammy Keyes and the Wild Things,*

and *Sammy Keyes and the Cold Hard Cash.* In *Sammy Keyes and the Art of Deception* Sammy is visiting an art gallery with her grandmother and Grans' elderly friend when a man enters, armed with a squirt gun, and steals several paintings. As Sammy and her grandmother attempt to get to the bottom of the theft, several sub-plots unfold: Sammy continues to battle her longtime nemesis Heather, while she feels oddly attracted to Heather's older brother Casey. *Sammy Keyes and the Psycho Kitty Queen* finds the young sleuth turning thirteen when a dead cat surfaces, portending bad luck. As other dead kitties turn up in other local dumpsters, Sammy's mom also appears with a bit of information that signals more bad luck. Diana Pierce, writing in *School Library Journal,* called *Sammy Keyes and the Psycho Kitty Queen* "another hit in a solid series," while Terrie Dorio wrote in the same periodical that *Sammy Keyes and the Art of Deception* is a "lively" story that finds Sammy's beloved Grans "just as bold, fearless, and gutsy as her granddaughter."

In *Sammy Keyes and the Dead Giveaway* Sammy is partly responsible for the disappearance of her teacher's pet bird, even though longtime enemy Heather gets the blame. While receiving anonymous threats regarding the missing bird, Sammy also decides to track down whoever it is who is throwing rocks through the windows of the homes of several elderly residents. *Sammy Keyes and the Wild Things* finds the young sleuth joining a Girl Scouts nature trip that inspires her to advocate on behalf of an injured condor, while a harsh word to an elderly thief results in a shocking demise and a burdensome financial windfall in *Sammy Keyes and the Cold Hard Cash* In her *Booklist* review of *Sammy Keyes and the Dead Giveaway* Francisca Goldsmith predicted that "the clever twist at the end of the story is sure to delight Sammy's fans," and *School Library Journal* critic Elizabeth Fernandez maintained that Van Draanen's "final cascade of stunning revelations will have readers on the edge of their seats." "Quick-witted banter makes [*Sammy Keyes and the Wild Things*] . . . a fast-paced joyride of a read," concluded *School Library Journal* reviewer Cheryl Ashton, and Stephanie Zvirin, writing in *Booklist,* dubbed *Sammy Keyes and the Cold Hard Cash* "an exceptionally good entry in an already remarkable series."

In *Secret Identity,* the first volume in her "Shredderman" series, Van Draanen introduces readers to Nolan Byrd, a nerdy fifth grader who sets out to expose school bully Bubba Bixby by disguising himself as cyber-hero Shredderman. Bubba not only picks on his classmates but also cheats and steals. With the use of a digital camera, Nolan uncovers the evidence he needs, sets up a Web site to expose the bully, and then tries to figure out how to get people to view the site. In a review for *Booklist,* Jennifer Mattson praised *Secret Identity,* writing: "Kudos [to Van Draanen]. . . for delivering a character-driven series that's spot-on for middle-graders and great for reluctant readers." A *Kirkus Reviews* writer

characterized the "Shredderman" series as "a Sammy Keyes for younger readers" that features "a supporting cast of unconventional characters."

The "Shredderman" series continues with *Attack of the Tagger, Meet the Gecko,* and *Enemy Spy,* which follow Nolan's further do-gooding, from tracking down a graffiti artist in *Attack of the Tagger* to assisting a popular television star who is being stalked by an evil reporter in *Meet the Gecko* Mattson called *Attack of the Tagger* a "balm for all those dweeby kids who will see themselves in Nolan and cheer him," while *Booklist* critic Todd Morning described *Meet the Gecko* as "a light-hearted, fast-moving story" that should appeal to reluctant readers.

Van Draanen has no plans to stop writing for adolescents. "They're growing, they're changing, and they're receptive to making the world a better place . . . ," she once explained. "Growing up's not easy. Everyone feels awkward through adolescence, but when you're a kid it seems that you're the only one who's not fitting in. Everyone else seems to have it together, or be comfortable

Van Draanan's heroic middle-grader stars in her "Shredderman" series of adventures that include **Enemy Spy,** *a novel featuring cover art by Brian Biggs.* (Yearling, 2005. Illustrations copyright © 2005 by Brian Biggs. Used by permission of Alfred A. Knopf, an imprint of Random House Children's Books, a division of Random House, Inc.)

with themselves. It's not true, but that's how we feel when we're kids. It's my goal to get kids through those awkward years and onto adulthood safely. The choices they make in the areas of honesty, convictions, friendships, and compassion now will affect them their entire lives."

Biographical and Critical Sources

PERIODICALS

Booklist, April 1, 1999, Kay Weisman, review of *Sammy Keyes and the Sisters of Mercy,* p. 1415; March 1, 2001, Gillian Engberg, review of *Sammy Keyes and the Hollywood Mummy,* p. 1272; February 1, 2004, Jennifer Mattson, review of *Secret Identity,* p. 975; September 1, 2004, Jennifer Mattson, review of *Attack of the Tagger,* p. 125; October 1, 2004, Kathleen Odean, review of *Sammy Keyes and the Psycho Kitty Queen,* p. 330; January 1, 2005, review of *Secret Identity,* p. 774; February 1, 2005, Todd Morning, review of *Meet the Gecko,* p. 962; May 1, 2005, Gillian Engberg, review of *Sammy Keyes and the Psycho Kitty Queen,* p. 1543; August, 2005, Carolyn Phelan, review of *Enemy Spy,* p. 2030; September 1, 2005, Francisca Goldsmith, review of *Sammy Keyes and the Dead Giveaway,* p. 137; September 1, 2006, GraceAnne A. DeCandido, review of *Runaway,* p. 112; May 1, 2007, Hazel Rochman, review of *Sammy Keyes and the Wild Things,* p. 45; October 1, 2008, Stephanie Zvirin, review of *Sammy Keyes and the Cold Hard Cash,* p. 43; December 1, 2008, Daniel Kraus, review of *Villain's Lair,* p. 52.

Horn Book, July-August, 1998, Martha V. Parravano, review of *Sammy Keyes and the Hotel Thief,* pp. 498-499; November-December, 1998, Martha V. Parravano, review of *Sammy Keyes and the Skeleton Man,* p. 743.

Kirkus Reviews, December 1, 1996, review of *How I Survived Being a Girl;* January 1, 2004, review of *Secret Identity,* p. 42; July 15, 2004, review of *Attack of the Tagger,* p. 694; December 15, 2004, review of *Meet the Gecko,* p. 1210; August 15, 2006, review of *Runaway,* p. 853; December 15, 2008, review of *Villain's Lair.*

Kliatt, September, 2006, Myrna Marler, review of *Runaway,* p. 19; May, 2008, Myrna Marler, review of *Confessions of a Serial Kisser,* p. 17.

Publishers Weekly, January 6, 1997, review of *How I Survived Being a Girl,* p. 73; April 27, 1998, review of *Sammy Keyes and the Hotel Thief,* p. 67; October 27, 2003, review of *Swear to Howdy,* p. 70; February 2, 2004, review of *Secret Identity,* p. 77; January 3, 2005, review of *Meet the Gecko,* p. 57; October 23, 2006, review of *Runaway,* p. 51; May 5, 2008, review of *Confessions of a Serial Kisser,* p. 62.

School Library Journal, February, 1997, Kathleen Odean, review of *How I Survived Being a Girl,* p. 106; September, 1998, Lynda Short, review of *Sammy Keyes and the Skeleton Man,* p. 211; July, 1999, Jennifer Ralston, review of *Sammy Keyes and the Sisters of Mercy,* p. 101; September, 1999, Linda Bindner, review of *Sammy Keyes and the Runaway Elf,* p. 229; February, 2001, Wanda Meyers-Hines, review of *Sammy Keyes and the Hollywood Mummy,* p. 122; March, 2001, Sarah Flowers, review of *Sammy Keyes and the Hotel Thief,* p. 87; March, 2003, Terrie Dorio, review of *Sammy Keyes and the Art of Deception,* p. 242; November, 2003, Amy Lilien-Harper, review of *Swear to Howdy,* p. 150; May, 2004, Edward Sullivan, review of *Secret Identity,* p. 158; October, 2004, Diana Pierce, review of *Sammy Keyes and the Psycho Kitty Queen,* p. 180; November, 2004, Christine McGinty, review of *Attack of the Tagger,* p. 156; January 1, 2005, Jennifer Cogan, review of *Meet the Gecko,* p. 774; July, 2005, Kim Carlson, review of *Enemy Spy,* p. 110; November, 2005, Elizabeth Fernandez, review of *Sammy Keyes and the Dead Giveaway,* p. 150; August 15, 2006, Jennifer Ralston, review of *Secret Identity,* p. 853; September, 2006, Faith Brautigam, review of *Runaway,* p. 220; June, 2007, Cheryl Ashton, review of *Sammy Keyes and the Wild Things,* p. 164; June, 2008, Amy S. Pattee, review of *Confessions of a Serial Kisser,* p. 152; December, 2008, Kathryn Kosiorek, review of *Sammy Keyes and the Cold Hard Cash,* p. 141; April, 2009, Misti Tidman, review of *The Greatest Power,* p. 118.

Voice of Youth Advocates, April, 2000, Beth E. Anderson, review of *Sammy Keyes and the Sisters of Mercy,* pp. 40-41.

ONLINE

KidsReads.com, http://www.kidsreads.com/ (November 15, 2009), Sarah A. Wood, review of *Secret Identity,* Tamara Penny, review of *Sammy Keyes and the Hollywood Mummy,* Marya Jansen-Gruber, review of *Sammy Keyes and the Art of Deception.*

Random House Web site, http://www.randomhouse.com/kids/ (November 15, 2009), "Wendelin van Draanen."

TeenLit.com, http://www.teenlit.com/ (November 15, 2009), review of *Sammy Keyes and the Search for Snake Eyes.**

*   *   *

VILA, Laura

Personal

Married. *Education:* Attended Chicago Art Institute and Pratt Institute; degree (communication design).

Addresses

Home—New York, NY. *E-mail*—laura@lauravila.com.

Career

Photographer, illustrator, graphic and Web designer, and author. Freelance book-jacket designer.

Laura Vila (Photo courtesy of Laura Vila Rawson.)

Writings

(Self-illustrated) *Building Manhattan*, Viking (New York, NY), 2008.

Sidelights

In *Building Manhattan*, which a *Kirkus Reviews* critic dubbed an "engaging debut" picture book, illustrator and graphic artist Laura Vila uses brilliant color and a variety of artistic styles to chronicle the history of New York City, the town that Vila calls home. Although *Building Manhattan* is her first published picture book, Vila is no stranger to the field of children's publishing. In addition to appearing on numerous book jackets, her graphic work encompasses color photography and Web design.

In *Building Manhattan* Vila describes the phases of development that occurred on the island of Manhattan over time. From a beautiful wilderness, the island changed when it became home to Native Americans, and then European colonists, eventually evolved into a cosmopolitan city that is noted for its architectural and cultural diversity. In her brief and nuanced text, Vila touches on history, sociology, and the shift in cultural demographics, then expands on her observations in what a *Publishers Weekly* contributor described as "radiantly dramatic mural-like paintings" that reflect a shifting visual perspective. Citing the artist/author's "folk-art style," Steven Engelfried added in *School Library Jour-*

nal that her "purposeful shifts in line, perspective, and composition . . . give each spread a distinct feel." In a *New York Times Book Review* appraisal of *Building Manhattan*, a critic described Vila's spare prose as akin to "a lightly skipping rock over a vast ocean of fact," noting that such restraint is appropriate for the book's intended audience. Citing the author/artist's use of "unconventional perspectives" in her colorful paintings, the *New York Times Book Review* contributor added that in *Building Manhattan* Vila's approach is "an ingenious way to suggest the acceleration of human activity."

Biographical and Critical Sources

PERIODICALS

Kirkus Reviews, April 15, 2008, review of *Building Manhattan*.
New York Times Book Review, September 14, 2008, review of *Building Manhattan*, p. 16.
School Library Journal, June, 2008, Steven Engelfried, review of *Building Manhattan*, p. 132.

ONLINE

Laura Vila Home Page, http://www.lauravila.com (November 10, 2009).

Illustration by Vila from her self-illustrated picture book **Building Manhattan.** (Illustration courtesy of Laura Vila Rawson.)

Little People Literature Web site, http://www.littlepeople literature.com/ (November 10, 2009), "Laura Vila."

* * *

VOHWINKEL, Astrid 1969-

Personal

Born 1969, in Essen, Germany. *Education:* Fachhochschule (Münster, Germany), degree (graphic design), 1996.

Addresses

Home—Münster, Germany. *E-mail*—vohwinkel@muen ster.de.

Career

Illustrator of children's books.

Writings

SELF-ILLUSTRATED

Lea geht zum Kinderarzt, Pestalozzi Verlag, 2002.
Jakob feiert Geburstag, Pestalozzi Verlag, 2002.
Lea darf bei Paula sclafen, Pestalozzi Verlag, 2002.
Jakob und sein kleiner Bruder, Pestalozzi Verlag, 2002.
Schau mal, ich spiele, Pestalozzi Verlag, 2003.
Mmmmh, das schmeckt mir!, Pestalozzi Verlag, 2003.
Plitsch-platsch, ich bade!, Pestalozzi Verlag, 2003.
Mein erster Besuch auf der Ritterburg, Coppenrath, 2006.

ILLUSTRATOR

Margot Hellmiß, *Im Wilden Westen,* Arena Verlag, 2002.
Christa Holtei, *Ein Tag auf der Ritterburg,* Carlsen Verlag, 2003.
Nina Schindler, *Im Dorf der Indianer,* Carlsen Verlag, 2004.
Christa Holtei, *Tom bei den Piraten,* Carlsen Verlag, 2004.
Christa Holtei, *Ein Tag bei den Wikingern,* Carlsen Verlag, 2004.
Julia Boehme, *Lesespatz: Ponydiebe im Indianerdorf,* Loewe Verlag (Bindlach, Germany), 2004.
Christa Holtei, *Nanuk will fliegen,* Thienemann Verlag, 2005, translated as *Nanuk Flies Home,* Eerdmans Books for Young Readers (Grand Rapids, MI), 2008.
Julia Boehme, *Kleine Wolke, großer Bär,* Carlsen Verlag, 2005.
Christa Holtei, *Jim bei den Cowboys,* Carlsen Verlag, 2005.
Julia Boehme, *Ein Pony im Garten,* Carlsen Verlag, 2005.
Imke Rudel, *Lesemaus: Pfeffer-Piet, der schlaute Pirate,* Carlsen Verlag, 2006.

Lydia Hauenschild, *Bidermaus Lesewörterbuch: Das weiß ich über den Bauernhof,* Loewe Verlag (Bindlach, Germany), 2006.
Werner Färber, *Bildermaus: Geschichten vom kleinen Indianer,* Loewe Verlag (Bindlach, Germany), 2007.
Christina Holtei, *Ein Tag in der Steinzeit,* Carlsen Verlag, 2007.
Manuela Mechtel, *Die Wikinger auf großer Fahrt,* Carlsen Verlag, 2007.
Christina Holtei, *Ein Tag im alten Ägypten,* Carlsen Verlag, 2008.
Sandra Grimm, *Silberwind: Jagd auf das Einhorn,* Loewe Verlag (Bindlach, Germany), 2008.
Marlene Jablonski, *Reitergeschichten,* Ravensburger (Ravensburg, Germany), 2008.
Fabian Lenk, *Die Kinder des Manitu: Indianergeschicten,* Ravensburger (Ravensburg, Germany), 2008.
Sandra Grimm, *Silberwind: Das blaue Einhorn,* Loewe Verlag (Bindlach, Germany), 2008.
Sandra Grimm, *Silberwind: Der Magische Feuerberg,* Loewe Verlag (Bindlach, Germany), 2008.
Annette Neubauer, *Zwei junge Samurai,* Carlsen Verlag, 2008.
Inga Huebner, *Der große Bauernhof,* Carlsen Verlag, 2008.
Susa Hämmerle, *Mein erstes Ballettbuch* (with CD), Betz (Vienna, Austria), 2009.
Cornelia Franz, *Ronni und Rasputin,* Carlsen Verlag, 2009.
Franziska Gehm, *Bidermaus: Geschichten vom kleinen Wikinger,* Loewe Verlag (Bindlach, Germany), 2009.
Sandra Grimm, *Silberwind die Eisprinzessin,* Loewe Verlag (Bindlach, Germany), 2009.
Sandra Grimm, *Silberwind: Das verzauberte Pferd,* Loewe Verlag (Bindlach, Germany), 2009.
Christa Holtei, *Ein Tag im alten Rom,* Carsen Verlag, 2009.
Julia Hofmann, *Bauernhof: Geschichten,* Carlsen Verlag, 2009.
Julia Hofmann, *Pony: Geschichten,* Carlsen Verlag, 2009.
Julia Hofmann, *Ritter: Geschichten,* Carlsen Verlag, 2009.
Christa Holtei, *Tom auf Piratenfahrt,* Carsen Verlag, 2009.
Imke Rudel, Ulrike Barzik, and others, *Tiergeschichten zum Lesenlernen,* Carlse Verlag, 2010.

Biographical and Critical Sources

PERIODICALS

Kirkus Reviews, July 15, 2008, review of *Nanuk Flies Home.*
School Library Journal, September, 2008, Ieva Bates, review of *Nanuk Flies Home,* p. 149.

ONLINE

Astrid Vohwinkel Home Page, http://vohwinkel.illustra tion.de (November 10, 2009).
Loewe Web site, http://www.loewe-verlag.de/ (November 10, 2009), "Astrid Vohwinkel."*

W-Z

WASSERMAN, Robin 1978-

Personal

Born May 31, 1978, in Philadelphia, PA. *Education:* Harvard University, bachelor's degree; University of California—Los Angeles, M.A. (history of science). *Hobbies and other interests:* Watching television.

Addresses

Home—Brooklyn, NY. *E-mail*—robin@robinwasserman. com.

Career

Novelist. Former associate editor at a New York, NY, publisher.

Writings

JUVENILE NOVELS

Search for Scooby Snacks ("Scooby-Doo! Picture Clue" series), illustrated by Duendes del Sur, Scholastic (New York, NY), 2000.

Vanishing Valentines ("Scooby-Doo! Picture Clue" series), illustrated by Duendes del Sur, Scholastic (New York, NY), 2001.

Snow Ghost ("Scooby-Doo! Picture Clue" series), illustrated by Duendes del Sur, Scholastic (New York, NY), 2001.

Ghost School ("Scooby-Doo! Picture Clue" series), illustrated by Duendes del Sur, Scholastic (New York, NY), 2002.

Stormy Night ("Scooby-Doo! Picture Clue" series), illustrated by Duendes del Sur, Scholastic (New York, NY), 2002.

Oh, No! Why Me? II, Scholastic (New York, NY), 2002.

Grind (adapted from a screenplay by Ralph Sall), Scholastic (New York, NY), 2003.

Oops! I Did It (Again)!, illustrated by Angela Martini, Scholastic (New York, NY), 2003.

A Cinderella Story (novelization; based on a screenplay by Leigh Dunlap), Scholastic (New York, NY), 2004.

Raise Your Voice (novelization; based on a screenplay by Sam Schreiber), Scholastic (New York, NY), 2004.

Just My Luck! Embarrassing Moments and the Girls Who Survive Them ("Friends 4 Ever" series), Scholastic (New York, NY), 2006.

Jinxed! ("Unfabulous" series), Scholastic (New York, NY), 2006.

Just Deal ("Unfabulous" series), Scholastic (New York, NY), 2006.

Meltdown ("Unfabulous" series), Scholastic (New York, NY), 2006.

So You Want to Be . . . ("Unfabulous" series), Scholastic (New York, NY), 2006.

Starstruck ("Unfabulous" series), Scholastic (New York, NY), 2006.

Callie for President ("Candy Apple" series), Scholastic (New York, NY), 2008.

Life, Starring Me! ("Candy Apple" series), Scholastic (New York, NY), 2009.

Wish You Were Here, Liza ("Candy Apple" series), Scholastic (New York, NY), 2010.

Bedtime Stories: School's Out?, Disney Press (New York, NY), 2011.

YOUNG-ADULT NOVELS

Hacking Harvard, Simon Pulse (New York, NY), 2007.

"SEVEN DEADLY SINS" SERIES; YOUNG-ADULT NOVELS

Lust, Simon Pulse (New York, NY), 2005.

Envy, Simon Pulse (New York, NY), 2006.

Pride, Simon Pulse (New York, NY), 2006.

Wrath, Simon Pulse (New York, NY), 2006.

Sloth, Simon Pulse (New York, NY), 2006.

Gluttony, Simon Pulse (New York, NY), 2007.

Greed, Simon Pulse (New York, NY), 2007.

"CHASING YESTERDAY" SERIES; YOUNG-ADULT NOVELS

Awakening, Scholastic (New York, NY), 2007.
Betrayal, Scholastic (New York, NY), 2007.
Truth, Scholastic (New York, NY), 2007.

"SKINNED" TRILOGY; YOUNG-ADULT NOVELS

Skinned, Simon Pulse (New York, NY), 2008.
Crashed, Simon Pulse (New York, NY), 2009.

OTHER

Sharks ("Face to Face" series), Scholastic (New York, NY), 2002.
Wolves ("Face to Face" series), Scholastic (New York, NY), 2002.
Night Creatures ("Face to Face" series), Scholastic (New York, NY), 2002.
Penguins ("Face to Face" series), Scholastic (New York, NY), 2002.
Insects ("Face to Face" series), Scholastic (New York, NY), 2002.
Extraordinary Dangerous Animals, Scholastic (New York, NY), 2003.
Extraordinary Sea Creatures, Scholastic (New York, NY), 2003.
Extraordinary Solar System, Scholastic (New York, NY), 2003.
Extraordinary Rain Forests, Scholastic (New York, NY), 2003.
Extraordinary Wild Weather, Scholastic (New York, NY), 2003.
Girl Talk: How to Deal with Friendship Conflicts, illustrated by Taia Marley, Scholastic (New York, NY), 2006.

Contributor to anthologies, including *First Kiss (Then Tell!): A Collection of True Lip-Locked Moments, 666: The Number of the Beast,* and *End Game,* Scholastic, 2005. Contributor to periodicals, including *Scholastic Choices.*

Adaptations

The "Seven Deadly Sins" novels were adapted for film by Lifetime.

Sidelights

Robin Wasserman got her start in children's books working as an assistant editor for a New York City publisher, and her experience there gave her a strong sense of what young readers WANT to read. Since making the break to author, she has produced books for both preteen and high-school readers and her "Chasing Yesterday" and "Seven Deadly Sins" novels, the latter which focus on problematic characters that socially savvy teens might enjoy vicariously but studiously avoid in real life. Wasserman's stand-alone novel, *Hack-*

ing Harvard, was inspired by personal experience: the daunting application process that culminated in her acceptance and ultimate graduation from the prestigious Harvard University. In *Booklist* Frances Bradburn dubbed *Hacking Harvard* a "harsh, funny, sophisticated, . . . and edgy" fictionalization of these experiences that also treats teens to a "memorable reading experience," while Debra Mitts-Smith wrote in *Kliatt* that Wasserman's "tale of high achievers with high ambitions is anything but predictable."

Wasserman's "Chasing Yesterday" series begins with *Awakening,* as a young teen is injured and knocked unconscious during an explosion, and then awakens without any memory of who she is. "Addictive and fast-paced," according to *Kliatt* contributor Stephanie Squicciarini, *Awakening* follows the girl—nicknamed J.D. for Jane Doe—as she begins to sense that her physical strength and aggressive tendencies mark her as someone with a less-than-typical home life. When a woman claims J.D. as her own lost daughter, the teen worries that this may not be the case; although her doctors think that she is skirting mental illness, J.D. knows that she must discover which of the vivid flashbacks she is experiencing are reality and which are something more sinister. The novels *Betrayal* and *Truth* round out Wasserman's "Chasing Yesterday" series.

Lust, Envy, Pride, Wrath, Sloth, Gluttony, and *Greed* chronicle the moral transgressions made by seven high-school seniors in Wasserman's popular "Seven Deadly Sins" series. Beginning in *Lust,* the author takes readers to the small California town of Grace where Beth, Kane, Harper, Adam, Miranda, Kaia, and Reed discard professed loyalties, stated promises, and common compassion in favor of sexual conquest and popularity during their final year at Haven High. In *Booklist* Bradburn characterized *Lust* as "a teen version of TV's 'Desperate Housewives,'" and *School Library Journal* critic Stephanie L. Petruso recommended the series to fans of YA writers Zoey Dean and Cecily von Ziegesar. Reviewing *Envy* in *School Library Journal,* Stephanie L. Petruso recommended the story as a "fast-paced," "compelling and frightening" view of contemporary adolescent culture, while *Pride* struck Rebecca M. Jones as an "addictive" chronicle of "cunning, lies, and emotional blackmail" in her review for the same periodical.

In *Skinned* Wasserman salts her teen drama with elements of science fiction as seventeen-year-old Lia Kahn finds herself downloaded into a mechanical body following a terrible automobile accident. Formerly considered among the most popular, accomplished, and pretty girls in school, Lia is now shunned by both her superficial former friends and her own younger sister. As Lia attempts to craft a new life from the wreckage of the old, the harsh reality of her "mech head" status—she no longer eats, sleeps, aspirates, or ages—forces her to accept her own failings and a less-than-promising future. Anticipating the "dystopian denouement" in *Skinned,* Francisca Goldsmith wrote in *Booklist* that Wasser-

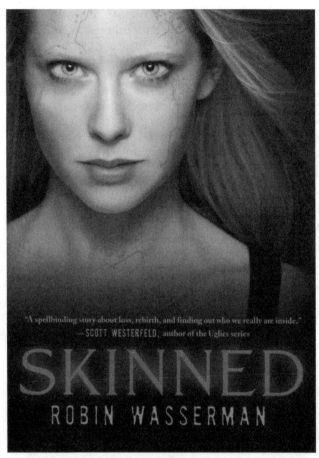

Cover of Robin Wasserman's futuristic drama Skinned, *in which a popular teen learns what life is like on the other side of adulation.* (Simon Pulse, 2008. Front cover photograph copyright © 2008 by Michael Frost. Reproduced by permission.)

man's story is "well composed and engaging," and *School Library Journal* critic Megan Honig stated that the fast-paced text contains "enough sarcasm, humor, and . . . momentum to engage reluctant readers." To a *Kirkus Reviews* writer, *Skinned* provides teens with more than a captivating story: it "intimately tackles tough ethical topics . . . through blunt dialogue and realistic characters."

Biographical and Critical Sources

PERIODICALS

Booklist, December 1, 2005, Frances Bradburn, review of *Lust,* p. 38; February 15, 2006, Gillian Engberg, review of *Pride,* p. 92; January 1, 2008, Frances Bradburn, review of *Hacking Harvard,* p. 58; October 15, 2008, Francisca Goldsmith, review of *Skinned,* p. 38.

Kirkus Reviews, August 1, 2008, review of *Skinned.*

Kliatt, September, 2007, Stephanie Squicciarini, review of *Awakening,* p. 26; January, 2008, Debra Mitts-Smith, review of *Hacking Harvard,* p. 17.

Publishers Weekly, December 5, 2005, review of *Lust,* p. 56; June 4, 2007, review of *Awakening,* p. 50.

School Library Journal, January, 2006, Stephanie L. Petruso, review of *Lust,* p. 145; February, 2006, Stephanie L. Petruso, review of *Envy,* p. 139; August, 2006, Rebecca M. Jones, review of *Pride,* p. 132; January, 2008, Vicki Reutter, review of *Hacking Harvard,* p. 128; January, 2009, Megan Honig, review of *Skinned,* p. 122.

ONLINE

Robin Wasserman Home Page, http://www.robinwasserman.com (November 10, 2009).*

*   *   *

WELLS, Rosemary 1943-

Personal

Born January 29, 1943, in New York, NY; married Thomas Moore Wells (an architect), 1963 (deceased); children: Victoria, Marguerite. *Education:* Attended Boston Museum School and a small private junior college (now defunct) in New York state. *Religion:* "Nominal Episcopalian."

Addresses

Home—Briarcliff Manor, NY.

Career

Author and illustrator of children's books. Allyn & Bacon, Inc., Boston, MA, art editor; Macmillan Publishing Co., Inc., New York, NY, art designer; freelance author and illustrator, 1968—. Also worked at various jobs, including buyer of women's shoes and accessories for a clothing store. Founder, with Susan Jeffers, of book design studio, New York, NY, early 1970s. Speaker for national literacy campaign "Twenty Minutes a Day," beginning 1994; founder of "Read to Your Bunny" campaign (part of "Prescription for Reading" program), 1998. *Exhibitions:* Work included in American Institute of Graphic Arts Children's Book shows.

Awards, Honors

Honor Book citation, *Book World* Spring Children's Book Festival, 1972, for *The Fog Comes on Little Pig Feet;* Children's Book Showcase Award, Children's Book Council, 1974, for *Noisy Nora;* Citation of Merit, Society of Illustrators, 1974, and Art Book for Children citation, Brooklyn Museum/Brooklyn Public Library, 1975, 1976, 1977, all for *Benjamin and Tulip;* Irma Simonton Black Award, Bank Street College of Education, 1975, for *Morris's Disappearing Bag;* Edgar Allan Poe Award runner-up, Mystery Writers of America, 1981, for *When No One Was Looking,* and 1988, for *Through the Hidden Door;* New Jersey Institute of Technology Award, 1983, for *A Lion for Lewis* and *Peabody;* Best Illustrated Books designation, *New York*

Times, 1985, for *Hazel's Amazing Mother;* Washington Irving Children's Book Choice Award, Westchester Library Association, 1986, for *Peabody,* 1988, for *Max's Christmas,* and 1992, for *Max's Chocolate Chicken;* Golden Sower Award, 1986, for *Peabody;* New Jersey Institute of Technology Award, 1987, for *Max's Christmas;* Virginia Young Readers Award, and New York Public Library Books for the Teen Age citation, both 1987, both for *The Man in the Woods;* Golden Kite Award, Society of Children's Books Writers, 1988, for *Forest of Dreams; Boston Globe/Horn Book* Award, and Parents' Choice Foundation Award, both 1989, both for *Shy Charles;* David McCord Children's Literature citation, 1991, for body of work; Missouri Building Blocks Picture Book Award nominations, Missouri Library Association, 1998, for both *Bunny Cakes* and *McDuff Moves In;* Oppenheim Toy Portfolio Platinum Award, 1999, for both *Old MacDonald* and *The Itsy-Bitsy Spider; Riverbank Review* Children's Book of Distinction Award, and Notable Children's Book in the Language Arts designation, National Council of Teachers of English/Children's Literature Assembly, both 1999, both for *Mary on Horseback;* Pick-of-the-List citations, American Bookseller Association, for *Abdul, Stanley and Rhoda, Timothy Goes to School, A Lion for Lewis, Forest of Dreams, Max's Chocolate Chicken,* and *Good Night, Fred;* Children's Books of the Year citations, Child Study Association, for both *Morris's Disappearing Bag* and *Don't Spill It Again, James;* Teacher's Choices listee, International Reading Association (IRA), for *Forest of Dreams;* Children's Choice citation, IRA, for *Max's Chocolate Chicken, Timothy Goes to School, A Lion for Lewis,* and *Peabody;* Best Books for Young Adults citation, American Library Association (ALA), for *Through the Hidden Door;* Notable Children's Book citations, ALA, for *Noisy Nora, Benjamin and Tulip, Morris's Disappearing Bag, Max's Breakfast, Max's Christmas, Max's Chocolate Chicken, Max's Dragon Shirt,* and *Red Moon at Sharpsburg.*

Writings

Forest of Dreams, illustrated by Susan Jeffers, Dial (New York, NY), 1988.

Waiting for the Evening Star, illustrated by Susan Jeffers, Dial (New York, NY), 1993.

Night Sounds, Morning Colors, illustrated by David McPhail, Dial (New York, NY), 1994.

Lucy Comes to Stay, illustrated by Mark Graham, Dial (New York, NY), 1994.

The Language of Doves, illustrated by Greg Shed, Dial (New York, NY), 1996.

Mary on Horseback: Three Mountain Stories (middle-grade nonfiction), illustrated by Peter McCarty, Dial (New York, NY), 1998.

Streets of Gold (nonfiction; based on Mary Antin's memoir *The Promised Land*), illustrated by Dan Andreasen, Dial (New York, NY), 1999.

(With husband, Tom Wells) *The House in the Mail,* illustrated by Dan Andreasen, Dial (New York, NY), 1999.

Wingwalker, illustrated by Brian Selznick, Hyperion Books for Children (New York, NY), 2002.

Adding It Up, illustrated by Michale Koelsch, Viking (New York, NY), 2002.

Ready to Read, illustrated by Michale Koelsch, Viking (New York, NY), 2002.

The Small World of Binky Braverman, illustrated by Richard Egielski, Viking (New York, NY), 2003.

The Miraculous Tale of the Two Maries, illustrated by Petra Mathers, Viking (New York, NY), 2006.

The Gulps, illustrated by Marc Brown, Little, Brown (New York, NY), 2007.

Lincoln and His Boys, illustrated by P.J. Lynch, Candlewick Press (Somerville, MA), 2009.

(With Dino Fernandez) *My Havana: Memories of a Cuban Boyhood,* illustrated by Peter Ferguson, Candlewick Press (Somerville, MA), 2010.

SELF-ILLUSTRATED

John and the Rarey, Funk, 1969.

Michael and the Mitten Test, Bradbury (New York, NY), 1969.

The First Child, Hawthorn, 1970.

Martha's Birthday, Bradbury (New York, NY), 1970.

Miranda's Pilgrims, Bradbury (New York, NY), 1970.

Unfortunately Harriet, Dial (New York, NY), 1972.

Benjamin and Tulip, Dial (New York, NY), 1973.

Noisy Nora, Dial (New York, NY), 1973, revised edition, with new illustrations, 1997.

Abdul, Dial (New York, NY), 1975.

Morris's Disappearing Bag: A Christmas Story, Dial (New York, NY), 1975.

Don't Spill It Again, James, Dial (New York, NY), 1977.

Stanley and Rhoda, Dial (New York, NY), 1978.

Good Night, Fred, Dial (New York, NY), 1981.

Timothy Goes to School, Dial (New York, NY), 1981.

A Lion for Lewis, Dial (New York, NY), 1982.

Peabody, Dial (New York, NY), 1983.

Hazel's Amazing Mother, Dial (New York, NY), 1985.

Shy Charles, Dial (New York, NY), 1988.

Fritz and the Mess Fairy, Dial (New York, NY), 1991.

(With Maria Tallchief) *Tallchief: America's Prima Ballerina* (nonfiction), Viking (New York, NY), 1999.

Emily's First 100 Days of School, Hyperion (New York, NY), 2000.

Timothy's Lost and Found Day, Viking (New York, NY), 2000.

Timothy Goes to School, Viking (New York, NY), 2000.

Lassie Come-Home, Henry Holt (New York, NY), 2000.

Felix Feels Better, Candlewick Press (Cambridge, MA), 2001.

Practice Makes Perfect, Hyperion Books for Children (New York, NY), 2002.

Timothy's Tales from Hilltop School, Viking (New York, NY), 2002.

Make New Friends, Volo (New York, NY), 2002.

Leave Well Enough Alone, Dial (New York, NY), 2002.

Bubble-Gum Radar, Hyperion Books for Children (New York, NY), 2002.

When I Grow Up, Hyperion Books for Children (New York, NY), 2003.

Only You, Viking (New York, NY), 2003.

Felix and the Worrier, Candlewick Press (Cambridge, MA), 2003.

Emily's World of Wonders, Hyperion Books for Children (New York, NY), 2003.

My Kindergarten, Hyperion (New York, NY), 2004.

Twinkle, Twinkle, Little Star, Scholastic (New York, NY), 2006.

Carry Me!, Scholastic (New York, NY), 2006.

My Shining Star: Raising a Child Who Is Ready to Learn, Scholastic (New York, NY), 2006.

Otto Runs for President, Scholastic (New York, NY), 2008.

Contributor to books, including *So I Shall Tell You a Story: The Magic World of Beatrix Potter,* edited by Judy Taylor, Warne, 1993, and *Stories and Fun for the Very Young,* Candlewick Press, 1998.

"MAX AND RUBY" SERIES; SELF-ILLUSTRATED

Max's First Word, Dial (New York, NY), 1979.

Max's New Suit, Dial (New York, NY), 1979.

Max's Ride, Dial (New York, NY), 1979.

Max's Toys: A Counting Book, Dial (New York, NY), 1979.

Max's Bath, Dial (New York, NY), 1985.

Max's Bedtime, Dial (New York, NY), 1985.

Max's Breakfast, Dial (New York, NY), 1985.

Max's Birthday, Dial (New York, NY), 1985.

Max's Christmas, Dial (New York, NY), 1986.

Hooray for Max, Dial (New York, NY), 1986.

Max's Chocolate Chicken, Dial (New York, NY), 1989.

Max's Dragon Shirt, Dial (New York, NY), 1991.

Max and Ruby's First Greek Myth: Pandora's Box, Dial (New York, NY), 1993.

Max and Ruby's Midas: Another Greek Myth, Dial (New York, NY), 1995.

Bunny Cakes, Dial (New York, NY), 1997.

Bunny Money, Dial (New York, NY), 1997.

Max's Chocolate Chicken, Dial (New York, NY), 1999.

Max Cleans Up, Viking (New York, NY), 2000.

Goodnight Max, Viking (New York, NY), 2000.

Bunny Party, Viking (New York, NY), 2001.

Max's Snowsuit, Grosset & Dunlap (New York, NY), 2001.

Play with Max and Ruby, Grosset & Dunlap (New York, NY), 2002.

Ruby's Beauty Shop, Viking (New York, NY), 2003.

Max's Christmas Stocking, Viking (New York, NY), 2003.

Max Drives Away, Viking (New York, NY), 2003.

Ruby's Tea for Two, Viking (New York, NY), 2003.

Bunny Mail, Viking (New York, NY), 2004.

Max's Halloween, Viking (New York, NY), 2004.

Max's ABC, Viking (New York, NY), 2006.

Max Counts His Chickens, Viking (New York, NY), 2007.

Max's Bunny Business, Viking (New York, NY), 2008.

Baby Max and Ruby: Clean-up Time, Viking (New York, NY), 2009.

Baby Max and Ruby: Red Boots, Viking (New York, NY), 2009.

"VOYAGE TO THE BUNNY PLANET" SERIES; SELF-ILLUSTRATED

Voyage to the Bunny Planet, Dial (New York, NY), 1992, reprinted, Viking (New York, NY), 2008.

First Tomato, Dial (New York, NY), 1992.

The Island Light, Dial (New York, NY), 1992.

Moss Pillows, Dial (New York, NY), 1992.

"EDWARD THE UNREADY" SERIES; SELF-ILLUSTRATED

Edward Unready for School, Dial (New York, NY), 1995.

Edward's Overwhelming Overnight, Dial (New York, NY), 1995.

Edward in Deep Water, Dial (New York, NY), 1995.

"MCDUFF" SERIES; ILLUSTRATED BY SUSAN JEFFERS

McDuff Moves In, Hyperion (New York, NY), 1997.

McDuff Comes Home, Hyperion (New York, NY), 1997.

McDuff and the Baby, Hyperion (New York, NY), 1997.

McDuff's New Friend, Hyperion (New York, NY), 1998.

McDuff, Hyperion (New York, NY), 1998.

McDuff's Birthday, Hyperion (New York, NY), 2000.

The McDuff Stories, Hyperion (New York, NY), 2000.

McDuff Goes to School, Hyperion (New York, NY), 2001.

McDuff Saves the Day, Hyperion (New York, NY), 2002.

McDuff Steps Out, Hyperion (New York, NY), 2004.

McDuff's Favorite Things, Hyperion (New York, NY), 2004.

McDuff's Hide-and-Seek, Hyperion (New York, NY), 2004.

McDuff's Wild Romp, Hyperion (New York, NY), 2005.

"BUNNY READS BACK" SERIES; SELF-ILLUSTRATED

Read to Your Bunny, Scholastic (New York, NY), 1998.

Old MacDonald, Scholastic (New York, NY), 1998.

The Bear Went over the Mountain, Scholastic (New York, NY), 1998.

Bingo, Scholastic (New York, NY), 1998.

The Itsy-Bitsy Spider, Scholastic (New York, NY), 1998.

"YOKO AND FRIENDS SCHOOL DAYS" SERIES; SELF-ILLUSTRATED, UNLESS OTHERWISE NOTED

Yoko, Hyperion (New York, NY), 1998.

Mama, Don't Go!, Hyperion (New York, NY), 2001.

The School Play, Hyperion (New York, NY), 2001.

The Halloween Parade, Hyperion (New York, NY), 2001.

Doris's Dinosaur, Hyperion (New York, NY), 2001.

Yoko's Paper Cranes, Hyperion (New York, NY), 2001.

The World around Us, illustrated by Lisa Koelsch, Hyperion (New York, NY), 2001.

Be My Valentine, illustrated by John Nez, Hyperion (New York, NY), 2001.

Read Me a Story, Hyperion (New York, NY), 2001.

The Germ Busters, illustrated by Jody Wheeler, Hyperion (New York, NY), 2002.

Yoko's World of Kindness: Golden Rules for a Happy Classroom, interior illustrated by John Nez and Jody Wheeler, Hyperion (New York, NY), 2005.

Yoko Writes Her Name, Japanese calligraphy by Masako Inkyo, Hyperion (New York, NY), 2008.

FICTION; FOR YOUNG ADULTS

The Fog Comes on Little Pig Feet, Dial (New York, NY), 1972.

None of the Above, Dial (New York, NY), 1974.

Leave Well Enough Alone, Dial (New York, NY), 1977.

When No One Was Looking, Dial (New York, NY), 1980, reprinted, Puffin (New York, NY), 2000.

The Man in the Woods, Dial (New York, NY), 1984.

Through the Hidden Door, Dial (New York, NY), 1987.

Red Moon at Sharpsburg, Viking (New York, NY), 2007.

RETELLER

The Little Lame Prince (based on the book by Dinash Mulock Craik), Dial (New York, NY), 1990.

Lassie Come-Home (based on the book by Eric Knight), illustrated by Susan Jeffers, Holt (New York, NY), 1995.

Alan Garner, *Jack and the Beanstalk,* Dorling Kindersley (New York, NY), 1997.

The Fisherman and His Wife: A Brand-New Version, illustrated by Eleanor Hubbard, Dial (New York, NY), 1998.

Hitty: Her First Hundred Years, with New Adventures (based on the book by Rachel Field), illustrated by Susan Jeffers, Simon & Schuster (New York, NY), 1999.

Alan Garner, *Little Red Riding Hood,* Dorling Kindersley (New York, NY), 1999.

ILLUSTRATOR

William Schwenck Gilbert and Arthur Sullivan, *A Song to Sing, O!* (from *The Yeoman of the Guard*), Macmillan (New York, NY), 1968.

Gilbert and Sullivan, *W.S. Gilbert's "The Duke of Plaza Toro"* (from *The Gondoliers*), Macmillan (New York, NY), 1969.

Paula Fox, *Hungry Fred,* Bradbury, 1969.

(With Susan Jeffers), Charlotte Pomerantz, *Why You Look like You Whereas I Tend to Look like Me,* Young Scott Books, 1969.

Robert W. Service, *The Shooting of Dan McGrew* [and] *The Cremation of Sam McGhee,* Young Scott Books, 1969.

Rudyard Kipling, *The Cat That Walked by Himself,* Hawthorn, 1970.

Winifred Rosen, *Marvin's Manhole,* Dial (New York, NY), 1970.

Marjorie Weinman Sharmat, *A Hot Thirsty Day,* Macmillan, 1971.

Ellen Conford, *Impossible, Possum,* Little, Brown (Boston, MA), 1971.

Beryl Epstein and Dorrit Davis, *Two Sisters and Some Hornets,* Holiday House (New York, NY), 1972.

Virginia A. Tashjian, editor, *With a Deep-Sea Smile: Story Hour Stretches for Large or Small Groups,* Little, Brown (Boston, MA), 1974.

Lore G. Segal, *Tell Me a Trudy,* Farrar, Straus (New York, NY), 1977.

Jostein Gaarder, *The Christmas Mystery,* translated by Elizabeth Rokkan, Farrar, Straus (New York, NY), 1996.

Iona Opie, editor, *My Very First Mother Goose,* Candlewick Press (Cambridge, MA), 1996.

Iona Opie, editor, *Humpty Dumpty and Other Rhymes,* Candlewick Press (Cambridge, MA), 1997.

Iona Opie, editor, *Little Boy Blue and Other Rhymes,* Candlewick Press (Cambridge, MA), 1997.

Iona Opie, editor, *Pussycat, Pussycat and Other Rhymes,* Candlewick Press (Cambridge, MA), 1997.

Iona Opie, editor, *Wee Willie Winkie and Other Rhymes,* Candlewick Press (Cambridge, MA), 1997.

(Watercolorist) E.B. White, *Stuart Little: Collector's Edition,* HarperCollins (New York, NY), 1999.

(Watercolorist) E.B. White, *Charlotte's Web: Collector's Edition,* HarperCollins (New York, NY), 1999.

Iona Opie, editor, *Here Comes Mother Goose,* Candlewick Press (Cambridge, MA), 1999.

(Watercolorist) Garth Williams, *Benjamin's Treasure* (excerpt from *The Adventures of Benjamin Pink*), Candlewick Press (Cambridge, MA), 2001.

Oscar Hammerstein and Richard Rogers, *Getting to Know You!: Rogers and Hammerstein Favorites,* HarperCollins (New York, NY), 2002.

(Watercolorist) Mary Stolz, *Emmett's Pig,* HarperCollins (New York, NY), 2003.

Frank Loesser, *I Love You! A Bushel and a Peck,* HarperCollins (New York, NY), 2005.

Iona Opie, editor, *Mother Goose's Little Treasures,* Candlewick Press (Cambridge, MA), 2007.

OTHER

Author, with Joanna Hurley, of *Cooking for Nitwits,* photographs by Barbara Olcott, Dutton, 1989. Contributor to *Worlds of Childhood: The Art and Craft of Writing for Children,* edited by William Zinsser, Houghton Mifflin, 1990.

Some of Wells' books have been translated into Spanish.

Adaptations

Morris's *Disappearing Bag* and *Max's Christmas* were adapted as short films by Weston Woods, 1982 and 1988, respectively; *Timothy Goes to School* was adapted as a filmstrip by Weston Woods, 1982; *Max's Christmas* was released as a filmstrip and on video by Weston Woods, 1987; *Timothy Goes to School* was adapted for television, 2000; the "Max and Ruby" characters appeared in sticker-book adaptations published by Grosset & Dunlap; the "Max and Ruby" books were adapted for an animated television series produced by Nickelodeon; Wells' characters have been produced as stuffed toys.

Sidelights

Rosemary Wells is a popular and versatile artist and writer who is noted for the realism, perception, and humor in both her picture books and young-adult novels. Wells is acclaimed for her originality, versatility, sensitivity, wry sense of humor, artistic talent, and understanding of both children and the human condition. She is also praised for her characterizations and is well known as the creator of many popular characters, such as sibling bunnies Max and Ruby, that are featured in her innovative board and picture books. As an illustrator, Wells has provided the pictures for works by such authors as Paula Fox, Rudyard Kipling, and Ellen Conford.

In her picture books, Wells takes a lighthearted but heartfelt approach to universal childhood experiences. Many of her works feature engaging anthropomorphic animal characters that are caught up in childhood dilemmas or comic predicaments involving sibling rivalry or distracted parents. Noted for accurately reflecting the feelings of children while emphasizing the child as an individual, Wells is also acknowledged for giving young readers and listeners the chance to laugh at themselves. As Janet Zarem observed in the *New York Times Book Review,* "Her respect and compassion for children's needs, feelings and dilemmas are boundless: for fear . . ., for embarrassment . . ., for anger . . ., for reassurance . . . and always for feeling cherished and for possessing a natural talent or ability worth acknowledging."

Wells' storybook art is a perfect match to Iona Opie's **My Very First Mother Goose.** *(. Candlewick Press, 1996. Text copyright © 1996 Iona Opie. Illustrations copyright © 1996 by Rosemary Wells. Reproduced by permission of the publisher Candlewick Press, Somerville, MA.)*

Wells' young-adult novels deal with ethical dilemmas such as betrayal, the pressures of competition, and the search for truth. Refusing to provide easy answers, she lets her characters tap their inner strength while establishing their identities and independence in a confusing world. Wells frequently creates a story-within-a-story and often concludes her books—some of which are written in verse—with unconventional endings. "Just as there are universal emotions and predicaments common to young childhood, so there are for teenagers as well," she remarked in *Worlds of Childhood: The Art and Craft of Writing for Children.* "In some ways, to be fourteen now is no different than it was for me or my mother. That part of writing for teenagers is familiar to me, and having those fragile and unstoppable joys and fears in my grasp is where I start."

As an artist, Wells favors line and water color; she is often praised for her rich use of color and for creating deceptively simple drawings that are filled with nuance and expression. "In a few lines and pale colors," noted Jennifer Farley Smith in the *Christian Science Monitor,* "Wells can speak volumes to her young audience." In *Booklist* Hazel Rochman also praised Wells' artwork, adding that the author/illustrator "has that rare ability to tell a funny story for very young children with domestic scenes of rising excitement and heartfelt emotion, and with not one word too many."

Born in New York City, Wells grew up in a home that was, as she recalled in an essay for *Something about the Author Autobiography Series* (*SAAS*), "always filled with books, dogs, nineteenth-century music, and other things my parents held in great esteem." Most of her childhood was spent on the New Jersey coast, where her maternal grandmother had a home right on the ocean. The author's parents—her father was a playwright and her mother was a ballet dancer—and her grandmother encouraged her early artistic endeavors. Wells' grandmother, to whom she was very close, was widely read and had been a great beauty in New York society. She often read to Rosemary from works by authors such as Longfellow, Kipling, and Poe. As Wells recalled on her home page, "Both my parents flooded me with books and stories. My grandmother took me on special trips to the theater and museums in New York."

From the age of two, Wells drew constantly. As she told Jean F. Mercier in *Publishers Weekly,* "I parlayed this [talent] into the sham of a school career. I discovered very early that making a picture of anything meant people saying 'Look at that!' and how else could I get that kind of attention?" Encouraged in her art in first grade, she decided early on that she wanted to be an artist when she grew up. As Wells recalled in *SAAS,* having a career goal during adolescence became increasingly important. "Because I could say artist, I had a reprieve from what, even then, I considered to be a life sentence of drudgery. When I became a teenager, the idea of being an artist was the only thing that stood between me and despair—I was gangly, underdevel-

Wells' original self-illustrated picture books include **Max Cleans Up,** *part of her popular "Max and Ruby" series.* (Puffin Books 2000. Copyright © 2000 by Rosemary Wells. Reproduced by permission of Rosemary Sandberg Ltd., and Puffin Books, a division of Penguin Putnam Books for Young Readers.)

oped, a social retard whose mother didn't like her watching 'American Bandstand.'" In addition to art, writing was also important to the young teen, and when she was not drawing or involved with friends and sports, Wells read and wrote stories.

At age thirteen, Wells was sent to an upscale boarding school for girls. "I reacted badly," the author/illustrator recalled in *SAAS:* "The school was a jail to me although the other girls seemed to be having a grand time." Wells found the regimentation, scrutiny, and constant supervision to be oppressive; in addition, "there was no privacy, no time to draw." Miserable, she was finally released from this torture when her parents took her out of the school. Back at home, Wells entered Red Bank High School, where she became an admittedly poor student. She was eventually accepted at a small private junior college in upstate New York, where she decided

to shed "the high school stigma of 'not being popular.'" At junior college she became a top student and made two lifelong friends. However, she soon got sidetracked by romance after meeting Tom Wells, a Dartmouth student. She left school after one year and moved to Boston.

In Boston, the nineteen-year-old Wells entered the Boston Museum School, where she studied anatomy, perspective, life drawing, and printing. In 1963, she and Tom Wells married, and she left school to enter the job market. On the strength of her portfolio, Wells landed a job as art editor with the publishers Allyn & Bacon. Then, as she wrote in *SAAS,* "all the laziness and reluctance to concentrate disappeared. I was assigned an American history book for Catholic high-school seniors. It was thirteen hundred pages long and I had to send away for all the prints and photos that would illus-

trate it. The book was wonderful. The Sisters of the Sacred Heart, who were involved in the editorial end, were splendid women. There was a party when it was published and I felt like a success at something for the first time in my life."

Two years later, when Tom was accepted at the Columbia University School of Architecture, the couple moved to New York City. While working as an art designer for Macmillan, Wells presented a small illustrated dummy of a Gilbert and Sullivan song, taken from their light opera *The Yeomen of the Guard,* to the company's editor-in-chief. This became her first published book, *A Song to Sing, O!,* and it was followed by *W.S. Gilbert's "The Duke of Plaza Toro,"* a picture book based on a Gilbert and Sullivan song from *The Gondoliers.*

After illustrating well-received volumes by Paula Fox and Robert W. Service, Wells created her first original work, *John and the Rarey.* Published in 1969, the picture book features a little boy who does not want to be an airplane pilot like his father. What John does want is a pet: he finds a fantastic, blue-eyed creature that takes him into the sky on its back. A reviewer in *Publishers Weekly* called Wells "a fresh new talent in children's books" and praised *John and the Rarey* as a "witty story," while *Horn Book* critic Sidney D. Long wrote that her book would "appeal to all children who have been faced with a frustrating family situation."

Throughout her career Wells has continued to illustrate the work of other authors while adding to a growing list of solo picture books. Inspired by the antics of her own two children, in 1979 she produced the first four books in her popular "Max and Ruby" series, including *Max's First Word* and *Max's Toys: A Counting Book.* Described by *Children's Books and Their Creators* contributor Maeve Visser Knoth as "the first funny board books for very young children," the "Max and Ruby" books use story, information, and humor to introduce preschoolers to topics such as prepositions, getting dressed, and the importance of individuality. Max is a white bunny; Ruby is an older sister who thinks she knows what is best for Max and tries to control him. Although Max is easygoing, he remains undaunted, innocently outsmarting his sister and always getting the last word. Featuring a minimal but lively text, the books feature pictures enlivened by vivid primary colors and featuring an uncluttered page layout.

Writing in *Booklist,* Judith Goldberger praised the series for "driv[ing] . . . a real wedge into the existing block of unnotable, overcute, didactic baby-toddler tomes." Wells has continued to produce board books in the "Max and Ruby" series, continuing the adventures of the brother-and-sister duo for new generations of pre-readers in books such as *Bunny Money* and *Ruby's Beauty Shop.* Reviewing *Ruby's Beauty Shop,* in which Ruby and friend Louie make Max their guinea pig in a game of beauty parlor that goes awry, a *Kirkus Reviews* critic noted that "Wells has an unerring ability to hit just the right note to tickle small-fry funny bones." "Each story portrays a typical preschool trauma resolved with humor and understanding," wrote Trev Jones in *School Library Journal,* while in a *Bulletin of the Center for Children's Books* review Zena Sutherland dubbed each book in the series "equally delectable, and they should be as useful for very young children as they are appealing."

Max's Christmas breaks with Wells' board-book tradition by presenting the first full-length picture-book treatment of the escapades of Max and Ruby. A bunny with an inquiring mind, Max has lots of unanswered questions about Santa Claus that Ruby answers curtly, prompting her little brother to take matters into his own hands. Calling Max "that epitome of the small child in rabbit guise," Judith Glover, wrote in *School Library Journal* that Wells "has an extraordinary talent for capturing a welter of thoughts and emotions with the placement of an eye or a turn of a smile." *Horn Book* critic Karen Jameyson concluded that, despite the book's longer format, "an uncanny perceptive simplicity, both in line and in word, is still Wells's most effective tool."

Other books about Max and Ruby adhere to the picture-book format. In *Bunny Cakes* the siblings have separate ideas for creating treats: Ruby wants to make an angel surprise cake while Max wants to present his grandmother with an earthworm cake decorated with red-hot marshmallow squirters. Max—who is too young to read and write—thinks of a way to communicate his shopping list to the grocer, and Grandma is thrilled when she receives two cakes. Pat Mathews, a reviewer for the *Bulletin of the Center for Children's Books,* claimed that, "in this take on written communication kidstyle, pudgy Max is at his winsome best."

Part of Wells' "Yoko and Friends" series, Make New Friends *features artwork by Jody Wheeler.* (Copyright © Rosemary Wells. Reproduced by permission of Disney Hyperion, an imprint of Disney Book Group, LLC. All rights reserved.)

Bunny Money finds the pair shopping to buy a birthday present for Grandma. The siblings' money goes fast—most of it is spent on Max, and Wells shows the gradual reduction of the contents of Ruby's wallet at the bottom of each page—but a compromise is reached: Grandma drives the pair home wearing musical earrings from Ruby and plastic vampire teeth from Max. A *Kirkus Reviews* critic called *Bunny Money* "a great adjunct to primary-grade math lessons," while Mathews concluded that Wells' "combination of gentle comedy, shrinking assets, and those expressive bunny eyes" will attract "old and new Max and Ruby fans."

Max Counts His Chickens is a counting book of sorts. Here the siblings hunt for ten marshmallow chicks on Easter morning, but Ruby's incredible success at ferreting out the hiding places leaves Max wanting. "Wells's artwork creates a warm, comfortable atmosphere in which counting to ten is a simple pleasure," a *Kirkus Reviews* critic observed, and Julie Cummins applauded the "perfect pairing of concept and story," noting that Wells' illustrations include "clever details that spill out across the Easter-egg-colored picture borders." Ruby and her brother engage in a heated competition in *Max's Bunny Business.* When Ruby and her best friend open a lemonade stand and refuse to let Max join the fun, he outwits them by creating a more profitable endeavor. "As always, Wells' Easter-bright artwork tells a dramatic story of sibling rivalry," Rochman stated in *Booklist.*

In addition to penning stories involving the irrepressible Max and Ruby, Wells has also created several other popular series. Her "Voyage to the Bunny Planet" books feature little bunnies that have bad days and imagine themselves transported to the Bunny Planet, where good times restore their equilibrium. The "Edward the Unready" series follows a little bear that is unenthusiastic about going to school or staying overnight at a friend's house and prefers to be at home among familiar surroundings. Other series feature Yoko, a little Asian kitten, and Felix, a young guinea pig. In *Yoko Writes Her Name,* the tiny feline, who is learning Japanese, grows anxious after two of her meddling classmates tease her about her penmanship. A critic in *Kirkus Reviews* observed that the work "teaches a subtle lesson on acceptance and maturity with great clarity," and in *School Library Journal,* Piper Nyman described *Yoko Writes Her Name* as "a carefully crafted picture book with Asian-inspired illustrations that delight the eye just as the gentle story soothes the soul." In *Felix Feels Better,* the title character is nursed back to health by Mom after overindulging in his favorite chocolate candy, and in *Felix and the Worrier* the protagonist discovers the courage to confront his fears, symbolized by an impish creature that invades Felix's dreams. Kay Weisman, writing in *Booklist,* noted that "Wells' watercolor-and-ink illustrations will charm and comfort young listeners," and *Horn Book* reviewer Kitty Flynn maintained that the author/illustrator's message "will come across loud and clear to young worrywarts."

A little guinea pig is a cute stand-in for young children in Wells' self-illustrated Felix and the Worrier. *(Candlewick Press 2003. Copyright © 2003 Rosemary Wells. Reproduced by permission of the publisher Candlewick Press, Inc., Somerville, MA.)*

In the "McDuff" series, a West Highland white terrier—based on Wells' own pet—escapes from a dogcatcher's truck and is adopted by a young couple. Written for three-to-six-year-old readers, the series takes up McDuff's problems and adventures, like getting lost while chasing a rabbit and dealing with a new baby in the house. In *McDuff Goes to School* the energetic terrier must attend obedience classes after he upsets his new canine companion's French owners. "Wells injects a warm humor into this brief story," a critic in *Kirkus Reviews* noted. A near-disastrous outing on the Fourth of July is the subject of *McDuff Saves the Day.* "The cozy, old-fashioned story is simple enough to be understood by younger preschoolers, with enough humor from McDuff's antics to entertain" readers of all ages, maintained a *Kirkus Reviews* contributor.

Stand-alone picture books by Wells include *Wingwalker* and *The House in the Mail,* the latter a collaboration with her husband. *Wingwalker,* which takes place during the Great Depression of the 1930s and finds a young Oklahoma boy and his family trying to make ends meet during the sustained drought that caused the Dust Bowl, was praised by a *Kirkus Reviews* critic who noted that "Wells' prose is spare but has both richness and freshness of simile and image." *The House in the Mail* takes readers back to an even earlier decade of the twentieth century, when houses could be ordered in kits from the Sears, Roebuck catalogue. The story is narrated by twelve-year-old Emily, whose father summons friends to help assemble the modern home. Complete with a refrigerator, running water, a washing machine, and other conveniences, the new six-room bungalow is put together piece, by piece, and the story is illustrated in scrap-book style by Dan Andreasen. Noting that "anec-

dotes and snatches of conversation flesh out the era," a *Publishers Weekly* contributor praised *The House in the Mail* as a story that "speaks . . . to the strong bond among the members of Emily's family." "This remarkable picture book . . . is like discovering a slice of American life in a family scrapbook," added Connie Fletcher in *Booklist.*

Wells has also enjoyed successful literary collaborations with other artists. In *The Small World of Binky Braverman,* a work illustrated by Richard Egielski, narrator Stanley "Binky" Braverman recalls the events of 1938, when a host of magical playmates helped ease his feelings of homesickness during a summer-long stay with relatives. "The watercolor illustrations complement Wells's imaginative text," Shawn Brommer wrote in *School Library Journal.* Based on French folklore, *The Miraculous Tale of the Two Maries* centers on a pair of girls who drown at sea but are given the chance to perform good deeds in the afterlife. "It's certainly an oddball tale, but it has its own logic and whimsical devoutness," noted *Horn Book* critic Roger Sutton, who also complimented the artwork of Petra Mathers. In *The Gulps* a family of junk-food junkies gets whipped into shape after its members find themselves stranded in the countryside during their summer vacation. "Wells' message, though couched in silliness and humor, is still ob-

P.J. Lynch captures the family drama in Wells' nonfiction profile **Lincoln and His Boys.** (Candlewick Press, 2009. Text copyright © Rosemary Wells. Illustrations copyright © 2009 by P.J. Lynch. All rights reserved. Reproduced by permission of the publisher Candlewick Press, Inc., Somerville, MA.)

vious," *Booklist* critic Shelle Rosenfeld maintained, and Gloria Koster, writing in *School Library Journal,* remarked that illustrator Marc Brown's "busily patterned cartoons in confectionery colors with cotton-candy clouds humorously depict the rotund characters in this tongue-in-cheek tale."

In addition to being a prolific author of picture books, Wells has written several well-respected novels for teen readers. The award-winning *When No One Was Looking* is a mystery novel that focuses on a highly competitive teen tennis player who is placed under suspicion when her arch rival conveniently drowns just before a face-off match. *The Fog Comes on Little Pig Feet,* which is based on Wells' boarding-school experience, takes the form of a diary written by thirteen-year-old Rachel Sakasian. A Brooklyn girl who wants to become a concert pianist, Rachel longs to attend Music and Art High, a New York City public school, but her parents instead enroll her at North Place, an elite boarding school. When she becomes friends with upper-classman Carlisle Duggett, who is rumored to be mentally unbalanced, Rachel finds herself covering for her new friend when the girl leaves school to live in Greenwich Village. After she learns that Carlisle has tried to commit suicide, Rachel is torn between protecting her friend and telling the truth. In a *School Library Journal* review, Alice Miller Bregman predicted that "teens will devour this fast-paced, adequately written entertainment." A contributor to *Best Sellers* applauded the novel's "priceless vignettes," concluding that Wells "brilliantly demonstrates [that] her writing abilities are an easy match for her already famous artistic talents."

None of the Above outlines five years in the life of Marcia, a teen who favors pink angora sweaters, reading movie magazines, and watching television. When her father remarries, Marcia feels out of place with her sophisticated stepmother and ambitious stepsister. In reaction, she decides to turn herself around: she switches to college prep classes and succeeds, although reluctantly, in school. However, she also becomes involved with Raymond, a good-looking though hoodish classmate. Calling Marcia an "unusual and oddly affecting heroine," *School Library Journal* critic Joni Brodart claimed that Wells "captures the girl's confusion in this timely, realistic, and moving novel which should reach a large audience." Writing in the *Bulletin of the Center for Children's Books,* Zena Sutherland noted that Wells' "characterization is strong and consistent, and the complexities of relationships within the family are beautifully developed. Wells is particularly adept at dialogue."

In addition to her work in fiction, Wells has also delved into nonfiction writing with several biographies of historical and contemporary women. *Mary on Horseback: Three Mountain Stories,* a book for middle graders, profiles Mary Breckinridge, founder of the Frontier Nursing Service in the Appalachian Mountains. Wells shows both the hardships and the triumphs experienced by the valiant nurse from the perspectives of three young

people whom Mary helped. Noting the "historical accuracy and elegance" of the volume, a reviewer in *Publishers Weekly* stated that the book's "well-honed first-person narratives add up to an outstanding biography." *Booklist* reviewer Helen Rosenberg added that "these beautifully written stories will remain with the reader long after the book is closed; Wells has given much deserved honor to a true heroine," while Peggy Morgan concluded in *School Library Journal* that *Mary on Horseback* is "a gem."

In *Streets of Gold* Wells presents a picture-book biography of Mary Antin, a Jewish girl who came to the United States from tsarist Russia in the early twentieth century. A year after her arrival, Antin wrote an epic poem about George Washington that was published in a Boston newspaper. A reviewer in *Publishers Weekly* claimed that, "among a profusion of books about turn-of-the-[twentieth-]century Russian-Jewish emigrants, Wells's . . . story about Mary Antin stands out for its exceptional economy and tenderness." Wells has also produced a well-received biography of American ballet dancer Maria Tallchief, collaborating with the noted Native American dancer on this project.

Wells examines life in Virginia's Shenandoah Valley during the U.S. Civil War in *Red Moon at Sharpsburg*. The novel centers on India Moody, a young woman who must fend for herself after the death of her father, a wagon driver for the Confederacy. The intelligent and sensitive India finds a companion in her neighbor, a scientist who tutors her after the local schools close, and she later risks her life by harboring a wounded Union soldier. "This powerful novel is unflinching in its depiction of war and the devastation it causes," Shannon Seglin commented in *School Library Journal*, and Claire Rosser, writing in *Kliatt*, stated that "India's character is a marvelous combination of vulnerability, strength and intelligence."

In *Lincoln and His Boys*, a fictional work based on an essay by Abraham Lincoln's son, Willie Lincoln, Wells looks at three events from the life of the U.S. president, focusing on the relationship between Lincoln and his sons, Willie and Tad. "Lincoln is shown to be a caring and fun-loving parent," Francisca Goldsmith observed in *Booklist*, and *School Library Journal* reviewer Janet S. Thompson acknowledged that viewing Lincoln "from his children's viewpoint brings both the family and the times to life."

Looking back on her long career, Wells wrote in *SAAS*, that "there are hard parts but no bad or boring parts, and that is more than can be said for any other line of work." In *Worlds of Childhood*, Wells further noted: "I believe that all stories and plays and paintings and songs and dances come from a palpable but unseen space in the cosmos. . . . According to how gifted we are, we are all given a large or small key to this treasury of wonders. I have been blessed with a small key to the world of the young."

Biographical and Critical Sources

BOOKS

Children's Books and Their Creators, edited by Anita Silvey, Houghton Mifflin (Boston, MA), 1995.
Children's Literature Review, Gale (Detroit, MI), Volume 16, 1989, Volume 69, 2001.
Contemporary Literary Criticism, Volume 12, Gale (Detroit, MI), 1980.
Sadker, Myra Pollack, and David Miller Sadker, *Now upon a Time: A Contemporary View of Children's Literature,* Harper (New York, NY), 1997.
St. James Guide to Children's Writers, Gale (Detroit, MI), 1999.
St. James Guide to Young-Adult Writers, Gale (Detroit, MI), 1999.
Something about the Author Autobiography Series, Volume 1, Gale (Detroit, MI), 1986.
Worlds of Childhood: The Art and Craft of Writing for Children, edited by William Zinsser, Houghton Mifflin (Boston, MA), 1990.

PERIODICALS

Best Sellers, July 15, 1972, review of *The Fog Comes on Little Pig Feet,* p. 200.
Booklist, October 15, 1978, Judith Goldberger, review of *Max's First Word, Max's New Suit, Max's Ride,* and *Max's Toys: A Counting Book,* p. 359; January 1, 1997, Hazel Rochman, review of *Bunny Cakes,* p. 857; September 1, 1998, Helen Rosenberg, review of *Mary on Horseback: Three Mountain Stories,* p. 113; February 1, 2001, Kathy Broderick, review of *Max Cleans Up,* p. 1059; February 15, 2001, Shelley Townsend Hudson, review of *Benjamin's Treasure,* p. 1142; May 1, 2001, Hazel Rochman, review of *Felix Feels Better,* p. 1693; November 1, 2001, Hazel Rochman, review of *Language of Doves,* p. 475; December 15, 2001, Stephanie Zvirin, review of *Felix Feels Better,* p. 728; March 1, 2002, Connie Fletcher, review of *The House in the Mail,* p. 1137; July, 2002, Shelle Rosenfeld, review of *McDuff Saves the Day,* p. 1861; August, 2002, Hazel Rochman, review of *Ruby's Beauty Shop,* p. 1977; November 1, 2003, Kay Weisman, review of *Felix and the Worrier,* p. 507; October 1, 2003, Gillian Engberg, review of *The Small World of Binky Braverman,* p. 329; August, 2004, Hazel Rochman, review of *My Kindergarten,* p. 1949; January 1, 2007, Julie Cummins, review of *Max Counts His Chickens,* p. 93; March 1, 2007, Shelle Rosenfeld, review of *The Gulps,* p. 90; March 1, 2008, Hazel Rochman, review of *Max's Bunny Business,* p. 73; January 1, 2009, Francisca Goldsmith, review of *Lincoln and His Boys,* p. 82.
Bulletin of the Center for Children's Books, April, 1975, Zena Sutherland, review of *None of the Above,* p. 139; April, 1985, Zena Sutherland, review of *Max's Bath,* p. 157; November, 1993, Betsy Hearne, review of *Max and Ruby's First Greek Myth: Pandora's Box,* p. 106; March, 1997, Pat Mathews, review of *Bunny*

Cakes, p. 261; October, 1997, Pat Mathews, review of *Bunny Money,* p. 71.

Childhood Education, winter, 2000, Susan A. Miller, review of *Goodnight Max,* p. 110.

Christian Science Monitor, March 6, 1974, Jennifer Farley Smith, "Animals Are Enduring Heroes," p. F2.

Horn Book, August, 1969, Sidney D. Long, review of *John and the Rarey,* pp. 399-400; March-April 1987, Rosemary Wells, "The Artist at Work: The Writer at Work," pp. 163-170; June, 1987, Roger Sutton, "A Second Look: 'None of the Above,'" pp. 368-371; July-August, 2002, Christine M. Heppermann, review of *Wingwalker,* p. 474; January-February, 2004, Kitty Flynn, review of *Felix and the Worrier,* p. 74; March-April, 2006, Roger Sutton, review of *The Miraculous Tale of the Two Maries,* p. 177; May-June, 2006, Joanna Rudge Long, review of *Max's ABC,* p. 307; May-June, 2008, Susan Dove Lempke, review of *Max's Bunny Business,* p. 301; July-August, 2008, Jennifer M. Brabander, review of *Otto Runs for President,* p. 435.

Kirkus Reviews, September 1, 1993, review of *Max and Ruby's First Greek Myth,* p 1154; July 15, 1997, review of *Bunny Money,* p. 1119; August 1, 2001, review of *McDuff Goes to School,* p. 1222; April 15, 2002, review of *Wingwalker,* p. 581; May 15, 2002, review of *McDuff Saves the Day,* p. 743; June 15, 2002, review of *Timothy's Tales from Hilltop School,* p. 890; July 15, 2002, review of *Ruby's Beauty Shop,* p. 1047; August 15, 2003, reviews of *Felix and the Worrier,* p. 1080, and *The Small World of Binky Braverman,* p. 1081; December 15, 2004, review of *I Love You! A Bushel and a Peck,* p. 1204; December 15, 2006, review of *Max Counts His Chickens,* p. 1274; August 1, 2007, review of *Mother Goose's Little Treasures;* June 15, 2008, review of *Yoko Writes Her Name.*

Kliatt, March, 2007, Claire Rosser, review of *Red Moon at Sharpsburg,* p. 20.

New York Times, April 20, 2003, Suzanne MacNeille, "He's Not Just a Bunny. He's My Brother," p. 55.

New York Times Book Review, November 24, 1974, Dale Carlson, review of *None of the Above,* p. 8; September 19, 2004, Janet Zarem, review of *My Kindergarten,* p. 16.

Publishers Weekly, April 21, 1969, review of *John and the Rarey,* p. 64; November 15, 1970, review of *Miranda's Pilgrims,* p. 1245; August 5, 1974, Jean F. Mercier, review of *None of the Above,* p. 58; October 9, 1978, review of *Stanley and Rhoda,* p. 76; February 29, 1980, Jean F. Mercier, interview, pp. 72-73; September 14, 1998, review of *Mary on Horseback: Three Mountain Stories,* p. 70; October 19, 1998, review of *Yoko,* p. 78; April 19, 1999, review of *Streets of Gold,* p. 73; June 4, 2001, review of *Felix Feels Better,* p. 79; January 14, 2002, review of *The House in the Mail,* p. 60; March 25, 2002, review of *Wingwalker,* p. 65; May 27, 2002, review of *Happy Anniversary, Charlotte and Wilbur,* p. 61; May 12, 2003, review of *Only You,* p. 65; August 18, 2003, review of *The Small World of Binky Braverman,* p. 78; September 1, 2003, review of *Felix and the Worrier,* p. 91; September 8, 2003, review of *Back to School,* p 78; November 14, 2005, review of *Carry Me!,* p. 67; April 9, 2007, review of *Red Moon at Sharpsburg,* p. 54; August 20, 2007, review of *Mother Goose's Little Treasures,* p. 67; June 2, 2008, review of *Otto Runs for President,* p. 45.

School Library Journal, May, 1972, Alice Miller Bregman, review of *The Fog Comes on Little Pig Feet,* p. 89; November, 1974, Joni Brodart, review of *None of the Above,* p. 69; March, 1985, Trev Jones, review of *Max's Bath,* pp. 159-160; October, 1986, Judith Glover, review of *Max's Christmas,* p. 112; July, 1997, Christy Norris, review of *McDuff Comes Home,* p. 78; October, 1998, Peggy Morgan, review of *Mary on Horseback,* p. 130; December, 2000, Christina F. Renaud, review of *Max Cleans Up,* p. 127; November, 2001, Rosalyn Pierini, review of *Yoko's Paper Cranes,* p. 138; December, 2001, Lisa Gangemi Kropp, review of *The World around Us,* p. 129; January, 2002, Marilyn Taniguchi, review of *Mama, Don't Go!,* p. 112; March, 2002, Rita Soltan, review of *Adding It Up,* p. 223; May, 2002, Heide Piehler, review of *Wingwalker,* p. 162; July, 2002, Janie Schomberg, review of *The Germ Busters,* p. 100; July, 2002, Shara Alpern, review of *Be My Valentine,* p. 100; August, 2002, Maryann H. Owen, review of *McDuff Saves the Day,* p. 172; October, 2002, Laurie von Mehren, review of *Timothy's Tales from Hilltop School,* p. 134; October, 2002, Shara Alpern, review of *Ruby's Beauty Shop,* p. 134; December, 2002, Anne Knickerbocker, review of *Read Me a Story,* p. 112; May, 2003, Heather E. Miller, review of *Only You,* p. 132; November, 2003, Shawn Brommer, review of *The Small World of Binky Braverman,* p. 118; August, 2004, Lisa Gangemi Kropp, review of *My Kindergarten,* p. 103; February, 2005, Bina Williams, review of *I Love You! A Bushel and a Peck,* p. 123; April, 2005, Bina Williams, review of *McDuff's Wild Romp,* p. 115; June 1, 2005, Shelle Rosenfeld, review of *McDuff's Wild Romp,* p. 1826; January, 2006, Maryann H. Owen, review of *Carry Me!,* p. 115; March, 2006, Catherine Callegari, review of *The Miraculous Tale of the Two Maries,* p. 204; May, 2006, Jacki Kellum, review of *Max's ABC,* p. 106; March, 2007, Gloria Koster, review of *The Gulps,* p. 190, and Shannon Seglin, review of *Red Moon at Sharpsburg,* p. 220; August, 2008, Piper Nyman, review of *Yoko Writes Her Name,* p. 105; January, 2009, Janet S. Thompson, review of *Lincoln and His Boys,* p. 122.

ONLINE

Children's Literature Comprehensive Database, http://www.childrenslit.com/ (November 15, 2009), "A Conversation with Rosemary Wells."

Reading Rockets Web site, http://www.readingrockets.org/ (November 15, 2009), "Meet Rosemary Wells" (transcript of video interview).

Rosemary Wells Home Page, http://www.rosemarywells.com (November 15, 2009).

Scholastic Web site, http://www2.scholastic.com/ (November 15, 2009), autobiographical essay by Wells.

OTHER

A Visit with Rosemary Wells (film), Penguin USA, 1994.*

WILCOX, Leah 1975(?)-

Personal

Born c. 1975, in WA; married; husband's name Mitch; children: four. *Hobbies and other interests:* Running.

Addresses

Home—Redmond, OR.

Career

Author and educator. Kindercare, Provo, UT, former teacher. Presenter at libraries.

Awards, Honors

International Reading Award Notable Book designation, Eloise Jarvis McGraw Award finalist, and Maryland Black-eyed Susan Picture Book Award, all 2003, all for *Falling for Rapunzel.*

Writings

Falling for Rapunzel, illustrated by Lydia Monks, G.P. Putnam's (New York, NY), 2003.
Waking Beauty, illustrated by Lydia Monks, G.P. Putnam's (New York, NY), 2008.

Sidelights

In her picture-book stories for young children, Leah Wilcox takes well-known fairy tales and reworks them with an eye toward fun. In *Falling for Rapunzel* the Oregon-based writer found her inspiration in the story of the beautiful princess who is freed from her prison in a tower by using her long, long hair as the rope that enables her rescue. In Wilcox's rhyming story, however, practical matters interfere: because Rapunzel is way up high in her ivory tower and the handsome prince is shouting from ground level, she has a difficult time hearing his well-known request to "let down your hair." A request for her hair results in a barrage of underwear, while a princely comment regarding the whereabouts of a ladder is misheard as a request for pancake batter. A *Kirkus Reviews* writer dubbed *Falling for Rapunzel* a "thoroughly silly, modernized, and thoroughly fractured" take on a favorite story, while Kitty Flynn described Wilcox's picture-book debut as an "irreverent spoof which plays with . . . fairy-tale conventions with obvious delight." The humor of Wilcox's wordplay is ratcheted up by Lydia Monks' colorful collage paintings, as she "conveys the addled antics in whimsical art," according to a *Publishers Weekly* critic. In *Booklist* Ilene Cooper also remarked on Monks' acrylic, colored pencil, and collage art, writing that the artist's "slapstick pictures . . . match the text in cheeky appeal."

The story of Sleeping Beauty receives a Wilcox makeover in *Waking Beauty,* which also features Monks' humorous illustrations. In this picture-book take on a well-

known story, Prince Charming discovers the slumbering princess by following the rhythmic sounds of her snoring to the gates of her enchanted palace. Although the maiden's guardian fairies urge the prince to awaken Beauty in the traditional manner (with a kiss), the enthusiastic royal opts to do things his own way, with humorous results. In *Publishers Weekly* a contributor described *Waking Beauty* as a "creatively warped" fairy tale "pairing [Wilcox's] chipper rhymed couplets with [Monk's] dynamic mixed-media art," and Kirsten Cutler wrote in *School Library Journal* that the "puns and lively wordplay" of the text are reflected in the story's "colorful, waggish illustrations."

Biographical and Critical Sources

PERIODICALS

Booklist, December 1, 2003, Ilene Cooper, review of *Falling for Rapunzel,* p. 686.
Horn Book, November-December, 2003, Kitty Flynn, review of *Falling for Rapunzel,* p. 737.
Kirkus Reviews, November 15, 2003, review of *Falling for Rapunzel,* p. 1365; December 1, 2007, review of *Waking Beauty.*

Lydia Wilcox creates the quirky illustrations that capture the fractured fairytale action of Leah Wilcox's **Falling for Rapunzel.** (Puffin Books, 2008. Illustrations copyright © Lydia Monds, 2008. All rights reserved. Reproduced by permission of Puffin Books, a division of Penguin Putnam Books for Young Readers.)

Publishers Weekly, January 5, 2004, review of *Falling for Rapunzel,* p. 61; December 17, 2007, review of *Waking Beauty,* p. 50.

School Library Journal, December, 2003, Nancy Menaldi-Scanlan, review of *Falling for Rapunzel,* p. 130; March, 2008, Kirsten Cutler, review of *Waking Beauty,* p. 179.*

* * *

WILLIAMS, Suzanne
See WILLIAMS, Suzanne Morgan

* * *

WILLIAMS, Suzanne M.
See WILLIAMS, Suzanne Morgan

* * *

WILLIAMS, Suzanne Morgan 1949-
(Suzanne Williams, Suzanne M. Williams)

Personal

Born 1949; married. *Education:* University of California, Davis, B.A.; University of Notre Dame, M.Ed.

Addresses

Home—Reno, NV. *E-mail*—suzanne@suzannemorgan williams.com.

Career

Author. Former teacher of elementary grades; presenter at schools and conferences.

Member

Society of Children's Book Writers and Illustrators (co-regional advisor of Nevada branch).

Awards, Honors

Texas Lone Star Reading List selection, and Texas Tayshas Reading List selection, both 2010, both for *Bull Rider.*

Writings

NONFICTION

(As Suzanne Williams) *Made in China: Ideas and Inventions from Ancient China,* illustrated by Andrea Fong, Pacific View Press (San Francisco, CA), 1997.

Suzanne Morgan Williams (Photograph by Zinser Photography, Reno, NV. Courtesy of Suzanne Morgan Williams.)

(As Suzanne Williams; with Zoe Harris) *Piñatas and Smiling Skeletons: Celebrating Mexican Festivals,* illustrated by Yolanda Garfias Woo, Pacific View Press (San Francisco, CA), 1998.

(As Suzanne M. Williams) *Kentucky,* Children's Press (New York, NY), 2001.

Powhatan Indians, Heinemann Library (Chicago, IL), 2003.

Chinook Indians, Heinemann Library (Chicago, IL), 2003.

(As Suzanne M. Williams) *The Inuit,* Franklin Watts (New York, NY), 2003.

Cherokee Indians, Heinemann Library (Chicago, IL), 2003.

Ojibwe Indians, Heinemann Library (Chicago, IL), 2003.

Tlingit Indians, Heinemann Library (Chicago, IL), 2003.

(As Suzanne M. Williams) *Nevada,* Children's Press (New York, NY), 2003.

China's Daughters, illustrated by Amber MacLean, Pacific View Press (San Francisco, CA), 2010.

FICTION

Bull Rider (middle-grade novel), Margaret K. McElderry (New York, NY), 2009.

Sidelights

In her novel *Bull Rider* Suzanne Morgan Williams draws readers into the life of a boy attempting to find his place amid the traditions of his Western past, a family tragedy, and his own dreams for his future. Prior to writing *Bull Rider,* Williams worked primarily in the

nonfiction genre, producing books on Native Americans and several of the United States for educational publishers. Travels to the regions she writes about give Williams' books immediacy; for example, in writing the text for *The Inuit,* she spent time in the Canadian Arctic among the Inuit people. For *Bull Rider,* the author spoke with professional bull riders as well as ranchers, and also familiarized herself with the lives of the wounded veterans returning from Iraq.

Williams sets *Bull Rider* in her home state of Nevada, and taps the ranch culture in the northern county, where bull riding is a respected skill. For fourteen-year-old Cam O'Mara, however, skateboarding is a more attractive challenge, and he works hard to perfect his skill on his board. When Cam's older brother Ben, a skilled bull rider, comes home from Iraq with injuries so severe that he will never compete again, the teen confronts his fears in order to inspire Ben with hope and keep alive his family's dreams of the future. According to *Booklist* contributor Hazel Rochman, Williams' "mix of wild macho action with family anguish and tenderness will grab teens," and in *School Library Journal* Madeline J. Bryant wrote that *Bull Rider* successfully "captur[es] . . . the small-town sense of community and pride." In *Bulletin of the Center for Children's Books* Deborah Stevenson praised the novel as "a gripping read" and a "sensitive and compelling exploration" of "the [Iraq] war's consequences."

"Writing a book is communication," Williams told *SATA.* "It changes the writer and the reader. My work has changed me. I have had the opportunity to work with tribal people across North America, to interview Chinese medicine specialists, to bump across the sea ice on Hudson Bay, and go behind the scenes at a rodeo. More than that, from Inuit people I learned to listen, from Chinook and Paiute people I learned patience, and from interviewing health-care specialists who work with severely injured veterans I gained a profound respect for the sacrifices our military and their families make every day.

"But writers need readers to complete that communication link. I hope my readers discover something new in my books and that in some way the reading will change them also."

Biographical and Critical Sources

PERIODICALS

Booklist, January 1, 2009, Hazel Rochman, review of *Bull Rider,* p. 64.
Bulletin of the Center for Children's Books, January, 2009, Deborah Stevenson, review of *Bull Rider,* pp. 222-223.
School Library Journal, April, 2009, Madeline J. Bryant, review of *Bull Rider,* p. 144.

ONLINE

Class of 2k9 Web site, http://classof2k9.com/ (November 10, 2009), "Suzanne Morgan Williams."
Suzanne Morgan Williams Home Page, http://www.suzannemorganwilliams.com (November 10, 2009).

*   *   *

WINGERTER, Linda S. 1973(?)-

Personal

Born c. 1973, in VT; father a graphic artist, mother a book designer. *Education:* Attended Community College of Vermont, 1990-92; Rhode Island School of Design, B.F.A., 1996. *Hobbies and other interests:* Figure skating, staff spinning, dancing, puppeteering, watching and playing roller derby, yoga, growing plants, doodling, writing, fire twirling, playing the musical saw.

Addresses

Home and office—New Haven, CT. *E-mail*—lindawingerter@gmail.com.

Career

Artist, performer, and children's book illustrator. Painter and muralist; designer of greeting cards, journals, and stationery; teaches puppetry at Quinnipiac University; performer for Puppetsweat (theater company), New Haven, CT; dollmaker and member of O.D.A.CT (Original Doll Artisans of Connecticut). Also performs as a fire dancer and works as a chauffeur. *Exhibitions:* Works have been shown at galleries and museums, including Cenci Gallery (Rome, Italy), Woods-Gerry Gallery (Providence, RI), Art on the Mountain (Dover, VT), Huntington House Museum (Windsor, CT), Eric Carle Museum (Amherst, MA), and Museum of American Illustration (New York, NY). Work has been exhibited in "The Original Art" exhibition, Society of Illustrators, New York, NY. Paintings reside in private collections.

Member

Society of Illustrators, Society of Children's Book Writers and Illustrators.

Awards, Honors

100 Titles for Reading and Sharing selection, New York Public Library, 2001, and Teachers' Choice Award, International Reading Association, 2002, both for *One Riddle, One Answer;* Lupine Award, Maine Library Association, 2003, Blue Ribbon selection, Bulletin of the Center for Children's Books, and "The Original Art" exhibition selection, Society of Illustrators, 2004, all for *The Water Gift and the Pig of the Pig;* three Magazine Merit Awards from Society of Children's Book Writers and Illustrators.

Illustrator

Susan Milord, reteller, *Bird Tales from Near and Far* ("Tales Alive!" series), Williamson Publishing (Charlotte, VT), 1998.

Lauren Thompson, *One Riddle, One Answer,* Scholastic (New York, NY), 2001.

Jacqueline Briggs Martin, *The Water Gift and the Pig of the Pig,* Houghton Mifflin (Boston, MA), 2003.

Pete Seeger, *One Grain of Sand: A Lullaby,* Little, Brown (New York, NY), 2003.

Josepha Sherman, reteller, *Magic Hoofbeats: Horse Tales from Many Lands,* Barefoot Books (Cambridge, MA), 2004.

Linda Ashman, *What Could Be Better than This?,* Dutton (New York, NY), 2005.

Also illustrator of school textbooks and book covers for science-fiction novels. Contributor of illustrations to periodicals, including *Cricket* and *Weekly Reader,* and to blogs.

Sidelights

Linda S. Wingerter is "a passionate artist whose forte is communing with things that exist between the lines—both in the books she illustrates and life in general," noted *Teaching Pre K-8* contributor Katherine Pierpont. A painter, doll maker, and puppeteer, Wingerter has also served as the illustrator for such highly regarded children's books as Jacqueline Briggs Martin's *The Water Gift and the Pig of the Pig* and Pete Seeger's *One Grain of Sand: A Lullaby.* In addition, Wingerter practices the art of fire twirling, skates with a roller derby team, and plays the musical saw. "Anything I can do to change someone's expectations, I love," she remarked to Pierpont.

Wingerter was born into an artistic family. Her great-grandfather painted church murals in Russia, her grandfather owned his own puppet theatre, and her grandmother painted miniatures. Wingerter's father, a graphic artist, and her mother, a book designer, encouraged her interest in the arts, and at the age of four Wingerter decided to become a children's book illustrator, inspired by artists such as Trina Schart Hyman. "I love the work of Gennady Spirin, Lisbeth Zwerger, S. Saelig Gallagher, Susan Gaber, [and] Mary GrandPré, among many others," Wingerter noted in an interview on the *Seven Impossible Things before Breakfast* Web site. "My all time favorite picture books are still the obscure and uniquely illustrated ones I've had since before I can remember, especially *The Forest of Lilacs* and *Jumping Julius.*" Wingerter also credits her grandparents with helping to develop her artistic tastes. "My grandfather had a marionette theater in New Jersey called The Stringpullers," she remarked in the *Seven Impossible Things* interview. "He and my grandmother and their daughters made all the puppets, sets, costumes from scratch. Growing up in his shop was a huge influence on me." Wingerter has remained active in the field, working as a puppet maker and performer for Pup-

petsweat, a company in New Haven, Connecticut, where she lives and works. "Their shows are shadow puppet oriented with exposed puppeteers and often live music, but expand into multiple puppet and theater disciplines with layers of dance, toy theater, shadows, video projections, music, and narration," she reported. "It's geared towards adults, the subject matter is often dark, and it's gorgeous."

Wingerter attended the Rhode Island School of Design, graduating in 1996 with a bachelor's degree in illustration. Her paintings have graced the covers of science-fiction novels and have appeared in financial magazines, on opera posters, and in computer software programs. In her works for young readers, Wingerter offers lush acrylic paintings that feature graceful, flowing brushstrokes and warm, soothing tones of blue and purple. Those colors hold a special significance for the artist, who was often cared for by her grandparents after her father died when she was just a child. Recalling the frequent car trips to and from her grandmother's house, Wingerter told Pierpont, "I remember the blue of the high beam light on the dashboard. I was transfixed on that for so long—I loved to get in the car at night just to watch that blue light. So, I think in every book I'm trying to capture that glow." She developed her textured brushstroke technique after a frustrating attempt to work with watercolors. One evening Wingerter added a layer of acrylics to a painting and then applied a distressing technique to weather it. "I thought it was really liberating that I could be destructive and let things happen on their own," she told Pierpont. "That element of chance and not planning ahead so far was just so pretty." From that point on, the artist has worked in acrylics.

Wingerter made her picture-book debut in 1998, providing the artwork for Susan Milord's *Bird Tales from Near and Far.* In the volume, Milord retells six stories from around the world, collecting works from Iroquois, Thai, Yemeni, Ukrainian, Ethiopian, and Japanese folklore. Additionally, the author includes directions for projects and crafts that relate to each tale. Wingerter drew praise for her contributions. "The rich illustrations for the individual tales fit the cultural roots of the story," stated *Booklist* contributors Karen Morgan and David Pitt, while Lisa Wu Stowe commented in *School Library Journal* that "Wingerter's richly colored and textured paintings transport readers" to diverse regions of the globe.

Wingerter's more recent collaborations include works with writer Lauren Thompson on the feminist fairy tale *One Riddle, One Answer.* The work concerns Aziza, a clever and independent Persian princess who convinces her father, the sultan, that she should choose her own husband. A lover of mathematical games and puzzles, Aziza devises a riddle that has only one correct response. After a scholar, a soldier, and a merchant all fail the test, a humble farmer solves the conundrum. "As the successful suitor explains his numerical solution to the riddle, Wingerter works the relevant num-

bers into her stylized acrylic paintings," a critic in *Publishers Weekly* stated. In *Booklist*, Carolyn Phelan observed that the artist's "lively acrylic paintings, sometimes reminiscent of Persian miniatures, dramatize the tale," and *School Library Journal* reviewer Barbara Scotto similarly noted that Wingerter's "fanciful Persian motifs and patterns set the mood for this original tale."

In Martin's *The Water Gift and the Pig of the Pig* a young girl shares a special talent with her grandfather. Isabel, a shy, sensitive child, loves to hear her grandfather's stories about his days as the captain of a schooner, and she spends her days playing with Pig of the Pig, a descendent of the creature that once sailed with Grandfather around Cape Horn. Isabel and her porcine pal often accompany Grandfather when he dowses for water using a divining rod, but when the elderly man takes ill and Pig of the Pig goes missing in a neighbor's woods, Isabel determines to set things right. According to *New York Times Book Review* contributor Stephanie Deutsch, Wingerter's "textured, subtly colored illustrations" for Martin's story "alternate between vast perspectives of sea or countryside and cozy interiors that emphasize both the story's drama and its very satisfying, quiet intimacy." Writing in *Horn Book*, Anita L. Burkam observed that the artist "matches the nostalgic feel with her acrylics in an antique palette, showing a coastal idyll of farm and sea, simple figures in a naive folk-art style," and a *Publishers Weekly* reviewer commented that her "paintings set an almost timeless mood, striking a balance between folk art and nods to some of the American masters."

A legendary folksinger, Seeger brings a 1956 tune, originally written for his youngest daughter, to the printed page in *One Grain of Sand*. In her *Seven Impossible Things before Breakfast* online interview, Wingerter recalled that creating visual images to pair with the work "was a turning point in the way I thought about illustrating, I was called on to put more of my personal self into that book then anything I'd ever done." A celebration of familial love, *One Grain of Sand* takes readers on a trip around the globe, beginning on a tropical beach where a family greets the sunrise and venturing to such exotic locales as the African plains and the Arctic before returning to the island setting as the day ends. "Working mostly in soothing hues of twilight blue," remarked a contributor in *Publishers Weekly*, Wingerter "riffs on the lullaby's subtext of connectedness," and a *Kirkus Reviews* critic applauded her "rich and warm acrylics." Writing in *Booklist*, Shelle Rosenfeld called *One Grain of Sand* "a lovely mesh of art and language that celebrates the beauty and diversity of the world—and family ties."

Josepha Sherman collects eight stories about animals with fantastic powers, such as the ability to fly or become invisible, in *Magic Hoofbeats: Horse Tales from Many Lands*. Sherman also provides information about the horse breeds featured in the stories, including the Marwari of India, the Colt Qeytas of Iran, and the pin-

tos of the Pawnee tribe. *Booklist* contributor Gillian Engberg complimented the "lively, multicultural collection, which is beautifully illustrated with Wingerter's fanciful acrylic artwork."

What Could Be Better than This?, a work by Linda Ashman, concerns the bonds between parents and their children. When a wealthy, dragon-slaying king meets a daring, seafaring maiden, they fall in love, marry, and decide to travel the earth. Despite lives filled with adventure and excitement, the pair only finds fulfillment after their infant son is born. Wingerter's "paintings—in a rich yet diverse palette—glow with warmth," a critic in *Kirkus Reviews* stated. Joy Fleishhacker, writing in *School Library Journal*, also praised the artwork. "Painted in rich hues," observed Fleishhacker, "the romanticized illustrations echo the once-upon-a-time tone of the rhyming tale." "*What Could Be Better than This?* has a very particular color pattern I constructed based on alchemical concepts, and I think my color sense is at its best in that book," Wingerter remarked in her *Seven Impossible Things before Breakfast* interview.

"As a children's book illustrator I think of myself as a director," Wingerter noted on her home page. "I cast characters, scout locations, choose costumes, and compose camera angles. I am dedicated to my script, but the passion is in stealing it from the author and making it my own."

Biographical and Critical Sources

PERIODICALS

Booklist, February 15, 1999, Karen Morgan and David Pitt, review of *Bird Tales from Near and Far*, p. 1066; February 1, 2001, Carolyn Phelan, review of *One Riddle, One Answer*, p. 1058; October 15, 2003, Shelle Rosenfeld, review of *One Grain of Sand: A Lullaby*, p. 409; November 1, 2004, Gillian Engberg, review of *Magic Hoofbeats: Horse Tales from Many Lands*, p. 487.

Horn Book, May-June, 2003, Anita L. Burkam, review of *The Water Gift and the Pig of the Pig*, p. 331.

Instructor, November-December, 2001, Judy Freeman, review of *One Riddle, One Answer*, p. 16.

Kirkus Reviews, April 1, 2003, review of *The Water Gift and the Pig of the Pig*, p. 537; July 1, 2003, review of *One Grain of Sand*, p. 915; July 15, 2006, review of *What Could Be Better than This?*, p. 719.

New York Times Book Review, September 21, 2003, Stephanie Deutsch, review of *The Water Gift and the Pig of the Pig*, p. 27.

Publishers Weekly, February 19, 2001, review of *One Riddle, One Answer*, p. 91; March 31, 2003, review of *The Water Gift and the Pig of the Pig*, p. 67; July 7, 2003, review of *One Grain of Sand*, p. 70.

Reading Teacher, November, 2002, review of *One Riddle, One Answer*, p. 260.

School Library Journal, November 1, 1998, Lisa Wu Stowe, review of *Bird Tales from Near and Far,* p. 108; April, 2001, Barbara Scotto, review of *One Riddle, One Answer,* p. 123; August, 2003, Jane Marino, review of *One Grain of Sand,* p. 152; June, 2003, Marianne Saccardi, review of *The Water Gift and the Pig of the Pig,* p. 112; February, 2005, Susan Hepler, review of *Magic Hoofbeats,* p. 153; April, 2007, Joy Fleishhacker, review of *What Could Be Better than This?,* p. 94.

Teaching Pre K-8, March, 2007, Katherine Pierpont, "Linda S. Wingerter: The Light Within."

ONLINE

Linda S. Wingerter Home Page, http://www.paintedbooks.com (April 1, 2008).

Seven Impossible Things before Breakfast Web site, http://blaine.org/sevenimpossiblethings/ (April 30, 2007), "Blue Rose Blogger, Fire-spinning and Puppeteering Rollergirl, and Illustrator Linda Wingerter."*

*   *   *

WOO, Howie 1974-

Personal

Born 1974, in Kentville, Nova Scotia, Canada. *Education:* Emily Carr Institute of Art and Design, degree. *Hobbies and other interests:* Crocheting amigurumi characters.

Addresses

Home—Coquitlam, British Columbia, Canada. *E-mail*—woo@wootoons.com.

Career

Illustrator and filmmaker.

Illustrator

Valerie Wyatt, *Who Discovered America?,* Kids Can Press (Tonawanda, NY), 2008.

Author and director of short films. Author of *WooWork* Web log.

Biographical and Critical Sources

PERIODICALS

Booklist, October 1, 2009, Carolyn Phelan, review of *Who Discovered America?,* p. 40.

School Library Journal, February, 2009, Anne Callaghan, review of *Who Discovered America?,* p. 128.

ONLINE

Howie Woo Home Page, http://www.wootoons.com (November 10, 2009).

WooFilms Web site, http://www.woofilms.com/ (November 10, 2009).

WooWork Web site, http://www.woowork.com/ (November 10, 2009).*

*   *   *

YOUNG, Judy 1956-

Personal

Born February 13, 1956, in Springfield, MO; daughter of Charles E. and Mary Anna Gottas; married Ross B. Young (an artist); children: Brett, Reid. *Education:* University of Tulsa, B.S., 1978, M.A., 1980. *Hobbies and other interests:* Hiking, camping, traveling, reading, fishing.

Addresses

Home and office—Springfield, MO. *E-mail*—judyyoungbooks@gmail.com.

Career

Author and poet. Speech and language pathologist, 1980-2004; writer, 1996—. Workshop presenter in schools and for professional organizations.

Member

Society of Children's Book Writers and Illustrators, National Federation of State Poetry Societies, Missouri Writers Guild, Missouri State Poetry Society (youth chair, 2001—), Missouri Poets and Friends (secretary, 2000-02), Springfield Writers' Guild (treasurer, 2001), Ozark Writers League.

Awards, Honors

Award of Merit for Outstanding Youth Activities, National Federation of State Poetry Societies; Springfield Writers' Guild award, 2000, for "The Whistler"; Missouri State Poetry Society Summer Poetry Contest award, 2000, for "Arch of Neck"; Missouri State Poetry Society Winter Poetry Contest award, 2001, for "White Rabbits with Red Wings"; National Parenting Publications Honor Award, and Best Juvenile Book Award, Missouri Writers' Guild, both 2006, and Mom's Choice Gold Award, and Educator's Choice award, both 2008, all for *R Is for Rhyme;* Choice designation, Missouri Center for the Book, 2008, for *S Is for Show Me; Storytelling World* Honor award, 2009, for *The Lucky Star; Storytelling World* Award for Pre-adolescent Listeners, 2010, for *Rose and Minnow.*

Writings

S Is for Show Me: A Missouri Alphabet, illustrated by husband, Ross B. Young, Sleeping Bear Press (Chelsea, MI), 2001.

Poetry and Paint: Selected Works, illustrated by Ross B. Young, Xlibris, 2003.

R Is for Rhyme: A Poetry Alphabet, illustrated by Victor Juhasz, Sleeping Bear Press (Chelsea, MI), 2006.

Lazy Days of Summer, illustrated by Kathy O'Malley, Sleeping Bear Press (Chelsea, MI), 2007.

Show Me the Number: A Missouri Number Book, illustrated by Ross B. Young, Sleeping Bear Press (Chelsea, MI), 2007.

H Is for Hook: A Fishing Alphabet, illustrated by Gary Palmer, Sleeping Bear Press (Chelsea, MI), 2008.

The Lucky Star, illustrated by Chris Ellison, Sleeping Bear Press (Chelsea, MI), 2008.

Minnow and Rose: An Oregon Trail Story, illustrated by Bill Farnsworth, Sleeping Bear Press (Chelsea, MI), 2009.

The Hidden Bestiary of Marvelous, Mysterious, and (Maybe Even) Magical Creatures, illustrated by Laura Francesca Filippucci, Sleeping Bear Press (Chelsea, MI), 2009.

Contributor to *How to Write Poetry: Ballad to Villanelle,* Night Owl Publications, 2000, and *Missouri,* Macmillan/McGraw Hill (New York, NY), 2007. Contributor of poetry to periodicals and annuals, including *Grist Anthology, Ozark Mountaineer, Hodgepodge Short Stories and Poetry,* and *Parnassus.*

Adaptations

R Is for Rhyme was adapted for the stage by University of Utah Creative Dance Program.

Sidelights

A former speech and language pathologist, Judy Young is also the author of children's books such as *R Is for Rhyme: A Poetry Alphabet,* an abecedarian anthology of verse and nonfiction prose, and *Minnow and Rose: An Oregon Trail Story,* a work of historical fiction. Young told *Kidlit Central News* online interviewer Susan Uhlig that she enjoys the variety each genre offers. "The creative process is the same for both, they're just written in different forms, but I really think writing poetry helps my prose," Young observed. "In poetry, each word plays an integral part. That should be the focus of prose, as well. Writers, especially for picture books, must be flexible."

In *R Is for Rhyme,* Young examines a host of poetic styles, including jingles, limericks, and tankas. Each selection introduces a term or technique that is embellished by one of the author's verses and an illustration by Victor Juhasz. A *Kirkus Reviews* contributor praised the "accessible sidebar lessons" in the collection. Young

describes a dozen familiar outdoor activities in *Lazy Days of Summer.* Hopscotch, relay races, and jacks are among the game described in rhyme; Young also presents the rules and history of each pastime. "Overall, this is an attractive package," Ilene Cooper noted in *Booklist.*

Set in 1933, Young's picture book *The Lucky Star* centers on Ruth, a nine year old whose life has been dramatically altered by the Great Depression. Ruth's father, a member of the Civilian Conservation Corps, works hundreds of miles away, and her school has closed because of a lack of funds. However, Ruth teaches her younger sister and her friends by using pebbles to learn basic arithmetic concepts and practicing their writing in flour residue. A critic in *Kirkus Reviews* described the work as a "positive, feel-good story," and Lucinda Snyder Whitehurst, writing in *School Library Journal,* commented that the tale "succeeds in capturing a particular time period as well as in delivering a timeless message."

The relationship between a Native American child and a pioneer girl is the focus of *Minnow and Rose.* While picking berries, Minnow discovers a group of covered wagons preparing to cross a river near her village. As her father helps the settlers with their journey, Minnow comes to the rescue when young Rose tumbles from

Judy Young's story of a young girl's life during the Great Depression is brought to life in Chris Ellison's paintings for **The Lucky Star.** (Sleeping Bear Press, 2008. Illustration copyright © 2008 Chris Ellison. Reproduced by permission of Chris Ellison and Will Sumpter Associates.)

one of the wagons into the raging current. The girls later celebrate their brief but life-altering encounter with an exchange of handmade gifts. In *Booklist* Shelle Rosenfeld described the story as "an appealing, child-centric story of communicating across language and culture and finding friendship despite differences."

In *The Hidden Bestiary of Marvelous, Mysterious, and (Maybe Even) Magical Creatures,* fictional naturalist Basil B. Barnswhitten travels the world looking for such strange animals as the Loch Ness Monster and Steller's Sea Cow, which are described in verse. Part of the fun of the book, Young told interviewer Phyllis Quigg, is identifying the beasts hidden in Laura Francesca Filippucci's illustrations. Audiences "read the poems that accompany each page and find a specific creature based on clues in the poem," Young explained. "Readers are also asked to determine, based on the poems' clues, whether the creature is endangered, extinct or never existed."

"My roots in writing are in the genre of poetry," Young told *SATA:* "Encouraged by my grandmother, and fascinated by words and language, I began writing poetry at a very young age and wrote all through my childhood. Upon entering college, my father strongly advised me to remember my interests, but to get a degree that has a 'job' attached. So, I received a B.S. and M.A. in speech and language pathology, which met his criterion but still focused on my interest in language. I worked in this field for twenty-four years, twenty of which were in the public schools, specializing in language development and impairment. Working in the school setting, PreK-12, also gave me firsthand experience with educational curricula and teaching strategies. This experience has played a great part in my writing for children, as well as in my school visit programs for students and workshops for teachers.

"I consciously decided to make writing a major part of my life when I was forty. I still wrote, but only inconsistently; the rigors of job and family had decreased the amount of time devoted to something I had always loved. I walk daily (another devotion) and decided to write a poem about each day's walk for an entire summer. This got me started writing on a regular basis. Then, I started submitting poems to contests and won some awards. In addition, I began submitting poems to magazines and literary journals and was honored at becoming published.

"In 2001, my first children's book, *S Is for Show Me: A Missouri Alphabet,* was published through a series of fortunate and lucky circumstances. Sleeping Bear Press had contracted my husband, Ross B. Young, a professional artist, to illustrate the "Missouri" book of their "Discover America" series. Upon learning that an author had not yet been contracted, I submitted and was accepted to be the author of this book, starting my career in childen's-book writing. In 2003, when queries for both *R Is for Rhyme: A Poetry Alphabet* and *Lazy Days of Summer* were both accepted on the same day, I resigned from my school job and became a full-time children's author. With time now totally devoted to writing, I continued writing poetry and nonfiction, but also began writing fiction. In 2007, my first piece of fiction, *The Lucky Star,* was published.

"An enjoyable outcome of becoming a published author is that I have been invited to speak nationwide at schools, literature festivals, young-author celebrations, professional educational conferences, libraries, and even nature centers. It is always a pleasure.

"From my grandmother who made me promise to keep on writing, to my father who told me to find a 'job' that included my interests, to my husband, without whom I would never have written my first book, to my editors who have had great faith in me, to all the teachers who use my books in their classrooms, to the parents who purchase my books for their children and most of all, to the children who enjoy reading my books, I can truly say that I that my sky is filled with lucky stars!"

Biographical and Critical Sources

PERIODICALS

Booklist, May 1, 2007, Ilene Cooper, review of *Lazy Days of Summer,* p. 94; March 1, 2009, Shelle Rosenfeld, review of *Minnow and Rose: An Oregon Trail Story,* p. 44.

Kirkus Reviews, February 15, 2006, review of *R Is for Rhyme: A Poetry Alphabet,* p. 191; April 1, 2008, review of *The Lucky Star.*

School Library Journal, June, 2007, Donna Cardon, review of *Lazy Days of Summer,* p. 137; July, 2008, Lucinda Snyder Whitehurst, review of *The Lucky Star,* p. 84; April, 2009, Nancy Baumann, review of *Minnow and Rose,* p. 119.

ONLINE

Judy Young Home Page, http://www.judyyoungpoetry.com (November 15, 2009).

Kidlit Central News Online, http://community.livejournal.com/kidlit_central/ (September 7, 2009), Susan Uhlig, interview with Young.

Phyllis Quigg Web log, http://phyllisquigg.blogspot.com/ (April 17, 2009), Phyllis Quigg, interview with Young.

*   *   *

ZECCA, Katherine

Personal

Born in Weisbaden, Germany; immigrated to United States. *Hobbies and other interests:* Camping, sketching, walking with her dogs.

Addresses

Home—Poultney, VT. *Agent*—Lori Nowicki, Painted-Words Literary Agency. *E-mail*—lori@painted-words.com

Career

Author, wildlife artist, illustrator, and art teacher. National Oceanic and Atmospheric Administration, former staff artist. Illustrator for institutions, including National Zoological Park, Smithsonian Institution, Alaska Fisheries Science Center, and National Marine Mammal Laboratory.

Member

Society of Children's Book Writers and Illustrators (New England chapter).

Awards, Honors

iParenting Media Award, and Moonbeam Children's Book Gold Award, both 2008, both for *River Song.*

Writings

SELF-ILLUSTRATED

(Self-illustrated) *A Puffin's Year,* Down East Books (Camden, ME), 2007.

ILLUSTRATOR

Steve Van Zandt, *River Song: With the Banana Slug String Band,* Dawn Publications (Nevada City, CA), 2007.
Valarie Giogas, *In My Backyard,* Sylvan Dell (Mount Pleasant, SC), 2007.

Katherine Zecca pairs her detailed paintings with a captivating text in the nature-themed **A Puffin's Year.** (Down East Books, 2007. Copyright © 2007 by Katherine Zecca. All rights reserved. Reproduced by permission of Down East Books.)

Tom Davis, *Why Puppies Do That: A Collection of Curious Puppy Behaviors,* Willow Creek Press (Minocqua, WI), 2007.

Sidelights

After working as a scientific illustrator for over two decades, Katherine Zecca made the decision to turn to fine-art painting. Moving from the Pacific northwest, she relocated to New England, and her home on a wildlife preserve provides her with many subjects for her paintings. In addition to working as an art teacher and wildlife artist, Zecca has contributed her detailed and scientifically accurate paintings to books such as Valarie Giogas's *In My Backyard* and Steve Van Zandt's *River Song: With the Banana Slug String Band,* in addition to creating the original self-illustrated picture book *A Puffin's Year.* Her "realistic" and "softly colored illustrations" for *In My Backyard* will inspire budding nature lovers, according to a *Kirkus Reviews* writer. On her home page, Zecca stated her goal as an illustrator: "To entertain . . . young readers while at the same time providing scientifically accurate information" in order to "instill in them a sense of awe about the world we live in."

In *A Puffin's Year* Zecca focuses on an intriguing summer visitor to the Atlantic coast. The Atlantic puffin stays ashore for only a few weeks, colonizing coastal islands while it mates, protects its eggs, and hatches its fluffy offspring. Zecca brings to life her "conversational narrative" in detailed paintings crafted in tones of sea blue and green, some of which possess a striking "intimacy and realism," according to a *Publishers Weekly* contributor. In *Booklist* Hazel Rochman cited Zecca's "clear text and bright, textured mixed-media art," while a *Kirkus Reviews* writer maintained that her large, "invitingly detailed gouache-and-colored-pencil" images will be irresistible to the book's intended readership. According to *School Library Journal* contributor Cynde Suite, *A Puffin's Year* ranks as a "beautiful, informative" source for young naturalists.

Biographical and Critical Sources

PERIODICALS

Booklist, May 1, 2007, Hazel Rochman, review of *A Puffin's Year,* p. 94.
Kirkus Reviews, May 15, 2007, review of *A Puffin's Year;* June 1, 2007, review of *In My Backyard.*
Publishers Weekly, June 4, 2007, review of *A Puffin's Year,* p. 52.
School Library Journal, August, 2007, Cynde Suite, review of *A Puffin's Year,* p. 108; November, 2007, Maura Bresnahan, review of *In My Backyard,* p. 108.

ONLINE

Katherine Zecca Home Page, http://www.katherinezecca.com (November 10, 2009).
Painted-Words.com, http://www.painted-words.com/ (November 10, 2009), "Katherine Zecca."
Society of Children's Book Writers and Illustrators—New England Web site, http://www.nescbwi.org/ (November 10, 2009), "Katherine Zecca."*

Illustrations Index

(In the following index, the number of the *volume* in which an illustrator's work appears is given *before* the colon, and the *page number* on which it appears is given *after* the colon. For example, a drawing by Adams, Adrienne appears in Volume 2 on page 6, another drawing by her appears in Volume 3 on page 80, another drawing in Volume 8 on page 1, and so on and so on. . . .)

YABC

Index references to *YABC* refer to listings appearing in the two-volume *Yesterday's Authors of Books for Children,* also published by Gale, Cengage Learning. *YABC* covers prominent authors and illustrators who died prior to 1960.

A

Aas, Ulf *5:* 174
Abbe, S. van
    See van Abbe, S.
Abel, Raymond *6:* 122; *7:* 195; *12:* 3; *21:* 86; *25:* 119
Abelliera, Aldo *71:* 120
Abolafia, Yossi *60:* 2; *93:* 163; *152:* 202
Abrahams, Hilary *26:* 205; *29:* 24, 25; *53:* 61
Abrams, Kathie *36:* 170
Abrams, Lester *49:* 26
Abulafia, Yossi *154:* 67; *177:* 3
Accardo, Anthony *191:* 3, 8
Accornero, Franco *184:* 8
Accorsi, William *11:* 198
Acs, Laszlo *14:* 156; *42:* 22
Acuna, Ed *198:* 79
Adams, Adrienne *2:* 6; *3:* 80; *8:* 1; *15:* 107; *16:* 180; *20:* 65; *22:* 134, 135; *33:* 75; *36:* 103, 112; *39:* 74; *86:* 54; *90:* 2, 3
Adams, Connie J. *129:* 68
Adams, John Wolcott *17:* 162
Adams, Lynn *96:* 44
Adams, Norman *55:* 82
Adams, Pam *112:* 1, 2
Adams, Sarah *98:* 126; *164:* 180
Adamson, George *30:* 23, 24; *69:* 64
Addams, Charles *55:* 5
Addison, Kenneth *192:* 173
Addy, Sean *180:* 8
Ade, Rene *76:* 198; *195:* 162
Adinolfi, JoAnn *115:* 42; *176:* 2
Adkins, Alta *22:* 250
Adkins, Jan *8:* 3; *69:* 4; *144:* 2, 3, 4
Adler, Kelynn *195:* 47
Adler, Peggy *22:* 6; *29:* 31
Adler, Ruth *29:* 29
Adlerman, Daniel *163:* 2
Adragna, Robert *47:* 145
Agard, Nadema *18:* 1
Agee, Jon *116:* 8, 9, 10; *157:* 4; *196:* 3, 4, 5, 6, 7, 8
Agre, Patricia *47:* 195
Aguirre, Alfredo *152:* 218
Ahjar, Brian *207:* 126
Ahl, Anna Maria *32:* 24
Ahlberg, Allan *68:* 6, 7, 9; *165:* 5
Ahlberg, Janet *68:* 6, 7, 9
Aicher-Scholl, Inge *63:* 127

Aichinger, Helga *4:* 5, 45
Aitken, Amy *31:* 34
Akaba, Suekichi *46:* 23; *53:* 127
Akasaka, Miyoshi *YABC 2:* 261
Akib, Jamel *181:* 13; *182:* 99
Akino, Fuku *6:* 144
Alain *40:* 41
Alajalov *2:* 226
Albert, Chris *200:* 64
Alborough, Jez *86:* 1, 2, 3; *149:* 3
Albrecht, Jan *37:* 176
Albright, Donn *1:* 91
Alcala, Alfredo *91:* 128
Alcantará, Felipe Ugalde *171:* 186
Alcorn, John *3:* 159; *7:* 165; *31:* 22; *44:* 127; *46:* 23, 170
Alcorn, Stephen *110:* 4; *125:* 106; *128:* 172; *150:* 97; *160:* 188; *165:* 48; *201:* 113; *203:* 39; *207:* 3
Alcott, May *100:* 3
Alda, Arlene *44:* 24; *158:* 2
Alden, Albert *11:* 103
Aldridge, Andy *27:* 131
Aldridge, George *105:* 125
Aldridge, Sheila *192:* 4
Alejandro, Cliff *176:* 75
Alex, Ben *45:* 25, 26
Alexander, Ellen *91:* 3
Alexander, Lloyd *49:* 34
Alexander, Martha *3:* 206; *11:* 103; *13:* 109; *25:* 100; *36:* 131; *70:* 6, 7; *136:* 3, 4, 5; *169:* 120
Alexander, Paul *85:* 57; *90:* 9
Alexeieff, Alexander *14:* 6; *26:* 199
Alfano, Wayne *80:* 69
Aliki
    See Brandenberg, Aliki
Allamand, Pascale *12:* 9
Allan, Judith *38:* 166
Alland, Alexandra *16:* 255
Allen, Gertrude *9:* 6
Allen, Graham *31:* 145
Allen, Jonathan *131:* 3, 4; *177:* 8, 9, 10
Allen, Joy *168:* 185
Allen, Pamela *50:* 25, 26, 27, 28; *81:* 9, 10; *123:* 4, 5
Allen, Raul *207:* 94
Allen, Rowena *47:* 75
Allen, Thomas B. *81:* 101; *82:* 248; *89:* 37; *104:* 9
Allen, Tom *85:* 176

Allender, David *73:* 223
Alley, R.W. *80:* 183; *95:* 187; *156:* 100, 153; *169:* 4, 5; *179:* 17
Allison, Linda *43:* 27
Allon, Jeffrey *119:* 174
Allport, Mike *71:* 55
Almquist, Don *11:* 8; *12:* 128; *17:* 46; *22:* 110
Aloise, Frank *5:* 38; *10:* 133; *30:* 92
Alsenas, Linas *186:* 2
Alter, Ann *206:* 4, 5
Althea
    See Braithwaite, Althea
Altschuler, Franz *11:* 185; *23:* 141; *40:* 48; *45:* 29; *57:* 181
Alvin, John *117:* 5
Ambrus, Victor G. *1:* 6, 7, 194; *3:* 69; *5:* 15; *6:* 44; *7:* 36; *8:* 210; *12:* 227; *14:* 213; *15:* 213; *22:* 209; *24:* 36; *28:* 179; *30:* 178; *32:* 44, 46; *38:* 143; *41:* 25, 26, 27, 28, 29, 30, 31, 32; *42:* 87; *44:* 190; *55:* 172; *62:* 30, 144, 145, 148; *86:* 99, 100, 101; *87:* 66, 137; *89:* 162; *134:* 160
Ames, Lee J. *3:* 12; *9:* 130; *10:* 69; *17:* 214; *22:* 124; *151:* 13
Amon, Aline *9:* 9
Amoss, Berthe *5:* 5
Amstutz, Andre *152:* 102
Amundsen, Dick *7:* 77
Amundsen, Richard E. *5:* 10; *24:* 122
Ancona, George *12:* 11; *55:* 144; *145:* 7
Anderson, Alasdair *18:* 122
Andersen, Bethanne *116:* 167; *162:* 189; *175:* 17; *191:* 4, 5
Anderson, Bob *139:* 16
Anderson, Brad *33:* 28
Anderson, C.W. *11:* 10
Anderson, Carl *7:* 4
Anderson, Catherine Corley *72:* 2
Anderson, Cecil *127:* 152
Anderson, David Lee *118:* 176
Anderson, Derek *169:* 9; *174:* 180
Anderson, Doug *40:* 111
Anderson, Erica *23:* 65
Anderson, Laurie *12:* 153, 155
Anderson, Lena *99:* 26
Anderson, Peggy Perry *179:* 2
Anderson, Sara *173:* 3
Anderson, Scoular *138:* 13; *201:* 6
Anderson, Susan *90:* 12
Anderson, Tara *188:* 132

Anderson, Wayne *23:* 119; *41:* 239; *56:* 7; *62:* 26; *147:* 6; *202:* 4, 5
Andreasen, Daniel *86:* 157; *87:* 104; *103:* 201, 202; *159:* 75; *167:* 106, 107; *168:* 184; *180:* 247; *186:* 9
Andrew, Ian *111:* 37; *116:* 12; *166:* 2
Andrew, John *22:* 4
Andrews, Benny *14:* 251; *31:* 24; *57:* 6, 7; *183:* 8
Andrews, Vaughn *166:* 28
Anelay, Henry *57:* 173
Angel, Marie *47:* 22
Angelo, Valenti *14:* 8; *18:* 100; *20:* 232; *32:* 70
Anglund, Joan Walsh *2:* 7, 250, 251; *37:* 198, 199, 200
Anholt, Catherine *74:* 8; *131:* 7; *141:* 5
Anholt, Laurence *141:* 4
Anno, Mitsumasa *5:* 7; *38:* 25, 26, 27, 28, 29, 30, 31, 32; *77:* 3, 4; *157:* 10, 11
Antal, Andrew *1:* 124; *30:* 145
Antram, David *152:* 133
Apostolou, Christy Hale
    See Hale, Christy
Apple, Margot *33:* 25; *35:* 206; *46:* 81; *53:* 8; *61:* 109; *64:* 21, 22, 24, 25, 27; *71:* 176; *77:* 53; *82:* 245; *92:* 39; *94:* 180; *96:* 107; *152:* 4, 5; *162:* 192, 194; *173:* 44
Appleyard, Dev *2:* 192
Aragones, Sergio *48:* 23, 24, 25, 26, 27
Araneus *40:* 29
Arbo, Cris *103:* 4
Archambault, Matt *85:* 173; *138:* 19, 20; *143:* 33; *145:* 144; *179:* 103; *187:* 7
Archer, Janet *16:* 69; *178:* 156
Ardizzone, Edward *1:* 11, 12; *2:* 105; *3:* 258; *4:* 78; *7:* 79; *10:* 100; *15:* 232; *20:* 69,178; *23:* 223; *24:* 125; *28:* 25, 26, 27, 28, 29, 30, 31,33, 34, 35, 36, 37; *31:* 192, 193; *34:* 215, 217; *60:* 173; *64:* 145; *87:* 176; *YABC 2:* 25
Arena, Jill *176:* 49
Arenella, Roy *14:* 9
Argemi, David *197:* 2
Argent, Kerry *103:* 56; *138:* 17; *158:* 134
Arihara, Shino *201:* 98
Arisman, Marshall *162:* 50
Armer, Austin *13:* 3
Armer, Laura Adams *13:* 3
Armer, Sidney *13:* 3
Armitage, David *47:* 23; *99:* 5; *155:* 4
Armitage, Eileen *4:* 16
Armstrong, George *10:* 6; *21:* 72
Armstrong, Shelagh *102:* 114
Armstrong-Ellis, Carey *185:* 196
Arno, Enrico *1:* 217; *2:* 22, 210; *4:* 9; *5:* 43; *6:* 52; *29:* 217, 219; *33:* 152; *35:* 99; *43:* 31, 32, 33; *45:* 212, 213, 214; *72:* 72; *74:* 166; *100:* 169
Arnold, Alli *187:* 40, 41
Arnold, Caroline *174:* 5
Arnold, Emily *76:* 7, 9, 10
Arnold, Katya *115:* 11; *168:* 2, 3
Arnold, Tedd *116:* 14; *133:* 152; *160:* 5
Arnosky, Jim *22:* 20; *70:* 9, 10, 11; *118:* 3, 5; *160:* 8, 10; *189:* 5, 7, 8, 9, 10
Arnsteen, Katy Keck *105:* 97; *116:* 145
Arnstein, Isabelle *207:* 7
Arrowood, Clinton *12:* 193; *19:* 11; *65:* 210
Artell, Mike *89:* 8
Arting, Fred J. *41:* 63
Artzybasheff, Boris *13:* 143; *14:* 15; *40:* 152, 155
Aruego, Ariane *6:* 4
Aruego, José *4:* 140; *6:* 4; *7:* 64; *33:* 195; *35:* 208; *68:* 16, 17; *75:* 46; *93:* 91, 92; *94:* 197; *109:* 65, 67; *125:* 2, 3, 4, 5; *127:* 188; *143:* 25; *178:* 17, 19, 74; *188:* 166; *202:* 164
Arzoumanian, Alik *177:* 12; *194:* 115
Asare, Meshack *86:* 9; *139:* 19
Ascensios, Natalie *105:* 139

Asch, Frank *5:* 9; *66:* 2, 4, 6, 7, 9, 10; *102:* 18, 19,21; *154:* 12
Ashby, Gail *11:* 135
Ashby, Gil *146:* 4
Ashby, Gwynneth *44:* 26
Ashley, C.W. *19:* 197
Ashmead, Hal *8:* 70
Aska, Warabe *56:* 10
Assel, Steven *44:* 153; *77:* 22, 97
Astrop, John *32:* 56
Atene, Ann *12:* 18
Atherton, Lisa *38:* 198
Atkinson, Allen *60:* 5
Atkinson, J. Priestman *17:* 275
Atkinson, Janet *86:* 147; *103:* 138
Atkinson, Mike *127:* 74
Atkinson, Wayne *40:* 46
Attard, Karl *196:* 22, 23
Attebery, Charles *38:* 170
Atwell, Debby *150:* 6
Atwood, Ann *7:* 9
Aubrey, Meg Kelleher *77:* 159
Auch, Herm *173:* 7, 8
Auch, Mary Jane *173:* 7
Augarde, Steve *25:* 22; *159:* 7
Austerman, Miriam *23:* 107
Austin, Margot *11:* 16
Austin, Robert *3:* 44
Austin, Virginia *81:* 205; *127:* 221
Auth, Tony *51:* 5; *192:* 18
Avendano, Dolores *158:* 74
Avedon, Richard *57:* 140
Averill, Esther *1:* 17; *28:* 39, 40, 41
Axeman, Lois *2:* 32; *11:* 84; *13:* 165; *22:* 8; *23:* 49; *61:* 116; *101:* 124
Axtel, David *155:* 110
Ayer, Jacqueline *13:* 7
Ayer, Margaret *15:* 12; *50:* 120
Ayers, Alan *91:* 58; *107:* 169
Ayliffe, Alex *95:* 164
Ayto, Russell *111:* 5; *112:* 54; *206:* 7, 8
Azarian, Mary *112:* 9, 10; *114:* 129; *117:* 171; *137:* 163; *171:* 4, 5; *181:* 161; *188:* 128

B

B.T.B.
    See Blackwell, Basil T.
Babbitt, Bradford *33:* 158
Babbitt, Natalie *6:* 6; *8:* 220; *68:* 20; *70:* 242, 243; *194:* 8, 9
Baca, Maria *104:* 5
Bacchus, Andy *94:* 87
Bacha, Andy *109:* 169
Bachelet, Gilles *196:* 18
Bachem, Paul *48:* 180; *67:* 65; *144:* 206
Back, Adam *63:* 125
Back, George *31:* 161
Backes, Nick *190:* 72
Backhouse, Colin *78:* 142
Bacon, Bruce *4:* 74
Bacon, Paul *7:* 155; *8:* 121; *31:* 55; *50:* 42; *56:* 175; *62:* 82, 84
Bacon, Peggy *2:* 11, 228; *46:* 44
Baek, Matthew J. *169:* 95; *202:* 8
Baer, Julie *161:* 2
Baicker-McKee, Carol *177:* 15; *180:* 215
Bailey, Peter *58:* 174; *87:* 221; *194:* 12
Bailey, Sheila *155:* 11
Baker, Alan *22:* 22; *61:* 134; *93:* 11, 12; *146:* 6, 7, 10
Baker, Charlotte *2:* 12
Baker, Garin *89:* 65
Baker, Jeannie *23:* 4; *88:* 18, 19, 20
Baker, Jim *22:* 24
Baker, Joe *82:* 188; *111:* 55; *124:* 70; *197:* 73
Baker, Keith *179:* 6, 7
Baker, Leslie *112:* 214; *132:* 103, 246; *180:* 74, 246

Baldacci, Rudy *184:* 9
Baldridge, Cyrus LeRoy *19:* 69; *44:* 50
Baldus, Zachary *152:* 231; *187:* 60
Balet, Jan *11:* 22
Balian, Lorna *9:* 16; *91:* 16
Balit, Christina *102:* 24; *159:* 9; *162:* 118, 119
Ballantyne, R.M. *24:* 34
Ballis, George *14:* 199
Balouch, Kristen *176:* 11
Baltzer, Hans *40:* 30
Banbery, Fred *58:* 15
Banfill, A. Scott *98:* 7; *112:* 59
Bang, Molly Garrett *24:* 37, 38; *69:* 8, 9, 10; *111:* 7,9, 10, 11; *140:* 11; *158:* 37, 38, 39; *195:* 3
Banik, Yvette Santiago *21:* 136
Banner, Angela
    See Maddison, Angela Mary
Bannerman, Helen *19:* 13, 14
Banning, Greg *202:* 98
Bannon, Laura *6:* 10; *23:* 8
Bantock, Nick *74:* 229; *95:* 6
Banyai, Istvan *185:* 209; *193:* 14, 16
Baptist, Michael *37:* 208
Baracca, Sal *135:* 206
Baranaski, Marcin *182:* 113
Barasch, Lynne *126:* 16; *186:* 15
Barbarin, Lucien C., Jr. *89:* 88
Barbour, Karen *96:* 5; *74:* 209; *170:* 16
Bare, Arnold Edwin *16:* 31
Bare, Colleen Stanley *32:* 33
Barger, Jan *147:* 11
Bargery, Geoffrey *14:* 258
Barkat, Jonathan *149:* 177; *164:* 254; *181:* 106; *184:* 186; *196:* 11; *198:* 148
Barker, Carol *31:* 27
Barker, Cicely Mary *49:* 50, 51
Barkley, James *4:* 13; *6:* 11; *13:* 112
Barks, Carl *37:* 27, 28, 29, 30, 31, 32, 33, 34
Barling, Joy *62:* 148
Barling, Tom *9:* 23
Barlow, Gillian *62:* 20
Barlow, Perry *35:* 28
Barlowe, Dot *30:* 223
Barlowe, Wayne *37:* 72; *84:* 43; *105:* 5
Barnard, Bryn *88:* 53; *13:* 55; *169:* 13; *193:* 194
Barneda, David *206:* 11
Barner, Bob *29:* 37; *128:* 33; *136:* 19, 20; *177:* 27
Barnes, Hiram P. *20:* 28
Barnes, Tim *137:* 28
Barnes-Murphy, Rowan *88:* 22
Barnett, Charles II *175:* 150
Barnett, Ivan *70:* 14
Barnett, Moneta *16:* 89; *19:* 142; *31:* 102; *33:* 30, 31, 32; *41:* 153; *61:* 94, 97
Barney, Maginel Wright *39:* 32, 33, 34; *YABC 2:* 306
Barnum, Jay Hyde *11:* 224; *20:* 5; *37:* 189, 190
Baron, Alan *80:* 3; *89:* 123
Barr, George *60:* 74; *69:* 64
Barragan, Paula S. *134:* 116; *186:* 158
Barrall, Tim *115:* 152
Barraud, Martin *189:* 38
Barrauds *33:* 114
Barrer-Russell, Gertrude *9:* 65; *27:* 31
Barret, Robert *85:* 134
Barrett, Angela *40:* 136, 137; *62:* 74; *75:* 10; *76:* 142; *144:* 137; *145:* 14
Barrett, Jennifer *58:* 149
Barrett, John E. *43:* 119
Barrett, Moneta *74:* 10
Barrett, Peter *55:* 169; *86:* 111
Barrett, Robert *62:* 145; *77:* 146; *82:* 35
Barrett, Ron *14:* 24; *26:* 35
Barron, John N. *3:* 261; *5:* 101; *14:* 220
Barrow, Ann *136:* 27
Barrows, Walter *14:* 268
Barry, Ethelred B. *37:* 79; *YABC 1:* 229

Barry, James *14:* 25
Barry, Katharina *2:* 159; *4:* 22
Barry, Robert E. *6:* 12
Barry, Scott *32:* 35
Barshaw, Ruth McNally *203:* 9
Bartenbach, Jean *40:* 31
Barth, Ernest Kurt *2:* 172; *3:* 160; *8:* 26; *10:* 31
Bartholomew, Marie *200:* 66
Bartlett, Alison *101:* 88; *165:* 93
Barton, Byron *8:* 207; *9:* 18; *23:* 66; *80:* 181; *90:* 18, 19, 20, 21; *126:* 29, 30
Barton, Harriett *30:* 71
Barton, Jill *129:* 108; *135:* 120; *145:* 185, 189; *184:* 177
Bartram, Robert *10:* 42
Bartsch, Jochen *8:* 105; *39:* 38
Bascove, Barbara *45:* 73
Base, Graeme *101:* 15, 16, 17, 18; *162:* 8, 10, 12
Baseman, Gary *174:* 12
Bash, Barbara *132:* 9
Baskin, Leonard *30:* 42, 43, 46, 47; *49:* 125, 126, 128, 129,133; *173:* 120
Bass, Saul *49:* 192
Bassett, Jeni *40:* 99; *64:* 30
Basso, Bill *99:* 139; *189:* 134
Batchelor, Joy *29:* 41, 47, 48
Bate, Norman *5:* 16
Bates, Amy June *188:* 170; *189:* 27, 28
Bates, Leo *24:* 35
Batet, Carmen *39:* 134
Batherman, Muriel *31:* 79; *45:* 185
Battaglia, Aurelius *50:* 44
Batten, John D. *25:* 161, 162
Batten, Mary *162:* 14, 15
Battles, Asa *32:* 94, 95
Bauer, Carla *193:* 6
Bauer, Jutta *150:* 32
Bauernschmidt, Marjorie *15:* 15
Baum, Allyn *20:* 10
Baum, Willi *4:* 24, 25; *7:* 173
Bauman, Leslie *61:* 121
Baumann, Jill *34:* 170
Baumhauer, Hans *11:* 218; *15:* 163, 165, 167
Baxter, Glen *57:* 100
Baxter, Leon *59:* 102
Baxter, Robert *87:* 129
Bayer, Herbert *181:* 16
Bayley, Dorothy *37:* 195
Bayley, Nicola *40:* 104; *41:* 34, 35; *69:* 15; *129:* 33, 34, 35
Baylin, Mark *158:* 233
Baynes, Pauline *2:* 244; *3:* 149; *13:* 133, 135,137, 141; *19:* 18, 19, 20; *32:* 208, 213, 214; *36:* 105, 108; *59:* 12, 13, 14, 16, 17, 18, 20; *100:* 158, 159, 243; *133:* 3, 4
Beach, Lou *150:* 150; *207:* 117, 118
Beame, Rona *12:* 40
Bean, Jonathan *196:* 102
Bear's Heart *73:* 215
Beard, Dan *22:* 31, 32
Beard, J.H. *YABC 1:* 158
Bearden, Romare *9:* 7; *22:* 35
Beardshaw, Rosalind *169:* 22; *190:* 22
Beardsley, Aubrey *17:* 14; *23:* 181; *59:* 130, 131
Bearman, Jane *29:* 38
Beaton, Cecil *24:* 208
Beaton, Clare *125:* 28
Beauce, J.A. *18:* 103
Beaujard, Sophie *81:* 54
Beccia, Carlyn *189:* 29
Beck, Charles *11:* 169; *51:* 173
Beck, Ian *138:* 27; *182:* 150; *190:* 25
Beck, Melinda *203:* 112
Beck, Ruth *13:* 11
Becker, Harriet *12:* 211
Beckett, Sheilah *25:* 5; *33:* 37, 38
Beckhoff, Harry *1:* 78; *5:* 163
Beckhorn, Susan Williams *189:* 32

Beckman, Kaj *45:* 38, 39, 40, 41
Beckman, Per *45:* 42, 43
Beddows, Eric *72:* 70
Bedford, F.D. *20:* 118, 122; *33:* 170; *41:* 220, 221,230, 233
Bee, Joyce *19:* 62
Bee, William *188:* 6
Beeby, Betty *25:* 36
Beech, Carol *9:* 149
Beech, Mark *192:* 122
Beek *25:* 51, 55, 59
Beeke, Tiphanie *177:* 127; *204:* 140
Beekman, Doug *125:* 146, 148
Beerbohm, Max *24:* 208
Beeson, Bob *108:* 57
Begin, Mary Jane *82:* 13; *206:* 13
Beha, Philippe *172:* 85
Behr, Joyce *15:* 15; *21:* 132; *23:* 161
Behrens, Hans *5:* 97
Beier, Ellen *135:* 170; *139:* 47; *183:* 164
Beinicke, Steve *69:* 18
Beisner, Monika *46:* 128, 131; *112:* 127
Belden, Charles J. *12:* 182
Belina, Renate *39:* 132
Bell, Corydon *3:* 20
Bell, Graham *54:* 48
Bell, Julia *151:* 214
Bell, Julie *159:* 172; *165:* 18
Bell, Thomas P. *76:* 182
Bellamy, Glen *127:* 15
Beltran, Alberto *43:* 37
Bemelmans, Ludwig *15:* 19, 21; *100:* 27
Ben-Ami, Doron *75:* 96; *84:* 107; *108:* 132; *110:* 63; *159:* 157; *197:* 142
Bendall-Brunello, John *150:* 4; *157:* 163; *185:* 3, 4; *203:* 5
Benda, Wladyslaw T. *15:* 256; *30:* 76, 77; *44:* 182
Bender, Robert *77:* 162; *79:* 13; *160:* 23
Bendick, Jeanne *2:* 24; *68:* 27, 28
Benioff, Carol *121:* 42; *175:* 23
Benner, Cheryl *80:* 11
Bennett, Charles H. *64:* 6
Bennett, Erin Susanne *165:* 216
Bennett, F.I. *YABC 1:* 134
Bennett, James *146:* 240
Bennett, Jill *26:* 61; *41:* 38, 39; *45:* 54
Bennett, Rainey *15:* 26; *23:* 53
Bennett, Richard *15:* 45; *21:* 11, 12, 13; *25:* 175
Bennett, Susan *5:* 55
Benny, Mike *142:* 78; *203:* 13, 14; *207:* 85
Benoit, Elise *77:* 74
Benson, Linda *60:* 130; *62:* 91; *75:* 101; *79:* 156; *134:* 129
Benson, Patrick *68:* 162; *147:* 17, 18, 19, 20
Bentley, Carolyn *46:* 153
Bentley, James *149:* 30
Bentley, Roy *30:* 162
Benton, Jim *172:* 22
Benton, Thomas Hart *2:* 99
Berelson, Howard *5:* 20; *16:* 58; *31:* 50
Berenstain, Jan *12:* 47; *64:* 33, 34, 36, 37, 38, 40, 42, 44; *135:* 25, 28, 31, 35
Berenstain, Stan *12:* 47; *64:* 33, 34, 36, 37, 38, 40, 42, 44; *135:* 25, 28, 31, 35
Berenzy, Alix *65:* 13; *73:* 6; *78:* 115
Berg, Joan *1:* 115; *3:* 156; *6:* 26, 58
Berg, Ron *36:* 48, 49; *48:* 37, 38; *67:* 72
Bergen, David *115:* 44; *207:* 34
Berger, Barbara *77:* 14
Berger, Carin *185:* 6
Berger, William M. *14:* 143; *YABC 1:* 204
Bergherr, Mary *74:* 170; *151:* 123
Bergin, Mark *114:* 8, 9; *143:* 95; *160:* 26, 27
Bergstreser, Douglas *69:* 76
Bergum, Constance R. *121:* 14, 15
Bering, Claus *13:* 14
Berkeley, Jon *139:* 218
Berkowitz, Jeanette *3:* 249
Berman, Paul *66:* 14

Bernal, Richard *154:* 176
Bernadette
　　See Watts, Bernadette
Bernardin, James *112:* 24; *167:* 94
Bernasconi, Pablo *183:* 10, 11
Bernath, Stefen *32:* 76
Bernhard, Durga *80:* 13
Bernstein, Michel J. *51:* 71
Bernstein, Ted *38:* 183; *50:* 131
Bernstein, Zena *23:* 46
Berridge, Celia *86:* 63
Berrill, Jacquelyn *12:* 50
Berry, Erick
　　See Best, Allena
Berry, Holly *205:* 116
Berry, William D. *14:* 29; *19:* 48
Berry, William A. *6:* 219
Berson, Harold *2:* 17, 18; *4:* 28, 29, 220; *9:* 10; *12:* 19; *17:* 45; *18:* 193; *22:* 85; *34:* 172; *44:* 120; *46:* 42; *80:* 240
Bertholf, Bret *187:* 9; *189:* 32, 33
Berton, Patsy *99:* 16
Bertschmann, Harry *16:* 1
Besco, Don *70:* 99
Beskow, Elsa *20:* 13, 14, 15
Bess, Clayton *63:* 94
Best, Allena *2:* 26; *34:* 76
Betera, Carol *74:* 68
Bethell, Thomas N. *61:* 169
Bethers, Ray *6:* 22
Bettina
　　See Ehrlich, Bettina
Betts, Ethel Franklin *17:* 161, 164, 165; *YABC 2:* 47
Betz, Rudolf *59:* 161
Bewick, Thomas *16:* 40, 41, 43, 44, 45, 47; *54:* 150; *YABC 1:* 107
Beyer, Paul J. III *74:* 24
Bezencon, Jacqueline *48:* 40
Biamonte, Daniel *40:* 90
Bianchi, John *91:* 19
Bianco, Pamela *15:* 31; *28:* 44, 45, 46
Bible, Charles *13:* 15
Bice, Clare *22:* 40
Biedrzycki, David *186:* 170
Bierman, Don *57:* 184
Biggers, John *2:* 123
Biggs, Brian *192:* 38; *196:* 15; *207:* 170
Bikadoroff, Roxanna *201:* 74
Bileck, Marvin *3:* 102; *40:* 36, 37
Bilibin, Ivan *61:* 8, 9, 12, 13, 14, 15, 151, 152, 154, 162
Billington, Patrick *98:* 71
Billout, Guy *144:* 38, 39
Bimen, Levent *5:* 179
Binch, Caroline *81:* 18; *140:* 15, 16; *144:* 115
Binder, Hannes *169:* 163
Bing, Christopher *126:* 34
Binger, Bill *121:* 46
Binks, Robert *25:* 150
Binzen, Bill *24:* 47
Birch, Reginald *15:* 150; *19:* 33, 34, 35, 36; *37:* 196,197; *44:* 182; *46:* 176; *YABC 1:* 84; *2:* 34, 39
Birchall, Mark *123:* 188
Bird, Esther Brock *1:* 36; *25:* 66
Birdsong, Keith *167:* 85
Birkett, Georgie *204:* 121
Birkett, Rachel *78:* 206
Birling, Paul *109:* 30
Birmingham, Christian *132:* 243; *143:* 114
Birmingham, Lloyd P. *12:* 51; *83:* 13
Biro, Val *1:* 26; *41:* 42; *60:* 178; *67:* 23, 24; *84:* 242, 243
Bischoff, Ilse *44:* 51
Bishop, Don *199:* 133
Bishop, Gavin *97:* 17, 18; *144:* 42, 44
Bishop, Kathleen Wong *115:* 67
Bishop, Rich *56:* 43
Bite, I. *60:* 14
Bittinger, Ned *93:* 117; *205:* 115

Bjorklund, Lorence *3:* 188, 252; *7:* 100; *9:* 113; *10:* 66; *19:* 178; *33:* 122, 123; *35:* 36, 37, 38, 39,41, 42, 43; *36:* 185; *38:* 93; *47:* 106; *66:* 194; *YABC 1:* 242
Bjorkman, Steve *91:* 199; *160:* 110; *198:* 18
Black Sheep *164:* 100
Blackburn, Loren H. *63:* 10
Blackall, Sophie *194:* 140
Blackford, John *137:* 105; *180:* 36
Blackwell, Basil T. *YABC 1:* 68, 69
Blackwood, Freya *199:* 9
Blackwood, Gary L. *118:* 17
Blades, Ann *16:* 52; *37:* 213; *50:* 41; *69:* 21; *99:* 215
Blair, Jay *45:* 46; *46:* 155
Blaisdell, Elinore *1:* 121; *3:* 134; *35:* 63
Blake, Anne Catharine *189:* 71
Blake, Francis *198:* 4
Blake, Quentin *3:* 170; *10:* 48; *13:* 38; *21:* 180; *26:* 60; *28:* 228; *30:* 29, 31; *40:* 108; *45:* 219; *46:* 165, 168; *48:* 196; *52:* 10, 11, 12,13, 14, 15, 16, 17; *73:* 41, 43; *78:* 84, 86; *80:* 250, 251; *84:* 210, 211, 212; *87:* 177; *96:* 24, 26, 28; *124:* 79; *125:* 32, 34; *181:* 139
Blake, Robert J. *37:* 90; *53:* 67; *54:* 23; *160:* 28, 29
Blake, William *30:* 54, 56, 57, 58, 59, 60
Blanchard, N. Taylor *82:* 140
Blass, Jacqueline *8:* 215
Blazek, Scott R. *91:* 71
Bleck, Cathie *118:* 116
Bleck, Linda *204:* 124
Blegvad, Erik *2:* 59; *3:* 98; *5:* 117; *7:* 131; *11:* 149; *14:* 34, 35; *18:* 237; *32:* 219; *60:* 106; *66:* 16, 17, 18, 19; *70:* 233; *76:* 18; *82:* 106; *87:* 45; *100:* 188; *129:* 125; *132:* 17, 18, 19, 20; *176:* 14; *200:* 100; *YABC 1:* 201
Blessen, Karen *93:* 126
Bliss, Corinne Demas *37:* 38
Bliss, Harry *196:* 27, 28, 29
Blitt, Barry *179:* 199; *187:* 13
Bloch, Lucienne *10:* 12
Blondon, Herve *129:* 48; *183:* 22
Bloom, Lloyd *35:* 180; *36:* 149; *47:* 99; *62:* 117; *68:* 231; *72:* 136; *75:* 185; *83:* 99; *108:* 19
Bloom, Suzanne *172:* 23, 24
Blossom, Dave *34:* 29
Blumenschein, E.L. *YABC 1:* 113, 115
Blumer, Patt *29:* 214
Blundell, Kim *29:* 36
Bluthenthal, Diana Cain *93:* 32; *104:* 106; *177:* 26
Blythe, Benjamin *128:* 7
Blythe, Gary *112:* 52; *181:* 166; *182:* 64; *185:* 7; *186:* 116, 117
Boake, Kathy *176:* 185
Board, Perry *171:* 99
Boardman, Gwenn *12:* 60
Bober, Richard *125:* 145; *132:* 40
Bobri *30:* 138; *47:* 27
Bock, Vera *1:* 187; *21:* 41
Bock, William Sauts *8:* 7; *14:* 37; *16:* 120; *21:* 141; *36:* 177; *62:* 203
Bodecker, N(iels) M(ogens) *8:* 13; *14:* 2; *17:* 55, 56, 57; *73:* 22, 23, 24
Boehm, Linda *40:* 31
Bogacki, Tomek *138:* 31, 32; *144:* 123; *202:* 13
Bogan, Paulette *197:* 152; *201:* 17
Bogdan, Florentina *107:* 43
Bohdal, Susi *22:* 44; *101:* 20
Bohlen, Nina *58:* 13
Boies, Alex *96:* 53
Bok, Chip *205:* 16
Bolam, Emily *101:* 216; *159:* 12; *205:* 59
Bolian, Polly *3:* 270; *4:* 30; *13:* 77; *29:* 197
Bolle, Frank *87:* 100
Bollen, Roger *79:* 186; *83:* 16
Bolling, Vickey *114:* 44

Bollinger, Peter *101:* 7; *128:* 198; *172:* 26
Bolognese, Don *2:* 147, 231; *4:* 176; *7:* 146; *17:* 43; *23:* 192; *24:* 50; *34:* 108; *36:* 133; *71:* 24, 25; *103:* 131; *129:* 39, 40
Bolster, Rob *186:* 169
Bolton, A.T. *57:* 158
Bond, Arnold *18:* 116
Bond, Barbara Higgins *21:* 102
Bond, Bruce *52:* 97
Bond, Felicia *38:* 197; *49:* 55, 56; *89:* 170; *90:* 171; *126:* 37
Bond, Higgins *177:* 22, 23
Bonn, Pat *43:* 40
Bonner, Hannah *197:* 13, 14
Bonners, Susan *41:* 40; *85:* 36; *94:* 99, 100; *151:* 105, 106
Bono, Mary *184:* 73
Bonsall, Crosby *23:* 6
Boon, Debbie *103:* 6; *144:* 188
Boon, Emilie *86:* 23, 24
Boone, Debbie *165:* 77
Boore, Sara *60:* 73
Bootman, Colin *155:* 13; *159:* 35; *174:* 192
Booth, Franklin *YABC 2:* 76
Booth, George *191:* 13
Booth, Graham *32:* 193; *37:* 41, 42
Borda, Juliette *102:* 188
Bordier, Georgette *16:* 54
Boren, Tinka *27:* 128
Borges, Jose Francisco *119:* 62
Borja, Robert *22:* 48
Born, Adolf *49:* 63
Bornstein, Ruth *14:* 44; *88:* 45, 46; *107:* 30
Borten, Helen *3:* 54; *5:* 24
Bosin, Blackbear *69:* 104
Bossom, Naomi *35:* 48
Bostock, Mike *83:* 221; *114:* 14; *188:* 205
Boston, Peter *19:* 42
Bosustow, Stephen *34:* 202
Boszko, Ron *75:* 47
Bottner, Barbara *14:* 46
Boucher, Joelle *41:* 138
Boulat, Pierre *44:* 40
Boulet, Susan Seddon *50:* 47
Bouma, Paddy *118:* 25; *128:* 16
Bour, Daniele *66:* 145
Bourke-White, Margaret *15:* 286, 287; *57:* 102
Boutavant, Marc *200:* 136
Boutet de Monvel, M. *30:* 61, 62, 63, 65
Bowen, Betsy *105:* 222
Bowen, Richard *42:* 134
Bowen, Ruth *31:* 188
Bower, Ron *29:* 33
Bowers, David *95:* 38; *115:* 20; *127:* 169, 170; *165:* 57; *207:* 11
Bowers, Tim *185:* 35; *201:* 41
Bowman, Claire *174:* 177
Bowman, Eric *151:* 23
Bowman, Leslie *85:* 203; *105:* 108; *116:* 76; *128:* 234; *182:* 24, 25
Bowman, Peter *146:* 214, 215; *150:* 115
Bowser, Carolyn Ewing *22:* 253
Boxall, Ed *178:* 28
Boyd, Aaron *158:* 242
Boyd, Patti *45:* 31
Boyle, Eleanor Vere *28:* 50, 51
Boynton, Sandra *57:* 13, 14, 15; *107:* 36, 37; *152:* 12, 13, 14
Bozzo, Frank *4:* 154
Brabbs, Derry *55:* 170
Brace, Eric *132:* 193, 194; *152:* 71; *184:* 195; *197:* 6; *201:* 54
Brackers de Hugo, Pierre *115:* 21
Bradford, June *158:* 138
Bradford, Ron *7:* 157
Bradley, David P. *69:* 105
Bradley, Richard D. *26:* 182
Bradley, William *5:* 164
Brady, Irene *4:* 31; *42:* 37; *68:* 191
Bragg, Michael *32:* 78; *46:* 31
Bragg, Ruth Gembicki *77:* 18

Brainerd, John W. *65:* 19
Braithwaite, Althea *23:* 12, 13; *119:* 16
Brak, Syd *146:* 187
Bralds, Braldt *90:* 28; *91:* 151
Bram, Elizabeth *30:* 67
Bramley, Peter *4:* 3
Brandenberg, Aliki *2:* 36, 37; *24:* 222; *35:* 49, 50, 51,52, 53, 54, 56, 57; *75:* 15, 17; *92:* 205; *113:* 18, 19, 20; *157:* 28; *156:* 111
Brandenburg, Alexa *75:* 19
Brandenburg, Jim *47:* 58; *150:* 212
Brandi, Lillian *31:* 158
Brandon, Brumsic, Jr. *9:* 25
Brannen, Sarah S. *202:* 15
Bransom, Paul *17:* 121; *43:* 44
Braren, Loretta Trezzo *87:* 193
Brassard, France *186:* 22
Braun, Wendy *80:* 17, 18
Brautigam, Don *115:* 175, 176
Brazell, Derek *75:* 105; *79:* 9
Breathed, Berkeley *86:* 27, 28, 29; *161:* 13, 14
Breckenreid, Julia *192:* 209
Breen, Steve *186:* 23
Brennan, Steve *83:* 230; *101:* 184
Brenner, Fred *22:* 85; *36:* 34; *42:* 34
Brett, Bernard *22:* 54
Brett, Harold M. *26:* 98, 99, 100
Brett, Jan *30:* 135; *42:* 39; *71:* 31, 32; *130:* 23, 24, 25, 26, 27; *171:* 15, 16
Brewer, Paul *106:* 115; *145:* 202
Brewer, Sally King *33:* 44
Brewster, Patience *40:* 68; *45:* 22, 183; *51:* 20; *66:* 144; *89:* 4; *97:* 30, 31
Brick, John *10:* 15
Brickman, Robin D. *131:* 88; *142:* 150; *155:* 18; *178:* 109; *184:* 32
Bridge, David R. *45:* 28
Bridgman, L.J. *37:* 77
Bridwell, Norman *4:* 37; *138:* 36, 37, 40
Brierley, Louise *91:* 22; *96:* 165; *183:* 51
Briggs, Harry *172:* 187
Briggs, Raymond *10:* 168; *23:* 20, 21; *66:* 29, 31, 32; *131:* 28, 29; *184:* 15, 16
Brigham, Grace A. *37:* 148
Bright, Robert *24:* 55
Brighton, Catherine *107:* 39; *206:* 23
Brinckloe, Julie *13:* 18; *24:* 79, 115; *29:* 35; *63:* 140; *81:* 131
Brion *47:* 116
Brisley, Joyce L. *22:* 57
Brisson, James F. *110:* 60
Brittingham, Geoffrey *88:* 37
Brix-Henker, Silke *81:* 194
Brock, Charles E. *15:* 97; *19:* 247, 249; *23:* 224, 225; *36:* 88; *42:* 41, 42, 43, 44, 45; *100:* 189; *YABC 1:* 194, 196, 203
Brock, Emma *7:* 21
Brock, Henry Matthew *15:* 81; *16:* 141; *19:* 71; *34:* 115; *40:* 164; *42:* 47, 48, 49; *49:* 66
Brocksopp, Arthur *57:* 157
Broda, Ron *136:* 180; *174:* 123
Brodkin, Gwen *34:* 135
Brodovitch, Alexi *52:* 22
Bromhall, Winifred *5:* 11; *26:* 38
Bromley, Lizzy *159:* 179
Bronson, Linda *150:* 210; *174:* 133; *203:* 16, 17
Brooke, L. Leslie *16:* 181, 182, 183, 186; *17:* 15, 16, 17; *18:* 194
Brooker, Christopher *15:* 251
Brooker, Kyrsten *111:* 94; *140:* 28; *162:* 111; *175:* 108; *186:* 42, 225; *199:* 12; *201:* 30
Brooks, Erik *166:* 52; *182:* 30
Brooks, Karen Stormer *186:* 110
Brooks, Maya Itzna *92:* 153
Brooks, Ron *94:* 15; *197:* 188
Brooks, S.G. *178:* 127
Broomfield, Maurice *40:* 141
Brotman, Adolph E. *5:* 21
Brown, Buck *45:* 48
Brown, Calef *179:* 18

Illustrations Index

Brown, Christopher 62: 124, 125, 127, 128
Brown, Craig McFarland 73: 28; 84: 65
Brown, Dan 61: 167; 115: 183, 184; 116: 28, 29; 193: 190; 200: 21, 23
Brown, David 7: 47; 48: 52
Brown, Denise 11: 213
Brown, Don 172: 29
Brown, Elbrite 195: 39; 198: 5
Brown, Ford Madox 48: 74
Brown, Hunter 191: 111, 112
Brown, Judith Gwyn 1: 45; 7: 5; 8: 167; 9: 182, 190; 20: 16, 17, 18; 23: 142; 29: 117; 33: 97; 36: 23, 26; 43: 184; 48: 201, 223; 49: 69; 86: 227; 110: 188; 153: 7
Brown, Kathryn 98: 26
Brown, Lisa 187: 175
Brown, Laurie Krasny 99: 30
Brown, Marc (Tolon) 10: 17, 197; 14: 263; 51: 18; 53: 11, 12, 13, 15, 16, 17; 75: 58; 80: 24, 25, 26; 82: 261; 99: 29; 145: 22, 23, 25, 27; 162: 198
Brown, Marcia 7: 30; 25: 203; 47: 31, 32, 33, 34, 35,36, 37, 38, 39, 40, 42, 43, 44; YABC 1: 27
Brown, Margery W. 5: 32, 33; 10: 3
Brown, Martin 101: 43
Brown, Mary Barrett 97: 74
Brown, Palmer 36: 40
Brown, Paul 25: 26; 26: 107
Brown, Richard 61: 18; 67: 30
Brown, Rick 78: 71; 150: 154
Brown, Robert S. 85: 33
Brown, Rod 157: 142
Brown, Ruth 55: 165; 86: 112, 113; 105: 16, 17, 18; 171: 178
Brown, Trevor 99: 160; 139: 247; 189: 206
Browne, Anthony 45: 50, 51, 52; 61: 21, 22, 23, 24, 25; 105: 21, 22, 23, 25
Browne, Dik 8: 212; 67: 32, 33, 35, 37, 39
Browne, Gordon 16: 97; 64: 114, 116, 117, 119, 121
Browne, Hablot K. 15: 65, 80; 21: 14, 15, 16, 17, 18, 19,20; 24: 25
Browne, Jane 165: 222
Browning, Coleen 4: 132
Browning, Mary Eleanor 24: 84
Bruce, Robert 23: 23
Brude, Dick 48: 215
Bruel, Nick 166: 41; 205: 17, 18
Brule, Al 3: 135
Brumbeau, Jeff 157: 29
Bruna, Dick 43: 48, 49, 50; 76: 27, 28
Brundage, Frances 19: 244
Brunhoff, Jean de 24: 57, 58
Brunhoff, Laurent de 24: 60; 71: 35, 36, 37
Brunkus, Denise 84: 50; 123: 117; 178: 209; 193: 99; 204: 10, 11, 12
Brunson, Bob 43: 135
Bryan, Ashley 31: 44; 72: 27, 28, 29; 107: 92; 116: 192; 132: 24; 178: 33, 34, 35
Bryant, Laura J. 176: 36; 183: 168
Bryant, Michael 93: 74
Brychta, Alex 21: 21
Bryer, Diana 107: 121
Bryson, Bernarda 3: 88, 146; 39: 26; 44: 185; 131: 40
Buba, Joy 12: 83; 30: 226; 44: 56
Buchanan, George 166: 198
Buchanan, Lilian 13: 16
Buchanan, Rachel 171: 71
Bucholtz-Ross, Linda 44: 137
Buchs, Thomas 40: 38
Buck, Margaret Waring 3: 30
Buckhardt, Marc 172: 59
Buckley, Mike 166: 180
Budwine, Greg 175: 172
Buehner, Mark 104: 12, 15; 105: 160; 119: 98; 157: 188; 159: 39, 40, 43; 192: 111
Buehr, Walter 3: 31
Buff, Conrad 19: 52, 53, 54
Buff, Mary 19: 52, 53

Bull, Charles Livingston 18: 207; 88: 175, 176
Bullen, Anne 3: 166, 167
Buller, Jon 205: 21
Bullock, Kathleen 77: 24
Bumgarner-Kirby, Claudia 77: 194
Burbank, Addison 37: 43
Burchard, Peter Duncan 3: 197; 5: 35; 6: 158, 218; 143: 17
Burckhardt, Marc 94: 48; 110: 89; 196: 41; 199: 116
Burger, Carl 3: 33; 45: 160, 162
Burgeson, Marjorie 19: 31
Burgess, Anne 76: 252
Burgess, Gelett 32: 39, 42
Burgess, Mark 157: 31
Burke, Jim 179: 19; 185: 63
Burke, Phillip 95: 117
Burkert, Nancy Ekholm 18: 186; 22: 140; 24: 62, 63,64, 65; 26: 53; 29: 60, 61; 46: 171; YABC 1: 46
Burkhardt, Bruce 142: 86
Burkhardt, Melissa A. 142: 86
Burleson, Joe 104: 35; 172: 139
Burn, Doris 6: 172
Burn, Jeffrey 89: 125; 152: 132
Burn, Ted
　See Burn, Thomas E.
Burn, Thomas E. 151: 41
Burnard, Damon 115: 23
Burnett, Virgil 44: 42
Burningham, John 9: 68; 16: 60, 61; 59: 28, 29, 30,31, 32, 33, 35; 111: 18, 19, 21; 160: 37
Burns, Howard M. 12: 173
Burns, Jim 47: 70; 86: 32; 91: 197; 123: 16
Burns, M.F. 26: 69
Burns, Raymond 9: 29
Burns, Robert 24: 106
Burr, Dan 65: 28; 108: 134; 164: 203; 182: 68
Burr, Dane 12: 2
Burra, Edward YABC 2: 68
Burrell, Galen 56: 76
Burri, Rene 41: 143; 54: 166
Burridge, Marge Opitz 14: 42
Burris, Burmah 4: 81
Burroughs, John Coleman 41: 64
Burroughs, Studley O. 41: 65
Burton, Marilee Robin 46: 33
Burton, Virginia Lee 2: 43; 44: 49, 51; 100: 46, 47; YABC 1: 24; 147: 56
Busoni, Rafaello 1: 186; 3: 224; 6: 126; 14: 5; 16: 62, 63
Butchkes, Sidney 50: 58
Butler, Geoff 94: 20
Butler, Ralph 116: 212
Butterfield, Ned 1: 153; 27: 128; 79: 63
Butterworth, Ian 184: 48, 49
Butterworth, Nick 106: 43, 44; 149: 34
Buxton, John 123: 12
Buzelli, Christopher 105: 149
Buzonas, Gail 29: 88
Buzzell, Russ W. 12: 177
Byard, Carole 39: 44; 57: 18, 19, 20; 60: 60; 61: 93, 96; 69: 210; 78: 246; 79: 227
Byars, Betsy 46: 35
Byfield, Barbara Ninde 8: 18
Byfield, Graham 32: 29
Bynum, Janie 176: 50
Byrd, Robert 13: 218; 33: 46; 158: 70
Byrd, Samuel 123: 104

C

Cabat, Erni 74: 38
Cabban, Vanessa 138: 73; 176: 39; 185: 65
Cabrera, Jane 103: 24; 152: 27; 182: 33, 34
Caceres, Ana Palmero 198: 106
Caddy, Alice 6: 41
Cady, Harrison 17: 21, 23; 19: 57, 58

Caffrey, Aileen 72: 223; 141: 154
Cairns, Julia 177: 37
Caldecott, Randolph 16: 98, 103; 17: 32, 33, 36, 38, 39; 26: 90; 100: 49, 50; YABC 2: 172
Calder, Alexander 18: 168
Calderón, Gloria 179: 5
Calderon, W. Frank 25: 160
Caldwell, Ben 105: 75; 149: 60; 195: 61
Caldwell, Clyde 98: 100; 116: 39
Caldwell, Doreen 23: 77; 71: 41
Caldwell, John 46: 225
Call, Greg 126: 135; 165: 49; 182: 105, 163; 197: 18, 19; 200: 159
Callahan, Kevin 22: 42
Callahan, Philip S. 25: 77
Callan, Jamie 59: 37
Calvin, James 61: 92
Camburn-Bracalente, Carol A. 118: 22
Cameron, Chad 190: 144
Cameron, Julia Margaret 19: 203
Cameron, Scott 99: 18
Camm, Martin 140: 208, 209, 210
Campbell, Ann 11: 43; 123: 182; 183: 68
Campbell, Bill 89: 39
Campbell, Ken 126: 143; 205: 162
Campbell, Robert 55: 120
Campbell, Rod 51: 27; 98: 34
Campbell, Walter M. YABC 2: 158
Camps, Luis 28: 120, 121; 66: 35
Canga, C.B. 187: 165
Caniglia, Jeremy 201: 89
Cann, Helen 124: 50; 141: 78; 170: 138; 179: 22, 23
Cannell, Jon 196: 43
Cannon, Janell 78: 25; 128: 40
Canright, David 36: 162
Cantone, AnnaLaura 182: 146; 196: 80
Canty, Thomas 85: 161; 92: 47; 113: 192; 134: 60; 185: 117
Canyon, Christopher 150: 44; 151: 112
Caparo, Antonio Javier 204: 128
Caporale, Wende 70: 42
Capp, Al 61: 28, 30, 31, 40, 41, 43, 44
Cappon, Manuela 154: 64
Caras, Peter 36: 64
Caraway, Caren 57: 22
Caraway, James 3: 200, 201
Carbe, Nino 29: 183
Cares, Linda 67: 176
Carigiet, Alois 24: 67
Carle, Eric 4: 42; 11: 121; 12: 29; 65: 32,33, 34, 36; 73: 63, 65; 163: 55, 56
Carling, Amelia Lau 164: 46
Carlino, Angela 168: 43; 188: 20
Carlson, Nancy L. 41: 116; 56: 25; 90: 45; 144: 48, 50
Carlluccio, Maria 175: 129
Carmi, Giora 79: 35; 149: 40
Carpenter, Nancy 76: 128; 86: 173; 89: 171; 131: 186; 134: 8; 138: 215; 153: 204; 159: 93; 165: 232
Carr, Archie 37: 225
Carrick, Donald 5: 194; 39: 97; 49: 70; 53: 156; 63: 15, 16, 17, 18, 19, 21; 80: 131; 86: 151; 118: 24
Carrick, Malcolm 28: 59, 60
Carrick, Paul 118: 26; 194: 28
Carrick, Valery 21: 47
Carrier, Lark 71: 43
Carroll, Jim 88: 211; 140: 177; 153: 99; 195: 75
Carroll, Lewis
　See Dodgson, Charles L.
Carroll, Michael 72: 5
Carroll, Pamela 84: 68; 128: 214; 199: 130
Carroll, Ruth 7: 41; 10: 68
Carter, Abby 81: 32; 97: 121; 102: 61; 163: 139; 164: 125; 184: 22, 23; 191: 85
Carter, Barbara 47: 167, 169
Carter, David A. 114: 24, 25; 170: 42, 43

Carter, Don *124:* 54; *184:* 100; *192:* 43, 44, 45
Carter, Harry *22:* 179
Carter, Helene *15:* 38; *22:* 202, 203; *YABC 2:* 220, 221
Carter, Penny *173:* 91
Cartlidge, Michelle *49:* 65; *96:* 50, 51
Cartwright, Reg *63:* 61, 62; *78:* 26; *143:* 4
Cartwright, Shannon *176:* 81
Carty, Leo *4:* 196; *7:* 163; *58:* 131
Cary *4:* 133; *9:* 32; *20:* 2; *21:* 143
Cary, Page *12:* 41
Casale, Paul *71:* 63; *109:* 122; *136:* 28
Case, Sandra E. *16:* 2
Caseley, Judith *87:* 36; *159:* 47, 48, 49
Casilla, Robert *78:* 7; *167:* 124
Casino, Steve *85:* 193
Cassel, Lili
   See Wronker, Lili Cassel
Cassel-Wronker, Lili
   See Wronker, Lili Cassel
Cassels, Jean *8:* 50; *150:* 119; *173:* 37; *186:* 182
Cassen, Melody *140:* 51
Cassity, Don *104:* 24
Cassler, Carl *75:* 137, 138; *82:* 162
Casson, Hugh *65:* 38, 40, 42, 43
Castellon, Federico *48:* 45, 46, 47, 48
Castle, Jane *4:* 80
Castro, Antonio *84:* 71
Casu, Danny "casroc" *201:* 10
Catalano, Dominic *94:* 79; *163:* 60, 61; *162:* 54
Catalanotto, Peter *63:* 170; *70:* 23; *71:* 182; *72:* 96; *74:* 114; *76:* 194, 195; *77:* 7; *79:* 157; *80:* 28, 67; *83:* 157; *85:* 27; *108:* 11; *113:* 30, 31, 33, 34, 36; *114:* 27, 28, 29; *117:* 53; *124:* 168; *159:* 54, 55; *195:* 19, 20, 21, 22, 24, 174; *200:* 156; *207:* 103
Catania, Tom *68:* 82
Cather, Carolyn *3:* 83; *15:* 203; *34:* 216
Catrow, David *117:* 179; *152:* 31, 33; *173:* 24; *206:* 29
Cauley, Lorinda Bryan *44:* 135; *46:* 49
Cayard, Bruce *38:* 67
Cazet, Denys *52:* 27; *99:* 39, 40; *163:* 65, 66; *191:* 25, 27, 28
Ceccoli, Nicoletta *181:* 39; *188:* 99; *199:* 118
Cecil, Randy *127:* 132, 133; *187:* 16, 17; *191:* 168
Cellini, Joseph *2:* 73; *3:* 35; *16:* 116; *47:* 103
Cepeda, Joe *90:* 62; *109:* 91; *134:* 172; *159:* 57, 58, 164; *197:* 157; *203:* 69, 95
Chabrian, Debbi *45:* 55
Chabrian, Deborah *51:* 182; *53:* 124; *63:* 107; *75:* 84; *79:* 85; *82:* 247; *89:* 93; *101:* 197
Chagnon, Mary *37:* 158
Chalmers, Mary *3:* 145; *13:* 148; *33:* 125; *66:* 214
Chamberlain, Christopher *45:* 57
Chamberlain, Margaret *46:* 51; *106:* 89; *188:* 193
Chamberlain, Nigel *78:* 140
Chambers, C.E. *17:* 230
Chambers, Dave *12:* 151
Chambers, Jill *134:* 110
Chambers, Mary *4:* 188
Chambliss, Maxie *42:* 186; *56:* 159; *93:* 163, 164; *103:* 178; *186:* 33, 34; *196:* 39
Champlin, Dale *136:* 124
Chan, Harvey *96:* 236; *99:* 153; *143:* 218; *179:* 144
Chan, Peter *207:* 21
Chandler, David P. *28:* 62
Chaney, Howard *139:* 27
Chang, Warren *101:* 209
Chapel, Jody *68:* 20
Chapman, C.H. *13:* 83, 85, 87
Chapman, Frederick T. *6:* 27; *44:* 28
Chapman, Gaye *203:* 133
Chapman, Gaynor *32:* 52, 53

Chapman, Jane *145:* 186; *150:* 56; *166:* 220; *174:* 202; *176:* 43, 44; *179:* 131; *202:* 189
Chapman, Lynne *175:* 31; *197:* 25
Chappell, Warren *3:* 172; *21:* 56; *27:* 125
Charles, Donald *30:* 154, 155
Charlip, Remy *4:* 48; *34:* 138; *68:* 53, 54; *119:* 29, 30
Charlot, Jean *1:* 137, 138; *8:* 23; *14:* 31; *48:* 151; *56:* 21
Charlot, Martin *64:* 72
Charlton, Michael *34:* 50; *37:* 39
Charmatz, Bill *7:* 45
Chartier, Normand *9:* 36; *52:* 49; *66:* 40; *74:* 220; *145:* 169; *168:* 91; *177:* 108
Chase, Lynwood M. *14:* 4
Chast, Roz *97:* 39, 40
Chastain, Madye Lee *4:* 50
Chateron, Ann *152:* 19
Chatterton, Martin *68:* 102; *152:* 19
Chau, Tungwai *140:* 35
Chauncy, Francis *24:* 158
Chayka, Doug *145:* 97; *177:* 150; *196:* 46
Chee, Cheng-Khee *79:* 42; *81:* 224; *180:* 245
Chen, Chih-sien *90:* 226
Chen, Tony *6:* 45; *19:* 131; *29:* 126; *34:* 160
Chen, Yong *183:* 34
Cheney, T.A. *11:* 47
Cheng, Andrea *205:* 28
Cheng, Judith *36:* 45; *51:* 16
Chermayeff, Ivan *47:* 53
Cherry, David *93:* 40
Cherry, Lynne *34:* 52; *65:* 184; *87:* 111; *99:* 46, 47
Chesak, Lina *135:* 118
Chess, Victoria *12:* 6; *33:* 42, 48, 49; *40:* 194; *41:* 145; *69:* 80; *72:* 100; *92:* 33, 34; *104:* 167
Chessare, Michele *41:* 50; *56:* 48; *69:* 145
Chesterton, G.K. *27:* 43, 44, 45, 47
Chestnutt, David *47:* 217
Chesworth, Michael *75:* 24, 152; *88:* 136; *94:* 25; *98:* 155; *160:* 42; *207:* 23, 24, 25
Chetham, Celia *134:* 34
Chetwin, Grace *86:* 40
Cheung, Irving *158:* 96
Chevalier, Christa *35:* 66
Chew, Ruth *7:* 46; *132:* 147
Chewning, Randy *92:* 206
Chichester Clark, Emma *72:* 121; *77:* 212; *78:* 209; *87:* 143; *117:* 37, 39, 40; *144:* 138; *156:* 24, 25
Chifflart *47:* 113, 127
Child, Lauren *119:* 32; *183:* 30, 31
Chin, Alex *28:* 54
Chitwood, Susan Tanner *163:* 16
Cho, Shinta *8:* 126
Chodos-Irvine, Margaret *52:* 102, 103, 107; *152:* 44
Choi, Yangsook *171:* 134; *173:* 135; *178:* 38, 39, 40
Chollat, Emilie *170:* 203
Chollick, Jay *25:* 175
Choma, Christina *99:* 169
Chomey, Steve *188:* 53
Chorao, Kay *7:* 200, 201; *8:* 25; *11:* 234; *33:* 187; *35:* 239; *69:* 35; *70:* 235; *123:* 174; *193:* 179
Chow, Frances J. Soo Ping *206:* 36
Chowdhury, Subrata *62:* 130; *162:* 22, 23
Christelow, Eileen *38:* 44; *83:* 198, 199; *90:* 57, 58; *184:* 26
Christensen, Bonnie *93:* 100; *153:* 67
Christensen, Gardell Dano *1:* 57
Christensen, James C. *140:* 226
Christiana, David *90:* 64; *135:* 13; *171:* 7; *195:* 26, 27
Christiansen, Per *40:* 24
Christie, R. Gregory *116:* 107; *127:* 20, 21; *162:* 179; *164:* 114; *165:* 137; *174:* 157; *179:* 172; *185:* 17, 18, 19; *200:* 2; *204:* 85

Christy, Howard Chandler *17:* 163, 164, 165, 168, 169; *19:* 186, 187; *21:* 22, 23, 24, 25
Christy, Jana *194:* 21
Chronister, Robert *23:* 138; *63:* 27; *69:* 167
Church, Caroline Jayne *179:* 27
Church, Frederick *YABC 1:* 155
Chute, Marchette *1:* 59
Chwast, Jacqueline *1:* 63; *2:* 275; *6:* 46, 47; *11:* 125; *12:* 202; *14:* 235
Chwast, Seymour *3:* 128, 129; *18:* 43; *27:* 152; *92:* 79; *96:* 56, 57, 58; *146:* 32, 33; *197:* 99
Cieslawksi, Steve *101:* 142; *127:* 116; *158:* 169, 171; *190:* 174
Cinelli, Lisa *146:* 253
Cirlin, Edgard *2:* 168
Clairin, Georges *53:* 109
Clapp, John *105:* 66; *109:* 58; *126:* 7; *129:* 148; *130:* 165; *195:* 48
Clark, Brenda *119:* 85; *153:* 55
Clark, David *77:* 164; *134:* 144, 145
Clark, Emma Chichester
   See Chichester Clark, Emma
Clark, Victoria *35:* 159
Clarke, Greg *169:* 134
Clarke, Gus *72:* 226; *134:* 31
Clarke, Harry *23:* 172, 173
Clarke, Peter *75:* 102
Claverie, Jean *38:* 46; *88:* 29
Clavis, Philippe Goossens *182:* 167
Clay, Wil *203:* 29
Clayton, Elaine *159:* 60
Clayton, Robert *9:* 181
Cleary, Brian P. *186:* 37
Cleaver, Elizabeth *8:* 204; *23:* 36
Cleland, T.M. *26:* 92
Clemens, Peter *61:* 125
Clement, Charles *20:* 38
Clement, Gary *186:* 79; *191:* 32
Clement, Janet *182:* 50
Clement, Nathan *200:* 30
Clement, Rod *97:* 42
Clement, Stephen *88:* 3
Clementson, John *84:* 213
Clemesha, David *192:* 49, 50
Clevin, Jorgen *7:* 50
Clifford, Judy *34:* 163; *45:* 198
Clokey, Art *59:* 44
Clouse, Dennis *187:* 158
Clouse, James *84:* 15
Clouse, Nancy L. *78:* 31; *114:* 90
Clover, Peter *152:* 45
Cneut, Carll *156:* 166; *165:* 67; *197:* 26
Coalson, Glo *9:* 72, 85; *25:* 155; *26:* 42; *35:* 212; *53:* 31; *56:* 154; *94:* 37, 38, 193
Cober, Alan E. *17:* 158; *32:* 77; *49:* 127
Cober-Gentry, Leslie *92:* 111
Cocca-Leffler, Maryann *80:* 46; *136:* 60; *139:* 193; *194:* 31, 33, 34
Cochran, Bobbye *11:* 52
CoConis, Ted *4:* 41; *46:* 41; *51:* 104
Cocozza, Chris *87:* 18; *110:* 173; *111:* 149
Cockroft, Jason *152:* 20
Coerr, Eleanor *1:* 64; *67:* 52
Coes, Peter *35:* 172
Cogancherry, Helen *52:* 143; *69:* 131; *77:* 93; *78:* 220; *109:* 204; *110:* 129; *203:* 92
Coggins, Jack *2:* 69
Cohen, Alix *7:* 53
Cohen, Miriam *155:* 23, 24
Cohen, Nancy R. *165:* 35
Cohen, Santiago *164:* 26
Cohen, Sheldon *105:* 33, 34; *166:* 46, 47
Cohen, Vincent O. *19:* 243
Cohen, Vivien *11:* 112
Coker, Paul *51:* 172
Colbert, Anthony *15:* 41; *20:* 193
Colby, C.B. *3:* 47
Cole, Babette *58:* 172; *96:* 63, 64; *155:* 29
Cole, Brock *68:* 223; *72:* 36, 37, 38, 192; *127:* 23; *136:* 64, 65; *197:*

Cole, Gwen *87:* 185
Cole, Henry *178:* 120; *181:* 42, 43; *189:* 60
Cole, Herbert *28:* 104
Cole, Michael *59:* 46
Cole, Olivia H.H. *1:* 134; *3:* 223; *9:* 111; *38:* 104
Colin, Paul *102:* 59; *123:* 118; *126:* 152; *192:* 129
Colley, Jacqui *202:* 20
Collicott, Sharleen *98:* 39; *143:* 29, 30
Collier, Bryan *126:* 54; *151:* 166; *174:* 16, 17, 18; *204:* 18, 19
Collier, David *13:* 127
Collier, John *27:* 179
Collier, Steven *50:* 52
Collier-Morales, Roberta *168:* 61
Collins, Heather *66:* 84; *67:* 68; *81:* 40; *98:* 192, 193; *129:* 95, 96, 98
Collins, Matt *167:* 90
Collins, Ross *140:* 23, 24; *200:* 36, 37
Colman, Audrey *146:* 161
Colón, Raul *108:* 112; *113:* 5; *117:* 167; *134:* 112; *146:* 23; *159:* 92; *166:* 73; *180:* 107; *186:* 156; *190:* 6; *193:* 24, 205; *202:* 21, 22, 23
Colonna, Bernard *21:* 50; *28:* 103; *34:* 140; *43:* 180; *78:* 150
Comport, Sally Wern *117:* 169; *169:* 104; *190:* 42; *207:* 50
Conde, J.M. *100:* 120
Condon, Grattan *54:* 85 Condon, Ken *161:* 44; *195:* 28, 29
Cone, Ferne Geller *39:* 49
Cone, J. Morton *39:* 49
Conklin, Paul *43:* 62
Connelly, James *198:* 12
Connolly, Howard *67:* 88
Connolly, Jerome P. *4:* 128; *28:* 52
Connolly, Peter *47:* 60
Conoly, Walle *110:* 224
Conover, Chris *31:* 52; *40:* 184; *41:* 51; *44:* 79
Constantin, Pascale *207:* 159
Contreras, Gerry *72:* 9
Converse, James *38:* 70
Conway *62:* 62
Conway, Michael *69:* 12; *81:* 3; *92:* 108
Cook, Ande *188:* 135
Cook, G.R. *29:* 165
Cook, Joel *108:* 160
Cookburn, W.V. *29:* 204
Cooke, Donald E. *2:* 77
Cooke, Tom *52:* 118
Coomaraswamy, A.K. *50:* 100
Coombs, Charles *43:* 65
Coombs, Deborah *139:* 175
Coombs, Patricia *2:* 82; *3:* 52; *22:* 119; *51:* 32, 33, 34, 35, 36, 37, 38, 39, 40, 42, 43
Cooney, Barbara *6:* 16, 17, 50; *12:* 42; *13:* 92; *15:* 145; *16:* 74, 111; *18:* 189; *23:* 38, 89, 93; *32:* 138; *38:* 105; *59:* 48, 49, 51, 52, 53; *74:* 222; *81:* 100; *91:* 25; *96:* 71, 72, 74; *100:* 149; *YABC2:* 10
Cooper, Elisha *157:* 38, 39
Cooper, Floyd *79:* 95; *81:* 45; *84:* 82; *85:* 74; *91:* 118; *96:* 77, 78; *103:* 149; *144:* 54; *145:* 151; *159:* 198; *176:* 133, 134; *187:* 26, 27, 28, 29; *188:* 22; *199:* 175
Cooper, Heather *50:* 39
Cooper, Helen *102:* 42, 43, 44
Cooper, Mario *24:* 107
Cooper, Marjorie *7:* 112
Cope, Jane *61:* 201; *108* 52
Copeland, Mark *180:* 12
Copelman, Evelyn *8:* 61; *18:* 25
Copley, Heather *30:* 86; *45:* 57
Corbett, Grahame *30:* 114; *43:* 67
Corbino, John *19:* 248
Corcos, Lucille *2:* 223; *10:* 27; *34:* 66
Cordell, Matthew *197:* 93; *199:* 20, 21
Corey, Robert *9:* 34
Corlass, Heather *10:* 7

Cornell, James *27:* 60
Cornell, Jeff *11:* 58
Cornell, Laura *94:* 179; *95:* 25
Corr, Christopher *204:* 98
Corrigan, Barbara *8:* 37
Corrigan, Patrick *145:* 149
Corwin, Judith Hoffman *10:* 28
Corwin, Oliver *191:* 119
Cory, Fanny Y. *20:* 113; *48:* 29
Cosentino, Ralph *169:* 32
Cosgrove, Margaret *3:* 100; *47:* 63; *82:* 133
Costabel, Eva Deutsch *45:* 66, 67
Costanza, John *58:* 7, 8, 9
Costello, Chris *86:* 78
Costello, David F. *23:* 55
Côté, Geneviéve *184:* 37, 39
Cote, Nancy *126:* 139; *156:* 101; *174:* 101; *182:* 53, 54, 55
Cottenden, Jeff *190:* 45
Couch, Greg *94:* 124; *110:* 13; *162:* 31; *168:* 149; *199:* 22
Councell, Ruth Tietjen *79:* 29
Courtney, Cathy *58:* 69, 144; *59:* 15; *61:* 20, 87
Courtney, R. *35:* 110
Counihan, Claire *133:* 106
Cousineau, Normand *89:* 180; *112:* 76
Cousins, Lucy *172:* 53, 54; *205:* 34, 35
Couture, Christin *41:* 209
Covarrubias, Miguel *35:* 118, 119, 123, 124, 125
Coville, Katherine *32:* 57; *36:* 167; *92:* 38
Covington, Neverne *113:* 87
Cowdrey, Richard *169:* 170; *178:* 205; *204:* 22, 23
Cowell, Cressida *140:* 39
Cowell, Lucinda *77:* 54
Cowles, Rose *203:* 164, 167
Cox *43:* 93
Cox, Charles *8:* 20
Cox, David *56:* 37; *90:* 63; *119:* 38
Cox, Palmer *24:* 76, 77
Cox, Steve *140:* 96
Coxe, Molly *69:* 44
Coxon, Michele *158:* 80
Crabb, Gordon *70:* 39
Crabtree, Judith *98:* 42
Craft, Kinuko *22:* 182; *36:* 220; *53:* 122, 123, 148,149; *74:* 12; *81:* 129; *86:* 31; *89:* 139; *127:* 27, 28, 29; *132:* 142; *139:* 38
Craig, Daniel *177:* 67; *180:* 11; *185:* 203
Craig, David *136:* 198; *205:* 37
Craig, Helen *49:* 76; *62:* 70, 71, 72; *69:* 141; *94:* 42, 43, 44; *112:* 53; *135:* 101, 102
Crane, Alan H. *1:* 217
Crane, H.M. *13:* 111
Crane, Jack *43:* 183
Crane, Jordan *174:* 21
Crane, Walter *18:* 46, 47, 48, 49, 53, 54, 56, 57, 59, 60, 61; *22:* 128; *24:* 210, 217; *100:* 70, 71
Cravath, Lynne W. *98:* 45; *182:* 58, 59
Crawford, Denise *137:* 213
Crawford, Will *43:* 77
Credle, Ellis *1:* 69
Czernecki, Stefan *154:* 104; *178:* 68, 69
Crespi, Francesca *87:* 90
Cressy, Michael *124:* 55; *203:* 132
Crews, Donald *32:* 59, 60; *76:* 42, 43, 44
Crews, Nina *97:* 49
Crichlow, Ernest *74:* 88; *83:* 203
Croft, James *150:* 57
Crofut, Bob *80:* 87; *81:* 47
Crofut, Susan *23:* 61
Croll, Carolyn *80:* 137; *102:* 52
Cross, Peter *56:* 78; *63:* 60, 65
Crowe, Elizabeth *88:* 144
Crowell, Pers *3:* 125
Cruikshank, George *15:* 76, 83; *22:* 74, 75, 76, 77, 78, 79,80, 81, 82, 84, 137; *24:* 22, 23
Crump, Fred H. *11:* 62

Cruz, Ray *6:* 55; *70:* 234; *123:* 173; *172:* 192
Csatari, Joe *44:* 82; *55:* 152; *63:* 25, 28; *102:* 58
Cuetara, Mittie *158:* 85
Cuffari, Richard *4:* 75; *5:* 98; *6:* 56; *7:* 13,84, 153; *8:* 148, 155; *9:* 89; *11:* 19; *12:* 55, 96,114; *15:* 51, 202; *18:* 5; *20:* 139; *21:* 197; *22:* 14, 192; *23:* 15, 106; *25:* 97; *27:* 133; *28:* 196; *29:* 54; *30:* 85; *31:* 35; *36:* 101; *38:* 171; *42:* 97; *44:* 92, 192; *45:* 212, 213; *46:* 36, 198; *50:* 164; *54:* 80, 136, 137, 145; *56:* 17; *60:* 63; *66:* 49, 50; *70:* 41; *71:* 132; *77:* 157; *78:* 58, 149; *79:* 120; *85:* 2, 152
Cugat, Xavier *19:* 120
Cumings, Art *35:* 160
Cummings, Chris *29:* 167
Cummings, Michael *159:* 142
Cummings, Pat *42:* 61; *61:* 99; *69:* 205; *71:* 57,58; *78:* 24, 25; *93:* 75; *107:* 49, 50; *164:* 259; *203:* 45, 46
Cummings, Richard *24:* 119
Cunette, Lou *20:* 93; *22:* 125
Cunningham, Aline *25:* 180
Cunningham, David *11:* 13
Cunningham, Imogene *16:* 122, 127
Cunningham, Kelley *176:* 159
Cupples, Pat *107:* 12; *126:* 109; *182:* 13; *198:* 68
Curlee, Lynn *98:* 48; *141:* 39; *190:* 48
Currey, Anna *190:* 145; *202:* 130, 132
Curry, John Steuart *2:* 5; *19:* 84; *34:* 36; *144:* 126
Curry, Tom *127:* 131; *185:* 25, 26
Curtis, Bruce *23:* 96; *30:* 88; *36:* 22
Curtis, Neil *167:* 30
Curtis, Stacy *205:* 38
Cusack, Margaret *58:* 49, 50, 51
Cushman, Doug *65:* 57; *101:* 39, 40; *133:* 179; *157:* 45; *186:* 157
Cutting, Ann *196:* 194
Cyrus, Kurt *132:* 39; *179:* 36, 37
Czechowski, Alicia *95:* 21; *171:* 37
Czernecki, Stefan *117:* 173

D

Dabcovich, Lydia *25:* 105; *40:* 114; *99:* 75, 76
Dacey, Bob *82:* 175; *152:* 65
d'Achille, Gino *127:* 175, 176
Dailey, Don *78:* 197
Dain, Martin J. *35:* 75
Dale, Penny *127:* 224; *151:* 57; *160:* 89; *197:* 75
Dale, Rae *72:* 197
Daley, Joann *50:* 22
Dalton, Anne *40:* 62; *63:* 119
Daly, Deborah M. *74:* 213
Daly, Jim *103:* 60; *150:* 48
Daly, Jude *138:* 118, 119
Daly, Nicholas *37:* 53; *76:* 48, 49
Daly, Niki *107:* 15; *114:* 38, 39, 40; *164:* 86; *192:* 53; *198:* 26, 27
Daly, Paul *97:* 205
Dalziel, Brothers *33:* 113
D'Amato, Alex *9:* 48; *20:* 25
D'Amato, Janet *9:* 48; *20:* 25; *26:* 118
D'Amico, Steve *170:* 52
Danalis, Johnny *167:* 27
D'Andrea, Domenick *183:* 108
Daniel, Alan *23:* 59; *29:* 110; *76:* 50, 53, 55, 56; *153:* 76 *115:* 74; *134:* 70
Daniel, Lea *76:* 53, 55; *153:* 76
Daniel, Lewis C. *20:* 216
Daniels, Beau *73:* 4
Daniels, Steve *22:* 16
Daniels, Stewart *56:* 12
Dann, Bonnie *31:* 83
Dann, Penny *82:* 128
Danska, Herbert *24:* 219

Danyell, Alice 20: 27
Darley, F.O.C. 16: 145; 19: 79, 86, 88, 185; 21: 28,36; 35: 76, 77, 78, 79, 80, 81; YABC 2: 175
Darling, Lois 3: 59; 23: 30, 31
Darling, Louis 1: 40, 41; 2: 63; 3: 59; 23: 30,31; 43: 54, 57, 59; 121: 53
Darrow, David R. 84: 101
Darrow, Whitney, Jr. 13: 25; 38: 220, 221
Darwin, Beatrice 43: 54
Darwin, Len 24: 82
Dastolfo, Frank 33: 179
Dauber, Liz 1: 22; 3: 266; 30: 49
Daugherty, James 3: 66; 8: 178; 13: 27, 28, 161; 18: 101; 19: 72; 29: 108; 32: 156; 42: 84; YABC 1: 256; 2: 174
d'Aulaire, Edgar Parin 5: 51; 66: 53
d'Aulaire, Ingri Parin 5: 51; 66: 53
Davalos, Felipe 99: 197; 159: 66; 174: 163
Davenier, Christine 125: 88; 127: 32; 128: 152; 179: 39, 40
Davick, Linda 151: 124
David, Jacques-Louis 193: 22
David, Jonathan 19: 37
Davidson, Kevin 28: 154
Davidson, Raymond 32: 61
Davie, Helen K. 77: 48, 49
Davies, Andy Robert 205: 169
Davis, Allen 20: 11; 22: 45; 27: 222; 29: 157; 41: 99; 47: 99; 50: 84; 52: 105
Davis, Bette J. 15: 53; 23: 95
Davis, Dimitris 45: 95
Davis, Hendon 151: 122
Davis, Jack E. 145: 139; 175: 84, 85
Davis, Jim 32: 63, 64
Davis, Katie 152: 52, 53, 54
Davis, Lambert 110: 23, 24; 176: 58
Davis, Marguerite 31: 38; 34: 69, 70; 100: 34; YABC 1: 126, 230
Davis, Nelle 69: 191
Davis, Paul 78: 214
Davis, Rich 206: 38
Davis, Yvonne LeBrun 94: 144
Davisson, Virginia H. 44: 178
DaVolls, Andy 85: 53
Dawson, Diane 24: 127; 42: 126; 52: 130; 68: 104
Day, Alexandra 67: 59; 97: 54; 166: 65; 169: 40; 197: 50, 51, 52, 54
Day, Larry 169: 88; 185: 59
Day, Rob 94: 110; 127: 24; 197: 32
Dean, Bob 19: 211
Dean, David 192: 55
de Angeli, Marguerite 1: 77; 27: 62, 65, 66, 67, 69, 70, 72; 100: 75, 76; YABC 1: 166
DeArmond, Dale 70: 47
Deas, Michael 27: 219, 221; 30: 156; 67: 134; 72: 24; 75: 155; 84: 206; 88: 124
Deas, Rich 191: 87; 193: 10
deBarros, Jim 196: 60
Debon, Nicolas 151: 60; 177: 46
de Bosschere, Jean 19: 252; 21: 4; 186: 44, 45
De Bruyn, M(onica) G. 13: 30, 31
Decker, C.B. 172: 120
De Cuir, John F. 1: 28, 29
Deeter, Catherine 74: 110; 103: 150; 137: 50
Degen, Bruce 40: 227, 229; 57: 28, 29; 56: 156; 75: 229; 76: 19; 81: 36, 37; 92: 26; 93: 199; 97: 56, 58, 59; 124: 40; 147: 39, 40, 41; 168: 23; 205: 45, 46
De Grazia 14: 59; 39: 56, 57
DeGrazio, George 88: 40
deGroat, Diane 9: 39; 18: 7; 23: 123; 28: 200, 201; 31: 58, 59; 34: 151; 41: 152; 43: 88; 46: 40, 200; 49: 163; 50: 89; 52: 30, 34; 54: 43; 63: 5; 70: 136; 71: 99; 73: 117,156; 77: 34; 85: 48; 86: 201; 87: 142; 90: 72, 73, 143; 95: 182; 111: 123; 118: 160; 126: 8; 130: 130; 138: 93, 94; 169: 46, 47
de Groot, Lee 6: 21
Deines, Brian 110: 139

DeJohn, Marie 89: 78
Dekhteryov, B. 61: 158
de Kiefte, Kees 94: 107
Delacre, Lulu 36: 66; 156: 35; 202: 10, 53
Delaney, A. 21: 78
Delaney, Michael 180: 16
Delaney, Molly 80: 43
Delaney, Ned 28: 68; 56: 80; 102: 11
DeLange, Alex Pardo 179: 128
DeLapine, Jim 79: 21
De La Roche Saint Andre, Anne 75: 37
de Larrea, Victoria 6: 119, 204; 29: 103; 72: 203; 87: 199
Delessert, Étienne 7: 140; 46: 61, 62, 63, 65, 67, 68; 130: 38, 39, 40, 41, 42; 179: 46, 47, 48, 49; YABC 2: 209
Delezenne, Christine 186: 126
Del Negro, Janice 196: 161
DeLorenzo, Christopher 154: 149
Delulio, John 15: 54
DeLuna, Tony 88: 95
Demarest, Chris L. 45: 68, 69, 70; 73: 172, 173, 176; 78: 106; 82: 48, 49; 89: 212; 92: 86; 128: 57, 58; 175: 46, 48
De Mejo, Oscar 40: 67
De Muth, Roger 205: 184
Demi 11: 135; 15: 245; 66: 129, 130; 89: 216; 102: 66, 67, 68
Denetsosie, Hoke 13: 126; 82: 34
Denise, Christopher 147: 43, 44; 176: 101; 193: 35, 36, 37; 201: 37
Dennis, Morgan 18: 68, 69; 64: 89
Dennis, Wesley 2: 87; 3: 111; 11: 132; 18: 71, 72, 73, 74; 22: 9; 24: 196, 200; 46: 178; 69: 94, 96; 129: 62
Denos, Julia 202: 26
Denslow, W.W. 16: 84, 85, 86, 87; 18: 19, 20, 24; 29: 211; 100: 21
Denton, Kady MacDonald 110: 82; 130: 70; 181: 54, 55, 56; 192: 75
Denton, Terry 72: 163; 174: 26; 186: 52; 196: 83, 84
DePalma, Mary Newell 132: 114; 139: 75; 185: 30, 31; 186: 121
dePaola, Tomie 8: 95; 9: 93; 11: 69; 25: 103; 28: 157; 29: 80; 39: 52, 53; 40: 226; 46: 187; 59: 61, 62, 63, 64, 65, 66, 67, 68, 69, 71, 72, 74; 62: 19; 108: 63, 67, 68, 70; 155: 62, 64, 66; 180: 105; 200: 47, 48, 49, 50
Deraney, Michael J. 77: 35; 78: 148
deRosa, Dee 70: 48; 71: 210; 91: 78
Dervaux, Isabelle 111: 117
DeSaix, Deborah Durland 180: 15; 188: 24
De Saulles, Tony 119: 39
de Seve, Peter 146: 261; 207: 78
Deshaprabhu, Meera Dayal 86: 192
Desimini, Lisa 86: 68; 94: 47; 96: 7; 104: 107; 125: 194; 131: 180; 172: 56
de St. Menin, Charles 70: 17
Detmold, Edward J. 22: 104, 105, 106, 107; 35: 120; 64: 5; YABC 2: 203
Detrich, Susan 20: 133
Deutermann, Diana 77: 175
DeVelasco, Joseph E. 21: 51
de Veyrac, Robert YABC 2: 19
DeVille, Edward A. 4: 235
de Visser, John 55: 119
Devito, Bert 12: 164
Devlin, Harry 11: 74; 74: 63, 65; 136: 77, 78
Dewan, Ted 108: 73; 157: 55; 165: 129
Dewar, Nick 133: 122
Dewdney, Anna 184: 43, 44
Dewey, Ariane 7: 64; 33: 195; 35: 208; 68: 16,17; 75: 46; 93: 91; 94: 197; 109: 65, 66, 67; 125: 2, 3, 4, 5; 127: 188; 143: 25; 178: 17, 19, 74; 188: 166; 202: 164
Dewey, Jennifer (Owings) 58: 54; 64: 214; 65: 207; 88: 169; 103: 45
Dewey, Kenneth 39: 62; 51: 23; 56: 163
de Zanger, Arie 30: 40
Diakité, Baba Wagué 174: 28

Diamond, Donna 21: 200; 23: 63; 26: 142; 35: 83, 84, 85, 86, 87, 88, 89; 38: 78; 40: 147; 44: 152; 50: 144; 53: 126; 69: 46, 47, 48, 201; 71: 133; 123: 19
Dias, Ron 71: 67
Diaz, David 80: 213; 96: 83, 84; 108: 228; 110: 29; 149: 106; 150: 63; 179: 160; 184: 95, 97; 189: 51, 52, 53
Dibley, Glin 138: 83; 141: 128
DiCesare, Joe 70: 38; 71: 63, 106; 79: 214; 93: 147; 116: 217; 143: 111; 166: 57
Dick, John Henry 8: 181
Dickens, Frank 34: 131
Dickey, Robert L. 15: 279
Dickson, Mora 84: 21
Didier, Sam 166: 114
Dietz, James 128: 223; 193: 136
di Fate, Vincent 37: 70; 90: 11; 93: 60; 109: 219, 220
Di Fiori, Lawrence 10: 51; 12: 190; 27: 97; 40: 219; 93: 57; 130: 45
Digby, Desmond 97: 180
Dignan, James 196: 143
Di Grazia, Thomas 32: 66; 35: 241
Dillard, Annie 10: 32
Dillard, Sarah 136: 186
Dillon, Corinne B. 1: 139
Dillon, Diane 4: 104, 167; 6: 23; 13: 29; 15: 99; 26: 148; 27: 136, 201; 51: 29, 48, 51, 52, 53, 54,55, 56, 57, 58, 59, 60, 61, 62; 54: 155; 56: 69; 58: 127,128; 61: 95; 62: 27; 64: 46; 68: 3; 69: 209; 74: 89; 79: 92; 86: 89; 92: 28, 177; 93: 7, 210; 94: 239, 240; 97: 167; 106: 58, 59,61, 64; 107: 3; 139: 246; 167: 77; 189: 202; 191: 191; 194: 45, 46, 48, 49
Dillon, Leo 4: 104, 167; 6: 23; 13: 29; 15: 99; 26: 148; 27: 136, 201; 51: 29, 48, 51, 52, 53, 54,55, 56, 57, 58, 59, 60, 61, 62; 54: 155; 56: 69; 58: 127,128; 61: 95; 62: 27; 64: 46; 68: 3; 69: 209; 74: 89; 79: 92; 86: 89; 92: 28, 177; 93: 7, 210; 94: 239, 240; 97: 167; 106: 58, 59,61, 64; 107: 3; 139: 246; 167: 77; 189: 202; 191: 191; 194: 45, 46, 48, 49
Dillon, Sharon Saseen 59: 179, 188
DiMaccio, Gerald 121: 80
DiMaggio, Joe 36: 22
DiMassi, Gina 169: 17
Dinan, Carol 25: 169; 59: 75
Dines, Glen 7: 66, 67
Dinesen, Thomas 44: 37
Dinh, Pham Viet 167: 184
Dinnerstein, Harvey 42: 63, 64, 65, 66, 67, 68; 50: 146
Dinsdale, Mary 10: 65; 11: 171
Dinyer, Eric 86: 148; 109: 163; 110: 239; 124: 11; 150: 69; 170: 4; 171: 30
Dion, Nathalie 170: 124
DiRocco, Carl 181: 23
DiSalvo-Ryan, DyAnne 59: 77; 62: 185; 117: 46; 144: 64; 150: 153; 186: 162
Disney, Walt 28: 71, 72, 73, 76, 77, 78, 79, 80, 81, 87, 88, 89,90, 91, 94
DiTerlizzi, Tony 105: 7; 147: 22; 154: 31, 32, 33
Divito, Anna 83: 159
Dixon, Don 74: 17; 109: 196
Dixon, Larry 127: 125
Dixon, Maynard 20: 165
Doares, Robert G. 20: 39
Dob, Bob 205: 14
Dobias, Frank 22: 162
Dobrin, Arnold 4: 68
Dobson, Steven Gaston 102: 103
Dockray, Tracy 139: 77
Docktor, Irv 43: 70
Dodd, Ed 4: 69
Dodd, Emma 203: 57
Dodd, Julie 74: 73
Dodd, Lynley 35: 92; 86: 71; 132: 45, 46, 47

Dodge, Bill 96: 36; 118: 7, 8, 9; 133: 135
Dodgson, Charles L. 20: 148; 33: 146; YABC 2: 98
Dodson, Bert 9: 138; 14: 195; 42: 55; 54: 8; 60: 49; 101: 125
Dodson, Liz Brenner 105: 117; 111: 15
Dohanos, Stevan 16: 10
Dolce, J. Ellen 74: 147; 75: 41
Dolch, Marguerite P. 50: 64
Dolesch, Susanne 34: 49
Dollar, Diane 57: 32
Dolobowsky, Mena 81: 54
Dolson, Hildegarde 5: 57
Domanska, Janina 6: 66, 67; YABC 1: 166
Domi 134: 113
Dominguez, El 53: 94
Domjan, Joseph 25: 93
Domm, Jeffrey C. 84: 69; 135: 70
Donahey, William 68: 209
Donahue, Dorothy 76: 170
Donahue, Vic 2: 93; 3: 190; 9: 44
Donald, Elizabeth 4: 18
Donalty, Alison 149: 195, 196, 197
Donato 85: 59; 149: 204; 191: 19
Donato, Michael A. 200: 143
Doney, Todd L.W. 87: 12; 93: 112; 98: 135; 101: 57; 104: 40; 118: 163; 135: 162, 163; 151: 18
Donna, Natalie 9: 52
Donohue, Dorothy 95: 2; 132: 30; 176: 54, 55; 178: 77, 78, 79
Dooling, Michael 82: 19; 105: 55; 106: 224; 125: 135; 171: 46; 172: 12; 176: 120; 197: 89
Doran, Ben-Ami 128: 189
Dore, Gustave 18: 169, 172, 175; 19: 93, 94, 95, 96, 97, 98, 99, 100, 101, 102, 103, 104, 105; 23: 188; 25: 197, 199
Doremus, Robert 6: 62; 13: 90; 30: 95, 96, 97; 38: 97
Dorfman, Ronald 11: 128
Doriau 86: 59; 91: 152
Dorman, Brandon 197: 35; 204: 6
Dormer, Frank W. 200: 55
Dorros, Arthur 78: 42, 43; 91: 28
Doruyter, Karel 165: 105
dos Santos, Joyce Audy 57: 187, 189
Doty, Roy 28: 98; 31: 32; 32: 224; 46: 157; 82: 71; 142: 7
Doucet, Bob 132: 238; 169: 159
Dougherty, Charles 16: 204; 18: 74
Doughty, Rebecca 177: 174
Doughty, Thomas 118: 31; 140: 60
Douglas, Aaron 31: 103
Douglas, Carole Nelson 73: 48
Douglas, Goray 13: 151
Dow, Brian 150: 92
Dowd, Jason 132: 51, 52; 164: 244
Dowd, Vic 3: 244; 10: 97
Dowden, Anne Ophelia 7: 70, 71; 13: 120
Dowdy, Mrs. Regera 29: 100
Downard, Barry 202: 32
Downes, Belinda 180: 29
Downing, Julie 60: 140; 81: 50; 86: 200; 99: 129
Doyle, Janet 56: 31
Doyle, Richard 21: 31, 32, 33; 23: 231; 24: 177; 31: 87
Draper, Angie 43: 84
Drath, Bill 26: 34
Drawson, Blair 17: 53; 126: 65
Dray, Matt 177: 47
Drescher, Henrik 105: 60, 62, 63; 172: 72
Drescher, Joan 30: 100, 101; 35: 245; 52: 168; 137: 52
Dressell, Peggy 186: 41
Drew, Janet 201: 177
Drew, Patricia 15: 100
Dronzek, Laura 199: 28, 29; 207: 69
Drummond, V.H. 6: 70
Drury, Christian Potter 105: 97; 186: 224

Dubanevich, Arlene 56: 44
Dubin, Jill 205: 56
Dubois, Claude K. 196: 2
Dubois, Gerard 182: 9
DuBurke, Randy 187: 89
Ducak, Danilo 99: 130; 108: 214
Duchesne, Janet 6: 162; 79: 8
Duda, Jana 102: 155
Dudash, Michael 32: 122; 77: 134; 82: 149
Duer, Douglas 34: 177
Duewell, Kristina 195: 76
Duffy, Daniel Mark 76: 37; 101: 196; 108: 147, 148
Duffy, Joseph 38: 203
Duffy, Pat 28: 153
Dugan, Karen 181: 26; 202: 35
Dugin, Andrej 77: 60
Dugina, Olga 77: 60
Duke, Chris 8: 195; 139: 164
Duke, Kate 87: 186; 90: 78, 79, 80, 81; 192: 21, 59, 60, 61, 63
Duke, Marion 165: 87
Dulac, Edmund 19: 108, 109, 110, 111, 112, 113, 114, 115, 117; 23: 187; 25: 152; YABC 1: 37; 2: 147
Dulac, Jean 13: 64
Dumas, Philippe 52: 36, 37, 38, 39, 40, 41, 42, 43, 45; 119: 40, 41, 42
Dunaway, Nancy 108: 161
Dunbar, James 76: 63
Dunbar, Polly 181: 60, 61
Duncan, Beverly 72: 92
Duncan, John 116: 94
Dunn, H.T. 62: 196
Dunn, Harvey 34: 78, 79, 80, 81
Dunn, Iris 5: 175
Dunn, Phoebe 5: 175
Dunne, Jeanette 72: 57, 173, 222
Dunnick, Regan 176: 51; 178: 83, 84
Dunnington, Tom 3: 36; 18: 281; 25: 61; 31: 159; 35: 168; 48: 195; 79: 144; 82: 230
Dunn-Ramsey, Marcy 117: 131
Dunrea, Olivier 59: 81; 118: 53, 54; 124: 43
Duntze, Dorothee 88: 28; 160: 76
Dupasquier, Philippe 86: 75; 104: 76; 151: 63
duPont, Lindsay Harper 207: 39
DuQuette, Keith 90: 83; 155: 73, 74
Durand, Delphine 200: 56
Durham, Sarah 192: 248
Duroussy, Nathalie 146: 150
Durrell, Julie 82: 62; 94: 62
Dutz 6: 59
Duvoisin, Roger 2: 95; 6: 76, 77; 7: 197; 28: 125; 30: 101, 102, 103, 104, 105, 107; 47: 205; 84: 254
Dyer, Dale 141: 71
Dyer, Jane 75: 219; 129: 28; 147: 49, 50, 51; 168: 121; 190: 4; 191: 57, 59, 60; 203: 4
Dypold, Pat 15: 37

E

E.V.B.
    See Boyle, Eleanor Vere (Gordon)
Eachus, Jennifer 29: 74; 82: 201; 164: 153
Eadie, Bob 63: 36
Eagle, Bruce 95: 119
Eagle, Ellen 82: 121; 89: 3
Eagle, Jeremy 141: 71
Eagle, Michael 11: 86; 20: 9; 23: 18; 27: 122; 28: 57; 34: 201; 44: 189; 73: 9; 78: 235; 85: 43
Earl-Bridges, Michele 159: 128
Earle, Edwin 56: 27
Earle, Olive L. 7: 75
Earle, Vana 27: 99
Earley, Lori 132: 2; 186: 4; 195: 8
Early, Margaret 72: 59
East, Stella 131: 223

Eastman, P.D. 33: 57
Easton, Reginald 29: 181
Eaton, Tom 4: 62; 6: 64; 22: 99; 24: 124
Ebbeler, Jeffrey 193: 62; 206: 45
Ebel, Alex 11: 89
Eberbach, Andrea 192: 115
Ebert, Len 9: 191; 44: 47
Echevarria, Abe 37: 69
Echo Hawk, Bunky 187: 192
Eckersley, Maureen 48: 62
Eckert, Horst 72: 62
Ede, Janina 33: 59
Edens, Cooper 49: 81, 82, 83, 84, 85; 112: 58
Edens, John 109: 115
Edgar, Sarah E. 41: 97
Edgerton, Perky 195: 144
Edliq, Emily S. 131: 107
Edrien 11: 53
Edwards, Freya 45: 102
Edwards, George Wharton 31: 155
Edwards, Gunvor 2: 71; 25: 47; 32: 71; 54: 106
Edwards, Jeanne 29: 257
Edwards, Linda Strauss 21: 134; 39: 123; 49: 88, 89
Edwards, Michelle 152: 62, 63
Edwards, Wallace 170: 55
Egan, Tim 155: 76, 77, 78
Egge, David 102: 71
Eggenhofer, Nicholas 2: 81
Eggleton, Bob 74: 40; 81: 190, 191; 105: 6; 121: 183; 149: 203; 166: 215
Egielski, Richard 11: 90; 16: 208; 33: 236; 38: 35; 49: 91, 92, 93, 95, 212, 213, 214, 216; 79: 122; 106: 67, 68, 69; 134: 135; 144: 244; 163: 82, 84; 207: 125
Ehlert, Lois 35: 97; 69: 51; 112: 7; 113: 208; 128: 63, 64, 65; 172: 77, 79, 80
Ehrlich, Bettina 1: 83
Eitan, Ora 160: 165
Eichenberg, Fritz 1: 79; 9: 54; 19: 248; 23: 170; 24: 200; 26: 208; 50: 67, 68, 69, 70, 71, 72, 73,74, 75, 77, 79, 80, 81; 60: 165; 100: 137; YABC 1: 104, 105; 2: 213
Einsel, Naiad 10: 35; 29: 136
Einsel, Walter 10: 37
Einzig, Susan 3: 77; 43: 78; 67: 155; 129: 154
Eisner, Will 165: 82, 83
Eitzen, Allan 9: 56; 12: 212; 14: 226; 21: 194; 38: 162; 76: 218
Eldridge, H. 54: 109
Eldridge, Harold 43: 83
Elgaard, Greta 19: 241
Elgin, Kathleen 9: 188; 39: 69
Ellacott, S.E. 19: 118
Elliot, David 192: 26
Elliott, Mark 93: 69; 105: 108; 107: 123; 140: 53; 165: 189; 173: 67; 195: 95; 203: 67
Elliott, Sarah M. 14: 58
Ellis, Dianne 130: 208
Ellis, Jan Davey 88: 50; 115: 80
Ellis, Richard 130: 47, 48
Ellison, Chris 196: 66; 199: 131; 207: 193
Ellison, Pauline 55: 21
Elmer, Richard 78: 5
Elmore, Larry 90: 8
Elschner, Géraldine 183: 38
Elwell, Peter 195: 150
Elwell, Tristan 110: 39; 121: 182; 127: 46; 137: 144; 141: 173; 151: 236; 158: 264; 167: 119, 120, 121; 169: 20; 190: 12; 202: 16
Elzbieta 88: 80, 81
Emberley, Ed 8: 53; 70: 53, 54; 146: 65, 69, 70
Emberley, Michael 34: 83; 80: 72; 119: 47, 48; 147: 100; 158: 115; 189: 62, 64; 203: 87, 89
Emerling, Dorothy 104: 27
Emery, Leslie 49: 187
Emmett, Bruce 49: 147; 80: 175; 101: 206

Emry-Perrott, Jennifer *61:* 57
Emshwiller, Ed *174:* 45
Endle, Kate *191:* 167; *207:* 41
Engel, Diana *70:* 57
Engle, Mort *38:* 64
Englebert, Victor *8:* 54
English, Mark *101:* 207
Enik, Ted *142:* 39
Enos, Randall *20:* 183
Enright, Maginel Wright *19:* 240, 243; *39:* 31, 35, 36
Enrique, Romeo *34:* 135
Ensor, Barbara *180:* 30
Epstein, Stephen *50:* 142, 148
Erdogan, Buket *174:* 179
Erdrich, Louise *141:* 62
Erhard, Walter *1:* 152
Erickson, Jim *196:* 190
Erickson, Phoebe *11:* 83; *59:* 85
Erikson, Mel *31:* 69
Eriksson, Eva *63:* 88, 90, 92, 93; *203:* 99; *207:* 44
Ering, Timothy Basil *131:* 100; *176:* 63, 64; *202:* 29; *204:* 8
Erlbruch, Wolf *181:* 66
Ernst, Lisa Campbell *47:* 147; *95:* 47; *154:* 46, 47, 48; *164:* 88
Esco, Jo *61:* 103
Escourido, Joseph *4:* 81
Escrivá, Viví *119:* 51; *181:* 36
Essakalli, Julie Klear *200:* 58
Este, Kirk *33:* 111
Estep, David *73:* 57
Estes, Eleanor *91:* 66
Estoril, Jean *32:* 27
Estrada, Pau *74:* 76
Estrada, Ric *5:* 52, 146; *13:* 174
Etchemendy, Teje *38:* 68
Etheredges, the *73:* 12
Etienne, Kirk-Albert *145:* 184
Ets, Marie Hall *2:* 102
Ettlinger, Doris *171:* 98; *186:* 106; *197:* 126
Eulalie *YABC 2:* 315
Evans, Greg *73:* 54, 55, 56; *143:* 40, 41
Evans, Katherine *5:* 64
Evans, Leslie *144:* 227; *207:* 57
Evans, Shane W. *159:* 142; *160:* 190; *168:* 39; *188:* 88; *189:* 66, 67, 68
Everitt, Betsy *151:* 110
Ewart, Claire *76:* 69; *145:* 59, 60
Ewing, Carolyn *66:* 143; *79:* 52
Ewing, Juliana Horatia *16:* 92
Eyolfson, Norman *98:* 154

F

Fabian, Limbert *136:* 114
Facklam, Paul *132:* 62
Falconer, Ian *125:* 66; *179:* 59
Falconer, Pearl *34:* 23
Falkenstern, Lisa *70:* 34; *76:* 133; *78:* 171; *127:* 16; *191:* 151
Falls, C.B. *1:* 19; *38:* 71, 72, 73, 74
Falter, John *40:* 169, 170
Falwell, Cathryn *118:* 77; *137:* 185; *196:* 71, 72
Fancher, Lou *138:* 219; *141:* 64; *144:* 199; *177:* 51
Fanelli, Sara *89:* 63; *126:* 69
Faria, Rosana *150:* 143
Faricy, Patrick *185:* 182
Farooqi, Musharraf Ali *207:* 46
Farmer, Andrew *49:* 102
Farmer, Peter *24:* 108; *38:* 75
Farnsworth, Bill *93:* 189; *116:* 147; *124:* 8; *135:* 52; *146:* 242, 243, 244; *182:* 176; *186:* 31, 83, 84, 85; *191:* 197
Farquharson, Alexander *46:* 75
Farrell, David *40:* 135

Farrell, Russell *196:* 38
Farris, David *74:* 42
Fasolino, Teresa *118:* 145
Fatigati, Evelyn *24:* 112
Fatus, Sophie *182:* 74; *190:* 218
Faul-Jansen, Regina *22:* 117
Faulkner, Jack *6:* 169
Faulkner, Matt *161:* 174; *167:* 75
Fava, Rita *2:* 29
Fax, Elton C. *1:* 101; *4:* 2; *12:* 77; *25:* 107
Fay *43:* 93
Fearnley, Jan *153:* 82, 83; *205:* 63, 64, 65
Fearrington, Ann *146:* 80
Federspiel, Marian *33:* 51
Fedorov, Nickolai Ivanovich *110:* 102
Feelings, Tom *5:* 22; *8:* 56; *12:* 153; *16:* 105; *30:* 196; *49:* 37; *61:* 101; *69:* 56, 57; *93:* 74; *105:* 88
Fehr, Terrence *21:* 87
Feiffer, Jules *3:* 91; *8:* 58; *61:* 66, 67, 70, 74, 76, 77, 78; *111:* 47, 48, 49, 50; *132:* 122; *157:* 62; *201:* 48, 49, 50
Feigeles, Neil *41:* 242
Feldman, Elyse *86:* 7
Feller, Gene *33:* 130
Fellows, Muriel H. *10:* 42
Felstead, Cathie *116:* 85
Felts, Shirley *33:* 71; *48:* 59
Fennell, Tracy *171:* 69
Fennelli, Maureen *38:* 181
Fenton, Carroll Lane *5:* 66; *21:* 39
Fenton, Mildred Adams *5:* 66; *21:* 39
Ferguson, Peter *177:* 30, 31; *181:* 154; *197:* 4; *199:* 40
Ferguson, Walter W. *34:* 86
Fernandes, Eugenie *77:* 67; *205:* 68
Fernandes, Stanislaw *70:* 28
Fernandez, Fernando *77:* 57
Fernandez, Laura *77:* 153; *101:* 117; *131:* 222; *170:* 119; *175:* 182
Ferrari, Alex *188:* 121
Ferrington, Susan *172:* 22
Fetz, Ingrid *11:* 67; *12:* 52; *16:* 205; *17:* 59; *29:* 105; *30:* 108, 109; *32:* 149; *43:* 142; *56:* 29; *60:* 34; *85:* 48; *87:* 146
Fiammenghi, Gioia *9:* 66; *11:* 44; *12:* 206; *13:* 57, 59; *52:* 126, 129; *66:* 64; *85:* 83; *91:* 161; *166:* 169
Fiedler, Joseph Daniel *96:* 42; *113:* 173; *129:* 164; *146:* 17; *159:* 68; *162:* 104
Field, Rachel *15:* 113
Fielding, David *70:* 124
Fieser, Stephen *152:* 36
Fine, Howard *145:* 159; *159:* 64; *165:* 134; *174:* 129; *181:* 68
Fine, Peter K. *43:* 210
Finger, Helen *42:* 81
Fink, Sam *18:* 119
Finlay, Winifred *23:* 72
Finney, Pat *79:* 215
Fiore, Peter *99:* 196; *125:* 139; *144:* 225; *160:* 169; *180:* 72
Fiorentino, Al *3:* 240
Firehammer, Karla *174:* 202
Firmin, Charlotte *29:* 75; *48:* 70
Firmin, Peter *58:* 63, 64, 65, 67, 68, 70, 71
Firth, Barbara *81:* 208; *127:* 218; *179:* 62
Fischel, Lillian *40:* 204
Fischer, Hans *25:* 202
Fischer, Scott *207:* 37
Fischer-Nagel, Andreas *56:* 50
Fischer-Nagel, Heiderose *56:* 50
Fisher, Carolyn *154:* 50
Fisher, Chris *79:* 62; *158:* 248; *188:* 195
Fisher, Cynthia *117:* 45; *137:* 118; *195:* 40
Fisher, Jeffrey *142:* 80
Fisher, Leonard Everett *3:* 6; *4:* 72, 86; *6:* 197; *9:* 59; *16:* 151, 153; *23:* 44; *27:* 134; *29:* 26; *34:* 87, 89, 90, 91, 93, 94, 95, 96; *40:* 206; *50:* 150; *60:* 158; *73:* 68, 70, 71, 72, 73; *176:* 71, 72, 73; *YABC 2:* 169

Fisher, Lois *20:* 62; *21:* 7
Fisher, Valorie *177:* 55
Fisk, Nicholas *25:* 112
Fitschen, Marilyn *2:* 20, 21; *20:* 48
Fitz-Maurice, Jeff *175:* 2
Fitzgerald, F.A. *15:* 116; *25:* 86, 87
Fitzgerald, Joanne *157:* 153, 154; *198:* 34, 35
Fitzgerald, Royce *205:* 5
Fitzhugh, Louise *1:* 94; *9:* 163; *45:* 75, 78
Fitzhugh, Susie *11:* 117
Fitzpatrick, Jim *109:* 130
Fitzpatrick, Marie-Louise *125:* 69, 70; *189:* 72, 73
Fitzsimmons, Arthur *14:* 128
Fix, Philippe *26:* 102
Flack, Marjorie *21:* 67; *100:* 93; *YABC 2:* 122
Flagg, James Montgomery *17:* 227
Flavin, Teresa *132:* 115; *186:* 119
Flax, Zeona *2:* 245
Fleetwood, Tony *171:* 51
Fleishman, Seymour *14:* 232; *24:* 87
Fleming, Denise *71:* 179; *81:* 58; *126:* 71, 72, 73; *173:* 52, 53
Fleming, Guy *18:* 41
Flesher, Vivienne *85:* 55
Fletcher, Claire *80:* 106; *157:* 159
Flint, Russ *74:* 80
Floate, Helen *111:* 163
Floca, Brian *155:* 88, 89; *190:* 10, 66, 67
Floethe, Richard *3:* 131; *4:* 90
Floherty, John J., Jr. *5:* 68
Flook, Helen *160:* 81
Flora, James *1:* 96; *30:* 111, 112
Florczak, Robert *166:* 51
Florian, Douglas *19:* 122; *83:* 64, 65; *125:* 71, 72, 74, 76; *128:* 130; *177:* 58, 60
Flory, Jane *22:* 111
Flower, Renee *125:* 109
Floyd, Gareth *1:* 74; *17:* 245; *48:* 63; *62:* 35,36, 37, 39, 40, 41; *74:* 245; *79:* 56
Fluchere, Henri A. *40:* 79
Flynn, Alice *183:* 2
Flynn, Barbara *7:* 31; *9:* 70
Fogarty, Thomas *15:* 89
Foley, Greg *190:* 69
Folger, Joseph *9:* 100
Folkard, Charles *22:* 132; *29:* 128, 257, 258
Foott, Jeff *42:* 202
Forberg, Ati *12:* 71, 205; *14:* 1; *22:* 113; *26:* 22; *48:* 64, 65
Ford, George *24:* 120; *31:* 70, 177; *58:* 126; *81:* 103; *107:* 91; *136:* 100; *194:* 47
Ford, Gilbert *199:* 10
Ford, H.J. *16:* 185, 186
Ford, Jason *174:* 119
Ford, Pamela Baldwin *27:* 104
Fordham, John *168:* 160, 161
Foreman, Michael *2:* 110, 111; *67:* 99; *73:* 78, 79, 80,81, 82; *93:* 146; *135:* 55, 56, 57; *184:* 58, 59
Forrester, Victoria *40:* 83
Forsey, Chris *140:* 210
Fortnum, Peggy *6:* 29; *20:* 179; *24:* 211; *26:* 76, 77, 78; *39:* 78; *58:* 19, 21, 23, 27; *YABC 1:* 148
Fortune, Eric *191:* 52
Foster, Brad W. *34:* 99
Foster, Genevieve *2:* 112
Foster, Gerald L. *7:* 78; *198:* 40
Foster, Jon *146:* 18; *198:* 7
Foster, Laura Louise *6:* 79
Foster, Marian Curtis *23:* 74; *40:* 42
Foster, Sally *58:* 73, 74
Foucher, Adele *47:* 118
Foust, Mitch *168:* 50
Fowler, Jim *184:* 190
Fowler, Mel *36:* 127
Fowler, Richard *87:* 219
Fowles, Shelley *165:* 127; *205:* 72
Fox, Charles Phillip *12:* 84
Fox, Christyan *188:* 36

Fox, Jim 6: 187
Fox-Davies, Sarah 76: 150; 182: 63; 199: 42, 43
Frace, Charles 15: 118
Frailey, Joy 72: 108
Frame, Paul 2: 45, 145; 9: 153; 10: 124; 21: 71; 23: 62; 24: 123; 27: 106; 31: 48; 32: 159; 34: 195; 38: 136; 42: 55; 44: 139; 60: 39, 40, 41, 42, 43, 44, 46; 73: 183
Frampton, David 85: 72; 102: 33; 139: 182; 152: 37; 189: 171
Francis, Guy 198: 164
Francois, Andre 25: 117
Francoise
    See Seignobosc, Francoise
Frank, Lola Edick 2: 199
Frank, Mary 4: 54; 34: 100
Franke, Phil 45: 91
Frankel, Alona 66: 70
Frankel, Julie 40: 84, 85, 202
Frankenberg, Robert 22: 116; 30: 50; 38: 92, 94, 95; 68: 111
Frankfeldt, Gwen 84: 223; 110: 92
Frankland, David 169: 137; 182: 164; 201: 159
Franklin, Ashton 165: 144
Franklin, John 24: 22
Franson, Leanne R. 111: 57, 58; 151: 7
Frascino, Edward 9: 133; 29: 229; 33: 190; 48: 80, 81, 82, 83, 84, 85, 86
Frasconi, Antonio 6: 80; 27: 208; 53: 41, 43, 45, 47,48; 68: 145; 73: 226; 131: 68
Fraser, Betty 2: 212; 6: 185; 8: 103; 31: 72,73; 43: 136; 111: 76
Fraser, Eric 38: 78; 41: 149, 151
Fraser, F.A. 22: 234
Fraser, James 171: 68
Fraser, Mary Ann 137: 63
Frasier, Debra 69: 60; 112: 67; 182: 81, 82, 83
Fraustino, Lisa Rowe 146: 87
Frazee, Marla 72: 98; 105: 79, 80; 151: 67, 68; 164: 165; 171: 190, 191; 187: 53, 54,55, 56, 143
Frazetta, Frank 41: 72; 58: 77, 78, 79, 80, 81, 82, 83
Frazier, Craig 177: 63
Freas, John 25: 207
Fredrickson, Mark 103: 33
Freeland, Michael J. 118: 115
Freeman, Don 2: 15; 13: 249; 17: 62, 63, 65, 67, 68; 18: 243; 20: 195; 23: 213, 217; 32: 155; 55: 129
Freeman, Irving 67: 150
Freeman, Laura 144: 111; 200: 62, 63
Freeman, Pietri 140: 223
Freeman, Tom 167: 118
Freeman, Tor 164: 93
Fregosi, Claudia 24: 117
Fremaux, Charlotte Murray 138: 29; 141: 95
French, Fiona 6: 82, 83; 75: 61; 109: 170; 132: 79, 80, 81, 82
French, Martin 163: 4
Frendak, Rodney 126: 97, 98
Freschet, Gina 175: 73
Freynet, Gilbert 72: 221
Fried, Janice 202: 121
Friedman, Judith 43: 197; 131: 221
Friedman, Marvin 19: 59; 42: 86
Frinta, Dagmar 36: 42
Frith, Michael K. 15: 138; 18: 120
Fritz, Ronald 46: 73; 82: 124
Fromm, Lilo 29: 85; 40: 197
Frost, A.B. 17: 6, 7; 19: 123, 124, 125, 126, 127, 128, 129,130; 100: 119; YABC 1: 156, 157, 160; 2: 107
Frost, Helen 183: 51
Frost, Kristi 118: 113
Frost, Michael 151: 209
Froud, Brian 150: 82, 83
Froud, Wendy 151: 237
Fry, Guy 2: 224

Fry, Rosalie 3: 72; YABC 2: 180, 181
Fry, Rosalind 21: 153, 168
Fryer, Elmer 34: 115
Fuchs, Bernie 110: 10; 162: 46
Fuchs, Erich 6: 84
Fuchshuber, Annegert 43: 96
Fufuka, Mahiri 32: 146
Fuge, Charles 144: 91, 93
Fujikawa, Gyo 39: 75, 76; 76: 72, 73, 74
Fulford, Deborah 23: 159
Fuller, Margaret 25: 189
Fulweiler, John 93: 99
Funai, Mamoru 38: 105
Funfhausen, Christian 196: 30
Funk, Tom 7: 17, 99
Furchgott, Terry 29: 86
Furness, William Henry, Jr. 94: 18
Furukawa, Mel 25: 42
Fusari, Erika 164: 227

G

Gaadt, David 78: 212; 121: 166; 201: 171
Gaadt, George 71: 9
Gaber, Susan 99: 33; 115: 57, 58; 164: 195; 169: 61, 62, 63; 185: 50, 51; 188: 124
Gaberell, J. 19: 236
Gable, Brian 195: 68, 69
Gabler, Mirko 99: 71; 195: 32
Gackenbach, Dick 19: 168; 41: 81; 48: 89, 90, 91, 92,93, 94; 54: 105; 79: 75, 76, 77
Gad, Victor 87: 161
Gaetano, Nicholas 23: 209
Gaffney-Kessell, Walter 94: 219; 174: 188
Gag, Flavia 17: 49, 52
Gag, Wanda 100: 101, 102; YABC 1: 135, 137, 138, 141, 143
Gagnon, Cecile 11: 77; 58: 87
Gaillard, Jason 200: 69; 204: 74
Gal, Laszlo 14: 127; 52: 54, 55, 56; 65: 142; 68: 150; 81: 185; 96: 104, 105
Galazinski, Tom 55: 13
Galbraith, Ben 200: 70
Galdone, Paul 1: 156, 181, 206; 2: 40, 241; 3: 42,144; 4: 141; 10: 109, 158; 11: 21; 12: 118, 210; 14: 16, 36, 37; 17: 70, 71, 72, 73, 74; 18: 111, 230; 19: 183; 21: 154; 22: 150, 245; 33: 126; 39: 136, 137; 42: 57; 51: 169; 55: 110; 66: 80, 82, 139; 72: 73; 100: 84
Gale, Cathy 140: 22; 143: 52
Gall, Chris 176: 79, 80
Gallagher, Jack 187: 100
Gallagher, S. Saelig 105: 154; 198: 91
Gallagher, Sears 20: 112Gallagher-Cole, Mernie 206: 56
Galloway, Ewing 51: 154
Galouchka, Annouchka Gravel 95: 55; 182: 40
Galster, Robert 1: 66
Galsworthy, Gay John 35: 232
Galvez, Daniel 125: 182
Gamble, Kim 112: 64, 65; 124: 77; 183: 40, 42, 43, 56, 57; 187: 170
Gammell, Stephen 7: 48; 13: 149; 29: 82; 33: 209; 41: 88; 50: 185, 186, 187; 53: 51, 52, 53, 54, 55, 56,57, 58; 54: 24, 25; 56: 147, 148, 150; 57: 27, 66; 81: 62, 63; 87: 88; 89: 10; 106: 223; 126: 2; 128: 71, 73, 74, 77; 154: 34
Gamper, Ruth 84: 198
Gampert, John 58: 94
Ganly, Helen 56: 56
Gannett, Ruth Chrisman 3: 74; 18: 254; 33: 77, 78
Gannon, Ned 205: 6
Gantschev, Ivan 45: 32
Garafano, Marie 73: 33
Garbot, Dave 131: 106
Garbutt, Bernard 23: 68

Garcia 37: 71
Garcia, Manuel 74: 145
Garcia-Franco, Rebecca 173: 46
Gardiner, Lindsey 178: 128; 186: 137
Gardner, Earle 45: 167
Gardner, Joan 40: 87
Gardner, Joel 40: 87, 92
Gardner, John 40: 87
Gardner, Lucy 40: 87
Gardner, Richard
    See Cummings, Richard
Gardner, Sally 171: 177; 177: 66, 68
Gargiulo, Frank 84: 158
Garland, Michael 36: 29; 38: 83; 44: 168; 48: 78, 221, 222; 49: 161; 60: 139; 71: 6, 11; 72: 229; 74: 142; 89: 187; 93: 183; 104: 110; 131: 55; 139: 209; 168: 56
Garland, Peggy 60: 139
Garland, Sarah 62: 45; 135: 67, 68; 171: 118
Garn, Aimee 75: 47
Garner, Joan 128: 170
Garneray, Ambroise Louis 59: 140
Garnett, Eve 3: 75
Garnett, Gary 39: 184
Garns, Allen 80: 125; 84: 39; 165: 231
Garófoli, Viviana 186: 123
Garraty, Gail 4: 142; 52: 106
Garrett, Agnes 46: 110; 47: 157
Garrett, Edmund H. 20: 29
Garrett, Tom 107: 194
Garrick, Jacqueline 67: 42, 43; 77: 94
Garrison, Barbara 19: 133; 104: 146; 109: 87
Garro, Mark 108: 131; 128: 210
Garvey, Robert 98: 222
Garza, Carmen Lomas 80: 211; 182: 86
Garza, Xavier 184: 64
Gates, Frieda 26: 80
Gaughan, Jack 26: 79; 43: 185
Gaver, Becky 20: 61
Gawing, Toby 72: 52
Gay, Marie-Louise 68: 76, 77, 78; 102: 136; 126: 76, 78, 81, 83; 127: 55, 56; 179: 70, 72, 73, 74
Gay, Zhenya 19: 135, 136
Gaydos, Tim 62: 201
Gazsi, Ed 80: 48
Gazso, Gabriel 73: 85
Geary, Clifford N. 1: 122; 9: 104; 51: 74
Geary, Rick 142: 44, 46
Gee, Frank 33: 26
Geehan, Wayne 157: 181
Geer, Charles 1: 91; 3: 179; 4: 201; 6: 168; 7: 96; 9: 58; 10: 72; 12: 127; 39: 156,157, 158, 159, 160; 42: 88, 89, 90, 91; 55: 111, 116
Geerinck, Manuel 173: 128
Gehm, Charlie 36: 65; 57: 117; 62: 60, 138
Geis, Alissa Imre 189: 77
Geisel, Theodor Seuss 1: 104, 105, 106; 28: 108, 109, 110,111, 112, 113; 75: 67, 68, 69, 70, 71; 89: 127, 128; 100: 106, 107, 108
Geisert, Arthur 92: 67, 68; 133: 72, 73, 74; 165: 97, 98; 171: 64, 65
Geldart, William 15: 121; 21: 202
Genia 4: 84
Gentry, Cyrille R. 12: 66
Genzo, John Paul 136: 74
George, Jean 2: 113
George, Lindsay Barrett 95: 57; 155: 97, 98
Geraghty, Paul 130: 60, 61
Gerard, Jean Ignace 45: 80
Gerard, Rolf 27: 147, 150
Gerber, Mark 61: 105
Gerber, Mary Jane 112: 124; 171: 56
Gerber, Stephanie 71: 195
Gerdstein, Mordecai 169: 105
Gergely, Tibor 54: 15, 16
Geritz, Franz 17: 135
Gerlach, Geff 42: 58
Gerrard, Roy 47: 78; 90: 96, 97, 98, 99
Gerritsen, Paula 177: 69
Gershinowitz, George 36: 27

Gerstein, Mordicai *31:* 117; *47:* 80, 81, 82, 83, 84, 85, 86; *51:* 173; *69:* 134; *107:* 122; *142:* 49, 52; *165:* 209; *176:* 119; *178:* 95, 97, 99
Gervase *12:* 27
Geter, Tyrone *146:* 249; *150:* 86
Getz, Arthur *32:* 148
Gévry, Claudine *188:* 47
Gewirtz, Bina *61:* 81
Giancola, Donato *95:* 146; *164:* 226
Gibala-Broxholm, Scott *205:* 76
Gibbons, Gail *23:* 78; *72:* 77, 78, 79; *82:* 182; *104:* 65; *160:* 99, 100; *201:* 59, 60, 62
Gibbs, Tony *40:* 95
Gibran, Kahlil *32:* 116
Gibson, Barbara Leonard *205:* 77
Gider, Iskender *81:* 193
Giebfried, Rosemary *170:* 135
Giesen, Rosemary *34:* 192, 193
Giffard, Hannah *83:* 70
Giguere, George *20:* 111
Gilbert, John *19:* 184; *54:* 115; *YABC 2:* 287
Gilbert, W.S. *36:* 83, 85, 96
Gilbert, Yvonne *116:* 70; *128:* 84; *149:* 119; *185:* 69; *192:* 25; *195:* 81
Gilchrist, Jan Spivey *72:* 82, 83, 84, 85, 87; *77:* 90; *105:* 89, 91; *130:* 63, 64; *155:* 105, 107; *182:* 67
Giles, Will *41:* 218
Gili, Phillida *70:* 73
Gill, Margery *4:* 57; *7:* 7; *22:* 122; *25:* 166; *26:* 146, 147
Gillen, Denver *28:* 216
Gillette, Henry J. *23:* 237
Gilliam, Stan *39:* 64, 81
Gillies, Chuck *62:* 31
Gilliland, Jillian *87:* 58
Gillman, Alec *98:* 105
Gilman, Esther *15:* 124
Gilman, Phoebe *104:* 70, 71
Ginsberg, Sari *111:* 184
Ginsburg, Max *62:* 59; *68:* 194 *Girard, Roge 161:* 30
Girouard, Patrick *155:* 100
Giovanopoulos, Paul *7:* 104; *60:* 36
Giovine, Sergio *79:* 12; *93:* 118; *139:* 118; *205:* 114
Gist, E.M. *206:* 60
Githens, Elizabeth M. *5:* 47
Gladden, Scott *99:* 108; *103:* 160; *193:* 46, 47
Gladstone, Gary *12:* 89; *13:* 190
Gladstone, Lise *15:* 273
Glanzman, Louis S. *2:* 177; *3:* 182; *36:* 97, 98; *38:* 120, 122; *52:* 141, 144; *71:* 191; *91:* 54, 56
Glaser, Byron *154:* 59, 60
Glaser, Milton *3:* 5; *5:* 156; *11:* 107; *30:* 26; *36:* 112; *54:* 141; *151:* 70
Glass, Andrew *36:* 38; *44:* 133; *48:* 205; *65:* 3; *68:* 43, 45; *90:* 104, 105; *150:* 89
Glass, Marvin *9:* 174
Glasser, Judy *41:* 156; *56:* 140; *69:* 79; *72:* 101
Glattauer, Ned *5:* 84; *13:* 224; *14:* 26
Glauber, Uta *17:* 76
Gleeson, J.M. *YABC 2:* 207
Glegg, Creina *36:* 100
Glienke, Amelie *63:* 150
Gliewe, Unada *3:* 78, 79; *21:* 73; *30:* 220
Gliori, Debi *72:* 91; *138:* 82; *162:* 37; *189:* 79, 81, 82
Glovach, Linda *7:* 105
Gobbato, Imero *3:* 180, 181; *6:* 213; *7:* 58; *9:* 150; *18:* 39; *21:* 167; *39:* 82, 83; *41:* 137, 251; *59:* 177
Goble, Paul *25:* 121; *26:* 86; *33:* 65; *69:* 68, 69; *131:* 79, 80
Goble, Warwick *46:* 78, 79; *194:* 143
Godal, Eric *36:* 93
Godkin, Celia *145:* 84, 86
Godfrey, Michael *17:* 279
Godon, Ingrid *166:* 163; *186:* 99

Goembel, Ponder *42:* 124
Goffe, Toni *61:* 83, 84, 85; *89:* 11; *90:* 124; *178:* 118
Goffstein, M.B. *8:* 71; *70:* 75, 76, 77
Golbin, Andre *15:* 125
Gold, Robert *166:* 151, 152
Goldfeder, Cheryl *11:* 191
Goldfinger, Jennifer P. *185:* 71
Goldsborough, June *5:* 154, 155; *8:* 92, *14:* 226; *19:* 139; *54:* 165
Goldsmith, Robert *110:* 77
Goldstein, Barry *198:* 147
Goldstein, Leslie *5:* 8; *6:* 60; *10:* 106
Goldstein, Nathan *1:* 175; *2:* 79; *11:* 41, 232; *16:* 55
Goldstrom, Robert *98:* 36; *145:* 51, 52
Golembe, Carla *79:* 80, 81; *136:* 91; *144:* 113; *193:* 53
Golin, Carlo *74:* 112
Gomez, Elena *188:* 122; *191:* 72
Gomez, Elizabeth *127:* 70; *133:* 76
Gomi, Taro *64:* 102; *103:* 74, 76
Gon, Adriano *101:* 112
Gonsalve, Ron *178:* 213
Gonzalez, Maya Christina *104:* 3; *136:* 92
Goodall, John S. *4:* 92, 93; *10:* 132; *66:* 92, 93; *YABC 1:* 198
Goode, Diane *15:* 126; *50:* 183; *52:* 114, 115; *76:* 195; *84:* 94; *99:* 141; *114:* 76, 77, 78; *170:* 99, 101
Goodelman, Aaron *40:* 203
Goodenow, Earle *40:* 97
Goodfellow, Peter *62:* 95; *94:* 202
Goodman, Joan Elizabeth *50:* 86
Goodman, Vivienne *82:* 251; *146:* 181, 182
Goodnow, Patti *117:* 33
Goodwin, Harold *13:* 74
Goodwin, Philip R. *18:* 206
Goor, Nancy *39:* 85, 86
Goor, Ron *39:* 85, 86
Goossens, Philippe *195:* 71
Gorbachev, Valeri *89:* 96; *112:* 97; *143:* 63, 64; *184:* 66, 67, 68, 101
Gordon, Gwen *12:* 151
Gordon, Margaret *4:* 147; *5:* 48, 49; *9:* 79
Gordon, Mike *101:* 62, 63, 64
Gordon, Russell *136:* 204; *137:* 214
Gordon, Walter *138:* 9
Gore, Leonid *89:* 51; *94:* 74; *136:* 8; *158:* 117; *166:* 136; *168:* 36; *170:* 107; *181:* 94; *185:* 73
Gorecka-Egan, Erica *18:* 35
Gorey, Edward *1:* 60, 61; *13:* 169; *18:* 192; *20:* 201; *29:* 90, 91, 92, 93, 94, 95, 96, 97, 98, 99, 100; *30:* 129; *32:* 90; *34:* 200, *65:* 48; *68:* 24, 25; *69:* 79; *70:* 80, 82, 83, 84; *85:* 136; *127:* 62
Gorsline, Douglas *1:* 98; *6:* 13; *11:* 113; *13:* 104; *15:* 14; *28:* 117, 118; *YABC 1:* 15
Gorton, Julia *108:* 94; *178:* 81, 82
Gosfield, Josh *118:* 165, 166; *149:* 67
Gosner, Kenneth *5:* 135
Gosney, Joy *167:* 142
Gotlieb, Jules *6:* 127
Goto, Scott *115:* 86; *136:* 69; *203:* 77, 78
Gott, Barry *197:* 95
Gottlieb, Dale *67:* 162; *107:* 16; *149:* 6
Goudey, Ray *97:* 86
Gough, Alan *91:* 57
Gough, Philip *23:* 47; *45:* 90
Gould, Chester *49:* 112, 113, 114, 116, 117, 118
Gould, Jason *151:* 232
Gourbault, Martine *177:* 159
Govern, Elaine R. *26:* 94
Gower, Teri *102:* 184
Gowing, Toby *60:* 25; *63:* 33; *78:* 70, 252; *83:* 228; *86:* 187; *93:* 145; *108:* 133; *110:* 217; *184:* 125
Grabianski *20:* 144
Grabianski, Janusz *39:* 92, 93, 94, 95

Graboff, Abner *35:* 103, 104
Graef, Renée *61:* 188; *72:* 207; *204:* 45
Grafe, Max *156:* 173; *178:* 237; *192:* 240; *198:* 51
Graham, A.B. *11:* 61
Graham, Bob *101:* 66, 67, 68; *151:* 74, 75; *187:* 65, 67, 68, 70
Graham, Georgia *188:* 3; *190:* 75
Graham, L. *7:* 108
Graham, Margaret Bloy *11:* 120; *18:* 305, 307
Graham, Mark *88:* 208; *159:* 153; *182:* 3
Grahame-Johnstone, Janet *13:* 61
Grahame-Johnstone, Anne *13:* 61
Grainger, Sam *42:* 95
Gralley, Jean *166:* 86
Gramatky, Hardie *1:* 107; *30:* 116, 119, 120, 122, 123
Gran, Julie *168:* 118
Granahan, Julie *84:* 84
GrandPré, Mary *84:* 131; *109:* 199; *118:* 76; *180:* 65; *184:* 70, 71, 180; *192:* 87
Grandström, Brita *176:* 139
Grandville, J.J. *45:* 81, 82, 83, 84, 85, 86, 87, 88; *47:* 125; *64:* 10
Granger, Paul *39:* 153
Granström, Brita *162:* 35; *167:* 46
Grant, (Alice) Leigh *10:* 52; *15:* 131; *20:* 20; *26:* 119; *48:* 202
Grant, Gordon *17:* 230, 234; *25:* 123, 124, 125, 126; *52:* 69; *YABC 1:* 164
Grant, Melvyn *159:* 186, 187; *170:* 48, 49
Grant, Renee *77:* 40
Grant, Shirley *109:* 45
Graves, Elizabeth *45:* 101
Graves, Keith *167:* 89; *191:* 74
Gray, Harold *33:* 87, 88
Gray, Les *82:* 76; *83:* 232
Gray, Reginald *6:* 69
Greco, Tony *184:* 6
Greder, Armin *76:* 235
Green, Ann Canevari *62:* 48
Green, Eileen *6:* 97
Green, Elizabeth Shippen *139:* 109
Green, Jonathan *86:* 135; *105:* 109
Green, Ken *111:* 68
Green, Michael *32:* 216
Green, Robina *87:* 138
Green, Jonathan *157:* 105
Greene, Jeffrey *117:* 93
Greenaway, Kate *17:* 275; *24:* 180; *26:* 107; *41:* 222, 232; *100:* 115, 116; *YABC 1:* 88, 89; *2:* 131, 133, 136,138, 139, 141
Greenberg, Melanie Hope *72:* 93; *80:* 125; *101:* 174; *133:* 180; *186:* 189
Greenseid, Diane *178:* 106, 107
Greenstein, Elaine *150:* 100
Greenwald, Sheila *1:* 34; *3:* 99; *8:* 72
Greger, Carol *76:* 86
Gregorian, Joyce Ballou *30:* 125
Gregory, Emilian *177:* 146; *187:* 10
Gregory, Fran *130:* 4; *140:* 93
Gregory, Frank M. *29:* 107
Greiffenhagen, Maurice *16:* 137; *27:* 57; *YABC 2:* 288
Greiner, Robert *6:* 86
Gretter, J. Clemens *31:* 134
Gretz, Susanna *7:* 114
Gretzer, John *1:* 54; *3:* 26; *4:* 162; *7:* 125; *16:* 247; *18:* 117; *28:* 66; *30:* 85, 211; *33:* 235; *56:* 16
Grey, Mini *166:* 90; *192:* 71
Grey Owl *24:* 41
Gri *25:* 90
Grieder, Walter *9:* 84
Griesbach/Martucci *59:* 3
Grifalconi, Ann *2:* 126; *3:* 248; *11:* 18; *13:* 182; *46:* 38; *50:* 145; *66:* 99, 100, 101, 104, 106; *69:* 38; *70:* 64; *87:* 128; *90:* 53; *93:* 49; *128:* 48; *133:* 79, 81
Griffin, Gillett Good *26:* 96
Griffin, James *30:* 166

Griffin, John Howard *59:* 186
Griffin, Rachel *131:* 23
Griffith, Gershom *94:* 214
Griffiths, Dave *29:* 76
Griffiths, Dean *168:* 180; *169:* 182
Grimly, Gris *186:* 102; *192:* 112; *197:* 86
Grimsdell, Jeremy *83:* 75
Grimwood, Brian *82:* 89
Gringhuis, Dirk *6:* 98; *9:* 196
Gripe, Harald *2:* 127; *74:* 98
Grisha *3:* 71
Grobler, Piet *201:* 100
Grohmann, Susan *84:* 97
Gropper, William *27:* 93; *37:* 193
Gros *60:* 199
Grose, Helen Mason *YABC 1:* 260; *2:* 150
Grossman, Nancy *24:* 130; *29:* 101
Grossman, Robert *11:* 124; *46:* 39
Groth, John *15:* 79; *21:* 53, 54; *83:* 230
Grover, Lorie Ann *168:* 59
Grubb, Lisa *160:* 116
Grue, Lisa *187:* 193
Gruelle, Johnny *35:* 107
Gschwind, William *11:* 72
Guarnaccia, Steven *201:* 170, 173
Guay-Mitchell, Rebecca *110:* 95, 96; *135:* 240;
   180: 76; *181:* 71, 73
Guback, Georgia *88:* 102
Guerguerion, Claudine *105:* 73
Guevara, Susan *97:* 87; *167:* 49; *194:* 54
Guggenheim, Hans *2:* 10; *3:* 37; *8:* 136
Guhathaakurta, Ajanta *183:* 199
Guida, Lisa Chauncy *172:* 188
Guilbeau, Honore *22:* 69
Guillette, Joseph *137:* 37
Guisewite, Cathy *57:* 52, 53, 54, 56, 57
Gukova, Julia *95:* 104; *154:* 103; *168:* 195
Gundersheimer, Karen *35:* 240; *82:* 100
Gunderson, Nick *57:* 120
Gunnella *192:* 144
Gurney, James *76:* 97; *86:* 32
Gurney, John Steven *75:* 39, 82; *110:* 175;
   143: 67, 68; *169:* 172
Gusman, Annie *38:* 62
Gustafson, Scott *34:* 111; *43:* 40
Gustavson, Adam *104:* 10; *171:* 183; *176:* 87;
   197: 94; *204:* 35
Guthridge, Bettina *108:* 79; *186:* 92
Guthrie, R. Dale *64:* 143
Guthrie, Robin *20:* 122
Gutierrez, Akemi *87:* 87; *205:* 135
Gutierrez, Alan *136:* 31, 32
Gutierrez, Rudy *97:* 162; *203:* 79
Gutmann, Bessie Pease *73:* 93, 94
Gwynne, Fred *41:* 94, 95
Gyberg, Bo-Erik *38:* 131

H

Haas, Irene *17:* 77; *87:* 46; *96:* 117
Hack, Konrad *51:* 127
Hader, Berta H. *16:* 126
Hader, Elmer S. *16:* 126
Haeffele, Deborah *76:* 99
Haemer, Alan *62:* 109
Hafner, Marylin *22:* 196, 216; *24:* 44; *30:* 51;
   35: 95; *51:* 25, 160, 164; *86:* 16; *105:* 196;
   121: 93, 94; *149:* 208, 209; *179:* 82, 83, 84,
   115; *190:* 200; *201:* 29
Hagerty, Sean *62:* 181
Hague, Michael *32:* 128; *48:* 98, 99, 100, 101,
   103, 105,106, 107, 108, 109, 110; *49:* 121;
   51: 105; *64:* 14, 15; *79:* 134; *80:* 91, 92; *83:*
   135; *100:* 241; *102:* 29; *129:* 101, 103, 104;
   185: 80, 81, 82
Hair, Jonathan *115:* 135
Halas, John *29:* 41, 47, 48
Haldane, Roger *13:* 76; *14:* 202
Hale, Bruce *203:* 83

Hale, Christy *79:* 124; *84:* 200; *114:* 201; *128:*
   2, 3; *146:* 203; *158:* 243; *167:* 99; *179:* 87
Hale, Irina *26:* 97
Hale, James Graham *88:* 207
Hale, Kathleen *17:* 79; *66:* 114, 116, 118
Haley, Amanda *205:* 82, 83
Haley, Gail E. *43:* 102, 103, 104, 105; *78:* 65,
   67; *136:* 106, 107
Hall, Amanda *96:* 110
Hall, Chuck *30:* 189
Hall, Douglas *15:* 184; *43:* 106, 107; *86:* 100;
   87: 82; *129:* 72
Hall, H. Tom *1:* 227; *30:* 210
Hall, Melanie *116:* 48, 49; *169:* 77, 78
Hall, Sydney P. *31:* 89
Hall, Tim *164:* 196; *202:* 41
Hall, Vicki *20:* 24
Hallinan, P.K. *39:* 98
Hallman, Tom *98:* 166
Hally, Greg *101:* 200; *151:* 224
Halperin, Wendy Anderson *96:* 151; *125:* 96,
   97, 98, 99; *139:* 22; *140:* 84; *200:* 77, 78
Halpern, Joan *10:* 25
Halpern, Shari *174:* 172
Halsey, Megan *96:* 172; *114:* 185; *180:* 8; *185:*
   85
Halstead, Virginia *125:* 105
Halverson, Janet *49:* 38, 42, 44
Hallensleben, Georg *134:* 5, 6; *172:* 17
Hamanaka, Sheila *71:* 100
Hamann, Brad *78:* 151
Hamann, Sigune *104:* 115
Hamberger, John *6:* 8; *8:* 32; *14:* 79; *34:* 136;
   88: 78
Hamil, Tom *14:* 80; *43:* 163
Hamilton, Bill and Associates *26:* 215
Hamilton, Helen S. *2:* 238
Hamilton, J. *19:* 83, 85, 87
Hamilton, Laurie *116:* 210
Hamilton, Todd Cameron *84:* 15
Hamlin, Janet *97:* 136; *124:* 90; *137:* 157;
   182: 117
Hamlin, Louise *71:* 135
Hammill, Matt *206:* 65
Hammond, Chris *21:* 37
Hammond, Elizabeth *5:* 36, 203
Hampshire, Michael *5:* 187; *7:* 110, 111; *48:*
   150; *51:* 129
Hampson, Denman *10:* 155; *15:* 130
Hampton, Blake *41:* 244
Handford, Martin *64:* 105, 106, 107, 109
Handforth, Thomas *42:* 100, 101, 102, 103,
   104, 105, 107
Handville, Robert *1:* 89; *38:* 76; *45:* 108, 109
Hane, Roger *17:* 239; *44:* 54
Haney, Elizabeth Mathieu *34:* 84
Hanke, Ted *71:* 10
Hankinson, Phil *181:* 164
Hanley, Catherine *8:* 161
Hann, Jacquie *19:* 144
Hanna, Cheryl *91:* 133
Hanna, Wayne A. *67:* 145
Hannon, Mark *38:* 37
Hanrahan, Kelly-Anne *203:* 142
Hansen, Gaby *159:* 11; *186:* 25
Hansen, Mia *149:* 76
Hanson, Joan *8:* 76; *11:* 139
Hanson, Peter E. *52:* 47; *54:* 99, 100; *73:* 21;
   84: 79; *116:* 144
Hansson, Gunilla *64:* 111, 112
Hardcastle, Nick *121:* 82; *175:* 185
Hardy, David A. *9:* 96; *119:* 74
Hardy, Paul *YABC 2:* 245 Haring, Keith *145:*
   65
Harlan, Jerry *3:* 96
Harlin, Greg *89:* 194; *103:* 82; *118:* 161; *121:*
   167; *182:* 76; *201:* 172
Harman, Dominic *206:* 48
Harness, Cheryl *106:* 80; *131:* 87; *178:* 111;
   200: 39
Harnischfeger *18:* 121

Harper, Arthur *YABC 2:* 121
Harper, Betty *126:* 90
Harper, Jamie *174:* 71
Harper, Piers *79:* 27; *105:* 102; *161:* 67
Harrington, Glenn *82:* 18; *94:* 66, 68; *185:*
   118
Harrington, Jack *83:* 162
Harrington, Richard *5:* 81
Harris, Andrew N. *191:* 78
Harris, Jim *127:* 130; *183:* 4
Harris, John *83:* 25
Harris, Nick *86:* 177
Harris, Susan Yard *42:* 121
Harrison, Florence *20:* 150, 152
Harrison, Harry *4:* 103
Harrison, Jack *28:* 149
Harrison, Mark *105:* 157; *165:* 190
Harrison, Ted *56:* 73
Harsh, Fred *72:* 107
Harston, Jerry *105:* 143
Hart, Lewis *98:* 115
Hart, Thomas *181:* 165
Hart, William *13:* 72
Hartland, Jessie *171:* 80, 81; *186:* 165
Hartung, Susan Kathleen *150:* 107, 108; *173:*
   106; *175:* 106; *192:* 78
Hartelius, Margaret *10:* 24
Hartshorn, Ruth *5:* 115; *11:* 129
Harvey, Amanda *145:* 44
Harvey, Bob *48:* 219
Harvey, Gerry *7:* 180
Harvey, Lisa *97:* 21
Harvey, Paul *88:* 74
Harvey, Roland *71:* 88; *123:* 63; *179:* 94
Haskamp, Steve *195:* 36
Hassall, Joan *43:* 108, 109
Hassell, Hilton *YABC 1:* 187
Hassett, John *162:* 59
Hasselriis, Else *18:* 87; *YABC 1:* 96
Hastings, Glenn *89:* 183
Hastings, Ian *62:* 67
Hauman, Doris *2:* 184; *29:* 58, 59; *32:* 85, 86,
   87
Hauman, George *2:* 184; *29:* 58, 59; *32:* 85,
   86, 87
Hausherr, Rosmarie *15:* 29
Hawkes, Kevin *78:* 72; *104:* 198; *105:* 197;
   112: 109; *126:* 87; *144:* 88; *149:* 210; *150:*
   110, 135; *156:* 94; *164:* 35; *186:* 18; *190:*
   197; *198:* 152; *201:* 70, 71, 72
Hawkins, Jacqui *112:* 86; *162:* 64
Hawkinson, John *4:* 109; *7:* 83; *21:* 64
Hawkinson, Lucy *21:* 64
Hawthorne, Mike *140:* 228
Haxton, Elaine *28:* 131
Haydock, Robert *4:* 95
Hayes, Geoffrey *26:* 111; *44:* 133; *91:* 85;
   207: 63
Hayes, Karel *207:* 65
Haynes, Max *72:* 107
Hays, Michael *73:* 207; *83:* 93; *139:* 197; *146:*
   202, 250; *202:* 47
Haywood, Carolyn *1:* 112; *29:* 104
Heale, Jonathan *104:* 117
Healy, Daty *12:* 143
Healy, Deborah *58:* 181, 182; *101:* 111
Heap, Sue *102:* 207; *150:* 113, 114; *187:* 84,
   85, 87
Hearn, Diane Dawson *79:* 99; *113:* 13
Hearon, Dorothy *34:* 69
Heaslip, William *57:* 24, 25
Hechtkopf, H. *11:* 110
Heck, Ed *173:* 81
Hector, Julian *205:* 85
Hedderwick, Mairi *30:* 127; *32:* 47; *36:* 104;
   77: 86; *145:* 91, 93, 95
Heffernan, Phil *146:* 197; *195:* 172
Hefter, Richard *28:* 170; *31:* 81, 82; *33:* 183
Hehenberger, Shelly *126:* 91
Heigh, James *22:* 98
Heighway, Richard *25:* 160; *64:* 4

Heighway-Bury, Robin *159:* 89
Heine, Helme *67:* 86; *135:* 91, 92
Heinly, John *45:* 113
Hellard, Susan *81:* 21; *204:* 82
Hellebrand, Nancy *26:* 57
Heller, Linda *46:* 86
Heller, Ruth M. *66:* 125; *77:* 30, 32
Hellmuth, Jim *38:* 164
Helms, Georgeann *33:* 62
Helquist, Brett *142:* 203; *146:* 133, 134; *156:* 10; *173:* 25; *180:* 106; *187:* 90, 91; *193:* 12
Helweg, Hans *41:* 118; *50:* 93; *58:* 22, 26
Hemphill, Helen *179:* 95
Henba, Bobbie *90:* 195
Henderson, Dave *73:* 76; *75:* 191, 192, 193, 194; *82:* 4
Henderson, Douglas *103:* 68
Henderson, Kathy *55:* 32; *155:* 118
Henderson, Keith *35:* 122
Henderson, Meryl *127:* 58, 60; *169:* 81
Hendrix, John *187:* 133
Hendry, Linda *80:* 104; *83:* 83; *164:* 216
Hengeveld, Dennis *142:* 86
Henkes, Kevin *43:* 111; *108:* 106, 107, 108
Henneberger, Robert *1:* 42; *2:* 237; *25:* 83
Henriksen, Harold *35:* 26; *48:* 68
Henriquez, Celeste *103:* 137
Henriquez, Elsa *82:* 260
Henriquez, Emile F. *89:* 88
Henry, Everett *29:* 191
Henry, Matthew *117:* 58
Henry, Paul *93:* 121; *194:* 125
Henry, Thomas *5:* 102
Hensel *27:* 119
Henshaw, Jacqui *141:* 127
Henstra, Friso *8:* 80; *36:* 70; *40:* 222; *41:* 250; *73:* 100, 101
Henterly, Jamichael *93:* 4
Heo, Yumi *89:* 85, 86; *94:* 89, 90; *146:* 40, 137, 138; *163:* 227; *201:* 192
Hepple, Norman *28:* 198
Herbert, Helen *57:* 70
Herbert, Jennifer *189:* 47
Herbert, Wally *23:* 101
Herbster, Mary Lee *9:* 33
Herder, Edwin *182:* 104
Herge
    See Remi, Georges
Hermansen, Pal *133:* 113
Hermanson, Dennis *10:* 55
Hermes, Gertrude *54:* 161
Herr, Margo *57:* 191
Herr, Susan *83:* 163
Herriman, George *140:* 74, 75, 76, 77, 78
Herriman, Lisa *87:* 190
Herring, Michael *121:* 76; *182:* 103
Herrington, Roger *3:* 161
Herscovici, C. *165:* 240
Hescox, Richard *85:* 86; *90:* 30; *139:* 35
Heslop, Mike *38:* 60; *40:* 130
Hess, Lydia J. *85:* 17
Hess, Mark *111:* 146; *113:* 207
Hess, Paul *134:* 47; *166:* 133; *193:* 13
Hess, Richard *42:* 31
Hester, Ronnie *37:* 85
Heuser, Olga J. *121:* 116
Heusser, Sibylle *168:* 195
Heustis, Louise L. *20:* 28
Hewgill, Jody *201:* 90
Hewitson, Jennifer *74:* 119; *124:* 167
Hewitt, Kathryn *80:* 126; *149:* 105; *184:* 93; *196:* 36
Hewitt, Margaret *84:* 112
Heyduck-Huth, Hilde *8:* 82
Heyer, Carol *74:* 122; *130:* 72, 73; *192:* 35; *203:* 78
Heyer, Hermann *20:* 114, 115
Heyer, Marilee *102:* 108
Heyman, Ken *8:* 33; *34:* 113
Heyne, Ulrike *146:* 151
Heywood, Karen *48:* 114

Hickling, P.B. *40:* 165
Hickman, Stephen *85:* 58; *136:* 33; *171:* 128
Hierstein, Judy *56:* 40; *162:* 168
Higashi, Sandra *154:* 59, 60
Higginbottom, J. Winslow *8:* 170; *29:* 105, 106
Higgins, Chester *101:* 79
Higham, David *50:* 104
Hilb, Nora *176:* 8
Hildebrandt, Greg *8:* 191; *55:* 35, 36, 38, 39, 40, 42, 46; *172:* 110
Hildebrandt, Tim *8:* 191; *55:* 44, 45, 46
Hilder, Rowland *19:* 207
Hill, Eric *66:* 127, 128; *133:* 91
Hill, Gregory *35:* 190
Hill, Pat *49:* 120
Hillenbrand, Will *84:* 115; *92:* 76, 80; *93:* 131; *104:* 168; *128:* 137; *145:* 187; *146:* 184; *147:* 105, 106, 107; *152:* 59; *184:* 179; *195:* 34, 180; *196:* 125
Hilliard, Richard *183:* 74
Hillier, Matthew *45:* 205
Hillman, Priscilla *48:* 115
Hills, Tad *113:* 4; *137:* 147; *173:* 83
Himler, Ronald *6:* 114; *7:* 162; *8:* 17, 84, 125; *14:* 76; *19:* 145; *26:* 160; *31:* 43; *38:* 116; *41:* 44, 79; *43:* 52; *45:* 120; *46:* 43; *54:* 44, 83; *58:* 180; *59:* 38; *68:* 146; *69:* 231; *70:* 98; *71:* 177, 178; *77:* 219; *79:* 212; *83:* 62; *89:* 5; *91:* 160; *92:* 91, 92, 93; *94:* 93; *95:* 69, 174, 194; *99:* 99, 112; *113:* 92; *118:* 114; *137:* 73, 74, 77, 167; *163:* 99; *165:* 138; *178:* 9, 220; *183:* 77, 79, 80, 81; *184:* 80, 83
Himmelman, John *47:* 109; *65:* 87; *94:* 96, 97; *159:* 85
Hinds, Bill *37:* 127, 130
Hines, Anna Grossnickle *51:* 90; *74:* 124; *95:* 78, 79,80, 81
Hines, Bob *135:* 149, 150
Hirao, Amiko *203:* 98
Hiroko *99:* 61
Hiroshige *25:* 71
Hirsh, Marilyn *7:* 126
Hiscock, Bruce *137:* 80, 81; *204:* 51, 53
Hissey, Jane *103:* 90; *130:* 81
Hitch, Jeff *99:* 206; *128:* 86
Hitz, Demi *11:* 135; *15:* 245; *66:* 129, 130; *152:* 94, 95
Hnizdovsky, Jacques *32:* 96; *76:* 187
Ho, Kwoncjan *15:* 132
Hoban, Lillian *1:* 114; *22:* 157; *26:* 72; *29:* 53; *40:* 105, 107, 195; *41:* 80; *69:* 107, 108; *71:* 98; *77:* 168; *106:* 50; *113:* 86; *136:* 118
Hoban, Tana *22:* 159; *104:* 82, 83, 85
Hobbie, Jocelyn *190:* 78; *196:* 92
Hobbie, Nathaniel *196:* 92
Hobbs, Leigh *166:* 95
Hoberman, Norman *5:* 82
Hobson, Sally *77:* 185
Hockerman, Dennis *39:* 22; *56:* 23
Hodgell, P.C. *42:* 114
Hodges, C. Walter *2:* 139; *11:* 15; *12:* 25; *23:* 34; *25:* 96; *38:* 165; *44:* 197; *45:* 95; *100:* 57; *YABC 2:* 62, 63
Hodges, David *9:* 98
Hodgetts, Victoria *43:* 132
Hofbauer, Imre *2:* 162
Hoff, Syd *9:* 107; *10:* 128; *33:* 94; *72:* 115,116, 117, 118; *138:* 114, 115
Hoffman, Rosekrans *15:* 133; *50:* 219; *63:* 97
Hoffman, Sanford *38:* 208; *76:* 174; *88:* 160, 161; *151:* 156
Hoffmann, Felix *9:* 109
Hoffnung, Gerard *66:* 76, 77
Hofsinde, Robert *21:* 70
Hogan, Inez *2:* 141
Hogan, Jamie *192:* 94; *198:* 177
Hogarth, Burne *41:* 58; *63:* 46, 48, 49, 50, 52, 53, 54, 55,56
Hogarth, Paul *41:* 102, 103, 104; *YABC 1:* 16
Hogarth, William *42:* 33

Hogenbyl, Jan *1:* 35
Hogner, Nils *4:* 122; *25:* 144
Hogrogian, Nonny *3:* 221; *4:* 106, 107; *5:* 166; *7:* 129; *15:* 2; *16:* 176; *20:* 154; *22:* 146; *25:* 217; *27:* 206; *74:* 127, 128, 129, 149, 152; *127:* 99; *YABC 2:* 84, 94
Hokanson, Lars *93:* 111; *172:* 137
Hokusai *25:* 71
Hol, Colby *126:* 96
Holberg, Richard *2:* 51
Holbrook, Kathy *107:* 114
Holdcroft, Tina *38:* 109
Holden, Caroline *55:* 159
Holder, Heidi *36:* 99; *64:* 9
Holder, Jim *204:* 163
Holder, Jimmy *151:* 224
Hole, Stian *204:* 55
Holiday, Henry *YABC 2:* 107
Holl, F. *36:* 91
Holland, Brad *45:* 59, 159
Holland, Gay W. *128:* 105
Holland, Janice *18:* 118
Holland, Marion *6:* 116
Holldobler, Turid *26:* 120
Holliday, Keaf *144:* 236
Holling, Holling C. *15:* 136, 137
Hollinger, Deanne *12:* 116
Holm, Sharon Lane *114:* 84; *115:* 52
Holmes, B. *3:* 82
Holmes, Bea *7:* 74; *24:* 156; *31:* 93
Holmes, Dave *54:* 22
Holmes, Lesley *135:* 96
Holmgren, George Ellen *45:* 112
Holmlund, Heather D. *150:* 140
Holt, Norma *44:* 106
Holt, Pater *151:* 188
Holtan, Gene *32:* 192
Holub, Joan *149:* 72
Holyfield, John *149:* 231
Holz, Loretta *17:* 81
Hom, Nancy *79:* 195
Homar, Lorenzo *6:* 2
Homer, Winslow *128:* 8; *YABC 2:* 87
Honey, Elizabeth *112:* 95, 96; *137:* 93, 94
Honeywood, Varnette P. *110:* 68, 70
Hong, Lily Toy *76:* 104
Honigman, Marian *3:* 2
Honore, Paul *42:* 77, 79, 81, 82
Hood, Alun *69:* 145, 218; *72:* 41; *80:* 226; *87:* 4; *95:* 139
Hood, Susan *12:* 43
Hook, Christian *104:* 103
Hook, Frances *26:* 188; *27:* 127
Hook, Jeff *14:* 137; *103:* 105
Hook, Richard *26:* 188
Hooks *63:* 30
Hooper, Hadley *177:* 145
Hoover, Carol A. *21:* 77
Hoover, Russell *12:* 95; *17:* 2; *34:* 156
Hope, James *141:* 116
Hopkins, Chris *99:* 127
Hopkinson, Leigh *202:* 70
Hopman, Philip *178:* 184
Hoppin, Augustus *34:* 66
Horacek, Petr *163:* 117
Horder, Margaret *2:* 108; *73:* 75
Horen, Michael *45:* 121
Horne, Daniel *73:* 106; *91:* 153; *109:* 127; *110:* 232; *164:* 176
Horne, Richard *111:* 80
Horowitz, Dave *204:* 58
Horse, Harry *128:* 195; *169:* 86
Horvat, Laurel *12:* 201
Horvath, David *192:* 95
Horvath, Ferdinand Kusati *24:* 176
Horvath, Maria *57:* 171
Horwitz, Richard *57:* 174
Hotchkiss, De Wolfe *20:* 49
Hough, Charlotte *9:* 112; *13:* 98; *17:* 83; *24:* 195
Houlihan, Ray *11:* 214

House, Caroline *183:* 121
Housman, Laurence *25:* 146, 147
Houston, James *13:* 107; *74:* 132, 134, 135
Hovland, Gary *88:* 172; *171:* 148
Hoyt, Eleanor *158:* 231
How, W.E. *20:* 47
Howard, Alan *16:* 80; *34:* 58; *45:* 114
Howard, Arthur *165:* 111, 112; *190:* 5
Howard, J.N. *15:* 234
Howard, John *33:* 179
Howard, Kim *116:* 71
Howard, Paul *142:* 126, 129; *144:* 187
Howard, Rob *40:* 161
Howarth, Daniel *170:* 34
Howe, John *79:* 101; *80:* 150; *115:* 47; *176:* 106; *207:* 32, 35
Howe, Phillip *79:* 117; *175:* 115
Howe, Stephen *1:* 232
Howell, Karen *119:* 123
Howell, Pat *15:* 139
Howell, Troy *23:* 24; *31:* 61; *36:* 158; *37:* 184; *41:* 76, 235; *48:* 112; *56:* 13; *57:* 3; *59:* 174; *63:* 5; *74:* 46; *89:* 188; *90:* 231; *95:* 97; *98:* 130; *99:* 189; *153:* 156, 157, 158; *176:* 104; *199:* 96, 98
Howes, Charles *22:* 17
Hoyt, Ard *145:* 141; *190:* 82; *207:* 148
Hranilovich, Barbara *127:* 51
Hu, Ying-Hwa *116:* 107; *152:* 236; *173:* 171
Huang, Benrei *137:* 55
Huang, Zhong-Yang *117:* 30, 32
Hubbard, Woodleigh Marx *98:* 67; *115:* 79; *160:* 138
Hubley, Faith *48:* 120, 121, 125, 130, 131, 132, 134
Hubley, John *48:* 125, 130, 131, 132, 134
Hudak, Michal *143:* 74
Hudnut, Robin *14:* 62
Huerta, Catherine *76:* 178; *77:* 44, 45; *90:* 182
Huffaker, Sandy *10:* 56
Huffman, Joan *13:* 33
Huffman, Tom *13:* 180; *17:* 212; *21:* 116; *24:* 132; *33:* 154; *38:* 59; *42:* 147
Hughes, Arthur *20:* 148, 149, 150; *33:* 114, 148, 149
Hughes, Darren *95:* 44
Hughes, David *36:* 197
Hughes, Shirley *1:* 20, 21; *7:* 3; *12:* 217; *16:* 163; *29:* 154; *63:* 118; *70:* 102, 103, 104; *73:* 169; *88:* 70; *110:* 118, 119; *159:* 103
Hugo, Victor *47:* 112
Huliska-Beith, Laura *204:* 108
Hull, Cathy *78:* 29
Hull, Richard *95:* 120; *123:* 175; *172:* 195
Hulsmann, Eva *16:* 166
Hume, Lachie *189:* 93
Hummel, Berta *43:* 137, 138, 139
Hummel, Lisl *29:* 109; *YABC 2:* 333, 334
Humphrey, Henry *16:* 167
Humphreys, Graham *25:* 168
Humphries, Tudor *76:* 66; *80:* 4; *124:* 4, 5
Huneck, Stephen *183:* 88, 89
Hunt, James *2:* 143
Hunt, Jonathan *84:* 120
Hunt, Paul *119:* 104; *129:* 135; *139:* 160; *173:* 112
Hunt, Robert *110:* 206, 235; *147:* 136, 137; *170:* 3
Hunt, Scott *190:* 143
Hunter, Anne *133:* 190; *178:* 150
Huntington, Amy *180:* 99
Hurd, Clement *2:* 148, 149; *64:* 127, 128, 129, 131, 133, 134,135, 136; *100:* 37, 38
Hurd, Peter *24:* 30, 31,; *YABC 2:* 56
Hurd, Thacher *46:* 88, 89; *94:* 114, 115, 116; *123:* 81, 82, 84
Hurlimann, Ruth *32:* 99
Hurst, Carol Otis *185:* 92
Hurst, Philip *196:* 79
Hurst, Tracey *192:* 238
Hussar, Michael *114:* 113; *117:* 159

Hustler, Tom *6:* 105
Hutchins, Laurence *55:* 22
Hutchins, Pat *15:* 142; *70:* 106, 107, 108; *178:* 131, 132
Hutchinson, Sascha *95:* 211
Hutchinson, William M. *6:* 3, 138; *46:* 70
Hutchison, Paula *23:* 10
Hutton, Clarke *YABC 2:* 335
Hutton, Kathryn *35:* 155; *89:* 91
Hutton, Warwick *20:* 91
Huyette, Marcia *29:* 188
Hyatt, John *54:* 7
Hyatt, Mitch *178:* 162
Hyde, Maureen *82:* 17; *121:* 145, 146
Hyman, David *117:* 64
Hyman, Trina Schart *1:* 204; *2:* 194; *5:* 153; *6:* 106; *7:* 138, 145; *8:* 22; *10:* 196; *13:* 96; *14:* 114; *15:* 204; *16:* 234; *20:* 82; *22:* 133; *24:* 151; *25:* 79, 82; *26:* 82; *29:* 83; *31:* 37, 39; *34:* 104; *38:* 84, 100, 128; *41:* 49; *43:* 146; *46:* 91, 92, 93, 95, 96, 97, 98, 99, 100, 101, 102, 103, 104, 105,108, 109, 111, 197; *48:* 60, 61; *52:* 32; *60:* 168; *66:* 38; *67:* 214; *72:* 74; *75:* 92; *79:* 57; *82:* 95, 238; *89:* 46; *95:* 91, 92, 93; *100:* 33, 199; *132:* 12; *147:* 33, 35, 36; *167:* 58, 60; *177:* 189, 190

I

Ibarra, Rosa *147:* 91
Ibatoulline, Bagram *156:* 48; *174:* 33, 82; *202:* 30
Ichikawa, Satomi *29:* 152; *41:* 52; *47:* 133, 134,135, 136; *78:* 93, 94; *80:* 81; *146:* 143, 145, 146
Ide, Jacqueline *YABC 1:* 39
Ilsley, Velma *3:* 1; *7:* 55; *12:* 109; *37:* 62; *38:* 184
Imai, Ayano *190:* 85, 86
in den Bosch, Nicole *150:* 204
Inga *1:* 142
Ingman, Bruce *134:* 50; *182:* 91, 92
Ingpen, Robert *109:* 103, 104; *132:* 138; *137:* 177; *166:* 103; *181:* 140
Ingraham, Erick *21:* 177; *84:* 256; *103:* 66
Inkpen, Mick *99:* 104, 105; *106:* 44
Innerst, Stacy *149:* 104
Innocenti, Roberto *21:* 123; *96:* 122; *159:* 111, 197; *199:* 176
Inoue, Yosuke *24:* 118
Iofin, Michael *97:* 157
Iosa, Ann *63:* 189
Ipcar, Dahlov *1:* 124, 125; *49:* 137, 138, 139, 140, 141, 142,143, 144, 145; *147:* 122, 124, 126
Irvin, Fred *13:* 166; *15:* 143, 144; *27:* 175
Irving, Jay *45:* 72
Irving, Laurence *27:* 50
Isaac, Joanne *21:* 76
Isaacs, Gary *170:* 188
Isadora, Rachel *43:* 159, 160; *54:* 31; *79:* 106, 107,108; *121:* 100, 102; *165:* 116, 117; *204:* 61, 63, 64
Ishmael, Woodi *24:* 111; *31:* 99
Ives, Ruth *15:* 257
Iwai, Melissa *149:* 233; *183:* 92; *199:* 115

J

Jabar, Cynthia *101:* 201
Jackness, Andrew *94:* 237
Jackson, Julian *91:* 104, 106
Jackson, Michael *43:* 42
Jackson, Shelley *79:* 71; *99:* 109; *187:* 82
Jacob, Murv *89:* 30
Jacobi, Kathy *62:* 118

Jacobs, Barbara *9:* 136
Jacobs, Lou, Jr. *9:* 136; *15:* 128
Jacobsen, Laura *176:* 98; *177:* 85, 86
Jacobson, Rick *131:* 222; *170:* 119
Jacobus, Tim *79:* 140; *109:* 126; *129:* 180
Jacques, Robin *1:* 70; *2:* 1; *8:* 46; *9:* 20; *15:* 187; *19:* 253; *32:* 102, 103, 104; *43:* 184; *73:* 135; *YABC 1:* 42
Jaeggi, Yoshiko *186:* 184
Jaffee, Al *66:* 131, 132
Jagr, Miloslav *13:* 197
Jahn-Clough, Lisa *88:* 114; *152:* 104; *193:* 70, 71
Jahnke, Robert *84:* 24
Jainschigg, Nicholas *80:* 64; *91:* 138; *95:* 63; *99:* 25; *108:* 50; *171:* 41
Jakesavic, Nenad *85:* 102
Jakobsen, Kathy *116:* 83
Jakubowski, Charles *14:* 192
Jambor, Louis *YABC 1:* 11
James, Ann *73:* 50; *82:* 113; *158:* 61; *183:* 44
James, Brian *140:* 91
James, Curtis E. *182:* 93
James, Derek *35:* 187; *44:* 91; *61:* 133; *74:* 2; *80:* 57; *86:* 88; *130:* 30; *179:* 29
James, Gilbert *YABC 1:* 43
James, Gordon C. *195:* 89
James, Harold *2:* 151; *3:* 62; *8:* 79; *29:* 113; *51:* 195; *74:* 90
James, Kennon *126:* 211
James, Robin *50:* 106; *53:* 32, 34, 35
James, Simon *202:* 73, 74
James, Will *19:* 150, 152, 153, 155, 163
Janosch
    See Eckert, Horst
Janovitch, Marilyn *68:* 168
Janovitz, Marilyn *87:* 187; *130:* 198; *194:* 91
Jansons, Inese *48:* 117
Jansson, Tove *3:* 90; *41:* 106, 108, 109, 110, 111, 113, 114
Jaques, Faith *7:* 11, 132, 133; *21:* 83, 84; *69:* 114,116; *73:* 170
Jaques, Frances Lee *29:* 224
Jarrett, Clare *201:* 77
Jauss, Anne Marie *1:* 139; *3:* 34; *10:* 57, 119; *11:* 205; *23:* 194
Jay, Alison *158:* 97, 98; *183:* 126, 127; *196:* 95, 96, 97, 98; *200:* 72, 73, 74
Jeffers, Oliver *175:* 111
Jeffers, Susan *17:* 86, 87; *25:* 164, 165; *26:* 112; *50:* 132, 134, 135; *70:* 111, 112, 113; *137:* 107, 108, 109, 110, 111; *202:* 77, 78
Jefferson, Louise E. *4:* 160
Jenkin-Pearce, Susie *78:* 16
Jenkins, Debra Reid *85:* 202; *114:* 89; *173:* 134
Jenkins, Jean *98:* 79, 102
Jenkins, Leonard *157:* 169; *167:* 128; *189:* 96, 97; *190:* 89
Jenkins, Patrick *72:* 126
Jenkins, Steve *124:* 177; *154:* 90, 91, 92, 93; *185:* 194; *188:* 81, 82, 83, 84, 85, 86
Jenks, Aleta *73:* 117; *124:* 225
Jenkyns, Chris *51:* 97
Jensen, Bruce *95:* 39
Jensinius, Kirsten *56:* 58
Jeram, Anita *89:* 135; *102:* 122, 123; *129:* 112; *154:* 96, 97, 98; *164:* 154; *203:* 123, 124
Jernigan, E. Wesley *85:* 92
Jerome, Karen A. *72:* 194
Jeruchim, Simon *6:* 173; *15:* 250
Jeschke, Susan *20:* 89; *39:* 161; *41:* 84; *42:* 120
Jessel, Camilla *29:* 115
Jessell, Tim *159:* 3; *177:* 87; *181:* 95; *205:* 4
Jeyaveeran, Ruth *182:* 100
Jiang, Cheng An *109:* 108
Jiang, Wei *109:* 108
Jimenez, Maria *77:* 158; *93:* 127
Jobling, Curtis *138:* 74

Jocelyn, Marthe *118:* 83; *137:* 219; *163:* 119, 120; *198:* 62
Joerns, Consuelo *38:* 36; *44:* 94
John, Diana *12:* 209
John, Helen *1:* 215; *28:* 204
Johns, Elizabeth *127:* 33
Johns, Jasper *61:* 172
Johns, Jeanne *24:* 114
Johnson, Adrian *143:* 50
Johnson, Bruce *9:* 47
Johnson, Cathy *92:* 136
Johnson, Crockett
See Leisk, David
Johnson, D. William *23:* 104
Johnson, D.B. *183:* 98, 139
Johnson, David *175:* 18; *191:* 91
Johnson, Gillian *119:* 175; *164:* 217
Johnson, Harper *1:* 27; *2:* 33; *18:* 302; *19:* 61; *31:* 181; *44:* 46, 50, 95
Johnson, Ingrid *37:* 118
Johnson, James Ralph *1:* 23, 127
Johnson, James David *12:* 195
Johnson, Jane *48:* 136
Johnson, Joel Peter *98:* 18; *128:* 111; *201:* 13
Johnson, John E. *34:* 133
Johnson, Kevin *72:* 44
Johnson, Kevin Eugene *109:* 215
Johnson, Larry *47:* 56; *123:* 107; *159:* 203
Johnson, Layne *187:* 94
Johnson, Margaret S. *35:* 131
Johnson, Meredith Merrell *71:* 181; *83:* 158; *89:* 103; *104:* 88
Johnson, Milton *1:* 67; *2:* 71; *26:* 45; *31:* 107; *60:* 112; *68:* 96
Johnson, Pamela *16:* 174; *52:* 145; *62:* 140; *73:* 116; *85:* 64
Johnson, Paul Brett *83:* 95; *132:* 119
Johnson, Stephen T. *80:* 15; *131:* 35; *141:* 96; *145:* 40; *164:* 187; *175:* 32; *189:* 99, 100
Johnson, Steve *138:* 219; *141:* 64; *144:* 199; *177:* 51
Johnson, William R. *38:* 91
Johnson-Petrov, Arden *115:* 206
Johnston, David McCall *50:* 131, 133
Johnston, Lynne *118:* 85, 87, 89
Johnstone, Anne *8:* 120; *36:* 89
Johnstone, Janet Grahame *8:* 120; *36:* 89
Jonas, Ann *50:* 107, 108, 109; *135:* 113
Jones, Bob *71:* 5; *77:* 199
Jones, Carol *5:* 131; *72:* 185, 186; *153:* 111, 112
Jones, Chuck *53:* 70, 71
Jones, Davy *89:* 176
Jones, Douglas B. *185:* 192; *202:* 82
Jones, Elizabeth Orton *18:* 124, 126, 128, 129
Jones, Harold *14:* 88; *52:* 50
Jones, Holly *127:* 3
Jones, Jeff *41:* 64
Jones, Laurian *25:* 24, 27
Jones, Margaret *74:* 57
Jones, Noah Z. *182:* 37; *203:* 159
Jones, Randy *131:* 104
Jones, Richard *127:* 222
Jones, Robert *25:* 67
Jones, Wilfred *35:* 115; *YABC 1:* 163
Jordan, Charles *89:* 58
Jordan, Jess *158:* 136; *203:* 111
Jordan, Martin George *84:* 127
Jordan, Richard *84:* 36
Jorgenson, Andrea *91:* 111
Jorisch, Stéphane *153:* 56, 193; *177:* 29; *178:* 138, 139; *187:* 23
Joseph, James *53:* 88
Joudrey, Ken *64:* 145; *78:* 6
Joyce, William *72:* 131, 132, 133, 134; *73:* 227; *145:* 37
Joyner, Jerry *34:* 138
Juan, Ana *175:* 38; *179:* 111, 112
Jucker, Sita *5:* 93
Judge, Lita *192:* 99
Judkis, Jim *37:* 38

Juhasz, Victor *31:* 67
Jullian, Philippe *24:* 206; *25:* 203
Jung, Tom *91:* 217
Junge, Alexandra *183:* 37
Junge, Walter *67:* 150
Jupo, Frank *7:* 148, 149
Jurisch, Stephane *154:* 105
Justice, Martin *34:* 72

K

Kabatova-Taborska, Zdenka *107:* 153
Kachik, John *165:* 230
Kaczman, James *156:* 98
Kadair, Deborah Ousley *184:* 45, 89
Kahl, David *74:* 95; *97:* 35; *109:* 174; *110:* 213; *198:* 15
Kahl, M.P. *37:* 83
Kahl, Virginia *48:* 138
Kahn, Katherine Janus *90:* 135
Kakimoo, Kozo *11:* 148
Kalett, Jim *48:* 159, 160, 161
Kalin, Victor *39:* 186
Kalis, Jennifer *207:* 82
Kalman, Maira *96:* 131, 132; *137:* 115
Kalmenoff, Matthew *22:* 191
Kalow, Gisela *32:* 105
Kamen, Gloria *1:* 41; *9:* 119; *10:* 178; *35:* 157; *78:* 236; *98:* 82
Kaminsky, Jef *102:* 153
Kandell, Alice *35:* 133
Kane, Henry B. *14:* 90; *18:* 219, 220
Kane, Robert *18:* 131
Kanfer, Larry *66:* 141
Kangas, Juli *200:* 88
Kappes, Alfred *28:* 104
Karalus, Bob *41:* 157
Karas, G. Brian *80:* 60; *99:* 179; *115:* 41; *118:* 50; *136:* 168; *145:* 166; *149:* 245; *159:* 65; *171:* 192; *178:* 142, 143; *202:* 38
Karasz, Ilonka *128:* 163
Karlin, Eugene *10:* 63; *20:* 131
Karlin, Nurit *63:* 78; *103:* 110
Karpinski, Tony *134:* 160
Kasamatsu, Shiro *139:* 155
Kasparavicius, Kestutis *139:* 210
Kassian, Olena *64:* 94
Kastner, Jill *79:* 135; *117:* 84, 85
Kasuya, Masahiro *41:* 206, 207; *51:* 100
Kasza, Keiko *191:* 99, 100, 101, 102, 103
Katona, Robert *21:* 85; *24:* 126
Katz, Avi *199:* 55
Katz, Karen *158:* 123
Kauffer, E. McKnight *33:* 103; *35:* 127; *63:* 67
Kaufman, Angelika *15:* 156
Kaufman, Joe *33:* 119
Kaufman, John *13:* 158
Kaufman, Stuart *62:* 64; *68:* 226; *137:* 44
Kaufmann, John *1:* 174; *4:* 159; *8:* 43, 1; *10:* 102; *18:* 133, 134; *22:* 251
Kaye, Graham *1:* 9; *67:* 7, 8
Kaye, M.M. *62:* 95
Kazalovski, Nata *40:* 205
Keane, Bil *4:* 135
Kearney, David *72:* 47; *121:* 83
Keating, Pamel T. *77:* 37
Keats, Ezra Jack *3:* 18, 105, 257; *14:* 101, 102; *33:* 129; *57:* 79, 80, 82, 83, 84, 87
Keegan, Charles *166:* 211
Keegan, Marcia *9:* 122; *32:* 93
Keeler, Patricia A. *81:* 56; *183:* 102, 103
Keely, Jack *119:* 95
Keely, John *26:* 104; *48:* 214
Keen, Eliot *25:* 213
Keep, Richard C. *170:* 122
Keeping, Charles *9:* 124, 185; *15:* 28, 134; *18:* 115; *44:* 194, 196; *47:* 25; *52:* 3; *54:* 156; *69:* 123, 124; *74:* 56; *155:* 9
Keeter, Susan *168:* 46; *183:* 192

Keith, Eros *4:* 98; *5:* 138; *31:* 29; *43:* 220; *52:* 91, 92, 93, 94; *56:* 64, 66; *60:* 37; *79:* 93
Keleinikov, Andrei *65:* 101, 102
Kelen, Emery *13:* 115
Keller, A.J. *62:* 198
Keller, Arthur I. *26:* 106
Keller, Dick *36:* 123, 125
Keller, Holly *45:* 79; *76:* 118, 119, 120, 121; *108:* 137, 138, 140; *157:* 117, 118, 119
Keller, Katie *79:* 222; *93:* 108
Keller, Laurie *196:* 105, 106
Keller, Ronald *45:* 208
Kelley, Gary *183:* 105
Kelley, True *41:* 114, 115; *42:* 137; *75:* 35; *92:* 104, 105; *124:* 62; *130:* 100, 101; *179:* 120, 121, 122; *192:* 251
Kellogg, Steven *8:* 96; *11:* 207; *14:* 130; *20:* ; *201:* 38 58; *29:* 140, 141; *30:* 35; *41:* 141; *57:* 89, 90, 92,93, 94, 96; *59:* 182; *73:* 141; *77:* 129; *130:* 105, 106; *177:* 94, 95, 96, 97; *199:* 57; *YABC 1:* 65, 73
Kelly, Billy *158:* 143
Kelly, Geoff *97:* 196; *112:* 25
Kelly, Irene *147:* 134
Kelly, John *194:* 186
Kelly, Joseph *174:* 94
Kelly, Kathleen M. *71:* 109
Kelly, Laura *89:* 217
Kelly, True *163:* 87
Kelly, Walt *18:* 136, 137, 138, 139, 140, 141, 144, 145, 146, 148, 149
Kemble, E.W. *34:* 75; *44:* 178; *YABC 2:* 54, 59
Kemp-Welsh, Lucy *24:* 197; *100:* 214
Kendall, Jane *150:* 105; *186:* 109
Kendall, Peter *152:* 85
Kendrick, Dennis *79:* 213
Kennaway, Adrienne *60:* 55, 56; *171:* 88, 89
Kennedy, Doug *189:* 104
Kennedy, Paul Edward *6:* 190; *8:* 132; *33:* 120
Kennedy, Richard *3:* 93; *12:* 179; *44:* 193; *100:* 15; *YABC 1:* 57
Kent, Jack *24:* 136; *37:* 37; *40:* 81; *84:* 89; *86:* 150; *88:* 77
Kent, Rockwell *5:* 166; *6:* 129; *20:* 225, 226, 227,229; *59:* 144
Kenyon, Tony *81:* 201; *127:* 74
Kepes, Juliet *13:* 119
Kerins, Anthony *76:* 84
Kerr, Judity *24:* 137
Kerr, Phyllis Forbes *72:* 141
Kessler, Leonard *1:* 108; *7:* 139; *14:* 107, 227; *22:* 101; *44:* 96; *67:* 79; *82:* 123
Kest, Kristin *168:* 99; *173:* 23
Kesteven, Peter *35:* 189
Ketcham, Hank *28:* 140, 141, 142
Kettelkamp, Larry *2:* 164
Key, Alexander *8:* 99
Khalsa, Dayal Kaur *62:* 99
Kiakshuk *8:* 59
Kid, Tom *207:* 54
Kidd, Chip *94:* 23
Kidd, Richard *152:* 110
Kidd, Tom *64:* 199; *81:* 189; *185:* 173
Kiddell-Monroe, Joan *19:* 201; *55:* 59, 60; *87:* 174; *121:* 112
Kidder, Harvey *9:* 105; *80:* 41
Kidwell, Carl *43:* 145
Kieffer, Christa *41:* 89
Kiesler, Kate *110:* 105; *136:* 142
Kiff, Ken *40:* 45
Kilbride, Robert *37:* 100
Kilby, Don *141:* 144
Kim, David *201:* 79; *202:* 97
Kim, Glenn *99:* 82
Kimball, Anton *78:* 114; *119:* 105
Kimball, Yeffe *23:* 116; *37:* 88
Kimber, Murray *171:* 91
Kimmel, Warren *176:* 112
Kincade, Orin *34:* 116
Kindersley, Barnabas *96:* 110

Kindred, Wendy 7: 151
King, Colin 53: 3
King, Robin 10: 164, 165
King, Stephen Michael 141: 31; 197: 191
King, Tara Calahan 139: 172
King, Tony 39: 121
Kingman, Dong 16: 287; 44: 100, 102, 104
Kingsley, Charles YABC 2: 182
Kingston, Julie 147: 14
Kingston, Maxine Hong 53: 92
Kinney, Jeff 187: 97
Kipling, John Lockwood YABC 2: 198
Kipling, Rudyard YABC 2: 196
Kipniss, Robert 29: 59
Kirchherr, Astrid 55: 23
Kirchhoff, Art 28: 136
Kirk, Daniel 153: 115, 116, 117; 173: 101;
    196: 113, 114, 115, 116
Kirk, David 117: 88, 89; 161: 97, 98
Kirk, Ruth 5: 96
Kirk, Steve 170: 37
Kirk, Tim 32: 209, 211; 72: 89; 83: 49
Kirmse, Marguerite 15: 283; 18: 153
Kirsch, Vincent X. 124: 207
Kirschner, Ruth 22: 154
Kirwan, Wednesday 198: 73
Kish, Ely 73: 119; 79: 2
Kitamura, Satoshi 62: 102; 98: 91; 101: 147;
    138: 2; 143: 83, 85, 86; 201: 83
Kiss, Andrew 168: 115
Kitchel, JoAnn E. 133: 32
Kitchen, Bert 70: 126; 193: 49
Kittelsen, Theodor 62: 14
Kiuchi, Tatsuro 114: 71
Kiwak, Barbara 172: 135
Klahr, Susan 176: 196
Klapholz, Mel 13: 35
Klein, Bill 89: 105
Klein, Robert 55: 77
Klein, Suzanna 63: 104
Kleinman, Zalman 28: 143
Kleven, Elisa 173: 96, 97
Kliban, B. 35: 137, 138
Kline, Michael 127: 66
Klise, M. Sarah 180: 117, 118; 181: 97
Knabel, Lonnie 73: 103; 75: 187, 228; 194:
    216
Kneen, Maggie 140: 139
Knight, Ann 34: 143
Knight, Christopher 13: 125
Knight, Hilary 1: 233; 3: 21; 15: 92, 158, 159;
    16: 258, 259, 260; 18: 235; 19: 169; 35:
    242; 46: 167; 52: 116; 69: 126, 127; 132:
    129; YABC 1: 168, 169, 172
Knorr, Laura 200: 91
Knorr, Peter 126: 92, 93
Knotts, Howard 20: 4; 25: 170; 36: 163
Knutson, Barbara 112: 134; 202: 108
Knutson, Kimberley 115: 90
Kobayashi, Ann 39: 58
Kochalka, James 196: 120, 121, 122
Kocsis, J.C.
    See Paul, James
Kodman, Stanislawa 201: 85
Koehler, Hanne Lore 176: 203
Koehn, Ilse 34: 198; 79: 123
Koelsch, Michael 99: 182; 107: 164; 109: 239;
    138: 142; 150: 94; 176: 105; 187: 63; 198:
    63
Koering, Ursula 3: 28; 4: 14; 44: 5; 64:
    140,141; 85: 46
Koerner, Henry
    See Koerner, W.H.D.
Koerner, W.H.D. 14: 216; 21: 88, 89, 90, 91;
    23: 211
Koetsch, Mike 166: 68
Koffler, Camilla 36: 113
Kogan, Deborah Ray 161: 101, 102
Koide, Yasuko 50: 114
Kolado, Karen 102: 228
Komoda, Kiyo 9: 128; 13: 214

Kompaneyets, Marc 169: 92
Konashevich, Vladimir 61: 160
Konashevicha, V. YABC 1: 26
Konigsburg, E.L. 4: 138; 48: 141, 142, 144,
    145; 94: 129, 130; 126: 129, 130, 131; 194:
    95, 98
Kono, Erin Eitter 177: 99
Kooiker, Leonie 48: 148
Koonook, Simon 65: 157
Koontz, Robin Michal 136: 155
Koopmans, Loek 101: 121
Kopelke, Lisa 154: 107
Kopper, Lisa 72: 152, 153; 105: 135, 136
Korach, Mimi 1: 128, 129; 2: 52; 4: 39; 5:
    159; 9: 129; 10: 21; 24: 69
Koren, Edward 5: 100; 65: 65, 67
Kosaka, Fumi 164: 130
Koscielniak, Bruce 99: 122; 153: 120, 121,
    122
Koshkin, Alexander 92: 180
Kossin, Sandy 10: 71; 23: 105
Kostin, Andrej 26: 204
Kosturko, Bob 164: 56
Kotzky, Brian 68: 184
Kovacevic, Zivojin 13: 247
Kovalski, Maryann 58: 120; 84: 88; 97: 124,
    125, 126; 158: 3; 186: 80
Krahn, Fernando 2: 257; 34: 206; 49: 152
Kramer, Anthony 33: 81
Kramer, David 96: 162; 109: 132; 150: 220
Kramer, Frank 6: 121
Krantz, Kathy 35: 83
Kratter, Paul 139: 65
Kraus, Robert 13: 217; 65: 113; 93: 93, 94
Krause, Jon 176: 62
Krauss, Trisha 174: 10
Kredel, Fritz 6: 35; 17: 93, 94, 95, 96; 22:
    147; 24: 175; 29: 130; 35: 77; YABC 2: 166,
    300
Kreloff, Eliot 189: 107, 108; 205: 182
Krementz, Jill 17: 98; 49: 41
Krenina, Katya 117: 106; 125: 133; 176: 117
Kresin, Robert 23: 19
Krieger, Salem 54: 164
Kriegler, Lyn 73: 29
Krinitz, Esther Nisenthal 193: 196
Krommes, Beth 128: 141; 149: 136; 181: 100,
    101; 184: 105; 188: 125
Krone, Mike 101: 71
Kronheimer, Ann 135: 119
Krosoczka, Jarrett J. 155: 142; 200: 93, 94
Kruck, Gerald 88: 181
Krudop, Walter Lyon 199: 19
Krupinski, Loretta 67: 104; 102: 131; 161:
    105, 106
Krupp, Robin Rector 53: 96, 98
Krush, Beth 1: 51, 85; 2: 233; 4: 115; 9: 61;
    10: 191; 11: 196; 18: 164, 165; 32: 72; 37:
    203; 43: 57; 60: 102, 103, 107, 108, 109
Krush, Joe 2: 233; 4: 115; 9: 61; 10: 191; 11:
    196; 18: 164, 165; 32: 72, 91; 37: 203; 43:
    57; 60: 102, 103, 107, 108, 109
Krych, Duane 91: 43
Krykorka, Vladyana 96: 147; 143: 90, 91;
    168: 14
Kubick, Dana 165: 91
Kubinyi, Laszlo 4: 116; 6: 113; 16: 118; 17:
    100; 28: 227; 30: 172; 49: 24, 28; 54: 23;
    167: 149
Kubricht, Mary 73: 118
Kucharik, Elena 139: 31
Kuchera, Kathleen 84: 5
Kuhn, Bob 17: 91; 35: 235
Kulikov, Boris 163: 185; 185: 23; 205: 99,
    100
Kulka, Joe 188: 110
Kukalis, Romas 90: 27; 139: 37
Kuklin, Susan 63: 82, 83, 84
Kunhardt, Dorothy 53: 101
Kunhardt, Edith 67: 105, 106
Kunstler, Mort 10: 73; 32: 143

Kurchevsky, V. 34: 61
Kurczok, Belinda 121: 118
Kurelek, William 8: 107
Kuriloff, Ron 13: 19
Kurisu, Jane 160: 120
Kuskin, Karla 2: 170; 68: 115, 116; 111: 116
Kutzer, Ernst 19: 249
Kuzma, Steve 57: 8; 62: 93
Kuznetsova, Berta 74: 45
Kvasnosky, Laura McGee 93: 103; 142: 83;
    182: 108
Kwas, Susan Estelle 179: 116
Kyong, Yunmee 165: 139

L

LaBlanc, Andre 24: 146
Laboccetta, Mario 27: 120
LaBrose, Darcie 157: 134
Labrosse, Darcia 58: 88; 108: 77; 178: 89
LaCava, Vince 95: 118
Laceky, Adam 32: 121
Lacis, Astra 85: 117
Lacome, Julie 174: 96, 97
La Croix YABC 2: 4
Ladd, London 206: 50
Ladwig, Tim 98: 212; 117: 76
La Farge, Margaret 47: 141
LaFave, Kim 64: 177; 72: 39; 97: 146; 99:
    172; 106: 123; 149: 126; 196: 128, 129
Lafontaine, Roger 167: 158
Lafrance, Marie 197: 109
Lagarrigue, Jerome 136: 102; 187: 81
Laimgruber, Monika 11: 153
Laite, Gordon 1: 130, 131; 8: 209; 31: 113;
    40: 63; 46: 117
Laliberté, Louise-Andrée 169: 98
LaMarche, Jim 46: 204; 61: 56; 94: 69; 114:
    22; 129: 163; 162: 78, 80
Lamb, Jim 10: 117
Lambase, Barbara 101: 185; 150: 221; 166:
    234
Lambert, J.K. 38: 129; 39: 24
Lambert, Sally Anne 133: 191
Lambert, Saul 23: 112; 33: 107; 54: 136
Lambert, Stephen 109: 33; 174: 99
Lambo, Don 6: 156; 35: 115; 36: 146
Lamontagne, Jacques 166: 227
Lamut, Sonja 57: 193
Lamut, Sonya 85: 102
Landa, Peter 11: 95; 13: 177; 53: 119
Landau, Jacob 38: 111
Landis, Joan 104: 23; 203: 32
Landon, Lucinda 79: 31
Landshoff, Ursula 13: 124
Landström, Lena 146: 165, 166
Landström, Olof 146: 166, 168; 170: 22
Lane, Daniel 112: 60
Lane, John R. 8: 145
Lane, John 15: 176, 177; 30: 146
Lane, Nancy 166: 74
Lang, G.D. 48: 56
Lang, Gary 73: 75
Lang, Jerry 18: 295
Langdo, Bryan 186: 187; 191: 113, 114, 115
Lange, Dorothea 50: 141
Langley, Jonathan 162: 128
Langner, Nola 8: 110; 42: 36
Lanino, Deborah 105: 148
Lantz, Paul 1: 82, 102; 27: 88; 34: 102; 45:
    123
Larkin, Bob 84: 225
Laroche, Giles 126: 140; 146: 81
LaRochelle, David 171: 97
Larrecq, John 44: 108; 68: 56
Larsen, Suzanne 1: 13
Larson, Gary 57: 121, 122, 123, 124, 125,
    126, 127

Larsson, Carl *35:* 144, 145, 146, 147, 148, 149, 150, 152, 153, 154
Larsson, Karl *19:* 177
Lartitegui, Ana G. *105:* 167
LaRue, Jenna *167:* 20
La Rue, Michael D. *13:* 215
Lasker, Joe *7:* 186, 187; *14:* 55; *38:* 115; *39:* 47; *83:* 113, 114, 115
Latham, Barbara *16:* 188, 189; *43:* 71
Lathrop, Dorothy *14:* 117, 118, 119; *15:* 109; *16:* 78, 79, 81; *32:* 201, 203; *33:* 112; *YABC 2:* 301
Lattimore, Eleanor Frances *7:* 156
Lauden, Claire *16:* 173
Lauden, George, Jr. *16:* 173
Laune, Paul *2:* 235; *34:* 31
Laure, Jason *49:* 53; *50:* 122
Lauter, Richard *63:* 29; *67:* 111; *77:* 198
Lavallee, Barbara *74:* 157; *92:* 154; *96:* 126; *145:* 193; *166:* 125, 126; *186:* 155; *192:* 172
Lave, Fitz Hugh *59:* 139
Lavis, Stephen *43:* 143; *87:* 137, 164, 165
Layton, Neal *152:* 120, 121; *182:* 65; *187:* 103, 105, 106
Law, Jenny *201:* 31
Lawrason, June *168:* 30
Lawrence, John *25:* 131; *30:* 141; *44:* 198, 200
Lawrence, Stephen *20:* 195
Lawson, Carol *6:* 38; *42:* 93, 131; *174:* 56; *189:* 89
Lawson, George *17:* 280
Lawson, Robert *5:* 26; *6:* 94; *13:* 39; *16:* 11; *20:* 100, 102, 103; *54:* 3; *66:* 12; *100:* 144, 145; *YABC 2:* 222, 224, 225, 227, 228, 229, 230, 231, 232, 233, 234, 235, 237, 238, 239, 240, 241
Layfield, Kathie *60:* 194
Lazare, Jerry *44:* 109; *74:* 28
Lazarevich, Mila *17:* 118
Lazarus, Claire *103:* 30
Lazarus, Keo Felker *21:* 94
Lazzaro, Victor *11:* 126
Lea, Bob *166:* 208; *203:* 108
Lea, Tom *43:* 72, 74
Leacroft, Richard *6:* 140
Leaf, Munro *20:* 99
Leake, Donald *70:* 41
Leander, Patricia *23:* 27
Lear, Edward *18:* 183, 184, 185
Lear, Rebecca *149:* 46
Lebenson, Richard *6:* 209; *7:* 76; *23:* 145; *44:* 191; *87:* 153
Le Cain, Errol *6:* 141; *9:* 3; *22:* 142; *25:* 198; *28:* 173; *68:* 128, 129; *86:* 49
Lechon, Daniel *113:* 211
Leder, Dora *129:* 172
Ledger, Bill *181:* 58
Leduc, Bernard *102:* 36
Lee, Alan *62:* 25, 28
Lee, Bryce *99:* 60; *101:* 195; *196:* 53
Lee, Chinlun *181:* 138; *182:* 112
Lee, Declan *191:* 20
Lee, Dom *83:* 118, 120; *93:* 123; *121:* 121, 126; *146:* 174, 175, 206, 207; *174:* 204
Lee, Doris *13:* 246; *32:* 183; *44:* 111
Lee, Hector Viveros *115:* 96
Lee, Ho Baek *200:* 160
Lee, Jeanne M. *158:* 56
Lee, Jared *93:* 200; *157:* 229
Lee, Jody *81:* 121; *82:* 225; *91:* 155; *100:* 182
Lee, Jody A. *127:* 124, 126, 127
See also Lee, Jody
Lee, Manning de V. *2:* 200; *17:* 12; *27:* 87; *37:* 102, 103, 104; *YABC 2:* 304
Lee, Marie G. *138:* 157
Lee, Paul *97:* 100; *105:* 72, 209; *109:* 177; *128:* 113; *202:* 45
Lee, Robert J. *3:* 97; *67:* 124
Lee, Victor *96:* 228; *105:* 182; *140:* 196
Leech, Dorothy *98:* 76

Leech, John *15:* 59
Leedy, Loreen *84:* 142; *128:* 144, 145, 146; *175:* 125, 126, 127
Leeman, Michael *44:* 157
Leeming, Catherine *87:* 39
Lees, Harry *6:* 112
LeFever, Bill *88:* 220, 221
Legenisel *47:* 111
Legrand, Edy *18:* 89, 93
Lehman, Barbara *73:* 123; *170:* 130
Lehrman, Rosalie *2:* 180
Leichman, Seymour *5:* 107
Leick, Bonnie *205:* 104
Leighton, Clare *25:* 130; *33:* 168; *37:* 105, 106, 108,109
Leisk, David *1:* 140, 141; *11:* 54; *30:* 137, 142, 143,144
Leister, Brian *89:* 45; *106:* 37; *114:* 67; *149:* 236
Leloir, Maurice *18:* 77, 80, 83, 99
Lemaître, Pascal *144:* 175; *176:* 130; *189:* 135
Lemieux, Michele *100:* 148; *139:* 153
Lemke, Horst *14:* 98; *38:* 117, 118, 119
Lemke, R.W. *42:* 162
Lemon, David Gwynne *9:* 1
LeMoult, Adolph *82:* 116
Lenn, Michael *136:* 89
Lennon, John *114:* 100
Lennox, Elsie *95:* 163; *143:* 160
Lenski, Lois *1:* 144; *26:* 135, 137, 139, 141; *100:* 153, 154
Lent, Blair *1:* 116, 117; *2:* 174; *3:* 206, 207; *7:* 168, 169; *34:* 62; *68:* 217; *133:* 101; *183:* 60
Leonard, Richard *91:* 128
Leonard, Tom *207:* 95
Leone, Leonard *49:* 190
Lerner, Carol *86:* 140, 141, 142
Lerner, Judith *116:* 138
Lerner, Sharon *11:* 157; *22:* 56
Leroux-Hugon, Helene *132:* 139
Leslie, Cecil *19:* 244
Lessac, Frané *80:* 182, 207; *96:* 182; *202:* 58
Lessing, Erich *167:* 52; *173:* 60
Lester, Alison *50:* 124; *90:* 147, 148; *129:* 130
Lethcoe, Jason *191:* 116, 117
Le Tord, Bijou *49:* 156; *95:* 112
Leutz, Emanuel *165:* 27
Levai, Blaise *39:* 130
Levin, Ted *12:* 148
Levine, David *43:* 147, 149, 150, 151, 152; *64:* 11
Levine, Joe *71:* 88
Levine, Marge *81:* 127
Levinson, David *178:* 232
Levit, Herschel *24:* 223
Levstek, Ljuba *131:* 192; *134:* 216; *149:* 65; *168:* 180
Levy, Jessica Ann *19:* 225; *39:* 191
Levy, Lina *117:* 126
Lewin, Betsy *32:* 114; *48:* 177; *90:* 151; *91:* 125; *92:* 85; *115:* 105; *169:* 110, 111; *178:* 47; *186:* 188; *194:* 201
Lewin, Ted *4:* 77; *8:* 168; *20:* 110; *21:* 99,100; *27:* 110; *28:* 96, 97; *31:* 49; *45:* 55; *48:* 223; *60:* 20, 119, 120; *62:* 139; *66:* 108; *71:* 12; *72:* 21; *74:* 226; *76:* 139, 140; *77:* 82; *79:* 87; *85:* 49, 177; *86:* 55; *88:* 182; *93:* 28, 29; *94:* 34, 182, 194; *99:* 156; *104:* 8; *115:* 123; *118:* 74; *119:* 114, 116; *131:* 54; *145:* 99; *165:* 151; *177:* 75; *178:* 42; *190:* 30; *192:* 86; *195:* 101, 102; *203:* 52
Lewis, Allen *15:* 112
Lewis, E.B. *88:* 143; *93:* 109; *119:* 79; *124:* 113; *128:* 49; *151:* 167; *168:* 110; *173:* 121; *174:* 66; *176:* 7; *184:* 150; *185:* 191
Lewis, H.B. *170:* 124
Lewis, J. Patrick *162:* 83
Lewis, Jan *81:* 22
Lewis, Kim *136:* 165
Lewis, Richard W. *52:* 25

Lewis, Robin Baird *98:* 193
Leydon, Rita Floden *21:* 101
Li, Xiojun *187:* 172
Liao, Jimmy *202:* 100
Lichtenheld, Tom *152:* 125, 126
Lieblich, Irene *22:* 173; *27:* 209, 214
Lieder, Rick *108:* 197; *199:* 58, 59, 60
Lies, Brian *92:* 40; *141:* 101; *150:* 138; *190:* 97, 98, 99,
Liese, Charles *4:* 222
Life, Kay *79:* 49
Lifton, Robert Jay *66:* 154
Lightburn, Ron *86:* 153; *91:* 122
Lightfoot, Norman R. *45:* 47
Lignell, Lois *37:* 114
Lill, Debra *121:* 70
Lilly, Charles *8:* 73; *20:* 127; *48:* 53; *72:* 9,16; *77:* 98; *102:* 94
Lilly, Ken *37:* 224
Lim, John *43:* 153
Limona, Mercedes *51:* 183
Lin, Grace *143:* 217; *162:* 86, 87; *174:* 185
Lincoln, Patricia Henderson *27:* 27; *78:* 127
Lindahl, Ron *84:* 17
Lindahl, Val *84:* 17
Lindberg, Howard *10:* 123; *16:* 190
Lindberg, Jeffrey *64:* 77; *77:* 71; *79:* 54; *80:* 149; *174:* 109; *179:* 52
Linden, Seymour *18:* 200, 201; *43:* 140
Lindenbaum, Pija *144:* 143; *183:* 113
Linder, Richard *27:* 119
Lindman, Maj *43:* 154
Lindsay, Norman *67:* 114
Lindsay, Vachel *40:* 118
Lindstrom, Jack *145:* 118
Line, Les *27:* 143
Linell
See Smith, Linell
Lionni, Leo *8:* 115; *72:* 159, 160, 161
Lipinsky, Lino *2:* 156; *22:* 175
Lippincott, Gary A. *70:* 35; *119:* 118
Lippman, Peter *8:* 31; *31:* 119, 120, 160
Lisi, Victoria *89:* 145
Lisker, Emily *169:* 114
Lisker, Sonia O. *16:* 274; *31:* 31; *44:* 113, 114
Lisowski, Gabriel *47:* 144; *49:* 157
Lissim, Simon *17:* 138
Little, Ed *89:* 145; *151:* 53
Little, Harold *16:* 72
Little, Mary E. *28:* 146
Littlewood, Karen *165:* 126
Litty, Julie *111:* 63
Litzinger, Rosanne *151:* 101; *176:* 118; *196:* 133, 134, 135
Liu, Lesley *143:* 72
Livesly, Lorna *19:* 216
Livingston, Susan *95:* 22
Liwska, Renata *164:* 113; *199:* 25, 69
Ljungkvist, Laura *180:* 120
Llerena, Carlos Antonio *19:* 181
Lloyd, Errol *11:* 39; *22:* 178
Lloyd, Megan *77:* 118; *80:* 113; *97:* 75; *117:* 94, 95; *189:* 121, 122
Lloyd, Sam *183:* 116, 117
Lo, Beth *165:* 154
Lo, Koon-chiu *7:* 134
Loates, Glen *63:* 76
Lobel, Anita *6:* 87; *9:* 141; *18:* 248; *55:* 85,86, 87, 88, 93, 104; *60:* 67; *78:* 263; *82:* 110; *96:* 157, 159; *101:* 84; *132:* 35; *162:* 93, 94
Lobel, Arnold *1:* 188, 189; *5:* 12; *6:* 147; *7:* 167, 209; *18:* 190, 191; *25:* 39, 43; *27:* 40; *29:* 174; *52:* 127; *55:* 89, 91, 94, 95, 97, 98, 99, 100, 101, 102,103, 105, 106; *60:* 18, 31; *66:* 181, 183; *75:* 57; *82:* 246; *136:* 146
Lobel, Gillian *190:* 21
Locker, Thomas *109:* 134
Lodge, Bernard *107:* 125, 126; *153:* 93
Loeb, Jeph *153:* 177
Lodge, Jo *112:* 119
Loefgren, Ulf *3:* 108

Illustrations Index

Loescher, Ann *20:* 108
Loescher, Gil *20:* 108
Loew, David *93:* 184; *171:* 120
Lofting, Hugh *15:* 182, 183; *100:* 161, 162
Lofts, Pamela *60:* 188
Loh, George *38:* 88
Lomberg, Jon *58:* 160
Lonette, Reisie *11:* 211; *12:* 168; *13:* 56; *36:* 122; *43:* 155
Long, Ethan *168:* 146; *178:* 12; *182:* 120, 121; *196:* 124
Long, Laurel *162:* 135; *190:* 11; *203:* 113, 114
Long, Loren *99:* 176; *172:* 65; *182:* 78; *188:* 114, 115
Long, Melinda *152:* 128
Long, Miles *115:* 174
Long, Sally *42:* 184
Long, Sylvia *74:* 168; *132:* 63; *179:* 134
Longoni, Eduardo *73:* 85
Longtemps, Ken *17:* 123; *29:* 221; *69:* 82
Looser, Heinz *YABC 2:* 208
Lopez, Loretta *190:* 100
López, Rafael *197:* 160; *198:* 85
Lopshire, Robert *6:* 149; *21:* 117; *34:* 166; *73:* 13
Lord, John Vernon *21:* 104; *23:* 25; *51:* 22
Lorenz, Albert *40:* 146; *115:* 127
Loretta, Sister Mary *33:* 73
Lorraine, Walter H. *3:* 110; *4:* 123; *16:* 192; *103:* 119
Los, Marek *146:* 22; *193:* 23
Loss, Joan *11:* 163
Louderback, Walt *YABC 1:* 164
Lousada, Sandra *40:* 138
Louth, Jack *149:* 252; *151:* 191, 192
Love, Judy *173:* 43; *196:* 40
Low, Joseph *14:* 124, 125; *18:* 68; *19:* 194; *31:* 166; *80:* 239
Low, William *62:* 175; *80:* 147; *112:* 194; *150:* 202; *169:* 175; *177:* 110; *192:* 27
Lowe, Vicky *177:* 130
Lowenheim, Alfred *13:* 65, 66
Lowenstein, Sallie *116:* 90, 91
Lowitz, Anson *17:* 124; *18:* 215
Lowrey, Jo *8:* 133
Lubach, Vanessa *142:* 152
Lubell, Winifred *1:* 207; *3:* 15; *6:* 151
Lubin, Leonard B. *19:* 224; *36:* 79, 80; *45:* 128, 129,131, 132, 133, 134, 135, 136, 137, 139, 140, 141; *70:* 95; *YABC2:* 96
Lucht, Irmgard *82:* 216
Ludwig, Helen *33:* 144, 145
Lufkin, Raymond *38:* 138; *44:* 48
Luhrs, Henry *7:* 123; *11:* 120
Lujan, Tonita *82:* 33
Lupo, Dom *4:* 204
Lustig, Loretta *30:* 186; *46:* 134, 135, 136, 137
Luthardt, Kevin *172:* 125, 126
Luxbacher, Irene *153:* 145
Luzak, Dennis *52:* 121; *99:* 142
Lydbury, Jane *82:* 98
Lydecker, Laura *21:* 113; *42:* 53
Lynch, Charles *16:* 33
Lynch, Marietta *29:* 137; *30:* 171
Lynch, P.J. *126:* 228; *129:* 110; *132:* 247; *183:* 64; *207:* 184
Lyne, Alison Davis *188:* 118, 198
Lyon, Carol *102:* 26
Lyon, Elinor *6:* 154
Lyon, Fred *14:* 16
Lyon, Tammie *175:* 170
Lyons, Oren *8:* 193
Lyster, Michael *26:* 41

M

Maas, Dorothy *6:* 175
Maas, Julie *47:* 61

Macaulay, David *46:* 139, 140, 141, 142, 143, 144, 145, 147, 149, 150; *72:* 167, 168, 169; *137:* 129, 130, 131, 132
MacCarthy, Patricia *69:* 141
Macdonald, Alister *21:* 55
Macdonald, Roberta *19:* 237; *52:* 164
MacDonald, Norman *13:* 99
MacDonald, Ross *201:* 103
MacDonald, Suse *54:* 41; *109* 138; *130:* 156; *193:* 106, 107, 109, 110
Mace, Varian *49:* 159
MacEachern, Stephen *206:* 2
Macguire, Robert Reid *18:* 67
Machetanz, Fredrick *34:* 147, 148
MacInnes, Ian *35:* 59
MacIntyre, Elisabeth *17:* 127, 128
Mack, Jeff *161:* 128; *194:* 119, 120
Mack, Stan *17:* 129; *96:* 33
Mackay, Donald *17:* 60
MacKaye, Arvia *32:* 119
Mackenzie, Robert *204:* 78
Mackenzie, Stuart *73:* 213
MacKenzie, Garry *33:* 159
Mackie, Clare *87:* 134
Mackinlay, Miguel *27:* 22
MacKinstry, Elizabeth *15:* 110; *42:* 139, 140, 141, 142, 143,144, 145
MacLeod, Lee *91:* 167
Maclise, Daniel *YABC 2:* 257
Macnaughton, Tina *182:* 145
MacRae, Tom *181:* 112
Madden, Don *3:* 112, 113; *4:* 33, 108, 155; *7:* 193; *78:* 12; *YABC 2:* 211
Maddison, Angela Mary *10:* 83
Madsen, Jim *146:* 259; *152:* 237; *184:* 106; *197:* 21; *202:* 103, 104
Maestro, Giulio *8:* 124; *12:* 17; *13:* 108; *25:* 182; *54:* 147; *59:* 114, 115, 116, 117, 118, 121, 123, 124, 125,126, 127; *68:* 37, 38; *106:* 129, 130, 131, 136, 137, 138
Maffia, Daniel *60:* 200
Maggio, Viqui *58:* 136, 181; *74:* 150; *75:* 90; *85:* 159; *90:* 158; *109:* 184; *193:* 113
Magnus, Erica *77:* 123
Magnuson, Diana *28:* 102; *34:* 190; *41:* 175
Magoon, Scott *181:* 104
Magovern, Peg *103:* 123
Maguire, Sheila *41:* 100
Magurn, Susan *91:* 30
Mahony, Will *37:* 120
Mahony, Will *85:* 116
Mahood, Kenneth *24:* 141
Mahurin, Matt *164:* 225; *175:* 95; *189:* 37; *196:* 14
Maik, Henri *9:* 102
Maione, Heather *106:* 5; *178:* 8; *189:* 126, 127; *193:* 58
Maisto, Carol *29:* 87
Maitland, Antony *1:* 100, 176; *8:* 41; *17:* 246; *24:* 46; *25:* 177, 178; *32:* 74; *60:* 65, 195; *67:* 156; *87:* 131; *101:* 110
Majewski, Dawn *169:* 95
Mak, Kam *72:* 25; *75:* 43; *87:* 186; *97:* 24; *102:* 154; *149:* 195; *186:* 28
Makie, Pam *37:* 117
Maktima, Joe *116:* 191
Maland, Nick *99:* 77
Male, Alan *132:* 64
Malone, James Hiram *84:* 161
Malone, Nola Langner *82:* 239
Malone, Peter *191:* 121, 122, 123
Malsberg, Edward *51:* 175
Malvern, Corinne *2:* 13; *34:* 148, 149
Manchess, Gregory *165:* 241; *203:* 119
Mancusi, Stephen *63:* 198, 199
Mandelbaum, Ira *31:* 115
Manders, John *138:* 152, 155; *188:* 171; *190:* 92; *199:* 5
Manet, Edouard *23:* 170
Mangiat, Jeff *173:* 127
Mangurian, David *14:* 133

Manham, Allan *42:* 109; *77:* 180; *80:* 227
Manley, Matt *103:* 167; *117:* 98; *172:* 49
Manna, Giovanni *178:* 44
Manniche, Lise *31:* 121
Manning, Jane *96:* 203
Manning, Jo *63:* 154
Manning, Lawrence *191:* 153
Manning, Mick *176:* 139
Manning, Samuel F. *5:* 75
Mantel, Richard *57:* 73; *63:* 106; *82:* 255
Mantha, John *205:* 164
Maraja *15:* 86; *YABC 1:* 28; *2:* 115
Marcellino, Fred *20:* 125; *34:* 222; *53:* 125; *58:* 205; *61:* 64, 121, 122; *68:* 154, 156, 157, 158, 159; *72:* 25; *86:* 184; *98:* 181; *118:* 129, 130, 131; *149:* 218; *194:* 7
Marchesi, Stephen *34:* 140; *46:* 72; *50:* 147; *66:* 239; *70:* 33; *73:* 18, 114, 163; *77:* 47, 76,147; *78:* 79; *80:* 30; *81:* 6; *89:* 66; *93:* 21,130; *94:* 94; *97:* 66; *98:* 96; *114:* 115, 116
Marchiori, Carlos *14:* 60
Marciano, John Bemelmans *118:* 133; *167:* 110, 111, 112
Marcus, Barry David *139:* 248; *145:* 18
Maren, Julie *199:* 73
Margules, Gabriele *21:* 120
Mariana
   See Foster, Marian Curtis
Mariano, Michael *52:* 108
Marino, Dorothy *6:* 37; *14:* 135
Mario, Heide Stetson *101:* 202
Maris, Ron *71:* 123
Maritz, Nicolaas *85:* 123
Mark, Mona *65:* 105; *68:* 205; *116:* 213
Markham, R.L. *17:* 240
Marks, Alan *104:* 104; *109:* 182; *164:* 92; *185:* 134; *187:* 120, 121, 122
Marks, Cara *54:* 9
Marks, Colin *203:* 129
Marokvia, Artur *31:* 122
Marquez, Susan *108:* 121
Marrella, Maria Pia *62:* 116
Marriott, Pat *30:* 30; *34:* 39; *35:* 164, 165, 166; *44:* 170; *48:* 186, 187, 188, 189, 191, 192, 193; *91:* 92
Mars, W.T. *1:* 161; *3:* 115; *4:* 208, 225; *5:* 92, 105, 186; *8:* 214; *9:* 12; *13:* 121; *27:* 151; *31:* 180; *38:* 102; *48:* 66; *62:* 164, 165; *64:* 62; *68:* 229; *79:* 55
Marschall, Ken *85:* 29
Marsh, Christine *3:* 164
Marsh, James *73:* 137
Marsh, Reginald *17:* 5; *19:* 89; *22:* 90, 96
Marshall, Anthony D. *18:* 216
Marshall, Felicia *170:* 190
Marshall, James *6:* 160; *40:* 221; *42:* 24, 25, 29; *51:* 111, 112, 113, 114, 115, 116, 117, 118, 119, 120, 121; *64:* 13; *75:* 126, 127, 128, 129; *102:* 10, 12
Marshall, Janet *97:* 154
Marstall, Bob *55:* 145; *84:* 153, 170; *104:* 145; *154:* 166, 167, 168
Martchenko, Michael *50:* 129, 153, 155, 156, 157; *83:* 144,145; *154:* 137, 138, 139
Marten, Ruth *129:* 52
Martin, Brad *186:* 186
Martin, Charles E. *70:* 144
Martin, David Stone *24:* 232; *62:* 4
Martin, Fletcher *18:* 213; *23:* 151
Martin, Rene *7:* 144; *42:* 148, 149, 150
Martin, Richard E. *51:* 157; *131:* 203
Martin, Ron *32:* 81
Martin, Stefan *8:* 68; *32:* 124, 126; *56:* 33
Martin, Whitney *166:* 137
Martinez, Ed *58:* 192; *72:* 231; *77:* 33; *80:* 214; *167:* 123
Martinez, John *6:* 113; *118:* 13; *139:* 143
Martinez, Sergio *158:* 190
Martini, Angela *183:* 161
Martiniere, Stephan *171:* 130

Marton, Jirina *95:* 127, 128; *144:* 145
Martorell, Antonio *84:* 6; *97:* 161
Martucci, Griesbach *52:* 106
Marvin, Frederic *83:* 86
Marx, Robert F. *24:* 143
Marzollo, Jean *190:* 127
Masefield, Judith *19:* 208, 209
Masheris, Robert *78:* 51
Masiello, Ralph *186:* 171
Mason, George F. *14:* 139
Mason, Robert *84:* 96
Massey, Barbara *68:* 142
Massie, Diane Redfield *16:* 194
Massie, Kim *31:* 43
Mataya, David *121:* 66
Mathers, Petra *119:* 135; *163:* 104; *176:* 143, 144; *187:* 142; *196:* 101
Mathewuse, James *51:* 143
Mathieu, Joseph *14:* 33; *39:* 206; *43:* 167; *56:* 180; *79:* 126; *94:* 147; *185:* 140
Matje, Martin *169:* 177, 178; *172:* 180
Matsubara, Naoko *12:* 121
Matsuda, Shizu *13:* 167
Matsuoka, Mei *192:* 135
Matte, L'Enc *22:* 183
Mattelson, Marvin *36:* 50, 51
Mattheson, Jenny *180:* 132
Matthews, Elizabeth *194:* 128
Matthews, F. Leslie *4:* 216
Matthews, Tina *190:* 130
Mattingly, David *71:* 76, 77; *82:* 64; *91:* 216, 217; *109:* 25
Matulay, Laszlo *5:* 18; *43:* 168
Matus, Greta *12:* 142
Maughan, William *181:* 31
Mauldin, Bill *27:* 23
Mauterer, Erin Marie *119:* 5
Mawicke, Tran *9:* 137; *15:* 191; *47:* 100
Mawson, Matt *74:* 115
Max, Peter *45:* 146, 147, 148, 149, 150
Maxie, Betty *40:* 135
Maxwell, John Alan *1:* 148
May, Steve *204:* 30
Mayan, Earl *7:* 193
Mayer, Bill *200:* 138
Mayer, Danuta *117:* 103
Mayer, Marianna *32:* 132
Mayer, Mercer *11:* 192; *16:* 195, 196; *20:* 55, 57; *32:* 129, 130, 132, 133, 134; *41:* 144, 248, 252; *58:* 186; *73:* 140, 142, 143; *137:* 137, 138
Mayforth, Hal *166:* 77
Mayhew, James *85:* 121; *138:* 187; *149:* 140; *204:* 81
Mayhew, Richard *3:* 106
Mayo, Gretchen Will *38:* 81; *84:* 166
Mays, Victor *5:* 127; *8:* 45, 153; *14:* 245; *23:* 50; *34:* 155; *40:* 79; *45:* 158; *54:* 91; *66:* 240
Mazal, Chanan *49:* 104
Maze, Deborah *71:* 83
Mazellan, Ron *75:* 97, 98
Mazetti, Alan *112:* 72
Mazille, Capucine *96:* 168
Mazza, Adriana Saviozzi *19:* 215
Mazzella, Mary Jo *82:* 165
Mazzetti, Alan *45:* 210
McAfee, Steve *135:* 146; *167:* 176; *191:* 84
McAlinden, Paul *112:* 128
McBride, Angus *28:* 49; *103:* 40
McBride, Will *30:* 110
McCaffery, Janet *38:* 145
McCallum, Graham *78:* 78
McCallum, Stephen *141:* 143; *156:* 5; *166:* 228
McCann, Gerald *3:* 50; *4:* 94; *7:* 54; *41:* 121
McCarthy, Dan *174:* 74
McCarthy, Linda *177:* 128
McCarthy, Meghan *168:* 134; *199:* 74
McCauley, Adam *157:* 36; *184:* 199; *193:* 100

McCay, Winsor *41:* 124, 126, 128, 129, 130, 131; *134:* 77, 79
McClary, Nelson *1:* 111
McClements, George *196:* 146
McClintock, Barbara *57:* 135; *95:* 130; *146:* 190
McClintock, Theodore *14:* 141
McCloskey, Robert *1:* 184, 185; *2:* 186, 187; *17:* 209; *39:* 139, 140, 141, 142, 143, 146, 147, 148; *85:* 150, 151; *100:* 172, 173, 174
McClung, Robert *2:* 189; *68:* 166, 167
McClure, Gillian *31:* 132; *150:* 53
McConnel, Jerry *31:* 75, 187
McConnell, Mary *102:* 49
McCord, Kathleen Garry *78:* 236
McCormack, John *66:* 193
McCormick, A.D. *35:* 119
McCormick, Dell J. *19:* 216
McCrady, Lady *16:* 198; *39:* 127
McCrea, James *3:* 122; *33:* 216
McCrea, Ruth *3:* 122; *27:* 102; *33:* 216
McCue, Lisa *65:* 148, 149; *77:* 54; *80:* 132; *175:* 33; *177:* 133, 135
McCully, Emily Arnold *2:* 89; *4:* 120, 121, 146, 197; *5:* 2, 129; *7:* 191; *11:* 122; *15:* 210; *33:* 23; *35:* 244; *37:* 122; *39:* 88; *40:* 103; *50:* 30,31, 32, 33, 34, 35, 36, 37; *52:* 89, 90; *57:* 6; *62:* 3; *70:* 195; *86:* 82; *96:* 192; *97:* 93; *110:* 143,144; *117:* 47; *167:* 96
McCurdy, Michael *13:* 153; *24:* 85; *81:* 160; *82:* 157, 158; *86:* 125; *97:* 92; *117:* 178; *132:* 6; *147:* 159, 160
McCusker, Paul *99:* 19
McDaniel, Jerry *132:* 135
McDaniel, Preston *160:* 206; *170:* 139
McDermott, Beverly Brodsky *11:* 180
McDermott, Gerald *16:* 201; *74:* 174, 175; *163:* 150, 151
McDermott, Mike *96:* 187
McDonald, Jill *13:* 155; *26:* 128
McDonald, Mercedes *169:* 118
McDonald, Ralph J. *5:* 123, 195
McDonnell, Flora *146:* 199, 200
McDonnell, Patrick *179:* 153, 154
McDonough, Don *10:* 163
McElligott, Matt *196:* 147
McElmurry, Jill *137:* 148; *163:* 141; *202:* 186
McElrath-Eslick, Lori *129:* 145; *142:* 21; *173:* 123; *202:* 194; *204:* 88, 89
McEntee, Dorothy *37:* 124
McEwan, Keith *88:* 116; *165:* 122, 123
McEwen, Katharine *169:* 34
McFall, Christie *12:* 144
McFeely, Daniel *160:* 213
McGaw, Laurie *109:* 243; *143:* 216
McGee, Barbara *6:* 165
McGee, Marni *163:* 153
McGillvray, Kim *158:* 171; *165:* 213; *186:* 183; *190:* 175
McGinley-Nally, Sharon *131:* 19
McGinnis, Robert *110:* 113; *177:* 80
McGovern, Tara *98:* 171
McGraw, Sheila *83:* 146
McGregor, Barbara *200:* 155
McGregor, Malcolm *23:* 27
McGrory, Anik *193:* 120
McGuire, Robert *204:* 57
McGuirk, Leslie *152:* 159
McHale, John *138:* 190
McHenry, E.B. *193:* 122
McHugh, Tom *23:* 64
McIntosh, Jon *42:* 56
McKay, Donald *2:* 118; *32:* 157; *45:* 151, 152
McKean, Dave *150:* 71; *174:* 156; *197:* 83, 118
McKeating, Eileen *44:* 58
McKee, David *10:* 48; *21:* 9; *70:* 154, 155; *107:* 139, 140, 141; *134:* 218; *158:* 148, 149, 150, 151
McKee, Diana *109:* 185
McKelvey, Patrick *164:* 141

McKendry, Joe *170:* 136
McKeveny, Tom *164:* 60; *173:* 79
McKie, Roy *7:* 44
McKie, Todd *205:* 181
McKillip, Kathy *30:* 153
McKinney, Ena *26:* 39
McKinnon, James *136:* 75
McKowen, Scott *172:* 63; *202:* 49
McLachlan, Edward *5:* 89
McLaren, Chesley *133:* 53
McLaren, Kirsty *123:* 99; *124:* 226
Mclean, Andrew *113:* 117, 118, 120, 121; *172:* 130, 131
Mclean, Janet *172:* 130
McLean, Meg *94:* 196
McLean, Sammis *32:* 197
McLean, Wilson *90:* 29; *113:* 195
McLoughlin, John C. *47:* 149
McLoughlin, Wayne *102:* 230; *134:* 178
McMahon, Robert *36:* 155; *69:* 169
McManus, Shawn *85:* 71
McMenemy, Sarah *156:* 139
McMillan, Bruce *22:* 184
McMullan, James *40:* 33; *67:* 172; *87:* 142; *99:* 63, 64; *189:* 133; *196:* 51
McMullen, Nigel *146:* 177
McNeely, Tom *162:* 55
McNaught, Harry *12:* 80; *32:* 136
McNaughton, Colin *39:* 149; *40:* 108; *92:* 144, 145, 146; *134:* 104, 106
McNicholas, Maureen *38:* 148
McNicholas, Shelagh *173:* 61; *191:* 125, 126
McPhail, David *14:* 105; *23:* 135; *37:* 217, 218, 220,221; *47:* 151, 152, 153, 154, 155, 156, 158, 159, 160, 162, 163, 164; *71:* 211; *81:* 139, 140, 142; *86:* 123; *132:* 150; *140:* 129, 131, 132; *182:* 134, 135, 137; *189:* 132
McPhee, Richard B. *41:* 133
McPheeters, Neal *78:* 132; *86:* 90; *99:* 162; *111:* 141; *142:* 162
McQuade, Jacqueline *124:* 223
McQueen, Lucinda *28:* 149; *41:* 249; *46:* 206; *53:* 103
McQuillan, Mary *153:* 97; *200:* 140
McVay, Tracy *11:* 68
McVicker, Charles *39:* 150
Mead, Ben Carlton *43:* 75
Meade, Holly *90:* 102; *94:* 101; *149:* 8; *151:* 107
Mecray, John *33:* 62
Meddaugh, Susan *20:* 42; *29:* 143; *41:* 241; *77:* 50; *84:* 173, 174, 175, 176, 177, 178; *125:* 160, 161, 162; *176:* 148, 149, 150, 151
Meehan, Dennis B. *56:* 144
Meents, Len W. *73:* 147, 150
Meers, Tony *99:* 113
Meisel, Paul *98:* 137; *124:* 18; *162:* 180; *179:* 16; *181:* 62; *194:* 154
Melanson, Luc *149:* 229; *198:* 97, 98
Melendez, Francisco *72:* 180
Melling, David *202:* 199
Melnychuk, Monika *153:* 65
Melo, Esperança *196:* 90
Melo, John *16:* 285; *58:* 203
Meloni, Maria Teresa *98:* 62
Meltzer, Ericka
    See O'Rourke, Ericka
Menasco, Milton *43:* 85
Menchin, Scott *188:* 129
Mendelson, Steven T. *86:* 154
Mendelssohn, Felix *19:* 170
Mendola, Christopher *88:* 223
Meng, Heinz *13:* 158
Merian, Maria Sibylla *140:* 88
Mero, Lee *34:* 68
Merrell, David *205:* 3
Merrill, Frank T. *16:* 147; *19:* 71; *YABC 1:* 226, 229,273
Merriman, Rachel *98:* 108; *114:* 122; *149:* 142
Merveille, David *200:* 142
Meryman, Hope *27:* 41

Meryweather, Jack *10:* 179
Meseldzija, Petar *168:* 97
Meserve, Jess *184:* 137
Messick, Dale *64:* 150, 151, 152
Meth, Harold *24:* 203
Meyer, Herbert *19:* 189
Meyer, Renate *6:* 170
Meyers, Bob *11:* 136
Meyers, Nancy *172:* 124
Meynell, Louis *37:* 76
Micale, Albert *2:* 65; *22:* 185
Miccuci, Charles *82:* 163; *144:* 150
Micich, Paul *164:* 163
Middleton, Jeffrey *177:* 173
Middleton-Sandford, Betty *2:* 125
Mieke, Anne *45:* 74
Mighell, Patricia *43:* 134
Miglio, Paige *101:* 203; *151:* 223; *201:* 118, 119; *204:* 162
Mikec, Larry *204:* 125
Mikolaycak, Charles *9:* 144; *12:* 101; *13:* 212; *21:* 121; *22:* 168; *30:* 187; *34:* 103, 150; *37:* 183; *43:* 179; *44:* 90; *46:* 115, 118, 119; *49:* 25; *78:* 121, 122, 205, 207; *81:* 4
Milelli, Pascal *129:* 66; *135:* 153; *187:* 45
Miles, Elizabeth *117:* 77
Miles, Jennifer *17:* 278
Milgrim, David *158:* 157; *187:* 125, 126, 128
Milhous, Katherine *15:* 193; *17:* 51
Millais, John E. *22:* 230, 231
Millar, H.R. *YABC 1:* 194, 195, 203
Millard, C.E. *28:* 186
Millard, Kerry *105:* 124; *204:* 93, 94
Miller, Don *15:* 195; *16:* 71; *20:* 106; *31:* 178
Miller, Edna *29:* 148
Miller, Edward *115:* 64; *183:* 140, 141
Miller, Frank J. *25:* 94
Miller, Grambs *18:* 38; *23:* 16
Miller, Ian *99:* 128
Miller, Jane *15:* 196
Miller, Marcia *13:* 233
Miller, Marilyn *1:* 87; *31:* 69; *33:* 157
Miller, Mitchell *28:* 183; *34:* 207
Miller, Phil *175:* 150
Miller, Shane *5:* 140
Miller, Virginia *81:* 206
Millman, Isaac *172:* 18
Mills, Elaine *72:* 181
Mills, Judith Christine *130:* 168, 169
Mills, Lauren *92:* 170
Mills, Yaroslava Surmach *35:* 169, 170; *46:* 114
Millsap, Darrel *51:* 102
Milone, Karen *89:* 169
Milord, Susan *147:* 163, 164; *200:* 144
Milton, Debbie *162:* 161
Mims, Ashley *170:* 51
Miner, Julia *98:* 69
Minor, Wendell *39:* 188; *52:* 87; *56:* 171; *58:* 116; *62:* 56; *66:* 109; *74:* 93; *78:* 129; *94:* 67; *117:* 12, 13; *124:* 84, 86; *136:* 121; *164:* 168, 169; *170:* 71; *199:* 79, 80, 81, 82
Minter, Daniel *176:* 154; *179:* 177
Mirocha, Paul *81:* 133; *192:* 148; *194:* 36
Misako Rocks! *192:* 149, 150
Mitchell, Judith *109:* 117
Mitchell, Mark *91:* 208
Mitchell, Tracy *190:* 15
Mitgutsch, Ali *76:* 161
Mitsuhashi, Yoko *45:* 153
Miyake, Yoshi *38:* 141
Mizumura, Kazue *10:* 143; *18:* 223; *36:* 159
Mochi, Ugo *8:* 122; *38:* 150
Mock, Paul *55:* 83; *123:* 32
Modarressi, Mitra *90:* 236; *126:* 168; *173:* 165, 166; *200:* 147, 148
Modell, Frank *39:* 152
Mogenson, Jan *74:* 183
Mohn, Susan *89:* 224
Mohr, Mark *133:* 201
Mohr, Nicholasa *8:* 139; *113:* 127

Molan, Christine *60:* 177; *84:* 183
Moldon, Peter L. *49:* 168
Molk, Laurel *92:* 150
Mollica, Gene *197:* 11
Momaday, N. Scott *48:* 159
Mombourquette, Paul *112:* 91; *126:* 142
Monk, Julie *165:* 231; *191:* 96
Monks, Lydia *189:* 136, 137
Monroy, Manuel *199:* 192
Montgomery, Lucy *150:* 126
Montgomery-Higham, Amanda *169:* 131
Monteiel, David *201:* 95
Montiel, David *69:* 106; *84:* 145
Montijo, Rhode *193:* 164
Montresor, Beni *2:* 91; *3:* 138; *38:* 152, 153, 154,155, 156, 157, 158, 159, 160; *68:* 63
Montserrat, Pep *128:* 135; *181:* 119; *184:* 53
Moon, Carl *25:* 183, 184, 185
Moon, Eliza *14:* 40
Moon, Ivan *22:* 39; *38:* 140
Moore, Adrienne *67:* 147
Moore, Agnes Kay Randall *43:* 187
Moore, Cyd *117:* 107, 108; *159:* 137, 138; *186:* 148, 149, 151; *203:* 15
Moore, Gustav *127:* 181, 182; *170:* 162, 163
Moore, Jackie *52:* 79
Moore, Janet *63:* 153
Moore, Margie *176:* 156
Moore, Mary *29:* 160
Moore, Patrick *184:* 121
Moore, Yvette *101:* 11, 12; *154:* 141
Mora, Giovanni *179:* 127; *184:* 11
Mora, Raul Mina *20:* 41
Moraes, Odilon *102:* 144
Morales, Yuyi *154:* 144
Moran, Rosslyn *111:* 26
Moran, Tom *60:* 100
Mordan, C.B. *193:* 115
Mordvinoff, Nicolas *15:* 179
Moreno, René King *169:* 59; *190:* 133, 209
Morgan, Barbara *169:* 116
Morgan, Jacqui *58:* 57
Morgan, Mary *114:* 133, 134, 135; *123:* 11
Morgan, Tom *42:* 157
Morgan, Pierr *173:* 148
Morgenstern, Michael *158:* 7, 57; *171:* 103; *174:* 60
Morice, Dave *93:* 142
Morin, Paul *73:* 132; *79:* 130; *88:* 140; *137:* 143
Moriuchi, Mique *177:* 203
Morning, Tuesday *205:* 25
Morozumi, Atsuko *110:* 155
Morrill, Leslie *18:* 218; *29:* 177; *33:* 84; *38:* 147; *42:* 127; *44:* 93; *48:* 164, 165, 167, 168, 169, 170,171; *49:* 162; *63:* 136, 180; *70:* 72; *71:* 70, 91,92; *72:* 228; *80:* 163, 164, 165; *90:* 121; *121:* 88; *178:* 117
Morrill, Rowena A. *84:* 16; *98:* 163
Morris *47:* 91
Morris, Frank *55:* 133; *60:* 28; *76:* 2
Morris, Harry O. *119:* 138
Morris, Jackie *128:* 194; *144:* 119; *151:* 146; *202:* 126, 127; *204:* 83
Morris, Jennifer E. *179:* 157
Morris, Oradel Nolen *128:* 180
Morris, Tony *62:* 146; *70:* 97
Morrison, Bill *42:* 116; *66:* 170; *69:* 40
Morrison, Gordon *87:* 150; *113:* 93; *128:* 181, 182; *183:* 144, 145, 146
Morrison, Frank *169:* 162; *205:* 156
Morrison, Taylor *159:* 144, 145; *187:* 131
Morrow, Gray *2:* 64; *5:* 200; *10:* 103, 114; *14:* 175
Morse, Scott *200:* 149, 150
Morton, Lee Jack *32:* 140
Morton, Marian *3:* 185
Mosberg, Hilary *117:* 195; *118:* 164; *149:* 55
Moser, Barry *56:* 68, 117, 118, 119, 120, 121, 122, 123, 124; *59:* 141; *60:* 160; *79:* 91, 147, 149, 151, 152; *82:* 81; *90:* 118; *91:* 35;

95: 210; *97:* 91, 93; *102:* 152; *126:* 4; *128:* 175; *133:* 141; *138:* 167, 171, 174; *153:* 205; *174:* 130; *185:* 152, 154; *195:* 163; *204:* 115
Moser, Cara *90:* 118; *138:* 167
Moses, Grandma *18:* 228
Moses, Will *178:* 170, 171
Moskof, Martin Stephen *27:* 152
Mosley, Francis *57:* 144
Moss, Donald *11:* 184
Moss, Geoffrey *32:* 198
Moss, Marissa *71:* 130; *104:* 127; *163:* 156
Most, Bernard *48:* 173; *91:* 142, 143; *134:* 120
Mowll, Joshua *188:* 133
Mowry, Carmen *50:* 62
Moxley, Sheila *96:* 174; *169:* 26; *206:* 16
Moyers, William *21:* 65
Moyler, Alan *36:* 142
Mozley, Charles *9:* 87; *20:* 176, 192, 193; *22:* 228; *25:* 205; *33:* 150; *43:* 170, 171, 172, 173, 174; *YABC2:* 89
Mueller, Hans Alexander *26:* 64; *27:* 52, 53
Mugnaini, Joseph *11:* 35; *27:* 52, 53; *35:* 62
Mujica, Rick *72:* 67; *88:* 95; *111:* 53; *180:* 185; *197:* 70
Mullen, Douglas *180:* 178
Muller, Robin *86:* 161
Muller, Steven *32:* 167
Muller, Jorg *35:* 215; *67:* 138, 139
Mulock, Julie *163:* 112
Mullins, Edward S. *10:* 101
Mullins, Patricia *51:* 68
Multer, Scott *80:* 108
Munari, Bruno *15:* 200
Munch, Edvard *140:* 143
Munowitz, Ken *14:* 148; *72:* 178, 179
Munro, Roxie *58:* 134; *136:* 177; *137:* 218; *184:* 133, 134
Munsinger, Lynn *33:* 161; *46:* 126; *71:* 92; *82:* 80; *89:* 218; *92:* 125; *94:* 157, 158, 159, 160; *98:* 196; *103:* 198; *142:* 143; *145:* 133, 134, 136; *153:* 203; *176:* 162; *177:* 140, 141, 142; *189:* 113, 114, 116, 117; *201:* 42
Munson, Russell *13:* 9
Munster, Sebastian *166:* 107
Munoz, William *42:* 160
Munzar, Barbara *149:* 75
Murdocca, Salvatore *73:* 212; *98:* 132; *111:* 168; *157:* 228; *164:* 257
Murphy, Bill *5:* 138; *130:* 170
Murphy, Jill *37:* 142; *70:* 166; *142:* 132, 134
Murphy, Kelly *130:* 212; *143:* 119; *176:* 158; *190:* 135
Murphy, Mary *196:* 158
Murphy, Tom *192:* 40
Murr, Karl *20:* 62
Murray, Joe *175:* 37
Murray, Ossie *43:* 176
Mussino, Attilio *29:* 131; *100:* 164
Mutchler, Dwight *1:* 25
Myers, Bernice *9:* 147; *36:* 75; *81:* 146, 147, 148
Muth, Jon J. *165:* 169; *167:* 109; *190:* 227; *193:* 59
Myers, Christopher *183:* 150; *193:* 139
Myers, Duane O. *99:* 145
Myers, Tim *147:* 168
Myers, V.G. *142:* 41
Myers, Lou *11:* 2

N

Nachreiner, Tom *29:* 182
Nacht, Merle *65:* 49
Nadler, Ellis *88:* 91
Nagle, Shane *180:* 223
Nagy, Ian *195:* 64
Najaka, Marlies *62:* 101
Nakai, Michael *30:* 217; *54:* 29

Nakata, Hiroe *157:* 156; *162:* 30; *205:* 124, 125
Nakatani, Chiyoko *12:* 124
Narahashi, Keiko *77:* 188; *82:* 213; *115:* 142, 143, 144
Nascimbene, Yan *133:* 128; *173:* 132, 133
Nash, Lesa *87:* 135
Nash, Linell *46:* 175
Nash, Scott *130:* 36; *188:* 196
Naso, John *33:* 183
Nason, Thomas W. *14:* 68
Nasser, Muriel *48:* 74
Nast, Thomas *21:* 29; *28:* 23; *51:* 132, 133, 134, 135,136, 137, 138, 139, 141
Nasta, Vincent *78:* 185
Natale, Vincent *76:* 3; *78:* 125; *112:* 47; *166:* 81; *174:* 189; *185:* 212; *197:* 59
Natchev, Alexi *96:* 177
Nathan, Charlott *125:* 151
Nathan, Cheryl *150:* 104; *186:* 112
Natti, Susanna *20:* 146; *32:* 141, 142; *35:* 178; *37:* 143; *71:* 49; *93:* 98; *125:* 166, 168; *126:* 228; *151:* 6; *178:* 8; *188:* 106
Navarra, Celeste Scala *8:* 142
Naylor, Penelope *10:* 104
Nazz, James *72:* 8
Nebel, M. *45:* 154
Neebe, William *7:* 93
Needham, Dave *196:* 85
Needler, Jerry *12:* 93
Neel, Alice *31:* 23
Neely, Beth *119:* 184
Neely, Keith R. *46:* 124
Neff, Leland *78:* 74
Negri, Rocco *3:* 213; *5:* 67; *6:* 91, 108; *12:* 159
Negrin, Fabian *174:* 125; *175:* 15
Neidigh, Sherry *128:* 53; *204:* 101, 102, 103
Neilan, Eujin Kim *180:* 241; *200:* 151, 152
Neill, John R. *18:* 8, 10, 11, 21, 30; *100:* 22
Neilsen, Cliff *158:* 131; *177:* 112, 121
Neilsen, Terese *116:* 74
Nelson, Craig *62:* 151; 153; *183:* 86
Nelson, Gail White *68:* 140
Nelson, Jennifer *129:* 152; *199:* 132
Nelson, Kadir *151:* 185; *154:* 146, 147; *157:* 189, 222; *181:* 122, 124; *197:* 155
Nelson, S.D. *131:* 34; *181:* 126, 127
Ness, Evaline *1:* 164, 165; *2:* 39; *3:* 8; *10:* 147; *12:* 53; *26:* 150, 151, 152, 153; *49:* 30, 31, 32; *56:* 30; *60:* 113
Neubecker, Robert *170:* 143
Neville, Vera *2:* 182
Nevins, Daniel *191:* 173
Nevwirth, Allan *79:* 168
Newberry, Clare Turlay *1:* 170
Newbold, Greg *108:* 125; *145:* 199; *151:* 23; *193:* 178; *197:* 10; *199:* 92, 93
Newfeld, Frank *14:* 121; *26:* 154
Newman, Andy *149:* 61; *195:* 63
Newman, Ann *43:* 90
Newman, Barbara Johansen *191:* 137, 138
Newsham, Ian *143:* 162
Newsom, Carol *40:* 159; *44:* 60; *47:* 189; *65:* 29; *70:* 192; *80:* 36; *85:* 137, 138; *92:* 167; *191:* 82
Newsom, Tom *49:* 149; *71:* 13, 62; *75:* 156; *91:* 113
Newton, Jill *83:* 105; *200:* 154
Ng, Michael *29:* 171
Ng, Simon *167:* 7
Nguyen, Vincent *189:* 49
Nicholson, William *15:* 33, 34; *16:* 48
Nickens, Bessie *104:* 153
Nicklaus, Carol *45:* 194; *62:* 132, 133
Nickle, John *181:* 128
Nickless, Will *16:* 139
Nicholas, Corasue *154:* 20
Nicolas *17:* 130, 132, 133; *YABC 2:* 215
Niebrugge, Jane *6:* 118

Nielsen, Cliff *95:* 207, 208; *105:* 58; *114:* 112; *124:* 12; *125:* 91, 92; *132:* 224; *135:* 187; *136:* 40; *137:* 168; *145:* 54; *149:* 28; *158:* 129; *165:* 64, 158; *168:* 169; *170:* 6; *175:* 114, 116; *187:* 75, 76; *194:* 107; *197:* 172; *201:* 14
Nielsen, Jon *6:* 100; *24:* 202
Nielsen, Kay *15:* 7; *16:* 211, 212, 213, 215, 217; *22:* 143; *YABC 1:* 32, 33
Niemann, Christoph *191:* 141
Nikola-Lisa, W. *180:* 180
Niland, Deborah *25:* 191; *27:* 156; *135:* 50; *172:* 143
Niland, Kilmeny *25:* 191; *75:* 143
Nino, Alex *59:* 145
Ninon *1:* 5; *38:* 101, 103, 108
Nissen, Rie *44:* 35
Nithael, Mark *158:* 237
Nivola, Claire A. *78:* 126; *140:* 147
Nixon, K. *14:* 152
Nobati, Eugenia *194:* 118
Noble, Louise *61:* 170
Noble, Marty *97:* 168; *125:* 171
Noble, Trinka Hakes *39:* 162; *84:* 157
Noda, Takayo *168:* 143
Noguchi, Yoshie *30:* 99
Nolan, Dennis *42:* 163; *67:* 163; *78:* 189; *82:* 225; *83:* 26; *92:* 169, 170; *103:* 166; *111:* 35; *112:* 213; *127:* 171; *166:* 161; *194:* 218
Noll, Sally *82:* 171
Nolte, Larry *121:* 63, 65
Nones, Eric Jon *61:* 111; *76:* 38; *77:* 177
Noonan, Daniel *100:* 224
Noonan, Julia *4:* 163; *7:* 207; *25:* 151; *91:* 29; *95:* 149
Norcia, Ernie *108:* 155; *140:* 47
Nordenskjold, Birgitta *2:* 208
Noreika, Robert *173:* 20
Norling, Beth *149:* 153, 154
Norman, Elaine *77:* 72, 176; *94:* 35; *136:* 63; *178:* 42
Norman, Mary *36:* 138, 147
Norman, Michael *12:* 117; *27:* 168
Northway, Jennifer *85:* 96
Nostlinger, Christiana *162:* 131
Novak, Linda *166:* 205
Novak, Matt *104:* 132, 133; *165:* 173, 174; *204:* 104, 106
Novelli, Luca *61:* 137
Nugent, Cynthia *106:* 189; *205:* 126, 127
Numeroff, Laura Joffe *28:* 161; *30:* 177
Nurse, Chris *164:* 91
Nussbaumer, Paul *16:* 219; *39:* 117
Nutt, Ken *72:* 69; *97:* 170
Nyce, Helene *19:* 219
Nygren, Tord *30:* 148; *127:* 164

O

Oakley, Graham *8:* 112; *30:* 164, 165; *84:* 188,189, 190, 191, 192
Oakley, Thornton *YABC 2:* 189
Oberheide, Heide *118:* 37
Obligado, Lilian *2:* 28, 66, 67; *6:* 30; *14:* 179; *15:* 103; *25:* 84; *61:* 138, 139, 140, 141, 143
Oblinski, Rafael *190:* 139
Obrant, Susan *11:* 186
O'Brien, Anne Sibley *53:* 116, 117; *155:* 115
O'Brien, John *41:* 253; *72:* 12; *89:* 59, 60; *98:* 16; *161:* 185; *169:* 16; *180:* 196
O'Brien, Patrick *193:* 142, 143, 144
O'Brien, Teresa *87:* 89
O'Brien, Tim *93:* 25; *136:* 94; *164:* 57; *169:* 57; *173:* 55; *175:* 86; *184:* 192; *191:* 134; *193:* 137
O'Clair, Dennis *127:* 25
O'Connor, George *183:* 153
Odell, Carole *35:* 47
Odem, Mel *99:* 164; *167:* 84, 87

O'Donohue, Thomas *40:* 89
Oechsli, Kelly *5:* 144, 145; *7:* 115; *8:* 83, 183; *13:* 117; *20:* 94; *81:* 199
Offen, Hilda *42:* 207
Ogden, Bill *42:* 59; *47:* 55
Ogg, Oscar *33:* 34
Ogle, Nancy Gray *163:* 144
Ohi, Ruth *90:* 175, 177; *131:* 63; *135:* 106; *175:* 107; *179:* 55
Ohlsson, Ib *4:* 152; *7:* 57; *10:* 20; *11:* 90; *19:* 217; *41:* 246; *82:* 106; *92:* 213
Ohtomo, Yasuo *37:* 146; *39:* 212, 213
O'Keefe, Jennifer *136:* 184
O'Kelley, Mattie Lou *36:* 150
Olbinski, Rafal *149:* 27; *158:* 77; *203:* 36
Oleynikov, Igor *202:* 134
Oliver, Isaac *171:* 182
Oliver, Jenni *23:* 121; *35:* 112
Oliver, Narelle *152:* 192; *197:* 129, 130
Oller, Erika *128:* 186; *134:* 126
Olschewski, Alfred *7:* 172
Olsen, Ib Spang *6:* 178, 179; *81:* 164
Olson, Alan *77:* 229
Olson-Brown, Ellen *183:* 154
Olugebefola, Ademola *15:* 205
O'Malley, Kevin *94:* 180; *106:* 8; *113:* 108; *136:* 70; *157:* 193; *191:* 146; *203:* 78
O'Neil, Dan IV *7:* 176
O'Neill, Catharine *72:* 113; *84:* 78; *134:* 153
O'Neill, Jean *22:* 146
O'Neill, Martin *187:* 39; *203:* 118
O'Neill, Michael J. *54:* 172
O'Neill, Rose *48:* 30, 31
O'Neill, Steve *21:* 118
Ono, Chiyo *7:* 97
Orbaan, Albert *2:* 31; *5:* 65, 171; *9:* 8; *14:* 241; *20:* 109
Orbach, Ruth *21:* 112
Orback, Craig *197:* 132
Orfe, Joan *20:* 81
Org, Ed *119:* 93
Ormai, Stella *72:* 129
Ormerod, Jan *55:* 124; *70:* 170, 171; *90:* 39; *132:* 172, 173, 174; *147:* 98
Ormsby, Virginia H. *11:* 187
O'Rourke, Ericka *108:* 216; *117:* 194; *111:* 142; *119:* 194; *137:* 152; *150:* 134; *167:* 64; *172:* 164; *188:* 163; *191:* 172; *201:* 15; *203:* 75
O'Rourke, Ericka Meltzer
  See O'Rourke, Ericka
Orozco, Jose Clemente *9:* 177
Orr, Forrest W. *23:* 9
Orr, N. *19:* 70
Ortiz, Vilma *88:* 158
Osborn, Kathy *152:* 232; *199:* 101, 102; *206:* 67
Osborn, Robert *65:* 49
Osborne, Billie Jean *35:* 209
Osmond, Edward *10:* 111
O'Sullivan, Tom *3:* 176; *4:* 55; *78:* 195
Otani, June *124:* 42; *156:* 53
Otis, Rebecca *185:* 92
Ottley, Matt *147:* 221; *171:* 133
Otto, Svend *22:* 130, 141; *67:* 188, 189
Oudry, J.B. *18:* 167
Oughton, Taylor *5:* 23; *104:* 136
Overeng, Johannes *44:* 36
Overlie, George *11:* 156
Owens, Carl *2:* 35; *23:* 521
Owens, Gail *10:* 170; *12:* 157; *19:* 16; *22:* 70; *25:* 81; *28:* 203, 205; *32:* 221, 222; *36:* 132; *46:* 40; *47:* 57; *54:* 66, 67, 68, 69, 70, 71, 72, 73; *71:* 100; *73:* 64; *77:* 157; *80:* 32; *82:* 3; *99:* 226
Owens, Mary Beth *113:* 202, 203; *191:* 148, 149
Owens, Nubia *84:* 74

Oxenbury, Helen *3:* 150, 151; *24:* 81; *68:* 174, 175,176; *81:* 209; *84:* 213, 245; *129:* 56; *149:* 159; *184:* 181
Oz, Robin *88:* 167; *185:* 181

P

Padgett, Jim *12:* 165
Page, Gail *205:* 128
Page, Homer *14:* 145
Page, Mark *162:* 70
Paget, Sidney *24:* 90, 91, 93, 95, 97
Paget, Walter *64:* 122
Paillot, Jim *173:* 89
Pajouhesh, Noushin *160:* 121
Pak *12:* 76
Pak, Yu Cha *86:* 174
Paladino, Lance *134:* 30
Palazzo, Tony *3:* 152, 153
Palecek, Josef *56:* 136; *89:* 158
Palen, Debbie *135:* 88; *195:* 148, 149
Palencar, John Jude *84:* 12, 45; *85:* 87; *92:* 187; *99:* 128; *110:* 204; *150:* 122; *171:* 86; *207:* 36
Palin, Nicki *81:* 201; *89:* 161
Palladini, David *4:* 113; *40:* 176, 177, 178, 179, 181,224, 225; *50:* 138; *78:* 186
Pallarito, Don *43:* 36
Palmer, Carol *158:* 230; *195:* 187
Palmer, Heidi *15:* 207; *29:* 102
Palmer, Jan *42:* 153; *82:* 161
Palmer, Judd *153:* 160, 161
Palmer, Juliette *6:* 89; *15:* 208
Palmer, Kate Salley *104:* 143; *154:* 169
Palmer, Lemuel *17:* 25, 29
Palmisciano, Diane *110:* 62; *162:* 26; *202:* 138, 139
Palmquist, Eric *38:* 133
Panesis, Nicholas *3:* 127
Panter, Gary *182:* 191
Panton, Doug *52:* 99
Paparone, Pamela *129:* 174
Papas, William *11:* 223; *50:* 160
Papin, Joseph *26:* 113
Papish, Robin Lloyd *10:* 80
Papp, Robert *198:* 41; *205:* 130
Paradis, Susan *40:* 216
Paraquin, Charles H. *18:* 166
Paris, Peter *31:* 127
Parisi, Elizabeth B. *141:* 82; *164:* 57
Park, Nick *113:* 143
Park, Seho *39:* 110
Park, W.B. *22:* 189
Parker, Ant *82:* 87, 88; *104:* 121
Parker, Lewis *2:* 179
Parker, Nancy Winslow *10:* 113; *22:* 164; *28:* 47, 144; *52:* 7; *69:* 153; *91:* 171, 174; *132:* 175
Parker, Robert *4:* 161; *5:* 74; *9:* 136; *29:* 39
Parker, Robert Andrew *11:* 81; *29:* 186; *39:* 165; *40:* 25; *41:* 78; *42:* 123; *43:* 144; *48:* 182; *54:* 140; *74:* 141; *91:* 24; *111:* 115; *151:* 201; *154:* 156; *200:* 163, 164
Parker-Rees, Guy *149:* 145; *193:* 149, 150
Parkin, Trevor *140:* 151
Parkins, David *114:* 123; *146:* 176; *176:* 168; *192:* 107
Parkinson, Kathy *71:* 143; *144:* 234
Parkinson, Keith *70:* 66
Parks, Gordon, Jr. *33:* 228
Parnall, Peter *5:* 137; *16:* 221; *24:* 70; *40:* 78; *51:* 130; *69:* 17, 155; *136:* 22, 23, 24
Parnall, Virginia *40:* 78
Parow, Lorraine *158:* 127
Parr, Todd *134:* 139, 140; *179:* 163, 164, 165
Parrish, Anne *27:* 159, 160
Parrish, Dillwyn *27:* 159

Parrish, Maxfield *14:* 160, 161, 164, 165; *16:* 109; *18:* 12, 13; *YABC 1:* 149, 152, 267; *2:* 146, 149
Parry, David *26:* 156
Parry, Marian *13:* 176; *19:* 179
Parsons, Garry *197:* 135
Partch, Virgil *45:* 163, 165
Pascal, David *14:* 174
Paschkis, Julie *177:* 153, 154
Pasquier, J.A. *16:* 91
Pastel, Elyse *201:* 123
Pasternak, Robert *119:* 53
Paterson, Diane *13:* 116; *39:* 163; *59:* 164, 165, 166,167; *72:* 51, 53; *129:* 175; *177:* 156, 157
Paterson, Helen *16:* 93
Patkau, Karen *112:* 123
Paton, Jane *15:* 271; *35:* 176
Patricelli, Leslie *207:* 129
Patrick, John *139:* 190
Patrick, Pamela *90:* 160; *93:* 211; *105:* 12
Patrick, Tom *190:* 103
Patterson, Geoffrey *54:* 75
Patterson, Robert *25:* 118
Patti, Joyce *187:* 145, 146
Patz, Nancy *111:* 40; *154:* 161
Paul, James *4:* 130; *23:* 161
Paul, Korky *102:* 85
Paull, Grace *24:* 157; *87:* 127
Paulsen, Ruth Wright *79:* 160, 164; *189:* 146
Pavlov, Elena *80:* 49
Payne, Adam S. *135:* 166
Payne, C.F. *145:* 138, 140; *179:* 168
Payne, Joan Balfour *1:* 118
Payne, Tom *170:* 27
Payson, Dale *7:* 34; *9:* 151; *20:* 140; *37:* 22
Payzant, Charles *21:* 147
Peacock, Ralph *64:* 118
Peake, Mervyn *22:* 136, 149; *23:* 162, 163, 164; *YABC2:* 307
Pearson, Larry *38:* 225
Pearson, Tracey Campbell *64:* 163, 164, 167, 168, 169; *118:* 51; *156:* 169, 171, 172; *163:* 140
Peat, Fern B. *16:* 115
Peck, Anne Merriman *18:* 241; *24:* 155
Peck, Beth *66:* 242; *79:* 166; *80:* 136; *91:* 34; *95:* 9; *101:* 77; *164:* 197; *190:* 170
Peddicord, Jane Ann *199:* 106
Pedersen, Janet *193:* 152
Pedersen, Judy *66:* 217; *121:* 36; *172:* 67
Pedersen, Vilhelm *YABC 1:* 40
Pederson, Sharleen *12:* 92
Pedlar, Elaine *161:* 45
Peek, Merle *39:* 168
Peet, Bill *2:* 203; *41:* 159, 160, 161, 162, 163; *78:* 158, 159, 160, 161
Peguero, Adrian *116:* 133
Peguero, Gerard *116:* 133
Pels, Winslow Pinney *55:* 126
Peltier, Leslie C. *13:* 178
Peltzer, Marc *202:* 92
Penberthy, Mark *171:* 78
Pendle, Alexy *7:* 159; *13:* 34; *29:* 161; *33:* 215; *86:* 62
Pendola, Joanne *76:* 203; *81:* 125; *105:* 181; *178:* 152, 153
Pene du Bois, William *4:* 70; *10:* 122; *26:* 61; *27:* 145, 211; *35:* 243; *41:* 216; *68:* 180, 181; *73:* 45
Penfound, David *102:* 185
Pennington, Eunice *27:* 162
Peppe, Mark *28:* 142
Peppe, Rodney *4:* 164, 165; *74:* 187, 188, 189
Pepper, Hubert *64:* 143
Percy, Graham *63:* 2
Pericoli, Matteo *178:* 177
Perini, Ben *173:* 77
Perkins, David *60:* 68
Perkins, Lucy Fitch *72:* 199
Perkins, Lynne Rae *172:* 146

Perl, Susan *2:* 98; *4:* 231; *5:* 44, 45, 118; *6:* 199; *8:* 137; *12:* 88; *22:* 193; *34:* 54, 55; *52:* 128; *YABC 1:* 176
Perrone, Donna *78:* 166
Perry, Marie Fritz *165:* 180
Perry, Patricia *29:* 137; *30:* 171
Perry, Roger *27:* 163
Perske, Martha *46:* 83; *51:* 108, 147
Persson, Stina *175:* 166
Pesek, Ludek *15:* 237
Petach, Heidi *149:* 166; *200:* 207
Peters, David *72:* 205; *182:* 116
Petersen, Jeff *181:* 95
Petersham, Maud *17:* 108, 147, 148, 149, 150, 151, 152, 153
Petersham, Miska *17:* 108, 147, 148, 149, 150, 151, 152, 153
Peterson, Eric *109:* 125
Peterson, Nisse *99:* 27
Peterson, R.F. *7:* 101
Peterson, Russell *7:* 130
Petie, Haris *2:* 3; *10:* 41, 118; *11:* 227; *12:* 70
Petricic, Dusan *153:* 75, 76, 77; *170:* 12; *172:* 13; *176:* 170; *179:* 56
Petrides, Heidrun *19:* 223
Petrone, Valeria *159:* 160; *171:* 92; *186:* 173; *204:* 49
Petrosino, Tamara *177:* 40; *193:* 154, 155
Petruccio, Steven James *67:* 159; *127:* 5
Pettingill, Ondre *64:* 181; *70:* 64
Peyo *40:* 56, 57
Peyton, K.M. *15:* 212
Pfeifer, Herman *15:* 262
Pfister, Marcus *83:* 165, 166, 167; *146:* 152; *150:* 160; *207:* 132, 134, 135, 136
Pfloog, Jan *124:* 60
Pham, LeUyen *160:* 48; *175:* 154, 156; *179:* 149; *201:* 124, 125, 126, 127; *204:* 28
Phelan, Matt *182:* 160; *184:* 222
Phillips, Craig *70:* 151; *207:* 74
Phillips, Douglas *1:* 19
Phillips, F.D. *6:* 202
Phillips, Louise *133:* 67
Phillips, Matt *184:* 173
Phillips, Thomas *30:* 55
Philpot, Glyn *54:* 46
Phiz
  See Browne, Hablot K.
Piatti, Celestino *16:* 223
Pica, Steve *115:* 181
Picarella, Joseph *13:* 147
Picart, Gabriel *121:* 165; *201:* 169
Pichon, Liz *174:* 139
Pickard, Charles *12:* 38; *18:* 203; *36:* 152
Picken, George A. *23:* 150
Pickens, David *22:* 156
Pickering, Jimmy *195:* 152; *197:* 163
Pienkowski, Jan *6:* 183; *30:* 32; *58:* 140, 141, 142,143, 146, 147; *73:* 3; *87:* 156, 157; *131:* 189
Pieper, Christiane *200:* 168
Pignataro, Anna *163:* 220 *Pileggi, Steve 145:* 122
Pilkey, Dav *68:* 186; *115:* 164, 166; *166:* 173, 174, 175
Pimlott, John *10:* 205
Pincus, Harriet *4:* 186; *8:* 179; *22:* 148; *27:* 164, 165; *66:* 202
Pini, Wendy *89:* 166
Pinkett, Neil *60:* 8
Pinkney, Brian *81:* 184, 185; *94:* 107; *113:* 146, 147; *117:* 121, 166; *132:* 145; *158:* 108, 191; *160:* 189; *200:* 8
Pinkney, Jerry *8:* 218; *10:* 40; *15:* 276; *20:* 66; *24:* 121; *33:* 109; *36:* 222; *38:* 200; *41:* 165, 166, 167, 168, 169, 170, 171, 173, 174; *44:* 198; *48:* 51; *53:* 20; *56:* 61, 68; *58:* 184; *60:* 59; *61:* 91; *71:* 146, 148, 149; *72:* 17; *73:* 149; *74:* 159,192; *75:* 45; *80:* 206; *81:* 44; *85:* 144; *95:* 50; *107:* 158, 159, 160; *108:* 164; *112:* 114, 115; *133:* 58; *195:* 140

Pinkwater, Daniel Manus *46:* 180, 181, 182, 185, 188, 189, 190; *151:* 161 *76:* 178, 179, 180
Pinkwater, Manus *8:* 156; *46:* 180
  See also Pinkwater, Daniel Manus
Pinkwater, Jill *114:* 160, 161; *158:* 179; *188:* 143, 145, 146
Pinto, Ralph *10:* 131; *45:* 93
Pinto, Sara *200:* 165
Pinon, Mark *74:* 22
Piven, Hanoch *173:* 142
Pistolesi *73:* 211
Pitcairn, Ansel *188:* 10
Pittman, Helena Clare *71:* 151
Pitz, Henry C. *4:* 168; *19:* 165; *35:* 128; *42:* 80; *YABC 2:* 95, 176
Pitzenberger, Lawrence J. *26:* 94
Pitzer, Susanna *181:* 131
Player, Stephen *82:* 190
Plecas, Jennifer *84:* 201; *106:* 124; *149:* 168; *205:* 180
Ploog, Mike *180:* 19
Plowden, David *52:* 135, 136
Plume, Ilse *170:* 149
Plummer, William *32:* 31
Podevin, Jean François *184:* 185
Podwal, Mark *56:* 170, 173; *101:* 154, 155, 157; *149:* 176; *160:* 194
Pogany, Willy *15:* 46, 49; *19:* 222, 256; *25:* 214; *44:* 142, 143, 144, 145, 146, 147, 148
Pohrt, Tom *67:* 116; *104:* 80; *152:* 199; *195:* 154; *199:* 85
Poirson, V.A. *26:* 89
Polacco, Patricia *74:* 195, 196, 197, 198; *123:* 121, 122, 123; *180:* 189, 190, 191, 193, 194
Polgreen, John *21:* 44
Politi, Leo *1:* 178; *4:* 53; *21:* 48; *47:* 173,174, 176, 178, 179, 180, 181
Pollema-Cahill, Phyllis *123:* 126
Pollen, Samson *64:* 80
Polonsky, Arthur *34:* 168
Polseno, Jo *1:* 53; *3:* 117; *5:* 114; *17:* 154; *20:* 87; *32:* 49; *41:* 245
Pomaska, Anna *117:* 148
Pons, Bernadette *184:* 100
Ponter, James *5:* 204
Poole, Colin *111:* 27
Poortvliet, Rien *6:* 212; *65:* 165, 166, 167
Pope, Kevin *183:* 158
Popp, Wendy *72:* 122; *158:* 68
Poppel, Hans *71:* 154, 155
Porfirio, Guy *76:* 134
Portal, Colette *6:* 186; *11:* 203
Porter, George *7:* 181
Porter, Janice Lee *136:* 175; *164:* 37
Porter, John *113:* 47
Porter, Pat Grant *84:* 112; *125:* 101
Porter, Sue *146:* 246, 247
Porter, Walter *124:* 175
Posada, Mia *187:* 151
Posen, Michael *175:* 82
Posthuma, Sieb *150:* 163
Postier, Jim *202:* 140; *204:* 25
Postma, Lidia *79:* 17
Potter, Beatrix *100:* 194, 195; *132:* 179, 180, 181, 182; *YABC 1:* 208, 209, 210, 212, 213
Potter, Giselle *117:* 123; *143:* 44; *144:* 170, 197; *149:* 7; *150:* 165; *187:* 152, 153; *190:* 198; *196:* 152; *200:* 12
Potter, Katherine *104:* 147; *171:* 135; *173:* 136
Potter, Miriam Clark *3:* 162
Poulin, Stephane *98:* 140, 141
Poullis, Nick *146:* 210
Powell, Constance Buffington *174:* 141
Powell, Gary *151:* 208
Powell, Ivan *67:* 219
Power, Margaret *105:* 122
Powers, Daniel *161:* 173
Powers, Richard M. *1:* 230; *3:* 218; *7:* 194; *26:* 186
Powledge, Fred *37:* 154

Powzyk, Joyce *74:* 214
Poydar, Nancy *96:* 149; *190:* 180, 181, 182
Pracher, Richard *91:* 166
Prachaticka, Marketa *126:* 126
Prange, Beckie *181:* 169
Prap, Lila *177:* 165
Prater, John *103:* 142, 143, 144; *149:* 172
Pratt, Charles *23:* 29
Pratt, George *116:* 208
Pratt, Pierre *150:* 73; *166:* 183; *168:* 172; *201:* 27
Prebenna, David *73:* 174
Preiss-Glasser, Robin *123:* 176; *152* 40; *172:* 194
Press, Jenny *116:* 95
Preston, Mark *152:* 162
Pretro, Korinna *91:* 126
Price, Christine *2:* 247; *3:* 163, 253; *8:* 166
Price, Cynthia *118:* 156
Price, Edward *33:* 34
Price, Garrett *1:* 76; *2:* 42
Price, Hattie Longstreet *17:* 13
Price, Norman *YABC 1:* 129
Price, Willard *48:* 184
Priceman, Marjorie *81:* 171; *136:* 169; *156:* 200; *168:* 153, 154; *188:* 45
Priestley, Alice *168:* 33
Priestley, Chris *198:* 144
Primavera, Elise *26:* 95; *58:* 151; *73:* 37; *80:* 79; *86:* 156; *105:* 161
Primrose, Jean *36:* 109
Prince, Alison *86:* 188, 189
Prince, Leonora E. *7:* 170
Pritchett, Shelley *116:* 148
Prittie, Edwin J. *YABC 1:* 120
Proimos, James *176:* 4
Proimos, John *173:* 144
Prosmitsky, Jenya *132:* 33
Provensen, Alice *37:* 204, 215, 222; *70:* 176, 177, 178, 180, *71:* 213; *147:* 184; *191:* 190
Provensen, Martin *37:* 204, 215, 222; *70:* 176, 177, 178, 180; *71:* 213; *191:* 190
Pucci, Albert John *44:* 154
Pudlo *8:* 59
Puggaard, Ulla *196:* 25
Pulver, Harry, Jr. *129:* 159
Pulver, Robin *160:* 4
Punchatz, Don *99:* 57
Purdy, Susan *8:* 162
Pursell, Weimer *55:* 18
Purtscher, Alfons *97:* 6
Puskas, James *5:* 141
Pyk, Jan *7:* 26; *38:* 123
Pyle, Chuck *99:* 149; *191:* 83
Pyle, Howard *16:* 225, 226, 227, 228, 230, 231, 232, 235; *24:* 27; *34:* 124, 125, 127, 128; *59:* 132; *100:* 198

Q

Quackenbush, Robert *4:* 190; *6:* 166; *7:* 175, 178; *9:* 86; *11:* 65, 221; *41:* 154; *43:* 157; *70:* 185, 186; *71:* 137; *85:* 47; *92:* 148; *133:* 154, 164, 169
Qualls, Sean *177:* 167, 168; *193:* 43
Quennell, Marjorie (Courtney) *29:* 163, 164
Quidor, John *19:* 82
Quirk, John *62:* 170
Quirk, Thomas *12:* 81

R

Rackham, Arthur *15:* 32, 78, 214-227; *17:* 105, 115; *18:* 233; *19:* 254; *20:* 151; *22:* 129, 131, 132, 133; *23:* 175; *24:* 161, 181; *26:* 91; *32:* 118; *64:* 18; *100:* 9, 16, 203, 204; *YABC 1:* 25, 45, 55, 147; *2:* 103, 142, 173, 210

Racz, Michael *56:* 134
Raczka, Bob *191:* 155, 156
Radcliffe, Andrew *82:* 215
Rader, Laura *101:* 219; *197:* 147; *203:* 53
Radunsky, Vladimir *177:* 170; *192:* 30
Rafilson, Sidney *11:* 172
Raglin, Tim *125:* 24
Raible, Alton *1:* 202, 203; *28:* 193; *35:* 181; *110:* 207
Raine, Patricia *82:* 74; *88:* 154
Ramá, Sue *173:* 45; *185:* 186; *190:* 184
Ramhorst, John *117:* 11
Ramirez, Gladys *177:* 19
Ramirez, Jose *207:* 27
Ramsey, James *16:* 41
Ramsey, Marcy Dunn *82:* 11; *180:* 186
Ramus, Michael *51:* 171
Rand, Paul *6:* 188
Rand, Ted *67:* 9, 10, 121, 123; *74:* 190; *84:* 170; *103:* 170; *112:* 6; *114:* 73; *139:* 168; *143:* 194; *156:* 154; *161:* 9, 10; *200:* 38; *204:* 7
Randazzo, Tony *81:* 98
Randell, William *55:* 54
Rane, Walter *93:* 144; *143:* 109; *184:* 126
Rankin, Joan *163:* 40
Rankin, Laura *176:* 173, 174; *179:* 150
Ransome, Arthur *22:* 201
Ransome, James E. *74:* 137; *75:* 80; *84:* 181; *94:* 108; *117:* 115; *123:* 128, 129, 130; *158:* 101, 102; *159:* 205; *178:* 188, 189, 190
Rantz, Don *119:* 184
Rao, Anthony *28:* 126
Raphael, Elaine *23:* 192; *71:* 24, 25
Rappaport, Eva *6:* 190
Raschka, Chris *80:* 187, 189, 190; *97:* 211; *115:* 210; *117:* 151, 152, 153, 154; *143:* 195; *145:* 153; *166:* 190, 191; *170:* 114; *207:* 140, 143, 144, 145
Rash, Andy *158:* 178; *162:* 172
Raskin, Ellen *2:* 208, 209; *4:* 142; *13:* 183; *22:* 68; *29:* 139; *36:* 134; *38:* 173, 174, 175, 176, 177, 178,179, 180, 181; *60:* 163; *86:* 81
Rathmann, Peggy *93:* 32; *94:* 168; *157:* 212, 214
Ratkus, Tony *77:* 133
Ratzkin, Lawrence *40:* 143
Rau, Margaret *9:* 157
Raverat, Gwen *YABC 1:* 152
Ravid, Joyce *61:* 73
Ravielli, Anthony *1:* 198; *3:* 168; *11:* 143
Ravilious, Robin *77:* 169
Rawlins, Donna *72:* 198; *73:* 15, 129
Rawlins, Janet *76:* 79
Rawlings, Steve *143:* 139; *151:* 54
Rawlinson, Debbie *75:* 132
Ray, Deborah Kogan *8:* 164; *29:* 238; *50:* 112, 113; *62:* 119; *78:* 191; *203:* 149, 150, 151
Ray, Jane *96:* 166; *97:* 104; *152:* 208; *190:* 221; *196:* 165
Ray, Ralph *2:* 239; *5:* 73
Rayann, Omar *162:* 205; *186:* 29, 30
Rayevsky, Robert *64:* 17; *70:* 173; *80:* 204; *117:* 79; *190:* 187, 188
Raymond, Larry *31:* 108; *97:* 109
Rayner, Hugh *151:* 170
Rayner, Mary *22:* 207; *47:* 140; *72:* 191; *87:* 171, 172; *192:* 104
Rayner, Shoo
  See Rayner, Hugh
Raynes, John *71:* 19
Raynor, Dorka *28:* 168
Raynor, Paul *24:* 73
Rayyan, Omar *110:* 222; *112:* 17; *125:* 131
Razzi, James *10:* 127
Read, Alexander D. *20:* 45
Reader, Dennis *71:* 157
Reasoner, Charles *53:* 33, 36, 37
Rebenschied, Shane *203:* 76
Reczuch, Karen *115:* 132; *145:* 131
Redlich, Ben *163:* 221; *198:* 193

Reddy, Mike *203:* 67
Reed, Joseph *116:* 139
Reed, Lynn Rowe *115:* 173; *171:* 146
Reed, Tom *34:* 171
Reeder, Colin *74:* 202; *77:* 113
Rees, Mary *134:* 219
Reese, Bob *60:* 135
Reeve, Philip *171:* 50
Reeves, Eira B. *130:* 173, 174; *141:* 151
Reeves, Rick *181:* 179
Reeves, Rosie *202:* 200
Regan, Dana *117:* 116
Regan, Laura *103:* 198; *153:* 206
Reichert, Renée *169:* 127
Reid, Barbara *82:* 178; *92:* 17; *93:* 169, 170
Reid, Stephen *19:* 213; *22:* 89
Reim, Melanie *104:* 151; *150:* 98
Reinert, Kirk *89:* 138; *195:* 129
Reinertson, Barbara *44:* 150; *62:* 103
Reiniger, Lotte *40:* 185
Reisberg, Mira *119:* 2
Reisch, Jesse *158:* 130
Reiser, Lynn *81:* 175; *138:* 184; *180:* 200
Reiss, John J. *23:* 193
Relf, Douglas *3:* 63
Relyea, C.M. *16:* 29; *31:* 153
Remi, Georges *13:* 184
Remington, Frederic *19:* 188; *41:* 178, 179, 180, 181, 183,184, 185, 186, 187, 188; *62:* 197
Remkiewicz, Frank *67:* 102; *77:* 171; *80:* 130; *113:* 107; *152:* 116; *152:* 211, 212; *157:* 148
Rendon, Maria *116:* 141; 192; *134:* 152
Renfro, Ed *79:* 176
Renier, Aaron *202:* 141; *207:* 119
Renlie, Frank *11:* 200
Reschofsky, Jean *7:* 118
Rethi *60:* 181
Rethi, Lili *2:* 153; *36:* 156
Reusswig, William *3:* 267
Revell, Cindy *195:* 93
Rex, Adam *156:* 172; *169:* 91; *186:* 178, 179
Rex, Michael *157:* 147; *191:* 159, 160
Rey, H.A. *1:* 182; *26:* 163, 164, 166, 167, 169; *69:* 172, 173, 174, 175; *86:* 195, 196, 197; *100:* 211; *YABC 2:* 17
Rey, Luis V. *201:* 162
Reynolds, Adrian *192:* 159, 160
Reynolds, Doris *5:* 71; *31:* 77
Reynolds, Peter H. *142:* 12; *179:* 175, 176; *202:* 113, 114
Rhead, Louis *31:* 91; *100:* 228
Rhodes, Andrew *38:* 204; *50:* 163; *54:* 76; *61:* 123, 124; *87:* 200
Ribbons, Ian *3:* 10; *37:* 161; *40:* 76
Ricci, Regolo *93:* 22; *164:* 148
Rice, Elizabeth *2:* 53, 214
Rice, Eve *34:* 174, 175; *91:* 172
Rice, James *22:* 210; *93:* 173
Rich, Martha *195:* 16
Richards, Chuck *170:* 154
Richards, George *40:* 116, 119, 121; *44:* 179
Richards, Henry *YABC 1:* 228, 231
Richardson, Ernest *2:* 144
Richardson, Frederick *18:* 27, 31
Richardson, John *110:* 88
Richman, Hilda *26:* 132
Richmond, George *24:* 179
Riddell, Chris *114:* 170, 195; *166:* 179; *199:* 164, 166, 167
Riddle, Tohby *74:* 204; *151:* 179
Riding, Peter *63:* 195
Rieniets, Judy King *14:* 28
Riger, Bob *2:* 166
Riggio, Anita *73:* 191; *85:* 63; *137:* 184; *172:* 165
Riley, Jon *74:* 70
Riley, Kenneth *22:* 230
Riley, Terry *203:* 100
Riley-Webb, Charlotte *153:* 143
Rinaldi, Angelo *165:* 60, 69

Ringgold, Faith *71:* 162; *114:* 173, 174, 176; *187:* 160, 161, 163
Ringi, Kjell *12:* 171
Rios, Tere
    See Versace, Marie
Ripper, Charles L. *3:* 175
Ripplinger, Henry *117:* 31
Ritchie, William *74:* 183
Ritter, John *175:* 14
Ritz, Karen *41:* 117; *72:* 239; *87:* 125; *102:* 7; *106:* 6
Rivers, Ruth *178:* 193
Rivkin, Jay *15:* 230
Rivoche, Paul *45:* 125
Roach, Marilynne *9:* 158
Robbin, Jodi *44:* 156, 159
Robbins, Frank *42:* 167
Robbins, Ken *147:* 191, 192
Robbins, Ruth *52:* 102
Roberts, Cliff *4:* 126
Roberts, David *154:* 4, 6; *191:* 162; *196:* 184; *197:* 105
Roberts, Doreen *4:* 230; *28:* 105
Roberts, Jim *22:* 166; *23:* 69; *31:* 110
Roberts, Tony *109:* 195, 214
Roberts, W. *22:* 2, 3
Robertson, M.P. *197:* 153
Robins, Arthur *137:* 172; *151:* 225; *204:* 161
Robinson, Aminah Brenda Lynn *86:* 205; *103:* 55; *159:* 175
Robinson, Charles [1870-1937] *17:* 157, 171, 172, 173, 175, 176; *24:* 207; *25:* 204; *YABC 2:* 308, 309, 310, 331
Robinson, Charles *3:* 53; *5:* 14; *6:* 193; *7:* 150; *7:* 183; *8:* 38; *9:* 81; *13:* 188; *14:* 248, 249; *23:* 149; *26:* 115; *27:* 48; *28:* 191; *32:* 28; *35:* 210; *36:* 37; *48:* 96; *52:* 33; *53:* 157; *56:* 15; *62:* 142; *77:* 41; *111:* 148
Robinson, Jerry *3:* 262
Robinson, Joan G. *7:* 184
Robinson, Lolly *90:* 227
Robinson, T.H. *17:* 179, 181, 182, 183; *29:* 254
Robinson, W. Heath *17:* 185, 187, 189, 191, 193, 195, 197, 199, 202; *23:* 167; *25:* 194; *29:* 150; *YABC 1:* 44; *2:* 183
Rocco, John *187:* 4; *188:* 151
Roche, Christine *41:* 98
Roche, Denis *99:* 184; *180:* 32; *196:* 168
Roche, P.K. *57:* 151, 152
Rocker, Fermin *7:* 34; *13:* 21; *31:* 40; *40:* 190,191
Rocklen, Margot *101:* 181
Rockwell, Anne *5:* 147; *33:* 171, 173; *71:* 166, 167,168; *114:* 183, 184; *194:* 152, 155
Rockwell, Gail *7:* 186
Rockwell, Harlow *33:* 171, 173, 175
Rockwell, Lizzy *114:* 182; *162:* 182; *185:* 189
Rockwell, Norman *23:* 39, 196, 197, 199, 200, 203, 204, 207; *41:* 140, 143; *123:* 47; *YABC 2:* 60
Rockwood, Richard *119:* 75
Rodanas, Kristina *156:* 183, 184
Rodegast, Roland *43:* 100
Rodgers, Frank *69:* 177
Rodriguez, Albert G. *182:* 50
Rodriguez, Christina *184:* 12
Rodriguez, Edel *204:* 86
Rodriguez, Joel *16:* 65
Rodriguez, Robert *145:* 145
Rodriguez-Howard, Pauline *177:* 18
Roeckelein, Katrina *134:* 223
Roennfeldt, Robert *66:* 243
Roever, J.M. *4:* 119; *26:* 170
Roffey, Maureen *33:* 142, 176, 177
Rogasky, Barbara *46:* 90
Rogé *173:* 160
Rogers, Carol *2:* 262; *6:* 164; *26:* 129
Rogers, Chris M. *150:* 59; *196:* 61
Rogers, Forest *87:* 160; *101:* 76
Rogers, Frances *10:* 130

Rogers, Gregory *104:* 76; *126:* 57; *171:* 26
Rogers, Jacqueline *78:* 249; *80:* 34; *86:* 54 *103:* 70; *115:* 72; *129:* 173; *131:* 57, 225; *143:* 211; *153:* 100; *193:* 186; *203:* 51
Rogers, Sherry *191:* 66
Rogers, Walter S. *31:* 135, 138; *67:* 65, 168; *100:* 81
Rogers, William A. *15:* 151, 153, 154; *33:* 35
Rogoff, Barbara *95:* 20
Rohmann, Eric *103:* 152; *198:* 151
Rojankovsky, Feodor *6:* 134, 136; *10:* 183; *21:* 128,129, 130; *25:* 110; *28:* 42; *68:* 120
Rolfsen, Alf *62:* 15
Romain, Trevor *134:* 157
Roman, Barbara J. *103:* 171
Romas *114:* 111; *165:* 63
Romano, Robert *64:* 68
Romero, Alejandro *187:* 185
Roos, Maryn *168:* 198
Root, Barry *80:* 212; *90:* 196; *146:* 78; *156:* 165; *159:* 161; *182:* 18, 172
Root, Kimberly Bulcken *86:* 72; *98:* 21; *108:* 111; *127:* 114; *159:* 162; *176:* 134; *192:* 163
Roper, Bob *65:* 153
Roraback, Robin *111:* 156
Rorer, Abigail *43:* 222; *85:* 155
Rosales, Melodye *80:* 35
Rosamilia, Patricia *36:* 120
Rose, Carl *5:* 62
Rose, David S. *29:* 109; *70:* 120
Rose, Gerald *68:* 200, 201; *86:* 48
Rose, Ted *93:* 178
Rosen, Elizabeth *205:* 137
Rosenbaum, Jonathan *50:* 46
Rosenberg, Amye *74:* 207, 208
Rosenberry, Vera *87:* 22, 26; *144:* 212, 213; *158:* 120
Rosenblum, Richard *11:* 202; *18:* 18
Rosenstiehl, Agnès *203:* 153
Rosier, Lydia *16:* 236; *20:* 104; *21:* 109; *22:* 125; *30:* 151, 158; *42:* 128; *45:* 214; *77:* 227, 228
Rosing, Jens *85:* 142
Ross
    See Thomson, Ross
Ross, Christine *83:* 172, 173
Ross, Clare Romano *3:* 123; *21:* 45; *48:* 199
Ross, Dave *32:* 152; *57:* 108
Ross, Graham *199:* 4
Ross, Herbert *37:* 78
Ross, John *3:* 123; *21:* 45
Ross, Johnny *32:* 190
Ross, Larry *47:* 168; *60:* 62
Ross, Ruth *109:* 233
Ross, Tony *17:* 204; *56:* 132; *65:* 176, 177, 179; *90:* 123; *123:* 186, 187, 190; *130:* 188, 190, 191, 192; *132:* 242; *174:* 159; *176:* 181, 182, 183; *202:* 198
Rossetti, Dante Gabriel *20:* 151, 153
Rostant, Larry *180:* 221; *194:* 108; *195:* 96; *197:* 12; *207:* 53
Roth, Arnold *4:* 238; *21:* 133
Roth, Julie Jersild *180:* 206
Roth, Marci *135:* 223
Roth, R.G. *184:* 50
Roth, Rob *105:* 98; *146:* 41
Roth, Robert *176:* 159
Roth, Roger *61:* 128; *190:* 192
Roth, Stephanie *136:* 171, 172
Roth, Susan L. *80:* 38; *93:* 78; *134:* 165, 166; *181:* 145, 146
Rothenberg, Joani Keller *162:* 190, 191
Rothman, Michael *139:* 62; *184:* 34 Rotman, Jeffrey L. *145:* 30
Rotondo, Pat *32:* 158
Roughsey, Dick *35:* 186
Rouille, M. *11:* 96
Rounds, Glen *8:* 173; *9:* 171; *12:* 56; *32:* 194; *40:* 230; *51:* 161, 162, 166; *56:* 149; *70:* 198, 199; *YABC 1:* 1, 2, 3; *112:* 163
Roundtree, Katherine *114:* 88; *168:* 102

Rovetch, Lissa *201:* 164
Rowan, Evadne *52:* 51
Rowe, Eric *111:* 161
Rowe, Gavin *27:* 144; *72:* 47; *88:* 201
Rowe, John *132:* 70, 71; *180:* 126
Rowell, Kenneth *40:* 72
Rowen, Amy *52:* 143
Rowena *116:* 101
Rowland, Andrew *164:* 136
Rowland, Jada *83:* 73
Rowles, Daphne *58:* 24
Roy, Jeroo *27:* 229; *36:* 110
Royo *118:* 32; *144:* 105, 106, 108; *165:* 19;
    166: 166
Rubel, Nicole *18:* 255; *20:* 59; *81:* 66, 67; *95:*
    169, 170; *119:* 60; *135:* 177, 179, 180; *169:*
    68; *181:* 150
Rubel, Reina *33:* 217
Rud, Borghild *6:* 15
Ruddell, Gary *110:* 238; *116:* 207
Rudolph, Norman Guthrie *17:* 13
Rue, Leonard Lee III *37:* 164
Rueda, Claudia *183:* 170, 171
Ruelle, Karen Gray *126:* 193
Ruff, Donna *50:* 173; *72:* 203; *78:* 49; *80:*
    120,121; *93:* 162; *164:* 121
Ruffins, Reynold *10:* 134, 135; *41:* 191, 192,
    193, 194, 195, 196; *125:* 187, 188, 189; *162:*
    197
Ruhlin, Roger *34:* 44
Ruiz, Art *95:* 154; *110:* 91
Rumford, James *193:* 167
Runnerstroem, Bengt Arne *75:* 161
Ruse, Margaret *24:* 155
Rush, Ken *98:* 74
Rush, Peter *42:* 75
Russell, Charles M. *167:* 171
Russell, E.B. *18:* 177, 182
Russell, Jim *53:* 134
Russell, P. Craig *80:* 196; *146:* 102; *162:* 186
Russo, Marisabina *84:* 51; *106:* 164; *151:* 183;
    188: 153, 154, 155, 156
Russo, Susan *30:* 182; *36:* 144
Russon, Mary *87:* 145
Ruth, Greg *183:* 125
Ruth, Rod *9:* 161
Rutherford, Alexa *110:* 108
Rutherford, Jenny *78:* 5
Rutherford, Meg *25:* 174; *34:* 178, 179; *69:*
    73; *72:* 31
Rutland, Jonathan *31:* 126
Ruurs, Margriet *147:* 195
Ruzzier, Sergio *159:* 176, 177; *163:* 184
Ryan, Amy *188:* 50
Ryan, Will *86:* 134
Ryden, Hope *8:* 176
Rylant, Cynthia *112:* 170, 172
Rymer, Alta M. *34:* 181
Ryniak, Christopher *178:* 11
Rystedt, Rex *49:* 80

S

Saaf, Chuck *49:* 179
Saaf, Donald *101:* 220; *124:* 180
Sabaka, Donna R. *21:* 172
Sabin, Robert *45:* 35; *60:* 30; *99:* 161
Sabuda, Robert *170:* 166, 167, 168
Sacker, Amy *16:* 100
Saelig, S.M. *129:* 73; *173:* 59
Saffiotti, Lino *36:* 176; *48:* 60
Saflund, Birgitta *94:* 2
Sagsoorian, Paul *12:* 183; *22:* 154; *33:* 106;
    87: 152
Sahara, Tony *168:* 106; *177:* 181; *178:* 228;
    186: 132; *207:* 89
Sahlberg, Myron *57:* 165
Saidens, Amy *145:* 162; *191:* 131
Saint Exupery, Antoine de *20:* 157

Saint James, Synthia *152:* 220; *188:* 90; *200:*
    7
Saldutti, Denise *39:* 186; *57:* 178
Sale, Morton *YABC 2:* 31
Sale, Tim *153:* 177
Salerno, Steven *150:* 79; *176:* 188; *202:* 39
Salter, George *72:* 128, 130
Saltzberg, Barney *135:* 184, 185; *194:* 160
Saltzman, David *86:* 209
Salwowski, Mark *71:* 54
Salzman, Yuri *86:* 12
Sambourne, Linley *YABC 2:* 181
Sampson, Katherine *9:* 197
Samson, Anne S. *2:* 216
San Souci, Daniel *40:* 200; *96:* 199, 200; *113:*
    171; *157:* 149; *170:* 69; *192:* 167, 168
Sancha, Sheila *38:* 185
Sanchez, Enrique O. *155:* 84
Sand, George X. *45:* 182
Sandberg, Lasse *15:* 239, 241
Sanders, Beryl *39:* 173
Sanderson, Ruth *21:* 126; *24:* 53; *28:* 63; *33:*
    67; *41:* 48, 198, 199, 200, 201, 202, 203; *43:*
    79; *46:* 36,44; *47:* 102; *49:* 58; *62:* 121, 122;
    85: 3; *109:* 207, 208, 209, 210; *172:* 157,
    158
Sandia *119:* 74
Sandin, Joan *4:* 36; *6:* 194; *7:* 177; *12:*
    145,185; *20:* 43; *21:* 74; *26:* 144; *27:* 142;
    28: 224, 225; *38:* 86; *41:* 46; *42:* 35; *59:* 6;
    80: 136; *94:* 188; *140:* 116; *153:* 179, 180;
    197: 168
Sandland, Reg *39:* 215
Sandoz, Edouard *26:* 45, 47
Sanford, John *66:* 96, 97
Sanger, Amy Wilson *205:* 140
Sankey, Tom *72:* 103
Sano, Kazuhiko *153:* 208; *195:* 171; *203:* 21
Santat, Dan *188:* 160
Santore, Charles *54:* 139; *200:* 171, 172
Santoro, Christopher *74:* 215
Santos, Jesse J. *99:* 24
Sapieha, Christine *1:* 180
Saport, Linda *123:* 137, 138
Sara
    See De La Roche Saint Andre, Anne
Sardinha, Rick *175:* 151
Sarg, Tony *YABC 2:* 236
Sargent, Claudia *64:* 181
Sargent, Robert *2:* 217
Saris *1:* 33
Sarony *YABC 2:* 170
Saroff, Phyllis V. *202:* 160
Sasaki, Goro *170:* 46
Sasek, Miroslav *16:* 239, 240, 241, 242
Sassman, David *9:* 79
Satty *29:* 203, 205
Sauber, Robert *40:* 183; *76:* 256; *78:* 154; *87:*
    92
Saunders, Dave *85:* 163, 164, 165
Savadier, Elivia *84:* 50; *145:* 45; *164:* 206
Savage, Naomi *56:* 172
Savage, Steele *10:* 203; *20:* 77; *35:* 28
Savage, Stephen *174:* 182
Savio *76:* 4
Savitt, Sam *8:* 66, 182; *15:* 278; *20:* 96; *24:*
    192; *28:* 98
Sawyer, Kem Knapp *84:* 228, 229
Say, Allen *28:* 178; *69:* 182, 183, 232; *110:*
    194, 195,196; *161:* 154, 155
Sayles, Elizabeth *82:* 93; *105:* 155; *109:* 116;
    180: 64
Scabrini, Janet *13:* 191; *44:* 128
Scanlan, Peter *83:* 27; *153:* 165; *187:* 149
Scanlon, Paul *83:* 87
Scannell, Reece *105:* 105
Scarry, Huck *35:* 204, 205
Scarry, Richard *2:* 220, 221; *18:* 20; *35:* 193,
    194, 195,196, 197, 198, 199, 200, 201, 202;
    75: 165, 167, 168

Schachner, Judith Byron *88:* 180; *92:* 163; *93:*
    102; *142:* 82; *178:* 199, 200; *190:* 140
Schade, Susan *205:* 21
Schaeffer, Mead *18:* 81, 94; *21:* 137, 138, 139;
    47: 128
Schaffer, Amanda *90:* 206
Schanzer, Rosalyn *138:* 192, 193
Scharl, Josef *20:* 132; *22:* 128
Scheel, Lita *11:* 230
Scheffler, Axel *180:* 23, 24
Scheib, Ida *29:* 28
Schermer, Judith *30:* 184
Schick, Eleanor *82:* 210, 211; *144:* 222
Schick, Joel *16:* 160; *17:* 167; *22:* 12; *27:*
    176; *31:* 147, 148; *36:* 23; *38:* 64; *45:* 116,
    117; *52:* 5, 85; *104:* 159
Schields, Gretchen *75:* 171, 203
Schindelman, Joseph *1:* 74; *4:* 101; *12:* 49;
    26: 51; *40:* 146; *56:* 158; *73:* 40
Schindler, Edith *7:* 22
Schindler, S.D. *38:* 107; *46:* 196; *74:* 162; *75:*
    172, 173; *99:* 133; *112:* 177; *118:* 185, 186;
    121: 71; *136:* 159; *143:* 45; *149:* 120; *156:*
    30; *169:* 135; *171:* 161, 162, 163; *172:* 9;
    186: 163; *194:* 109; *195:* 35; *198:* 170, 171,
    172
Schlesinger, Bret *7:* 77
Schmid, Eleanore *12:* 188; *126:* 196, 197
Schmiderer, Dorothy *19:* 224
Schmidt, Bill *73:* 34; *76:* 220, 222, 224
Schmidt, Elizabeth *15:* 242
Schmidt, George Paul *132:* 122
Schmidt, Karen Lee *54:* 12; *71:* 174; *92:* 56;
    94: 190, 191; *127:* 103
Schmidt, Lynette *76:* 205
Schmitz, Tamara *207:* 147
Schneider, Christine M. *171:* 165
Schneider, Howie *181:* 159
Schneider, Rex *29:* 64; *44:* 171
Schnurr, Edward *170:* 62
Schoberle, Cecile *80:* 200; *92:* 134
Schoenherr, Ian *32:* 83; *173:* 41
Schoenherr, John *1:* 146, 147, 173; *3:* 39, 139;
    17: 75; *29:* 72; *32:* 83; *37:* 168, 169, 170;
    43: 164, 165; *45:* 160, 162; *51:* 127; *66:*
    196, 197, 198; *68:* 83; *72:* 240; *75:* 225; *88:*
    176
Scholder, Fritz *69:* 103
Schomburg, Alex *13:* 23
Schongut, Emanuel *4:* 102; *15:* 186; *47:* 218,
    219; *52:* 147, 148, 149, 150; *185:* 27
Schoonover, Frank *17:* 107; *19:* 81, 190, 233;
    22: 88,129; *24:* 189; *31:* 88; *41:* 69; *YABC
    2:* 282, 316
Schories, Pat *164:* 210
Schottland, Miriam *22:* 172
Schramm, Ulrik *2:* 16; *14:* 112
Schreiber, Elizabeth Anne *13:* 193
Schreiber, Ralph W. *13:* 193
Schreiter, Rick *14:* 97; *23:* 171; *41:* 247; *49:*
    131
Schroeder, Binette *56:* 128, 129
Schroeder, E. Peter *12:* 112
Schroeder, Ted *11:* 160; *15:* 189; *30:* 91; *34:*
    43
Schrotter, Gustav *22:* 212; *30:* 225
Schubert, Dieter *101:* 167, 168
Schubert-Gabrys, Ingrid *101:* 167, 168
Schucker, James *31:* 163
Schuett, Stacey *72:* 137
Schulder, Lili *146:* 29
Schulke, Debra *57:* 167
Schulke, Flip *57:* 167
Schulz, Barbara *167:* 24
Schulz, Charles M. *10:* 137, 138, 139, 140,
    141, 142; *118:* 192, 193, 194, 196, 199
Schutzer, Dena *109:* 32
Schwark, Mary Beth *51:* 155; *72:* 175
Schwartz, Amy *47:* 191; *82:* 100; *83:* 178,
    179, 180,181; *129:* 107; *131:* 197, 198; *189:*
    166, 168

Schwartz, Carol *124:* 41; *130:* 199
Schwartz, Charles *8:* 184
Schwartz, Daniel *46:* 37
Schwartz, Joanie *124:* 170
Schwartzberg, Joan *3:* 208
Schwarz, Viviane *204:* 132
Schweitzer, Iris *2:* 137; *6:* 207
Schweninger, Ann *29:* 172; *82:* 246; *159:* 202; *168:* 166
Schwinger, Laurence *84:* 44; *91:* 61
Scofield, Penrod *61:* 107; *62:* 160
Scott, Anita Walker *7:* 38
Scott, Art *39:* 41
Scott, Frances Gruse *38:* 43
Scott, Julian *34:* 126
Scott, Roszel *33:* 238
Scott, Sally *87:* 27
Scott, Steve *166:* 230, 231; *171:* 93
Scott, Trudy *27:* 172
Scrace, Carolyn *143:* 95, 96
Scrambly, Crab *198:* 196
Scribner, Joanne *14:* 236; *29:* 78; *33:* 185; *34:* 208; *78:* 75; *164:* 237; *203:* 73
Scrofani, Joseph *31:* 65; *74:* 225
Scroggs, Kirk *187:* 169
Seaman, Mary Lott *34:* 64
Searle, Ronald *24:* 98; *42:* 172, 173, 174, 176, 177, 179; *66:* 73, 74; *70:* 205, 206, 207
Searle, Townley *36:* 85
Sebree, Charles *18:* 65
Sedacca, Joseph M. *11:* 25; *22:* 36
Seder, Jason *108:* 102
Seeger, Laura Vaccaro *172:* 162
Seegmiller, Don *174:* 57
Seely, David *164:* 173
Seeley, Laura L. *97:* 105
Segal, John *178:* 202
Segar, E.C. *61:* 179, 181
Segur, Adrienne *27:* 121
Seibold, J. Otto *83:* 188, 190, 191; *149:* 212, 214, 215, 216; *196:* 177, 179
Seignobosc, Francoise *21:* 145, 146
Sejima, Yoshimasa *8:* 187
Selig, Sylvie *13:* 199
Seltzer, Isadore *6:* 18; *133:* 59
Seltzer, Meyer *17:* 214
Selven, Maniam *144:* 133
Selway, Martina *169:* 157
Selznick, Brian *79:* 192; *104:* 25; *117:* 175; *126:* 156; *134:* 171; *158:* 76, 78; *169:* 70; *171:* 172, 173; *191:* 106; *192:* 130; *197:* 158; *203:* 35; *205:* 92
Sempe, Jean-Jacques *47:* 92; *YABC 2:* 109
Sendak, Maurice *1:* 135, 190; *3:* 204; *7:* 142; *15:* 199; *17:* 210; *27:* 181, 182, 183, 185, 186, 187, 189,190, 191, 192, 193, 194, 195, 197, 198, 199, 203; *28:* 181, 182; *32:* 108; *33:* 148, 149; *35:* 238; *44:* 180, 181; *45:* 97, 99; *46:* 174; *73:* 225; *91:* 10, 11 *YABC1:* 167; *113:* 163, 165, 167, 168; *118:* 153; *127:* 161
Senders, Marci *180:* 79
Sengler, Johanna *18:* 256
Senn, Steve *60:* 145
Seredy, Kate *1:* 192; *14:* 20, 21; *17:* 210
Sergeant, John *6:* 74
Servello, Joe *10:* 144; *24:* 139; *40:* 91; *70:* 130, 131; *146:* 159
Seton, Ernest Thompson *18:* 260-269, 271
Seuss, Dr.
    See Geisel, Theodor
Severin, John Powers *7:* 62
Sewall, Marcia *15:* 8; *22:* 170; *37:* 171, 172, 173; *39:* 73; *45:* 209; *62:* 117; *69:* 185, 186; *71:* 212; *90:* 232; *96:* 127; *102:* 101; *107:* 129; *119:* 176, 177, 178, 180
Seward, James *70:* 35
Seward, Prudence *16:* 243
Sewell, Helen *3:* 186; *15:* 308; *33:* 102; *38:* 189, 190, 191, 192
Seymour, Stephen *54:* 21

Sfar, Joann *182:* 183
Shachat, Andrew *82:* 179
Shadbolt, Robert *203:* 68
Shahn, Ben *39:* 178; *46:* 193
Shalansky, Len *38:* 167
Shanks, Anne Zane *10:* 149
Shannon, David *57:* 137; *107:* 184; *112:* 216; *135:* 12; *152:* 223, 224, 225; *158:* 192
Sharp, Paul *52:* 60
Sharp, William *6:* 131; *19:* 241; *20:* 112; *25:* 141
Sharratt, Nick *102:* 207, 208; *104:* 163; *153:* 198; *175:* 176; *192:* 208; *199:* 141, 142, 143, 184, 187, 188
Shaw, Barclay *74:* 14, 16; *118:* 138
Shaw, Charles *21:* 135; *38:* 187; *47:* 124; *126:* 219
Shaw, Charles G. *13:* 200
Shaw-Smith, Emma *144:* 117
Shea, Edmund *56:* 19
Shearer, Ted *43:* 193, 194, 195, 196
Sheban, Chris *182:* 185; *190:* 102, 104; *202:* 28; *204:* 112, 114
Shecter, Ben *16:* 244; *25:* 109; *33:* 188, 191; *41:* 77
Shed, Greg *74:* 94; *84:* 204; *129:* 149, 167: 91; *179:* 192
Sheeban, Chris *144:* 190; *158:* 163
Shefcik, James *48:* 221, 222; *60:* 141
Shefelman, Karl *58:* 168
Shefelman, Tom *204:* 137
Shefts, Joelle *48:* 210
Shein, Bob *139:* 189
Sheinkin, Stephen *204:* 139
Shekerjian, Haig *16:* 245
Shekerjian, Regina *16:* 245; *25:* 73
Sheldon, David *184:* 174; *185:* 204
Shelley, John *186:* 223
Shemie, Bonnie *96:* 207
Shenton, Edward *45:* 187, 188, 189; *YABC 1:* 218, 219, 221
Shepard, Ernest H. *3:* 193; *4:* 74; *16:* 101; *17:* 109; *25:* 148; *33:* 152, 199, 200, 201, 202, 203, 204, 205, 206,207; *46:* 194; *98:* 114; *100:* 111, 178, 179, 217, 219, 220,221; *YABC 1:* 148, 153, 174, 176, 180, 181
Shepard, Mary *4:* 210; *22:* 205; *30:* 132, 133; *54:* 150, 152, 153, 157, 158; *59:* 108, 109, 111; *100:* 246
Shepherd, Amanda *198:* 14
Shepherd, Irana *171:* 112
Sheppard, Kate *195:* 176
Shepperson, Rob *96:* 153; *177:* 163; *178:* 204; *197:* 34; *205:* 108
Sheridan, Brian *196:* 193
Sherman, Theresa *27:* 167
Sherwan, Earl *3:* 196
Shields, Charles *10:* 150; *36:* 63
Shields, Leonard *13:* 83, 85, 87
Shiffman, Lena *139:* 167; *168:* 136
Shigley, Neil K. *66:* 219
Shillabeer, Mary *35:* 74
Shilston, Arthur *49:* 61; *62:* 58
Shimin, Symeon *1:* 93; *2:* 128, 129; *3:* 202; *7:* 85; *11:* 177; *12:* 139; *13:* 202, 203; *27:* 138; *28:* 65; *35:* 129; *36:* 130; *48:* 151; *49:* 59; *56:* 63, 65, 153
Shine, Andrea *104:* 165; *128:* 34
Shinn, Everett *16:* 148; *18:* 229; *21:* 149, 150, 151; *24:* 218
Shinn, Florence Scovel *63:* 133, 135
Shore, Robert *27:* 54; *39:* 192, 193; *YABC 2:* 200
Shortall, Leonard *4:* 144; *8:* 196; *10:* 166; *19:* 227, 228, 229, 230; *25:* 78; *28:* 66, 167; *33:* 127; *52:* 125; *73:* 12, 212
Shortt, T.M. *27:* 36
Shpitalnik, Vladimir *83:* 194
Shropshire, Sandy *170:* 191
Shtainments, Leon *32:* 161

Shulevitz, Uri *3:* 198, 199; *17:* 85; *22:* 204; *27:* 212; *28:* 184; *50:* 190, 191, 192, 193, 194, 195, 196,197, 198, 199, 201; *106:* 181, 182, 183; *165:* 203, 205; *166:* 138
Shulman, Dee *180:* 140
Shupe, Bobbi *139:* 80, 81
Shute, A.B. *67:* 196
Shute, Linda *46:* 59; *74:* 118
Siberell, Anne *29:* 193
Sibley, Don *1:* 39; *12:* 196; *31:* 47
Sibthorp, Fletcher *94:* 111, 112
Sidjakov, Nicolas *18:* 274
Siebel, Fritz *3:* 120; *17:* 145
Siebold, J. Otto *158:* 227
Siegel, Hal *74:* 246
Sieger, Ted *189:* 172
Siegl, Helen *12:* 166; *23:* 216; *34:* 185, 186
Silin-Palmer, Pamela *184:* 102
Sill, John *140:* 194; *141:* 157
Sills, Joyce *5:* 199
Silva, Simon *108:* 122
Silver, Maggie *85:* 210
Silveria, Gordon *96:* 44
Silverstein, Alvin *8:* 189
Silverstein, Shel *33:* 211; *92:* 209, 210
Silverstein, Virginia *8:* 189
Silvey, Joe *135:* 203
Simard, Remy *95:* 156
Simmons, Elly *110:* 2; *127:* 69; *134:* 181
Simon, Eric M. *7:* 82
Simon, Hilda *28:* 189
Simon, Howard *2:* 175; *5:* 132; *19:* 199; *32:* 163, 164, 165
Simont, Marc *2:* 119; *4:* 213; *9:* 168; *13:* 238,240; *14:* 262; *16:* 179; *18:* 221; *26:* 210; *33:* 189, 194; *44:* 132; *58:* 122; *68:* 117; *73:* 204, 205, 206; *74:* 221; *126:* 199, 200; *133:* 195; *164:* 128
Sims, Agnes *54:* 152
Sims, Blanche *44:* 116; *57:* 129; *75:* 179, 180; *77:* 92; *104:* 192; *152:* 117; *156:* 160; *160:* 70; *168:* 174, 175; *198:* 17
Singer, Edith G. *2:* 30
Singer, Gloria *34:* 56; *36:* 43
Singer, Julia *28:* 190
Singh, Jen *178:* 146
Siomades, Lorianne *134:* 45; *204:* 48
Simont, Marc *163:* 40
Siracusa, Catherine *68:* 135; *82:* 218
Sís, Peter *67:* 179, 181, 183, 184, 185; *96:* 96, 98; *106:* 193, 194, 195; *149:* 224, 226; *180:* 177; *192:* 180, 182
Sivard, Robert *26:* 124
Sivertson, Liz *116:* 84
Skardinski, Stanley *23:* 144; *32:* 84; *66:* 122; *84:* 108
Slack, Michael *185:* 108; *189:* 173, 174
Slackman, Charles B. *12:* 201
Slade, Christian *193:* 187; *204:* 134
Slade, Paul *61:* 170
Slark, Albert *99:* 212; *205:* 161
Slater, Rod *25:* 167
Slavin, Bill *182:* 14, 15; *196:* 90; *199:* 148, 149, 150
Sloan, Joseph *16:* 68
Sloane, Eric *21:* 3; *52:* 153, 154, 155, 156, 157, 158, 160
Sloat, Teri *164:* 231
Slobodkin, Louis *1:* 200; *3:* 232; *5:* 168; *13:* 251; *15:* 13, 88; *26:* 173, 174, 175, 176, 178, 179; *60:* 180
Slobodkina, Esphyr *1:* 201
Slonim, David *166:* 167, 168
Small, David *50:* 204, 205; *79:* 44; *95:* 189, 190, 191; *126:* 203, 204; *136:* 119; *143:* 201, 202, 203; *144:* 246; *150:* 5; *161:* 176; *183:* 181, 182, 183, 184; *200:* 211
Small, W. *33:* 113
Smalley, Janet *1:* 154
Smath, Jerry *198:* 179, 180
Smedley, William T. *34:* 129

Smee, David *14:* 78; *62:* 30
Smee, Nicola *167:* 156
Smith, A.G., Jr. *35:* 182
Smith, Ali *204:* 68
Smith, Alvin *1:* 31, 229; *13:* 187; *27:* 216; *28:* 226; *48:* 149; *49:* 60
Smith, Andy *188:* 20; *207:* 151
Smith, Anne *194:* 147
Smith, Anne Warren *41:* 212
Smith, Barry *75:* 183
Smith, Brian *200:* 183
Smith, Carl *36:* 41
Smith, Cat Bowman *146:* 39; *164:* 219; *201:* 55, 184
Smith, Craig *97:* 197; *172:* 175; *206:* 40
Smith, Donald A. *178:* 7
Smith, Doris Susan *41:* 139
Smith, Douglas *189:* 159
Smith, Duane *171:* 152
Smith, E. Boyd *19:* 70; *22:* 89; *26:* 63; *YABC 1:* 4, 5, 240, 248, 249
Smith, Edward J. *4:* 224
Smith, Elwood H. *157:* 231; *181:* 79; *203:* 160, 161, 162
Smith, Eunice Young *5:* 170
Smith, Gary *113:* 216
Smith, George *102:* 169
Smith, Howard *19:* 196
Smith, J. Gerard *95:* 42
Smith, Jacqueline Bardner *27:* 108; *39:* 197
Smith, Jay J. *61:* 119
Smith, Jeff *93:* 191
Smith, Jessie Willcox *15:* 91; *16:* 95; *18:* 231; *19:* 57, 242; *21:* 29, 156, 157, 158, 159, 160, 161; *34:* 65; *100:* 223; *YABC 1:* 6; *2:* 180, 185, 191, 311, 325
Smith, Jos. A. *52:* 131; *72:* 120; *74:* 151; *84:* 147, 148; *85:* 146; *87:* 96; *94:* 219; *96:* 97; *104:* 33; *108:* 126, 127, 128; *111:* 140; *136:* 145; *181:* 173; *200:* 213; *201:* 94
Smith, Kenneth R. *47:* 182
Smith, Kevin Warren *89:* 112
Smith, L.H. *35:* 174
Smith, Lane *76:* 211, 213; *88:* 115; *105:* 202, 203,204, 205; *131:* 207; *160:* 217, 221; *179:* 183, 184, 185, 186; *199:* 122, 123, 124, 126
Smith, Lee *29:* 32
Smith, Linell Nash *2:* 195
Smith, Maggie Kaufman *13:* 205; *35:* 191; *110:* 158; *178:* 226; *190:* 204
Smith, Mavis *101:* 219
Smith, Moishe *33:* 155
Smith, Philip *44:* 134; *46:* 203
Smith, Ralph Crosby *2:* 267; *49:* 203
Smith, Robert D. *5:* 63
Smith, Sally J. *84:* 55
Smith, Susan Carlton *12:* 208
Smith, Terry *12:* 106; *33:* 158
Smith, Virginia *3:* 157; *33:* 72
Smith, William A. *1:* 36; *10:* 154; *25:* 65
Smith-Moore, J.J. *98:* 147
Smolinski, Dick *84:* 217
Smoljan, Joe *112:* 201
Smollin, Mike *39:* 203
Smyth, Iain *105:* 207
Smyth, M. Jane *12:* 15
Smythe, Fiona *151:* 213
Smythe, Theresa *141:* 37
Snair, Andy *176:* 4
Sneed, Brad *125:* 25; *191:* 175, 176
Snyder, Andrew A. *30:* 212
Snyder, Jerome *13:* 207; *30:* 173
Snyder, Joel *28:* 163
So, Meilo *162:* 201
Soentpiet, Chris K. *97:* 208; *110:* 33; *159:* 184; *161:* 10; *163:* 130
Sofia *1:* 62; *5:* 90; *32:* 166; *86:* 43
Sofilas, Mark *93:* 157
Sogabe, Aki *207:* 153
Sohn, Jiho *182:* 78
Sokol, Bill *37:* 178; *49:* 23

Sokolov, Kirill *34:* 188
Solbert, Ronni *1:* 159; *2:* 232; *5:* 121; *6:* 34; *17:* 249
Solomon, Michael *174:* 115
Solonevich, George *15:* 246; *17:* 47
Soma, Liana *81:* 118
Soman, David *90:* 122; *102:* 126; *140:* 120; *93*; *188:* 43, 89; *200:* 180, 181
Sommer, Robert *12:* 211
Song, Jae *203:* 27
Soo, Kean *201:* 185
Sorel, Edward *4:* 61; *36:* 82; *65:* 191, 193; *126:* 214
Sorensen, Henri *196:* 58
Sorensen, Henrik *62:* 16
Sorensen, Svend Otto *22:* 130, 141; *67:* 188, 189
Sorra, Kristin *155:* 80
Sosa, Hernan *198:* 66
Sostre, Maria *187:* 36
Sotomayor, Antonio *11:* 215
Souhami, Jessica *112:* 128; *176:* 193
Souza, Diana *71:* 139
Sovak, Jan *115:* 190
Soyer, Moses *20:* 177
Spaenkuch, August *16:* 28
Spafford, Suzy *160:* 228
Spain, Valerie *105:* 76
Spain, Sunday Sahara *133:* 204
Spalenka, Greg *149:* 69; *151:* 228; *184:* 195; *191:* 21; *196:* 12; *198:* 181, 182, 201
Spanfeller, James *1:* 72, 149; *2:* 183; *19:* 230, 231,232; *22:* 66; *36:* 160, 161; *40:* 75; *52:* 166; *76:* 37
Sparks, Mary Walker *15:* 247
Spears, Rick *182:* 187
Speidel, Sandra *78:* 233; *94:* 178; *134:* 180
Speirs, John *67:* 178
Spence, Geraldine *21:* 163; *47:* 196
Spence, Jim *38:* 89; *50:* 102
Spencer, Laurie *113:* 12
Spencer, Mark *57:* 170
Spengler, Kenneth J. *146:* 256
Sperling, Andrea *133:* 182
Spiegel, Beth *184:* 203
Spiegel, Doris *29:* 111
Spiegelman, Art *109:* 227
Spier, Jo *10:* 30
Spier, Peter *3:* 155; *4:* 200; *7:* 61; *11:* 78; *38:* 106; *54:* 120, 121, 122, 123, 124, 125, 126, 127, 128, 129, 130,131, 132, 133, 134
Spilka, Arnold *5:* 120; *6:* 204; *8:* 131
Spirin, Gennady *95:* 196, 197; *113:* 172; *128:* 9; *129:* 49; *134:* 210; *153:* 9; *204:* 143, 144, 145
Spivak, I. Howard *8:* 10; *13:* 172
Spohn, David *72:* 233
Spohn, Kate *87:* 195; *147:* 201, 202
Spollen, Christopher J. *12:* 214
Spooner, Malcolm *40:* 142
Spowart, Robin *82:* 228; *92:* 149; *133:* 131; *176:* 163; *177:* 183, 184
Sprague, Kevin *150:* 60; *196:* 62
Spranger, Nina *201:* 199
Sprattler, Rob *12:* 176
Spring, Bob *5:* 60
Spring, Ira *5:* 60
Springer, Harriet *31:* 92
Spudvilas, Anne *110:* 74; *197:* 192; *199:* 154
Spurll, Barbara *78:* 199; *88:* 141, 142; *99:* 215
Spurrier, Steven *28:* 198
Spuvilas, Anne *85:* 114
Spy
    See Ward, Leslie
Squires, Stuart *127:* 74
St. Aubin, Bruno *179:* 54
St. John, J. Allen *41:* 62
Stabin, Victor *101:* 131; *164:* 158
Stadler, John *62:* 33; *204:* 149
Staffan, Alvin E. *11:* 56; *12:* 187

Stahl, Ben *5:* 181; *12:* 91; *49:* 122; *71:* 128; *87:* 206; *112:* 107
Stair, Gobin *35:* 214
Stallwood, Karen *73:* 126
Stamaty, Mark Alan *12:* 215
Stammen, JoEllen McAllister *113:* 14
Stampnick, Ken *51:* 142
Stanbridge, Joanne *150:* 91
Stanley, Diane *3:* 45; *37:* 180; *80:* 217, 219
Stanley, Sanna *145:* 228
Starcke, Helmut *86:* 217
Stark, Ken *197:* 102
Starr, Branka *73:* 25
Stasiak, Krystyna *49:* 181; *64:* 194
Staub, Leslie *103:* 54
Staunton, Ted *112:* 192
Stawicki, Matt *164:* 250
Stead, L. *55:* 51, 56
Steadman, Broeck *97:* 185, 186; *99:* 56; *121:* 48
Steadman, Ralph *32:* 180; *123:* 143, 145
Stearn, Nick *183:* 26
Steckler, June *90:* 178
Steele, Robert Gantt *169:* 174
Steichen, Edward *30:* 79
Steig, William *18:* 275, 276; *70:* 215, 216, 217, 218; *111:* 173, 174, 175, 176, 177
Stein, Harve *1:* 109
Steinberg, Saul *47:* 193
Steinel, William *23:* 146
Steiner, Charlotte *45:* 196
Steiner, Joan *110:* 219; *199:* 160, 161
Steirnagel, Michael *80:* 56
Stemp, Eric *60:* 184
Stephens, Alice Barber *66:* 208, 209
Stephens, Charles H. *YABC 2:* 279
Stephens, Pam *198:* 69
Stephens, Pat *126:* 110; *128:* 101
Stephens, William M. *21:* 165
Steptoe, Javaka *151:* 203, 204; *190:* 169
Steptoe, John *8:* 197; *57:* 9; *63:* 158, 159, 160, 161,163, 164, 165, 166, 167; *96:* 4; *105:* 87
Stern, Simon *15:* 249, 250; *17:* 58; *34:* 192, 193
Sterret, Jane *53:* 27
Stetsios, Debbie *165:* 108, 109
Steven, Kat *158:* 237
Stevens, David *62:* 44
Stevens, Helen *189:* 31; *207:* 83
Stevens, Janet *40:* 126; *57:* 10, 11; *80:* 112; *90:* 221, 222; *109:* 156; *130:* 34; *166:* 202; *176:* 53, 116; *193:* 199, 200, 202
Stevens, Mary *11:* 193; *13:* 129; *43:* 95
Stevenson, Harvey *66:* 143; *80:* 201, 221; *153:* 60; *191:* 166
Stevenson, James *42:* 182, 183; *51:* 163; *66:* 184; *71:* 185, 187, 188; *78:* 262; *87:* 97; *113:* 182, 183,184, 185; *161:* 182, 183
Stevenson, Sucie *92:* 27; *104:* 194, 195; *112:* 168; *160:* 202; *194:* 172, 173; *195:* 166
Stewart, April Blair *75:* 210
Stewart, Arvis *33:* 98; *36:* 69; *60:* 118; *75:* 91; *127:* 4
Stewart, Charles *2:* 205
Stewart, Joel *151:* 205
Stieg, William *172:* 58
Stiles, Fran *26:* 85; *78:* 56; *82:* 150
Stillman, Susan *44:* 130; *76:* 83
Stimpson, Tom *49:* 171
Stinemetz, Morgan *40:* 151
Stinson, Paul *110:* 86
Stirnweis, Shannon *10:* 164
Stites, Joe *86:* 96
Stobbs, William *1:* 48, 49; *3:* 68; *6:* 20; *17:* 117, 217; *24:* 150; *29:* 250; *60:* 179; *87:* 204, 205,206
Stock, Catherine *37:* 55; *65:* 198; *72:* 7; *99:* 225; *114:* 197, 198, 199; *126:* 3; *145:* 161; *161:* 82; *173:* 149
Stockman, Jack *113:* 24

Stoeke, Janet Morgan *90:* 225; *136:* 196; *202:* 182, 183
Stoerrle, Tom *55:* 147
Stolp, Jaap *49:* 98
Stolp, Todd *89:* 195
Stone, David L. *87:* 154
Stone, David *9:* 173
Stone, David K. *4:* 38; *6:* 124; *9:* 180; *43:* 182; *60:* 70
Stone, Helen V. *6:* 209
Stone, Helen *44:* 121, 122, 126
Stone, Kazuko G. *134:* 43
Stone, Kyle M. *202:* 185
Stone, Phoebe *86:* 212; *134:* 213; *162:* 188; *205:* 145
Stone, Steve *166:* 213
Stone, Tony *150:* 34, 35
Storrings, Michael *191:* 108
Stoud, Virginia A. *89:* 31
Stover, Jill *82:* 234
Strachan, Bruce *205:* 146
Stratton, Helen *33:* 151
Stratton-Porter, Gene *15:* 254, 259, 263, 264, 268, 269
Straub, Matt *192:* 176
Straub, Phillip *197:* 22
Streano, Vince *20:* 173
Street, Janet Travell *84:* 235
Streeter, Clive *121:* 2
Stringer, Lauren *129:* 187; *154:* 172, 173; *161:* 127; *183:* 187, 188
Strodl, Daniel *47:* 95
Strogart, Alexander *63:* 139
Stromoski, Rick *111:* 179; *124:* 161, 190
Strong, Joseph D., Jr. *YABC 2:* 330
Stroyer, Poul *13:* 221
Strugnell, Ann *27:* 38
Struzan, Drew *117:* 6
Stubbs, William *73:* 196
Stubis, Talivaldis *5:* 182, 183; *10:* 45; *11:* 9; *18:* 304; *20:* 127
Stubley, Trevor *14:* 43; *22:* 219; *23:* 37; *28:* 61; *87:* 26
Stuck, Marion *104:* 44
Stuecklen, Karl W. *8:* 34, 65; *23:* 103
Stull, Betty *11:* 46
Stutzman, Mark *119:* 99
Stutzmann, Laura *73:* 185
Suarez, Maribel *162:* 208; *200:* 202
Suba, Susanne *4:* 202, 203; *14:* 261; *23:* 134; *29:* 222; *32:* 30
Sueling, Barbara *98:* 185
Sueling, Gwenn *98:* 186
Sugarman, Tracy *3:* 76; *8:* 199; *37:* 181, 182
Sugimoto, Yugo *170:* 144
Sugita, Yutaka *36:* 180, 181
Suh, John *80:* 157
Sullivan, Dorothy *89:* 113
Sullivan, Edmund J. *31:* 86
Sullivan, James F. *19:* 280; *20:* 192
Sully, Tom *104:* 199, 200; *182:* 77
Sumichrast, Jozef *14:* 253; *29:* 168, 213
Sumiko *46:* 57
Summers, Leo *1:* 177; *2:* 273; *13:* 22
Summers, Mark *118:* 144
Summers, Mike *190:* 176
Sutton, Judith *94:* 164
Svarez, Juan *56:* 113
Svendsen, Mark *181:* 176
Svolinsky, Karel *17:* 104
Swain, Carol *172:* 182
Swain, Su Zan Noguchi *21:* 170
Swan, Susan *22:* 220, 221; *37:* 66; *60:* 146; *145:* 205; *181:* 168
Swann, Susan *86:* 55
Swanson, Karl *79:* 65; *89:* 186
Swarner, Kristina *203:* 62
Swayne, Sam *53:* 143, 145
Swayne, Zoa *53:* 143, 145
Swearingen, Greg *152:* 56; *165:* 135; *173:* 2

Sweat, Lynn *25:* 206; *57:* 176; *73:* 184; *168:* 178
Sweet, Darrell K. *60:* 9; *69:* 86; *74:* 15; *75:* 215; *76:* 130, 131; *81:* 96, 122; *82:* 253; *83:* 11; *84:* 14; *85:* 37; *89:* 140; *90:* 6; *91:* 137,139; *95:* 160, 161; *126:* 25; *185:* 175; *195:* 132
Sweet, Darrell K. *1:* 163; *4:* 136; *164:* 175
Sweet, Melissa *71:* 94; *72:* 172; *111:* 82; *139:* 53, 58; *141:* 88; *142:* 231; *155:* 121; *159:* 121, 122; *172:* 185; *188:* 127
Sweet, Ozzie *31:* 149, 151, 152
Sweetland, Robert *12:* 194
Swiatkowska, Gabi *132:* 43; *175:* 139; *180:* 218; *183:* 176
Swope, Martha *43:* 160; *56:* 86, 87, 89
Sylvada, Peter *154:* 174
Sylvester, Natalie G. *22:* 222
Szafran, Gene *24:* 144
Szasz, Susanne *13:* 55, 226; *14:* 48
Szekeres, Cyndy *2:* 218; *5:* 185; *8:* 85; *11:* 166; *14:* 19; *16:* 57, 159; *26:* 49, 214; *34:* 205; *60:* 150, 151, 152, 153, 154; *73:* 224; *74:* 218; *131:* 213, 215
Szpura, Beata *81:* 68; *119:* 65; *168:* 201

T

Taback, Simms *40:* 207; *52:* 120; *57:* 34; *80:* 241; *104:* 202, 203; *170:* 176, 177; *205:* 183
Taber, Patricia *75:* 124
Tabor, Nancy Maria Grande *89:* 210; *161:* 188
Taddei, Richard *112:* 13, 14
Tadgell, Nicole *150:* 77; *161:* 20; *177:* 186
Tadiello, Ed *133:* 200
Tafuri, Nancy *39:* 210; *75:* 199, 200; *92:* 75; *130:* 215, 216, 217
Tailfeathers, Gerald *86:* 85
Tait, Douglas *12:* 220; *74:* 105, 106
Takabayashi, Mari *113:* 112; *130:* 22; *156:* 169
Takahashi, Hideko *136:* 160; *187:* 6
Takakjian, Portia *15:* 274
Takashima, Shizuye *13:* 228
Talarczyk, June *4:* 173
Talbott, Hudson *84:* 240; *163:* 100
Tallarico, Tony *116:* 197
Tallon, Robert *2:* 228; *43:* 200, 201, 202, 203, 204, 205,206, 207, 209
Tamaki, Jillian *201:* 188
Tamas, Szecsko *29:* 135
Tamburine, Jean *12:* 222
Tandy, H.R. *13:* 69
Tandy, Russell H. *65:* 9; *100:* 30, 131
Tang, Charles *81:* 202; *90:* 192
Tang, Susan *80:* 174; *108:* 158
Tang, You-shan *63:* 100
Tankersley, Paul *69:* 206; *133:* 219
Tannenbaum, Robert *48:* 181
Tanner, Jane *87:* 13; *97:* 37
Tanner, Tim *72:* 192; *84:* 35
Tanobe, Miyuki *23:* 221
Tarabay, Sharif *110:* 149; *113:* 123; *169:* 83
Tarkington, Booth *17:* 224, 225
Tarlow, Phyllis *61:* 198
Tate, Don *159:* 141, 191; *183:* 69; *186:* 120
Tauss, Herbert *95:* 179
Tauss, Marc *117:* 160; *126:* 155; *178:* 221; *197:* 7
Tavares, Matt *159:* 192, 193; *198:* 188, 189, 190; *199:* 86
Taylor, Ann *41:* 226
Taylor, Dahl *129:* 157
Taylor, Geoff *93:* 156; *197:* 173, 175; *204:* 151, 152
Taylor, Isaac *41:* 228
Taylor, Mike *143:* 99, 100
Teague, Mark *83:* 6; *139:* 241; *170:* 180, 181; *205:* 150, 151
Teale, Edwin Way *7:* 196

Teason, James *1:* 14
Teckentrup, Britta *200:* 191, 192
Teeple, Lyn *33:* 147
Tee-Van, Helen Damrosch *10:* 176; *11:* 182
Teicher, Dick *50:* 211
Teichman, Mary *77:* 220; *124:* 208; *127:* 22; *197:* 33
Temertey, Ludmilla *96:* 232; *104:* 43, 45; *109:* 244
Tempest, Margaret *3:* 237, 238; *88:* 200
Temple, Frances *85:* 185, 186, 187
Temple, Herbert *45:* 201
Templeton, Owen *11:* 77
ten Cate, Marijke *183:* 193
Tenggren, Gustaf *18:* 277, 278, 279; *19:* 15; *28:* 86; *YABC2:* 145
Tennent, Julie *81:* 105
Tenneson, Joyce *153:* 166
Tenney, Gordon *24:* 204
Tenniel, John *74:* 234, 235; *100:* 89; *YABC 2:* 99; *153:* 63
Tepper, Matt *116:* 80
Terkel, Ari *103:* 162
Terry, Michael *180:* 209
Terry, Will *131:* 73; *205:* 155
Teskey, Donald *71:* 51
Tessler, Manya *200:* 193
Thacher, Mary M. *30:* 72
Thackeray, William Makepeace *23:* 224, 228
Thamer, Katie *42:* 187
Tharlet, Eve *146:* 149
Thelwell, Norman *14:* 201
Theobalds, Prue *40:* 23
Theurer, Marilyn Churchill *39:* 195
Thiesing, Lisa *89:* 134; *95:* 202; *156:* 190; *159:* 195
Thiewes, Sam *133:* 114
Thistlethwaite, Miles *12:* 224
Thollander, Earl *11:* 47; *18:* 112; *22:* 224
Thomas, Allan *2:* 13
Thomas, Art *48:* 217
Thomas, Eric *28:* 49
Thomas, Harold *20:* 98
Thomas, Jacqui *125:* 95
Thomas, Jan *197:* 180
Thomas, Mark *42:* 136
Thomas, Martin *14:* 255
Thomas, Middy *177:* 114
Thompson, Arthur *34:* 107
Thompson, Carol *85:* 189; *95:* 75; *102:* 86; *147:* 166; *189:* 179, 180, 181; *190:* 84; *207:* 18
Thompson, Colin *95:* 204
Thompson, Ellen *51:* 88, 151; *60:* 33; *67:* 42; *77:* 148; *78:* 75, 219; *79:* 122, 170; *84:* 219; *85:* 97; *87:* 37; *88:* 192, 194; *89:* 80; *93:* 37; *98:* 59; *132:* 14
Thompson, George W. *22:* 18; *28:* 150; *33:* 135
Thompson, John *58:* 201; *102:* 226; *124:* 154; *128:* 228; *129:* 157; *150:* 49; *185:* 160; *191:* 192
Thompson, Julie *44:* 158
Thompson, Katherine *132:* 146
Thompson, K. Dyble *84:* 6
Thompson, Miles *152:* 77
Thompson, Sharon *74:* 113; *158:* 60; *165:* 87
Thomson, Arline K. *3:* 264
Thomson, Bill *186:* 160
Thomson, Hugh *26:* 88
Thomson, Ross *36:* 179
Thorkelson, Gregg *95:* 183, 184; *98:* 58; *165:* 30, 31
Thorn, Lori *189:* 119
Thornberg, Dan *104:* 125
Thornburgh, Rebecca McKillip *143:* 37
Thorne, Diana *25:* 212
Thornhill, Jan *77:* 213
Thorpe, Peter *58:* 109
Thorvall, Kerstin *13:* 235
Threadgall, Colin *77:* 215

Thurber, James *13:* 239, 242, 243, 245, 248, 249
Thurman, Mark *63:* 173; *168:* 116
Tibbles, Jean-Paul *115:* 200
Tibbles, Paul *45:* 23
Tibo, Gilles *67:* 207; *107:* 199, 201
Tichenor, Tom *14:* 207
Tichnor, Richard *90:* 218
Tiegreen, Alan *36:* 143; *43:* 55, 56, 58; *77:* 200; *94:* 216, 217; *121:* 54, 59
Tierney, Tom *113:* 198, 200, 201
Tilley, Debbie *102:* 134; *133:* 226; *137:* 101; *159:* 96; *190:* 211, 212
Tilney, F.C. *22:* 231
Timbs, Gloria *36:* 90
Timmins, Harry *2:* 171
Timmons, Bonnie *194:* 189
Tinkelman, Murray *12:* 225; *35:* 44
Titherington, Jeanne *39:* 90; *58:* 138; *75:* 79; *135:* 161
Tobin, Nancy *145:* 197
Toddy, Irving *172:* 144
Tokunbo, Dimitrea *181:* 183; *187:* 182, 183
Tolbert, Jeff *128:* 69
Toledo, Francisco *197:* 182; *198:* 199
Toledo, Natalia *197:* 182
Tolford, Joshua *1:* 221
Tolkien, J.R.R. *2:* 243; *32:* 215
Tolman, Marije *195:* 43
Tolmie, Ken *15:* 292
Tomei, Lorna *47:* 168, 171
Tomes, Jacqueline *2:* 117; *12:* 139
Tomes, Margot *1:* 224; *2:* 120, 121; *16:* 207; *18:* 250; *20:* 7; *25:* 62; *27:* 78, 79; *29:* 81, 199; *33:* 82; *36:* 186, 187, 188, 189, 190; *46:* 129; *56:* 71; *58:* 183; *70:* 228; *75:* 73, 75; *80:* 80; *83:* 97; *90:* 205
Tommaso, Rich *200:* 198
Toner, Raymond John *10:* 179
Tong, Gary *66:* 215
Tongier, Stephen *82:* 32
Tooke, Susan *173:* 162
Toothill, Harry *6:* 54; *7:* 49; *25:* 219; *42:* 192
Toothill, Ilse *6:* 54
Topolski, Feliks *44:* 48
Torbert, Floyd James *22:* 226
Torgersen, Don *55:* 157
Torline, Kevin *169:* 171
Tormey, Bertram M. *75:* 3, 4
Torrecilla, Pablo *176:* 207
Torres, Leyla *156:* 199, 201
Torrey, Helen *87:* 41
Torrey, Marjorie *34:* 105
Torrey, Richard *189:* 182; *205:* 24
Toschik, Larry *6:* 102
Totten, Bob *13:* 93
Toy, Julie *128:* 112
Trachok, Cathy *131:* 16
Tracy, Libba *82:* 24
Trago, Keith *158:* 253
Trail, Lee *55:* 157
Trang, To Ngoc *167:* 180
Trang, Winson *89:* 151
Trapani, Iza *116:* 202
Travers, Bob *49:* 100; *63:* 145
Treatner, Meryl *95:* 180
Tremain, Ruthven *17:* 238
Tresilian, Stuart *25:* 53; *40:* 212
Trez, Alain *17:* 236
Trezzo, Loretta *86:* 45
Trier, Walter *14:* 96
Trimby, Elisa *47:* 199
Trinkle, Sally *53:* 27
Triplett, Gina *182:* 193; *188:* 100; *198:* 38
Tripp, F.J. *24:* 167
Tripp, Wallace *2:* 48; *7:* 28; *8:* 94; *10:* 54,76; *11:* 92; *31:* 170, 171; *34:* 203; *42:* 57; *60:* 157; *73:* 182
Trivas, Irene *53:* 4; *54:* 168; *82:* 46, 101
Trnka, Jiri *22:* 151; *43:* 212, 213, 214, 215; *YABC 1:* 30, 31

Trondheim, Lewis *182:* 183
Troughton, Joanna *37:* 186; *48:* 72
Troyer, Johannes *3:* 16; *7:* 18
Trudeau, G.B. *35:* 220, 221, 222; *48:* 119, 123, 126, 127,128, 129, 133; *168:* 189
Trueman, Matthew *165:* 208; *183:* 191
Truesdell, Sue *55:* 142; *108:* 219, 220
Tryon, Leslie *84:* 7; *139:* 214; *143:* 10; *181:* 10
Tseng, Jean *72:* 195; *94:* 102; *119:* 126; *151:* 106; *173:* 138, 139; *200:* 158
Tseng, Mou-sien *72:* 195; *94:* 102; *119:* 126; *151:* 106; *173:* 138, 139; *200:* 158
Tsinajinie, Andy *2:* 62
Tsinganos, Jim *180:* 142
Tsugami, Kyuzo *18:* 198, 199
Tucker, Ezra *156:* 31
Tuckwell, Jennifer *17:* 205
Tudor, Bethany *7:* 103
Tudor, Tasha *18:* 227; *20:* 185, 186, 187; *36:* 111; *69:* 196, 198; *100:* 44; *YABC 2:* 46, 314; *160:* 234
Tuerk, Hanne *71:* 201
Tugeau, Jeremy *199:* 170; *203:* 96
Tulloch, Maurice *24:* 79
Tunis, Edwin *1:* 218, 219; *28:* 209, 210, 211, 212
Tunnicliffe, C.F. *62:* 176; 177; 178, 179; 181
Turkle, Brinton *1:* 211, 213; *2:* 249; *3:* 226; *11:* 3; *16:* 209; *20:* 22; *50:* 23; *67:* 50; *68:* 65; *79:* 205, 206, 207; *128:* 47; *YABC 1:* 79
Turnbull, Christopher J. *143:* 99, 100
Turner, Gwenda *59:* 195
Turner, Helen *203:* 154
Turska, Krystyna *12:* 103; *31:* 173, 174, 175; *56:* 32,34; *100:* 66
Tusa, Tricia *72:* 242; *111:* 180, 181; *157:* 165; *164:* 186; *189:* 40; *201:* 9; *207:* 163, 164
Tusan, Stan *6:* 58; *22:* 236, 237
Tworkov, Jack *47:* 207
Tyers, Jenny *89:* 220
Tylden-Wright, Jenny *114:* 119
Tyrol, Adelaide Murphy *103:* 27
Tyrrell, Frances *107:* 204
Tzimoulis, Paul *12:* 104

U

Uchida, Yoshiko *1:* 220
Uderzo *47:* 88
Udovic, David *189:* 185; *195:* 201
Ueno, Noriko *59:* 155
Ugliano, Natascia *196:* 186
Ulm, Robert *17:* 238
Ulrich, George *73:* 15; *75:* 136, 139; *99:* 150
Ulriksen, Mark *101:* 58; *182:* 43
Unada *84:* 67
  See Gliewe, Unada
Underhill, Liz *53:* 159
Underwood, Beck *192:* 36
Underwood, Clarence *40:* 166
Unger, Jim *67:* 208
Ungerer, Tomi *5:* 188; *9:* 40; *18:* 188; *29:* 175; *33:* 221, 222, 223, 225; *71:* 48; *106:* 209, 210, 211, 212
Unwin, Nora S. *3:* 65, 234, 235; *4:* 237; *44:* 173, 174; *YABC 1:* 59; *2:* 301
Upitis, Alvis *145:* 179
Urban, Helle *149:* 243
Urbanovic, Jackie *86:* 86; *189:* 186, 187
Uris, Jill *49:* 188, 197
Ursell, Martin *50:* 51
Utpatel, Frank *18:* 114
Utz, Lois *5:* 190

V

Vagin, Vladimir *66:* 10; *142:* 215
Vaillancourt, Francois *107:* 199
Vainio, Pirkko *123:* 157, 158
Valério, Geraldo *180:* 225; *194:* 116
Vallejo, Boris *62:* 130; *72:* 212; *91:* 38; *93:* 61
Van Abbe, S. *16:* 142; *18:* 282; *31:* 90; *YABC 2:* 157, 161
Van Allsburg, Chris *37:* 205, 206; *53:* 161, 162, 163, 165,166, 167, 168, 169, 170, 171; *105:* 215, 216, 217, 218; *156:* 176, 177, 178
Vance, James *65:* 28
Van Der Linde, Henry *99:* 17
van der Meer, Ron *98:* 204, 205
van der Meer, Atie *98:* 204, 205
Vandivert, William *21:* 175
Van Dongen, H.R. *81:* 97
Van Dusen, Chris W. *173:* 169
Van Everen, Jay *13:* 160; *YABC 1:* 121
Van Fleet, John *165:* 12, 13
Van Frankenhuyzen, Gijsbert *145:* 230; *149:* 164; *184:* 151
van Genechten, Guido *165:* 226
van Haeringen, Annemarie *193:* 206
Van Horn, William *43:* 218
van Hout, Mies *195:* 191; *207:* 58
van Kampen, Vlasta *194:* 217
van Lawick, Hugo *62:* 76, 79
Van Lieshout, Maria *201:* 196
Van Loon, Hendrik Willem *18:* 285, 289, 291
Van Munching, Paul *83:* 85
van Ommen, Sylvia *186:* 192
Van Patter, Bruce *183:* 195
Van Rynbach, Iris *102:* 192
Van Sciver, Ruth *37:* 162
VanSeveren, Joe *63:* 182
Van Stockum, Hilda *5:* 193
Van Wassenhove, Sue *202:* 193
Van Wely, Babs *16:* 50; *79:* 16
Van Wright, Cornelius *72:* 18; *102:* 208; *116:* 107; *152:* 236; *173:* 170, 171; *199:* 185
Van Zyle, Jon *103:* 125; *160:* 181, 182; *176:* 199, 200
Vardzigulyants, Ruben *90:* 54
Varga, Judy *29:* 196
Vargo, Kurt *79:* 224
Varley, Susan *61:* 199; *63:* 176, 177; *101:* 148; *134:* 220
Varon, Sara *195:* 208
Vasconcellos, Daniel *80:* 42
Vasiliu, Mircea *2:* 166, 253; *9:* 166; *13:* 58; *68:* 42
Vaughn, Frank *34:* 157
Vavra, Robert *8:* 206
Vawter, Will *17:* 163
Vayas, Diana *71:* 61
Vazquez, Carlos *125:* 184
Veeder, Larry *18:* 4
Velasquez, Eric *45:* 217; *61:* 45; *63:* 110, 111; *88:* 162; *90:* 34, 144; *94:* 213; *107:* 147; *132:* 192; *138:* 213; *159:* 126; *181:* 184; *184:* 96; *191:* 16; *192:* 234
Velasquez, Jose A. *63:* 73
Velez, Walter *71:* 75; *91:* 154; *121:* 181; *168:* 49; *207:* 52
Velthuijs, Max *110:* 228, 229
Vendrell, Carme Sole *42:* 205
Venezia, Mike *54:* 17
Venti, Anthony Bacon *124:* 103; *126:* 26
Venturo, Piero *61:* 194, 195
Ver Beck, Frank *18:* 16, 17
Verkaaik, Ben *110:* 209
Verling, John *71:* 27
Verney, John *14:* 225; *75:* 8
Vernon, Ursula *204:* 157
Verrier, Suzanne *5:* 20; *23:* 212
Versace, Marie *2:* 255
Verstraete, Randy *108:* 193
Vestal, H.B. *9:* 134; *11:* 101; *27:* 25; *34:* 158

Vestergaard, Hope *190:* 203
Vicatan *59:* 146
Vickrey, Robert *45:* 59, 64
Victor, Joan Berg *30:* 79
Viereck, Ellen *3:* 242; *14:* 229
Vigna, Judith *15:* 293; *102:* 194, 195, 196, 197
Vila, Laura *207:* 172
Vilato, Gaspar E. *5:* 41
Villiard, Paul *51:* 178
Vimnera, A. *23:* 154
Vincent, Eric *34:* 98
Vincent, Felix *41:* 237
Vincent, Gabrielle *121:* 175
Vip *45:* 164
Viskupic, Gary *83:* 48
Vitale, Stefano *109:* 71, 107; *114:* 219, 220; *123:* 106; *138:* 232; *180:* 228, 229
Vivas, Julie *51:* 67, 69; *96:* 225; *197:* 190; *199:* 71
Voake, Charlotte *114:* 221, 222; *180:* 232
Vo-Dinh, Mai *16:* 272; *60:* 191
Vogel, Ilse-Margret *14:* 230
Voigt, Erna *35:* 228
Vojnar, Kamil *95:* 31; *114:* 4; *115:* 62; *121:* 90; *124:* 72; *130:* 31; *141:* 81; *146:* 196; *150:* 123; *158:* 5, 6; *158:* 154; *171:* 119, 188; *179:* 15; *180:* 112; *203:* 74
Vojtech, Anna *42:* 190; *108:* 222, 223; *150:* 203; *174:* 173
von Buhler, Cynthia *149:* 237; *162:* 177; *177:* 205; *180:* 77; *185:* 214, 215, 216
von Roehl, Angela *126:* 191
von Schmidt, Eric *8:* 62; *50:* 209, 210
von Schmidt, Harold *30:* 80
Vosburgh, Leonard *1:* 161; *7:* 32; *15:* 295, 296; *23:* 110; *30:* 214; *43:* 181
Voss, Tom *127:* 104
Voter, Thomas W. *19:* 3, 9
Vroman, Tom *10:* 29
Vulliamy, Clara *72:* 65

W

Waber, Bernard *47:* 209, 210, 211, 212, 213, 214; *95:* 215, 216, 217; *156:* 203, 205, 206, 207
Wachenje, Benjamin *194:* 170
Wack, Jeff *95:* 140; *110:* 90
Wagner, John *8:* 200; *52:* 104
Wagner, Ken *2:* 59
Waide, Jan *29:* 225; *36:* 139
Wainwright, Jerry *14:* 85
Waites, Joan C. *171:* 2
Wakeen, Sandra *47:* 97
Wakiyama, Hanako *171:* 96; *192:* 236; *200:* 16
Waldherr, Kris *81:* 186
Waldman, Bruce *15:* 297; *43:* 178
Waldman, Neil *35:* 141; *50:* 163; *51:* 180; *54:* 78, 77; *79:* 162; *82:* 174; *84:* 5, 56, 106; *94:* 232, 233, 234; *96:* 41; *111:* 139; *113:* 9; *118:* 30; *142:* 220, 223; *203:* 173, 174
Waldrep, Richard *111:* 147; *198:* 202
Walker, Brian *144:* 128
Walker, Charles *1:* 46; *4:* 59; *5:* 177; *11:* 115; *19:* 45; *34:* 74; *62:* 168; *72:* 218
Walker, Dugald Stewart *15:* 47; *32:* 202; *33:* 112
Walker, Gil *8:* 49; *23:* 132; *34:* 42
Walker, Jeff *55:* 154; *123:* 116
Walker, Jim *10:* 94
Walker, Mort *8:* 213
Walker, Norman *41:* 37; *45:* 58
Walker, Stephen *12:* 229; *21:* 174
Wallace, Beverly Dobrin *19:* 259
Wallace, Cly *87:* 93
Wallace, Ian *53:* 176, 177; *56:* 165, 166; *58:* 4; *98:* 4; *101:* 191; *112:* 124; *141:* 197, 198, 199, 200; *151:* 212

Wallace, John *105:* 228
Wallace, Nancy Elizabeth *141:* 204; *186:* 195, 197, 199
Wallenta, Adam *123:* 180
Waller, S.E. *24:* 36
Wallner, Alexandra *15:* 120; *156:* 183
Wallner, John C. *9:* 77; *10:* 188; *11:* 28; *14:* 209; *31:* 56, 118; *37:* 64; *51:* 186, 187, 188, 189, 190, 191,192, 193, 194, 195; *52:* 96; *53:* 23, 26; *71:* 99; *73:* 158; *89:* 215; *141:* 9
Wallner, John *162:* 17
Wallower, Lucille *11:* 226
Walotsky, Ron *93:* 87
Walsh, Ellen Stoll *99:* 209; *147:* 219; *194:* 194, 195, 196
Walsh, Rebecca *158:* 193
Walsh, Vivian *149:* 215; *158:* 227
Walters, Anita *205:* 163
Walters, Audrey *18:* 294
Walther, Tom *31:* 179
Walton, Garry *69:* 149
Walton, Tony *11:* 164; *24:* 209; *153:* 8; *177:* 73
Waltrip, Lela *9:* 195
Waltrip, Mildred *3:* 209; *37:* 211
Waltrip, Rufus *9:* 195
Wan *12:* 76
Wang, Suling *191:* 183
Warburton, Sarah *154:* 187
Wappers, G. *121:* 40
Ward, Fred *52:* 19
Ward, Helen *72:* 244; *144:* 240, 242
Ward, John *42:* 191; *96:* 54; *97:* 110; *123:* 105; *124:* 71; *173:* 66
Ward, Keith *2:* 107; *132:* 69
Ward, Leslie *34:* 126; *36:* 87
Ward, Lynd *1:* 99, 132, 133, 150; *2:* 108, 158, 196, 259; *18:* 86; *27:* 56; *29:* 79, 187, 253, 255; *36:* 199,200, 201, 202, 203, 204, 205, 206, 207, 209; *43:* 34; *56:* 28; *60:* 116; *100:* 65
Ward, Peter *37:* 116
Waring, Geoff *172:* 84
Warhola, James *92:* 5; *115:* 85, 87; *118:* 174, 175, 177; *176:* 84; *187:* 189, 190
Warner, Ben *159:* 171
Warner, Peter *14:* 87
Warnes, Tim *175:* 159; *202:* 188
Warnick, Elsa *113:* 223
Warren, Betsy *2:* 101
Warren, Jim *85:* 81
Warren, Marion Cray *14:* 215
Warshaw, Jerry *30:* 197, 198; *42:* 165
Wasden, Kevin *102:* 162
Washington, Nevin *20:* 123
Washington, Phyllis *20:* 123
Wasserman, Amy L. *92:* 110
Waterman, Stan *11:* 76
Watkins-Pitchford, D.J. *6:* 215, 217
Watling, James *67:* 210; *78:* 112; *101:* 81; *117:* 189, 190; *127:* 119, 120
Watson, Aldren A. *2:* 267; *5:* 94; *13:* 71; *19:* 253; *32:* 220; *42:* 193, 194, 195, 196, 197, 198, 199, 200, 201; *YABC 2:* 202
Watson, G. *83:* 162
Watson, Gary *19:* 147; *36:* 68; *41:* 122; *47:* 139
Watson, J.D. *22:* 86
Watson, Jesse Joshua *197:* 124; *199:* 181; *202:* 136
Watson, Karen *11:* 26
Watson, Mary *117:* 193
Watson, Richard Jesse *62:* 188, 189
Watson, Wendy *5:* 197; *13:* 101; *33:* 116; *46:* 163; *64:* 12; *74:* 242, 243; *91:* 21; *142:* 228
Watt, Mélanie *136:* 206; *193:* 211
Wattenberg, Jane *174:* 200; *185:* 46; *187:* 108
Watterson, Bill *66:* 223, 225, 226
Watts, Bernadette *4:* 227; *103:* 182, 183
Watts, James *59:* 197; *74:* 145; *86:* 124
Watts, John *37:* 149

Watts, Leslie Elizabeth *150:* 207; *165:* 106
Watts, Stan *116:* 205
Weatherby, Mark Alan *77:* 141
Webb, Jennifer *110:* 79
Webb, Lanny *142:* 175
Webb, Sophie *135:* 214
Webber, Helen *3:* 141
Webber, Irma E. *14:* 238
Weber, Erik *56:* 19, 20
Weber, Florence *40:* 153
Weber, Jill *127:* 227, 228; *189:* 163
Weber, Roland *61:* 204
Weber, Sam *190:* 227
Weber, William J. *14:* 239
Webster, Jean *17:* 241
Weeks, Sarah *162:* 39
Wegman, William *78:* 243
Wegner, Fritz *14:* 250; *20:* 189; *44:* 165; *86:* 62
Weidenear, Reynold H. *21:* 122
Weigel, Jeff *170:* 193
Weihs, Erika *4:* 21; *15:* 299; *72:* 201; *107:* 207, 208
Weil, Lisl *7:* 203; *10:* 58; *21:* 95; *22:* 188,217; *33:* 193
Weiman, Jon *50:* 162, 165; *52:* 103; *54:* 78, 79, 81; *78:* 80; *82:* 107; *93:* 82; *97:* 69; *105:* 179; *193:* 65
Weiner, Sandra *14:* 240
Weiner, Scott *55:* 27
Weinhaus, Karen Ann *53:* 90; *71:* 50; *86:* 124
Weinman, Brad *197:* 20
Weinstock, Robert *204:* 165, 166
Weisgard, Leonard *1:* 65; *2:* 191, 197, 204, 264, 265; *5:* 108; *21:* 42; *30:* 200, 201, 203, 204; *41:* 47; *44:* 125; *53:* 25; *85:* 196, 198, 200, 201; *100:* 139,207; *YABC 2:* 13
Weisman, David *173:* 47
Weiss, Ellen *44:* 202
Weiss, Emil *1:* 168; *7:* 60
Weiss, Harvey *1:* 145, 223; *27:* 224, 227; *68:* 214; *76:* 245, 246, 247
Weiss, Nicki *33:* 229
Weissman, Bari *49:* 72; *90:* 125; *139:* 142
Weitzman, David L. *172:* 199
Welch, Sheila Kelly *130:* 221
Welkes, Allen *68:* 218
Wellington, Monica *99:* 223; *157:* 259, 260, 261
Welliver, Norma *76:* 94
Wellner, Fred *127:* 53
Wells, Frances *1:* 183
Wells, H.G. *20:* 194, 200
Wells, Haru *53:* 120, 121
Wells, Robert E. *184:* 208
Wells, Rosemary *6:* 49; *18:* 297; *60:* 32; *66:* 203; *69:* 215, 216; *114:* 227; *118:* 149, 150; *156:* 188, 189, 190, 191; *207:* 180, 181, 182, 183
Wells, Rufus III *56:* 111, 113
Wells, Susan *22:* 43
Wendelin, Rudolph *23:* 234
Wengenroth, Stow *37:* 47
Weninger, Brigitte *189:* 192, 194
Werenskiold, Erik *15:* 6; *62:* 17
Werner, Honi *24:* 110; *33:* 41; *88:* 122
Werth, Kurt *7:* 122; *14:* 157; *20:* 214; *39:* 128
Wesson,
West, Harry A. *124:* 38
Westcott, Nadine Bernard *68:* 46; *84:* 49; *86:* 133; *106:* 199; *111:* 78; *113:* 111; *130:* 224; *139:* 54; *158:* 256; *194:* 199
Westerberg, Christine *29:* 226
Westerduin, Anne *105:* 229
Westerman, Johanna *162:* 206
Weston, Martha *29:* 116; *30:* 213; *33:* 85, 100; *53:* 181, 182, 183, 184; *77:* 95; *80:* 152; *119:* 196,197, 198, 199; *127:* 189; *133:* 196
Wetherbee, Margaret *5:* 3
Wexler, Jerome *49:* 73; *150:* 129
Whalley, Peter *50:* 49

Whatley, Bruce *186:* 93, 95; *207:* 127
Wheatley, Arabelle *11:* 231; *16:* 276
Wheeler, Cindy *49:* 205
Wheeler, Dora *44:* 179
Wheelright, Rowland *15:* 81; *YABC 2:* 286
Whelan, Michael *56:* 108; *70:* 27, 29, 67, 68, 148; *74:* 18; *84:* 14; *91:* 195, 196; *95:* 147; *98:* 150, 151; *106:* 157; *113:* 218, 220; *116:* 99, 100
Whelan, Patrick *135:* 145
Whistler, Rex *16:* 75; *30:* 207, 208
White, Craig *110:* 130; *119:* 193; *130:* 33; *179:* 31
White, David Omar *5:* 56; *18:* 6
White, Joan *83:* 225
White, Martin *51:* 197; *85:* 127
Whitear *32:* 26
Whitehead, Beck *86:* 171
Whitehead, S.B. *154:* 132
Whithorne, H.S. *7:* 49
Whitney, George Gillett *3:* 24
Whitney, Jean *99:* 53
Whitson, Paul *102:* 161
Whittam, Geoffrey *30:* 191
Whyte, Mary *96:* 127
Wiberg, Harald *38:* 127; *93:* 215
Wick, Walter *77:* 128
Wickstrom, Sylvie *106:* 87; *169:* 180
Wickstrom, Thor *200:* 205
Widener, Terry *105:* 230; *106:* 7; *163:* 23; *200:* 17
Wiese, Kurt *3:* 255; *4:* 206; *14:* 17; *17:* 18, 19; *19:* 47; *24:* 152; *25:* 212; *32:* 184; *36:* 211,213, 214, 215, 216, 217, 218; *45:* 161; *100:* 92
Wiesner, David *33:* 47; *51:* 106; *57:* 67; *58:* 55; *64:* 78, 79, 81; *69:* 233; *72:* 247, 248, 249, 251,252, 253, 254; *83:* 134; *104:* 31; *117:* 197, 199, 200, 202; *139:* 223, 224; *151:* 51; *181:* 189, 190
Wiesner, William *4:* 100; *5:* 200, 201; *14:* 262
Wiggins, George *6:* 133
Wijngaard, Juan *111:* 36; *114:* 124
Wikkelsoe, Otto *45:* 25, 26
Wikland, Ilon *5:* 113; *8:* 150; *38:* 124, 125, 130; *127:* 162
Wikler, Madeline *114:* 233
Wilbur, C. Keith, M.D. *27:* 228
Wilburn, Kathy *53:* 102; *68:* 234
Wilcox, Cathy *105:* 123
Wilcox, J.A.J. *34:* 122
Wilcox, Lydia *207:* 187
Wilcox, R. Turner *36:* 219
Wild, Jocelyn *46:* 220, 221, 222; *80:* 117
Wilde, George *7:* 139
Wildsmith, Brian *16:* 281, 282; *18:* 170, 171; *66:* 25; *69:* 224, 225, 227; *77:* 103; *83:* 218; *124:* 214,217, 219
Wildsmith, Mike *140:* 229
Wilhelm, Hans *58:* 189, 191; *73:* 157; *77:* 127; *135:* 229, 230, 233, 234; *196:* 209
Wilkin, Eloise *36:* 173; *49:* 208, 209, 210
Wilkinson, Barry *50:* 213
Wilkinson, Gerald *3:* 40
Wilkon, Jozef *31:* 183, 184; *71:* 206, 207, 209; *133:* 222
Wilks, Mike *34:* 24; *44:* 203
Willems, Mo *154:* 245, 246, 247; *180:* 236, 237, 239
Willey, Bee *103:* 129; *139:* 159; *173:* 115
Willhoite, Michael A. *71:* 214
William, Maria *168:* 51
Williams, Berkeley, Jr. *64:* 75
Williams, Ferelith Eccles *22:* 238
Williams, Garth *1:* 197; *2:* 49, 270; *4:* 205; *15:* 198, 302, 304, 307; *16:* 34; *18:* 283, 298, 299, 300, 301; *29:* 177, 178, 179, 232, 233, 241, 242, 243, 244, 245, 248; *40:* 106; *66:* 229, 230, 231, 233, 234; *71:* 192; *73:* 218, 219, 220; *78:* 261; *100:* 251, 252, 255; *136:* 117; *YABC 2:* 15, 16, 19

Williams, J. Scott *48:* 28
Williams, Jennifer *102:* 201
Williams, Jenny *60:* 202; *81:* 21; *88:* 71
Williams, Kent *180:* 18
Williams, Kit *44:* 206, 207, 208, 209, 211, 212
Williams, Marcia *97:* 214; *159:* 208, 209
Williams, Maureen *12:* 238
Williams, Patrick *14:* 218
Williams, Richard *44:* 93; *72:* 229; *74:* 133; *78:* 155, 237; *91:* 178; *110:* 212; *136:* 201, 202, 203; *152:* 115
Williams, Sam *124:* 222; *153:* 11; *177:* 201, 202; *180:* 34
Williams, Sophy *135:* 236
Williams, Vera B. *53:* 186, 187, 188, 189; *102:* 201, 202, 203
Williamson, Alex *177:* 180; *205:* 50
Williamson, Mel *60:* 9
Willingham, Fred *104:* 206; *154:* 157
Willis, Adam *181:* 75
Willmore, J.T. *54:* 113, 114
Wilsdorf, Anne *180:* 122; *189:* 124; *191:* 195
Wilson, Anne *160:* 114
Wilson, Charles Banks *17:* 92; *43:* 73
Wilson, Connie *113:* 179
Wilson, Dagmar *10:* 47
Wilson, Dawn *67:* 161; *81:* 120; *113:* 158
Wilson, Edward A. *6:* 24; *16:* 149; *20:* 220, 221; *22:* 87; *26:* 67; *38:* 212, 214, 215, 216, 217
Wilson, Forrest *27:* 231
Wilson, Gahan *35:* 234; *41:* 136
Wilson, George *76:* 87
Wilson, Helen Miranda *140:* 61
Wilson, Jack *17:* 139
Wilson, Janet *77:* 154; *96:* 114; *99:* 219, 220; *153:* 64 *106:* 122; *130:* 210; *145:* 178; *173:* 64
Wilson, John *22:* 240
Wilson, Maurice *46:* 224
Wilson, Patten *35:* 61
Wilson, Peggy *15:* 4; *84:* 20
Wilson, Phil *181:* 29
Wilson, Rowland B. *30:* 170
Wilson, Sarah *50:* 215
Wilson, Tom *33:* 232
Wilson, W.N. *22:* 26
Wilson-Max, Ken *170:* 196; *180:* 181
Wilton, Nicholas *103:* 52; *183:* 111
Wilwerding, Walter J. *9:* 202
Wimmer, Mike *63:* 6; *70:* 121; *75:* 186; *76:* 21,22, 23; *91:* 114; *97:* 45, 68; *98:* 28; *107:* 130; *146:* 21; *149:* 47; *173:* 126; *193:* 21, 25; *194:* 204, 205
Winborn, Marsha *78:* 34; *99:* 70; *192:* 20
Winch, John *165:* 233
Winchester, Linda *13:* 231
Wind, Betty *28:* 158
Windham, Kathryn Tucker *14:* 260
Windham, Sophie *184:* 212
Winfield, Alison *115:* 78
Winfield, Wayne *72:* 23
Wing, Gary *64:* 147
Wing, Ron *50:* 85
Wingerter, Linda S. *132:* 199; *174:* 181; *200:* 196
Winick, Judd *124:* 227, 228, 229
Winn-Lederer, Ilene *202:* 91
Winslow, Will *21:* 124
Winstead, Rosie *180:* 243
Winsten, Melanie Willa *41:* 41
Winter, Jeanette *151:* 240, 241, 242; *184:* 215, 217, 218, 219
Winter, Milo *15:* 97; *19:* 221; *21:* 181, 203, 204, 205; *64:* 19; *YABC 2:* 144
Winter, Paula *48:* 227
Winter, Susan *163:* 177; *182:* 201
Winters, Greg *70:* 117
Winters, Nina *62:* 194
Wise, Louis *13:* 68
Wiseman, Ann *31:* 187

Wiseman, B. *4:* 233
Wishnefsky, Phillip *3:* 14
Wiskur, Darrell *5:* 72; *10:* 50; *18:* 246
Wisniewski, David *95:* 220, 221
Wisniewski, Robert *95:* 10; *119:* 192
Witschonke, Alan *153:* 149, 150
Witt, Dick *80:* 244
Wittmann, Patrick *162:* 204
Wittman, Sally *30:* 219
Wittner, Dale *99:* 43
Wittwer, Hala *158:* 267; *195:* 80
Woehr, Lois *12:* 5
Wohlberg, Meg *12:* 100; *14:* 197; *41:* 255
Wohnoutka, Mike *137:* 68; *190:* 199; *195:* 218; *205:* 132
Wojtowycz, David *167:* 168
Woldin, Beth Weiner *34:* 211
Wolf, Elizabeth *133:* 151
Wolf, J. *16:* 91
Wolf, Janet *78:* 254
Wolf, Linda *33:* 163
Wolfe, Corey *72:* 213
Wolfe, Gillian *199:* 193
Wolff, Ashley *50:* 217; *81:* 216; *156:* 216, 217; *170:* 57; *174:* 174; *184:* 72; *203:* 181, 182, 183, 184
Wolff, Glenn *178:* 230
Wolfsgruber, Linda *166:* 61
Wondriska, William *6:* 220
Wong, Janet S. *98:* 225; *152:* 43
Wong, Nicole *174:* 13
Wonsetler, John C. *5:* 168
Wood, Audrey *50:* 221, 222, 223; *81:* 219, 221; *198:* 206
Wood, Don *50:* 220, 225, 226, 228, 229; *81:* 218, 220; *139:* 239, 240
Wood, Grant *19:* 198
Wood, Heather *133:* 108
Wood, Ivor *58:* 17
Wood, Muriel *36:* 119; *77:* 167; *171:* 55; *187:* 46
Wood, Myron *6:* 220
Wood, Owen *18:* 187; *64:* 202, 204, 205, 206, 208, 210
Wood, Rob *193:* 48
Wood, Ruth *8:* 11
Woodbridge, Curtis *133:* 138; *204:* 113
Wooding, Sharon L. *66:* 237
Woodruff, Liza *132:* 239; *182:* 46, 204
Woodruff, Thomas *171:* 73
Woods, John, Jr. *109:* 142
Woodson, Jack *10:* 201
Woodson, Jacqueline *94:* 242
Woodward, Alice *26:* 89; *36:* 81
Wool, David *26:* 27
Woolley, Janet *112:* 75
Woolman, Steven *106:* 47; *163:* 73
Wooten, Vernon *23:* 70; *51:* 170
Worboys, Evelyn *1:* 166, 167
Word, Reagan *103:* 204
Wormell, Christopher *154:* 251; *202:* 206
Worth, Jo *34:* 143
Worth, Wendy *4:* 133
Wosmek, Frances *29:* 251
Wrenn, Charles L. *38:* 96; *YABC 1:* 20, 21
Wright, Barbara Mullarney *98:* 161
Wright, Cliff *168:* 203
Wright, Dare *21:* 206
Wright-Frierson, Virginia *58:* 194; *110:* 246
Wright, George *YABC 1:* 268
Wright, Joseph *30:* 160
Wronker, Lili Cassel *3:* 247; *10:* 204; *21:* 10
Wu, Donald *200:* 18
Wummer, Amy *154:* 181; *168:* 150; *176:* 85; *201:* 202, 203
Wyant, Alexander Helwig *110:* 19
Wyatt, David *97:* 9; *101:* 44; *114:* 194; *140:* 20; *167:* 13; *188:* 48
Wyatt, Stanley *46:* 210
Wyeth, Andrew *13:* 40; *YABC 1:* 133, 134
Wyeth, Jamie *41:* 257

Wyeth, N.C. *13:* 41; *17:* 252, 253, 254, 255, 256, 257, 258, 259, 264, 265, 266, 267, 268; *18:* 181; *19:* 80, 191, 200; *21:* 57, 183; *22:* 91; *23:* 152; *24:* 28, 99; *35:* 61; *41:* 65; *100:* 206; *YABC1:* 133, 223; *2:* 53, 75, 171, 187, 317
Wyman, Cherie R. *91:* 42

X

Xuan, YongSheng *119:* 202, 207, 208; *140:* 36; *187:* 21

Y

Yaccarino, Dan *141:* 208, 209; *147:* 171; *192:* 244, 245; *207:* 168
Yakovetic, Joe *59:* 202; *75:* 85
Yalowitz, Paul *93:* 33
Yamaguchi, Marianne *85:* 118
Yamasaki, James *167:* 93
Yang, Belle *170:* 198
Yang, Jay *1:* 8; *12:* 239
Yap, Weda *6:* 176
Yaroslava
    See Mills, Yaroslava Surmach
Yashima, Taro *14:* 84
Yates, John *74:* 249, 250
Yayo *178:* 88
Yee, Cora *166:* 233
Yee, Wong Herbert *115:* 216, 217; *172:* 204, 205; *194:* 59
Yelchin, Eugene *204:* 4
Yeo, Brad *135:* 121; *192:* 106
Yerxa, Leo *181:* 195
Yezerski, Thomas F. *162:* 29
Ylla
    See Koffler, Camilla
Yohn, F.C. *23:* 128; *YABC 1:* 269
Yoo, Taeeun *191:* 198
Yorinks, Adrienne *144:* 248; *200:* 214

Yorke, David *80:* 178
Yoshida, Toshi *77:* 231
Yoshikawa, Sachiko *168:* 104; *177:* 28; *181:* 196, 197
Youll, Paul *91:* 218
Youll, Stephen *92:* 227; *118:* 136, 137; *164:* 248; *202:* 92
Young, Amy L. *185:* 218; *190:* 46
Young, Cybéle *167:* 9
Young, Ed *7:* 205; *10:* 206; *40:* 124; *63:* 142; *74:* 250, 251, 252, 253; *75:* 227; *81:* 159; *83:* 98; *94:* 154; *115:* 160; *137:* 162; *YABC 2:* 242; *173:* 174, 175, 176; *205:* 29
Young, Mary O'Keefe *77:* 95; *80:* 247; *134:* 214; *140:* 213
Young, Noela *8:* 221; *89:* 231; *97:* 195
Young, Paul *190:* 222
Young, Selina *153:* 12; *201:* 204, 205
Yun, Cheng Mung *60:* 143

Z

Zacharow, Christopher *88:* 98
Zacks, Lewis *10:* 161
Zadig *50:* 58
Zaffo, George *42:* 208
Zagwyn, Deborah Turney *138:* 227
Zahares, Wade *193:* 219
Zaid, Barry *50:* 127; *51:* 201
Zaidenberg, Arthur *34:* 218, 219, 220
Zalben, Jane Breskin *7:* 211; *79:* 230, 231, 233; *170:* 202
Zallinger, Jean *4:* 192; *8:* 8, 129; *14:* 273; *68:* 36; *80:* 254; *115:* 219, 220, 222
Zallinger, Rudolph F. *3:* 245
Zakrajsek, Molly *177:* 146
Zappa, Ahmet *180:* 250
Zebot, George *83:* 214
Zecca, Katherine *207:* 195
Zeck, Gerry *40:* 232
Zeff, Joe *181:* 98
Zeifert, Harriet *154:* 265, 267
Zeiring, Bob *42:* 130
Zeldich, Arieh *49:* 124; *62:* 120

Zeldis, Malcah *86:* 239; *94:* 198; *146:* 265, 266
Zelinsky, Paul O. *14:* 269; *43:* 56; *49:* 218-223; *53:* 111; *68:* 195; *102:* 219, 222, 221, 222; *154:* 255, 256, 257; *171:* 141; *185:* 96
Zelvin, Diana *72:* 190; *76:* 101; *93:* 207
Zemach, Kaethe *149:* 250
Zemach, Margot *3:* 270; *8:* 201; *21:* 210, 211; *27:* 204, 205, 210; *28:* 185; *49:* 22, 183, 224; *53:* 151; *56:* 146; *70:* 245, 246; *92:* 74
Zeman, Ludmila *153* 212
Zemsky, Jessica *10:* 62
Zepelinsky, Paul *35:* 93
Zerbetz, Evon *127:* 34; *158:* 109
Zezejl, Daniel *197:* 74
Zhang, Ange *101:* 190; *172:* 41
Zhang, Son Nang *163:* 113; *170:* 206
Ziegler, Jack *84:* 134
Zimdars, Berta *129:* 155
Zimet, Jay *147:* 94; *152:* 74; *196:* 75
Zimic, Tricia *72:* 95
Zimmer, Dirk *38:* 195; *49:* 71; *56:* 151; *65:* 214; *84:* 159; *89:* 26; *147:* 224
Zimmer, Tracie Vaughn *169:* 183
Zimmerman, Andrea *192:* 49, 50
Zimmermann, H. Werner *101:* 223; *112:* 197
Zimnik, Reiner *36:* 224
Zingone, Robin *180:* 134
Zinkeisen, Anna *13:* 106
Zinn, David *97:* 97
Zoellick, Scott *33:* 231
Zollars, Jaime *190:* 190
Zonia, Dhimitri *20:* 234, 235
Zorn, Peter A., Jr. *142:* 157
Zudeck, Darryl *58:* 129; *63:* 98; *80:* 52
Zug, Mark *88:* 131; *204:* 169
Zulewski, Tim *164:* 95
Zuma *99:* 36
Zvorykin, Boris *61:* 155
Zweifel, Francis *14:* 274; *28:* 187
Zwerger, Lisbeth *54:* 176, 178; *66:* 246, 247, 248; *130:* 230, 231, 232, 233; *181:* 92; *194:* 224, 225, 226
Zwinger, Herman H. *46:* 227
Zwolak, Paul *67:* 69, 71, 73, 74

Author Index

The following index gives the number of the volume in which an author's biographical sketch, Autobiography Feature, Brief Entry, or Obituary appears.

This index includes references to all entries in the following series, which are also published by The Gale Group.

YABC—*Yesterday's Authors of Books for Children: Facts and Pictures about Authors and Illustrators of Books for Young People from Early Times to 1960*

CLR—*Children's Literature Review: Excerpts from Reviews, Criticism, and Commentary on Books for Children*

SAAS—*Something about the Author Autobiography Series*

A

Aardema, Verna 1911-2000 .... *107*
　Obituary *119*
　Earlier sketches in SATA *:4, 68*
　See also CLR *17*
　See also SAAS *8*
Aaron, Chester 1923- *74*
　Earlier sketch in SATA *9*
　See also SAAS *12*
Aaseng, Nate
　See Aaseng, Nathan
Aaseng, Nathan 1953- *172*
　Brief entry *38*
　Earlier sketches in SATA *51, 88*
　See also CLR *54*
　See also SAAS *12*
Abadzis, Nick 1965- *193*
abalos, Rafael 1956- *197*
Abbas, Jailan 1952- *91*
Abbey, Lynn
　See Abbey, Marilyn Lorraine
Abbey, Marilyn Lorraine 1948- *156*
Abbott, Alice
　See Borland, Kathryn Kilby
　and Speicher, Helen Ross S(mith)
Abbott, Jacob 1803-1879 .... *22*
Abbott, Manager Henry
　See Stratemeyer, Edward L.
Abbott, R(obert) Tucker 1919-1995 .... *61*
　Obituary *87*
Abbott, Sarah
　See Zolotow, Charlotte
Abbott, Tony 1952- *205*
　Earlier sketch in SATA *159*
Abdelsayed, Cindy 1962- *123*
Abdul, Raoul 1929- *12*
Abeele, Veronique van den *196*
Abel, Raymond 1911- *12*
Abell, Kathleen 1938- *9*
Abelove, Joan *110*
Abels, Harriette S(heffer) 1926- *50*
Abercrombie, Barbara 1939- *182*
　Earlier sketch in SATA *16*
Abercrombie, Barbara Mattes
　See Abercrombie, Barbara
Abercrombie, Lynn
　See Sorrells, Walter
Abernethy, Robert G(ordon) 1927- *5*

Abisch, Roslyn Kroop 1927- *9*
Abisch, Roz
　See Abisch, Roslyn Kroop
Ablow, Gail 1962- *198*
Abodaher, David J. (Naiph) 1919- *17*
Abolafia, Yossi 1944-
　See Abulafia, Yossi
Abouzeid, Chris *175*
Abrahall, Clare Hoskyns
　See Hoskyns-Abrahall, Clare (Constance Drury)
Abrahams, Hilary (Ruth) 1938- *29*
Abrahams, Peter 1947- *194*
Abrahams, Robert David 1905-1998 .... *4*
Abramovitz, Anita (Zeltner Brooks) 1914- *5*
Abrams, Joy 1941- *16*
Abrams, Lawrence F. *58*
　Brief entry *47*
Abrashkin, Raymond 1911-1960 .... *50*
Abulafia, Yossi 1944- *177*
　Brief entry *46*
　Earlier sketch in SATA *60*
Acampora, Paul *175*
Accardo, Anthony *191*
Acer, David *206*
Achebe, Albert Chinualumogu
　See Achebe, Chinua
Achebe, Chinua 1930- *40*
　Brief entry *38*
　Earlier sketch in SATA *38*
　See also CLR *20*
Ackerman, Diane 1948- *102*
Ackerman, Eugene (Francis) 1888-1974 ...... *10*
Ackerman, Karen 1951- *126*
Ackerman, Susan Yoder 1945- *92*
Ackison, Wendy Wassink 1956- *103*
Ackley, Peggy Jo 1955- *58*
Ackroyd, Peter 1949- *153*
Acorn, John (Harrison) 1958- *79*
Acredolo, Linda (Potter) 1947- *159*
Acs, Laszlo (Bela) 1931- *42*
　Brief entry *32*
Acuff, Selma Boyd 1924- *45*
Ada, Alma Flor 1938- *181*
　Earlier sketches in SATA *43, 84, 143*
　See also CLR *62*
Adair, Gilbert 1944- *98*
Adair, Ian 1942- *53*
Adair, Margaret Weeks (?)-1971 .... *10*

Adam, Cornel
　See Lengyel, Cornel Adam
Adam, Mark
　See Alexander, Marc
Adam, Robert 1948- *93*
Adams, Adrienne 1906- *90*
　Earlier sketch in SATA *8*
　See also CLR *73*
Adams, Andy 1859-1935
　See YABC *1*
Adams, Barbara Johnston 1943- *60*
Adams, Bruin
　See Ellis, Edward S.
Adams, Captain Bruin
　See Ellis, Edward S.
Adams, Captain J. F. C.
　See Ellis, Edward S.
Adams, Dale
　See Quinn, Elisabeth
Adams, Daniel
　See Nicole, Christopher (Robin)
Adams, Debra
　See Speregen, Devra Newberger
Adams, Douglas 1952-2001 .... *116*
　Obituary *128*
Adams, Douglas Noel
　See Adams, Douglas
Adams, Edith
　See Shine, Deborah
Adams, Florence 1932- *61*
Adams, Harriet S(tratemeyer) 1892(?)-1982 .. *1*
　Obituary *29*
Adams, Harrison
　See Rathborne, St. George (Henry)
　and Stratemeyer, Edward L.
Adams, Hazard 1926- *6*
Adams, Hazard Simeon
　See Adams, Hazard
Adams, John Anthony 1944- *67*
Adams, Laurie 1941- *33*
Adams, Lowell
　See Joseph, James (Herz)
Adams, Nicholas
　See Pine, Nicholas
Adams, Nicholas
　See Smith, Sherwood
Adams, Nicholas
　See Doyle, Debra
　and Macdonald, James D.

Adams, Pam 1919- *112*
Adams, Pamela
   See Adams, Pam
Adams, Richard 1920- *69*
   Earlier sketch in SATA 7
   See also CLR *121*
Adams, Richard George
   See Adams, Richard
Adams, Ruth Joyce *14*
Adams, Tricia
   See Kite, Pat
Adams, William Taylor 1822-1897 .... *28*
Adam Smith, Janet (Buchanan) 1905-1999 .. *63*
Adamson, Gareth 1925-1982(?) *46*
   Obituary *30*
Adamson, George 1906-1989
   Obituary *63*
Adamson, George (Worsley) 1913-2005 ...... *30*
Adamson, Graham
   See Groom, Arthur William
Adamson, Joy(-Friederike Victoria)
   1910-1980 .... *11*
   Obituary *22*
Adamson, Wendy Writson 1942- *22*
Addasi, Maha 1968- *205*
Addison, Kenneth 1949(?)-2005 .... *187*
Addison, Kenneth L.
   See Addison, Kenneth
Addona, Angelo F. 1925- *14*
Addy, Sharon Hart 1943- *192*
   Earlier sketch in SATA *108*
Addy, Ted
   See Winterbotham, R(ussell) R(obert)
Adelberg, Doris
   See Orgel, Doris
Adelson, Leone 1908- *11*
Adinolfi, JoAnn *176*
Adkins, Jan 1944- *144*
   Earlier sketches in SATA 8, 69
   See also CLR 77
   See also SAAS 19
Adler, C(arole) S(chwerdtfeger) 1932- *126*
   Earlier sketches in SATA 26, 63, 102
   See also CLR 78
   See also SAAS 15
Adler, David A. 1947- *178*
   Earlier sketches in SATA 14, 70, 106, 151
   See also CLR 108
Adler, Irene
   See Penzler, Otto
   and Storr, Catherine (Cole)
Adler, Irving 1913- *29*
   Autobiography Feature *164*
   Earlier sketch in SATA 1
   See also CLR 27
   See also SAAS 15
Adler, Larry 1939- *36*
Adler, Peggy *22*
Adler, Ruth 1915-1968 .... *1*
Adlerman, Daniel (Ezra) 1963- *163*
   Earlier sketch in SATA 96
Adlerman, Kim
   See Adlerman, Kimberly M(arie)
Adlerman, Kimberly M(arie) 1964- *163*
   Earlier sketch in SATA 96
Adoff, Arnold 1935- *96*
   Earlier sketches in SATA 5, 57
   See also CLR 7
   See also SAAS 15
Adoff, Jaime *163*
Adoff, Jaime Levi
   See Adoff, Jaime
Adorjan, Carol (Madden) 1934- *71*
   Earlier sketch in SATA 10
Adrian, Frances
   See Polland, Madeleine A(ngela Cahill)
Adrian, Mary
   See Jorgensen, Mary Venn
Adshead, Gladys L(ucy) 1896-1985 .... *3*
Aesop 620(?)B.C.-560(?)B.C. *64*
   See also CLR *14*

Aesop, Abraham
   See Newbery, John
Affabee, Eric
   See Stine, R.L.
Agapida, Fray Antonio
   See Irving, Washington
Agard, John 1949- *138*
Agard, Nadema 1948- *18*
Agarwal, Deepa 1947- *141*
Agee, Jon 1960- *196*
   Earlier sketches in SATA *116, 157*
Agell, Charlotte 1959- *150*
   Earlier sketch in SATA *99*
Agent Orange
   See Moseley, James W(illett)
Aghill, Gordon
   See Garrett, Randall
   and Silverberg, Robert
Agle, Nan Hayden 1905- *3*
   See also SAAS 10
Agnew, Edith J(osephine) 1897-1988 .... *11*
Agonito, Joseph *177*
Agonito, Rosemary 1937- *177*
Ahern, Margaret McCrohan 1921- *10*
Ahl, Anna Maria 1926- *32*
Ahlberg, Allan 1938- *165*
   Brief entry *35*
   Earlier sketches in SATA 68, 120
   See also CLR 18
Ahlberg, Janet 1944-1994 .... *120*
   Brief entry *32*
   Obituary *83*
   Earlier sketch in SATA 68
   See also CLR 18
Aho, Julia Kay
   See Kay, Julia
Aichinger, Helga 1937- *4*
Aiken, Clarissa (M.) Lorenz 1899-1992 ...... *12*
   Obituary *109*
Aiken, Conrad 1889-1973 .... *30*
   Earlier sketch in SATA 3
Aiken, Conrad Potter
   See Aiken, Conrad
Aiken, Joan (Delano) 1924-2004 .... *73*
   Autobiography Feature *109*
   Obituary *152*
   Earlier sketches in SATA 2, 30
   See also CLR 90
   See also SAAS 1
Aillaud, Cindy Lou 1955- *184*
Ainsley, Alix
   See Steiner, Barbara A(nnette)
Ainsworth, Catherine Harris 1910- *56*
Ainsworth, Norma 1911-1987 .... *9*
Ainsworth, Ruth (Gallard) 1908- *73*
   Earlier sketch in SATA 7
Ainsworth, William Harrison 1805-1882 .... *24*
Aistrop, Jack 1916- *14*
Aitken, Amy 1952- *54*
   Brief entry *40*
Aitken, Dorothy 1916- *10*
Aitmatov, Chingiz 1928-2008 .... *56*
Aitmatov, Chingiz Torekulovich
   See Aitmatov, Chingiz
Akaba, Suekichi 1910- *46*
Akers, Floyd
   See Baum, L. Frank
Akib, Jamel *181*
Aks, Patricia 1926-1994 .... *68*
Alagoa, Ebiegberi Joe 1933- *108*
Alain
   See Brustlein, Daniel
Alajalov, Constantin 1900-1987
   Obituary *53*
Alalou, Ali *203*
Alalou, Elizabeth *203*
Alan, David
   See Horsfield, Alan
Alan, Robert
   See Silverstein, Robert Alan
Alarcon, Francisco X. 1954- *104*

Alarcon, Francisco Xavier
   See Alarcon, Francisco X.
Alarcon, Karen Beaumont
   See Beaumont, Karen
Albert, Burton 1936- *22*
Albert, Louise 1928- *157*
Albert, Michael 1966- *202*
Albert, Richard E. 1909-1999 .... *82*
Albert, Susan Wittig 1940- *107*
Alberts, Frances Jacobs 1907-1989 .... *14*
Albertson, Susan
   See Wojciechowski, Susan
Albion, Lee Smith *29*
Alborough, Jez 1959- *149*
   Earlier sketch in SATA 86
Albrecht, Lillie (Vanderveer H.)
   1894-1985 .... *12*
Albyn, Carole Lisa 1955- *83*
Alchemy, Jack
   See Gershator, David
Alcock, Gudrun 1908- *56*
   Brief entry *33*
Alcock, Vivien (Dolores) 1924-2003 .... *76*
   Brief entry *38*
   Obituary *148*
   Earlier sketch in SATA 45
   See also CLR 26
Alcorn, John 1935- *31*
   Brief entry *30*
Alcorn, Stephen 1958- *207*
   Earlier sketch in SATA *110*
Alcott, Louisa May 1832-1888 .... *100*
   See also YABC *1*
   See also CLR *109*
Alda, Arlene 1933- *205*
   Brief entry *36*
   Earlier sketches in SATA 44, 106, 158
   See also CLR 93
Alden, Isabella (Macdonald) 1841-1930 ..... *115*
   See also YABC *2*
Alden, Sue
   See Francis, Dorothy
Alderman, Clifford Lindsey 1902-1988 .... *3*
Alderson, Sue Ann 1940- *59*
   Brief entry *48*
Alding, Peter
   See Jeffries, Roderic
Aldis, Dorothy (Keeley) 1896-1966 .... *2*
Aldiss, Brian W. 1925- *34*
Aldiss, Brian Wilson
   See Aldiss, Brian W.
Aldon, Adair
   See Meigs, Cornelia Lynde
Aldous, Allan (Charles) 1911- *27*
Aldrich, Ann
   See Meaker, Marijane
Aldrich, Bess Streeter 1881-1954
   See CLR 70
Aldrich, Thomas (Bailey) 1836-1907 .... *114*
   Earlier sketch in SATA 17
Aldridge, (Harold Edward) James 1918- *87*
Aldridge, Josephine Haskell *14*
Aldridge, Sheila 1974- *192*
Aleas, Richard
   See Appelt, Kathi
Alegria, Malin 1974(?)- *190*
Alegria, Ricardo E(nrique) 1921- *6*
Aleksin, Anatolii Georgievich 1924- *36*
Alenov, Lydia 1948- *61*
Alex, Ben (a pseudonym) 1946- *45*
Alex, Marlee (a pseudonym) 1948- *45*
Alexander, Anna B(arbara Cooke) 1913- *1*
Alexander, Anne
   See Alexander, Anna B(arbara Cooke)
Alexander, Ellen 1938- *91*
Alexander, Frances (Laura) 1888-1979 .... *4*
Alexander, Janet 1907-1994 .... *97*
   Earlier sketch in SATA 1
Alexander, Jocelyn Anne Arundel 1930- *22*
Alexander, Linda 1935- *2*

Alexander, Lloyd 1924-2007 .... *135*
  Obituary *182*
  Earlier sketches in SATA *3, 49, 81, 129*
  See also CLR *48*
  See also SAAS *19*
Alexander, Lloyd Chudley
  See Alexander, Lloyd
Alexander, Marc 1929- *117*
Alexander, Martha 1920- *136*
  Earlier sketches in SATA *11, 70*
Alexander, Rae Pace
  See Alexander, Raymond Pace
Alexander, Raymond Pace 1898-1974 .... *22*
Alexander, Robert *200*
Alexander, Rod
  See Pellowski, Michael (Joseph)
Alexander, Sally Hobart 1943- *84*
Alexander, Sue 1933-2008 .... *136*
  Obituary *195*
  Earlier sketches in SATA *12, 89*
  See also SAAS *15*
Alexander, Vincent Arthur 1925-1980
  Obituary *23*
Alexeieff, Alexandre A. 1901-1979 .... *14*
Alger, Horatio, Jr.
  See Stratemeyer, Edward L.
Alger, Horatio, Jr. 1832-1899 .... *16*
  See also CLR *87*
Alger, Leclaire (Gowans) 1898-1969 .... *15*
Aliki
  See Brandenberg, Aliki
Alkema, Chester Jay 1932- *12*
Al-Khalili, Jim 1962- *124*
Alkiviades, Alkis 1953- *105*
Alkouatli, Claire *186*
Allaby, John Michael
  See Allaby, Michael
Allaby, Michael 1933- *167*
Allamand, Pascale 1942- *12*
Allan, Mabel Esther 1915-1998 .... *75*
  Earlier sketches in SATA *5, 32*
  See also CLR *43*
  See also SAAS *11*
Allan, Nicholas 1956- *123*
  Earlier sketch in SATA *79*
Allan-Meyer, Kathleen 1918- *51*
  Brief entry *46*
Allard, Harry
  See Allard, Harry G(rover), Jr.
Allard, Harry G(rover), Jr. 1928- *102*
  Earlier sketch in SATA *42*
  See also CLR *85*
Allee, Marjorie Hill 1890-1945 .... *17*
Allen, Adam
  See Epstein, Beryl
  and Epstein, Samuel
Allen, Alex B.
  See Heide, Florence Parry
Allen, Allyn
  See Eberle, Irmengarde
Allen, Betsy
  See Harrison, Elizabeth (Allen) Cavanna
Allen, Bob 1961- *76*
Allen, Gertrude E(lizabeth) 1888-1984 .... *9*
Allen, Grace
  See Hogarth, Grace (Weston Allen)
Allen, Jeffrey (Yale) 1948- *42*
Allen, John
  See Perry, Ritchie (John Allen)
Allen, Jonathan 1957- *177*
  Earlier sketch in SATA *131*
Allen, Jonathan Dean
  See Allen, Jonathan
Allen, Judy (Christina) 1941- *124*
  Earlier sketch in SATA *80*
Allen, Kenneth S. 1913-1981 .... *56*
Allen, Leroy 1912- *11*
Allen, Linda 1925- *33*
Allen, Marjorie 1931- *22*
Allen, Maury 1932- *26*
Allen, Merritt Parmelee 1892-1954 .... *22*

Allen, Nancy Kelly 1949- *171*
  Earlier sketch in SATA *127*
Allen, Nina (Stroemgren) 1935- *22*
Allen, Pamela (Kay) 1934- *123*
  Earlier sketches in SATA *50, 81*
  See also CLR *44*
Allen, Raul *205*
Allen, Rodney F. 1938-1999 .... *27*
Allen, Roger MacBride 1957- *105*
Allen, Ruth
  See Peterson, Esther (Allen)
Allen, Samuel W(ashington) 1917- *9*
Allen, T. D.
  See Allen, Terril Diener
Allen, Terril Diener 1908- *35*
Allen, Terry D.
  See Allen, Terril Diener
Allen, Thomas B. 1929- *193*
  Earlier sketches in SATA *45, 140*
Allen, Thomas B. 1929- *193*
Allen, Thomas Benton
  See Allen, Thomas B.
Allen, Tom
  See Allen, Thomas B.
Allende, Isabel 1942- *163*
  See also CLR *99*
Allerton, Mary
  See Govan, (Mary) Christine Noble
Alley, Robert W.
  See Alley, R.W.
Alley, R.W. *169*
Alleyn, Ellen
  See Rossetti, Christina
Allington, Richard L(loyd) 1947- *39*
  Brief entry *35*
Allison, Amy 1956- *138*
Allison, Bob *14*
Allison, Diane Worfolk *78*
Allison, Jennifer *173*
Allison, Linda 1948- *43*
Allison, Margaret
  See Klam, Cheryl
Allman, Barbara 1950- *137*
Allmendinger, David F(rederick), Jr. 1938- . *35*
Allred, Alexandra Powe 1965- *144*
Allred, Gordon T(hatcher) 1930- *10*
Allsop, Kenneth 1920-1973 .... *17*
Allsopp, Sophie *188*
Alma, Ann 1946- *201*
Almedingen, E. M.
  See Almedingen, Martha Edith von
Almedingen, Martha Edith von 1898-1971 .... *3*
Almon, Russell
  See Clevenger, William R.
  and Downing, David A(lmon)
Almond, David 1951- *158*
  Earlier sketch in SATA *114*
  See also CLR *85*
Almond, Linda Stevens 1881(?)-1987
  Obituary *50*
Almquist, Don 1929- *11*
Alonzo, Sandra *199*
Alphin, Elaine Marie 1955- *139*
  Autobiography Feature *139*
  Earlier sketches in SATA *80, 130*
Alsenas, Linas 1979- *186*
Alsop, Mary O'Hara 1885-1980 .... *34*
  Obituary *24*
  Earlier sketch in SATA *2*
Alter, Anna 1974- *206*
  Earlier sketch in SATA *135*
Alter, Judith (MacBain) 1938- *101*
  Earlier sketch in SATA *52*
Alter, Judy
  See Alter, Judith (MacBain)
Alter, Robert Edmond 1925-1965 .... *9*
Alter, Stephen 1956- *187*
Althea
  See Braithwaite, Althea
Altman, Linda Jacobs 1943- *21*

Altman, Suzanne
  See Orgel, Doris
  and Schecter, Ellen
Alton, Steve *169*
Altshuler, Franz 1923- *45*
Altsheler, Joseph A(lexander) 1862-1919
  See YABC *1*
Alvarez, John
  See del Rey, Lester
Alvarez, Joseph A. 1930- *18*
Alvarez, Julia 1950- *129*
al-Windawi, Thura
  See Windawi, Thura al-
Alyer, Philip A.
  See Stratemeyer, Edward L.
Amado, Elisa *193*
Amann, Janet 1951- *79*
Amato, Carol A. 1942- *92*
Amato, Mary 1961- *178*
  Earlier sketch in SATA *140*
Ambrose, Stephen E. 1936-2002 .... *138*
  Earlier sketch in SATA *40*
Ambrose, Stephen Edward
  See Ambrose, Stephen E.
Ambrus, Gyozo Laszlo 1935- *1*
  See also SAAS *4*
Ambrus, Victor G.
  See Ambrus, Gyozo Laszlo
Amend, Bill 1962- *147*
Amerman, Lockhart 1911-1969 .... *3*
Ames, Evelyn 1908-1990 .... *13*
  Obituary *64*
Ames, Gerald 1906-1993 .... *11*
  Obituary *74*
Ames, Lee J(udah) 1921- *151*
  Earlier sketch in SATA *3*
Ames, Mildred 1919-1994 .... *85*
  Earlier sketches in SATA *22, 81*
Amico, Tom 1960(?)- *176*
Amit, Ofra 1966- *205*
Ammon, Richard 1942- *124*
Amon, Aline 1928- *9*
Amoss, Berthe 1925- *112*
  Earlier sketch in SATA *5*
Anastasio, Dina 1941- *94*
  Brief entry *30*
  Earlier sketch in SATA *37*
Anaya, Rudolfo 1937-
  See CLR *129*
Anaya, Rudolfo A.
  See Anaya, Rudolfo
Anaya, Rudolpho Alfonso
  See Anaya, Rudolfo
Anckarsvard, Karin Inez Maria 1915-1969 .... *6*
Ancona, George 1929- *192*
  Earlier sketches in SATA *12, 85, 145*
  See also SAAS *18*
Anders, C. J.
  See Bennett, Cherie
Anders, Isabel 1946- *101*
Anders, Lou *176*
Andersdatter, Karla M(argaret) 1938- *34*
Andersen, Bethanne 1954- *191*
Andersen, Hans Christian 1805-1875 .... *100*
  See also YABC *1*
  See also CLR *113*
Andersen, Ted
  See Boyd, Waldo T.
Andersen, Yvonne 1932- *27*
Anderson, Bernice G(oudy) 1894-1997 .... *33*
Anderson, Bob 1944- *139*
  Earlier sketch in SATA *136*
Anderson, Brad(ley Jay) 1924- *33*
  Brief entry *31*
Anderson, C. C.
  See Anderson, Catherine Corley
Anderson, C(larence) W(illiam) 1891-1971 . *11*
Anderson, Catherine C.
  See Anderson, Catherine Corley
Anderson, Catherine Corley 1909-2001 .... *72*

Anderson, Clifford
  See Gardner, Richard (M.)
Anderson, Daryl Shon 1963- *93*
Anderson, Dave
  See Anderson, David
Anderson, David 1929- *60*
Anderson, Derek 1969- *169*
Anderson, Eloise Adell 1927- *9*
Anderson, George
  See Groom, Arthur William
Anderson, Grace Fox 1932- *43*
Anderson, J(ohn) R(ichard) L(ane)
  1911-1981 .... *15*
  Obituary *27*
Anderson, Jodi Lynn *182*
Anderson, John David 1975- *197*
Anderson, John L. 1905- *2*
Anderson, Joy 1928- *1*
Anderson, Kevin J. 1962- *117*
  Earlier sketch in SATA *74*
Anderson, Kevin James
  See Anderson, Kevin J.
Anderson, Kirsty 1978- *108*
Anderson, K.J.
  See Moesta, Rebecca
Anderson, Laurie Halse 1961- *186*
  Earlier sketches in SATA *95, 132*
  See also CLR *138*
Anderson, LaVere Francis Shoenfelt
  1907-1998 .... *27*
Anderson, Leone Castell 1923- *53*
  Brief entry *49*
Anderson, Lisa G. 1963- *108*
Anderson, Lonzo
  See Anderson, John L.
Anderson, Lucia (Lewis) 1922- *10*
Anderson, Madelyn Klein 1926-2005 .... *28*
Anderson, Margaret J(ean) 1931- *27*
  See also SAAS *8*
Anderson, Marilyn D. 1943- *144*
Anderson, Mary 1939- *82*
  Earlier sketch in SATA *7*
  See also SAAS *23*
Anderson, Matthew Tobin
  See Anderson, M.T.
Anderson, Mona 1910-2004 .... *40*
Anderson, Mrs. Melvin
  See Anderson, Catherine Corley
Anderson, M.T. 1968- *182*
  Earlier sketches in SATA *97, 146*
Anderson, Norman Dean 1928- *22*
Anderson, Peggy Perry 1953- *179*
  Earlier sketch in SATA *84*
Anderson, Poul 1926-2001 .... *90*
  Autobiography Feature *106*
  Brief entry *39*
  See also CLR *58*
Anderson, Poul William
  See Anderson, Poul
Anderson, Rachel 1943- *86*
  Earlier sketch in SATA *34*
  See also SAAS *18*
Anderson, Rebecca M.
  See Moesta, Rebecca
Anderson, Rebecca Moesta
  See Moesta, Rebecca
Anderson, Richard
  See Anderson, J(ohn) R(ichard) L(ane)
Anderson, Sara *173*
Anderson, Scoular *201*
Anderson, (Tom) Scoular *138*
Anderson, Susan 1952- *90*
Anderson, Thomas Scoular
  See Anderson, Scoular
Anderson, W. B.
  See Schultz, James Willard
Anderson, Wayne 1946- *202*
  Earlier sketches in SATA *56, 147*
Andersson, Kenneth 1970- *200*
Andre, Evelyn M(arie) 1924- *27*
Andreasen, Dan *186*

Andreassen, Karl
  See Boyd, Waldo T.
Andreassi, K. Robert
  See DeCandido, Keith R.A.
Andree, Louise
  See Coury, Louise Andree
Andrew, Ian 1962- *166*
  Earlier sketch in SATA *116*
Andrew, Ian Peter
  See Andrew, Ian
Andrew, Prudence (Hastings) 1924- *87*
Andrews, Benny 1930-2006 .... *31*
  Obituary *178*
Andrews, Eleanor Lattimore
  See Lattimore, Eleanor Frances
Andrews, Elton V.
  See Pohl, Frederik
Andrews, F(rank) Emerson 1902-1978 .... *22*
Andrews, J(ames) S(ydney) 1934- *4*
Andrews, Jan 1942- *167*
  Brief entry *49*
  Earlier sketches in SATA *58, 98*
Andrews, Julie 1935- *153*
  Earlier sketch in SATA *7*
  See also CLR *85*
Andrews, Laura
  See Coury, Louise Andree
Andrews, Roy Chapman 1884-1960 .... *19*
Andrews, Tamra 1959- *129*
Andrews, V(irginia) C(leo) 1924(?)-1986
  Obituary *50*
Andrews, Wendy
  See Sharmat, Marjorie Weinman
Andrews, William G(eorge) 1930- *74*
Andrezel, Pierre
  See Blixen, Karen
Andriani, Renee
  See Williams-Andriani, Renee
Andriola, Alfred J. 1912-1983
  Obituary *34*
Andrist, Ralph K. 1914-2004 .... *45*
Andronik, Catherine M. *189*
Andryszewski, Tricia 1956- *148*
  Earlier sketch in SATA *88*
Angel, Ann 1952- *192*
Angel, Carl *178*
Angel, Marie 1923- *47*
Angeles, Peter A. 1931- *40*
Angeletti, Roberta 1964- *124*
Angeli, Marguerite (Lofft) de
  See de Angeli, Marguerite (Lofft)
Angell, Judie 1937- *78*
  Earlier sketch in SATA *22*
  See also CLR *33*
Angell, Madeline 1919- *18*
Angelo, Valenti 1897- *14*
Angelou, Maya 1928- *136*
  Earlier sketch in SATA *49*
  See also CLR *53*
Angier, Bradford -1997 .... *12*
Angle, Kimberly Greene *203*
Angle, Paul M(cClelland) 1900-1975
  Obituary *20*
Anglund, Joan Walsh 1926- *2*
  See also CLR *94*
Ango, Fan D.
  See Longyear, Barry B(rookes)
Angrist, Stanley W(olff) 1933- *4*
Anholt, Catherine 1958- *131*
  Earlier sketch in SATA *74*
Anholt, Laurence 1959- *141*
  Earlier sketch in SATA *74*
Anita
  See Daniel, Anita
Anmar, Frank
  See Nolan, William F(rancis)
Annett, Cora
  See Scott, Cora Annett (Pipitone)
Annie-Jo
  See Blanchard, Patricia
  and Suhr, Joanne

Annixter, Jane
  See Sturtzel, Jane Levington
Annixter, Paul
  See Sturtzel, Howard A(llison)
Anno, Mitsumasa 1926- *157*
  Earlier sketches in SATA *5, 38, 77*
  See also CLR *122*
Anrooy, Francine Van
  See Van Anrooy, Francine
Ansary, Mir Tamim 1948- *140*
Anstey, Caroline 1958- *81*
Antell, Will D. 1935- *31*
Anthony, Barbara
  See Barber, Antonia
Anthony, C. L.
  See Smith, Dorothy Gladys
Anthony, Edward 1895-1971 .... *21*
Anthony, John
  See Beckett, Ronald Brymer
  and Ciardi, John (Anthony)
  and Sabini, John Anthony
Anthony, Joseph Patrick 1964- *103*
Anthony, Patricia 1947- *109*
Anthony, Piers 1934- *129*
  Autobiography Feature *129*
  Earlier sketch in SATA *84*
  See also CLR *118*
  See also SAAS *22*
Anthony, Susan C(arol) 1953- *87*
Anticaglia, Elizabeth 1939- *12*
Antilles, Kem
  See Moesta, Rebecca
Antle, Nancy 1955- *102*
Antolini, Margaret Fishback 1904-1985
  Obituary *45*
Anton, Michael J(ames) 1940- *12*
Antonacci, Robert J(oseph) 1916- *45*
  Brief entry *37*
Anvil, Christopher 1925-2009 .... *102*
Anzaldua, Gloria (Evanjelina) 1942-2004
  Obituary *154*
Aoki, Hisako 1942- *45*
Apfel, Necia H(alpern) 1930- *51*
  Brief entry *41*
Aphrodite, J.
  See Livingston, Carole
Apikuni
  See Schultz, James Willard
Apostolina, M. *184*
Apostolina, Michael
  See Apostolina, M.
Apostolou, Christine Hale 1955- *179*
  Earlier sketches in SATA *82, 128*
Appel, Allen (R.) 1945- *115*
Appel, Benjamin 1907-1977 .... *39*
  Obituary *21*
Appel, Martin 1948- *45*
Appel, Martin Eliot
  See Appel, Martin
Appel, Marty
  See Appel, Martin
Appelbaum, Diana Muir Karter 1953- *132*
Appelt, Kathi 1954- *190*
  Earlier sketches in SATA *83, 129*
Apperley, Dawn 1969- *135*
Appiah, Peggy 1921-2006 .... *84*
  Earlier sketch in SATA *15*
  See also SAAS *19*
Apple, Margot *152*
  Brief entry *42*
  Earlier sketch in SATA *64*
Applebaum, Stan 1922- *45*
Applegate, K.A.
  See Applegate, Katherine
Applegate, Katherine 1956- *196*
  Earlier sketches in SATA *109, 162*
  See also CLR *90*
Applegate, Katherine Alice
  See Applegate, Katherine

Appleton, Victor
  See Barrett, Neal, Jr.
  and Doyle, Debra
  and Macdonald, James D.
  and Stratemeyer, Edward L.
  and Vardeman, Robert E(dward)
Appleton, Victor II
  See Goulart, Ron
Apsler, Alfred 1907-1982 .... *10*
Aragones, Sergio 1937- *48*
  Brief entry *39*
Araujo, Frank P. 1937- *86*
Arbo, Cris 1950- *103*
Arbuckle, Dorothy Fry 1910-1982
  Obituary *33*
Arbuthnot, May Hill 1884-1969 .... *2*
Archambault, John *163*
  Earlier sketches in SATA *67, 112*
Archbold, Rick 1950- *97*
Archer, Colleen Rutherford 1949- *164*
Archer, Frank
  See O'Connor, Richard
Archer, Jules 1915- *85*
  Earlier sketch in SATA *4*
  See also SAAS *5*
Archer, Lily 1981- *193*
Archer, Marion Fuller 1917- *11*
Archer, Nathan
  See Watt-Evans, Lawrence
Archer, Peggy 1947- *199*
Archibald, Joe
  See Archibald, Joseph S(topford)
Archibald, Joseph S(topford) 1898-1986 .... *3*
  Obituary *47*
Ard, William
  See Jakes, John
Ardagh, Philip 1961- *154*
Ardai, Charles 1969- *85*
Arden, Barbi
  See Stoutenburg, Adrien (Pearl)
Arden, William
  See Lynds, Dennis
Ardizzone, Edward (Jeffrey Irving)
  1900-1979 .... *28*
  Obituary *21*
  Earlier sketch in SATA *1*
  See also CLR *3*
Ardley, Neil (Richard) 1937- *121*
  Earlier sketch in SATA *43*
Arehart-Treichel, Joan 1942- *22*
Arena, Felice 1968- *151*
Arenella, Roy 1939- *14*
Argent, Kerry 1960- *138*
Argueta, Jorge *179*
Arihara, Shino 1973- *201*
Arkin, Alan 1934- *59*
  Brief entry *32*
Arkin, Alan Wolf
  See Arkin, Alan
Arksey, Neil *158*
Arlen, Leslie
  See Nicole, Christopher (Robin)
Arley, Robert
  See Jackson, Mike
Armer, Alberta (Roller) 1904-1986 .... *9*
Armer, Laura Adams 1874-1963 .... *13*
Armistead, John 1941- *130*
Armitage, David 1943- *155*
  Brief entry *38*
  Earlier sketch in SATA *99*
Armitage, Frank
  See Carpenter, John
Armitage, Ronda (Jacqueline) 1943- *155*
  Brief entry *38*
  Earlier sketches in SATA *47, 99*
Armour, Richard (Willard) 1906-1989 .... *14*
  Obituary *61*
Armstrong, Alan 1939- *172*
Armstrong, Alan W.
  See Armstrong, Alan
Armstrong, George D. 1927- *10*

Armstrong, Gerry (Breen) 1929- *10*
Armstrong, Jeannette (C.) 1948- *102*
Armstrong, Jennifer 1961- *165*
  Autobiography Feature *120*
  Earlier sketches in SATA *77, 111*
  See also CLR *66*
  See also SAAS *24*
Armstrong, Louise *43*
  Brief entry *33*
Armstrong, Martin Donisthorpe
  1882-1974 .... *115*
Armstrong, Matthew 1975- *188*
Armstrong, Matthew S.
  See Armstrong, Matthew
Armstrong, Ralph Richard
  See Armstrong, Richard
Armstrong, Richard 1903-1986 .... *11*
Armstrong, William H(oward) 1914-1999 ..... *4*
  Obituary *111*
  See also CLR *117*
  See also SAAS *7*
Armstrong-Ellis, Carey (Fraser) 1956- *145*
Arndt, Ursula (Martha H.) *56*
  Brief entry *39*
Arneson, D(on) J(on) 1935- *37*
Arnett, Caroline
  See Cole, Lois Dwight
Arnett, Jack
  See Goulart, Ron
Arnette, Robert
  See Silverberg, Robert
Arno, Enrico 1913-1981 .... *43*
  Obituary *28*
Arnold, Ann 1953(?)- *207*
Arnold, Caroline 1944- *174*
  Brief entry *34*
  Earlier sketches in SATA *36, 85, 131*
  See also CLR *61*
  See also SAAS *23*
Arnold, Elizabeth 1944- *164*
Arnold, Elliott 1912-1980 .... *5*
  Obituary *22*
Arnold, Emily 1939- *134*
  Autobiography Feature *134*
  Earlier sketches in SATA *5, 50, 76, 110*
  See also CLR *46*
  See also SAAS *7*
Arnold, Gillian Clare
  See Cross, Gillian
Arnold, Katya 1947- *168*
  Earlier sketches in SATA *82, 115*
Arnold, Louise *175*
Arnold, Marsha Diane 1948- *147*
  Earlier sketch in SATA *93*
Arnold, Nick 1961- *113*
Arnold, Oren 1900-1980 .... *4*
Arnold, Susan (Riser) 1951- *58*
Arnold, Tedd 1949- *160*
  Earlier sketches in SATA *69, 116*
Arnoldy, Julie
  See Bischoff, Julia Bristol
Arnosky, James Edward 1946- *189*
  Earlier sketches in SATA *70, 118*
  See also CLR *93*
Arnosky, Jim
  See Arnosky, James Edward
Arnott, Kathleen 1914- *20*
Arnov, Boris, Jr. 1926- *12*
Arnow, Harriette (Louisa) Simpson
  1908-1986 .... *42*
  Obituary *47*
Arnsteen, Katy Keck 1934- *68*
Arnstein, Helene S(olomon) 1915- *12*
Arntson, Herbert E(dward) 1911-1982 .... *12*
Aroner, Miriam *82*
Aronin, Ben 1904-1980
  Obituary *25*
Aronson, Marc 1950- *189*
  Autobiography Feature *189*
  Earlier sketches in SATA *126, 175*

Aronson, Marc Henry
  See Aronson, Marc
Aronson, Sarah *196*
Aronson, Virginia 1954- *122*
Arora, Shirley (Lease) 1930- *2*
Arrasmith, Patrick *176*
Arrick, Fran
  See Angell, Judie
Arrigan, Mary 1943- *142*
Arrington, Aileen *183*
Arrington, Stephen L. 1948- *97*
Arrington, Stephen Lee
  See Arrington, Stephen L.
Arrley, Richmond
  See Delany, Samuel R., Jr.
Arrowood, (McKendrick Lee) Clinton
  1939- *19*
Arrowsmith, Pat 1930- *59*
Arsenault, Isabelle 1978- *207*
Artell, Mike 1948- *183*
  Earlier sketches in SATA *89, 134*
Arthur, Robert (Andrew) 1909-1969
  See Arthur, Robert, (Jr.)
Arthur, Robert, (Jr.) 1909-1969 .... *118*
Arthur, Ruth M(abel) 1905-1979 .... *26*
  Earlier sketch in SATA *7*
Artis, Vicki Kimmel 1945- *12*
Artzybasheff, Boris (Miklailovich)
  1899-1965 .... *14*
Aruego, Ariane
  See Dewey, Ariane
Aruego, Jose 1932- *178*
  Earlier sketches in SATA *6, 68, 125*
  See also CLR *5*
Aruego, Jose Espiritu
  See Aruego, Jose
Arundel, Honor (Morfydd) 1919-1973 .... *4*
  Obituary *24*
  See also CLR *35*
Arundel, Jocelyn
  See Alexander, Jocelyn Anne Arundel
Arvey, Michael 1948- *79*
Arzoumanian, Alik *177*
Asare, Meshack (Yaw) 1945- *139*
  Earlier sketch in SATA *86*
Asaro, Catherine 1955- *165*
  Earlier sketch in SATA *101*
Asaro, Catherine Ann 1955-
  See Asaro, Catherine
Asay, Donna Day 1945- *127*
Asbjornsen, Peter Christen 1812-1885 .... *15*
  See also CLR *104*
Asch, Frank 1946- *154*
  Earlier sketches in SATA *5, 66, 102*
Ash, Jutta 1942- *38*
Ashabranner, Brent 1921- *166*
  Earlier sketches in SATA *1, 67, 130*
  See also CLR *28*
  See also SAAS *14*
Ashabranner, Brent Kenneth
  See Ashabranner, Brent
Ashbless, William
  See Blaylock, James P.
  and Powers, Tim
Ashby, Gil 1958- *146*
Ashby, Gwynneth 1922- *44*
Ashby, Ruth *170*
Ashby, Yvonne 1955- *121*
Ashe, Arthur (Robert, Jr.) 1943-1993 .... *65*
  Obituary *87*
Ashe, Geoffrey (Thomas) 1923- *17*
  Autobiography Feature *125*
Ashe, Mary Ann
  See Lewis, Mary
Asher, Bridget
  See Baggott, Julianna
Asher, Sandra Fenichel
  See Asher, Sandy

Asher, Sandy 1942- 71
    Autobiography Feature 158
    Brief entry 34
    Earlier sketch in SATA 36
    See also SAAS 13
Asheron, Sara
    See Moore, Lilian
Ashey, Bella
    See Breinburg, Petronella
Ashford, Daisy
    See Ashford, Margaret Mary
Ashford, Jeffrey
    See Jeffries, Roderic
Ashford, Margaret Mary 1881-1972 10
Ashland, Monk 1972- 207
Ashley, Bernard (John) 1935- 155
    Brief entry 39
    Earlier sketches in SATA 47, 79
    See also CLR 4
Ashley, Elizabeth
    See Salmon, Annie Elizabeth
Ashley, Ray
    See Abrashkin, Raymond
Ashman, Linda 1960- 203
    Earlier sketch in SATA 150
Ashton, Lorayne
    See Gottfried, Theodore Mark
Ashton, Warren T.
    See Adams, William Taylor
Asimov, Isaac 1920-1992 74
    Earlier sketches in SATA 1, 26
    See also CLR 79
Asinof, Eliot 1919-2008 6
Asinof, Eliot Tager
    See Asinof, Eliot
Aska, Warabe
    See Masuda, Takeshi
Asprin, Robert L. 1946-2008 92
Asprin, Robert Lynn
    See Asprin, Robert L.
Asquith, Cynthia Mary Evelyn (Charteris)
    1887-1960 107
Asquith, Ros 153
Astley, Juliet
    See Lofts, Norah (Robinson)
Aston, Dianna Hutts 1964- 176
Aston, James
    See White, T(erence) H(anbury)
Ata, Te 1895-1995 119
Atene, Ann
    See Atene, (Rita) Anna
Atene, (Rita) Anna 1922- 12
Atheling, William, Jr.
    See Blish, James
Atkins, Catherine 160
Atkins, Jeannine 1953- 172
    Earlier sketch in SATA 113
Atkinson, Allen G. 1953(?)-1987 60
    Brief entry 46
    Obituary 55
Atkinson, M. E.
    See Frankau, Mary Evelyn Atkinson
Atkinson, Margaret Fleming 14
Atteberry, Kevan J. 186
Attema, Martha 1949- 156
    Earlier sketch in SATA 94
Atticus
    See Davies, Hunter
    and Fleming, Ian
    and Pawle, Gerald Strachan
    and Wilson, (Thomas) Woodrow
Atwater, Florence (Hasseltine Carroll)
    1896-1979 66
    Earlier sketch in SATA 16
    See also CLR 19
Atwater, Montgomery Meigs 1904-1976 15
Atwater, Richard (Tupper) 1892-1948 66
    Brief entry 27
    Earlier sketch in SATA 54
    See also CLR 19

Atwater-Rhodes, Amelia 1984- 170
    Earlier sketch in SATA 124
Atwell, Debby 1953- 150
    Earlier sketch in SATA 87
Atwood, Ann (Margaret) 1913-1992 7
Atwood, Margaret 1939- 170
    Earlier sketch in SATA 50
Atwood, Margaret Eleanor
    See Atwood, Margaret
Aubrey, Meg Kelleher 1963- 83
Aubry, Claude B. 1914-1984 29
    Obituary 40
Auch, Herm 173
Auch, Mary Jane 173
    Earlier sketch in SATA 138
Auch, M.J.
    See Auch, Mary Jane
Auclair, Joan 1960- 68
Auel, Jean 1936- 91
Auel, Jean M.
    See Auel, Jean
Auel, Jean Marie
    See Auel, Jean
Auer, Martin 1951- 77
Augarde, Steve 1950- 159
    Earlier sketch in SATA 25
Augelli, John P(at) 1921- 46
Augustine, Mildred
    See Benson, Mildred
Ault, Phil
    See Ault, Phillip H(alliday)
Ault, Phillip H(alliday) 1914- 23
Ault, Rosalie Sain 1942- 38
Ault, Roz
    See Ault, Rosalie Sain
Aung, (Maung) Htin 1909- 21
Auntie Deb
    See Coury, Louise Andree
Auntie Louise
    See Coury, Louise Andree
Aunt Weedy
    See Alcott, Louisa May
Auseon, Andrew 1976- 166
Austen, Carrie
    See Bennett, Cherie
Austin, Carrie
    See Seuling, Barbara
Austin, Elizabeth S. 1907-1977 5
Austin, Harry
    See McInerny, Ralph
Austin, Margot 1909(?)-1990 11
    Obituary 66
Austin, Michael 178
Austin, Oliver L(uther), Jr. 1903-1988 7
    Obituary 59
Austin, Patricia 1950- 137
Austin, R. G.
    See Gelman, Rita Golden
    and Lamb, Nancy
Austin, Virginia 1951- 152
    Earlier sketch in SATA 80
Auteur, Hillary
    See Gottfried, Theodore Mark
Auth, Tony
    See Auth, William Anthony, Jr.
Auth, William Anthony, Jr. 1942- 192
Autry, Gloria Diener
    See Allen, Terril Diener
Auvil, Peggy A 1954- 122
Auvil, Peggy Appleby
    See Auvil, Peggy A
Aveni, Anthony F. 1938- 181
Aveni, Anthony Francis
    See Aveni, Anthony F.
Averbeck, Jim 1963- 201
Averill, Esther (Holden) 1902-1992 28
    Obituary 72
    Earlier sketch in SATA 1
Avery, A. A.
    See Montgomery, Rutherford George

Avery, Al
    See Montgomery, Rutherford George
Avery, Gillian (Elise) 1926- 137
    Autobiography Feature 137
    Earlier sketches in SATA 7, 75
    See also SAAS 6
Avery, Kay 1908- 5
Avery, Lorraine
    See Older, Effin
    and Older, Jules
Avery, Lynn
    See Cole, Lois Dwight
Avi 1937- 190
    Earlier sketches in SATA 14, 71, 108, 156
    See also CLR 68
Avishai, Susan 1949- 82
Avril, Francois 1961- 191
Avril, Lynne
    See Cravath, Lynne W.
Awdry, Christopher Vere 1940- 67
Awdry, Wilbert Vere 1911-1997 94
    See also CLR 23
Axelrod, Amy 131
Axelsen, Stephen 1953- 165
Axton, David
    See Koontz, Dean
Ayars, James S(terling) 1898-1986 4
Aye, A. K.
    See Edwards, Hazel (Eileen)
Ayer, Eleanor H. 1947-1998 121
    Earlier sketch in SATA 78
Ayer, Jacqueline 1930- 13
Ayer, Margaret (?)-1981 15
Aylesworth, Jim 1943- 139
    Earlier sketches in SATA 38, 89
    See also CLR 89
Aylesworth, Thomas G(ibbons) 1927-1995 .. 88
    Earlier sketch in SATA 4
    See also CLR 6
    See also SAAS 17
Ayliffe, Alex 190
Aylward, Marcus
    See Alexander, Marc
Aymar, Brandt 1911- 22
Ayme, Marcel (Andre) 1902-1967 91
    See also CLR 25
Ayres, Becky
    See Hickox, Rebecca (Ayres)
Ayres, Katherine 1947- 187
Ayres, Pam 1947- 90
Ayres, Patricia Miller 1923-1985
    Obituary 46
Aytmatov, Chingiz
    See Aitmatov, Chingiz
Ayto, Russell 1960- 206
    Earlier sketches in SATA 111, 166
Azaid
    See Zaidenberg, Arthur
Azar, Penny 1952- 121
Azarian, Mary 1940- 171
    Earlier sketch in SATA 112
Azore, Barbara 1934- 188

                            B

Baastad, Babbis Friis
    See Friis-Baastad, Babbis Ellinor
Bab
    See Gilbert, W(illiam) S(chwenck)
Babbis, Eleanor
    See Friis-Baastad, Babbis Ellinor
Babbitt, Lucy Cullyford 1960- 85
Babbitt, Natalie 1932- 194
    Earlier sketches in SATA 6, 68, 106
    See also CLR 141
    See also SAAS 5
Babbitt, Natalie Zane Moore
    See Babbitt, Natalie
Babcock, Chris 1963- 83

Babcock, Dennis 1948- 22
Babcock, Dennis Arthur
   See Babcock, Dennis
Baber, Carolyn Stonnell 1936- 96
Baboni, Elena 198
Baca, Ana 1967- 191
Baca, Maria 1951- 104
Bach, Alice (Hendricks) 1942- 93
   Brief entry 27
   Earlier sketch in SATA 30
Bach, Bellamy
   See Windling, Terri
Bach, Mary 1960- 125
Bach, Richard 1936- 13
Bach, Richard David
   See Bach, Richard
Bache, Ellyn 1942- 124
Bachel, Beverly K. 1957- 142
Bachelet, Gilles 1952- 196
Bachman, Fred 1949- 12
Bachman, Richard
   See King, Stephen
Bachrach, Deborah 80
Backus, James Gilmore 1913-1989
   Obituary 63
Backus, Jim
   See Backus, James Gilmore
Bacmeister, Rhoda W(arner) 1893-1991 11
Bacon, Betty
   See Bacon, Elizabeth
Bacon, Elizabeth 1914-2001 3
   Obituary 131
Bacon, Joan Chase
   See Bowden, Joan Chase
Bacon, Josephine Dodge (Daskam)
   1876-1961 48
Bacon, Margaret Frances
   See Bacon, Peggy
Bacon, Margaret Hope 1921- 6
Bacon, Martha Sherman 1917-1981 18
   Obituary 27
   See also CLR 3
Bacon, Melvin 1950- 93
Bacon, Melvin L.
   See Bacon, Melvin
Bacon, Peggy 1895-1987 50
Bacon, R(onald) L(eonard) 1924- 84
   Earlier sketch in SATA 26
Baden, Robert 1936- 70
Baden-Powell, Robert (Stephenson Smyth)
   1857-1941 16
Badt, Karin L(uisa) 1963- 91
Bae, Hyun-Joo 186
Baehr, Kingsley M. 1937- 89
Baehr, Patricia 1952- 65
Baehr, Patricia Goehner
   See Baehr, Patricia
Baek, Matthew J. 1971- 202
Baer, Jill
   See Gilbert, (Agnes) Joan (Sewell)
Baer, Judy 1951- 71
Baer, Julie 1960- 161
Baer-Block, Roxanna 172
Baerg, Harry J(ohn) 1909-1996 12
Baeten, Lieve 1954- 83
Bagert, Brod 1947- 191
   Earlier sketch in SATA 80
Baggette, Susan K. 1942- 126
Baggott, Julianna 1969- 197
Bagnold, Enid 1889-1981 25
   Earlier sketch in SATA 1
Baguley, Elizabeth 1959- 199
Bahlke, Valerie Worth -1994
   See Worth, Valerie
Bahous, Sally 1939- 86
Bahr, Mary (Madelyn) 1946- 95
Bahr, Robert 1940- 38
Bahti, Tom 1926-1972 57
   Brief entry 31
Baicker-McKee, Carol 1958- 177
Bailey, Alice Cooper 1890-1978 12

Bailey, Anne 1958- 71
Bailey, Bernadine (Freeman) 1901-1995 14
Bailey, Carolyn Sherwin 1875-1961 14
Bailey, Debbie 1954- 123
Bailey, Donna (Veronica Anne) 1938- 68
Bailey, Jane H(orton) 1916- 12
Bailey, John (Robert) 1940- 52
Bailey, Len 193
Bailey, Linda 1948- 182
   Earlier sketch in SATA 107
Bailey, Maralyn Collins (Harrison) 1941- 12
Bailey, Matilda
   See Radford, Ruby L(orraine)
Bailey, Maurice Charles 1932- 12
Bailey, Pearl (Mae) 1918-1990 81
Bailey, Peter 1946- 194
Bailey, Ralph Edgar 1893-1982 11
Bailey, Sheila (Lucas) 1960- 155
Baillie, Allan 1943- 151
   Earlier sketch in SATA 87
   See also CLR 49
   See also SAAS 21
Baillie, Allan Stuart
   See Baillie, Allan
Baines, John (David) 1943- 71
Bains, Larry
   See Sabin, Louis
Baird, Alison 1963- 138
Baird, Bil 1904-1987 30
   Obituary 52
Baird, Thomas (P.) 1923-1990 45
   Brief entry 39
   Obituary 64
Baird, William Britton
   See Baird, Bil
Baity, Elizabeth Chesley 1907-1989 1
Baiul, Oksana 1977- 108
Bajoria, Paul 1964- 187
Bakeless, John (Edwin) 1894-1978 9
Bakeless, Katherine Little 1895-1992 9
Baker, Alan 1951- 146
   Earlier sketches in SATA 22, 93
Baker, Augusta 1911-1998 3
Baker, Barbara 1947- 192
Baker, Betty Lou 1928-1987 73
   Obituary 54
   Earlier sketch in SATA 5
Baker, Carin Greenberg 1959- 79
Baker, Charlotte 1910- 2
Baker, Christina
   See Kline, Christina Baker
Baker, Christopher W. 1952- 144
Baker, Deirdre 1955- 195
Baker, E.D. 190
Baker, (Mary) Elizabeth (Gillette) 1923- 7
Baker, Gayle Cunningham 1950- 39
Baker, James W. 1924- 65
   Earlier sketch in SATA 22
Baker, James W. 1926- 122
Baker, Janice E(dla) 1941- 22
Baker, Jeanette 178
Baker, Jeannie 1950- 156
   Earlier sketches in SATA 23, 88
   See also CLR 28
Baker, Jeffrey J(ohn) W(heeler) 1931- 5
Baker, Jim
   See Baker, James W.
Baker, Keith 1953- 179
Baker, Ken 1962- 133
Baker, Laura Nelson 1911- 3
Baker, Margaret 1890-1965 4
Baker, Margaret J(oyce) 1918- 12
   See also SAAS 8
Baker, Mary Gladys Steel 1892-1974 12
Baker, (Robert) Michael (Graham) 1938- 4
Baker, Nina (Brown) 1888-1957 15
Baker, Pamela J. 1947- 66
Baker, Rachel 1904-1978 2
   Obituary 26
Baker, Roberta 206
Baker, Rosalie F. 1945- 166

Baker, Samm Sinclair 1909-1997 12
   Obituary 96
Baker, Sharon Reiss 1962- 207
Baker, Susan (Catherine) 1942-1991 29
Balaam
   See Lamb, G(eoffrey) F(rederick)
Balan, Bruce 1959- 113
Balcavage, Dynise 1965- 137
Balch, Glenn 1902-1989 3
   Obituary 83
   See also SAAS 11
Baldacci, David 1960- 184
Baldacci, David G.
   See Baldacci, David
   and Baldacci, David
Balderose, Nancy Ward 1952- 93
Balderson, Margaret 1935- 151
Baldini, Michelle 205
Baldry, Cherith 1947- 167
   Earlier sketch in SATA 72
Balducci, Carolyn 1946- 5
Balducci, Carolyn Feleppa
   See Balducci, Carolyn
Baldwin, Alex
   See Griffin, W.E.B.
Baldwin, Anne Norris 1938- 5
Baldwin, Clara 11
Baldwin, Gordo
   See Baldwin, Gordon C(ortis)
Baldwin, Gordon C(ortis) 1908-1983 12
Baldwin, James 1841-1925 24
Baldwin, James 1924-1987 9
   Obituary 54
Baldwin, Louis 1919- 110
Baldwin, Margaret
   See Weis, Margaret
Baldwin, Stan(ley C.) 1929- 62
   Brief entry 28
Bales, Carol Ann 1940- 57
   Brief entry 29
Balet, Jan (Bernard) 1913- 11
Balgassi, Haemi 1971- 131
Balian, Lorna 1929- 91
   Earlier sketch in SATA 9
Balit, Christina 1961- 159
   Earlier sketch in SATA 102
Ball, Duncan 1941- 73
Ball, Zachary
   See Janas, Frankie-Lee
   and Masters, Kelly R(ay)
Ballantine, Lesley Frost
   See Frost, Lesley
Ballantyne, R(obert) M(ichael) 1825-1894 ... 24
   See also CLR 137
Ballard, James G.
   See Ballard, J.G.
Ballard, James Graham
   See Ballard, J.G.
Ballard, Jane
   See Gorman, Carol
Ballard, J.G. 1930-2009 93
   Obituary 203
Ballard, Jim G.
   See Ballard, J.G.
Ballard, John 1945- 110
Ballard, Lowell C(lyne) 1904-1986 12
   Obituary 49
Ballard, (Charles) Martin 1929- 1
Ballard, Mignon F. 1934- 64
   Brief entry 49
Ballard, Mignon Franklin
   See Ballard, Mignon F.
Ballard, Robert D(uane) 1942- 85
   See also CLR 60
Ballard, Robin 1965- 126
Balliett, Blue 1955- 156
Ballinger, Bryan 1968- 161
Ballouhey, Pierre 1944- 90
Balogh, Penelope 1916-1975 1
   Obituary 34
Balouch, Kristen 176

Balow, Tom 1931- *12*
Baltazzi, Evan S(erge) 1921- *90*
Balterman, Marcia Ridlon 1942- *22*
Baltimore, J.
    See Catherall, Arthur
Baltzer, Hans (Adolf) 1900- *40*
Balzano, Jeanne (Koppel) 1912- *7*
Bambara, Toni Cade 1939-1995 .... *112*
Bamfylde, Walter
    See Bevan, Tom
Bamman, Henry A. 1918- *12*
Banat, D. R.
    See Bradbury, Ray
Bancroft, Griffing 1907-1999 .... *6*
Bancroft, Laura
    See Baum, L. Frank
Bandel, Betty 1912- *47*
Baner, Skulda Vanadis 1897-1964 .... *10*
Banerjee, Anjali *174*
Banfill, A. Scott 1956- *98*
Bang, Betsy 1912- *48*
    Brief entry *37*
Bang, Garrett
    See Bang, Molly
Bang, Molly 1943- *158*
    Earlier sketches in SATA *24, 69, 111*
    See also CLR 8
Bang, Molly Garrett
    See Bang, Molly
Bang-Campbell, Monika 1975(?)- *195*
    Earlier sketch in SATA *140*
Banjo, The
    See Paterson, A(ndrew) B(arton)
Banke, Cecile de
    See de Banke, Cecile
Banks, Kate 1960- *200*
    Earlier sketches in SATA *134, 172*
Banks, Laura Stockton Voorhees 1908(?)-1980
    Obituary *23*
Banks, Lynne Reid
    See Reid Banks, Lynne
Banks, Merry *197*
Banks, Michael A. 1951- *101*
Banks, Paul 1952- *174*
Banks, Sara (Jeanne Gordon Harrell) *26*
    See Harrell, Sara (Jeanne) Gordon
Bannatyne-Cugnet, Elizabeth Jo-Anne
    See Bannatyne-Cugnet, Jo
Bannatyne-Cugnet, Jo 1951- *101*
Banner, Angela
    See Maddison, Angela Mary
Bannerman, Helen (Brodie Cowan Watson)
    1862(?)-1946 .... *19*
    See also CLR *144*
Banning, Evelyn I. 1903-1993 .... *36*
Bannon, Laura (?)-1963 .... *6*
Bannor, Brett 1959- *143*
Banta, Susan *181*
Bantock, Nick 1950(?)- *95*
Banyai, Istvan *193*
Barakat, Ibtisam 1963- *186*
Barasch, Lynne 1939- *186*
    Earlier sketches in SATA *74, 126*
Barbalet, Margaret 1949- *77*
Barbary, James
    See Baumann, Amy Beeching
    and Beeching, Jack
Barbash, Shepard 1957- *84*
Barbe, Walter Burke 1926- *45*
Barber, Antonia 1932- *163*
    Earlier sketch in SATA *29*
Barber, Atiim Kiambu
    See Barber, Tiki
Barber, Lynda
    See Graham-Barber, Lynda
Barber, Lynda Graham
    See Graham-Barber, Lynda
Barber, Richard (William) 1941- *35*
Barber, Ronde 1975- *182*
Barber, Tiki 1975- *182*

Barbera, Joe 1911-2006 .... *51*
    Obituary *179*
Barbera, Joseph
    See Barbera, Joe
Barbera, Joseph Roland
    See Barbera, Joe
Barberis, Juan C(arlos) 1920- *61*
Barbour, Karen 1956- *170*
    Earlier sketches in SATA *63, 121*
Barbour, Ralph Henry 1870-1944 .... *16*
Barclay, Bill
    See Moorcock, Michael
Barclay, Isabel
    See Dobell, I(sabel) M(arian) B(arclay)
Barclay, William Ewert
    See Moorcock, Michael
Bardhan-Quallen, Sudipta *168*
Bardoe, Cheryl *181*
Bare, Arnold Edwin 1920- *16*
Bare, Colleen Stanley *32*
Bar-el, Dan *199*
Barenholtz, Bernard 1914-1989
    Obituary *64*
Bargar, Gary W. 1947-1985 .... *63*
Barger, Jan 1948- *147*
Barish, Matthew 1907-2000 .... *12*
Barkan, Joanne *127*
    Earlier sketch in SATA *77*
Barker, Albert W. 1900- *8*
Barker, Carol (Minturn) 1938- *31*
Barker, Cicely Mary 1895-1973 .... *49*
    Brief entry *39*
    See also CLR *88*
Barker, Melvern 1907-1989 .... *11*
Barker, S. Omar 1894-1985 .... *10*
Barker, Squire Omar
    See Barker, S. Omar
Barker, Will 1913-1983 .... *8*
Barkin, Carol 1944- *52*
    Earlier sketch in SATA *42*
Barklem, Jill 1951- *96*
    See also CLR *31*
Barkley, Brad *178*
Barkley, James Edward 1941- *6*
Barks, Carl 1901-2000 .... *37*
Barley, Janet Crane 1934- *95*
Barnaby, Ralph S(tanton) 1893-1986 .... *9*
Barnard, A. M.
    See Alcott, Louisa May
Barnard, Bryn 1956- *169*
    Earlier sketch in SATA *115*
Barne, Kitty
    See Barne, Marion Catherine
Barne, Marion Catherine 1883-1957 .... *97*
Barneda, David *206*
Barner, Bob 1947- *136*
    Earlier sketch in SATA *29*
Barnes, Dawn 1957- *175*
Barnes, Derrick *191*
Barnes, Derrick D.
    See Barnes, Derrick
Barnes, (Frank) Eric Wollencott 1907-1962 . *22*
Barnes, Joyce Annette 1958- *85*
Barnes, Laura T. 1958- *119*
Barnes, Loutricia
    See Barnes-Svarney, Patricia L(ou)
Barnes, Malcolm 1909(?)-1984
    Obituary *41*
Barnes, Michael 1934- *55*
Barnes-Murphy, Frances 1951- *88*
Barnes-Murphy, Rowan 1952- *88*
Barnes-Svarney, Patricia L(ou) 1953- *67*
Barnet, Nancy 1954- *84*
Barnett, Ivan 1947- *70*
Barnett, Lincoln (Kinnear) 1909-1979 .... *36*
Barnett, Moneta 1922-1976 .... *33*
Barnett, Naomi 1927- *40*
Barney, Maginel Wright 1881(?)-1966 .... *39*
    Brief entry *32*
Barnhart, Clarence L(ewis) 1900-1993 .... *48*
    Obituary *78*

Barnouw, Adriaan Jacob 1877-1968
    Obituary *27*
Barnouw, Victor 1915-1989 .... *43*
    Brief entry *28*
Barnstone, Willis 1927- *20*
Barnum, Jay Hyde 1888(?)-1962 .... *20*
Barnum, P. T., Jr.
    See Stratemeyer, Edward L.
Barnum, Richard *67*
    Earlier sketch in SATA *1*
Barnum, Theodore
    See Stratemeyer, Edward L.
Barnwell, Ysaye M. 1946- *200*
Baron, Kathy 1954- *90*
Baron, Virginia Olsen 1931- *46*
    Brief entry *28*
Barr, Donald 1921-2004 .... *20*
    Obituary *152*
Barr, George 1907-1992 .... *2*
Barr, Jene 1922-1985 .... *16*
    Obituary *42*
Barr, Nevada 1952- *126*
    Earlier sketch in SATA *115*
Barrer, Gertrude
    See Barrer-Russell, Gertrude
Barrer-Russell, Gertrude 1921- *27*
Barrett, Angela (Jane) 1955- *145*
    Earlier sketch in SATA *75*
Barrett, Ethel *87*
    Brief entry *44*
Barrett, Joyce Durham 1943- *138*
Barrett, Judi *204*
    See Barrett, Judith
Barrett, Judith 1941- *26*
    See also CLR *98*
    See Barrett, Judi
Barrett, Robert T(heodore) 1949- *92*
Barrett, Ron 1937- *14*
Barrett, Susan (Mary) 1938- *113*
Barrett, Tracy 1955- *207*
    Earlier sketches in SATA *84, 115, 156*
Barrett, William E(dmund) 1900-1986
    Obituary *49*
Barretta, Gene *176*
Barretton, Grandall
    See Garrett, Randall
Barrie, Baronet
    See Barrie, J. M.
Barrie, J. M. 1860-1937 .... *100*
    See also YABC *1*
    See also CLR *124*
Barrie, James Matthew
    See Barrie, J. M.
Barringer, William 1940-1996 .... *153*
Barrington, Michael
    See Moorcock, Michael
Barris, George 1925- *47*
Barrol, Grady
    See Bograd, Larry
Barron, Rex 1951- *84*
Barron, T.A. 1952- *192*
    Earlier sketches in SATA *83, 126*
    See also CLR *86*
Barron, Thomas Archibald
    See Barron, T.A.
Barron, Tom
    See Barron, T.A.
Barrow, Lloyd H. 1942- *73*
Barrows, Annie 1962- *180*
Barry, Dan 1958- *177*
Barry, Dana (Marie Malloy) 1949- *139*
Barry, James P(otvin) 1918- *14*
Barry, Katharina Watjen 1936- *4*
Barry, Robert (Everett) 1931- *6*
Barry, Scott 1952- *32*
Barry, Sheila Anne -2003 .... *91*
Barshaw, Ruth McNally *203*
Bartell, Susan S. *175*
Bartenbach, Jean 1918- *40*
Barth, Edna 1914-1980 .... *7*
    Obituary *24*

Barth, Kelly L. 1964- *152*
Barthelme, Donald 1931-1989 7
　Obituary 62
Barth-Grozinger, Inge 1950- *185*
Bartholomew, Barbara 1941- *86*
　Brief entry *42*
Bartholomew, Jean
　See Beatty, Patricia (Robbins)
Bartlett, Alison *153*
Bartlett, Philip A. *1*
Bartlett, Robert Merrill 1899-1995 .... *12*
Bartoletti, Susan Campbell 1958- *173*
　Earlier sketches in SATA *88, 129, 135*
Barton, Byron 1930- *126*
　Earlier sketches in SATA *9, 90*
Barton, Jill(ian) 1940- *75*
Barton, May Hollis *67*
　Earlier sketch in SATA *1*
Barton, Pat
　See Arrowsmith, Pat
Bartos-Hoeppner, Barbara 1923- *5*
Bartram, Simon *156*
Bartsch, Jochen 1906- *39*
Baruch, Dorothy W(alter) 1899-1962 .... *21*
Barunga, Albert 1912(?)-1977 .... *120*
Baryshnikov, Mikhail 1948- *192*
Bas, Rutger
　See Rutgers van der Loeff-Basenau, An(na)
　Maria Margaretha
Base, Graeme 1958- *162*
　Earlier sketches in SATA *67, 101*
　See also CLR 22
Base, Graeme Rowland
　See Base, Graeme
Baseman, Gary 1960- *174*
Bash, Barbara 1948- *132*
Bashevis, Isaac
　See Singer, Isaac Bashevis
Bashevis, Yitskhok
　See Singer, Isaac Bashevis
Bashista, Adrienne Ehlert *203*
Basile, Gloria Vitanza 1929- *180*
Baskin, Leonard 1922-2000 .... *120*
　Brief entry *27*
　Earlier sketch in SATA *30*
Baskin, Nora Raleigh 1961- *189*
　Earlier sketch in SATA *129*
Bason, Lillian 1913- *20*
Bass, L. G.
　See Geringer, Laura
Bassett, Jeni 1959- *64*
　Brief entry *43*
Bassett, John Keith
　See Keating, Lawrence A.
Bassett, Lisa 1958- *61*
Bassil, Andrea
　See Nilsen, Anna
Bastyra, Judy *108*
Basye, Dale E. *205*
Bat-Ami, Miriam 1950- *150*
　Autobiography Feature *150*
　Earlier sketches in SATA *82, 122*
Bate, Lucy 1939-1993 .... *18*
Bate, Norman (Arthur) 1916- 5
Bateman, Colin 1962- *172*
Bateman, Donna M. *190*
Bateman, Teresa 1957- *168*
　Earlier sketch in SATA *112*
Bates, Amy June *189*
Bates, Barbara S(nedeker) 1919- *12*
Bates, Betty
　See Bates, Elizabeth
Bates, Dianne 1948- *147*
Bates, Elizabeth 1921- *19*
Bates, Ivan *175*
Bates, Katharine Lee 1859-1929 .... *113*
Bates, Martine
　See Leavitt, Martine
Bateson, Catherine 1960- *197*
　Earlier sketch in SATA *157*

Batey, Tom 1946- *52*
　Brief entry *41*
Bath, Kevin P.
　See Bath, K.P.
Bath, K.P. 1959- *171*
Batherman, Muriel
　See Sheldon, Muriel
Batson, Larry 1930- *35*
Batt, Tanya Robyn 1970- *131*
Battaglia, Aurelius 1910- *50*
　Brief entry *33*
Batten, H(arry) Mortimer 1888-1958 .... *25*
Batten, Mary 1937- *162*
　Earlier sketches in SATA *5, 102*
Batterberry, Ariane Ruskin 1935- *13*
Batterberry, Michael Carver 1932- *32*
Battle-Lavert, Gwendolyn 1951- *155*
　Earlier sketches in SATA *85, 131*
Battles, (Roxy) Edith 1921- 7
Baudouy, Michel-Aime 1909- 7
Bauer, A.C.E. *201*
Bauer, Caroline Feller 1935- *98*
　Brief entry *46*
　Earlier sketch in SATA *52*
　See also SAAS 24
Bauer, Fred 1934- *36*
Bauer, Helen 1900-1988 2
Bauer, Joan 1951- *160*
　Earlier sketch in SATA *117*
Bauer, Jutta 1955- *150*
Bauer, Marion Dane 1938- *192*
　Autobiography Feature *144*
　Earlier sketches in SATA *20, 69, 113, 144*
　See also SAAS 9
Bauer, Michael Gerard 1955(?)- *167*
Bauer, Steven 1948- *125*
Bauerschmidt, Marjorie 1926- *15*
Baughman, Dorothy 1940- *61*
Baum, Allyn Z(elton) 1924-1997 .... *98*
　Earlier sketch in SATA *20*
Baum, L. Frank
　See Thompson, Ruth Plumly
Baum, L. Frank 1856-1919 .... *100*
　Earlier sketch in SATA *18*
　See also CLR *107*
Baum, Louis 1948- *182*
　Brief entry *52*
　Earlier sketch in SATA *64*
Baum, Louis F.
　See Baum, L. Frank
Baum, Lyman Frank
　See Baum, L. Frank
Baum, Maxie *188*
Baum, Willi 1931- 4
Baumann, Amy Beeching 1922- *10*
Baumann, Amy Brown Beeching
　See Baumann, Amy Beeching
Baumann, Hans 1914- 2
　See also CLR 35
Baumann, Kurt 1935- *21*
Baumgartner, Barbara 1939- *86*
Baurys, Flo(rence) 1938- *122*
Bausum, Ann *173*
Bawden, Nina 1925- *132*
　Earlier sketches in SATA *4, 72*
　See also CLR *51*
　See also SAAS 16
Bawden, Nina Mary Mabey
　See Bawden, Nina
Baxter, Valerie
　See Meynell, Laurence Walter
Bay, Jeanette Graham 1928- *88*
Bayer, Harold
　See Gregg, Andrew K.
Bayer, Jane E. (?)-1985
　Obituary *44*
Bayley, Nicola 1949- *129*
　Earlier sketches in SATA *41, 69*
Baylor, Byrd 1924- *136*
　Earlier sketches in SATA *16, 69*
　See also CLR 3

Baynes, Pauline 1922-2008 .... *133*
　Obituary *196*
　Earlier sketches in SATA *19, 59*
Baynes, Pauline Diana
　See Baynes, Pauline
Bayoc, Cbabi *186*
BB
　See Watkins-Pitchford, Denys James
Beach, Charles
　See Reid, (Thomas) Mayne
Beach, Charles Amory *1*
Beach, Edward L. 1918-2002 .... *12*
　Obituary *140*
Beach, Edward Latimer
　See Beach, Edward L.
Beach, Lisa 1957- *111*
Beach, Lynn
　See Lance, Kathryn
Beach, Stewart T(aft) 1899-1979 .... *23*
Beachcroft, Nina 1931- *18*
Beagle, Peter S. 1939- *130*
　Earlier sketch in SATA *60*
Beagle, Peter Soyer
　See Beagle, Peter S.
Beaglehole, Helen 1946- *117*
Beale, Fleur *107*
Bealer, Alex W(inkler III) 1921-1980 .... *8*
　Obituary *22*
Beales, Valerie 1915- *74*
Beals, Carleton 1893-1979 .... *12*
Beals, Frank Lee 1881-1972
　Obituary *26*
Beam, Matt 1970- *187*
Beame, Rona 1934- *12*
Beamer, (George) Charles (Jr.) 1942- *43*
Bean, Jonathan 1979- *194*
Bean, Normal
　See Burroughs, Edgar Rice
Beaney, Jan
　See Udall, Jan Beaney
Beaney, Jane
　See Udall, Jan Beaney
Bear, Carolyn
　See Rayban, Chloe
Bear, Greg 1951- *105*
　Earlier sketch in SATA *65*
Bear, Gregory Dale
　See Bear, Greg
Bearanger, Marie
　See Messier, Claire
Beard, Charles A(ustin) 1874-1948 .... *18*
Beard, Dan(iel Carter) 1850-1941 .... *22*
Beard, Darleen Bailey 1961- *96*
Bearden, Romare (Howard) 1914(?)-1988 ... *22*
　Obituary *56*
Beardmore, Cedric
　See Beardmore, George
Beardmore, George 1908-1979 .... *20*
Beardshaw, Rosalind 1969- *190*
Beardsley, Martyn R. 1957- *150*
Bearman, Jane (Ruth) 1917- *29*
Beaton, Clare 1947- *125*
Beatty, Elizabeth
　See Holloway, Teresa (Bragunier)
Beatty, Hetty Burlingame 1907-1971 .... *5*
Beatty, Jerome, Jr. 1918- *5*
Beatty, John (Louis) 1922-1975 .... *6*
　Obituary *25*
Beatty, Patricia (Robbins) 1922-1991 .... *73*
　Obituary *68*
　Earlier sketches in SATA *1, 30*
　See also SAAS 4
Beaty, Andrea *186*
Beaty, Mary (T.) 1947- *146*
Beaumont, Karen 1954- *204*
Beccia, Carlyn *189*
Bechard, Margaret 1953- *164*
　Earlier sketch in SATA *85*
Bechtel, Louise Seaman 1894-1985 .... *4*
　Obituary *43*
Beck, Barbara L. 1927- *12*

Beck, Ian 1947- *190*
  Earlier sketch in SATA *138*
  See Beck, Ian Archibald
Beck, Peggy 1949- *171*
Beck, Scott *197*
Becker, Beril 1901-1999 .... *11*
Becker, Bonny *184*
Becker, Deborah Zimmett 1955- *138*
Becker, Helaine 1961- *142*
Becker, John (Leonard) 1901- *12*
Becker, John E(mil) 1942- *148*
Becker, Joyce 1936- *39*
Becker, May Lamberton 1873-1958 .... *33*
Becker, Neesa 1951- *123*
Becker, Shari *174*
Beckerman, Chad W. *198*
Beckett, Sheilah 1913- *33*
Beckhorn, Susan Williams 1953- *189*
Beckles Willson, Robina 1930- *27*
Beckman, Delores 1914-1994 .... *51*
Beckman, Gunnel 1910- *6*
  See also CLR *25*
  See also SAAS *9*
Beckman, Kaj
  See Beckman, Karin
Beckman, Karin 1913- *45*
Beckman, Per (Frithiof) 1913- *45*
Bedard, Michael 1949- *154*
  Earlier sketch in SATA *93*
  See also CLR *35*
Beddor, Frank *194*
Beddows, Eric
  See Nutt, Ken
Bedford, A. N.
  See Watson, Jane Werner
Bedford, Annie North
  See Watson, Jane Werner
Bedford, David *159*
Bedoukian, Kerop 1907-1981 .... *53*
Bee, Jay
  See Brainerd, John W(hiting)
Bee, William *188*
Beebe, B. F.
  See Johnson, B. F.
Beebe, (Charles) William 1877-1962 .... *19*
Beeby, Betty 1923- *25*
Beech, Mark 1971- *191*
Beech, Webb
  See Griffin, W.E.B.
Beecham, Jahnna *161*
Beechcroft, William
  See Hallstead, William F(inn III)
Beeching, Jack 1922- *14*
Beeke, Tiphanie *163*
Beeler, Janet
  See Shaw, Janet
Beeler, Nelson F(rederick) 1910-1978 .... *13*
Beere, Peter 1951- *97*
Beers, Dorothy Sands 1917- *9*
Beers, Lorna 1897-1989 .... *14*
Beers, V(ictor) Gilbert 1928- *130*
  Earlier sketch in SATA *9*
Beeton, Max
  See Redding, Robert Hull
Begay, Shonto 1954- *137*
Begaye, Lisa Shook
  See Beach, Lisa
Begin, Mary Jane 1963- *82*
Begin-Callanan, Mary Jane
  See Begin, Mary Jane
Begley, Kathleen A. 1948- *21*
Begley, Kathleen Anne
  See Begley, Kathleen A.
Behan, Leslie
  See Gottfried, Theodore Mark
Behler, Deborah A. 1947- *145*
Behler, John L. 1943-2006 .... *145*
  Obituary *173*
Behler, John Luther
  See Behler, John L.

Behn, Harry 1898-1973 .... *2*
  Obituary *34*
Behnke, Frances L. *8*
Behr, Joyce 1929- *15*
Behrens, June York 1925- *19*
Behrman, Carol H(elen) 1925- *144*
  Earlier sketch in SATA *14*
Beifuss, John, (Jr.) 1959- *92*
Beil, Karen Magnuson 1950- *124*
Beiler, Edna 1923- *61*
Beinicke, Steve 1956- *69*
Beirne, Barbara 1933- *71*
Beiser, Arthur 1931- *22*
Beiser, Germaine 1931- *11*
Belair, Richard L. 1934- *45*
Belaney, Archibald Stansfeld 1888-1938 ...... *24*
  See also CLR *32*
Belbin, David 1958- *164*
  Earlier sketch in SATA *106*
Belden, Wilanne Schneider 1925- *56*
Belfrage, Sally 1936-1994 .... *65*
  Obituary *79*
Belknap, B. H.
  See Ellis, Edward S.
Belknap, Boynton
  See Ellis, Edward S.
Belknap, Boynton M.D.
  See Ellis, Edward S.
Bell, Anthea 1936- *148*
  Earlier sketch in SATA *88*
Bell, Cathleen Davitt 1971- *203*
Bell, Cece *202*
Bell, Clare (Louise) 1952- *99*
Bell, Corydon Whitten 1894-1980 .... *3*
Bell, David Owen 1949- *99*
Bell, Emerson
  See Stratemeyer, Edward L.
Bell, Emily Mary
  See Cason, Mabel Earp
Bell, Frank
  See Benson, Mildred
Bell, Gertrude (Wood) 1911-1987 .... *12*
Bell, Gina
  See Balzano, Jeanne (Koppel)
Bell, Hilari 1958- *197*
  Earlier sketch in SATA *151*
Bell, Jadrien
  See Golden, Christie
Bell, Janet
  See Clymer, Eleanor
Bell, Janet Cheatham 1937- *127*
Bell, Krista 1950- *126*
Bell, Krista Anne Blakeney
  See Bell, Krista
Bell, Margaret E(lizabeth) 1898-1990 .... *2*
Bell, Mary Reeves 1946- *88*
Bell, Norman (Edward) 1899- *11*
Bell, Raymond Martin 1907-1999 .... *13*
Bell, Siobhan *177*
Bell, Thelma Harrington 1896-1985 .... *3*
Bell, William 1945- *90*
  See also CLR *91*
Bellairs, John (Anthony) 1938-1991 .... *160*
  Obituary *66*
  Earlier sketches in SATA *2, 68*
  See also CLR *37*
Beller, Susan Provost 1949- *128*
  Earlier sketch in SATA *84*
  See also CLR *106*
Bellingham, Brenda 1931- *99*
  Brief entry *51*
Bello, Rosario de
  See De Bello, Rosario
Belloc, Hilaire 1870-1953 .... *112*
  See also YABC *1*
  See also CLR *102*
Belloc, Joseph Hilaire Pierre Sebastien Rene
  Swanton
  See Belloc, Hilaire
Belloc, Joseph Peter Rene Hilaire
  See Belloc, Hilaire

Belloc, Joseph Pierre Hilaire
  See Belloc, Hilaire
Belloli, Andrea P. A. 1947- *86*
Bell-Rehwoldt, Sheri 1962- *199*
Bellville, Cheryl Walsh 1944- *54*
  Brief entry *49*
Bell-Zano, Gina
  See Balzano, Jeanne (Koppel)
Belpre, Pura 1899-1982 .... *16*
  Obituary *30*
Belting, Natalia Maree 1915-1997 .... *6*
Belton, John Raynor 1931- *22*
Belton, Sandra 1939- *186*
  Earlier sketches in SATA *85, 134*
Belton, Sandra Yvonne
  See Belton, Sandra
Belton, Sandra Yvonne
  See Belton, Sandra
Beltran, Alberto 1923- *43*
Beltran-Hernandez, Irene 1945- *74*
Belvedere, Lee
  See Grayland, Valerie (Merle Spanner)
Bemelmans, Ludwig 1898-1962 .... *100*
  Earlier sketch in SATA *15*
  See also CLR *93*
Benander, Carl D. 1941- *74*
Benary, Margot
  See Benary-Isbert, Margot
Benary-Isbert, Margot 1889-1979 .... *2*
  Obituary *21*
  See also CLR *12*
Benasutti, Marion 1908-1992 .... *6*
Benatar, Raquel 1955- *167*
Benchley, Nathaniel (Goddard) 1915-1981 .. *25*
  Obituary *28*
  Earlier sketch in SATA *3*
Benchley, Peter 1940-2006 .... *164*
  Earlier sketches in SATA *3, 89*
Benchley, Peter Bradford
  See Benchley, Peter
Bendall-Brunello, John *185*
Bender, Edna 1941- *92*
Bender, Esther 1942- *88*
Bender, Lucy Ellen 1942- *22*
Bender, Robert 1962- *160*
  Earlier sketch in SATA *79*
Bendick, Jeanne 1919- *135*
  Earlier sketches in SATA *2, 68*
  See also CLR *5*
  See also SAAS *4*
Bendick, Robert L(ouis) 1917- *11*
Benedetto, William R. 1928- *180*
Benedetto, William Ralph
  See Benedetto, William R.
Benedict, Andrew
  See Arthur, Robert, (Jr.)
Benedict, Dorothy Potter 1889-1979 .... *11*
  Obituary *23*
Benedict, Lois Trimble 1902-1967 .... *12*
Benedict, Rex 1920-1995 .... *8*
Benedict, Stewart H(urd) 1924- *26*
Beneduce, Ann Keay *128*
Benet, Laura 1884-1979 .... *3*
  Obituary *23*
Benet, Stephen Vincent 1898-1943
  See YABC *1*
Benet, Sula 1906-1982 .... *21*
  Obituary *33*
Ben-Ezer, Ehud 1936- *122*
Benezra, Barbara (Beardsley) 1921- *10*
Benham, Leslie 1922- *48*
Benham, Lois (Dakin) 1924- *48*
Benham, Mary Lile 1914-1991 .... *55*
Benjamin, E. M. J.
  See Bache, Ellyn
Benjamin, Floella 1949- *206*
Benjamin, Nora
  See Kubie, Nora Gottheil Benjamin
Benjamin, Saragail Katzman 1953- *86*
Benner, Cheryl 1962- *80*
Benner, Judith Ann 1942- *94*

Bennett, Alice
  See Ziner, Florence
Bennett, Cherie 1960- 158
  Earlier sketch in SATA 97
Bennett, Dorothea
  See Young, Dorothea Bennett
Bennett, Holly 1957- 181
Bennett, Holly 1957- 181
Bennett, James (W.) 1942- 153
  Autobiography Feature 153
  Earlier sketches in SATA 93, 148
Bennett, Jay 1912- 87
  Brief entry 27
  Earlier sketch in SATA 41
  See also SAAS 4
Bennett, Jill (Crawford) 1934- 41
Bennett, John 1865-1956
  See YABC 1
Bennett, Penelope (Agnes) 1938- 94
Bennett, Rachel
  See Hill, Margaret (Ohler)
Bennett, Rainey 1907-1998 15
  Obituary 111
Bennett, Richard 1899- 21
Bennett, Russell H(oradley) 1896- 25
Bennett, Veronica 1953- 178
Bennett, William (John) 1943- 102
Benning, Elizabeth
  See Rice, Bebe Faas
Benny, Mike 1964- 203
Benson, Elizabeth P(olk) 1924- 65
Benson, Kathleen 1947- 183
  Earlier sketches in SATA 62, 111
Benson, Linda M(aria) 1959- 84
Benson, Mildred 1905-2002 100
  Obituary 135
  Earlier sketches in SATA 1, 65, 67
Benson, Mildred Augustine Wirt
  See Benson, Mildred
Benson, Mildred Wirt
  See Benson, Mildred
Benson, Millie
  See Benson, Mildred
Benson, Patrick 1956- 147
Benson, Sally 1900-1972 35
  Obituary 27
  Earlier sketch in SATA 1
Bentley, Judith (McBride) 1945- 89
  Earlier sketch in SATA 40
Bentley, Karen
  See Taschek, Karen
Bentley, Nancy (L.) 1946- 78
Bentley, Nicolas Clerihew 1907-1978
  Obituary 24
Bentley, Phyllis Eleanor 1894-1977 6
  Obituary 25
Bentley, Roy 1947- 46
Bentley, William (George) 1916- 84
Benton, Jim 1963- 172
ben Uzair, Salem
  See Horne, Richard Henry Hengist
Bercaw, Edna Coe 1961- 124
Berck, Judith 1960- 75
Berelson, Howard 1940- 5
Berends, Polly Berrien 1939- 50
  Brief entry 38
Berenstain, Jan 1923- 135
  Earlier sketches in SATA 12, 64, 129
  See also CLR 19
  See also SAAS 20
Berenstain, Janice
  See Berenstain, Jan
Berenstain, Michael 1951- 45
Berenstain, Mike
  See Berenstain, Michael
Berenstain, Stan 1923-2005 135
  Obituary 169
  Earlier sketches in SATA 12, 64, 129
  See also CLR 19
  See also SAAS 20

Berenstain, Stanley
  See Berenstain, Stan
Berenzy, Alix 1957- 168
  Earlier sketch in SATA 65
Beresford, Elisabeth 1928- 141
  Earlier sketches in SATA 25, 86
  See also SAAS 20
Berg, Adriane G(ilda) 1948- 152
Berg, Dave
  See Berg, David
Berg, David 1920-2002 27
  Obituary 137
Berg, Elizabeth 1948- 104
Berg, Jean Horton 1913-1995 6
Berg, Joan
  See Victor, Joan Berg
Berg, Ron 1952- 48
Bergaust, Erik 1925-1978 20
Bergel, Colin J. 1963- 137
Bergen, Joyce 1949- 95
Berger, Barbara (Helen) 1945- 77
Berger, Carin 185
Berger, Gilda 1935- 88
  Brief entry 42
Berger, Josef 1903-1971 36
Berger, Melvin H. 1927- 158
  Autobiography Feature 124
  Earlier sketches in SATA 5, 88
  See also CLR 32
  See also SAAS 2
Berger, Phil 1942-2001 62
Berger, Samantha (Allison) 1969- 140
Berger, Terry 1933- 8
Bergey, Alyce (Mae) 1934- 45
Bergin, Mark 1961- 160
  Earlier sketch in SATA 114
Berglin, Ruth Marie 1970- 181
Bergman, Donna 1934- 73
Bergman, Mara 1956- 196
Bergman, Tamar 1939- 95
Bergren, Lisa T.
  See Bergren, Lisa Tawn
Bergren, Lisa Tawn 200
Bergsma, Jody Lynn 163
Bergum, Constance R. 1952- 121
Berkebile, Fred D(onovan) 1900-1978
  Obituary 26
Berkeley, Jon 1962- 204
Berkes, Marianne 173
Berkey, Barry Robert 1935- 24
Berkowitz, Freda Pastor 1908-1994 12
Berkus, Clara Widess 1909- 78
Berlan, Kathryn Hook 1946- 78
Berlfein, Judy Reiss 1958- 79
Berlin, Eric 195
Berliner, Don 1930- 33
Berliner, Franz 1930- 13
Berlitz, Charles (L. Frambach) 1914-2003 ... 32
  Obituary 151
Berman, Linda 1948- 38
Berman, Paul (Lawrence) 1949- 66
Berna, Paul 1910-1994 15
  Obituary 78
  See also CLR 19
Bernadette
  See Watts, (Anna) Bernadette
Bernard, Bruce 1928-2000 78
  Obituary 124
Bernard, George I. 1949- 39
Bernard, Jacqueline (de Sieyes) 1921-1983 ... 8
  Obituary 45
Bernard, Patricia 1942- 181
  Earlier sketch in SATA 106
Bernard, Trish
  See Bernard, Patricia
Bernardin, James (B.) 1966- 112
Bernardo, Anilu 184
Bernards, Neal 1963- 71
Bernasconi, Pablo 1973- 183
Bernays, Anne 1930- 32
Bernhard, Durga T. 1961- 80

Bernhard, Emery 1950- 80
Bernheimer, Kate 201
Bernier-Grand, Carmen T. 1947- 202
Bernstein, Daryl (Evan) 1976- 81
Bernstein, Joanne E(ckstein) 1943- 15
Bernstein, Margery 1933- 114
Bernstein, Nina 1949- 180
Bernstein, Theodore M(enline) 1904-1979 ... 12
  Obituary 27
Berrien, Edith Heal
  See Heal, Edith
Berrill, Jacquelyn (Batsel) 1905- 12
Berrington, John
  See Brownjohn, Alan
Berry, B. J.
  See Berry, Barbara J.
Berry, Barbara J. 1937- 7
Berry, Erick
  See Best, (Evangel) Allena Champlin
Berry, James 1924- 110
  Earlier sketch in SATA 67
  See also CLR 143
Berry, Jane Cobb 1915(?)-1979
  Obituary 22
Berry, Joy
  See Berry, Joy Wilt
Berry, Joy Wilt 1944- 58
  Brief entry 46
Berry, Lynne 190
Berry, William D(avid) 1926- 14
Bersani, Shennen 1961- 164
Berson, Harold 1926- 4
Bertagna, Julie 1962- 151
Bertholf, Bret 189
Bertin, Charles-Francois
  See Berlitz, Charles (L. Frambach)
Bertolet, Paul
  See McLaughlin, Frank
Berton, Pierre (Francis de Marigny)
  1920-2004 99
  Obituary 158
Bertrand, Cecile 1953- 76
Bertrand, Diane Gonzales 1956- 177
  Earlier sketch in SATA 106
Bertrand, Lynne 1963- 164
  Earlier sketch in SATA 81
Beskow, Elsa (Maartman) 1874-1953 20
  See also CLR 17
Bess, Clayton
  See Locke, Robert
Besson, Luc 1959- 199
Best, (Evangel) Allena Champlin 1892-1974 . 2
  Obituary 25
Best, Cari 1951- 200
  Earlier sketches in SATA 107, 149
Best, (Oswald) Herbert 1894-1980 2
Bestall, A(lfred) E(dmeades) 1892-1986 97
  Obituary 48
Betancourt, Jeanne 1941- 148
  Brief entry 43
  Earlier sketches in SATA 55, 96
Beth, Mary
  See Miller, Mary Beth
Bethancourt, T. Ernesto
  See Paisley, Tom
Bethel, Dell 1929- 52
Bethell, Jean (Frankenberry) 1922- 8
Bethers, Ray 1902-1973 6
Bethke, Bruce Raymond 1955- 114
Bethlen, T.D.
  See Silverberg, Robert
Bethune, J. G.
  See Ellis, Edward S.
Bethune, J. H.
  See Ellis, Edward S.
Betteridge, Anne
  See Potter, Margaret
Bettina
  See Ehrlich, Bettina Bauer
Bettmann, Otto Ludwig 1903-1998 46
Bettoli, Delana 187

Betts, James
  See Haynes, Betsy
Betz, Eva Kelly 1897-1968 .... *10*
Bevan, Tom 1868-1930(?)
  See YABC 2
Bevis, Mary 1939- *202*
Bewick, Thomas 1753-1828 .... *16*
Beyer, Audrey White 1916- *9*
Beyer, Paul J. III 1950- *74*
Beynon, John
  See Harris, John (Wyndham Parkes Lucas)
  Beynon
Bezencon, Jacqueline (Buxcel) 1924- *48*
Bhatia, Jamunadevi 1919- *48*
Bhatia, June
  See Bhatia, Jamunadevi
Bial, Morrison David 1917- *62*
Bial, Raymond 1948- *165*
  Earlier sketches in SATA *76, 116*
Biala
  See Brustlein, Janice Tworkov
Biale, Rachel 1952- *99*
Bialk, Elisa
  See Krautter, Elisa (Bialk)
Bianchi, John 1947- *91*
Bianchi, Robert S(teven) 1943- *92*
Bianco, Margery
  See Bianco, Margery Williams
Bianco, Margery Williams 1881-1944 .... *15*
  See also CLR *146*
Bianco, Pamela 1906- *28*
Bibby, Violet 1908-1996 .... *24*
Bible, Charles 1937- *13*
Bibo, Bobette
  See Gugliotta, Bobette
Bice, Clare 1909-1976 .... *22*
Bickerstaff, Isaac
  See Swift, Jonathan
Bidner, Jenni 1963- *193*
Biegel, Paul 1925- *79*
  Earlier sketch in SATA *16*
  See also CLR *27*
  See also SAAS *18*
Biemiller, Carl L(udwig), Jr.) 1912-1979 ..... *40*
  Obituary *21*
Bienenfeld, Florence L(ucille) 1929- *39*
Bierhorst, John (William) 1936- *149*
  Autobiography Feature *149*
  Earlier sketches in SATA *6, 91*
  See also SAAS *10*
Biggar, Joan R(awlins) 1936- *120*
Biggle, Lloyd, Jr. 1923-2002 .... *65*
Biggs, Brian 1968- *192*
Bilal, Abdel W(ahab) 1970- *92*
Bilbrough, Norman 1941- *111*
Bildner, Phil *173*
Bileck, Marvin 1920- *40*
Bilibin, Ivan (Iakolevich) 1876-1942 .... *61*
Bill, Alfred Hoyt 1879-1964 .... *44*
Billam, Rosemary 1952- *61*
Billings, Charlene W(interer) 1941- *41*
Billingsley, Franny 1954- *132*
Billington, Elizabeth T(hain) *50*
  Brief entry *43*
Billout, Guy (Rene) 1941- *144*
  Earlier sketch in SATA *10*
  See also CLR *33*
Bilson, Geoffrey 1938-1987 .... *99*
Binch, Caroline (Lesley) 1947- *140*
  Earlier sketch in SATA *81*
Bing, Christopher (H.) *126*
Bingham, Caroline 1962- *158*
Bingham, Jane M. 1941- *163*
Bingham, Jane Marie
  See Bingham, Jane M.
Bingham, Janet 1959- *200*
Bingham, Kelly 1967- *207*
Bingham, Sam(uel A.) 1944- *96*
Bingley, Margaret (Jane Kirby) 1947- *72*
Binkley, Anne
  See Rand, Ann (Binkley)

Binzen, Bill
  See Binzen, William
Binzen, William *24*
Birch, David (W.) 1913-1996 .... *89*
Birch, Reginald B(athurst) 1856-1943 .... *19*
Birchman, David 1949- *72*
Birchmore, Daniel A. 1951- *92*
Bird, Carmel 1940- *124*
Bird, E(lzy) J(ay) 1911- *58*
Birdsall, Jeanne 1952(?)- *170*
Birdseye, Tom 1951- *148*
  Earlier sketches in SATA *66, 98*
Birenbaum, Barbara 1941- *65*
Birmingham, Lloyd P(aul) 1924- *83*
  Earlier sketch in SATA *12*
Birmingham, Ruth
  See Sorrells, Walter
Birney, Betty G. 1947- *169*
  Earlier sketch in SATA *98*
Biro, B.
  See Biro, B. S.
Biro, B. S. 1921- *1*
  See also CLR *28*
  See also SAAS *13*
Biro, Val
  See Biro, B. S.
Bischoff, Julia Bristol 1899-1970 .... *12*
Bishop, Bonnie 1943- *37*
Bishop, Claire Huchet 1899(?)-1993 .... *14*
  Obituary *74*
  See also CLR *80*
Bishop, Courtney
  See Ruemmler, John D(avid)
Bishop, Curtis (Kent) 1912-1967 .... *6*
Bishop, Elizabeth 1911-1979
  Obituary *24*
Bishop, Gavin 1946- *144*
  Earlier sketch in SATA *97*
Bishop, Kathleen Wong 1954- *120*
Bishop, Kathy
  See Bishop, Kathleen Wong
Bishop, Nic 1955- *161*
  Earlier sketch in SATA *107*
Bisset, Donald 1910-1995 .... *86*
  Earlier sketch in SATA *7*
Bisson, Terry 1942- *99*
Bisson, Terry Ballantine
  See Bisson, Terry
Bitter, Gary G(len) 1940- *22*
Bixby, William (Courtney) 1920-1986 .... *6*
  Obituary *47*
Bjoerk, Christina 1938- *99*
  Earlier sketch in SATA *67*
  See also CLR *22*
Bjork, Christina
  See Bjoerk, Christina
Bjorklund, Lorence F. 1913-1978 .... *35*
  Brief entry *32*
Bjorkman, Steve *163*
Black, Algernon David 1900-1993 .... *12*
  Obituary *76*
Black, Holly 1971- *147*
Black, Irma Simonton 1906-1972 .... *2*
  Obituary *25*
Black, Mansell
  See Trevor, Elleston
Black, MaryAnn
  See Easley, MaryAnn
Black, Susan Adams 1953- *40*
Blackall, Bernie 1956- *126*
Blackall, Sophie *182*
Blackburn, Claire
  See Altman, Linda Jacobs
Blackburn, John(ny) Brewton 1952- *15*
Blackburn, Joyce Knight 1920- *29*
Blacker, Terence 1948- *194*
Blacker, Tina
  See Louise, Tina
Blackett, Veronica Heath 1927- *12*
Blackie, Jean Cutler 1943- *79*

Blacklin, Malcolm
  See Chambers, Aidan
Blacklock, Dyan 1951- *112*
Blackman, Malorie 1962- *196*
  Earlier sketches in SATA *83, 128*
Blackton, Peter
  See Wilson, Lionel
Blackwood, Alan 1932- *70*
Blackwood, Freya *199*
Blackwood, Gary L. 1945- *169*
  Earlier sketches in SATA *72, 118*
Blade, Alexander
  See Garrett, Randall
  and Hamilton, Edmond
  and Silverberg, Robert
Blades, Ann (Sager) 1947- *69*
  Earlier sketch in SATA *16*
  See also CLR *15*
Bladow, Suzanne Wilson 1937- *14*
Blaine, Chris
  See Gardner, Craig Shaw
Blaine, John
  See Goodwin, Harold L(eland)
Blaine, Marge
  See Blaine, Margery Kay
Blaine, Margery Kay 1937- *11*
Blair, Alison
  See Lerangis, Peter
Blair, Anne Denton 1914-1993 .... *46*
Blair, David Nelson 1954- *80*
Blair, Eric
  See Orwell, George
Blair, Jay 1953- *45*
Blair, Lucile
  See Yeakley, Marjory Hall
Blair, Margaret Whitman 1951- *124*
Blair, Mary 1911-1978 .... *195*
Blair, Pauline Hunter
  See Clarke, Pauline
Blair, Ruth Van Ness 1912-1999 .... *12*
Blair, Shannon
  See Kaye, Marilyn
Blair, Walter 1900-1992 .... *12*
  Obituary *72*
Blaisdell, Bob
  See Blaisdell, Robert
Blaisdell, Robert 1959- *105*
Blake, Bronwyn 1940- *149*
Blake, Francis *198*
Blake, Jon 1954- *171*
  Earlier sketch in SATA *78*
Blake, Olive
  See Supraner, Robyn
Blake, Quentin (Saxby) 1932- *125*
  Earlier sketches in SATA *9, 52, 96*
  See also CLR *31*
Blake, Robert 1949- *42*
Blake, Robert J. *160*
Blake, Walker E.
  See Griffin, W.E.B.
Blake, William 1757-1827 .... *30*
  See also CLR *52*
Blakely, Gloria 1950- *139*
Blakely, Roger K. 1922- *82*
Blakeney, Jay D.
  See Chester, Deborah
Blakey, Nancy 1955- *94*
Blanc, Esther S. 1913-1997 .... *66*
Blanc, Mel 1908-1989
  Obituary *64*
Blanchard, Patricia *125*
Blanchet, M(uriel) Wylie 1891-1961 .... *106*
Blanco, Richard L(idio) 1926- *63*
Bland, E.
  See Nesbit, E.
Bland, Edith Nesbit
  See Nesbit, E.
Bland, Fabian
  See Nesbit, E.
Blane, Gertrude
  See Blumenthal, Gertrude

Blank, Clarissa Mabel 1915-1965 .... *62*
Blankenship, LeeAnn 1944- *181*
Blassingame, Wyatt Rainey 1909-1985 .... *34*
    Obituary *41*
    Earlier sketch in SATA *1*
Blatchford, Claire H. 1944- *94*
Blauer, Ettagale 1940- *49*
Bleck, Linda *207*
Bledsoe, Glen L. 1951- *108*
Bledsoe, Glen Leonard
    See Bledsoe, Glen L.
Bledsoe, Karen E. 1962- *167*
    Earlier sketch in SATA *108*
Bledsoe, Karen Elizabeth
    See Bledsoe, Karen E.
Bledsoe, Lucy Jane 1957- *162*
    Earlier sketch in SATA *97*
Bleeker, Sonia
    See Zim, Sonia Bleeker
Blegen, Daniel M. 1950- *92*
Blegvad, Erik 1923- *132*
    Earlier sketches in SATA *14, 66*
Blegvad, Lenore 1926- *176*
    Earlier sketches in SATA *14, 66*
Bley, Anette 1967- *188*
Blish, James 1921-1975 .... *66*
Blish, James Benjamin
    See Blish, James
Blishen, Edward (William) 1920-1996 .... *66*
    Obituary *93*
    Earlier sketch in SATA *8*
Bliss, Corinne Demas 1947- *131*
    Earlier sketch in SATA *37*
    See Demas, Corinne
Bliss, Frederick
    See Card, Orson Scott
Bliss, Gillian
    See Paton Walsh, Jill
Bliss, Harry 1964- *196*
    Earlier sketch in SATA *156*
Bliss, Reginald
    See Wells, H. G.
Bliss, Ronald G(ene) 1942- *12*
Blitt, Barry *187*
Bliven, Bruce, Jr. 1916-2002 .... *2*
Blixen, Karen 1885-1962 .... *44*
Blizzard, Gladys S. (?)-1992 .... *79*
Blobaum, Cindy 1966- *123*
Bloch, Lucienne 1909-1999 .... *10*
Bloch, Marie Halun 1910-1998 .... *6*
    See also SAAS *9*
Bloch, Robert (Albert) 1917-1994 .... *12*
    Obituary *82*
Blochman, Lawrence G(oldtree)
    1900-1975 .... *22*
Block, Francesca Lia 1962- *158*
    Earlier sketches in SATA *80, 116*
    See also CLR *116*
    See also SAAS *21*
Block, Irvin 1917- *12*
Blomgren, Jennifer (Alice) 1954- *136*
Blood, Charles Lewis 1929- *28*
Bloom, Barbara Lee 1943- *146*
Bloom, Freddy 1914-2000 .... *37*
    Obituary *121*
Bloom, Lloyd 1947- *108*
    Brief entry *43*
Bloom, Suzanne 1950- *172*
Bloomfield, Michaela 1966- *70*
Bloor, Edward 1950- *201*
    Earlier sketches in SATA *98, 155*
Bloor, Edward William
    See Bloor, Edward
Blos, Joan W. 1928- *153*
    Autobiography Feature *153*
    Brief entry *27*
    Earlier sketches in SATA *33, 69, 109*
    See also CLR *18*
    See also SAAS *11*
Blos, Joan Winsor
    See Blos, Joan W.

Blough, Glenn O(rlando) 1907-1995 .... *1*
Blue, Rose 1931- *166*
    Autobiography Feature *117*
    Earlier sketches in SATA *5, 91, 93*
    See also SAAS *24*
Blue, Zachary
    See Stine, R.L.
Bluggage, Oranthy
    See Alcott, Louisa May
Blumberg, Leda 1956- *59*
Blumberg, Rhoda 1917- *123*
    Earlier sketches in SATA *35, 70*
    See also CLR *21*
Blume, Judy 1938- *195*
    Earlier sketches in SATA *2, 31, 79, 142*
    See also CLR *69*
Blume, Judy Sussman
    See Blume, Judy
Blume, Lesley M.M. 1975- *180*
Blumenthal, Deborah *204*
    Earlier sketch in SATA *161*
Blumenthal, Gertrude 1907-1971
    Obituary *27*
Blumenthal, Shirley 1943- *46*
Blutig, Eduard
    See Gorey, Edward (St. John)
Bly, Janet (Chester) 1945- *43*
Bly, Stephen A(rthur) 1944- *116*
    Earlier sketch in SATA *43*
Blyler, Allison Lee 1966- *74*
Blythe, Gary 1959- *185*
Blyton, Carey 1932-2002 .... *9*
    Obituary *138*
Blyton, Enid 1897-1968 .... *25*
    See also CLR *31*
Blyton, Enid Mary
    See Blyton, Enid
Bo, Ben
    See Richardson, V.A.
Boardman, Fon Wyman, Jr. 1911-2000 .... *6*
Boardman, Gwenn R.
    See Petersen, Gwenn Boardman
Boase, Wendy 1944-1999 .... *28*
    Obituary *110*
Boatner, Mark Mayo III 1921- *29*
Bobbe, Dorothie de Bear 1905-1975 .... *1*
    Obituary *25*
Bober, Natalie S. 1930- *134*
    Earlier sketch in SATA *87*
    See also SAAS *23*
Bobette, Bibo
    See Gugliotta, Bobette
Bobri, Vladimir V. 1898-1986 .... *47*
    Brief entry *32*
Bobritsky, Vladimir
    See Bobri, Vladimir V.
Bochak, Grayce 1956- *76*
Bock, Hal
    See Bock, Harold I.
Bock, Harold I. 1939- *10*
Bock, William Sauts Netamux'we 1939- *14*
Bodanis, David *179*
Bode, Janet 1943-1999 .... *96*
    Obituary *118*
    Earlier sketch in SATA *60*
Bode, N.E.
    See Baggott, Julianna
Bodecker, N(iels) M(ogens) 1922-1988 .... *73*
    Obituary *54*
    Earlier sketch in SATA *8*
Boden, Hilda
    See Bodenham, Hilda Morris
Bodenham, Hilda Morris 1901- *13*
Bodett, Thomas Edward 1955- *70*
Bodett, Tom
    See Bodett, Thomas Edward
Bodie, Idella F(allaw) 1925- *89*
    Earlier sketch in SATA *12*
Bodker, Cecil
    See Bodker, Cecil

Bodker, Cecil 1927- *133*
    Earlier sketch in SATA *14*
    See also CLR *23*
Bodsworth, (Charles) Fred(erick) 1918- *27*
Boeckman, Charles 1920- *12*
Boegehold, Betty (Doyle) 1913-1985
    Obituary *42*
Boelts, Maribeth 1964- *200*
    Earlier sketches in SATA *78, 163*
Boerst, William J. 1939- *170*
    Earlier sketch in SATA *121*
Boesch, Mark J(oseph) 1917- *12*
Boesen, Victor 1908- *16*
Bogacki, Tomek 1950- *138*
Bogaerts, Gert 1965- *80*
Bogan, Paulette 1960- *201*
    Earlier sketch in SATA *129*
Bogart, Jo Ellen 1945- *92*
    See also CLR *59*
Boggs, Ralph Steele 1901-1994 .... *7*
Bograd, Larry 1953- *89*
    Earlier sketch in SATA *33*
    See also SAAS *21*
Bogue, Gary 1938- *195*
Bogue, Gary L.
    See Bogue, Gary
Bohdal, Susi 1951- *101*
    Earlier sketch in SATA *22*
Bohlen, Nina 1931- *58*
Bohlmeijer, Arno 1956- *94*
Bohner, Charles (Henry) 1927- *62*
Bohnhoff, Maya Kaathryn 1954- *88*
Boiger, Alexandra *178*
Boissard, Janine 1932- *59*
Bojunga, Lygia
    See Nunes, Lygia Bojunga
Bojunga-Nunes, Lygia
    See Nunes, Lygia Bojunga
Bok, Arthur
    See Bok, Chip
Bok, Chip 1952- *205*
Bolam, Emily 1969- *206*
Boland, Janice *98*
Bolden, Tonya 1959- *188*
    Earlier sketches in SATA *79, 138*
Bolden, Tonya Wilyce
    See Bolden, Tonya
Boles, Paul Darcy 1916-1984 .... *9*
    Obituary *38*
Bolian, Polly 1925- *4*
Bollen, Roger 1941(?)- *83*
    Brief entry *29*
Bolliger, Max 1929- *7*
Bollinger, Max 1929- *167*
Bollinger, Peter *172*
Bolognese, Don(ald Alan) 1934- *129*
    Earlier sketches in SATA *24, 71*
Bolognese, Elaine 1933- *23*
Bolotin, Norman (Phillip) 1951- *93*
Bolton, Carole 1926- *6*
Bolton, Elizabeth
    See St. John, Nicole
Bolton, Evelyn
    See Bunting, Eve
Bonar, Veronica
    See Bailey, Donna (Veronica Anne)
Bond, B. J.
    See Heneghan, James
Bond, Bruce 1939- *61*
Bond, Felicia 1954- *126*
    Earlier sketch in SATA *49*
Bond, Gladys Baker 1912- *14*
Bond, Higgins 1951- *177*
    Earlier sketch in SATA *83*
Bond, J. Harvey
    See Winterbotham, R(ussell) R(obert)
Bond, (Thomas) Michael 1926- *157*
    Earlier sketches in SATA *6, 58*
    See also CLR *95*
    See also SAAS *3*

Bond, Nancy 1945- *159*
  Autobiography Feature *159*
  Earlier sketches in SATA *22, 82*
  See also CLR *11*
  See also SAAS *13*
Bond, Nancy Barbara
  See Bond, Nancy
Bond, Rebecca 1972- *130*
Bond, Ruskin 1934- *87*
  Earlier sketch in SATA *14*
Bondie, J. D.
  See Cunningham, Chet
Bondoux, Anne-Laure 1971- *175*
Bone, Ian 1956- *158*
  Earlier sketch in SATA *117*
Bonehill, Captain Ralph
  See Stratemeyer, Edward L.
Bonestell, Chesley 1888-1986
  Obituary *48*
Bonham, Barbara Thomas 1926- *7*
Bonham, Frank 1914-1989 .... *49*
  Obituary *62*
  Earlier sketch in SATA *1*
  See also SAAS *3*
Boniface, William 1963- *182*
  Earlier sketch in SATA *102*
Bonino, Louise
  See Williams, Louise Bonino
Bonk, John J. *189*
Bonn, Pat
  See Bonn, Patricia Carolyn
Bonn, Patricia Carolyn 1948- *43*
Bonner, Hannah *197*
Bonner, Mary Graham 1890-1974 .... *19*
Bonner, Mike 1951- *121*
Bonners, Susan 1947- *85*
  Brief entry *48*
Bonnett-Rampersaud, Louise *173*
Bonning, Tony 1948- *169*
Bonsall, Crosby Barbara (Newell)
  1921-1995 .... *23*
  Obituary *84*
Bonsall, Joseph S. 1948- *119*
Bonsignore, Joan 1959- *140*
Bontemps, Arna 1902-1973 .... *44*
  Obituary *24*
  Earlier sketch in SATA *2*
  See also CLR *6*
Bontemps, Arnaud Wendell
  See Bontemps, Arna
Bonzon, Paul-Jacques 1908-1978 .... *22*
Boock, Paula 1964- *134*
Booher, Dianna Daniels 1948- *33*
Book, Rick 1949- *119*
Book, Rita
  See Holub, Joan
Bookman, Charlotte
  See Zolotow, Charlotte
Boon, Debbie 1960- *103*
Boon, Emilie (Laetitia) 1958- *86*
Boone, Charles Eugene
  See Boone, Pat
Boone, Pat 1934- *7*
Boorman, Linda (Kay) 1940- *46*
Boorstin, Daniel J(oseph) 1914-2004 .... *52*
Boos, Ben 1971- *206*
Booth, Coe *187*
Booth, Ernest Sheldon 1915-1984 .... *43*
Booth, George 1926- *191*
Booth, Graham (Charles) 1935- *37*
Bootman, Colin *159*
Borden, Louise 1949- *190*
  Autobiography Feature *141*
  Earlier sketches in SATA *68, 104, 141*
Bordier, Georgette 1924- *16*
Borgman, James
  See Borgman, Jim
Borgman, James Mark
  See Borgman, Jim
Borgman, Jim 1954- *122*
Borgo, Lacy Finn 1972- *194*

Boring, Mel 1939- *168*
  Earlier sketch in SATA *35*
Borja, Corinne 1929- *22*
Borja, Robert 1923- *22*
Borland, Hal
  See Borland, Harold Glen
Borland, Harold Glen 1900-1978 .... *5*
  Obituary *24*
Borland, Kathryn Kilby 1916- *16*
Borlenghi, Patricia 1951- *79*
Born, Adolf 1930- *49*
Bornstein, Ruth Lercher
  See Bornstein-Lercher, Ruth
Bornstein-Lercher, Ruth 1927- *88*
  Autobiography Feature *107*
  Earlier sketch in SATA *14*
Borski, Lucia Merecka *18*
Borten, Helen Jacobson 1930- *5*
Bortolotti, Dan 1969- *157*
Borton, Elizabeth
  See Trevino, Elizabeth B(orton) de
Borton, Lady 1942- *98*
Borton de Trevino, Elizabeth
  See Trevino, Elizabeth B(orton) de
Bortstein, Larry 1942- *16*
Bortz, Alfred B(enjamin) 1944- *139*
  Earlier sketch in SATA *74*
Bortz, Fred
  See Bortz, Alfred B(enjamin)
Bosch, Pseudonymous *199*
Bosco, Jack
  See Holliday, Joseph
Boshell, Gordon 1908-1991 .... *15*
Boshinski, Blanche 1922- *10*
Bosman, Paul 1929- *107*
Bosse, Malcolm (Joseph, Jr.) 1926-2002 .... *136*
  Earlier sketch in SATA *35*
Bosserman, (Charles) Phillip 1931- *84*
Bossom, Naomi 1933- *35*
Bostock, Mike 1962- *114*
Boston, L(ucy) M(aria Wood) 1892-1990 .... *19*
  Obituary *64*
  See also CLR *3*
Bostrom, Kathleen (Susan) Long 1954- *139*
Bostrom, Kathy
  See Bostrom, Kathleen (Susan) Long
Bosworth, J. Allan 1925- *19*
Bothwell, Jean (?)-1977 .... *2*
Botkin, B(enjamin) A(lbert) 1901-1975 .... *40*
Botsford, Ward 1927-2004 .... *66*
Botting, Douglas (Scott) 1934- *43*
Bottner, Barbara 1943- *170*
  Autobiography Feature *121*
  Earlier sketches in SATA *14, 93*
  See also SAAS *26*
Bottone, Frank G., Jr. 1969- *141*
Bouchard, David 1952- *117*
Boucher, (Clarence) Carter 1954- *129*
Boudelang, Bob
  See Pell, Ed(ward)
Boughton, Richard 1954- *75*
Boulet, Susan Seddon 1941- *50*
Boulle, Pierre (Francois Marie-Louis)
  1912-1994 .... *22*
  Obituary *78*
Boulton, Jane 1921- *91*
Bouma, Paddy 1947- *128*
Bour, Daniele 1939- *62*
Bourbonniere, Sylvie 1966- *182*
Bourdon, David 1934-1998 .... *46*
Bourgeois, Paulette 1951- *153*
Bourne, Lesley
  See Marshall, Evelyn
Bourne, Miriam Anne 1931-1989 .... *16*
  Obituary *63*
Boutavant, Marc 1970- *200*
Boutet de Monvel, (Louis) M(aurice)
  1850(?)-1913 .... *30*
  See also CLR *32*

Bova, Ben 1932- *133*
  Earlier sketches in SATA *6, 68*
  See also CLR *96*
Bova, Benjamin William
  See Bova, Ben
Bovaird, Anne E(lizabeth) 1960- *90*
Bow, Patricia 1946- *168*
Bowden, Joan Chase 1925- *51*
  Brief entry *38*
Bowe, Julie 1962- *194*
Bowen, Alexandria Russell *97*
Bowen, Andy Russell
  See Bowen, Alexandria Russell
Bowen, Anne 1952- *202*
  Earlier sketch in SATA *170*
Bowen, Betty Morgan
  See West, Betty
Bowen, Catherine (Shober) Drinker
  1897-1973 .... *7*
Bowen, David
  See Bowen, Joshua David
Bowen, Fred 1953- *136*
Bowen, Joshua David 1930- *22*
Bowen, Rhys
  See Quin-Harkin, Janet
Bowen, Robert Sydney 1900-1977 .... *52*
  Obituary *21*
Bowermaster, Jon 1954- *135*
  Earlier sketch in SATA *77*
Bowers, Terrell L. 1945- *101*
Bowers, Terry
  See Bowers, Terrell L.
Bowers, Tim *185*
Bowie, C. W.
  See Old, Wendie C(orbin)
  and Wirths, Claudine (Turner) G(ibson)
Bowie, Jim
  See Norwood, Victor G(eorge) C(harles)
  and Stratemeyer, Edward L.
Bowkett, Stephen 1953- *67*
Bowler, Jan Brett
  See Brett, Jan
Bowler, Tim 1953- *149*
Bowman, Catherine
  See Smith, Cat Bowman
Bowman, Crystal 1951- *105*
Bowman, James Cloyd 1880-1961 .... *23*
Bowman, John S(tewart) 1931- *16*
Bowman, Kathleen (Gill) 1942- *52*
  Brief entry *40*
Bowman, Leslie
  See Bowman, Leslie W.
Bowman, Leslie W. *182*
Bowsher, Melodie *195*
Boxall, Ed *178*
Boyce, Frank Cottrell *182*
Boyce, George A(rthur) 1898- *19*
Boyd, Candy Dawson 1946- *72*
  See also CLR *50*
Boyd, Pauline
  See Schock, Pauline
Boyd, Selma
  See Acuff, Selma Boyd
Boyd, Waldo T. 1918- *18*
Boyden, Linda 1948- *143*
Boyer, Allen B. 1963- *153*
Boyer, Robert E(rnst) 1929- *22*
Boyes, Vivien 1952- *106*
Boyes, Vivien Elizabeth
  See Boyes, Vivien
Boyle, Ann (Peters) 1916- *10*
Boyle, Eleanor Vere (Gordon) 1825-1916 .... *28*
Boyle, Robert H. 1928- *65*
Boylston, Helen Dore 1895-1984 .... *23*
  Obituary *39*
Boyne, John 1971- *181*
Boynton, Sandra (Keith) 1953- *152*
  Brief entry *38*
  Earlier sketches in SATA *57, 107*
  See also CLR *105*

Boz
See Dickens, Charles
Braasch, Gary 201
Bracken, Charles
See Pellowski, Michael (Joseph)
Brackers de Hugo, Pierre 1960- 115
Brackett, Dolli Tingle 1911-1993 137
Brackett, Virginia 1950- 166
Earlier sketch in SATA 121
Brackett, Virginia Roberts Meredith
See Brackett, Virginia
Bradbury, Bianca (Ryley) 1908-1982 56
Earlier sketch in SATA 3
Bradbury, Edward P.
See Moorcock, Michael
Bradbury, Ray 1920- 123
Earlier sketches in SATA 11, 64
Bradbury, Ray Douglas
See Bradbury, Ray
Bradby, Marie 161
Bradfield, Carl 1942- 91
Bradford, Ann (Liddell) 1917- 56
Brief entry 38
Bradford, Barbara Taylor 1933- 66
Bradford, Karleen 1936- 96
Earlier sketch in SATA 48
Bradford, Lois J(ean) 1936- 36
Bradford, Richard (Roark) 1932-2002 59
Obituary 135
Bradley, Duane
See Sanborn, Duane
Bradley, Kimberly Brubaker 1967- 179
Bradley, Marion Zimmer 1930-1999 139
Obituary 116
Earlier sketch in SATA 90
Bradley, Timothy J. 193
Bradley, Virginia 1912- 23
Bradley, Will
See Strickland, Brad
Bradman, Tony 1954- 152
Earlier sketch in SATA 81
Bradshaw, Gillian (Joan) 1949- 118
Bradshaw, Gillian 1956- 127
Bradshaw, Gillian Marucha
See Bradshaw, Gillian
Bradstreet, T. J.
See Thesman, Jean
Brady, Esther Wood 1905-1987 31
Obituary 53
Brady, Irene 1943- 4
Brady, Kimberley S. 1953- 101
Brady, Kimberley Smith
See Brady, Kimberley S.
Brady, Lillian 1902- 28
Bragdon, Elspeth MacDuffie 1897-1980 6
Bragdon, Lillian Jacot 24
Brager, Bruce L. 1949- 146
Bragg, Mabel Caroline 1870-1945 24
Bragg, Michael 1948- 46
Bragg, Ruth Gembicki 1943- 77
Brahm, Sumishta 1954- 58
Brailsford, Frances
See Wosmek, Frances
Brainerd, John W(hiting) 1918- 65
Braithwaite, Althea 1940- 23
Autobiography Feature 119
See also SAAS 24
Bram, Elizabeth 1948- 30
Brancato, Robin F(idler) 1936- 97
See also CLR 32
See also SAAS 9
Branch, Muriel Miller 1943- 152
Earlier sketch in SATA 94
Brand, Christianna
See Lewis, Mary
Brand, Rebecca
See Charnas, Suzy McKee
Brande, Robin 194
Brandel, Marc 1919- 71
Brandenberg, Alexa (Demetria) 1966- 97

Brandenberg, Aliki 1929- 157
Earlier sketches in SATA 2, 35, 75, 113
See also CLR 71
Brandenberg, Franz 1932- 75
Earlier sketches in SATA 8, 35
Brandenburg, Jim 1945- 87
Brandhorst, Carl T(heodore) 1898-1988 23
Brandis, Marianne 1938- 149
Earlier sketches in SATA 59, 96
Brandon, Brumsic, Jr. 1927- 9
Brandon, Curt
See Bishop, Curtis (Kent)
Brandreth, Gyles 1948- 28
Brandreth, Gyles Daubeney
See Brandreth, Gyles
Brandt, Catharine 1905-1997 40
Brandt, Keith
See Sabin, Louis
Brandt, Sue R(eading) 1916- 59
Branfield, John (Charles) 1931- 11
Branford, Henrietta 1946-1999 106
Branley, Franklyn M(ansfield) 1915-2002 .. 136
Earlier sketches in SATA 4, 68
See also CLR 13
See also SAAS 16
Brannen, Sarah S. 202
Branscum, Robbie (Tilley) 1937-1997 72
Obituary 96
Earlier sketch in SATA 23
See also SAAS 17
Bransom, (John) Paul 1885-1979 43
Brashares, Ann 1967- 188
Earlier sketch in SATA 145
See also CLR 113
Brassard, France 1963- 186
Braswell, E.J.
See Lynn, Tracy
Braswell, Elizabeth J.
See Lynn, Tracy
Braswell, Liz
See Lynn, Tracy
Bratton, Helen 1899-1986 4
Bratun, Katy 1950- 160
Earlier sketch in SATA 83
Braude, Michael 1936- 23
Braun, Lilian Jackson 1916(?)- 109
Brautigan, Richard 1935-1984 56
Brautigan, Richard Gary
See Brautigan, Richard
Bray, Libba 203
Earlier sketch in SATA 159
Bray, Martha E.
See Bray, Libba
Braymer, Marjorie Elizabeth 1911-1988 6
Breathed, Berke 1957- 161
Earlier sketch in SATA 86
Breathed, Guy Berkeley
See Breathed, Berke
Brecht, Edith 1895-1975 6
Obituary 25
Breck, Vivian
See Breckenfeld, Vivian Gurney
Breckenfeld, Vivian Gurney 1895-1992 1
Breda, Tjalmar
See DeJong, David C(ornel)
Bredeson, Carmen 1944- 163
Earlier sketch in SATA 98
Breen, Steve 1970- 186
Breinburg, Petronella 1927- 11
See also CLR 31
Breisky, William J(ohn) 1928- 22
Brenaman, Miriam 172
Brennan, Caitlin
See Tarr, Judith
Brennan, Gale (Patrick) 1927- 64
Brief entry 53
Brennan, Herbie 1940- 183
Earlier sketch in SATA 140
Brennan, James Herbert
See Brennan, Herbie

Brennan, Jan
See Brennan, Herbie
Brennan, J.H.
See Brennan, Herbie
Brennan, Joseph Lomas 1903-2000 6
Brennan, Linda Crotta 1952- 130
Brennan, Tim
See Conroy, John Wesley
Brennan-Nelson, Denise 203
Brenner, Anita 1905-1974 56
Brenner, Barbara (Johnes) 1925- 124
Earlier sketches in SATA 4, 42, 76
See also SAAS 14
Brenner, Fred 1920- 36
Brief entry 34
Brent, Hope 1935(?)-1984
Obituary 39
Brent, Stuart 14
Breskin, Jane
See Zalben, Jane Breskin
Breslin, Theresa 128
Autobiography Feature 128
Earlier sketch in SATA 70
Breslow, Maurice 1935- 72
Breslow, Maurice A
See Breslow, Maurice
Breslow, Susan 1951- 69
Brett, Bernard 1925- 22
Brett, Grace N(eff) 1900-1975 23
Brett, Jan 1949- 171
Earlier sketches in SATA 42, 71, 130
See also CLR 27
Brett, Jan Churchill
See Brett, Jan
Brett Bowler, Jan
See Brett, Jan
Brewer, Heather 1973- 196
Brewer, James D. 1951- 108
Brewer, Sally King 1947- 33
Brewster, Benjamin
See Folsom, Franklin (Brewster)
Brewster, Hugh 1950- 191
Earlier sketch in SATA 95
Brewster, Patience 1952- 97
Brewton, John E(dmund) 1898-1982 5
Brian, Janeen (Paulette) 1948- 141
Briant, Ed 180
Brick, John 1922-1973 10
Brickman, Robin D. 1954- 155
Bride, Nadja
See Nobisso, Josephine
Bridgers, Sue Ellen 1942- 90
Autobiography Feature 109
Earlier sketch in SATA 22
See also CLR 18
See also SAAS 1
Bridges, Laurie
See Bruck, Lorraine
Bridges, Ruby (Nell) 1954- 131
Bridges, William (Andrew) 1901-1984 5
Bridwell, Norman (Ray) 1928- 138
Earlier sketches in SATA 4, 68
See also CLR 96
Brier, Howard M(axwell) 1903-1969 8
Brierley, (Louise) 1958- 59
Briggs, Katharine Mary 1898-1980 101
Obituary 25
Briggs, Peter 1921-1975 39
Obituary 31
Briggs, Raymond 1934- 184
Earlier sketches in SATA 23, 66, 131
See also CLR 10
Briggs, Raymond Redvers
See Briggs, Raymond
Bright, Paul 1949- 182
Bright, Robert Sr.) 1902-1988 63
Obituary 60
Earlier sketch in SATA 24
Bright, Robert Douglas
See Bright, Robert Sr.)

Bright, Sarah
  See Shine, Deborah
Brightfield, Richard 1927- 65
  Brief entry 53
Brightfield, Rick
  See Brightfield, Richard
Brighton, Catherine 1943- 206
  Earlier sketches in SATA 65, 107
Brill, Marlene Targ 1945- 124
  Earlier sketch in SATA 77
Brimberg, Stanlee 1947- 9
Brimner, Larry Dane 1949- 170
  Autobiography Feature 112
  Earlier sketch in SATA 79
Brin, David 1950- 65
Brin, Ruth Firestone 1921- 22
Brinckloe, Julie 1950- 13
Brinckloe, Julie Lorraine
  See Brinckloe, Julie
Brindel, June (Rachuy) 1919- 7
Brindle, Max
  See Fleischman, Sid
Brindze, Ruth 1903-1984 23
Brink, Carol Ryrie 1895-1981 100
  Obituary 27
  Earlier sketches in SATA 1, 31
  See also CLR 149
Brinsmead, H. F(ay)
  See Brinsmead, H(esba) F(ay)
Brinsmead, H. F.
  See Brinsmead, H(esba) F(ay)
Brinsmead, H(esba) F(ay) 1922- 78
  Earlier sketch in SATA 18
  See also CLR 47
  See also SAAS 5
Briquebec, John
  See Rowland-Entwistle, (Arthur) Theodore
  (Henry)
Brisbane, Henry R.
  See Ellis, Edward S.
Brisco, P. A.
  See Matthews, Patricia
Brisco, Patty
  See Matthews, Patricia
  and Matthews, Clayton (Hartley)
Briscoe, Jill (Pauline) 1935- 56
  Brief entry 47
Brisley, Joyce Lankester 1896-1978 22
  Obituary 84
Brissenden, Connie
  See Brissenden, Constance
Brissenden, Constance 1947- 150
Brisson, Pat 1951- 177
  Autobiography Feature 133
  Earlier sketches in SATA 67, 128, 133
Britt, Albert 1874-1969
  Obituary 28
Britt, Dell 1934- 1
Brittain, Bill
  See Brittain, William
Brittain, C. Dale 1948- 82
Brittain, William 1930- 76
  Earlier sketch in SATA 36
  See also SAAS 7
Brittingham, Geoffrey (Hugh) 1959- 76
Britton, Kate
  See Stegeman, Janet Allais
Britton, Louisa
  See McGuire, Leslie (Sarah)
Britton, Rick 1952- 82
Bro, Margueritte (Harmon) 1894-1977 19
  Obituary 27
Broach, Elise 1963- 173
Broadhead, Helen Cross 1913- 25
Brochmann, Elizabeth 1938- 41
Brock, Betty (Carter) 1923-2003 4
  Obituary 150
Brock, C(harles) E(dmund) 1870-1938 42
  Brief entry 32
Brock, Delia
  See Ephron, Delia

Brock, Emma L(illian) 1886-1974 8
Brock, H(enry) M(atthew) 1875-1960 42
Brockett, Eleanor Hall 1913-1967 10
Brockman, C(hristian) Frank 1902-1985 26
Brockmeier, Kevin 1972- 176
Broderick, Dorothy M. 1929- 5
Brodeur, Ruth Wallace
  See Wallace-Brodeur, Ruth
Brodie, Sally
  See Cavin, Ruth (Brodie)
Brodsky, Beverly
  See McDermott, Beverly Brodsky
Brody, Wendy
  See Staub, Wendy Corsi
Broeger, Achim 1944- 31
Broekel, Rainer Lothar 1923- 38
Broekel, Ray
  See Broekel, Rainer Lothar
Broekstra, Lorette 1964- 189
  Earlier sketch in SATA 124
Brogden, Sherryl
  See Jordan, Sherryl
Broger, Achim
  See Broeger, Achim
Broida, Marian 154
Brokamp, Marilyn 1920- 10
Broman, Fred
  See Moseley, James W(illett)
Bromhall, Winifred 26
Brommer, Gerald F(rederick) 1927- 28
Brondfield, Jerome 1913-1998 22
Brondfield, Jerry
  See Brondfield, Jerome
Bronner, Stephen Eric 1949- 101
Bronowski, Jacob 1908-1974 55
Bronson, Alice
  See Watkins, Dawn L.
Bronson, Linda 203
Bronson, Lynn
  See Lampman, Evelyn Sibley
Bronson, Wilfrid Swancourt 1894-1985
  Obituary 43
Brook, Judith (Penelope) 1926- 59
  Brief entry 51
Brook, Judy
  See Brook, Judith (Penelope)
Brooke, L(eonard) Leslie 1862-1940 17
  See also CLR 20
Brooke, William J. 1946- 139
Brooke-Haven, P.
  See Wodehouse, P. G.
Brooker, Kyrsten 199
Brookins, Dana 1931- 28
Brooks, Anita
  See Abramovitz, Anita (Zeltner Brooks)
Brooks, Bill 1939- 59
Brooks, Bruce 1950- 112
  Brief entry 53
  Earlier sketch in SATA 72
  See also CLR 25
Brooks, Caryl 1924- 84
Brooks, Charlotte K(endrick) 1918-1998 24
  Obituary 112
Brooks, Erik 1972- 182
  Earlier sketch in SATA 152
Brooks, George
  See Baum, L. Frank
Brooks, Gwendolyn 1917-2000 6
  Obituary 123
  See also CLR 27
Brooks, Gwendolyn Elizabeth
  See Brooks, Gwendolyn
Brooks, Jerome 1931- 23
Brooks, Kevin 1959- 197
  Earlier sketch in SATA 150
Brooks, Kevin M.
  See Brooks, Kevin
Brooks, Lester 1924- 7
Brooks, Martha 1944- 134
  Autobiography Feature 134
  Earlier sketches in SATA 68, 121

Brooks, Maurice (Graham) 1900- 45
Brooks, Polly Schoyer 1912- 12
Brooks, Ron 1948- 94
  Brief entry 33
Brooks, Ronald George
  See Brooks, Ron
Brooks, Terry 1944- 60
Brooks, Walter R(ollin) 1886-1958 17
Brooks-Hill, Helen (Mason) 1908-1994 59
Broome, Errol 1937- 158
  Earlier sketch in SATA 105
Brophy, Nannette 1963- 73
Brosnan, James Patrick 1929- 14
Brosnan, Jim
  See Brosnan, James Patrick
Brostoff, Anita 1931- 132
Brothers Grimm
  See Grimm, Jacob Ludwig Karl
  and Grimm, Wilhelm Karl
Brothers Hildebrandt, The
  See Hildebrandt, Greg
  and Hildebrandt, Tim
Broun, Emily
  See Sterne, Emma Gelders
Brouwer, S. W.
  See Brouwer, Sigmund (W.)
Brouwer, Sigmund (W.) 1959- 109
Brow, Thea 1934- 60
Brower, Millicent 8
Brower, Pauline 1929- 22
Browin, Frances Williams 1898-1986 5
Brown, Alexis
  See Baumann, Amy Beeching
Brown, Anne Ensign 1937- 61
Brown, Beverly Swerdlow 97
Brown, Bill
  See Brown, William L(ouis)
Brown, Billye Walker
  See Cutchen, Billye Walker
Brown, Bob
  See Brown, Robert Joseph
Brown, Buck 1936- 45
Brown, Calef 179
Brown, Cassie 1919-1986 55
Brown, Charlotte Lewis 181
Brown, Conrad 1922- 31
Brown, Craig McFarland 1947- 73
Brown, David
  See Brown, David A(lan)
  and Myller, Rolf
Brown, Dee 1908-2002 110
  Obituary 141
  Earlier sketch in SATA 5
Brown, Dee Alexander
  See Brown, Dee
Brown, Don 1949- 200
  Earlier sketch in SATA 172
Brown, Drew T. III 1955- 83
Brown, Drollene P. 1939- 53
Brown, Elbrite 198
Brown, Eleanor Frances 1908-1987 3
Brown, Elizabeth Ferguson 1937- 153
Brown, Elizabeth M(yers) 1915- 43
Brown, Fern G. 1918- 34
Brown, (Robert) Fletch 1923- 42
Brown, Fornan 1901-1996 71
  Obituary 88
Brown, George Earl 1883-1964 11
Brown, George Mackay 1921-1996 35
Brown, Irene Bennett 1932- 3
Brown, Irving
  See Adams, William Taylor
Brown, Ivor (John Carnegie) 1891-1974 5
  Obituary 26
Brown, Jane Clark 1930- 81
Brown, Janet Mitsui 87
Brown, Jo 1964- 170
Brown, Joanne 1933- 147
Brown, Joe David 1915-1976 44
Brown, Joseph E(dward) 1929- 59
  Brief entry 51

Brown, Judith Gwyn 1933- 20
Brown, Kathryn 1955- 168
Earlier sketch in SATA 98
Brown, Kathy
See Brown, Kathryn
Brown, Ken (James) 129
Brown, Kevin 1960- 101
Brown, Laurene Krasny 1945- 99
Earlier sketch in SATA 54
Brown, Laurie Krasny
See Brown, Laurene Krasny
Brown, Lloyd Arnold 1907-1966 36
Brown, Mahlon A.
See Ellis, Edward S.
Brown, Marc (Tolon) 1946- 145
Earlier sketches in SATA 10, 53, 80
See also CLR 29
Brown, Marcia (Joan) 1918- 47
Earlier sketch in SATA 7
See also CLR 12
Brown, Margaret Wise 1910-1952 100
See also YABC 2
See also CLR 107
Brown, Margery (Wheeler) 78
Earlier sketch in SATA 5
Brown, Marion Marsh 1908-2001 6
Brown, Myra Berry 1918- 6
Brown, Palmer 1919- 36
Brown, Pamela (Beatrice) 1924-1989 5
Obituary 61
Brown, Peter 1979- 178
Brown, Rachel W.N. 1947- 203
Brown, Reeve Lindbergh
See Lindbergh, Reeve
Brown, Richard E. 1946- 61
Brown, Robert Joseph 1907-1989 14
Brown, Roderick (Langmere) Haig-
See Haig-Brown, Roderick (Langmere)
Brown, Rosalie
See Moore, Rosalie (Gertrude)
Brown, Roswell
See Webb, Jean Francis (III)
Brown, Roy (Frederick) 1921-1982 51
Obituary 39
Brown, Ruth 1941- 170
Earlier sketch in SATA 105
Brown, Scott 1971- 134
Brown, Sue Ellen 1954- 81
Brown, Tricia 1954- 114
Brown, Vinson 1912-1991 19
Brown, Walter R(eed) 1929- 19
Brown, Will
See Ainsworth, William Harrison
Brown, William L(ouis) 1910-1964 5
Browne, Anthony 1946- 163
Brief entry 44
Earlier sketches in SATA 45, 61, 105
See also CLR 19
Browne, Anthony Edward Tudor
See Browne, Anthony
Browne, Dik
See Browne, Richard Arthur Allen
Browne, Hablot Knight 1815-1882 21
Browne, Matthew
See Rands, William Brighty
Browne, Nicki M.
See Browne, N.M.
Browne, Nicky Matthews
See Browne, N.M.
Browne, N.M. 1960- 167
Browne, Richard Arthur Allen 1917-1989 ... 67
Brief entry 38
Browne, Vee F(rances) 1956- 90
Browning, Robert 1812-1889
See YABC 1
See also CLR 97
Brownjohn, Alan 1931- 6
Brownlee, Walter 1930- 62
Brownlie, Betty 1946- 159
Brownlow, Kevin 1938- 65
Brownlow, Mike 183

Brownridge, William R(oy) 1932- 94
Broyles, Anne 1953- 201
Bruce, Dorita Fairlie 1885-1970
Obituary 27
Bruce, (William) Harry 1934- 77
Bruce, Mary 1927- 1
Bruchac, Joseph III
See Bruchac, Joseph
Bruchac, Joseph 1942- 176
Autobiography Feature 176
Earlier sketches in SATA 42, 89, 131
See also CLR 46
Bruchac, Margaret M.
See Bruchac, Marge
Bruchac, Marge 181
Bruck, Lorraine 1921- 55
Brief entry 46
Bruel, Nick 205
Earlier sketch in SATA 166
Bruel, Robert O. 1929-2002 189
Bruemmer, Fred 1929- 47
Brugman, Alyssa (F.) 1974- 152
Brumbeau, Jeff 1955- 157
Bruna, Dick 1927- 76
Brief entry 30
Earlier sketch in SATA 43
See also CLR 7
Brunhoff, Jean de 1899-1937 24
See also CLR 116
Brunhoff, Laurent de 1925- 150
Earlier sketches in SATA 24, 71
See also CLR 116
Brunkus, Denise 204
Brunskill, Elizabeth Ann Flatt
See Flatt, Lizann
Brush, Karen A(lexandra) 1960- 85
Brussel-Smith, Bernard 1914- 58
Brust, Steven 1955- 121
Earlier sketch in SATA 86
Brust, Steven K. Zoltan
See Brust, Steven
Brustlein, Daniel 1904- 40
Brustlein, Janice Tworkov -2000 40
Obituary 126
Brutschy, Jennifer 1960- 84
Bryan, Ashley 1923- 178
Earlier sketches in SATA 31, 72, 132
See also CLR 66
Bryan, Ashley F.
See Bryan, Ashley
Bryan, Dorothy M. 1896(?)-1984
Obituary 39
Bryan, Jennifer 190
Bryan, Sean 192
Bryant, Bernice (Morgan) 1908-1976 11
Bryant, Jen 1960- 175
Earlier sketch in SATA 94
Bryant, Jennifer
See Bryant, Jen
Bryant, Jennifer Fisher
See Bryant, Jen
Bryant, Laura J. 176
Brychta, Alex 1956- 21
Brynie, Faith H. 1946- 113
Brynie, Faith Hickman
See Brynie, Faith H.
Bryson, Bernarda 1903-2004 9
Buba, Joy Flinsch 1904- 44
Buchan, Bryan 1945- 36
Buchan, John 1875-1940
See YABC 2
Buchan, Stuart 1942-1987
Obituary 54
Buchanan, Debby 1952- 82
Buchanan, Deborah Leevonne
See Buchanan, Debby
Buchanan, Jane 1956- 160
Buchanan, Paul 1959- 116
Buchanan, Sue 1939- 139
Buchheimer, Naomi Barnett
See Barnett, Naomi

Buchignani, Walter 1965- 84
Buchmann, Stephen L. 194
Buchwald, Art 1925-2007 10
Buchwald, Arthur
See Buchwald, Art
Buchwald, Emilie 1935- 7
Buck, Gisela 1941- 101
Buck, Lewis 1925- 18
Buck, Margaret Waring 1905-1997 3
Buck, Nola
See Godwin, Laura
Buck, Pearl S. 1892-1973 25
Earlier sketch in SATA 1
Buck, Pearl Sydenstricker
See Buck, Pearl S.
Buck, Siegfried 1941- 101
Buckalew, Clare B.
See Dunkle, Clare B.
Buckeridge, Anthony (Malcolm)
1912-2004 85
Earlier sketch in SATA 6
Buckholtz, Eileen (Garber) 1949- 54
Brief entry 47
Buckler, Ernest 1908-1984 47
Buckless, Andrea K. 1968- 117
Buckley, Helen E(lizabeth) 1918- 90
Earlier sketch in SATA 2
Buckley, James, Jr. 1963- 166
Earlier sketch in SATA 114
Buckley, Michael 177
Buckley, Susan 184
Buckley, Susan Washburn
See Buckley, Susan
Buckley-Archer, Linda 185
Buckmaster, Henrietta
See Stephens, Henrietta Henkle
Bucks, Brad
See Holub, Joan
Budd, E. S.
See Sirimarco, Elizabeth
Budd, Lillian (Peterson) 1897-1989 7
Budhos, Marina 173
Buehler, Stephanie Jona 1956- 83
Buehner, Caralyn (M.) 1963- 159
Earlier sketch in SATA 104
Buehner, Mark 1959- 159
Earlier sketch in SATA 104
Buehr, Walter Franklin 1897-1971 3
Buell, Ellen Lewis
See Cash, Ellen Lewis Buell
Buell, Janet 1952- 185
Earlier sketch in SATA 106
Buergel, Paul-Hermann H. 1949- 83
Buettner, Dan 1960- 95
Buff, Conrad 1886-1975 19
Buff, Mary (E. Marsh) 1890-1970 19
Buffett, Jimmy 1946- 110
Earlier sketch in SATA 76
Buffie, Margaret 1945- 161
Earlier sketches in SATA 71, 107
See also CLR 39
Bugbee, Emma 1888(?)-1981
Obituary 29
Bugni, Alice 1951- 122
Buhhos, Marina Tamar
See Budhos, Marina
Bujold, Lois McMaster 1949- 136
Bulfinch, Thomas 1796-1867 35
Bulion, Leslie 1958- 161
Bull, Angela (Mary) 1936- 45
Bull, Emma 1954- 190
Autobiography Feature 103
Earlier sketch in SATA 99
Bull, Norman John 1916- 41
Bull, Peter (Cecil) 1912-1984
Obituary 39
Bull, Schuyler M. 1974- 138
Bulla, Clyde R. 1914-2007 139
Obituary 182
Earlier sketches in SATA 2, 41, 91
See also SAAS 6

Bullard, Lisa 1961- *142*
Buller, Jon *205*
Bullock, Kathleen (Mary) 1946- *77*
Bullock, Robert (D.) 1947- *92*
Bulpin, (Barbara) Vicki *92*
Bumstead, Kathleen Mary 1918-1987 .... *53*
Bundles, A'Lelia Perry 1952- *76*
Bunge, Daniela 1973- *207*
Bunin, Catherine 1967- *30*
Bunin, Sherry 1925- *30*
Bunkers, Suzanne L. 1950- *136*
Bunting, A.E.
    See Bunting, Eve
Bunting, Anne Evelyn
    See Bunting, Eve
Bunting, Eve 1928- *196*
    Earlier sketches in SATA *18, 64, 110, 158*
    See also CLR *82*
Bunting, Glenn (Davison) 1957- *22*
Bunyan, John 1628-1688
    See CLR *124*
Bupp, Walter
    See Garrett, Randall
Burack, Sylvia K. 1916-2003 .... *35*
    Obituary *143*
Burbank, Addison (Buswell) 1895-1961 ...... *37*
Burch, Joann J(ohansen) *75*
Burch, Robert J(oseph) 1925- *74*
    Earlier sketch in SATA *1*
    See also CLR *63*
Burchard, Peter Duncan 1921- *143*
    Earlier sketches in SATA *5, 74*
    See also SAAS *13*
Burchard, S. H.
    See Burchard, Sue
Burchard, Sue 1937- *22*
Burchardt, Nellie 1921- *7*
Burckhardt, Marc 1962- *196*
Burdett, Lois *117*
Burdick, Eugene (Leonard) 1918-1965 .... *22*
Burford, Eleanor
    See Hibbert, Eleanor Alice Burford
Burg, Shana 1968- *204*
Burgan, Michael 1960- *167*
    Earlier sketch in SATA *118*
Burger, Carl 1888-1967 .... *9*
Burgess, Ann Marie
    See Gerson, Noel Bertram
Burgess, Barbara Hood 1926- *69*
Burgess, Em
    See Burgess, Mary Wyche
Burgess, (Frank) Gelett 1866-1951 .... *32*
    Brief entry *30*
Burgess, Mark *157*
Burgess, Mary Wyche 1916- *18*
Burgess, Melvin 1954- *198*
    Earlier sketches in SATA *96, 146*
Burgess, Michael
    See Gerson, Noel Bertram
Burgess, Robert F(orrest) 1927- *4*
Burgess, Starling
    See Tudor, Tasha
Burgess, Thornton Waldo 1874-1965 .... *17*
Burgess, Trevor
    See Trevor, Elleston
Burgwyn, Mebane Holoman 1914-1992 .... *7*
Burke, David 1927- *46*
Burke, Diana G.
    See Gallagher, Diana G.
Burke, Diana Gallagher
    See Gallagher, Diana G.
Burke, Dianne O'Quinn 1940- *89*
Burke, Janine 1952- *139*
Burke, Jim 1973- *179*
Burke, John
    See O'Connor, Richard
Burke, Katie 1953- *168*
Burke, Patrick 1958- *114*
Burke, Ralph
    See Garrett, Randall
    and Silverberg, Robert

Burkert, Nancy Ekholm 1933- *24*
    See also SAAS *14*
Burkett, D. Brent *194*
Burke-Weiner, Kimberly 1962- *95*
Burks, Brian 1955- *95*
Burland, Brian (Berkeley) 1931- *34*
Burland, C. A.
    See Burland, Cottie (Arthur)
Burland, Cottie (Arthur) 1905-1983 .... *5*
Burleigh, Robert 1936- *193*
    Earlier sketches in SATA *55, 98, 146*
Burlingame, (William) Roger 1889-1967 .... *2*
Burman, Alice Caddy 1896(?)-1977
    Obituary *24*
Burman, Ben Lucien 1896-1984 .... *6*
    Obituary *40*
Burn, Doris 1923- *1*
Burn, Ted
    See Burn, Thomas E.
Burn, Thomas E. 1940- *150*
Burnard, Damon 1963- *115*
Burnett, Constance Buel 1893-1975 .... *36*
Burnett, Frances Eliza Hodgson
    See Burnett, Frances Hodgson
Burnett, Frances Hodgson 1849-1924 .... *100*
    See also YABC *2*
    See also CLR *122*
Burnett Bossi, Lisa *193*
Burney, Anton
    See Hopkins, (Hector) Kenneth
Burnford, Sheila (Philip Cochrane Every)
    1918-1984 .... *3*
    Obituary *38*
    See also CLR *2*
Burnham, Gretchen
    See Sprague, Gretchen
Burnham, Nicole 1970- *161*
Burnham, Niki
    See Burnham, Nicole
Burnham, Sophy 1936- *65*
Burningham, John 1936- *160*
    Earlier sketches in SATA *16, 59, 111*
    See also CLR *9*
Burningham, Robin Yoko
    See Racoma, Robin Yoko
Burns, Diane L. 1950- *81*
    See also SAAS *24*
Burns, Eloise Wilkin
    See Wilkin, Eloise
Burns, Florence M. 1905-1988 .... *61*
Burns, Khephra 1950- *92*
Burns, Loree Griffin *193*
Burns, Marilyn 1941- *96*
    Brief entry *33*
Burns, Olive Ann 1924-1990 .... *65*
Burns, Paul C. *5*
Burns, Ray
    See Burns, Raymond (Howard)
Burns, Raymond (Howard) 1924- *9*
Burns, Theresa 1961- *84*
Burns, William A. 1909-1999 .... *5*
Burr, Dan 1951- *65*
Burr, Lonnie 1943- *47*
Burrell, Roy E(ric) C(harles) 1923- *72*
Burroughs, Edgar Rice 1875-1950 .... *41*
Burroughs, Jean Mitchell 1908- *28*
Burroughs, Polly 1925- *2*
Burroway, Janet (Gay) 1936- *23*
Burstein, Chaya M(alamud) 1923- *64*
Burstein, Fred 1950- *83*
Burstein, John 1949- *54*
    Brief entry *40*
Burstein, Stanley M.
    See Burstein, Stanley Mayer
Burstein, Stanley Mayer 1941- *175*
Bursztynski, Sue 1953- *114*
Burt, Jesse Clifton 1921-1976 .... *46*
    Obituary *20*
Burt, Olive Woolley 1894-1981 .... *4*
Burtinshaw, Julie *185*
Burton, Gennett 1945- *95*

Burton, Hester (Wood-Hill) 1913-2000 .... *74*
    Earlier sketch in SATA *7*
    See also CLR *1*
    See also SAAS *8*
Burton, Leslie
    See McGuire, Leslie (Sarah)
Burton, Marilee Robin 1950- *82*
    Earlier sketch in SATA *46*
Burton, Maurice 1898-1992 .... *23*
Burton, Rebecca 1970- *183*
Burton, Robert (Wellesley) 1941- *22*
Burton, Virginia Lee 1909-1968 .... *100*
    Earlier sketch in SATA *2*
    See also CLR *11*
Burton, William H(enry) 1890-1964 .... *11*
Busby, Ailie *192*
Busby, Cylin 1970- *118*
Busby, Edith (A. Lake) (?)-1964
    Obituary *29*
Buscaglia, (Felice) Leo(nardo) 1924-1998 ... *65*
Buscaglia, Leo F.
    See Buscaglia, (Felice) Leo(nardo)
Busch, Phyllis S. 1909- *30*
Bush, Anne Kelleher
    See Kelleher, Anne
Bush, Catherine 1961- *128*
Bushmiller, Ernest Paul 1905-1982 .... *31*
Bushmiller, Ernie
    See Bushmiller, Ernest Paul
Bushnell, Jack 1952- *86*
Busoni, Rafaello 1900-1962 .... *16*
Buss, Helen M.
    See Clarke, Margaret
Busse, Sarah Martin *194*
Busselle, Rebecca 1941- *80*
Bustard, Anne 1951- *173*
Butcher, Kristin 1951- *140*
Butenko, Bohdan 1931- *90*
Butler, Beverly Kathleen 1932- *7*
Butler, Bill
    See Butler, William Vivian
    and Butler, Ernest Alton
    and Butler, William Huxford
Butler, Charles 1963- *175*
    Earlier sketch in SATA *121*
Butler, Charles Cadman
    See Butler, Charles
Butler, Dori Hillestad 1965- *207*
    Earlier sketch in SATA *164*
Butler, Dorothy 1925- *73*
Butler, Geoff 1945- *94*
Butler, M. Christina 1934- *170*
    Earlier sketch in SATA *72*
Butler, Octavia 1947-2006 .... *84*
    See also CLR *65*
Butler, Octavia E.
    See Butler, Octavia
Butler, Octavia Estelle
    See Butler, Octavia
Butler, Vivian
    See Butler, William Vivian
Butler, William
    See Butler, William Vivian
Butler, William Vivian 1927-1987 .... *79*
Butters, Dorothy Gilman
    See Gilman, Dorothy
Butterworth, Emma Macalik 1928- *43*
Butterworth, Nick 1946- *149*
    Earlier sketch in SATA *106*
Butterworth, Oliver 1915-1990 .... *1*
    Obituary *66*
Butterworth, W.E.
    See Griffin, W.E.B.
Butterworth, William E.
    See Griffin, W.E.B.
Butterworth, William Edmund III
    See Griffin, W.E.B.
Butts, Ed 1951- *177*
Butts, Edward P.
    See Butts, Ed
Butts, Ellen R(ubinstein) 1942- *93*

Buxton, Ralph
　See Silverstein, Alvin
　and Silverstein, Virginia B.
Buzzeo, Toni 1951- *135*
Byalick, Marcia 1947- *141*
　Earlier sketch in SATA *97*
Byard, Carole (Marie) 1941- *57*
Byars, Betsy 1928- *163*
　Autobiography Feature *108*
　Earlier sketches in SATA *4, 46, 80*
　See also CLR *72*
　See also SAAS *1*
Byars, Betsy Cromer
　See Byars, Betsy
Byfield, Barbara Ninde 1930- *8*
Byman, Jeremy 1944- *129*
Bynum, Janie *133*
Byrd, Elizabeth 1912-1989 .... *34*
Byrd, Nicole
　See Zach, Cheryl (Byrd)
Byrd, Robert (John) 1942- *158*
　Earlier sketches in SATA *33, 112*
Byrne, Mary Gregg 1951- *162*

C

C. 3. 3.
　See Wilde, Oscar
C. E. M.
　See Mastrangelo, Charles E(lmer)
Cabaniss, J(ames) Allen 1911-1997 .... *5*
Cabat, Erni 1914- *74*
Cabban, Vanessa 1971- *176*
Cable, Mary 1920- *9*
Cabot, Meg 1967- *175*
　Earlier sketch in SATA *127*
　See also CLR *85*
Cabot, Meggin
　See Cabot, Meg
Cabot, Meggin Patricia
　See Cabot, Meg
Cabot, Patricia
　See Cabot, Meg
Cabral, O. M.
　See Cabral, Olga
Cabral, Olga 1909- *46*
Cabrera, Cozbi A. 1963- *177*
Cabrera, Jane 1968- *182*
　Earlier sketches in SATA *103, 152*
Cabrera, Marcela 1966- *90*
Caddy, Alice
　See Burman, Alice Caddy
Cade, Toni
　See Bambara, Toni Cade
Cadmus and Harmonia
　See Buchan, John
Cadnum, Michael 1949- *165*
　Earlier sketches in SATA *87, 121*
　See also CLR *78*
Caduto, Michael J. 1955- *103*
Cadwallader, Sharon 1936- *7*
Cady, (Walter) Harrison 1877(?)-1970 .... *19*
Caffey, Donna (J.) 1954- *110*
Cagle, Malcolm W(infield) 1918- *32*
Cahn, Rhoda 1922- *37*
Cahn, William 1912-1976 .... *37*
Cain, Arthur H(omer) 1913-1981 .... *3*
Cain, Christopher
　See Fleming, Thomas
Cain, Sheridan 1952- *186*
Caine, Geoffrey
　See Walker, Robert W.
Caines, Jeannette (Franklin) 1938- *78*
　Brief entry *43*
　See also CLR *24*
Cairns, Trevor 1922- *14*
Calabro, Marian 1954- *79*
Caldecott, Moyra 1927- *22*

Caldecott, Randolph (J.) 1846-1886 .... *100*
　Earlier sketch in SATA *17*
　See also CLR *110*
Calder, Charlotte 1952- *125*
Calder, David 1932-1997 .... *105*
Calder, Lyn
　See Calmenson, Stephanie
Calder, Marie D(onais) 1948- *96*
Calderone-Stewart, Lisa
　See Calderone-Stewart, Lisa-Marie
Calderone-Stewart, Lisa-Marie 1958- *123*
Caldwell, Doreen (Mary) 1942- *71*
Caldwell, John C(ope) 1913-1984 .... *7*
Caletti, Deb 1963- *171*
Calhoun, B. B. 1961- *98*
Calhoun, Chad
　See Barrett, Neal, Jr.
　and Cunningham, Chet
　and Goulart, Ron
Calhoun, Dia 1959- *183*
　Earlier sketch in SATA *129*
Calhoun, Mary
　See Wilkins, Mary Huiskamp
Calhoun, T.B.
　See Bisson, Terry
Cali, Davide 1972- *190*
Calif, Ruth 1922- *67*
Calkins, Franklin
　See Stratemeyer, Edward L.
Call, Greg *197*
Call, Hughie Florence 1890-1969 .... *1*
Callahan, Dorothy M(onahan) 1934- *39*
　Brief entry *35*
Callahan, Philip Serna 1923- *25*
Callan, Jamie 1954- *59*
Callan, Jim 1951- *181*
Callaway, Bernice (Anne) 1923- *48*
Callaway, Kathy 1943- *36*
Callen, Larry
　See Callen, Lawrence Willard, Jr.
Callen, Lawrence Willard, Jr. 1927- *19*
Calley, Karin 1965- *92*
Calmenson, Stephanie 1952- *139*
　Brief entry *37*
　Earlier sketches in SATA *51, 84*
Calvert, Elinor H.
　See Lasell, Elinor H.
Calvert, John
　See Leaf, (Wilbur) Munro
Calvert, Pam 1966- *205*
Calvert, Patricia 1931- *132*
　Earlier sketches in SATA *45, 69*
　See also SAAS *17*
Camburn, Carol A.
　See Camburn-Bracalente, Carol A.
Camburn-Bracalente, Carol A. 1962- *118*
Cameron, Ann 1943- *129*
　Earlier sketches in SATA *27, 89*
　See also SAAS *20*
Cameron, Edna M. 1905-1999 .... *3*
Cameron, Eleanor (Frances) 1912-1996 .... *25*
　Obituary *93*
　Earlier sketch in SATA *1*
　See also CLR *72*
　See also SAAS *10*
Cameron, Elizabeth
　See Nowell, Elizabeth Cameron
Cameron, Elizabeth Jane 1910-1976 .... *32*
　Obituary *30*
Cameron, Ian
　See Payne, Donald Gordon
Cameron, M(alcolm) G(ordon) Graham
　See Graham-Cameron, M(alcolm) G(ordon)
Cameron, M. Graham
　See Graham-Cameron, M(alcolm) G(ordon)
Cameron, Mike Graham
　See Graham-Cameron, M(alcolm) G(ordon)
Cameron, Polly 1928- *2*
Cameron, Scott 1962- *84*
Camp, Charles L. 1893-1975
　Obituary *31*

Camp, Lindsay 1957- *133*
Camp, Madeleine L'Engle
　See L'Engle, Madeleine
Camp, Walter (Chauncey) 1859-1925
　See YABC *1*
Campbell, (Elizabeth) Andrea 1963- *50*
Campbell, Ann R. 1925- *11*
Campbell, Bill 1960- *89*
Campbell, Bruce
　See Epstein, Samuel
Campbell, Camilla 1905-1992 .... *26*
Campbell, Carole R. 1939- *125*
Campbell, Hope 1925- *20*
Campbell, Hugh 1930- *90*
Campbell, Jane
　See Edwards, Jane Campbell
Campbell, Julie
　See Tatham, Julie Campbell
Campbell, Patricia J(ean) 1930- *45*
Campbell, Patty
　See Campbell, Patricia J(ean)
Campbell, Peter A. 1948- *99*
Campbell, R. W.
　See Campbell, Rosemae Wells
Campbell, Robin
　See Strachan, Ian
Campbell, Rod 1945- *98*
　Brief entry *44*
　Earlier sketch in SATA *51*
Campbell, Rosemae Wells 1909- *1*
Campbell, Sarah C. 1966- *207*
Camper, Cathy 1956- *170*
Campion, Nardi Reeder 1917-2007 .... *22*
Campling, Elizabeth 1948- *53*
Campoy, F. Isabel 1946- *181*
　Earlier sketch in SATA *143*
Camps, Luis 1928- *66*
Canales, Viola 1957- *141*
Candell, Victor 1903-1977
　Obituary *24*
Canfield, Dorothea F.
　See Fisher, Dorothy (Frances) Canfield
Canfield, Dorothea Frances
　See Fisher, Dorothy (Frances) Canfield
Canfield, Dorothy
　See Fisher, Dorothy (Frances) Canfield
Canfield, Jack 1944- *164*
Canfield, Jane White 1897-1984 .... *32*
　Obituary *38*
Canfield, Muriel 1935- *94*
Caniff, Milton 1907-1988
　Obituary *58*
Caniff, Milton Arthur Paul
　See Caniff, Milton
Cann, Helen 1969- *179*
　Earlier sketch in SATA *124*
Cann, Kate 1954- *152*
　Earlier sketch in SATA *103*
Cannan, Joanna
　See Pullein-Thompson, Joanna Maxwell
Cannell, Jon *196*
Cannell, Jonathan C.
　See Cannell, Jon
Cannon, A.E. *202*
　Earlier sketches in SATA *93, 163*
Cannon, Ann Edwards
　See Cannon, A.E.
Cannon, Bettie (Waddell) 1922- *59*
Cannon, Curt
　See Hunter, Evan
Cannon, Eileen E(mily) 1948- *119*
Cannon, Frank
　See Mayhar, Ardath
Cannon, Janell 1957- *128*
　Earlier sketch in SATA *78*
　See also CLR *120*
Cannon, Marian G. 1923- *85*
Cannon, Taffy
　See Cannon, Eileen E(mily)
Cantone, AnnaLaura *182*

Canusi, Jose
See Barker, S. Omar
Canyon, Christopher 1966- 150
Earlier sketch in SATA 104
Caparo, Antonio
See Caparo, Antonio Javier
Caparo, Antonio Javier 205
Capek, Michael 1947- 142
Earlier sketch in SATA 96
Capes, Bernard (Edward Joseph)
1854-1918 116
Caple, Kathy 193
Caple, Laurie 1958- 201
Caplin, Alfred Gerald 1909-1979 61
Obituary 21
Caponigro, John Paul 1965- 84
Capote, Truman 1924-1984 91
Capp, Al
See Caplin, Alfred Gerald
Cappel, Constance 1936- 22
Cappetta, Cynthia 1949- 125
Cappo, Nan Willard 1955- 143
Capps, Benjamin (Franklin) 1922- 9
Cappy Dick
See Cleveland, George
Captain Kangaroo
See Keeshan, Robert J.
Captain Wheeler
See Ellis, Edward S.
Captain Young of Yale
See Stratemeyer, Edward L.
Capucilli, Alyssa Satin 1957- 203
Earlier sketches in SATA 115, 163
Capucine
See Mazille, Capucine
Caraher, Kim(berley Elizabeth) 1961- 105
Caraker, Mary 1929- 74
Caras, Roger A(ndrew) 1928-2001 12
Obituary 127
Caravantes, Peggy 1935- 140
Caraway, Caren 1939- 57
Carbone, Elisa 1954- 173
Earlier sketches in SATA 81, 137
Carbone, Elisa Lynn
See Carbone, Elisa
Carbonnier, Jeanne 1894-1974 3
Obituary 34
Card, Orson Scott 1951- 127
Earlier sketch in SATA 83
See also CLR 116
Care, Felicity
See Coury, Louise Andree
Carew, Jan 1925- 51
Brief entry 40
Carew, Jan Rynveld
See Carew, Jan
Carey, Bonnie
See Marshall, Bonnie C.
Carey, Charles W., Jr. 1951- 170
Carey, Ernestine Gilbreth 1908-2006 2
Obituary 177
Carey, Janet Lee 1954(?)- 185
Carey, Lisa 110
Carey, M. V.
See Carey, Mary V(irginia)
Carey, Mary V(irginia) 1925-1994 44
Brief entry 39
Carey, Peter 1943- 94
Carey, Peter Philip
See Carey, Peter
Carey, Valerie Scho 1949- 60
Carheden, Goorel Kristina
See Naaslund, Goorel Kristina
Carigiet, Alois 1902-1985 24
Obituary 47
See also CLR 38
Carini, Edward 1923- 9
Carkeet, David 1946- 75

Carle, Eric 1929- 163
Earlier sketches in SATA 4, 65, 120
See also CLR 72
See also SAAS 6
Carleton, Captain L. C.
See Ellis, Edward S.
Carleton, Captain Latham C.
See Ellis, Edward S.
Carleton, Latham C.
See Ellis, Edward S.
Carley, V(an Ness) Royal 1906-1976
Obituary 20
Carling, Amelia Lau 1949- 164
Earlier sketch in SATA 119
Carlisle, Carolyn
See Hawes, Louise
Carlisle, Clark
See Holding, James (Clark Carlisle, Jr.)
Carlisle, Olga Andreyev 1930- 35
Carlock, Miriam
See Eyerly, Jeannette
Carls, Claudia 1978- 198
Carlsen, G(eorge) Robert 1917- 30
Carlsen, Ruth C(hristoffer) 1918- 2
Carlson, Bernice Wells 1910- 8
Carlson, Christopher C. 202
Carlson, Dale (Bick) 1935- 1
Carlson, Daniel (Bick) 1960- 27
Carlson, Kirsten 1968- 192
Carlson, Kirsten M.
See Carlson, Kirsten
Carlson, Laurie 1952- 173
Earlier sketch in SATA 101
Carlson, Laurie Winn
See Carlson, Laurie
Carlson, Melody 1956- 171
Earlier sketch in SATA 113
Carlson, Nancy L.
See Carlson, Nancy L(ee)
Carlson, Nancy L(ee) 1953- 144
Brief entry 45
Earlier sketches in SATA 56, 90
Carlson, Natalie Savage 1906-1997 68
Earlier sketch in SATA 2
See also SAAS 4
Carlson, Susan Johnston 1953- 88
Carlson, Vada F. 1897- 16
Carlstrom, Nancy White 1948- 156
Brief entry 48
Earlier sketches in SATA 53, 92
Carlton, Keith
See Robertson, Keith (Carlton)
Carlton, Susan 1960- 195
Carlyon, Richard 55
Carman, Patrick 1966- 197
Earlier sketch in SATA 161
Carmer, Carl (Lamson) 1893-1976 37
Obituary 30
Carmer, Elizabeth Black 1904- 24
Carmi, Giora 1944- 149
Earlier sketch in SATA 79
Carmichael, Carrie
See Carmichael, Harriet
Carmichael, Harriet 40
Carmody, Isobelle 1958- 191
Earlier sketch in SATA 161
Carmody, Isobelle Jane
See Carmody, Isobelle
Carney, Elizabeth 1981- 199
Carney, Jeff 1962- 196
Carney, Mary Lou 1949- 170
Carol, Bill J.
See Knott, William C(ecil, Jr.)
Caron, Romi
See Caron-Kyselkova', Romana
Caron-Kyselkova', Romana 1967- 94
Caroselli, Remus F(rancis) 1916- 36
Carpelan, Bo 1926- 8
Carpelan, Bo Gustaf Bertelsson
See Carpelan, Bo

Carpenter, (John) Allan 1917- 81
Earlier sketch in SATA 3
Carpenter, Angelica Shirley 1945- 153
Earlier sketch in SATA 71
Carpenter, Frances 1890-1972 3
Obituary 27
Carpenter, John 1948- 58
Carpenter, John Howard
See Carpenter, John
Carpenter, Johnny
See Carpenter, John
Carpenter, Patricia (Healy Evans) 1920- 11
Carr, Glyn
See Styles, (Frank) Showell
Carr, Harriett H(elen) 1899-1977 3
Carr, Jan 1953- 132
Earlier sketch in SATA 89
Carr, M. J.
See Carr, Jan
Carr, Mary Jane 1899-1988 2
Obituary 55
Carr, Philippa
See Hibbert, Eleanor Alice Burford
Carr, Roger Vaughan 1937- 95
Carrel, Annette Felder 1929- 90
Carrick, Carol (Hatfield) 1935- 118
Earlier sketches in SATA 7, 63
See also SAAS 18
Carrick, Donald (F.) 1929-1989 63
Earlier sketch in SATA 7
Carrick, Malcolm 1945- 28
Carrick, Paul 1972- 194
Carrier, Lark 1947- 71
Brief entry 50
Carrier, Roch 1937- 166
Earlier sketch in SATA 105
Carrighar, Sally 1898-1985 24
Carrington, G. A.
See Cunningham, Chet
Carrington, Marsha Gray 1954- 168
Earlier sketch in SATA 111
Carris, Joan 1938- 182
Brief entry 42
Earlier sketch in SATA 44
Carris, Joan Davenport
See Carris, Joan
Carroll, Curt
See Bishop, Curtis (Kent)
Carroll, Elizabeth
See Barkin, Carol
and James, Elizabeth
Carroll, Jaye
See Carroll, Michael
Carroll, Jenny
See Cabot, Meg
Carroll, (Archer) Latrobe 1894-1996 7
Carroll, Laura
See Parr, Lucy
Carroll, Lewis 1832-1898 100
See also YABC 2
See also CLR 108
Carroll, Michael 1966- 203
Carroll, Raymond 1924- 86
Brief entry 47
Carruth, Hayden 1921-2008 47
Obituary 197
Carryl, Charles E. 1841-1920 114
Carryl, Charles Edward
See Carryl, Charles E.
Carse, Robert 1902-1971 5
Carson, J(ohn) Franklin 1920-1981 1
Obituary 107
Carson, Mary Kay 1964- 200
Earlier sketch in SATA 150
Carson, Rachel 1907-1964 23
Carson, Rachel Louise
See Carson, Rachel
Carson, Rosalind
See Chittenden, Margaret
Carson, S. M.
See Gorsline, (Sally) Marie

Carson, William C. 1928- *154*
Carter, Abby *184*
Carter, Alden R 1947- *137*
  Earlier sketch in SATA *67*
  See also CLR *22*
  See also SAAS *18*
Carter, Alden Richardson
  See Carter, Alden R
Carter, Andy 1948- *134*
Carter, Angela 1940-1992 .... *66*
  Obituary *70*
Carter, Angela Olive
  See Carter, Angela
Carter, Anne Laurel 1953- *135*
Carter, Asa Earl
  See Carter, Forrest
Carter, Avis Murton
  See Allen, Kenneth S.
Carter, Bruce
  See Hough, Richard (Alexander)
Carter, Carol S(hadis) 1948- *124*
Carter, David A. 1957- *170*
  Earlier sketch in SATA *114*
Carter, Don 1958- *192*
  Earlier sketch in SATA *124*
Carter, Dorothy Sharp 1921- *8*
Carter, Forrest 1927(?)-1979 .... *32*
Carter, Helene 1887-1960 .... *15*
Carter, (William) Hodding, Jr. 1907-1972 ..... *2*
  Obituary *27*
Carter, James Earl, Jr.
  See Carter, Jimmy
Carter, Jimmy 1924- *79*
Carter, Katharine J(ones) 1905-1984 .... *2*
Carter, Lin(wood Vrooman) 1930-1988 .... *91*
Carter, Mike 1936- *138*
Carter, Nick
  See Avallone, Michael (Angelo, Jr.)
  and Ballard, (Willis) Todhunter
  and Crider, Bill
  and Cassiday, Bruce (Bingham)
  and Chastain, Thomas
  and Dey, Frederic (Merrill) Van Rensselaer
  and Garside, Jack
  and Hayes, Ralph E(ugene)
  and Henderson, M(arilyn) R(uth)
  and Lynds, Dennis
  and Lynds, Gayle (Hallenbeck)
  and Randisi, Robert J.
  and Rasof, Henry
  and Stratemeyer, Edward L.
  and Smith, Martin Cruz
  and Swain, Dwight V(reeland)
  and Vardeman, Robert E(dward)
  and Wallmann, Jeffrey M(iner)
  and White, Lionel
Carter, Peter 1929- *57*
Carter, Phyllis Ann
  See Eberle, Irmengarde
Carter, Samuel (Thomson) III 1904-1988 .... *37*
  Obituary *60*
Carter, William E. 1926-1983 .... *1*
  Obituary *35*
Cartlidge, Michelle 1950- *96*
  Brief entry *37*
  Earlier sketch in SATA *49*
Cartner, William Carruthers 1910- *11*
Cartwright, Ann 1940- *78*
Cartwright, Reg(inald Ainsley) 1938- *64*
Cartwright, Sally 1923- *9*
Carusone, Al 1949- *89*
Carvell, Marlene *172*
Carver, John
  See Gardner, Richard (M.)
Carwell, L'Ann
  See McKissack, Patricia C.
Cary
  See Cary, Louis F(avreau)
Cary, Barbara Knapp 1912(?)-1975
  Obituary *31*
Cary, Kate 1967(?)- *174*

Cary, Louis F(avreau) 1915- *9*
Caryl, Jean
  See Kaplan, Jean Caryl Korn
Casanova, Mary 1957- *186*
  Earlier sketches in SATA *94, 136*
Cascone, A.G.
  See Cascone, Annette
  and Cascone, Gina
Cascone, Annette 1960- *103*
Cascone, Gina 1955- *103*
Case, Marshal T(aylor) 1941- *9*
Case, Michael
  See Howard, Robert West
Caseley, Judith 1951- *159*
  Brief entry *53*
  Earlier sketch in SATA *87*
Casewit, Curtis W(erner) 1922-2002 .... *4*
Casey, Barbara (Louise) 1944- *147*
  Earlier sketch in SATA *79*
Casey, Brigid 1950- *9*
Casey, Tina 1959- *141*
Cash, Ellen Lewis Buell 1905-1989
  Obituary *64*
Cash, Megan Montague *160*
Cashore, Kristin 1976(?)- *206*
Casilla, Robert 1959- *146*
  Earlier sketch in SATA *75*
Cason, Mabel Earp 1892-1965 .... *10*
Cass, Joan E(velyn) *1*
Cass-Beggs, Barbara 1904- *62*
Cassedy, Patrice (Rinaldo) 1953- *149*
Cassedy, Sylvia 1930-1989 .... *77*
  Obituary *61*
  Earlier sketch in SATA *27*
  See also CLR *26*
Cassel, Lili
  See Wronker, Lili Cassel
Cassels, Jean *173*
Cassidy, Anne 1952- *166*
Cassidy, Cathy 1962- *183*
Casson, Hugh Maxwell 1910-1999 .... *65*
  Obituary *115*
Cassutt, Michael 1954- *78*
Cassutt, Michael Joseph
  See Cassutt, Michael
Castaldi, Elicia *194*
Castaldo, Nancy Fusco 1962- *151*
  Earlier sketch in SATA *93*
Castaneda, Omar S. 1954- *71*
Castell, Megan
  See Williams, Jeanne
Castellanos, Jane Mollie Robinson
  1913-2001 .... *9*
Castellon, Federico 1914-1971 .... *48*
Castellucci, Cecil 1969- *176*
Castillo, Edmund L. 1924-2005 .... *1*
  Obituary *167*
Castillo, Lauren *195*
Castle, Lee
  See Ogan, George F.
  and Ogan, Margaret E. (Nettles)
Castle, Paul
  See Howard, Vernon (Linwood)
Castle, Robert
  See Hamilton, Edmond
Castrovilla, Selene 1966- *186*
Caswell, Brian 1954- *171*
  Earlier sketch in SATA *97*
Caswell, Helen (Rayburn) 1923- *12*
Catalano, Dominic 1956- *163*
  Earlier sketch in SATA *76*
Catalano, Grace (A.) 1961- *99*
Catalanotto, Peter 1959- *195*
  Autobiography Feature *113*
  Earlier sketches in SATA *70, 114, 159*
  See also CLR *68*
  See also SAAS *25*
Catanese, P.W. 1961- *179*
Cate, Annette LeBlanc *196*
Cate, Dick
  See Cate, Richard Edward Nelson

Cate, Richard Edward Nelson 1932- *28*
Cather, Willa 1873-1947 .... *30*
  See also CLR *98*
Catherall, Arthur 1906-1980 .... *74*
  Earlier sketches in SATA *3, 4*
Cathon, Laura E(lizabeth) 1908-1991 .... *27*
Catlett, Elizabeth 1919(?)- *82*
Catlin, Wynelle 1930- *13*
Catlow, Nikalas
  See Catlow, Niki
Catlow, Niki 1975- *193*
Cato, Heather *105*
Cato, Sheila *114*
Catran, Ken 1944- *190*
Catrow, David *206*
  See Catrow, David J. III
Catrow, David J. III *152*
  See Catrow, David
Catt, Louis
  See French, Vivian
Cattell, James 1954- *123*
Catton, (Charles) Bruce 1899-1978 .... *2*
  Obituary *24*
Catz, Max
  See Glaser, Milton
Caudell, Marian 1930- *52*
Caudill, Rebecca 1899-1985 .... *1*
  Obituary *44*
Cauley, Lorinda Bryan 1951- *46*
  Brief entry *43*
Caulfield, Peggy F. 1926-1987
  Obituary *53*
Cauman, Samuel 1910-1971 .... *48*
Causley, Charles (Stanley) 1917-2003 .... *66*
  Obituary *149*
  Earlier sketch in SATA *3*
  See also CLR *30*
Cavallaro, Ann (Abelson) 1918- *62*
Cavallo, Diana 1931- *7*
Cavanagh, Helen (Carol) 1939- *98*
  Brief entry *37*
  Earlier sketch in SATA *48*
Cavanah, Frances 1899-1982 .... *31*
  Earlier sketch in SATA *1*
Cavanna, Betty
  See Harrison, Elizabeth (Allen) Cavanna
Cavanna, Elizabeth
  See Harrison, Elizabeth (Allen) Cavanna
Cave, Kathryn 1948- *123*
  Earlier sketch in SATA *76*
Cavendish, Peter
  See Horler, Sydney
Cavin, Ruth (Brodie) 1918- *38*
Cavoukian, Raffi 1948- *68*
Cawley, Winifred 1915- *13*
Caxton, Pisistratus
  See Lytton, Edward G(eorge) E(arle) L(ytton)
  Bulwer-Lytton Baron
Cazeau, Charles J(ay) 1931- *65*
Cazet, Denys 1938- *191*
  Brief entry *41*
  Earlier sketches in SATA *52, 99, 163*
Cazzola, Gus 1934- *73*
Cebulash, Mel 1937- *91*
  Earlier sketch in SATA *10*
Ceccoli, Nicoletta *181*
Cecil, Randy 1968- *187*
Cecka, Melanie *199*
Ceder, Georgiana Dorcas -1985 .... *10*
Celenza, Anna Harwell *133*
Celestino, Martha Laing
  See Laing, Martha
Cepeda, Joe *159*
Cerf, Bennett (Alfred) 1898-1971 .... *7*
Cerf, Christopher (Bennett) 1941- *2*
Cermak, Martin
  See Duchacek, Ivo D(uka)
Cerullo, Mary M. 1949- *145*
  Earlier sketch in SATA *86*
Cervon, Jacqueline
  See Moussard, Jacqueline

Cetin, Frank Stanley 1921- 2
Chabon, Michael 1963- 145
Chaconas, D.J.
  See Chaconas, Dori
Chaconas, Dori 1938- 175
  Earlier sketch in SATA 145
Chaconas, Doris J.
  See Chaconas, Dori
Chadwick, Lester 67
  Earlier sketch in SATA 1
Chaffee, Allen 3
Chaffin, Lillie D(orton) 1925- 4
Chaikin, Miriam 1924- 152
  Earlier sketches in SATA 24, 102
Chall, Marsha Wilson 150
Challand, Helen J(ean) 1921- 64
Challans, Mary
  See Renault, Mary
Chalmers, Mary (Eileen) 1927- 6
  See also SAAS 14
Chamberlain, Barbara A.
  See Azore, Barbara
Chamberlain, Margaret 1954- 46
Chamberlin, Kate 1945- 105
Chamberlin, Mary 1960- 177
Chamberlin, Rich 177
Chamberlin, Richard
  See Chamberlin, Rich
Chambers, Aidan 1934- 171
  Earlier sketches in SATA 1, 69, 108
  See also SAAS 12
Chambers, Bradford 1922-1984
  Obituary 39
Chambers, Catherine E.
  See St. John, Nicole
Chambers, John W. 1933- 57
  Brief entry 46
Chambers, Kate
  See St. John, Nicole
Chambers, Margaret Ada Eastwood 1911- 2
Chambers, Peggy
  See Chambers, Margaret Ada Eastwood
Chambers, Robert W(illiam) 1865-1933 107
Chambliss, Maxie 186
Chan, Gillian 1954- 147
  Earlier sketch in SATA 102
Chan, Peter 1980(?)- 207
Chance, James T.
  See Carpenter, John
Chance, John T.
  See Carpenter, John
Chance, Stephen
  See Turner, Philip (William)
Chandler, Caroline A(ugusta) 1906-1979 22
  Obituary 24
Chandler, David P(orter) 1933- 28
Chandler, Edna Walker 1908-1982 11
  Obituary 31
Chandler, Jennifer
  See Westwood, Jennifer
Chandler, Karen 1959- 122
Chandler, Linda S(mith) 1929- 39
Chandler, Pauline 175
Chandler, Robert 1953- 40
Chandler, Ruth Forbes 1894-1978 2
  Obituary 26
Chandonnet, Ann F. 1943- 92
Chaney, Jill 1932- 87
Chang, Chih-Wei 1966- 111
Chang, Cindy 1968- 90
Chang, Margaret 1941- 71
Chang, Margaret Scrogin
  See Chang, Margaret
Chang, Raymond 1939- 142
  Earlier sketches in SATA 71, 142 PEN
Chanin, Michael 1952- 84
Channel, A. R.
  See Catherall, Arthur
Chapian, Marie 1938- 29
Chapin, Alene Olsen Dalton 1915(?)-1986
  Obituary 47

Chapin, Tom 1945- 83
Chapman, Allen 67
  Earlier sketch in SATA 1
Chapman, Cheryl O(rth) 1948- 80
Chapman, (Constance) Elizabeth (Mann)
  1919- 10
Chapman, Gaye 1970- 200
Chapman, Gaye Coralie
  See Chapman, Gaye
Chapman, Gaynor 1935- 32
Chapman, Gillian 1955- 120
Chapman, Jane 1970- 176
  Earlier sketch in SATA 122
Chapman, Jean 104
  Earlier sketch in SATA 34
  See also CLR 65
Chapman, John Stanton Higham 1891-1972
  Obituary 27
Chapman, Lee
  See Bradley, Marion Zimmer
Chapman, Lynne 1960- 197
Chapman, Lynne F(erguson) 1963- 150
  Earlier sketch in SATA 94
Chapman, Maristan
  See Chapman, John Stanton Higham
Chapman, Vera (Ivy May) 1898-1996 33
Chapman, Walker
  See Silverberg, Robert
Chappell, Audrey 1954- 72
Chappell, Crissa-Jean 198
Chappell, Warren 1904-1991 68
  Obituary 67
  Earlier sketch in SATA 6
  See also SAAS 10
Chapra, Mimi 182
Charbonneau, Eileen 1951- 118
  Earlier sketch in SATA 84
Charbonnet, Gabrielle 1961- 81
Chardiet, Bernice (Kroll) 1927(?)- 27
Charest, Emily MacLachlan 198
Charles, Donald
  See Meighan, Donald Charles
Charles, Louis
  See Stratemeyer, Edward L.
Charles, Nicholas
  See Kuskin, Karla
Charles, Nicholas J.
  See Kuskin, Karla
Charles, Norma 153
Charles, Veronika Martenova 182
Charlip, Remy 1929- 119
  Earlier sketches in SATA 4, 68
  See also CLR 8
Charlot, Jean 1898-1979 8
  Obituary 31
Charlot, Martin (Day) 1944- 64
Charlton, Michael (Alan) 1923- 34
Charlton-Trujillo, e.E. 189
Charmatz, Bill 1925-2005 7
Charnas, Suzy McKee 1939- 110
  Earlier sketch in SATA 61
Charosh, Mannis 1906- 5
Chartier, Normand L. 1945- 66
Chase, Alice
  See McHargue, Georgess
Chase, Alyssa 1965- 92
Chase, Andra 1942- 91
Chase, Emily
  See Aks, Patricia
  and Garwood, Julie
  and Sachs, Judith
  and White, Carol
Chase, Mary (Coyle) 1907-1981 17
  Obituary 29
Chase, Mary Ellen 1887-1973 10
Chase, Richard 1904-1988 64
  Obituary 56
Chase, Samantha
  See Glick, Ruth (Burtnick)
Chast, Roz 1954- 97
Chastain, Madye Lee 1908-1989 4

Chataway, Carol 1955- 140
Chatterjee, Debjani 1952- 83
Chauncy, Nan(cen Beryl Masterman)
  1900-1970 6
  See also CLR 6
Chaundler, Christine 1887-1972 1
  Obituary 25
Chayka, Doug 196
Chbosky, Stephen 1972- 164
Cheaney, Janie B.
  See Cheaney, J.B.
Cheaney, J.B. 1950- 188
Chee, Cheng-Khee 1934- 79
Cheese, Chloe 1952- 118
Chekhonte, Antosha
  See Chekhov, Anton
Chekhov, Anton 1860-1904 90
Chekhov, Anton Pavlovich
  See Chekhov, Anton
Chelushkin, Kirill 1968- 186
Chen, Anthony 1929- 6
Chen, Chih-Yuan 1975- 155
Chen, Ju-Hong 1941- 78
Chen, Pauline 1966- 202
Chen, Sara
  See Odgers, Sally Farrell
Chen, Tony
  See Chen, Anthony
Chen, Yong 1963- 183
Chen, Yuan-tsung 1932- 65
Chenault, Nell
  See Smith, Linell Nash
Chenery, Janet (Dai) 1923- 25
Cheney, Cora 1916-1999 3
  Obituary 110
Cheney, Glenn (Alan) 1951- 99
Cheney, Lynne V. 1941- 152
Cheney, Lynne Vincent
  See Cheney, Lynne V.
Cheney, Ted
  See Cheney, Theodore Albert
Cheney, Theodore A. Rees
  See Cheney, Theodore Albert
Cheney, Theodore Albert 1928- 11
Cheng, Andrea 1957- 205
  Earlier sketches in SATA 128, 172
Cheng, Christopher 1959- 173
  Earlier sketch in SATA 106
Cheng, Judith 1955- 36
Cheng, Shan
  See Jiang, Cheng An
Cheripko, Jan 1951- 155
  Earlier sketch in SATA 83
Chermayeff, Ivan 1932- 47
Chernenko, Dan
  See Chernenko, Dan
Chernoff, Dorothy A.
  See Ernst, (Lyman) John
Chernoff, Goldie Taub 1909- 10
Cherry, Carolyn Janice
  See Cherryh, C.J.
Cherry, Lynne 1952- 99
  Earlier sketch in SATA 34
Cherryh, C.J. 1942- 172
  Earlier sketch in SATA 93
Cherryholmes, Anne
  See Price, Olive
Cheshire, Simon 172
Chesler, Bernice 1932-2002 59
Chess, Victoria (Dickerson) 1939- 92
  Earlier sketch in SATA 33
Chessa, Francesca 191
Chester, Deborah 1957- 85
Chester, Kate
  See Guccione, Leslie Davis
Chesterton, G. K. 1874-1936 27
Chesterton, Gilbert Keith
  See Chesterton, G. K.
Chesworth, Michael 207
  Earlier sketch in SATA 160
Chetin, Helen 1922- 6

Chetwin, Grace 86
  Brief entry 50
Chevalier, Christa 1937- 35
Chevalier, Tracy 1962- 128
Chew, Ruth 1920- 7
Chichester Clark, Emma 1955- 69
  Earlier sketches in SATA *117, 156*
Chidsey, Donald Barr 1902-1981 3
  Obituary 27
Chiefari, Janet D. 1942- 58
Chien, Catia 193
Chien-min, Lin
  See Rumford, James
Child, L. Maria
  See Child, Lydia Maria
Child, Lauren 1965- 183
  Earlier sketches in SATA *119, 160*
Child, Lincoln 1957- 113
Child, Lincoln B.
  See Child, Lincoln
Child, Lydia Maria 1802-1880 67
Child, Mrs.
  See Child, Lydia Maria
Child, Philip 1898-1978 47
Children's Shepherd, The
  See Westphal, Arnold Carl
Childress, Alice 1920-1994 81
  Earlier sketches in SATA *7, 48*
  See also CLR *14*
Childs, H(alla) Fay (Cochrane) 1890-1971 1
  Obituary 25
Chilton, Charles (Frederick William)
  1917- 102
Chima, Cinda Williams 192
Chimaera
  See Farjeon, Eleanor
Chin, Richard (M.) 1946- 52
Chinery, Michael 1938- 26
Chin-Lee, Cynthia 1958- 102
Chin-Lee D., Cynthia
  See Chin-Lee, Cynthia
Chippendale, Lisa A. 158
Chipperfield, Joseph Eugene 1912-1980(?) .. 87
  Earlier sketch in SATA *2*
Chisholm, P. F.
  See Finney, Patricia
Chislett, Gail (Elaine) 1948- 58
Chittenden, Elizabeth F. 1903-1999 9
Chittenden, Margaret 1935- 28
Chittum, Ida 1918- 7
Chitwood, Suzanne Tanner 1958- 160
Chmielarz, Sharon Lee 1940- 72
Choate, Judith (Newkirk) 1940- 30
Chocolate, Debbi 1954- 96
Chocolate, Deborah M. Newton
  See Chocolate, Debbi
Chodos-Irvine, Margaret 152
Choi, Sook Nyul 1937- 73
  Autobiography Feature 126
  See also CLR *53*
Choi, Yangsook 178
Choldenko, Gennifer 1957- 182
  Earlier sketch in SATA *135*
Chorao, (Ann Mc)Kay (Sproat) 1936- 162
  Earlier sketches in SATA *8, 69*
Choron, Sandra (Zena Samelson) 1950- 146
Choung, Eun-hee 199
Chown, Marcus 1959- 137
Choyce, Lesley 1951- 165
  Earlier sketch in SATA *94*
Chrisman, Arthur Bowie 1889-1953 124
  See also YABC *1*
Christelow, Eileen 1943- 184
  Autobiography Feature 120
  Brief entry 35
  Earlier sketches in SATA *38, 90*
Christensen, Bonnie 1951- 157
  Earlier sketch in SATA *110*
Christensen, Gardell Dano 1907-1991 1
Christensen, Laurie
  See Steding, Laurie

Christesen, Barbara 1940- 40
Christgau, Alice Erickson 1902-1977 13
Christian, Mary Blount 1933- 9
Christiana, David 195
Christie, Agatha 1890-1976 36
Christie, Agatha Mary Clarissa
  See Christie, Agatha
Christie, Ann Philippa
  See Pearce, Philippa
Christie, Gregory
  See Christie, R. Gregory
Christie, Philippa
  See Pearce, Philippa
Christie, R. Gregory 1971- 185
  Earlier sketch in SATA *127*
Christopher, John
  See Youd, Samuel
Christopher, Louise
  See Hale, Arlene
Christopher, Matt(hew Frederick)
  1917-1997 80
  Obituary 99
  Earlier sketches in SATA *2, 47*
  See also CLR *119*
  See also SAAS *9*
Christopher, Milbourne 1914(?)-1984 46
Christy, Howard Chandler 1873-1952 21
Chrustowski, Rick 176
Chrystie, Frances N(icholson) 1904-1986 60
Chu, Daniel 1933- 11
Chukovsky, Kornei (Ivanovich) 1882-1969 . 34
  Earlier sketch in SATA *5*
Church, Caroline Jayne 179
Church, Richard 1893-1972 3
Churchill, E(lmer) Richard 1937- 11
Churchill, Elizabeth
  See Hough, Richard (Alexander)
Chute, B(eatrice) J(oy) 1913-1987 2
  Obituary 53
Chute, Marchette (Gaylord) 1909-1994 1
Chwast, Jacqueline 1932- 6
Chwast, Seymour 1931- 146
  Earlier sketches in SATA *18, 96*
Ciardi, John (Anthony) 1916-1986 65
  Obituary 46
  Earlier sketch in SATA *1*
  See also CLR *19*
  See also SAAS *26*
Ciccone, Madonna Louise Veronica
  See Madonna
Ciment, James D. 1958- 140
Cirrone, Dorian 182
Cisneros, Sandra 1954-
  See CLR *123*
Citra, Becky 1954- 137
Citrin, Michael 1965(?)- 183
Clair, Andree 19
Clampett, Bob 1914(?)-1985 44
  Obituary 38
Clampett, Robert
  See Clampett, Bob
Clapp, John 1968- 109
Clapp, Patricia 1912- 74
  Earlier sketch in SATA *4*
  See also SAAS *4*
Clare, Ellen
  See Sinclair, Olga
Clare, Helen
  See Clarke, Pauline
Claremont, Chris 1950- 87
Claremont, Christopher Simon
  See Claremont, Chris
Clark, Ann Nolan 1896-1995 82
  Obituary 87
  Earlier sketch in SATA *4*
  See also CLR *16*
  See also SAAS *16*
Clark, Champ 1923-2002 47
Clark, Christopher (Anthony) Stuart
  See Stuart-Clark, Christopher (Anthony)

Clark, Clara Gillow 1951- 154
  Earlier sketch in SATA *84*
Clark, David
  See Hardcastle, Michael
Clark, David Allen
  See Ernst, (Lyman) John
Clark, Emma Chichester
  See Chichester Clark, Emma
Clark, Frank J(ames) 1922- 18
Clark, Garel
  See Garelick, May
Clark, Halsey
  See Deming, Richard
Clark, Joan
  See Benson, Mildred
Clark, Joan 1934- 182
  Earlier sketches in SATA *59, 96*
Clark, Leonard 1905-1981 30
  Obituary 29
Clark, M. R.
  See Clark, Mavis Thorpe
Clark, Margaret (D.) 1943- 126
Clark, Margaret Goff 1913- 82
  Earlier sketch in SATA *8*
Clark, Mary Higgins 1929- 46
Clark, Mavis Thorpe 1909-1999 74
  Earlier sketch in SATA *8*
  See also CLR *30*
  See also SAAS *5*
Clark, Merle
  See Gessner, Lynne
Clark, Patricia Denise 1921- 117
Clark, Patricia Finrow 1929- 11
Clark, Ronald Harry 1904-1999 193
Clark, Ronald William 1916-1987 2
  Obituary 52
Clark, Sherryl 1956- 149
Clark, Van D(eusen) 1909-1974 2
Clark, Virginia
  See Gray, Patricia (Clark)
Clark, Walter Van Tilburg 1909-1971 8
Clarke, Arthur
  See Clarke, Arthur C.
Clarke, Arthur C. 1917-2008 115
  Obituary 191
  Earlier sketches in SATA *13, 70*
  See also CLR *119*
Clarke, Arthur Charles
  See Clarke, Arthur C.
Clarke, Clorinda 1917- 7
Clarke, Gus 1948- 134
Clarke, J.
  See Clarke, Judith
Clarke, James Hall
  See Rowland-Entwistle, (Arthur) Theodore
  (Henry)
Clarke, Joan B. 1921- 42
  Brief entry 27
Clarke, John
  See Laklan, Carli
  and Sontup, Dan(iel)
Clarke, Judith 1943- 164
  Earlier sketches in SATA *75, 110*
  See also CLR *61*
Clarke, Julia 1950- 138
Clarke, Kenneth 1957- 107
Clarke, Lea
  See Rowland-Entwistle, (Arthur) Theodore
  (Henry)
Clarke, Margaret 1941-
  See CLR *99*
Clarke, Mary Stetson 1911-1994 5
Clarke, Michael
  See Newlon, (Frank) Clarke
Clarke, Pauline 1921- 131
  Earlier sketch in SATA *3*
  See also CLR *28*
Clarke-Rich, Elizabeth L. 1934- 103
Clarkson, E(dith) Margaret 1915- 37
Clarkson, Ewan 1929- 9

Claudia, Susan
  See Goulart, Ron
  and Johnston, William
Claverie, Jean 1946- 38
Clay, Patrice 1947- 47
Clay, Wil 203
Clayman, Deborah Paula
  See Da Costa, Deborah
Claypool, Jane
  See Miner, Jane Claypool
Clayton, Elaine 1961- 159
  Earlier sketch in SATA 94
Clayton, Lawrence (Otto, Jr.) 1945- 75
Clayton, Sandra 1951- 110
Cle, Troy 202
Clea, Super
  See Hantman, Clea
Cleary, Beverly 1916- 121
  Earlier sketches in SATA 2, 43, 79
  See also CLR 72
  See also SAAS 20
Cleary, Beverly Atlee Bunn
  See Cleary, Beverly
Cleary, Brian P. 1959- 186
  Earlier sketches in SATA 93, 132
Cleaver, Bill
  See Cleaver, William J.
Cleaver, Carole 1934- 6
Cleaver, Elizabeth (Ann Mrazik)
  1939-1985 23
  Obituary 43
  See also CLR 13
Cleaver, Hylton Reginald 1891-1961 49
Cleaver, Vera 1919-1993 76
  Earlier sketch in SATA 22
  See also CLR 6
Cleaver, Vera Allen
  See Cleaver, Vera
Cleaver, William J. 1920-1981 22
  Obituary 27
  See also CLR 6
Cleishbotham, Jebediah
  See Scott, Sir Walter
Cleland, Mabel
  See Widdemer, Mabel Cleland
Clem, Margaret H(ollingsworth) 1923- 90
Clemens, Samuel
  See Twain, Mark
Clemens, Samuel Langhorne
  See Twain, Mark
Clemens, Virginia Phelps 1941- 35
Clement, Gary 191
Clement, Janet 182
Clement, Nathan 1966- 200
Clement, Priscilla Ferguson 1942- 171
Clement, Rod 97
Clement-Moore, Rosemary 188
Clements, Andrew 1949- 203
  Earlier sketches in SATA 104, 158
Clements, Bruce 1931- 178
  Earlier sketches in SATA 27, 94
Clemesha, David 192
Clemons, Elizabeth
  See Nowell, Elizabeth Cameron
Clerk, N. W.
  See Lewis, C. S.
Cleveland, Bob
  See Cleveland, George
Cleveland, George 1903(?)-1985
  Obituary 43
Cleveland-Peck, Patricia 80
Cleven, Cathrine
  See Cleven, Kathryn Seward
Cleven, Kathryn Seward 2
Clevenger, William R. 1954- 84
Clevenger, William Russell
  See Clevenger, William R.
Clevin, Joergen 1920- 7
Clevin, Jorgen
  See Clevin, Joergen

Clewes, Dorothy (Mary) 1907-2003 86
  Obituary 138
  Earlier sketch in SATA 1
Clifford, David
  See Rosenberg, Eth Clifford
Clifford, Eth
  See Rosenberg, Eth Clifford
Clifford, Harold B(urton) 1893-1988 10
Clifford, Margaret Cort 1929- 1
Clifford, Martin
  See Hamilton, Charles (Harold St. John)
Clifford, Mary Louise Beneway 1926- 23
Clifford, Peggy
  See Clifford, Margaret Cort
Clifford, Rachel Mark
  See Lewis, Brenda Ralph
Clifton, Lucille 1936- 128
  Earlier sketches in SATA 20, 69
  See also CLR 5
Clifton, Thelma Lucille
  See Clifton, Lucille
Climo, Shirley 1928- 166
  Autobiography Feature 110
  Brief entry 35
  Earlier sketches in SATA 39, 77
  See also CLR 69
Cline-Ransome, Lesa 201
Clinton, Catherine 1952- 203
Clinton, Cathryn 1957- 136
Clinton, Dirk
  See Silverberg, Robert
Clinton, Jon
  See Prince, J(ack) H(arvey)
Clippinger, Carol 193
Clish, (Lee) Marian 1946- 43
Clive, Clifford
  See Hamilton, Charles (Harold St. John)
Clokey, Art 1921- 59
Cloudsley-Thompson, J(ohn) L(eonard)
  1921- 19
Clouse, Nancy L. 1938- 78
Clover, Peter 1952- 152
Clutha, Janet Paterson Frame
  See Frame, Janet
Clymer, Eleanor 1906-2001 85
  Obituary 126
  Earlier sketch in SATA 9
  See also SAAS 17
Clyne, Patricia (Edwards) 31
Cneut, Carll 1969- 197
Coalson, Glo 1946- 94
  Earlier sketch in SATA 26
Coates, Anna 1958- 73
Coates, Belle 1896-1986 2
Coates, Ruth Allison 1915- 11
Coats, Alice M(argaret) 1905-1976 11
Coatsworth, Elizabeth (Jane) 1893-1986 100
  Obituary 49
  Earlier sketches in SATA 2, 56
  See also CLR 2
Cobalt, Martin
  See Mayne, William (James Carter)
Cobb, Jane
  See Berry, Jane Cobb
Cobb, Mary 1931- 88
Cobb, Vicki 1938- 136
  Autobiography Feature 136
  Earlier sketches in SATA 8, 69, 131
  See also CLR 2
  See also SAAS 6
Cobbett, Richard
  See Pluckrose, Henry (Arthur)
Cober, Alan E(dwin) 1935-1998 7
  Obituary 101
Cobham, Sir Alan
  See Hamilton, Charles (Harold St. John)
Coburn, Jake 1978- 155
Cocagnac, Augustin Maurice(-Jean) 1924- 7
Cocca-Leffler, Maryann 1958- 194
  Earlier sketches in SATA 80, 136
Cochran, Bill 187

Cochran, Bobbye A. 1949- 11
Cochran, Thomas 1955- 198
Cockett, Mary 3
Cocks, Peter 204
Cocovini, Abby 202
Coddell, Esme Raji
  See Codell, Esme Raji
Codell, Esme Raji 1968- 160
Cody, C. S.
  See Waller, Leslie
Cody, Jess
  See Cunningham, Chet
Coe, Anne (E.) 1949- 95
Coe, Douglas
  See Epstein, Beryl
  and Epstein, Samuel
Coe, Lloyd 1899(?)-1976
  Obituary 30
Coen, Rena Neumann 1925- 20
Coerr, Eleanor (Beatrice) 1922- 67
  Earlier sketch in SATA 1
Cofer, Judith Ortiz 1952- 164
  Earlier sketch in SATA 110
Coffelt, Nancy 1961- 189
Coffey, Brian
  See Koontz, Dean
Coffin, Geoffrey
  See Mason, F(rancis) van Wyck
Coffin, M. T.
  See Stanley, George Edward
Coffman, Ramon Peyton 1896-1989 4
Cogan, Karen 1954- 125
Coggins, Jack (Banham) 1911-2006 2
Cohen, Barbara 1932-1992 77
  Obituary 74
  Earlier sketch in SATA 10
  See also SAAS 7
Cohen, Daniel (E.) 1936- 70
  Earlier sketch in SATA 8
  See also CLR 43
  See also SAAS 4
Cohen, Deborah Bodin 1968- 180
Cohen, Jan Barger
  See Barger, Jan
Cohen, Jene Barr
  See Barr, Jene
Cohen, Joan Lebold 1932- 4
Cohen, Judith Love 1933- 78
Cohen, Miriam 1926-1955 155
  Earlier sketches in SATA 29, 106
  See also SAAS 11
Cohen, Nora 75
Cohen, Paul S. 1945- 58
Cohen, Peter Zachary 1931- 150
  Earlier sketch in SATA 4
Cohen, Robert Carl 1930- 8
Cohen, Sholom 1951- 94
Cohn, Angelo 1914-1997 19
Cohn, Diana 194
Cohn, Rachel 1968- 161
Coit, Margaret Louise 1922-2003 2
  Obituary 142
Colato Lainez, Rene 1970- 176
Colbert, Anthony 1934-2007 15
Colbert, Nancy A. 1936- 139
Colby, C(arroll) B(urleigh) 1904-1977 35
  Earlier sketch in SATA 3
Colby, Jean Poindexter 1909-1993 23
Cole, Annette
  See Steiner, Barbara A(nnette)
Cole, Babette 1949- 155
  Earlier sketches in SATA 61, 96
Cole, Betsy 1940- 83
Cole, Brock 1938- 200
  Earlier sketches in SATA 72, 136
  See also CLR 18
Cole, Davis
  See Elting, Mary
Cole, Hannah 1954- 74
Cole, Henry 1955- 181

Cole, Jack -1974
See Stewart, John
Cole, Jackson
See Curry, Thomas Albert
and Germano, Peter B.
and Heckelmann, Charles N(ewman)
and Newton, D(wight) B(ennett)
and Schisgall, Oscar
Cole, Jennifer
See Zach, Cheryl (Byrd)
Cole, Joanna 1944- 168
Brief entry 37
Earlier sketches in SATA 49, 81, 120
See also CLR 40
Cole, Lois Dwight 1903-1979 10
Obituary 26
Cole, Michael 1947- 59
Cole, Samantha
See Cole, Stephen
Cole, Sheila 1939- 171
Earlier sketches in SATA 24, 95
Cole, Sheila R.
See Cole, Sheila
Cole, Sheila Rotenberg
See Cole, Sheila
Cole, Stephen 1971- 161
Cole, William (Rossa) 1919-2000 71
Earlier sketch in SATA 9
See also SAAS 9
Coleman, Andrew
See Pine, Nicholas
Coleman, Clare
See Bell, Clare (Louise)
and Easton, M(alcolm) Coleman
Coleman, Janet Wyman 184
Coleman, Loren 1947- 164
Coleman, Loren Elwood, Jr.
See Coleman, Loren
Coleman, Mary Ann 1928- 83
Coleman, Michael
See Jones, Allan Frewin
Coleman, Michael 1946- 199
Autobiography Feature 133
Earlier sketches in SATA 108, 133
Coleman, Rowan 187
Coleman, William L(eRoy) 1938- 49
Brief entry 34
Coles, Robert (Martin) 1929- 23
Colfer, Eoin 1965- 197
Earlier sketch in SATA 148
See also CLR 112
Colin, Ann
See Ure, Jean
Collard, Sneed B. III 1959- 184
Earlier sketches in SATA 84, 139
Colledge, Anne 1939- 142
Colley, Jacqui 1965- 202
Collicott, Sharleen 1937- 143
Earlier sketch in SATA 98
Collier, Bryan 204
Earlier sketches in SATA 126, 174
Collier, Christopher 1930- 70
Earlier sketch in SATA 16
See also CLR 126
Collier, Ethel 1903-1999 22
Collier, James Lincoln 1928- 166
Earlier sketches in SATA 8, 70
See also CLR 126
See also SAAS 21
Collier, Jane
See Collier, Zena
Collier, Kristi 182
Collier, Steven 1942- 61
Collier, Zena 1926- 23
Collings, Gillian 1939- 102
Collington, Peter 1948- 99
Earlier sketch in SATA 59
Collins, Ace 1953- 82
Collins, Andrew J.
See Collins, Ace

Collins, David R(aymond) 1940-2001 121
Earlier sketch in SATA 7
Collins, Heather 1946- 81
Collins, Hunt
See Hunter, Evan
Collins, Michael
See Lynds, Dennis
Collins, Michael 1930- 58
Collins, Pat(ricia) Lowery 1932- 151
Earlier sketch in SATA 31
Collins, Paul 1954- 126
Collins, Ross 1972- 200
Collins, Ruth Philpott 1890-1975
Obituary 30
Collins, Suzanne 180
Collins, Yvonne 194
Collinson, A. S.
See Collinson, Alan S.
Collinson, Alan S. 1934- 80
Collinson, Roger (Alfred) 1936- 133
Collison, Linda 1953- 185
Collodi, Carlo
See Lorenzini, Carlo
Colloms, Brenda 1919- 40
Colman, Hila 53
Earlier sketch in SATA 1
See also SAAS 14
Colman, Morris 1899(?)-1981
Obituary 25
Colman, Penny (Morgan) 1944- 160
Autobiography Feature 160
Earlier sketches in SATA 77, 114
Colman, Warren (David) 1944- 67
Colombo, John Robert 1936- 50
Colon, Raul 156
Colon, Raul 1952- 202
Colonius, Lillian 1911-1992 3
Colorado, Antonio J.
See Colorado (Capella), Antonio J(ulio)
Colorado (Capella), Antonio J(ulio)
1903-1994 23
Obituary 79
Colquhoun, Glenn 1964- 165
Colston, Fifi E. 1960- 150
Colt, Martin
See Epstein, Beryl
and Epstein, Samuel
Colum, Padraic 1881-1972 15
See also CLR 36
Columbus, Chris 1959- 97
Columbus, Christopher
See Columbus, Chris
Columella
See Moore, Clement Clarke
Colver, Anne 1908- 7
Colvin, James
See Moorcock, Michael
Colwell, Eileen (Hilda) 1904-2002 2
Colwyn, Stewart
See Pepper, Frank S.
Coman, Carolyn 1951- 197
Earlier sketch in SATA 127
Combs, Lisa M.
See McCourt, Lisa
Combs, Robert
See Murray, John
Comfort, Jane Levington
See Sturtzel, Jane Levington
Comfort, Mildred Houghton 1886-1976 3
Comins, Ethel M(ae) 11
Comins, Jeremy 1933- 28
Commager, Henry Steele 1902-1998 23
Obituary 102
Comora, Madeleine 190
Compere, Mickie
See Davidson, Margaret
Compestine, Ying Chang 1963- 187
Earlier sketch in SATA 140
Comport, Sally Wern 190
Compton, Patricia A. 1936- 75

Comte, The Great
See Hawkesworth, Eric
Comus
See Ballantyne, R(obert) M(ichael)
Comyns, Nance
See Comyns-Toohey, Nantz
Comyns-Toohey, Nantz 1956- 86
Conan Doyle, Arthur
See Doyle, Sir Arthur Conan
Condie, Ally 204
Condie, Allyson B.
See Condie, Ally
Condit, Martha Olson 1913- 28
Condon, Bill 1949- 142
Condon, Judith 83
Condon, Ken 195
Condy, Roy 1942- 96
Cone, Ferne Geller 1921- 39
Cone, Molly (Lamken) 1918- 151
Autobiography Feature 151
Earlier sketches in SATA 1, 28, 115
See also SAAS 11
Cone, Patrick 1954- 89
Coney, Michael G. 1932-2005 61
Obituary 170
Coney, Michael Greatrex
See Coney, Michael G.
Coney, Mike
See Coney, Michael G.
Conford, Ellen 1942- 162
Earlier sketches in SATA 6, 68, 110
See also CLR 71
Conger, Lesley
See Suttles, Shirley (Smith)
Conklin, Gladys Plemon 1903- 2
Conklin, Paul S. 1929(?)-2003 43
Brief entry 33
Obituary 147
Conkling, Hilda 1910-1986 23
Conlan, Kathleen Elizabeth 1950- 145
Conlan, Kathy
See Conlan, Kathleen Elizabeth
Conley, Robyn 1963- 125
Conley-Weaver, Robyn
See Conley, Robyn
Conlon-McKenna, Marita 1956- 71
Conly, Jane Leslie 1948- 164
Earlier sketches in SATA 80, 112
Conly, Robert Leslie 1918(?)-1973 23
See also CLR 2
Connell, Kirk
See Chapman, John Stanton Higham
Connell, Tom 206
Connelly, Marc(us Cook) 1890-1980
Obituary 25
Connolly, Jerome P(atrick) 1931- 8
Connolly, Pat 1943- 74
Connolly, Peter 1935- 105
Earlier sketch in SATA 47
Conover, Chris 1950- 31
Conquest, Owen
See Hamilton, Charles (Harold St. John)
Conrad, Joseph 1857-1924 27
Conrad, Pam 1947-1996 133
Brief entry 49
Obituary 90
Earlier sketches in SATA 52, 80
See also CLR 18
See also SAAS 19
Conroy, Jack
See Conroy, John Wesley
Conroy, John Wesley 1899-1990 19
Obituary 65
Conroy, Robert
See Goldston, Robert (Conroy)
Constable, Kate 1966- 172
Constant, Alberta Wilson 1908-1981 22
Obituary 28
Constantin, Pascale 185
Conway, Diana C(ohen) 1943- 91

Conway, Gordon
  See Hamilton, Charles (Harold St. John)
Cook, Ande 192
Cook, Bernadine 1924- 11
Cook, Fred J(ames) 1911-2003 2
  Obituary 145
Cook, Glen 1944- 171
  Earlier sketch in SATA 108
Cook, Glen Charles
  See Cook, Glen
Cook, Hugh 1956- 85
Cook, Hugh, Walter Gilbert
  See Cook, Hugh
Cook, Jean Thor 1930- 94
Cook, Joel 1934- 79
Cook, Joseph Jay 1924- 8
Cook, Lisa Broadie 157
Cook, Lyn
  See Waddell, Evelyn Margaret
Cook, Roy
  See Silverberg, Robert
Cook, Sally 207
Cook, Trish 175
Cooke, Ann
  See Cole, Joanna
Cooke, Arthur
  See Lowndes, Robert A(ugustine) W(ard)
Cooke, Barbara
  See Alexander, Anna B(arbara Cooke)
Cooke, David Coxe 1917- 2
Cooke, Donald Ewin 1916-1985 2
  Obituary 45
Cooke, Frank E. 1920- 87
Cooke, Jean (Isobel Esther) 1929- 74
Cooke, John Estes
  See Baum, L. Frank
Cooke, Trish 1962- 129
Cookson, Catherine (McMullen) 1906-1998 .. 9
  Obituary 116
Cooley, Regina Francoise 1940- 177
Coolidge, Olivia E(nsor) 1908- 26
  Earlier sketch in SATA 1
Cooling, Wendy 169
  Earlier sketch in SATA 111
Coombs, Charles I(ra) 1914-1994 43
  Earlier sketch in SATA 3
  See also SAAS 15
Coombs, Chick
  See Coombs, Charles I(ra)
Coombs, Jonathan 204
Coombs, Kate 190
Coombs, Patricia 1926- 51
  Earlier sketch in SATA 3
  See also SAAS 22
Cooney, Barbara 1917-2000 96
  Obituary 123
  Earlier sketches in SATA 6, 59
  See also CLR 23
Cooney, Caroline B. 1947- 179
  Brief entry 41
  Earlier sketches in SATA 48, 80, 113, 130
Cooney, Doug 181
Cooney, Nancy Evans 1932- 42
Coontz, Otto 1946- 33
Cooper, Ann (Catharine) 1939- 104
Cooper, Dutch
  See Kuyper, Sjoerd
Cooper, Elisha 1971- 157
  Earlier sketch in SATA 99
Cooper, Elizabeth Keyser -1992 47
Cooper, Floyd 187
  Earlier sketches in SATA 96, 144
  See also CLR 60
Cooper, Gordon 1932- 23
Cooper, Helen 1963- 169
  Earlier sketch in SATA 102
Cooper, Henry S(potswood) F(enimore), Jr.
  1933- 65
Cooper, Ilene 1948- 145
  Earlier sketches in SATA 66, 97

Cooper, James Fenimore 1789-1851 19
  See also CLR 105
Cooper, John R. 1
Cooper, Kay 1941- 11
Cooper, Lee Pelham 1926- 5
Cooper, Lester (Irving) 1919-1985 32
  Obituary 43
Cooper, Lettice (Ulpha) 1897-1994 35
  Obituary 82
Cooper, Louise 1952-2009 152
Cooper, M.E.
  See Lerangis, Peter
Cooper, M.E.
  See Davis, Maggie S.
Cooper, Melrose
  See Kroll, Virginia L.
Cooper, Michael L. 1950- 181
  Earlier sketches in SATA 79, 117
Cooper, Patrick 1949- 134
Cooper, Susan 1935- 151
  Earlier sketches in SATA 4, 64, 104
  See also CLR 67
  See also SAAS 6
Cooper, Susan Mary
  See Cooper, Susan
Cope, Jane U(rsula) 1949- 108
Copeland, Helen 1920- 4
Copeland, Mark 1956- 180
Copeland, Paul W. 23
Coplans, Peta 1951- 84
Copley (Diana) Heather Pickering 1918- 45
Coppard, A(lfred) E(dgar) 1878-1957
  See YABC 1
Copper, Melinda 1952- 172
Copper, Melinda McConnaughey
  See Copper, Melinda
Coralie
  See Anderson, Catherine Corley
Corbett, Grahame 43
  Brief entry 36
Corbett, Scott 1913- 42
  Earlier sketch in SATA 2
  See also CLR 1
  See also SAAS 2
Corbett, Sue 174
Corbett, W(illiam) J(esse) 1938- 102
  Brief entry 44
  Earlier sketch in SATA 50
  See also CLR 19
Corbin, Sabra Lee
  See Malvern, Gladys
Corbin, William
  See McGraw, William Corbin
Corbman, Marjorie 1987- 179
Corby, Dan
  See Catherall, Arthur
Corcoran, Barbara (Asenath) 1911- 77
  Autobiography Feature 125
  Earlier sketch in SATA 3
  See also CLR 50
  See also SAAS 20
Corcos, Lucille 1908-1973 10
Cordell, Alexander
  See Graber, Alexander
Cordell, Matthew 1975- 199
Corder, Zizou
  See Young, Louisa
Corella, Joseph
  See Odgers, Sally Farrell
Coren, Alan 1938-2007 32
  Obituary 187
Corey, Dorothy 23
Corey, Shana 1974- 133
Corfe, Thomas Howell 1928- 27
Corfe, Tom
  See Corfe, Thomas Howell
Corfield, Robin Bell 1952- 74
Corlett, William 1938-2005 46
  Brief entry 39
Cormack, M(argaret) Grant 1913- 11
Cormack, Maribelle B. 1902-1984 39

Cormier, Robert 1925-2000 83
  Obituary 122
  Earlier sketches in SATA 10, 45
  See also CLR 55
Cormier, Robert Edmund
  See Cormier, Robert
Cornelius, Carol 1942- 40
Cornelius, Kay 1933- 157
Cornell, J.
  See Cornell, Jeffrey
Cornell, James (Clayton, Jr.) 1938- 27
Cornell, Jean Gay 1920- 23
Cornell, Jeffrey 1945- 11
Cornell, Laura 189
Cornish, D.M. 1972- 185
Cornish, Sam(uel James) 1935- 23
Cornwall, Nellie
  See Sloggett, Nellie
Cornwell, Autumn 195
Corr, Christopher 1955- 189
Correy, Lee
  See Stine, G(eorge) Harry
Corrick, James A. 1945- 76
Corrigan, (Helen) Adeline 1909- 23
Corrigan, Barbara 1922- 8
Corrigan, Eireann 1977- 163
Corrin, Sara 1918- 86
  Brief entry 48
Corrin, Stephen 86
  Brief entry 48
Corsi, Wendy
  See Staub, Wendy Corsi
Cort, M. C.
  See Clifford, Margaret Cort
Cort, Margaret
  See Clifford, Margaret Cort
Corwin, Judith H(offman) 1946- 10
Corwin, Oliver
  See Corwin, Oliver J.
Corwin, Oliver J. 206
Cory, Rowena
  See Lindquist, Rowena Cory
Cosby, Bill 1937- 110
  Earlier sketch in SATA 66
Cosby, William Henry, Jr.
  See Cosby, Bill
  and Cosby, Bill
Cosentino, Ralph 169
Cosgrave, John O'Hara II 1908-1968
  Obituary 21
Cosgrove, Margaret (Leota) 1926- 47
Cosgrove, Stephen E(dward) 1945- 53
  Brief entry 40
Coskey, Evelyn 1932- 7
Cosner, Shaaron 1940- 43
Cossi, Olga 1921- 102
  Earlier sketch in SATA 67
Costabel, Eva Deutsch 1924- 45
Costabel-Deutsch, Eva
  See Costabel, Eva Deutsch
Coste, Marion 1938- 183
Costello, David 174
Costello, David F(rancis) 1904-1990 23
Cte, Genevieve 1964- 184
Cote, Nancy 1952- 182
Cott, Jonathan 1942- 23
Cottam, Clarence 1899-1974 25
Cotten, Cynthia 188
Cottle, Joan 1960- 135
Cottler, Joseph 1899-1996 22
Cottonwood, Joe 1947- 92
Cottrell, Leonard 1913-1974 24
Cottringer, Anne 1952- 150
  Earlier sketch in SATA 97
Couch, Greg 199
Coulman, Valerie 1969- 161
Couloumbis, Audrey 173
Counsel, June 1926- 70
Countryman, The
  See Whitlock, Ralph

Courlander, Harold 1908-1996 .... *6*
  Obituary *88*
Coursen, Valerie 1965(?)- *102*
Courtis, Stuart Appleton 1874-1969
  Obituary *29*
Courtland, Tyler
  See Stevens, Serita
Courtney, Dayle
  See Goldsmith, Howard
Coury, Louise Andree 1895(?)-1983
  Obituary *34*
Cousins, Linda 1946- *90*
Cousins, Lucy 1964- *205*
  Earlier sketch in SATA *172*
Cousins, Margaret 1905-1996 .... *2*
  Obituary *92*
Cousteau, Jacques-Yves 1910-1997 .... *98*
  Earlier sketch in SATA *38*
Couture, Christin 1951- *73*
Couvillon, Jacques *195*
Covert, Ralph 1968- *197*
Coville, Bruce 1950- *155*
  Autobiography Feature *155*
  Earlier sketches in SATA *32, 77, 118*
Covington, Dennis *109*
Covington, Linda
  See Windsor, Linda
Cowan, Catherine *121*
Cowan, Rebecca M.
  See Moesta, Rebecca
Cowan, Rebecca Moesta
  See Moesta, Rebecca
Coward, Fiona 1963- *178*
Cowdrey, Richard 1959- *204*
Cowell, Cressida 1966- *140*
Cowen, Eve
  See Werner, Herma
Cowen, Ida 1898-1993 .... *64*
Cowie, Leonard W(allace) 1919- *4*
Cowles, Kathleen
  See Krull, Kathleen
Cowley, Cassia Joy
  See Cowley, Joy
Cowley, Joy 1936- *164*
Cowley, (Cassia) Joy 1936- *90*
  Autobiography Feature *118*
  Earlier sketch in SATA *4*
  See also CLR *55*
  See also SAAS *26*
Cowley, Marjorie 1925- *111*
Cox, (Christopher) Barry 1931- *62*
Cox, Clinton 1934- *108*
  Earlier sketch in SATA *74*
Cox, David (Dundas) 1933- *56*
Cox, Donald William 1921- *23*
Cox, Jack
  See Cox, John Roberts
Cox, John Roberts 1915-1981 .... *9*
Cox, Judy 1954- *198*
  Earlier sketches in SATA *117, 160*
Cox, Marion Monroe 1898-1983
  Obituary *34*
Cox, Palmer 1840-1924 .... *24*
  See also CLR *24*
Cox, Vic 1942- *88*
Cox, Vicki 1945- *158*
Cox, Victoria
  See Garretson, Victoria Diane
Cox, Wallace 1924-1973 .... *25*
Cox, Wally
  See Cox, Wallace
Cox, William R(obert) 1901-1988 .... *46*
  Brief entry *31*
  Obituary *57*
Coxe, Molly 1959- *101*
  Earlier sketch in SATA *69*
Coxon, Michele 1950- *158*
  Earlier sketch in SATA *76*
Coy, Harold 1902-1986 .... *3*
Coy, John 1958- *171*
  Earlier sketch in SATA *120*

Craats, Rennay 1973- *131*
Crabtree, Judith 1928- *98*
  Earlier sketch in SATA *63*
Cracker, Edward E.B.
  See Odgers, Sally Farrell
Craft, Elizabeth 1971(?)- *204*
Craft, K. Y.
  See Craft, Kinuko Y(amabe)
Craft, Kinuko
  See Craft, Kinuko Y(amabe)
Craft, Kinuko Y(amabe) 1940- *127*
  Earlier sketch in SATA *65*
Craft, Ruth 1935- *87*
  Brief entry *31*
Craig, A. A.
  See Anderson, Poul
Craig, Alisa
  See MacLeod, Charlotte (Matilda)
Craig, David *205*
  See James, Bill
Craig, Helen 1934- *94*
  Earlier sketches in SATA *46, 49*
Craig, Joe 1979- *198*
Craig, Joe Alexander
  See Craig, Joe
Craig, John Eland
  See Chipperfield, Joseph Eugene
Craig, John Ernest 1921- *23*
Craig, Kit
  See Reed, Kit
Craig, M. F.
  See Craig, Mary (Francis) Shura
Craig, M. Jean *17*
Craig, M. S.
  See Craig, Mary (Francis) Shura
Craig, Margaret (Maze) 1911-1964 .... *9*
Craig, Mary
  See Craig, Mary (Francis) Shura
Craig, Mary Shura
  See Craig, Mary (Francis) Shura
Craig, Mary (Francis) Shura 1923-1991 .... *86*
  Obituary *65*
  Earlier sketch in SATA *6*
  See also SAAS *7*
Craig, Ruth 1922- *95*
Craik, Mrs.
  See Craik, Dinah Maria (Mulock)
Craik, Dinah Maria (Mulock) 1826-1887 ..... *34*
Crandall, Court 1965- *175*
Crandell, Rachel 1943- *152*
Crane, Barbara (Joyce) 1934- *31*
Crane, Caroline 1930- *11*
Crane, Jordan 1973- *174*
Crane, M. A.
  See Wartski, Maureen (Ann Crane)
Crane, Royston Campbell 1901-1977
  Obituary *22*
Crane, Stephen 1871-1900
  See YABC *2*
  See also CLR *132*
Crane, Stephen Townley
  See Crane, Stephen
Crane, Walter 1845-1915 .... *100*
  Earlier sketch in SATA *18*
  See also CLR *56*
Crane, William D(wight) 1892-1976 .... *1*
Cranfield, Ingrid 1945- *74*
Cranshaw, Stanley
  See Fisher, Dorothy (Frances) Canfield
Crary, Elizabeth (Ann) 1942- *99*
  Brief entry *43*
Crary, Margaret (Coleman) 1906-1986 .... *9*
Craste, Marc *201*
Cravath, Lynne Avril
  See Cravath, Lynne W.
Cravath, Lynne W. 1951- *182*
  Earlier sketches in SATA *98, 148*
Craven, Thomas 1889-1969 .... *22*
Crawford, Charles P. 1945- *28*
Crawford, Deborah 1922- *6*
Crawford, John E(dmund) 1904-1971 .... *3*

Crawford, K(aren) Michael 1959- *155*
Crawford, Mel 1925- *44*
  Brief entry *33*
Crawford, Phyllis 1899- *3*
Crawley, Dave *177*
Cray, Roberta
  See Emerson, Ru
Crayder, Dorothy *7*
Crayder, Teresa
  See Colman, Hila
Crayon, Geoffrey
  See Irving, Washington
Craz, Albert G. 1926- *24*
Crebbin, June 1938- *169*
  Earlier sketch in SATA *80*
Crecy, Jeanne
  See Williams, Jeanne
Credle, Ellis 1902-1998 .... *1*
Creech, Sharon 1945- *172*
  Earlier sketches in SATA *94, 139*
  See also CLR *89*
Creeden, Sharon 1938- *91*
Creel, Ann Howard 1953- *187*
Creighton, (Mary) Helen 1899-1989
  Obituary *64*
Creighton, Jill 1949- *96*
Crenson, Victoria 1952- *159*
  Earlier sketch in SATA *88*
Cresp, Gael 1954- *119*
Crespo, George 1962- *82*
Cresswell, Helen 1934-2005 .... *79*
  Obituary *168*
  Earlier sketches in SATA *1, 48*
  See also CLR *18*
  See also SAAS *20*
Cressy, Michael 1955- *124*
Cressy, Mike
  See Cressy, Michael
Cretan, Gladys (Yessayan) 1921- *2*
Cretzmeyer, Stacy (Megan) 1959- *124*
Crew, Gary 1947- *163*
  Earlier sketches in SATA *75, 110*
  See also CLR *42*
Crew, Helen (Cecilia) Coale 1866-1941
  See YABC *2*
Crew, Linda (Jean) 1951- *137*
  Earlier sketch in SATA *71*
Crews, Donald 1938- *76*
  Brief entry *30*
  Earlier sketch in SATA *32*
  See also CLR *7*
Crews, Nina 1963- *158*
  Earlier sketch in SATA *97*
Crichton, John Michael
  See Crichton, Michael
Crichton, Michael 1942-2008 .... *88*
  Obituary *199*
  Earlier sketch in SATA *9*
Crider, Allen Billy
  See Crider, Bill
Crider, Bill 1941- *99*
Crilley, Mark 1966- *148*
  Autobiography Feature *148*
  Earlier sketch in SATA *120*
Crimi, Carolyn 1959- *176*
Cripps, Enid Margaret
  See Appiah, Peggy
Crisler, Curtis L. *188*
Crisman, Ruth 1914- *73*
Crisp, Marta Marie 1947- *128*
Crisp, Marty
  See Crisp, Marta Marie
Crispin, A(nn) C(arol) 1950- *86*
Crist, James J. 1961- *168*
Cristall, Barbara *79*
Crist-Evans, Craig 1954- *153*
Crocker, Carter *193*
Crocker, Nancy 1956- *185*
Crofford, Emily (Ardell) 1927- *61*
Crofut, William E. III 1934- *23*
Croggon, Alison 1962- *194*

Croll, Carolyn 1945- 102
   Brief entry 52
   Earlier sketch in SATA 56
Croman, Dorothy Young
   See Rosenberg, Dorothy
Cromie, Alice Hamilton 1914-2000 24
Cromie, William J(oseph) 1930- 4
Crompton, Anne Eliot 1930- 73
   Earlier sketch in SATA 23
Crompton, Richmal
   See Lamburn, Richmal Crompton
Cronbach, Abraham 1882-1965 11
Crone, Ruth 1919-2003 4
Cronin, A(rchibald) J(oseph) 1896-1981 47
   Obituary 25
Cronin, Doreen (A.) 125
Cronin, Doreen 1966(?)- 178
   See also CLR 136
Cronin, Doreen A.
   See Cronin, Doreen
Crook, Beverly Courtney 38
   Brief entry 35
Crook, Connie Brummel 1930- 168
   Earlier sketch in SATA 98
Crook, Constance
   See Crook, Connie Brummel
Crosby, Alexander L. 1906-1980 2
   Obituary 23
Crosby, Harry C.
   See Anvil, Christopher
Crosby, Margaret
   See Rathmann, Peggy
Crosher, G. R. 14
Cross, Gilbert B. 1939- 60
   Brief entry 51
Cross, Gillian 1945- 178
   Autobiography Feature 178
   Earlier sketches in SATA 38, 71, 110, 165
   See also CLR 28
Cross, Gillian Clare
   See Cross, Gillian
Cross, Helen Reeder
   See Broadhead, Helen Cross
Cross, Peter 1951- 95
Cross, Shauna 1976(?)- 196
Cross, Tom 1954- 146
Cross, Verda 1914- 75
Cross, Wilbur Lucius III 1918- 2
Crossland, Caroline 1964- 83
Crossley-Holland, Kevin 1941- 165
   Earlier sketches in SATA 5, 74, 120
   See also CLR 84
   See also SAAS 20
Crossley-Holland, Kevin John William
   See Crossley-Holland, Kevin
Crouch, Marcus 1913-1996 4
Crout, George C(lement) 1917- 11
Crow, Donna Fletcher 1941- 40
Crow, Francis Luther
   See Luther, Frank
Crowe, Andrew 111
Crowe, Carole 1943- 204
Crowe, Chris 206
Crowe, Ellie 203
Crowe, John
   See Lynds, Dennis
Crowe, (Bettina) Peter Lum 1911- 6
Crowell, Grace Noll 1877-1969 34
Crowell, Pers 1910-1990 2
Crowell, Robert Leland 1909-2001 63
Crowfield, Christopher
   See Stowe, Harriet Beecher
Crowley, Arthur McBlair 1945- 38
Crowley, John 1942- 140
   Earlier sketch in SATA 65
Crowley, Suzanne 1963- 196
Crowley, Suzanne Carlisle
   See Crowley, Suzanne
Crownfield, Gertrude 1867-1945
   See YABC 1
Crowther, James Gerald 1899-1983 14

Crowther, Robert 1948- 163
Cruikshank, George 1792-1878 22
   See also CLR 63
Cruise, Robin 1951- 179
Crum, Shutta 192
   Earlier sketch in SATA 134
Crummel, Susan Stevens 1949- 176
   Earlier sketch in SATA 130
Crump, Fred H., Jr. 1931- 76
   Earlier sketch in SATA 11
Crump, J(ames) Irving 1887-1979 57
   Obituary 21
Crump, William D(rake) 1949- 138
Crunden, Reginald
   See Cleaver, Hylton Reginald
Crunk, T.
   See Crunk, Tony
Crunk, Tony 1956- 130
Crutcher, Chris 1946- 196
   Earlier sketches in SATA 52, 99, 153
   See also CLR 28
Crutcher, Christopher C.
   See Crutcher, Chris
Cruz, Ray(mond) 1933- 6
Cruz Martinez, Alejandro (?)-1987 74
Crystal, Billy 1947- 154
Ctvrtek, Vaclav 1911-1976
   Obituary 27
Cuetara, Mittie 1957- 158
   Earlier sketch in SATA 106
Cuffari, Richard 1925-1978 66
   Obituary 25
   Earlier sketch in SATA 6
Cuffe-Perez, Mary 1946- 199
Cullen, Countee 1903-1946 18
Cullen, Lynn 190
Culliford, Pierre 1928-1992 40
   Obituary 74
Cullinan, Bernice E(llinger) 1926- 135
Culp, Louanna McNary 1901-1965 2
Culper, Felix
   See McCaughrean, Geraldine
Cumbaa, Stephen 1947- 72
Cumming, Peter 1951- 168
Cumming, Primrose Amy 1915- 24
Cumming, Robert 1945- 65
Cummings, Betty Sue 1918- 15
   See also SAAS 9
Cummings, Mary 1951- 185
Cummings, Parke 1902-1987 2
   Obituary 53
Cummings, Pat 1950- 203
   Earlier sketches in SATA 42, 71, 107
   See also CLR 48
   See also SAAS 13
Cummings, Phil 1957- 123
   Earlier sketch in SATA 74
Cummings, Priscilla 1951- 170
   Earlier sketch in SATA 129
Cummings, Richard
   See Gardner, Richard (M.)
Cummins, Julie 200
Cummins, Maria Susanna 1827-1866
   See YABC 1
Cumpliano, Ina 207
Cuneo, Mary Louise -2001 85
Cunliffe, John Arthur 1933- 86
   Earlier sketch in SATA 11
Cunliffe, Marcus (Falkner) 1922-1990 37
   Obituary 66
Cunnane, Kelly 175
Cunningham, Bob
   See May, Julian
Cunningham, Captain Frank
   See Glick, Carl (Cannon)
Cunningham, Cathy
   See Cunningham, Chet
Cunningham, Chet 1928- 23
Cunningham, Dale S(peers) 1932- 11
Cunningham, Dru 91

Cunningham, E. V.
   See Fast, Howard
Cunningham, Julia (Woolfolk) 1916- 132
   Earlier sketches in SATA 1, 26
   See also SAAS 2
Cunningham, Lawrence J. 1943- 125
Cunningham, Virginia
   See Holmgren, Virginia C(unningham)
Curiae, Amicus
   See Fuller, Edmund (Maybank)
Curie, Eve 1904-2007 1
   Obituary 188
Curlee, Lynn 1947- 190
   Earlier sketches in SATA 98, 141
Curley, Daniel 1918-1988 23
   Obituary 61
Curley, Marianne 1959- 175
   Earlier sketch in SATA 131
Currey, Anna 194
Currie, Robin 1948- 120
Currie, Stephen 1960- 132
   Earlier sketch in SATA 82
Curry, Ann (Gabrielle) 1934- 72
Curry, Jane L(ouise) 1932- 138
   Autobiography Feature 138
   Earlier sketches in SATA 1, 52, 90
   See also CLR 31
   See also SAAS 6
Curry, Peggy Simson 1911-1987 8
   Obituary 50
Curry, Tom 185
Curtis, Bruce (Richard) 1944- 30
Curtis, Chara M(ahar) 1950- 78
Curtis, Christopher Paul 1954(?)- 187
   Earlier sketches in SATA 93, 140
   See also CLR 68
Curtis, Gavin 1965- 107
Curtis, Jamie Lee 1958- 144
   Earlier sketch in SATA 95
   See also CLR 88
Curtis, Jennifer Keats 185
Curtis, Marci 160
Curtis, Munzee
   See Caseley, Judith
Curtis, Neil 1950-2006 202
Curtis, Patricia 1921- 101
   Earlier sketch in SATA 23
Curtis, Peter
   See Lofts, Norah (Robinson)
Curtis, Philip (Delacourt) 1920- 62
Curtis, Richard 1937- 29
Curtis, Richard Alan
   See Curtis, Richard
Curtis, Richard Hale
   See Deming, Richard
   and Levinson, Leonard
   and Rothweiler, Paul Roger
Curtis, Stacy 205
Curtis, Wade
   See Pournelle, Jerry (Eugene)
Curtiss, A(rlene) B. 1934- 90
Cusack, Margaret 1945- 58
Cushman, Doug 1953- 157
   Earlier sketches in SATA 65, 101
Cushman, Jerome 2
Cushman, Karen 1941- 147
   Earlier sketch in SATA 89
   See also CLR 55
Cusick, Richie Tankersley 1952- 140
   Earlier sketch in SATA 67
Cutbill, Andy 1972- 201
Cutchen, Billye Walker 1930- 15
Cutchins, Judy 1947- 59
Cutler, Daniel S(olomon) 1951- 78
Cutler, Ebbitt 1923- 9
Cutler, Ivor 1923-2006 24
   Obituary 174
Cutler, Jane 1936- 162
   Earlier sketches in SATA 75, 118
Cutler, May Ebbitt
   See Cutler, Ebbitt

Cutler, Samuel
  See Folsom, Franklin (Brewster)
Cutlip, Kimbra L(eigh-Ann) 1964- *128*
Cutrate, Joe
  See Spiegelman, Art
Cutt, W(illiam) Towrie 1898-1981 .... *16*
  Obituary *85*
Cuyler, Margery 1948- *195*
  Earlier sketches in SATA *39, 99, 156*
Cuyler, Margery Stuyvesant
  See Cuyler, Margery
Cuyler, Stephen
  See Bates, Barbara S(nedeker)
Cyrus, Kurt 1954- *179*
  Earlier sketch in SATA *132*
Czernecki, Stefan 1946- *178*

D

Dabba Smith, Frank *174*
Dabcovich, Lydia *99*
  Brief entry *47*
  Earlier sketch in SATA *58*
Dace, Dolores B(oelens) 1929- *89*
Da Costa, Deborah *193*
Daddo, Andrew 1967- *198*
Dadey, Debbie 1959- *136*
  Earlier sketch in SATA *73*
Dahl, Borghild (Margarethe) 1890-1984 .... *7*
  Obituary *37*
Dahl, Roald 1916-1990 .... *73*
  Obituary *65*
  Earlier sketches in SATA *1, 26*
  See also CLR *111*
Dahlberg, Maurine F. 1951- *171*
Dahlstedt, Marden (Stewart) 1921-1983 .... *8*
  Obituary *110*
Dahme, Joanne *206*
Dain, Martin J. 1924-2000 .... *35*
Dakos, Kalli 1950- *115*
  Earlier sketch in SATA *80*
Dale, Anna 1971- *170*
Dale, Gary
  See Reece, Colleen L.
Dale, George E.
  See Asimov, Isaac
Dale, Jack
  See Holliday, Joseph
Dale, Kim 1957- *123*
Dale, Margaret J(essy) Miller 1911- *39*
Dale, Mitzi
  See Hemstock, Gillian
Dale, Norman
  See Denny, Norman (George)
Dale, Penny 1954- *151*
  Earlier sketch in SATA *70*
Daley, Michael J. *170*
Dalgliesh, Alice 1893-1979 .... *17*
  Obituary *21*
  See also CLR *62*
Dalkey, Kara 1953- *132*
Dalkey, Kara Mia
  See Dalkey, Kara
Dallas, Ruth 1919- *86*
Dalmas, John
  See Jones, John R(obert)
Dalton, Alene
  See Chapin, Alene Olsen Dalton
Dalton, Annie 1948- *140*
  Earlier sketch in SATA *40*
Dalton, Kit
  See Cunningham, Chet
Dalton, Pamela
  See Johnson, Pamela
Dalton, Sean
  See Chester, Deborah
Dalton, Sheila 1949- *108*
D'Aluisio, Faith 1957- *205*

Daly, Jim
  See Stratemeyer, Edward L.
Daly, Jude 1951- *177*
Daly, Kathleen N(orah) *124*
  Brief entry *37*
Daly, Maureen 1921-2006 .... *129*
  Obituary *176*
  Earlier sketch in SATA *2*
  See also CLR *96*
  See also SAAS *1*
Daly, Nicholas 1946- *164*
  Earlier sketches in SATA *37, 76, 114*
  See also CLR *41*
  See also SAAS *21*
  See Daly, Niki
Daly, Niki *198*
  See Daly, Nicholas
D'Amato, Alex 1919- *20*
D'Amato, Janet (Potter) 1925- *9*
Damerow, Gail 1944- *83*
Damerow, Gail Jane
  See Damerow, Gail
D'Amico, Carmela *170*
D'Amico, Steve *170*
Damrell, Liz 1956- *77*
Damrosch, Helen
  See Tee-Van, Helen Damrosch
Dana, Barbara 1940- *22*
Dana, Richard Henry, Jr. 1815-1882 .... *26*
Danachair, Caoimhin O
  See Danaher, Kevin
Danaher, Kevin 1913-2002 .... *22*
Danakas, John 1963- *94*
Dandi
  See Mackall, Dandi Daley
D'Andrea, Kate
  See Steiner, Barbara A(nnette)
Dangerfield, Balfour
  See McCloskey, (John) Robert
Daniel, Alan 1939- *76*
  Brief entry *53*
Daniel, Anita 1893(?)-1978 .... *23*
  Obituary *24*
Daniel, Anne
  See Steiner, Barbara A(nnette)
Daniel, Becky 1947- *56*
Daniel, Claire 1949- *164*
Daniel, Colin
  See Windsor, Patricia
Daniel, Hawthorne 1890- *8*
Daniel, (Donna) Lee 1944- *76*
Daniel, Rebecca
  See Daniel, Becky
Daniels, Guy 1919-1989 .... *11*
  Obituary *62*
Daniels, Lucy
  See Oldfield, Jenny
Daniels, Max
  See Gellis, Roberta
Daniels, Olga
  See Sinclair, Olga
Daniels, Patricia 1955- *93*
Daniels, Zoe
  See Laux, Constance
Dank, Gloria Rand 1955- *56*
  Brief entry *46*
Dank, Leonard D(ewey) 1929- *44*
Dank, Milton 1920- *31*
Dann, Max 1955- *62*
Danneberg, Julie 1958- *173*
Dantz, William R.
  See Philbrick, Rodman
Danziger, Paula 1944-2004 .... *149*
  Brief entry *30*
  Obituary *155*
  Earlier sketches in SATA *36, 63, 102*
  See also CLR *20*
Darby, Gene Kegley
  See Darby, Jean (Kegley)
Darby, J. N.
  See Govan, (Mary) Christine Noble

Darby, Jean (Kegley) 1921- *68*
Darby, Patricia (Paulsen) *14*
Darby, Ray(mond) 1912-1982 .... *7*
d'Arcy, Willard
  See Cox, William R(obert)
Dare, Geena
  See McNicoll, Sylvia (Marilyn)
Darian, Shea 1959- *97*
Daringer, Helen Fern 1892-1986 .... *1*
Darke, Marjorie 1929- *87*
  Earlier sketch in SATA *16*
Darley, F(elix) O(ctavius) C(arr)
  1822-1888 .... *35*
Darling, David J. 1953- *60*
  Brief entry *44*
Darling, Kathy
  See Darling, Mary Kathleen
Darling, Lois (MacIntyre) 1917-1989 .... *3*
  Obituary *64*
Darling, Louis, (Jr.) 1916-1970 .... *3*
  Obituary *23*
Darling, Mary Kathleen 1943- *124*
  Earlier sketches in SATA *9, 79*
Darling, Sandra Louise Woodward
  See Day, Alexandra
Darnell, K(athryn) L(ynne) 1955- *150*
Darroll, Sally
  See Odgers, Sally Farrell
Darrow, Sharon *181*
Darrow, Whitney, (Jr.) 1909-1999 .... *13*
  Obituary *115*
Darwin, Len
  See Darwin, Leonard
Darwin, Leonard 1916- *24*
Dasent, Sir George Webbe 1817-1896 .... *62*
  Brief entry *29*
Dash, Joan 1925- *142*
Daskam, Josephine Dodge
  See Bacon, Josephine Dodge (Daskam)
D'ath, Justin 1953- *174*
  Earlier sketch in SATA *106*
Dauer, Rosamond 1934- *23*
Daugherty, Charles Michael 1914- *16*
Daugherty, James (Henry) 1889-1974 .... *13*
  See also CLR *78*
Daugherty, Richard D(eo) 1922- *35*
Daugherty, Sonia Medwedeff (?)-1971
  Obituary *27*
d'Aulaire, Edgar Parin 1898-1986 .... *66*
  Obituary *47*
  Earlier sketch in SATA *5*
  See also CLR *21*
d'Aulaire, Ingri 1904-1980 .... *66*
  Obituary *24*
  Earlier sketch in SATA *5*
  See also CLR *21*
d'Aulaire, Ingri Mortenson Parin
  See d'Aulaire, Ingri
Dave, Dave
  See Berg, David
Daveluy, Paule Cloutier 1919- *11*
Davenier, Christine 1961- *179*
  Earlier sketch in SATA *127*
Davenport, John 1960- *156*
Daves, Michael 1938- *40*
David, A. R.
  See David, A(nn) Rosalie
David, A(nn) Rosalie 1946- *103*
David, Jonathan
  See Ames, Lee J(udah)
David, Lawrence 1963- *165*
  Earlier sketch in SATA *111*
David, Peter 1956- *72*
David, Peter Allen
  See David, Peter
David, Rosalie
  See David, A(nn) Rosalie
Davidson, Alice Joyce 1932- *54*
  Brief entry *45*
Davidson, Basil 1914- *13*
Davidson, (Marie) Diane 1924- *91*

Davidson, Hugh
  See Hamilton, Edmond
Davidson, Jessica 1915-1986 5
Davidson, Judith 1953- 40
Davidson, Lionel 1922-2009 87
Davidson, Margaret 1936- 5
Davidson, Marion
  See Garis, Howard R.
Davidson, Mary R. 1885-1973 9
Davidson, Mary S. 1940- 61
Davidson, Mickie
  See Davidson, Margaret
Davidson, Nicole
  See Jensen, Kathryn
Davidson, R.
  See Davidson, Raymond
Davidson, Raymond 1926- 32
Davidson, Rosalie 1921- 23
Davie, Helen K(ay) 1952- 148
  Earlier sketch in SATA 77
Davies, Andrew (Wynford) 1936- 27
Davies, Andy Robert 200
Davies, Bettilu D(onna) 1942- 33
Davies, Hunter 1936- 55
  Brief entry 45
Davies, Jacqueline 1962- 186
  Earlier sketch in SATA 155
Davies, Joan 1934- 50
  Brief entry 47
Davies, Nicola 1958- 182
  Earlier sketches in SATA 99, 150
Davies, Peter J(oseph) 1937- 52
Davies, Sumiko 1942- 46
Davis, (A.) Aubrey 1949- 153
Davis, Barbara Steincrohn
  See Davis, Maggie S.
Davis, Bette J. 1923- 15
Davis, Burke 1913- 4
Davis, Christopher 1928- 6
Davis, D(elbert) Dwight 1908-1965 33
Davis, Daniel S(heldon) 1936- 12
Davis, David R. 1948- 106
Davis, Donald 1944- 169
  Earlier sketch in SATA 93
Davis, Donald D.
  See Davis, Donald
Davis, Emma
  See Davis, Maggie S.
Davis, Gibbs 1953- 102
  Brief entry 41
  Earlier sketch in SATA 46
Davis, Grania 1943- 88
  Brief entry 50
Davis, H(arold) L(enoir) 1896-1960 114
Davis, Hubert J(ackson) 1904-1997 31
Davis, Jacky 204
Davis, James Robert 1945- 32
Davis, Jenny 1953- 74
Davis, Jim
  See Davis, James Robert
Davis, Julia 1900(?)-1993 6
  Obituary 75
Davis, Karen (Elizabeth) 1944- 109
Davis, Katie 1959(?)- 152
Davis, Lambert 176
Davis, Leslie
  See Guccione, Leslie Davis
Davis, Louise Littleton 1921- 25
Davis, Maggie S. 1943- 57
Davis, Marguerite 1889- 34
Davis, Mary L(ee) 1935- 9
Davis, Mary Octavia 1901-1976 6
Davis, Nelle 1961- 73
Davis, Ossie 1917-2005 81
  See also CLR 56
Davis, Paxton 1925-1994 16
Davis, Rich 1958- 206
Davis, Robert 1881-1949
  See YABC 1
Davis, Robin W(orks) 1962- 87
Davis, Russell Gerard 1922- 3

Davis, Tim(othy N.) 1957- 94
Davis, Verne Theodore 1889-1973 6
Davis, Yvonne 1927- 115
Davol, Marguerite W. 1928- 146
  Earlier sketch in SATA 82
DaVolls, Andy (P.) 1967- 85
DaVolls, Linda 1966- 85
Davys, Sarah
  See Manning, Rosemary
Dawes, Claiborne 1935- 111
Dawson, Arthur L. 207
Dawson, Elmer A. 67
  Earlier sketch in SATA 1
Dawson, Imogen (Zoe) 1948- 126
  Earlier sketch in SATA 90
Dawson, Janine 1957- 196
Dawson, Mary 1919- 11
Day, A(rthur) Grove 1904-1994 59
Day, Alexandra 1941- 197
  Autobiography Feature 197
  Earlier sketches in SATA 67, 97, 169
  See also CLR 22
  See also SAAS 19
Day, Beth (Feagles) 1924- 33
Day, Donna
  See Asay, Donna Day
Day, Edward C. 1932- 72
Day, Jon 1936(?)- 79
Day, Karen 187
Day, Larry 1956- 181
Day, Nancy 1953- 140
Day, Nancy Raines 1951- 148
  Earlier sketch in SATA 93
Day, Shirley 1962- 94
Day, Thomas 1748-1789
  See YABC 1
Day, Trevor 1955- 124
Dazey, Agnes J(ohnston) 2
Dazey, Frank M. 2
Deacon, Alexis 1978- 139
Deacon, Eileen
  See Geipel, Eileen
Deacon, Richard
  See McCormick, (George) Donald (King)
Deadman, Ronald 1919-1988(?)
  Obituary 56
Deak, Erzsi 1959- 152
Dean, Anabel 1915- 12
Dean, Carolee 1962- 148
Dean, David 1976- 192
Dean, Karen Strickler 1923- 49
Dean, Ruth (Brigham) 1947- 145
Dean, Zoey
  See Bennett, Cherie
de Angeli, Marguerite (Lofft) 1889-1987 ... 100
  Obituary 51
  Earlier sketches in SATA 1, 27
  See also CLR 1
Deans, Karen 195
Deans, Sis Boulos 1955- 136
  Earlier sketch in SATA 78
DeArmand, Frances Ullmann 1904(?)-1984 . 10
  Obituary 38
DeArmond, Dale 1914- 70
DeArmond, Dale Burlison
  See DeArmond, Dale
Deary, Terry 1946- 171
  Brief entry 41
  Earlier sketches in SATA 51, 101
Deaver, Julie Reece 1953- 68
de Banke, Cecile 1889-1965 11
De Bello, Rosario 1923- 89
Debon, Nicolas 186
  Earlier sketch in SATA 151
de Bono, Edward 1933- 66
de Brissac, Malcolm
  See Dickinson, Peter
de Brunhoff, Jean
  See Brunhoff, Jean de
De Brunhoff, Laurent
  See Brunhoff, Laurent de

De Bruyn, Monica G. 1952- 13
De Bruyn, Monica Jean Grembowicz
  See De Bruyn, Monica G.
DeBry, Roger K. 1942- 91
de Camp, Catherine Crook 1907-2000 83
  Earlier sketch in SATA 12
de Camp, L. Sprague 1907-2000 83
  Earlier sketch in SATA 9
de Camp, Lyon Sprague
  See de Camp, L. Sprague
DeCandido, Keith R.A. 112
Dechausay, Sonia E. 94
Decker, C.B. 172
Decker, Cynthia B.
  See Decker, C.B.
Decker, Duane 1910-1964 5
Decker, Timothy 1974- 197
DeClements, Barthe (Faith) 1920- 131
  Earlier sketches in SATA 35, 71
  See also CLR 23
de Clercq Zubli, Rita la Fontaine 1929- 199
de Conte, Sieur Louis
  See Twain, Mark
Dedman, Stephen 108
Dee, Catherine 1964- 138
Dee, Ruby
  See Wallace, Ruby Ann
Deedy, Carmen Agra 1960- 196
Deedy, John 1923- 24
Deegan, Paul Joseph 1937- 48
  Brief entry 38
Deem, James M. 1950- 191
  Autobiography Feature 191
  Earlier sketches in SATA 75, 134
Deem, James Morgan
  See Deem, James M.
Deeter, Catherine 1947- 137
DeFelice, Cynthia 1951- 165
  Earlier sketches in SATA 79, 121
DeFelice, Cynthia C.
  See DeFelice, Cynthia
Defoe, Daniel 1660(?)-1731 22
  See also CLR 61
DeFord, Deborah H. 123
deFrance, Anthony
  See DiFranco, Anthony (Mario)
Degen, Bruce 1945- 205
  Brief entry 47
  Earlier sketches in SATA 57, 97, 147
DeGering, Etta (Belle) Fowler 1898-1996 7
De Goldi, Kate
  See De Goldi, Kathleen Domenica
De Goldi, Kathleen Domenica 1959- 123
de Goursac, Olivier 1959- 184
De Grazia, Ettore 1909-1982 39
De Grazia, Ted
  See De Grazia, Ettore
deGroat, Diane 1947- 169
  Earlier sketches in SATA 31, 90
deGros, J. H.
  See Villiard, Paul
de Grummond, Lena Young 62
  Earlier sketch in SATA 6
de Hamel, Joan Littledale 1924- 86
De Haven, Tom 1949- 72
de Hugo, Pierre
  See Brackers de Hugo, Pierre
Deiss, Joseph Jay 1915- 12
de Jenkins, Lyll Becerra 1925-1997 102
DeJong, David C(ornel) 1905-1967 10
de Jong, Dola 1911-2003
  See de Jong, Dorothea Rosalie
de Jong, Dorothea Rosalie 1911-2003 7
  Obituary 149
DeJong, Meindert 1906-1991 2
  Obituary 68
  See also CLR 73
DeJonge, Joanne E. 1943- 56
Deka, Connie
  See Laux, Constance

de Kay, Ormonde (Jr.) 1923-1998 7
  Obituary 106
de Kiriline, Louise
  See Lawrence, Louise de Kiriline
Dekker, Carl
  See Laffin, John (Alfred Charles)
  and Lynds, Dennis
deKruif, Paul (Henry) 1890-1971 50
  Earlier sketch in SATA 5
Delacre, Lulu 1957- 156
  Earlier sketch in SATA 36
DeLaCroix, Alice 1940- 195
  Earlier sketch in SATA 75
de la Cruz, Melissa 1971- 179
De la Garza, Phyllis 1942- 169
De Lage, Ida 1918- 11
de la Mare, Walter (John) 1873-1956 16
  See also CLR 23
Delaney, Harry 1932- 3
Delaney, Joseph 1945- 172
Delaney, M.C.
  See Delaney, Michael
Delaney, Michael 1955- 180
  Earlier sketch in SATA 96
Delaney, Michael Clark
  See Delaney, Michael
Delaney, Ned
  See Delaney, Thomas Nicholas III
Delaney, Thomas Nicholas III 1951- 28
Delano, Hugh 1933- 20
Delany, Samuel R., Jr. 1942- 92
Delany, Samuel Ray
  See Delany, Samuel R., Jr.
de la Pena, Matt 205
De La Ramee, Marie Louise 1839-1908 20
de la Roche, Mazo 1879-1961 64
De La Roche Saint Andre, Anne 1950- 75
Delaune, (Jewel) Lynn (de Grummond) 7
DeLaurentis, Louise Budde 1920- 12
del Barco, Lucy Salamanca 1900(?)-1989
  Obituary 64
Delderfield, Eric R(aymond) 1909-1995 14
Delderfield, Ronald Frederick 1912-1972 20
DeLeeuw, Adele (Louise) 1899-1988 30
  Obituary 56
  Earlier sketch in SATA 1
De Leon, Nephtali 1945- 97
Delessert, Etienne 1941- 179
  Brief entry 27
  Earlier sketches in SATA 46, 130
  See also CLR 81
Delgado, James P. 1958- 122
de Lint, Charles 1951- 207
  Earlier sketches in SATA 115, 157
de Lint, Charles Henri Diederick Hofsmit
  See de Lint, Charles
Delmar, Roy
  See Wexler, Jerome (LeRoy)
Del Negro, Janice M. 197
Deloria, Vine, Jr. 1933-2005 21
  Obituary 171
Deloria, Vine Victor, Jr.
  See Deloria, Vine, Jr.
del Rey, Lester 1915-1993 22
  Obituary 76
Delrio, Martin
  See Doyle, Debra
  and Macdonald, James D.
Delton, Judy 1931-2001 77
  Obituary 130
  Earlier sketch in SATA 14
  See also SAAS 9
Delulio, John 1938- 15
Delving, Michael
  See Williams, Jay
de Marcken, Gail 186
Demarest, Chris L. 1951- 175
  Brief entry 44
  Earlier sketches in SATA 45, 82, 128
Demarest, Christopher Lynn
  See Demarest, Chris L.

Demarest, Doug
  See Barker, Will
De Mari, Silvana 1953- 193
Demas, Corinne 203
  See Bliss, Corinne Demas
Demas, Vida 1927- 9
Dematons, Charlotte 1957- 203
DeMatteis, J.M. 1953- 180
DeMatteis, John Marc
  See DeMatteis, J.M.
De Mejo, Oscar 1911-1992 40
Demers, Dominique 1956- 177
de Messieres, Nicole 1930- 39
Demi
  See Hitz, Demi
Demijohn, Thom
  See Disch, Thomas M.
  and Sladek, John
Deming, Richard 1915-1983 24
Deming, Sarah 191
de Monfreid, Dorothee 1973- 189
Demuth, Patricia Brennan 1948- 84
  Brief entry 51
Dendinger, Roger E. 1952- 158
Denenberg, Barry 1940- 175
Dengler, Marianna (Herron) 1935- 103
Dengler, Sandy 1939- 54
  Brief entry 40
Denim, Sue
  See Pilkey, Dav
Denise, Christopher 1968- 193
  Earlier sketch in SATA 147
Denman, K.L. 1957- 186
Denmark, Harrison
  See Zelazny, Roger
Dennard, Deborah 1953- 136
  Earlier sketch in SATA 78
Denney, Diana 1910-2000 25
  Obituary 120
Dennis, Morgan 1891(?)-1960 18
Dennis, Wesley 1903-1966 18
Denniston, Elinore 1900-1978
  Obituary 24
Denny, Norman (George) 1901-1982 43
Denos, Julia 202
Denslow, Sharon Phillips 1947- 142
  Earlier sketch in SATA 68
Denslow, W(illiam) W(allace) 1856-1915 16
  See also CLR 15
Dent, Grace 1973- 187
Denton, Kady MacDonald 181
  Earlier sketches in SATA 66, 110
  See also CLR 71
Denton, Terry 1950- 186
Denver, Walt
  See Redding, Robert Hull
  and Sherman, Jory (Tecumseh)
Denzel, Justin F(rancis) 1917-1999 46
  Brief entry 38
Denzer, Ann Wiseman
  See Wiseman, Ann (Sayre)
DePalma, Mary Newell 1961- 185
  Earlier sketch in SATA 139
De Palma, Toni 199
dePaola, Thomas Anthony 1934- 155
  Earlier sketches in SATA 11, 59, 108
  See also CLR 81
  See also SAAS 15
  See dePaola, Tomie
dePaola, Tomie 200
  See dePaola, Thomas Anthony
dePaParrie, Paul 1949- 74
DePauw, Linda Grant 1940- 24
DeRan, David 1946- 76
Derby, Ken 1956- 181
Derby, Kenneth R.
  See Derby, Ken
Derby, Pat 1942- 172
Derby, Sally 1934- 189
  Earlier sketches in SATA 89, 132

de Regniers, Beatrice Schenk (Freedman)
  1914-2000 68
  Obituary 123
  Earlier sketch in SATA 2
  See also SAAS 6
Dereske, Jo 1947- 72
Derleth, August (William) 1909-1971 5
Derman, Martha (Winn) 74
Derman, Sarah Audrey 1915- 11
DeRoberts, Lyndon
  See Silverstein, Robert Alan
de Roo, Anne Louise 1931-1997 84
  Earlier sketch in SATA 25
  See also CLR 63
deRosa, Dee 70
Derrick, Lionel
  See Cunningham, Chet
Derrickson, Jim 1959- 141
Derry Down Derry
  See Lear, Edward
Dervaux, Isabelle 1961- 106
Derwent, Lavinia 14
Desai, Anita 1937- 126
  Earlier sketch in SATA 63
DeSaix, Deborah Durland 188
De Saulles, Tony 1958- 119
Desbarats, Peter 1933- 39
de Selincourt, Aubrey 1894-1962 14
de Seve, Randall 198
Deshpande, Chris 1950- 69
Desimini, Lisa 1964- 148
  Earlier sketch in SATA 86
Desjarlais, John 1953- 71
Desjarlais, John J.
  See Desjarlais, John
Desmoinaux, Christel 1967- 149
  Earlier sketch in SATA 103
Desmond, Adrian J(ohn) 1947- 51
Desmond, Alice Curtis 1897-1990 8
Desnoettes, Caroline 183
DeSpain, Pleasant 1943- 87
Desputeaux, Helene 1959- 95
Dessen, Sarah 1970- 172
  Earlier sketch in SATA 120
Detine, Padre
  See Olsen, Ib Spang
de Trevino, Elizabeth B.
  See Trevino, Elizabeth B(orton) de
de Trevino, Elizabeth Borton
  See Trevino, Elizabeth B(orton) de
Detwiler, Susan Dill 1956- 58
Deuker, Carl 1950- 196
  Earlier sketches in SATA 82, 150
Deutsch, Babette 1895-1982 1
  Obituary 33
Deutsch, Eva Costabel
  See Costabel, Eva Deutsch
Deutsch, Helen 1906-1992 76
Deutsch, Kurt
  See Singer, Kurt D.
De Valera, Sinead 1879(?)-1975
  Obituary 30
Devaney, John 1926-1994 12
de Varennes, Monique 1947- 168
de Varona, Frank J. 1943- 83
Devereux, Frederick L(eonard), Jr.
  1914-1993 9
Devi, Nila
  See Woody, Regina Jones
deVinck, Christopher 1951- 85
DeVita, James 195
DeVito, Cara 1956- 80
Devlin, Dorothy Wende
  See Devlin, Wende
Devlin, Harry 1918-2001 136
  Earlier sketches in SATA 11, 74
Devlin, Wende 1918-2002 74
  Earlier sketch in SATA 11
Devon, Paddie 1953- 92
Devons, Sonia 1974- 72
Devorah-Leah 111

de Vos, Gail 1949- *122*
DeVries, Douglas 1933- *122*
De Waard, E(lliott) John 1935- *7*
Dewan, Ted 1961- *157*
  Earlier sketch in SATA *108*
Dewdney, Anna *184*
Dewdney, Selwyn (Hanington) 1909-1979 ... *64*
DeWeese, Gene
  See DeWeese, Thomas Eugene
DeWeese, Jean
  See DeWeese, Thomas Eugene
DeWeese, Thomas Eugene 1934- *46*
  Brief entry *45*
Dewey, Ariane 1937- *178*
  Earlier sketches in SATA *7, 109*
Dewey, Jennifer (Owings) 1941- *103*
  Brief entry *48*
  Earlier sketch in SATA *58*
Dewey, Kenneth Francis 1940- *39*
De Wire, Elinor 1953- *180*
deWit, Dorothy (May Knowles) 1916-1980 . *39*
  Obituary *28*
Dexter, Alison 1966- *125*
Dexter, John
  See Bradley, Marion Zimmer
Deyneka, Anita 1943- *24*
Deyrup, Astrith Johnson 1923- *24*
Dezern, Chad *201*
Dhami, Narinder 1958- *152*
Dhondy, Farrukh 1944- *152*
  Earlier sketch in SATA *65*
  See also CLR *41*
Diakite, Baba Wague 1961- *174*
Diakite, Penda 1993(?)- *174*
Diamond, Arthur 1957- *76*
Diamond, Donna 1950- *69*
  Brief entry *30*
  Earlier sketch in SATA *35*
Diamond, Petra
  See Sachs, Judith
Diamond, Rebecca
  See Sachs, Judith
Dias, Earl Joseph 1916- *41*
Dias, Ron 1937- *71*
Diaz, David 1959(?)- *189*
  Earlier sketches in SATA *96, 150*
  See also CLR *65*
Dibley, Glin *188*
DiCamillo, Kate 1964- *202*
  Earlier sketches in SATA *121, 163*
  See also CLR *117*
Di Certo, J(oseph) J(ohn) 1933- *60*
DiCianni, Ron 1952- *107*
Dick, Trella Lamson 1889-1974 .... *9*
Dickens, Charles 1812-1870 .... *15*
  See also CLR *95*
Dickens, Charles John Huffam
  See Dickens, Charles
Dickens, Frank
  See Huline-Dickens, Frank William
Dickens, Monica (Enid) 1915-1992 .... *4*
  Obituary *74*
Dickerson, Roy Ernest 1886-1965
  Obituary *26*
Dickinson, Emily 1830-1886 .... *29*
Dickinson, Emily Elizabeth
  See Dickinson, Emily
Dickinson, Mary 1949- *48*
  Brief entry *41*
Dickinson, Mary-Anne
  See Rodda, Emily
Dickinson, Peter 1927- *150*
  Earlier sketches in SATA *5, 62, 95*
  See also CLR *125*
Dickinson, Peter Malcolm de Brissac
  See Dickinson, Peter
Dickinson, Susan 1931- *8*
Dickinson, Terence 1943- *102*
Dickinson, W(illiam) Croft 1897-1963 .... *13*
Dickson, Gordon R. 1923-2001 .... *77*

Dickson, Gordon Rupert
  See Dickson, Gordon R.
Dickson, Helen
  See Reynolds, Helen Mary Greenwood Campbell
Dickson, Naida 1916- *8*
Diehn, Gwen 1943- *80*
Dierssen, Andreas 1962- *190*
Diesen, Deborah 1967- *200*
Dieterich, Michele M. 1962- *78*
Dietz, David H(enry) 1897-1984 .... *10*
  Obituary *41*
Dietz, Lew 1907-1997 .... *11*
  Obituary *95*
Diffily, Deborah *159*
Di Fiori, Larry
  See Di Fiori, Lawrence
Di Fiori, Lawrence 1934- *130*
DiFranco, Anthony (Mario) 1945- *42*
Digby, Anne 1935- *72*
Digges, Jeremiah
  See Berger, Josef
Digman, Kristina 1959- *176*
D'Ignazio, Fred(erick) 1949- *39*
  Brief entry *35*
Di Grazia, Thomas (?)-1983 .... *32*
Dijkstra, Lida 1961- *195*
Dikty, Julian May
  See May, Julian
Dillard, Annie 1945- *140*
  Earlier sketch in SATA *10*
Dillard, Kristine 1964- *113*
Dillard, Polly Hargis 1916- *24*
Diller, Harriett 1953- *78*
Dillon, Barbara 1927- *44*
  Brief entry *39*
Dillon, Diane 1933- *194*
  Earlier sketches in SATA *15, 51, 106*
  See also CLR *44*
Dillon, Diane Claire
  See Dillon, Diane
Dillon, Eilis 1920-1994 .... *74*
  Autobiography Feature *105*
  Obituary *83*
  Earlier sketch in SATA *2*
  See also CLR *26*
Dillon, Jana (a pseudonym) 1952- *117*
Dillon, Leo 1933- *194*
  Earlier sketches in SATA *15, 51, 106*
  See also CLR *44*
Dillon, Sharon Saseen
  See Saseen, Sharon (Dillon)
Dils, Tracey E. 1958- *83*
Dilson, Jesse 1914-1988 .... *24*
Dinan, Carolyn *59*
  Brief entry *47*
Dines, Carol 1956- *175*
Dines, (Harry) Glen 1925-1996 .... *7*
Dinesen, Isak
  See Blixen, Karen
Dinessi, Alex
  See Schembri, Jim
Dinneen, Betty 1929- *61*
Dinnerstein, Harvey 1928- *42*
Dinsdale, Tim(othy Kay) 1924-1987 .... *11*
Diop, Birago (Ismael) 1906-1989
  Obituary *64*
Diouf, Sylviane A. *168*
Diouf, Sylviane Anna
  See Diouf, Sylviane A.
DiPucchio, Kelly *204*
  Earlier sketch in SATA *159*
Dirk
  See Gringhuis, Richard H.
Dirks, Wilhelmina 1916- *59*
Dirks, Willy
  See Dirks, Wilhelmina
Dirtmeister
  See Tomecek, Steve
DiSalvo, DyAnne 1960- *144*
  Earlier sketch in SATA *59*

DiSalvo-Ryan, DyAnne
  See DiSalvo, DyAnne
Disch, Thomas M. 1940-2008 .... *92*
  Obituary *195*
  See also CLR *18*
  See also SAAS *15*
Disch, Thomas Michael
  See Disch, Thomas M.
Disch, Tom
  See Disch, Thomas M.
Disher, Garry 1949- *125*
  Earlier sketch in SATA *81*
Disney, Walt(er Elias) 1901-1966 .... *28*
  Brief entry *27*
Ditchfield, Christin 1973- *189*
DiTerlizzi, Tony 1969- *154*
Divakaruni, Chitra Banerjee 1956- *160*
Di Valentin, Maria (Amelia) Messuri
  1911-1985 .... *7*
Divine, Arthur Durham 1904-1987
  Obituary *52*
Divine, David
  See Divine, Arthur Durham
Dixon, Ann R. 1954- *127*
  Earlier sketch in SATA *77*
Dixon, Ann Renee
  See Dixon, Ann R.
Dixon, Dougal 1947- *190*
  Earlier sketches in SATA *45, 127*
Dixon, Franklin W.
  See Barrett, Neal, Jr.
  and Goulart, Ron
  and Lantz, Francess L(in)
  and Lerangis, Peter
  and McFarlane, Leslie
  and Stanley, George Edward
  and Stratemeyer, Edward L.
Dixon, Jeanne 1936- *31*
Dixon, Paige
  See Corcoran, Barbara (Asenath)
Dixon, Peter L(ee) 1931- *6*
Dixon, Rachel 1952- *74*
Djoleto, (Solomon Alexander) Amu 1929- ... *80*
d'lacey, Chris 1949- *165*
Doak, Annie
  See Dillard, Annie
Doane, Pelagie 1906-1966 .... *7*
Dob, Bob *207*
Dobell, I(sabel) M(arian) B(arclay)
  1909-1998 .... *11*
Dobie, J(ames) Frank 1888-1964 .... *43*
Dobkin, Alexander 1908-1975
  Obituary *30*
Dobler, Lavinia G. 1910- *6*
Dobrin, Arnold 1928- *4*
Dobson, Jill 1969- *140*
Dobson, Julia 1941- *48*
Dobson, Mary 1954- *117*
Docherty, James
  See Docherty, Jimmy
Docherty, Jimmy 1976- *204*
Dockery, Wallene T. 1941- *27*
Dockray, Tracy 1962- *139*
Dockrey, Karen 1955- *103*
Doctor, Bernard
  See Doctor, Bernard Aquina
Doctor, Bernard Aquina 1950- *81*
Doctor X
  See Nourse, Alan E(dward)
Dodd, Ed(ward Benton) 1902-1991 .... *4*
  Obituary *68*
Dodd, Emma 1969- *203*
Dodd, Lynley (Stuart) 1941- *132*
  Earlier sketches in SATA *35, 86*
  See also CLR *62*
Dodd, Marty 1921- *142*
Dodd, Quentin 1972- *137*
Dodds, Bill 1952- *78*
Dodds, Dayle Ann 1952- *201*
  Earlier sketches in SATA *75, 150*
Doder, Josh 1968- *187*

Dodge, Bertha S(anford) 1902-1995 .... *8*
Dodge, Fremont
 See Grimes, Lee
Dodge, Gil
 See Hano, Arnold
Dodge, Mary (Elizabeth) Mapes
 1831(?)-1905 .... *100*
 Earlier sketch in SATA *21*
 See also CLR *62*
Dodgson, Charles Lutwidge
 See Carroll, Lewis
Dodson, Kenneth MacKenzie 1907-1999 ..... *11*
Dodson, Susan 1941- *50*
 Brief entry *40*
Dogyear, Drew
 See Gorey, Edward (St. John)
Doherty, Berlie 1943- *111*
 Earlier sketch in SATA *72*
 See also CLR *21*
 See also SAAS *16*
Doherty, Charles Hugh 1913- *6*
Doherty, Craig A. 1951- *169*
 Earlier sketch in SATA *83*
Doherty, Katherine M(ann) 1951- *83*
Doherty, Kieran 1945- *164*
Dokey, Cameron 1956- *97*
Dolan, Edward F(rancis), Jr. 1924- *94*
 Brief entry *31*
 Earlier sketch in SATA *45*
Dolan, Ellen M(eara) 1929-1998 .... *88*
Dolan, Sean J. 1958- *74*
Dolce, J. Ellen 1948- *75*
Dolch, Edward William 1889-1961 .... *50*
Dolch, Marguerite Pierce 1891-1978 .... *50*
Dollar, Diane (Hills) 1933- *57*
Dolson, Hildegarde
 See Lockridge, Hildegarde (Dolson)
Domanska, Janina 1913(?)-1995 .... *68*
 Obituary *84*
 Earlier sketch in SATA *6*
 See also CLR *40*
 See also SAAS *18*
Dominguez, Angel 1953- *76*
Domino, John
 See Averill, Esther (Holden)
Domjan, Joseph (Spiri) 1907-1992 .... *25*
Domm, Jeffrey C. 1958- *84*
Donahue, Dorothy *178*
Donald, Rhonda Lucas 1962- *147*
Donalds, Gordon
 See Shirreffs, Gordon D(onald)
Donaldson, Bryna
 See Stevens, Bryna
Donaldson, Gordon 1913-1993 .... *64*
 Obituary *76*
Donaldson, Joan 1953- *78*
Donaldson, Julia 1948- *180*
 Earlier sketches in SATA *82, 132*
Donaldson, Stephen R. 1947- *121*
Donaldson, Stephen Reeder
 See Donaldson, Stephen R.
Doner, Kim 1955- *91*
Doney, Todd L. W. 1959- *104*
Dong-Sung, Kim 1970- *195*
Dong-Sung Kim
 See Dong-Sung, Kim
Donkin, Nance (Clare) 1915- *95*
Donna, Natalie 1934-1979 .... *9*
Donnelly, Elfie 1950-
 See CLR *104*
Donnelly, Jennifer 1963- *154*
Donnelly, Matt 1972- *148*
Donnio, Sylviane *188*
Donoghue, Emma 1969- *101*
Donohue, Moira Rose 1954- *201*
Donoughue, Carol 1935- *139*
Donovan, Frank (Robert) 1906-1975
 Obituary *30*
Donovan, John 1928-1992 .... *72*
 Brief entry *29*
 See also CLR *3*

Donovan, Mary Lee 1961- *86*
Donovan, William
 See Berkebile, Fred D(onovan)
Donze, Mary Terese 1911- *89*
Doob, Leonard W(illiam) 1909-2000 .... *8*
Dooley, Norah 1953- *74*
Dooling, Michael 1958- *105*
Dor, Ana
 See Ceder, Georgiana Dorcas
Dore, (Louis Christophe Paul) Gustave
 1832-1883 .... *19*
Doremus, Robert 1913- *30*
Doren, Marion (Walker) 1928- *57*
Dorenkamp, Michelle 1957- *89*
Dorflinger, Carolyn 1953- *91*
Dorfman, Joaquin 1979- *180*
Dorfman, Joaquin Emiliano
 See Dorfman, Joaquin
Dorian, Edith M(cEwen) 1900-1983 .... *5*
Dorian, Harry
 See Hamilton, Charles (Harold St. John)
Dorian, Marguerite *7*
Dorin, Patrick C(arberry) 1939- *59*
 Brief entry *52*
Dorman, Brandon *194*
Dorman, Michael 1932- *7*
Dorman, N. B. 1927- *39*
Dormer, Frank W. *200*
Dorris, Michael 1945-1997 .... *75*
 Obituary *94*
 See also CLR *58*
Dorris, Michael A.
 See Dorris, Michael
Dorris, Michael Anthony
 See Dorris, Michael
Dorritt, Susan
 See Schlein, Miriam
Dorros, Alex 1991- *194*
Dorros, Arthur 1950- *168*
 Earlier sketches in SATA *78, 122*
 See also CLR *42*
 See also SAAS *20*
Dorros, Arthur M.
 See Dorros, Arthur
Dorson, Richard M(ercer) 1916-1981 .... *30*
Doss, Helen (Grigsby) 1918- *20*
Doss, Margot Patterson *6*
dos Santos, Joyce Audy 1949- *57*
 Brief entry *42*
Dothers, Anne
 See Chess, Victoria (Dickerson)
Dotlich, Rebecca Kai 1951- *182*
Dottig
 See Grider, Dorothy
Dotts, Maryann J. 1933- *35*
Doty, Jean Slaughter 1929- *28*
Doty, Roy 1922- *28*
Doubtfire, Dianne (Abrams) 1918- *29*
Doucet, Sharon Arms 1951- *144*
 Autobiography Feature *144*
 Earlier sketch in SATA *125*
Dougherty, Charles 1922- *18*
Dougherty, Terri (L.) 1964- *146*
Doughty, Rebecca 1955- *174*
Douglas, Blaise 1960- *101*
Douglas, Carole Nelson 1944- *73*
Douglas, Garry
 See Kilworth, Garry
Douglas, James McM.
 See Griffin, W.E.B.
Douglas, Kathryn
 See Ewing, Kathryn
Douglas, Leonard
 See Bradbury, Ray
Douglas, Lola
 See Zeises, Lara M.
Douglas, Marjory Stoneman 1890-1998 .... *10*
Douglas, Michael
 See Bright, Robert Sr.)
Douglas, Michael
 See Crichton, Michael

Douglas, Shirley Stewart
 See Tepper, Sheri S.
Douglass, Barbara 1930- *40*
Douglass, Frederick 1817(?)-1895 .... *29*
Douglass, Keith
 See Cunningham, Chet
Douty, Esther M(orris) 1909-1978 .... *8*
 Obituary *23*
Dow, Emily R. 1904-1987 .... *10*
Dow, Vicki
 See McVey, Vicki
Dowd, John David 1945- *78*
Dowd, Siobhan 1960-2007 .... *204*
Dowdell, Dorothy (Florence) Karns 1910- ... *12*
Dowden, Anne Ophelia Todd 1907-2007 .... *7*
 Obituary *180*
 See also SAAS *10*
Dowdey, Landon Gerald 1923- *11*
Dowdy, Mrs. Regera
 See Gorey, Edward (St. John)
Dowell, Frances O'Roark *205*
 Earlier sketch in SATA *157*
Dower, Laura *185*
Dowling, Terry 1947- *101*
Downard, Barry 1956- *202*
Downer, Ann 1960- *155*
Downer, Marion 1892(?)-1971 .... *25*
Downes, Belinda 1962- *180*
Downey, Fairfax D(avis) 1893-1990 .... *3*
 Obituary *66*
Downey, Lynn 1961- *185*
Downham, Jenny 1964- *192*
Downie, John 1931- *87*
Downie, Mary Alice 1934- *171*
 Earlier sketches in SATA *13, 87*
Downie, Mary Alice Dawe
 See Downie, Mary Alice
Downing, David A(lmon) 1958- *84*
Downing, Johnette *184*
Downing, Julie 1956- *148*
 Earlier sketch in SATA *81*
Downing, Paula E. 1951- *80*
Downing, Warwick 1931- *138*
Downing, Wick
 See Downing, Warwick
Dowswell, Paul 1957- *184*
Doyle, A. Conan
 See Doyle, Sir Arthur Conan
Doyle, Sir Arthur Conan 1859-1930 .... *24*
 See also CLR *106*
Doyle, Brian 1935- *156*
 Earlier sketches in SATA *67, 104*
 See also CLR *22*
 See also SAAS *16*
Doyle, Charlotte 1937- *178*
 Earlier sketch in SATA *94*
Doyle, Charlotte Lackner
 See Doyle, Charlotte
Doyle, Conan
 See Doyle, Sir Arthur Conan
Doyle, Debra 1952- *165*
 Earlier sketch in SATA *105*
Doyle, Donovan
 See Boegehold, Betty (Doyle)
Doyle, John
 See Graves, Robert
Doyle, Malachy 1954- *165*
 Earlier sketch in SATA *120*
 See also CLR *83*
Doyle, Richard 1824-1883 .... *21*
Doyle, Sir A. Conan
 See Doyle, Sir Arthur Conan
Dr. A
 See Asimov, Isaac
 and Silverstein, Alvin
 and Silverstein, Virginia B.
Dr. Alphabet
 See Morice, Dave
Dr. Fred
 See Bortz, Alfred B(enjamin)

Dr. Laura
    See Schlessinger, Laura (Catherine)
Dr. Seuss 1904-1991 100
    Obituary 67
    Earlier sketches in SATA *1, 28, 75*
    See also CLR *100*
Dr. Zed
    See Penrose, Gordon
Drabble, Margaret 1939- 48
Drackett, Phil(ip Arthur) 1922- 53
Draco, F.
    See Davis, Julia
Dracup, Angela 1943- 74
Dragisic, Patricia 116
Dragonwagon, Crescent 1952- 186
    Autobiography Feature 186
    Earlier sketches in SATA *11, 41, 75, 133*
    See also SAAS *14*
Drake, David 1945- 85
Drake, David Allen
    See Drake, David
Drake, Frank
    See Hamilton, Charles (Harold St. John)
Drake, Jane 1954- 82
Drakeford, Dale B 1952- 113
Drakeford, Dale Benjamin
    See Drakeford, Dale B
Draper, Hastings
    See Jeffries, Roderic
Draper, Sharon
    See Draper, Sharon M.
Draper, Sharon M. 1948- 195
    Autobiography Feature 146
    Earlier sketches in SATA *98, 146*
    See also CLR *57*
Draper, Sharon Mills
    See Draper, Sharon M.
Drapier, M. B.
    See Swift, Jonathan
Drawson, Blair 1943- 126
    Earlier sketch in SATA *17*
Dray, Matt 1967- 177
Dray, Matthew Frederick
    See Dray, Matt
Dresang, Eliza (Carolyn Timberlake) 1941- . 19
Drescher, Henrik 1955- 172
    Earlier sketches in SATA *67, 105*
    See also CLR *20*
Drescher, Joan E(lizabeth) 1939- 137
    Earlier sketch in SATA *30*
Dressen-McQueen, Stacey 191
Dreves, Veronica R. 1927-1986
    Obituary 50
Drew, Patricia (Mary) 1938- 15
Drewery, Mary 1918- 6
Drewery, Melanie 1970- 165
Drewry, Henry N(athaniel) 1924- 138
Dreyer, Ellen 177
Drial, J. E.
    See Laird, Jean E(louise)
Drimmer, Frederick 1916-2000 60
    Obituary 124
Driskill, J. Lawrence 1920- 90
Driskill, Larry
    See Driskill, J. Lawrence
Driving Hawk, Virginia
    See Sneve, Virginia Driving Hawk
Dron, Laura
    See Matthews, L.S.
Dronzek, Laura 199
Drucker, Malka 1945- 111
    Brief entry 29
    Earlier sketch in SATA *39*
Drucker, Olga Levy 1927- 79
Druitt, Tobias
    See Purkiss, Diane
Drummond, V(iolet) H(ilda) 1911-2000 6
Drummond, Walter
    See Silverberg, Robert

Drury, Clare Marie
    See Hoskyns-Abrahall, Clare (Constance
    Drury)
Drury, Roger W(olcott) 1914-1996 15
Druse, Eleanor
    See King, Stephen
Dryden, Pamela
    See St. John, Nicole
D.T., Hughes
    See Hughes, Dean
Duane, Diane (Elizabeth) 1952- 145
    Brief entry 46
    Earlier sketches in SATA *58, 95*
Dubanevich, Arlene 1950- 56
Dubelaar, Thea 1947- 60
Dubin, Jill 205
du Blane, Daphne
    See Groom, Arthur William
Duble, Kathleen Benner 1958- 164
Dubois, Claude K. 1960- 196
DuBois, Rochelle Holt 1946- 41
Du Bois, Shirley Graham 1907(?)-1977 24
    See Graham, Shirley
Du Bois, W. E. B. 1868-1963 42
Du Bois, William Edward Burghardt
    See Du Bois, W. E. B.
du Bois, William Pene
    See Pene du Bois, William (Sherman)
Duboise, Novella 1911-1999 88
Dubosarsky, Ursula 1961- 193
    Earlier sketches in SATA *107, 147*
DuBose, LaRocque (Russ) 1926- 2
Dubrovin, Vivian 1931- 139
    Earlier sketch in SATA *65*
DuBurke, Randy 172
Ducey, Jean Sparks 1915- 93
Duchacek, Ivo D(uka) 1913-1988
    Obituary 55
Du Chaillu, Paul (Belloni) 1835(?)-1903 26
Ducharme, Dede Fox
    See Ducharme, Lilian Fox
Ducharme, Lilian Fox 1950- 122
Ducornet, Erica 1943- 7
Ducornet, Rikki
    See Ducornet, Erica
Duden, Jane 1947- 136
Duder, Tessa 1940- 117
    Earlier sketch in SATA *80*
    See also CLR *43*
    See also SAAS *23*
Dudley, Helen
    See Hope Simpson, Jacynth
Dudley, Martha Ward 1909(?)-1985
    Obituary 45
Dudley, Nancy
    See Cole, Lois Dwight
Dudley, Robert
    See Baldwin, James
Dudley, Ruth H(ubbell) 1905-2001 11
Dudley-Smith, T.
    See Trevor, Elleston
Due, Linnea A. 1948- 64
Dueck, Adele 1955- 97
Dueland, Joy V(ivian) 27
Duerr, Gisela 1968- 89
Duey, Kathleen 1950- 199
    Earlier sketch in SATA *132*
Dufault, Joseph Ernest Nephtali
    See James, Will(iam Roderick)
Duff, Annis (James) 1904(?)-1986
    Obituary 49
Duff, Maggie
    See Duff, Margaret K(app)
Duff, Margaret K(app) 1916-2003 37
    Obituary 144
Duffey, Betsy (Byars) 1953- 131
    Earlier sketch in SATA *80*
Duffie, Charles 1960- 144
Duffield, Katy S. 1961- 147
Duffy, Carol Ann 1955- 165
    Earlier sketch in SATA *95*

Dugan, Jack
    See Griffin, W.E.B.
Dugan, John Kevin
    See Griffin, W.E.B.
Dugan, Karen 202
Dugan, Karen M.
    See Dugan, Karen
Dugan, Michael (Gray) 1947- 15
Duggan, Alfred Leo 1903-1964 25
Duggan, Maurice 1922-1974 40
    Obituary 30
Duggan, Maurice Noel
    See Duggan, Maurice
Duggleby, John 1952- 94
Dugin, Andrej 1955- 77
Dugina, Olga 1964- 77
du Jardin, Rosamond Neal 1902-1963 2
Duka, Ivo
    See Duchacek, Ivo D(uka)
Duke, Kate 1956- 192
    Earlier sketches in SATA *90, 148*
    See also CLR *51*
Duke, Will
    See Gault, William Campbell
Dulac, Edmund 1882-1953 19
Dumas, Alexandre (pere) 1802-1870 18
    See also CLR *134*
Dumas, Jacqueline 1946- 55
Dumas, Philippe 1940- 119
    Earlier sketch in SATA *52*
du Maurier, Daphne 1907-1989 27
    Obituary 60
Dumbleton, Mike 1948- 206
    Earlier sketches in SATA *73, 124*
Dunbar, Fiona 1961- 167
Dunbar, Joyce 1944- 162
    Earlier sketches in SATA *76, 112*
Dunbar, Paul Laurence 1872-1906 34
Dunbar, Polly 1980(?)- 181
Dunbar, Robert E(verett) 1926- 32
Duncan, Alexandra
    See Moore, Ishbel (Lindsay)
Duncan, Alice Faye 1967- 168
    Earlier sketch in SATA *95*
Duncan, Gregory
    See McClintock, Marshall
Duncan, Jane
    See Cameron, Elizabeth Jane
Duncan, Julia K.
    See Benson, Mildred
Duncan, Lois 1934- 141
    Autobiography Feature 141
    Earlier sketches in SATA *1, 36, 75, 133*
    See also CLR *129*
    See also SAAS *2*
Duncan, Norman 1871-1916
    See YABC *1*
Duncan, Terence
    See Nolan, William F(rancis)
Duncombe, Frances (Riker) 1900-1994 25
    Obituary 82
Dungy, Anthony
    See Dungy, Tony
Dungy, Tony 1955- 206
Dunham, Montrew 1919- 162
Dunham, Montrew Goetz
    See Dunham, Montrew
Dunkle, Clare B. 1964- 155
Dunlap, Julie 1958- 84
Dunleavy, Deborah 1951- 133
Dunlop, Agnes M. R. (?)-1982 87
Dunlop, Eileen (Rhona) 1938- 76
    Earlier sketch in SATA *24*
    See also SAAS *12*
Dunmore, Helen 1952- 201
Dunn, Anne M. 1940- 107
Dunn, Harvey T(homas) 1884-1952 34
Dunn, Herb
    See Gutman, Dan
Dunn, John M. (III) 1949- 93

Dunn, Judy
  See Spangenberg, Judith Dunn
Dunn, Mary Lois 1930- 6
Dunnahoo, Terry Janson 1927- 7
Dunne, Jeanette 1952- 72
Dunne, Kathleen 1933- *126*
Dunne, Marie
  See Clark, Ann Nolan
Dunne, Mary Collins 1914- *11*
Dunne, Mary Jo
  See Dunne, Mary Collins
Dunnett, Kaitlyn
  See Emerson, Kathy Lynn
Dunnett, Margaret (Rosalind) 1909-1977 ..... *42*
Dunnick, Regan *178*
Dunrea, Olivier 1953- *160*
  Brief entry *46*
  Earlier sketches in SATA *59, 118*
Dunrea, Olivier Jean-Paul Dominique
  See Dunrea, Olivier
Dunton, Dorothy 1912- 92
Dupasquier, Philippe 1955- *151*
  Earlier sketch in SATA *86*
duPont, Lindsay 207
duPont, Lindsay Harper
  See duPont, Lindsay
DuPrau, Jeanne 1944- *144*
Dupuy, T(revor) N(evitt) 1916-1995 4
  Obituary *86*
DuQuette, Keith 1960- *155*
  Earlier sketch in SATA *90*
Duran, Gloria 1924- *171*
Duran, Gloria Bradley
  See Duran, Gloria
Duranceau, Suzanne 1952- *162*
Durand, Delphine 1971- *200*
Durango, Julia 1967- *173*
Durant, Alan 1958- *165*
  Earlier sketch in SATA *121*
Durant, John 1902- 27
Durbin, William 1951- *174*
  Earlier sketch in SATA *143*
Durell, Ann 1930- 66
Durkee, Sarah *173*
Durney, Ryan *205*
Durrant, Lynda 1954- *148*
  Earlier sketch in SATA *96*
Durrell, Gerald (Malcolm) 1925-1995 8
  Obituary *84*
Durrell, Julie 1955- *94*
Durrett, Deanne 1940- *144*
  Earlier sketch in SATA *92*
Durst, Sarah Beth 1974- 203
Du Soe, Robert C. 1892-1958
  See YABC 2
Dussling, Jennifer 1970- *143*
  Earlier sketch in SATA *96*
DuTemple, Lesley A. 1952- *113*
Dutton, Sandra *191*
Dutz
  See Davis, Mary Octavia
Duval, Katherine
  See James, Elizabeth
Duval, Kathy 1946- *181*
Duvall, Aimee
  See Thurlo, Aimee
  and Thurlo, David
Duvall, Evelyn Millis 1906- 9
Duvall, Jill D(onovan) 1932- *102*
Duvoisin, Roger (Antoine) 1904-1980 30
  Obituary 23
  Earlier sketch in SATA *2*
  See also CLR *23*
Dwiggins, Don(ald J.) 1913-1988 4
  Obituary 60
Dwight, Allan
  See Cole, Lois Dwight
Dwyer, Deanna
  See Koontz, Dean
Dwyer, K.R.
  See Koontz, Dean

Dyck, Peter J. 1914- 75
Dyer, James (Frederick) 1934- 37
Dyer, Jane *191*
  Earlier sketch in SATA *147*
Dyess, John (Foster) 1939- 76
Dygard, Thomas J. 1931-1996 97
  Obituary 92
  Earlier sketch in SATA *24*
  See also SAAS *15*
Dyke, John 1935- 35

E

E. V. L.
  See Lucas, E(dward) V(errall)
Eagar, Frances (Elisabeth Stuart)
  1940-1978 .... *11*
  Obituary 55
Eager, Edward (McMaken) 1911-1964 .... *17*
  See also CLR *43*
Eager, George 1921- 56
Eager, George B.
  See Eager, George
Eagle, Ellen 1953- 61
Eagle, Kin
  See Adlerman, Daniel (Ezra)
  and Adlerman, Kimberly M(arie)
Eagle, Mike 1942- *11*
Earle, Olive L(ydia) 1888-1982 7
Earle, William
  See Johns, W(illiam) E(arle)
Earls, Nick 1963- *156*
  Earlier sketch in SATA *95*
Early, Jack
  See Scoppettone, Sandra
Early, Jon
  See Johns, W(illiam) E(arle)
Early, Margaret 1951- 72
Earnshaw, Brian 1929- *17*
Earnshaw, Micky
  See Earnshaw, Spencer Wright
Earnshaw, Spencer Wright 1939- 88
Easley, MaryAnn 94
Eason, Alethea 1957- *197*
Eastman, Charles A(lexander) 1858-1939
  See YABC *1*
Eastman, P(hilip) D(ey) 1909-1986 33
  Obituary 46
Easton, Kelly 1960- *192*
  Earlier sketch in SATA *141*
Eastwick, Ivy (Ethel) O(live) 3
Eaton, Anne T(haxter) 1881-1971 32
Eaton, Anthony 1971- *167*
Eaton, George L.
  See Verral, Charles Spain
Eaton, Janet
  See Givens, Janet E(aton)
Eaton, Jeanette 1886-1968 24
Eaton, Maxwell III 1981- *199*
Eaton, Tom 1940- 22
Ebbeler, Jeff
  See Ebbeler, Jeffrey
Ebbeler, Jeffrey 1974- *206*
Ebel, Alex 1927- *11*
Eber, Dorothy (Margaret) Harley 1930- 27
Eberhart, Sheri S.
  See Tepper, Sheri S.
Eberle, Irmengarde 1898-1979 2
  Obituary 23
Eble, Diane 1956- 74
Eboch, Chris *113*
Eccles Williams, Ferelith 1920- 22
Echlin, Kim 1955- *166*
Eckblad, Edith Berven 1923- 23
Ecke, Wolfgang 1927-1983
  Obituary 37

Eckert, Allan W. 1931- *91*
  Brief entry 27
  Earlier sketch in SATA *29*
  See also SAAS *21*
Eckert, Horst 1931- 72
  Earlier sketch in SATA *8*
  See also CLR *26*
Ecklar, Julia (Marie) 1964- *112*
Eddings, David 1931-2009 .... *91*
Eddings, David Carroll
  See Eddings, David
Ede, Janina 1937- 33
Edell, Celeste 12
Edelman, Lily (Judith) 1915-1981 22
Edelson, Edward 1932- 51
Edens, Cooper 1945- *166*
  Earlier sketches in SATA *49, 112*
Edens, (Bishop) David 1926- 39
Edey, Maitland A(rmstrong) 1910-1992 25
  Obituary 71
Edgerton, Perky *196*
Edgeworth, Maria 1768-1849 21
Edgy, Wardore
  See Gorey, Edward (St. John)
Edison, Theodore
  See Stratemeyer, Edward L.
Edler, Tim(othy) 1948- 56
Edmiston, Jim 1948- 80
Edmonds, I(vy) G(ordon) 1917- 8
Edmonds, Walter D(umaux) 1903-1998 27
  Obituary 99
  Earlier sketch in SATA *1*
  See also SAAS *4*
Edmund, Sean
  See Pringle, Laurence
Edsall, Marian (Stickney) 1920- 8
Edwards, Al
  See Nourse, Alan E(dward)
Edwards, Anne 1927- 35
Edwards, Audrey 1947- 52
  Brief entry 31
Edwards, Becky (Jane) 1966- *125*
Edwards, Bertram
  See Edwards, Herbert Charles
Edwards, Bronwen Elizabeth
  See Rose, Wendy
Edwards, Cecile Pepin 1916- 25
Edwards, David 1962- *198*
Edwards, Dorothy 1914-1982 88
  Obituary 31
  Earlier sketch in SATA *4*
Edwards, F. E.
  See Nolan, William F(rancis)
Edwards, Frank B. 1952- 93
Edwards, Gunvor 32
Edwards, Harvey 1929- 5
Edwards, Hazel (Eileen) 1945- *135*
Edwards, Herbert Charles 1912- 12
Edwards, Jane Campbell 1932- 10
Edwards, Julia
  See Stratemeyer, Edward L.
Edwards, Julie
  See Andrews, Julie
Edwards, Julie Andrews
  See Andrews, Julie
Edwards, June
  See Bhatia, Jamunadevi
Edwards, Linda Strauss 1948- 49
  Brief entry 42
Edwards, Margaret (Alexander) 1902-1988
  Obituary 56
Edwards, Michelle 1955- *152*
  Earlier sketch in SATA *70*
Edwards, Monica le Doux Newton
  1912-1998 12
Edwards, Olwen
  See Gater, Dilys
Edwards, Page (Lawrence, Jr.) 1941-1999 ... 59
Edwards, Pamela Duncan *189*
Edwards, R. T.
  See Goulart, Ron

Edwards, Sally (Cary) 1929- 7
Edwards, Samuel
  See Gerson, Noel Bertram
Edwards, Wallace 1957(?)- 170
Egan, E(dward) W(elstead) 1922- 35
Egan, Kerry 175
Egan, Lorraine Hopping 1960- 134
  Earlier sketch in SATA 91
Egan, Tim 1957- 191
  Earlier sketches in SATA 89, 155
Egermeier, Elsie E(milie) 1890-1986 65
Eggenberger, David 1918- 6
Eggleston, Edward 1837-1902 27
Egielski, Richard 1952- 163
  Earlier sketches in SATA 11, 49, 106
Egypt, Ophelia Settle 1903-1984 16
  Obituary 38
Ehlert, Lois 1934- 172
  Earlier sketches in SATA 35, 69, 128
  See also CLR 28
Ehlert, Lois Jane
  See Ehlert, Lois
Ehling, Katalin Olah 1941- 93
Ehrenfreund, Norbert 1921- 86
Ehrenhaft, Daniel 1970- 185
Ehrhardt, Karen 1963- 184
Ehrlich, Amy 1942- 132
  Earlier sketches in SATA 25, 65, 96
Ehrlich, Bettina Bauer 1903-1985 1
Ehrlich, Fred 205
Ehrlich, Fred M.D.
  See Ehrlich, Fred
Ehrlich, H. M.
  See Ziefert, Harriet
Eichenberg, Fritz 1901-1990 50
  Earlier sketch in SATA 9
Eichler, Margrit 1942- 35
Eichner, James A. 1927- 4
Eidson, Thomas 1944- 112
Eifert, Virginia (Louise) S(nider) 1911-1966 . 2
Eige, (Elizabeth) Lillian 1915- 65
Eiken, J. Melia 1967- 125
Einhorn, Edward 1970- 204
Einsel, Naiad 10
Einsel, Walter 1926- 10
Einzig, Susan 1922- 43
Eiseman, Alberta 1925- 15
Eisenberg, Azriel (Louis) 1903-1985 12
Eisenberg, Lisa 1949- 155
  Brief entry 50
  Earlier sketch in SATA 57
Eisenberg, Phyllis Rose 1924- 41
Eisner, Vivienne
  See Margolis, Vivienne
Eisner, Will 1917-2005 165
  Earlier sketch in SATA 31
Eisner, William Erwin
  See Eisner, Will
Eitzen, Allan 1928- 9
Eitzen, Ruth (Carper) 1924- 9
Ekwensi, C. O. D.
  See Ekwensi, Cyprian
Ekwensi, Cyprian 1921-2007 66
Ekwensi, Cyprian Odiatu Duaka
  See Ekwensi, Cyprian
Elam, Richard M(ace, Jr.) 1920- 9
Elborn, Andrew
  See Clements, Andrew
  and Clements, Andrew
Elboz, Stephen 1956- 152
Eldin, Peter 1939- 154
Eldon, Kathy 1946- 107
Eldridge, Marion 199
Elfman, Blossom 1925- 8
Elgin, Kathleen 1923- 39
Elia
  See Lamb, Charles
Eliot, A. D.
  See Jewett, Sarah Orne
Eliot, Alice
  See Jewett, Sarah Orne

Eliot, Anne
  See Cole, Lois Dwight
Eliot, Dan
  See Silverberg, Robert
Elish, Dan 1960- 204
  Earlier sketches in SATA 68, 129
Elisha, Ron 1951- 104
Elisofon, Eliot 1911-1973
  Obituary 21
Elkeles, Simone 1970- 187
Elkin, Benjamin 1911-1995 3
Elkins, Dov Peretz 1937- 5
Ellacott, S(amuel) E(rnest) 1911- 19
Elleman, Barbara 1934- 147
Ellen, Jaye
  See Nixon, Joan Lowery
Eller, Scott
  See Holinger, William (Jacques)
  and Shepard, Jim
Ellestad, Myrvin
  See Ellestad, Myrvin H.
Ellestad, Myrvin H. 1921- 120
Elliot, David 1952- 122
Elliott, Bruce
  See Field, Edward
Elliott, David 1947- 201
  Earlier sketch in SATA 163
Elliott, Don
  See Silverberg, Robert
Elliott, Elizabeth Shippen Green
  See Green, Elizabeth Shippen
Elliott, Janice 1931-1995 119
Elliott, Joey
  See Houk, Randy
Elliott, Laura Malone 1957- 197
Elliott, Louise 111
Elliott, Odette 1939- 75
Elliott, Patricia 1946- 176
Elliott, Sarah M(cCarn) 1930- 14
Elliott, (Robert) Scott 1970- 153
Elliott, William
  See Bradbury, Ray
Elliott, Zetta 206
Ellis, (Mary) Amabel (Nassau Strachey)
  Williams
  See Williams-Ellis, (Mary) Amabel (Nassau
  Strachey)
Ellis, Anyon
  See Rowland-Entwistle, (Arthur) Theodore
  (Henry)
Ellis, Carson 1975- 190
Ellis, Carson Friedman
  See Ellis, Carson
Ellis, Deborah 1960- 187
  Earlier sketch in SATA 129
Ellis, E. S.
  See Ellis, Edward S.
Ellis, Edward S. 1840-1916
  See YABC 1
Ellis, Edward Sylvester
  See Ellis, Edward S.
Ellis, Ella Thorp 1928- 127
  Earlier sketch in SATA 7
  See also SAAS 9
Ellis, Harry Bearse 1921-2004 9
Ellis, Herbert
  See Wilson, Lionel
Ellis, Mel(vin Richard) 1912-1984 7
  Obituary 39
Ellis, Richard 1938- 130
Ellis, Sarah 1952- 179
  Earlier sketches in SATA 68, 131
  See also CLR 42
Ellison, Chris 196
Ellison, Emily 114
Ellison, Lucile Watkins 1907(?)-1979 50
  Obituary 22
Ellison, Virginia H(owell) 1910- 4
Ellsberg, Edward 1891-1983 7
Ellsworth, Loretta 1954- 199
Ellsworth, Mary Ellen (Tressel) 1940- 146

Elmer, Robert 1958- 154
  Earlier sketch in SATA 99
Elmore, (Carolyn) Patricia 1933- 38
  Brief entry 35
El-Moslimany, Ann P(axton) 1937- 90
Elschner, Geraldine 1954- 183
Elspeth
  See Bragdon, Elspeth MacDuffie
Elster, Jean Alicia 1953- 150
Elting, Mary 1906- 88
  Earlier sketch in SATA 2
  See also SAAS 20
Elvgren, Jennifer Riesmeyer 179
Elwart, Joan Potter 1927- 2
Elwood, Ann 1931- 55
  Brief entry 52
Elwood, Roger 1943-2007 58
Elya, Susan Middleton 1955- 202
  Earlier sketches in SATA 106, 159
Elzbieta 88
Ember, Kathi 190
Emberley, Barbara A. 1932- 146
  Earlier sketches in SATA 8, 70
  See also CLR 5
Emberley, Barbara Anne
  See Emberley, Barbara A.
Emberley, Ed 1931- 146
  Earlier sketches in SATA 8, 70
  See also CLR 81
Emberley, Edward Randolph
  See Emberley, Ed
Emberley, Michael 1960- 189
  Earlier sketches in SATA 34, 80, 119
Embry, Margaret Jacob 1919-1975 5
Emecheta, Buchi 1944- 66
Emecheta, Florence Onye Buchi
  See Emecheta, Buchi
Emerson, Alice B.
  See Benson, Mildred
Emerson, Kathy Lynn 1947- 63
Emerson, Ru 1944- 107
  Earlier sketch in SATA 70
Emerson, Sally 1952- 111
Emerson, William K(eith) 1925- 25
Emert, Phyllis R(aybin) 1947- 93
Emery, Anne (McGuigan) 1907- 33
  Earlier sketch in SATA 1
Emmens, Carol Ann 1944- 39
Emmett, Jonathan 1965- 188
  Earlier sketch in SATA 138
Emmons, Della (Florence) Gould 1890-1983
  Obituary 39
Emory, Jerry 1957- 96
Emrich, Duncan (Black Macdonald)
  1908-1970(?) 11
Emshwiller, Carol 1921- 174
  Autobiography Feature 174
Emshwiller, Carol Fries
  See Emshwiller, Carol
Emslie, M. L.
  See Simpson, Myrtle L(illias)
Ende, Michael (Andreas Helmuth)
  1929-1995 130
  Brief entry 42
  Obituary 86
  Earlier sketch in SATA 61
  See also CLR 138
Enderle, Dotti 1954- 203
  Earlier sketch in SATA 145
Enderle, Judith (Ann) Ross 1941- 89
  Autobiography Feature 114
  Earlier sketch in SATA 38
  See also SAAS 26
Endle, Kate 207
Enell, Trinka (Gochenour) 1951- 79
Enfield, Carrie
  See Smith, Susan Vernon
Engdahl, Sylvia Louise 1933- 4
  Autobiography Feature 122
  See also CLR 2
  See also SAAS 5

Engel, Diana 1947- 70
Engelbreit, Mary 1952- 169
Engelhart, Margaret S. 1924- 59
Engelmann, Kim (V.) 1959- 87
England, George Allan 1877-1936 102
Englart, Mindi Rose 1965- 146
Engle, Eloise
    See Paananen, Eloise (Katherine)
Engle, Margarita 1951- 193
Englebert, Victor 1933- 8
English, James W(ilson) 1915- 37
English, Karen 202
Engstrom, Elizabeth 1951- 110
Enright, D(ennis) J(oseph) 1920-2002 25
    Obituary 140
Enright, Dominique 194
Enright, Elizabeth (Wright) 1909-1968 9
    See also CLR 4
Ensor, Barbara 180
Ensor, Robert (T.) 1922- 93
Enthoven, Sam 1974- 187
Entwistle, (Arthur) Theodore (Henry) Rowland
    See Rowland-Entwistle, (Arthur) Theodore
    (Henry)
Enys, Sarah L.
    See Sloggett, Nellie
Epanya, Christian A(rthur Kingue) 1956- 91
Ephraim, Shelly S(chonebaum) 1952- 97
Ephron, Delia 1944- 197
    Brief entry 50
    Earlier sketch in SATA 65
Epler, Doris M. 1928- 73
Epp, Margaret A(gnes) 1913- 20
Eppenstein, Louise (Kohn) 1892-1987
    Obituary 54
Epple, Anne Orth 1927- 20
Epstein, Anne Merrick 1931- 20
Epstein, Beryl 1910- 31
    Earlier sketch in SATA 1
    See also CLR 26
    See also SAAS 17
Epstein, Beryl M. Williams
    See Epstein, Beryl
Epstein, Perle S(herry) 1938- 27
Epstein, Rachel S. 1941- 102
Epstein, Samuel 1909-2000 31
    Earlier sketch in SATA 1
    See also CLR 26
    See also SAAS 17
Erdman, Loula Grace 1905(?)-1976 1
Erdoes, Richard 1912- 33
    Brief entry 28
Erdogan, Buket 187
Erdrich, Karen Louise
    See Erdrich, Louise
Erdrich, Louise 1954- 141
    Earlier sketch in SATA 94
Erickson, Betty J. 1923- 97
Erickson, Betty Jean
    See Erickson, Betty J.
Erickson, John R. 1943- 136
    Earlier sketch in SATA 70
Erickson, Jon 1948- 141
Erickson, Phoebe 59
Erickson, Russell E(verett) 1932- 27
Erickson, Sabra Rollins 1912-1995 35
Erickson, Walter
    See Fast, Howard
Ericson, Walter
    See Fast, Howard
Ericsson, Jennifer A. 170
Erikson, Mel 1937- 31
Eriksson, Eva 1949- 207
Ering, Timothy Basil 176
Erlanger, Baba
    See Trahey, Jane
Erlbach, Arlene 1948- 160
    Earlier sketches in SATA 78, 115
Erlbruch, Wolf 1948- 181
Erlich, Lillian (Feldman) 1910-1983 10
Erlings, Fridrik 1962- 196

Erlingsson, Frierik
    See Erlings, Fridrik
Ermatinger, James W. 1959- 170
Ernest, William
    See Berkebile, Fred D(onovan)
Ernst, (Lyman) John 1940- 39
Ernst, Kathleen
    See Ernst, Kathleen A.
Ernst, Kathleen A. 1959- 162
Ernst, Kathryn (Fitzgerald) 1942- 25
Ernst, Lisa Campbell 1957- 154
    Brief entry 44
    Earlier sketches in SATA 55, 95
Erskine, Kathryn 193
Ervin, Janet Halliday 1923- 4
Erwin, Will
    See Eisner, Will
Esbaum, Jill 174
Esbensen, Barbara J(uster) 1925-1996 97
    Brief entry 53
    Earlier sketch in SATA 62
Eschbacher, Roger 160
Eschmeyer, R. E. 1898-1989 29
Escriva, Vivi 182
Eseki, Bruno
    See Mphahlele, Es'kia
Esekie, Bruno
    See Mphahlele, Es'kia
Eshmeyer, Reinhart Ernst
    See Eschmeyer, R. E.
Eskridge, Ann E. 1949- 84
Espeland, Pamela (Lee) 1951- 128
    Brief entry 38
    Earlier sketch in SATA 52
Espinosa, Laura 203
Espinosa, Leo 203
Espriella, Don Manuel Alvarez
    See Southey, Robert
Espy, Willard R(ichardson) 1910-1999 38
    Obituary 113
Essakalli, Julie Klear 200
Essrig, Harry 1912- 66
Estep, Irene Compton 5
Esterl, Arnica 1933- 77
Estes, Eleanor (Ruth) 1906-1988 91
    Obituary 56
    Earlier sketch in SATA 7
    See also CLR 70
Estoril, Jean
    See Allan, Mabel Esther
Estrada, Pau 1961- 200
    Earlier sketch in SATA 74
Etchemendy, Nancy 1952- 166
    Earlier sketch in SATA 38
Etchemendy, Nancy Elise Howell
    See Etchemendy, Nancy
Etchison, Birdie L(ee) 1937- 38
Etchison, Craig 1945- 133
Etherington, Frank 1945- 58
Eton, Robert
    See Meynell, Laurence Walter
Ets, Marie Hall 1893-1984 2
    See also CLR 33
Ettlinger, Doris 1950- 173
Eunson, (John) Dale 1904-2002 5
    Obituary 132
Evan, Frances Y. 1951- 167
Evanoff, Vlad 1916- 59
Evans, Cambria 1981- 178
Evans, Douglas 1953- 144
    Earlier sketch in SATA 93
Evans, Eva (Knox) 1905-1998 27
Evans, Freddi Williams 1957- 134
Evans, Greg 1947- 143
    Earlier sketch in SATA 73
Evans, Hubert Reginald 1892-1986 118
    Obituary 48
Evans, Katherine (Floyd) 1901-1964 5
Evans, Larry
    See Evans, Laurence Chubb
Evans, Laurence Chubb 1939- 88

Evans, Lawrence Watt
    See Watt-Evans, Lawrence
Evans, Lezlie 180
Evans, Mari 1923- 10
Evans, Mark 19
Evans, Nancy 1950- 65
Evans, Nate 201
Evans, Patricia Healy
    See Carpenter, Patricia (Healy Evans)
Evans, (Alice) Pearl 1927- 83
Evans, Shane W. 189
Evans, Shirlee 1931- 58
Evans, Tabor
    See Cameron, Lou
    and Knott, William C(ecil, Jr.)
    and Wallmann, Jeffrey M(iner)
    and Whittington, Harry (Benjamin)
Evarts, Esther
    See Benson, Sally
Evarts, Hal G., (Jr.) 1915-1989 6
Everett, Gail
    See Hale, Arlene
Evernden, Margery 1916- 5
Eversole, Robyn 1971- 74
Eversole, Robyn H.
    See Eversole, Robyn
Eversole, Robyn Harbert
    See Eversole, Robyn
Evslin, Bernard 1922-1993 83
    Brief entry 28
    Obituary 77
    Earlier sketch in SATA 45
Ewart, Claire 1958- 145
    Earlier sketch in SATA 76
Ewart, Franzeska G. 1950- 205
Ewen, David 1907-1985 4
    Obituary 47
Ewing, Juliana (Horatia Gatty) 1841-1885 ... 16
    See also CLR 78
Ewing, Kathryn 1921- 20
Eyerly, Jeannette 1908-2008 86
    Obituary 196
    Earlier sketch in SATA 4
    See also SAAS 10
Eyerly, Jeannette Hyde
    See Eyerly, Jeannette
Eyre, Dorothy
    See McGuire, Leslie (Sarah)
Eyre, Frank 1910-1988
    Obituary 62
Eyre, Katherine Wigmore 1901-1970 26
Ezzell, Marilyn 1937- 42
    Brief entry 38

F

Fabe, Maxene 1943- 15
Faber, Doris (Greenberg) 1924- 78
    Earlier sketch in SATA 3
Faber, Harold 1919- 5
Fabre, Jean Henri (Casimir) 1823-1915 22
Fabry, Glenn 1961- 205
Facklam, Margaret
    See Thomas, Peggy
Facklam, Margery (Metz) 1927- 132
    Earlier sketches in SATA 20, 85
Fadden, David Kanietakeron 196
Fadiman, Clifton (Paul) 1904-1999 11
    Obituary 115
Fagan, Cary 1957- 186
Fahs, Sophia Blanche Lyon 1876-1978 102
Failing, Barbara Larmon 182
Fain, Sarah 1971- 204
Fair, David 1952- 96
Fair, Sylvia 1933- 13
Fairfax-Lucy, Brian (Fulke Cameron-Ramsay)
    1898-1974 6
    Obituary 26

Fairfield, Flora
  See Alcott, Louisa May
Fairlie, Gerard 1899-1983
  Obituary 34
Fairman, Joan A(lexandra) 1935- 10
Faithfull, Gail 1936- 8
Falcone, L(ucy) M. 1951- 155
Falconer, Ian 1959- 179
  Earlier sketch in SATA 125
  See also CLR 146
Falconer, James
  See Kirkup, James
Falconer, Lee N.
  See May, Julian
Falkner, Brian 1962- 206
Falkner, Leonard 1900-1977 12
Fall, Andrew
  See Arthur, Robert, (Jr.)
Fall, Thomas
  See Snow, Donald Clifford
Faller, Regis 1968- 187
Falls, C(harles) B(uckles) 1874-1960 38
  Brief entry 27
Falstein, Louis 1909-1995 37
Falwell, Cathryn 1952- 196
Fancher, Lou 1960- 177
Fanelli, Sara 1969- 126
  Earlier sketch in SATA 89
Fanning, Leonard M(ulliken) 1888-1967 5
Faralla, Dana 1909- 9
Faralla, Dorothy W.
  See Faralla, Dana
Farb, Peter 1929-1980 12
  Obituary 22
Farber, Norma 1909-1984 75
  Obituary 38
  Earlier sketch in SATA 25
Fardell, John 1967- 195
Farish, Terry 1947- 146
  Earlier sketch in SATA 82
Farjeon, (Eve) Annabel 1919-2004 11
  Obituary 153
Farjeon, Eleanor 1881-1965 2
  See also CLR 34
Farley, Carol (J.) 1936- 137
  Earlier sketch in SATA 4
Farley, Terri 165
Farley, Walter (Lorimer) 1915-1989 132
  Earlier sketches in SATA 2, 43
Farlow, James O(rville, Jr.) 1951- 75
Farmer, Nancy 1941- 161
  Earlier sketches in SATA 79, 117
Farmer, Patti 1948- 79
Farmer, Penelope (Jane) 1939- 105
  Brief entry 39
  Earlier sketch in SATA 40
  See also CLR 8
  See also SAAS 22
Farmer, Peter 1950- 38
Farmer, Philip Jose
  See Farmer, Philip Jose
Farmer, Philip Jose 1918-2009 93
  Obituary 201
Farmer, Philipe Jos
  See Farmer, Philip Jose
Farnham, Burt
  See Clifford, Harold B(urton)
Farnsworth, Bill 1958- 186
  Earlier sketches in SATA 84, 135
Farooqi, Musharraf Ali 1968- 207
Farquhar, Margaret C(utting) 1905-1988 13
Farquharson, Alexander 1944- 46
Farquharson, Martha
  See Finley, Martha
Farr, Diana 82
  Earlier sketch in SATA 3
Farr, Finis (King) 1904-1982 10
Farrar, Jill
  See Morris, Jill
Farrar, Susan Clement 1917- 33

Farrell, Ben
  See Cebulash, Mel
Farrell, John 1951- 204
Farrell, Patrick
  See Odgers, Sally Farrell
Farrell, Sally
  See Odgers, Sally Farrell
Farrer, Vashti 167
Farrington, Benjamin 1891-1974
  Obituary 20
Farrington, S(elwyn) Kip, Jr. 1904-1983 20
Farris, Christine King 1927- 206
Farshtey, Greg(ory T.) 1965- 148
Farthing, Alison 1936- 45
  Brief entry 36
Farthing-Knight, Catherine 1933- 92
Fassler, Joan (Grace) 1931- 11
Fast, Howard 1914-2003 7
  Autobiography Feature 107
Fast, Howard Melvin
  See Fast, Howard
Fasulo, Michael 1963- 83
Fatchen, Max 1920- 84
  Earlier sketch in SATA 20
  See also SAAS 20
Fate, Marilyn
  See Collins, Paul
Father Goose
  See Ghigna, Charles
Fatigati, (Frances) Evelyn 1948- 24
Fatio, Louise 1904-1993 6
Fatus, Sophie 1957- 182
Faulhaber, Martha 1926- 7
Faulkner, Anne Irvin 1906- 23
Faulkner, Frank
  See Ellis, Edward S.
Faulkner, Nancy
  See Faulkner, Anne Irvin
Faulknor, Cliff(ord Vernon) 1913- 86
Favole, Robert J(ames) 1950- 125
Fax, Elton Clay 1909-1993 25
Faxon, Lavinia
  See Russ, Lavinia (Faxon)
Feagles, Anita M(acRae) 1927- 9
Feagles, Elizabeth
  See Day, Beth (Feagles)
Feague, Mildred H. 1915- 14
Fearnley, Jan 1965- 205
  Earlier sketch in SATA 153
Fearrington, Ann (Peyton) 1945- 146
Fecher, Constance
  See Heaven, Constance (Christina)
Feder, Chris Welles 1938- 81
Feder, Harriet K. 1928- 73
Feder, Paula (Kurzband) 1935- 26
Federici, Debbie 1965- 175
Federici, Debbie Tanner
  See Federici, Debbie
Feelings, Muriel 1938- 16
  See also CLR 5
  See also SAAS 8
Feelings, Muriel Lavita Grey
  See Feelings, Muriel
Feelings, Thomas 1933-2003 69
  Obituary 148
  Earlier sketch in SATA 8
  See also CLR 58
  See also SAAS 19
Feelings, Tom
  See Feelings, Thomas
Fehler, Gene 1940- 201
  Earlier sketch in SATA 74
Fehrenbach, T(heodore) R(eed, Jr.) 1925- 33
Feiffer, Jules 1929- 201
  Earlier sketches in SATA 8, 61, 111, 157
Feiffer, Jules Ralph
  See Feiffer, Jules
Feiffer, Kate 1964- 206
  Earlier sketch in SATA 170
Feig, Barbara Krane 1937- 34

Feikema, Feike
  See Manfred, Frederick (Feikema)
Feil, Hila 1942- 12
Feilen, John
  See May, Julian
Feinberg, Barbara Jane 1938- 123
  Earlier sketch in SATA 58
Feinberg, Barbara Silberdick
  See Feinberg, Barbara Jane
Feinstein, John 1956- 195
  Earlier sketch in SATA 163
Feldman, Anne (Rodgers) 1939- 19
Feldman, Elane 79
Feldman, Jody 200
Felin, M. Sindy 194
Felix
  See Vincent, Felix
Fell, Derek 1939- 167
Fell, Derek John
  See Fell, Derek
Fellowes, Julian 1950- 198
Fellows, Muriel H. 10
Fellows, Stan 1957- 177
Fellows, Stanley
  See Fellows, Stan
Felsen, Henry Gregor 1916-1995 1
  See also SAAS 2
Felstead, Cathie 1954- 192
Feltenstein, Arlene (H.) 1934- 119
Felton, Harold William 1902-1991 1
Felton, Ronald Oliver 1909- 3
Felts, Shirley 1934- 33
Fenderson, Lewis H., Jr. 1907-1983 47
  Obituary 37
Fenner, Carol (Elizabeth) 1929-2002 89
  Obituary 132
  Earlier sketch in SATA 7
  See also SAAS 24
Fenner, Phyllis R(eid) 1899-1982 1
  Obituary 29
Fensham, Elizabeth 169
Fenten, Barbara D(oris) 1935- 26
Fenten, D(onald) X. 1932- 4
Fenton, Carroll Lane 1900-1969 5
Fenton, Edward 1917-1995 7
  Obituary 89
Fenton, Mildred Adams 1899-1995 21
Fenwick, Patti
  See Grider, Dorothy
Feravolo, Rocco Vincent 1922- 10
Ferber, Brenda A. 1967- 184
Ferber, Edna 1887-1968 7
Fergus, Charles 114
Ferguson, Alane 1957- 182
  Earlier sketch in SATA 85
Ferguson, Bob
  See Ferguson, Robert Bruce
Ferguson, Cecil 1931- 45
Ferguson, Peter 1968- 199
Ferguson, Robert Bruce 1927-2001 13
Ferguson, Sarah 1959- 180
  Earlier sketches in SATA 66, 110
Ferguson, Sarah Margaret
  See Ferguson, Sarah
Ferguson, Walter (W.) 1930- 34
Fergusson, Erna 1888-1964 5
Fermi, Laura 1907-1977 6
  Obituary 28
Fern, Eugene A. 1919-1987 10
  Obituary 54
Fern, Tracey E. 202
Fernandes, Eugenie 1943- 205
  Earlier sketches in SATA 77, 139
Fernandez, Laura 1960- 171
Ferrari, Maria 123
Ferreiro, Carmen 1958- 158
Ferrell, Nancy Warren 1932- 70
Ferri, Giuliano 1965- 197
Ferrier, Lucy
  See Penzler, Otto
Ferris, Helen Josephine 1890-1969 21

Ferris, James Cody
  See McFarlane, Leslie
Ferris, Jean 1939- 202
  Brief entry 50
  Earlier sketches in SATA *56, 105, 149*
Ferris, Jeri Chase 1937- 84
Ferry, Charles 1927- 92
  Earlier sketch in SATA *43*
  See also CLR *34*
  See also SAAS *20*
Fetz, Ingrid 1915- 30
Feydy, Anne Lindbergh
  See Sapiyevski, Anne Lindbergh
Fiammenghi, Gioia 1929- 66
  Earlier sketch in SATA *9*
Fiarotta, Noel
  See Ficarotta, Noel
Fiarotta, Phyllis
  See Ficarotta, Phyllis
Ficarotta, Noel 1944- 15
Ficarotta, Phyllis 1942- 15
Fichter, George S. 1922-1993 7
Ficocelli, Elizabeth 189
Fidler, Kathleen (Annie) 1899-1980 87
  Obituary 45
  Earlier sketch in SATA *3*
Fiedler, Jean(nette Feldman) 4
Fiedler, Joseph Daniel 159
Fiedler, Lisa 185
Field, Dorothy 1944- 97
Field, Edward 1924- 109
  Earlier sketch in SATA *8*
Field, Elinor Whitney 1889-1980
  Obituary 28
Field, Eugene 1850-1895 16
Field, Gans T.
  See Wellman, Manly Wade
Field, James 1959- 113
Field, Peter
  See Drago, Harry Sinclair
  and Dresser, Davis
  and Mann, E(dward) B(everly)
Field, Rachel (Lyman) 1894-1942 15
  See also CLR *21*
Fielding, Kate
  See Oldfield, Jenny
Fields, Bryan W. 1958(?)- 188
Fields, Terri 1948- 191
Fields, T.S.
  See Fields, Terri
Fienberg, Anna 1956- 183
  Earlier sketch in SATA *112*
Fiery, Ann
  See Barrows, Annie
Fife, Dale (Odile Hollerbach) 1901- 18
Fighter Pilot, A
  See Johnston, H(ugh) A(nthony) S(tephen)
Figler, Jeanie 1949- 123
Figley, Marty Rhodes 1948- 158
  Earlier sketch in SATA *88*
Figueredo, D(anilo) H. 1951- 155
Figueroa, Pablo 1938- 9
Fijan, Carol 1918- 12
Filderman, Diane E(lizabeth) 1959- 87
Files, Meg 1946- 107
Fillmore, Parker H(oysted) 1878-1944
  See YABC *1*
Filstrup, Chris
  See Filstrup, E(dward) Christian
Filstrup, E(dward) Christian 1942- 43
Filstrup, Janie
  See Merrill, Jane
Finchler, Judy 1943- 93
Finder, Martin
  See Salzmann, Siegmund
Findlay, Jamieson 1958- 169
Findon, Joanne 1957- 161
Fine, Anne 1947- 197
  Earlier sketches in SATA *29, 72, 111, 160*
  See also CLR *25*
  See also SAAS *15*

Fine, Edith Hope 169
Fine, Howard 1961- 181
Fine, Jane
  See Ziefert, Harriet
Finger, Charles J(oseph) 1869(?)-1941 42
Fink, William B(ertrand) 1916- 22
Finke, Blythe Foote 1922- 26
Finkel, George (Irvine) 1909-1975 8
Finkelstein, Norman H. 1941- 137
  Earlier sketch in SATA *73*
Finkelstein, Norman Henry
  See Finkelstein, Norman H.
Finlay, Alice Sullivan 1946- 82
Finlay, Winifred Lindsay Crawford
  (McKissack) 1910-1989 23
Finlayson, Ann 1925- 8
Finley, Martha 1828-1909 43
Finley, Mary Peace 1942- 83
Finney, Jack 1911-1995 109
Finney, Patricia 1958- 163
Finney, Shan 1944- 65
Finney, Walter Braden
  See Finney, Jack
Firer, Ben Zion
  See Firer, Benzion
Firer, Benzion 1914- 64
Fireside, Bryna J. 1932- 73
Firmin, Charlotte 1954- 29
Firmin, Peter 1928- 58
  Earlier sketch in SATA *15*
Firth, Barbara 179
Fischbach, Julius 1894-1988 10
Fischer, John
  See Fluke, Joanne
Fischer, R.J.
  See Fluke, Joanne
Fischer, Scott M. 1971- 195
Fischer-Nagel, Andreas 1951- 56
Fischer-Nagel, Heiderose 1956- 56
Fischler, Shirley (Walton) 66
Fischler, Stan(ley I.) 66
  Brief entry 36
Fischtrom, Harvey 1933-1974 3
Fishback, Margaret
  See Antolini, Margaret Fishback
Fishbone, Greg R. 195
Fisher, Aileen (Lucia) 1906-2002 73
  Obituary 143
  Earlier sketches in SATA *1, 25*
  See also CLR *49*
Fisher, Barbara 1940- 44
  Brief entry 34
Fisher, Carolyn 1968- 154
Fisher, Catherine 1957- 155
Fisher, Chris G. 1958- 80
Fisher, Clavin C(argill) 1912- 24
Fisher, Cynthia 195
Fisher, Dorothy (Frances) Canfield 1879-1958
  See YABC *1*
  See also CLR *71*
Fisher, Gary L. 1949- 86
Fisher, John 1909-1996 15
Fisher, John Oswald Hamilton
  See Fisher, John
Fisher, Laura Harrison 1934- 5
Fisher, Leonard Everett 1924- 176
  Autobiography Feature 122
  Earlier sketches in SATA *4, 34, 73, 120*
  See also CLR *18*
  See also SAAS *1*
Fisher, Lois I. 1948- 38
  Brief entry 35
Fisher, Margery (Turner) 1913-1992 20
  Obituary 74
Fisher, Marshall Jon 1963- 113
Fisher, Nikki
  See Strachan, Ian
Fisher, Robert (Tempest) 1943- 47
Fisher, Suzanne
  See Staples, Suzanne Fisher
Fisher, Valorie 177

Fishman, Cathy Goldberg 1951- 106
Fisk, Nicholas
  See Higginbottom, David
Fisk, Pauline 1948- 160
  Earlier sketch in SATA *66*
Fiske, Tarleton
  See Bloch, Robert (Albert)
Fisscher, Catharina G. M. 1958- 142
Fisscher, Tiny
  See Fisscher, Catharina G. M.
Fitch, Clarke
  See Sinclair, Upton
Fitch, John IV
  See Cormier, Robert
Fitch, Sheree 1956- 178
  Earlier sketch in SATA *108*
Fitschen, Dale 1937- 20
Fitzalan, Roger
  See Trevor, Elleston
Fitzgerald, Captain Hugh
  See Baum, L. Frank
FitzGerald, Cathleen 1932-1987
  Obituary 50
Fitzgerald, Dawn 175
Fitzgerald, Edward Earl 1919-2001 20
Fitzgerald, F(rancis) A(nthony) 1940- 15
Fitzgerald, Joanne 1956- 198
Fitzgerald, John D(ennis) 1907(?)-1988 20
  Obituary 56
  See also CLR *1*
Fitzgerald, Merni Ingrassia 1955- 53
Fitzgibbon, Terry 1948- 121
Fitzhardinge, Joan Margaret 1912- 73
  Earlier sketch in SATA *2*
  See also CLR *5*
  See also SAAS *3*
Fitzhugh, Louise (Perkins) 1928-1974 45
  Obituary 24
  Earlier sketch in SATA *1*
  See also CLR *72*
Fitzhugh, Percy Keese 1876-1950 65
Fitzpatrick, Marie-Louise 1962- 189
  Earlier sketch in SATA *125*
FitzRalph, Matthew
  See McInerny, Ralph
Fitz-Randolph, Jane (Currens) 1915- 51
Fitzsimons, Cecilia 1952- 97
Fitzsimons, Cecilia A.L.
  See Fitzsimons, Cecilia
Flack, Marjorie 1897-1958 100
  See also YABC *2*
  See also CLR *28*
Flack, Naomi John White -1999 40
  Brief entry 35
Flake, Sharon G. 166
Flanagan, John 1944- 180
Flanagan, John Anthony
  See Flanagan, John
Flannery, Kate
  See De Goldi, Kathleen Domenica
Flatt, Lizann 1966- 88
Fleagle, Gail S(hatto) 1940- 117
Fleetwood, Jenni 1947- 80
Fleischer, Jane
  See Oppenheim, Joanne
Fleischauer-Hardt, Helga 1936- 30
Fleischman, Albert Sidney
  See Fleischman, Sid
Fleischman, John 1948- 145
Fleischman, Paul 1952- 156
  Brief entry 32
  Earlier sketches in SATA *39, 72, 110*
  See also CLR *66*
  See also SAAS *20*
Fleischman, Sid 1920- 185
  Earlier sketches in SATA *8, 59, 96, 148*
  See also CLR *15*
Fleischner, Jennifer 1956- 188
  Earlier sketch in SATA *93*
Fleisher, Paul 1948- 132
  Earlier sketch in SATA *81*

Fleisher, Robbin 1951-1977 52
  Brief entry 49
Fleishman, Seymour 1918- 66
  Brief entry 32
Fleming, A. A.
  See Arthur, Robert, (Jr.)
Fleming, Alice Mulcahey 1928- 9
Fleming, Candace 1962- 190
  Earlier sketches in SATA 94, 143
Fleming, Denise 1950- 173
  Earlier sketches in SATA 81, 126
Fleming, Elizabeth P. 1888-1985
  Obituary 48
Fleming, Ian 1908-1964 9
Fleming, Ian Lancaster
  See Fleming, Ian
Fleming, Ronald Lee 1941- 56
Fleming, Sally
  See Walker, Sally M(acArt)
Fleming, Stuart
  See Knight, Damon (Francis)
Fleming, Susan 1932- 32
Fleming, Thomas 1927- 8
Fleming, Thomas James
  See Fleming, Thomas
Fleming, Virginia (Edwards) 1923- 84
Flesch, Y.
  See Flesch, Yolande (Catarina)
Flesch, Yolande (Catarina) 1950- 55
Fletcher, Charlie May Hogue 1897-1977 3
Fletcher, Colin 1922-2007 28
Fletcher, Dirk
  See Cunningham, Chet
Fletcher, George U.
  See Pratt, (Murray) Fletcher
Fletcher, Helen Jill 1910- 13
Fletcher, Ralph 1953- 195
  Earlier sketches in SATA 105, 149
  See also CLR 104
Fletcher, Ralph J.
  See Fletcher, Ralph
Fletcher, Richard E. 1917(?)-1983
  Obituary 34
Fletcher, Rick
  See Fletcher, Richard E.
Fletcher, Susan 1951- 181
  Earlier sketches in SATA 70, 110
Fletcher, Susan Clemens
  See Fletcher, Susan
Fleur, Paul
  See Pohl, Frederik
Flexner, James Thomas 1908-2003 9
Flinn, Alex 1966- 198
  Earlier sketch in SATA 159
Flint, Helen 1952- 102
Flint, Russ 1944- 74
Flitner, David P(erkins), Jr. 1949- 7
Floca, Brian 190
  Earlier sketch in SATA 155
Floethe, Louise Lee 1913-1988 4
Floethe, Richard 1901-1998 4
Floherty, John Joseph 1882-1964 25
Flood, Bo
  See Flood, Nancy Bo
Flood, Nancy Bo 1945- 130
Flood, Pansie Hart 1964- 140
Flood, William 1942- 129
Flooglebuckle, Al
  See Spiegelman, Art
Flora, James (Royer) 1914-1998 30
  Obituary 103
  Earlier sketch in SATA 1
  See also SAAS 6
Flores-Galbis, Enrique 1952- 186
Florian, Douglas 1950- 177
  Earlier sketches in SATA 19, 83, 125
Flory, Jane Trescott 1917- 22
Flournoy, Valerie 1952- 95
Flournoy, Valerie Rose
  See Flournoy, Valerie
Flowerdew, Phyllis -1994 33

Flowers, Pam 1946- 136
Flowers, Sarah 1952- 98
Floyd, Gareth 1940- 62
  Brief entry 31
Fluchere, Henri 1914-1991 40
Fluke, Joanne 1943- 88
Flutsztejn-Gruda, Ilona 1930- 170
Flynn, Barbara 1928- 9
Flynn, Jackson
  See Bensen, Donald R.
  and Shirreffs, Gordon D(onald)
Flynn, Nicholas
  See Odgers, Sally Farrell
Flynn, Rachel 1953- 171
  Earlier sketch in SATA 109
Flynn, Warren (G.) 1950- 154
Fodor, R(onald) V(ictor) 1944- 25
Fogelin, Adrian 1951- 175
  Earlier sketch in SATA 129
Foley, (Anna) Bernice Williams 1902-1987 . 28
Foley, Greg E. 1969- 190
Foley, June 1944- 44
Foley, (Mary) Louise Munro 1933- 106
  Brief entry 40
  Earlier sketch in SATA 54
Foley, Rae
  See Denniston, Elinore
Folke, Will
  See Bloch, Robert (Albert)
Follett, Helen Thomas 1884(?)-1970
  Obituary 27
Folsom, Franklin (Brewster) 1907-1995 5
  Obituary 88
Folsom, Michael (Brewster) 1938-1990 40
  Obituary 88
Fontenot, Mary Alice 1910-2003 91
  Earlier sketch in SATA 34
Fontes, Justine 172
Fontes, Ron 1952- 183
Foon, Dennis 1951- 119
Fooner, Michael 22
Foote, Timothy (Gilson) 1926- 52
Forberg, Ati
  See Forberg, Beate Gropius
Forberg, Beate Gropius 1925- 22
Forbes, Anna 1951- 101
Forbes, Bryan 1926- 37
Forbes, Cabot L.
  See Hoyt, Edwin P(almer), Jr.
Forbes, Esther 1891-1967 100
  Earlier sketch in SATA 2
  See also CLR 147
Forbes, Graham B. 1
Forbes, Kathryn
  See McLean, Kathryn (Anderson)
Forbes, Robert
  See Arthur, Robert, (Jr.)
Ford, Albert Lee
  See Stratemeyer, Edward L.
Ford, Barbara 56
  Brief entry 34
Ford, Brian J(ohn) 1939- 49
Ford, Carolyn (Mott) 1938- 98
Ford, Christine 1953- 176
Ford, David
  See Baldacci, David
  and Baldacci, David
Ford, David B.
  See Baldacci, David
Ford, David Baldacci
  See Baldacci, David
Ford, Elbur
  See Hibbert, Eleanor Alice Burford
Ford, Ellen 1949- 89
Ford, George (Jr.) 31
Ford, Hilary
  See Youd, Samuel
Ford, Hildegarde
  See Morrison, Velma Ford
Ford, Jerome W. 1949- 78

Ford, Jerry
  See Ford, Jerome W.
Ford, Juwanda G(ertrude) 1967- 102
Ford, Marcia
  See Radford, Ruby L(orraine)
Ford, Nancy K(effer) 1906-1961
  Obituary 29
Ford, Peter 1936- 59
Ford, S. M.
  See Uhlig, Susan
Forde, Catherine 1961- 170
Foreman, Mark 199
Foreman, Michael 1938- 184
  Earlier sketches in SATA 2, 73, 129, 135
  See also CLR 32
  See also SAAS 21
Foreman, Wilmoth 1939- 153
Forest, Antonia 1915-2003 29
  Obituary 149
Forest, Dial
  See Gault, William Campbell
Forest, Heather 1948- 185
  Earlier sketch in SATA 120
Forester, C. S. 1899-1966 13
Forester, Cecil Scott
  See Forester, C. S.
Forman, Brenda 1936- 4
Forman, James
  See Forman, James D.
Forman, James D. 1932- 70
  Earlier sketch in SATA 8
Forman, James Douglas
  See Forman, James D.
Forman, Ruth 1970- 186
Forrest, Elizabeth
  See Salsitz, Rhondi Vilott
Forrest, Mary
  See Pausacker, Jenny
Forrest, Sybil
  See Markun, Patricia Maloney
Forrestal, Elaine 1941- 165
  Earlier sketch in SATA 117
Forrester, Frank H. 1919(?)-1986
  Obituary 52
Forrester, Helen
  See Bhatia, Jamunadevi
Forrester, Jade
  See Pausacker, Jenny
Forrester, Marian
  See Schachtel, Roger
Forrester, Sandra 1949- 166
  Earlier sketch in SATA 90
Forrester, Victoria 1940- 40
  Brief entry 35
Forsee, (Frances) Aylesa -1986 1
Forsey, Chris 1950- 59
Forshay-Lunsford, Cin 1965- 60
Forster, E. M. 1879-1970 57
Forster, Edward Morgan
  See Forster, E. M.
Forsyth, Kate 1966- 154
Fort, Paul
  See Stockton, Francis Richard
Forte, Maurizio 1961- 110
Fortey, Richard 1946- 109
Fortey, Richard A.
  See Fortey, Richard
Fortey, Richard Alan
  See Fortey, Richard
Forth, Melissa D(eal) 96
Fortnum, Peggy
  See Nuttall-Smith, Margaret Emily Noel
Fortune, Eric 182
Forward, Robert L(ull) 1932-2002 82
Foster, Alan Dean 1946- 70
Foster, Brad W. 1955- 34
Foster, Doris Van Liew 1899-1993 10
Foster, E(lizabeth) C(onnell) 1902- 9
Foster, Elizabeth 1902- 12
Foster, Elizabeth 1905-1963 10
Foster, F. Blanche 1919- 11

Foster, G(eorge) Allen 1907-1969 .... *26*
Foster, Genevieve (Stump) 1893-1979 .... *2*
  Obituary *23*
  See also CLR 7
Foster, Gerald L. *198*
Foster, Hal
  See Foster, Harold
Foster, Harold 1892-1982 .... *31*
Foster, Jeanne
  See Williams, Jeanne
Foster, John
  See Foster, John L(ouis)
  and Furcolo, Foster
Foster, John (Thomas) 1925- *8*
Foster, John L(ouis) 1941- *102*
Foster, Juliana *196*
Foster, Laura Louise (James) 1918- *6*
Foster, Leila Merrell 1929- *73*
Foster, Lynne 1937- *74*
Foster, Margaret Lesser 1899(?)-1979
  Obituary *21*
Foster, Marian Curtis 1909-1978 .... *23*
Foster, Mark 1961- *197*
Foster, Sally *58*
Fotheringham, Edwin *201*
Foulds, E. V.
  See Foulds, Elfrida Vipont
Foulds, Elfrida Vipont 1902-1992 .... *52*
Fountas, Angela Jane *180*
Fourie, Corlia 1944- *91*
Fourth Brother, The
  See Aung, (Maung) Htin
Fowke, Edith (Margaret) 1913-1996 .... *14*
Fowles, John 1926-2005 .... *22*
  Obituary *171*
Fowles, John Robert
  See Fowles, John
Fowles, Shelley 1956- *205*
Fox, Aileen 1907-2005 .... *58*
  Obituary *170*
Fox, Aileen Mary
  See Fox, Aileen
Fox, Annie 1950- *175*
Fox, Charles Philip 1913-2003 .... *12*
  Obituary *150*
Fox, Christyan *188*
Fox, Diane *188*
Fox, Eleanor
  See St. John, Wylly Folk
Fox, Fontaine Talbot, Jr. 1884-1964
  Obituary *23*
Fox, Fred 1903(?)-1981
  Obituary *27*
Fox, Freeman
  See Hamilton, Charles (Harold St. John)
Fox, Geoffrey 1941- *73*
Fox, Grace
  See Anderson, Grace Fox
Fox, Helen 1962- *181*
Fox, Larry *30*
Fox, Lorraine 1922-1976 .... *27*
  Earlier sketch in SATA *11*
Fox, Louisa
  See Kroll, Virginia L.
Fox, Mary Virginia 1919- *152*
  Brief entry *39*
  Earlier sketches in SATA *44, 88*
Fox, Mem
  See Fox, Merrion Frances
Fox, Merrion Frances 1946- *155*
  Earlier sketches in SATA *51, 103*
  See also CLR 80
Fox, Michael W(ilson) 1937- *15*
Fox, Norma Diane
  See Mazer, Norma Fox
Fox, Paula 1923- *167*
  Earlier sketches in SATA *17, 60, 120*
  See also CLR 96
Fox, Robert J. 1927- *33*
Fox-Davies, Sarah 1956- *199*
Foyt, Victoria .... *187.*

Fradin, Dennis
  See Fradin, Dennis Brindell
Fradin, Dennis Brindell 1945- *185*
  Earlier sketches in SATA *29, 90, 135*
Fradin, Judith Bloom 1945- *185*
  Earlier sketches in SATA *90, 152*
Frailey, Paige (Menefee) 1965- *82*
Frame, Janet 1924-2004 .... *119*
Frame, Paul 1913-1994 .... *60*
  Brief entry *33*
  Obituary *83*
Frances, Miss
  See Horwich, Frances R(appaport)
Franchere, Ruth *18*
Francis, Charles
  See Holme, Bryan
Francis, Dee
  See Haas, Dorothy F.
Francis, Dorothy 1926- *127*
  Earlier sketch in SATA *10*
Francis, Dorothy B.
  See Francis, Dorothy
Francis, Dorothy Brenner
  See Francis, Dorothy
Francis, Jaye
  See Pausacker, Jenny
Francis, Pamela (Mary) 1926- *11*
Franck, Eddie
  See Cooke, Frank E.
Franco, Betsy *188*
  Earlier sketch in SATA *150*
Franco, Eloise (Bauder) 1910- *62*
Franco, Johan (Henri Gustave) 1908-1988 ... *62*
Franco, Marjorie *38*
Francois, Andre 1915-2005 .... *25*
Francoise
  See Seignobosc, Francoise
Frank, Anne 1929-1945 .... *87*
  Brief entry *42*
  See also CLR 101
Frank, Annelies Marie
  See Frank, Anne
Frank, Daniel B. 1956- *55*
Frank, Emily R.
  See Frank, E.R.
Frank, E.R. 1967- *157*
Frank, Helene
  See Vautier, Ghislaine
Frank, Hillary 1976- *148*
Frank, John *199*
Frank, Josette 1893-1989 .... *10*
  Obituary *63*
Frank, Lucy 1947- *166*
  Earlier sketch in SATA *94*
Frank, Mary 1933- *34*
Frank, R., Jr.
  See Ross, Frank (Xavier), Jr.
Frankau, Mary Evelyn Atkinson 1899-1974 .. *4*
Frankel, Alona 1937- *66*
Frankel, Bernice *9*
Frankel, Edward 1910- *44*
Frankel, Ellen 1951- *78*
Frankel, Julie 1947- *40*
  Brief entry *34*
Frankenberg, Robert 1911- *22*
Frankland, David *207*
Franklin, Cheryl J. 1955- *70*
Franklin, Harold 1926- *13*
Franklin, Kristine L. 1958- *124*
  Earlier sketch in SATA *80*
Franklin, Lance
  See Lantz, Francess L(in)
Franklin, Madeleine
  See L'Engle, Madeleine
Franklin, Madeleine L'Engle
  See L'Engle, Madeleine
Franklin, Madeleine L'Engle Camp
  See L'Engle, Madeleine
Franklin, Max
  See Deming, Richard

Franklin, Steve
  See Stevens, Franklin
Franson, Leanne R. 1963- *111*
Franson, Scott E. 1966- *192*
Franzen, Nils-Olof 1916- *10*
Frascino, Edward *48*
  Brief entry *33*
  See also SAAS 9
Frasconi, Antonio 1919- *131*
  Earlier sketches in SATA *6, 53*
  See also SAAS 11
Fraser, Betty
  See Fraser, Elizabeth Marr
Fraser, Elizabeth Marr 1928- *31*
Fraser, Eric (George) 1902-1983 .... *38*
Fraser, Mary Ann 1959- *137*
  Earlier sketch in SATA *76*
  See also SAAS 23
Fraser, Wynnette (McFaddin) 1925- *90*
Frasier, Debra 1953- *182*
  Earlier sketches in SATA *69, 112*
Fraustino, Lisa Rowe 1961- *146*
  Autobiography Feature *146*
  Earlier sketch in SATA *84*
Frazee, Marla 1958- *187*
  Earlier sketches in SATA *105, 151*
Frazetta, Frank 1928- *58*
Frazier, Craig 1955- *177*
Frazier, Neta (Osborn) Lohnes 1890-1990 ..... *7*
Frazier, Sundee T. 1968- *198*
Frazier, Sundee Tucker
  See Frazier, Sundee T.
Frederic, Mike
  See Cox, William R(obert)
Frederick, Heather Vogel *207*
Fredericks, Anthony D. 1947- *113*
Freed, Alvyn M. 1913-1993 .... *22*
Freedman, Benedict 1919- *27*
Freedman, Claire *185*
Freedman, Deborah 1960- *191*
Freedman, Jeff 1953- *90*
Freedman, Nancy 1920- *27*
Freedman, Russell 1929- *175*
  Earlier sketches in SATA *16, 71, 123*
  See also CLR 71
Freedman, Russell Bruce
  See Freedman, Russell
Freeman, Barbara C. 1906-1999 .... *28*
Freeman, Barbara Constance
  See Freeman, Barbara C.
Freeman, Bill
  See Freeman, William Bradford
Freeman, Don 1908-1978 .... *17*
  See also CLR 90
Freeman, Ira Maximilian 1905-1987 .... *21*
Freeman, Kimberley
  See Wilkins, Kim
Freeman, Laura *200*
Freeman, Lucy (Greenbaum) 1916-2004 ...... *24*
Freeman, Mae 1907-1985 .... *25*
Freeman, Mae Blacker
  See Freeman, Mae
Freeman, Marcia S. 1937- *102*
Freeman, Martha 1956- *201*
  Earlier sketches in SATA *101, 152*
Freeman, Nancy 1932- *61*
Freeman, Peter J.
  See Calvert, Patricia
Freeman, Sarah (Caroline) 1940- *66*
Freeman, Tor 1977- *164*
Freeman, VicToria
  See Freeman, Tor
Freeman, William Bradford 1938- *58*
  Brief entry *48*
Fregosi, Claudia (Anne Marie) 1946- *24*
Freitas, Donna 1972- *205*
French, Allen 1870-1946
  See YABC 1
French, Dorothy Kayser 1926- *5*

French, Fiona 1944- 132
    Earlier sketches in SATA 6, 75
    See also CLR 37
    See also SAAS 21
French, Jackie 186
    Autobiography Feature 139
    Earlier sketches in SATA 108, 139
    See French, Jackie Anne
    and French, Jacqueline Anne
French, Kathryn
    See Mosesson, Gloria R(ubin)
French, Martin 176
French, Michael 1944- 49
    Brief entry 38
French, Paul
    See Asimov, Isaac
French, Simon 1957- 147
    Earlier sketch in SATA 86
French, Vivian 165
Frenette, Liza 126
Freschet, Gina 1960- 175
    Earlier sketch in SATA 139
Frewer, Glyn (M.) 1931- 11
Frey, Darcy 98
Freymann, Saxton 1958(?)- 178
Freymann-Weyr, (Rhoda) Garret (Michaela)
    1965- 145
Frick, C. H.
    See Irwin, Constance (H.) Frick
Frick, Constance
    See Irwin, Constance (H.) Frick
Fricke, Aaron 1962- 89
Fridell, Ron 1943- 124
Fried, Janice 197
Friedlander, Joanne K(ohn) 1930- 9
Friedman, Aimee 1979- 189
Friedman, D. Dina 1957- 180
Friedman, Debra 1955- 150
Friedman, Estelle (Ehrenwald) 1920- 7
Friedman, Frieda 1905- 43
Friedman, Ina R(osen) 1926- 136
    Brief entry 41
    Earlier sketch in SATA 49
Friedman, Jerrold David
    See Gerrold, David
Friedman, Judi 1935- 59
Friedman, Laurie 1964- 179
    Earlier sketch in SATA 138
Friedman, Marvin 1930- 42
    Brief entry 33
Friedman, Robin 1968- 162
Friedmann, Stan 1953- 80
Friedrich, Otto (Alva) 1929-1995 33
Friedrich, Priscilla 1927- 39
Friend, Catherine 1957(?)- 194
Friend, David Michael 1975- 195
Friend, Natasha 1972- 184
Friendlich, Dick
    See Friendlich, Richard J.
Friendlich, Richard J. 1909- 11
Friermood, Elisabeth Hamilton 1903-1992 5
Friesen, Bernice (Sarah Anne) 1966- 105
Friesen, Gayle 1960- 200
    Earlier sketch in SATA 109
Friesen, Jonathan 1967(?)- 206
Friesner, Esther 1951- 207
    Earlier sketches in SATA 71, 168
Friesner, Esther M.
    See Friesner, Esther
Friis-Baastad, Babbis Ellinor 1921-1970 7
Frimmer, Steven 1928- 31
Frischmuth, Barbara 1941- 114
Friskey, Margaret (Richards) 1901-1995 5
Fritts, Mary Bahr
    See Bahr, Mary (Madelyn)
Fritz, Jean (Guttery) 1915- 163
    Autobiography Feature 122
    Earlier sketches in SATA 1, 29, 72, 119
    See also CLR 96
    See also SAAS 2
Froehlich, Margaret W(alden) 1930- 56

Frois, Jeanne 1953- 73
Froissart, Jean 1338(?)-1410(?) 28
Froman, Elizabeth Hull 1920-1975 10
Froman, Robert (Winslow) 1917- 8
Fromm, Lilo 1928- 29
Frommer, Harvey 1937- 41
Frost, A(rthur) B(urdett) 1851-1928 19
Frost, Elizabeth
    See Frost-Knappman, Elizabeth
Frost, Erica
    See Supraner, Robyn
Frost, Helen 1949- 194
    Autobiography Feature 194
    Earlier sketches in SATA 157, 183
Frost, Helen Marie
    See Frost, Helen
Frost, Lesley 1899-1983 14
    Obituary 34
Frost, Robert 1874-1963 14
    See also CLR 67
Frost, Robert Lee
    See Frost, Robert
Frost, Shelley 1960- 138
Frost-Knappman, Elizabeth 1943- 179
Froud, Brian 1947- 150
Fry, Annette R(iley) 89
Fry, Christopher 1907-2005 66
Fry, Edward Bernard 1925- 35
Fry, Rosalie Kingsmill 1911-1992 3
    See also SAAS 11
Fry, Virginia Lynn 1952- 95
Frye, Sally
    See Moore, Elaine
Fuchs, Bernie 1932- 162
    Earlier sketch in SATA 95
Fuchs, Erich 1916- 6
Fuchshuber, Annegert 1940- 43
Fuerst, Jeffrey B. 1956- 143
Fuertes, Gloria 1918-1998 115
Fuge, Charles 1966- 144
    Earlier sketch in SATA 74
Fujikawa, Gyo 1908-1998 76
    Brief entry 30
    Obituary 110
    Earlier sketch in SATA 39
    See also CLR 25
    See also SAAS 16
Fujita, Tamao 1905-1999 7
Fujiwara, Kim 1957- 81
Fujiwara, Michiko 1946- 15
Fuka, Vladimir 1926-1977
    Obituary 27
Fulcher, Jennifer
    See Westwood, Jennifer
Fuller, Catherine Leuthold 1916- 9
Fuller, Edmund (Maybank) 1914- 21
Fuller, Iola
    See McCoy, Iola Fuller
Fuller, John G(rant, Jr.) 1913-1990 65
Fuller, Kathleen
    See Gottfried, Theodore Mark
Fuller, Lois Hamilton 1915- 11
Fuller, Margaret 1810-1850 25
Fuller, Maud
    See Petersham, Maud
Fuller, Roy (Broadbent) 1912-1991 87
Fuller, Sarah Margaret
    See Fuller, Margaret
Fults, John Lee 1932- 33
Funk, Thompson 1911- 7
Funk, Tom
    See Funk, Thompson
Funke, Cornelia 1958- 174
    Earlier sketch in SATA 154
    See also CLR 145
Funke, Cornelia Caroline
    See Funke, Cornelia
Funke, Lewis 1912-1992 11
Fuqua, Jonathon Scott 1966- 141
Furbee, Mary R.
    See Furbee, Mary Rodd

Furbee, Mary Rodd 1954- 138
Furchgott, Terry 1948- 29
Furlong, Monica (Mavis) 1930-2003 86
    Obituary 142
Furman, Gertrude Lerner Kerman 1909- 21
Furniss, Tim 1948- 49
Furrow, Robert 1985- 172
Furukawa, Toshi 1924- 24
Fusillo, Archimede 1962- 137
Futcher, Jane P. 1947- 76
Futehali, Zahida
    See Whitaker, Zai
Fyleman, Rose (Amy) 1877-1957 21
Fyson, Jenny Grace
    See Fyson, J.G.
Fyson, J.G. 1904-1998 42

                          G

Gaan, Margaret 1914- 65
Gaber, Susan 1956- 169
    Earlier sketch in SATA 115
Gaberman, Judie Angell
    See Angell, Judie
Gabhart, Ann
    See Gabhart, Ann H.
Gabhart, Ann H. 1947- 75
Gable, Brian 1949- 195
Gabler, Mirko 1951- 77
Gabriel, Adriana
    See Rojany, Lisa
Gabrys, Ingrid Schubert
    See Schubert-Gabrys, Ingrid
Gackenbach, Dick 1927- 79
    Brief entry 30
    Earlier sketch in SATA 48
Gadd, Jeremy 1949- 116
Gaddis, Vincent H. 1913-1997 35
Gadler, Steve J. 1905-1985 36
Gaeddert, Lou Ann (Bigge) 1931- 103
    Earlier sketch in SATA 20
Gaeddert, Louann
    See Gaeddert, Lou Ann (Bigge)
Gaer, Joseph 1897-1969 118
Gaer, Yossef
    See Gaer, Joseph
Gaetz, Dayle Campbell 1947- 138
Gaffney, Timothy R. 1951- 170
    Earlier sketch in SATA 69
Gaffron, Norma (Bondeson) 1931- 97
Gag, Flavia 1907-1979
    Obituary 24
Gag, Wanda (Hazel) 1893-1946 100
    See also YABC 1
    See also CLR 4
Gage, Brian 162
Gage, Wilson
    See Steele, Mary Q(uintard Govan)
Gagliano, Eugene M. 1946- 150
Gagliardo, Ruth Garver 1895(?)-1980
    Obituary 22
Gagnon, Cecile 1936- 58
Gaillard, Jason 1965- 200
Gaiman, Neil 1960- 197
    Earlier sketches in SATA 85, 146
    See also CLR 109
Gaiman, Neil Richard
    See Gaiman, Neil
Gainer, Cindy 1962- 74
Gaines, Ernest J. 1933- 86
    See also CLR 62
Gaines, Ernest James
    See Gaines, Ernest J.
Gaither, Gloria 1942- 127
Gal, Laszlo 1933- 96
    Brief entry 32
    Earlier sketch in SATA 52
    See also CLR 61
Galbraith, Ben 1980- 200

Galbraith, Kathryn O(sebold) 1945- *85*
Galdone, Paul 1907(?)-1986 .... *66*
    Obituary *49*
    Earlier sketch in SATA *17*
    See also CLR *16*
Galindo, Claudia 1979- *203*
Galinsky, Ellen 1942- *23*
Gall, Chris 1961- *176*
Gallagher, Diana G. 1946- *153*
Gallagher, Lurlene Nora
    See McDaniel, Lurlene
Gallagher-Cole, Mernie 1958- *206*
Gallant, Roy A(rthur) 1924- *110*
    Earlier sketches in SATA *4, 68*
    See also CLR *30*
Gallardo, Evelyn 1948- *78*
Gallaz, Christophe 1948- *162*
    See also CLR *126*
Gallego Garcia, Laura 1977- *173*
Gallico, Paul (William) 1897-1976 .... *13*
Gallo, Donald R. 1938- *112*
    Autobiography Feature *104*
Gallo, Donald Robert
    See Gallo, Donald R.
Galloway, Owateka (S.) 1981- *121*
Galloway, Priscilla 1930- *112*
    Earlier sketch in SATA *66*
Gallup, Joan 1957- *128*
Galouchko, Annouchka Gravel 1960- *95*
Galt, Thomas Franklin, Jr. 1908-1989 .... *5*
Galt, Tom
    See Galt, Thomas Franklin, Jr.
Galvin, Matthew R. 1950- *93*
Galvin, Matthew Reppert
    See Galvin, Matthew R.
Gamble, Kim 1952- *183*
    Earlier sketches in SATA *81, 124*
Gambrell, Jamey *82*
Gamerman, Martha 1941- *15*
Gammell, Stephen 1943- *128*
    Earlier sketches in SATA *53, 81*
    See also CLR *83*
Ganly, Helen (Mary) 1940- *56*
Gannett, Ruth Chrisman (Arens)
    1896-1979 .... *33*
Gannett, Ruth Stiles 1923- *3*
Gannon, Ned 1974- *205*
Gannon, Robert Haines 1931- *8*
Gano, Lila 1949- *76*
Gans, Roma 1894-1996 .... *45*
    Obituary *93*
Gant, Matthew
    See Hano, Arnold
Gantner, Susan (Verble) 1939- *63*
Gantos, Jack 1951- *169*
    Earlier sketches in SATA *20, 81, 119*
    See also CLR *85*
Gantos, John Bryan, Jr.
    See Gantos, Jack
Ganz, Yaffa 1938- *61*
    Brief entry *52*
Garafano, Marie 1942- *84*
Garant, Andre J. 1968- *123*
Garbe, Ruth Moore
    See Moore, Ruth (Ellen)
Garber, Esther
    See Lee, Tanith
Garcia, Emma 1969- *198*
Garcia, Yolanda P. 1952- *113*
Garcia, Yolanda Pacheco
    See Garcia, Yolanda P.
Gard, Janice
    See Latham, Jean Lee
Gard, Joyce
    See Reeves, Joyce
Gard, Robert Edward 1910-1992 .... *18*
    Obituary *74*
Gard, (Sanford) Wayne 1899-1986
    Obituary *49*

Gardam, Jane 1928- *130*
    Brief entry *28*
    Earlier sketches in SATA *39, 76*
    See also CLR *12*
    See also SAAS *9*
Gardam, Jane Mary
    See Gardam, Jane
Gardella, Tricia 1944- *96*
Garden, Nancy 1938- *147*
    Autobiography Feature *147*
    Earlier sketches in SATA *12, 77, 114*
    See also CLR *51*
    See also SAAS *8*
Gardiner, John Reynolds 1944-2006 .... *64*
    Obituary *174*
Gardiner, Lindsey 1971- *144*
Gardner, Craig Shaw 1949- *99*
Gardner, Dic
    See Gardner, Richard (M.)
Gardner, Graham *159*
Gardner, Hugh 1910-1986
    Obituary *49*
Gardner, Jane Mylum 1946- *83*
Gardner, Jeanne LeMonnier 1925- *5*
Gardner, John, Jr. 1933-1982 .... *40*
    Obituary *31*
Gardner, John Champlin, Jr.
    See Gardner, John, Jr.
Gardner, John E(dward) 1917- *192*
Gardner, Lyn *192*
Gardner, Martin 1914- *142*
    Earlier sketch in SATA *16*
Gardner, Miriam
    See Bradley, Marion Zimmer
Gardner, Richard (M.) 1931- *24*
Gardner, Richard A(lan) 1931-2003 .... *13*
    Obituary *144*
Gardner, Sally *177*
Gardner, Sandra 1940- *70*
Gardner, Scot 1968- *143*
Gardner, Sheldon 1934- *33*
Gardner, Ted
    See Gardner, Theodore Roosevelt II
Gardner, Theodore Roosevelt
    See Gardner, Theodore Roosevelt II
Gardner, Theodore Roosevelt II 1934- *84*
Garelick, May 1910-1989 .... *19*
Garfield, James B. 1881-1984 .... *6*
    Obituary *38*
Garfield, Leon 1921-1996 .... *76*
    Obituary *90*
    Earlier sketches in SATA *1, 32*
    See also CLR *21*
Garfinkle, Debra L.
    See Garfinkle, D.L.
Garfinkle, D.L. *187*
Garis, Howard R. 1873-1962 .... *13*
Garis, Howard Roger
    See Garis, Howard R.
Garland, Mark 1953- *79*
Garland, Mark A.
    See Garland, Mark
Garland, Michael 1952- *168*
Garland, Sarah 1944- *135*
    Earlier sketch in SATA *62*
Garland, Sherry 1948- *145*
    Autobiography Feature *145*
    Earlier sketches in SATA *73, 114*
Garner, Alan 1934- *69*
    Autobiography Feature *108*
    Earlier sketch in SATA *18*
    See also CLR *130*
Garner, David 1958- *78*
Garner, Eleanor Ramrath 1930- *122*
Garner, James Finn 1960(?)- *92*
Garnet, A. H.
    See Slote, Alfred
Garnett, Eve C. R. 1900-1991 .... *3*
    Obituary *70*
Garofoli, Viviana 1970- *186*

Garou, Louis P.
    See Bowkett, Stephen
Garraty, John A. 1920-2007 .... *23*
    Obituary *189*
Garraty, John Arthur
    See Garraty, John A.
Garren, Devorah-Leah
    See Devorah-Leah
Garret, Maxwell R. 1917- *39*
Garretson, Victoria Diane 1945- *44*
Garrett, Helen 1895- *21*
Garrett, Randall 1927-1987 .... *180*
Garrett, Richard 1920- *82*
Garrigue, Sheila 1931- *21*
Garrison, Barbara 1931- *163*
    Earlier sketch in SATA *19*
Garrison, Frederick
    See Sinclair, Upton
Garrison, Mary 1952- *146*
Garrison, Peter
    See Gardner, Craig Shaw
Garrison, Webb B(lack) 1919-2000 .... *25*
Garrity, Jennifer Johnson 1961- *124*
Garrity, Linda K. 1947- *128*
Garsee, Jeannine *199*
Garst, Doris Shannon 1894-1981 .... *1*
Garst, Shannon
    See Garst, Doris Shannon
Garth, Will
    See Hamilton, Edmond
    and Kuttner, Henry
Garthwaite, Marion H(ook) 1893-1981 .... *7*
Garton, Malinda D(ean) (?)-1976
    Obituary *26*
Garvie, Maureen 1944- *175*
Garvie, Maureen McCallum
    See Garvie, Maureen
Garza, Carmen Lomas 1948- *182*
Garza, Xavier *184*
Gascoigne, Bamber 1935- *62*
Gaskins, Pearl Fuyo 1957- *134*
Gasperini, Jim 1952- *54*
    Brief entry *49*
Gater, Dilys 1944- *41*
Gates, Doris 1901-1987 .... *34*
    Obituary *54*
    Earlier sketch in SATA *1*
    See also SAAS *1*
Gates, Frieda 1933- *26*
Gates, Susan 1950- *153*
Gates, Viola R. 1931- *101*
Gathorne-Hardy, Jonathan G. 1933- *124*
    Earlier sketch in SATA *26*
Gatti, Anne 1952- *103*
Gatty, Juliana Horatia
    See Ewing, Juliana (Horatia Gatty)
Gauch, Patricia Lee 1934- *80*
    Earlier sketch in SATA *26*
    See also CLR *56*
    See also SAAS *21*
Gaudasinska, Elzbieta 1943- *190*
Gaul, Randy 1959- *63*
Gault, Clare 1925- *36*
Gault, Frank 1926-1982 .... *36*
    Brief entry *30*
Gault, William Campbell 1910-1995 .... *8*
Gauthier, Gail 1953- *203*
    Earlier sketches in SATA *118, 160*
Gaver, Becky
    See Gaver, Rebecca
Gaver, Rebecca 1952- *20*
Gavin, Jamila 1941- *125*
    Earlier sketch in SATA *96*
Gay, Amelia
    See Hogarth, Grace (Weston Allen)
Gay, Francis
    See Gee, H(erbert) L(eslie)
Gay, Kathlyn 1930- *144*
    Earlier sketch in SATA *9*

Gay, Marie-Louise 1952- 179
  Earlier sketches in SATA 68, 126
  See also CLR 27
  See also SAAS 21
Gay, Michel 1947- 162
Gay, Zhenya 1906-1978 19
Gaze, Gillian
  See Barklem, Jill
Gear, Kathleen M. O'Neal
  See Gear, Kathleen O'Neal
Gear, Kathleen O'Neal 1954- 166
  Earlier sketch in SATA 71
Gear, W. Michael 1955- 166
  Earlier sketch in SATA 71
Geary, Rick 1946- 142
Geason, Susan 1946- 122
Gedalof, Robin
  See McGrath, Robin
Gedge, Pauline (Alice) 1945- 101
Gee, H(erbert) L(eslie) 1901-1977
  Obituary 26
Gee, Maurice 1931- 101
  Earlier sketch in SATA 46
  See also CLR 56
Gee, Maurice Gough
  See Gee, Maurice
Geehan, Wayne (E.) 1947- 107
Geer, Charles 1922- 42
  Brief entry 32
Geeslin, Campbell 1925- 163
  Earlier sketch in SATA 107
Gehman, Mary W. 1923- 86
Gehr, Mary 1910(?)-1997 32
  Obituary 99
Geipel, Eileen 1932- 30
Geis, Alissa Imre 1976- 189
Geis, Darlene Stern 1918(?)-1999 7
  Obituary 111
Geisel, Helen 1898-1967 26
Geisel, Theodor Seuss
  See Dr. Seuss
Geisert, Arthur 1941- 171
  Brief entry 52
  Earlier sketches in SATA 56, 92, 133
  See also CLR 87
  See also SAAS 23
Geisert, Arthur Frederick
  See Geisert, Arthur
Geisert, Bonnie 1942- 165
  Earlier sketch in SATA 92
Geist, Ken 191
Geldart, William 1936- 15
Gelinas, Paul J. 1904-1996 10
Gellis, Roberta 1927- 128
Gellis, Roberta Leah Jacobs
  See Gellis, Roberta
Gellman, Marc 112
Gelman, Amy 1961- 72
Gelman, Jan 1963- 58
Gelman, Rita Golden 1937- 131
  Brief entry 51
  Earlier sketch in SATA 84
Gelman, Steve 1934- 3
Gemming, Elizabeth 1932- 11
Gendel, Evelyn W. 1916(?)-1977
  Obituary 27
Gennaro, Joseph F(rancis), Jr. 1924- 53
Gentieu, Penny 204
Gentile, Petrina 1969- 91
Gentle, Mary 1956- 48
Gentleman, David (William) 1930- 7
Geoghegan, Adrienne 1962- 143
George, Barbara
  See Katz, Bobbi
George, Emily
  See Katz, Bobbi
George, Gail
  See Katz, Bobbi
George, Jean
  See George, Jean Craighead

George, Jean C.
  See George, Jean Craighead
George, Jean Craighead 1919- 170
  Earlier sketches in SATA 2, 68, 124
  See also CLR 136
George, John L(othar) 1916- 2
George, Kristine O'Connell 1954- 156
  Earlier sketch in SATA 110
George, Lindsay Barrett 1952- 206
  Earlier sketches in SATA 95, 155
George, S(idney) C(harles) 1898- 11
George, Sally
  See Orr, Wendy
George, Twig C. 1950- 114
George, W(illiam) Lloyd 1900(?)-1975
  Obituary 30
Georgiou, Constantine 1927- 7
Georgiou, Theo
  See Odgers, Sally Farrell
Geraghty, Paul 1959- 130
Gerard, Jean Ignace Isidore 1803-1847 45
Geras, Adele 1944- 180
  Autobiography Feature 180
  Earlier sketches in SATA 23, 87, 129, 173
  See also SAAS 21
Geras, Adele Daphne Weston
  See Geras, Adele
Gerber, Carole 1947- 207
Gerber, Merrill Joan 1938- 170
  Autobiography Feature 170
  Earlier sketches in SATA 64, 127
Gerber, Perren 1933- 104
Gerberg, Mort 1931- 64
Gergely, Tibor 1900-1978 54
  Obituary 20
Geringer, Laura 1948- 164
  Earlier sketches in SATA 29, 94
Gerler, William R(obert) 1917-1996 47
Gerrard, Jean 1933- 51
Gerrard, Roy 1935-1997 90
  Brief entry 45
  Obituary 99
  Earlier sketch in SATA 47
  See also CLR 23
Gerritsen, Paula 1956- 177
Gerrold, David 1944- 144
  Earlier sketch in SATA 66
Gershator, David 1937- 180
Gershator, Phillis 1942- 188
  Earlier sketches in SATA 90, 158
Gershon, Dann 1955- 187
Gershon, Gina 1962- 187
Gerson, Corinne 1927- 37
Gerson, Mary-Joan 136
  Earlier sketch in SATA 79
Gerson, Noel Bertram 1914-1988 22
  Obituary 60
Gerstein, Mordicai 1935- 178
  Brief entry 36
  Earlier sketches in SATA 47, 81, 142
  See also CLR 102
Gertridge, Allison 1967- 132
Gervais, Bernadette 1959- 80
Gervay, Susanne 183
Gesner, Clark 1938-2002 40
  Obituary 143
Gessner, Lynne 1919- 16
Geter, Tyrone 150
Getz, David 1957- 91
Getzinger, Donna 1968- 128
Geus, Mireille 1964- 207
Gevirtz, Eliezer 1950- 49
Gevry, Claudine 188
Gewe, Raddory
  See Gorey, Edward (St. John)
Ghan, Linda (R.) 1947- 77
Ghent, Natale 1962- 148
Gherman, Beverly 1934- 123
  Earlier sketch in SATA 68
Ghigna, Charles 1946- 153
  Earlier sketch in SATA 108

Giacobbe, Beppe 1953- 174
Giambastiani, Kurt R. A. 1958- 141
Giannini, Enzo 1946- 68
Gibala-Broxholm, Scott 1959(?)- 205
Gibbons, Alan 1953- 198
  Earlier sketch in SATA 124
Gibbons, Faye 1938- 103
  Earlier sketch in SATA 65
Gibbons, Gail 1944- 201
  Earlier sketches in SATA 23, 72, 104, 160
  See also CLR 8
  See also SAAS 12
Gibbons, Gail Gretchen
  See Gibbons, Gail
Gibbons, Kaye 1960- 117
Gibbs, Adrea 1960- 126
Gibbs, Alonzo (Lawrence) 1915-1992 5
Gibbs, (Cecilia) May 1877-1969
  Obituary 27
Gibbs, Tony
  See Gibbs, Wolcott, Jr.
Gibbs, Wolcott, Jr. 1935- 40
Giblin, James Cross 1933- 197
  Earlier sketches in SATA 33, 75, 122
  See also CLR 29
  See also SAAS 12
Gibson, Andrew (William) 1949- 72
Gibson, Barbara L. 205
Gibson, Barbara Leonard
  See Gibson, Barbara L.
Gibson, Betty 1911- 75
Gibson, Jo
  See Fluke, Joanne
Gibson, Josephine
  See Hine, Sesyle Joslin
  and Hine, Al(fred Blakelee)
Gibson, William 1914-2008 66
  Obituary 199
Gibson, William Ford
  See Gibson, William
Gidal, Nachum
  See Gidal, Tim Nachum
Gidal, Sonia (Epstein) 1922- 2
Gidal, Tim Nachum 1909-1996 2
Gidalewitsch, Nachum
  See Gidal, Tim Nachum
Gideon, Melanie 1963- 175
Giegling, John A(llan) 1935- 17
Gifaldi, David 1950- 76
Giff, Patricia Reilly 1935- 203
  Earlier sketches in SATA 33, 70, 121, 160
Giffard, Hannah 1962- 83
Gifford, Clive 1966- 198
Gifford, Griselda 1931- 171
  Earlier sketch in SATA 42
Gifford, Kerri 1961- 91
Gifford, Peggy 1952- 191
Gilbert, Ann
  See Taylor, Ann
Gilbert, Anne Yvonne 1951- 185
Gilbert, Barbara Snow 1954- 97
Gilbert, Catherine
  See Murdock, Catherine Gilbert
Gilbert, Frances
  See Collings, Gillian
Gilbert, Harriett 1948- 30
Gilbert, (Agnes) Joan (Sewell) 1931- 10
Gilbert, John (Raphael) 1926- 36
Gilbert, Nan
  See Gilbertson, Mildred Geiger
Gilbert, Roby Goodale 1966- 90
Gilbert, Ruth Gallard Ainsworth
  See Ainsworth, Ruth (Gallard)
Gilbert, Sara (Dulaney) 1943- 82
  Earlier sketch in SATA 11
Gilbert, Sheri L. 157
Gilbert, Suzie 1956- 97
Gilbert, W(illiam) S(chwenck) 1836-1911 ... 36
Gilbert, Yvonne
  See Gilbert, Anne Yvonne
Gilbertson, Mildred Geiger 1908-1988 2

Gilbreath, Alice 1921- *12*
Gilbreth, Frank B., Jr. 1911-2001 .... *2*
Gilbreth, Frank Bunker
  See Gilbreth, Frank B., Jr.
Gilchrist, Jan Spivey 1949- *130*
  Earlier sketch in SATA *72*
Gilden, Mel 1947- *97*
Giles, Gail *196*
  Earlier sketch in SATA *152*
Gilfond, Henry *2*
Gilge, Jeanette 1924- *22*
Gili, Phillida 1944- *70*
Gill, Derek (Lewis Theodore) 1919-1997 ...... *9*
Gill, Margery Jean 1925- *22*
Gill, Shelley *176*
Gill, Stephen 1932- *63*
Gillespie, Carol Ann 1951- *158*
Gillett, Mary (Bledsoe) *7*
Gillette, Henry Sampson 1915- *14*
Gillette, J(an) Lynett 1946- *103*
Gilley, Jeremy 1969- *174*
Gillham, Bill
  See Gillham, W(illiam) E(dwin) C(harles)
Gillham, W(illiam) E(dwin) C(harles)
  1936- *42*
Gilliam, Stan 1946- *39*
  Brief entry *35*
Gilliland, Alexis A(rnaldus) 1931- *72*
Gilliland, (Cleburne) Hap 1918- *92*
Gilliland, Judith Heide *180*
Gillmor, Don 1954- *127*
Gilman, Dorothy 1923- *5*
Gilman, Esther 1925- *15*
Gilman, Laura Anne *178*
Gilman, Phoebe 1940-2002 .... *104*
  Obituary *141*
  Earlier sketch in SATA *58*
Gilmore, Iris 1900-1982 .... *22*
Gilmore, Kate 1931- *87*
Gilmore, Mary (Jean Cameron) 1865-1962 . *49*
Gilmore, Susan 1954- *59*
Gilpin, Stephen *177*
Gilroy, Beryl (Agatha) 1924- *80*
Gilson, Barbara
  See Gilson, Charles James Louis
Gilson, Charles James Louis 1878-1943
  See YABC 2
Gilson, Jamie 1933- *176*
  Brief entry *34*
  Earlier sketches in SATA *37, 91*
Ginsburg, Mirra 1909-2000 .... *92*
  Earlier sketch in SATA *6*
  See also CLR *45*
Giovanni, Nikki 1943- *107*
  Earlier sketch in SATA *24*
  See also CLR *73*
Giovanni, Yolanda Cornelia
  See Giovanni, Nikki
Giovanni, Yolande Cornelia
  See Giovanni, Nikki
Giovanni, Yolande Cornelia, Jr.
  See Giovanni, Nikki
Giovanopoulos, Paul (Arthur) 1939- *7*
Gipson, Billie
  See Letts, Billie
Gipson, Fred(erick Benjamin) 1908-1973 ...... *2*
  Obituary *24*
Girard, Linda (Walvoord) 1942- *41*
Girion, Barbara 1937- *78*
  Earlier sketch in SATA *26*
  See also SAAS *14*
Girl, Nerdy
  See Castellucci, Cecil
Girouard, Patrick 1957- *155*
Girzone, Joseph F. 1930- *76*
Girzone, Joseph Francis
  See Girzone, Joseph F.
Gise, Joanne
  See Mattern, Joanne
Gist, E.M. *206*
Gittings, Jo (Grenville) Manton 1919- *3*

Gittings, Robert (William Victor) 1911-1992 . *6*
  Obituary *70*
Givens, Janet E(aton) 1932- *60*
Givner, Joan 1936- *171*
Givner, Joan Mary
  See Givner, Joan
Gladstone, Eve
  See Werner, Herma
Gladstone, Gary 1935- *12*
Gladstone, M(yron) J. 1923- *37*
Glanville, Brian (Lester) 1931- *42*
Glanzman, Louis S. 1922- *36*
Glaser, Byron 1954- *154*
Glaser, Dianne E(lizabeth) 1937- *50*
  Brief entry *31*
Glaser, Isabel Joshlin 1929- *94*
Glaser, Milton 1929- *151*
  Earlier sketch in SATA *11*
Glaser, Shirley *151*
Glaspell, Susan 1882(?)-1948
  See YABC 2
Glass, Andrew 1949- *150*
  Brief entry *46*
  Earlier sketch in SATA *90*
Glass, Linzi *175*
Glass, Linzi Alex
  See Glass, Linzi
Glasscock, Amnesia
  See Steinbeck, John
Glassman, Bruce 1961- *76*
Glauber, Uta (Heil) 1936- *17*
Glazer, Thomas (Zachariah) 1914-2003 .... *9*
Glazer, Tom
  See Glazer, Thomas (Zachariah)
Gleasner, Diana (Cottle) 1936- *29*
Gleason, Judith 1929- *24*
Gleason, Katherine (A.) 1960- *104*
Gleeson, Libby 1950- *142*
  Autobiography Feature *142*
  Earlier sketches in SATA *82, 118*
Gleiter, Jan 1947- *111*
Gleitzman, Morris 1953- *156*
  Earlier sketch in SATA *88*
  See also CLR *88*
Glen, Maggie 1944- *88*
Glendinning, Richard 1917-1988 .... *24*
Glendinning, Sally
  See Glendinning, Sara W(ilson)
Glendinning, Sara W(ilson) 1913-1993 .... *24*
Glenn, John W. *195*
Glenn, Mel 1943- *93*
  Brief entry *45*
  Earlier sketch in SATA *51*
  See also CLR *51*
Glenn, Patricia Brown 1953- *86*
Glenn, Sharlee *159*
Glenn, Sharlee Mullins
  See Glenn, Sharlee
Glennon, Karen M. 1946- *85*
Gles, Margaret Breitmaier 1940- *22*
Glick, Carl (Cannon) 1890-1971 .... *14*
Glick, Ruth (Burtnick) 1942- *125*
Glick, Virginia Kirkus 1893-1980
  Obituary *23*
Gliewe, Unada (Grace) 1927- *3*
Glimmerveen, Ulco 1958- *85*
Glines, Carroll V(ane), Jr. 1920- *19*
Gliori, Debi 1959- *189*
  Earlier sketches in SATA *72, 138*
Globe, Leah Ain 1900- *41*
Glori Ann
  See Blakely, Gloria
Glovach, Linda 1947- *105*
  Earlier sketch in SATA *7*
Glover, Denis (James Matthews) 1912-1980 . *7*
Glubok, Shirley (Astor) *146*
  Autobiography Feature *146*
  Earlier sketches in SATA *6, 68*
  See also CLR *1*
  See also SAAS *7*

Gluck, Felix 1923-1981
  Obituary *25*
Glyman, Caroline A. 1967- *103*
Glynne-Jones, William 1907-1977 .... *11*
Gobbato, Imero 1923- *39*
Gobbletree, Richard
  See Quackenbush, Robert M(ead)
Goble, Dorothy *26*
Goble, Paul 1933- *131*
  Earlier sketches in SATA *25, 69*
  See also CLR *21*
Goble, Warwick (?)-1943 .... *46*
Godden, (Margaret) Rumer 1907-1998 .... *36*
  Obituary *109*
  Earlier sketch in SATA *3*
  See also CLR *20*
  See also SAAS *12*
Gode, Alexander
  See Gode von Aesch, Alexander (Gottfried
    Friedrich)
Gode von Aesch, Alexander (Gottfried
  Friedrich) 1906-1970 .... *14*
Godfrey, Jane
  See Bowden, Joan Chase
Godfrey, Martyn
  See Godfrey, Martyn N.
  and Godfrey, Martyn N.
Godfrey, Martyn N. 1949-2000 .... *95*
  See also CLR *57*
Godfrey, William
  See Youd, Samuel
Godin, Celia (Marilyn) 1948- *145*
  Earlier sketch in SATA *66*
Godon, Ingrid 1958- *186*
Godwin, Laura 1956- *179*
Godwin, Sam
  See Pirotta, Saviour
Goedecke, Christopher (John) 1951- *81*
Goekler, Susan
  See Wooley, Susan Frelick
Goembel, Ponder *204*
Goertzen, Glenda *172*
Goettel, Elinor 1930- *12*
Goetz, Delia 1898-1996 .... *22*
  Obituary *91*
Goffe, Toni 1936- *61*
Goffstein, Brooke
  See Goffstein, M(arilyn) B(rooke)
Goffstein, M(arilyn) B(rooke) 1940- *70*
  Earlier sketch in SATA *8*
  See also CLR *3*
Goforth, Ellen
  See Francis, Dorothy
Gogol, Sara 1948-2004 .... *80*
Goh, Chan Hon 1969- *145*
Going, Kelly L.
  See Going, K.L.
Going, Kelly Louise
  See Going, K.L.
Going, K.L. *199*
  Earlier sketch in SATA *156*
Golann, Cecil Paige 1921-1995 .... *11*
Golbin, Andree 1923- *15*
Gold, Alison Leslie 1945- *104*
Gold, Bernice *150*
Gold, Phyllis
  See Goldberg, Phyllis
Gold, Robert S(tanley) 1924- *63*
Gold, Sharlya *9*
Gold, Susan
  See Gold, Susan Dudley
Gold, Susan Dudley 1949- *147*
Goldberg, Grace 1956- *78*
Goldberg, Herbert S. 1926- *25*
Goldberg, Jacob 1943- *94*
Goldberg, Jake
  See Goldberg, Jacob
Goldberg, Phyllis 1941- *21*
Goldberg, Stan J. 1939- *26*
Goldberg, Susan 1948- *71*
Goldberg, Whoopi 1955- *119*

Goldberger, Judith M. 1948- 80
Goldblatt, Stacey 1969(?)- 191
Golden, Christie 1963- 167
Earlier sketch in SATA 116
Goldentyer, Debra 1960- 84
Goldfeder, Cheryl
See Pahz, Cheryl Suzanne
Goldfeder, James
See Pahz, James Alon
Goldfeder, Jim
See Pahz, James Alon
Goldfinger, Jennifer P. 1963- 185
Goldfrank, Helen Colodny 1912- 6
Goldin, Augusta 1906-1999 13
Goldin, Barbara Diamond 1946- 129
Autobiography Feature 129
Earlier sketch in SATA 92
See also SAAS 26
Goldin, David 1963- 101
Golding, Julia 1969- 188
Golding, Theresa Martin 1960- 150
Golding, William 1911-1993
See CLR 130
Golding, William Gerald
See Golding, William
Goldman, Alex J. 1917- 65
Goldman, Arthur Steven
See Goldman, Steven
Goldman, E(leanor) M(aureen) 1943- 103
Goldman, Elizabeth 1949- 90
Goldman, Steven 1964- 207
Goldring, Ann 1937- 149
Goldsborough, June 1923- 19
Goldschmidt, Judy 202
Goldsmith, Connie 1945- 147
Goldsmith, Howard 1943- 108
Earlier sketch in SATA 24
Goldsmith, John Herman Thorburn 1903-1987
Obituary 52
Goldsmith, Oliver 1730(?)-1774 26
Goldsmith, Ruth M. 1919- 62
Goldstein, Nathan 1927- 47
Goldstein, Philip 1910-1997 23
Goldston, Robert (Conroy) 1927- 6
Goldstone, Bruce 183
Goldstone, Lawrence A.
See Treat, Lawrence
Goldszmit, Henryk 1878-1942 65
Golembe, Carla 1951- 79
Golenbock, Peter 1946- 99
Goll, Reinhold W(eimar) 1897-1993 26
Gollub, Matthew 1960- 134
Earlier sketch in SATA 83
Gomes, Filomena 1965- 183
Gomez, Elena 191
Gomez, Elizabeth 133
Gomez-Freer, Elizabeth
See Gomez, Elizabeth
Gomi, Taro 1945- 103
Earlier sketch in SATA 64
See also CLR 57
Gondosch, Linda 1944- 58
Gonyea, Mark 194
Gonzalez, Catherine Troxell 1917-2000 87
Gonzalez, Christina
See Gonzalez, Maya Christina
Gonzalez, Gloria 1940- 23
Gonzalez, Julie 1958- 174
Gonzalez, Julie Sehers
See Gonzalez, Julie
Gonzalez, Lucia M. 1957- 202
Gonzalez, Maya
See Gonzalez, Maya Christina
Gonzalez, Maya Christina 1964- 175
Earlier sketch in SATA 115
Gonzalez, Rigoberto 1970- 147
Goobie, Beth 1959- 128
Good, Alice 1950- 73
Good, Clare
See Romano, Clare

Goodall, Daphne Machin
See Machin Goodall, Daphne (Edith)
Goodall, Jane 1934- 111
Goodall, John S(trickland) 1908-1996 66
Obituary 91
Earlier sketch in SATA 4
See also CLR 25
Goodbody, Slim
See Burstein, John
Goode, Diane 1949- 170
Earlier sketches in SATA 15, 84, 114
Goode, Diane Capuozzo
See Goode, Diane
Goode, Stephen Ray 1943- 55
Brief entry 40
Goodenow, Earle 1913- 40
Goodhart, Pippa 1958- 196
Earlier sketch in SATA 153
Goodhue, Thomas W. 1949- 143
Goodin, Sallie (Brown) 1953- 74
Goodman, Alison 1966- 111
Goodman, Deborah Lerme 1956- 50
Brief entry 49
Goodman, Elaine 1930- 9
Goodman, Joan Elizabeth 1950- 162
Earlier sketches in SATA 50, 94
Goodman, Susan E. 1952- 181
Goodman, Walter 1927-2002 9
Goodrich, Samuel Griswold 1793-1860 23
Goodsell, Jane Neuberger 1921(?)-1988
Obituary 56
GoodWeather, Hartley
See King, Thomas
Goodweather, Hartley
See King, Thomas
Goodwin, Hal
See Goodwin, Harold L(eland)
Goodwin, Harold L(eland) 1914-1990 51
Obituary 65
Earlier sketch in SATA 13
Goodwin, William 1943- 117
Goor, Nancy (Ruth Miller) 1944- 39
Brief entry 34
Goor, Ron(ald Stephen) 1940- 39
Brief entry 34
Goossen, Agnes
See Epp, Margaret A(gnes)
Goossens, Philippe 1963- 195
Gootman, Marilyn E. 1944- 179
Gopnik, Adam 1956- 171
Gorbachev, Valeri 1944- 184
Autobiography Feature 143
Earlier sketches in SATA 98, 143
Gordion, Mark
See Turtledove, Harry
Gordon, Ad
See Hano, Arnold
Gordon, Amy 1949- 197
Earlier sketches in SATA 115, 156
Gordon, Bernard Ludwig 1931- 27
Gordon, Colonel H. R.
See Ellis, Edward S.
Gordon, David
See Garrett, Randall
Gordon, Donald
See Payne, Donald Gordon
Gordon, Dorothy 1893-1970 20
Gordon, Esther S(aranga) 1935- 10
Gordon, Frederick 1
Gordon, Gaelyn 1939-1997
See CLR 75
Gordon, Garrett
See Garrett, Randall
Gordon, Gary
See Edmonds, I(vy) G(ordon)
Gordon, Hal
See Goodwin, Harold L(eland)
Gordon, Jeffie Ross
See Enderle, Judith (Ann) Ross
and Gordon, Stephanie Jacob

Gordon, John
See Gesner, Clark
Gordon, John (William) 1925- 84
Gordon, Lew
See Baldwin, Gordon C(ortis)
Gordon, Margaret (Anna) 1939- 9
Gordon, Mike 1948- 101
Gordon, Mildred 1912-1979
Obituary 24
Gordon, Selma
See Lanes, Selma Gordon
Gordon, Sheila 1927- 88
See also CLR 27
Gordon, Shirley 1921- 48
Brief entry 41
Gordon, Sol 1923- 11
Gordon, Stephanie Jacob 1940- 89
Autobiography Feature 114
Earlier sketch in SATA 64
See also SAAS 26
Gordon, Stewart
See Shirreffs, Gordon D(onald)
Gordons, The
See Gordon, Mildred
and Gordon, Gordon
Gore, Leonid 185
Gorelick, Molly C(hernow) 1920-2003 9
Obituary 153
Gorey, Edward (St. John) 1925-2000 70
Brief entry 27
Obituary 118
Earlier sketch in SATA 29
See also CLR 36
Gorham, Charles Orson 1868-1936 36
Gorham, Michael
See Folsom, Franklin (Brewster)
Gorman, Carol 187
Earlier sketch in SATA 150
Gorman, Jacqueline Laks 1955- 148
Gorman, Mike 206
Gormley, Beatrice 1942- 202
Brief entry 35
Earlier sketches in SATA 39, 127
Gorog, Judith (Katharine Allen) 1938- 75
Earlier sketch in SATA 39
Gorrell, Gena K. 1946- 170
Gorsline, Douglas (Warner) 1913-1985 11
Obituary 43
Gorsline, (Sally) Marie 1928- 28
Gorsline, S. M.
See Gorsline, (Sally) Marie
Gorton, Kaitlyn
See Emerson, Kathy Lynn
Gorton, Kathy Lynn
See Emerson, Kathy Lynn
Goryan, Sirak
See Saroyan, William
Goscinny, Rene 1926-1977 47
Brief entry 39
See also CLR 37
Goss, Clay(ton E.) 1946- 82
Goss, Gary 1947- 124
Goss, Mini 1963- 186
Goto, Scott 203
Gott, Barry 197
Gottesman, S. D.
See Kornbluth, C(yril) M.
and Lowndes, Robert A(ugustine) W(ard)
and Pohl, Frederik
Gottfried, Ted
See Gottfried, Theodore Mark
Gottfried, Theodore Mark 1928- 150
Earlier sketch in SATA 85
Gottlieb, Gerald 1923- 7
Gottlieb, William P. 1917-2006 24
Gottlieb, William Paul
See Gottlieb, William P.
Goudey, Alice E(dwards) 1898-1993 20
Goudge, Eileen 1950- 88

Goudge, Elizabeth (de Beauchamp)
  1900-1984 2
  Obituary 38
  See also CLR 94
Gough, Catherine
  See Mulgan, Catherine
Gough, Philip 1908-1986 45
Gough, Sue 1940- 106
Goulart, Ron 1933- 67
  Earlier sketch in SATA 1
Goulart, Ronald Joseph
  See Goulart, Ron
Gould, Alberta 1945- 96
Gould, Chester 1900-1985 49
  Obituary 43
Gould, Jean R(osalind) 1909-1993 11
  Obituary 77
Gould, Lilian 6
Gould, Marilyn 1928- 76
  Earlier sketch in SATA 15
Gould, Robert 154
Gould, Steven 1955- 95
Gould, Steven Charles
  See Gould, Steven
Gourley, Catherine 1950- 190
  Earlier sketch in SATA 95
Gourse, Leslie 1939-2004 89
Govan, (Mary) Christine Noble 1898-1985 ... 9
Gove, Doris 1944- 72
Govenar, Alan 1952- 189
Govenar, Alan Bruce
  See Govenar, Alan
Govern, Elaine 1939- 26
Gowen, L. Kris 1968- 156
Graaf, Peter
  See Youd, Samuel
Graber, Alexander 1914-1997 98
  Earlier sketch in SATA 7
Graber, George Alexander
  See Graber, Alexander
Graber, Janet 1942- 170
Graber, Richard (Fredrick) 1927- 26
Grabianski, Janusz 1928-1976 39
  Obituary 30
Graboff, Abner 1919-1986 35
Grace, Fran(ces Jane) 45
Grace, N.B.
  See Harper, Suzanne
Grace, Theresa
  See Mattern, Joanne
Gracza, Margaret Young 1928- 56
Graduate of Oxford, A
  See Ruskin, John
Grady, Denise 1952- 189
Graeber, Charlotte Towner 106
  Brief entry 44
  Earlier sketch in SATA 56
Graef, Renee 1956- 204
Graeme, Roderic
  See Jeffries, Roderic
Graf, Michael
  See Graf, Mike
Graf, Mike 1960- 164
Grafe, Max 198
Graff, Lisa 1981- 188
Graff, Polly Anne Colver
  See Colver, Anne
Graff, (S.) Stewart 1908- 9
Graham, Ada 1931- 11
Graham, Alastair 1945- 74
Graham, Arthur Kennon
  See Harrison, David L.
Graham, Bob 1942- 187
  Earlier sketches in SATA 63, 101, 151
  See also CLR 31
Graham, Brenda Knight 1942- 32
Graham, Charlotte
  See Bowden, Joan Chase
Graham, Eleanor 1896-1984 18
  Obituary 38

Graham, Ennis
  See Molesworth, Mary Louisa
Graham, Frank, Jr. 1925- 11
Graham, Georgia 1959- 190
Graham, Ian 1953- 112
Graham, John 1926-2007 11
Graham, Kennon
  See Harrison, David L.
Graham, Larry
  See Graham, Lawrence
Graham, Lawrence 1962- 63
Graham, Lawrence Otis
  See Graham, Lawrence
Graham, Linda
  See Graham-Barber, Lynda
Graham, Lorenz (Bell) 1902-1989 74
  Obituary 63
  Earlier sketch in SATA 2
  See also CLR 10
  See also SAAS 5
Graham, Margaret Bloy 1920- 11
Graham, Robin Lee 1949- 7
Graham, Shirley 1896(?)-1977
  See Du Bois, Shirley Graham
Graham-Barber, Lynda 1944- 159
  Earlier sketch in SATA 42
Graham-Cameron, M.
  See Graham-Cameron, M(alcolm) G(ordon)
Graham-Cameron, M(alcolm) G(ordon)
  1931- 53
  Brief entry 45
Graham-Cameron, Mike
  See Graham-Cameron, M(alcolm) G(ordon)
Grahame, Kenneth 1859-1932 100
  See also YABC 1
  See also CLR 135
Gralley, Jean 166
Gramatky, Hardie 1907-1979 30
  Obituary 23
  Earlier sketch in SATA 1
  See also CLR 22
Grambling, Lois G. 1927- 206
  Earlier sketches in SATA 71, 148
Grambo, Rebecca L(ynn) 1963- 109
Grammer, June Amos 1927- 58
Grand, Samuel 1912-1988 42
Grandits, John 1949- 192
GrandPre, Mary 1954- 184
Grandville, J. J.
  See Gerard, Jean Ignace Isidore
Grandville, Jean Ignace Isidore Gerard
  See Gerard, Jean Ignace Isidore
Granfield, Linda 1950- 160
  Earlier sketch in SATA 96
Grange, Peter
  See Nicole, Christopher (Robin)
Granger, Margaret Jane 1925(?)-1977
  Obituary 27
Granger, Michele 1949- 88
Granger, Peggy
  See Granger, Margaret Jane
Granowsky, Alvin 1936- 101
Granstaff, Bill 1925- 10
Granstrom, Brita 1969- 167
  Earlier sketch in SATA 111
Grant, Bruce 1893-1977 5
  Obituary 25
Grant, Cynthia D. 1950- 147
  Earlier sketches in SATA 33, 77
Grant, Eva 1907-1996 7
Grant, Evva H. 1913-1977
  Obituary 27
Grant, Gordon 1875-1962 25
Grant, Gwen(doline Ellen) 1940- 47
Grant, Katie M.
  See Grant, K.M.
Grant, K.M. 175
Grant, (Alice) Leigh 1947- 10
Grant, Matthew G.
  See May, Julian

Grant, Maxwell
  See Gibson, Walter B(rown)
  and Lynds, Dennis
Grant, Melvyn 183
Grant, Myrna (Lois) 1934- 21
Grant, Neil 1938- 154
  Earlier sketch in SATA 14
Grant, Nicholas
  See Nicole, Christopher (Robin)
Grant, Richard 1948- 80
Grant, Skeeter
  See Spiegelman, Art
Grater, Michael 1923- 57
Gravel, Fern
  See Hall, James Norman
Gravelle, Karen 1942- 166
  Earlier sketch in SATA 78
Graves, Charles Parlin 1911-1972 4
Graves, Keith 191
  Earlier sketch in SATA 156
Graves, Robert 1895-1985 45
Graves, Robert von Ranke
  See Graves, Robert
Graves, Valerie
  See Bradley, Marion Zimmer
Gravett, Emily 1972(?)- 189
Gray, Betsy
  See Poole, Gray Johnson
Gray, Caroline
  See Nicole, Christopher (Robin)
Gray, Dianne E. 183
Gray, Elizabeth Janet
  See Vining, Elizabeth Gray
Gray, Genevieve S(tuck) 1920-1995 4
Gray, Harold (Lincoln) 1894-1968 33
  Brief entry 32
Gray, Jenny
  See Gray, Genevieve S(tuck)
Gray, John Lee
  See Jakes, John
Gray, Judith A. 1949- 93
Gray, Judith Anne
  See Gray, Judith A.
Gray, Keith 151
Gray, Kes 1960- 153
Gray, Les 1929- 82
Gray, Libba Moore 1937- 83
Gray, Luli 1945- 149
  Earlier sketch in SATA 90
Gray, Marian
  See Pierce, Edith Gray
Gray, Nicholas Stuart 1922-1981 4
  Obituary 27
Gray, Nigel 1941- 104
  Earlier sketch in SATA 33
Gray, (Lucy) Noel (Clervaux) 1898-1983 47
Gray, Patricia (Clark) 7
Gray, Patsey
  See Gray, Patricia (Clark)
Gray, Rita 184
Graydon, Shari 1958- 158
Grayland, V. Merle
  See Grayland, Valerie (Merle Spanner)
Grayland, Valerie (Merle Spanner) 7
Grayson, Devin (Kalile) 1970- 119
Grayson, Kristine
  See Rusch, Kristine Kathryn
Grayson, Paul 1946- 79
Graystone, Lynn
  See Brennan, Joseph Lomas
Great Comte, The
  See Hawkesworth, Eric
Greaves, Margaret 1914-1995 87
  Earlier sketch in SATA 7
Greaves, Nick 1955- 77
Gree, Alain 1936- 28
Green, Adam
  See Weisgard, Leonard (Joseph)
Green, Anne Canevari 1943- 62
Green, Brian
  See Card, Orson Scott

Green, Cliff(ord) 1934- *126*
Green, Connie Jordan 1938- *80*
Green, D.
  See Casewit, Curtis W(erner)
Green, Elizabeth Shippen 1871-1954 .... *139*
Green, Hannah
  See Greenberg, Joanne (Goldenberg)
Green, Jane 1937- *9*
Green, John 1977(?)- *170*
Green, Mary Moore 1906- *11*
Green, Morton 1937- *8*
Green, Norma B(erger) 1925- *11*
Green, Phyllis 1932- *20*
Green, Roger (Gilbert) Lancelyn 1918-1987 . *2*
  Obituary *53*
Green, (James Le)Roy 1948- *89*
Green, Sheila Ellen 1934- *148*
  Earlier sketches in SATA *8, 87*
Green, Timothy 1953- *91*
Greenaway, Kate 1846-1901 .... *100*
  See also YABC *2*
  See also CLR *111*
Greenbank, Anthony Hunt 1933- *39*
Greenberg, David 1954- *171*
Greenberg, David T.
  See Greenberg, David
Greenberg, Harvey R. 1935- *5*
Greenberg, Jan 1942- *125*
  Earlier sketch in SATA *61*
Greenberg, Joanne (Goldenberg) 1932- *25*
Greenberg, Melanie Hope 1954- *72*
Greenberg, Polly 1932- *52*
  Brief entry *43*
Greenblat, Rodney Alan 1960- *106*
Greenburg, Dan 1936- *175*
  Earlier sketch in SATA *102*
Greene, Bette 1934- *161*
  Earlier sketches in SATA *8, 102*
  See also CLR *140*
  See also SAAS *16*
Greene, Carla 1916- *67*
  Earlier sketch in SATA *1*
Greene, Carol *102*
  Brief entry *44*
  Earlier sketch in SATA *66*
Greene, Constance C(larke) 1924- *72*
  Earlier sketch in SATA *11*
  See also CLR *62*
  See also SAAS *11*
Greene, Edgar
  See Papademetriou, Lisa
Greene, Ellin 1927- *23*
Greene, Graham 1904-1991 .... *20*
Greene, Graham Henry
  See Greene, Graham
Greene, Jacqueline Dembar 1946- *131*
  Earlier sketch in SATA *76*
Greene, Laura Offenhartz 1935- *38*
Greene, Meg
  See Malvasi, Meg Greene
Greene, Michele 1962- *178*
Greene, Michele Dominguez
  See Greene, Michele
Greene, Rhonda Gowler 1955- *160*
  Earlier sketch in SATA *101*
Greene, Stephanie 1953- *173*
  Earlier sketch in SATA *127*
Greene, Wade 1933- *11*
Greene, Yvonne
  See Flesch, Yolande (Catarina)
Greenfeld, Howard (Scheinman) 1928- *140*
  Earlier sketch in SATA *19*
Greenfeld, Josh(ua Joseph) 1928- *62*
Greenfield, Eloise 1929- *155*
  Earlier sketches in SATA *19, 61, 105*
  See also CLR *38*
  See also SAAS *16*
Greenhaus, Thelma Nurenberg 1903-1984
  Obituary *45*
Greenhut, Josh
  See Mercer, Sienna

Greenhut, Josh
  See Mercer, Sienna
Greening, Hamilton
  See Hamilton, Charles (Harold St. John)
Greenlaw, M. Jean 1941- *107*
Greenleaf, Barbara Kaye 1942- *6*
Greenleaf, Peter 1910-1997 .... *33*
Greenlee, Sharon 1935- *77*
Greeno, Gayle 1949- *81*
Greenseid, Diane 1948- *178*
  Earlier sketch in SATA *93*
Greenspun, Adele Aron 1938- *142*
  Earlier sketch in SATA *76*
Greenstein, Elaine 1959- *150*
  Earlier sketch in SATA *82*
Greenwald, Sheila
  See Green, Sheila Ellen
Greenwood, Barbara 1940- *129*
  Earlier sketch in SATA *90*
Greenwood, Mark 1958- *202*
Greenwood, Pamela D. 1944- *115*
Greer, Richard
  See Garrett, Randall
  and Silverberg, Robert
Gregg, Andrew K. 1929- *81*
Gregg, Charles T(hornton) 1927- *65*
Gregg, Walter H(arold) 1919- *20*
Gregor, Arthur 1923- *36*
Gregor, Lee
  See Pohl, Frederik
Gregori, Leon 1919- *15*
Gregorian, Joyce Ballou 1946-1991 .... *30*
  Obituary *83*
Gregorich, Barbara 1943- *184*
  Earlier sketch in SATA *66*
Gregorowski, Christopher 1940- *30*
Gregory, Diana (Jean) 1933- *49*
  Brief entry *42*
Gregory, Harry
  See Gottfried, Theodore Mark
Gregory, Jean
  See Ure, Jean
Gregory, Kristiana 1951- *136*
  Earlier sketch in SATA *74*
Gregory, Nan 1944- *192*
  Earlier sketch in SATA *148*
Gregory, Philippa 1954- *122*
Gregory, Stephen
  See Penzler, Otto
Gregory, Valiska 1940- *82*
Greif, Jean-Jacques 1944- *195*
Greisman, Joan Ruth 1937- *31*
Grendon, Stephen
  See Derleth, August (William)
Grenville, Pelham
  See Wodehouse, P. G.
Gretz, Susanna 1937- *7*
Gretzer, John *18*
Grewdead, Roy
  See Gorey, Edward (St. John)
Grey, Carol
  See Lowndes, Robert A(ugustine) W(ard)
Grey, Christopher *191*
Grey, Christopher Peter
  See Grey, Christopher
Grey, Jerry 1926- *11*
Grey, Mini *205*
  Earlier sketch in SATA *166*
Greybeard the Pirate
  See Macintosh, Brownie
Grey Owl
  See Belaney, Archibald Stansfeld
Gri
  See Denney, Diana
Gribbin, John 1946- *159*
Gribbin, John R.
  See Gribbin, John
Grice, Frederick 1910-1983 .... *6*
Grider, Dorothy 1915- *31*
Gridley, Marion E(leanor) 1906-1974 .... *35*
  Obituary *26*

Grieco-Tiso, Pina 1954- *108*
Grieder, Walter 1924- *9*
Griego, Tony A. 1955- *77*
Griese, Arnold A(lfred) 1921- *9*
Griessman, Annette 1962- *170*
  Earlier sketch in SATA *116*
Grieve, James 1934- *146*
Grifalconi, Ann 1929- *133*
  Earlier sketches in SATA *2, 66*
  See also CLR *35*
  See also SAAS *16*
Griffin, Adele 1970- *195*
  Earlier sketches in SATA *105, 153*
Griffin, Elizabeth May 1985- *89*
Griffin, Gillett Good 1928- *26*
Griffin, Judith Berry *34*
Griffin, Kitty 1951- *137*
Griffin, Peni R. 1961- *193*
  Earlier sketches in SATA *67, 99*
Griffin, Steven A. 1953- *89*
Griffin, Steven Arthur
  See Griffin, Steven A.
Griffin, W.E.B. 1929- *5*
Griffith, Connie 1946- *89*
Griffith, Gershom 1960- *85*
Griffith, Helen V(irginia) 1934- *87*
  Autobiography Feature *107*
  Earlier sketch in SATA *39*
Griffith, Jeannette
  See Eyerly, Jeannette
Griffith, Saul 1974- *200*
Griffiths, Andy 1961- *196*
  Earlier sketch in SATA *152*
Griffiths, G(ordon) D(ouglas) 1910-1973
  Obituary *20*
Griffiths, Helen 1939- *86*
  Earlier sketch in SATA *5*
  See also CLR *75*
  See also SAAS *5*
Grigson, Jane (McIntire) 1928-1990 .... *63*
Grimes, Lee 1920- *68*
Grimes, Nikki 1950- *174*
  Earlier sketches in SATA *93, 136*
  See also CLR *42*
Grimly, Gris *186*
Grimm, Jacob Ludwig Karl 1785-1863 .... *22*
  See also CLR *112*
Grimm, Wilhelm Karl 1786-1859 .... *22*
  See also CLR *112*
Grimm, William C(arey) 1907-1992 .... *14*
Grimm and Grim
  See Grimm, Jacob Ludwig Karl
  and Grimm, Wilhelm Karl
Grimm Brothers
  See Grimm, Jacob Ludwig Karl
  and Grimm, Wilhelm Karl
Grimsdell, Jeremy 1942- *83*
Grimshaw, Nigel (Gilroy) 1925- *23*
Grimsley, Gordon
  See Groom, Arthur William
Grindley, Jane Sally
  See Grindley, Sally
Grindley, Sally 1953- *148*
Gringhuis, Dirk
  See Gringhuis, Richard H.
Gringhuis, Richard H. 1918-1974 .... *6*
  Obituary *25*
Grinnell, David
  See Wollheim, Donald A(llen)
Grinnell, George Bird 1849-1938 .... *16*
Grinspoon, David
  See Grinspoon, David H.
Grinspoon, David H. 1959- *156*
Grinspoon, David Harry
  See Grinspoon, David H.
Gripe, Maria 1923- *74*
  Earlier sketch in SATA *2*
  See also CLR *5*
Gripe, Maria Kristina
  See Gripe, Maria
Grobler, Piet 1959- *201*

Groch, Judith (Goldstein) 1929- 25
Grode, Redway
   See Gorey, Edward (St. John)
Groener, Carl
   See Lowndes, Robert A(ugustine) W(ard)
Groening, Matt 1954- 116
   Earlier sketch in SATA *81*
Grohmann, Susan 1948- 84
Grohskopf, Bernice 7
Grol, Lini R(icharda) 1913- 9
Grollman, Earl A. 1925- 22
Groom, Arthur William 1898-1964 10
Grooms, Duffy 1964- 169
Gross, Alan 1947- 54
   Brief entry 43
Gross, Ernie 1913- 67
Gross, Philip 1952- 164
   Earlier sketch in SATA *84*
Gross, Philip John
   See Gross, Philip
Gross, Ruth Belov 1929- 33
Gross, Sarah Chokla 1906-1976 9
   Obituary 26
Grosser, Morton 1931- 74
Grosser, Vicky 1958- 83
Grossman, Bill 1948- 126
   Earlier sketch in SATA *72*
Grossman, Nancy 1940- 29
Grossman, Patricia 1951- 73
Grossman, Robert 1940- 11
Grote, JoAnn A. 1951- 113
Groten, Dallas 1951- 64
Groth, John (August) 1908-1988 21
   Obituary 56
Groth-Fleming, Candace
   See Fleming, Candace
Grove, Vicki 1948- 151
   Autobiography Feature 151
   Earlier sketch in SATA *122*
Grover, Lorie Ann 1964- 168
Grover, Wayne 1934- 69
Groves, Georgina
   See Symons, (Dorothy) Geraldine
Groves, Maketa 1950- 107
Groves, Seli 77
Grubb, Lisa 160
Gruber, Michael 1940- 173
Gruber, Terry (deRoy) 1953- 66
Gruelle, John 1880-1938 35
   Brief entry 32
   See also CLR *34*
Gruelle, Johnny
   See Gruelle, John
Gruenberg, Sidonie Matsner 1881-1974 2
   Obituary 27
Gruhzit-Hoyt, Olga (Margaret) 1922- 127
   Earlier sketch in SATA *16*
Grummer, Arnold E(dward) 1923- 49
Grunewalt, Pine
   See Kunhardt, Edith
Grunwell, Jeanne Marie 1971- 147
Grupper, Jonathan 137
Gryski, Camilla 1948- 72
Guarino, Dagmar
   See Guarino, Deborah
Guarino, Deborah 1954- 68
Guay, Georgette (Marie Jeanne) 1952- 54
Guback, Georgia 88
Guccione, Leslie Davis 1946- 111
   Earlier sketch in SATA *72*
Guck, Dorothy 1913-2002 27
Guerny, Gene
   See Gurney, Gene
Guest, Elissa Haden 1953- 125
Guest, Jacqueline 1952- 135
Guevara, Susan 167
   Earlier sketch in SATA *97*
Gugler, Laurel Dee 95
Gugliotta, Bobette 1918-1994 7
Guianan, Eve 1965- 102

Guiberson, Brenda Z. 1946- 124
   Earlier sketch in SATA *71*
Guibert, Emmanuel 1964- 181
Guile, Melanie 1949- 152
   Earlier sketch in SATA *104*
Guillaume, Jeanette G. Flierl 1899-1990 8
Guillot, Rene 1900-1969 7
   See also CLR *22*
Guisewite, Cathy (Lee) 1950- 57
Gulbis, Stephen 1959- 142
Gulley, Judie 1942- 58
Gump, P. Q.
   See Card, Orson Scott
Gump, P.Q.
   See Card, Orson Scott
Gundrey, Elizabeth 1924- 23
Gunn, James E. 1923- 35
Gunn, James Edwin
   See Gunn, James E.
Gunn, Robin Jones 1955- 84
Gunnella 1956- 197
Gunning, Monica Olwen 1930- 161
Gunston, Bill
   See Gunston, William Tudor
Gunston, William Tudor 1927- 9
Gunterman, Bertha Lisette 1886(?)-1975
   Obituary 27
Gunther, John 1901-1970
Guravich, Dan 1918- 74
Gurko, Leo 1914- 9
Gurko, Miriam 1910(?)-1988 9
   Obituary 58
Gurney, Gene 1924- 65
Gurney, James 1958- 120
   Earlier sketch in SATA *76*
Gurney, John Steven 1962- 143
   Earlier sketch in SATA *75*
Gustafson, Sarah R.
   See Riedman, Sarah R(egal)
Gustafson, Scott 1956- 34
Gustavson, Adam 176
Guthrie, A(lfred) B(ertram), Jr. 1901-1991 .. 62
   Obituary 67
Guthrie, Anne 1890-1979 28
Guthrie, Donna W. 1946- 105
   Earlier sketch in SATA *63*
Gutierrez, Akemi 172
Gutierrez, Rudy 203
Gutman, Bill 128
   Brief entry 43
   Earlier sketch in SATA *67*
Gutman, Dan 1955- 188
   Earlier sketches in SATA *77, 139*
Gutman, Naham 1899(?)-1981
   Obituary 25
Gutmann, Bessie Pease 1876-1960 73
Guy, Geoffrey 1942- 153
Guy, Ginger Foglesong 1954- 171
Guy, Rosa (Cuthbert) 1925- 122
   Earlier sketches in SATA *14, 62*
   See also CLR *137*
Guy, Susan 1948- 149
Guymer, (Wilhelmina) Mary 1909- 50
Guzman, Lila 1952- 168
Guzman, Rick 1957- 168
Gwaltney, Doris 1932- 181
Gwynne, Fred(erick Hubbard) 1926-1993 41
   Brief entry 27
   Obituary 75
Gwynne, Oscar A.
   See Ellis, Edward S.
Gwynne, Oswald A.
   See Ellis, Edward S.

H

Haab, Sherri 1964- 169
   Earlier sketch in SATA *91*
Haar, Jaap ter
   See ter Haar, Jaap
Haarsma, P.J. 183
Haas, Carolyn Buhai 1926- 43
Haas, Dan 1957- 105
Haas, Dorothy F. 46
   Brief entry 43
   See also SAAS *17*
Haas, Irene 1929- 96
   Earlier sketch in SATA *17*
Haas, James E(dward) 1943- 40
Haas, (Katherine) Jessie 1959- 135
   Autobiography Feature 135
   Earlier sketch in SATA *98*
Haas, Merle S. 1896(?)-1985
   Obituary 41
Habenstreit, Barbara 1937- 5
Haber, Karen 1955- 78
Haber, Louis 1910-1988 12
Hacker, Randi 1951- 185
Hacker, Randi Dawn
   See Hacker, Randi
Hackett, John Winthrop 1910-1997 65
Hacks, Peter 1928-2003
   Obituary 151
Haddix, Margaret Peterson 1964- 187
   Earlier sketches in SATA *94, 125*
Haddon, Mark 1962- 155
Hader, Berta (Hoerner) 1891(?)-1976 16
Hader, Elmer (Stanley) 1889-1973 16
Hadithi, Mwenye
   See Hobson, Bruce
Hadley, Franklin
   See Winterbotham, R(ussell) R(obert)
Hadley, Lee 1934-1995 89
   Brief entry 38
   Obituary 86
   Earlier sketch in SATA *47*
   See also CLR *40*
   See also SAAS *14*
Haeffele, Deborah 1954- 76
Haenel, Wolfram 1956- 89
   See also CLR *64*
Hafner, Marylin 1925- 179
   Earlier sketches in SATA *7, 121*
Haft, Erin
   See Ehrenhaft, Daniel
Hager, Alan 1940- 176
Hager, Alice Rogers 1894-1969
   Obituary 26
Hager, Betty 1923- 89
Hager, Sarah 171
Hager, Thomas 1953- 119
Hager, Tom
   See Hager, Thomas
Hagerup, Klaus 1946- 186
Haggard, H(enry) Rider 1856-1925 16
Haggerty, James J(oseph) 1920- 5
Hagon, Priscilla
   See Allan, Mabel Esther
Hague, (Susan) Kathleen 1949- 49
   Brief entry 45
Hague, Michael 1948- 185
   Brief entry 32
   Earlier sketches in SATA *48, 80, 129*
Hague, Michael R.
   See Hague, Michael
Hahn, Emily 1905-1997 3
   Obituary 96
Hahn, Hannelore 8
Hahn, James (Sage) 1947- 9
Hahn, (Mona) Lynn 1949- 9
Hahn, Mary Downing 1937- 157
   Autobiography Feature 157
   Brief entry 44
   Earlier sketches in SATA *50, 81, 138*
   See also SAAS *12*

Hahn, Michael T. 1953- 92
Haig-Brown, Roderick (Langmere)
  1908-1976 12
  See also CLR 31
Haight, Anne Lyon 1895-1977
  Obituary 30
Haight, Rip
  See Carpenter, John
Haight, Sandy 1949- 79
Haij, Vera
  See Jansson, Tove (Marika)
Haines, Gail Kay 1943- 11
Haines, Margaret Ann Beck
  See Beck, Peggy
Haining, Peter 1940-2007 14
  Obituary 188
Haining, Peter Alexander
  See Haining, Peter
Hains, Harriet
  See Watson, Carol
Hajdusiewicz, Babs Bell 163
Hakim, Joy 1931- 173
  Earlier sketch in SATA 83
Halacy, D. S., Jr. 1919-2002 36
  See also SAAS 8
Halacy, Dan
  See Halacy, D. S., Jr.
Halam, Ann
  See Jones, Gwyneth A(nn)
Haldane, Roger John 1945- 13
Hale, Arlene 1924-1982 49
Hale, Bruce 1957- 203
  Earlier sketch in SATA 123
Hale, Christy
  See Apostolou, Christine Hale
Hale, Edward Everett 1822-1909 16
Hale, Glenn
  See Walker, Robert W.
Hale, Helen
  See Mulcahy, Lucille Burnett
Hale, Irina 1932- 26
Hale, Kathleen 1898-2000 66
  Obituary 121
  Earlier sketch in SATA 17
Hale, Linda (Howe) 1929- 6
Hale, Lucretia P.
  See Hale, Lucretia Peabody
Hale, Lucretia Peabody 1820-1900 26
  See also CLR 105
Hale, Marian 194
Hale, Nancy 1908-1988 31
  Obituary 57
Hale, Shannon 200
  Earlier sketch in SATA 158
Haley, Amanda 205
Haley, Gail E(inhart) 1939- 161
  Autobiography Feature 161
  Brief entry 28
  Earlier sketches in SATA 43, 78, 136
  See also CLR 21
  See also SAAS 13
Haley, Neale 52
Hall, Adam
  See Trevor, Elleston
Hall, Adele 1910- 7
Hall, Anna Gertrude 1882-1967 8
Hall, August 207
Hall, Barbara 1960- 68
Hall, Becky 1950- 186
Hall, Beverly B. 1918- 95
Hall, Borden
  See Yates, Raymond F(rancis)
Hall, Brian P(atrick) 1935- 31
Hall, Cameron
  See del Rey, Lester
Hall, Caryl
  See Hansen, Caryl (Hall)
Hall, Donald 1928- 97
  Earlier sketch in SATA 23
Hall, Donald Andrew, Jr.
  See Hall, Donald

Hall, Douglas 1931- 43
Hall, Elizabeth 1929- 77
Hall, Elvajean 1910-1984 6
Hall, Francie 1940- 166
Hall, James Norman 1887-1951 21
Hall, Jesse
  See Boesen, Victor
Hall, Katy
  See McMullan, Kate
Hall, Kirsten Marie 1974- 67
Hall, Lynn 1937- 79
  Earlier sketches in SATA 2, 47
  See also SAAS 4
Hall, Malcolm 1945- 7
Hall, Marcellus 203
Hall, Marjory
  See Yeakley, Marjory Hall
Hall, Melanie W. 1949- 169
  Earlier sketches in SATA 78, 116
Hall, Patricia 1940- 136
Hall, Rosalys Haskell 1914- 7
Hall, Willis 1929-2005 66
Hallard, Peter
  See Catherall, Arthur
Hallas, Richard
  See Knight, Eric
Hall-Clarke, James
  See Rowland-Entwistle, (Arthur) Theodore
  (Henry)
Hallensleben, Georg 1958- 173
Haller, Dorcas Woodbury 1946- 46
Hallett, Mark 1947- 83
Halliburton, Richard 1900-1939(?) 81
Halliburton, Warren J. 1924- 19
Halliday, Brett
  See Dresser, Davis
  and Johnson, (Walter) Ryerson
  and Terrall, Robert
Halliday, William R(oss) 1926- 52
Hallin, Emily Watson 1916-1995 6
Hallinan, P(atrick) K(enneth) 1944- 39
  Brief entry 37
Hallman, Ruth 1929- 43
  Brief entry 28
Hallowell, Tommy
  See Hill, Thomas
Hall-Quest, (Edna) Olga W(ilbourne)
  1899-1986 11
  Obituary 47
Halls, Kelly Milner 1957- 131
Hallstead, William F(inn III) 1924- 11
Hallward, Michael 1889-1982 12
Halperin, Michael 156
Halperin, Wendy Anderson 1952- 200
  Earlier sketches in SATA 80, 125
Halpern, Julie 1975- 198
Halpin, Brendan 1968- 193
Halpin, Marlene 1927- 88
Halsell, Grace (Eleanor) 1923-2000 13
Halsey, Megan 185
Halsted, Anna Roosevelt 1906-1975
  Obituary 30
Halter, Jon C(harles) 1941- 22
Halverson, Deborah 202
Halvorson, Marilyn 1948- 123
Hamalian, Leo 1920- 41
Hamberger, John 1934- 14
Hamblin, Dora Jane 1920- 36
Hambly, Barbara 1951- 108
Hambly, Barbara Joan
  See Hambly, Barbara
Hamer, Martyn
  See Eldin, Peter
Hamerstrom, Frances 1907-1998 24
Hamil, Thomas Arthur 1928- 14
Hamill, Ethel
  See Webb, Jean Francis (III)
Hamilton, (John) Alan 1943- 66
Hamilton, Alice
  See Cromie, Alice Hamilton
Hamilton, Anita 1919- 92

Hamilton, Buzz
  See Hemming, Roy G.
Hamilton, Carol (Jean Barber) 1935- 94
Hamilton, Charles (Harold St. John)
  1876-1961 13
Hamilton, Charles 1913-1996 65
  Obituary 93
Hamilton, Clive
  See Lewis, C. S.
Hamilton, Dorothy (Drumm) 1906-1983 12
  Obituary 35
Hamilton, Edith 1867-1963 20
Hamilton, Edmond 1904-1977 118
Hamilton, (Muriel) Elizabeth (Mollie)
  1906- 23
Hamilton, Emma Walton 1962- 177
Hamilton, Franklin
  See Silverberg, Robert
Hamilton, Gail
  See Corcoran, Barbara (Asenath)
  and Dodge, Mary Abigail
Hamilton, Kersten 1958- 204
  Earlier sketch in SATA 134
Hamilton, K.R.
  See Hamilton, Kersten
Hamilton, Martha 1953- 183
  Earlier sketch in SATA 123
Hamilton, Mary (E.) 1927- 55
Hamilton, Mollie
  See Kaye, M.M.
Hamilton, Morse 1943-1998 101
  Earlier sketch in SATA 35
Hamilton, Peter F. 1960- 109
Hamilton, Priscilla
  See Gellis, Roberta
Hamilton, Ralph
  See Stratemeyer, Edward L.
Hamilton, Virginia 1936-2002 123
  Obituary 132
  Earlier sketches in SATA 4, 56, 79
  See also CLR 127
Hamilton, Virginia Esther
  See Hamilton, Virginia
Hamilton-Paterson, James 1941- 82
Hamlet, Ova
  See Lupoff, Richard A(llen)
Hamley, D. C.
  See Hamley, Dennis
Hamley, Dennis 1935- 69
  Earlier sketch in SATA 39
  See also CLR 47
  See also SAAS 22
Hamley, Dennis C.
  See Hamley, Dennis
Hamlin, Peter J. 1970- 84
Hamm, Diane Johnston 1949- 78
Hammer, Charles 1934- 58
Hammer, Richard 1928- 6
Hammerman, Gay M(orenus) 1926- 9
Hammill, Matt 1982- 206
Hammond, Andrew 1970- 181
Hammond, Ralph
  See Hammond Innes, Ralph
Hammond, Winifred G(raham) 1899-1992 ... 29
  Obituary 107
Hammond Innes, Ralph 1913-1998 116
Hammontree, Marie (Gertrude) 1913- 13
Hample, Zack 1977- 161
Hampshire, Joyce Gregorian
  See Gregorian, Joyce Ballou
Hampshire, Susan 1942- 98
Hampson, (Richard) Denman 1929- 15
Hampson, Frank 1918(?)-1985
  Obituary 46
Hampton, Wilborn 1940- 196
  Earlier sketch in SATA 156
Hamre, Leif 1914- 5
Hamsa, Bobbie 1944- 52
  Brief entry 38
Han, Jenny 1981- 175

Han, Lu
  See Stickler, Soma Han
Han, Soma
  See Stickler, Soma Han
Han, Suzanne Crowder 1953- 89
Hancock, Mary A. 1923- 31
Hancock, Sibyl 1940- 9
Hand, Elizabeth 1957- 167
  Earlier sketch in SATA *118*
Handford, Martin (John) 1956- 64
  See also CLR 22
Handforth, Thomas (Schofield) 1897-1948 .. 42
Handler, Daniel
  See Snicket, Lemony
Handville, Robert (Tompkins) 1924- 45
Hane, Roger 1940-1974
  Obituary 20
Hanel, Wolfram
  See Haenel, Wolfram
Haney, Lynn 1941- 23
Hanff, Helene 1916-1997 97
  Earlier sketch in SATA *11*
Hanft, Josh 1956- 197
Hanft, Joshua E.
  See Hanft, Josh
Hanley, Boniface Francis 1924- 65
Hanlon, Emily 1945- 15
Hann, Jacquie 1951- 19
Hann, Judith 1942- 77
Hanna, Bill
  See Hanna, William (Denby)
Hanna, Cheryl 1951- 84
Hanna, Dan 200
Hanna, Jack (Bushnell) 1947- 74
Hanna, Nell(ie L.) 1908- 55
Hanna, Paul R(obert) 1902-1988 9
Hanna, William (Denby) 1910-2001 51
  Obituary 126
Hannam, Charles 1925- 50
Hannan, Peter 1954- 187
Hannigan, Katherine 170
Hannon, Ezra
  See Hunter, Evan
Hann-Syme, Marguerite 127
Hano, Arnold 1922- 12
Hano, Renee Roth
  See Roth-Hano, Renee
Hanover, Terri
  See Huff, Tanya
Hansen, Ann Larkin 1958- 96
Hansen, Brooks 1965- 104
Hansen, Caryl (Hall) 1929- 39
Hansen, Ian V. 1929- 113
Hansen, Jennifer 1972- 156
Hansen, Joyce 1942- 172
  Autobiography Feature 172
  Brief entry 39
  Earlier sketches in SATA *46, 101*
  See also CLR 21
  See also SAAS 15
Hansen, Joyce Viola
  See Hansen, Joyce
Hansen, Mark Victor 112
Hansen, Ron 1947- 56
Hansen, Ronald Thomas
  See Hansen, Ron
Hanser, Richard (Frederick) 1909-1981 13
Hanson, Joan 1938- 8
Hanson, Joseph E. 1894(?)-1971
  Obituary 27
Hanson, Mary Elizabeth 188
Hanson, Warren 1949- 155
Hansson, Gunilla 1939- 64
Hantman, Clea 200
Harald, Eric
  See Boesen, Victor
Harcourt, Ellen Knowles 1890(?)-1984
  Obituary 36
Hard, Charlotte (Ann) 1969- 98
Hardcastle, Michael 1933- 47
  Brief entry 38

Harding, Lee 1937- 32
  Brief entry 31
Hardt, Helga Fleischhauer
  See Fleischhauer-Hardt, Helga
Hardwick, Richard Holmes, Jr. 1923- 12
Hardy, Alice Dale 67
  Earlier sketch in SATA *1*
Hardy, David A(ndrews) 1936- 9
Hardy, Jon 1958- 53
Hardy, LeAnne 1951- 154
Hardy, Stuart
  See Schisgall, Oscar
Hare, Norma Q(uarles) 1924- 46
  Brief entry 41
Harel, Nira 1936- 154
Harford, Henry
  See Hudson, W(illiam) H(enry)
Hargrave, Leonie
  See Disch, Thomas M.
Hargreaves, (Charles) Roger 1935-1988
  Obituary 56
Hargrove, James 1947- 57
  Brief entry 50
Hargrove, Jim
  See Hargrove, James
Harik, Elsa
  See Marston, Elsa
Harik, Elsa M.
  See Marston, Elsa
Harik, Elsa Marston
  See Marston, Elsa
Hariton, Anca I. 1955- 79
Hark, Mildred
  See McQueen, Mildred Hark
Harkaway, Hal
  See Stratemeyer, Edward L.
Harkins, Philip 1912-1997 6
  Obituary 129
Harlan, Elizabeth 1945- 41
  Brief entry 35
Harlan, Glen
  See Cebulash, Mel
Harlan, Judith 1949- 135
  Earlier sketch in SATA *74*
  See also CLR 81
Harland, Richard 1947- 152
Harlee, J. V.
  See Leese, Jennifer L.B.
Harler, Ann
  See Van Steenwyk, Elizabeth (Ann)
Harley, Avis 183
Harley, Bill 1954- 87
Harlow, Joan Hiatt 1932- 157
Harman, Fred 1902(?)-1982
  Obituary 30
Harman, Hugh 1903-1982
  Obituary 33
Harmelink, Barbara (Mary) 9
Harmer, Mabel 1894-1992 45
Harmon, Dan
  See Harmon, Daniel E(lton)
Harmon, Daniel E(lton) 1949- 157
Harmon, Margaret 1906- 20
Harmon, Michael 1969- 189
Harmon, Michael B.
  See Harmon, Michael
Harmon, William (Ruth) 1938- 65
Harnan, Terry 1920- 12
Harness, Cheryl 1951- 178
  Earlier sketch in SATA *131*
Harnett, Cynthia (Mary) 1893-1981 5
  Obituary 32
Harper, Anita 1943- 41
Harper, Betty 1946- 126
Harper, Charise
  See Harper, Charise Mericle
Harper, Charise Mericle 179
Harper, Elaine
  See Hallin, Emily Watson
Harper, Ellen
  See Noble, Marty

Harper, Jamie 174
Harper, Jessica 1949- 148
Harper, Jo 1932- 169
  Earlier sketch in SATA 97
Harper, Lee 201
Harper, Mary Wood
  See Dixon, Jeanne
Harper, Piers 1966- 161
  Earlier sketch in SATA 105
Harper, Suzanne 194
Harper, Wilhelmina 1884-1973 4
  Obituary 26
Harrah, Madge 1931- 154
Harrah, Michael 1940- 41
Harrah, Monique
  See Harrah, Madge
Harrar, George E. 1949- 124
Harrell, Beatrice Orcutt 1943- 93
Harrell, Janice 1945- 70
Harries, Joan 1922- 39
Harrill, Ronald 1950- 90
Harrington, Denis J(ames) 1932- 88
Harrington, Evelyn Davis 1911- 5
Harrington, Janice N. 1956- 187
Harrington, Lyn
  See Harrington, Evelyn Davis
Harris, Alan 1944- 71
Harris, Aurand 1915-1996 37
  Obituary 91
Harris, Bob
  See Harris, Robert J.
Harris, Carol Flynn 1933- 135
Harris, Catherine
  See Ainsworth, Catherine Harris
Harris, Christie
  See Harris, Christie (Lucy) Irwin
Harris, Christie (Lucy) Irwin 1907-2002 74
  Autobiography Feature 116
  Earlier sketch in SATA 6
  See also CLR 47
  See also SAAS 10
Harris, Christine 1955- 105
Harris, Colver
  See Colver, Anne
Harris, David 1942- 118
Harris, David William
  See Harris, David
Harris, Dorothy Joan 1931- 153
  Earlier sketch in SATA 13
Harris, Geraldine (Rachel) 1951- 54
Harris, Jacqueline L. 1929- 62
Harris, Janet 1932-1979 4
  Obituary 23
Harris, Jesse
  See Standiford, Natalie
Harris, Joan 1946- 146
Harris, Joe 1928- 201
Harris, Joel Chandler 1848-1908 100
  See also YABC 1
  See also CLR 128
Harris, John (Wyndham Parkes Lucas) Beynon
  1903-1969 118
Harris, Johnson
  See Harris, John (Wyndham Parkes Lucas)
  Beynon
Harris, Jonathan 1921-1997 52
Harris, Larry Vincent 1939- 59
Harris, Lavinia
  See St. John, Nicole
Harris, Leon A., Jr. 1926-2000 4
Harris, Lois V. 199
Harris, Lorle K(empe) 1912-2001 22
Harris, Marilyn
  See Springer, Marilyn Harris
Harris, Mark Jonathan 1941- 84
  Earlier sketch in SATA 32
Harris, Mary K(athleen) 1905-1966 119
Harris, Robert J. 1955- 195
Harris, Robie H. 1940- 203
  Brief entry 53
  Earlier sketches in SATA 90, 147

Harris, Robin
    See Shine, Deborah
Harris, Rosemary (Jeanne) 82
    Earlier sketch in SATA 4
    See also CLR 30
    See also SAAS 7
Harris, Ruth Elwin 1935- 164
Harris, Sherwood 1932-2009 25
Harris, Steven Michael 1957- 55
Harris, Trudy 1949- 191
    Earlier sketch in SATA 128
Harris-Filderman, Diane
    See Filderman, Diane E(lizabeth)
Harrison, C(hester) William 1913-1994 35
Harrison, Carol
    See Harrison, Carol Thompson
Harrison, Carol Thompson 113
Harrison, David L. 1937- 186
    Earlier sketches in SATA 26, 92, 150
Harrison, Deloris 1938- 9
Harrison, Edward Hardy 1926- 56
Harrison, Elizabeth (Allen) Cavanna
    1909-2001 30
    Earlier sketch in SATA 1
    See also SAAS 4
Harrison, Harry 1925- 4
Harrison, Harry Max
    See Harrison, Harry
Harrison, Mette Ivie 1970- 202
    Earlier sketch in SATA 149
Harrison, Michael 1939- 106
Harrison, Molly (Hodgett) 1909-2002 41
Harrison, Sarah 1946- 63
Harrison, Ted
    See Harrison, Edward Hardy
Harsh, Fred (T.) 1925- 72
Harshaw, Ruth H(etzel) 1890-1968 27
Harshman, Marc 1950- 109
    Earlier sketch in SATA 71
Hart, Alexandra 1939- 14
Hart, Alison
    See Leonhardt, Alice
Hart, Bruce 1938-2006 57
    Brief entry 39
Hart, Carole 1943- 57
    Brief entry 39
Hart, Carolyn 1936- 74
Hart, Carolyn G.
    See Hart, Carolyn
Hart, Carolyn Gimpel
    See Hart, Carolyn
Hart, Jan Siegel 1940- 79
Hart, Joyce 1954- 148
Hart, Karen 185
Hart, Lenore 171
Hart, Philip S. 1944- 180
Hart, Virginia 1949- 83
Harte, Bret 1836(?)-1902 26
Harte, Francis Brett
    See Harte, Bret
Harter, Debbie 1963- 107
Hartfield, Claire 1957- 147
Hartinger, Brent 1964- 174
    Earlier sketch in SATA 145
Hartland, Jessie 171
Hartley, Ellen (Raphael) 1915-1980 23
Hartley, Fred Allan III 1953- 41
Hartley, William B(rown) 1913-1980 23
Hartling, Peter
    See Hartling, Peter
Hartling, Peter 1933- 66
    See also CLR 29
Hartman, Cassie 202
Hartman, Dan 1955- 202
Hartman, Evert 1937- 38
    Brief entry 35
Hartman, Jane E(vangeline) 1928- 47
Hartman, Louis F(rancis) 1901-1970 22
Hartman, Rachel 174
Hartman, Victoria 1942- 91

Hartnett, Sonya 1968- 176
    Earlier sketches in SATA 93, 130
Hartshorn, Ruth M. 1928- 11
Hartung, Susan Kathleen 192
    Earlier sketch in SATA 150
Hartwig, Manfred 1950- 81
Harvey, Brett 1936- 61
Harvey, Edith 1908(?)-1972
    Obituary 27
Harvey, Gill 189
Harvey, Karen D. 1935- 88
Harvey, Roland 1945- 179
    Earlier sketches in SATA 71, 123
Harvey-Fitzhenry, Alyxandra 1974- 189
Harwick, B. L.
    See Keller, Beverly L(ou)
Harwin, Brian
    See Henderson, LeGrand
Harwood, Pearl Augusta (Bragdon)
    1903-1998 9
Haseley, Dennis 1950- 157
    Brief entry 44
    Earlier sketches in SATA 57, 105
Hashmi, Kerri 1955- 108
Haskell, Arnold L(ionel) 1903-1981(?) 6
Haskins, James
    See Haskins, James S.
Haskins, James S. 1941-2005 132
    Autobiography Feature 132
    Earlier sketches in SATA 9, 69, 105
    See also CLR 39
    See also SAAS 4
Haskins, Jim
    See Haskins, James S.
Hasler, Eveline 1933- 181
Hasler, Joan 1931- 28
Hass, Robert 1941- 94
Hassall, Joan 1906-1988 43
    Obituary 56
Hassett, Ann 1958- 162
Hassett, John 162
Hassler, Jon 1933-2008 19
    Obituary 191
Hassler, Jon Francis
    See Hassler, Jon
Hastings, Beverly
    See Barkin, Carol
    and James, Elizabeth
Hastings, Graham
    See Jeffries, Roderic
Hastings, Ian 1912- 62
Hastings, Victor
    See Disch, Thomas M.
Haszard, Patricia Moyes 1923-2000 63
Hatch, Lynda S. 1950- 90
Hathaway, Barbara 164
Hathorn, Elizabeth
    See Hathorn, Elizabeth Helen
Hathorn, Elizabeth Helen 1943- 156
    Autobiography Feature 156
    Earlier sketches in SATA 74, 120
Hathorn, Libby 1943-
    See Hathorn, Elizabeth Helen
Hatkoff, Craig 1954- 192
Hatlo, Jimmy 1898-1963
    Obituary 23
Hatton, Caroline 1957- 205
Haugaard, Erik Christian 1923- 68
    Earlier sketch in SATA 4
    See also CLR 11
    See also SAAS 12
Haugaard, Kay 117
Haugen, Hayley Mitchell 1968- 172
Haugen, Tormod 1945- 66
Hauman, Doris 1898-1984 32
Hauman, George 1890-1961 32
Hauptly, Denis J(ames) 1945- 57
Hauser, Jill Frankel 1950- 127
Hauser, Margaret L(ouise) 1909- 10
Hausherr, Rosmarie 1943- 86

Hausman, Gerald 1945- 180
    Earlier sketches in SATA 13, 90, 132
    See also CLR 89
Hausman, Gerry
    See Hausman, Gerald
Hauth, Katherine B. 1940- 99
Hautman, Pete 1952- 173
    Earlier sketches in SATA 82, 128
Hautman, Peter Murray
    See Hautman, Pete
Hautzig, Deborah 1956- 106
    Earlier sketch in SATA 31
Hautzig, Esther Rudomin 1930-2009 148
    Earlier sketches in SATA 4, 68
    See also CLR 22
    See also SAAS 15
Havel, Geoff 1955- 152
Havel, Jennifer
    See Havill, Juanita
Havelin, Kate 1961- 143
Havighurst, Walter (Edwin) 1901-1994 1
    Obituary 79
Haviland, Virginia 1911-1988 6
    Obituary 54
Havill, Juanita 1949- 155
    Earlier sketch in SATA 74
Hawes, Judy 1913- 4
Hawes, Louise 1943- 180
    Earlier sketch in SATA 60
Hawke, Rosanne 1953- 165
    Earlier sketch in SATA 124
Hawke, Rosanne Joy
    See Hawke, Rosanne
Hawkes, Kevin 1959- 201
    Earlier sketches in SATA 78, 150
Hawkes, Nigel 1943- 119
Hawkesworth, Eric 1921- 13
Hawking, Lucy 1969- 197
Hawkins, Arthur 1903-1985 19
Hawkins, Colin 1945- 162
    Earlier sketch in SATA 112
Hawkins, Jacqui 162
    Earlier sketch in SATA 112
Hawkins, Jimmy 1941- 188
Hawkins, Laura 1951- 74
Hawkins, (Helena Ann) Quail 1905-2002 6
    Obituary 141
Hawkinson, John (Samuel) 1912-1994 4
Hawkinson, Lucy (Ozone) 1924-1971 21
Hawks, Robert 1961- 85
Hawley, Mabel C. 67
    Earlier sketch in SATA 1
Haworth, Danette 207
Hawthorne, Captain R. M.
    See Ellis, Edward S.
Hawthorne, Nathaniel 1804-1864
    See YABC 2
    See also CLR 103
Hay, Jeff T. 154
Hay, John 1915- 13
Hay, Timothy
    See Brown, Margaret Wise
Hayashi, Leslie Ann 1954- 115
Hayashi, Nancy 1939- 186
    Earlier sketch in SATA 80
Haycak, Cara 1961- 180
Haycock, Kate 1962- 77
Haycraft, Howard 1905-1991 6
    Obituary 70
Haycraft, Molly Costain 1911- 6
Hayden, Gwendolen Lampshire 1904- 35
Hayden, Robert
    See Hayden, Robert Earl
Hayden, Robert C(arter), Jr. 1937- 47
    Brief entry 28
Hayden, Robert E.
    See Hayden, Robert Earl
Hayden, Robert Earl 1913-1980 19
    Obituary 26
Hayden, Torey L. 1951- 163
    Earlier sketch in SATA 65

Hayden, Torey Lynn
  See Hayden, Torey L.
Hayes, Carlton J(oseph) H(untley)
  1882-1964 .... *11*
Hayes, Daniel 1952- *109*
  Earlier sketch in SATA *73*
Hayes, Geoffrey 1947- *207*
  Earlier sketches in SATA *26, 91*
Hayes, Joe 1945- *131*
  Earlier sketch in SATA *88*
Hayes, John F. 1904-1980 .... *11*
Hayes, Karel 1949- *207*
Hayes, Rosemary *158*
Hayes, Sheila 1937- *51*
  Brief entry *50*
Hayes, Will *7*
Hayes, William D(imitt) 1913-1976 .... *8*
Haynes, Betsy 1937- *94*
  Brief entry *37*
  Earlier sketch in SATA *48*
  See also CLR *90*
Haynes, David 1955- *97*
Haynes, Linda
  See Swinford, Betty (June Wells)
Haynes, Mary 1938- *65*
Haynes, Max 1956- *72*
Hays, H(offmann) R(eynolds) 1904-1980 .... *26*
Hays, Thomas Anthony 1957- *84*
Hays, Tony
  See Hays, Thomas Anthony
Hays, Wilma Pitchford 1909- *28*
  Earlier sketch in SATA *1*
  See also CLR *59*
  See also SAAS *3*
Hayward, Linda 1943- *185*
  Brief entry *39*
  Earlier sketch in SATA *101*
Haywood, Carolyn 1898-1990 .... *75*
  Obituary *64*
  Earlier sketches in SATA *1, 29*
  See also CLR *22*
Hazell, Rebecca (Eileen) 1947- *141*
Hazen, Barbara Shook 1930- *178*
  Earlier sketches in SATA *27, 90*
Hazen, Lynn E. *202*
Head, Gay
  See Hauser, Margaret L(ouise)
Head, Tom 1978- *167*
Headley, Elizabeth
  See Harrison, Elizabeth (Allen) Cavanna
Headley, Justina Chen 1968- *176*
Headstrom, (Birger) Richard 1902-1985 .... *8*
Heady, Eleanor B(utler) 1917-1979 .... *8*
Heagy, William D. 1964- *76*
Heal, Edith 1903-1995 .... *7*
Heal, Gillian 1934- *89*
Heale, Jay (Jeremy Peter Wingfield) 1937- .. *84*
Healey, Brooks
  See Albert, Burton
Healey, Larry 1927- *44*
  Brief entry *42*
Heap, Sue 1954- *187*
  Earlier sketch in SATA *150*
Heaps, Willard A(llison) 1908-1987 .... *26*
Hearn, Diane Dawson 1952- *79*
Hearn, Emily
  See Valleau, Emily
Hearn, Julie 1958- *152*
Hearn, Lian
  See Rubinstein, Gillian
Hearn, Sneed
  See Gregg, Andrew K.
Hearne, Betsy 1942- *146*
  Earlier sketches in SATA *38, 95*
Heath, Charles D(ickinson) 1941- *46*
Heath, Veronica
  See Blackett, Veronica Heath
Heaven, Constance (Christina) 1911- *7*
Hebert-Collins, Sheila 1948- *111*
Hecht, George J(oseph) 1895-1980
  Obituary *22*

Hecht, Henri Joseph 1922- *9*
Hechtkopf, Henryk 1910- *17*
Heck, Bessie (Mildred) Holland 1911-1995 . *26*
Heck, Ed 1963- *173*
Heckert, Connie K(aye Delp) 1948- *82*
Hector, Julian *205*
Hedderwick, Mairi 1939- *145*
  Earlier sketches in SATA *30, 77*
Hedges, Sid(ney) G(eorge) 1897-1974 .... *28*
Hedrick, Irene Hope 1920- *175*
Heelan, Jamee Riggio 1965- *146*
Heerboth, Sharon
  See Leon, Sharon
Heffernan, John 1949- *168*
  Earlier sketch in SATA *121*
Heffron, Dorris 1944- *68*
Hefter, Richard 1942- *31*
Hegarty, Reginald Beaton 1906-1973 .... *10*
Hehenberger, Shelly 1968- *126*
Heidbreder, Robert 1947- *196*
  Earlier sketch in SATA *130*
Heidbreder, Robert K.
  See Heidbreder, Robert
Heide, Florence Parry 1919- *192*
  Earlier sketches in SATA *32, 69, 118*
  See also CLR *60*
  See also SAAS *6*
Heiderstadt, Dorothy 1907-2001 .... *6*
Heidi Louise
  See Erdrich, Louise
Heidler, David S(tephen) 1955- *132*
Heidler, Jeanne T. 1956- *132*
Heilbroner, Joan Knapp 1922- *63*
Heilbrun, Lois Hussey 1922(?)-1987
  Obituary *54*
Heiligman, Deborah 1958- *193*
  Earlier sketches in SATA *90, 144*
Heilman, Joan Rattner *50*
Heimann, Rolf 1940- *164*
  Earlier sketch in SATA *120*
Hein, Lucille Eleanor 1915-1994 .... *20*
Heine, Helme 1941- *135*
  Earlier sketch in SATA *67*
  See also CLR *18*
Heinlein, Robert A. 1907-1988 .... *69*
  Obituary *56*
  Earlier sketch in SATA *9*
  See also CLR *75*
Heinlein, Robert Anson
  See Heinlein, Robert A.
Heins, Ethel L(eah) 1918-1997 .... *101*
Heins, Paul 1909- *13*
Heintze, Carl 1922- *26*
Heinz, Bill
  See Heinz, W. C.
Heinz, Brian J. 1946- *181*
  Earlier sketch in SATA *95*
Heinz, Brian James
  See Heinz, Brian J.
Heinz, W. C. 1915-2008 .... *26*
Heinz, Wilfred Charles
  See Heinz, W. C.
Heinzen, Mildred
  See Masters, Mildred
Heisel, Sharon E(laine) 1941- *125*
  Earlier sketch in SATA *84*
Heitzmann, William Ray 1948- *73*
Heitzmann, Wm. Ray
  See Heitzmann, William Ray
Helakoski, Leslie *178*
Helberg, Shirley Adelaide Holden 1919- ... *138*
Helfer, Andrew *187*
Helfer, Ralph 1937- *177*
Helfman, Elizabeth S(eaver) 1911-2001 .... *3*
Helfman, Harry Carmozin 1910-1995 .... *3*
Helgerson, Joseph 1950- *181*
Hellard, Susan *182*
Hellberg, Hans-Eric 1927- *38*
Heller, Linda 1944- *46*
  Brief entry *40*

Heller, Mike
  See Hano, Arnold
Heller, Ruth M. 1924- *112*
  Earlier sketch in SATA *66*
Hellman, Hal
  See Hellman, Harold
Hellman, Harold 1927- *4*
Helman, Andrea (Jean) 1946- *160*
  Earlier sketch in SATA *107*
Helmer, Diana Star 1962- *86*
Helmer, Marilyn *160*
  Earlier sketch in SATA *112*
Helps, Racey 1913-1971 .... *2*
  Obituary *25*
Helquist, Brett *187*
  Earlier sketch in SATA *146*
Helweg, Hans H. 1917- *50*
  Brief entry *33*
Helyar, Jane Penelope Josephine 1933- *5*
  Autobiography Feature *138*
  See also SAAS *2*
Hemmant, Lynette 1938- *69*
Hemming, Roy G. 1928-1995 .... *11*
  Obituary *86*
Hemphill, Helen 1955- *179*
Hemphill, Kris (Harrison) 1963- *118*
Hemphill, Martha Locke 1904-1973 .... *37*
Hemphill, Stephanie *190*
Hemstock, Gillian 1956- *173*
Henba, Bobbie 1926- *87*
Henbest, Nigel 1951- *55*
  Brief entry *52*
Henderley, Brooks *1*
Henderson, Aileen Kilgore 1921- *178*
Henderson, Aileen Mary
  See Fox, Aileen
Henderson, Gordon 1950- *53*
Henderson, Kathy 1949- *155*
  Brief entry *53*
  Earlier sketches in SATA *55, 95*
Henderson, Lauren 1966- *201*
Henderson, LeGrand 1901-1965 .... *9*
Henderson, Nancy Wallace 1916- *22*
Henderson, Zenna (Chlarson) 1917-1983 .... *5*
Hendrickson, Walter Brookfield, Jr. 1936- *9*
Hendry, Diana 1941- *106*
  Earlier sketch in SATA *68*
Hendry, Frances Mary 1941- *171*
  Earlier sketch in SATA *110*
Hendry, Linda (Gail) 1961- *83*
Heneghan, James 1930- *160*
  Earlier sketches in SATA *53, 97*
Henkes, Kevin 1960- *207*
  Earlier sketches in SATA *43, 76, 108, 154*
  See also CLR *108*
Hennessy, Barbara G.
  See Hennessy, B.G.
Hennessy, Barbara Gulbrandsen
  See Hennessy, B.G.
Hennessy, B.G. 1951- *175*
Henney, Carolee Wells 1928- *102*
Henriod, Lorraine 1925- *26*
Henriquez, Emile F. 1937- *170*
  Earlier sketch in SATA *89*
Henry, April 1959- *174*
Henry, Ernest 1948- *107*
Henry, Joanne Landers 1927- *6*
Henry, Maeve 1960- *75*
Henry, Marguerite 1902-1997 .... *100*
  Obituary *99*
  See also CLR *4*
  See also SAAS *7*
Henry, Marie H. 1935- *65*
Henry, Marilyn 1939- *117*
Henry, Marion
  See del Rey, Lester
Henry, O. 1862-1910
  See YABC *2*
Henry, Oliver
  See Henry, O.

Henry, T. E.
See Rowland-Entwistle, (Arthur) Theodore
(Henry)
Henschel, Elizabeth Georgie 56
Henson, Heather 206
Henson, James Maury
See Henson, Jim
Henson, Jim 1936-1990 43
Obituary 65
Henstra, Friso 1928- 73
Earlier sketch in SATA 8
See also SAAS 14
Hentoff, Nat(han Irving) 1925- 133
Brief entry 27
Earlier sketches in SATA 42, 69
See also CLR 52
Henty, G(eorge) A(lfred) 1832-1902 64
See also CLR 76
Heo, Yumi 1964- 206
Earlier sketches in SATA 94, 146
Hepler, Heather 177
Herald, Kathleen
See Peyton, Kathleen Wendy
Herb, Angela M. 1970- 92
Herbert, Cecil
See Hamilton, Charles (Harold St. John)
Herbert, Don 1917-2007 2
Obituary 184
Herbert, Donald Jeffrey
See Herbert, Don
Herbert, Frank 1920-1986 37
Obituary 47
Earlier sketch in SATA 9
Herbert, Frank Patrick
See Herbert, Frank
Herbert, Helen (Jean) 1947- 57
Herbert, Janis 1956- 139
Herbert, Wally 1934-2007 23
Herbert, Walter William
See Herbert, Wally
Herbst, Judith 1947- 74
Herda, D.J. 1948- 80
Herge
See Remi, Georges
Heritage, Martin
See Horler, Sydney
Herkimer, L(awrence) R(ussell) 1925(?)- 42
Herlihy, Dirlie Anne 1935- 73
Herman, Charlotte 1937- 203
Earlier sketches in SATA 20, 99
Hermanson, Dennis (Everett) 1947- 10
Hermes, Jules 1962- 92
Hermes, Patricia 1936- 191
Earlier sketches in SATA 31, 78, 141
Hermes, Patricia Mary
See Hermes, Patricia
Hernandez, Natalie Nelson 1929- 123
Herndon, Ernest 91
Herold, Ann Bixby 1937- 72
Herrera, Juan Felipe 1948- 127
Herrick, Steven 1958- 156
Earlier sketch in SATA 103
Herriman, George (Joseph) 1880-1944 140
Herriot, James 1916-1995
See Wight, James Alfred
Herrmanns, Ralph 1933- 11
Herrold, Tracey
See Dils, Tracey E.
Herron, Carolivia 1947- 203
Herron, Edward A(lbert) 1912- 4
Herschler, Mildred Barger 130
Hersey, John 1914-1993 25
Obituary 76
Hersey, John Richard
See Hersey, John
Hershberger, Priscilla (Gorman) 1951- 81
Hershenhorn, Esther 1945- 151
Hershey, Kathleen M. 1934- 80
Hershey, Mary 173
Hersom, Kathleen 1911- 73
Hertz, Grete Janus 1915- 23

Herzig, Alison Cragin 1935- 87
Herzog, Brad 1968- 131
Heslewood, Juliet 1951- 82
Hess, Lilo 1916- 4
Hess, Paul 1961- 134
Hesse, Hermann 1877-1962 50
Hesse, Karen 1952- 158
Autobiography Feature 113
Earlier sketches in SATA 74, 103
See also CLR 141
See also SAAS 25
Hest, Amy 1950- 193
Earlier sketches in SATA 55, 82, 129
Heuer, Karsten 1968(?)- 202
Heuer, Kenneth John 1927- 44
Heuman, William 1912-1971 21
Heuston, Kimberley 1960- 167
Heuston, Kimberley Burton
See Heuston, Kimberley
Hewes, Agnes Danforth 1874-1963 35
Hewett, Anita 1918-1989 13
Hewett, Joan 1930- 140
Earlier sketch in SATA 81
Hewett, Richard 1929- 81
Hewitson, Jennifer 1961- 97
Hewitt, Margaret 1961- 84
Hewitt, Sally 1949- 127
Hext, Harrington
See Phillpotts, Eden
Hey, Nigel S(tewart) 1936- 20
Heyduck-Huth, Hilde 1929- 8
Heyer, Carol 1950- 130
Earlier sketch in SATA 74
Heyer, Marilee 1942- 102
Earlier sketch in SATA 64
Heyerdahl, Thor 1914-2002 52
Earlier sketch in SATA 2
Heyes, (Nancy) Eileen 1956- 150
Earlier sketch in SATA 80
Heyliger, William 1884-1955
See YABC 1
Heyman, Ken(neth Louis) 1930- 114
Earlier sketch in SATA 34
Heyward, (Edwin) DuBose 1885-1940 21
Heywood, Karen 1946- 48
Hezlep, William (Earl) 1936- 88
Hibbert, Arthur Raymond
See Hibbert, Christopher
Hibbert, Christopher 1924-2008 4
Obituary 201
Hibbert, Eleanor Alice Burford 1906-1993 2
Obituary 74
Hickman, Estella (Lee) 1942- 111
Hickman, Janet 1940- 127
Earlier sketch in SATA 12
Hickman, Martha Whitmore 1925- 26
Hickman, Pamela 1958- 186
Earlier sketch in SATA 128
Hickock, Will
See Harrison, C(hester) William
Hickok, Lorena A. 1893-1968 20
Hickox, Rebecca (Ayres) 116
Hicks, Barbara Jean 1953- 165
Hicks, Betty 191
Hicks, Clifford B. 1920- 50
Hicks, Eleanor B.
See Coerr, Eleanor (Beatrice)
Hicks, Harvey
See Stratemeyer, Edward L.
Hicks, Peter 1952- 111
Hicyilmaz, Gaye 1947- 157
Earlier sketch in SATA 77
Hieatt, Constance B(artlett) 1928- 4
Hiebert, Ray Eldon 1932- 13
Higdon, Hal 1931- 4
Higginbottom, David 1923- 87
Earlier sketch in SATA 25
Higginbottom, J(effrey) Winslow 1945- 29
Higgins, Joanna 1945- 125
Higgins, Simon (Richard) 1958- 105
Higginsen, Vy 79

High, Linda Oatman 1958- 188
Autobiography Feature 188
Earlier sketches in SATA 94, 145
High, Philip E. 1914- 119
High, Philip Empson
See High, Philip E.
Higham, David (Michael) 1949- 50
Higham, Jon Atlas
See Higham, Jonathan Huw
Higham, Jonathan Huw 1960- 59
Highet, Helen
See MacInnes, Helen (Clark)
Hightman, Jason 1971(?)- 189
Hightman, J.P.
See Hightman, Jason
Hightower, Florence Cole 1916-1981 4
Obituary 27
Highwater, Jamake (Mamake)
1942(?)-2001 69
Brief entry 30
Earlier sketch in SATA 32
See also CLR 17
Hilb, Nora 1953- 178
Hildebrandt, Greg 1939- 172
Brief entry 33
Earlier sketch in SATA 55
Hildebrandt, Tim 1939-2006 55
Brief entry 33
Hildebrandt, Timothy
See Hildebrandt, Tim
Hildebrandts, The
See Hildebrandt, Greg
and Hildebrandt, Tim
Hilder, Rowland 1905-1993 36
Obituary 77
Hildick, E. W.
See Hildick, Wallace
Hildick, Wallace 1925-2001 68
Earlier sketch in SATA 2
See also SAAS 6
Hilgartner, Beth 1957- 58
Hill, Alexis
See Craig, Mary (Francis) Shura
and Glick, Ruth (Burtnick)
Hill, Anthony R. 1942- 164
Earlier sketch in SATA 91
Hill, Anthony Robert
See Hill, Anthony R.
Hill, David 1942- 152
Earlier sketch in SATA 103
Hill, Donna (Marie) 1921- 124
Earlier sketch in SATA 24
Hill, Douglas 1935-2007 78
Earlier sketch in SATA 39
Hill, Douglas Arthur
See Hill, Douglas
Hill, Elizabeth Starr 1925- 143
Earlier sketch in SATA 24
Hill, Eric 1927- 133
Brief entry 53
Earlier sketch in SATA 66
See also CLR 13
Hill, Gordon
See Eldin, Peter
Hill, Grace Brooks 67
Earlier sketch in SATA 1
Hill, Grace Livingston 1865-1947
See YABC 2
Hill, Helen M(orey) 1915- 27
Hill, John
See Koontz, Dean
Hill, Johnson
See Kunhardt, Edith
Hill, Judy I. R.
See Roberts, Judy I.
Hill, Kathleen Louise 1917- 4
Hill, Kay
See Hill, Kathleen Louise
Hill, Kirkpatrick 1938- 188
Earlier sketches in SATA 72, 126

Hill, Laban
  See Hill, Laban Carrick
Hill, Laban Carrick 170
Hill, Lee Sullivan 1958- 96
Hill, Lorna 1902-1991 12
Hill, Margaret (Ohler) 1915- 36
Hill, Meg
  See Hill, Margaret (Ohler)
Hill, Meredith
  See Craig, Mary (Francis) Shura
Hill, Monica
  See Watson, Jane Werner
Hill, Pamela Smith 1954- 112
Hill, Ralph Nading 1917-1987 65
Hill, Robert W(hite) 1919-1982 12
  Obituary 31
Hill, Ruth A.
  See Viguers, Ruth Hill
Hill, Ruth Livingston
  See Munce, Ruth Hill
Hill, Stuart 1958- 186
Hill, Susan 1942- 183
Hill, Susan Elizabeth
  See Hill, Susan
Hill, Susanna Leonard 1965- 193
Hill, Thomas 1960- 82
Hillcourt, William 1900-1992 27
Hillenbrand, Will 1960- 147
  Earlier sketch in SATA 84
Hiller, Ilo (Ann) 1938- 59
Hillerman, Anthony Grove
  See Hillerman, Tony
Hillerman, Tony 1925-2008 6
  Obituary 198
Hillert, Margaret 1920- 91
  Earlier sketch in SATA 8
Hilliard, Richard 183
Hillman, Ben 1957- 202
Hillman, Elizabeth 1942- 75
Hillman, John 1952- 120
Hillman, Martin
  See Hill, Douglas
Hillman, Priscilla 1940- 48
  Brief entry 39
Hillman, Shane 200
Hills, C.A.R. 1955- 39
Hills, Charles Albert Reis
  See Hills, C.A.R.
Hills, Tad 173
Hilton, Irene Pothus -1979 7
Hilton, James 1900-1954 34
Hilton, Margaret Lynette 1946- 105
  Earlier sketch in SATA 68
  See also CLR 25
  See also SAAS 21
Hilton, Nette
  See Hilton, Margaret Lynette
Hilton, Ralph 1907-1982 8
Hilton, Suzanne 1922- 4
Hilton-Bruce, Anne
  See Hilton, Margaret Lynette
Him, George 1937-1982
  Obituary 30
Himelblau, Linda -2005 179
Himelstein, Shmuel 1940- 83
Himler, Ann 1946- 8
Himler, Ronald 1937- 183
  Earlier sketches in SATA 6, 92, 137
Himler, Ronald Norbert
  See Himler, Ronald
Himmelman, John C(arl) 1959- 159
  Earlier sketches in SATA 47, 94
Hinckley, Helen
  See Jones, Helen Hinckley
Hind, Dolores (Ellen) 1931- 53
  Brief entry 49
Hindin, Nathan
  See Bloch, Robert (Albert)
Hindley, Judy 1940- 179
  Earlier sketch in SATA 120
Hinds, P(atricia) Mignon 98

Hine, Sesyle Joslin 1929- 2
Hines, Anna Grossnickle 1946- 141
  Brief entry 45
  Earlier sketches in SATA 51, 95
  See also SAAS 16
Hines, Gary (Roger) 1944- 136
  Earlier sketch in SATA 74
Hinojosa, Maria (de Lourdes) 1961- 88
Hinton, Nigel 1941- 166
Hinton, S. E. 1950- 160
  Earlier sketches in SATA 19, 58, 115
  See also CLR 23
Hinton, Sam 1917-2009 43
Hinton, Susan Eloise
  See Hinton, S. E.
Hintz, Martin 1945- 128
  Brief entry 39
  Earlier sketch in SATA 47
Hintz, Stephen V. 1975- 129
Hippopotamus, Eugene H.
  See Kraus, (Herman) Robert
Hirano, Cathy 1957- 68
Hirao, Amiko 203
Hirsch, Karen 1941- 61
Hirsch, Odo 157
  Earlier sketch in SATA 111
Hirsch, Phil 1926- 35
Hirsch, S. Carl 1913-1990 2
  See also SAAS 7
Hirschfelder, Arlene B. 1943- 138
  Earlier sketch in SATA 80
Hirschi, Ron 1948- 192
  Earlier sketches in SATA 56, 95
Hirschmann, Linda (Ann) 1941- 40
Hirsh, Marilyn 1944-1988 7
  Obituary 58
Hirshberg, Al(bert Simon) 1909-1973 38
Hiscock, Bruce 1940- 204
  Earlier sketches in SATA 57, 137
Hiser, Constance 1950- 71
Hiser, Iona Seibert -1998 4
Hislop, Julia Rose Catherine 1962- 74
Hissey, Jane 1952- 130
  Autobiography Feature 130
  Earlier sketches in SATA 58, 103
Hissey, Jane Elizabeth
  See Hissey, Jane
Hitchcock, Alfred (Joseph) 1899-1980 27
  Obituary 24
Hite, Sid 1954- 175
  Earlier sketches in SATA 75, 136
Hitte, Kathryn 1919- 16
Hitz, Demi 1942- 152
  Earlier sketches in SATA 11, 66, 102
  See also CLR 58
Hitzeroth, Deborah L. 1961- 78
Hnizdovsky, Jacques 1915- 32
Ho, Louise 185
Ho, Minfong 1951- 151
  Earlier sketches in SATA 15, 94
  See also CLR 28
Hoagland, Edward (Morley) 1932- 51
Hoare, Robert J(ohn) 1921-1975 38
Hoban, Lillian 1925-1998 69
  Obituary 104
  Earlier sketch in SATA 22
  See also CLR 67
Hoban, Russell 1925- 136
  Earlier sketches in SATA 1, 40, 78
  See also CLR 139
Hoban, Russell Conwell
  See Hoban, Russell
Hoban, Tana 1917(?)-2006 104
  Obituary 173
  Earlier sketches in SATA 22, 70
  See also CLR 76
  See also SAAS 12
Hobart, Lois (Elaine) 7
Hobbie, Holly 1944- 178
  See also CLR 88
Hobbie, Jocelyn 190

Hobbie, Nathaniel 196
Hobbs, Leigh 1953- 166
Hobbs, Valerie 1941- 193
  Autobiography Feature 145
  Earlier sketches in SATA 93, 145
Hobbs, Will 1947- 177
  Autobiography Feature 127
  Earlier sketches in SATA 72, 110
  See also CLR 59
Hobbs, William Carl
  See Hobbs, Will
Hoberman, Mary Ann 1930- 158
  Earlier sketches in SATA 5, 72, 111
  See also CLR 22
  See also SAAS 18
Hobson, Bruce 1950- 62
Hobson, Burton (Harold) 1933- 28
Hobson, Laura Z(ametkin) 1900-1986 52
Hobson, Sally 1967- 172
  Earlier sketch in SATA 84
Hoce, Charley E. 174
Hochman, David 202
Hochschild, Arlie Russell 1940- 11
Hockaby, Stephen
  See Mitchell, Gladys (Maude Winifred)
Hockenberry, Hope
  See Newell, Hope Hockenberry
Hodge, Deborah 1954- 163
  Earlier sketch in SATA 122
Hodge, P. W.
  See Hodge, Paul W(illiam)
Hodge, Paul W(illiam) 1934- 12
Hodgell, P(atricia) C(hristine) 1951- 42
Hodges, C. Walter 1909-2004 2
  Obituary 158
Hodges, Carl G. 1902-1964 10
Hodges, Cyril Walter
  See Hodges, C. Walter
Hodges, Elizabeth Jamison 1
Hodges, Margaret 1911-2005 167
  Obituary 172
  Earlier sketches in SATA 1, 33, 75, 117
  See also SAAS 9
Hodges, Margaret Moore
  See Hodges, Margaret
Hodgetts, Blake Christopher 1967- 43
Hodgkins, Fran 1964- 199
Hodgkinson, Leigh 1975- 202
Hodgman, Ann 1956- 198
Hodgson, Harriet (W.) 1935- 84
Hoehne, Marcia 1951- 89
Hoellwarth, Cathryn Clinton
  See Clinton, Cathryn
Hoestlandt, Jo 1948- 94
Hoestlandt, Jocelyne
  See Hoestlandt, Jo
Hoexter, Corinne K. 1927- 6
Hoeye, Michael 1947- 136
Hoff, Carol 1900-1979 11
Hoff, Mary (King) 1956- 157
  Earlier sketch in SATA 74
Hoff, Syd(ney) 1912-2004 138
  Obituary 154
  Earlier sketches in SATA 9, 72
  See also CLR 83
  See also SAAS 4
Hoffman, Edwin D. 49
Hoffman, Elizabeth P(arkinson) 1921-2003
  Obituary 153
Hoffman, Mary 1945- 144
  Earlier sketches in SATA 59, 97
  See also SAAS 24
Hoffman, Mat 1972- 150
Hoffman, Nina Kiriki 1955- 160
Hoffman, Phyllis M(iriam) 1944- 4
Hoffman, Rosekrans 1926- 15
Hoffmann, E(rnst) T(heodor) A(madeus)
  1776-1822 27
  See also CLR 133
Hoffmann, Felix 1911-1975 9

Hoffmann, Heinrich 1809-1894
  See CLR 122
Hoffmann, Margaret Jones 1910- 48
Hoffmann, Peggy
  See Hoffmann, Margaret Jones
Hofher, Catherine Baxley 1954- 130
Hofher, Cathy
  See Hofher, Catherine Baxley
Hofmeyr, Dianne (Louise) 138
Hofsepian, Sylvia A. 1932- 74
Hofsinde, Robert 1902-1973 21
Hogan, Bernice Harris 1929- 12
Hogan, Inez 1895-1973 2
Hogan, James P(atrick) 1941- 81
Hogan, Jamie 192
Hogan, Linda 1947- 132
Hogarth, Burne 1911-1996 89
  Earlier sketch in SATA 63
Hogarth, Grace (Weston Allen) 1905-1995 .. 91
Hogarth, Jr.
  See Kent, Rockwell
Hogarth, (Arthur) Paul 1917-2001 41
Hogg, Garry 1902-1976 2
Hogg, Gary 1957- 172
  Earlier sketch in SATA 105
Hogner, Dorothy Childs 4
Hogner, Nils 1893-1970 25
Hogrogian, Nonny 1932- 74
  Autobiography Feature 127
  Earlier sketch in SATA 7
  See also CLR 95
  See also SAAS 1
Hoh, Diane 1937- 102
  Brief entry 48
  Earlier sketch in SATA 52
Hoke, Helen
  See Watts, Helen L. Hoke
Hoke, Helen L.
  See Watts, Helen L. Hoke
Hoke, John (Lindsay) 1925- 7
Hokenson, Terry 1948- 193
Hol, Coby 1943- 126
Holabird, Katharine 1948- 135
  Earlier sketch in SATA 62
Holaday, Bobbie 1922- 153
Holbeach, Henry
  See Rands, William Brighty
Holberg, Ruth L(angland) 1889-1984 1
Holbrook, Kathy 1963- 107
Holbrook, Peter
  See Glick, Carl (Cannon)
Holbrook, Sabra
  See Erickson, Sabra Rollins
Holbrook, Sara 131
Holbrook, Stewart Hall 1893-1964 2
Holcomb, Jerry (Leona) Kimble 1927- 113
Holcomb, Nan
  See McPhee, Norma H.
Holden, Elizabeth Rhoda
  See Lawrence, Louise
Holding, James (Clark Carlisle, Jr.)
  1907-1997 3
Hole, Stian 1969- 204
Holeman, Linda 1949- 136
  Autobiography Feature 136
  Earlier sketch in SATA 102
Holinger, William (Jacques) 1944- 90
Holisher, Desider 1901-1972 6
Holl, Adelaide Hinkle 1910- 8
Holl, Kristi D(iane) 1951- 51
Holland, Gay W. 1941- 128
Holland, Isabelle (Christian) 1920-2002 70
  Autobiography Feature 103
  Obituary 132
  Earlier sketch in SATA 8
  See also CLR 57
Holland, Janice 1913-1962 18
Holland, John L(ewis) 1919- 20
Holland, Joyce
  See Morice, Dave
Holland, Julia 1954- 106

Holland, Lynda (H.) 1959- 77
Holland, Lys
  See Gater, Dilys
Holland, Marion 1908-1989 6
  Obituary 61
Hollander, John 1929- 13
Hollander, Nicole 1940(?)- 101
Hollander, Paul
  See Silverberg, Robert
Hollander, Phyllis 1928- 39
Hollander, Zander 1923- 63
Holldobler, Turid 1939- 26
Holliday, Joe
  See Holliday, Joseph
Holliday, Joseph 1910- 11
Holling, Holling C(lancy) 1900-1973 15
  Obituary 26
  See also CLR 50
Hollingsworth, Alvin C(arl) 1930- 39
Hollingsworth, Mary 1947- 166
  Earlier sketch in SATA 91
Holloway, Teresa (Bragunier) 1906- 26
Hollyer, Belinda 204
Holm, (Else) Anne (Lise) 1922-1998 1
  See also CLR 75
  See also SAAS 7
Holm, Jennifer L. 1968(?)- 183
  Earlier sketches in SATA 120, 163
Holm, Matthew 1974- 174
Holm, Sharon Lane 1955- 114
  Earlier sketch in SATA 78
Holman, Felice 1919- 82
  Earlier sketch in SATA 7
  See also SAAS 17
Holm and Hamel
  See Holm, Jennifer L.
Holmberg, Bo R. 1945- 203
Holme, Bryan 1913-1990 26
  Obituary 66
Holmes, Barbara Ware 1945- 127
  Earlier sketch in SATA 65
Holmes, Elizabeth 1957- 191
Holmes, Elizabeth Ann
  See Holmes, Elizabeth
Holmes, John
  See Souster, (Holmes) Raymond
Holmes, Marjorie (Rose) 1910-2002 43
Holmes, Martha 1961- 72
Holmes, Mary Tavener 1954- 199
Holmes, Mary Z(astrow) 1943- 80
Holmes, Oliver Wendell 1809-1894 34
Holmes, Peggy 1898- 60
Holmes, Raymond
  See Souster, (Holmes) Raymond
Holmes, Rick
  See Hardwick, Richard Holmes, Jr.
Holmes, Sara Lewis 186
Holmgren, Helen Jean 1930- 45
Holmgren, Sister George Ellen
  See Holmgren, Helen Jean
Holmgren, Virginia C(unningham) 1909- 26
Holmquist, Eve 1921- 11
Holt, Kimberly Willis 1960- 179
  Earlier sketch in SATA 122
Holt, Margaret 1937- 4
Holt, Margaret Van Vechten (Saunders)
  1899-1963 32
Holt, Michael (Paul) 1929- 13
Holt, Rackham
  See Holt, Margaret Van Vechten (Saunders)
Holt, Rochelle L.
  See DuBois, Rochelle Holt
Holt, Stephen
  See Thompson, Harlan
Holt, Victoria
  See Hibbert, Eleanor Alice Burford
Holton, Leonard
  See Wibberley, Leonard
Holtz, Thomas R., Jr. 1965- 203
Holtze, Sally Holmes 1952- 64

Holtzman, Jerome 1926-2008 57
  Obituary 194
Holub, Joan 1956- 149
  Earlier sketch in SATA 99
Holub, Josef 1926- 175
Holubitsky, Katherine 1955- 165
  Earlier sketch in SATA 121
Holyer, Erna Maria 1925- 22
Holyer, Ernie
  See Holyer, Erna Maria
Holz, Loretta (Marie) 1943- 17
Homel, David 1952- 97
Homze, Alma C. 1932- 17
Honey, Elizabeth 1947- 137
  Autobiography Feature 137
  Earlier sketch in SATA 112
Honeycutt, Natalie 1945- 97
Hong, Lily Toy 1958- 76
Hong, Maxine Ting Ting
  See Kingston, Maxine Hong
Honig, Donald 1931- 18
Honness, Elizabeth H. 1904- 2
Hoobler, Dorothy 1941- 161
  Earlier sketches in SATA 28, 109
Hoobler, Thomas 161
  Earlier sketches in SATA 28, 109
Hood, Joseph F. 1925- 4
Hood, Robert E. 1926- 21
Hood, Sarah
  See Killough, (Karen) Lee
Hook, Brendan 1963- 105
Hook, Frances 1912-1983 27
Hook, Geoffrey R(aynor) 1928- 103
Hook, Jeff
  See Hook, Geoffrey R(aynor)
Hook, Martha 1936- 27
Hooker, Richard
  See Heinz, W. C.
Hooker, Ruth 1920-1998 21
hooks, bell 1952(?)- 170
  Earlier sketch in SATA 115
Hooks, William H(arris) 1921- 94
  Earlier sketch in SATA 16
Hoon, Patricia Easterly 1954- 90
Hooper, Byrd
  See St. Clair, Byrd Hooper
Hooper, Mary 1948- 205
  Earlier sketch in SATA 160
Hooper, Maureen Brett 1927- 76
Hooper, Meredith 1939- 159
  Earlier sketches in SATA 28, 101
Hooper, Meredith Jean
  See Hooper, Meredith
Hooper, Patricia 1941- 95
Hoopes, Lyn Littlefield 1953- 49
  Brief entry 44
Hoopes, Ned E(dward) 1932- 21
Hoopes, Roy 1922-2009 11
Hoose, Phillip M. 1947- 137
Hoover, H(elen) M(ary) 1935- 132
  Brief entry 33
  Earlier sketches in SATA 44, 83
  See also SAAS 8
Hoover, Helen (Drusilla Blackburn)
  1910-1984 12
  Obituary 39
Hope, Christopher 1944- 62
Hope, Christopher David Tully
  See Hope, Christopher
Hope, Laura Lee
  See Goulart, Ron
  and Stanley, George Edward
Hope Simpson, Jacynth 1930- 12
Hopf, Alice (Martha) L(ightner) 1904-1988 ... 5
  Obituary 55
Hopkins, A. T.
  See Turngren, Annette
Hopkins, C. M.
  See Hopkins, Cathy
Hopkins, Cathy 1953- 165

Hopkins, Cathy M.
  See Hopkins, Cathy
Hopkins, Clark 1895-1976
  Obituary 34
Hopkins, Ellen 1955- 128
  See Hopkins, Ellen L.
Hopkins, Ellen L.
  See Hopkins, Ellen
Hopkins, Jackie
  See Hopkins, Jackie Mims
Hopkins, Jackie Mims 1952- 178
  Earlier sketch in SATA 92
Hopkins, Joseph G(erard) E(dward) 1909- .. 11
Hopkins, (Hector) Kenneth 1914-1988
  Obituary 58
Hopkins, Lee Bennett 1938- 168
  Earlier sketches in SATA 3, 68, 125
  See also CLR 44
  See also SAAS 4
Hopkins, Lyman
  See Folsom, Franklin (Brewster)
Hopkins, Marjorie 1911-1999 9
Hopkins, Mary R(ice) 1956- 97
Hopkinson, Amanda 1948- 84
Hopkinson, Deborah 1952- 180
  Autobiography Feature 180
  Earlier sketches in SATA 76, 108, 159
  See also CLR 118
Hopman, Philip 1961- 177
Hoppe, Joanne 1932- 42
Hoppe, Matthias 1952- 76
Hopper, Nancy J. 1937- 38
  Brief entry 35
Hopping, Lorraine Jean
  See Egan, Lorraine Hopping
Horacek, Petr 163
Horenstein, Henry 1947- 108
Horgan, Paul (George Vincent O'Shaughnessy)
  1903-1995 13
  Obituary 84
Horlak, E.E.
  See Tepper, Sheri S.
Horler, Sydney 1888-1954 102
Horn, Sandra Ann 1944- 154
Hornblow, Arthur, Jr. 1893-1976 15
Hornblow, Leonora 1920-2005 18
  Obituary 171
Hornblow, Leonora Schinasi
  See Hornblow, Leonora
Horne, Constance 1927- 149
Horne, Richard 1960-2007 169
  Obituary 180
  Earlier sketch in SATA 111
Horne, Richard Henry Hengist
  1802(?)-1884 29
Horner, Althea (Jane) 1926- 36
Horner, Dave 1934- 12
Horner, Jack
  See Horner, John R(obert)
Horner, John R(obert) 1946- 106
Hornik, Laurie Miller 159
Horniman, Joanne 1951- 167
  Earlier sketch in SATA 98
Hornos, Axel 1907-1994 20
Hornstein, Reuben Aaron 1912- 64
Horowitz, Anthony 1955- 195
  Earlier sketch in SATA 137
Horowitz, Dave 1970- 204
  Earlier sketch in SATA 172
Horowitz, Ruth 1957- 136
Horrocks, Anita 1958- 169
Horse, Harry
  See Horne, Richard
Horsfield, Alan 1939- 153
Hort, Lenny 179
Horton, James O. 1943- 173
Horton, James Oliver
  See Horton, James O.
Horton, Madelyn (Stacey) 1962- 77
Horvath, Betty 1927- 4
Horvath, David 1972(?)- 192

Horvath, Polly 1957- 194
  Earlier sketches in SATA 85, 140
  See also CLR 90
Horwich, Frances R(appaport) 1908-2001 11
  Obituary 130
Horwitz, Elinor Lander 45
  Brief entry 33
Horwood, William 1944- 85
Hosford, Dorothy (Grant) 1900-1952 22
Hosford, Jessie 1892-1990 5
Hoshi, Shin'ichi 1926- 101
Hoshino, Felicia 1968- 189
Hoskyns-Abrahall, Clare (Constance
  Drury) 13
Hosler, Danamarie 1978- 184
Hossack, Sylvia 1939- 83
Hossack, Sylvie Adams
  See Hossack, Sylvia
Hosseini, Khaled 1965- 156
Hossell, Karen Price
  See Price, Karen
Hosta, Dar 192
Hostetler, Marian 1932- 91
Houck, Carter 1924- 22
Hough, Charlotte 1924-2008 9
  Obituary 202
Hough, Helen Charlotte
  See Hough, Charlotte
Hough, Judy Taylor 1932- 63
  Brief entry 51
  Earlier sketch in SATA 56
Hough, Richard (Alexander) 1922-1999 17
Houghton, Eric 1930- 7
Houk, Randy 1944- 97
Houlehen, Robert J. 1918- 18
Houlton, Peggy Mann 1925(?)-1990 6
Household, Geoffrey (Edward West)
  1900-1988 14
  Obituary 59
Housman, Laurence 1865-1959 25
Houston, Dick 1943- 74
Houston, Gloria 138
  Autobiography Feature 138
  Earlier sketch in SATA 81
Houston, James A(rchibald) 1921-2005 74
  Obituary 163
  Earlier sketch in SATA 13
  See also CLR 3
  See also SAAS 17
Houston, James D. 1933-2009 78
  Obituary 203
Houston, James Dudley
  See Houston, James D.
Houston, James Dudley
  See Houston, James D.
Houston, Jeanne Toyo Wakatsuki
  See Houston, Jeanne Wakatsuki
Houston, Jeanne Wakatsuki 1934- 168
  Autobiography Feature 168
  Earlier sketch in SATA 78
Houston, Juanita C. 1921- 129
Houton, Kathleen
  See Kilgore, Kathleen
Houts, Amy F. 164
Hovey, Kate 158
Howard, Alan 1922- 45
Howard, Alyssa
  See Buckholtz, Eileen (Garber)
  and Glick, Ruth (Burtnick)
  and Titchener, Louise
Howard, Arthur 1948- 165
Howard, Arthur Charles
  See Howard, Arthur
Howard, Elizabeth Fitzgerald 1927- 119
  Earlier sketch in SATA 74
Howard, Ellen 1943- 184
  Earlier sketches in SATA 67, 99
Howard, Jane R(uble) 1924- 87
Howard, Norman Barry 1949- 90
Howard, P. M.
  See Howard, Pauline Rodriguez

Howard, Paul 1967- 190
  Earlier sketch in SATA 118
Howard, Pauline Rodriguez 1951- 124
Howard, Prosper
  See Hamilton, Charles (Harold St. John)
Howard, Robert West 1908-1988 5
Howard, Todd 1964- 135
Howard, Tristan
  See Currie, Stephen
Howard, Vernon (Linwood) 1918-1992 40
  Obituary 73
Howard, Warren F.
  See Pohl, Frederik
Howarth, Daniel 188
Howarth, David (Armine) 1912-1991 6
  Obituary 68
Howarth, Lesley 1952- 94
Howe, Deborah 1946-1978 29
Howe, James 1946- 161
  Earlier sketches in SATA 29, 71, 111
  See also CLR 9
Howe, John F. 1957- 79
Howe, Norma 1930- 126
Howell, Pat 1947- 15
Howell, S.
  See Styles, (Frank) Showell
Howell, Virginia
  See Ellison, Virginia H(owell)
Howes, Barbara 1914-1996 5
Howie, Diana 1945- 122
Howie, Diana Melson
  See Howie, Diana
Howker, Janni 1957- 72
  Brief entry 46
  See also CLR 14
  See also SAAS 13
Howland, Ethan 1963- 131
Hoy, Linda 1946- 65
Hoy, Nina
  See Roth, Arthur J(oseph)
Hoyle, Geoffrey 1942- 18
Hoyt, Ard 190
Hoyt, Edwin P(almer), Jr. 1923- 28
Hoyt, Erich 1950- 140
  Earlier sketch in SATA 65
Hoyt, Olga
  See Gruhzit-Hoyt, Olga (Margaret)
Hrdlitschka, Shelley 1956- 167
  Earlier sketch in SATA 111
Hrdlitschka, Shelley Joanne
  See Hrdlitschka, Shelley
Htin Aung, U.
  See Aung, (Maung) Htin
Hu, Ying-Hwa 173
Huang, Benrei 1959- 86
Hubalek, Linda K. 1954- 111
Hubbard, Margaret Ann
  See Priley, Margaret (Ann) Hubbard
Hubbard, Michelle Calabro 1953- 122
Hubbard, Patricia 1945- 124
Hubbard, Woodleigh Marx 160
  Earlier sketch in SATA 98
Hubbell, Patricia 1928- 186
  Earlier sketches in SATA 8, 132
Hubery, Julia 195
Hubley, Faith Elliot 1924-2001 48
  Obituary 133
Hubley, John 1914-1977 48
  Obituary 24
Huck, Charlotte S. 1922- 136
  Earlier sketch in SATA 82
Hudak, Michal 1956- 143
Hudson, Cheryl Willis 1948- 160
  Earlier sketch in SATA 81
Hudson, Jan 1954-1990 77
  See also CLR 40
Hudson, Jeffery
  See Crichton, Michael
Hudson, Jeffrey
  See Crichton, Michael
Hudson, (Margaret) Kirsty 1947- 32

Hudson, Margaret
   See Shuter, Jane (Margaret)
Hudson, W(illiam) H(enry) 1841-1922 35
Hudson, Wade 1946- 162
   Earlier sketch in SATA 74
Huelsmann, Eva 1928- 16
Huerlimann, Bettina 1909-1983 39
   Obituary 34
Huerlimann, Ruth 1939- 32
   Brief entry 31
Huff, Barbara A. 1929- 67
Huff, Tanya 1957- 171
   Earlier sketch in SATA 85
Huff, Tanya Sue
   See Huff, Tanya
Huff, T.S.
   See Huff, Tanya
Huff, Vivian 1948- 59
Huffaker, Sandy 1943- 10
Huffman, Tom 24
Huggins, Nathan Irvin 1927-1989 63
Huggins, Peter 1951- 178
Hughes, Carol 1955- 108
Hughes, Dean 1943- 139
   Earlier sketches in SATA 33, 77
   See also CLR 76
Hughes, Eden
   See Griffin, W.E.B.
Hughes, Edward James
   See Hughes, Ted
Hughes, James Langston
   See Hughes, Langston
Hughes, Langston 1902-1967 33
   Earlier sketch in SATA 4
   See also CLR 17
Hughes, Libby 71
Hughes, Matilda
   See MacLeod, Charlotte (Matilda)
Hughes, Monica 1925-2003 162
   Earlier sketches in SATA 15, 70, 119
   See also CLR 60
   See also SAAS 11
Hughes, Monica Ince
   See Hughes, Monica
Hughes, Pat 197
Hughes, Richard (Arthur Warren)
   1900-1976 8
   Obituary 25
Hughes, Sara
   See Saunders, Susan
Hughes, Shirley 1927- 159
   Earlier sketches in SATA 16, 70, 110
   See also CLR 15
Hughes, Ted 1930-1998 49
   Brief entry 27
   Obituary 107
   See also CLR 131
Hughes, Thomas 1822-1896 31
Hughes, Virginia
   See Campbell, Hope
Hughes, Walter (Llewellyn) 1910-1993 26
Hughey, Roberta 1942- 61
Hugo, Pierre Brackers de
   See Brackers de Hugo, Pierre
Hugo, Victor 1802-1885 47
Hugo, Victor Marie
   See Hugo, Victor
Huline-Dickens, Frank William 1931- 34
Huling, Jan 172
Huliska-Beith, Laura 175
Hull, Eleanor (Means) 1913- 21
Hull, Eric Traviss
   See Harnan, Terry
Hull, H. Braxton
   See Jacobs, Helen Hull
Hull, Jesse Redding
   See Hull, Jessie Redding
Hull, Jessie Redding 1932- 51
Hull, Katharine 1921-1977 23
Hull, Lise (E.) 1954- 148
Hull, Maureen 1949- 142

Hulme, Joy N. 1922- 161
   Earlier sketches in SATA 74, 112
Hults, Dorothy Niebrugge 1898-2000 6
Humble, Richard 1945- 60
Hume, Lachie 189
Hume, Lotta Carswell 7
Hume, Ruth Fox 1922-1980 26
   Obituary 22
Hume, Stephen Eaton 1947- 136
Hummel, Berta 1909-1946 43
Hummel, Sister Maria Innocentia
   See Hummel, Berta
Humphrey, Carol Sue 1956- 167
Humphrey, Henry (III) 1930- 16
Humphrey, Kate
   See Forsyth, Kate
Humphrey, Sandra McLeod 1936- 95
Humphreys, Martha 1943- 71
Humphreys, Susan L.
   See Lowell, Susan
Hundal, Nancy 1957- 128
Huneck, Stephen 1949- 183
   Earlier sketch in SATA 129
Hungerford, Hesba Fay
   See Brinsmead, H(esba) F(ay)
Hungerford, Pixie
   See Brinsmead, H(esba) F(ay)
Hunkin, Timothy Mark Trelawney 1950- 53
Hunt, Angela Elwell 1957- 159
   Earlier sketch in SATA 75
Hunt, Bernice 1920- 4
Hunt, Francesca
   See Holland, Isabelle (Christian)
Hunt, Irene 1907-2001 91
   Earlier sketch in SATA 2
   See also CLR 1
Hunt, Janie Louise 1963- 102
Hunt, Jonathan 1966- 84
Hunt, Joyce 1927- 31
Hunt, Linda 1940- 39
Hunt, Lisa B(ehnke) 1967- 84
Hunt, Mabel Leigh 1892-1971 1
   Obituary 26
Hunt, Morton M(agill) 1920- 22
Hunt, Nigel
   See Greenbank, Anthony Hunt
Hunt, Peter (Leonard) 1945- 76
Hunter, Anne B. 1966- 118
Hunter, Bernice Thurman 1922-2002 85
   Brief entry 45
Hunter, Bobbi Dooley 1945- 89
Hunter, Captain Marcy
   See Ellis, Edward S.
Hunter, Chris
   See Fluke, Joanne
Hunter, Clingham M.D.
   See Adams, William Taylor
Hunter, Edith Fisher 1919- 31
Hunter, Erin
   See Cary, Kate
Hunter, Evan 1926-2005 25
   Obituary 167
Hunter, George E.
   See Ellis, Edward S.
Hunter, Hilda 1921- 7
Hunter, Jana
   See Hunter, Jana Novotny
Hunter, Jana Novotny 190
Hunter, Jim 1939- 65
Hunter, Kristin
   See Lattany, Kristin Hunter
Hunter, Leigh
   See Etchison, Birdie L(ee)
Hunter, Lieutenant Ned
   See Ellis, Edward S.
Hunter, Mel 1927-2004 39
Hunter, Mollie 1922- 139
   Autobiography Feature 139
   Earlier sketches in SATA 2, 54, 106
   See also CLR 25
   See also SAAS 7

Hunter, Ned
   See Ellis, Edward S.
Hunter, Norman (George Lorimer)
   1899-1995 84
   Earlier sketch in SATA 26
Hunter, Ryan Ann
   See Greenwood, Pamela D.
   and Macalaster, Elizabeth G.
Hunter, Sara Hoagland 1954- 98
Hunter Blair, Pauline
   See Clarke, Pauline
Huntington, Amy 1956- 180
   Earlier sketch in SATA 138
Huntington, Geoffrey 145
Huntington, Harriet E(lizabeth) 1909- 1
Huntsberry, William E(mery) 1916- 5
Hurd, Clement (G.) 1908-1988 64
   Obituary 54
   Earlier sketch in SATA 2
   See also CLR 49
Hurd, Edith Thacher 1910-1997 64
   Obituary 95
   Earlier sketch in SATA 2
   See also CLR 49
   See also SAAS 13
Hurd, (John) Thacher 1949- 94
   Autobiography Feature 123
   Brief entry 45
   Earlier sketch in SATA 46
Hurley, Jo
   See Dower, Laura
Hurley, Tonya 207
Hurlimann, Bettina
   See Huerlimann, Bettina
Hurlimann, Ruth
   See Huerlimann, Ruth
Hurmence, Belinda 1921- 77
   See also CLR 25
   See also SAAS 20
Hurst, Carol Otis 1933-2007 185
   Earlier sketch in SATA 130
Hurt-Newton, Tania 1968- 84
Hurwin, Davida Wills 1950- 180
Hurwitz, Johanna 1937- 175
   Earlier sketches in SATA 20, 71, 113
   See also SAAS 18
Hurwood, Bernhardt J. 1926-1987 12
   Obituary 50
Husain, Shahrukh 1950- 108
Huser, Glen 1943- 151
Hutchens, Paul 1902-1977 31
Hutchins, Carleen M.
   See Hutchins, Carleen Maley
Hutchins, Carleen Maley 1911-2009 9
   Obituary 206
Hutchins, Hazel J. 1952- 175
   Brief entry 51
   Earlier sketches in SATA 81, 135
   See also SAAS 24
Hutchins, Pat 1942- 178
   Earlier sketches in SATA 15, 70, 111
   See also CLR 20
   See also SAAS 16
Hutchins, Ross Elliott 1906- 4
Hutchison, Linda 1942- 152
Huthmacher, J. Joseph 1929- 5
Hutto, Nelson (Allen) 1904-1985 20
Hutton, Kathryn 1915- 89
Hutton, Sam
   See Jones, Allan Frewin
Hutton, Warwick 1939-1994 20
   Obituary 83
   See also SAAS 17
Huxley, Aldous 1894-1963 63
Huxley, Aldous Leonard
   See Huxley, Aldous
Huxley, Elspeth (Josceline Grant)
   1907-1997 62
   Obituary 95
Hyde, Catherine R.
   See Hyde, Catherine Ryan

Hyde, Catherine Ryan 1955- *141*
Hyde, Dayton O(gden) *9*
Hyde, Hawk
  See Hyde, Dayton O(gden)
Hyde, Jeannette
  See Eyerly, Jeannette
Hyde, Margaret O. 1917- *139*
  Earlier sketches in SATA *1, 42, 76*
  See also CLR 23
  See also SAAS 8
Hyde, Margaret Oldroyd
  See Hyde, Margaret O.
Hyde, Shelley
  See Reed, Kit
Hyde, Wayne Frederick 1922- *7*
Hylander, Clarence J(ohn) 1897-1964 .... *7*
Hyman, Robin P(hilip) 1931- *12*
Hyman, Trina Schart 1939-2004 .... *95*
  Obituary *158*
  Earlier sketches in SATA *7, 46*
  See also CLR 50
Hymes, Lucia M(anley) 1907-1998 .... *7*
Hyndman, Jane Andrews Lee 1912-1978 ..... *46*
  Obituary *23*
  Earlier sketch in SATA *1*
Hyndman, Robert Utley 1906-1973 .... *18*
Hynes, Pat *98*

I

Iannone, Jeanne
  See Balzano, Jeanne (Koppel)
Ibatoulline, Bagram 1965(?)- *174*
Ibbitson, John Perrie 1955- *102*
Ibbotson, Eva 1925- *156*
  Earlier sketches in SATA *13, 103*
Ibbotson, M. C(hristine) 1930- *5*
Icenoggle, Jodi 1967- *168*
Icenoggle, Jodi O.
  See Icenoggle, Jodi
Ichikawa, Satomi 1949- *146*
  Brief entry *36*
  Earlier sketches in SATA *47, 78*
  See also CLR 62
Iggulden, Hal 1972- *196*
Ignoffo, Matthew 1945- *92*
Igus, Toyomi 1953- *112*
  Earlier sketch in SATA *76*
Ihimaera, Witi (Tame) 1944- *148*
Ikeda, Daisaku 1928- *77*
Ilowite, Sheldon A. 1931- *27*
Ilsey, Dent
  See Chapman, John Stanton Higham
Ilsley, Dent
  See Chapman, John Stanton Higham
Ilsley, Velma (Elizabeth) 1918- *12*
Imai, Ayano 1980- *190*
Imai, Miko 1963- *90*
Imershein, Betsy 1953- *62*
Immel, Mary Blair 1930- *28*
Immell, Myra H. 1941- *92*
Impey, Rose 1947- *152*
  Earlier sketch in SATA *69*
Ingelow, Jean 1820-1897 .... *33*
Ingermanson, Randall 1958- *134*
Ingermanson, Randy
  See Ingermanson, Randall
Ingersoll, Norman 1928- *79*
Ingham, Colonel Frederic
  See Hale, Edward Everett
Ingman, Bruce 1963- *182*
  Earlier sketch in SATA *134*
Ingman, Nicholas 1948- *52*
Ingold, Jeanette *128*
Ingpen, Robert 1936- *166*
  Earlier sketch in SATA *109*
Ingpen, Robert Roger
  See Ingpen, Robert
Ingraham, Erick 1950- *145*

Ingraham, Leonard W(illiam) 1913-2003 .... *4*
Ingram, Scott 1948- *167*
  Earlier sketch in SATA *92*
Ingram, W. Scott
  See Ingram, Scott
Ingrams, Doreen 1906-1997 .... *97*
  Earlier sketch in SATA *20*
Ingrid, Charles
  See Salsitz, Rhondi Vilott
Ingves, Gunilla (Anna Maria Folkesdotter)
  1939- *101*
Inkpen, Mick 1952- *154*
  Earlier sketch in SATA *99*
Innes, (Ralph) Hammond
  See Hammond Innes, Ralph
Innes, Ralph Hammond
  See Hammond Innes, Ralph
Innocenti, Roberto 1940- *159*
  Earlier sketch in SATA *96*
  See also CLR 126
Innocenti and Gallaz
  See Gallaz, Christophe
  and Innocenti, Roberto
Inyart, Gene
  See Namovicz, Gene Inyart
Ionesco, Eugene 1909-1994 .... *7*
  Obituary *79*
Ipcar, Dahlov (Zorach) 1917- *147*
  Autobiography Feature *147*
  Earlier sketches in SATA *1, 49*
  See also SAAS 8
Ireland, Karin *151*
  Earlier sketch in SATA *101*
Ironside, Jetske 1940- *60*
Irvin, Fred 1914- *15*
Irvine, Georgeanne 1955- *72*
Irvine, Joan 1951- *80*
Irving, Alexander
  See Hume, Ruth Fox
Irving, Robert
  See Adler, Irving
Irving, Washington 1783-1859
  See YABC 2
  See also CLR 97
Irwin, Ann(abelle Bowen) 1915-1998 .... *89*
  Brief entry *38*
  Obituary *106*
  Earlier sketch in SATA *44*
  See also CLR 40
  See also SAAS 14
Irwin, Constance (H.) Frick 1913-1995 .... *6*
Irwin, Hadley
  See Hadley, Lee
  and Irwin, Ann(abelle Bowen)
Irwin, Keith Gordon 1885-1964 .... *11*
Isaac, Joanne 1934- *21*
Isaacs, Anne 1949- *185*
  Earlier sketch in SATA *90*
Isaacs, Jacob
  See Kranzler, George G(ershon)
Isaacson, Philip M(arshal) 1924- *87*
Isadora, Rachel 1953(?)- *204*
  Brief entry *32*
  Earlier sketches in SATA *54, 79, 121, 165*
  See also CLR 7
Isbell, Rebecca T(emple) 1942- *125*
Isham, Charlotte H(ickock) 1912- *21*
Ishida, Jui *176*
Ish-Kishor, Judith 1892-1972 .... *11*
Ish-Kishor, Sulamith 1896-1977 .... *17*
Ishmael, Woodi 1914-1995 .... *31*
  Obituary *109*
Isle, Sue 1963- *105*
Israel, Elaine 1945- *12*
Israel, Marion Louise 1882-1973
  Obituary *26*
Iterson, S(iny) R(ose) Van
  See Van Iterson, S(iny) R(ose)
Ivanko, John D. 1966- *111*
Ivanko, John Duane
  See Ivanko, John D.

Iversen, Jeremy 1980(?)- *174*
Iversen, Jeremy Watt
  See Iversen, Jeremy
Iverson, Carol (L.) 1941- *145*
Iverson, Diane 1950- *122*
Iverson, Eric G.
  See Turtledove, Harry
Ivery, Martha M. 1948- *124*
Ives, David 1951- *173*
Ives, Morgan
  See Bradley, Marion Zimmer
Iwai, Melissa *183*
Iwamatsu, Jun Atsushi 1908-1994 .... *81*
  Earlier sketch in SATA *14*
  See also CLR 4
Iwasaki (Matsumoto), Chihiro 1918-1974
  See CLR 18

J

Jablonski, Carla *184*
Jac, Lee
  See Morton, Lee Jack, Jr.
Jacka, Martin 1943- *72*
Jackson, Alison 1953- *160*
  Earlier sketches in SATA *73, 108*
Jackson, Anne 1896(?)-1984
  Obituary *37*
Jackson, Barry
  See Jackson, Barry E.
Jackson, Barry E. *200*
Jackson, C(aary) Paul 1902-1991 .... *6*
Jackson, Caary
  See Jackson, C(aary) Paul
Jackson, Charlotte E. (Cobden) 1903(?)-1989
  Obituary *62*
Jackson, Dave
  See Jackson, J. David
Jackson, Donna M. 1959- *206*
Jackson, Ellen B. 1943- *167*
  Earlier sketches in SATA *75, 115*
Jackson, Garnet Nelson 1944- *87*
Jackson, Geoffrey (Holt Seymour) 1915-1987
  Obituary *53*
Jackson, Gina
  See Fluke, Joanne
Jackson, Guida M. 1930- *71*
Jackson, J. David 1944- *91*
Jackson, Jacqueline 1928- *65*
Jackson, Jacqueline Dougan
  See Jackson, Jacqueline
Jackson, Jesse 1908-1983 .... *29*
  Obituary *48*
  Earlier sketch in SATA *2*
  See also CLR 28
Jackson, Marjorie 1928- *127*
Jackson, Melanie 1956- *141*
Jackson, Mike 1946- *91*
Jackson, Neta J. 1944- *91*
Jackson, O. B.
  See Jackson, C(aary) Paul
Jackson, Rob 1961- *176*
Jackson, Robert B(lake) 1926- *8*
Jackson, Robert Bradley
  See Jackson, Rob
Jackson, Sally
  See Kellogg, Jean (Defrees)
Jackson, Shirley 1919-1965 .... *2*
Jackson, Woody 1948- *92*
Jackson Issa, Kai *205*
Jacob, Helen Pierce 1927- *21*
Jacobin
  See Bisson, Terry
Jacobs, Deborah Lynn *187*
Jacobs, Flora Gill 1918-2006 .... *5*
  Obituary *178*
Jacobs, Francine 1935- *150*
  Brief entry *42*
  Earlier sketch in SATA *43*

Jacobs, Frank 1929- *30*
Jacobs, Helen Hull 1908-1997 .... *12*
Jacobs, Joseph 1854-1916 .... *25*
Jacobs, Judy 1952- *69*
Jacobs, Laurie A. 1956- *89*
Jacobs, Leah
  See Gellis, Roberta
Jacobs, Leland Blair 1907-1992 .... *20*
  Obituary *71*
Jacobs, Linda
  See Altman, Linda Jacobs
Jacobs, Lou(is), Jr. 1921- *2*
Jacobs, Shannon K. 1947- *77*
Jacobs, Susan
  See Quinn, Susan
Jacobs, William Jay 1933- *89*
  Earlier sketch in SATA 28
Jacobsen, Laura *177*
Jacobson, Daniel 1923- *12*
Jacobson, Jennifer
  See Jacobson, Jennifer Richard
Jacobson, Jennifer Richard 1958- *170*
Jacobson, Morris K(arl) 1906- *21*
Jacobson, Rick *170*
Jacopetti, Alexandra
  See Hart, Alexandra
Jacques, Brian 1939- *176*
  Earlier sketches in SATA 62, 95, 138
  See also CLR 21
Jacques, Robin 1920-1995 .... *32*
  Brief entry *30*
  Obituary *86*
  See also SAAS 5
Jaekel, Susan M. 1948- *89*
Jaffe, Michele *179*
Jaffe, Michele Sharon
  See Jaffe, Michele
Jaffee, Al(lan) 1921- *66*
  Earlier sketch in SATA 37
Jagendorf, Moritz (Adolf) 1888-1981 .... *2*
  Obituary *24*
Jahn, Joseph Michael
  See Jahn, Michael
Jahn, Michael 1943- *28*
Jahn, Mike
  See Jahn, Michael
Jahn-Clough, Lisa 1967- *193*
  Earlier sketches in SATA 88, 152
Jahsmann, Allan Hart 1916- *28*
Jakes, John 1932- *62*
Jakes, John William
  See Jakes, John
James, Andrew
  See Kirkup, James
James, Ann 1952- *168*
  Earlier sketches in SATA 82, 117
James, Betsy *183*
James, Brian 1976- *140*
James, Bronte
  See Nash, Renea Denise
James, Captain Lew
  See Stratemeyer, Edward L.
James, Charlie 1961- *185*
James, Curtis E. *182*
James, Dynely
  See Mayne, William (James Carter)
James, Edwin
  See Gunn, James E.
James, Elizabeth 1942- *97*
  Earlier sketches in SATA 39, 45, 52
James, Emily
  See Standiford, Natalie
James, Gordon C. 1973- *195*
James, Harry Clebourne 1896-1978 .... *11*
James, J. Alison 1962- *146*
  Earlier sketch in SATA 83
James, Josephine
  See Sterne, Emma Gelders
James, Mary
  See Meaker, Marijane
James, Matt *201*

James, Philip
  See del Rey, Lester
  and Moorcock, Michael
James, Robin 1953- *50*
James, Robin Irene
  See James, Robin
James, Simon *202*
  See Kunen, James Simon
James, T. F.
  See Fleming, Thomas
James, Tegan
  See Odgers, Sally Farrell
James, Will(iam Roderick) 1892-1942 .... *19*
Jameson, W. C. 1942- *93*
Jamieson, Ian R.
  See Goulart, Ron
Jamiolkowski, Raymond M. 1953- *81*
Jane, Mary Childs 1909- *6*
Jane, Pamela *158*
Janeczko, Paul B(ryan) 1945- *155*
  Earlier sketches in SATA 53, 98
  See also CLR 47
  See also SAAS 18
Janes, Edward C. 1908-1984 .... *25*
Janes, J(oseph) Robert 1935- *148*
  Brief entry *50*
  Earlier sketch in SATA 101
Janeway, Elizabeth (Hall) 1913-2005 .... *19*
Janger, Kathleen N. 1940- *66*
Janice
  See Brustlein, Janice Tworkov
Janisch, Heinz 1960- *181*
Janosch
  See Eckert, Horst
Janover, Caroline (Davis) 1943- *141*
  Earlier sketch in SATA 89
Janovitz, Marilyn *194*
Jansen, Jared
  See Cebulash, Mel
Janson, Dora Jane (Heineberg) 1916- *31*
Janson, H(orst) W(oldemar) 1913-1982 .... *9*
Jansson, Tove (Marika) 1914-2001 .... *41*
  Earlier sketch in SATA 3
  See also CLR 125
Janus, Grete
  See Hertz, Grete Janus
Jaques, Faith 1923-1997 .... *97*
  Earlier sketches in SATA 21, 69
Jaquith, Priscilla 1908- *51*
Jaramillo, Mari-Luci 1928- *139*
Jarman, Julia 1946- *198*
  Earlier sketch in SATA 133
Jarman, Rosemary Hawley 1935- *7*
Jarrell, Mary Von Schrader 1914- *35*
Jarrell, Randall 1914-1965 .... *7*
  See also CLR 111
Jarrett, Clare 1952- *201*
Jarrett, Roxanne
  See Werner, Herma
Jarrow, Gail 1952- *185*
  Earlier sketch in SATA 84
Jarvis, E.K.
  See Ellison, Harlan
  and Silverberg, Robert
Jarvis, Robin 1963- *181*
Jaskol, Julie 1958- *127*
Jasner, W. K.
  See Watson, Jane Werner
Jassem, Kate
  See Oppenheim, Joanne
Jauss, Anne Marie 1902(?)-1991 .... *10*
  Obituary *69*
Javernick, Ellen 1938- *89*
Jay, Alison *196*
Jayne, Lieutenant R. H.
  See Ellis, Edward S.
Jaynes, Clare
  See Mayer, Jane Rothschild
Jeake, Samuel, Jr.
  See Aiken, Conrad
Jean-Bart, Leslie 1954- *121*

Jeapes, Ben 1965- *174*
Jecan, Gavriel 1962- *200*
Jefferds, Vincent H(arris) 1916- *59*
  Brief entry *49*
Jefferies, (John) Richard 1848-1887 .... *16*
Jeffers, Dawn *189*
Jeffers, Oliver 1977- *175*
Jeffers, Susan 1942- *202*
  Earlier sketches in SATA 17, 70, 129, 137
  See also CLR 30
Jefferson, Sarah
  See Farjeon, (Eve) Annabel
Jeffries, Roderic 1926- *4*
Jeffries, Roderic Graeme
  See Jeffries, Roderic
Jenkin-Pearce, Susie 1943- *80*
Jenkins, A.M. 1961- *174*
Jenkins, Amanda McRaney
  See Jenkins, A.M.
Jenkins, Debra Reid
  See Reid Jenkins, Debra
Jenkins, Emily 1967- *174*
  Earlier sketch in SATA 144
Jenkins, Jean *98*
Jenkins, Jerry B. 1949- *149*
Jenkins, Jerry Bruce
  See Jenkins, Jerry B.
Jenkins, Leonard *189*
Jenkins, Marie M(agdalen) 1909- *7*
Jenkins, Patrick 1955- *72*
Jenkins, Steve 1952- *188*
  Earlier sketch in SATA 154
Jenkins, William A(twell) 1922-1998 .... *9*
Jenkyns, Chris 1924- *51*
Jennings, Christopher S. 1971(?)- *201*
Jennings, Coleman A(lonzo) 1933- *64*
Jennings, C.S.
  See Jennings, Christopher S.
Jennings, Dana Andrew 1957- *93*
Jennings, Elizabeth (Joan) 1926-2001 .... *66*
Jennings, Gary 1928-1999 .... *9*
  Obituary *117*
Jennings, Gary Gayne
  See Jennings, Gary
Jennings, Patrick 1962- *205*
  Earlier sketches in SATA 96, 160
Jennings, Paul 1943- *165*
  Earlier sketch in SATA 88
  See also CLR 40
Jennings, Richard W. 1945- *185*
  Earlier sketch in SATA 136
Jennings, Robert
  See Hamilton, Charles (Harold St. John)
Jennings, S. M.
  See Meyer, Jerome Sydney
Jennings, Sharon 1954- *95*
Jennings, Sharon Elizabeth
  See Jennings, Sharon
Jennison, C. S.
  See Starbird, Kaye
Jennison, Keith Warren 1911-1995 .... *14*
Jensen, Kathryn 1949- *81*
Jensen, Kristine Mary 1961- *78*
Jensen, Niels 1927- *25*
Jensen, Vickie (Dee) 1946- *81*
Jensen, Virginia Allen 1927- *8*
Jenson-Elliott, Cynthia L(ouise) 1962- *143*
Jeram, Anita 1965- *154*
  Earlier sketches in SATA 71, 102
Jerman, Jerry 1949- *89*
Jernigan, E. Wesley 1940- *85*
Jernigan, Gisela (Evelyn) 1948- *85*
Jeschke, Susan 1942- *42*
  Brief entry *27*
Jessel, Camilla (Ruth) 1937- *143*
  Earlier sketch in SATA 29
Jessell, Tim *177*
Jessey, Cornelia
  See Sussman, Cornelia Silver
Jewel
  See Kilcher, Jewel

Jewell, Nancy 1940- *109*
  Brief entry *41*
Jewett, Eleanore Myers 1890-1967 .... *5*
Jewett, Sarah Orne 1849-1909 .... *15*
Jewett, Theodora Sarah Orne
  See Jewett, Sarah Orne
Jezard, Alison 1919- *57*
  Brief entry *34*
Jiang, Cheng An 1943- *109*
Jiang, Ji-li 1954- *101*
Jiang, Zheng An
  See Jiang, Cheng An
Jiler, John 1946- *42*
  Brief entry *35*
Jimenez, Francisco 1943- *108*
Jinks, Catherine 1963- *207*
  Earlier sketches in SATA *94, 155*
Jobb, Jamie 1945- *29*
Jobling, Curtis *131*
Jocelyn, Ann Henning 1948- *92*
Jocelyn, Marthe 1956- *198*
  Earlier sketches in SATA *118, 163*
Joerns, Consuelo *44*
  Brief entry *33*
Joey D
  See Macaulay, Teresa (E.)
Johansen, Krista V.
  See Johansen, K.V.
Johansen, K.V 1968- *186*
Johansen, K.V. 1968- *186*
  Earlier sketch in SATA *129*
Johansson, Philip *163*
John, Antony 1972- *206*
John, Joyce *59*
Johns, Avery
  See Cousins, Margaret
Johns, Elizabeth 1943- *88*
Johns, Janetta
  See Quin-Harkin, Janet
Johns, Linda 1945- *173*
Johns, W(illiam) E(arle) 1893-1968 .... *55*
Johns, Captain W. E.
  See Johns, W(illiam) E(arle)
Johnson, A.
  See Johnson, Annabell
Johnson, A. E.
  See Johnson, Annabell
  and Johnson, Edgar (Raymond)
Johnson, Angela 1961- *188*
  Earlier sketches in SATA *69, 102, 150*
  See also CLR *33*
Johnson, Annabel
  See Johnson, Annabell
Johnson, Annabell 1921- *72*
  Earlier sketch in SATA *2*
Johnson, Art 1946- *123*
Johnson, B. F. 1920- *1*
Johnson, Benjamin F., of Boone
  See Riley, James Whitcomb
Johnson, Bettye 1858-1919
  See Rogers, Bettye
Johnson, Caryn
  See Goldberg, Whoopi
Johnson, Caryn E.
  See Goldberg, Whoopi
Johnson, Caryn Elaine
  See Goldberg, Whoopi
Johnson, Charles R. 1925- *11*
Johnson, Charlotte Buel
  See von Wodtke, Charlotte Buel Johnson
Johnson, Chuck
  See Johnson, Charles R.
Johnson, Crockett
  See Leisk, David (Johnson)
Johnson, D(ana) William 1945- *23*
Johnson, Daniel Shahid 1954- *73*
Johnson, David
  See Johnson, David A.
Johnson, David A. 1951- *191*
Johnson, D.B. 1944- *183*
  Earlier sketch in SATA *146*

Johnson, Dianne 1960- *130*
Johnson, Dinah
  See Johnson, Dianne
Johnson, Dolores 1949- *69*
Johnson, Donald B.
  See Johnson, D.B.
Johnson, Dorothy M(arie) 1905-1984 .... *6*
  Obituary *40*
Johnson, E(ugene) Harper *44*
Johnson, Edgar (Raymond) 1912-1990 .... *72*
  Earlier sketch in SATA *2*
Johnson, Eleanor Murdock 1892-1987
  Obituary *54*
Johnson, Elizabeth 1911-1984 .... *7*
  Obituary *39*
Johnson, Eric W(arner) 1918-1994 ....
  Obituary *82*
  Earlier sketch in SATA *8*
Johnson, Evelyne 1922- *20*
Johnson, Fred 19(?)-1982 .... *63*
Johnson, Gaylord 1884-1972 .... *7*
Johnson, Gerald White 1890-1980 .... *19*
  Obituary *28*
Johnson, Harper
  See Johnson, E(ugene) Harper
Johnson, Harriett 1908-1987
  Obituary *53*
Johnson, James Ralph 1922- *1*
Johnson, James Weldon 1871-1938 .... *31*
  See also CLR *32*
Johnson, Jane 1951- *48*
Johnson, Joan J. 1942- *59*
Johnson, John E(mil) 1929- *34*
Johnson, Johnny 1901-1995
  See Johnson, (Walter) Ryerson
Johnson, Kathleen Jeffrie 1950- *186*
Johnson, La Verne B(ravo) 1925- *13*
Johnson, Layne *187*
Johnson, Lee Kaiser 1962- *78*
Johnson, Lissa H(alls) 1955- *65*
Johnson, Lois Smith 1894-1993 .... *6*
Johnson, Lois Walfrid 1936- *130*
  Earlier sketches in SATA *22, 91*
Johnson, Margaret S(weet) 1893-1964 .... *35*
Johnson, Marguerite Annie
  See Angelou, Maya
Johnson, Mary Frances K. 1929(?)-1979
  Obituary *27*
Johnson, Maud Battle 1918(?)-1985
  Obituary *46*
Johnson, Maureen 1973- *200*
Johnson, Meredith Merrell 1952- *104*
Johnson, Milton 1932- *31*
Johnson, Neil 1954- *135*
  Earlier sketch in SATA *73*
Johnson, Pamela 1949- *71*
Johnson, Patricia Polin 1956- *84*
Johnson, Paul Brett 1947- *132*
  Earlier sketch in SATA *83*
Johnson, Rebecca L. 1956- *147*
  Earlier sketch in SATA *67*
Johnson, Rick L. 1954- *79*
Johnson, (Walter) Ryerson 1901-1995 .... *10*
  Obituary *106*
Johnson, Scott 1952- *119*
  Earlier sketch in SATA *76*
Johnson, Sherrie 1948- *87*
Johnson, Shirley K(ing) 1927- *10*
Johnson, Siddie Joe 1905-1977
  Obituary *20*
Johnson, Spencer 1938- *145*
  Brief entry *38*
Johnson, Stacie
  See Myers, Walter Dean
Johnson, Stephen T. 1964- *189*
  Earlier sketches in SATA *84, 141*
Johnson, Steve 1960- *177*
Johnson, Sue Kaiser 1963- *78*
Johnson, Sylvia A. *166*
  Brief entry *52*
  Earlier sketch in SATA *104*

Johnson, William R. *38*
Johnson, William Weber 1909-1992 .... *7*
Johnson-Feelings, Dianne
  See Johnson, Dianne
Johnston, Agnes Christine
  See Dazey, Agnes J(ohnston)
Johnston, Annie Fellows 1863-1931 .... *37*
Johnston, Dorothy Grunbock 1915-1979 ...... *54*
Johnston, Ginny 1946- *60*
Johnston, H(ugh) A(nthony) S(tephen)
  1913-1967 .... *14*
Johnston, Janet 1944- *71*
Johnston, Jeffry W. *188*
Johnston, Johanna 1914(?)-1982 .... *12*
  Obituary *33*
Johnston, Julie 1941- *110*
  Autobiography Feature *128*
  Earlier sketch in SATA *78*
  See also CLR *41*
  See also SAAS *24*
Johnston, Lynn 1947- *118*
Johnston, Lynn Beverley
  See Johnston, Lynn
Johnston, Mark *194*
Johnston, Norma
  See St. John, Nicole
Johnston, Portia
  See Takakjian, Portia
Johnston, Susan Taylor 1942- *180*
  Earlier sketches in SATA *8, 83, 128*
Johnston, Tim(othy Patrick) 1962- *146*
Johnston, Tony
  See Johnston, Susan Taylor
Joinson, Carla *160*
Jolin, Paula *186*
Jonas, Ann 1932- *135*
  Brief entry *42*
  Earlier sketch in SATA *50*
  See also CLR *74*
Jonell, Lynne 1956- *196*
  Earlier sketch in SATA *109*
Jones, Adrienne 1915-2000 .... *82*
  Earlier sketch in SATA *7*
  See also SAAS *10*
Jones, Allan Frewin 1954- *204*
Jones, Annabel
  See Lewis, Mary
Jones, Betty Millsaps 1940- *54*
Jones, Carol 1942- *153*
  Earlier sketch in SATA *79*
Jones, Carrie 1971- *191*
Jones, Charles M. 1912-2002 .... *53*
  Obituary *133*
Jones, Charlotte Foltz 1945- *122*
  Earlier sketch in SATA *77*
Jones, Chuck
  See Jones, Charles M.
Jones, Constance *112*
Jones, Constance A.
  See Jones, Constance
Jones, David 1956- *202*
Jones, Diana Wynne 1934- *160*
  Earlier sketches in SATA *9, 70, 108*
  See also CLR *120*
  See also SAAS *7*
Jones, Douglas B. *202*
Jones, Douglas C(lyde) 1924-1998 .... *52*
Jones, Elizabeth McDavid *155*
Jones, Elizabeth Orton 1910-2005 .... *18*
  Obituary *164*
Jones, Evan 1915-1996 .... *3*
Jones, Frewin
  See Jones, Allan Frewin
Jones, Geraldine
  See McCaughrean, Geraldine
Jones, Gillingham
  See Hamilton, Charles (Harold St. John)
Jones, Gwyneth A(nn) 1952- *159*
Jones, Harold 1904-1992 .... *14*
  Obituary *72*
Jones, Helen Hinckley 1903-1991 .... *26*

Jones, Helen L(ouise) 1903-1973
  Obituary 22
Jones, Hettie 1934- 42
  Brief entry 27
Jones, Hortense P. 1918- 9
Jones, J. Sydney 1948- 101
Jones, Jasmine
  See Papademetriou, Lisa
Jones, Jennifer (Berry) 1947- 90
Jones, Jessie Mae Orton 1887(?)-1983
  Obituary 37
Jones, John R(obert) 1926- 76
Jones, Jon Sydney
  See Jones, J. Sydney
Jones, Kimberly K. 1957- 187
Jones, Marcia Thornton 1958- 115
  Earlier sketch in SATA 73
Jones, Martha T(annery) 1931- 130
Jones, Mary Alice 1898(?)-1980 6
Jones, McClure 34
Jones, Noah Z. 182
Jones, Patrick 1961- 136
Jones, Penelope 1938- 31
Jones, Rebecca C(astaldi) 1947- 99
  Earlier sketch in SATA 33
Jones, Robin D(orothy) 1959- 80
Jones, Sanford W.
  See Thorn, John
Jones, Sylvie 185
Jones, Sylvie Michelle
  See Jones, Sylvie
Jones, Terence Graham Parry 1942- 127
  Brief entry 51
  Earlier sketch in SATA 67
Jones, Terry
  See Jones, Terence Graham Parry
Jones, Tim Wynne
  See Wynne-Jones, Tim
Jones, Traci L. 186
Jones, V(ictoria) M(ary) 1958- 147
Jones, Veda Boyd 1948- 119
Jones, Volcano
  See Mitchell, Adrian
Jones, Weyman (B.) 1928- 4
  See also SAAS 11
Jones, William Glynne
  See Glynne-Jones, William
Jonk, Clarence 1906-1987 10
Jonsberg, Barry 1951- 168
Joos, Francoise 1956- 78
Joos, Frederic 1953- 78
Joosse, Barbara M. 1949- 164
  Earlier sketches in SATA 52, 96
Joosse, Barbara Monnot
  See Joosse, Barbara M.
Jordan, Alexis Hill
  See Glick, Ruth (Burtnick)
  and Titchener, Louise
Jordan, Anne Devereaux 1943- 80
Jordan, Chris
  See Philbrick, Rodman
Jordan, Deloris 191
Jordan, Don
  See Howard, Vernon (Linwood)
Jordan, Hope Dahle 1905-1995 15
Jordan, Jael (Michal) 1949- 30
Jordan, June 1936-2002 136
  Earlier sketch in SATA 4
  See also CLR 10
Jordan, June Meyer
  See Jordan, June
Jordan, Lee
  See Scholefield, Alan
Jordan, Martin George 1944- 84
Jordan, Robert 1948-2007 95
Jordan, Robert K.
  See Jordan, Robert
Jordan, Rosa 1939- 191
Jordan, Roslyn M. 189

Jordan, Sherryl 1949- 122
  Earlier sketch in SATA 71
  See also SAAS 23
Jordan, Shirley 1930- 154
Jordan, Tanis 1946- 84
Jorgensen, Ivar
  See Ellison, Harlan
  and Garrett, Randall
Jorgensen, Mary Venn -1995 36
Jorgensen, Norman 1954- 157
Jorgenson, Ivar
  See Silverberg, Robert
Jorisch, Stephane 178
Joseph, Anne
  See Coates, Anna
Joseph, James (Herz) 1924- 53
Joseph, Joan 1939- 34
Joseph, Joseph M(aron) 1903-1979 22
Joseph, Patrick
  See O'Malley, Kevin
Josephs, Rebecca
  See Talbot, Toby
Josephson, Judith Pinkerton 1943- 198
Josh
  See Twain, Mark
Joshua, Peter
  See Stone, Peter
Joslin, Mary 1953- 176
Joslin, Sesyle
  See Hine, Sesyle Joslin
Joubert, Beverly 1957- 204
Joubert, Dereck 204
Journet, Mireille
  See Marokvia, Mireille
Joyce, Bill
  See Joyce, William
Joyce, J(ames) Avery 1902-1987 11
  Obituary 50
Joyce, Peter 1937- 127
Joyce, William 1957- 118
  Brief entry 46
  Earlier sketch in SATA 72
  See also CLR 26
Joyner, Jerry 1938- 34
Juan, Ana 1961- 179
Jubert, Herve 185
Juby, Susan 1969- 202
  Earlier sketch in SATA 156
Jucker, Sita 1921- 5
Judah, Aaron 1923- 118
Judd, Cyril
  See Kornbluth, C(yril) M.
  and Merril, Judith
  and Pohl, Frederik
Judd, Denis (O'Nan) 1938- 33
Judd, Frances K.
  See Benson, Mildred
Jude, Conny 81
Judge, Lita 192
Judson, Clara Ingram 1879-1960 38
  Brief entry 27
Judy, Stephen
  See Tchudi, Stephen N.
Judy, Stephen N.
  See Tchudi, Stephen N.
Juhasz, Victor 1954- 177
Jukes, Mavis 1947- 111
  Brief entry 43
  Earlier sketch in SATA 72
  See also SAAS 12
Jules, Jacqueline 1956- 183
  Earlier sketch in SATA 148
Julesberg, Elizabeth Rider Montgomery
  1902-1985 34
  Obituary 41
  Earlier sketch in SATA 3
Julian, Jane
  See Wiseman, David
Jumpp, Hugo
  See MacPeek, Walter G.
Jungman, Ann 165

Jupo, Frank J. 1904-1981 7
Jurmain, Suzanne 1945- 169
  Earlier sketch in SATA 72
Jurmain, Suzanne Tripp
  See Jurmain, Suzanne
Juster, Norton 1929- 132
  Earlier sketch in SATA 3
  See also CLR 112
Justus, May 1898-1989 1
  Obituary 106
Juvenilia
  See Taylor, Ann

K

Kaaberbol, Lene
  See Kaaberbol, Lene
Kaaberbol, Lene 1960- 159
Kabdebo, Tamas
  See Kabdebo, Thomas
Kabdebo, Thomas 1934- 10
Kabibble, Osh
  See Jobb, Jamie
Kacer, Kathy 1954- 184
  Earlier sketch in SATA 142
Kaczman, James 156
Kadair, Deborah Ousley 184
Kadesch, Robert R(udstone) 1922- 31
Kadohata, Cynthia 1956(?)- 180
  Earlier sketch in SATA 155
  See also CLR 121
Kaempfert, Wade
  See del Rey, Lester
Kaestner, Erich 1899-1974 14
  See also CLR 4
Kahl, Jonathan (D.) 1959- 77
Kahl, M(arvin) P(hilip) 1934- 37
Kahl, Virginia (Caroline) 1919-2004 48
  Brief entry 38
  Obituary 158
Kahn, Joan 1914-1994 48
  Obituary 82
Kahn, Katherine Janus 1942- 167
  Earlier sketch in SATA 90
Kahn, Peggy
  See Katz, Bobbi
Kahn, Roger 1927- 37
Kahukiwa, Robyn 1940- 134
Kains, Josephine
  See Goulart, Ron
Kaizuki, Kiyonori 1950- 72
Kakimoto, Kozo 1915- 11
Kalashnikoff, Nicholas 1888-1961 16
Kalb, Jonah 1926- 23
Kalbacken, Joan 1925- 96
Kalechofsky, Roberta 1931- 92
Kaler, James Otis 1848-1912 15
Kalis, Jennifer 207
Kalish, Claire M. 1947- 92
Kallen, Stuart A(rnold) 1955- 126
  Earlier sketch in SATA 86
Kallevig, Christine Petrell 1955- 164
Kalman, Bobbie 1947- 63
Kalman, Maira 1949- 137
  Earlier sketch in SATA 96
  See also CLR 32
Kalnay, Francis 1899-1992 7
Kaloustian, Rosanne 1955- 93
Kalow, Gisela 1946- 32
Kalstein, Dave 175
Kamen, Gloria 1923- 98
  Earlier sketch in SATA 9
Kamerman, Sylvia E.
  See Burack, Sylvia K.
Kamm, Josephine (Hart) 1905-1989 24
Kammerman, Sylvia K.
  See Burack, Sylvia K.
Kandel, Michael 1941- 93
Kandell, Alice S. 1938- 35

Kane, Bob 1916-1998 .... *120*
Kane, Henry Bugbee 1902-1971 .... *14*
Kane, L. A.
  See Mannetti, Lisa
Kane, Robert W. 1910- *18*
Kane, Wilson
  See Bloch, Robert (Albert)
Kanefield, Teri 1960- *135*
Kaner, Etta 1947- *198*
  Earlier sketch in SATA *126*
Kanetzke, Howard W(illiam) 1932- *38*
Kangas, Juli 1958- *200*
Kann, Elizabeth *180*
Kann, Victoria *180*
Kanninen, Barbara *196*
Kanninen, Barbara J.
  See Kanninen, Barbara
Kanoza, Muriel Canfield
  See Canfield, Muriel
Kantner, Seth 1965- *179*
Kanzawa, Toshiko
  See Furukawa, Toshi
Kanzler, John 1963- *188*
Kaplan, Andrew 1960- *78*
Kaplan, Anne Bernays
  See Bernays, Anne
Kaplan, Bess 1927- *22*
Kaplan, Boche 1926- *24*
Kaplan, Elizabeth 1956- *83*
Kaplan, Elizabeth A.
  See Kaplan, Elizabeth
Kaplan, Irma 1900- *10*
Kaplan, Jean Caryl Korn 1926- *10*
Kaplow, Robert 1954- *70*
Karageorge, Michael
  See Anderson, Poul
Karas, G. Brian 1957- *178*
Karas, George Brian
  See Karas, G. Brian
Karasz, Ilonka 1896-1981
  Obituary *29*
Karen, Ruth 1922-1987 .... *9*
  Obituary *54*
Kark, Nina Mary
  See Bawden, Nina
Karl, Herb 1938- *73*
Karl, Jean E(dna) 1927-2000 .... *122*
  Earlier sketch in SATA *34*
  See also SAAS *10*
Karlin, Bernie 1927- *68*
Karlin, Eugene 1918- *10*
Karlin, Nurit *103*
  Earlier sketch in SATA *63*
Karnes, Frances A. 1937- *110*
Karp, Naomi J. 1926- *16*
Karpinski, J. Rick
  See Karpinski, John Eric
Karpinski, John Eric 1952- *81*
Karpinski, Rick
  See Karpinski, John Eric
Karr, Kathleen 1946- *127*
  Earlier sketch in SATA *82*
Karr, Phyllis Ann 1944- *119*
Karwoski, Gail 1949- *127*
Karwoski, Gail Langer
  See Karwoski, Gail
Kashiwagi, Isami 1925- *10*
Kaslik, Ibi
  See Kaslik, Ibolya Emma
Kaslik, Ibolya Emma 1973- *185*
Kassem, Lou 1931- *62*
  Brief entry *51*
Kastel, Warren
  See Silverberg, Robert
Kastner, Erich
  See Kaestner, Erich
Kastner, Jill (Marie) 1964- *117*
  Earlier sketch in SATA *70*
Kasuya, Masahiro 1937- *51*
Kasza, Keiko 1951- *191*
  Earlier sketch in SATA *124*

Kataphusin
  See Ruskin, John
Katchen, Carole 1944- *9*
Katcher, Brian 1975- *203*
Kathryn
  See Searle, Kathryn Adrienne
Kato, Aya 1982- *202*
Katona, Robert 1949- *21*
Katsarakis, Joan Harries
  See Harries, Joan
Katz, Alan *185*
Katz, Avi 1949- *199*
Katz, Avner 1939- *103*
Katz, Bobbi 1933- *179*
  Earlier sketch in SATA *12*
Katz, Fred(eric Phillip) 1938- *6*
Katz, Jane B(resler) 1934- *33*
Katz, Karen 1947- *195*
  Earlier sketch in SATA *158*
Katz, Marjorie P.
  See Weiser, Marjorie P(hillis) K(atz)
Katz, Susan 1945- *156*
Katz, Welwyn Wilton 1948- *96*
  Autobiography Feature *118*
  Earlier sketch in SATA *62*
  See also CLR *45*
Katz, William 1940- *98*
Katz, William Loren 1927- *13*
Kaufman, Bel *57*
Kaufman, Jeff 1955- *84*
Kaufman, Joe 1911-2001 .... *33*
Kaufman, Joseph
  See Kaufman, Joe
Kaufman, Mervyn D. 1932- *4*
Kaufmann, Angelika 1935- *15*
Kaufmann, John 1931- *18*
Kaula, Edna Mason 1906-1987 .... *13*
Kaur Khalsa, Dayal
  See Khalsa, Dayal Kaur
Kavaler, Lucy 1930- *23*
Kavanagh, Jack 1920- *85*
Kavanagh, P(atrick) J(oseph Gregory)
  1931- *122*
Kavanaugh, Ian
  See Webb, Jean Francis (III)
Kay, Alan N. 1965- *144*
Kay, Elizabeth 1949- *165*
Kay, Guy Gavriel 1954- *167*
  Earlier sketch in SATA *121*
Kay, Helen
  See Goldfrank, Helen Colodny
Kay, Jackie 1961- *165*
  Earlier sketch in SATA *97*
Kay, Jacqueline Margaret
  See Kay, Jackie
Kay, Julia *205*
Kay, Mara *13*
Kay, Verla 1946- *120*
Kaye, Danny 1913-1987
  Obituary *50*
Kaye, Geraldine (Hughesdon) 1925- *85*
  Earlier sketch in SATA *10*
Kaye, Judy
  See Baer, Judy
Kaye, Marilyn 1949- *110*
  Earlier sketch in SATA *56*
Kaye, Mary Margaret
  See Kaye, M.M.
Kaye, M.M. 1908-2004 .... *62*
  Obituary *152*
Kaye, Mollie
  See Kaye, M.M.
Kaye, Peggy 1948- *143*
Keach, James P. 1950- *125*
Keams, Geri 1951- *117*
Keane, Bil 1922- *4*
Keaney, Brian 1954- *188*
  Earlier sketch in SATA *106*
Kearney, Meg 1964- *178*
Kearny, Jillian
  See Goulart, Ron

Keating, Bern
  See Keating, Leo Bernard
Keating, Frank 1944- *143*
Keating, Lawrence A. 1903-1966 .... *23*
Keating, Leo Bernard 1915- *10*
Keats, Emma 1899(?)-1979(?) *68*
Keats, Ezra Jack 1916-1983 .... *57*
  Obituary *34*
  Earlier sketch in SATA *14*
  See also CLR *35*
Keefer, Catherine
  See Ogan, George F.
  and Ogan, Margaret E. (Nettles)
Keefer, Janice Kulyk
  See Kulyk Keefer, Janice
Keegan, Marcia 1943- *104*
  Earlier sketch in SATA *9*
Keehn, Sally M. 1947- *165*
  Earlier sketch in SATA *87*
Keel, Frank
  See Keeler, Ronald F(ranklin)
Keeler, Patricia *183*
Keeler, Patricia A.
  See Keeler, Patricia
Keeler, Ronald F(ranklin) 1913-1983 .... *47*
Keely, Jack 1951- *119*
Keen, Martin L. 1913-1992 .... *4*
Keenan, Sheila 1953- *95*
Keene, Ann T(odd) 1940- *86*
Keene, Carolyn
  See Benson, Mildred
  and Goulart, Ron
  and Lerangis, Peter
  and McFarlane, Leslie
  and Stanley, George Edward
  and Stratemeyer, Edward L.
Keens-Douglas, Richardo 1953- *154*
  Earlier sketch in SATA *95*
Keep, Linda Lowery
  See Lowery, Linda
Keep, Richard 1949- *170*
Keep, Richard Cleminson
  See Keep, Richard
Keeping, Charles (William James)
  1924-1988 .... *69*
  Obituary *56*
  Earlier sketch in SATA *9*
  See also CLR *34*
Keeshan, Robert J. 1927-2004 .... *32*
  Obituary *151*
Kehlenbeck, Angela 1959- *186*
Kehret, Peg 1936- *149*
  Autobiography Feature *149*
  Earlier sketches in SATA *73, 108*
Keillor, Garrison 1942- *58*
Keillor, Gary Edward
  See Keillor, Garrison
Keir, Christine
  See Pullein-Thompson, Christine
Keister, Douglas 1948- *88*
Keith, Doug 1952- *81*
Keith, Eros 1942- *52*
Keith, Hal 1934- *36*
Keith, Harold (Verne) 1903-1998 .... *74*
  Earlier sketch in SATA *2*
Keith, Robert
  See Applebaum, Stan
Keleinikov, Andrei 1924- *65*
Kelemen, Julie 1959- *78*
Kelen, Emery 1896-1978 .... *13*
  Obituary *26*
Kelleam, Joseph E(veridge) 1913-1975 .... *31*
Kelleher, Anne 1959- *97*
Kelleher, Annette 1950- *122*
Kelleher, Daria Valerian 1955- *79*
Kelleher, Victor (Michael Kitchener)
  1939- *129*
  Brief entry *52*
  Earlier sketch in SATA *75*
  See also CLR *36*

Keller, Beverly L(ou) 91
  Earlier sketch in SATA 13
Keller, Charles 1942- 82
  Earlier sketch in SATA 8
Keller, Debra 1958- 94
Keller, Dick 1923- 36
Keller, Emily 96
Keller, Gail Faithfull
  See Faithfull, Gail
Keller, Holly 1942- 157
  Brief entry 42
  Earlier sketches in SATA 76, 108
  See also CLR 45
Keller, Irene (Barron) 1927-2002 36
  Obituary 139
Keller, Laurie 1961(?)- 196
Kelley, Ellen A. 185
Kelley, Ellen Chavez
  See Kelley, Ellen A.
Kelley, Gary 1945- 183
Kelley, Leo P(atrick) 1928- 32
  Brief entry 31
Kelley, Patrick (G.) 1963- 129
Kelley, Patte 1947- 93
Kelley, True 1946- 179
Kelley, True (Adelaide) 1946- 130
  Brief entry 39
  Earlier sketches in SATA 41, 92
Kelley, True Adelaide
  See Kelley, True
Kellin, Sally Moffet 1932- 9
Kelling, Furn L. 1914-2000 37
Kellogg, Gene
  See Kellogg, Jean (Defrees)
Kellogg, Jean (Defrees) 1916-1978 10
Kellogg, Steven 1941- 177
  Earlier sketches in SATA 8, 57, 130
  See also CLR 6
Kellogg, Steven Castle
  See Kellogg, Steven
Kellow, Kathleen
  See Hibbert, Eleanor Alice Burford
Kelly, C. M. O.
  See Gibbs, (Cecilia) May
Kelly, Clint 1950- 140
Kelly, Eric P(hilbrook) 1884-1960
  See YABC 1
Kelly, Fiona
  See Coleman, Michael
  and Hendry, Frances Mary
  and Oldfield, Jenny
  and Welford, Sue
Kelly, Fiona
  See Jones, Allan Frewin
Kelly, Irene 1957- 147
Kelly, Jeff
  See Kelly, Jeffrey
Kelly, Jeffrey 1946- 65
Kelly, Joanne (W.) 1934- 87
Kelly, Kate 1958- 91
Kelly, Kathleen M. 1964- 71
Kelly, Katy 1955- 169
Kelly, Lauren
  See Oates, Joyce Carol
Kelly, Laurene 1954- 123
Kelly, Martha Rose 1914-1983 37
Kelly, Marty
  See Kelly, Martha Rose
Kelly, Mij 166
Kelly, Ralph
  See Geis, Darlene Stern
Kelly, Regina Z(immerman) 1898-1986 5
Kelly, Rosalie (Ruth) 43
Kelly, Tom 1961- 191
Kelly, Walt(er Crawford) 1913-1973 18
Kelsey, Alice Geer 1896-1982 1
Kelsey, Elin 1961- 159
Kemly, Kathleen 1958- 197
Kemnitz, Thomas Milton, Jr. 1984- 152
Kemnitz, Tom, Jr.
  See Kemnitz, Thomas Milton, Jr.

Kemp, Gene 1926- 75
  Earlier sketch in SATA 25
  See also CLR 29
Kempner, Mary Jean 1913-1969 10
Kempter, Christa 1945- 187
Kempton, Jean Welch 1914- 10
Kenah, Katharine 1949- 182
Kenda, Margaret 1942- 71
Kendall, Carol (Seeger) 1917- 74
  Earlier sketch in SATA 11
  See also SAAS 7
Kendall, Katherine
  See Applegate, Katherine
Kendall, Lace
  See Stoutenburg, Adrien (Pearl)
Kendall, Martha E. 87
Kendall, Russ 1957- 83
Kenealy, James P. 1927- 52
  Brief entry 29
Kenealy, Jim
  See Kenealy, James P.
Kennaway, Adrienne 1945- 171
  Earlier sketch in SATA 60
Kennedy, Anne 1955- 198
Kennedy, Anne Vittur
  See Kennedy, Anne
Kennedy, Brendan 1970- 57
Kennedy, Dana Forrest 1917- 74
Kennedy, Dorothy M(intzlaff) 1931- 53
Kennedy, Doug 1963- 189
  Earlier sketch in SATA 122
Kennedy, Frances 1937- 192
Kennedy, John F. 1917-1963 11
Kennedy, John Fitzgerald
  See Kennedy, John F.
Kennedy, Joseph Charles 1929- 130
  Autobiography Feature 130
  Earlier sketches in SATA 14, 86
  See also CLR 27
  See also SAAS 22
  See Kennedy, X. J.
Kennedy, Kim 189
Kennedy, Pamela (J.) 1946- 87
Kennedy, Paul E(dward) 1929- 113
  Earlier sketch in SATA 33
Kennedy, Richard (Pitt) 1910-1989
  Obituary 60
Kennedy, (Jerome) Richard 1932- 22
Kennedy, Robert 1938- 63
Kennedy, T.A. 1953- 42
  Brief entry 35
Kennedy, Teresa
  See Kennedy, T.A.
Kennedy, Teresa A.
  See Kennedy, T.A.
Kennedy, William 1928- 57
Kennedy, William Joseph
  See Kennedy, William
Kennedy, X. J.
  See CLR 27
  See also SAAS 22
  See Kennedy, Joseph Charles
Kennell, Ruth Epperson 1893-1977 6
  Obituary 25
Kennemore, Tim 1957- 133
Kennen, Ally 190
Kennett, David 1959- 206
  Earlier sketch in SATA 121
Kennison, Ruth 202
Kenny, Ellsworth Newcomb 1909-1971
  Obituary 26
Kenny, Herbert Andrew 1912-2002 13
Kenny, Jude
  See Daly, Jude
Kenny, Kathryn
  See Bowden, Joan Chase
  and Krull, Kathleen
  and Sanderlin, Owenita (Harrah)
  and Stack, Nicolete Meredith
Kenny, Kevin
  See Krull, Kathleen

Kensinger, George
  See Fichter, George S.
Kensington, Kathryn Wesley
  See Rusch, Kristine Kathryn
Kent, Alexander
  See Reeman, Douglas Edward
Kent, David
  See Lambert, David
Kent, Deborah Ann 1948- 155
  Brief entry 41
  Earlier sketches in SATA 47, 104
Kent, Jack
  See Kent, John Wellington
Kent, John Wellington 1920-1985 24
  Obituary 45
Kent, Lisa 1942- 90
Kent, Mallory
  See Lowndes, Robert A(ugustine) W(ard)
Kent, Margaret 1894- 2
Kent, Rockwell 1882-1971 6
Kent, Rose 188
Kent, Sherman 1903-1986 20
  Obituary 47
Kenward, Jean 1920- 42
Kenworthy, Leonard S. 1912-1991 6
Kenyon, Karen (Smith) 1938- 145
Kenyon, Kate
  See Adorjan, Carol (Madden)
  and Ransom, Candice F.
Kenyon, Ley 1913-1990 6
Keown, Elizabeth 78
Kepes, Juliet A(ppleby) 1919-1999 13
Kephart, Beth 1960- 196
Kerby, Mona 1951- 202
  Earlier sketch in SATA 75
Kerigan, Florence 1896-1984 12
Kerley, Barbara 1960- 191
  Earlier sketch in SATA 138
Kerman, Gertrude
  See Furman, Gertrude Lerner Kerman
Kerns, Thelma 1929- 116
Kerr, Anne Louise
  See Mackey, Weezie Kerr
Kerr, Bob 1951- 120
Kerr, Jessica 1901-1991 13
Kerr, (Anne-)Judith 1923-1970 24
Kerr, M. E.
  See Meaker, Marijane
Kerr, P.B.
  See Kerr, Philip
Kerr, Philip 1956- 168
Kerr, Phyllis Forbes 1942- 72
Kerr, Tom 1950- 77
Kerrin, Jessica Scott 174
Kerry, Frances
  See Kerigan, Florence
Kerry, Lois
  See Duncan, Lois
Kershen, (L.) Michael 1982- 82
Kerven, Rosalind 1954- 83
Ker Wilson, Barbara 1929- 121
  Earlier sketches in SATA 20, 70
  See also SAAS 18
Keselman, Gabriela 1953- 128
Kesey, Ken 1935-2001 66
  Obituary 131
Kesey, Ken Elton
  See Kesey, Ken
Kesler, Jay 1935- 65
Kessel, Joyce Karen 1937- 41
Kessler, Cristina 190
Kessler, Ethel 1922- 44
  Brief entry 37
Kessler, Leonard P. 1921- 14
Kessler, Liz 1966- 206
Kest, Kristin 1967- 168
  Earlier sketch in SATA 118
Kesteven, G. R.
  See Crosher, G. R.
Ketcham, Hank
  See Ketcham, Henry King

Ketcham, Henry King 1920-2001 .... *28*
　Brief entry *27*
　Obituary *128*
Ketcham, Sallie 1963- *124*
Ketchum, Liza 1946-
　See Murrow, Liza Ketchum
Ketner, Mary Grace 1946- *75*
Kettelkamp, Larry (Dale) 1933- *2*
　See also SAAS *3*
Ketteman, Helen 1945- *167*
　Earlier sketches in SATA *73, 115*
Kettle, Peter
　See Glover, Denis (James Matthews)
Kevles, Bettyann Holtzmann 1938- *23*
Key, Alexander (Hill) 1904-1979 .... *8*
　Obituary *23*
Key, Samuel M.
　See de Lint, Charles
Key, Watt 1970- *189*
Keyes, Daniel 1927- *37*
Keyes, Diane *207*
Keyes, Fenton 1915-1999 .... *34*
Keyes, Greg 1963- *116*
Keyes, J. Gregory
　See Keyes, Greg
Keyser, Marcia 1933- *42*
Keyser, Sarah
　See McGuire, Leslie (Sarah)
Khalid, Mohamed Nor
　See Lat
Khalsa, Dayal Kaur 1943-1989 .... *62*
　See also CLR *30*
Khan, Rukhsana 1962- *165*
　Earlier sketch in SATA *118*
Khanshendel, Chiron
　See Rose, Wendy
Kheirabadi, Masoud 1951- *158*
Khemir, Sabiha *87*
Kherdian, David 1931- *74*
　Autobiography Feature *125*
　Earlier sketch in SATA *16*
　See also CLR *24*
Khing, T.T. 1933- *192*
Kibbe, Pat (Hosley) *60*
Kidd, Diana 1933-2000 .... *150*
Kidd, Richard 1952-2008 .... *152*
　Obituary *194*
Kidd, Ronald 1948- *173*
　Earlier sketches in SATA *42, 92*
Kiddell, John 1922- *3*
Kiddell-Monroe, Joan 1908-1972 .... *55*
Kidwell, Carl 1910- *43*
Kiefer, Irene 1926- *21*
Kiefer, Kathleen Balmes 1957- *142*
Kiepper, Shirley Morgan 1933- *10*
Kierstead, Vera M.
　See Kierstead-Farber, Vera M.
Kierstead-Farber, Vera M. 1913- *121*
Kierstead-Farber, Vera May
　See Kierstead-Farber, Vera M.
Kiesel, Stanley 1925- *35*
Kiesler, Kate (A.) 1971- *152*
　Earlier sketch in SATA *90*
Kihn, Greg 1952- *110*
Kikukawa, Cecily H(arder) 1919- *44*
　Brief entry *35*
Kilcher, Jewel 1974- *109*
Kile, Joan 1940- *78*
Kilgore, Kathleen 1946- *42*
Kilian, Crawford 1941- *35*
Killdeer, John
　See Mayhar, Ardath
Killien, Christi 1956- *73*
Killilea, Marie (Lyons) 1913-1991 .... *2*
Killingback, Julia 1944- *63*
Killough, (Karen) Lee 1942- *64*
Kilpatrick, Don *206*
Kilreon, Beth
　See Walker, Barbara (Jeanne) K(erlin)
Kilworth, Garry 1941- *94*

Kilworth, Garry D.
　See Kilworth, Garry
Kilworth, Garry Douglas
　See Kilworth, Garry
Kim, David 1977- *201*
Kim, Helen 1899-1970 .... *98*
Kim, Joung Un 1970- *205*
Kimball, Gayle 1943- *90*
Kimball, Violet T(ew) 1932- *126*
Kimball, Yeffe 1914-1978 .... *37*
Kimber, Murray 1964- *171*
Kimble, Warren *176*
Kimbrough, Emily 1899-1989 .... *2*
　Obituary *59*
Kimeldorf, Martin 1948- *121*
Kimeldorf, Martin R.
　See Kimeldorf, Martin
Kimenye, Barbara 1940(?)- *121*
Kimmel, Elizabeth Cody *170*
Kimmel, Eric A. 1946- *176*
　Earlier sketches in SATA *13, 80, 125*
Kimmel, Margaret Mary 1938- *43*
　Brief entry *33*
Kimmelman, Burt 1947- *180*
Kimmelman, Leslie (Grodinsky) 1958- *156*
　Earlier sketch in SATA *85*
Kincaid, Jamaica 1949-
　See CLR *63*
Kincher, Jonni 1949- *79*
Kindl, Patrice 1951- *128*
　Earlier sketch in SATA *82*
　See also CLR *132*
Kindred, Wendy (Good) 1937- *7*
Kinerk, Robert *199*
Kines, Pat Decker 1937- *12*
King, Adam
　See Hoare, Robert J(ohn)
King, Alison
　See Martini, Teri
King, (Maria) Anna 1964- *72*
King, Billie Jean 1943- *12*
King, Christopher (L.) 1945- *84*
King, (David) Clive 1924- *144*
　Earlier sketch in SATA *28*
King, Colin 1943- *76*
King, Cynthia 1925- *7*
King, Daniel (John) 1963- *130*
King, Daren 1972- *197*
King, Elizabeth 1953- *83*
King, Frank O. 1883-1969
　Obituary *22*
King, Frank R. 1904-1999 .... *127*
King, Jane
　See Currie, Stephen
King, Jeanette (Margaret) 1959- *105*
King, Larry L. 1929- *66*
King, Laurie R. 1952- *88*
King, Marian 1900(?)-1986 .... *23*
　Obituary *47*
King, Martin Luther, Jr. 1929-1968 .... *14*
King, Mary Ellen 1958- *93*
King, Paul
　See Drackett, Phil(ip Arthur)
King, Paula
　See Downing, Paula E.
King, Stephen 1947- *161*
　Earlier sketches in SATA *9, 55*
　See also CLR *124*
King, Stephen Edwin
　See King, Stephen
King, Stephen Michael *157*
King, Steve
　See King, Stephen
King, Thomas 1943- *96*
King, Thomas Hunt
　See King, Thomas
King, Tony 1947- *39*
King, Willie Christine
　See Farris, Christine King
Kingman, Dong (Moy Shu) 1911-2000 .... *44*

Kingman, Lee
　See Natti, Lee
Kingsland, Leslie William 1912- *13*
Kingsley, Charles 1819-1875
　See YABC *2*
　See also CLR *77*
Kingsley, Emily Perl 1940- *33*
Kingsley, Kaza *193*
King-Smith, Dick 1922- *192*
　Brief entry *38*
　Earlier sketches in SATA *47, 80, 135*
　See also CLR *40*
Kingston, Maxine Hong 1940- *53*
Kingston, Maxine Ting Ting Hong
　See Kingston, Maxine Hong
Kinney, C. Cle(land) 1915- *6*
Kinney, Harrison 1921- *13*
Kinney, Jean Stout 1912- *12*
Kinney, Jeff 1971- *187*
Kinsey, Elizabeth
　See Clymer, Eleanor
Kinsey, Helen 1948- *82*
Kinsey-Warnock, Natalie 1956- *167*
　Earlier sketch in SATA *71, 116*
Kinzel, Dorothy 1950- *57*
Kinzel, Dottie
　See Kinzel, Dorothy
Kipling, Joseph Rudyard
　See Kipling, Rudyard
Kipling, Rudyard 1865-1936 .... *100*
　See also YABC *2*
　See also CLR *65*
Kippax, Frank
　See Needle, Jan
Kirby, David K. 1944- *78*
Kirby, David Kirk
　See Kirby, David K.
Kirby, Margaret
　See Bingley, Margaret (Jane Kirby)
Kirby, Susan E. 1949- *62*
Kirk, Connie Ann 1957- *167*
Kirk, Daniel 1952- *196*
　Earlier sketches in SATA *107, 153*
Kirk, David 1955- *161*
　Earlier sketch in SATA *117*
Kirk, Heather 1949- *166*
Kirk, Ruth (Kratz) 1925- *5*
Kirkham, Dinah
　See Card, Orson Scott
Kirkland, Will
　See Hale, Arlene
Kirkpatrick, Katherine (Anne) 1964- *113*
Kirkup, James 1918-2009 .... *12*
Kirkus, Virginia
　See Glick, Virginia Kirkus
Kirkwood, Kathryn
　See Fluke, Joanne
Kirshenbaum, Binnie *79*
Kirshner, David S. 1958- *123*
Kirtland, G. B.
　See Hine, Sesyle Joslin
　and Hine, Al(fred Blakelee)
Kirwan, Wednesday *198*
Kish, Eleanor M(ary) 1924- *73*
Kish, Ely
　See Kish, Eleanor M(ary)
Kishida, Eriko 1929- *12*
Kisinger, Grace Gelvin (Maze) 1913-1965 .. *10*
Kissin, Eva H. 1923- *10*
Kissinger, Rosemary K.
　See Updyke, Rosemary K.
Kistler, John M. 1967- *160*
Kitamura, Satoshi 1956- *201*
　Earlier sketches in SATA *62, 98, 143*
　See also CLR *60*
Kitchen, Bert
　See Kitchen, Herbert Thomas
Kitchen, Herbert Thomas 1940- *70*
Kite, L. Patricia
　See Kite, Pat
Kite, Pat 1940- *78*

Kitt, Tamara
  See de Regniers, Beatrice Schenk (Freedman)
Kittinger, Jo S(usenbach) 1955- *148*
  Earlier sketch in SATA *96*
Kituomba
  See Odaga, Asenath (Bole)
Kitzinger, Sheila 1929- *57*
Kiwak, Barbara 1966- *103*
Kjelgaard, James Arthur 1910-1959 .... *17*
  See also CLR *81*
  See Kjelgaard, Jim
Kjelgaard, Jim
  See Kjelgaard, James Arthur
Kjelle, Marylou Morano 1954- *146*
Klages, Ellen 1954- *196*
Klagsbrun, Francine (Lifton) *36*
Klaits, Barrie 1944- *52*
Klam, Cheryl *191*
Klaperman, Gilbert 1921- *33*
Klaperman, Libby Mindlin 1921-1982 .... *33*
  Obituary *31*
Klass, David 1960- *207*
  Earlier sketches in SATA *88, 142*
Klass, Morton 1927-2001 .... *11*
Klass, Sheila Solomon 1927- *99*
  Autobiography Feature *126*
  Earlier sketch in SATA *45*
  See also SAAS *26*
Klause, Annette Curtis 1953- *175*
  Earlier sketch in SATA *79*
  See also CLR *104*
Klaveness, Jan O'Donnell 1939- *86*
Kleberger, Ilse 1921- *5*
Kleeberg, Irene (Flitner) Cumming 1932- *65*
Klein, Aaron E. 1930-1998 .... *45*
  Brief entry *28*
Klein, Bill 1945- *89*
Klein, David 1919-2001 .... *59*
Klein, Frederick C. 1938- *154*
Klein, Gerda Weissmann 1924- *44*
Klein, H(erbert) Arthur *8*
Klein, James 1932- *115*
Klein, Leonore (Glotzer) 1916- *6*
Klein, Mina C(ooper) 1906-1979 .... *8*
Klein, Norma 1938-1989 .... *57*
  Earlier sketch in SATA *7*
  See also CLR *19*
  See also SAAS *1*
Klein, Rachel S. 1953- *105*
Klein, Robin 1936- *164*
  Brief entry *45*
  Earlier sketches in SATA *55, 80*
  See also CLR *21*
Klemin, Diana *65*
Klemm, Barry 1945- *104*
Klemm, Edward G., Jr. 1910-2001 .... *30*
Klemm, Roberta K(ohnhorst) 1884-1975 .... *30*
Kleven, Elisa 1958- *173*
  Earlier sketch in SATA *76*
  See also CLR *85*
Klevin, Jill Ross 1935- *39*
  Brief entry *38*
Kliban, B(ernard) 1935-1990 .... *35*
  Obituary *66*
Klimowicz, Barbara 1927- *10*
Kline, Christina Baker 1964- *101*
Kline, James
  See Klein, James
Kline, Jim
  See Kline, Jim
Kline, Lisa Williams 1954- *143*
Kline, Suzy 1943- *193*
  Autobiography Feature *193*
  Brief entry *48*
  Earlier sketches in SATA *67, 99, 152*
Kliros, Thea 1935- *106*
Klise, Kate *181*
Klise, M. Sarah 1961- *180*
  Earlier sketch in SATA *128*
Klots, Alexander Barrett 1903-1989
  Obituary *62*

Klug, Ron(ald) 1939- *31*
Knaak, Richard A. 1961- *166*
  Earlier sketch in SATA *86*
Knaak, Richard Allen
  See Knaak, Richard A.
Knapman, Timothy *200*
Knapp, Edward
  See Kunhardt, Edith
Knapp, Ron 1952- *34*
Knebel, Fletcher 1911-1993 .... *36*
  Obituary *75*
Kneeland, Linda Clarke 1947- *94*
Knickerbocker, Diedrich
  See Irving, Washington
Knifesmith
  See Cutler, Ivor
Knigge, Robert (R.) 1921(?)-1987 .... *50*
Knight, Anne (Katherine) 1946- *34*
Knight, Brenda *112*
Knight, Christopher G. 1943- *96*
Knight, Damon (Francis) 1922-2002 .... *9*
  Obituary *139*
Knight, David C(arpenter) 1925-1984 .... *14*
  See also CLR *38*
Knight, Eric 1897-1943 .... *18*
Knight, Eric Mowbray
  See Knight, Eric
Knight, Francis Edgar 1905- *14*
Knight, Frank
  See Knight, Francis Edgar
Knight, Hilary 1926- *132*
  Earlier sketches in SATA *15, 69*
Knight, Joan (MacPhail) *159*
  Earlier sketch in SATA *82*
Knight, Joan
  See Knight, Joan (MacPhail)
Knight, Kathryn Lasky
  See Lasky, Kathryn
Knight, Mallory T.
  See Hurwood, Bernhardt J.
Knight, Ruth Adams 1898-1974
  Obituary *20*
Knight, Theodore O. 1946- *77*
Knobloch, Dorothea 1951- *88*
Knoepfle, John (Ignatius) 1923- *66*
Knorr, Laura 1971- *200*
Knott, Bill
  See Knott, William C(ecil, Jr.)
Knott, William C(ecil, Jr.) 1927- *3*
Knotts, Howard (Clayton, Jr.) 1922- *25*
Knowles, Anne 1933- *37*
Knowles, Jo 1970- *197*
Knowles, Johanna Beth
  See Knowles, Jo
Knowles, John 1926-2001 .... *89*
  Obituary *134*
  Earlier sketch in SATA *8*
  See also CLR *98*
Knox, Calvin M.
  See Silverberg, Robert
Knox, (Mary) Eleanor Jessie 1909-2000 ...... *59*
  Earlier sketch in SATA *30*
Knox, Elizabeth 1959- *176*
Knox, Elizabeth Fiona
  See Knox, Elizabeth
Knox, James
  See Brittain, William
Knox, Jolyne 1937- *76*
Knudsen, James 1950- *42*
Knudsen, Michelle *171*
Knudson, R. R.
  See Knudson, Rozanne
Knudson, Richard L(ewis) 1930- *34*
Knudson, Rozanne 1932-2008 .... *79*
  Earlier sketch in SATA *7*
  See also SAAS *18*
Knutson, Barbara 1959-2005 .... *166*
Knutson, Kimberley *115*
Knye, Cassandra
  See Disch, Thomas M.
Kobayashi, Masako Matsuno 1935- *6*

Koch, Dorothy Clarke 1924- *6*
Koch, Kenneth 1925-2002 .... *65*
Koch, Kenneth Jay
  See Koch, Kenneth
Koch, Phyllis (Mae) McCallum 1911- *10*
Kochalka, James 1967- *196*
Kocsis, J. C.
  See Paul, James
Koda-Callan, Elizabeth 1944- *140*
  Earlier sketch in SATA *67*
Kodman, Stanislawa *201*
Koehler, Phoebe 1955- *85*
Koehler-Pentacoff, Elizabeth 1957- *160*
  Earlier sketch in SATA *96*
Koehn, Ilse
  See Van Zwienen, Ilse Charlotte Koehn
Koeller, Carol *192*
Koenig, Viviane 1950- *80*
Koering, Ursula 1921-1976 .... *64*
Koerner, W(illiam) H(enry) D(avid)
  1878-1938 .... *21*
Koertge, Ronald 1940- *131*
  Earlier sketches in SATA *53, 92*
Koestler-Grack, Rachel A. 1973- *156*
Koff, Richard Myram 1926- *62*
Koffinke, Carol 1949- *82*
Kogan, Deborah
  See Kogan Ray, Deborah
Kogan Ray, Deborah 1940- *203*
  Earlier sketches in SATA *8, 50, 161*
Kogawa, Joy 1935- *99*
Kogawa, Joy Nozomi
  See Kogawa, Joy
Kogler, Jennifer Anne 1982(?)- *174*
Kohara, Kazuno *207*
Kohl, Herbert 1937- *47*
Kohl, Herbert R.
  See Kohl, Herbert
Kohl, MaryAnn F(aubion) 1947- *144*
  Earlier sketch in SATA *74*
Kohler, Julilly H(ouse) 1908-1976
  Obituary *20*
Kohn, Bernice
  See Hunt, Bernice
Kohn, Rita (T.) 1933- *89*
Kohner, Frederick 1905-1986 .... *10*
  Obituary *48*
Koide, Tan 1938-1986 .... *50*
Koike, Kay 1940- *72*
Koja, Kathe 1960- *199*
  Earlier sketch in SATA *155*
Koja, Stephan *198*
Kolar, Bob 1960(?)- *206*
Kolb, Larry J. 1953- *175*
Kolba, St. Tamara *22*
Kolibalova, Marketa
  See Kolibalova, Marketa
Kolibalova, Marketa 1953- *126*
Koller, Jackie French 1948- *157*
  Earlier sketches in SATA *72, 109*
  See also CLR *68*
Kolodny, Nancy J. 1946- *76*
Kolosov, Jacqueline 1967- *199*
Komaiko, Leah 1954- *164*
  Earlier sketch in SATA *97*
Komisar, Lucy 1942- *9*
Komoda, Beverly 1939- *25*
Komoda, Kiyo 1937- *9*
Kompaneyets, Marc 1974- *169*
Komroff, Manuel 1890-1974 .... *2*
  Obituary *20*
Konigsberg, Bill 1970- *207*
Konigsburg, E.L. 1930- *194*
  Earlier sketches in SATA *4, 48, 94, 126*
  See also CLR *81*
Konigsburg, Elaine Lobl
  See Konigsburg, E.L.
Koning, Hans 1921-2007 .... *5*
  Obituary *182*
Koningsberger, Hans
  See Koning, Hans

Konkle, Janet Everest 1917- *12*
Kono, Erin Eitter 1973- *177*
Konzak, Burt 1946- *151*
Koob, Theodora (J. Foth) 1918- *23*
Kooiker, Leonie
    See Kooyker-Romijn, Johanna Maria
Koons, James
    See Pernu, Dennis
Koontz, Dean 1945- *165*
    Earlier sketch in SATA *92*
Koontz, Dean R.
    See Koontz, Dean
Koontz, Dean Ray
    See Koontz, Dean
Koontz, Robin Michal 1954- *136*
    Earlier sketch in SATA *70*
Kooyker, Leonie
    See Kooyker-Romijn, Johanna Maria
Kooyker-Romijn, Johanna Maria 1927- *48*
Kooyker-Romyn, Johanna Maria
    See Kooyker-Romijn, Johanna Maria
Kopelke, Lisa 1963- *154*
Kopper, Lisa (Esther) 1950- *105*
    Brief entry *51*
Koppes, Steven N. 1957- *169*
Koppes, Steven Nelson
    See Koppes, Steven N.
Korach, Mimi 1922- *9*
Koralek, Jenny 1934- *140*
    Earlier sketch in SATA *71*
Korczak, Janusz
    See Goldszmit, Henryk
Koren, Edward (Benjamin) 1935- *148*
    Earlier sketch in SATA *5*
Koren, Edward 1935- *206*
Korinets, Iurii Iosifovich
    See Korinetz, Yuri (Iosifovich)
Korinetz, Yuri (Iosifovich) 1923- *9*
    See also CLR *4*
Korman, Bernice 1937- *78*
Korman, Gordon 1963- *167*
    Brief entry *41*
    Earlier sketches in SATA *49, 81, 119*
    See also CLR *25*
Korman, Gordon Richard
    See Korman, Gordon
Korman, Justine 1958- *70*
Kornblatt, Marc 1954- *147*
    Earlier sketch in SATA *84*
Kornprobst, Jacques 1937- *177*
Korte, Gene J. 1950- *74*
Korthues, Barbara 1971- *203*
Korty, Carol 1937- *15*
Koscielniak, Bruce 1947- *153*
    Earlier sketches in SATA *67, 99*
Koshin, Alexander (A.) 1952- *86*
Kositsky, Lynne 1947- *158*
Koskenmaki, Rosalie
    See Maggio, Rosalie
Koss, Amy Goldman 1954- *158*
    Earlier sketch in SATA *115*
Kossin, Sandy (Sanford) 1926- *10*
Kossman, Nina 1959- *84*
Kostecki-Shaw, Jenny Sue *203*
Kostick, Conor 1964- *186*
Kotzwinkle, William 1938- *146*
    Earlier sketches in SATA *24, 70*
    See also CLR *6*
Kouhi, Elizabeth 1917- *54*
    Brief entry *49*
Kouts, Anne 1945- *8*
Koutsky, Jan Dale 1955- *146*
Kovacs, Deborah 1954- *132*
    Earlier sketch in SATA *79*
Kovalski, Maryann 1951- *175*
    Earlier sketches in SATA *58, 97*
    See also CLR *34*
    See also SAAS *21*
Kowalski, Kathiann M. 1955- *151*
    Earlier sketch in SATA *96*
Kraft, Betsy Harvey 1937- *157*

Kraft, Erik P. *193*
Krahn, Fernando 1935- *49*
    Brief entry *31*
    See also CLR *3*
Krakauer, Hoong Yee Lee 1955- *86*
Krakauer, Jon 1954- *108*
Kramer, George
    See Heuman, William
Kramer, Nora 1896(?)-1984 .... *26*
    Obituary *39*
Kramer, Remi (Thomas) 1935- *90*
Krantz, Hazel (Newman) *12*
Kranzler, George G(ershon) 1916- *28*
Kranzler, Gershon
    See Kranzler, George G(ershon)
Krasilovsky, Phyllis 1926- *38*
    Earlier sketch in SATA *1*
    See also CLR *83*
    See also SAAS *5*
Krasne, Betty
    See Levine, Betty K(rasne)
Krasner, Steven 1953- *154*
Krasno, Rena 1923- *104*
Kratman, Tom *175*
Kraus, Joanna Halpert 1937- *87*
Kraus, (Herman) Robert 1925-2001 .... *93*
    Obituary *130*
    Earlier sketches in SATA *4, 65*
    See also SAAS *11*
Krauss, Ruth (Ida) 1911-1993 .... *30*
    Obituary *75*
    Earlier sketch in SATA *1*
    See also CLR *42*
Krautter, Elisa (Bialk) 1912(?)-1990 .... *1*
    Obituary *65*
Krautwurst, Terry 1946- *79*
Kray, Robert Clement 1930- *82*
Krech, Bob 1956- *185*
Krech, Robert
    See Krech, Bob
Kredel, Fritz 1900-1973 .... *17*
Kreikemeier, Gregory Scott 1965- *85*
Kreloff, Elliot *189*
Krementz, Jill 1940- *134*
    Earlier sketches in SATA *17, 71*
    See also CLR *5*
    See also SAAS *8*
Kremer, Marcie
    See Sorenson, Margo
Krenina, Katya 1968- *101*
Krensky, Stephen 1953- *188*
    Brief entry *41*
    Earlier sketches in SATA *47, 93, 136*
Krensky, Stephen Alan
    See Krensky, Stephen
Kresh, Paul 1919-1997 .... *61*
    Obituary *94*
Kress, Nancy 1948- *147*
    Autobiography Feature *147*
    Earlier sketch in SATA *85*
Kricher, John C. 1944- *113*
Krieger, Melanie *96*
Krinitz, Esther Nisenthal 1927-2001 .... *194*
Kripke, Dorothy Karp *30*
Krisher, Trudy 1946- *160*
    Earlier sketch in SATA *86*
Krisher, Trudy B.
    See Krisher, Trudy
Krishnaswami, Uma 1956- *182*
    Earlier sketch in SATA *144*
Kristof, Jane 1932- *8*
Kroeber, Theodora (Kracaw) 1897-1979 .... *1*
Kroeger, Mary Kay 1950- *92*
Krohn, Katherine E(lizabeth) 1961- *125*
    Earlier sketch in SATA *84*
Kroll, Francis Lynde 1904-1973 .... *10*
Kroll, Steven 1941- *135*
    Autobiography Feature *135*
    Earlier sketches in SATA *19, 66, 125*
    See also SAAS *7*

Kroll, Virginia L. 1948- *168*
    Earlier sketches in SATA *76, 114*
Kroll, Virginia Louisa
    See Kroll, Virginia L.
Kromhout, Rindert 1958- *189*
Krommes, Beth 1956- *181*
    Earlier sketch in SATA *128*
Kronenwetter, Michael 1943- *62*
Kroniuk, Lisa
    See Berton, Pierre (Francis de Marigny)
Kropp, Paul 1948- *38*
    Brief entry *34*
    See also CLR *96*
Kropp, Paul Stephan
    See Kropp, Paul
Krosoczka, Jarrett J. 1977- *200*
    Earlier sketch in SATA *155*
Krovatin, Christopher 1985- *171*
Kruess, James
    See Kruss, James
Kruglik, Gerald *187*
Krull, Kathleen 1952- *184*
    Autobiography Feature *106*
    Brief entry *39*
    Earlier sketches in SATA *52, 80, 149*
    See also CLR *44*
Krumgold, Joseph (Quincy) 1908-1980 .... *48*
    Obituary *23*
    Earlier sketch in SATA *1*
Krupinski, Loretta 1940- *161*
    Earlier sketches in SATA *67, 102*
Krupnick, Karen 1947- *89*
Krupp, E(dwin) C(harles) 1944- *123*
    Earlier sketch in SATA *53*
Krupp, Robin Rector 1946- *53*
Krush, Beth 1918- *18*
Krush, Joe 1918-
    See Krush, Joseph P.
Krush, Joseph P. 1918- *18*
Kruss, James 1926-1997 .... *8*
    See also CLR *9*
Kruusval, Catarina 1951- *201*
Krykorka, Vladyana 1945- *96*
Krystoforski, Andrej 1943- *196*
Kubie, Eleanor Gottheil
    See Kubie, Nora Gottheil Benjamin
Kubie, Nora Benjamin
    See Kubie, Nora Gottheil Benjamin
Kubie, Nora Gottheil Benjamin 1899-1988 . *39*
    Obituary *59*
Kubinyi, Laszlo 1937- *94*
    Earlier sketch in SATA *17*
Kudlinski, Kathleen V. 1950- *150*
Kuehnert, Stephanie 1979- *205*
Kuenstler, Morton 1927- *10*
Kuh, Charlotte 1892(?)-1985
    Obituary *43*
Kuharski, Janice 1947- *128*
Kuhn, Dwight *199*
Kuijer, Guus 1942- *179*
Kujoth, Jean Spealman 1935-1975
    Obituary *30*
Kuklin, Susan 1941- *163*
    Earlier sketches in SATA *63, 95*
    See also CLR *51*
Kulikov, Boris 1966- *205*
    Earlier sketch in SATA *170*
Kulka, Joe *188*
Kulling, Monica 1952- *89*
Kullman, Harry 1919-1982 .... *35*
Kulyk Keefer, Janice 1952- *132*
Kumin, Maxine 1925- *12*
Kumin, Maxine Winokur
    See Kumin, Maxine
Kunhardt, Dorothy (Meserve) 1901-1979 .... *53*
    Obituary *22*
Kunhardt, Edith 1937- *67*
Kunjufu, Jawanza 1953- *73*
Kunstler, Morton
    See Kuenstler, Morton
Kuntz, J(ohn) L. 1947- *91*

Kuntz, Jerry 1956- *133*
Kupferberg, Herbert 1918-2001 .... *19*
Kuratomi, Chizuko 1939- *12*
  See also CLR *32*
Kurczok, Belinda 1978- *121*
Kurelek, William 1927-1977 .... *8*
  Obituary *27*
  See also CLR *2*
Kurian, George 1928- *65*
Kurjian, Judi(th M.) 1944- *127*
Kurland, Gerald 1942- *13*
Kurland, Michael 1938- *118*
  Earlier sketch in SATA *48*
Kurland, Michael Joseph
  See Kurland, Michael
Kuroi, Ken 1947- *120*
Kurokawa, Mitsuhiro 1954- *88*
Kurten, Bjorn (Olof) 1924-1988 .... *64*
Kurtz, Jane 1952- *139*
  Earlier sketch in SATA *91*
  See also CLR *123*
Kurtz, Katherine 1944- *182*
  Earlier sketches in SATA *76, 126*
Kurtz, Katherine Irene
  See Kurtz, Katherine
Kurz, Rudolf 1952- *95*
Kushner, Donn (J.) 1927- *52*
  See also CLR *55*
Kushner, Ellen 1955- *202*
  Earlier sketch in SATA *98*
Kushner, Ellen Ruth
  See Kushner, Ellen
Kushner, Jill Menkes 1951- *62*
Kushner, Lawrence 1943- *169*
  Earlier sketch in SATA *83*
Kushner, Tony 1956- *160*
Kuskin, Karla 1932-2009 .... *164*
  Obituary *206*
  Earlier sketches in SATA *2, 68, 111*
  See also CLR *4*
  See also SAAS *3*
Kuskin, Karla Seidman
  See Kuskin, Karla
Kusugak, Michael 1948- *143*
Kusugak, Michael Arvaarluk
  See Kusugak, Michael
Kutner, Merrily 1948- *196*
Kuttner, Paul 1922- *18*
Kuyper, Sjoerd 1952- *177*
Kuzma, Kay 1941- *39*
Kvale, Velma R(uth) 1898-1979 .... *8*
Kvasnosky, Laura McGee 1951- *182*
  Earlier sketches in SATA *93, 142*
Kwasney, Michelle D. 1960- *162*
Kyle, Benjamin
  See Gottfried, Theodore Mark
Kyle, Elisabeth
  See Dunlop, Agnes M. R.
Kyte, Kathy S. 1946- *50*
  Brief entry *44*

L

L., Barry
  See Longyear, Barry B(rookes)
L., Tommy
  See Lorkowski, Thomas V(incent)
Labouisse, Eve Curie
  See Curie, Eve
Labouisse, Eve Denise
  See Curie, Eve
Lace, William W. 1942- *126*
Lacey, Joshua
  See Doder, Josh
Lachner, Dorothea
  See Knobloch, Dorothea
Lachtman, Ofelia Dumas 1919- *179*
Lackey, Mercedes R. 1950- *127*
  Earlier sketch in SATA *81*

Lackey, Mercedes Ritchie
  See Lackey, Mercedes R.
Lacoe, Addie *78*
Lacombe, Benjamin 1982- *198*
Lacome, Julie 1961- *174*
  Earlier sketch in SATA *80*
Lacy, Leslie Alexander 1937- *6*
Ladd, Cheryl (Jean) 1951- *113*
Ladd, London 1972(?)- *206*
Ladd, Louise 1943- *97*
Ladd, Veronica
  See Miner, Jane Claypool
Laden, Nina 1962- *148*
  Earlier sketch in SATA *85*
Lader, Lawrence 1919-2006 .... *6*
  Obituary *178*
LaDoux, Rita C. 1951- *74*
Lady, A
  See Taylor, Ann
Lady Mears
  See Tempest, Margaret Mary
Lady of Quality, A
  See Bagnold, Enid
La Farge, Oliver 1901-1963 .... *19*
La Farge, Oliver Hazard Perry
  See La Farge, Oliver
La Farge, Phyllis *14*
LaFave, Kim *196*
LaFaye, A. 1970- *156*
  Earlier sketch in SATA *105*
LaFaye, Alexandria R.T.
  See LaFaye, A.
LaFevers, R.L. *191*
LaFevers, Robin L.
  See LaFevers, R.L.
Laffin, John (Alfred Charles) 1922- *31*
LaFontaine, Bruce 1948- *176*
  Earlier sketch in SATA *114*
La Fontaine, Jean de 1621-1695 .... *18*
Lafrance, Marie 1955- *197*
Lager, Claude
  See Lapp, Christiane (Germain)
Lager, Marilyn 1939- *52*
Lagercrantz, Rose (Elsa) 1947- *39*
Lagerloef, Selma
  See Lagerlof, Selma
Lagerlof, Selma 1858-1940 .... *15*
  See also CLR *7*
Laguna, Sofie 1968- *158*
LaHaye, Tim F. 1926- *149*
LaHaye, Timothy F.
  See LaHaye, Tim F.
Laidlaw, Rob *205*
Laiken, Deirdre S(usan) 1948- *48*
  Brief entry *40*
Laimgruber, Monika 1946- *11*
Lain, Anna
  See Lamb, Nancy
Laing, Alexander (Kinnan) 1903-1976 .... *117*
Laing, Martha 1951- *39*
Laird, Christa 1944- *108*
  Autobiography Feature *120*
  See also SAAS *26*
Laird, Elizabeth (Mary Risk) 1943- *159*
  Earlier sketches in SATA *77, 114*
  See also CLR *65*
Laird, Jean E(louise) 1930- *38*
Laite, Gordon 1925- *31*
Lake, Harriet
  See Taylor, Paula (Wright)
Lakin, Patricia 1944- *190*
Laklan, Carli 1907-1988 .... *5*
Laliberte, Louise-Andree 1958- *169*
Lalicki, Barbara *61*
Lalicki, Tom 1949- *186*
Lally, Soinbhe 1945- *119*
LaMarche, Jim *162*
Lamb, Albert *187*
Lamb, Beatrice Pitney 1904-1997 .... *21*
Lamb, Charles 1775-1834 .... *17*
Lamb, Elizabeth Searle 1917- *31*

Lamb, G(eoffrey) F(rederick) *10*
Lamb, Harold (Albert) 1892-1962 .... *53*
Lamb, Lynton (Harold) 1907-1977 .... *10*
Lamb, Mary Ann 1764-1847 .... *17*
Lamb, Nancy 1939- *80*
Lamb, Robert (Boyden) 1941- *13*
Lamba, Marie *195*
Lambert, David 1932- *84*
  Brief entry *49*
Lambert, David Compton
  See Lambert, David
Lambert, Janet 1895(?)-1973 .... *25*
Lambert, Martha L. *113*
Lambert, Saul 1928- *23*
Lambert, Stephen *174*
Lamburn, Richmal Crompton 1890-1969 .... *5*
Lamensdorf, Len 1930- *120*
Lamensdorf, Leonard
  See Lamensdorf, Len
Laminack, Lester L. 1956- *163*
  Earlier sketch in SATA *120*
Lamont, Priscilla *200*
Lamorisse, Albert (Emmanuel) 1922-1970 ... *23*
Lampert, Emily 1951- *52*
  Brief entry *49*
Lamplugh, Lois 1921- *17*
Lampman, Evelyn Sibley 1907-1980 .... *87*
  Obituary *23*
  Earlier sketch in SATA *4*
Lamprey, Louise 1869-1951
  See YABC *2*
Lampton, Chris
  See Lampton, Christopher F.
Lampton, Christopher
  See Lampton, Christopher F.
Lampton, Christopher F. *67*
  Brief entry *47*
Lamstein, Sarah 1943- *174*
  Earlier sketch in SATA *126*
Lamstein, Sarah Marwil
  See Lamstein, Sarah
Lanagan, Margo 1960- *201*
  Earlier sketch in SATA *163*
Lancaster, Bruce 1896-1963 .... *9*
Lancaster, Matthew 1973(?)-1983
  Obituary *45*
Lance, Kathryn 1943- *76*
Land, Barbara (Neblett) 1923- *16*
Land, Jane
  See Borland, Kathryn Kilby
  and Speicher, Helen Ross S(mith)
Land, Myrick (Ebben) 1922-1998 .... *15*
Land, Ross
  See Borland, Kathryn Kilby
  and Speicher, Helen Ross S(mith)
Landau, Elaine 1948- *141*
  Earlier sketches in SATA *10, 94*
Landau, Jacob 1917- *38*
Landeck, Beatrice 1904-1978 .... *15*
Landin, Les 1923- *2*
Landis, J(ames) D(avid) 1942- *60*
  Brief entry *52*
Landis, James D.
  See Landis, J(ames) D(avid)
Landis, Jill Marie 1948- *101*
Landman, Tanya *207*
Landmann, Bimba 1968- *176*
Landon, Dena 1978(?)- *168*
Landon, Lucinda 1950- *56*
  Brief entry *51*
Landon, Margaret (Dorothea Mortenson)
  1903-1993 .... *50*
Landry, Leo *202*
Landshoff, Ursula 1908-1989 .... *13*
Landstrom, Lena 1943- *206*
  Earlier sketch in SATA *146*
Landstrom, Olof 1943- *146*
Lane, Carolyn 1926-1993 .... *10*
Lane, Connie
  See Laux, Constance

Lane, Dakota 1959- *166*
  Earlier sketch in SATA *105*
Lane, Jerry
  See Martin, Patricia Miles
Lane, John (Richard) 1932- *15*
Lane, Leena *199*
Lane, Margaret 1907-1994 .... *65*
  Brief entry *38*
  Obituary *79*
Lane, Rose Wilder 1887-1968 .... *29*
  Brief entry *28*
Lanes, Selma Gordon 1929- *3*
Lanfredi, Judy 1964- *83*
Lang, Andrew 1844-1912 .... *16*
  See also CLR *101*
Lang, Aubrey *169*
Lang, Paul 1948- *83*
Lang, Susan S. 1950- *68*
Lang, T.T.
  See Taylor, Theodore
Langart, Darrell T.
  See Garrett, Randall
Langdo, Bryan 1973- *191*
  Earlier sketch in SATA *138*
Lange, John
  See Crichton, Michael
Lange, Karen E. *190*
Lange, Suzanne 1945- *5*
Langley, Andrew 1949- *166*
  Earlier sketch in SATA *104*
Langley, Charles P(itman) III 1949- *103*
Langley, Jonathan 1952- *122*
Langley, Noel 1911-1980
  Obituary *25*
Langley, Wanda *173*
Langner, Nola
  See Malone, Nola Langner
Langone, John (Michael) 1929- *46*
  Brief entry *38*
Langreuter, Jutta 1944- *122*
Langrish, Katherine *177*
Langsen, Richard C. 1953- *95*
Langstaff, John 1920-2005 .... *68*
  Obituary *172*
  Earlier sketch in SATA *6*
  See also CLR *3*
Langstaff, John Meredith
  See Langstaff, John
Langstaff, Launcelot
  See Irving, Washington
Langston, Laura 1958- *186*
Langton, Jane 1922- *200*
  Autobiography Feature *140*
  Earlier sketches in SATA *3, 68, 129, 140*
  See also CLR *33*
  See also SAAS *5*
Lanier, Sidney 1842-1881 .... *18*
Lanier, Sterling E. 1927-2007 .... *109*
Lanier, Sterling Edmund
  See Lanier, Sterling E.
Lanino, Deborah 1964- *123*
Lankford, Mary D. 1932- *112*
  Earlier sketch in SATA *77*
Lannin, Joanne 1951- *121*
Lannin, Joanne A.
  See Lannin, Joanne
Lansdale, Joe R. 1951- *116*
Lansdale, Joe Richard
  See Lansdale, Joe R.
Lansing, Alfred 1921-1975 .... *35*
Lansing, Karen E. 1954- *71*
Lansky, Vicki 1942- *177*
Lanthier, Jennifer 1964- *204*
Lantier-Sampon, Patricia 1952- *92*
Lantz, Fran
  See Lantz, Francess L(in)
Lantz, Francess L(in) 1952-2004 .... *153*
  Autobiography Feature *153*
  Obituary *159*
  Earlier sketches in SATA *63, 109*
Lantz, Paul 1908- *45*

Lantz, Walter 1900-1994 .... *37*
  Obituary *79*
Lanza, Barbara 1945- *101*
Lapp, Christiane (Germain) 1948- *74*
Lappin, Peter 1911-1999 .... *32*
Larbalestier, Justine *178*
Lardy, Philippe 1963- *168*
LaReau, Jenna *181*
LaReau, Kara 1949- *181*
Larios, Julie 1949- *178*
Larios, Julie Hofstrand
  See Larios, Julie
Larkin, Amy
  See Burns, Olive Ann
Larkin, Maia
  See Wojciechowska, Maia (Teresa)
Laroche, Giles 1956- *126*
  Earlier sketch in SATA *71*
LaRochelle, David 1960- *171*
  Earlier sketch in SATA *115*
Larom, Henry V. 1903(?)-1975
  Obituary *30*
LaRose, Linda *125*
Larrabee, Lisa 1947- *84*
Larrecq, John M(aurice) 1926-1980 .... *44*
  Obituary *25*
Larrick (Crosby), Nancy 1910-2004 .... *4*
Larsen, Anita 1942- *78*
Larsen, Egon 1904- *14*
Larsen, Rebecca 1944- *54*
Larson, Eve
  See St. John, Wylly Folk
Larson, Gary 1950- *57*
Larson, Hope 1982- *205*
Larson, Ingrid D(ana) 1965- *92*
Larson, Jean Russell 1930- *121*
Larson, Kirby 1954- *181*
  Earlier sketch in SATA *96*
Larson, Norita D(ittberner) 1944- *29*
Larson, William H. 1938- *10*
Larsson, Carl (Olof) 1853-1919 .... *35*
LaSalle, Charles A.
  See Ellis, Edward S.
LaSalle, Charles E.
  See Ellis, Edward S.
Lasell, Elinor H. 1929- *19*
Lasell, Fen H.
  See Lasell, Elinor H.
Lasenby, Jack 1931- *172*
  Earlier sketches in SATA *65, 103*
Laser, Michael 1954- *117*
Lash, Joseph P. 1909-1987 .... *43*
Lasher, Faith B. 1921- *12*
Lasker, David 1950- *38*
Lasker, Joe
  See Lasker, Joseph Leon
Lasker, Joseph Leon 1919- *83*
  Earlier sketch in SATA *9*
  See also SAAS *17*
Laski, Marghanita 1915-1988 .... *55*
Laskin, Pamela L. 1954- *75*
Lasky, Kathryn 1944- *157*
  Earlier sketches in SATA *13, 69, 112*
  See also CLR *140*
Lasky Knight, Kathryn
  See Lasky, Kathryn
Lass, Bonnie *131*
Lassalle, C. E.
  See Ellis, Edward S.
Lassiter, Mary
  See Hoffman, Mary
Lassiter, Rhiannon 1977- *157*
Lat 1951- *196*
Latham, Barbara 1896- *16*
Latham, Frank B(rown) 1910-2000 .... *6*
Latham, Jean Lee 1902-1995 .... *68*
  Earlier sketch in SATA *2*
  See also CLR *50*
Latham, Mavis
  See Clark, Mavis Thorpe

Latham, Philip
  See Richardson, Robert S(hirley)
Lathrop, Dorothy P(ulis) 1891-1980 .... *14*
  Obituary *24*
Lathrop, Francis
  See Leiber, Fritz (Reuter, Jr.)
Latimer, Jim 1943- *80*
Latta, Rich
  See Latta, Richard
Latta, Richard 1946- *113*
Latta, Sara L. 1960- *174*
Lattany, Kristin
  See Lattany, Kristin Hunter
Lattany, Kristin (Eggleston) Hunter 1931- . *154*
  Autobiography Feature *154*
  Earlier sketch in SATA *132*
Lattany, Kristin Hunter 1931- *132*
  Earlier sketch in SATA *12*
  See also CLR *3*
  See also SAAS *10*
Lattimore, Eleanor Frances 1904-1986 .... *7*
  Obituary *48*
Lattin, Ann
  See Cole, Lois Dwight
Lauber, Patricia (Grace) 1924- *138*
  Earlier sketches in SATA *1, 33, 75*
  See also CLR *16*
Laugesen, Malene *207*
Laugesen, Malene Reynolds
  See Laugesen, Malene
Laugesen, Mary E(akin) 1906-1995 .... *5*
Laughbaum, Steve 1945- *12*
Laughlin, Florence Young 1910-2001 .... *3*
Laughlin, Rosemary 1941- *123*
Launder, Sally *206*
Laure, Ettagale
  See Blauer, Ettagale
Laure, Jason 1940- *50*
  Brief entry *44*
Laurence, Ester Hauser 1935- *7*
Laurence, Jean Margaret Wemyss
  See Laurence, Margaret
Laurence, Margaret 1926-1987
  Obituary *50*
Laurie, Rona 1916- *55*
Laurin, Anne
  See McLaurin, Anne
Lauritzen, Jonreed 1902-1979 .... *13*
Lauscher, Hermann
  See Hesse, Hermann
Lauture, Denize 1946- *86*
Laux, Connie
  See Laux, Constance
Laux, Constance 1952- *97*
Laux, Dorothy 1920- *49*
Lavallee, Barbara 1941- *166*
  Earlier sketch in SATA *74*
Lavender, David (Sievert) 1910-2003 .... *97*
  Obituary *145*
  Earlier sketch in SATA *64*
Lavender, William D. 1921- *143*
Laverne, Christine *175*
Lavert, Gwendolyn Battle 1951-
  See Battle-Lavert, Gwendolyn
Laverty, Donald
  See Blish, James
  and Knight, Damon (Francis)
Lavigne, Louis-Dominique *107*
Lavine, David 1928- *31*
Lavine, Sigmund Arnold 1908-1986 .... *82*
  Earlier sketch in SATA *3*
  See also CLR *35*
Lavond, Paul Dennis
  See Kornbluth, C(yril) M.
  and Lowndes, Robert A(ugustine) W(ard)
  and Pohl, Frederik
Lawford, Paula Jane 1960- *57*
  Brief entry *53*
Lawhead, Stephen R. 1950- *109*
Lawhead, Steve
  See Lawhead, Stephen R.

Lawlor, Laurie 1953- 137
  Earlier sketch in SATA 80
Lawlor, William
  See Lawlor, William T.
Lawlor, William T. 1951- 183
Lawrence, Ann (Margaret) 1942-1987 41
  Obituary 54
Lawrence, Caroline 1954- 203
Lawrence, Iain 1955- 183
  Earlier sketch in SATA 135
Lawrence, J. T.
  See Rowland-Entwistle, (Arthur) Theodore
  (Henry)
Lawrence, Jerome 1915-2004 65
Lawrence, John 1933- 30
Lawrence, Josephine 1890(?)-1978
  Obituary 24
Lawrence, Louise 1943- 119
  Earlier sketches in SATA 38, 78
Lawrence, Louise de Kiriline 1894-1992 13
Lawrence, Lynn
  See Garland, Sherry
Lawrence, Margery H. 1889-1969 120
Lawrence, Michael 1943- 132
Lawrence, Mildred Elwood 1907-1997 3
Lawrence, R(onald) D(ouglas) 1921- 55
Lawrinson, Julia 1969- 141
Lawson, Amy
  See Gordon, Amy
Lawson, Carol (Antell) 1946- 42
Lawson, Don(ald Elmer) 1917-1990 9
Lawson, Joan 1906- 55
Lawson, Julie 1947- 126
  Earlier sketch in SATA 79
  See also CLR 89
Lawson, Marion Tubbs 1896-1994 22
Lawson, Robert 1892-1957 100
  See also YABC 2
  See also CLR 73
Lawton, Clive A. 1951- 145
Laxdal, Vivienne 1962- 112
Laybourn, Emma 193
Laycock, George (Edwin) 1921- 5
Layne, Laura
  See Knott, William C(ecil, Jr.)
Layne, Steven L. 171
Layton, Neal 1971- 187
  Earlier sketch in SATA 152
Layton, Neal Andrew
  See Layton, Neal
Lazare, Gerald John 1927- 44
Lazare, Jerry
  See Lazare, Gerald John
Lazarevich, Mila 1942- 17
Lazarus, Keo Felker 1913-1993 21
  Obituary 129
Lea, Alec 1907- 19
Lea, Bob 1952- 203
Lea, Joan
  See Neufeld, John (Arthur)
Leach, Maria 1892-1977 39
  Brief entry 28
Leacock, Elspeth 1946- 131
Leacroft, Helen (Mabel Beal) 1919- 6
Leacroft, Richard (Vallance Becher) 1914- 6
Leaf, Margaret P. 1909(?)-1988
  Obituary 55
Leaf, (Wilbur) Munro 1905-1976 20
  See also CLR 25
Leaf, VaDonna Jean 1929- 26
Leah, Devorah
  See Devorah-Leah
Leakey, Richard E(rskine Frere) 1944- 42
Leander, Ed
  See Richelson, Geraldine
Lear, Edward 1812-1888 100
  Earlier sketch in SATA 18
  See also CLR 75
Lears, Laurie 1955- 127
Leasor, James 1923-2007 54

Leasor, Thomas James
  See Leasor, James
Leavitt, Jerome E(dward) 1916- 23
Leavitt, Martine 1953- 170
LeBar, Mary E(velyn) 1910-1982 35
LeBlanc, Annette M. 1965- 68
LeBlanc, L(ee) 1913- 54
LeBox, Annette 1943- 145
Lebrun, Claude 1929- 66
Le Cain, Errol (John) 1941-1989 68
  Obituary 60
  Earlier sketch in SATA 6
Lechner, Jack 201
Lechner, John 1966- 200
Lecourt, Nancy (Hoyt) 1951- 73
Ledbetter, Suzann 1953- 119
Leder, Jane Mersky 1945- 61
  Brief entry 51
Lederer, Muriel 1929- 48
Lederer, William J(ulius) 1912- 62
Lee, Amanda
  See Baggett, Nancy
  and Buckholtz, Eileen (Garber)
  and Glick, Ruth (Burtnick)
Lee, Benjamin 1921- 27
Lee, Betsy 1949- 37
Lee, Carol
  See Fletcher, Helen Jill
Lee, Carol Ann 1969- 185
Lee, Chinlun 182
Lee, Cora
  See Anderson, Catherine Corley
Lee, Dennis (Beynon) 1939- 102
  Earlier sketch in SATA 14
  See also CLR 3
Lee, Dom 1959- 146
  Autobiography Feature 121
  Earlier sketch in SATA 83
  See also SAAS 26
Lee, Doris Emrick 1905-1983 44
  Obituary 35
Lee, Edward
  See Lee, J. Edward
Lee, Elizabeth Rogers 1940- 90
Lee, Harper 1926- 11
Lee, Hector Viveros 1962- 115
Lee, Howard N.
  See Goulart, Ron
Lee, Huy Voun 1969- 129
Lee, J. Edward 1953- 130
Lee, Jeanne M. 1943- 138
Lee, John R(obert) 1923-1976 27
Lee, Jordan
  See Scholefield, Alan
Lee, Joseph Edward
  See Lee, J. Edward
Lee, Julian
  See Latham, Jean Lee
Lee, Linda
  See Eyerly, Jeannette
Lee, Liz
  See Lee, Elizabeth Rogers
Lee, Lucy
  See Talbot, Charlene Joy
Lee, Lyn 1953- 128
Lee, Manning de Villeneuve 1894-1980 37
  Obituary 22
Lee, Marian
  See Clish, (Lee) Marian
Lee, Marie G. 1964- 178
  Earlier sketches in SATA 81, 130
Lee, Marie Myung-Ok
  See Lee, Marie G.
Lee, Mary Price 1934- 82
  Earlier sketch in SATA 8
Lee, Mildred
  See Scudder, Mildred Lee
Lee, Nelle Harper
  See Lee, Harper
Lee, Richard S. 1927- 82
Lee, Robert C. 1931- 20

Lee, Robert Edwin 1918-1994 65
  Obituary 82
Lee, Robert J. 1921- 10
Lee, Roy
  See Hopkins, Clark
Lee, Sally 1943- 67
Lee, Suzy 193
Lee, Tammie
  See Townsend, Thomas L.
Lee, Tanith 1947- 185
  Earlier sketches in SATA 8, 88, 134
Leech, Ben
  See Bowkett, Stephen
Leeds, Contance 188
Leedy, Loreen 1959- 175
  Brief entry 50
  Earlier sketches in SATA 54, 84, 128
Leedy, Loreen Janelle
  See Leedy, Loreen
Lee-Hostetler, Jeri 1940- 63
Leekley, Thomas B(riggs) 1910-2001 23
Leeming, Jo Ann
  See Leeming, Joseph
Leeming, Joseph 1897-1968 26
Leemis, Ralph B. 1954- 72
Leese, Jennifer L.B. 1970- 163
Leeson, Muriel 1920- 54
Leeson, R. A.
  See Leeson, Robert (Arthur)
Leeson, Robert (Arthur) 1928- 76
  Earlier sketch in SATA 42
Lee Tae-Jun 1904-1956(?) 194
Lee-Tai, Amy 1964- 189
Leffland, Ella 1931- 65
Leffler, Silke 197
Lefler, Irene (Whitney) 1917- 12
LeFrak, Karen 182
Le Gallienne, Eva 1899-1991 9
  Obituary 68
Legg, Gerald 1947- 143
Legg, Sarah Martha Ross Bruggeman (?)-1982
  Obituary 40
LeGrand
  See Henderson, LeGrand
Le Guin, Ursula K. 1929- 194
  Earlier sketches in SATA 4, 52, 99, 149
  See also CLR 91
Le Guin, Ursula Kroeber
  See Le Guin, Ursula K.
Legum, Colin 1919-2003 10
Lehman, Barbara 1963- 170
  Earlier sketch in SATA 115
Lehman, Bob 91
Lehman, Elaine 91
Lehmann, Debra Lynn
  See Vanasse, Deb
Lehn, Cornelia 1920- 46
Lehne, Judith Logan 1947- 93
Lehr, Delores 1920- 10
Lehr, Norma 1930- 71
Leiber, Fritz (Reuter, Jr.) 1910-1992 45
  Obituary 73
Leibold, Jay 1957- 57
  Brief entry 52
Leichman, Seymour 1933- 5
Leick, Bonnie 205
Leigh, Nila K. 1981- 81
Leigh, Tom 1947- 46
Leigh-Pemberton, John 1911-1997 35
Leighton, Clare (Veronica Hope)
  1899-1989 37
Leighton, Margaret (Carver) 1896-1987 1
  Obituary 52
Leiner, Al(an) 1938- 83
Leiner, Katherine 1949- 93
Leipold, L. Edmond 1902-1983 16
Leisk, David (Johnson) 1906-1975 30
  Obituary 26
  Earlier sketch in SATA 1
  See also CLR 98
Leister, Mary 1917- 29

Leitch, Patricia 1933- 98
  Earlier sketch in SATA *11*
Leitner, Isabella 1924- 86
Lekich, John 202
Leland, Bob 1956- 92
Leland, Robert E.
  See Leland, Bob
Lematre, Pascal 1967- 176
Lember, Barbara Hirsch 1941- 92
LeMieux, A.C. 1954- 125
  Earlier sketch in SATA *90*
LeMieux, Anne
  See LeMieux, A.C.
LeMieux, Anne Connelly
  See LeMieux, A.C.
Lemieux, Michele 1955- 139
Lemke, Horst 1922- 38
Lenain, Thierry 1959- 201
Lenanton, Carola Mary Anima Oman
  See Oman, Carola (Mary Anima)
Lenard, Alexander 1910-1972
  Obituary 21
Lendroth, Susan 207
L'Engle, Madeleine 1918-2007 128
  Obituary 186
  Earlier sketches in SATA *1, 27, 75*
  See also CLR *57*
  See also SAAS *15*
L'Engle, Madeleine Camp Franklin
  See L'Engle, Madeleine
Lengyel, Cornel Adam 1915- 27
Lengyel, Emil 1895-1985 3
  Obituary 42
Lennon, John 1940-1980 114
Lennon, John Ono
  See Lennon, John
Leno, Jay 1950- 154
LeNoir, Janice 1941- 89
Lens, Sidney 1912-1986 13
  Obituary 48
Lenski, Lois 1893-1974 100
  Earlier sketches in SATA *1, 26*
  See also CLR *26*
Lent, Blair 1930-2009 133
  Obituary 200
  Earlier sketch in SATA *2*
Lent, Henry Bolles 1901-1973 17
Lent, John 1948- 108
Leodhas, Sorche Nic
  See Alger, Leclaire (Gowans)
Leokum, Arkady 1916(?)- 45
Leon, Sharon 1959- 79
Leonard, Alison 1944- 70
Leonard, Constance (Brink) 1923- 42
  Brief entry 40
Leonard, Dutch
  See Leonard, Elmore
Leonard, Elmore 1925- 163
Leonard, Elmore John, Jr.
  See Leonard, Elmore
Leonard, Jonathan N(orton) 1903-1975 36
Leonard, Laura 1923- 75
Leonard, Tom 1955- 207
Leonetti, Mike 1958- 202
Leong, Gor Yun
  See Ellison, Virginia H(owell)
Leonhardt, Alice 1950- 152
Lerangis, Peter 1955- 171
  Earlier sketch in SATA *72*
Lerner, Aaron 1920-2007 35
  Obituary 179
Lerner, Aaron Bunsen
  See Lerner, Aaron
Lerner, Carol 1927- 86
  Earlier sketch in SATA *33*
  See also CLR *34*
  See also SAAS *12*
Lerner, Gerda 1920- 65
Lerner, Harriet 1944- 101
Lerner, Marguerite Rush 1924-1987 11
  Obituary 51

Lerner, Sharon (Ruth) 1938-1982 11
  Obituary 29
Leroe, Ellen W(hitney) 1949- 99
  Brief entry 51
  Earlier sketch in SATA *61*
Leroux, Gaston 1868-1927 65
Leroux-Hugon, Helene 1955- 132
LeRoy, Gen 52
  Brief entry 36
Lerrigo, Marion Olive 1898-1968
  Obituary 29
LeShan, Eda J(oan) 1922-2002 21
  See also CLR *6*
LeSieg, Theo.
  See Dr. Seuss
Lesinski, Jeanne M. 1960- 120
Leslie, Robert Franklin 1911-1990 7
Leslie, Roger 1961- 168
Leslie, Roger James
  See Leslie, Roger
Leslie, Sarah
  See McGuire, Leslie (Sarah)
LeSourd, Catherine
  See Marshall, (Sarah) Catherine (Wood)
Lessac, Frane
  See Lessac, Frane
Lessac, Frane 1954- 148
  Earlier sketch in SATA *61*
Lessem, Dino Don
  See Lessem, Don
Lessem, Don 1951- 182
  Earlier sketches in SATA *97, 155*
Lesser, Margaret 1899(?)-1979
  Obituary 22
Lesser, Rika 1953- 53
Lester, Alison 1952- 129
  Earlier sketches in SATA *50, 90*
Lester, Helen 1936- 189
  Earlier sketches in SATA *46, 92, 145*
Lester, Julius 1939- 157
  Earlier sketches in SATA *12, 74, 112*
  See also CLR *143*
Lester, Julius Bernard
  See Lester, Julius
Lester, Mike 1955- 206
  Earlier sketch in SATA *131*
Le Sueur, Meridel 1900-1996 6
Lethcoe, Jason 191
Le Tord, Bijou 1945- 95
  Earlier sketch in SATA *49*
Letts, Billie 1938- 121
Letts, Elizabeth
  See Alalou, Elizabeth
Leuck, Laura 1962- 192
  Earlier sketches in SATA *85, 146*
Leutscher, Alfred (George) 1913- 23
Levai, Blaise 1919- 39
Levenkron, Steven 1941- 86
Leverich, Kathleen 1948- 103
LeVert, (William) John 1946- 55
Levete, Sarah 1961- 153
Levin, Betty 1927- 201
  Earlier sketches in SATA *19, 84, 137*
  See also SAAS *11*
Levin, Ira 1929-2007 66
  Obituary 187
Levin, Ira Marvin
  See Levin, Ira
Levin, Ira Marvin
  See Levin, Ira
Levin, Marcia Obrasky 1918- 13
Levin, Meyer 1905-1981 21
  Obituary 27
Levin, Miriam (Ramsfelder) 1962- 97
Levine, Abby 1943- 54
  Brief entry 52
Levine, Betty K(rasne) 1933- 66
Levine, David 1926-2009 43
  Brief entry 35
Levine, Edna S(imon) 35
Levine, Ellen 1939- 190

Levine, Evan 1962- 77
  Earlier sketch in SATA *74*
Levine, Gail Carson 1947- 195
  Earlier sketches in SATA *98, 161*
  See also CLR *85*
Levine, I(srael) E. 1923-2003 12
  Obituary 146
Levine, Joan Goldman 11
Levine, Joseph 1910- 33
Levine, Marge 1934- 81
Levine, Rhoda 14
Levine, Sarah 1970- 57
Levine, Shar 1953- 131
Levine-Freidus, Gail
  See Provost, Gail Levine
Levinson, Nancy Smiler 1938- 140
  Earlier sketches in SATA *33, 80*
Levinson, Riki 99
  Brief entry 49
  Earlier sketch in SATA *52*
Levithan, David 1972- 166
Levitin, Sonia 1934- 192
  Autobiography Feature 131
  Earlier sketches in SATA *4, 68, 119, 131*
  See also CLR *53*
  See also SAAS *2*
Levitt, Sidney (Mark) 1947- 68
Levon, O. U.
  See Kesey, Ken
Levoy, Myron 49
  Brief entry 37
Levy, Barrie 112
Levy, Constance 1931- 140
  Earlier sketch in SATA *73*
  See also SAAS *22*
Levy, Elizabeth 1942- 169
  Earlier sketches in SATA *31, 69, 107*
  See also SAAS *18*
Levy, Janice 172
Levy, Marilyn 1937- 67
Levy, Nathan 1945- 63
Levy, Robert 1945- 82
Lewees, John
  See Stockton, Francis Richard
Lewin, Betsy 1937- 169
  Autobiography Feature 115
  Earlier sketches in SATA *32, 90*
Lewin, Hugh 1939- 72
  Brief entry 40
  See also CLR *9*
Lewin, Ted 1935- 195
  Autobiography Feature 115
  Earlier sketches in SATA *21, 76, 119, 165*
Lewis, Alice C. 1936- 46
Lewis, Alice Hudson 1895(?)-1971
  Obituary 29
Lewis, Amanda 1955- 80
Lewis, Anthony 1927- 27
Lewis, Anthony 1966- 120
Lewis, Barbara A. 1943- 73
Lewis, Beverly 1949- 80
Lewis, Brenda Ralph 1932- 72
Lewis, Brian 1963- 128
Lewis, C. S. 1898-1963 100
  Earlier sketch in SATA *13*
  See also CLR *109*
Lewis, Claudia (Louise) 1907-2001 5
Lewis, Clive Staples
  See Lewis, C. S.
Lewis, Cynthia Copeland 1960- 111
Lewis, E. M. 123
  Earlier sketch in SATA *20*
Lewis, Earl Bradley
  See Lewis, E.B.
Lewis, E.B. 1956- 168
  Earlier sketches in SATA *93, 124*
Lewis, Elizabeth Foreman 1892-1958 121
  See also YABC *2*
Lewis, Francine
  See Wells, Helen

Lewis, Harry Sinclair
  See Lewis, Sinclair
Lewis, Hilda (Winifred) 1896-1974
  Obituary 20
Lewis, J. Patrick 1942- 205
  Earlier sketches in SATA *69, 104, 162*
Lewis, Jack P(earl) 1919- 65
Lewis, Jean 1924- 61
Lewis, Jon Samuel
  See Lewis, J.S.
Lewis, Joseph Anthony
  See Lewis, Anthony
Lewis, J.S. 1972- 203
Lewis, Julinda
  See Lewis-Ferguson, Julinda
Lewis, Kevin 173
Lewis, Kim 1951- 136
  Earlier sketch in SATA *84*
Lewis, Linda (Joy) 1946- 67
Lewis, Lucia Z.
  See Anderson, Lucia (Lewis)
Lewis, Marjorie 1929- 40
  Brief entry 35
Lewis, Mary 1907(?)-1988 64
  Obituary 56
Lewis, Mervyn
  See Frewer, Glyn (M.)
Lewis, Michael
  See Untermeyer, Louis
Lewis, Naomi 1911-2009 144
  Earlier sketch in SATA *76*
Lewis, Paeony 1960- 173
Lewis, Paul
  See Gerson, Noel Bertram
Lewis, Richard 1935- 3
Lewis, Rob 1962- 72
Lewis, Roger
  See Zarchy, Harry
Lewis, Shannon
  See Llywelyn, Morgan
Lewis, Shari 1934-1998 35
  Brief entry 30
  Obituary 104
Lewis, Sylvan R.
  See Aronson, Virginia
Lewis, Thomas P(arker) 1936- 27
Lewis, Wendy A. 1966- 150
Lewis-Ferguson, Julinda 1955- 85
Lewison, Wendy Cheyette 177
Lewiton, Mina 1904-1970 2
Lew-Vriethoff, Joanne 186
Lexau, Joan M. 130
  Earlier sketches in SATA *1, 36*
Ley, Willy 1906-1969 2
Leydon, Rita (Floden) 1949- 21
Leyland, Eric (Arthur) 1911- 37
L'Hommedieu, Dorothy Keasley 1885-1961
  Obituary 29
Li, Xiao Jun 1952- 86
Liao, Jimmy 1958- 202
Liatsos, Sandra Olson 1942- 103
Libby, Alisa M. 189
Libby, Barbara M. 153
Libby, Bill
  See Libby, William M.
Libby, William M. 1927-1984 5
  Obituary 39
Liberty, Gene 1924- 3
Lichtenheld, Tom 152
Lichtman, Wendy 1946- 193
Liddell, Kenneth 1912-1975 63
Lidz, Jane 120
Lieberman, E(dwin) James 1934- 62
Liebers, Arthur 1913-1984 12
Lieblich, Irene 1923- 22
Liers, Emil E(rnest) 1890-1975 37
Lies, Brian 1963- 190
  Earlier sketch in SATA *131*
Liestman, Vicki 1961- 72
Lietz, Gerald S. 1918- 11
Life, Kay (Guinn) 1930- 83

Lifton, Betty Jean 118
  Earlier sketch in SATA *6*
Lifton, Robert Jay 1926- 66
Lightburn, Ron 1954- 91
Lightburn, Sandra 1955- 91
Lightner, A. M.
  See Hopf, Alice (Martha) L(ightner)
Lightner, Alice
  See Hopf, Alice (Martha) L(ightner)
Lignell, Lois 1911- 37
Liles, Maurine Walpole 1935- 81
Lillegard, Dee 184
Lilley, Stephen R. 1950- 97
Lilley, Stephen Ray
  See Lilley, Stephen R.
Lillington, Kenneth (James) 1916-1998 39
Lilly, Nate 182
Lilly, Ray
  See Curtis, Richard
Lim, John 1932- 43
Liman, Ellen (Fogelson) 1936- 22
Limb, Sue 1946- 203
  Earlier sketch in SATA *158*
Limburg, Peter R(ichard) 1929- 13
Lin, Grace 1974- 198
  Earlier sketches in SATA *111, 162*
Lincoln, C(harles) Eric 1924-2000 5
Lincoln, Hazel 187
Lincoln, James
  See Bates, Katharine Lee
Lindbergh, Anne
  See Sapieyevski, Anne Lindbergh
Lindbergh, Anne Morrow 1906-2001 33
  Obituary 125
Lindbergh, Anne Spencer Morrow
  See Lindbergh, Anne Morrow
Lindbergh, Charles A(ugustus, Jr.)
  1902-1974 33
Lindbergh, Reeve 1945- 163
  Earlier sketch in SATA *116*
Lindblom, Steven (Winther) 1946- 94
  Brief entry 39
  Earlier sketch in SATA *42*
Linde, Gunnel 1924- 5
Lindenbaum, Pija 1955- 183
  Earlier sketches in SATA *77, 144*
Lindgren, Astrid (Anna Emilia Ericsson)
  1907-2002 38
  Obituary 128
  Earlier sketch in SATA *2*
  See also CLR *119*
Lindgren, Barbro 1937- 207
  Brief entry 46
  Earlier sketches in SATA *63, 120*
  See also CLR *86*
Lindman, Maj (Jan) 1886-1972 43
Lindop, Edmund 1925- 5
Lindquist, Jennie Dorothea 1899-1977 13
Lindquist, Rowena Cory 1958- 98
Lindquist, Willis 1908-1988 20
Lindsay, Nicholas Vachel
  See Lindsay, Vachel
Lindsay, Norman Alfred William
  1879-1969 67
  See also CLR *8*
Lindsay, Vachel 1879-1931 40
Lindsey, Kathleen D(orothy) 1949- 153
Line, David
  See Davidson, Lionel
Line, Les 1935- 27
Lines, Kathleen Mary 1902-1988
  Obituary 61
Linfield, Esther 40
Lingard, Joan (Amelia) 1932- 130
  Autobiography Feature 130
  Earlier sketches in SATA *8, 74, 114*
  See also CLR *89*
  See also SAAS *5*
Link, Martin 1934- 28
Linn, Margot
  See Ziefert, Harriet

Linnea, Sharon 1956- 82
Lion, Melissa 1976- 176
Lionni, Leo(nard) 1910-1999 72
  Obituary 118
  Earlier sketch in SATA *8*
  See also CLR *71*
Lipinsky de Orlov, Lino S. 1908- 22
Lipkind, William 1904-1974 15
Lipman, David 1931-2008 21
Lipman, Matthew 1923- 14
Lipp, Frederick 204
Lippincott, Bertram 1898(?)-1985
  Obituary 42
Lippincott, Gary A. 1953- 119
  Earlier sketch in SATA *73*
Lippincott, Joseph W(harton) 1887-1976 17
Lippincott, Sarah Lee 1920- 22
Lippman, Peter J. 1936- 31
Lipsyte, Robert 1938- 198
  Earlier sketches in SATA *5, 68, 113, 161*
  See also CLR *76*
Lipsyte, Robert Michael
  See Lipsyte, Robert
Lisandrelli, Elaine Slivinski 1951- 94
Lisker, Sonia O. 1933- 44
Lisle, Holly 1960- 98
Lisle, Janet Taylor 1947- 150
  Brief entry 47
  Earlier sketches in SATA *59, 96*
  See also SAAS *14*
Lisle, Rebecca 162
Lisle, Seward D.
  See Ellis, Edward S.
Lisowski, Gabriel 1946- 47
  Brief entry 31
Liss, Howard 1922-1995 4
  Obituary 84
Lissiat, Amy
  See Thompson, Colin
Lisson, Deborah 1941- 110
  Earlier sketch in SATA *71*
List, Ilka Katherine 1935- 6
Liston, Robert A. 1927- 5
Litchfield, Ada B(assett) 1916-1999 5
Litchfield, Jo 1973- 116
Lithgow, John (Arthur) 1945- 145
Litowinsky, Olga (Jean) 1936- 26
Littke, Lael J. 1929- 140
  Earlier sketches in SATA *51, 83*
Little, A. Edward
  See Klein, Aaron E.
Little, Douglas 1942- 96
Little, (Flora) Jean 1932- 149
  Earlier sketches in SATA *2, 68, 106*
  See also CLR *4*
  See also SAAS *17*
Little, Lessie Jones 1906-1986 60
  Obituary 50
Little, Mary E. 1912-1999 28
Littlechild, George 1958- 85
Littledale, Freya (Lota) 1929-1992 74
  Earlier sketch in SATA *2*
Littlefield, Bill 1948- 83
Littlefield, Holly 1963- 97
Littlesugar, Amy 1953- 176
  Earlier sketch in SATA *122*
Littleton, Mark R. 1950- 142
  Earlier sketch in SATA *89*
Littman, Sarah Darer 175
Litty, Julie 1971- 181
Litzinger, Rosanne 1948- 196
Lively, Penelope 1933- 164
  Earlier sketches in SATA *7, 60, 101*
  See also CLR *7*
Lively, Penelope Margaret
  See Lively, Penelope
Liverakos, L.A.
  See Gilman, Laura Anne
Liversidge, (Henry) Douglas 1913- 8
Livesey, Claire (Warner) 1927- 127
Livingston, Carole 1941- 42

Livingston, (M.) Irene 1932- *150*
Livingston, Myra Cohn 1926-1996 .... *68*
  Obituary *92*
  Earlier sketch in SATA *5*
  See also CLR *7*
  See also SAAS *1*
Livingston, Richard R(oland) 1922- *8*
Livo, Norma J. 1929- *76*
Liwska, Renata *199*
Ljungkvist, Laura *180*
Llerena Aguirre, Carlos 1952- *19*
Llerena Aguirre, Carlos Antonio
  See Llerena Aguirre, Carlos
Llewellyn, Claire 1954- *196*
  Earlier sketches in SATA *77, 143*
Llewellyn, Grace 1964- *110*
Llewellyn, Richard
  See Llewellyn Lloyd, Richard Dafydd Vivian
Llewellyn, Sam 1948- *185*
  Earlier sketch in SATA *95*
Llewellyn Lloyd, Richard Dafydd Vivian
  1906-1983 .... *11*
  Obituary *37*
Llewelyn, T. Harcourt
  See Hamilton, Charles (Harold St. John)
Lloyd, Alan
  See Lloyd, A.R.
Lloyd, Alan Richard
  See Lloyd, A.R.
Lloyd, A.R. 1927- *168*
  Earlier sketch in SATA *97*
Lloyd, David
  See Lloyd, David T.
Lloyd, David T. 1954- *167*
Lloyd, E. James
  See James, Elizabeth
Lloyd, Errol 1943- *22*
Lloyd, Hugh
  See Fitzhugh, Percy Keese
Lloyd, James
  See James, Elizabeth
Lloyd, Megan 1958- *189*
  Earlier sketches in SATA *77, 117*
Lloyd, Norman 1909-1980
  Obituary *23*
Lloyd, (Mary) Norris 1908-1993 .... *10*
  Obituary *75*
Lloyd, Sam *183*
Lloyd-Jones, Sally 1960- *179*
Lloyd Webber, Andrew 1948- *56*
Llywelyn, Morgan 1937- *109*
Lo, Ginnie *165*
Lo, Virginia M.
  See Lo, Ginnie
Lobato, Jose Bento Monteiro 1882-1948 ... *114*
Lobel, Anita (Kempler) 1934- *162*
  Earlier sketches in SATA *6, 55, 96*
Lobel, Arnold (Stark) 1933-1987 .... *55*
  Obituary *54*
  Earlier sketch in SATA *6*
  See also CLR *5*
Lobel, Gillian *181*
Lobsenz, Amelia *12*
Lobsenz, Norman M(itchell) 1919- *6*
Lochak, Michele 1936- *39*
Lochlons, Colin
  See Jackson, C(aary) Paul
Locke, Clinton W. *1*
Locke, Elsie (Violet) 1912-2001 .... *87*
Locke, Gary 1963- *197*
Locke, Lucie 1904-1989 .... *10*
Locke, Robert 1944- *63*
  See also CLR *39*
Locker, Thomas 1937- *109*
  Earlier sketch in SATA *59*
  See also CLR *14*
Lockhart, E.
  See Jenkins, Emily
Lockridge, Hildegarde (Dolson)
  1908-1981 .... *121*
  Earlier sketch in SATA *5*

Lockwood, Mary
  See Spelman, Mary
Lodge, Bernard 1933- *107*
  Earlier sketch in SATA *33*
Lodge, Jo 1966- *173*
  Earlier sketch in SATA *112*
Loeb, Jeffrey 1946- *57*
Loeb, Robert H., Jr. 1917- *21*
Loefgren, Ulf 1931- *3*
Loehfelm, Bill 1969- *153*
Loehr, Mallory *184*
Loehr, Patrick 1968(?)- *194*
Loeper, John J(oseph) 1929- *118*
  Earlier sketch in SATA *10*
Loescher, Ann Dull 1942- *20*
Loescher, Gil(burt Damian) 1945- *20*
Loewer, Jean Jenkins
  See Jenkins, Jean
Loewer, (Henry) Peter 1934- *98*
LoFaro, Jerry 1959- *77*
Lofo
  See Heimann, Rolf
Lofthouse, Liz *199*
Lofting, Hugh (John) 1886-1947 .... *100*
  Earlier sketch in SATA *15*
  See also CLR *143*
Lofts, Norah (Robinson) 1904-1983 .... *8*
  Obituary *36*
Logan, Jake
  See Knott, William C(ecil, Jr.)
  and Krepps, Robert W(ilson)
  and Pearl, Jacques Bain
  and Riefe, Alan
  and Rifkin, Shepard
  and Smith, Martin Cruz
Logan, Mark
  See Nicole, Christopher (Robin)
Logan, Rochelle 1954- *169*
Logston, Anne 1962- *112*
Logue, Christopher 1926- *23*
Logue, Mary 1952- *161*
  Earlier sketch in SATA *112*
Logue, Mary Louise
  See Logue, Mary
Loh, Morag 1935- *73*
Lohans, Alison 1949- *101*
Loizeaux, William *185*
Loken, Newton Clayton 1919- *26*
Lomas, Steve
  See Brennan, Joseph Lomas
Lomask, Milton (Nachman) 1909-1991 .... *20*
Lombard, Jenny *178*
Lombino, Salvatore
  See Hunter, Evan
LoMonaco, Palmyra 1932- *102*
London, Jack 1876-1916 .... *18*
  See also CLR *108*
London, Jane
  See Geis, Darlene Stern
London, John Griffith
  See London, Jack
London, Jonathan (Paul) 1947- *157*
  Earlier sketches in SATA *74, 113*
Lonergan, (Pauline) Joy (MacLean) 1909- ... *10*
Lonette, Reisie (Dominee) 1924- *43*
Long, Cathryn J. 1946- *89*
Long, Earlene (Roberta) 1938- *50*
Long, Emmett
  See Leonard, Elmore
Long, Ethan 1968(?)- *182*
Long, Helen Beecher *1*
Long, Judith Elaine 1953- *20*
Long, Judy
  See Long, Judith Elaine
Long, Kim 1949- *69*
Long, Laura Mooney 1892-1967
  Obituary *29*
Long, Laurel *203*
Long, Loren 1966(?)- *188*
  Earlier sketch in SATA *151*
Long, Melinda 1960- *152*

Long, Sylvia 1948- *179*
  Earlier sketch in SATA *120*
Longbeard, Frederick
  See Longyear, Barry B(rookes)
Longfellow, Henry Wadsworth 1807-1882 ... *19*
  See also CLR *99*
Longfellow, Layne (A.) 1937- *102*
Longman, Harold S. 1919- *5*
Longsworth, Polly 1933- *28*
Longtemps, Kenneth 1933- *17*
Longway, A. Hugh
  See Lang, Andrew
Longyear, Barry B(rookes) 1942- *117*
Look, Lenore *180*
Loomans, Diane 1955- *90*
Loomis, Christine *160*
  Earlier sketch in SATA *113*
Loomis, Jennifer A. 1942- *101*
Loomis, Robert D. *5*
Lopez, Angelo (Cayas) 1967- *83*
Lopez, Barry 1945- *67*
Lopez, Barry Holstun
  See Lopez, Barry
Lopez, Jack 1950- *178*
Lopez, Loretta 1963- *190*
Lopez, Lorraine 1956- *181*
Lopez, Lorraine M.
  See Lopez, Lorraine
Lopez, Rafael 1961(?)- *198*
Lopshire, Robert M(artin) 1927- *6*
Loraine, Connie
  See Reece, Colleen L.
Lorbiecki, Marybeth 1959- *172*
  Earlier sketch in SATA *121*
Lord, Athena V. 1932- *39*
Lord, Beman 1924-1991 .... *5*
  Obituary *69*
Lord, Bette Bao 1938- *58*
Lord, Cynthia *182*
Lord, Doreen Mildred Douglas
  See Lord, Douglas
Lord, Douglas 1904-1992 .... *12*
Lord, Janet *204*
Lord, John Vernon 1939- *21*
Lord, Michele *201*
Lord, Nancy
  See Titus, Eve
Lord, Patricia C. 1927-1988
  Obituary *58*
Lord, Walter 1917-2002 .... *3*
Lorde, Diana
  See Reno, Dawn E(laine)
Lorenz, Albert 1941- *115*
Lorenzini, Carlo 1826-1890 .... *100*
  Earlier sketch in SATA *29*
  See also CLR *120*
Lorey, Dean 1967- *193*
Lorimer, Janet 1941- *60*
Loring, Emilie (Baker) 1864(?)-1951 .... *51*
Lorkowski, Thomas V(incent) 1950- *92*
Lorkowski, Tom
  See Lorkowski, Thomas V(incent)
Lorraine, Walter (Henry) 1929- *16*
Lorrimer, Claire
  See Clark, Patricia Denise
Loss, Joan 1933- *11*
Lothrop, Harriet Mulford Stone 1844-1924 . *20*
Lottridge, Celia Barker 1936- *157*
  Earlier sketch in SATA *112*
LoTurco, Laura 1963- *84*
Lotz, Wolfgang 1912-1981 .... *65*
Louie, Ai-Ling 1949- *40*
  Brief entry *34*
Louis, Catherine 1963- *186*
Louis, Pat
  See Francis, Dorothy
Louisburgh, Sheila Burnford
  See Burnford, Sheila (Philip Cochrane Every)
Louise, Anita
  See Riggio, Anita
Louise, Tina 1934- *191*

Lourie, Helen
  See Storr, Catherine (Cole)
Lourie, Peter 1952- *183*
  Earlier sketches in SATA *82, 142*
Lourie, Peter King
  See Lourie, Peter
Love, Ann 1947- *168*
  Earlier sketch in SATA *79*
Love, D. Anne 1949- *180*
  Earlier sketches in SATA *96, 145*
Love, Douglas 1967- *92*
Love, Judith Dufour
  See Love, Judy
Love, Judy *188*
Love, Katherine (Isabel) 1907- *3*
Love, Kathleen Ann
  See Love, Ann
Love, Sandra (Weller) 1940- *26*
Lovejoy, Jack 1937- *116*
Lovelace, Delos Wheeler 1894-1967 .... *7*
Lovelace, Maud Hart 1892-1980 .... *2*
  Obituary *23*
Lovell, Ingraham
  See Bacon, Josephine Dodge (Daskam)
Loverseed, Amanda (Jane) 1965- *75*
Lovett, Margaret (Rose) 1915- *22*
Low, Alice 1926- *156*
  Earlier sketches in SATA *11, 76*
Low, Elizabeth Hammond 1898-1991 .... *5*
Low, Joseph 1911-2007 .... *14*
Low, Penelope Margaret
  See Lively, Penelope
Low, William *177*
Lowe, Helen 1961- *206*
Lowe, Jay, Jr.
  See Loeper, John J(oseph)
Lowell, Pamela *187*
Lowell, Susan 1950- *206*
  Earlier sketches in SATA *81, 127*
Lowenstein, Dyno 1914-1996 .... *6*
Lowenstein, Sallie 1949- *116*
Lowery, Linda 1949- *151*
  Earlier sketch in SATA *74*
Lowitz, Anson C. 1901(?)-1978 .... *18*
Lowitz, Sadyebeth Heath 1901-1969 .... *17*
Lowndes, Robert A(ugustine) W(ard)
  1916-1998 .... *117*
Lowrey, Janette Sebring 1892-1986 .... *43*
Lowry, Lois 1937- *177*
  Autobiography Feature *127*
  Earlier sketches in SATA *23, 70, 111*
  See also CLR *72*
  See also SAAS *3*
Lowry, Lois Hammersberg
  See Lowry, Lois
Lowry, Peter 1953- *7*
Lowther, George F. 1913-1975
  Obituary *30*
Loyie, Larry 1933- *150*
Lozansky, Edward D. 1941- *62*
Lozier, Herbert 1915- *26*
Lubar, David 1954- *190*
  Earlier sketch in SATA *133*
Lubell, Cecil 1912-2000 .... *6*
Lubell, Winifred (A. Milius) 1914- *6*
Lubin, Leonard
  See Lubin, Leonard B.
Lubin, Leonard B. 1943-1994 .... *45*
  Brief entry *37*
Lubka, S. Ruth 1948- *154*
Lubner, Susan *185*
Luby, Thia 1954- *124*
Lucado, Max (Lee) 1955- *104*
Lucas, Cedric 1962- *101*
Lucas, E(dward) V(errall) 1868-1938 .... *20*
Lucas, Eileen 1956- *113*
  Earlier sketch in SATA *76*
Lucas, George 1944- *56*
Lucas, Jerry 1940- *33*
Lucas, Margeaux *186*

Lucas, Victoria
  See Plath, Sylvia
Lucashenko, Melissa 1967- *104*
Luccarelli, Vincent 1923- *90*
Luce, Celia (Geneva Larsen) 1914- *38*
Luce, Willard (Ray) 1914-1990 .... *38*
Lucht, Irmgard 1937- *82*
Lucke, Deb *202*
Luckett, Dave 1951- *167*
  Earlier sketch in SATA *106*
Luckhardt, Mildred Corell 1898-1990 .... *5*
Ludden, Allen (Ellsworth) 1918(?)-1981
  Obituary *27*
Ludel, Jacqueline 1945- *64*
Ludlow, Geoffrey
  See Meynell, Laurence Walter
Ludlum, Mabel Cleland
  See Widdemer, Mabel Cleland
Ludwig, Helen *33*
Ludwig, Lyndell 1923- *63*
Ludwig, Trudy 1959- *166*
Lueders, Edward (George) 1923- *14*
Luenn, Nancy 1954- *79*
  Earlier sketch in SATA *51*
Lufkin, Raymond H. 1897- *38*
Lugard, Flora Louisa Shaw 1852-1929 .... *21*
Luger, Harriett Mandelay 1914- *23*
Luhrmann, Winifred B(ruce) 1934- *11*
Luis, Earlene W. 1929- *11*
Lujan, Jorge *201*
Luke, Pauline *178*
Luke, Pauline R.
  See Luke, Pauline
Lum, Peter
  See Crowe, (Bettina) Peter Lum
Lumry, Amanda (R.) *159*
Lund, Deb *157*
Lund, Doris Herold 1919- *12*
Lunde, Darrin *202*
Lung, Chang
  See Jordan, Robert
Lunge-Larsen, Lise 1955- *184*
  Earlier sketch in SATA *138*
Lunn, Carolyn (Kowalczyk) 1960- *67*
Lunn, Janet (Louise Swoboda) 1928- *110*
  Earlier sketches in SATA *4, 68*
  See also CLR *18*
  See also SAAS *12*
Lunsford, Cin Forshay
  See Forshay-Lunsford, Cin
Lupica, Michael
  See Lupica, Mike
Lupica, Michael Thomas
  See Lupica, Mike
Lupica, Mike 1952- *177*
Lupoff, Dick
  See Lupoff, Richard A(llen)
Lupoff, Richard A(llen) 1935- *60*
Lurie, Alison 1926- *112*
  Earlier sketch in SATA *46*
Lurie, Morris 1938- *72*
Lussert, Anneliese 1929- *101*
Lusted, Marcia Amidon 1962- *143*
Lustig, Arnost 1926- *56*
Lustig, Loretta 1944- *46*
Luthardt, Kevin 1973- *172*
Luther, Frank 1905-1980
  Obituary *25*
Luther, Rebekah (Lyn) S(tiles) 1960- *90*
Luttmann, Gail
  See Damerow, Gail
Luttrell, Guy L. 1938- *22*
Luttrell, Ida (Alleene) 1934- *91*
  Brief entry *35*
  Earlier sketch in SATA *40*
Luttrell, William (J. III) 1954- *149*
Lutz, John 1939- *180*
Lutz, John Thomas
  See Lutz, John
Lutz, Norma Jean 1943- *122*
Lutzeier, Elizabeth 1952- *72*

Lutzker, Edythe 1904-1991 .... *5*
Luxbacher, Irene M. 1970- *153*
Luzadder, Patrick 1954- *89*
Luzzati, Emanuele 1921-2007 .... *7*
Luzzatto, Paola Caboara 1938- *38*
Lybbert, Tyler 1970- *88*
Lydon, Michael 1942- *11*
Lyfick, Warren
  See Reeves, Lawrence F.
Lyle, Katie Letcher 1938- *8*
Lynch, Chris 1962- *171*
  Earlier sketches in SATA *95, 131*
  See also CLR *58*
Lynch, Jay 1945- *204*
Lynch, Lorenzo 1932- *7*
Lynch, Marietta 1947- *29*
Lynch, P(atrick) J(ames) 1962- *122*
  Earlier sketch in SATA *79*
Lynch, Patricia (Nora) 1898-1972 .... *9*
Lynds, Dennis 1924-2005 .... *47*
  Brief entry *37*
Lyne, Alison Davis *188*
Lyngseth, Joan
  See Davies, Joan
Lynn, Elizabeth A(nne) 1946- *99*
Lynn, Mary
  See Brokamp, Marilyn
Lynn, Patricia
  See Watts, Mabel Pizzey
Lynn, Tracy *175*
Lyon, Elinor 1921-2008 .... *6*
  Obituary *192*
Lyon, Elinor Bruce
  See Lyon, Elinor
Lyon, George Ella 1949- *207*
  Autobiography Feature *148*
  Earlier sketches in SATA *68, 119, 148*
Lyon, Lyman R.
  See de Camp, L. Sprague
Lyons, Dorothy M(arawee) 1907-1997 .... *3*
Lyons, Grant 1941- *30*
Lyons, Marcus
  See Blish, James
Lyons, Mary E. 1947- *195*
  Autobiography Feature *195*
  Earlier sketches in SATA *93, 142*
Lyons, Mary Evelyn
  See Lyons, Mary E.
Lystad, Mary (Hanemann) 1928- *11*
Lytle, Elizabeth Stewart 1949- *79*
Lytle, Robert A. 1944- *119*
Lyttle, Richard B(ard) 1927- *23*
Lytton, Edward G(eorge) E(arle) L(ytton)
  Bulwer-Lytton Baron 1803-1873 .... *23*

M

Ma, Wenhai 1954- *84*
Maar, Leonard (Frank, Jr.) 1927- *30*
Maartens, Maretha 1945- *73*
Maas, Selve -1997 .... *14*
Maass, Robert *195*
Mabie, Grace
  See Mattern, Joanne
Mac
  See MacManus, Seumas
  and Maccari, Ruggero
Macalaster, Elizabeth G. 1951- *115*
MacAlister, Katie *159*
MacAllan, Andrew
  See Leasor, James
MacAodhagain, Eamon
  See Egan, E(dward) W(elstead)
MacArthur-Onslow, Annette Rosemary
  1933- *26*
Macaulay, David (Alexander) 1946- *137*
  Brief entry *27*
  Earlier sketches in SATA *46, 72*
  See also CLR *14*

Author Index

Macaulay, Teresa (E.) 1947- 95
Macavinta, Courtney 176
MacBeth, George (Mann) 1932-1992 4
   Obituary 70
MacBride, Roger Lea 1929-1995 85
MacCarter, Don 1944- 91
MacClintock, Dorcas 1932- 8
MacCready, Robin Merrow 1959(?)- 190
MacCullough, Carolyn 174
MacDonald, Alan 1958- 192
MacDonald, Amy 1951- 156
   Autobiography Feature 156
   Earlier sketches in SATA 76, 136
MacDonald, Anne Elizabeth Campbell Bard
   -1958
   See MacDonald, Betty
MacDonald, Anson
   See Heinlein, Robert A.
MacDonald, Betty 1908-1958
   See YABC 1
Macdonald, Blackie
   See Emrich, Duncan (Black Macdonald)
Macdonald, Caroline 1948- 86
   Obituary 111
   See also CLR 60
Macdonald, Dwight 1906-1982 29
   Obituary 33
MacDonald, George 1824-1905 100
   Earlier sketch in SATA 33
   See also CLR 67
MacDonald, Golden
   See Brown, Margaret Wise
Macdonald, Guy 195
Macdonald, James D. 1954- 67
   Earlier sketches in SATA 81, 114, 165, 1
Macdonald, Marcia
   See Hill, Grace Livingston
MacDonald, Margaret Read 1940- 194
   Earlier sketches in SATA 94, 164
Macdonald, Marianne 1934- 113
Macdonald, Mary
   See Gifford, Griselda
Macdonald, Maryann 1947- 189
   Earlier sketch in SATA 72
MacDonald, Ross 1957- 201
Macdonald, Shelagh 1937- 25
MacDonald, Suse 1940- 193
   Brief entry 52
   Earlier sketches in SATA 54, 109
Macdonald, Zillah K(atherine) 1885-1979 ... 11
MacDonnell, Megan
   See Stevens, Serita
MacDougal, John
   See Blish, James
Mace, Elisabeth 1933- 27
Mace, Varian 1938- 49
MacEachern, Stephen 206
MacEwen, Gwendolyn (Margaret)
   1941-1987 50
   Obituary 55
Macfarlan, Allan A. 1892-1982 35
MacFarlane, Iris 1922- 11
MacGill-Callahan, Sheila 1926-2000 78
MacGregor, Carol Lynn 153
MacGregor, Ellen 1906-1954 39
   Brief entry 27
MacGregor-Hastie, Roy (Alasdhair Niall)
   1929- 3
MacGrory, Yvonne 1948- 142
Machado, Ana Maria 1941- 150
MacHale, D.J. 1956- 175
MacHale, Donald James
   See MacHale, D.J.
Machetanz, Frederick 1908- 34
Machin Goodall, Daphne (Edith) 37
Macht, Norm
   See Macht, Norman L.
Macht, Norman L. 1929- 122
Macht, Norman Lee
   See Macht, Norman L.

MacInnes, Helen (Clark) 1907-1985 22
   Obituary 44
Macintosh, Brownie 1950- 98
MacIntyre, Elisabeth 1916- 17
MacIntyre, Rod
   See MacIntyre, R.P.
MacIntyre, R.P. 1947- 203
MacIntyre, R.P. 1947- 203
MacIntyre, Wendy 1947- 196
Mack, Jeff 194
Mack, L.V.
   See Kimmelman, Burt
Mack, Stan(ley) 17
Mack, Todd 168
Mack, Tracy 1968- 183
   Earlier sketch in SATA 128
Mackall, Dandi D.
   See Mackall, Dandi Daley
Mackall, Dandi Daley 1949- 182
   Earlier sketches in SATA 118, 177
Mackay, Claire 1930- 97
   Autobiography Feature 124
   Earlier sketch in SATA 40
   See also CLR 43
Mackay, Constance D'Arcy (?)-1966 125
Mackay, Donald 1914-2005 81
   Obituary 173
Mackay, Donald Alexander
   See Mackay, Donald
MacKaye, Percy (Wallace) 1875-1956 32
Mackel, Kathryn 1950- 162
Mackel, Kathy
   See Mackel, Kathryn
MacKellar, William 1914- 4
Macken, JoAnn Early 1953- 201
Macken, Walter 1915-1967 36
MacKenzie, Jill (Kelly) 1947- 75
Mackenzie, Robert 1974- 204
Mackey, Ernan
   See McInerny, Ralph
Mackey, Weezie Kerr 188
Mackie, Maron
   See McNeely, Jeannette
Mackin, Edward
   See McInerny, Ralph
MacKinnon, Bernie 1957- 69
MacKinnon Groomer, Vera 1915- 57
MacKinstry, Elizabeth 1879-1956 42
Mackler, Carolyn 1973- 156
MacLachlan, Emily
   See Charest, Emily MacLachlan
MacLachlan, Patricia 1938- 168
   Brief entry 42
   Earlier sketches in SATA 62, 107
   See also CLR 14
MacLane, Jack
   See Crider, Bill
MacLean, Alistair 1922(?)-1987 23
   Obituary 50
MacLean, Alistair Stuart
   See MacLean, Alistair
Maclean, Art
   See Shirreffs, Gordon D(onald)
MacLean, Christine Kole 1962- 177
MacLean, Glynne 1964- 150
MacLeod, Beatrice 1910- 162
   Earlier sketch in SATA 10
MacLeod, Beatrice Beach
   See MacLeod, Beatrice
MacLeod, Charlotte (Matilda) 1922-2005 28
   Obituary 160
MacLeod, Doug 1959- 201
   Earlier sketch in SATA 60
MacLeod, Elizabeth 184
   Earlier sketch in SATA 158
MacLeod, Ellen Jane (Anderson) 1916- 14
MacManus, James
   See MacManus, Seumas
MacManus, Seumas 1869-1960 25
MacMaster, Eve (Ruth) B(owers) 1942- 46

MacMillan, Annabelle
   See Quick, Annabelle
MacMillan, Dianne M(arie) 1943- 125
   Earlier sketch in SATA 84
Macnaughton, Tina 182
Macneill, Janet
   See McNeely, Jeannette
MacPeek, Walter G. 1902-1973 4
   Obituary 25
MacPhail, Catherine 1946- 197
   Earlier sketch in SATA 130
MacPherson, Margaret 1908-2001 9
   See also SAAS 4
MacPherson, Thomas George 1915-1976
   Obituary 30
MacPherson, Winnie 1930- 107
MacRae, Tom 1980- 181
Macrae, Travis
   See Feagles, Anita M(acRae)
MacRaois, Cormac 1944- 72
Macumber, Mari
   See Sandoz, Mari(e Susette)
Macy, Sue 1954- 134
   Earlier sketch in SATA 88
Madaras, Lynda 1947- 151
Madden, Don 1927- 3
Madden, Kerry 1961- 168
Madden-Lunsford, Kerry
   See Madden, Kerry
Maddern, Eric 1950- 166
Maddigan, Beth 1967- 174
Maddison, Angela Mary 1923- 10
   See also CLR 24
Maddock, Reginald (Bertram) 1912-1994 15
Madenski, Melissa (Ann) 1949- 77
Madian, Jon 1941- 9
Madison, Alan 182
Madison, Arnold 1937- 6
Madison, Winifred 5
Madonna 1958- 149
Madsen, Gunnar 171
Madsen, Jim 1964- 202
Madsen, Ross Martin 1946- 82
Madsen, Susan A. 1954- 90
Madsen, Susan Arrington
   See Madsen, Susan A.
Maehlqvist, Stefan 1943- 30
Maestro, Betsy (Crippen) 1944- 106
   Brief entry 30
   Earlier sketch in SATA 59
   See also CLR 45
Maestro, Giulio 1942- 106
   Earlier sketches in SATA 8, 59
   See also CLR 45
Maeterlinck, Maurice 1862-1949 66
Magee, Doug 1947- 78
Magee, Wes 1939- 64
Maggio, Rosalie 1943- 69
Magid, Ken(neth Marshall) 65
Magnus, Erica 1946- 77
Magoon, Scott 182
Magorian, James 1942- 92
   Earlier sketch in SATA 32
Magorian, Michelle 1947- 128
   Earlier sketch in SATA 67
Magorian, Michelle Jane
   See Magorian, Michelle
Magovern, Peg 103
Maguire, Anne
   See Nearing, Penny
Maguire, Gregory 1954- 200
   Autobiography Feature 200
   Earlier sketches in SATA 28, 84, 129
   See also SAAS 22
Maguire, Gregory Peter
   See Maguire, Gregory
Maguire, Jack 1920-2000 74
Maguire, Jesse
   See Smith, Sherwood
Maguire, Jessie
   See Smith, Sherwood

Maher, Ramona 1934- *13*
Mahlqvist, Stefan
  See Maehlqvist, Stefan
Mahon, Julia C(unha) 1916- *11*
Mahony, Elizabeth Winthrop
  See Winthrop, Elizabeth
Mahood, Kenneth 1930- *24*
Mahy, Margaret 1936- *171*
  Earlier sketches in SATA *14, 69, 119*
  See also CLR *78*
Mahy, Margaret May
  See Mahy, Margaret
Maiden, Cecil (Edward) 1902-1981 .... *52*
Maidoff, Ilka
  See List, Ilka Katherine
Maifair, Linda Lee 1947- *83*
Maik, Henri
  See Hecht, Henri Joseph
Maillu, David G(ian) 1939- *111*
Maine, Trevor
  See Catherall, Arthur
Mains, Randolph P. 1946- *80*
Maione, Heather *189*
Maiorano, Robert 1946- *43*
Maisner, Heather 1947- *89*
Maison, Della
  See Katz, Bobbi
Maitland, Antony Jasper 1935- *25*
Maitland, Barbara *102*
Mai-Wyss, Tatjana 1972- *187*
Major, Kevin (Gerald) 1949- *134*
  Earlier sketches in SATA *32, 82*
  See also CLR *11*
Majure, Janet 1954- *96*
Makhijani, Pooja *188*
Makie, Pam 1943- *37*
Makowski, Silk
  See Makowski, Silvia Ann
Makowski, Silvia Ann 1940- *101*
Malam, John 1957- *152*
  Earlier sketch in SATA *89*
Maland, Nick *195*
Malcolm, Dan
  See Silverberg, Robert
Malcolm, Jahnna N.
  See Beecham, Jahnna
Malcolmson, Anne
  See von Storch, Anne B.
Malcolmson, David 1899-1978 .... *6*
Maletta, Dr. Arlene
  See Feltenstein, Arlene (H.)
Maley, Carleen
  See Hutchins, Carleen Maley
Mali, Jane Lawrence 1937-1995 .... *51*
  Brief entry *44*
  Obituary *86*
Malkin, Nina 1959(?)- *179*
Mallett, Jerry J. 1939- *76*
Malley, Gemma *198*
Malley, G.R.
  See Malley, Gemma
Mallory, Kenneth 1945- *185*
  Earlier sketch in SATA *128*
Mallowan, Agatha Christie
  See Christie, Agatha
Malmberg, Carl 1904-1979 .... *9*
Malmgren, Dallin 1949- *65*
Malo, John W. 1911-2000 .... *4*
Malone, James Hiram 1930- *84*
Malone, Nola Langner 1930-2003 .... *8*
  Obituary *151*
Malone, Patricia 1932- *155*
Malone, Peter 1953- *191*
Maloney, Pat
  See Markun, Patricia Maloney
Malory, Sir Thomas 1410(?)-1471(?) *59*
  Brief entry *33*
Maltese, Michael 1909(?)-1981
  Obituary *24*
Malvasi, Meg Greene *143*
Malvern, Corinne 1905-1956 .... *34*

Malvern, Gladys (?)-1962 .... *23*
Mama G.
  See Davis, Grania
Mammano, Julie 1962- *202*
  Earlier sketch in SATA *107*
Mamonova, Tatyana 1943- *93*
Manchel, Frank 1935- *10*
Manchess, Gregory 1955- *203*
Manchester, William (Raymond)
  1922-2004 .... *65*
Mandabach, Brian 1962(?)- *197*
Mandel, Brett H. 1969- *108*
Mandel, Peter 1957- *87*
Mandel, Sally (Elizabeth) 1944- *64*
Mandell, Muriel (Hortense Levin) 1921- *63*
Manders, John 1957- *175*
Manes, Stephen 1949- *99*
  Brief entry *40*
  Earlier sketch in SATA *42*
Manfred, Frederick (Feikema) 1912-1994 .... *30*
Mangin, Marie France 1940- *59*
Mangione, Gerlando 1909-1998 .... *6*
  Obituary *104*
Mangione, Jerre
  See Mangione, Gerlando
Mango, Karin N. 1936- *52*
Mangurian, David 1938- *14*
Mania, Cathy 1950- *102*
Mania, Robert 1952- *102*
Mania, Robert C., Jr.
  See Mania, Robert
Maniatty, Taramesha 1978- *92*
Maniscalco, Joseph 1926- *10*
Manley, Deborah 1932- *28*
Manley, Seon 1921- *15*
  See also CLR *3*
  See also SAAS *2*
Mann, Elizabeth 1948- *153*
Mann, Josephine
  See Pullein-Thompson, Josephine (Mary Wedderburn)
Mann, Kenny 1946- *91*
Mann, Pamela 1946- *91*
Mann, Patrick
  See Waller, Leslie
Mann, Peggy
  See Houlton, Peggy Mann
Mannetti, Lisa 1953- *57*
  Brief entry *51*
Mannheim, Grete (Salomon) 1909-1986 ...... *10*
Manniche, Lise 1943- *31*
Manning, Jane K. *185*
Manning, Mick 1959- *176*
Manning, Rosemary 1911-1988 .... *10*
Manning, Sarra *162*
Manning-Sanders, Ruth (Vernon)
  1895(?)-1988 .... *73*
  Obituary *57*
  Earlier sketch in SATA *15*
Mannion, Diane
  See Paterson, Diane
Mannis, Celeste Davidson *173*
Mannon, Warwick
  See Hopkins, (Hector) Kenneth
Manos, Helen *199*
Mansir, A. Richard 1932- *170*
Manson, Ainslie Kertland 1938- *115*
Manson, Beverlie 1945- *57*
  Brief entry *44*
Manthorpe, Helen 1958- *122*
Mantinband, Gerda (B.) 1917- *74*
Manton, Jo
  See Gittings, Jo (Grenville) Manton
Manuel, Lynn 1948- *179*
  Earlier sketch in SATA *99*
Manushkin, Fran 1942- *205*
  Earlier sketches in SATA *7, 54, 93, 166*
Manushkin, Frances
  See Manushkin, Fran
Man Without a Spleen, A
  See Chekhov, Anton

Manzano, Sonia 1950- *167*
Mapes, Mary A.
  See Ellison, Virginia H(owell)
Maple, Marilyn 1931- *80*
Mappin, Strephyn 1956- *109*
Mara, Barney
  See Roth, Arthur J(oseph)
Mara, Jeanette
  See Cebulash, Mel
Marais, Josef 1905-1978
  Obituary *24*
Marasmus, Seymour
  See Rivoli, Mario
Marbach, Ethel
  See Pochocki, Ethel (Frances)
Marcal, Annette B.
  See Callaway, Bernice (Anne)
Marcelino
  See Agnew, Edith J(osephine)
Marcellino, Fred 1939-2001 .... *118*
  Obituary *127*
  Earlier sketch in SATA *68*
March, Carl
  See Fleischman, Sid
Marchant, Bessie 1862-1941
  See YABC *2*
Marchant, Catherine
  See Cookson, Catherine (McMullen)
Marcher, Marion Walden 1890-1987 ...... *10*
Marchesi, Stephen 1951- *114*
Marchesi, Steve
  See Marchesi, Stephen
  and Older, Effin
  and Older, Jules
Marchetta, Melina 1965- *170*
Marciano, John Bemelmans 1970- *167*
  Earlier sketch in SATA *118*
  See also CLR *93*
Marco, Lou
  See Gottfried, Theodore Mark
Marcus, Leonard S. 1950- *187*
  Earlier sketch in SATA *133*
Marcus, Paul 1953- *82*
Marcus, Rebecca B(rian) 1907- *9*
Marcuse, Aida E. 1934- *89*
Marek, Margot L. 1934(?)-1987
  Obituary *54*
Maren, Julie 1970- *199*
Margaret, Karla
  See Andersdatter, Karla M(argaret)
Margolin, Harriet
  See Ziefert, Harriet
Margolis, Jeffrey A. 1948- *108*
Margolis, Leslie *187*
Margolis, Richard J(ules) 1929-1991 ...... *86*
  Obituary *67*
  Earlier sketch in SATA *4*
Margolis, Vivienne 1922- *46*
Mariana
  See Foster, Marian Curtis
Marie, Geraldine 1949- *61*
Mariner, Scott
  See Pohl, Frederik
Marino, Dorothy Bronson 1912- *14*
Marino, Jan 1936- *114*
Marino, Nick
  See Deming, Richard
Marino, Peter 1960- *179*
Mario, Anna
  See Odgers, Sally Farrell
Marion, Henry
  See del Rey, Lester
Maris, Ron *71*
  Brief entry *45*
Mark, Jan 1943-2006 .... *164*
  Obituary *173*
  Earlier sketches in SATA *22, 69, 114*
  See also CLR *11*
Mark, Janet Marjorie
  See Mark, Jan
Mark, Joan T. 1937- *122*

Mark, Pauline (Dahlin) 1913-1997 .... *14*
Mark, Polly
  See Mark, Pauline (Dahlin)
Mark, Ted
  See Gottfried, Theodore Mark
Markel, Michelle *169*
Marker, Sherry 1941- *76*
Markert, Jennifer 1965- *83*
Markert, Jenny
  See Markert, Jennifer
Markham, Lynne 1947- *102*
Markham, Marion M. 1929- *60*
Markham, Wendy
  See Staub, Wendy Corsi
Markins, W. S.
  See Jenkins, Marie M(agdalen)
Markle, Sandra L. 1946- *185*
  Brief entry *41*
  Earlier sketches in SATA *57, 92, 148*
Markle, Sandra Lee
  See Markle, Sandra L.
Marko, Katherine D(olores) *28*
Markoosie
  See Patsauq, Markoosie
Marks, Alan 1957- *187*
  Earlier sketches in SATA *77, 151*
Marks, Burton 1930- *47*
  Brief entry *43*
Marks, Graham *158*
Marks, Hannah K.
  See Trivelpiece, Laurel
Marks, J.
  See Highwater, Jamake (Mamake)
Marks, J(ames) M(acdonald) 1921- *13*
Marks, Laurie J. 1957- *68*
Marks, Margaret L. 1911(?)-1980
  Obituary *23*
Marks, Mickey Klar -1986 .... *12*
Marks, Peter
  See Smith, Robert Kimmel
Marks, Rita 1938- *47*
Marks, Stan(ley) *14*
Marks-Highwater, J.
  See Highwater, Jamake (Mamake)
Markun, Patricia Maloney 1924- *15*
Markusen, Bruce (Stanley Rodriguez)
  1965- *141*
Marley, Louise 1952- *173*
  Earlier sketch in SATA *120*
Marlin, Hilda
  See Van Stockum, Hilda
Marlow, Layne *204*
Marlow, Max
  See Nicole, Christopher (Robin)
Marlow, Susan K. 1953- *178*
Marlowe, Amy Bell *67*
  Earlier sketch in SATA *1*
Marlowe, Jack
  See Deary, Terry
Marney, Dean 1952- *90*
Marokvia, Artur 1909- *31*
Marokvia, Mireille 1908-2008 .... *5*
  Obituary *197*
Marokvia, Mireille Journet
  See Marokvia, Mireille
Marol, Jean-Claude 1946- *125*
Marr, John S(tuart) 1940- *48*
Marr, Melissa 1972- *189*
Marric, J. J.
  See Butler, William Vivian
  and Creasey, John
Marrin, Albert 1936- *193*
  Brief entry *43*
  Earlier sketches in SATA *53, 90, 126*
  See also CLR *53*
Marriott, Alice Lee 1910-1992 .... *31*
  Obituary *71*
Marriott, Janice 1946- *134*
Marriott, Pat(ricia) 1920- *35*
Marroquin, Patricio
  See Markun, Patricia Maloney

Mars, W. T.
  See Mars, Witold Tadeusz J.
Mars, Witold Tadeusz J. 1912-1985 .... *3*
Marsden, Carolyn 1950- *175*
  Earlier sketch in SATA *140*
Marsden, John 1950- *146*
  Earlier sketches in SATA *66, 97*
  See also CLR *34*
  See also SAAS *22*
Marsh, Carole 1946- *127*
Marsh, Dave 1950- *66*
Marsh, J. E.
  See Marshall, Evelyn
Marsh, James 1946- *73*
Marsh, Jean
  See Marshall, Evelyn
Marsh, Joan F. 1923- *83*
Marsh, Paul
  See Hopkins, (Hector) Kenneth
Marsh, Valerie 1954- *89*
Marshall, Anthony D(ryden) 1924- *18*
Marshall, Bonnie C. 1941- *141*
  Earlier sketch in SATA *18*
Marshall, Bridget M(ary) 1974- *103*
Marshall, (Sarah) Catherine (Wood)
  1914-1983 .... *2*
  Obituary *34*
Marshall, Douglas
  See McClintock, Marshall
Marshall, Edmund
  See Hopkins, (Hector) Kenneth
Marshall, Edward
  See Marshall, James
Marshall, Evelyn 1897-1991 .... *11*
Marshall, Felicity 1950- *116*
Marshall, Garry 1934- *60*
Marshall, H. H.
  See Jahn, Michael
Marshall, James 1942-1992 .... *75*
  Earlier sketches in SATA *6, 51*
  See also CLR *21*
Marshall, James Edward
  See Marshall, James
Marshall, James Vance
  See Payne, Donald Gordon
Marshall, Janet (Perry) 1938- *97*
Marshall, Jeff
  See Laycock, George (Edwin)
Marshall, Kim
  See Marshall, Michael (Kimbrough)
Marshall, Michael (Kimbrough) 1948- *37*
Marshall, Percy
  See Young, Percy M(arshall)
Marshall, S(amuel) L(yman) A(twood)
  1900-1977 .... *21*
Marsoli, Lisa Ann 1958- *101*
  Brief entry *53*
Marsten, Richard
  See Hunter, Evan
Marston, Elsa 1933- *156*
Marston, Hope Irvin 1935- *127*
  Earlier sketch in SATA *31*
Marszalek, John F. 1939- *167*
Marszalek, John Francis, Jr.
  See Marszalek, John F.
Marszalek, John Francis 1939-
  See Marszalek, John F.
Martchenko, Michael 1942- *154*
  Earlier sketches in SATA *50, 95*
Martel, Aimee
  See Thurlo, Aimee
  and Thurlo, David
Martel, Suzanne 1924- *99*
Martignoni, Margaret E. 1908(?)-1974
  Obituary *27*
Martin, Ann M. 1955- *192*
  Brief entry *41*
  Earlier sketches in SATA *44, 70, 126*
  See also CLR *32*

Martin, Bill, Jr. 1916-2004 .... *145*
  Brief entry *40*
  Earlier sketches in SATA *40, 67*
  See also CLR *97*
Martin, Charles E(lmer)
  See Mastrangelo, Charles E(lmer)
Martin, Christopher
  See Hoyt, Edwin P(almer), Jr.
Martin, C.K. Kelly *207*
Martin, Claire 1933- *76*
Martin, Courtney Autumn 1984- *205*
Martin, David Stone 1913-1992 .... *39*
Martin, Del 1921-2008 .... *47*
Martin, Donald
  See Honig, Donald
Martin, Dorothy
  See Martin, Del
Martin, Dorothy L.
  See Martin, Del
Martin, Eugene *1*
Martin, Eva M. 1939- *65*
Martin, Frances M(cEntee) 1906-1998 .... *36*
Martin, Francesca 1947- *101*
Martin, Fred 1948- *119*
Martin, Fredric
  See Christopher, Matt(hew Frederick)
Martin, George Raymond Richard
  See Martin, George R.R.
Martin, George R.R. 1948- *118*
Martin, J(ohn) P(ercival) 1880(?)-1966 .... *15*
Martin, Jacqueline Briggs 1945- *188*
  Earlier sketches in SATA *98, 149*
Martin, Jane Read 1957- *84*
Martin, Jeremy
  See Levin, Marcia Obrasky
Martin, Les
  See Schulman, L(ester) M(artin)
Martin, Linda 1961- *82*
Martin, Lynne 1923- *21*
Martin, Marcia
  See Levin, Marcia Obrasky
Martin, Marvin 1926- *126*
Martin, Melanie
  See Pellowski, Michael (Joseph)
Martin, Nancy
  See Salmon, Annie Elizabeth
Martin, Patricia *200*
Martin, Patricia A.
  See Martin, Patricia
Martin, Patricia Miles 1899-1986 .... *43*
  Obituary *48*
  Earlier sketch in SATA *1*
Martin, Peter
  See Chaundler, Christine
Martin, Rafe 1946- *175*
Martin, Rene 1891-1977 .... *42*
  Obituary *20*
Martin, Rupert (Claude) 1905- *31*
Martin, S. R.
  See Mappin, Strephyn
Martin, Stefan 1936- *32*
Martin, Vicky
  See Storey, Victoria Carolyn
Martin, Webber
  See Silverberg, Robert
Martin, Wendy
  See Martini, Teri
Martin, William Ivan, Jr.
  See Martin, Bill, Jr.
Martineau, Diane 1940- *178*
Martineau, Harriet 1802-1876
  See YABC *2*
Martinet, Jeanne 1958- *80*
Martinez, Agnes *167*
Martinez, Arturo O. 1933- *192*
Martinez, Ed(ward) 1954- *98*
Martinez, Elizabeth Coonrod 1954- *85*
Martinez, Victor 1954- *95*
Martini, Teri 1930- *3*
Martini, Therese
  See Martini, Teri

Martino, Alfred C. 1964- *174*
Martinson, Janis
  See Herbert, Janis
Marton, Jirina 1946- *144*
  Earlier sketch in SATA *95*
Marton, Pierre
  See Stone, Peter
Martson, Del
  See Lupoff, Richard A(llen)
Martyr, Paula (Jane)
  See Lawford, Paula Jane
Maruki, Toshi 1912-2000 .... *112*
  See also CLR *19*
Marvin, Isabel R(idout) 1924- *84*
Marx, Patricia Windschill
  See Marx, Trish
Marx, Robert F(rank) 1936- *24*
Marx, Trish 1948- *202*
  Earlier sketches in SATA *112, 160*
Marzani, Carl (Aldo) 1912-1994 .... *12*
Marzollo, Jean 1942- *190*
  Autobiography Feature *190*
  Earlier sketches in SATA *29, 77, 130*
  See also SAAS *15*
Masefield, John (Edward) 1878-1967 .... *19*
Masoff, Joy 1951- *118*
Mason, Adrienne 1962- *163*
Mason, Cherie *170*
Mason, Edwin A. 1905-1979
  Obituary *32*
Mason, Ernst
  See Pohl, Frederik
Mason, F(rancis) van Wyck 1901-1978 .... *3*
  Obituary *26*
Mason, Frank W.
  See Mason, F(rancis) van Wyck
Mason, George Frederick 1904-2000 .... *14*
Mason, Miriam E(vangeline) 1900-1973 .... *2*
  Obituary *26*
Mason, Prue *195*
Mason, Simon 1962- *178*
Mason, Tally
  See Derleth, August (William)
Mason, Van Wyck
  See Mason, F(rancis) van Wyck
Mass, Wendy 1967- *196*
  Earlier sketch in SATA *158*
Mass, William
  See Gibson, William
Masselman, George 1897-1971 .... *19*
Massie, Dianne Redfield 1938- *125*
  Earlier sketch in SATA *16*
Massie, Elizabeth *108*
Masson, Sophie 1959- *179*
  Earlier sketch in SATA *133*
Masters, Anthony (Richard) 1940-2003 ...... *112*
  Obituary *145*
Masters, Kelly R(ay) 1897-1987 .... *3*
Masters, Mildred 1932- *42*
Masters, William
  See Cousins, Margaret
Masters, Zeke
  See Bensen, Donald R.
  and Goulart, Ron
Mastrangelo, Charles E(lmer) 1910-1995 ..... *70*
  Earlier sketch in SATA *69*
Masuda, Takeshi 1944- *56*
Matas, Carol 1949- *194*
  Autobiography Feature *112*
  Earlier sketch in SATA *93*
  See also CLR *52*
Matchette, Katharine E. 1941- *38*
Math, Irwin 1940- *42*
Mathabane, Mark 1960- *123*
Mather, Kirtley F(letcher) 1888-1978 .... *65*
Mathers, Petra 1945- *176*
  Earlier sketch in SATA *119*
  See also CLR *76*
Matheson, Richard (Christian) 1953- *119*
Matheson, Shirlee Smith 1942- *155*

Mathews, Eleanor
  See Mathews, Ellie
Mathews, Ellie 1946(?)- *193*
Mathews, Janet 1914-1992 .... *41*
Mathews, Judith
  See Goldberger, Judith M.
Mathews, Louise
  See Tooke, Louise Mathews
Mathiesen, Egon 1907-1976
  Obituary *28*
Mathieu, Joe 1949- *185*
  Brief entry *36*
  Earlier sketches in SATA *43, 94*
Mathieu, Joseph P.
  See Mathieu, Joe
Mathis, Sharon Bell 1937- *58*
  Earlier sketch in SATA *7*
  See also CLR *147*
  See also SAAS *3*
Matlin, Marlee 1965- *181*
Matlin, Marlee Beth
  See Matlin, Marlee
Matloff, Gregory 1945- *73*
Matott, Justin 1961- *109*
Matranga, Frances Carfi 1922- *78*
Matray, James I. 1948- *161*
Matray, James Irving
  See Matray, James I.
Matson, Emerson N(els) 1926- *12*
Matsui, Tadashi 1926- *8*
Matsuno, Masako
  See Kobayashi, Masako Matsuno
Matsuoka, Mei 1981- *192*
Matte, (Encarnacion) L'Enc 1936- *22*
Mattern, Joanne 1963- *122*
Matheson, Jenny *180*
Matthew, James
  See Barrie, J. M.
Matthews, Aline
  See De Wire, Elinor
Matthews, Andrew 1948- *138*
Matthews, Caitlin 1952- *122*
Matthews, Downs 1925- *71*
Matthews, Elizabeth 1978- *194*
Matthews, Ellen
  See Bache, Ellyn
Matthews, Ellen 1950- *28*
Matthews, Harold Downs
  See Matthews, Downs
Matthews, Jacklyn Meek
  See Meek, Jacklyn O'Hanlon
Matthews, John (Kentigern) 1948- *116*
Matthews, Laura S.
  See Matthews, L.S.
Matthews, Liz
  See Pellowski, Michael (Joseph)
Matthews, L.S. *183*
Matthews, Morgan
  See Pellowski, Michael (Joseph)
Matthews, Nicola
  See Browne, N.M.
Matthews, Patricia 1927-2006 .... *28*
Matthews, Patricia Anne
  See Matthews, Patricia
Matthews, Tina 1961- *190*
Matthews, Tom L.
  See Lalicki, Tom
Matthews, William Henry III 1919- *45*
  Brief entry *28*
Matthiessen, Peter 1927- *27*
Mattingley, Christobel (Rosemary) 1931- *85*
  Earlier sketch in SATA *37*
  See also CLR *24*
  See also SAAS *18*
Matulay, Laszlo 1912- *43*
Matus, Greta 1938- *12*
Maugham, W. S.
  See Maugham, W. Somerset
Maugham, W. Somerset 1874-1965 .... *54*
Maugham, William S.
  See Maugham, W. Somerset

Maugham, William Somerset
  See Maugham, W. Somerset
Maurer, Diane Philippoff
  See Maurer-Mathison, Diane V(ogel)
Maurer, Diane Vogel
  See Maurer-Mathison, Diane V(ogel)
Maurer-Mathison, Diane V(ogel) 1944- *89*
Mauser, Pat Rhoads
  See McCord, Patricia
Mauser, Patricia Rhoads
  See McCord, Patricia
Maves, Mary Carolyn 1916- *10*
Maves, Paul B(enjamin) 1913-1994 .... *10*
Mavor, Salley 1955- *125*
Mawicke, Tran 1911- *15*
Max 1906-1989
  See Diop, Birago (Ismael)
Max, Peter 1939- *45*
Maxon, Anne
  See Best, (Evangel) Allena Champlin
Maxwell, Arthur S. 1896-1970 .... *11*
Maxwell, Edith 1923- *7*
Maxwell, Gavin 1914-1969 .... *65*
Maxwell, Katie
  See MacAlister, Katie
Maxwell, William (Keepers, Jr.) 1908-2000
  Obituary *128*
Maxwell-Hyslop, Miranda 1968- *154*
May, Charles Paul 1920- *4*
May, Elaine Tyler 1947- *120*
May, J. C.
  See May, Julian
May, Julian 1931- *11*
May, Robert Lewis 1905-1976
  Obituary *27*
May, Robert Stephen 1929-1996 .... *46*
May, Robin
  See May, Robert Stephen
Mayall, Beth *171*
Mayberry, Florence V(irginia) Wilson *10*
Maybury, Richard J. 1946- *72*
Maybury, Rick
  See Maybury, Richard J.
Mayer, Agatha
  See Maher, Ramona
Mayer, Albert Ignatius, Jr. 1906-1994
  Obituary *29*
Mayer, Ann M(argaret) 1938- *14*
Mayer, Bill *200*
Mayer, Danuta 1958- *117*
Mayer, Hannelore Valencak 1929- *42*
Mayer, Jane Rothschild 1903-2001 .... *38*
Mayer, Marianna 1945- *132*
  Earlier sketches in SATA *32, 83*
Mayer, Mercer 1943- *137*
  Earlier sketches in SATA *16, 32, 73, 129*
  See also CLR *11*
Mayerson, Charlotte Leon *36*
Mayerson, Evelyn Wilde 1935- *55*
Mayfield, Katherine 1958- *118*
Mayfield, Sue 1963- *146*
  Earlier sketch in SATA *72*
Mayhar, Ardath 1930- *38*
Mayhew, James 1964- *204*
  Earlier sketches in SATA *85, 149*
Maynard, Olga 1920- *40*
Mayne, William (James Carter) 1928- *122*
  Earlier sketches in SATA *6, 68*
  See also CLR *123*
  See also SAAS *11*
Maynes, J. O. Rocky, Jr.
  See Maynes, J. Oscar, Jr.
Maynes, J. Oscar, Jr. 1929- *38*
Mayo, Gretchen Will 1936- *163*
  Earlier sketch in SATA *84*
Mayo, Margaret 1935- *165*
  Earlier sketches in SATA *38, 96*
Mayo, Margaret Mary
  See Mayo, Margaret
Mayr, Diane 1949- *197*
Mays, Lucinda L(a Bella) 1924- *49*

Mays, (Lewis) Victor (Jr.) 1927- 5
Mazer, Anne 1953- 192
Earlier sketches in SATA 67, 105
Mazer, Harry 1925- 167
Earlier sketches in SATA 31, 67, 105
See also CLR 16
See also SAAS 11
Mazer, Norma Fox 1931-2009 198
Earlier sketches in SATA 24, 67, 105, 168
See also CLR 23
See also SAAS 1
Mazille, Capucine 1953- 96
Mazza, Adriana 1928- 19
Mazzio, Joann 1926- 74
Mbugua, Kioi Wa 1962- 83
McAfee, Carol 1955- 81
McAllister, Amanda
See Dowdell, Dorothy (Florence) Karns
and Hager, Jean
and Meaker, Eloise
McAllister, Angela 182
McAllister, Margaret I. 1956- 169
Earlier sketch in SATA 117
McAllister, M.I.
See McAllister, Margaret I.
McArdle, Paula 1971- 198
McArthur, Nancy 96
McAvoy, Jim 1972- 142
McBain, Ed
See Hunter, Evan
McBain, Georgina 189
McBratney, Sam 1943- 203
Earlier sketches in SATA 89, 164
See also CLR 44
McBrier, Michael
See Older, Effin
and Older, Jules
McCafferty, Jim 1954- 84
McCaffery, Janet 1936- 38
McCaffrey, Anne 1926- 152
Autobiography Feature 152
Earlier sketches in SATA 8, 70, 116
See also CLR 130
See also SAAS 11
McCaffrey, Anne Inez
See McCaffrey, Anne
McCaffrey, Mary
See Szudek, Agnes S(usan) P(hilomena)
McCain, Becky Ray 1954- 138
McCain, Murray (David, Jr.) 1926-1981 7
Obituary 29
McCall, Edith (Sansom) 1911- 6
McCall, Virginia Nielsen 1909-2000 13
McCall, Wendell
See Pearson, Ridley
McCall Smith, Alexander
See Smith, Alexander McCall
McCallum, Phyllis
See Koch, Phyllis (Mae) McCallum
McCallum, Stephen 1960- 91
McCampbell, Darlene Z. 1942- 83
McCann, Edson
See del Rey, Lester
and Pohl, Frederik
McCann, Gerald 1916- 41
McCann, Helen 1948- 75
McCannon, Dindga 41
McCants, William D. 1961- 82
McCarter, Neely Dixon 1929- 47
McCarthy, Agnes 1933- 4
McCarthy, Colin (John) 1951- 77
McCarthy, Mary 1951- 203
McCarthy, Meghan 199
Earlier sketch in SATA 168
McCarthy, Ralph F. 1950- 139
McCarthy-Tucker, Sherri N. 1958- 83
McCarty, Peter 1966- 182
McCarty, Rega Kramer 1904-1986 10
McCaslin, Nellie 1914-2005 12

McCaughrean, Geraldine 1951- 173
Earlier sketches in SATA 87, 139
See also CLR 38
McCaughren, Tom 1936- 75
McCauley, Adam 1965- 128
McCay, (Zenas) Winsor 1869-1934 134
Earlier sketch in SATA 41
McClafferty, Carla Killough 1958- 137
McClary, Jane Stevenson 1919-1990
Obituary 64
McCleery, Patsy R. 1925- 133
Earlier sketch in SATA 88
McClements, George 196
McClintock, Barbara 1955- 146
Earlier sketches in SATA 57, 95
McClintock, Marshall 1906-1967 3
McClintock, May Garelick
See Garelick, May
McClintock, Mike
See McClintock, Marshall
McClintock, Norah 178
McClintock, Theodore 1902-1971 14
McClinton, Leon 1933- 11
McCloskey, Kevin 1951- 79
McCloskey, (John) Robert 1914-2003 100
Obituary 146
Earlier sketches in SATA 2, 39
See also CLR 7
McCloy, James F(loyd) 1941- 59
McClung, Robert M(arshall) 1916- 135
Earlier sketches in SATA 2, 68
See also CLR 11
See also SAAS 15
McClure, Gillian Mary 1948- 31
McColley, Kevin 1961- 80
See also SAAS 23
McConduit, Denise Walter 1950- 89
McConnell, James Douglas Rutherford
1915-1988 40
Obituary 56
McCord, Anne 1942- 41
McCord, David (Thompson Watson)
1897-1997 18
Obituary 96
See also CLR 9
McCord, Jean 1924- 34
McCord, Pat Mauser
See McCord, Patricia
McCord, Patricia 1943- 159
Earlier sketch in SATA 37
McCord, Patricia Sue Rhoads Mauser
See McCord, Patricia
McCormick, Brooks
See Adams, William Taylor
McCormick, Dell J. 1892-1949 19
McCormick, (George) Donald (King)
1911-1998 14
McCormick, Edith (Joan) 1934- 30
McCormick, Kimberly A. 1960- 153
McCormick, Patricia 1956- 181
Earlier sketch in SATA 128
McCourt, Edward (Alexander) 1907-1972
Obituary 28
McCourt, Lisa 1964- 159
Earlier sketch in SATA 117
McCourt, Malachy 1931- 126
McCoy, Iola Fuller 3
McCoy, J(oseph) J(erome) 1917- 8
McCoy, Karen Kawamoto 1953- 82
McCoy, Lois (Rich) 1941- 38
McCrady, Lady 1951- 16
McCrea, James (Craig, Jr.) 1920- 3
McCrea, Ruth (Pirman) 1921- 3
McCreigh, James
See Pohl, Frederik
McCrumb, Sharyn 1948- 109
McCue, Lisa 1959- 177
Earlier sketch in SATA 65
McCue, Lisa Emiline
See McCue, Lisa

McCullen, Andrew
See Arthur, Robert, (Jr.)
McCullers, Carson 1917-1967 27
McCullers, Lula Carson Smith
See McCullers, Carson
McCulloch, Derek (Ivor Breashur) 1897-1967
Obituary 29
McCulloch, John Tyler
See Burroughs, Edgar Rice
McCulloch, Sarah
See Ure, Jean
McCullough, David 1933- 62
McCullough, David Gaub
See McCullough, David
McCullough, Frances Monson 1938- 8
McCullough, Sharon Pierce 1943- 131
McCully, Emily Arnold
See Arnold, Emily
McCune, Dan
See Haas, Dorothy F.
McCunn, Ruthanne Lum 1946- 63
McCurdy, Michael (Charles) 1942- 147
Earlier sketches in SATA 13, 82
McCutcheon, Elsie (Mary Jackson) 1937- ... 60
McCutcheon, John 1952- 97
McDaniel, Becky Bring 1953- 61
McDaniel, Lurlene 1944- 146
Earlier sketch in SATA 71
McDaniels, Pellom III 1968- 121
McDaniels, Preston 1952- 192
McDearmon, Kay 20
McDermott, Beverly Brodsky 1941- 11
McDermott, Eleni 156
McDermott, Gerald (Edward) 1941- 163
Earlier sketches in SATA 16, 74
See also CLR 9
McDermott, Michael 1962- 76
McDevitt, Jack 1935- 155
Earlier sketch in SATA 94
McDevitt, John Charles
See McDevitt, Jack
McDole, Carol
See Farley, Carol (J.)
McDonald, Collin 1943- 79
McDonald, Gerald D(oan) 1905-1970 3
McDonald, Jamie
See Heide, Florence Parry
McDonald, Janet 1953-2007 204
Earlier sketch in SATA 148
McDonald, Jill (Masefield) 1927-1982 13
Obituary 29
McDonald, Joyce 1946- 164
Earlier sketch in SATA 101
McDonald, Lucile Saunders 1898-1992 10
McDonald, Mary Ann 1956- 84
McDonald, Megan 1958- 202
Autobiography Feature 151
Earlier sketches in SATA 67, 99, 148, 151
See also CLR 94
McDonald, Meme 1954- 112
McDonald, Mercedes 1956- 169
Earlier sketch in SATA 97
McDonald, Rae A. 1952- 201
McDonell, Chris 1960- 138
McDonnell, Christine 1949- 115
Earlier sketch in SATA 34
McDonnell, Flora (Mary) 1963- 146
Earlier sketch in SATA 90
McDonnell, Kathleen 1947- 186
McDonnell, Lois Eddy 1914-2001 10
McDonnell, Patrick 1956- 179
McDonough, Yona Zeldis 1957- 73
McElligott, Matt 1968- 196
Earlier sketch in SATA 135
McElligott, Matthew
See McElligott, Matt
McElmeel, Sharron L. 1942- 128
McElmurry, Jill 198
Earlier sketch in SATA 159
McElrath, William N. 1932- 65

McElrath-Eslick, Lori 1960- 204
 Earlier sketch in SATA 96
McEntee, Dorothy (Layng) 1902- 37
McEwen, Katherine 183
McEwen, Robert (Lindley) 1926-1980
 Obituary 23
McFadden, Kevin Christopher
 See Pike, Christopher
McFall, Christie 1918- 12
McFall, Gardner 1952- 183
McFarlan, Donald M(aitland) 1915- 59
McFarland, Henry "Hammer"
 See McFarland, Henry O.
McFarland, Henry O. 1934- 143
McFarland, Kenton D(ean) 1920- 11
McFarland, Martha
 See Smith-Ankrom, M. E.
McFarlane, Leslie 1902-1977 100
 Earlier sketches in SATA 31, 1, 65, 67
 See also CLR 118
McFarlane, Leslie Charles
 See McFarlane, Leslie
McFarlane, Peter (William) 1940- 95
McFarlane, Sheryl P. 1954- 86
McFarlane, Todd 1961- 117
McGaw, Jessie Brewer 1913-1997 10
McGee, Barbara 1943- 6
McGee, Marni 163
McGhee, Alison 1960- 196
McGiffin, (Lewis) Lee (Shaffer) 1908-1978 ... 1
McGill, Alice 159
McGill, Ormond 1913- 92
McGinley, Jerry 1948- 116
McGinley, Phyllis 1905-1978 44
 Obituary 24
 Earlier sketch in SATA 2
McGinnis, Lila S(prague) 1924- 44
McGinty, Alice B. 1963- 202
 Earlier sketch in SATA 134
McGivern, Justin 1985- 129
McGivern, Maureen Daly
 See Daly, Maureen
McGivern, Maureen Patricia Daly
 See Daly, Maureen
McGough, Elizabeth (Hemmes) 1934- 33
McGovern, Ann 1930- 132
 Earlier sketches in SATA 8, 69, 70
 See also CLR 50
 See also SAAS 17
McGowen, Thomas E. 1927- 109
 Earlier sketch in SATA 2
McGowen, Tom
 See McGowen, Thomas E.
McGrady, Mike 1933- 6
McGrath, Barbara Barbieri 1953- 169
 Earlier sketch in SATA 108
McGrath, Robin 1949- 121
McGrath, Thomas (Matthew) 1916-1990 41
 Obituary 66
McGraw, Eloise Jarvis 1915-2000 67
 Obituary 123
 Earlier sketch in SATA 1
 See also SAAS 6
McGraw, William Corbin 1916-1999 3
McGreal, Elizabeth
 See Yates, Elizabeth
McGregor, Barbara 1959- 82
McGregor, Craig 1933- 8
McGregor, Iona 1929- 25
McGrory, Anik 193
McGuffey, Alexander Hamilton 1816-1896 . 60
McGuigan, Mary Ann 1949- 106
McGuire, Edna 1899- 13
McGuire, Leslie (Sarah) 1945- 94
 Brief entry 45
 Earlier sketch in SATA 52
McGuire, Robert 187
McGuirk, Leslie (A.) 1960- 152
McGurk, Slater
 See Roth, Arthur J(oseph)

McHargue, Georgess 1941- 77
 Earlier sketch in SATA 4
 See also CLR 2
 See also SAAS 5
McHenry, E.B. 1963(?)- 193
McHugh, (Berit) Elisabet 1941- 55
 Brief entry 44
McIlvaine, Jane
 See McClary, Jane Stevenson
McIlwraith, Maureen Mollie Hunter
 See Hunter, Mollie
McInerney, Judith W(hitelock) 1945- 49
 Brief entry 46
McInerny, Ralph 1929- 93
McInerny, Ralph Matthew
 See McInerny, Ralph
McKaughan, Larry (Scott) 1941- 75
McKay, Donald 1895- 45
McKay, Hilary (Jane) 1959- 145
 Earlier sketch in SATA 92
 See also SAAS 23
McKay, Lawrence, Jr. 1948- 114
McKay, Robert W. 1921- 15
McKay, Sharon E. 1954- 165
McKay, Simon
 See Nicole, Christopher (Robin)
McKean, Dave 1963- 197
McKean, David Jeff
 See McKean, Dave
McKeating, Eileen 1957- 81
McKee, David (John) 1935- 158
 Earlier sketches in SATA 70, 107
 See also CLR 38
McKee, Tim 1970- 111
McKeever, Marcia
 See Laird, Jean E(louise)
McKelvey, Carole A. 1942- 78
McKelvy, Charles 1950- 124
McKendrick, Melveena (Christine) 1941- 55
McKendry, Joe 1972- 170
McKenna, Colleen O'Shaughnessy 1948- .. 136
 Earlier sketch in SATA 76
McKenzie, Dorothy Clayton 1910-1981
 Obituary 28
McKenzie, Ellen Kindt 1928- 80
McKernan, Victoria 1957- 171
McKie, Robin 112
McKillip, Patricia A. 1948- 174
 Earlier sketches in SATA 30, 80, 126
McKillip, Patricia Anne
 See McKillip, Patricia A.
McKim, Audrey Margaret 1909-1999 47
McKimmie, Chris 194
McKinley, Jennifer Carolyn Robin
 See McKinley, Robin
McKinley, Robin 1952- 195
 Brief entry 32
 Earlier sketches in SATA 50, 89, 130
 See also CLR 127
McKinney, Barbara Shaw 1951- 116
McKinney, Nadine 1938- 91
McKinty, Adrian 186
McKissack, Fredrick L. 1939- 162
 Brief entry 53
 Earlier sketches in SATA 73, 117
 See also CLR 55
McKissack, Fredrick Lemuel
 See McKissack, Fredrick L.
McKissack, Patricia C. 1944- 195
 Earlier sketches in SATA 51, 73, 117, 162
 See also CLR 129
McKissack, Patricia L'Ann Carwell
 See McKissack, Patricia C.
McKissack and McKissack
 See McKissack, Fredrick L.
 and McKissack, Patricia C.
McKown, Robin (?)-1976 6
McKy, Katie 1956- 184
McLaren, Clemence 1938- 158
 Earlier sketch in SATA 105
McLaughlin, Frank 1934- 73

McLaurin, Anne 1953- 27
McLean, Andrew 1946- 172
 Earlier sketch in SATA 113
McLean, J. Sloan
 See Gillette, Virginia M(ary)
 and Wunsch, Josephine (McLean)
McLean, Jacqueline
 See Kolosov, Jacqueline
McLean, Janet 1946- 113
McLean, Kathryn (Anderson) 1909-1966 9
McLean, Virginia Overton 1946- 90
McLean-Carr, Carol 1948- 122
McLeish, Kenneth 1940-1997 35
McLenighan, Valjean 1947- 46
 Brief entry 40
McLennan, Connie 171
McLennan, Will
 See Wisler, G(ary) Clifton
McLeod, Bob 1951- 173
McLeod, Chum 1955- 95
McLeod, Emilie Warren 1926-1982 23
 Obituary 31
McLeod, Kirsty
 See Hudson, (Margaret) Kirsty
McLeod, Margaret Vail
 See Holloway, Teresa (Bragunier)
McLerran, Alice 1933- 137
 Earlier sketch in SATA 68
McLimans, David 1949- 182
McLoughlin, John C. 1949- 47
McManus, Patrick F. 1933- 46
McManus, Patrick Francis
 See McManus, Patrick F.
McMeekin, Clark
 See McMeekin, Isabel McLennan
McMeekin, Isabel McLennan 1895-1973 3
McMenemy, Sarah 1965- 156
McMillan, Bruce 1947- 192
 Earlier sketches in SATA 22, 70, 129
 See also CLR 47
McMillan, Naomi
 See Grimes, Nikki
McMorey, James L.
 See Moyer, Terry J.
McMorrow, Annalisa 1969- 104
McMullan, Jim 1934- 150
 Earlier sketch in SATA 87
McMullan, K. H.
 See McMullan, Kate
McMullan, Kate 1947- 189
 Brief entry 48
 Earlier sketches in SATA 52, 87, 132
McMullan, Kate Hall
 See McMullan, Kate
McMullan, Margaret 1960- 203
McMurtrey, Martin A(loysias) 1921- 21
McNabb, Linda 1963- 147
McNair, Kate 3
McNair, Sylvia 1924-2002 74
McNamara, Margaret C(raig) 1915-1981
 Obituary 24
McNaught, Harry 32
McNaughton, Colin 1951- 134
 Earlier sketches in SATA 39, 92
 See also CLR 54
McNaughton, Janet 1953- 162
 Earlier sketch in SATA 110
McNeal, Laura 194
McNeal, Tom 194
McNeely, Jeannette 1918- 25
McNeer, May (Yonge) 1902-1994 81
 Earlier sketch in SATA 1
McNeese, Tim 1953- 139
McNeill, Janet
 See Alexander, Janet
McNicholas, Shelagh 191
McNickle, D'Arcy 1904-1977
 Obituary 22
McNickle, William D'Arcy
 See McNickle, D'Arcy

McNicoll, Sylvia (Marilyn) 1954- *113*
    See also CLR 99
McNulty, Faith 1918-2005 .... *168*
    Earlier sketches in SATA *12, 84, 139*
McPhail, David 1940- *183*
    Brief entry *32*
    Earlier sketches in SATA *47, 81, 140*
McPhail, David M.
    See McPhail, David
McPhail, David Michael
    See McPhail, David
McPhee, Norma H. 1928- *95*
McPhee, Richard B(yron) 1934- *41*
McPherson, James M. 1936- *141*
    Earlier sketch in SATA *16*
McPherson, James Munro
    See McPherson, James M.
McQueen, Lucinda 1950- *58*
    Brief entry *48*
McQueen, Mildred Hark 1908-1978 .... *12*
McQuillan, Mary *200*
McRae, Russell (William) 1934- *63*
McShean, Gordon 1936- *41*
Mc Swigan, Marie 1907-1962 .... *24*
McTavish, Sandy
    See Eyerly, Jeannette
McVeity, Jen *148*
McVey, Vicki 1946- *80*
McVicker, Charles (Taggart) 1930- *39*
McVicker, Chuck
    See McVicker, Charles (Taggart)
McWhirter, A(lan) Ross 1925-1975 .... *37*
    Obituary *31*
McWhirter, Norris (Dewar) 1925-2004 .... *37*
McWilliams, Karen 1943- *65*
Mdurvwa, Hajara E. 1962- *92*
Meacham, Margaret 1952- *203*
    Earlier sketch in SATA *95*
Meachum, Virginia 1918- *133*
    Earlier sketch in SATA *87*
Mead, Alice 1952- *146*
    Earlier sketch in SATA *94*
Mead, Margaret 1901-1978
    Obituary *20*
Mead, Russell (M., Jr.) 1935- *10*
Mead, Stella (?)-1981
    Obituary *27*
Meade, Ellen
    See Roddick, Ellen
Meade, Holly *207*
Meade, Marion 1934- *127*
    Earlier sketch in SATA *23*
Meader, Stephen W(arren) 1892-1977 .... *1*
Meadmore, Susan
    See Sallis, Susan (Diana)
Meadow, Charles T(roub) 1929- *23*
Meadowcroft, Enid LaMonte
    See Wright, Enid Meadowcroft (LaMonte)
Meadows, Graham (W.) 1934- *161*
Meadows, Michelle *202*
Meaker, M. J.
    See Meaker, Marijane
Meaker, Marijane 1927- *160*
    Autobiography Feature *111*
    Earlier sketches in SATA *20, 61, 99*
    See also CLR 29
    See also SAAS *1*
Meaker, Marijane Agnes
    See Meaker, Marijane
Means, Florence Crannell 1891-1980 .... *1*
    Obituary *25*
    See also CLR 56
Mearian, Judy Frank 1936- *49*
Mecca, Judy Truesdell 1955- *127*
Mechling, Lauren 1978(?)- *194*
Mechner, Jordan 1964- *205*
Medary, Marjorie 1890-1980 .... *14*
Meddaugh, Susan 1944- *176*
    Earlier sketches in SATA *29, 84, 125*
Medearis, Angela Shelf 1956- *123*
    Earlier sketch in SATA *72*

Medearis, Mary 1915- *5*
Medina, Jane 1953- *167*
    Earlier sketch in SATA *122*
Medina, Nico 1982- *193*
Medlicott, Mary 1946- *88*
Mee, Charles L., Jr. 1938- *72*
    Earlier sketch in SATA *8*
Meehl, Brian *204*
Meek, Jacklyn O'Hanlon 1933- *51*
    Brief entry *34*
Meek, S(terner St.) P(aul) 1894-1972
    Obituary *28*
Meeker, Clare Hodgson 1952- *96*
Meeker, Oden 1919(?)-1976 .... *14*
Meeker, Richard
    See Brown, Fornan
Meeks, Esther MacBain *1*
Meggs, Libby Phillips 1943- *130*
Mehdevi, Alexander (Sinclair) 1947- *7*
Mehdevi, Anne (Marie) Sinclair 1947- *8*
Meidell, Sherry 1951- *73*
Meier, Minta 1906- *55*
Meighan, Donald Charles 1929- *30*
Meigs, Cornelia Lynde 1884-1973 .... *6*
    See also CLR 55
Meilach, Dona Z(weigoron) 1926- *34*
Meilman, Philip W(arren) 1951- *79*
Meinstereifel, Ronald L. 1960- *134*
Meisel, Paul *184*
Meister, Cari *204*
Melanson, Luc *198*
Melcher, Daniel 1912-1985
    Obituary *43*
Melcher, Frederic Gershom 1879-1963
    Obituary *22*
Melcher, Marguerite Fellows 1879-1969 ...... *10*
Meldrum, Christina *206*
Melendez, Francisco 1964- *72*
Melhuish, Eva *199*
Melin, Grace Hathaway 1892-1973 .... *10*
Mellersh, H(arold) E(dward) L(eslie)
    1897- *10*
Melling, David *186*
Melmoth, Sebastian
    See Wilde, Oscar
Melnikoff, Pamela (Rita) *97*
Meltzer, Amy 1968- *202*
Meltzer, Milton 1915-2009 .... *201*
    Autobiography Feature *124*
    Earlier sketches in SATA *1, 50, 80, 128*
    See also CLR 13
    See also SAAS *1*
Melville, Anne
    See Potter, Margaret
Melville, Herman 1819-1891 .... *59*
Melwood, Mary
    See Lewis, E. M.
Melzack, Ronald 1929- *5*
Memling, Carl 1918-1969 .... *6*
Menchin, Scott *188*
Mendel, Jo
    See Bond, Gladys Baker
    and Gilbertson, Mildred Geiger
Mendelson, Steven T. 1958-1995 .... *86*
Mendelson-Stevens, Serita Deborah
    See Stevens, Serita
Mendes, Valerie 1939- *157*
Mendez, Raymond A. 1947- *66*
Mendonca, Susan
    See Smith, Susan Vernon
Mendoza, George 1934- *41*
    Brief entry *39*
    See also SAAS *7*
Menendez, Shirley (C.) 1937- *146*
Meng, Cece *194*
Meng, Heinz (Karl) 1924- *13*
Mennen, Ingrid 1954- *85*
Menotti, Gian Carlo 1911-2007 .... *29*
    Obituary *180*
Menuhin, Sir Yehudi 1916-1999 .... *40*
    Obituary *113*

Menville, Douglas 1935- *64*
Menzel, Barbara Jean 1946- *63*
Menzel, Peter 1948- *207*
Mercati, Cynthia *164*
Mercati, Cynthia J.
    See Mercati, Cynthia
Mercer, Charles (Edward) 1917-1988 .... *16*
    Obituary *61*
Mercer, Jessie *21*
Mercer, Sienna *192*
Meredith, Arnold
    See Hopkins, (Hector) Kenneth
Meredith, David William
    See Miers, Earl Schenck
Meringoff, Laurene Krasny
    See Brown, Laurene Krasny
Meriwether, Louise 1923- *52*
    Brief entry *31*
Merlin, Arthur
    See Blish, James
Merlin, Christina
    See Heaven, Constance (Christina)
Merriam, Eve 1916-1992 .... *73*
    Earlier sketches in SATA *3, 40*
    See also CLR 14
Merrill, Jane 1946- *42*
Merrill, Jane Merrill
    See Merrill, Jane
Merrill, Jean (Fairbanks) 1923- *82*
    Earlier sketch in SATA *1*
    See also CLR 52
Merrill, Phil
    See Merrill, Jane
Merriman, Alex
    See Silverberg, Robert
Merriman, Rachel 1971- *149*
    Earlier sketch in SATA *98*
Merrit, Elizabeth
    See Goudge, Eileen
Merski, Patricia K.
    See Merski, P.K.
Merski, P.K. *172*
Mertz, Barbara
    See Peters, Elizabeth
Mertz, Barbara Gross
    See Peters, Elizabeth
Merveille, David *200*
Merz, Jennifer J. *196*
Meschel, Susan V. 1936- *83*
Messenger, Charles (Rynd Milles) 1942- *59*
Messick, Dale 1906-2005 .... *64*
    Brief entry *48*
Messier, Claire 1956- *103*
Messieres, Nicole de
    See de Messieres, Nicole
Messinger, Carla *198*
Messmer, Otto 1892(?)-1983 .... *37*
Mesta, Gabriel
    See Moesta, Rebecca
Metcalf, Doris H(unter) *91*
Metcalf, Suzanne
    See Baum, L. Frank
Metos, Thomas H(arry) 1932- *37*
Metter, Bert(ram Milton) 1927- *56*
Metzenthen, David 1958- *167*
    Earlier sketch in SATA *106*
Meunier, Brian 1954- *195*
Meyer, Barbara 1939- *77*
Meyer, Carolyn 1935- *142*
    Autobiography Feature *142*
    Earlier sketches in SATA *9, 70, 118*
    See also SAAS 9
Meyer, Carolyn Mae
    See Meyer, Carolyn
Meyer, Edith Patterson 1895-1993 .... *5*
Meyer, F(ranklyn) E(dward) 1932- *9*
Meyer, Jean Shepherd *11*
Meyer, Jerome Sydney 1895-1975 .... *3*
    Obituary *25*
Meyer, June
    See Jordan, June

Meyer, Kerstin 1966- 190
Meyer, L. A.
  See Meyer, Louis A(lbert), Jr.
Meyer, Louis A(lbert), Jr. 1942- 144
  Earlier sketch in SATA *12*
Meyer, Renate 1930- 6
Meyer, Stephenie 1973- 193
  See also CLR *142*
Meyer, Susan E. 1940- 64
Meyers, Susan 1942- 164
  Earlier sketches in SATA *19, 108*
Meynell, Laurence Walter 1899-1989
  Obituary 61
Meynier, Yvonne (Pollet) 1908- 14
Mezey, Robert 1935- 33
Micale, Albert 1913- 22
Michael, James
  See Scagnetti, Jack
Michael, Livi 1960- 172
Michael, Manfred
  See Winterfeld, Henry
Michael, Olivia
  See Michael, Livi
Michaels, Barbara
  See Peters, Elizabeth
Michaels, Jamie 195
Michaels, Joanne Louise
  See Teitelbaum, Michael
Michaels, Kristin
  See Williams, Jeanne
Michaels, Molly
  See Untermeyer, Louis
Michaels, Neal
  See Teitelbaum, Michael
Michaels, Rune 194
Michaels, Ski
  See Pellowski, Michael (Joseph)
Michaels, Steve 1955- 71
Michaels, William M. 1917- 77
Michel, Anna 1943- 49
  Brief entry 40
Michel, Francois 1948- 82
Michelin, Linda 183
Michelson, Richard 198
  Earlier sketch in SATA *173*
Micich, Paul 74
Micklish, Rita 1931- 12
Micklos, John, Jr. 1956- 173
  Earlier sketch in SATA *129*
Micklos J., John, Jr. 1956-
  See Micklos, John, Jr.
Micucci, Charles (Patrick, Jr.) 1959- 144
  Earlier sketch in SATA *82*
Middleton, Haydn 1955- 152
  Earlier sketch in SATA *85*
Miers, Earl Schenck 1910-1972 1
  Obituary 26
Migdale, Lawrence 1951- 89
Miglio, Paige 1966- 201
Mikaelsen, Ben 1952- 173
  Earlier sketches in SATA *73, 107*
Mikaelsen, Benjamin John
  See Mikaelsen, Ben
Miklowitz, Gloria D. 1927- 129
  Earlier sketches in SATA *4, 68*
  See also SAAS *17*
Mikolaycak, Charles 1937-1993 78
  Obituary 75
  Earlier sketch in SATA *9*
  See also SAAS *4*
Mild, Warren (Paul) 1922- 41
Milelli, Pascal 1965- 135
Miles, Betty 1928- 78
  Earlier sketch in SATA *8*
  See also SAAS *9*
Miles, Miska
  See Martin, Patricia Miles
Miles, (Mary) Patricia 1930- 29
Miles, Patricia A.
  See Martin, Patricia Miles
Miles, Victoria 1966- 188

Milgrim, David 187
  Earlier sketch in SATA *158*
Milgrom, Harry 1912-1978 25
Milhous, Katherine 1894-1977 15
Milich, Zoran 174
Milios, Rita 1949- 79
Militant
  See Sandburg, Carl
Millais, Raoul 1901- 77
Millar, Barbara F. 1924- 12
Millar, Margaret (Ellis Sturm) 1915-1994 61
  Obituary 79
Millard, Glenda 203
Millard, Kerry 204
Millbank, Captain H. R.
  See Ellis, Edward S.
Millen, C(ynthia) M. 1955- 114
Miller, Albert G(riffith) 1905-1982 12
  Obituary 31
Miller, Alice Ann 1958- 150
Miller, Alice P(atricia McCarthy) 22
Miller, Debbie 1951- 160
  Earlier sketch in SATA *103*
Miller, Debbie S.
  See Miller, Debbie
Miller, Deborah Uchill 1944- 61
Miller, Don 1923- 15
Miller, Doris R.
  See Mosesson, Gloria R(ubin)
Miller, Eddie
  See Miller, Edward
Miller, Edna Anita 1920- 29
Miller, Edward 1905-1974 8
Miller, Edward 1964- 183
Miller, Elizabeth 1933- 41
Miller, Ellanita 1957- 87
Miller, Eugene 1925- 33
Miller, Frances A. 1937- 52
  Brief entry 46
Miller, Helen M(arkley) -1984 5
Miller, Helen Topping 1884-1960
  Obituary 29
Miller, Jane (Judith) 1925-1989 15
Miller, Jewel 1956- 73
Miller, John
  See Samachson, Joseph
Miller, Judi 117
Miller, Kate 1948- 193
Miller, Kirsten 1973- 185
Miller, Louise (Rolfe) 1940- 76
Miller, M. L. 85
Miller, Madge 1918- 63
Miller, Margaret J.
  See Dale, Margaret J(essy) Miller
Miller, Marilyn (Jean) 1925- 33
Miller, Marvin 65
Miller, Mary
  See Northcott, (William) Cecil
Miller, Mary Beth 1942- 9
Miller, Mary Beth 1964- 185
Miller, Maryann 1943- 73
Miller, Natalie 1917-1976 35
Miller, Robert H. 1944- 91
Miller, Ron 1947- 185
Miller, Ruth White
  See White, Ruth C.
Miller, Sandra
  See Miller, Sandy
Miller, Sandra Peden
  See Miller, Sandy
Miller, Sandy 1948- 41
  Brief entry 35
Miller, Sarah 1969- 175
Miller, Virginia
  See Austin, Virginia
Miller, William R. 1959- 116
Milligan, Bryce 1953- 170
Milligan, Spike
  See Milligan, Terence Alan

Milligan, Terence Alan 1918-2002 29
  Obituary 134
  See also CLR *92*
Millington, Ada
  See Deyneka, Anita
Millman, Isaac 1933- 140
Mills, Adam
  See Stanley, George Edward
Mills, Claudia 1954- 191
  Brief entry 41
  Earlier sketches in SATA *44, 89, 145*
Mills, Elaine (Rosemary) 1941- 72
Mills, G. Riley 196
Mills, Joyce C. 1944- 102
Mills, Judith Christine 1956- 130
Mills, Yaroslava Surmach 1925- 35
Millspaugh, Ben P. 1936- 77
Millstead, Thomas E. 30
Millward, Gwen 202
Milne, A. A. 1882-1956 100
  See also YABC *1*
  See also CLR *108*
Milne, Alan Alexander
  See Milne, A. A.
Milne, Lorus J. 5
  See also CLR *22*
  See also SAAS *18*
Milne, Margery 5
  See also CLR *22*
  See also SAAS *18*
Milne, Terry
  See Milne, Theresa Ann
Milne, Theresa Ann 1964- 84
Milnes, Irma McDonough 1924- 101
Milonas, Rolf
  See Myller, Rolf
Milone, Karen
  See Dugan, Karen
Milone-Dugan, Karen
  See Dugan, Karen
Milord, Susan 1954- 200
  Earlier sketches in SATA *74, 147*
Milotte, Alfred G(eorge) 1904-1989 11
  Obituary 62
Milstein, Linda 1954- 80
Milton, Ann 134
Milton, Hilary (Herbert) 1920- 23
Milton, John R(onald) 1924- 24
Milton, Joyce 1946- 101
  Brief entry 41
  Earlier sketch in SATA *52*
Milverton, Charles A.
  See Penzler, Otto
Milway, Katie Smith 1960- 203
Minahan, John A. 1956- 92
Minar, Barbra (Goodyear) 1940- 79
Minard, Rosemary 1939- 63
Minarik, Else Holmelund 1920- 127
  Earlier sketch in SATA *15*
  See also CLR *33*
Miner, Jane Claypool 1933- 103
  Brief entry 37
  Earlier sketch in SATA *38*
Miner, Lewis S. 1909-1971 11
Mines, Jeanette 1948- 61
Mines, Jeanette Marie
  See Mines, Jeanette
Minier, Nelson
  See Stoutenburg, Adrien (Pearl)
Minnitt, Ronda Jacqueline
  See Armitage, David
Minor, Wendell 1944- 199
  Earlier sketches in SATA *78, 109, 164*
Minter, Daniel 1961- 176
Mintonye, Grace 4
Miranda, Anne 1954- 109
  Earlier sketch in SATA *71*
Miranda, Inaki 1983(?)- 207
Mirocha, Paul 192
Mirsky, Jeannette 1903-1987 8
  Obituary 51

Mirsky, Reba Paeff 1902-1966 .... *1*
Misako Rocks! *192*
Mishica, Clare 1960- *91*
Miskovits, Christine 1939- *10*
Miss Frances
  See Horwich, Frances R(appaport)
Miss Read
  See Saint, Dora Jessie
Mister Rogers
  See Rogers, Fred McFeely
Mitchard, Jacquelyn 1956- *168*
  Earlier sketch in SATA *98*
Mitchell, Adrian 1932-2008 .... *166*
  Obituary *200*
  Earlier sketch in SATA *104*
Mitchell, Allison
  See Griffin, W.E.B.
Mitchell, Betty Jo
  See Mitchell, B.J.
Mitchell, B.J. 1931- *120*
Mitchell, Clyde
  See Ellison, Harlan
  and Silverberg, Robert
Mitchell, Cynthia 1922- *29*
Mitchell, (Sibyl) Elyne (Keith) 1913- *10*
Mitchell, Gladys (Maude Winifred)
  1901-1983 .... *46*
  Obituary *35*
Mitchell, Jay
  See Roberson, Jennifer
Mitchell, Joyce Slayton 1933- *142*
  Brief entry *43*
  Earlier sketch in SATA *46*
Mitchell, K. L.
  See Lamb, Elizabeth Searle
Mitchell, Kathy 1948- *59*
Mitchell, Lori 1961- *128*
Mitchell, Margaree King 1953- *84*
Mitchell, Marianne 1947- *145*
Mitchell, Rhonda *89*
Mitchell, Stephen 1943- *199*
Mitchell, Todd 1974- *191*
Mitchell, Yvonne 1925-1979
  Obituary *24*
Mitchelson, Mitch
  See Mitchelson, Peter Richard
Mitchelson, Peter Richard 1950- *104*
Mitchison, Naomi (Margaret Haldane)
  1897-1999 .... *24*
  Obituary *112*
Mitchnik, Helen 1901-1982 .... *41*
  Brief entry *35*
Mitchum, Hank
  See Knott, William C(ecil, Jr.)
  and Murray, Stuart A. P.
  and Newton, D(wight) B(ennett)
  and Sherman, Jory (Tecumseh)
Mitgutsch, Ali 1935- *76*
Mitsuhashi, Yoko *45*
  Brief entry *33*
Mitton, Jacqueline 1948- *162*
  Earlier sketches in SATA *66, 115*
Mitton, Simon 1946- *66*
Mitton, Tony 1951- *203*
  Earlier sketches in SATA *104, 149*
Miura, Taro 1968- *181*
Mizner, Elizabeth Howard 1907- *27*
Mizumura, Kazue *18*
Mlynowski, Sarah 1977(?)- *180*
Mobin-Uddin, Asma *172*
Mobley, Joe A. 1945- *91*
Moche, Dinah (Rachel) L(evine) 1936- *44*
  Brief entry *40*
Mochi, Ugo (A.) 1889-1977 .... *38*
Mochizuki, Ken 1954- *146*
  Earlier sketch in SATA *81*
  See also SAAS *22*
Modarressi, Mitra 1967- *200*
  Earlier sketch in SATA *126*
Modell, Frank B. 1917- *39*
  Brief entry *36*

Modesitt, Jeanne 1953- *143*
  Earlier sketch in SATA *92*
Modesitt, L.E., Jr. 1943- *164*
  Earlier sketch in SATA *91*
Modesitt, Leland Exton, Jr.
  See Modesitt, L.E., Jr.
Modrell, Dolores 1933- *72*
Moe, Barbara 1937- *20*
Moe, Jorgen (Ingebretsen) 1813-1882
  See CLR *104*
Moed-Kass, Pnina *169*
Moerbeek, Kees 1955- *98*
Moeri, Louise 1924- *93*
  Earlier sketch in SATA *24*
  See also SAAS *10*
Moesta, Rebecca 1956- *182*
Moffett, Jami 1952- *84*
Moffett, Mark W. 1957(?)- *203*
Moffett, Martha (Leatherwood) 1934- *8*
Mogensen, Suzanne A(ncher) 1946- *129*
Mohammed, Khadra *197*
Mohn, Peter B(urnet) 1934- *28*
Mohn, Viola Kohl 1914- *8*
Mohr, Nicholasa 1938- *97*
  Autobiography Feature *113*
  Earlier sketch in SATA *8*
  See also CLR *22*
  See also SAAS *8*
Mok, Esther 1953- *93*
Molan, Christine 1943- *84*
Molarsky, Osmond 1909- *16*
Moldon, Peter L(eonard) 1937- *49*
Mole, John 1941- *103*
  Earlier sketch in SATA *36*
  See also CLR *61*
Molesworth, Mary Louisa 1839-1921 .... *98*
Molin, Charles
  See Mayne, William (James Carter)
Molina, Silvia 1946- *97*
Molk, Laurel 1957- *162*
  Earlier sketch in SATA *92*
Mollel, Tololwa M. 1952- *88*
Molloy, Anne Baker 1907-1999 .... *32*
Molloy, Michael (John) 1940- *162*
Molloy, Paul (George) 1924- *5*
Moloney, James 1954- *202*
  Autobiography Feature *144*
  Earlier sketches in SATA *94, 144*
Momaday, N. Scott 1934- *48*
  Brief entry *30*
Momaday, Navarre Scott
  See Momaday, N. Scott
Monaco, Octavia 1963- *169*
Monagle, Bernie 1957- *121*
Moncure, Jane Belk 1926- *23*
Monjo, F(erdinand) N(icholas III)
  1924-1978 .... *16*
  See also CLR *2*
Monk, Isabell 1952- *136*
Monks, Lydia *189*
Monroe, Lyle
  See Heinlein, Robert A.
Monroe, Marion
  See Cox, Marion Monroe
Monroy, Manuel 1970- *196*
Monsell, Helen Albee 1895-1971 .... *24*
Monson-Burton, Marianne 1975- *139*
Montana, Bob 1920-1975
  Obituary *21*
Montecalvo, Janet *177*
Montenegro, Laura Nyman 1953- *95*
Montero, Gloria 1933- *109*
Montes, Marisa 1951- *144*
Montgomerie, Norah (Mary) 1913- *26*
Montgomery, Constance
  See Cappel, Constance
Montgomery, Elizabeth
  See Julesberg, Elizabeth Rider Montgomery
Montgomery, Elizabeth Rider
  See Julesberg, Elizabeth Rider Montgomery
Montgomery, Hugh (Edward) 1962- *146*

Montgomery, L. M. 1874-1942 .... *100*
  See also YABC *1*
  See also CLR *145*
Montgomery, Lucy Maud
  See Montgomery, L. M.
Montgomery, Raymond A. (Jr.) 1936- *39*
Montgomery, Rutherford George 1894-1985 . *3*
Montgomery, Sy 1958- *184*
  Autobiography Feature *132*
  Earlier sketches in SATA *114, 132*
Montgomery, Vivian *36*
Monthei, Betty *179*
Montijo, Rhode *179*
Montileaux, Donald F. 1948- *183*
Montpetit, Charles 1958- *101*
Montresor, Beni 1926-2001 .... *38*
  Earlier sketch in SATA *3*
  See also SAAS *4*
Montserrat, Pep *181*
Monty Python
  See Chapman, Graham
  and Cleese, John (Marwood)
  and Gilliam, Terry
  and Idle, Eric
  and Jones, Terence Graham Parry
  and Palin, Michael
Moodie, Craig 1956- *172*
Moodie, Fiona 1952- *133*
Moody, Minerva
  See Alcott, Louisa May
Moody, Ralph Owen 1898-1982 .... *1*
Moon, Carl 1879(?)-1948 .... *25*
Moon, Grace (Purdie) 1877(?)-1947 .... *25*
Moon, Lily
  See Warnes, Tim
Moon, Nicola 1952- *147*
  Earlier sketch in SATA *96*
Moon, Pat 1946- *113*
Moon, Sheila 1910-1991 .... *5*
  Obituary *114*
Moon, Sheila Elizabeth
  See Moon, Sheila
Mooney, Bel 1946- *95*
Mooney, Bill 1936- *122*
Mooney, Elizabeth C(omstock) 1918-1986
  Obituary *48*
Mooney, William
  See Mooney, Bill
Moor, Emily
  See Deming, Richard
Moorcock, Michael 1939- *166*
  Earlier sketch in SATA *93*
Moorcock, Michael John
  See Moorcock, Michael
Moore, Anne Carroll 1871-1961 .... *13*
Moore, Cheri
  See Ladd, Cheryl (Jean)
Moore, Clement Clarke 1779-1863 .... *18*
Moore, Cyd 1957- *186*
  Earlier sketches in SATA *83, 133*
Moore, Don W. 1905(?)-1986
  Obituary *48*
Moore, Elaine 1944- *86*
Moore, Eva 1942- *103*
  Earlier sketch in SATA *20*
Moore, Ishbel (Lindsay) 1954- *140*
Moore, Jack (William) 1941- *46*
  Brief entry *32*
Moore, Janet Gaylord 1905-1992 .... *18*
Moore, Jim 1946- *42*
Moore, John Travers 1908- *12*
Moore, Lilian 1909-2004 .... *137*
  Obituary *155*
  Earlier sketch in SATA *52*
  See also CLR *15*
Moore, Liz
  See Moore, M. Elizabeth
Moore, M. Elizabeth 1959- *156*
Moore, Margaret R(umberger) 1903- *12*
Moore, Margie *176*
Moore, Marianne 1887-1972 .... *20*

Moore, Marianne Craig
  See Moore, Marianne
Moore, Patrick (Alfred Caldwell) 1923- 49
  Brief entry 39
  See also SAAS 8
Moore, Patrick 1959- 184
Moore, Perry 193
Moore, Peter 1963- 175
Moore, Peter G.
  See Moore, Peter
Moore, Ray (S.) 1905(?)-1984
  Obituary 37
Moore, Regina
  See Dunne, Mary Collins
Moore, Rosalie (Gertrude) 1910-2001 9
Moore, Ruth (Ellen) 1908-1989 23
Moore, Ruth Nulton 1923- 38
Moore, S(arah) E. 23
Moore, Sarah Margaret
  See Hodges, Margaret
Moore, Tara 1950- 61
Moore, Yvette 1958- 154
  Earlier sketches in SATA 69, 70
Moores, Dick
  See Moores, Richard (Arnold)
Moores, Richard (Arnold) 1909-1986
  Obituary 48
Mooser, Stephen 1941- 75
  Earlier sketch in SATA 28
Mora, Francisco X(avier) 1952- 90
Mora, Pat 1942- 186
  Earlier sketches in SATA 92, 134
  See also CLR 58
Mora, Patricia
  See Mora, Pat
Morais, Flavio 207
Morales, Yuyi 180
  Earlier sketch in SATA 154
Moran, Tom 1943- 60
Moranville, Sharelle Byars 196
  Earlier sketch in SATA 152
Moray Williams, Ursula 1911-2006 3
  Obituary 177
  See also SAAS 9
Mordvinoff, Nicolas 1911-1973 17
More, Caroline
  See Cone, Molly (Lamken)
  and Strachan, Margaret Pitcairn
Moreno, Rene King 190
Moreton, Andrew Esq.
  See Defoe, Daniel
Morey, Charles
  See Fletcher, Helen Jill
Morey, Walt(er Nelson) 1907-1992 51
  Obituary 70
  Earlier sketch in SATA 3
  See also SAAS 9
Morgan, Alfred P(owell) 1889-1972 33
Morgan, Alison (Mary) 1930- 85
  Earlier sketch in SATA 30
Morgan, Anne 1954- 121
Morgan, Christopher 1956- 199
Morgan, Clay 1950- 198
Morgan, Douglas
  See Macdonald, James D.
Morgan, Ellen
  See Bumstead, Kathleen Mary
Morgan, Geoffrey 1916- 46
Morgan, Helen (Gertrude Louise)
  1921-1990 29
Morgan, Jane
  See Cooper, James Fenimore
  and Franklin, Jane (Morgan)
  and Moren, Sally M(oore)
Morgan, Lenore H. 1908-1976 8
Morgan, Mary 1957- 114
  Earlier sketch in SATA 81
Morgan, McKayla
  See Basile, Gloria Vitanza
Morgan, Michaela
  See Basile, Gloria Vitanza

Morgan, Nicola 1961- 161
Morgan, Nina 1953- 110
Morgan, Pierr 1952- 122
  Earlier sketch in SATA 77
Morgan, Robin (Evonne) 1941- 80
Morgan, Roxanne
  See Gentle, Mary
Morgan, Sarah (Nicola) 1959- 68
Morgan, Shirley
  See Kiepper, Shirley Morgan
Morgan, Stacy T(owle) 1959- 104
Morgan, Stevie
  See Davies, Nicola
Morgan, Tom 1942- 42
Morgan, Wendy
  See Staub, Wendy Corsi
Morgan-Vanroyen, Mary
  See Morgan, Mary
Morgenstern, Susie Hoch 1945- 133
Mori, Hana 1909-1990(?) 88
Mori, Kyoko 1957- 122
  Autobiography Feature 126
  See also CLR 64
  See also SAAS 26
Moriarty, Jaclyn 162
Moriarty, William J. 1930- 127
Morice, Dave 1946- 93
Morin, Isobel V. 1928- 110
Morine, Hoder
  See Conroy, John Wesley
Morley, Taia 199
Morley, Wilfred Owen
  See Lowndes, Robert A(ugustine) W(ard)
Morningstar, Mildred (Whaley) 1912-1997 .. 61
  Obituary 114
Morozumi, Atsuko 110
Morpurgo, Michael 1943- 184
  Earlier sketches in SATA 93, 143
  See also CLR 51
Morrah, Dave
  See Morrah, David Wardlaw, Jr.
Morrah, David Wardlaw, Jr. 1914-1991 10
Morreale-de la Garza, Phyllis
  See De la Garza, Phyllis
Morressy, John 1930-2006 23
Morrill, Leslie H(olt) 1934-2003 48
  Brief entry 33
  Obituary 148
  See also SAAS 22
Morris, Chris(topher Crosby) 1946- 66
Morris, Deborah 1956- 91
Morris, Desmond 1928- 14
Morris, Desmond John
  See Morris, Desmond
Morris, Don 1954- 83
Morris, Gerald 1963- 207
  Earlier sketches in SATA 107, 150
Morris, Gerald Paul
  See Morris, Gerald
Morris, Gilbert (Leslie) 1929- 104
Morris, Jackie 202
  Earlier sketch in SATA 151
Morris, Janet (Ellen) 1946- 66
Morris, Jay
  See Tatham, Julie Campbell
Morris, (Margaret) Jean 1924- 98
Morris, Jeffrey B(randon) 1941- 92
Morris, Jennifer E. 1969- 179
Morris, Jill 1936- 165
  Earlier sketch in SATA 119
Morris, Juddi 85
Morris, Judy K. 1936- 61
Morris, Oradel Nolen 128
Morris, Robert A(da) 1933- 7
Morris, William 1913-1994 29
Morrison, Bill 1935- 66
  Brief entry 37
Morrison, Chloe Anthony Wofford
  See Morrison, Toni
Morrison, Dorothy Nafus 29
Morrison, Frank 1971- 185

Morrison, Gordon 1944- 183
  Earlier sketches in SATA 87, 128
Morrison, Joan 1922- 65
Morrison, Lillian 1917- 108
  Earlier sketch in SATA 3
Morrison, Lucile Phillips 1896- 17
Morrison, Martha A. 1948- 77
Morrison, Meighan 1966- 90
Morrison, P.R. 196
Morrison, Richard
  See Lowndes, Robert A(ugustine) W(ard)
Morrison, Robert
  See Lowndes, Robert A(ugustine) W(ard)
Morrison, Roberta
  See Webb, Jean Francis (III)
Morrison, Susan Dudley
  See Gold, Susan Dudley
Morrison, Taylor 1971- 187
  Earlier sketches in SATA 95, 159
Morrison, Toni 1931- 144
  Earlier sketch in SATA 57
  See also CLR 99
Morrison, Velma Ford 1909- 21
Morrison, Wilbur Howard 1915- 64
Morrison, William
  See Samachson, Joseph
Morriss, James E(dward) 1932- 8
Morrissey, Dean 183
Morrow, Barbara Olenyik 1952- 167
Morrow, Betty
  See Bacon, Elizabeth
Morse, C. Scott
  See Morse, Scott
Morse, Carol
  See Yeakley, Marjory Hall
Morse, C.S.
  See Morse, Scott
Morse, Dorothy B(ayley) 1906-1979
  Obituary 24
Morse, Flo 1921- 30
Morse, Scott 1973- 200
Morse, Tony 1953- 129
Mort, Vivian
  See Cromie, Alice Hamilton
Mortensen, Denise Dowling 179
Mortimer, Anne 1958- 206
  Earlier sketch in SATA 116
Mortimer, Mary H.
  See Coury, Louise Andree
Morton, Alexandra (Hubbard) 1957- 144
Morton, Anthony
  See Arthur, Robert, (Jr.)
Morton, Jane 1931- 50
Morton, Joseph C. 1932- 156
Morton, Lee Jack, Jr. 1928- 32
Morton, Miriam 1918(?)-1985 9
  Obituary 46
Mosatche, Harriet
  See Mosatche, Harriet
Mosatche, Harriet 1949- 122
Moscow, Alvin 1925- 3
Mosel, Arlene (Tichy) 1921-1996 7
Moseley, James W(illett) 1931- 139
Moseng, Elisabeth 1967- 90
Moser, Barry 1940- 185
  Earlier sketches in SATA 56, 79, 138
  See also CLR 49
  See also SAAS 15
Moser, Don(ald Bruce) 1932- 31
Moser, Laura 194
Moser, Lisa 192
Moses, Sheila P. 1961- 168
Moses, Will 1956- 178
  Earlier sketch in SATA 120
Mosesson, Gloria R(ubin) 24
Mosher, Richard 1949- 120
Moskin, Marietta D(unston) 1928- 23
Moskof, Martin Stephen 1930- 27
Mosley, Francis 1957- 57
Moss, Don(ald) 1920- 11

Moss, Elaine (Dora) 1924- 57
   Brief entry 31
Moss, Jeff(rey) 1942-1998 73
   Obituary 106
Moss, Marissa 1959- 163
   Earlier sketches in SATA *71, 104*
   See also CLR *134*
Moss, Miriam 1955- 202
   Earlier sketches in SATA *76, 140*
Moss, Thylias 1954- 108
Moss, Thylias Rebecca Brasier
   See Moss, Thylias
Most, Bernard 1937- 134
   Brief entry 40
   Earlier sketches in SATA *48, 91*
Mosz, Gosia 1972- 194
Mott, Evelyn Clarke 1962- 133
   Earlier sketch in SATA *75*
Motz, Lloyd 1909-2004 20
Mould, Chris 205
Mould, Edwin
   See Whitlock, Ralph
Mouly, Francoise 155
Mountain, Robert
   See Montgomery, Raymond A. (Jr.)
Mountfield, David
   See Grant, Neil
Mourlevat, Jean-Claude 1952- 187
Mourning, Tuesday 206
Moussard, Jacqueline 1924- 24
Mowat, Claire 1933- 123
Mowat, Claire Angel Wheeler
   See Mowat, Claire
Mowat, Farley 1921- 55
   Earlier sketch in SATA *3*
   See also CLR *20*
Mowat, Farley McGill
   See Mowat, Farley
Mowll, Joshua 1970(?)- 188
Mowry, Jess 1960- 131
   Autobiography Feature 131
   Earlier sketch in SATA *109*
   See also CLR *65*
Moxley, Sheila 1966- 96
Moyer, Terry J. 1937- 94
Moyes, Patricia
   See Haszard, Patricia Moyes
Moyler, Alan (Frank Powell) 1926- 36
Mozelle, Shirley 179
Mozley, Charles 1915- 43
   Brief entry 32
Mphahlele, Es'kia 1919-2008 119
   Obituary 198
Mphahlele, Ezekiel
   See Mphahlele, Es'kia
Mphahlele, Zeke
   See Mphahlele, Es'kia
Mr. McGillicuddy
   See Abisch, Roslyn Kroop
Mr. Sniff
   See Abisch, Roslyn Kroop
Mr. Tivil
   See Lorkowski, Thomas V(incent)
Mr. Wizard
   See Herbert, Don
Mrs. Fairstar
   See Horne, Richard Henry Hengist
Muchamore, Robert 1972- 175
Muchmore, Jo Ann 1937- 103
Mude, O.
   See Gorey, Edward (St. John)
Mudgeon, Apeman
   See Mitchell, Adrian
Mueller, Jorg 1942- 67
   See also CLR *43*
Mueller, Miranda R. 201
Mueller, Virginia 1924- 28
Muggs
   See Watkins, Lois
Muir, Diana
   See Appelbaum, Diana Muir Karter

Muir, Frank (Herbert) 1920-1998 30
Muir, Helen 1937- 65
Mukerji, Dhan Gopal 1890-1936 40
   See also CLR *10*
Mulcahy, Lucille Burnett 12
Mulford, Philippa G. 1948- 112
   Earlier sketch in SATA *43*
Mulford, Philippa Greene
   See Mulford, Philippa G.
Mulgan, Catherine 1931- 24
Mulila, Vigad G.
   See Maillu, David G(ian)
Mull, Brandon 1974- 190
Mullen, Michael 1937- 122
Muller, Billex
   See Ellis, Edward S.
Muller, Jorg
   See Mueller, Jorg
Muller, (Lester) Robin 1953- 86
Mullin, Caryl Cude 1969- 130
Mullins, Edward S(wift) 1922- 10
Mullins, Hilary 1962- 84
Mulock, Dinah Maria
   See Craik, Dinah Maria (Mulock)
Mulvihill, William Patrick 1923- 8
Mumford, Ruth
   See Dallas, Ruth
Mumy, Bill 1954- 112
Mun
   See Leaf, (Wilbur) Munro
Munari, Bruno 1907-1998 15
   See also CLR *9*
Munce, Ruth Hill 1898- 12
Mundy, Simon 1954- 64
Mundy, Simon Andrew James Hainault
   See Mundy, Simon
Munger, Nancy 170
Munowitz, Ken 1935-1977 14
Munoz, William 1949- 92
   Earlier sketch in SATA *42*
Munro, Alice 1931- 29
Munro, Alice Anne
   See Munro, Alice
Munro, Eleanor 1928- 37
Munro, Roxie 1945- 184
   Earlier sketches in SATA *58, 136*
Munsch, Bob
   See Munsch, Robert (Norman)
Munsch, Robert (Norman) 1945- 120
   Brief entry 48
   Earlier sketches in SATA *50, 83*
   See also CLR *19*
Munsinger, Lynn 1951- 177
   Earlier sketches in SATA *33, 94*
Munson, Derek 1970- 139
Munson, R. W.
   See Karl, Jean E(dna)
Munson-Benson, Tunie 1946- 15
Munsterberg, Peggy 1921- 102
Muntean, Michaela 182
Munthe, Nelly 1947- 53
Munves, James (Albert) 1922- 30
Munzer, Martha E. 1899-1999 4
Murawski, Darlyne A. 193
Murch, Mel
   See Manes, Stephen
Murdoch, David H(amilton) 1937- 96
Murdoch, Patricia 1957- 192
Murdock, Catherine Gilbert 185
Murhall, J(acqueline) J(ane) 1964- 143
Murphy, Barbara Beasley 1933- 130
   Earlier sketch in SATA *5*
Murphy, Claire Rudolf 1951- 137
   Earlier sketch in SATA *76*
Murphy, E(mmett) Jefferson 1926- 4
Murphy, Jill (Frances) 1949- 142
   Earlier sketches in SATA *37, 70*
   See also CLR *39*

Murphy, Jim 1947- 185
   Brief entry 32
   Earlier sketches in SATA *37, 77, 124*
   See also CLR *53*
Murphy, Joseph E., Jr. 1930- 65
Murphy, Kelly 1977- 190
   Earlier sketch in SATA *143*
Murphy, Louise 1943- 155
Murphy, Mary 1961- 196
Murphy, Pat
   See Murphy, E(mmett) Jefferson
Murphy, Patricia J. 1963- 132
Murphy, Rita 180
Murphy, Robert (William) 1902-1971 10
Murphy, Shirley Rousseau 1928- 126
   Earlier sketches in SATA *36, 71*
   See also SAAS *18*
Murphy, Stuart J. 1942- 157
   Earlier sketch in SATA *115*
Murphy, Thomas Basil, Jr. 1935- 191
Murphy, Tim
   See Murphy, Jim
Murphy, Tom
   See Murphy, Thomas Basil, Jr.
Murray, John 1923- 39
Murray, Kirsty 1960- 165
   Earlier sketch in SATA *108*
Murray, Marguerite 1917- 63
Murray, Marian 5
Murray, Martine 1965- 125
Murray, (Judith) Michele (Freedman)
   1933-1974 7
Murray, Ossie 1938- 43
Murray, Peter
   See Hautman, Pete
Murrow, Liza Ketchum 1946- 132
   Earlier sketch in SATA *78*
Musgrave, Florence 1902-1999 3
Musgrove, Margaret W(ynkoop) 1943- 124
   Earlier sketch in SATA *26*
Musgrove, Marianne 207
Mussey, Virginia Howell
   See Ellison, Virginia H(owell)
Mussey, Virginia T.H.
   See Ellison, Virginia H(owell)
Mussi, Sarah 206
Mutel, Cornelia F. 1947- 74
Muth, Jon J. 206
   Earlier sketch in SATA *165*
Mutz
   See Kuenstler, Morton
Mwangi, Meja 1948- 174
My Brother's Brother
   See Chekhov, Anton
Myers, Anna 160
Myers, Arthur 1917- 91
   Earlier sketch in SATA *35*
Myers, Bernice 81
   Earlier sketch in SATA *9*
Myers, Caroline Elizabeth Clark
   1887-1980 28
Myers, Christopher 1975- 183
   See also CLR *97*
Myers, Edward 1950- 172
   Earlier sketch in SATA *96*
Myers, Elisabeth P(erkins) 1918- 36
Myers, (Mary) Hortense (Powner)
   1913-1987 10
Myers, Jack 1913-2006 83
   Obituary 178
Myers, Jack Edgar
   See Myers, Jack
Myers, Lou 1915-2005 81
   Obituary 171
Myers, Louis
   See Myers, Lou
Myers, R.E. 1924- 119
Myers, Robert Eugene
   See Myers, R.E.
Myers, Tim 1953- 176
   Earlier sketch in SATA *147*

Myers, Timothy Joseph
　See Myers, Tim
Myers, Walter Dean 1937- 193
　Brief entry 27
　Earlier sketches in SATA *41, 71, 109, 157*
　See also CLR *110*
　See also SAAS *2*
Myers, Walter M.
　See Myers, Walter Dean
Myller, Rolf 1926-2006 27
　Obituary 175
Myra, Harold L(awrence) 1939- 46
　Brief entry 42
Myracle, Lauren 1969- 204
　Earlier sketch in SATA *162*
Myrus, Donald (Richard) 1927- 23
Mysterious Traveler, The
　See Arthur, Robert, (Jr.)

N

Na, An 149
Naaslund, Goorel Kristina 1940- 170
Nadel, Laurie 1948- 74
Naden, Corinne J. 1930- 166
　Earlier sketch in SATA *79*
Nadimi, Suzan 188
Nagda, Ann Whitehead 199
Nagel, Andreas Fischer
　See Fischer-Nagel, Andreas
Nagel, Heiderose Fischer
　See Fischer-Nagel, Heiderose
Nagle, Shane 176
Naidoo, Beverley 1943- 180
　Earlier sketches in SATA *63, 135*
　See also CLR *29*
Nakae, Noriko 1940- 59
Nakata, Hiroe 205
Nakatani, Chiyoko 1930-1981 55
　Brief entry 40
　See also CLR *30*
Nally, Susan W. 1947- 90
Namioka, Lensey 1929- 157
　Autobiography Feature 116
　Earlier sketches in SATA *27, 89*
　See also CLR *48*
　See also SAAS *24*
Namovicz, Gene Inyart 1927- 6
Nanji, Shenaaz 1954- 204
　Earlier sketch in SATA *131*
Nanogak Agnes 1925- 61
Napier, Mark
　See Laffin, John (Alfred Charles)
Napoli, Donna Jo 1948- 190
　Earlier sketches in SATA *92, 137*
　See also CLR *51*
　See also SAAS *23*
Napp, Daniel 1974- 204
Narahashi, Keiko 1959- 115
　Earlier sketch in SATA *79*
Narayan, R. K. 1906-2001 62
Narayan, Rasipuram Krishnaswami
　See Narayan, R. K.
Nascimbene, Yan 1949- 173
　Earlier sketch in SATA *133*
Nash, Bruce M(itchell) 1947- 34
Nash, Frediric Ogden
　See Nash, Ogden
Nash, Linell
　See Smith, Linell Nash
Nash, Mary (Hughes) 1925- 41
Nash, Ogden 1902-1971 46
　Earlier sketch in SATA *2*
Nash, Renea Denise 1963- 81
Nast, Elsa Ruth
　See Watson, Jane Werner
Nast, Thomas 1840-1902 51
　Brief entry 33
Nastick, Sharon 1954- 41

Natale, Vince 196
Natarajan, Srividya 187
Nathan, Adele (Gutman) 1900(?)-1986
　Obituary 48
Nathan, Amy 155
　Earlier sketch in SATA *104*
Nathan, Dorothy (Goldeen) (?)-1966 15
Nathan, Robert (Gruntal) 1894-1985 6
　Obituary 43
Nathanson, Laura Walther 1941- 57
Natti, Lee 1919- 67
　Earlier sketch in SATA *1*
　See also SAAS *3*
Natti, Susanna 1948- 125
　Earlier sketch in SATA *32*
Nau, Thomas 186
Naughtie, Eleanor
　See Updale, Eleanor
Naughton, Bill
　See Naughton, William John (Francis)
Naughton, James Franklin 1957- 85
Naughton, Jim
　See Naughton, James Franklin
Naughton, William John (Francis)
　1910-1992 86
Navarra, John Gabriel 1927- 8
Naylor, Penelope 1941- 10
Naylor, Phyllis 1933- 152
　Autobiography Feature 152
　Earlier sketches in SATA *12, 66, 102*
　See also CLR *135*
　See also SAAS *10*
Naylor, Phyllis Reynolds 1933-
　See Naylor, Phyllis
Nazarian, Nikki
　See Nichols, Cecilia Fawn
Nazaroff, Alexander I(vanovich) 1898-1981 .. 4
Nazoa, Aquiles 1920-1976 198
Neal, Harry Edward 1906-1993 5
　Obituary 76
Neal, Michael
　See Teitelbaum, Michael
Nearing, Penny 1916- 47
　Brief entry 42
Nebel, Gustave E. 45
　Brief entry 33
Nebel, Mimouca
　See Nebel, Gustave E.
Nee, Kay Bonner 10
Needham, Kate 1962- 95
Needle, Jan 1943- 98
　Earlier sketch in SATA *30*
　See also CLR *43*
　See also SAAS *23*
Needleman, Jacob 1934- 6
Neel, David 1960- 82
Neel, Preston 1959- 93
Negri, Rocco 1932- 12
Negrin, Fabian 1963- 189
Neidigh, Sherry 1956- 204
Neier, Aryeh 1937- 59
Neigoff, Anne 13
Neigoff, Mike 1920- 13
Neilan, Eujin Kim 1969- 200
Neilson, Frances Fullerton (Jones)
　1910-2001 14
Neimark, Anne E. 1935- 145
　Earlier sketch in SATA *4*
Neimark, Paul G. 1934- 80
　Brief entry 37
Neitzel, Shirley 1941- 134
　Earlier sketch in SATA *77*
Nell
　See Hanna, Nell(ie L.)
Nelscott, Kris
　See Rusch, Kristine Kathryn
Nelson, Blake 1960- 177
Nelson, Catherine Chadwick 1926- 87
Nelson, Cordner 1918-2009 54
　Brief entry 29
Nelson, Drew 1952- 77

Nelson, Esther L. 1928- 13
Nelson, Jim A.
　See Stotter, Mike
Nelson, Julie L. 1970- 117
Nelson, Kadir 181
　Earlier sketch in SATA *154*
Nelson, Kris
　See Rusch, Kristine Kathryn
Nelson, Lawrence E(rnest) 1928-1977
　Obituary 28
Nelson, Marilyn 1946- 60
　Autobiography Feature 180
Nelson, Mary Carroll 1929- 23
Nelson, O. Terry 1941- 62
Nelson, Peter N. 1953- 73
Nelson, R.A. 197
Nelson, Richard K(ing) 1941- 65
Nelson, Robin Laura 1971- 141
Nelson, Roy Paul 1923- 59
Nelson, S.D. 181
Nelson, Sharlene (P.) 1933- 96
Nelson, Suzanne 1976- 184
Nelson, Ted (W.) 1931- 96
Nelson, Theresa 1948- 143
　Autobiography Feature 143
　Earlier sketch in SATA *79*
Nemeth, Sally 187
Neri, G. 197
Neri, Greg
　See Neri, G.
Neri, Gregory
　See Neri, G.
Nerlove, Miriam 1959- 53
　Brief entry 49
Nesbit, E. 1858-1924 100
　See also YABC *1*
　See also CLR *70*
Nesbit, Edith
　See Nesbit, E.
Nesbit, Troy
　See Folsom, Franklin (Brewster)
Nespojohn, Katherine V(eronica) 1912-1975 . 7
Ness, Evaline (Michelow) 1911-1986 26
　Obituary 49
　Earlier sketch in SATA *1*
　See also CLR *6*
　See also SAAS *1*
Ness, Patrick 1971- 207
Nestor, Larry 1940- 149
Nestor, William P(rodromos) 1947- 49
Nethery, Mary 93
Neubecker, Robert 170
Neuberger, Julia (Babette Sarah) 1950- 142
　Earlier sketch in SATA *78*
Neufeld, John (Arthur) 1938- 131
　Autobiography Feature 131
　Earlier sketches in SATA *6, 81*
　See also CLR *52*
　See also SAAS *3*
Neuhaus, David 1958- 83
Neumeyer, Peter F(lorian) 1929- 13
Neurath, Marie (Reidemeister) 1898-1986 1
Neuschwander, Cindy 1953- 157
　Earlier sketch in SATA *107*
Neusner, Jacob 1932- 38
Neville, Charles
　See Bodsworth, (Charles) Fred(erick)
Neville, Emily Cheney 1919- 1
　See also SAAS *2*
Neville, Mary
　See Woodrich, Mary Neville
Nevins, Albert (Francis) J(erome)
　1915-1997 20
Nevius, Carol 1955- 186
Newberger, Devra
　See Speregen, Devra Newberger
Newberry, Clare Turlay 1903-1970 1
　Obituary 26
Newbery, John 1713-1767 20
　See also CLR *147*

Author Index

Newbery, Linda 1952- *184*
  Earlier sketch in SATA *142*
Newbigging, Martha *198*
Newbold, Greg *199*
Newcomb, Ellsworth
  See Kenny, Ellsworth Newcomb
Newcombe, Eugene A. 1923-1990 .... *45*
  Brief entry *33*
Newcombe, Jack
  See Newcombe, Eugene A.
Newcome, Robert 1955- *91*
Newcome, Zita 1959- *88*
Newell, Crosby
  See Bonsall, Crosby Barbara (Newell)
Newell, Edythe W(eatherford) 1910-1989 .... *11*
Newell, Hope Hockenberry 1896-1965 .... *24*
Newfeld, Frank 1928- *26*
Newgarden, Mark 1959- *194*
Newlon, (Frank) Clarke 1905(?)-1982 .... *6*
  Obituary *33*
Newman, Barbara Johansen *191*
Newman, C.J.
  See Newman, Coleman J.
Newman, Coleman J. 1935- *82*
Newman, Daisy 1904-1994 .... *27*
  Obituary *78*
Newman, Gerald 1939- *46*
  Brief entry *42*
Newman, Jerry
  See Newman, Coleman J.
Newman, Leslea 1955- *134*
  Earlier sketches in SATA *71, 128*
Newman, Margaret
  See Potter, Margaret
Newman, Marjorie *146*
Newman, Matthew (Harrison) 1955- *56*
Newman, Nanette 1934- *162*
Newman, Robert (Howard) 1909-1988 .... *87*
  Obituary *60*
  Earlier sketch in SATA *4*
Newman, Shirlee P(etkin) *144*
  Earlier sketches in SATA *10, 90*
Newsom, Carol 1948- *92*
  Earlier sketch in SATA *40*
Newsom, Tom 1944- *80*
Newth, Mette 1942- *140*
Newton, David E(dward) 1933- *67*
Newton, James R(obert) 1935- *23*
Newton, Jill 1964- *200*
Newton, Robert 1965- *191*
Newton, Suzanne 1936- *77*
  Earlier sketch in SATA *5*
Newton, Vanessa
  See Newton, Vanessa Brantley
Newton, Vanessa Brantley 1962(?)- *206*
Ney, John 1923- *43*
  Brief entry *33*
Nez, John *155*
Ng, Franklin *82*
Nguyen, Vincent *187*
Nichol, B(arrie) P(hillip) 1944-1988 .... *66*
Nicholas, Louise D.
  See Watkins, Dawn L.
Nicholls, Judith (Ann) 1941- *61*
Nichols, Cecilia Fawn 1906-1987 .... *12*
Nichols, Grace 1950- *164*
  Earlier sketch in SATA *98*
Nichols, Janet (Louise) 1952- *67*
Nichols, Judy 1947- *124*
Nichols, Leigh
  See Koontz, Dean
Nichols, Paul
  See Hawks, Robert
Nichols, Peter
  See Youd, Samuel
Nichols, (Joanna) Ruth 1948- *15*
  See also CLR *149*
Nichols, Travis *206*
Nicholson, C. R.
  See Nicole, Christopher (Robin)

Nicholson, Christina
  See Nicole, Christopher (Robin)
Nicholson, Joyce Thorpe 1919- *35*
Nicholson, Lois P. 1949- *88*
Nicholson, Robin
  See Nicole, Christopher (Robin)
Nicholson, William *180*
Nicholson, William 1872-1949
  See CLR *76*
Nickel, Barbara 1966- *188*
Nickell, Joe 1944- *167*
  Earlier sketch in SATA *73*
Nickelsburg, Janet 1893-1983 .... *11*
Nickerson, Betty 1922- *14*
Nickerson, Elizabeth
  See Nickerson, Betty
Nickl, Barbara (Elisabeth) 1939- *56*
Nicklaus, Carol *62*
  Brief entry *33*
Nickle, John *181*
Nickless, Will 1902-1979(?) *66*
Nic Leodhas, Sorche
  See Alger, Leclaire (Gowans)
Nicol, Ann
  See Turnbull, Ann
Nicolas
  See Mordvinoff, Nicolas
Nicolay, Helen 1866-1954
  See YABC *1*
Nicole, Christopher (Robin) 1930- *5*
Nicoll, Helen 1937- *87*
Nicolson, Cynthia Pratt 1949- *141*
Ni Dhuibhne, Eilis 1954- *91*
Niehaus, Paddy Bouma
  See Bouma, Paddy
Nields, Nerissa 1967- *166*
Nielsen, Kay (Rasmus) 1886-1957 .... *16*
  See also CLR *16*
Nielsen, Laura F. 1960- *93*
Nielsen, Laura Farnsworth
  See Nielsen, Laura F.
Nielsen, Nancy J. 1951- *77*
Nielsen, Susin 1964- *195*
Nielsen, Virginia
  See McCall, Virginia Nielsen
Nielsen-Fernlund, Susin
  See Nielsen, Susin
Niemann, Christoph 1970- *191*
Nieuwsma, Milton J(ohn) 1941- *142*
Nightingale, Sandy 1953- *76*
Nikolajeva, Maria 1952- *127*
Nikola-Lisa, W. 1951- *180*
  Earlier sketch in SATA *71*
Niland, Deborah 1951- *172*
  Earlier sketch in SATA *27*
Niland, Kilmeny *75*
Nilsen, Anna 1948- *174*
  Earlier sketch in SATA *96*
Nilsson, Eleanor 1939- *117*
  Earlier sketch in SATA *81*
  See also SAAS *23*
Nilsson, Per 1954- *159*
Nimmo, Jenny 1944- *144*
  Earlier sketch in SATA *87*
  See also CLR *44*
Nishimura, Kae *196*
Niven, Larry 1938- *171*
  Earlier sketch in SATA *95*
Niven, Laurence VanCott
  See Niven, Larry
Nivola, Claire A. 1947- *140*
  Earlier sketch in SATA *84*
Nix, Garth 1963- *143*
  Earlier sketch in SATA *97*
  See also CLR *68*
Nixon, Hershell Howard 1923- *42*
Nixon, Joan Lowery 1927-2003 .... *115*
  Obituary *146*
  Earlier sketches in SATA *8, 44, 78*
  See also CLR *24*
  See also SAAS *9*

Nixon, K.
  See Nixon, Kathleen Irene (Blundell)
Nixon, Kathleen Irene (Blundell)
  1894-1988(?) *14*
  Obituary *59*
Nobati, Eugenia 1968- *201*
Nobisso, Josephine 1953- *121*
  Earlier sketch in SATA *78*
Noble, Iris (Davis) 1922-1986 .... *5*
  Obituary *49*
Noble, Marty 1947- *125*
  Earlier sketch in SATA *97*
Noble, Trinka Hakes 1944- *197*
  Brief entry *37*
  Earlier sketch in SATA *123*
Nobleman, Marc Tyler 1972- *203*
Noda, Takayo 1961- *168*
Nodelman, Perry 1942- *101*
Nodset, Joan L.
  See Lexau, Joan M.
Noel Hume, Ivor 1927- *65*
Noestlinger, Christine
  See Nostlinger, Christine
Noguere, Suzanne 1947- *34*
Nolan, Dennis 1945- *166*
  Brief entry *34*
  Earlier sketches in SATA *42, 92*
Nolan, Han 1956- *157*
  Earlier sketch in SATA *109*
Nolan, Janet 1956- *191*
  Earlier sketch in SATA *145*
Nolan, Jeannette Covert 1897-1974 .... *2*
  Obituary *27*
Nolan, Paul T(homas) 1919- *48*
Nolan, William F(rancis) 1928- *88*
  Brief entry *28*
Nolen, Jerdine 1953- *157*
  Earlier sketch in SATA *105*
Noll, Sally 1946- *82*
Noonan, Brandon 1979- *184*
Noonan, Diana 1960- *146*
Noonan, Julia 1946- *148*
  Earlier sketches in SATA *4, 95*
Norac, Carl 1960- *166*
Norcross, John
  See Conroy, John Wesley
Nordan, Robert W(arren) 1934-2004 .... *133*
Nordhoff, Charles Bernard 1887-1947 .... *23*
Nordlicht, Lillian *29*
Nordstrom, Ursula 1910-1988 .... *3*
  Obituary *57*
Nordtvedt, Matilda 1926- *67*
Norling, Beth 1969- *149*
Norman, Charles 1904-1996 .... *38*
  Obituary *92*
Norman, Howard
  See Norman, Howard A.
Norman, Howard A. 1949- *81*
Norman, James
  See Schmidt, James Norman
Norman, Jay
  See Arthur, Robert, (Jr.)
Norman, Lilith 1927- *120*
  Earlier sketch in SATA *86*
Norman, Mary 1931- *36*
Norman, Steve
  See Pashko, Stanley
Norment, Lisa 1966- *91*
Norris, Gunilla Brodde 1939- *20*
North, Andrew
  See Norton, Andre
North, Anthony
  See Koontz, Dean
North, Captain George
  See Stevenson, Robert Louis
North, Captain George
  See Stevenson, Robert Louis
North, Howard
  See Trevor, Elleston
North, Joan 1920- *16*

North, Milou
  See Erdrich, Louise
North, Robert
  See Withers, Carl A.
North, Sara
  See Bonham, Barbara Thomas
  and Hager, Jean
North, Sherry 201
North, Sterling 1906-1974 45
  Obituary 26
  Earlier sketch in SATA *1*
Northcott, (William) Cecil 1902-1987
  Obituary 55
Northeast, Brenda V(ictoria) 1948- 106
Northmore, Elizabeth Florence 1906-1974 . 122
Norton, Alice Mary
  See Norton, Andre
Norton, Andre 1912-2005 91
  Earlier sketches in SATA *1, 43*
  See also CLR 50
Norton, Browning
  See Norton, Frank R. B(rowning)
Norton, Frank R. B(rowning) 1909-1989 10
Norton, Mary 1903-1992 60
  Obituary 72
  Earlier sketch in SATA *18*
  See also CLR 140
Nosredna, Trebor
  See Anderson, Bob
Nostlinger, Christine 1936- 162
  Brief entry 37
  Earlier sketch in SATA *64*
  See also CLR 12
Nourse, Alan E(dward) 1928-1992 48
  See also CLR 33
Novak, Matt 1962- 204
  Brief entry 52
  Earlier sketches in SATA *60, 104, 165*
Novelli, Luca 1947- 61
Nowell, Elizabeth Cameron 12
Noyes, Deborah 1965- 194
  Earlier sketch in SATA *145*
Nugent, Cynthia 1954- 205
Nugent, Nicholas 1949- 73
Numeroff, Laura 1953- 206
  Earlier sketches in SATA *28, 90, 142*
  See also CLR 85
Numeroff Joffe, Laura
  See Numeroff, Laura
Nunes, Lygia Bojunga 1932- 154
  Earlier sketch in SATA *75*
Nunn, Laura (Donna) Silverstein 1968- 124
Nurenberg, Thelma
  See Greenhaus, Thelma Nurenberg
Nurnberg, Maxwell 1897-1984 27
  Obituary 41
Nussbaumer, Paul (Edmund) 1934- 16
Nutt, Ken 1951- 163
  Earlier sketch in SATA *97*
Nuttall-Smith, Margaret Emily Noel 1919- .. 26
Nuygen, Mathieu 1967- 80
Nuzum, K.A. 195
Nyberg, (Everett Wayne) Morgan 1944- 87
Nyce, (Nellie) Helene von Strecker
  1885-1969 19
Nyce, Vera 1862-1925 19
Nye, Naomi Shihab 1952- 198
  Earlier sketches in SATA *86, 147*
  See also CLR 59
Nye, Robert 1939- 6
Nyeu, Tao 206
Nyikos, Stacy A. 1969- 164
Nystrom, Carolyn 1940- 130
  Earlier sketch in SATA *67*

O

O. Henry
  See Henry, O.
Oakes, Elizabeth H. 1964- 132
Oakes, Vanya 1909-1983 6
  Obituary 37
Oakley, Don(ald G.) 1927- 8
Oakley, Graham 1929- 84
  Earlier sketch in SATA *30*
  See also CLR 7
Oakley, Helen (McKelvey) 1906- 10
Oana, Katherine 1929- 53
  Brief entry 37
Oates, Eddie H. 1943- 88
Oates, Joyce Carol 1938- 159
Oates, Stephen B(aery) 1936- 59
Obed, Ellen Bryan 1944- 74
Oberle, Joseph 1958- 69
Oberman, Sheldon 1949-2004 85
  Autobiography Feature 114
  Obituary 153
  See also CLR 54
  See also SAAS 26
Obligado, Lilian (Isabel) 1931- 61
  Brief entry 45
Obrant, Susan 1946- 11
O'Brian, E.G.
  See Clarke, Arthur C.
O'Brien, Anne Sibley 1952- 80
  Brief entry 48
  Earlier sketch in SATA *53*
O'Brien, E.G.
  See Clarke, Arthur C.
O'Brien, Esse Forrester 1895(?)-1975
  Obituary 30
O'Brien, Patrick 1960- 193
O'Brien, Robert C.
  See Conly, Robert Leslie
O'Brien, Thomas C(lement) 1938- 29
O'Callaghan, Julie 1954- 113
O'Callahan, Jay 1938- 88
O'Carroll, Ryan
  See Markun, Patricia Maloney
Ochiltree, Dianne 1953- 117
Ockham, Joan Price
  See Price, Joan
O'Connell, Margaret F(orster) 1935-1977 30
  Obituary 30
O'Connell, Peg
  See Ahern, Margaret McCrohan
O'Connell, Rebecca 1968- 130
O'Connor, Barbara 1950- 193
  Earlier sketch in SATA *154*
O'Connor, Francine M(arie) 1930- 90
O'Connor, Genevieve A. 1914- 75
O'Connor, George 183
O'Connor, Ian 1965- 188
O'Connor, Jane 1947- 186
  Brief entry 47
  Earlier sketches in SATA *59, 103, 150*
O'Connor, Karen 1938- 89
  Earlier sketch in SATA *34*
O'Connor, Patrick
  See Wibberley, Leonard
O'Connor, Richard 1915-1975
  Obituary 21
O'Conor, Jane 1958- 78
Odaga, Asenath (Bole) 1937- 130
  Earlier sketch in SATA *67*
  See also SAAS 19
O Danachair, Caoimhin
  See Danaher, Kevin
Odanaka, Barbara 159
O'Daniel, Janet 1921- 24
O'Day, Cathy
  See Crane, Barbara (Joyce)
O'Dell, Scott 1898-1989 134
  Earlier sketches in SATA *12, 60*
  See also CLR 126
Odenwald, Robert P(aul) 1899-1965 11

Odgers, Sally
  See Odgers, Sally Farrell
Odgers, Sally Farrell 1957- 139
  Earlier sketch in SATA *72*
O'Donnell, Dick
  See Lupoff, Richard A(llen)
  and Thompson, Don(ald Arthur)
Odriozola, Elena 186
Oechsli, Kelly 1918-1999 5
Oesterle, Virginia Rorby
  See Rorby, Ginny
Ofek, Uriel 1926- 36
  See also CLR 28
Ofer, Avi 1975- 207
Offenbacher, Ami 1958- 91
Offit, Sidney 1928- 10
Ofosu-Appiah, L(awrence) H(enry) 1920- ... 13
Ogan, George F. 1912-1983 13
Ogan, M. G.
  See Ogan, George F.
  and Ogan, Margaret E. (Nettles)
Ogan, Margaret E. (Nettles) 1923-1979 13
Ogburn, Charlton (Jr.) 1911-1998 3
  Obituary 109
Ogburn, Jacqueline K. 162
Ogilvie, Elisabeth May 1917-2006 40
  Brief entry 29
  Obituary 176
Ogilvy, Gavin
  See Barrie, J. M.
Ogilvy, Ian 1943- 177
Ogilvy, Ian Raymond
  See Ogilvy, Ian
Ogle, Lucille Edith 1904-1988
  Obituary 59
Ogletree, Charles J. 1952- 175
O'Green, Jennifer
  See Roberson, Jennifer
O'Green, Jennifer Roberson
  See Roberson, Jennifer
O'Hagan, Caroline 1946- 38
O'Hanlon, Jacklyn
  See Meek, Jacklyn O'Hanlon
O'Hara, Elizabeth
  See Ni Dhuibhne, Eilis
O'Hara, Kenneth
  See Morris, (Margaret) Jean
O'Hara, Mary
  See Alsop, Mary O'Hara
O'Hara (Alsop), Mary
  See Alsop, Mary O'Hara
O'Hare, Jeff(rey A.) 1958- 105
Ohi, Ruth 1964- 95
Ohiyesa
  See Eastman, Charles A(lexander)
Ohlsson, Ib 1935- 7
Ohmi, Ayano 1959- 115
Ohtomo, Yasuo 1946- 37
o huigin, sean 1942- 138
  See also CLR 75
Oiseau
  See Moseley, James W(illett)
Oke, Janette 1935- 97
O'Keefe, Susan Heyboer 176
  Earlier sketch in SATA *133*
O'Keeffe, Frank 1938- 99
O'Kelley, Mattie Lou 1908-1997 97
  Earlier sketch in SATA *36*
Okimoto, Jean Davies 1942- 103
  Earlier sketch in SATA *34*
Okomfo, Amasewa
  See Cousins, Linda
olafsdottir, Gudrun Elin
  See Gunnella
Olaleye, Isaac O. 1941- 96
  See also SAAS 23
Olcott, Frances Jenkins 1872(?)-1963 19
Old, Wendie C(orbin) 1943- 154
Old Boy
  See Hughes, Thomas
Oldenburg, E(gbert) William 1936-1974 35

Older, Effin 1942- *114*
Older, Jules 1940- *156*
  Earlier sketch in SATA *114*
Oldfield, Jenny 1949- *140*
Oldfield, Margaret J(ean) 1932- *56*
Oldfield, Pamela 1931- *86*
Oldham, June *70*
Oldham, Mary 1944- *65*
Olds, Elizabeth 1896-1991 .... *3*
  Obituary *66*
Olds, Helen Diehl 1895-1981 .... *9*
  Obituary *25*
Oldstyle, Jonathan
  See Irving, Washington
O'Leary, Brian (Todd) 1940- *6*
O'Leary, Patsy B(aker) 1937- *97*
Oleynikov, Igor 1953- *202*
Oliphant, B.J.
  See Tepper, Sheri S.
Oliver, Burton
  See Burt, Olive Woolley
Oliver, Chad
  See Oliver, Symmes C.
Oliver, John Edward 1933- *21*
Oliver, Lin *202*
Oliver, Marilyn Tower 1935- *89*
Oliver, Narelle 1960- *197*
  Earlier sketch in SATA *152*
Oliver, Shirley (Louise Dawkins) 1958- *74*
Oliver, Symmes C. 1928-1993 .... *101*
Oliviero, Jamie 1950- *84*
Olmsted, Lorena Ann 1890-1989 .... *13*
Olney, Ross R. 1929- *13*
Olschewski, Alfred (Erich) 1920- *7*
Olsen, Barbara *148*
Olsen, Carol 1945- *89*
Olsen, Ib Spang 1921- *81*
  Earlier sketch in SATA *6*
Olsen, Violet (Mae) 1922-1991 .... *58*
Olson, Arielle North 1932- *67*
Olson, David J. 1974- *198*
Olson, Gene 1922- *32*
Olson, Gretchen *187*
Olson, Helen Kronberg *48*
Olson, Kay Melchisedech 1948- *175*
Olson, Marianne
  See Mitchell, Marianne
Olson-Brown, Ellen 1967- *183*
Olten, Manuela 1970- *197*
Olugebefola, Ademole 1941- *15*
Oluonye, Mary N(kechi) 1955- *111*
Om
  See Gorey, Edward (St. John)
O'Malley, Kevin 1961- *191*
  Earlier sketch in SATA *157*
Oman, Carola (Mary Anima) 1897-1978 ..... *35*
O'Mara, Carmel 1965- *166*
O'Mara-Horwitz, Carmel
  See O'Mara, Carmel
O'Meara, Walter (Andrew) 1897-1989 .... *65*
Ommanney, F(rancis) D(ownes) 1903-1980 . *23*
O Mude
  See Gorey, Edward (St. John)
Oneal, Elizabeth 1934- *82*
  Earlier sketch in SATA *30*
  See also CLR *13*
O'Neal, Katherine Pebley 1957- *204*
O'Neal, Reagan
  See Jordan, Robert
O'Neal, Regan
  See Jordan, Robert
Oneal, Zibby
  See Oneal, Elizabeth
O'Neill, Amanda 1951- *111*
O'Neill, Catharine *203*
O'Neill, Gerard K(itchen) 1927-1992 .... *65*
O'Neill, Judith (Beatrice) 1930- *34*
O'Neill, Mary L(e Duc) 1908(?)-1990 .... *2*
  Obituary *64*
O'Neill, Reagan
  See Jordan, Robert

Onslow, Annette Rosemary MacArthur
  See MacArthur-Onslow, Annette Rosemary
Onslow, John 1906-1985
  Obituary *47*
Onyefulu, Ifeoma 1959- *157*
  Earlier sketches in SATA *81, 115*
Opie, Iona (Margaret Balfour) 1923- *118*
  Earlier sketches in SATA *3, 63*
  See also SAAS *6*
Opie, Peter (Mason) 1918-1982 .... *118*
  Obituary *28*
  Earlier sketches in SATA *3, 63*
Oppel, Kenneth 1967- *199*
  Earlier sketches in SATA *99, 153*
Oppel, Kenneth Kerry
  See Oppel, Kenneth
Oppenheim, Joanne 1934- *174*
  Earlier sketches in SATA *5, 82, 136*
Oppenheim, Shulamith Levey 1928- *177*
Oppenheimer, Joan L(etson) 1925- *28*
Oppong, Joseph Ransford 1953- *160*
Optic, Oliver
  See Adams, William Taylor
  and Stratemeyer, Edward L.
Oram, Hiawyn 1946- *101*
  Earlier sketch in SATA *56*
Orbach, Ruth Gary 1941- *21*
Orback, Craig *197*
Orczy, Emma
  See Orczy, Baroness Emmuska
Orczy, Emma Magdalena Rosalia Maria Josefa
  See Orczy, Baroness Emmuska
Orczy, Emmuska
  See Orczy, Baroness Emmuska
Orczy, Baroness Emmuska 1865-1947 .... *40*
Orde, A.J.
  See Tepper, Sheri S.
O'Reilly, Jackson
  See Jordan, Robert
Orenstein, Denise Gosliner 1950- *157*
Orgad, Dorit 1936- *199*
Orgel, Doris 1929- *148*
  Earlier sketches in SATA *7, 85*
  See also CLR *48*
  See also SAAS *19*
Orgill, Roxane *198*
Oriolo, Joe
  See Oriolo, Joseph D.
Oriolo, Joseph D. 1913-1985
  Obituary *46*
Orleans, Ilo 1897-1962 .... *10*
Orlev, Uri 1931- *135*
  Earlier sketch in SATA *58*
  See also CLR *30*
  See also SAAS *19*
Ormai, Stella *57*
  Brief entry *48*
Ormerod, Jan 1946- *132*
  Brief entry *44*
  Earlier sketches in SATA *55, 70*
  See also CLR *20*
Ormes, Jackie
  See Ormes, Zelda J.
Ormes, Zelda J. 1914-1986
  Obituary *47*
Ormondroyd, Edward 1925- *14*
Ormsby, Virginia H(aire) 1906-1990 .... *11*
Orona-Ramirez, Kristy 1964- *189*
Orozco, Jose-Luis 1948- *179*
Orr, Katherine S(helley) 1950- *72*
Orr, Wendy 1953- *206*
  Earlier sketches in SATA *90, 141*
Orris
  See Ingelow, Jean
Orth, Richard
  See Gardner, Richard (M.)
Ortiz Cofer, Judith
  See Cofer, Judith Ortiz
Orwell, George 1903-1950 .... *29*
  See also CLR *68*
Orwin, Joanna 1944- *141*

Osborn, Elinor 1939- *145*
Osborn, Kathy 1955(?)- *199*
Osborn, Lois D(orothy) 1915- *61*
Osborne, Charles 1927- *59*
Osborne, Chester G(orham) 1915-1987 .... *11*
Osborne, David
  See Silverberg, Robert
Osborne, George
  See Silverberg, Robert
Osborne, Leone Neal 1914-1996 .... *2*
Osborne, Mary Pope 1949- *144*
  Earlier sketches in SATA *41, 55, 98*
  See also CLR *88*
Osceola
  See Blixen, Karen
Osgood, William E(dward) 1926- *37*
O'Shaughnessy, Darren
  See Shan, Darren
O'Shaughnessy, Ellen Cassels 1937- *78*
O'Shea, Catherine Patricia Shiels
  See O'Shea, Pat
O'Shea, Pat 1931-2007 .... *87*
  See also CLR *18*
Osmond, Edward 1900- *10*
Ossoli, Sarah Margaret
  See Fuller, Margaret
Ostendorf, (Arthur) Lloyd, (Jr.) 1921-2000 .. *65*
  Obituary *125*
Ostow, Micol 1976- *170*
Otfinoski, Steven 1949- *116*
  Earlier sketch in SATA *56*
Otis, James
  See Kaler, James Otis
O'Toole, Thomas 1941- *71*
O'Trigger, Sir Lucius
  See Horne, Richard Henry Hengist
Otten, Charlotte
  See Otten, Charlotte F.
Otten, Charlotte F. 1926- *98*
Otten, Charlotte Fennema
  See Otten, Charlotte F.
Ottley, Matt 1962- *171*
  Earlier sketch in SATA *102*
Ottley, Reginald Leslie 1909-1985 .... *26*
  See also CLR *16*
Otto, Margaret Glover 1909-1976
  Obituary *30*
Otto, Svend
  See Soerensen, Svend Otto
Oughton, Jerrie (Preston) 1937- *131*
  Earlier sketch in SATA *76*
Oughton, (William) Taylor 1925- *104*
Ouida
  See De La Ramee, Marie Louise
Ousley, Odille 1896-1976 .... *10*
Outcalt, Todd 1960- *123*
Overmyer, James E. 1946- *88*
Overton, Jenny (Margaret Mary) 1942- *52*
  Brief entry *36*
Owen, Ann
  See Qualey, Marsha
Owen, Annie 1949- *75*
Owen, Caroline Dale
  See Snedeker, Caroline Dale (Parke)
Owen, Clifford
  See Hamilton, Charles (Harold St. John)
Owen, Dilys
  See Gater, Dilys
Owen, (Benjamin) Evan 1918-1984 .... *38*
Owen, (John) Gareth 1936-2002 .... *162*
  Earlier sketch in SATA *83*
  See also CLR *31*
  See also SAAS *14*
Owen, James A. *185*
Owens, Bryant 1968- *116*
Owens, Dana Elaine
  See Queen Latifah
Owens, Gail 1939- *54*
Owens, Mary Beth *191*
Owens, Thomas S(heldon) 1960- *86*

Owens, Tom
  See Owens, Thomas S(heldon)
Oxenbury, Helen 1938- 149
  Earlier sketches in SATA *3, 68*
  See also CLR *70*
Oxendine, Bess Holland 1933- 90
Oz, Frank (Richard) 1944- 60
Ozer, Jerome S. 1927- 59

P

Paananen, Eloise (Katherine) 1923-1993 9
Pace, Lorenzo 1943- 131
Pace, Mildred Mastin 1907- 46
  Brief entry 29
Pachter, Hedwig (?)-1988 63
Pack, Janet 1952- 77
Pack, Robert 1929- 118
Packard, Edward 1931- 148
  Earlier sketches in SATA *47, 90*
Packer, Kenneth L. 1946- 116
Packer, Vin
  See Meaker, Marijane
Pad, Peter
  See Stratemeyer, Edward L.
Page, Eileen
  See Heal, Edith
Page, Eleanor
  See Coerr, Eleanor (Beatrice)
Page, Gail 1950- 205
Page, Jake 1936- 81
Page, James Keena, Jr.
  See Page, Jake
Page, Lou Williams 1912-1997 38
Page, Mary
  See Heal, Edith
Page, Robin 1943- 154
Pagnucci, Susan 1944- 90
Pahlen, Kurt 1907-2003
  Obituary 147
Pahz, Cheryl
  See Pahz, Cheryl Suzanne
Pahz, Cheryl Suzanne 1949- 11
Pahz, James Alon 1943- 11
Paice, Margaret 1920- 10
Paige, Harry W(orthington) 1922- 41
  Brief entry 35
Paige, Richard
  See Koontz, Dean
Paige, Robin
  See Albert, Susan Wittig
Paine, Penelope Colville 1946- 87
Paine, Roberta M. 1925- 13
Paisley, Tom 1932- 11
  See also CLR *3*
Palatini, Margie 207
  Earlier sketches in SATA *134, 174*
Palazzo, Anthony D.
  See Palazzo, Tony
Palazzo, Tony 1905-1970 3
Palder, Edward L. 1922- 5
Palecek, Josef 1932- 56
Palecek, Libuse 1937- 89
Palen, Debbie 195
Palin, Michael 1943- 67
Palin, Michael Edward
  See Palin, Michael
Palladini, David (Mario) 1946- 40
  Brief entry 32
Pallas, Norvin 1918-1983 23
Pallister, John C(lare) 1891-1980
  Obituary 26
Pallotta, Gerard Larry
  See Pallotta, Jerry
Pallotta, Jerry 1953- 186
Pallotta-Chiarolli, Maria 1960- 117
Palmer, Bernard (Alvin) 1914-1998 26
Palmer, C. Everard 1930- 14
Palmer, (Ruth) Candida 1926- 11

Palmer, Cyril Everard
  See Palmer, C. Everard
Palmer, Don
  See Benson, Mildred
Palmer, Hap 1942- 68
Palmer, Heidi 1948- 15
Palmer, Helen Marion
  See Geisel, Helen
Palmer, Jessica 1953- 120
Palmer, Judd 1972- 153
Palmer, Juliette 1930- 15
Palmer, Kate Salley 1946- 97
Palmer, Maria
  See Strachan, Ian
Palmer, Maria
  See Brennan, Herbie
Palmer, Robin 1909-2000 43
Palmero Caceres, Ana 198
Palmisciano, Diane 202
Paltrowitz, Donna 1950- 61
  Brief entry 50
Paltrowitz, Donna Milman
  See Paltrowitz, Donna
Paltrowitz, Stuart 1946- 61
  Brief entry 50
Pamela, Todd 1950- 124
Pamintuan, Macky 178
Panagopoulos, Janie Lynn 149
Panati, Charles 1943- 65
Panchyk, Richard 1970- 138
Panetta, George 1915-1969 15
Panetta, Joseph N. 1953- 96
Pang, YaWen Ariel 206
Panik, Sharon 1952- 82
Panowski, Eileen Thompson 1920- 49
Pansy
  See Alden, Isabella (Macdonald)
Pantell, Dora (Fuchs) 39
Panter, Carol 1936- 9
Paolini, Christopher 1983- 157
  See also CLR *102*
Papademetriou, Lisa 175
Paparone, Pam 185
Paparone, Pamela
  See Paparone, Pam
Papas, Bill
  See Papas, William
Papas, William 1927-2000 50
Papashvily, George 1898-1978 17
Papashvily, Helen (Waite) 1906-1996 17
Pape, D. L.
  See Pape, Donna (Lugg)
Pape, Donna (Lugg) 1930- 82
  Earlier sketch in SATA *2*
Paperny, Myra (Green) 1932- 51
  Brief entry 33
Papp, Robert 1967- 205
Paradis, Adrian A(lexis) 1912- 67
  Earlier sketch in SATA *1*
  See also SAAS *8*
Paradis, Marjorie Bartholomew
  1886(?)-1970 17
Paradiz, Valerie 1963- 176
Paratore, Coleen
  See Paratore, Coleen Murtagh
Paratore, Coleen Murtagh 1958- 200
Parenteau, Shirley 1935- 199
  Brief entry 40
  Earlier sketch in SATA *47*
Parish, Margaret 1927-1988 73
  Obituary 59
  Earlier sketch in SATA *17*
  See also CLR *22*
Parish, Margaret Holt
  See Holt, Margaret
Parish, Peggy
  See Parish, Margaret
Park, Barbara 1947- 123
  Brief entry 35
  Earlier sketches in SATA *40, 78*
  See also CLR *34*

Park, Bill
  See Park, W(illiam) B(ryan)
Park, Frances 1955- 171
Park, Ginger 173
Park, Janie Jaehyun 150
Park, Jordan
  See Kornbluth, C(yril) M.
  and Pohl, Frederik
Park, Linda Sue 1960- 200
  Earlier sketches in SATA *127, 173*
  See also CLR *84*
Park, Nick 1958- 113
Park, (Rosina) Ruth (Lucia) 1923(?)- 93
  Earlier sketch in SATA *25*
  See also CLR *51*
Park, W(illiam) B(ryan) 1936- 22
Parke, Marilyn 1928- 82
Parker, Barbara Keevil 1938- 157
Parker, Daniel
  See Ehrenhaft, Daniel
Parker, Elinor Milnor 1906- 3
Parker, Julie F. 1961- 92
Parker, Kim 1963- 174
Parker, Kristy 1957- 59
Parker, Lois M(ay) 1912-1996 30
Parker, Margot M. 1937- 52
Parker, Marjorie Blain 1960- 205
  Earlier sketch in SATA *145*
Parker, Mary Jessie 1948- 71
Parker, Nancy Winslow 1930- 132
  Earlier sketches in SATA *10, 69*
  See also SAAS *20*
Parker, Richard 1915-1990 14
Parker, Robert
  See Boyd, Waldo T.
  and Parker, Robert Andrew
Parker, Robert Andrew 1927- 200
Parker, Toni Trent 1947-2005 142
  Obituary 169
Parker-Rees, Guy 193
Parkes, Lucas
  See Harris, John (Wyndham Parkes Lucas)
  Beynon
Parkhill, John
  See Cox, William R(obert)
Parkins, David 1955- 176
Parkinson, Ethelyn M(inerva) 1906-1999 11
Parkinson, Kathryn N. 1954- 71
Parkinson, Kathy
  See Parkinson, Kathryn N.
Parkinson, Siobhan
  See Parkinson, Siobhan
Parkinson, Siobhan 1954- 178
Parks, Deborah A. 1948- 133
  Earlier sketch in SATA *91*
Parks, Edd Winfield 1906-1968 10
Parks, Gordon 1912-2006 108
  Obituary 175
  Earlier sketch in SATA *8*
Parks, Gordon Roger Alexander
  See Parks, Gordon
Parks, Peggy J. 1951- 143
Parks, PJ
  See Parks, Peggy J.
Parks, Rosa 1913-2005 83
  Obituary 169
Parks, Rosa Louise Lee
  See Parks, Rosa
Parks, Van Dyke 1943- 62
Parley, Peter
  See Goodrich, Samuel Griswold
Parlin, John
  See Graves, Charles Parlin
Parme, Fabrice 1966- 191
Parnall, Peter 1936- 69
  Earlier sketch in SATA *16*
  See also SAAS *11*
Parotti, Phillip (Elliott) 1941- 109
Parr, Ann 1943- 144
Parr, Danny
  See Parr, Ann

Parr, Letitia (Evelyn) 1906-1985(?) *37*
Parr, Lucy 1924- *10*
Parr, Todd *179*
　Earlier sketch in SATA *134*
Parrish, Anne 1888-1957 .... *27*
Parrish, Mary
　See Cousins, Margaret
Parrish, Maxfield
　See Parrish, (Frederick) Maxfield
Parrish, (Frederick) Maxfield 1870-1966 ..... *14*
Parry, Marian 1924- *13*
Parson Lot
　See Kingsley, Charles
Parsons, Alexandra 1947- *92*
Parsons, Ellen
　See Dragonwagon, Crescent
Parsons, Garry *197*
Parsons, Martin 1951- *116*
Parsons, Martin Leslie
　See Parsons, Martin
Parsons, Tom
　See MacPherson, Thomas George
Parsons-Yazzi, Evangeline *172*
Partch, Virgil Franklin II 1916-1984 .... *39*
　Obituary *39*
Parton, Dolly 1946- *94*
Parton, Dolly Rebecca
　See Parton, Dolly
Partridge, Benjamin W., Jr. 1915-2005 .... *28*
　Obituary *163*
Partridge, Benjamin Waring, Jr.
　See Partridge, Benjamin W., Jr.
Partridge, Cora Cheney
　See Cheney, Cora
Partridge, Elizabeth *134*
Partridge, Jenny (Lilian) 1947- *52*
　Brief entry *37*
Pasachoff, Naomi 1947- *147*
Pascal, David 1918- *14*
Pascal, Francine 1938- *143*
　Brief entry *37*
　Earlier sketches in SATA *51, 80*
　See also CLR *25*
Paschal, Nancy
　See Trotter, Grace V(iolet)
Paschkis, Julie 1957- *177*
Pascudniak, Pascal
　See Lupoff, Richard A(llen)
Pashko, Stanley 1913-1982 .... *29*
Passailaigue, Thomas E.
　See Paisley, Tom
Pastel, Elyse *201*
Pateman, Robert 1954- *84*
Patent, Dorothy Hinshaw 1940- *162*
　Autobiography Feature *162*
　Earlier sketches in SATA *22, 69, 120*
　See also CLR *19*
　See also SAAS *13*
Paterson, A(ndrew) B(arton) 1864-1941 .... *97*
Paterson, Banjo
　See Paterson, A(ndrew) B(arton)
Paterson, Diane 1946- *177*
　Brief entry *33*
　Earlier sketch in SATA *59*
Paterson, John (Barstow) 1932- *114*
Paterson, Katherine 1932- *204*
　Earlier sketches in SATA *13, 53, 92, 133*
　See also CLR *127*
Paterson, Katherine Womeldorf
　See Paterson, Katherine
Patience, John 1949- *90*
Patneaude, David 1944- *159*
　Earlier sketch in SATA *85*
Paton, Alan 1903-1988 .... *11*
　Obituary *56*
Paton, Alan Stewart
　See Paton, Alan
Paton, Jane (Elizabeth) 1934- *35*
Paton, Priscilla 1952- *98*
Paton Walsh, Gillian
　See Paton Walsh, Jill

Paton Walsh, Jill 1937- *190*
　Autobiography Feature *190*
　Earlier sketches in SATA *4, 72, 109*
　See also CLR *128*
　See also SAAS *3*
Patricelli, Leslie *207*
Patrick, Susan
　See Clark, Patricia Denise
Patron, Susan 1948- *182*
　Earlier sketch in SATA *76*
Patsauq, Markoosie 1942-
　See CLR *23*
Patschke, Steve 1955- *125*
Patten, Brian 1946- *152*
　Earlier sketch in SATA *29*
Patterson, Charles 1935- *59*
Patterson, Geoffrey 1943- *54*
　Brief entry *44*
Patterson, James 1947- *197*
　Earlier sketch in SATA *164*
Patterson, James B.
　See Patterson, James
Patterson, Lillie G. -1999 .... *88*
　Earlier sketch in SATA *14*
Patterson, Nancy Ruth 1944- *148*
　Earlier sketch in SATA *72*
Pattison, Darcy (S.) 1954- *126*
　Earlier sketch in SATA *72*
Pattou, Edith *164*
Patz (Blaustein), Nancy *154*
Paul, Aileen 1917- *12*
Paul, Alison *196*
Paul, Ann Whitford 1941- *168*
　Earlier sketches in SATA *76, 110*
Paul, David (Tyler) 1934-1988
　Obituary *56*
Paul, Dominique 1973- *184*
Paul, Elizabeth
　See Crow, Donna Fletcher
Paul, Hamish Vigne Christie 1951- *151*
　See also CLR *87*
Paul, James 1936- *23*
Paul, Korky
　See Paul, Hamish Vigne Christie
Paul, Robert
　See Roberts, John G(aither)
Paul, Tessa 1944- *103*
Pauli, Hertha (Ernestine) 1909-1973 .... *3*
　Obituary *26*
Paull, Grace A. 1898- *24*
Paulsen, Gary 1939- *189*
　Earlier sketches in SATA *22, 50, 54, 79, 111,*
　158
　See also CLR *82*
Paulson, Jack
　See Jackson, C(aary) Paul
Pauquet, Gina Ruck
　See Ruck-Pauquet, Gina
Pausacker, Jenny 1948- *72*
　See also SAAS *23*
Pausewang, Gudrun 1928- *165*
　Earlier sketch in SATA *104*
Pavel, Frances 1907- *10*
Paver, Michelle *170*
Paxton, Thomas R. 1937- *70*
Paxton, Tom
　See Paxton, Thomas R.
Paye, Won-Ldy *185*
Payne, Alan
　See Jakes, John
Payne, Bernal C., Jr. 1941- *60*
Payne, C. Douglas
　See Payne, C.D.
Payne, C.D. 1949- *133*
Payne, C.F. 1956- *179*
Payne, Chris Fox
　See Payne, C.F.
Payne, Donald Gordon 1924- *37*
Payne, Emmy
　See West, Emily Govan
Payne, Nina *135*

Payne, Rachel Ann
　See Jakes, John
Payson, Dale 1943- *9*
Payzant, Charles *18*
Paz, A.
　See Pahz, James Alon
Paz, Natalia Toledo
　See Toledo, Natalia
Paz, Zan
　See Pahz, Cheryl Suzanne
Peace, Mary
　See Finley, Mary Peace
Peacock, Shane 1957- *192*
Peake, Mervyn 1911-1968 .... *23*
Peale, Norman Vincent 1898-1993 .... *20*
　Obituary *78*
Pearce, Ann Philippa
　See Pearce, Philippa
Pearce, Emily Smith 1975- *199*
Pearce, Jacqueline 1962- *146*
Pearce, Margaret *104*
Pearce, Philippa 1920-2006 .... *129*
　Obituary *179*
　Earlier sketches in SATA *1, 67*
　See also CLR *9*
Peare, Catherine Owens 1911- *9*
Pearle, Ida *207*
Pearsall, Shelley 1966- *190*
Pearson, Gayle 1947- *119*
　Earlier sketch in SATA *53*
Pearson, Jean Mary
　See Gardam, Jane
Pearson, Kit 1947- *77*
　Autobiography Feature *117*
　See also CLR *26*
Pearson, Mary E. 1955- *134*
Pearson, Ridley 1953- *182*
Pearson, Susan 1946- *166*
　Brief entry *27*
　Earlier sketches in SATA *39, 91*
Pearson, Tracey Campbell 1956- *155*
　Earlier sketch in SATA *64*
Pease, (Clarence) Howard 1894-1974 .... *2*
　Obituary *25*
Peavy, Linda 1943- *54*
Peck, Anne Merriman 1884-1976 .... *18*
Peck, Beth 1957- *190*
　Earlier sketch in SATA *79*
Peck, Jan *159*
Peck, Jeanie J. 1967- *147*
Peck, Marshall III 1951- *92*
Peck, Richard 1934- *190*
　Autobiography Feature *110*
　Earlier sketches in SATA *18, 55, 97, 110, 158*
　See also CLR *142*
　See also SAAS *2*
Peck, Richard Wayne
　See Peck, Richard
Peck, Robert Newton 1928- *156*
　Autobiography Feature *108*
　Earlier sketches in SATA *21, 62, 111*
　See also CLR *45*
　See also SAAS *1*
Peck, Sylvia 1953- *133*
Peck-Whiting, Jeanie J.
　See Peck, Jeanie J.
Peddicord, Jane Ann *199*
Pedersen, Janet *193*
Pederson, Sharleen
　See Collicott, Sharleen
Pedler, Caroline *197*
Peebles, Anne
　See Galloway, Priscilla
Peek, Merle 1938- *39*
Peel, John 1954- *79*
Peel, Norman Lemon
　See Hirsch, Phil
Peeples, Edwin A(ugustus, Jr.) 1915-1994 ..... *6*
Peers, Judi 1956- *119*
Peers, Judith May West
　See Peers, Judi

Peet, Bill
See Peet, William Bartlett
Peet, Creighton B. 1899-1977 30
Peet, Mal 171
Peet, Malcolm
See Peet, Mal
Peet, William Bartlett 1915-2002 78
Obituary 137
Earlier sketches in SATA 2, 41
See also CLR 12
Peguero, Leone 116
Pelaez, Jill 1924- 12
Pelham, David 1938- 70
Pell, Ed(ward) 1950- 157
Pelletier, Andrew T. 195
Pelletier, Andrew Thomas
See Pelletier, Andrew T.
Pellowski, Anne 1933- 20
Pellowski, Michael (Joseph) 1949- 151
Brief entry 48
Earlier sketch in SATA 88
Pellowski, Michael Morgan
See Pellowski, Michael (Joseph)
Pelta, Kathy 1928- 18
Peltier, Leslie C(opus) 1900-1980 13
Pemberton, Bonnie 191
Pemberton, John Leigh
See Leigh-Pemberton, John
Pembury, Bill
See Groom, Arthur William
Pemsteen, Hans
See Manes, Stephen
Pendennis, Arthur Esquir
See Thackeray, William Makepeace
Pender, Lydia Podger 1907- 61
Pendery, Rosemary (Schmitz) 7
Pendle, Alexy 1943- 29
Pendle, George 1906-1977
Obituary 28
Pendleton, Don
See Cunningham, Chet
and Garside, Jack
and Jagninski, Tom
and Krauzer, Steven M(ark)
and Obstfeld, Raymond
Pendleton, Thomas 1965- 206
Pendziwol, Jean E. 1965- 177
Pene du Bois, William (Sherman)
1916-1993 68
Obituary 74
Earlier sketch in SATA 4
See also CLR 1
Penn, Audrey 1950- 22
Penn, Ruth Bonn
See Rosenberg, Eth Clifford
Pennac, Daniel 1944- 155
Pennage, E. M.
See Finkel, George (Irvine)
Penner, Fred 1946- 169
Earlier sketch in SATA 67
Penner, Frederick Ralph Cornelius
See Penner, Fred
Penney, Grace Jackson 1904-2000 35
Penney, Ian 1960- 76
Penney, Sue 1957- 152
Earlier sketch in SATA 102
Pennington, Eunice 1923- 27
Pennington, Lillian Boyer 1904-2003 45
Pennypacker, Sara 1951- 187
Penrose, Gordon 1925- 66
Penson, Mary E. 1917- 78
Penzler, Otto 1942- 38
Pepe, Phil 1935- 20
Pepe, Philip
See Pepe, Phil
Peppe, Rodney (Darrell) 1934- 74
Earlier sketch in SATA 4
See also SAAS 10
Pepper, Frank S. 1910-1988
Obituary 61

Percy, Charles Henry
See Smith, Dorothy Gladys
Percy, Rachel 1930- 63
Perdrizet, Marie-Pierre 1952- 79
Perenyi, Constance 1954- 93
Perenyi, Constance Marie
See Perenyi, Constance
Perera, Hilda 1926- 105
Perera, Thomas Biddle 1938- 13
Peretti, Frank E. 1951- 141
Earlier sketch in SATA 80
Perez, L. King 1940- 199
Perez, Lana
See Perez, Marlene
Perez, Lucia Angela 1973- 182
Perez, Marlene 170
Pericoli, Matteo 1968- 178
Perkins, Al(bert Rogers) 1904-1975 30
Perkins, Lucy Fitch 1865-1937 72
Perkins, Lynne Rae 1956- 172
Earlier sketch in SATA 131
Perkins, (Richard) Marlin 1905-1986 21
Obituary 48
Perkins, Mitali 1963- 188
Earlier sketch in SATA 88
Perks, Anne-Marie 1955- 122
Perl, Erica S. 188
Perl, Lila 72
Earlier sketch in SATA 6
Perl, Susan 1922-1983 22
Obituary 34
Perlman, Rhea 1948- 183
Perlmutter, O(scar) William 1920-1975 8
Pernu, Dennis 1970- 87
Perrault, Charles 1628-1703 25
See also CLR 134
Perret, Delphine 1980- 190
Perret, Gene (Richard) 1937- 76
Perrine, Mary 1913-1976 2
Perrins, Lesley 1953- 56
Perrow, Angeli 1954- 121
Perry, Andrea 1956- 190
Earlier sketch in SATA 148
Perry, Barbara Fisher
See Fisher, Barbara
Perry, Elizabeth 1959- 174
Perry, Elizabeth Goodwin
See Perry, Elizabeth
Perry, Marie Fritz 165
Perry, Patricia 1949- 30
Perry, Phyllis J(ean) 1933- 152
Earlier sketches in SATA 60, 101
Perry, Ritchie (John Allen) 1942- 105
Perry, Roger 1933- 27
Perry, Steve(n Carl) 1947- 76
Pershall, Mary K. 1951- 172
Earlier sketch in SATA 70
Pershing, Marie
See Schultz, Pearle Henriksen
Perske, Robert 1927- 57
Persun, Morgan Reed
See Watkins, Dawn L.
Petach, Heidi 149
Peter
See Stratemeyer, Edward L.
Peters, Alexander
See Hollander, Zander
Peters, Andrew Fusek 1965- 169
Earlier sketch in SATA 107
Peters, Caroline
See Betz, Eva Kelly
Peters, David
See David, Peter
Peters, Elizabeth 1927- 49
Peters, Emma
See Price, Karen
Peters, Gabriel
See Matott, Justin
Peters, Julie Anne 1952- 197
Earlier sketches in SATA 82, 128

Peters, Linda
See Catherall, Arthur
Peters, Lisa Westberg 1951- 161
Earlier sketches in SATA 74, 115
Peters, Patricia 1953- 84
Peters, Russell M. 1929- 78
Peters, S. H.
See Henry, O.
and Proffitt, Nicholas
Petersen, David 1946- 109
Earlier sketch in SATA 62
Petersen, Gwenn Boardman 1924- 12
Petersen, P(eter) J(ames) 1941- 118
Brief entry 43
Earlier sketches in SATA 48, 83
Petersen, Palle 1943- 85
Petersham, Maud 1890-1971 17
See also CLR 24
Petersham, Maud Sylvia Fuller
See Petersham, Maud
Petersham, Miska 1888-1960 17
See also CLR 24
Peterson, Cris 1952- 174
Earlier sketches in SATA 84, 145
Peterson, Dawn 1934- 86
Peterson, Esther (Allen) 1934- 35
Peterson, Hans 1922- 8
Peterson, Harold L(eslie) 1922-1978 8
Peterson, Helen Stone 1910- 8
Peterson, Jean Sunde 1941- 108
Peterson, Jeanne Whitehouse 1939- 159
Earlier sketch in SATA 29
Peterson, Kathleen B. 1951- 119
Peterson, Lorraine 1940- 56
Brief entry 44
Peterson, Shelley 1952- 146
Peterson, Will
See Cocks, Peter
Petie, Haris
See Petty, Roberta
Petricic, Dusan 1946- 176
Petrides, Heidrun 1944- 19
Petrie, Catherine 1947- 52
Brief entry 41
Petrone, Valeria 186
Petrosino, Tamara 193
Petroski, Catherine (Ann Groom) 1939- 48
Petrovich, Michael B(oro) 1922- 40
Petrovskaya, Kyra
See Wayne, Kyra Petrovskaya
Petruccio, Steven James 1961- 67
Petry, Ann 1908-1997 5
Obituary 94
See also CLR 12
Petry, Ann Lane
See Petry, Ann
Pettit, Jayne 1932- 108
Petty, J.T. 1977- 189
Petty, Kate 1951-2007 204
Petty, Roberta 1915- 10
Pevsner, Stella 131
Earlier sketches in SATA 8, 77
See also SAAS 14
Peyo
See Culliford, Pierre
Peyton, K. M.
See Peyton, Kathleen Wendy
Peyton, Kathleen Wendy 1929- 157
Earlier sketches in SATA 15, 62
See also CLR 3
See also SAAS 17
Pfanner, (Anne) Louise 1955- 68
Pfeffer, Susan Beth 1948- 180
Earlier sketches in SATA 4, 83
See also CLR 11
See also SAAS 17
Pfeffer, Wendy 1929- 204
Earlier sketches in SATA 78, 142
Pfeiffer, Janet (B.) 1949- 96

Pfister, Marcus 207
  Earlier sketches in SATA *83, 150*
  See also CLR *42*
Pfitsch, Patricia Curtis 1948- 148
Pflieger, Pat 1955- 84
Pham, LeUyen 1973- 201
  Earlier sketch in SATA *175*
Phelan, Mary Kay 1914- 3
Phelan, Matt 1970- 172
Phelan, Terry Wolfe 1941- 56
Phelps, Ethel Johnston 1914-1984 35
Philbrick, Rodman 1951- 163
Philbrick, W. R.
  See Philbrick, Rodman
Philbrick, W. Rodman
  See Philbrick, Rodman
Philbrook, Clem(ent E.) 1917- 24
Phillips, Aileen Paul
  See Paul, Aileen
Phillips, Betty Lou
  See Phillips, Elizabeth Louise
Phillips, Bob 1940- 95
Phillips, Douglas A. 1949- 161
Phillips, Elizabeth Louise 58
  Brief entry 48
Phillips, Irv(ing W.) 1905-2000 11
  Obituary 125
Phillips, Jack
  See Sandburg, Carl
Phillips, Leon
  See Gerson, Noel Bertram
Phillips, Loretta (Hosey) 1893-1987 10
Phillips, Louis 1942- 102
  Earlier sketch in SATA *8*
Phillips, Mark
  See Garrett, Randall
  and Janifer, Laurence M(ark)
Phillips, Mary Geisler 1881-1964 10
Phillips, Michael
  See Nolan, William F(rancis)
Phillips, (Woodward) Prentice 1894-1981 10
Phillpotts, Eden 1862-1960 24
Phin
  See Thayer, Ernest Lawrence
Phipson, Joan
  See Fitzhardinge, Joan Margaret
Phiz
  See Browne, Hablot Knight
Phleger, Fred B. 1909-1993 34
Phleger, Marjorie Temple 1908(?)-1986 1
  Obituary 47
Piaget, Jean 1896-1980
  Obituary 23
Piatti, Celestino 1922- 16
Picard, Barbara Leonie 1917- 89
  Earlier sketch in SATA *2*
  See also SAAS *10*
Pichon, Liz 174
Pickard, Charles 1932- 36
Pickering, James Sayre 1897-1969 36
  Obituary 28
Pickering, Jimmy 195
Pickering, Robert B. 1950- 93
Pielichaty, Helena 1955- 142
Pienkowski, Jan (Michal) 1936- 131
  Earlier sketches in SATA *6, 58*
  See also CLR *6*
Pierce, Edith Gray 1893-1977 45
Pierce, Katherine
  See St. John, Wylly Folk
Pierce, Meredith Ann 1958- 127
  Brief entry 48
  Earlier sketch in SATA *67*
  See also CLR *20*
Pierce, Ruth (Ireland) 1936- 5
Pierce, Sharon
  See McCullough, Sharon Pierce
Pierce, Tamora 1954- 187
  Brief entry 49
  Earlier sketches in SATA *51, 96, 153*
Pierce, Terry 178

Pierik, Robert 1921- 13
Piernas-Davenport, Gail 199
Piers, Robert
  See Anthony, Piers
Pig, Edward
  See Gorey, Edward (St. John)
Pike, Bob
  See Pike, Robert W(ilson)
Pike, Christopher 1954(?)- 156
  Earlier sketch in SATA *68*
  See also CLR *29*
Pike, Deborah 1951- 89
Pike, E(dgar) Royston 1896-1980 22
  Obituary 56
Pike, R. William 1956- 92
Pike, Robert W(ilson) 1931- 102
Pilarski, Laura 1926- 13
Pilgrim, Anne
  See Allan, Mabel Esther
Pilkey, Dav 1966- 166
  Earlier sketches in SATA *68, 115*
  See also CLR *48*
Pilkey, David Murray, Jr.
  See Pilkey, Dav
Pilkington, Francis Meredyth 1907-1993 4
Pilkington, Roger (Windle) 1915-2003 10
  Obituary 144
Pin, Isabel 1975- 183
Pinchot, David 1914(?)-1983
  Obituary 34
Pincus, Harriet 1938- 27
Pinczes, Elinor J(ane) 1940- 81
Pine, Nicholas 1951- 91
Pine, Tillie S(chloss) 1896-1999 13
Pini, Richard (Alan) 1950- 89
Pini, Wendy 1951- 89
Pinkerton, Kathrene Sutherland (Gedney)
  1887-1967
  Obituary 26
Pinkett, Jada
  See Smith, Jada Pinkett
Pinkney, Andrea Davis 1963- 160
  Earlier sketch in SATA *113*
Pinkney, Brian 1961- 206
  Earlier sketches in SATA *74, 148*
  See also CLR *54*
Pinkney, Gloria Jean 1941- 85
Pinkney, J. Brian
  See Pinkney, Brian
Pinkney, Jerry 1939- 198
  Autobiography Feature 198
  Brief entry 32
  Earlier sketches in SATA *41, 71, 107, 151*
  See also CLR *43*
  See also SAAS *12*
Pinkney, John 97
Pinkney, Sandra L. 193
  Earlier sketch in SATA *128*
Pinkwater, D. Manus
  See Pinkwater, Daniel
Pinkwater, Daniel 1941- 158
  Earlier sketches in SATA *8, 46, 76, 114*
  See also CLR *4*
  See also SAAS *3*
Pinkwater, Daniel M.
  See Pinkwater, Daniel
Pinkwater, Daniel Manus
  See Pinkwater, Daniel
Pinkwater, Jill 188
Pinkwater, Manus
  See Pinkwater, Daniel
Pinner, Joma
  See Werner, Herma
Pinto, Sara 200
Pioneer
  See Yates, Raymond F(rancis)
Piowaty, Kim Kennelly 1957- 49
Piper, Roger
  See Fisher, John
Pirner, Connie White 1955- 72
Piro, Richard 1934- 7

Pirot, Alison Lohans
  See Lohans, Alison
Pirotta, Saviour 184
Pirsig, Robert M(aynard) 1928- 39
Pita
  See Rendon, Maria
Pitcher, C.
  See Pitcher, Caroline
Pitcher, Caroline 1948- 128
Pitcher, Caroline Nell
  See Pitcher, Caroline
Pitman, (Isaac) James 1901-1985
  Obituary 46
Pitre, Felix 1949- 84
Pitrone, Jean Maddern 1920- 4
Pittman, Helena Clare 1945- 71
Pitz, Henry C(larence) 1895-1976 4
  Obituary 24
Pitzer, Susanna 1958- 181
Piven, Hanoch 1963- 173
Pixley, Marcella 194
Pizer, Vernon 1918- 21
Place, Marian T(empleton) 1910- 3
Place, Robin (Mary) 1926- 71
Plaidy, Jean
  See Hibbert, Eleanor Alice Burford
Plain, Belva 1919- 62
Plaine, Alfred R. 1898(?)-1981
  Obituary 29
Plath, Sylvia 1932-1963 96
Platt, Chris 1959- 185
Platt, Kin 1911- 86
  Earlier sketch in SATA *21*
  See also SAAS *17*
Platt, Randall 1948- 95
Platt, Randall Beth
  See Platt, Randall
Platt, Richard 1953- 166
  Earlier sketch in SATA *120*
Playfellow, Robin
  See Ellis, Edward S.
Playsted, James
  See Wood, James Playsted
Plecas, Jennifer 1966- 149
  Earlier sketch in SATA *84*
Plimpton, George 1927-2003 10
  Obituary 150
Plimpton, George Ames
  See Plimpton, George
Plomer, William Charles Franklin
  1903-1973 24
Plotz, Helen Ratnoff 1913-2000 38
Plourde, Lynn 1955- 168
  Earlier sketch in SATA *122*
Plowden, David 1932- 52
Plowden, Martha Ward 1948- 98
Plowhead, Ruth Gipson 1877-1967 43
Plowman, Stephanie 1922- 6
Pluckrose, Henry (Arthur) 1931- 141
  Earlier sketch in SATA *13*
Plum, J.
  See Wodehouse, P. G.
Plum, Jennifer
  See Kurland, Michael
Plumb, Charles P. 1900(?)-1982
  Obituary 29
Plume, Ilse 170
  Brief entry 43
Plumme, Don E.
  See Katz, Bobbi
Plummer, Margaret 1911- 2
Plum-Ucci, Carol 184
Pochocki, Ethel (Frances) 1925- 76
Podendorf, Illa (E.) 1903(?)-1983 18
  Obituary 35
Podwal, Mark 1945- 160
  Earlier sketch in SATA *101*
Podwal, Mark H.
  See Podwal, Mark
Poe, Edgar Allan 1809-1849 23
Poe, Ty (Christopher) 1975- 94

Pogany, William Andrew 1882-1955 .... *44*
   Brief entry *30*
Pogany, Willy
   See Pogany, William Andrew
Pohl, Frederik 1919- *24*
Pohlmann, Lillian (Grenfell) 1902-1997 .... *11*
Pohrt, Tom 1953- *195*
   Earlier sketches in SATA *67, 152*
Pointon, Robert
   See Rooke, Daphne
Points, Larry G. 1945- *177*
   Earlier sketch in SATA *133*
Points, Larry Gene
   See Points, Larry G.
Pokeberry, P.J.
   See Mitchell, B.J.
POLA
   See Watson, Pauline
Polacco, Patricia 1944- *180*
   Earlier sketches in SATA *74, 123*
   See also CLR *40*
Polacco, Patricia Ann
   See Polacco, Patricia
Polak, Monique 1960- *178*
Polatnick, Florence T. 1923- *5*
Polder, Markus
   See Kruss, James
Polese, Carolyn 1947- *58*
Polese, James 1914- *87*
Polette, Nancy (Jane) 1930- *42*
Polhamus, Jean Burt 1928- *21*
Policoff, Stephen Phillip 1948- *77*
Polikoff, Barbara G. 1929- *162*
   Earlier sketch in SATA *77*
Polikoff, Barbara Garland
   See Polikoff, Barbara G.
Polisar, Barry Louis 1954- *134*
   Earlier sketch in SATA *77*
Politi, Leo 1908-1996 .... *47*
   Obituary *88*
   Earlier sketch in SATA *1*
   See also CLR *29*
Polking, Kirk 1925- *5*
Pollack, Jill S. 1963- *88*
Pollack, Merrill S. 1924-1988
   Obituary *55*
Polland, Barbara K(ay) 1939- *44*
Polland, Madeleine A(ngela Cahill) 1918- ... *68*
   Earlier sketch in SATA *6*
   See also SAAS *8*
Pollema-Cahill, Phyllis 1958- *123*
Pollock, Bruce 1945- *46*
Pollock, Mary
   See Blyton, Enid
Pollock, Penny 1935- *137*
   Brief entry *42*
   Earlier sketch in SATA *44*
Pollowitz, Melinda Kilborn 1944- *26*
Polner, Murray 1928- *64*
Polonsky, Arthur 1925- *34*
Polseno, Jo *17*
Pomaska, Anna 1946- *117*
Pomerantz, Charlotte 1930- *177*
   Earlier sketches in SATA *20, 80*
Pomeroy, Pete
   See Roth, Arthur J(oseph)
Pond, Alonzo W(illiam) 1894-1986 .... *5*
Pontiflet, Ted 1932- *32*
Poole, Gray Johnson 1906- *1*
Poole, Josephine
   See Helyar, Jane Penelope Josephine
Poole, (Jane Penelope) Josephine
   See Helyar, Jane Penelope Josephine
Poole, Lynn 1910-1969 .... *1*
Poole, Peggy 1925- *39*
Poortvliet, Rien 1932- *65*
   Brief entry *37*
Pope, Elizabeth Marie 1917-1992 .... *38*
   Brief entry *36*
Pope, Kevin 1958- *183*

Popescu, Christine
   See Pullein-Thompson, Christine
Poploff, Michelle 1956- *67*
Popp, K. Wendy *91*
Poppel, Hans 1942- *71*
Porfirio, Guy 1958- *197*
Portal, Colette 1936- *6*
Porte, Barbara Ann 1943- *152*
   Brief entry *45*
   Earlier sketches in SATA *57, 93*
Porter, A(nthony) P(eyton) 1945- *68*
Porter, Connie (Rose) 1959(?)- *129*
   Earlier sketch in SATA *81*
Porter, Donald Clayton
   See Gerson, Noel Bertram
Porter, Eleanor H(odgman) 1868-1920
   See CLR *110*
Porter, Gene Stratton
   See Stratton-Porter, Gene
Porter, Janice Lee 1953- *108*
   Earlier sketch in SATA *68*
Porter, Katherine Anne 1890-1980 .... *39*
   Obituary *23*
Porter, Kathryn
   See Swinford, Betty (June Wells)
Porter, Pamela 1956- *193*
Porter, Sheena 1935- *24*
   See also SAAS *10*
Porter, Sue
   See Limb, Sue
Porter, Sue 1951- *76*
Porter, Tracey *191*
Porter, William Sydney
   See Henry, O.
Portis, Antoinette *189*
Porto, Tony 1960- *153*
Portteus, Eleanora Marie Manthei (?)-1983
   Obituary *36*
Posada, Mia *187*
Posell, Elsa Z(eigerman) -1995 .... *3*
Posten, Margaret L(ois) 1915- *10*
Posthuma, Sieb 1960- *150*
Postier, Jim 1965- *202*
Potok, Chaim 1929-2002 .... *106*
   Obituary *134*
   Earlier sketch in SATA *33*
   See also CLR *92*
Potok, Herbert Harold
   See Potok, Chaim
Potok, Herman Harold
   See Potok, Chaim
Potter, Beatrix 1866-1943 .... *132*
   Earlier sketch in SATA *100*
   See also YABC *1*
   See also CLR *73*
Potter, Giselle *187*
   Earlier sketch in SATA *150*
Potter, Helen Beatrix
   See Potter, Beatrix
Potter, Margaret 1926-1998 .... *21*
   Obituary *104*
Potter, Marian 1915- *9*
Potter, Miriam Clark 1886-1965 .... *3*
Poulin, Stephane 1961- *98*
   See also CLR *28*
Poulton, Kimberly 1957(?)- *136*
Pournelle, Jerry (Eugene) 1933- *161*
   Earlier sketches in SATA *26, 91*
Povelite, Kay 1955- *102*
Pow, Tom 1950- *163*
Powe-Allred, Alexandra
   See Allred, Alexandra Powe
Powell, A. M.
   See Morgan, Alfred P(owell)
Powell, Consie *174*
Powell, E. Sandy 1947- *72*
Powell, E.S.
   See Powell, E. Sandy
Powell, Pamela 1960- *78*
Powell, Patricia Hruby 1951- *136*
Powell, Randy 1956- *118*

Powell, Richard Stillman
   See Barbour, Ralph Henry
Powell, Robert (Stephenson Smyth) Baden
   See Baden-Powell, Robert (Stephenson
   Smyth)
Powell, Stephanie 1953- *93*
Power, Margaret (M.) 1945- *125*
   Earlier sketch in SATA *75*
Powers, Anne
   See Schwartz, Anne Powers
Powers, Bill 1931- *52*
   Brief entry *31*
Powers, Daniel 1959- *164*
Powers, Jessica Lynn
   See Powers, J.L.
Powers, J.L. 1974- *195*
Powers, Margaret
   See Heal, Edith
Powers, Tim 1952- *107*
Powers, Timothy Thomas
   See Powers, Tim
Powledge, Fred 1935- *37*
Poydar, Nancy *190*
Poynter, Margaret 1927- *27*
Prachaticka, Marketa
   See Kolibalova, Marketa
Prachatika, Marketa
   See Kolibalova, Marketa
Prager, Arthur *44*
Prager, Ellen J. 1962- *136*
Prange, Beckie *172*
Prap, Lila 1955- *177*
Praprotnik-Zupancic, Lilijana
   See Prap, Lila
Pratchett, Terence David John
   See Pratchett, Terry
Pratchett, Terry 1948- *185*
   Earlier sketches in SATA *82, 139*
   See also CLR *64*
Prater, John 1947- *149*
   Earlier sketches in SATA *72, 103*
Prato, Rodica *184*
Pratt, (Murray) Fletcher 1897-1956 .... *102*
Pratt, Kristin Joy 1976- *87*
Pratt, Pierre 1962- *166*
   Earlier sketch in SATA *95*
Preiss, Byron 1953-2005 .... *166*
   Brief entry *42*
   Earlier sketch in SATA *47*
Preiss, Byron Cary
   See Preiss, Byron
Preller, James 1961- *88*
Prelutsky, Jack 1940- *171*
   Earlier sketches in SATA *22, 66, 118*
   See also CLR *115*
Prentice, Amy
   See Kaler, James Otis
Prescott, Casey
   See Morris, Chris(topher Crosby)
Presnall, Judith (Ann) Janda 1943- *96*
Pressler, Mirjam 1940- *155*
Preston, Douglas 1956- *113*
Preston, Edna Mitchell *40*
Preston, Lillian Elvira 1918- *47*
Preussler, Otfried 1923- *24*
Prevert, Jacques (Henri Marie) 1900-1977
   Obituary *30*
Prevost, Guillaume 1964- *192*
Prevost, Mikela *203*
Price, Beverley Joan 1931- *98*
Price, Charlie *187*
Price, Christine (Hilda) 1928-1980 .... *3*
   Obituary *23*
Price, Garrett 1896-1979
   Obituary *22*
Price, Jennifer
   See Hoover, Helen (Drusilla Blackburn)
Price, Joan 1931- *124*
Price, Jonathan (Reeve) 1941- *46*
Price, Karen 1957- *125*
Price, Kathy Z. 1957- *172*

Price, Lucie Locke
　See Locke, Lucie
Price, Olive 1903-1991 8
Price, Susan 1955- 128
　Earlier sketches in SATA 25, 85
Price, Willard 1887-1983 48
　Brief entry 38
Price-Groff, Claire 127
Priceman, Marjorie 1958- 168
　Earlier sketches in SATA 81, 120
Prichard, Katharine Susannah 1883-1969 66
Prideaux, Tom 1908-1993 37
　Obituary 76
Priestley, Alice 1962- 95
Priestley, Chris 1958- 198
Priestley, Lee (Shore) 1904-1999 27
Priestly, Doug 1954- 122
Priestly, Douglas Michael
　See Priestly, Doug
Prieto, Mariana Beeching 1912-1999 8
Priley, Margaret (Ann) Hubbard 1909-1992
　Obituary 130
Primavera, Elise 1954- 185
　Brief entry 48
　Earlier sketches in SATA 58, 109
Prime, Derek (James) 1931- 34
Prince, Alison (Mary) 1931- 86
　Earlier sketch in SATA 28
Prince, April Jones 1975- 180
Prince, J(ack) H(arvey) 1908- 17
Prince, Joshua 188
Prince, Maggie 102
Prineas, Sarah 204
Pringle, Eric 138
Pringle, Laurence 1935- 201
　Autobiography Feature 201
　Earlier sketches in SATA 4, 68, 104, 154
　See also CLR 57
　See also SAAS 6
Pringle, Laurence Patrick
　See Pringle, Laurence
Prinz, Yvonne 1960- 175
Prior, Natalie Jane 1963- 106
Pritchett, Elaine H(illyer) 1920- 36
Pritchett, Laura 1971- 178
Pritchett, Laura Rose
　See Pritchett, Laura
Pritts, Kim Derek 1953- 83
Prochazkova, Iva 1953- 68
Proctor, Everitt
　See Montgomery, Rutherford George
Proeysen, Alf 1914-1970 67
　See also CLR 24
Professor Scribbler
　See Hollingsworth, Mary
Proimos, James 1955- 173
Prose, Francine 1947- 198
　Earlier sketches in SATA 101, 149
Protopopescu, Orel 186
Protopopescu, Orel Odinov
　See Protopopescu, Orel
Provensen, Alice 1918- 147
　Earlier sketches in SATA 9, 70
　See also CLR 11
Provensen, Martin 1916-1987 70
　Obituary 51
　Earlier sketch in SATA 9
　See also CLR 11
Provensen, Martin Elias
　See Provensen, Martin
Provenzo, Eugene (F., Jr.) 1949- 142
　Earlier sketch in SATA 78
Provist, d'Alain 1906-1989
　See Diop, Birago (Ismael)
Provost, Gail Levine 1944- 65
Provost, Gary (Richard) 1944-1995 66
Proysen, Alf
　See Proeysen, Alf
Pruett, Candace (J.) 1968- 157
Pryor, Bonnie H. 1942- 69
Pryor, Boori (Monty) 1950- 112

Pryor, Helen Brenton 1897-1972 4
Pryor, Michael 1957- 153
Pucci, Albert John 1920- 44
Pudney, John (Sleigh) 1909-1977 24
Pugh, Ellen (Tiffany) 1920- 7
Pullein-Thompson, Christine 1925-2005 82
　Obituary 172
　Earlier sketch in SATA 3
Pullein-Thompson, Diana
　See Farr, Diana
Pullein-Thompson, Joanna Maxwell
　1898-1961 82
Pullein-Thompson, Josephine (Mary
　Wedderburn) 82
　Earlier sketch in SATA 3
Pullen, Zachary 189
Pullman, Philip 1946- 198
　Earlier sketches in SATA 65, 103, 150
　See also CLR 84
　See also SAAS 17
Pullman, Philip Nicholas
　See Pullman, Philip
Pulver, Harry, Jr. 1960- 129
Pulver, Robin 1945- 133
　Earlier sketch in SATA 76
Puner, Helen W(alker) 1915-1989 37
　Obituary 63
Purdy, Carol 1943- 120
　Earlier sketch in SATA 66
Purdy, Susan G(old) 1939- 8
Purkiss, Diane 1961- 194
Purmell, Ann 1953- 206
　Earlier sketch in SATA 147
Purnell, Idella 1901-1982 120
Purscell, Phyllis 1934- 7
Purtill, Richard L. 1931- 53
Pushker, Gloria 1927- 162
　Earlier sketch in SATA 75
Pushker, Gloria Teles
　See Pushker, Gloria
Pushkin, Aleksandr Sergeevich
　See Pushkin, Alexander
Pushkin, Alexander 1799-1837 61
Putnam, Alice 1916- 61
Putnam, Arthur Lee
　See Alger, Horatio, Jr.
Putnam, Peter B(rock) 1920-1998 30
　Obituary 106
Puttapipat, Niroot 199
Puttock, Simon 178
Puvilland, Alex 205
Puvilland, Alexandre
　See Puvilland, Alex
Puybaret, Eric 1976- 195
Pyle, Howard 1853-1911 100
　Earlier sketch in SATA 16
　See also CLR 117
Pyle, Katharine 1863-1938 66
Pyne, Mable Mandeville 1903-1969 9
Pyrnelle, Louise-Clarke 1850-1907 114

Quackenbush, Robert M(ead) 1929- 133
　Autobiography Feature 133
　Earlier sketches in SATA 7, 70
　See also CLR 122
　See also SAAS 7
Qualey, Marsha 1953- 124
　Earlier sketch in SATA 79
Qualls, Sean 177
Quammen, David 1948- 7
Quark, Jason
　See Eldin, Peter
Quarles, Benjamin 1904-1996 12
Quarles, Benjamin Arthur
　See Quarles, Benjamin
Quatermass, Martin
　See Carpenter, John

Quattlebaum, Mary 1958- 185
　Earlier sketches in SATA 88, 134
Quay, Emma 173
　Earlier sketch in SATA 119
Queen, Ellery
　See Deming, Richard
　and Dannay, Frederic
　and Davidson, Avram (James)
　and Fairman, Paul W.
　and Flora, Fletcher
　and Holding, James (Clark Carlisle, Jr.)
　and Hoch, Edward D.
　and Kane, Henry
　and Lee, Manfred B.
　and Marlowe, Stephen
　and Powell, (Oval) Talmage
　and Sheldon, Walter J(ames)
　and Sturgeon, Theodore (Hamilton)
　and Tracy, Don(ald Fiske)
　and Vance, Jack
Queen Latifah 1970- 185
Quennell, Marjorie Courtney 1884-1972 29
Quentin
　See Sheldon, David
Quentin, Brad
　See Bisson, Terry
Quest, (Edna) Olga W(ilbourne) Hall
　See Hall-Quest, (Edna) Olga W(ilbourne)
Quick, Annabelle 1922-1986 2
Quigg, Jane (Hulda) (?)-1986
　Obituary 49
Quill, Monica
　See McInerny, Ralph
Quin-Harkin, Janet 1941- 165
　Earlier sketches in SATA 18, 90, 119
Quin-Harkin, Janet Elizabeth
　See Quin-Harkin, Janet
Quinlan, Susan E. 1954- 88
Quinlan, Susan Elizabeth
　See Quinlan, Susan E.
Quinn, Elisabeth 1881-1962 22
Quinn, Pat 1947- 130
Quinn, Patrick 1950- 73
Quinn, Rob 1972- 138
Quinn, Susan 1940- 30
Quinn, Susan Taft
　See Quinn, Susan
Quinn, Theodora K.
　See Kroeber, Theodora (Kracaw)
Quinn, Vernon
　See Quinn, Elisabeth
Quintano, D.M.
　See Sheldon, Dyan
Quirk, Anne (E.) 1956- 99
Quixley, Jim 1931- 56
Quyth, Gabriel
　See Jennings, Gary

Ra, Carol F. 1939- 76
Raab, Evelyn 1951- 129
Rabb, Margo 1972- 188
Rabb, M.E.
　See Rabb, Margo
Rabe, Berniece (Louise) 1928- 148
　Autobiography Feature 148
　Earlier sketches in SATA 7, 77
　See also SAAS 10
Rabe, Olive H(anson) (?)-1968 13
Rabin, Staton 1958- 162
　Earlier sketch in SATA 84
Rabinowich, Ellen 1946- 29
Rabinowitz, Sandy 1954- 52
　Brief entry 39
Rachlin, Carol K(ing) 1919- 64
Rachlin, Harvey 1951- 47
Rachlin, Harvey Brant
　See Rachlin, Harvey

Q

R

Rachlin, Nahid 64
Rachlis, Eugene (Jacob) 1920-1986
  Obituary 50
Rackham, Arthur 1867-1939 100
  Earlier sketch in SATA 15
  See also CLR 57
Racoma, Robin Yoko 1953- 207
Raczka, Bob 1963- 191
  Earlier sketch in SATA 163
Radencich, Marguerite C. 1952-1998 79
Rader, Laura 197
Radford, Ruby L(orraine) 1891-1971 6
Radin, Ruth Yaffe 1938- 107
  Brief entry 52
  Earlier sketch in SATA 56
Radlauer, David 1952- 28
Radlauer, Edward 1921- 15
Radlauer, Ruth Shaw 1926- 98
  Earlier sketch in SATA 15
Radley, Gail 1951- 112
  Earlier sketch in SATA 25
Radunsky, Vladimir 177
Rae, Gwynedd 1892-1977 37
Raebeck, Lois 1921- 5
Rael, Elsa Okon 1927-
  See CLR 84
Raffi
  See Cavoukian, Raffi
Raftery, Gerald (Bransfield) 1905-1986 11
Ragan-Reid, Gale 1956- 90
Rahaman, Vashanti 1953- 98
Rahn, Joan Elma 1929- 27
Rai, Bali 1971- 152
Raible, Alton (Robert) 1918- 35
Raiff, Stan 1930- 11
Raines, Shirley C(arol) 1945- 128
Rainey, W. B.
  See Blassingame, Wyatt Rainey
Rake, Jody 1961- 157
Rallison, Janette 1966- 183
Ralston, Jan
  See Dunlop, Agnes M. R.
Rama, Sue 190
Ramal, Walter
  See de la Mare, Walter (John)
Ramanujan, A(ttipat) K(rishnaswami)
  1929-1993 86
Rame, David
  See Divine, Arthur Durham
Ramirez, Jose 1967- 198
Ramirez, Orlando L. 1972- 194
Ramos, Jorge 1958- 205
Ramstad, Ralph L. 1919- 115
Rana, Indi
  See Rana, Indira Higham
Rana, Indira Higham 1944- 82
Rana, J.
  See Bhatia, Jamunadevi
Ranadive, Gail 1944- 10
Rand, Ann (Binkley) 30
Rand, Gloria 1925- 156
  Earlier sketch in SATA 101
Rand, Paul 1914-1996 6
Randall, Carrie
  See Ransom, Candice F.
Randall, David 1972- 167
Randall, Florence Engel 1917-1997 5
Randall, Janet
  See Young, Janet Randall
  and Young, Robert W(illiam)
Randall, Robert
  See Garrett, Randall
  and Silverberg, Robert
Randall, Ruth (Elaine) Painter 1892-1971 3
Randell, Beverley
  See Price, Beverley Joan
Randle, Kristen D. 1952- 92
  Autobiography Feature 119
  See also SAAS 24
Randle, Kristen Downey
  See Randle, Kristen D.

Randolph, Boynton M.D.
  See Ellis, Edward S.
Randolph, Ellen
  See Rawn, Melanie
Randolph, Geoffrey
  See Ellis, Edward S.
Randolph, J. H.
  See Ellis, Edward S.
Randolph, Lieutenant J. H.
  See Ellis, Edward S.
Rands, William Brighty 1823-1882 17
Raney, Ken 1953- 74
Rankin, Joan 1940- 148
  Earlier sketch in SATA 88
Rankin, Laura 1953(?)- 176
Ranney, Agnes V. 1916-1985 6
Ransom, Candice F. 1952- 183
  Brief entry 49
  Earlier sketches in SATA 52, 89, 135
Ransom, Jeanie Franz 1957- 187
Ransome, Arthur (Michell) 1884-1967 22
  See also CLR 8
Ransome, James E. 1961- 178
  Earlier sketches in SATA 76, 123
  See also CLR 86
Rant, Tol E.
  See Longyear, Barry B(rookes)
Raphael, Elaine
  See Bolognese, Elaine
Raposo, Joseph Guilherme 1938-1989
  Obituary 61
Rapp, Adam 1968- 148
Rappaport, Doreen 151
Rappoport, Eva 1924- 6
Rappoport, Ken 1935- 167
  Earlier sketch in SATA 89
Rarick, Carrie 1911-2002 41
Raschka, Chris 1959- 207
  Earlier sketches in SATA 80, 117, 166
Raschka, Christopher
  See Raschka, Chris
Rascol, Sabina I. 159
Rash, Andy 162
Raskin, Edith Lefkowitz 1908-1987 9
Raskin, Ellen 1928-1984 139
  Earlier sketches in SATA 2, 38
  See also CLR 12
Raskin, Joseph 1897-1982 12
  Obituary 29
Rathjen, Carl Henry 1909-1984 11
Rathmann, Peggy 1953- 157
  Earlier sketch in SATA 94
  See also CLR 77
Ratliff, Thomas M. 1948- 118
Ratner, Sue Lynn
  See Alexander, Sue
Rattigan, Jama Kim 1951- 99
Ratto, Linda Lee 1952- 79
Rattray, Simon
  See Trevor, Elleston
Ratz de Tagyos, Paul 1958- 198
  Earlier sketch in SATA 76
Rau, Dana Meachen 1971- 167
  Earlier sketch in SATA 94
Rau, Margaret 1913- 168
  Earlier sketch in SATA 9
  See also CLR 8
Rauch, Mabel Thompson 1888-1972
  Obituary 26
Raucher, Herman 1928- 8
Raude, Karina 199
Rauh, Sherry
  See North, Sherry
Raum, Elizabeth 1949- 155
Raven, Margot Theis 184
RavenWolf, Silver 1956- 155
Ravielli, Anthony 1916-1997 3
  Obituary 95
Ravilious, Robin 1944- 77
Ravishankar, Anushka 1961- 200
Rawding, F(rederick) W(illiam) 1930- 55

Rawlings, Marjorie Kinnan 1896-1953 100
  See also YABC 1
  See also CLR 63
Rawlins, Donna 1956- 206
Rawlinson, Julia 175
Rawls, (Woodrow) Wilson 1913-1984 22
  See also CLR 81
Rawlyk, George Alexander 1935- 64
Rawn, Melanie 1954- 98
Rawn, Melanie Robin
  See Rawn, Melanie
Rawson, Katherine 1955- 190
Ray, Carl 1943-1978 63
Ray, Deborah
  See Kogan Ray, Deborah
Ray, Delia 1963- 179
  Earlier sketch in SATA 70
Ray, Irene
  See Sutton, Margaret Beebe
Ray, Jane 1960- 196
  Earlier sketches in SATA 72, 152
Ray, JoAnne 1935- 9
Ray, Mary (Eva Pedder) 1932- 127
  Earlier sketch in SATA 2
Ray, Mary Lyn 1946- 154
  Earlier sketch in SATA 90
Rayban, Chloe 1944- 167
Rayevsky, Robert 1955- 190
  Earlier sketch in SATA 81
Raymond, James Crossley 1917-1981
  Obituary 29
Raymond, Robert
  See Alter, Robert Edmond
Rayner, Catherine 204
Rayner, Hugh 151
Rayner, Mary 1933- 87
  Earlier sketch in SATA 22
  See also CLR 41
Rayner, Shoo
  See Rayner, Hugh
Rayner, William 1929- 55
  Brief entry 36
Raynor, Dorka 28
Rayson, Steven 1932- 30
Razzell, Arthur (George) 1925- 11
Razzell, Mary (Catherine) 1930- 102
Razzi, James 1931- 10
Read, Elfreida 1920- 2
Read, Nicholas 1956- 146
Read, Piers Paul 1941- 21
Reade, Deborah 1949- 69
Reader, Dennis 1929- 71
Reading, Richard P(atrick) 1962- 161
Readman, Jo 1958- 89
Ready, Kirk L(ewis) 1943- 39
Reaney, James 1926-2008 43
Reaney, James Crerar
  See Reaney, James
Reardon, Joyce
  See Pearson, Ridley
Reaver, Chap 1935-1993 69
  Obituary 77
Reaver, Herbert R.
  See Reaver, Chap
Reaves, J. Michael
  See Reaves, (James) Michael
Reaves, (James) Michael 1950- 99
Reber, Deborah 189
Recorvits, Helen 191
Redding, Robert Hull 1919- 2
Redekopp, Elsa 61
Redlich, Ben 1977- 181
Redsand, Anna 1948- 184
Redway, Ralph
  See Hamilton, Charles (Harold St. John)
Redway, Ridley
  See Hamilton, Charles (Harold St. John)
Reece, Colleen L. 1935- 116
Reece, Gabrielle 1970- 108
Reed, Betty Jane 1921- 4

Reed, Dallas
　　See Pendleton, Thomas
Reed, E.
　　See Evans, Mari
Reed, Gwendolyn E(lizabeth) 1932- 21
Reed, Kit 1932- 184
　Autobiography Feature 184
　Earlier sketches in SATA *34, 116*
Reed, Lynn Rowe 171
Reed, Neil 1961- 99
Reed, Talbot Baines 1852-1893
　　See CLR *76*
Reed, Thomas (James) 1947- 34
Reed, William Maxwell 1871-1962 15
Reeder, Carolyn 1937- 97
　Earlier sketch in SATA *66*
　　See also CLR *69*
Reeder, Colin (Dawson) 1938- 74
Reeder, Colonel Red
　　See Reeder, Russell P(otter), Jr.
Reeder, Russell P(otter), Jr. 1902-1998 4
　Obituary 101
Reeder, Stephanie Owen 1951- 102
Reed-Jones, Carol 1955- 112
Reef, Catherine 1951- 189
　Earlier sketches in SATA *73, 128*
Reekie, Jocelyn (Margaret) 1947- 145
Reeman, Douglas Edward 1924- 63
　Brief entry 28
Rees, Celia 1949- 124
Rees, David (Bartlett) 1936-1993 69
　Obituary 76
　Earlier sketch in SATA *36*
　　See also SAAS *5*
Rees, Douglas 1947- 169
Rees, Ennis (Samuel, Jr.) 1925- 3
Rees, (George) Leslie (Clarence)
　1905-2000 105
　Obituary 135
Reese, Bob
　　See Reese, Robert A.
Reese, Carolyn Johnson 1938- 64
Reese, Della 1931(?)- 114
Reese, Lyn
　　See Reese, Carolyn Johnson
Reese, Robert A. 1938- 60
　Brief entry 53
Reese, (John) Terence 1913-1996 59
Reeve, Joel
　　See Cox, William R(obert)
Reeve, Kirk 1934- 117
Reeve, Philip 201
　Earlier sketch in SATA *170*
Reeve, Rosie 186
Reeve, Rosie 188
Reeves, Faye Couch 1953- 76
Reeves, James
　　See Reeves, John Morris
Reeves, Jeni 1947- 111
Reeves, John Morris 1909-1978 87
　Earlier sketch in SATA *15*
Reeves, Joyce 1911- 17
Reeves, Lawrence F. 1926- 29
Reeves, Ruth Ellen
　　See Ranney, Agnes V.
Regan, Dian Curtis 1950- 149
　Autobiography Feature 149
　Earlier sketches in SATA *75, 133*
Regehr, Lydia 1903-1991 37
Reger, James P. 1952- 106
Reggiani, Renee 1925- 18
Rehm, Karl M. 1935- 72
Reich, Ali
　　See Katz, Bobbi
Reich, Susanna 1954- 113
Reiche, Dietlof 1941- 159
Reichert, Edwin C(lark) 1909-1988
　Obituary 57
Reichert, Mickey Zucker
　　See Reichert, Miriam Zucker
Reichert, Miriam Zucker 1962- 85

Reichert, Renee 172
Reichhold, Jane(t E.) 1937- 147
Reid, Alastair 1926- 46
Reid, Barbara 1922- 21
Reid, Barbara (Jane) 1957- 93
　See also CLR *64*
Reid, Desmond
　　See Moorcock, Michael
　　and McNeilly, Wilfred (Glassford)
Reid, Eugenie Chazal 1924- 12
Reid, John Calvin 21
Reid, (Thomas) Mayne 1818-1883 24
Reid, Meta Mayne 1905-1991 58
　Brief entry 36
Reid, Robin (Nicole) 1969- 145
Reid Banks, Lynne 1929- 165
　Earlier sketches in SATA *22, 75, 111*
　　See also CLR *86*
Reider, Katja 1960- 126
Reid Jenkins, Debra 1955- 87
Reiff, Stephanie Ann 1948- 47
　Brief entry 28
Reig, June 1933- 30
Reigot, Betty Polisar 1924- 55
　Brief entry 41
Reilly, Joan 195
Reim, Melanie (K.) 1956- 104
Reinach, Jacquelyn (Krasne) 1930-2000 28
Reiner, Carl 1922- 151
Reiner, William B(uck) 1910-1976 46
　Obituary 30
Reinfeld, Fred 1910-1964 3
Reinhardt, Dana 1971- 175
Reinhart, Matthew 1971- 197
　Earlier sketch in SATA *161*
Reiniger, Lotte 1899-1981 40
　Obituary 33
Reinsma, Carol 1949- 91
Reinstedt, Randall A. 1935- 101
Reinstedt, Randy
　　See Reinstedt, Randall A.
Reisberg, Mira 1955- 82
Reisberg, Veg
　　See Reisberg, Mira
Reiser, Lynn 1944- 180
　Earlier sketches in SATA *81, 138*
Reiser, Lynn Whisnant
　　See Reiser, Lynn
Reisgies, Teresa (Maria) 1966- 74
Reiss, Johanna (de Leeuw) 1929(?)- 18
　　See also CLR *19*
Reiss, John J. 23
Reiss, Kathryn 1957- 144
　Earlier sketch in SATA *76*
Reit, Seymour Victory 1918-2001 21
　Obituary 133
Reit, Sy
　　See Reit, Seymour Victory
Relf, Patricia 1954- 134
　Earlier sketch in SATA *71*
Remi, Georges 1907-1983 13
　Obituary 32
　　See also CLR *114*
Remington, Frederic S(ackrider)
　1861-1909 41
Remkiewicz, Frank 1939- 152
　Earlier sketch in SATA *77*
Rempt, Fiona 1973- 198
Remy, Georges
　　See Remi, Georges
Renaud, Bernadette 1945- 66
Renault, Mary 1905-1983 23
　Obituary 36
Rendell, Joan 28
Rendina, Laura (Jones) Cooper 1902- 10
Rendon, Marcie R. 1952- 97
Rendon, Maria 1965- 116
Renee, Janina 1956- 140
Renfro, Ed 1924- 79
Renick, Marion (Lewis) 1905-1983 1
Renier, Aaron 1977- 202

Renken, Aleda 1907- 27
Renlie, Frank H. 1936- 11
Rennert, Richard Scott 1956- 67
Rennison, Louise 1951- 149
Reno, Dawn E(laine) 1953- 130
Rensie, Willis
　　See Eisner, Will
Renton, Cam
　　See Armstrong, Richard
Renvoize, Jean 5
Resau, Laura 1973- 190
Resciniti, Angelo G. 1952- 75
Resnick, Michael David
　　See Resnick, Mike
Resnick, Mike 1942- 159
　Earlier sketches in SATA *38, 106*
Resnick, Seymour 1920- 23
Retla, Robert
　　See Alter, Robert Edmond
Rettig, Liz 199
Rettstatt, Chris
　　See Ashland, Monk
Reuter, Bjarne (B.) 1950- 142
　Earlier sketch in SATA *68*
Reuter, Carol (Joan) 1931- 2
Revena
　　See Wright, Betty Ren
Revsbech, Vicki
　　See Liestman, Vicki
Rex, Adam 186
Rex, Michael 191
Rey, H. A. 1898-1977 100
　Earlier sketches in SATA *1, 26, 69*
　　See also CLR *93*
Rey, Hans Augusto
　　See Rey, H. A.
Rey, Luis V. 1955- 201
Rey, Margret 1906-1996 86
　Obituary 93
　Earlier sketch in SATA *26*
　　See also CLR *93*
Rey, Margret Elisabeth
　　See Rey, Margret
Reyher, Becky
　　See Reyher, Rebecca Hourwich
Reyher, Rebecca Hourwich 1897-1987 18
　Obituary 50
Reynold, Ann
　　See Bernardo, Anilu
Reynolds, Aaron 1970- 197
Reynolds, Adrian 1963- 192
Reynolds, C. Buck 1957- 107
Reynolds, Dickson
　　See Reynolds, Helen Mary Greenwood Campbell
Reynolds, Helen Mary Greenwood Campbell
　1884-1969
　Obituary 26
Reynolds, Jan 1956- 180
Reynolds, John
　　See Whitlock, Ralph
Reynolds, Madge
　　See Whitlock, Ralph
Reynolds, Malvina 1900-1978 44
　Obituary 24
Reynolds, Marilyn 1935- 121
　　See also SAAS *23*
Reynolds, Marilyn M.
　　See Reynolds, Marilyn
Reynolds, Marilynn 1940- 141
　Earlier sketch in SATA *80*
Reynolds, Pamela 1923- 34
Reynolds, Peter H. 1961- 128
Reynolds, Peter J. 1961- 179
Reynolds, Susan 179
Rhine, Richard
　　See Silverstein, Alvin
　　and Silverstein, Virginia B.
Rhoades, Diane 1952- 90
Rhodes, Bennie (Loran) 1927- 35
Rhodes, Donna McKee 1962- 87

Rhodes, Frank Harold Trevor 1926- 37
Rhue, Morton
    See Strasser, Todd
Rhyne, Nancy 1926- 66
Rhynes, Martha E. 1939- 141
Ribbons, Ian 1924- 37
    Brief entry 30
    See also SAAS 3
Ricciuti, Edward R(aphael) 1938- 10
Rice, Alice (Caldwell) Hegan 1870-1942 63
Rice, Bebe Faas 1932- 89
Rice, Charles D(uane) 1910-1971
    Obituary 27
Rice, Dale R. 1948- 42
Rice, Dale Richard
    See Rice, Dale R.
Rice, Dick
    See Rice, R. Hugh
Rice, Earle (Wilmont), Jr. 1928- 151
    Earlier sketch in SATA 92
Rice, Edward 1918-2001 47
    Brief entry 42
Rice, Elizabeth 1913-1976 2
Rice, Eve 1951- 91
    Earlier sketch in SATA 34
Rice, Eve Hart
    See Rice, Eve
Rice, Inez 1907- 13
Rice, James 1934- 93
    Earlier sketch in SATA 22
Rice, John F. 1958- 82
Rice, R. Hugh 1929- 115
Rice, Richard H.
    See Rice, R. Hugh
Rich, Barbara
    See Graves, Robert
Rich, Elaine Sommers 1926- 6
Rich, Josephine Bouchard 1912- 10
Rich, Louise Dickinson 1903-1991 54
    Obituary 67
Richard, Adrienne 1921- 5
    See also SAAS 9
Richard, James Robert
    See Bowen, Robert Sydney
Richards, Chuck 1957- 170
Richards, Frank
    See Hamilton, Charles (Harold St. John)
Richards, Hilda
    See Hamilton, Charles (Harold St. John)
Richards, Jackie 1925- 102
Richards, Jean 1940- 135
Richards, Justin 169
Richards, Kay
    See Baker, Susan (Catherine)
Richards, Laura E(lizabeth Howe) 1850-1943
    See YABC 1
    See also CLR 54
Richards, Leigh
    See King, Laurie R.
Richards, Marlee
    See Brill, Marlene Targ
Richards, Norman 1932- 48
Richards, R(onald) C(harles) W(illiam)
    1923- 59
    Brief entry 43
Richards, Walter Alden (Jr.) 1907-1988
    Obituary 56
Richardson, Andrew (William) 1986- 120
Richardson, Carol 1932- 58
Richardson, Frank Howard 1882-1970
    Obituary 27
Richardson, Grace Lee
    See Dickson, Naida
Richardson, Jean (Mary) 59
Richardson, Judith Benet 1941- 77
Richardson, Nigel 1957- 187
Richardson, Robert S(hirley) 1902-1981 8
Richardson, Sandy 1949- 116
Richardson, V.A. 189
Richardson, Willis 1889-1977 60
Richelson, Geraldine 1922- 29

Richemont, Enid 1940- 82
Richler, Mordecai 1931-2001 98
    Brief entry 27
    Earlier sketch in SATA 44
    See also CLR 17
Richman, Sophia 1941- 142
Rich-McCoy, Lois
    See McCoy, Lois (Rich)
Richmond, Robin 1951- 75
Richoux, Pat(ricia) 1927- 7
Richter, Alice 1941- 30
Richter, Conrad (Michael) 1890-1968 3
Richter, Hans Peter 1925-1993 6
    See also CLR 21
    See also SAAS 11
Richter, Jutta 1955- 184
Rickard, Graham 1949- 71
Rico, Don(ato) 1917-1985
    Obituary 43
Riddell, Chris 1962- 166
    Earlier sketch in SATA 114
Riddell, Christopher Barry
    See Riddell, Chris
Riddell, Edwina 1955- 82
Ridden, Brian (John) 1934- 123
Riddle, Tohby 1965- 151
    Earlier sketch in SATA 74
Riddleburger, Sam 202
Riddles, Libby 1956- 140
Rideout, Sandy 194
Ridge, Antonia (Florence) (?)-1981 7
    Obituary 27
Ridge, Martin 1923-2003 43
Ridley, Philip 171
    Earlier sketch in SATA 88
Ridlon, Marci
    See Balterman, Marcia Ridlon
Riedman, Sarah R(egal) 1902-1995 1
Riehecky, Janet 1953- 164
Ries, Lori 185
Riesenberg, Felix, Jr. 1913-1962 23
Rieu, E(mile) V(ictor) 1887-1972 46
    Obituary 26
Riffenburgh, Beau 1955- 175
Rigg, Sharon
    See Creech, Sharon
Riggio, Anita 1952- 148
    Earlier sketch in SATA 73
Riggs, Shannon 190
Riggs, Sidney Noyes 1892-1975
    Obituary 28
Riggs, Stephanie 1964- 138
Riglietti, Serena 1969- 189
Rigney, James Oliver, Jr.
    See Jordan, Robert
Rikhoff, Jean 1928- 9
Rikki
    See Ducornet, Erica
Riley, James A. 1939- 97
Riley, James Whitcomb 1849-1916 17
Riley, Jocelyn 1949- 60
    Brief entry 50
Riley, Jocelyn Carol
    See Riley, Jocelyn
Riley, Linda Capus 1950- 85
Riley, Martin 1948- 81
Rimbauer, Steven
    See Pearson, Ridley
Rimes, (Margaret) LeAnn 1982- 154
Rinaldi, Ann 1934- 202
    Brief entry 50
    Earlier sketches in SATA 51, 78, 117, 161
    See also CLR 46
Rinard, Judith E(llen) 1947- 140
    Earlier sketch in SATA 44
Rinder, Lenore 1949- 92
Ring, Elizabeth 1920- 79
Ringdahl, Mark
    See Longyear, Barry B(rookes)

Ringgold, Faith 1930- 187
    Earlier sketches in SATA 71, 114
    See also CLR 30
Ringi, Kjell (Arne Soerensen) 1939- 12
Rinkoff, Barbara Jean (Rich) 1923-1975 4
    Obituary 27
Rinn, Miriam 1946- 127
Riordan, James 1936- 95
Riordan, Rick 174
Rios, Tere
    See Versace, Marie Teresa Rios
Ripken, Cal, Jr. 1960- 114
Ripken, Calvin Edward, Jr.
    See Ripken, Cal, Jr.
Ripley, Catherine 1957- 82
Ripley, Elizabeth Blake 1906-1969 5
Ripper, Charles L(ewis) 1929- 3
Ripper, Chuck
    See Ripper, Charles L(ewis)
Riq
    See Atwater, Richard (Tupper)
Rish, David 1955- 110
Riskind, Mary 1944- 60
Rissinger, Matt 1956- 93
Rissman, Art
    See Sussman, Susan
Rissman, Susan
    See Sussman, Susan
Ritchie, Barbara Gibbons 14
Ritter, Felix
    See Kruss, James
Ritter, John H. 1951- 137
    Earlier sketch in SATA 129
Ritter, Lawrence S(tanley) 1922-2004 58
    Obituary 152
Ritthaler, Shelly 1955- 91
Ritts, Paul 1920(?)-1980
    Obituary 25
Ritz, Karen 1957- 202
    Earlier sketch in SATA 80
Rivera, Geraldo (Miguel) 1943- 54
    Brief entry 28
Rivers, Elfrida
    See Bradley, Marion Zimmer
Rivers, Karen 1970- 131
Riverside, John
    See Heinlein, Robert A.
Rivkin, Ann 1920- 41
Rivoli, Mario 1943- 10
Roach, Marilynne K. 1946- 9
Roach, Marilynne Kathleen
    See Roach, Marilynne K.
Roach, Portia
    See Takakjian, Portia
Robb, Don 1937- 194
Robb, Laura 1937- 95
Robberecht, Thierry 1960- 182
Robbins, Frank 1917-1994(?) 42
    Brief entry 32
Robbins, Ken 1945- 147
    Brief entry 53
    Earlier sketch in SATA 94
Robbins, Raleigh
    See Hamilton, Charles (Harold St. John)
Robbins, Ruth 1917(?)- 14
Robbins, Tony
    See Pashko, Stanley
Robbins, Wayne
    See Cox, William R(obert)
Robel, S. L.
    See Fraustino, Lisa Rowe
Roberson, Jennifer 1953- 72
Roberson, John R(oyster) 1930- 53
Robert, Adrian
    See St. John, Nicole
Roberts, Bethany 202
    Earlier sketch in SATA 133
Roberts, Bruce (Stuart) 1930- 47
    Brief entry 39

Author Index

Roberts, Charles G(eorge) D(ouglas) 1860-1943 88
  Brief entry 29
  See also CLR *33*
Roberts, David
  See Cox, John Roberts
Roberts, David 1970- *191*
Roberts, Diane 1937- *184*
Roberts, Elizabeth 1944- *80*
Roberts, Elizabeth Madox 1886-1941 .... *33*
  Brief entry 27
  See also CLR *100*
Roberts, Jim
  See Bates, Barbara S(nedeker)
Roberts, John G(aither) 1913-1993 27
Roberts, Judy I. 1957- *93*
Roberts, Katherine 1962- *152*
Roberts, M. L.
  See Mattern, Joanne
Roberts, Nancy Correll 1924- *52*
  Brief entry 28
Roberts, Priscilla 1955- *184*
Roberts, Terence
  See Sanderson, Ivan T(erence)
Roberts, Willo Davis 1928-2004 .... *150*
  Autobiography Feature *150*
  Obituary *160*
  Earlier sketches in SATA *21, 70, 133*
  See also CLR *95*
  See also SAAS *8*
Robertson, Barbara (Anne) 1931- *12*
Robertson, Don 1929-1999 .... *8*
  Obituary *113*
Robertson, Dorothy Lewis 1912- *12*
Robertson, Ellis
  See Ellison, Harlan
  and Silverberg, Robert
Robertson, James I., Jr. 1930- *182*
Robertson, James Irvin
  See Robertson, James I., Jr.
Robertson, Janet (E.) 1935- *68*
Robertson, Jennifer Sinclair 1942-1998 .... *12*
Robertson, Jenny
  See Robertson, Jennifer Sinclair
Robertson, Keith (Carlton) 1914-1991 .... *85*
  Obituary *69*
  Earlier sketch in SATA *1*
  See also SAAS *15*
Robertson, Mark
  See Robertson, M.P.
Robertson, M.P. 1965- *197*
Robertson, Stephen
  See Walker, Robert W.
Robertus, Polly M. 1948- *73*
Robeson, Kenneth
  See Dent, Lester
  and Goulart, Ron
Robeson, Kenneth
  See Johnson, (Walter) Ryerson
Robinet, Harriette Gillem 1931- *104*
  Earlier sketch in SATA *27*
  See also CLR *64*
Robins, Deri 1958- *166*
  Earlier sketch in SATA *117*
Robins, Patricia
  See Clark, Patricia Denise
Robins, Rollo, Jr.
  See Ellis, Edward S.
Robins, Seelin
  See Ellis, Edward S.
Robinson, Adjai 1932- *8*
Robinson, Aminah Brenda Lynn 1940- *159*
  Earlier sketch in SATA *77*
Robinson, Barbara (Webb) 1927- *84*
  Earlier sketch in SATA *8*
Robinson, C(harles) A(lexander), Jr. 1900-1965 .... *36*
Robinson, Charles 1870-1937 .... *17*
Robinson, Charles 1931- *6*
Robinson, Dorothy W. 1929- *54*
Robinson, Elizabeth Keeler 1959- *204*

Robinson, Eve
  See Tanselle, Eve
Robinson, Glen 1953- *92*
Robinson, Glendal P.
  See Robinson, Glen
Robinson, Jan M. 1933- 6
Robinson, Jean O. 1934- 7
Robinson, Joan (Mary) G(ale Thomas) 1910-1988 7
Robinson, Kim Stanley 1952- *109*
Robinson, Lee 1948- *110*
Robinson, Lloyd
  See Silverberg, Robert
Robinson, Lynda S(uzanne) 1951- *107*
Robinson, Marileta 1942- *32*
Robinson, Maudie Millian Oller 1914- *11*
Robinson, Maurice R(ichard) 1895-1982
  Obituary 29
Robinson, Nancy K(onheim) 1942-1994 .... *91*
  Brief entry *31*
  Obituary *79*
  Earlier sketch in SATA *32*
Robinson, Ray 1920- *23*
Robinson, Raymond Kenneth
  See Robinson, Ray
Robinson, Shari
  See McGuire, Leslie (Sarah)
Robinson, Sharon 1950- *197*
  Earlier sketch in SATA *162*
Robinson, Spider 1948- *118*
Robinson, Sue
  See Robinson, Susan Maria
Robinson, Susan Maria 1955- *105*
Robinson, Susan Patricia
  See Gates, Susan
Robinson, Suzanne
  See Robinson, Lynda S(uzanne)
Robinson, T(homas) H(eath) 1869-1950 .... *17*
Robinson, Tim 1963- *205*
Robinson, (Wanda) Veronica 1926- *30*
Robinson, W(illiam) Heath 1872-1944 .... *17*
Robison, Bonnie 1924- *12*
Robison, Nancy L(ouise) 1934- *32*
Robles, Harold E. 1948- *87*
Robottom, John 1934- 7
Robson, Eric 1939- *82*
Roca, Francois 1971- *200*
Rocco, John 1967- *188*
Roche, A. K.
  See Abisch, Roslyn Kroop
  and Kaplan, Boche
Roche, Denis 1967- *196*
  Earlier sketch in SATA *99*
Roche, Denis Mary
  See Roche, Denis
Roche, Luane 1937- *170*
Roche, P(atricia) K. 1935- *57*
  Brief entry *34*
Roche, Terry
  See Poole, Peggy
Rochman, Hazel 1938- *105*
Rock, Lois
  See Joslin, Mary
Rock, Maxine 1940- *108*
Rocker, Fermin 1907- *40*
Rocklin, Joanne 1946- *134*
  Earlier sketch in SATA *86*
Rockwell, Anne F. 1934- *194*
  Earlier sketches in SATA *33, 71, 114, 162*
  See also SAAS *19*
Rockwell, Anne Foote
  See Rockwell, Anne F.
Rockwell, Bart
  See Pellowski, Michael (Joseph)
Rockwell, Harlow 1910-1988 .... *33*
  Obituary *56*
Rockwell, Lizzy 1961- *185*
Rockwell, Norman (Percevel) 1894-1978 .... *23*
Rockwell, Thomas 1933- *70*
  Earlier sketch in SATA *7*
  See also CLR *6*

Rockwood, Joyce 1947- *39*
Rockwood, Roy
  See McFarlane, Leslie
  and Stratemeyer, Edward L.
Rodanas, Kristina 1952- *155*
Rodari, Gianni 1920-1980
  See CLR *24*
Rodd, Kathleen Tennant
  See Rodd, Kylie Tennant
Rodd, Kylie Tennant 1912-1988 .... *57*
  Obituary *55*
  Earlier sketch in SATA *6*
Rodda, Emily 1948- *146*
  Earlier sketch in SATA *97*
  See also CLR *32*
Roddenberry, Eugene Wesley 1921-1991 .... *45*
  Obituary *69*
Roddenberry, Gene
  See Roddenberry, Eugene Wesley
Roddick, Ellen 1936- 5
Roddie, Shen *153*
Roddy, Lee 1921- *57*
Rodenas, Paula *73*
Rodgers, Frank 1944- *69*
Rodgers, Mary 1931- *130*
  Earlier sketch in SATA *8*
  See also CLR *20*
Rodman, Emerson
  See Ellis, Edward S.
Rodman, Eric
  See Silverberg, Robert
Rodman, Maia
  See Wojciechowska, Maia (Teresa)
Rodman, Mary Ann *185*
Rodman, (Cary) Selden 1909-2002 9
Rodowsky, Colby 1932- *164*
  Earlier sketches in SATA *21, 77, 120*
  See also SAAS *22*
Rodowsky, Colby F.
  See Rodowsky, Colby
Rodriguez, Alejo 1941- *83*
Rodriguez, Alex 1975- *189*
Rodriguez, Christina 1981- *177*
Rodriguez, Edel 1971- *196*
Rodriguez, Luis J. 1954- *125*
Rodriguez, Rachel *180*
Rodriguez, Rachel Victoria
  See Rodriguez, Rachel
Roeder, Virginia Marsh 1926- *98*
Roehrig, Catharine H. 1949- *67*
Roennfeldt, Robert 1953- *78*
Roessel-Waugh, C. C.
  See Waugh, Carol-Lynn Rossel
  and Waugh, Charles G(ordon)
Roets, Lois F. 1937- *91*
Roever, J(oan) M(arilyn) 1935- *26*
Rofes, Eric 1954-2006 .... *52*
Rofes, Eric Edward 1954-2006
  See Rofes, Eric
Roffey, Maureen 1936- *33*
Rogak, Lisa 1962- *80*
Rogak, Lisa Angowski
  See Rogak, Lisa
Rogan, S. Jones *199*
Rogan, Sally Jones
  See Rogan, S. Jones
Rogasky, Barbara 1933- *144*
  Earlier sketch in SATA *86*
Rogers, (Thomas) Alan (Stinchcombe) 1937- *81*
  Earlier sketch in SATA *2*
Rogers, Bettye 1858-1919 .... *103*
Rogers, Cindy 1950- *89*
Rogers, Emma 1951- *74*
Rogers, Frances 1888-1974 .... *10*
Rogers, Fred McFeely 1928-2003 .... *33*
  Obituary *138*
Rogers, Hal
  See Sirimarco, Elizabeth
Rogers, Jean 1919- *55*
  Brief entry *47*

Rogers, Matilda 1894-1976 5
  Obituary 34
Rogers, Pamela 1927- 9
Rogers, Paul 1950- 98
  Earlier sketch in SATA 54
Rogers, Robert
  See Hamilton, Charles (Harold St. John)
Rogers, Sherry 193
Rogers, W(illiam) G(arland) 1896-1978 23
Rohan, M. S.
  See Rohan, Michael Scott
Rohan, Michael Scott 1951- 98
Rohan, Mike Scott
  See Rohan, Michael Scott
Rohmann, Eric 1957- 171
  See also CLR 100
Rohmer, Harriet 1938- 56
Rohrer, Doug 1962- 89
Rojan
  See Rojankovsky, Feodor (Stepanovich)
Rojankovsky, Feodor (Stepanovich)
  1891-1970 21
Rojany, Lisa 94
Rokeby-Thomas, Anna E(lma) 1911- 15
Roland, Albert 1925-2002 11
Roland, Mary
  See Lewis, Mary
Roleff, Tamara L. 1959- 143
Rolerson, Darrell A(llen) 1946- 8
Roll, Winifred 1909-1998 6
Rollins, Charlemae Hill 1897-1979 3
  Obituary 26
Rollock, Barbara T(herese) 1924- 64
Romack, Janice Reed
  See LeNoir, Janice
Romain, Trevor 134
Romanenko, Vitaliy 1962- 101
Romano, Clare 1922- 111
  Earlier sketch in SATA 48
Romano, Louis G. 1921- 35
Romano, Melora A. 1966- 118
Romano, Ray 1957- 170
Romano, Raymond
  See Romano, Ray
Romijn, Johanna Maria Kooyker
  See Kooyker-Romijn, Johanna Maria
Romyn, Johanna Maria Kooyker
  See Kooyker-Romijn, Johanna Maria
Rong, Yu 1970- 174
Rongen, Bjoern 1906- 10
Rongen, Bjorn
  See Rongen, Bjoern
Ronson, Mark
  See Alexander, Marc
Rood, Ronald (N.) 1920- 12
Rook, Sebastian
  See Jeapes, Ben
Rooke, Daphne 1914-2009 12
Rooke, Daphne Marie
  See Rooke, Daphne
Roop, Connie 1951- 167
  Brief entry 49
  Earlier sketches in SATA 54, 116
Roop, Constance Betzer
  See Roop, Connie
Roop, Peter 1951- 167
  Brief entry 49
  Earlier sketches in SATA 54, 116
Roop, Peter G.
  See Roop, Peter
Roop, Peter Geiger
  See Roop, Peter
Roos, Stephen 1945- 128
  Brief entry 41
  Earlier sketches in SATA 47, 77
Roose-Evans, James 1927- 65
Roosevelt, Eleanor 1884-1962 50
Root, Barry 182
Root, Betty 84
Root, Kimberly Bulcken 192

Root, Phyllis 1949- 184
  Brief entry 48
  Earlier sketches in SATA 55, 94, 145
Root, Shelton L., Jr. 1923-1986
  Obituary 51
Roper, Laura (Newbold) Wood 1911-2003 .. 34
  Obituary 150
Roper, Robert 1946- 142
  Earlier sketch in SATA 78
Roraback, Robin (Ellan) 1964- 111
Rorby, Ginny 1944- 94
Rorer, Abigail 1949- 85
Rosamel, Godeleine de 1968- 151
Roscoe, D(onald) T(homas) 1934- 42
Rose, Anne 8
Rose, Deborah Lee 1955- 185
  Earlier sketches in SATA 71, 124
Rose, Elizabeth (Jane Pretty) 1933- 68
  Brief entry 28
Rose, Florella
  See Carlson, Vada F.
Rose, Gerald (Hembdon Seymour) 1935- 68
  Brief entry 30
Rose, Malcolm 1953- 168
  Earlier sketch in SATA 107
Rose, Nancy A.
  See Sweetland, Nancy A(nn)
Rose, Ted 1940- 93
Rose, Wendy 1948- 12
Rosen, Elizabeth 1961- 205
Rosen, Lillian (Diamond) 1928- 63
Rosen, Marvin 1933- 161
Rosen, Michael 1946- 181
  Brief entry 40
  Earlier sketches in SATA 48, 84, 137
  See also CLR 45
Rosen, Michael J. 1954- 199
  Earlier sketch in SATA 86
Rosen, Michael Wayne
  See Rosen, Michael
Rosen, Sidney 1916- 1
Rosen, Winifred 1943- 8
Rosenbaum, Maurice 1907-1987 6
Rosenberg, Amye 1950- 74
Rosenberg, Dorothy 1906- 40
Rosenberg, Eth Clifford 1915- 92
  See also SAAS 22
Rosenberg, Jane 1949- 58
Rosenberg, Liz 1958- 129
  Earlier sketch in SATA 75
Rosenberg, Maxine B(erta) 1939- 93
  Brief entry 47
  Earlier sketch in SATA 55
Rosenberg, Nancy (Sherman) 1931- 4
Rosenberg, Sharon 1942- 8
Rosenberry, Vera 1948- 144
  Earlier sketch in SATA 83
Rosenblatt, Arthur
  See Rosenblatt, Arthur S.
Rosenblatt, Arthur S. 1938- 68
  Brief entry 45
Rosenblatt, Lily 1956- 90
Rosenbloom, Joseph 1928- 21
Rosenblum, Richard 1928- 11
Rosenburg, John M. 1918- 6
Rosenfeld, Dina 1962- 99
Rosenstiehl, Agnes 1941- 203
Rosenthal, Amy Krouse 1965- 177
Rosenthal, Betsy R. 1957- 178
Rosenthal, Harold 1914-1999 35
Rosenthal, M(acha) L(ouis) 1917-1996 59
Rosenthal, Marc 1949- 193
Rosenthal, Mark A(lan) 1946- 64
Rosing, Norbert 1953- 196
Rosman, Steven M 1956- 81
Rosman, Steven Michael
  See Rosman, Steven M
Rosoff, Meg 1956- 160
Ross, Alan
  See Warwick, Alan R(oss)

Ross, Christine 1950- 172
  Earlier sketch in SATA 83
Ross, Clare
  See Romano, Clare
Ross, Dana Fuller
  See Cockrell, Amanda
  and Gerson, Noel Bertram
Ross, Dave
  See Ross, David
Ross, David 1896-1975 49
  Obituary 20
Ross, David 1949- 133
  Earlier sketch in SATA 32
Ross, Deborah J.
  See Wheeler, Deborah
Ross, Diana
  See Denney, Diana
Ross, Edward S(hearman) 1915- 85
Ross, Eileen 1950- 115
Ross, Frank (Xavier), Jr. 1914- 28
Ross, Jane 1961- 79
Ross, John 1921- 45
Ross, Judy 1942- 54
Ross, Katharine Reynolds
  See Ross, Kathy
Ross, Kathy 1948- 169
  Earlier sketch in SATA 89
Ross, Kent 1956- 91
Ross, Lillian Hammer 1925- 72
Ross, Michael Elsohn 1952- 170
  Earlier sketches in SATA 80, 127
Ross, Pat(ricia Kienzle) 1943- 53
  Brief entry 48
Ross, Ramon R(oyal) 1930- 62
Ross, Stewart 1947- 134
  Earlier sketch in SATA 92
  See also SAAS 23
Ross, Tom 1958- 84
Ross, Tony 1938- 176
  Earlier sketches in SATA 17, 65, 130
Ross, Wilda 1915- 51
  Brief entry 39
Rossel, Seymour 1945- 28
Rossell, Judith 1953- 187
Rossel-Waugh, C. C.
  See Waugh, Carol-Lynn Rossel
Rossetti, Christina 1830-1894 20
  See also CLR 115
Rossetti, Christina Georgina
  See Rossetti, Christina
Rossi, Joyce 1943- 116
Rossotti, Hazel Swaine 1930- 95
Rostkowski, Margaret I. 1945- 59
Roth, Arnold 1929- 21
Roth, Arthur J(oseph) 1925-1993 43
  Brief entry 28
  Obituary 75
  See also SAAS 11
Roth, David 1940- 36
Roth, Julie Jersild 180
Roth, Matthue 1978(?)- 174
Roth, Roger 190
Roth, Stephanie 202
Roth, Susan L. 181
  Earlier sketch in SATA 134
Rothberg, Abraham 1922- 59
Roth-Hano, Renee 1931- 85
Rothkopf, Carol Z. 1929- 4
Rothman, Joel 1938- 7
Rotner, Shelley 1951- 169
  Earlier sketch in SATA 76
Rottman, S.L. 1970- 157
  Earlier sketch in SATA 106
Rottman, Susan Lynn
  See Rottman, S.L.
Roueche, Berton 1911-1994 28
Roughsey, Dick 1921(?)-1985 35
  See also CLR 41
Roughsey, Goobalathaldin
  See Roughsey, Dick

Rounds, Glen (Harold) 1906-2002 .... *112*
  Obituary *141*
  Earlier sketches in SATA *8, 70*
Rourke, Constance Mayfield 1885-1941
  See YABC *1*
Rovetch, Gerda 1925(?)- *202*
Rovetch, L. Bob
  See Rovetch, Lissa
Rovetch, Lissa *201*
Rowan, Deirdre
  See Williams, Jeanne
Rowe, Jennifer
  See Rodda, Emily
Rowe, John A. 1949- *198*
  Earlier sketch in SATA *146*
Rowe, Viola Carson 1903-1969
  Obituary *26*
Rowh, Mark 1952- *90*
Rowland, Florence Wightman 1900-1997 ...... *8*
  Obituary *108*
Rowland-Entwistle, (Arthur) Theodore (Henry)
  1925- *94*
  Earlier sketch in SATA *31*
Rowling, J. K. 1965- *174*
  Earlier sketch in SATA *109*
  See also CLR *112*
Rowling, Joanne Kathleen
  See Rowling, J. K.
Rowsome, Frank (Howard), Jr. 1914-1983 .. *36*
Roy, Gabrielle 1909-1983 .... *104*
Roy, Jacqueline 1954- *74*
Roy, Jennifer
  See Roy, Jennifer Rozines
Roy, Jennifer Rozines 1967- *178*
Roy, Jessie Hailstalk 1895-1986
  Obituary *51*
Roy, Liam
  See Scarry, Patricia (Murphy)
Roy, Ron(ald) 1940- *110*
  Brief entry *35*
  Earlier sketch in SATA *40*
Roybal, Laura 1956- *85*
Roybal, Laura Husby
  See Roybal, Laura
Royds, Caroline 1953- *55*
Royston, Angela 1945- *169*
  Earlier sketch in SATA *120*
Rozakis, Laurie E. 1952- *84*
Rozen, Anna 1960- *206*
Rubel, Nicole 1953- *181*
  Earlier sketches in SATA *18, 95, 135*
Rubin, Eva Johanna 1925- *38*
Rubin, Susan Goldman 1939- *182*
  Earlier sketches in SATA *84, 132*
Rubin, Vicky 1964- *193*
Rubinetti, Donald 1947- *92*
Rubinstein, Gillian 1942- *158*
  Autobiography Feature *116*
  Earlier sketches in SATA *68, 105*
  See also CLR *35*
  See also SAAS *25*
Rubinstein, Gillian Margaret
  See Rubinstein, Gillian
Rubinstein, Patricia -2003
  See Forest, Antonia
Rubinstein, Robert E(dward) 1943- *49*
Rublowsky, John M(artin) 1928- *62*
Rubright, Lynn 1936- *171*
Ruby, Laura *181*
  Earlier sketch in SATA *155*
Ruby, Lois 1942- *184*
  Autobiography Feature *105*
  Brief entry *34*
  Earlier sketches in SATA *35, 95*
Ruby, Lois F.
  See Ruby, Lois
Ruchlis, Hy(man) 1913-1992 .... *3*
  Obituary *72*
Rucker, Mike 1940- *91*
Ruckman, Ivy 1931- *93*
  Earlier sketch in SATA *37*

Ruck-Pauquet, Gina 1931- *40*
  Brief entry *37*
Ruditis, Paul *190*
Rudley, Stephen 1946- *30*
Rudolph, Marguerita 1908- *21*
Rudomin, Esther
  See Hautzig, Esther Rudomin
Rue, Leonard Lee III 1926- *142*
  Earlier sketch in SATA *37*
Rueda, Claudia *183*
Ruedi, Norma Paul
  See Ainsworth, Norma
Ruelle, Karen Gray 1957- *126*
  Earlier sketch in SATA *84*
Ruemmler, John D(avid) 1948- *78*
Ruepp, Krista 1947- *143*
Ruffell, Ann 1941- *30*
Ruffins, Reynold 1930- *125*
  Earlier sketch in SATA *41*
Rugg, Jim *206*
Rugoff, Milton 1913- *30*
Ruhen, Olaf 1911-1989 .... *17*
Rukeyser, Muriel 1913-1980
  Obituary *22*
Rumbaut, Hendle 1949- *84*
Rumford, James 1948- *193*
  Earlier sketch in SATA *116*
Rumsey, Marian (Barritt) 1928- *16*
Rumstuckle, Cornelius
  See Brennan, Herbie
Runnerstroem, Bengt Arne 1944- *75*
Runyan, John
  See Palmer, Bernard (Alvin)
Runyon, Catherine 1947- *62*
Ruoff, A. LaVonne Brown 1930- *76*
Rupp, Rebecca *185*
Rusch, Elizabeth 1966- *198*
Rusch, Kris
  See Rusch, Kristine Kathryn
Rusch, Kristine Kathryn 1960- *113*
Rush, Alison 1951- *41*
Rush, Peter 1937- *32*
Rushdie, Ahmed Salman
  See Rushdie, Salman
Rushdie, Salman 1947-
  See CLR *125*
Rushford, Patricia H(elen) 1943- *134*
Rushmore, Helen 1898-1994 .... *3*
Rushmore, Robert (William) 1926-1986 .... *8*
  Obituary *49*
Ruskin, Ariane
  See Batterberry, Ariane Ruskin
Ruskin, John 1819-1900 .... *24*
Russ, Lavinia (Faxon) 1904-1992 .... *74*
Russell, Charlotte
  See Rathjen, Carl Henry
Russell, Ching Yeung 1946- *107*
Russell, Don(ald Bert) 1899-1986
  Obituary *47*
Russell, Franklin (Alexander) 1926- *11*
Russell, Gertrude Barrer
  See Barrer-Russell, Gertrude
Russell, Helen Ross 1915- *8*
Russell, James 1933- *53*
Russell, Jim
  See Russell, James
Russell, Joan Plummer 1930- *139*
Russell, P(hilip) Craig 1951- *162*
  Earlier sketch in SATA *80*
Russell, Patrick
  See Sammis, John
Russell, Paul (Gary) 1942- *57*
Russell, Sarah
  See Laski, Marghanita
Russell, Sharman Apt 1954- *123*
Russell, Solveig Paulson 1904-1985 .... *3*
Russo, Marisabina 1950- *188*
  Earlier sketches in SATA *106, 151*
Russo, Monica J. 1950- *83*
Russo, Susan 1947- *30*
Russon, Penni 1974- *179*

Rutgers van der Loeff, An
  See Rutgers van der Loeff-Basenau, An(na)
  Maria Margaretha
Rutgers van der Loeff-Basenau, An(na) Maria
  Margaretha 1910- *22*
Ruth, Rod 1912-1987 .... *9*
Rutherford, Douglas
  See McConnell, James Douglas Rutherford
Rutherford, Meg 1932- *34*
Ruthin, Margaret
  See Catherall, Arthur
Rutledge, Jill Zimmerman 1951- *155*
Rutz, Viola Larkin 1932- *12*
Ruurs, Margriet 1952- *147*
  Earlier sketch in SATA *97*
Ruzicka, Rudolph 1883-1978
  Obituary *24*
Ruzzier, Sergio 1966- *159*
, Ryan
  See Ryan, John
Ryan, Betsy
  See Ryan, Elizabeth (Anne)
Ryan, Cheli Duran *20*
Ryan, Darlene 1958- *176*
Ryan, Elizabeth (Anne) 1943- *30*
Ryan, Jeanette
  See Mines, Jeanette
Ryan, John 1921-2009 .... *22*
Ryan, Margaret 1950- *166*
  Earlier sketch in SATA *78*
Ryan, Mary E. 1953- *61*
Ryan, Mary Elizabeth
  See Ryan, Mary E.
Ryan, Pam Munoz 1951- *197*
  Earlier sketch in SATA *134*
Ryan, Patrick 1957- *138*
Ryan, Peter (Charles) 1939- *15*
Ryan-Lush, Geraldine 1949- *89*
Rybakov, Anatoli (Naumovich) 1911-1998 .. *79*
  Obituary *108*
Rybakov, Anatolii (Naumovich)
  See Rybakov, Anatoli (Naumovich)
Rybolt, Thomas R. 1954- *62*
Rybolt, Thomas Roy
  See Rybolt, Thomas R.
Rybolt, Tom
  See Rybolt, Thomas R.
Rydberg, Ernest E(mil) 1901-1993 .... *21*
Rydberg, Lou(isa Hampton) 1908- *27*
Rydell, Katy 1942- *91*
Rydell, Wendell
  See Rydell, Wendy
Rydell, Wendy *4*
Ryden, Hope *91*
  Earlier sketch in SATA *8*
Ryder, Joanne (Rose) 1946- *163*
  Brief entry *34*
  Earlier sketches in SATA *65, 122*
  See also CLR *37*
Ryder, Pamela
  See Lamb, Nancy
Rye, Anthony
  See Youd, Samuel
Rylant, Cynthia 1954- *195*
  Brief entry *44*
  Earlier sketches in SATA *50, 76, 112, 160*
  See also CLR *86*
  See also SAAS *13*
Rymer, Alta May 1925- *34*
Rymond, Lynda Gene *199*

                              S

S. L. C.
  See Twain, Mark
S., Svend Otto
  See Soerensen, Svend Otto
Saaf, Donald W(illiam) 1961- *124*

Saal, Jocelyn
  See Sachs, Judith
Sabbeth, Carol (Landstrom) 1957- *125*
Saberhagen, Fred 1930-2007 .... *89*
  Obituary *184*
  Earlier sketch in SATA *37*
Saberhagen, Fred T.
  See Saberhagen, Fred
Saberhagen, Fred Thomas
  See Saberhagen, Fred
Saberhagen, Frederick Thomas
  See Saberhagen, Fred
Sabin, Edwin L(egrand) 1870-1952
  See YABC *2*
Sabin, Francene *27*
Sabin, Lou
  See Sabin, Louis
Sabin, Louis 1930- *27*
Sabre, Dirk
  See Laffin, John (Alfred Charles)
Sabuda, Robert (James) 1965- *120*
  Earlier sketch in SATA *81*
Sabuda, Robert 1965- *170*
Sabuda, Robert James
  See Sabuda, Robert
Sachar, Louis 1954- *154*
  Brief entry *50*
  Earlier sketches in SATA *63, 104*
  See also CLR *79*
Sachs, Elizabeth-Ann 1946- *48*
Sachs, Judith 1947- *52*
  Brief entry *51*
Sachs, Marilyn 1927- *164*
  Autobiography Feature *110*
  Earlier sketches in SATA *3, 68*
  See also CLR *2*
  See also SAAS *2*
Sachs, Marilyn Stickle
  See Sachs, Marilyn
Sackett, S(amuel) J(ohn) 1928- *12*
Sackson, Sid 1920- *16*
Sacre, Antonio 1968- *152*
Saddler, Allen
  See Richards, R(onald) C(harles) W(illiam)
Saddler, K. Allen
  See Richards, R(onald) C(harles) W(illiam)
Sadie, Stanley 1930-2005 .... *14*
Sadie, Stanley John
  See Sadie, Stanley
Sadiq, Nazneen 1944- *101*
Sadler, Catherine Edwards 1952- *60*
  Brief entry *45*
Sadler, Marilyn (June) 1950- *79*
Sadler, Mark
  See Lynds, Dennis
Saffer, Barbara *144*
Sagan, Carl 1934-1996 .... *58*
  Obituary *94*
Sagan, Carl Edward
  See Sagan, Carl
Sage, Angie 1952- *197*
Sage, Juniper
  See Brown, Margaret Wise
  and Hurd, Edith Thacher
Sagsoorian, Paul 1923- *12*
Said, S.F. 1967- *174*
Saidman, Anne 1952- *75*
Saint, Dora Jessie 1913- *10*
St. Anthony, Jane *175*
St. Antoine, Sara L. 1966- *84*
St. Clair, Byrd Hooper 1905-1976
  Obituary *28*
Saint-Exupery, Antoine de 1900-1944 .... *20*
  See also CLR *142*
Saint-Exupery, Antoine Jean Baptiste Marie
  Roger de
  See Saint-Exupery, Antoine de
St. George, Judith 1931- *161*
  Earlier sketches in SATA *13, 99*
  See also CLR *57*
  See also SAAS *12*

St. George, Judith Alexander
  See St. George, Judith
St. James, Blakely
  See Gottfried, Theodore Mark
  and Platt, Charles
St. James, Blakely
  See Griffin, W.E.B.
St. James, Sierra
  See Rallison, Janette
Saint James, Synthia 1949- *152*
  Earlier sketch in SATA *84*
St. John, Nicole *143*
  Autobiography Feature *143*
  Earlier sketches in SATA *29, 89*
  See also CLR *46*
  See also SAAS *7*
St. John, Patricia Mary 1919-1993
  Obituary *79*
St. John, Philip
  See del Rey, Lester
St. John, Wylly Folk 1908-1985 .... *10*
  Obituary *45*
St. Max, E. S.
  See Ellis, Edward S.
St. Meyer, Ned
  See Stratemeyer, Edward L.
St. Mox, E. A.
  See Ellis, Edward S.
St. Myer, Ned
  See Stratemeyer, Edward L.
St. Tamara
  See Kolba, St. Tamara
Saito, Michiko
  See Fujiwara, Michiko
Sakaki, Ichiro 1969- *192*
Sakamoto, Miki *198*
Sakers, Don 1958- *72*
Sakharnov, S.
  See Sakharnov, Svyatoslav
Sakharnov, Svyatoslav 1923- *65*
Sakharnov, Svyatoslav Vladimirovich
  See Sakharnov, Svyatoslav
Saksena, Kate *148*
Sakurai, Gail 1952- *153*
  Earlier sketch in SATA *87*
Salamanca, Lucy
  See del Barco, Lucy Salamanca
Salassi, Otto R(ussell) 1939-1993 .... *38*
  Obituary *77*
Salat, Cristina *82*
Saldana, Rene, Jr. *186*
Saldutti, Denise 1953- *39*
Sale, Tim 1956- *153*
Salem, Kay 1952- *92*
Salerno, Steven *176*
Salinger, J.D. 1919-2010 .... *67*
  See also CLR *18*
Salinger, Jerome David
  See Salinger, J.D.
Salisbury, Graham 1944- *195*
  Earlier sketches in SATA *76, 108, 161*
Salisbury, Joyce E(llen) 1944- *138*
Salkey, (Felix) Andrew (Alexander)
  1928-1995 .... *118*
  Earlier sketch in SATA *35*
Salley, Coleen *166*
Sallis, Susan (Diana) 1929- *55*
Salmon, Annie Elizabeth 1899- *13*
Salonen, Roxane Beauclair 1968- *184*
Salsi, Lynn 1947- *130*
Salsitz, R. A. V.
  See Salsitz, Rhondi Vilott
Salsitz, Rhondi Vilott *115*
Salten, Felix
  See Salzmann, Siegmund
Salter, Cedric
  See Knight, Francis Edgar
Saltman, Judith 1947- *64*
Saltzberg, Barney 1955- *194*
  Earlier sketch in SATA *135*

Saltzman, David (Charles Laertes)
  1967-1990 .... *86*
Salvadori, Mario (George) 1907-1997 .... *97*
  Earlier sketch in SATA *40*
Salwood, F.K.
  See Kilworth, Garry
Salzer, L. E.
  See Wilson, Lionel
Salzman, Marian 1959- *77*
Salzmann, Siegmund 1869-1945 .... *25*
Samachson, Dorothy (Mirkin) 1914-1997 ...... *3*
Samachson, Joseph 1906-1980 .... *3*
  Obituary *52*
Sammis, John 1942- *4*
Sampson, Emma (Keats) Speed 1868-1947 . *68*
Sampson, Fay (Elizabeth) 1935- *151*
  Brief entry *40*
  Earlier sketch in SATA *42*
Sampson, Michael 1952- *143*
  Earlier sketch in SATA *95*
Samson, Anne S(tringer) 1933- *2*
Samson, Joan 1937-1976 .... *13*
Samson, Suzanne M. 1959- *91*
Samuels, Barbara *199*
Samuels, Charles 1902-1982 .... *12*
Samuels, Cynthia K(alish) 1946- *79*
Samuels, Gertrude 1910(?)-2003 .... *17*
  Obituary *147*
Sanborn, Duane 1914-1996 .... *38*
Sancha, Sheila 1924- *38*
Sanchez, Alex 1957- *151*
Sanchez, Sonia 1934- *136*
  Earlier sketch in SATA *22*
  See also CLR *18*
Sanchez-Silva, Jose Maria 1911- *132*
  Earlier sketch in SATA *16*
  See also CLR *12*
Sand, George X. *45*
Sandak, Cass R(obert) 1950-2001 .... *51*
  Brief entry *37*
Sandberg, (Karin) Inger 1930- *15*
Sandberg, Karl C. 1931- *35*
Sandberg, Lasse (E. M.) 1924- *15*
Sandburg, Carl 1878-1967 .... *8*
  See also CLR *67*
Sandburg, Carl August
  See Sandburg, Carl
Sandburg, Charles
  See Sandburg, Carl
Sandburg, Charles A.
  See Sandburg, Carl
Sandburg, Helga 1918- *3*
  See also SAAS *10*
Sandell, Lisa Ann 1977- *175*
Sander, Heather L. 1947- *157*
Sanderlin, George 1915- *4*
Sanderlin, Owenita (Harrah) 1916- *11*
Sanders, Betty Jane
  See Monthei, Betty
Sanders, Nancy I. 1960- *141*
  Earlier sketch in SATA *90*
Sanders, Scott Russell 1945- *109*
  Earlier sketch in SATA *56*
Sanders, Winston P.
  See Anderson, Poul
Sanderson, Irma 1912- *66*
Sanderson, Ivan T(erence) 1911-1973 .... *6*
Sanderson, Margaret Love
  See Keats, Emma
  and Sampson, Emma (Keats) Speed
Sanderson, Ruth 1951- *172*
  Earlier sketches in SATA *41, 109*
Sanderson, Ruth L.
  See Sanderson, Ruth
Sandin, Joan 1942- *197*
  Earlier sketches in SATA *12, 94, 153*
Sandison, Janet
  See Cameron, Elizabeth Jane
Sandler, Martin W. *160*
Sandom, J. Gregory
  See Welsh, T.K.

Sandom, J.G.
  See Welsh, T.K.
Sandoz, Mari(e Susette) 1900-1966 5
Sanford, Agnes (White) 1897-1976 61
Sanford, Doris 1937- 69
Sanford, Rose
  See Simmonds, Posy
Sanger, Amy Wilson 1967- 205
Sanger, Marjory Bartlett 1920- 8
San Jose, Christine 1929- 167
Sankey, Alice (Ann-Susan) 1910- 27
San Souci, Daniel 192
  Earlier sketch in SATA *96*
San Souci, Robert D. 1946- 158
  Earlier sketches in SATA *40, 81, 117*
  See also CLR *43*
Santamaria, Benjamin 1955- 184
Santat, Dan 188
Santesson, Hans Stefan 1914(?)-1975
  Obituary 30
Santiago, Esmeralda 1948- 129
Santore, Charles 1935- 200
Santos, Helen
  See Griffiths, Helen
Santrey, Louis
  See Sabin, Louis
Santucci, Barbara 1948- 130
Sapergia, Barbara 1943- 181
Sapieyevski, Anne Lindbergh 1940-1993 81
  Brief entry 32
  Earlier sketches in SATA *35, 78*
Saport, Linda 1954- 123
Sapp, Allen 1929- 151
Sarac, Roger
  See Caras, Roger A(ndrew)
Sarah, Duchess of York
  See Ferguson, Sarah
Sarasin, Jennifer
  See Sachs, Judith
Sardinha, Rick 192
Sarg, Anthony Frederick
  See Sarg, Tony
Sarg, Tony 1882-1942
  See YABC *1*
Sargent, Pamela 1948- 78
  Earlier sketch in SATA *29*
Sargent, Robert 1933- 2
Sargent, Sarah 1937- 44
  Brief entry 41
Sargent, Shirley 1927-2004 11
Sarnoff, Jane 1937- 10
Saroff, Phyllis V. 202
Saroyan, William 1908-1981 23
  Obituary 24
Sarton, Eleanor May
  See Sarton, May
Sarton, May 1912-1995 36
  Obituary 86
Sasaki, Chris 182
Sasaki, Ellen Joy 206
Saseen, Sharon (Dillon) 1949- 59
Sasek, Miroslav 1916-1980 16
  Obituary 23
  See also CLR *4*
Sasso, Sandy Eisenberg 1947- 162
  Earlier sketches in SATA *86, 116*
Sathre, Vivian 1952- 133
  Earlier sketch in SATA *79*
Satterfield, Charles
  See del Rey, Lester
  and Pohl, Frederik
Sattgast, L. J.
  See Sattgast, Linda J.
Sattgast, Linda J. 1953- 91
Sattler, Helen Roney 1921-1992 74
  Earlier sketch in SATA *4*
  See also CLR *24*
Sauer, Julia Lina 1891-1983 32
  Obituary 36
Sauerwein, Leigh 1944- 155

Saul, Carol P. 1947- 117
  Earlier sketch in SATA *78*
Saul, John III
  See Saul, John
Saul, John 1942- 98
Saul, John W.
  See Saul, John
Saul, John W. III
  See Saul, John
Saul, John Woodruff III
  See Saul, John
Saul, (Ellen) Wendy 1946- 42
Saulnier, Karen Luczak 1940- 80
Saunders, Caleb
  See Heinlein, Robert A.
Saunders, Dave 1939- 85
Saunders, Julie 1939- 85
Saunders, (William) Keith 1910-1994 12
Saunders, Rubie (Agnes) 1929- 21
Saunders, Steven
  See Jones, Allan Frewin
Saunders, Susan 1945- 96
  Brief entry 41
  Earlier sketch in SATA *46*
Saunders-Smith, Gail 1952- 169
Sauvain, Philip Arthur 1933- 111
Savadier, Elivia 1950- 164
  Earlier sketch in SATA *79*
Savage, Alan
  See Nicole, Christopher (Robin)
Savage, Blake
  See Goodwin, Harold L(eland)
Savage, Candace 1949- 142
Savage, Deborah 1955- 76
Savage, Jeff 1961- 97
Savage, Katharine James 1905-1989
  Obituary 61
Savage, Stephen 1965- 194
Savage, Thomas 1915-2003
  Obituary 147
Savageau, Cheryl 1950- 96
Savery, Constance (Winifred) 1897-1999 1
Saville, Andrew
  See Taylor, Andrew
Saville, (Leonard) Malcolm 1901-1982 23
  Obituary 31
Saviozzi, Adriana
  See Mazza, Adriana
Savitt, Sam 1917-2000 8
  Obituary 126
Savitz, Harriet May 1933- 72
  Earlier sketch in SATA *5*
  See also SAAS *26*
Sawicki, Mary 1950- 90
Sawyer, (Frederick) Don(ald) 1947- 72
Sawyer, Kem Knapp 1953- 84
Sawyer, Robert J. 1960- 149
  Earlier sketch in SATA *81*
Sawyer, Robert James
  See Sawyer, Robert J.
Sawyer, Ruth 1880-1970 17
  See also CLR *36*
Saxby, H.M.
  See Saxby, (Henry) Maurice
Saxby, (Henry) Maurice 1924- 71
Saxon, Andrew
  See Arthur, Robert, (Jr.)
Saxon, Antonia
  See Sachs, Judith
Say, Allen 1937- 161
  Earlier sketches in SATA *28, 69, 110*
  See also CLR *135*
Sayers, Frances Clarke 1897-1989 3
  Obituary 62
Sayles, Elizabeth 1956- 163
  Earlier sketch in SATA *108*
Saylor-Marchant, Linda 1963- 82
Sayre, April Pulley 1966- 191
  Earlier sketches in SATA *88, 131*
Sazer, Nina 1949- 13
Scabrini, Janet 1953- 13

Scagell, Robin 1946- 107
Scagnetti, Jack 1924- 7
Scamander, Newt
  See Rowling, J. K.
Scamell, Ragnhild 1940- 180
  Earlier sketch in SATA *77*
Scanlon, Marion Stephany 11
Scannel, John Vernon
  See Scannell, Vernon
Scannell, Vernon 1922-2007 59
  Obituary 188
Scarborough, Elizabeth
  See Scarborough, Elizabeth Ann
Scarborough, Elizabeth Ann 1947- 171
  Earlier sketch in SATA *98*
Scarf, Maggi
  See Scarf, Maggie
Scarf, Maggie 1932- 5
Scariano, Margaret M. 1924- 86
Scarlett, Susan
  See Streatfeild, Noel
Scarry, Huck
  See Scarry, Richard McClure, Jr.
Scarry, Patricia (Murphy) 1924- 2
Scarry, Patsy
  See Scarry, Patricia (Murphy)
Scarry, Richard (McClure) 1919-1994 75
  Obituary 90
  Earlier sketches in SATA *2, 35*
  See also CLR *41*
Scarry, Richard McClure, Jr. 1953- 35
Schachner, Judith Byron 1951- 178
  Earlier sketch in SATA *88*
Schachner, Judy
  See Schachner, Judith Byron
Schachtel, Roger 1949- 38
Schachtel, Roger Bernard
  See Schachtel, Roger
Schade, Susan 189
Schaedler, Sally 116
Schaefer, Carole Lexa 173
Schaefer, Jack (Warner) 1907-1991 66
  Obituary 65
  Earlier sketch in SATA *3*
Schaefer, Lola M. 1950- 183
  Earlier sketches in SATA *91, 144*
Schaeffer, Mead 1898- 21
Schaeffer, Susan Fromberg 1941- 22
Schaer, Brigitte 1958- 112
Schaller, George
  See Schaller, George B.
Schaller, George B. 1933- 30
Schaller, George Beals
  See Schaller, George B.
Schanzer, Rosalyn (Good) 1942- 138
  Earlier sketch in SATA *77*
Schatell, Brian 66
  Brief entry 47
Schechter, Betty (Goodstein) 1921- 5
Schechter, Simone
  See Elkeles, Simone
Schecter, Ellen 1944- 85
Scheeder, Louis 1946- 141
Scheer, Julian (Weisel) 1926-2001 8
Scheffler, Victor B(lanchard) 1906- 6
Scheffler, Axel 1957- 180
Scheffler, Ursel 1938- 81
Scheffrin-Falk, Gladys 1928- 76
Scheidl, Gerda Marie 1913- 85
Scheier, Michael 1943- 40
  Brief entry 36
Schell, Mildred 1922- 41
Schell, Orville (Hickok) 1940- 10
Scheller, Melanie 1953- 77
Schellie, Don 1932- 29
Schembri, Jim 1962- 124
Schembri, Pamela 1969- 195
Schemm, Mildred Walker 1905-1998 21
  Obituary 103
Schenker, Dona 1947- 133
  Earlier sketch in SATA *68*

Scher, Paula 1948- *47*
Scherer, Jeffrey *194*
Scherf, Margaret 1908-1979 .... *10*
Schermer, Judith (Denise) 1941- *30*
Schertle, Alice 1941- *192*
  Earlier sketches in SATA *36, 90, 145*
Schick, Alice 1946- *27*
Schick, Eleanor 1942- *144*
  Earlier sketches in SATA *9, 82*
Schick, Joel 1945- *31*
  Brief entry *30*
Schields, Gretchen 1948- *75*
Schiff, Ken(neth Roy) 1942- *7*
Schiller, Andrew 1919- *21*
Schiller, Barbara (Heyman) 1928- *21*
Schiller, Pamela (Byrne) *127*
Schindel, John 1955- *115*
  Earlier sketch in SATA *77*
Schindelman, Joseph 1923- *67*
  Brief entry *32*
Schindler, S.D. 1952- *198*
  Brief entry *50*
  Earlier sketches in SATA *75, 118, 171*
Schindler, Steven D.
  See Schindler, S.D.
Schinto, Jeanne 1951- *93*
Schisgall, Oscar 1901-1984 .... *12*
  Obituary *38*
Schlaepfer, Gloria G. 1931- *154*
Schlee, Ann 1934- *44*
  Brief entry *36*
Schleichert, Elizabeth 1945- *77*
Schlein, Miriam 1926-2004 .... *130*
  Obituary *159*
  Earlier sketches in SATA *2, 87*
  See also CLR *41*
Schlesinger, Arthur M., Jr. 1917-2007 .... *61*
  Obituary *181*
  See Schlesinger, Arthur Meier
Schlesinger, Arthur Meier 1888-1965
Schlessinger, Laura (Catherine) 1947- *160*
  Earlier sketch in SATA *110*
Schlitz, Laura Amy *184*
Schloat, G. Warren, Jr. 1914-2000 .... *4*
Schmatz, Pat *197*
Schmid, Eleonore 1939- *126*
  Earlier sketches in SATA *12, 84*
Schmiderer, Dorothy 1940- *19*
Schmidt, Annie M. G. 1911-1995 .... *67*
  Obituary *91*
  See also CLR *22*
Schmidt, C.A. *196*
Schmidt, Diane 1953- *70*
Schmidt, Elizabeth 1915- *15*
Schmidt, Gary D. 1957- *193*
  Earlier sketches in SATA *93, 135*
Schmidt, James Norman 1912-1983 .... *21*
Schmidt, Karen Lee 1953- *185*
  Earlier sketch in SATA *94*
Schmidt, Lynette 1952- *76*
Schmitz, Tamara *207*
Schneider, Antonie 1954- *167*
  Earlier sketch in SATA *89*
Schneider, Christine M. 1972(?)- *171*
  Earlier sketch in SATA *120*
Schneider, Dick
  See Schneider, Richard H.
Schneider, Elisa
  See Kleven, Elisa
Schneider, Herman 1905-2003 .... *7*
  Obituary *148*
Schneider, Howie -2007 .... *181*
Schneider, Josh 1980- *196*
Schneider, Laurie
  See Adams, Laurie
Schneider, Nina 1913-2007 .... *2*
  Obituary *186*
Schneider, Nina Zimet
  See Schneider, Nina
Schneider, Rex 1937- *44*
Schneider, Richard H. 1922- *171*

Schneider, Richard Henry
  See Schneider, Richard H.
Schneider, Robyn 1986- *187*
Schnirel, James R. 1931- *14*
Schnitter, Jane T. 1958- *88*
Schnitzlein, Danny *134*
Schnur, Steven 1952- *144*
  Earlier sketch in SATA *95*
Schnurre, Wolfdietrich 1920-1989
  Obituary *63*
Schoberle, Cecile 1949- *80*
Schock, Pauline 1928- *45*
Schoell, William 1951- *160*
Schoen, Barbara (Taylor) 1924-1993 .... *13*
Schoenherr, Ian *177*
Schoenherr, John (Carl) 1935- *66*
  Earlier sketch in SATA *37*
  See also SAAS *13*
Schofield, Sandy
  See Rusch, Kristine Kathryn
Scholastica, Sister Mary
  See Jenkins, Marie M(agdalen)
Scholefield, A. T.
  See Scholefield, Alan
Scholefield, Alan 1931- *66*
Scholefield, Edmund O.
  See Griffin, W.E.B.
Scholey, Arthur 1932- *28*
Scholz, Jackson Volney 1897-1986
  Obituary *49*
Schone, Virginia *22*
Schongut, Emanuel 1936- *184*
  Brief entry *36*
  Earlier sketch in SATA *52*
Schoonover, Frank (Earle) 1877-1972 .... *24*
Schoor, Gene 1921- *3*
Schories, Pat 1952- *164*
  Earlier sketch in SATA *116*
Schorr, Melissa 1972- *194*
Schorr, Melissa Robin
  See Schorr, Melissa
Schott, Jane A. 1946- *172*
Schotter, Roni *190*
  Earlier sketches in SATA *105, 149*
Schraff, Anne E(laine) 1939- *92*
  Earlier sketch in SATA *27*
Schram, Peninnah 1934- *119*
Schrank, Joseph 1900-1984
  Obituary *38*
Schrecengost, Maity 1938- *118*
Schrecengost, S. Maitland
  See Schrecengost, Maity
Schreck, Karen
  See Schreck, Karen Halvorsen
Schreck, Karen Halvorsen 1962- *185*
Schrecker, Judie 1954- *90*
Schreiber, Elizabeth Anne (Ferguson)
  1947- *13*
Schreiber, Ralph W(alter) 1942- *13*
Schreiner, Samuel A(gnew), Jr. 1921- *70*
Schroeder, Alan 1961- *98*
  Earlier sketch in SATA *66*
Schroeder, Binette
  See Nickl, Barbara (Elisabeth)
Schroeder, Russell (K.) 1943- *146*
Schroeder, Ted 1931(?)-1973
  Obituary *20*
Schubert, Dieter 1947- *101*
  Earlier sketch in SATA *62*
Schubert, Leda 1950(?)- *181*
Schubert-Gabrys, Ingrid 1953- *101*
  Earlier sketch in SATA *62*
Schuelein-Steel, Danielle
  See Steel, Danielle
Schuelein-Steel, Danielle Fernande
  See Steel, Danielle
Schuerger, Michele R. *110*
Schuett, Stacey 1960- *168*
  Earlier sketch in SATA *75*
Schulke, Flip Phelps Graeme 1930- *57*
Schulman, Arlene 1961- *105*

Schulman, Janet 1933- *137*
  Earlier sketch in SATA *22*
Schulman, L(ester) M(artin) 1934- *13*
Schulte, Elaine L(ouise) 1934- *36*
Schultz, Betty K(epka) 1932- *125*
Schultz, Gwendolyn *21*
Schultz, James Willard 1859-1947
  See YABC *1*
Schultz, Pearle Henriksen 1918- *21*
Schulz, Charles M. 1922-2000 .... *10*
  Obituary *118*
Schulz, Charles Monroe
  See Schulz, Charles M.
Schumacher, Julie 1958- *191*
Schumaker, Ward 1943- *96*
Schuman, Michael A. 1953- *134*
  Earlier sketch in SATA *85*
Schur, Maxine
  See Schur, Maxine Rose
Schur, Maxine Rose 1948- *135*
  Autobiography Feature *135*
  Brief entry *49*
  Earlier sketches in SATA *53, 98*
Schurfranz, Vivian 1925- *13*
Schutzer, A. I. 1922- *13*
Schuyler, Pamela R. 1948- *30*
Schwabach, Karen *185*
Schwager, Tina 1964- *110*
Schwandt, Stephen (William) 1947- *61*
Schwark, Mary Beth 1954- *51*
Schwartz, Alvin 1927-1992 .... *56*
  Obituary *71*
  Earlier sketch in SATA *4*
  See also CLR *89*
Schwartz, Amy 1954- *189*
  Brief entry *41*
  Earlier sketches in SATA *47, 83, 131*
  See also CLR *25*
  See also SAAS *18*
Schwartz, Anne Powers 1913-1987 .... *10*
Schwartz, Carol 1954- *77*
Schwartz, Charles W(alsh) 1914- *8*
Schwartz, David M. 1951- *110*
  Earlier sketch in SATA *59*
Schwartz, David Martin
  See Schwartz, David M.
Schwartz, Elizabeth Reeder 1912- *8*
Schwartz, Ellen 1949- *117*
Schwartz, Jerome L.
  See Lawrence, Jerome
Schwartz, Joel L. 1940- *54*
  Brief entry *51*
Schwartz, Joyce R. 1950- *93*
Schwartz, Julius 1907-2004 .... *45*
Schwartz, Perry 1942- *75*
Schwartz, Sheila (Ruth) 1929- *27*
Schwartz, Stephen (Lawrence) 1948- *19*
Schwartz, Virginia Frances 1950- *184*
  Earlier sketch in SATA *131*
Schwarz, Silvia Tessa Viviane
  See Schwarz, Viviane
Schwarz, Viviane 1977- *204*
Schwarz, (Silvia Tessa) Viviane 1977- *141*
Schweitzer, Byrd Baylor
  See Baylor, Byrd
Schweitzer, Iris *59*
  Brief entry *36*
Schweninger, Ann 1951- *168*
  Earlier sketches in SATA *29, 98*
Schwerin, Doris H(alpern) 1922- *64*
Schy, Yael *197*
Scieszka, Jon 1954- *199*
  Earlier sketches in SATA *68, 105, 160*
  See also CLR *107*
Scillian, Devin *199*
  Earlier sketch in SATA *128*
Scioscia, Mary (Hershey) 1926- *63*
Sciurba, Katie 1957- *196*
Scofield, Penrod 1933- *62*
  Obituary *78*

Scoggin, Margaret C(lara) 1905-1968 .... *47*
   Brief entry *28*
Scoltock, Jack 1942- *141*
   Earlier sketch in SATA *72*
Scoppettone, Sandra 1936- *92*
   Earlier sketch in SATA *9*
Scot, Michael
   See Rohan, Michael Scott
Scot-Bernard, P.
   See Bernard, Patricia
Scotland, Jay
   See Jakes, John
Scott, Alastair
   See Allen, Kenneth S.
Scott, Ann Herbert 1926- *140*
   Autobiography Feature *140*
   Brief entry *29*
   Earlier sketches in SATA *56, 94*
Scott, Bill
   See Scott, William N(eville)
Scott, Bill 1920(?)-1985
   Obituary *46*
Scott, Cora Annett (Pipitone) 1931- *11*
Scott, Dan
   See Barker, S. Omar
Scott, Elaine 1940- *198*
   Earlier sketches in SATA *36, 90, 164*
Scott, Elizabeth *194*
Scott, Jack Denton 1915-1995 .... *83*
   Earlier sketch in SATA *31*
   See also CLR *20*
   See also SAAS *14*
Scott, Jane (Harrington) 1931- *55*
Scott, Jessica
   See De Wire, Elinor
Scott, John 1912-1976 .... *14*
Scott, John Anthony 1916- *23*
Scott, John M(artin) 1913- *12*
Scott, Mary
   See Mattern, Joanne
Scott, Melissa 1960- *109*
Scott, Richard
   See Rennert, Richard Scott
Scott, Roney
   See Gault, William Campbell
Scott, Sally 1909-1978 .... *43*
Scott, Sally 1948- *44*
Scott, Sally Elisabeth
   See Scott, Sally
Scott, W. N.
   See Scott, William N(eville)
Scott, Sir Walter 1771-1832
   See YABC *2*
Scott, Warwick
   See Trevor, Elleston
Scott, William N(eville) 1923- *87*
Scotti, Anna
   See Coates, Anna
Scotton, Rob 1960- *177*
Scribner, Charles, Jr. 1921-1995 .... *13*
   Obituary *87*
Scribner, Joanne L. 1949- *33*
Scribner, Kimball 1917- *63*
Scrimger, Richard 1957- *164*
   Earlier sketch in SATA *119*
Scrimsher, Lila Gravatt 1897-1974
   Obituary *28*
Scroder, Walter K. 1928- *82*
Scroggs, Kirk *187*
Scruggs, Sandy 1961- *89*
Scudder, Brooke 1959- *154*
Scudder, Mildred Lee 1908- *6*
   See also SAAS *12*
Scull, Marie-Louise 1943-1993 .... *77*
Scuro, Vincent 1951- *21*
Seabrooke, Brenda 1941- *148*
   Earlier sketches in SATA *30, 88*
Seaman, Augusta Huiell 1879-1950 .... *31*
Seamands, Ruth 1916- *9*
Searcy, Margaret Zehmer 1926- *54*
   Brief entry *39*

Searight, Mary W(illiams) 1918- *17*
Searle, Kathryn Adrienne 1942- *10*
Searle, Ronald (William Fordham) 1920- *70*
   Earlier sketch in SATA *42*
Sears, Stephen W. 1932- *4*
Seaskull, Cecil
   See Castellucci, Cecil
Sebastian, Lee
   See Silverberg, Robert
Sebestyen, Igen
   See Sebestyen, Ouida
Sebestyen, Ouida 1924- *140*
   Earlier sketch in SATA *39*
   See also CLR *17*
   See also SAAS *10*
Sebrey, Mary Ann 1951- *62*
Sechrist, Elizabeth Hough 1903-1991 .... *2*
Sedges, John
   See Buck, Pearl S.
Sedgwick, Marcus 1968- *197*
   Earlier sketch in SATA *160*
Seed, Cecile Eugenie 1930- *86*
   Earlier sketch in SATA *8*
   See also CLR *76*
Seed, Jenny
   See Seed, Cecile Eugenie
Seed, Sheila Turner 1937(?)-1979
   Obituary *23*
Seeger, Elizabeth 1889-1973
   Obituary *20*
Seeger, Laura Vaccaro *200*
   Earlier sketch in SATA *172*
Seeger, Pete 1919- *139*
   Earlier sketch in SATA *13*
Seeger, Peter R.
   See Seeger, Pete
Seeley, Laura L. 1958- *71*
Seever, R.
   See Reeves, Lawrence F.
Sefozo, Mary 1925- *82*
Sefton, Catherine
   See Waddell, Martin
Segal, John *178*
Segal, Joyce 1940- *35*
Segal, Lore 1928- *163*
   Earlier sketches in SATA *4, 66*
   See also SAAS *11*
Segal, Lore Groszmann
   See Segal, Lore
Segar, E(lzie) C(risler) 1894-1938 .... *61*
Segovia, Andres 1893(?)-1987
   Obituary *52*
Seguin, Marilyn W(eymouth) 1951- *91*
Seguin-Fontes, Marthe 1924- *109*
Seibold, J. Otto 1960- *196*
   Earlier sketches in SATA *83, 149*
   See also SAAS *22*
Seidel, Ross *95*
Seidelman, James Edward 1926- *6*
Seiden, Art(hur) *107*
   Brief entry *42*
Seidensticker, John 1944- *200*
Seidler, Ann (G.) 1925- *131*
Seidler, Tor 1952- *149*
   Brief entry *46*
   Earlier sketches in SATA *52, 98*
Seidman, Karla
   See Kuskin, Karla
Seidman, Laurence Ivan 1925- *15*
Seigel, Kalman 1917-1998 .... *12*
   Obituary *103*
Seignobosc, Francoise 1897-1961 .... *21*
Seinfeld, Jerry 1954- *146*
Seitz, Jacqueline 1931- *50*
Seixas, Judith S. 1922- *17*
Sejima, Yoshimasa 1913- *8*
Selberg, Ingrid (Maria) 1950- *68*
Selden, George
   See Thompson, George Selden
Selden, Neil R(oy) 1931- *61*
Self, Margaret Cabell 1902-1996 .... *24*

Selfors, Suzanne 1963- *193*
Selick, Henry 1952- *183*
Selig, Sylvie 1942- *13*
Selkirk, Jane
   See Chapman, John Stanton Higham
Sellers, Naomi
   See Flack, Naomi John White
Selman, LaRue W. 1927- *55*
Selsam, Millicent E(llis) 1912-1996 .... *29*
   Obituary *92*
   Earlier sketch in SATA *1*
   See also CLR *1*
Seltzer, Meyer 1932- *17*
Seltzer, Richard 1946- *41*
Seltzer, Richard Warren, Jr.
   See Seltzer, Richard
Selvadurai, Shyam 1965(?)- *171*
Selway, Martina 1940- *169*
   Earlier sketch in SATA *74*
Selzer, Adam 1980- *192*
Selznick, Brian 1966- *171*
   Earlier sketches in SATA *79, 117*
Semel, Nava 1954- *107*
Semloh
   See Holmes, Peggy
Sendak, Jack 1924(?)-1995 .... *28*
Sendak, Maurice 1928- *165*
   Earlier sketches in SATA *1, 27, 113*
   See also CLR *131*
Sendak, Maurice Bernard
   See Sendak, Maurice
Sender, Ruth M(insky) 1926- *62*
Sengler, Johanna 1924- *18*
Senisi, Ellen B. 1951- *116*
Senisi, Ellen Babinec
   See Senisi, Ellen B.
Senn, J(oyce) A(nn) 1941- *115*
Senn, Steve 1950- *60*
   Brief entry *48*
Sensel, Joni 1962- *204*
Serafini, Frank *201*
Serage, Nancy 1924- *10*
Seredy, Kate 1899-1975 .... *1*
   Obituary *24*
   See also CLR *10*
Serfozo, Mary 1925- *194*
Seroff, Victor I(ilyitch) 1902-1979 .... *12*
   Obituary *26*
Serra, Sebastia 1966- *202*
Serraillier, Ian (Lucien) 1912-1994 .... *73*
   Obituary *83*
   Earlier sketch in SATA *1*
   See also CLR *2*
   See also SAAS *3*
Serros, Michele *175*
Serros, Michele M.
   See Serros, Michele
Servello, Joe 1932- *10*
Service, Pamela F. 1945- *64*
Service, Robert
   See Service, Robert W.
Service, Robert W. 1874(?)-1958 .... *20*
Serwadda, W(illiam) Moses 1931- *27*
Serwer-Bernstein, Blanche L(uria)
   1910-1997 .... *10*
Sescoe, Vincent E. 1938- *123*
Seth, Mary
   See Lexau, Joan M.
Seton, Anya 1904(?)-1990 .... *3*
   Obituary *66*
Seton, Ernest (Evan) Thompson 1860-1946 . *18*
   See also CLR *59*
Seton-Thompson, Ernest
   See Seton, Ernest (Evan) Thompson
Seuling, Barbara 1937- *193*
   Earlier sketches in SATA *10, 98, 145*
   See also SAAS *24*
Seuss, Dr.
   See Dr. Seuss
Severn, Bill
   See Severn, William Irving

Severn, David
  See Unwin, David S(torr)
Severn, William Irving 1914- *1*
Sewall, Marcia 1935- *119*
  Earlier sketches in SATA *37, 69*
Seward, Prudence 1926- *16*
Sewell, Anna 1820-1878 .... *100*
  Earlier sketch in SATA *24*
  See also CLR *17*
Sewell, Helen (Moore) 1896-1957 .... *38*
Sexton, Anne 1928-1974 .... *10*
Sexton, Anne Harvey
  See Sexton, Anne
Seymour, Alta Halverson *10*
Seymour, Jane 1951- *139*
Seymour, Tres 1966- *164*
  Earlier sketch in SATA *82*
Sfar, Joann 1971- *182*
Shachtman, Tom 1942- *49*
Shackleton, C.C.
  See Aldiss, Brian W.
Shader, Rachel
  See Sofer, Barbara
Shadow, Jak
  See Sutherland, Jon
Shadyland, Sal
  See Cooper, Louise
Shafer, Audrey *183*
Shafer, Robert E(ugene) 1925- *9*
Shaffer, Terea 1968- *79*
Shahan, Sherry 1949- *134*
  Earlier sketch in SATA *92*
Shahn, Ben(jamin) 1898-1969
  Obituary *21*
Shahn, Bernarda Bryson
  See Bryson, Bernarda
Shaik, Fatima *114*
Shalant, Phyllis 1949- *150*
Shan, Darren 1972- *199*
  Earlier sketches in SATA *129, 168*
Shan, D.B.
  See Shan, Darren
Shanahan, Lisa *199*
Shanberg, Karen
  See Shragg, Karen (I.)
Shane, Harold Gray 1914-1993 .... *36*
  Obituary *76*
Shange, Ntozake 1948- *157*
Shanks, Ann Zane (Kushner) *10*
Shannon, David 1959- *152*
  Earlier sketch in SATA *107*
  See also CLR *87*
Shannon, George 1952- *202*
  Earlier sketches in SATA *35, 94, 143*
Shannon, George William Bones
  See Shannon, George
Shannon, Jacqueline *63*
Shannon, Margaret
  See Silverwood, Margaret Shannon
Shannon, Monica 1905(?)-1965 .... *28*
Shannon, Terry
  See Mercer, Jessie
Shannon, Terry Miller 1951- *148*
Shapiro, Irwin 1911-1981 .... *32*
Shapiro, Jody Fickes 1940- *193*
Shapiro, Karen Jo 1964- *186*
Shapiro, Michelle 1961- *196*
Shapiro, Milton J. 1926- *32*
Shapiro, Tricia
  See Andryszewski, Tricia
Shapp, Charles M(orris) 1906-1989
  Obituary *61*
Shapp, Martha Glauber 1910- *3*
Sharenow, Robert *193*
Sharfman, Amalie *14*
Sharma, Partap 1939- *15*
Sharma, Rashmi
  See Singh, Rashmi Sharma
Sharman, Alison
  See Leonard, Alison

Sharmat, Marjorie Weinman 1928- *133*
  Earlier sketches in SATA *4, 33, 74*
Sharmat, Mitchell 1927- *127*
  Earlier sketch in SATA *33*
Sharp, Anne Wallace 1947- *144*
Sharp, Luke
  See Alkiviades, Alkis
Sharp, Margery 1905-1991 .... *29*
  Obituary *67*
  Earlier sketch in SATA *1*
  See also CLR *27*
Sharp, Zerna A. 1889-1981
  Obituary *27*
Sharpe, Jon
  See Duncan, Alice
  and Knott, William C(ecil, Jr.)
  and Messman, Jon
Sharpe, Mitchell R(aymond) 1924- *12*
Sharpe, Susan 1946- *71*
Sharratt, Nick 1962- *199*
  Earlier sketches in SATA *104, 153*
Shasha, Mark 1961- *80*
Shattuck, Roger 1923-2005 .... *64*
  Obituary *174*
Shattuck, Roger Whitney
  See Shattuck, Roger
Shaw, Arnold 1909-1989 .... *4*
  Obituary *63*
Shaw, Carolyn V. 1934- *91*
Shaw, Charles (Green) 1892-1974 .... *13*
Shaw, Evelyn S. 1927- *28*
Shaw, Flora Louisa
  See Lugard, Flora Louisa Shaw
Shaw, Janet 1937- *146*
  Earlier sketch in SATA *61*
  See also CLR *96*
Shaw, Janet Beeler
  See Shaw, Janet
Shaw, Lisa
  See Rogak, Lisa
Shaw, Margret 1940- *68*
Shaw, Mary 1965- *180*
Shaw, Nancy 1946- *162*
  Earlier sketch in SATA *71*
Shaw, Ray *7*
Shaw, Richard 1923- *12*
Shawn, Frank S.
  See Goulart, Ron
Shay, Art
  See Shay, Arthur
Shay, Arthur 1922- *4*
Shay, Lacey
  See Shebar, Sharon Sigmond
Shea, Bob *188*
Shea, George 1940- *54*
  Brief entry *42*
Shea, Pegi Deitz 1960- *172*
  Earlier sketches in SATA *77, 137*
Shearer, Alex 1949- *204*
Shearer, John 1947- *43*
  Brief entry *27*
  See also CLR *34*
Shearer, Ted 1919- *43*
Shearing, Leonie 1972- *184*
Sheban, Chris *182*
Shebar, Sharon Sigmond 1945- *36*
Shecter, Ben 1935- *16*
Shedd, Warner 1934- *147*
  Earlier sketch in SATA *87*
Sheedy, Alexandra Elizabeth 1962- *39*
  Earlier sketch in SATA *19*
Sheehan, Ethna 1908-2000 .... *9*
Sheehan, Patty 1945- *77*
Sheehan, Sean 1951- *154*
  Earlier sketch in SATA *86*
Sheen, Barbara 1949- *143*
Shefelman, Janice 1930- *205*
  Earlier sketches in SATA *58, 129*
Shefelman, Janice Jordan
  See Shefelman, Janice

Shefelman, Tom 1927- *204*
  Earlier sketch in SATA *58*
Sheffer, H. R.
  See Abels, Harriette S(heffer)
Sheffield, Charles 1935-2002 .... *109*
Sheffield, Janet N. 1926- *26*
Sheikh, Nazneen
  See Sadiq, Nazneen
Sheinkin, Steve 1968- *204*
Shekerjian, Regina Tor *16*
Shelby, Anne 1948- *85*
  Autobiography Feature *121*
  See also SAAS *26*
Sheldon, Ann
  See Antle, Nancy
Sheldon, Ann *67*
  Earlier sketch in SATA *1*
Sheldon, Aure 1917-1976 .... *12*
Sheldon, David *185*
Sheldon, Dyan *181*
Sheldon, John
  See Bloch, Robert (Albert)
Sheldon, Muriel 1926- *45*
  Brief entry *39*
Shell, Barry 1951- *176*
Shelley, Frances
  See Wees, Frances Shelley
Shelley, John 1959- *202*
Shelley, Mary
  See Shelley, Mary Wollstonecraft
Shelley, Mary Wollstonecraft 1797-1851 ..... *29*
  See also CLR *133*
Shelton, William Roy 1919-1995 .... *5*
  Obituary *129*
Shemie, Bonnie (Jean Brenner) 1949- *96*
Shemin, Margaretha (Hoeneveld) 1928- *4*
Shen, Michele 1953- *173*
Shenker, Michele
  See Shen, Michele
Shenton, Edward 1895-1977 .... *45*
Shepard, Aaron 1950- *187*
  Earlier sketches in SATA *75, 113*
Shepard, Ernest Howard 1879-1976 .... *100*
  Obituary *24*
  Earlier sketches in SATA *3, 33*
  See also CLR *27*
Shepard, James R.
  See Shepard, Jim
Shepard, Jim 1956- *164*
  Earlier sketch in SATA *90*
Shepard, Mary
  See Knox, (Mary) Eleanor Jessie
Shephard, Esther 1891-1975 .... *5*
  Obituary *26*
Shepherd, Amanda *201*
Shepherd, Donna Walsh
  See Walsh Shepherd, Donna
Shepherd, Elizabeth *4*
Shepherd, Irana *173*
Shepherd, Roni
  See Shepherd, Irana
Sheppard, Kate *195*
Shepperson, Rob *178*
Sherburne, Zoa (Lillian Morin) 1912-1995 .... *3*
  See also SAAS *18*
Sherk-Savage, Candace
  See Savage, Candace
Sherlock, Patti *71*
Sherman, D(enis) R(onald) 1934- *48*
  Brief entry *29*
Sherman, Diane (Finn) 1928- *12*
Sherman, Elizabeth
  See Friskey, Margaret (Richards)
Sherman, Harold (Morrow) 1898-1987 .... *37*
  Obituary *137*
Sherman, Josepha *163*
  Earlier sketch in SATA *75*
Sherman, Michael
  See Lowndes, Robert A(ugustine) W(ard)
Sherman, Nancy
  See Rosenberg, Nancy (Sherman)

Sherman, Pat *174*
Sherman, Peter Michael
  See Lowndes, Robert A(ugustine) W(ard)
Sherrard, Valerie (Anne) 1957- *141*
Sherrod, Jane
  See Singer, Jane Sherrod
Sherry, Clifford J. 1943- *84*
Sherry, (Dulcie) Sylvia 1932- *122*
  Earlier sketch in SATA *8*
Sherwan, Earl 1917- *3*
Sherwood, Jonathan
  See London, Jonathan (Paul)
Sheth, Kashmira *186*
Shetterly, Will 1955- *78*
  Autobiography Feature *106*
Shetterly, William Howard
  See Shetterly, Will
Shiefman, Vicky 1942- 22
Shields, Brenda Desmond (Armstrong)
  1914- *37*
Shields, Carol Diggory *174*
Shields, Charles 1944- *10*
Shields, Gillian *203*
Shiels, Barbara
  See Adams, Barbara Johnston
Shiffman, Lena 1957- *101*
Shiina, Makoto 1944- *83*
Shimin, Symeon 1902-1984 .... *13*
Shimko, Bonnie 1941- *191*
Shine, Andrea 1955- *104*
Shine, Deborah 1932- *71*
Shinn, Everett 1876-1953 .... *21*
Shinn, Sharon 1957- *164*
  Earlier sketch in SATA *110*
Shippen, Katherine B(inney) 1892-1980 .... *1*
  Obituary *23*
  See also CLR *36*
Shippey, T. A. 1943- *143*
Shippey, Thomas Alan
  See Shippey, T. A.
Shipton, Eric Earle 1907-1977 .... *10*
Shipton, Paul 1963- *196*
Shiraz, Yasmin *173*
Shirer, William L(awrence) 1904-1993 .... *45*
  Obituary *78*
Shirley, Debra *203*
Shirley, Gayle C 1955- *96*
Shirley, Gayle Corbett
  See Shirley, Gayle C
Shirley, Jean 1919- *70*
Shirreffs, Gordon D(onald) 1914-1996 .... *11*
Shirts, Morris A(lpine) 1922- *63*
Shlichta, Joe 1968- *84*
Shmurak, Carole B. 1944- *118*
Sholokhov, Mikhail 1905-1984
  Obituary *36*
Sholokhov, Mikhail Aleksandrovich
  See Sholokhov, Mikhail
Shore, Diane Z. *179*
Shore, Diane ZuHone
  See Shore, Diane Z.
Shore, June Lewis *30*
Shore, Nancy 1960- *124*
Shore, Robert 1924- *39*
Short, Michael 1937- *65*
Short, Roger
  See Arkin, Alan
Shortall, Leonard W. *19*
Shortt, Tim(othy Donald) 1961- *96*
Shotwell, Louisa Rossiter 1902-1993 .... *3*
Shoup, Barbara 1947- *156*
  Earlier sketch in SATA *86*
  See also SAAS *24*
Shoveller, Herb *184*
Showalter, Jean B(reckinridge) *12*
Showell, Ellen Harvey 1934- *33*
Showers, Paul C. 1910-1999 .... *92*
  Obituary *114*
  Earlier sketch in SATA *21*
  See also CLR *6*
  See also SAAS *7*

Shpakow, Tanya 1959(?)- *94*
Shpitalnik, Vladimir 1964- *83*
Shragg, Karen (I.) 1954- *142*
Shreeve, Elizabeth 1956- *156*
Shreve, Susan
  See Shreve, Susan Richards
Shreve, Susan Richards 1939- *152*
  Brief entry *41*
  Earlier sketches in SATA *46, 95*
Shriver, Jean Adair 1932- *75*
Shriver, Maria 1955- *134*
Shriver, Maria Owings
  See Shriver, Maria
Shrode, Mary
  See Hollingsworth, Mary
Shtainmets, Leon *32*
Shub, Elizabeth 1915(?)-2004 .... *5*
Shuken, Julia 1948- *84*
Shulevitz, Uri 1935- *165*
  Earlier sketches in SATA *3, 50, 106*
  See also CLR *61*
Shulman, Alix Kates 1932- *7*
Shulman, Dee 1957- *146*
Shulman, Irving 1913-1995 .... *13*
Shulman, Lisa *202*
Shulman, Mark 1962- *184*
Shulman, Max 1919-1988
  Obituary *59*
Shulman, Milton 1913-2004
  Obituary *154*
Shulman, Neil B(arnett) 1945- *89*
Shumsky, Zena
  See Collier, Zena
Shura, Mary Francis
  See Craig, Mary (Francis) Shura
Shusterman, Neal 1962- *201*
  Autobiography Feature *140*
  Earlier sketches in SATA *85, 121, 140*
Shuter, Jane (Margaret) 1955- *151*
  Earlier sketch in SATA *90*
Shuttlesworth, Dorothy Edwards *3*
Shwartz, Susan (Martha) 1949- *94*
Shyer, Christopher 1961- *98*
Shyer, Marlene Fanta *13*
Siberell, Anne *29*
Sibley, Don 1922- *12*
Siburt, Ruth 1951- *121*
Siculan, Daniel 1922- *12*
Siddon, Barbara
  See Bradford, Barbara Taylor
Sidgwick, Ethel 1877-1970 .... *116*
Sidjakov, Nicolas 1924- *18*
Sidman, Joyce 1956- *181*
  Earlier sketch in SATA *145*
Sidney, Frank
  See Warwick, Alan R(oss)
Sidney, Margaret
  See Lothrop, Harriet Mulford Stone
Siebert, Diane 1948- *189*
Siegal, Aranka 1930- *88*
  Brief entry *37*
Siegel, Beatrice *36*
Siegel, Helen
  See Siegl, Helen
Siegel, Robert 1939- *39*
Siegel, Robert Harold
  See Siegel, Robert
Siegel, Siena Cherson 1967(?)- *185*
Siegelson, Kim L. 1962- *114*
Sieger, Ted 1958- *189*
Siegl, Helen 1924- *34*
Siepmann, Mary Aline
  See Wesley, Mary (Aline)
Sierra, Judy 1945- *195*
  Earlier sketches in SATA *104, 162*
Sieswerda, Paul L. 1942- *147*
Sievert, Terri
  See Dougherty, Terri (L.)
Silas
  See McCay, (Zenas) Winsor
Silcock, Sara Lesley 1947- *12*

Silin-Palmer, Pamela *184*
Sill, Cathryn 1953- *141*
  Earlier sketch in SATA *74*
Sill, John 1947- *140*
  Earlier sketch in SATA *74*
Sillitoe, Alan 1928- *61*
Sills, Leslie (Elka) 1948- *129*
Silly, E. S.
  See Kraus, (Herman) Robert
Silsbe, Brenda 1953- *73*
Silva, Joseph
  See Goulart, Ron
Silver, Ruth
  See Chew, Ruth
Silverberg, Robert 1935- *91*
  Autobiography Feature *104*
  Earlier sketch in SATA *13*
  See also CLR *59*
Silverman, Erica 1955- *165*
  Earlier sketches in SATA *78, 112*
Silverman, Janis L. 1946- *127*
Silverman, Mel(vin Frank) 1931-1966 .... *9*
Silverman, Robin L. 1954- *96*
Silverman, Robin Landew
  See Silverman, Robin L.
Silverstein, Alvin 1933- *124*
  Earlier sketches in SATA *8, 69*
  See also CLR *25*
Silverstein, Herma 1945- *106*
Silverstein, Robert Alan 1959- *124*
  Earlier sketch in SATA *77*
Silverstein, Shel 1932-1999 .... *92*
  Brief entry *27*
  Obituary *116*
  Earlier sketch in SATA *33*
  See also CLR *96*
Silverstein, Sheldon Allan
  See Silverstein, Shel
Silverstein, Virginia B. 1937- *124*
  Earlier sketches in SATA *8, 69*
  See also CLR *25*
Silverstein, Virginia Barbara Opshelor
  See Silverstein, Virginia B.
Silverthorne, Elizabeth 1930- *35*
Silverwood, Margaret Shannon 1966- *137*
  Earlier sketch in SATA *83*
Silvey, Diane F. 1946- *135*
Sim, David 1953- *162*
Sim, Dorrith M. 1931- *96*
Simak, Clifford D(onald) 1904-1988
  Obituary *56*
Simard, Remy 1959- *168*
Simmie, Lois (Ann) 1932- *106*
Simmonds, Posy 1945- *130*
  See also CLR *23*
Simmonds, Rosemary Elizabeth
  See Simmonds, Posy
Simmons, Andra 1939- *141*
Simmons, Elly 1955- *134*
Simmons, Michael 1970- *185*
Simms, Laura 1947- *117*
Simner, Janni Lee *113*
Simon, Charlie May
  See Fletcher, Charlie May Hogue
Simon, Francesca 1955- *111*
Simon, Gabriel 1972- *118*
Simon, Hilda Rita 1921- *28*
  See also CLR *39*
Simon, Howard 1903-1979 .... *32*
  Obituary *21*
Simon, Joe
  See Simon, Joseph H.
Simon, Joseph H. 1913- *7*
Simon, Martin P(aul William) 1903-1969 .... *12*
Simon, Mina Lewiton
  See Lewiton, Mina
Simon, Norma (Feldstein) 1927- *129*
  Earlier sketches in SATA *3, 68*
Simon, Seymour 1931- *202*
  Earlier sketches in SATA *4, 73, 138*
  See also CLR *63*

Simon, Shirley (Schwartz) 1921- *11*
Simon, Solomon 1895-1970 .... *40*
Simonetta, Linda 1948- *14*
Simonetta, Sam 1936- *14*
Simons, Barbara B(rooks) 1934- *41*
Simont, Marc 1915- *126*
  Earlier sketches in SATA *9, 73*
Simpson, Harriette
  See Arnow, Harriette (Louisa) Simpson
Simpson, Jacynth Hope
  See Hope Simpson, Jacynth
Simpson, Lesley 1963- *150*
Simpson, Margaret 1943- *128*
Simpson, Myrtle L(illias) 1931- *14*
Sims, Blanche *168*
  Earlier sketch in SATA *75*
Sims, Blanche L.
  See Sims, Blanche
Simundsson, Elva 1950- *63*
Sinclair, Clover
  See Gater, Dilys
Sinclair, Emil
  See Hesse, Hermann
Sinclair, Jeff 1958- *77*
Sinclair, Olga 1923- *121*
Sinclair, Rose
  See Smith, Susan Vernon
Sinclair, Upton 1878-1968 .... *9*
Sinclair, Upton Beall
  See Sinclair, Upton
Singer, A.L.
  See Lerangis, Peter
Singer, Arthur 1917-1990 .... *64*
Singer, Isaac
  See Singer, Isaac Bashevis
Singer, Isaac Bashevis 1904-1991 .... *27*
  Obituary *68*
  Earlier sketch in SATA *3*
  See also CLR *1*
Singer, Jane Sherrod 1917-1985 .... *4*
  Obituary *42*
Singer, Julia 1917- *28*
Singer, Kurt D. 1911-2005 .... *38*
  Obituary *172*
Singer, Marilyn 1948- *201*
  Autobiography Feature *158*
  Brief entry *38*
  Earlier sketches in SATA *48, 80, 125, 158*
  See also CLR *48*
  See also SAAS *13*
Singer, Muff 1942-2005 .... *104*
  Obituary *160*
Singer, Nicky 1956- *194*
Singer, Susan (Mahler) 1941- *9*
Singh, Rashmi Sharma 1952- *90*
Singleton, Linda Joy 1957- *166*
  Earlier sketch in SATA *88*
Singleton, L.J.
  See Singleton, Linda Joy
Sinykin, Sheri
  See Sinykin, Sheri Cooper
Sinykin, Sheri Cooper 1950- *142*
  Autobiography Feature *142*
  Earlier sketches in SATA *72, 133*
Sinykin, Sheril Terri Cooper
  See Sinykin, Sheri Cooper
Sipiera, Paul P., (Jr.) 1948- *144*
  Earlier sketch in SATA *89*
Siracusa, Catherine (Jane) 1947- *82*
Sirett, Dawn (Karen) 1966- *88*
Sirimarco, Elizabeth 1966- *158*
Sirof, Harriet 1930- *94*
  Earlier sketch in SATA *37*
Sirois, Allen L. 1950- *76*
Sirvaitis (Chernyaev), Karen (Ann) 1961- ... *79*
Sis, Peter 1949- *192*
  Earlier sketch in SATA *149*
  See also CLR *110*
Sisson, Rosemary Anne 1923- *11*

Sister Mary Terese
  See Donze, Mary Terese
Sita, Lisa 1962- *87*
Sitarski, Anita *200*
Sitomer, Alan Lawrence *174*
Sitomer, Harry 1903-1985 .... *31*
Sitomer, Mindel 1903-1987 .... *31*
Sittenfeld, Curtis 1975(?)- *164*
Sive, Helen R(obinson) 1951- *30*
Sivulich, Sandra (Jeanne) Stroner 1941- *9*
Siy, Alexandra *193*
Skarmeta, Antonio 1940- *57*
Skeers, Linda 1958- *207*
Skelly, James R(ichard) 1927- *17*
Skelton, Matthew 1971- *185*
Skinner, Constance Lindsay 1877-1939
  See YABC *1*
Skinner, Cornelia Otis 1901-1979 .... *2*
Skipper, G. C. 1939- *46*
  Brief entry *38*
Sklansky, Amy E. 1971- *204*
Sklansky, Amy E(dgar) 1971- *145*
Skofield, James *95*
  Brief entry *44*
Skold, Betty Westrom 1923- *41*
Skorpen, Liesel Moak 1935- *3*
Skott, Maria
  See Nikolajeva, Maria
Skrypuch, Marsha Forchuk 1954- *134*
Skultety, Nancy Laney 1960- *175*
Skurzynski, Gloria 1930- *145*
  Autobiography Feature *145*
  Earlier sketches in SATA *8, 74, 122*
  See also SAAS *9*
Skurzynski, Gloria Joan
  See Skurzynski, Gloria
Skutch, Robert 1925- *89*
Skye, Maggie
  See Werner, Herma
Skye, Obert *200*
  Earlier sketch in SATA *170*
Slack, Michael 1969- *189*
Slackman, Charles B. 1934- *12*
Slade, Arthur G. 1967- *149*
  Earlier sketch in SATA *106*
Slade, Arthur Gregory
  See Slade, Arthur G.
Slade, Christian 1974- *193*
Slade, Richard 1910-1971 .... *9*
Slangerup, Erik Jon 1969- *130*
Slate, Joseph 1928- *174*
  Earlier sketches in SATA *38, 122*
Slate, Joseph Frank
  See Slate, Joseph
Slater, Dashka 1963- *179*
Slater, Ray
  See Lansdale, Joe R.
Slaughter, Hope 1940- *84*
Slaughter, Jean
  See Doty, Jean Slaughter
Slaughter, Tom 1955- *152*
Slavicek, Louise Chipley 1956- *144*
Slavin, Bill 1959- *199*
  Earlier sketches in SATA *76, 148*
Slaymaker, Melissa Eskridge 1958- *158*
Sleator, William 1945- *161*
  Earlier sketches in SATA *3, 68, 118*
  See also CLR *128*
Sleator, William Warner III
  See Sleator, William
Slegers, Liesbet 1975- *154*
Sleigh, Barbara 1906-1982 .... *86*
  Obituary *30*
  Earlier sketch in SATA *3*
Slepian, Jan 1921- *85*
  Brief entry *45*
  Earlier sketch in SATA *51*
  See also SAAS *8*
Slepian, Janice B.
  See Slepian, Jan
Slicer, Margaret O. 1920- *4*

Slier, Debby
  See Shine, Deborah
Sloan, Brian 1966- *172*
Sloan, Carolyn 1937- *116*
  Earlier sketch in SATA *58*
Sloan, Glenna (Davis) 1930- *120*
Sloane, Eric 1910(?)-1985 .... *52*
  Obituary *42*
Sloane, Todd 1955- *88*
Sloat, Teri 1948- *164*
  Earlier sketches in SATA *70, 106*
Slobodkin, Florence Gersh 1905-1994 .... *5*
  Obituary *107*
Slobodkin, Louis 1903-1975 .... *26*
  Earlier sketch in SATA *1*
Slobodkina, Esphyr 1908-2002 .... *1*
  Obituary *135*
  See also SAAS *8*
Sloggett, Nellie 1851-1923 .... *44*
Slonim, David 1966- *207*
Sloss, Lesley Lord 1965- *72*
Slote, Alfred 1926- *72*
  Earlier sketch in SATA *8*
  See also CLR *4*
  See also SAAS *21*
Slote, Elizabeth 1956- *80*
Small, Charlie
  See Ward, Nick
Small, David 1945- *183*
  Brief entry *46*
  Earlier sketches in SATA *50, 95, 126*
  See also CLR *53*
Small, Ernest
  See Lent, Blair
Small, Mary 1932- *165*
Small, Terry 1942- *75*
Smallcomb, Pam 1954- *159*
Smallman, Steve *197*
Smalls, Irene
  See Smalls-Hector, Irene
Smalls-Hector, Irene 1950- *146*
  Earlier sketch in SATA *73*
  See also CLR *103*
Smallwood, Norah (Evelyn) 1910(?)-1984
  Obituary *41*
Smaridge, Norah (Antoinette) 1903-1994 ...... *6*
Smath, Jerry 1933- *198*
Smee, Nicola 1948- *167*
  Earlier sketch in SATA *76*
Smiley, Virginia Kester 1923- *2*
Smit, Noelle 1972- *199*
Smith, Alexander McCall 1948- *179*
  Earlier sketch in SATA *73*
Smith, Andy J. 1975- *207*
Smith, Anne Warren 1938- *41*
  Brief entry *34*
Smith, Barry (Edward Jervis) 1943- *75*
Smith, Beatrice S(chillinger) *12*
Smith, Betsy Covington 1937- *55*
  Earlier sketch in SATA *43*
Smith, Betty (Wehner) 1904-1972 .... *6*
Smith, Bradford 1909-1964 .... *5*
Smith, Brenda 1946- *82*
Smith, C. Pritchard
  See Hoyt, Edwin P(almer), Jr.
Smith, Caesar
  See Trevor, Elleston
Smith, Cat Bowman 1939- *201*
Smith, Charles R., Jr. 1969- *203*
  Earlier sketch in SATA *159*
Smith, Craig 1955- *172*
  Earlier sketches in SATA *81, 117*
Smith, Cynthia Leitich 1967- *152*
Smith, Datus C(lifford), Jr. 1907-1999 .... *13*
  Obituary *116*
Smith, Debra 1955- *89*
Smith, Derek 1943- *141*
Smith, Dick King
  See King-Smith, Dick
Smith, Dodie
  See Smith, Dorothy Gladys

Smith, Doris Buchanan 1934-2002 .... *75*
   Obituary *140*
   Earlier sketch in SATA *28*
   See also SAAS *10*
Smith, Dorothy Gladys 1896-1990 .... *82*
   Obituary *65*
Smith, Dorothy Stafford 1905- *6*
Smith, Duane 1974- *202*
Smith, E(lmer) Boyd 1860-1943
   See YABC *1*
Smith, E(dric) Brooks 1917- *40*
Smith, Elwood H. 1941- *203*
Smith, Emma 1923- *52*
   Brief entry *36*
Smith, (Katherine) Eunice (Young)
   1902-1993 .... *5*
Smith, Frances C(hristine) 1904-1986 .... *3*
Smith, Gary R. 1932- *14*
Smith, Geof 1969- *102*
Smith, George Harmon 1920- *5*
Smith, Gordon 1951- *184*
Smith, Greg Leitich *152*
Smith, H(arry) Allen 1907-1976
   Obituary *20*
Smith, Helene 1937- *142*
Smith, Hope Anita *202*
Smith, Howard E(verett), Jr. 1927- *12*
Smith, Hugh L(etcher) 1921-1968 .... *5*
Smith, Imogene Henderson 1922- *12*
Smith, Jacqueline B. 1937- *39*
Smith, Jada Pinkett 1971- *161*
Smith, James D. 1955- *176*
Smith, James Noel 1950- *193*
Smith, Janet (Buchanan) Adam
   See Adam Smith, Janet (Buchanan)
Smith, Janice Lee 1949- *155*
   Earlier sketch in SATA *54*
Smith, Jean
   See Smith, Frances C(hristine)
Smith, Jean Pajot 1945- *10*
Smith, Jeff 1958- *161*
   Earlier sketch in SATA *93*
Smith, Jeff Allen
   See Smith, Jeff
Smith, Jenny 1963- *90*
Smith, Jessie
   See Kunhardt, Edith
Smith, Jessie Willcox 1863-1935 .... *21*
   See also CLR *59*
Smith, Joan (Mary) 1933- *54*
   Brief entry *46*
Smith, Johnston
   See Crane, Stephen
Smith, Jos A. 1936- *181*
   Earlier sketches in SATA *73, 120*
Smith, Joseph Arthur
   See Smith, Jos A.
Smith, Judie R. 1936- *80*
Smith, Lafayette
   See Higdon, Hal
Smith, Lane 1959- *179*
   Earlier sketches in SATA *76, 131*
   See also CLR *47*
Smith, Lee
   See Albion, Lee Smith
Smith, Lendon H(oward) 1921- *64*
Smith, Lillian H(elena) 1887-1983
   Obituary *32*
Smith, Linda 1949- *177*
Smith, Linell Nash 1932- *2*
Smith, Lucia B. 1943- *30*
Smith, Maggie 1965- *190*
Smith, Margaret Emily Noel Nuttall
   See Nuttall-Smith, Margaret Emily Noel
Smith, Marion Hagens 1913- *12*
Smith, Marion Jaques 1899-1987 .... *13*
Smith, Mary Ellen *10*
Smith, Marya 1945- *78*
Smith, Mike
   See Smith, Mary Ellen
Smith, Nancy Covert 1935- *12*

Smith, Norman F. 1920- *70*
   Earlier sketch in SATA *5*
Smith, Patricia Clark 1943- *96*
Smith, Pauline C.
   See Arthur, Robert, (Jr.)
Smith, Pauline C(oggeshall) 1908-1994 .... *27*
Smith, Philip Warren 1936- *46*
Smith, R. Alexander McCall
   See Smith, Alexander McCall
Smith, Rebecca 1946- *123*
Smith, Robert Kimmel 1930- *77*
   Earlier sketch in SATA *12*
Smith, Robert Paul 1915-1977 .... *52*
   Obituary *30*
Smith, Roland 1951- *193*
   Earlier sketches in SATA *115, 161*
Smith, Rosamond
   See Oates, Joyce Carol
Smith, Ruth Leslie 1902- *2*
Smith, Samantha 1972-1985
   Obituary *45*
Smith, Sandra Lee 1945- *75*
Smith, Sarah Stafford
   See Smith, Dorothy Stafford
Smith, Sharon 1947- *82*
Smith, Sherri L. 1971- *156*
Smith, Sherwood 1951- *206*
   Autobiography Feature *206*
   Earlier sketches in SATA *82, 140*
Smith, Shirley Raines
   See Raines, Shirley C(arol)
Smith, Susan Carlton 1923- *12*
Smith, Susan Mathias 1950- *43*
   Brief entry *35*
Smith, Susan Vernon 1950- *48*
   Brief entry *45*
Smith, Tim(othy R.) 1945- *151*
Smith, Ursula 1934- *54*
Smith, Vian (Crocker) 1920-1969 .... *11*
Smith, Wanda VanHoy 1926- *65*
Smith, Ward
   See Goldsmith, Howard
Smith, William A. 1918- *10*
Smith, William Jay 1918- *154*
   Autobiography Feature *154*
   Earlier sketches in SATA *2, 68*
   See also SAAS *22*
Smith, Winsome 1935- *45*
Smith, Z.Z.
   See Westheimer, David
Smith-Ankrom, M. E. 1942- *130*
Smith-Griswold, Wendy 1955- *88*
Smith-Rex, Susan J. 1950- *94*
Smithsen, Richard
   See Pellowski, Michael (Joseph)
Smits, Teo
   See Smits, Theodore R(ichard)
Smits, Theodore R(ichard) 1905-1996 .... *45*
   Brief entry *28*
Smolinski, Dick 1932- *86*
Smothers, Ethel Footman 1944- *149*
   Earlier sketch in SATA *76*
Smucker, Barbara 1915-2003 .... *130*
   Earlier sketches in SATA *29, 76*
   See also CLR *10*
   See also SAAS *11*
Smucker, Barbara Claassen
   See Smucker, Barbara
Smyth, Iain 1959- *105*
Snedeker, Caroline Dale (Parke) 1871-1956
   See YABC *2*
Sneed, Brad *191*
Sneider, Marian 1932-2005 .... *197*
Snell, Nigel (Edward Creagh) 1936- *57*
   Brief entry *40*
Snellgrove, L(aurence) E(rnest) 1928- *53*
Snelling, Dennis (Wayne) 1958- *84*
Sneve, Virginia Driving Hawk 1933- *95*
   Earlier sketch in SATA *8*
   See also CLR *2*

Snicket, Lemony 1970- *187*
   Earlier sketch in SATA *126*
   See also CLR *79*
Sniegoski, Thomas E. *195*
Sniegoski, Tom
   See Sniegoski, Thomas E.
Snodgrass, Mary Ellen 1944- *75*
Snodgrass, Quentin Curtius
   See Twain, Mark
Snodgrass, Thomas Jefferson
   See Twain, Mark
Snook, Barbara (Lillian) 1913-1976 .... *34*
Snow, Alan 1959- *190*
Snow, Donald Clifford 1917-1979 .... *16*
Snow, Dorothea J(ohnston) 1909- *9*
Snow, Richard F(olger) 1947- *52*
   Brief entry *37*
Snyder, Anne 1922-2001 .... *4*
   Obituary *125*
Snyder, Bernadette McCarver 1930- *97*
Snyder, Carol 1941- *35*
Snyder, Gerald S(eymour) 1933- *48*
   Brief entry *34*
Snyder, Jerome 1916-1976
   Obituary *20*
Snyder, Midori 1954- *106*
Snyder, Paul A. 1946- *125*
Snyder, Zilpha Keatley 1927- *163*
   Autobiography Feature *163*
   Earlier sketches in SATA *1, 28, 75, 110*
   See also CLR *121*
   See also SAAS *2*
Snyderman, Reuven K. 1922- *5*
So, Meilo *162*
Sobel, June 1950- *149*
Soble, Jennie
   See Cavin, Ruth (Brodie)
Sobol, Donald J. 1924- *132*
   Earlier sketches in SATA *1, 31, 73*
   See also CLR *4*
Sobol, Harriet Langsam 1936- *47*
   Brief entry *34*
Sobol, Rose 1931- *76*
Sobott-Mogwe, Gaele 1956- *97*
Soderlind, Arthur E(dwin) 1920- *14*
Soentpiet, Chris K. 1970- *159*
   Earlier sketch in SATA *97*
Soerensen, Svend Otto 1916- *67*
Sofer, Barbara 1949- *109*
Sofer, Rachel
   See Sofer, Barbara
Softly, Barbara Frewin 1924- *12*
Sogabe, Aki *207*
Soglow, Otto 1900-1975
   Obituary *30*
Sohl, Frederic J(ohn) 1916- *10*
Sohr, Daniel 1973- *190*
Sokol, Bill
   See Sokol, William
Sokol, William 1923- *37*
Sokolov, Kirill 1930- *34*
Solbert, Romaine G. 1925- *2*
Solbert, Ronni
   See Solbert, Romaine G.
Solheim, James *133*
Solomon, Heather M. *188*
Solomon, Joan 1930- *51*
   Brief entry *40*
Solomons, Ikey Esquir
   See Thackeray, William Makepeace
Solonevich, George 1915-2003 .... *15*
Solot, Mary Lynn 1939- *12*
Soman, David 1965- *200*
Somerlott, Robert 1928-2001 .... *62*
Somers, Kevin *205*
Somervill, Barbara A(nn) 1948- *140*
Sommer, Angela
   See Sommer-Bodenburg, Angela
Sommer, Carl 1930- *175*
   Earlier sketch in SATA *126*
Sommer, Elyse 1929- *7*

Sommer, Robert 1929- *12*
Sommer-Bodenburg, Angela 1948- *113*
  Earlier sketch in SATA *63*
Sommerdorf, Norma 1926- *131*
Sommerdorf, Norma Jean
  See Sommerdorf, Norma
Sommerfelt, Aimee 1892-1975 .... *5*
Son, John *160*
Sones, Sonya *131*
Sonneborn, Ruth (Cantor) 1899-1974 .... *4*
  Obituary *27*
Sonnenblick, Jordan 1969- *185*
  See also CLR *144*
Sonnenmark, Laura A. 1958- *73*
Soo, Kean *201*
Sopko, Eugen 1949- *58*
Sorel, Edward 1929- *126*
  Brief entry *37*
  Earlier sketch in SATA *65*
Sorensen, Henri 1950- *115*
  Earlier sketch in SATA *77*
Sorensen, Svend Otto
  See Soerensen, Svend Otto
Sorensen, Virginia 1912-1991 .... *2*
  Obituary *72*
  See also SAAS *15*
Sorenson, Jane 1926- *63*
Sorenson, Margo 1946- *96*
Sorley Walker, Kathrine *41*
Sorra, Kristin *185*
Sorrells, Walter *177*
Sorrentino, Joseph N. 1937- *6*
Sortor, June Elizabeth 1939- *12*
Sortor, Toni
  See Sortor, June Elizabeth
Sosa, Hernan 1977- *203*
Soskin, V. H.
  See Ellison, Virginia H(owell)
Soto, Gary 1952- *174*
  Earlier sketches in SATA *80, 120*
  See also CLR *38*
Sotomayor, Antonio 1902-1985 .... *11*
Souci, Robert D. San
  See San Souci, Robert D.
Soudley, Henry
  See Wood, James Playsted
Souhami, Jessica *176*
Soule, Gardner (Bosworth) 1913-2000 .... *14*
Soule, Jean Conder 1919- *10*
Souster, (Holmes) Raymond 1921- *63*
South, Sheri Cobb 1959- *82*
Southall, Ivan 1921-2008 .... *134*
  Autobiography Feature *134*
  Earlier sketches in SATA *3, 68*
  See also CLR *2*
  See also SAAS *3*
Southall, Ivan Francis
  See Southall, Ivan
Southey, Robert 1774-1843 .... *54*
Southgate, Vera *54*
Sovak, Jan 1953- *115*
Sowden, Celeste
  See Walters, Celeste
Sowter, Nita *69*
Spafford, Suzy 1945- *160*
Spagnoli, Cathy 1950- *134*
  Earlier sketch in SATA *79*
Spain, Sahara Sunday 1991- *133*
Spain, Susan Rosson *185*
Spalding, Andrea 1944- *150*
  Earlier sketch in SATA *101*
Spalenka, Greg 1958- *198*
Spanfeller, James J. 1930- *19*
  See also SAAS *8*
Spanfeller, Jim
  See Spanfeller, James J.
Spangenberg, Judith Dunn 1942- *5*
Spanyol, Jessica 1965- *206*
  Earlier sketch in SATA *137*
Spar, Jerome 1918- *10*
Sparks, Barbara 1942- *78*

Sparks, Beatrice (Mathews) 1918- *44*
  Brief entry *28*
  See also CLR *139*
Sparks, Mary W. 1920- *15*
Spaulding, Douglas
  See Bradbury, Ray
Spaulding, Leonard
  See Bradbury, Ray
Spaulding, Norma *107*
Speare, Elizabeth George 1908-1994 .... *62*
  Obituary *83*
  Earlier sketch in SATA *5*
  See also CLR *8*
Spearing, Judith (Mary Harlow) 1922- *9*
Spears, Rick *182*
Speck, Katie *196*
Speck, Nancy 1959- *104*
Specking, Inez 1890-1960(?) *11*
Speed, Nell
  See Keats, Emma
  and Sampson, Emma (Keats) Speed
Speed, Nell (Ewing) 1878-1913 .... *68*
Speer, Bonnie Stahlman 1929- *113*
Speer-Lyon, Tammie L. 1965- *89*
Speicher, Helen Ross S(mith) 1915- *8*
Speir, Nancy 1958- *81*
Spellman, John W(illard) 1934- *14*
Spellman, Roger G.
  See Cox, William R(obert)
Spelman, Cornelia Maude 1946- *144*
  Earlier sketch in SATA *96*
Spelman, Mary 1934- *28*
Spelvin, George
  See Lerangis, Peter
  and Phillips, David Atlee
Spence, Cynthia
  See Eble, Diane
Spence, Eleanor (Rachel) 1928- *21*
  See also CLR *26*
Spence, Geraldine 1931- *47*
Spencer, Ann 1918- *10*
Spencer, Britt *206*
Spencer, Cornelia
  See Yaukey, Grace S(ydenstricker)
Spencer, Donald D(ean) 1931- *41*
Spencer, Elizabeth 1921- *14*
Spencer, Leonard G.
  See Garrett, Randall
  and Silverberg, Robert
Spencer, William 1922- *9*
Spencer, Zane A(nn) 1935- *35*
Sper, Emily 1957- *142*
Speregen, Devra Newberger 1964- *84*
Sperling, Dan(iel Lee) 1949- *65*
Sperry, Armstrong W. 1897-1976 .... *1*
  Obituary *27*
Sperry, Raymond
  See Garis, Howard R.
Sperry, Raymond, Jr. *1*
Spetter, Jung-Hee 1969- *134*
Spicer, Dorothy Gladys -1975 .... *32*
Spiegel, Beth *184*
Spiegelman, Art 1948- *158*
  Earlier sketch in SATA *109*
Spiegelman, Judith M. *5*
Spielberg, Steven 1947- *32*
Spier, Peter (Edward) 1927- *54*
  Earlier sketch in SATA *4*
  See also CLR *5*
Spilhaus, Athelstan (Frederick) 1911-1998 .. *13*
  Obituary *102*
Spilka, Arnold 1917- *6*
Spillane, Frank Morrison
  See Spillane, Mickey
Spillane, Mickey 1918-2006 .... *66*
  Obituary *176*
Spinelli, Eileen 1942- *186*
  Earlier sketches in SATA *38, 101, 150*
Spinelli, Jerry 1941- *195*
  Earlier sketches in SATA *39, 71, 110, 158*
  See also CLR *82*

Spink, Reginald (William) 1905-1994 .... *11*
Spinka, Penina Keen 1945- *72*
Spinner, Stephanie 1943- *132*
  Earlier sketches in SATA *38, 91*
Spinossimus
  See White, William, Jr.
Spiotta-DiMare, Loren *173*
Spires, Ashley 1978- *183*
Spires, Elizabeth 1952- *111*
  Earlier sketch in SATA *71*
Spiridellis, Gregg 1971(?)- *199*
Spirin, Gennadii
  See Spirin, Gennady
Spirin, Gennadij
  See Spirin, Gennady
Spirin, Gennady 1948- *204*
  Earlier sketches in SATA *95, 134*
  See also CLR *88*
Spivak, Dawnine *101*
Spizman, Robyn Freedman *194*
Spohn, David 1948- *72*
Spohn, Kate 1962- *147*
  Earlier sketch in SATA *87*
Spollen, Christopher 1952- *12*
Spooner, Michael (Tim) 1954- *92*
Spowart, Robin 1947- *177*
  Earlier sketch in SATA *82*
Spradlin, Michael P. *204*
Sprague, Gretchen 1926-2003 .... *27*
Spranger, Nina 1969- *203*
Sprengel, Artie
  See Lerangis, Peter
Sprigge, Elizabeth (Miriam Squire)
  1900-1974 .... *10*
Spring, (Robert) Howard 1889-1965 .... *28*
Springer, Margaret 1941- *78*
Springer, Marilyn Harris 1931- *47*
Springer, Nancy 1948- *172*
  Earlier sketches in SATA *65, 110*
Springstubb, Tricia 1950- *78*
  Brief entry *40*
  Earlier sketch in SATA *46*
Spudvilas, Anne 1951- *199*
  Earlier sketch in SATA *94*
Spurll, Barbara 1952- *78*
Spurr, Elizabeth *172*
Spykman, E(lizabeth) C(hoate) 1896-1965 .. *10*
  See also CLR *35*
Spyri, Johanna (Heusser) 1827-1901 .... *100*
  Earlier sketch in SATA *19*
  See also CLR *115*
Squires, Phil
  See Barker, S. Omar
Srba, Lynne *98*
Sreenivasan, Jyotsna 1964- *101*
S-Ringi, Kjell
  See Ringi, Kjell (Arne Soerensen)
Stacey, Cherylyn 1945- *96*
Stacy, Donald
  See Pohl, Frederik
Stadler, John *204*
Stadtler, Bea 1921- *17*
Stafford, Jean 1915-1979
  Obituary *22*
Stafford, Liliana 1950- *141*
Stafford, Paul 1966- *116*
Stahl, Ben(jamin) 1910-1987 .... *5*
  Obituary *54*
Stahl, Hilda 1938-1993 .... *48*
  Obituary *77*
Stahler, David, Jr. *162*
Stainton, Sue *187*
Stair, Gobin (John) 1912- *35*
Stalder, Valerie *27*
Stamaty, Mark Alan 1947- *12*
Stambler, Irwin 1924- *5*
Standiford, Natalie 1961- *169*
  Earlier sketch in SATA *81*
Stanek, Lou Willett 1931- *63*
Stang, Judit 1921-1977 .... *29*

Stang, Judy
See Stang, Judit
Stangl, (Mary) Jean 1928- 67
Stanhope, Eric
See Hamilton, Charles (Harold St. John)
Stankevich, Boris 1928- 2
Stanley, Diane 1943- 164
Brief entry 32
Earlier sketches in SATA 37, 80, 115
See also CLR 46
See also SAAS 15
Stanley, Elizabeth 1947- 206
Stanley, George Edward 1942- 67
Earlier sketches in SATA 53, 111, 157, 1
Stanley, Jerry 1941- 127
Earlier sketch in SATA 79
Stanley, Mandy 165
Stanley, Robert
See Hamilton, Charles (Harold St. John)
Stanley, Sanna 1962- 145
Stanli, Sue
See Meilach, Dona Z(weigoron)
Stanstead, John
See Groom, Arthur William
Stanton, Karen 1960- 190
Stanton, Schuyler
See Baum, L. Frank
Staples, Suzanne Fisher 1945- 207
Earlier sketches in SATA 70, 105, 151
See also CLR 137
Stapleton, Marjorie (Winifred) 1932- 28
Stapp, Arthur D(onald) 1906-1972 4
Starbird, Kaye 1916- 6
See also CLR 60
Stark, Evan 1942- 78
Stark, James
See Goldston, Robert (Conroy)
Stark, Ken 1943- 199
Stark, Ulf 1944- 124
Starke, Ruth (Elaine) 1946- 129
Starkey, Marion L(ena) 1901-1991 13
Starr, Ward
See Manes, Stephen
Starret, William
See McClintock, Marshall
Starr Taylor, Bridget 1959- 99
Stasiak, Krystyna 49
Staub, Frank 1949- 116
Staub, Frank Jacob
See Staub, Frank
Staub, Wendy Corsi 1964- 114
Stauffacher, Sue 1961- 199
Earlier sketch in SATA 155
Stauffer, Don
See Berkebile, Fred D(onovan)
Staunton, Schuyler
See Baum, L. Frank
Staunton, Ted 1956- 167
Earlier sketch in SATA 112
Stead, Rebecca 1968(?)- 188
Steadman, Ralph 1936- 123
Earlier sketch in SATA 32
Steadman, Ralph Idris
See Steadman, Ralph
Stearman, Kaye 1951- 118
Stearns, Monroe (Mather) 1913-1987 5
Obituary 55
Steckler, Arthur 1921-1985 65
Steding, Laurie 1953- 119
Steel, Danielle 1947- 66
Steel, Danielle Fernande
See Steel, Danielle
Steele, Addison II
See Lupoff, Richard A(llen)
Steele, Alexander 1958- 116
Steele, Henry Maxwell
See Steele, Max
Steele, Mary 1930- 94
Steele, Mary Q(uintard Govan) 1922-1992 .. 51
Obituary 72
Earlier sketch in SATA 3

Steele, Max 1922-2005 168
Earlier sketch in SATA 10
Steele, Philip 1948- 140
Earlier sketch in SATA 81
Steele, William O(wen) 1917-1979 51
Obituary 27
Earlier sketch in SATA 1
Steelhammer, Ilona 1952- 98
Steelsmith, Shari 1962- 72
Stefanik, Alfred T. 1939- 55
Steffanson, Con
See Cassiday, Bruce (Bingham)
and Goulart, Ron
Steffens, Bradley 1955- 166
Earlier sketch in SATA 77
Steffensmeier, Alexander 1977- 195
Stegeman, Janet Allais 1923- 49
Brief entry 49
Steggall, Susan 1967- 182
Steig, William 1907-2003 111
Obituary 149
Earlier sketches in SATA 18, 70
See also CLR 103
Steig, William H.
See Steig, William
Stein, David Ezra 180
Stein, M(eyer) L(ewis) 1920- 6
Stein, Mathilde 1969- 195
Stein, Mini 2
Stein, R(ichard) Conrad 1937- 154
Earlier sketches in SATA 31, 82
Stein, Wendy 1951- 77
Steinbeck, John 1902-1968 9
Steinbeck, John Ernst
See Steinbeck, John
Steinberg, Alfred 1917-1995 9
Steinberg, David 1962- 200
Steinberg, D.J.
See Steinberg, David
Steinberg, Fannie 1899-1990 43
Steinberg, Fred J. 1933- 4
Steinberg, Phillip Orso 1921- 34
Steinberg, Rafael (Mark) 1927- 45
Steinberg, Saul 1914-1999 67
Steincrohn, Maggie
See Davis, Maggie S.
Steiner, Barbara A(nnette) 1934- 83
Earlier sketch in SATA 13
See also SAAS 13
Steiner, Charlotte 1900-1981 45
Steiner, George 1929- 62
Steiner, Joan 199
Earlier sketch in SATA 110
Steiner, Jorg
See Steiner, Jorg
Steiner, Jorg 1930- 35
Steiner, K. Leslie
See Delany, Samuel R., Jr.
Steiner, Stan(ley) 1925-1987 14
Obituary 50
Steins, Richard 1942- 79
Stem, Jacqueline 1931- 110
Stemple, Jason 179
Steneman, Shep 1945- 132
Stengel, Joyce A. 1938- 158
Stephanie, Gordon
See Gordon, Stephanie Jacob
Stephens, Alice Barber 1858-1932 66
Stephens, Casey
See Wagner, Sharon B.
Stephens, Henrietta Henkle 1909-1993 6
Stephens, J.B.
See Lynn, Tracy
Stephens, Mary Jo 1935- 8
Stephens, Rebecca 1961- 141
Stephens, Reed
See Donaldson, Stephen R.
Stephens, Suzanne
See Kirby, Susan E.
Stephens, William M(cLain) 1925- 21

Stephensen, A. M.
See Manes, Stephen
Stephenson, Lynda 1941- 179
Stephenson, Lynda A.
See Stephenson, Lynda
Stepp, Ann 1935- 29
Stepto, Michele 1946- 61
Steptoe, Javaka 1971- 151
Steptoe, John (Lewis) 1950-1989 63
Earlier sketch in SATA 8
See also CLR 12
Sterling, Brett
See Bradbury, Ray
and Hamilton, Edmond
and Samachson, Joseph
Sterling, Dorothy 1913-2008 83
Autobiography Feature 127
Obituary 200
Earlier sketch in SATA 1
See also CLR 1
See also SAAS 2
Sterling, Helen
See Watts, Helen L. Hoke
Sterling, Philip 1907-1989 8
Obituary 63
Sterling, Shirley (Anne) 1948- 101
Stern, Ellen Norman 1927- 26
Stern, Judith M. 1951- 75
Stern, Madeleine
See Stern, Madeleine B.
Stern, Madeleine B. 1912-2007 14
Stern, Madeleine Bettina
See Stern, Madeleine B.
Stern, Maggie 1953- 156
Stern, Philip Van Doren 1900-1984 13
Obituary 39
Stern, Simon 1943- 15
Sterne, Emma Gelders 1894- 6
Steurt, Marjorie Rankin 1888-1978 10
Stevens, Bryna 1924- 65
Stevens, Carla M(cBride) 1928- 13
Stevens, Chambers 1968- 128
Stevens, Diane 1939- 94
Stevens, Franklin 1933- 6
Stevens, Greg
See Cook, Glen
Stevens, Gwendolyn 1944- 33
Stevens, Jan Romero 1953- 95
Stevens, Janet 1953- 193
Earlier sketches in SATA 90, 148
Stevens, Kathleen 1936- 49
Stevens, Leonard A. 1920- 67
Stevens, Lucile Vernon 1899-1994 59
Stevens, Margaret Dean
See Aldrich, Bess Streeter
Stevens, Patricia Bunning 1931- 27
Stevens, Peter
See Geis, Darlene Stern
Stevens, Serita 1949- 70
Stevens, Serita Deborah
See Stevens, Serita
Stevens, Serita Mendelson
See Stevens, Serita
Stevens, Shira
See Stevens, Serita
Stevenson, Anna (M.) 1905- 12
Stevenson, Augusta 1869(?)-1976 2
Obituary 26
Stevenson, Burton Egbert 1872-1962 25
Stevenson, Drew 1947- 60
Stevenson, Emma 207
Stevenson, Harvey 1960- 148
Earlier sketch in SATA 80
Stevenson, James 1929- 195
Brief entry 34
Earlier sketches in SATA 42, 71, 113, 161
See also CLR 17
Stevenson, Janet 1913- 8
Stevenson, Robert Louis 1850-1894 100
See also YABC 2
See also CLR 107

Stevenson, Robert Louis Balfour
  See Stevenson, Robert Louis
Stevenson, Sucie
  See Stevenson, Sucie
Stevenson, Sucie 1956- *194*
  Earlier sketch in SATA *104*
Stewart, A(gnes) C(harlotte) *15*
Stewart, Amber *181*
Stewart, Chantal 1945- *173*
  Earlier sketch in SATA *121*
Stewart, Charles
  See Zurhorst, Charles (Stewart, Jr.)
Stewart, Eleanor
  See Porter, Eleanor H(odgman)
Stewart, Elisabeth J(ane) 1927- *93*
Stewart, Elizabeth Laing 1907- *6*
Stewart, Gail B. 1949- *141*
Stewart, George Rippey 1895-1980 .... *3*
  Obituary *23*
Stewart, Jennifer J(enkins) 1960- *128*
Stewart, Joel *151*
Stewart, John 1920- *14*
Stewart, Mary (Florence Elinor) 1916- *12*
Stewart, Mary Rainbow
  See Stewart, Mary (Florence Elinor)
Stewart, Melissa 1968- *167*
  Earlier sketch in SATA *111*
Stewart, Paul 1955- *199*
  Earlier sketches in SATA *114, 163*
Stewart, Robert Neil 1891-1972 .... *7*
Stewart, Sarah *143*
Stewart, Scott
  See Zaffo, George J.
Stewart, W(alter) P. 1924- *53*
Stewart, Whitney 1959- *167*
  Earlier sketch in SATA *92*
Stewig, John Warren 1937- *162*
  Earlier sketches in SATA *26, 110*
Stickler, Soma Han 1942- *128*
Stidworthy, John 1943- *63*
Stiegemeyer, Julie *180*
Stier, Catherine *198*
Stiles, Martha Bennett *108*
  Earlier sketch in SATA *6*
Still, James 1906-2001 .... *29*
  Obituary *127*
Stille, Darlene R. 1942- *170*
  Earlier sketch in SATA *126*
Stille, Darlene Ruth
  See Stille, Darlene R.
Stillerman, Marci *104*
Stillerman, Robbie 1947- *12*
Stilley, Frank 1918- *29*
Stilton, Geronimo *158*
Stimpson, Gerald
  See Mitchell, Adrian
Stine, Catherine *165*
Stine, G(eorge) Harry 1928-1997 .... *136*
  Earlier sketch in SATA *10*
Stine, Jovial Bob
  See Stine, R.L.
Stine, R.L. 1943- *194*
  Earlier sketches in SATA *31, 76, 129*
  See also CLR *111*
Stine, Robert Lawrence
  See Stine, R.L.
Stinetorf, Louise (Allender) 1900-1992 .... *10*
Stinson, Kathy 1952- *98*
Stirling, Arthur
  See Sinclair, Upton
Stirling, Ian 1941- *77*
Stirling, Nora B(romley) 1900-1997 .... *3*
Stirnweis, Shannon 1931- *10*
Stobbs, William 1914-2000 .... *17*
  Obituary *120*
Stock, Carolmarie 1951- *75*
Stock, Catherine 1952- *158*
  Earlier sketches in SATA *65, 114*
Stockdale, Susan 1954- *206*
  Earlier sketch in SATA *98*
Stockham, Peter (Alan) 1928- *57*

Stockton, Francis Richard 1834-1902 .... *44*
  Brief entry *32*
Stockton, Frank R.
  See Stockton, Francis Richard
Stockwell-Moniz, Marc J. 1954- *164*
Stoddard, Edward G. 1923- *10*
Stoddard, Hope 1900-1987 .... *6*
Stoddard, Sandol 1927- *98*
  Earlier sketch in SATA *14*
Stoehr, Shelley 1969- *107*
Stoeke, Janet Morgan 1957- *202*
  Earlier sketches in SATA *90, 136*
Stohner, Anu 1952- *179*
Stoiko, Michael 1919- *14*
Stojic, Manya 1967- *156*
Stoker, Abraham
  See Stoker, Bram
Stoker, Bram 1847-1912 .... *29*
Stokes, Cedric
  See Beardmore, George
Stokes, Jack (Tilden) 1923- *13*
Stokes, Olivia Pearl 1916- *32*
Stolarz, Laurie Faria *203*
Stolz, Mary 1920-2006 .... *133*
  Obituary *180*
  Earlier sketches in SATA *10, 71*
  See also SAAS *3*
Stolz, Mary Slattery
  See Stolz, Mary
Stone, Alan
  See Svenson, Andrew E(dward)
Stone, David K(arl) 1922- *9*
Stone, David Lee 1978- *166*
Stone, Eugenia 1879-1971 .... *7*
Stone, Gene
  See Stone, Eugenia
Stone, Helen V(irginia) *6*
Stone, Idella Purnell
  See Purnell, Idella
Stone, Ikey
  See Purnell, Idella
Stone, Irving 1903-1989 .... *3*
  Obituary *64*
Stone, Jeff *178*
Stone, Jon 1931-1997 .... *39*
  Obituary *95*
Stone, Josephine Rector
  See Dixon, Jeanne
Stone, Kyle M. 1972- *202*
Stone, Lesley
  See Trevor, Elleston
Stone, Peter 1930-2003 .... *65*
  Obituary *143*
Stone, Phoebe *205*
  Earlier sketch in SATA *134*
Stone, Raymond *1*
Stone, Rosetta
  See Dr. Seuss
Stone, Tanya Lee 1965- *182*
Stonehouse, Bernard 1926- *140*
  Earlier sketches in SATA *13, 80*
Stones, (Cyril) Anthony 1934- *72*
Stong, Phil(ip Duffield) 1899-1957 .... *32*
Stoops, Erik D(aniel) 1966- *142*
  Earlier sketch in SATA *78*
Stoppelmoore, Cheryl Jean
  See Ladd, Cheryl (Jean)
Stops, Sue 1936- *86*
Storace, Patricia *193*
Storad, Conrad J. 1957- *119*
Storey, Margaret 1926- *9*
Storey, Victoria Carolyn 1945- *16*
Storme, Peter
  See Stern, Philip Van Doren
Storr, Catherine (Cole) 1913-2001 .... *87*
  Obituary *122*
  Earlier sketch in SATA *9*
Story, Josephine
  See Loring, Emilie (Baker)
Stotko, Mary-Ann 1960- *154*

Stott, Dorothy (M.) 1958- *99*
  Earlier sketch in SATA *67*
Stott, Dot
  See Stott, Dorothy (M.)
Stotter, Mike 1957- *108*
Stout, William 1949- *132*
Stoutenburg, Adrien (Pearl) 1916-1982 .... *3*
Stoutland, Allison 1963- *130*
Stover, Allan C(arl) 1938- *14*
Stover, Jill (Griffin) 1958- *82*
Stover, Marjorie Filley 1914- *9*
Stowe, Harriet Beecher 1811-1896
  See YABC *1*
  See also CLR *131*
Stowe, Harriet Elizabeth Beecher
  See Stowe, Harriet Beecher
Stowe, Leland 1899-1994 .... *60*
  Obituary *78*
Stowe, Rosetta
  See Ogan, George F.
  and Ogan, Margaret E. (Nettles)
Stower, Adam *195*
Strachan, Bruce 1959- *205*
Strachan, Ian 1938- *85*
Strachan, Linda *167*
Strachan, Margaret Pitcairn 1908-1998 .... *14*
Strahinich, H. C.
  See Strahinich, Helen C.
Strahinich, Helen C. 1949- *78*
Strait, Treva Adams 1909-2002 .... *35*
Strand, Mark 1934- *41*
Strange, Philippa
  See Coury, Louise Andree
Stranger, Joyce
  See Wilson, Joyce M.
Strangis, Joel 1948- *124*
Strannigan, Shawn 1956- *93*
Strannigan, Shawn Alyne
  See Strannigan, Shawn
Strasser, Todd 1950- *153*
  Earlier sketches in SATA *41, 45, 71, 107*
  See also CLR *11*
Stratemeyer, Edward L. 1862-1930 .... *100*
  Earlier sketches in SATA *1, 67*
  See Adams, Harrison
Stratford, Philip 1927- *47*
Stratton, Allan 1951- *178*
Stratton, J. M.
  See Whitlock, Ralph
Stratton, Thomas
  See Coulson, Robert S(tratton)
  and DeWeese, Thomas Eugene
Stratton-Porter, Gene 1863-1924 .... *15*
  See also CLR *87*
Strauss, Gwen 1963- *77*
Strauss, Joyce 1936- *53*
Strauss, Linda Leopold 1942- *127*
Strauss, Susan (Elizabeth) 1954- *75*
Strayer, E. Ward
  See Stratemeyer, Edward L.
Streano, Vince(nt Catello) 1945- *20*
Streatfeild, Mary Noel
  See Streatfeild, Noel
Streatfeild, Noel 1897(?)-1986 .... *20*
  Obituary *48*
  See also CLR *83*
Street, Janet Travell 1959- *84*
Street, Julia Montgomery 1898-1993 .... *11*
Streissguth, Thomas 1958- *116*
Strelkoff, Tatiana 1957- *89*
Stren, Patti 1949- *88*
  Brief entry *41*
  See also CLR *5*
Strete, Craig Kee 1950- *96*
  Earlier sketch in SATA *44*
Stretton, Barbara (Humphrey) 1936- *43*
  Brief entry *35*
Strickland, Brad 1947- *200*
  Earlier sketches in SATA *83, 137, 142*
Strickland, Craig (A.) 1956- *102*
Strickland, Dorothy S(alley) 1933- *89*

Strickland, Michael R. 1965- *144*
  Earlier sketch in SATA *83*
Strickland, Tessa *173*
Strickland, William Bradley
  See Strickland, Brad
Striegel, Jana 1955- *140*
Striegel-Wilson, Jana
  See Striegel, Jana
Striker, Lee
  See Clark, Margaret (D.)
Striker, Susan 1942- *63*
Stringer, Lauren 1957- *183*
  Earlier sketch in SATA *129*
Stroeyer, Poul 1923- *13*
Stromoski, Rick 1958- *111*
Strong, Charles
  See Epstein, Beryl
  and Epstein, Samuel
Strong, David
  See McGuire, Leslie (Sarah)
Strong, Jeremy 1949- *175*
  Earlier sketches in SATA *36, 105*
Strong, J.J.
  See Strong, Jeremy
Strong, Pat
  See Hough, Richard (Alexander)
Strong, Stacie 1965- *74*
Stroud, Bettye 1939- *165*
  Earlier sketch in SATA *96*
Stroud, Jonathan 1970- *159*
  Earlier sketch in SATA *102*
  See also CLR *134*
Stroyer, Poul
  See Stroeyer, Poul
Strug, Kerri 1977- *108*
Stryer, Andrea Stenn 1938- *192*
Stryker, Daniel
  See Morris, Chris(topher Crosby)
  and Stump, Jane Barr
Stuart, David
  See Hoyt, Edwin P(almer), Jr.
Stuart, Derek
  See Foster, John L(ouis)
Stuart, Forbes 1924- *13*
Stuart, Ian
  See MacLean, Alistair
Stuart, Jesse (Hilton) 1906-1984 .... *2*
  Obituary *36*
Stuart, Ruth McEnery 1849(?)-1917 .... *116*
Stuart, Sheila
  See Baker, Mary Gladys Steel
Stuart-Clark, Christopher (Anthony) 1940- .. *32*
Stubis, Talivaldis 1926- *5*
Stubley, Trevor (Hugh) 1932- *22*
Stucky, Naomi R. 1922- *72*
Stucley, Elizabeth
  See Northmore, Elizabeth Florence
Stultifer, Morton
  See Curtis, Richard
Sture-Vasa, Mary
  See Alsop, Mary O'Hara
Sturges, Philemon *174*
Sturtevant, Katherine 1950- *180*
  Earlier sketch in SATA *130*
Sturton, Hugh
  See Johnston, H(ugh) A(nthony) S(tephen)
Sturtzel, Howard A(llison) 1894-1985 .... *1*
Sturtzel, Jane Levington 1903-1996 .... *1*
Stutley, D(oris) J(ean) 1959- *142*
Stutson, Caroline 1940- *104*
Stuve-Bodeen, Stephanie 1965- *158*
  Earlier sketch in SATA *114*
Stux, Erica 1929- *140*
Styles, (Frank) Showell 1908- *10*
Stynes, Barbara White *133*
Suarez, Maribel 1952- *201*
Suba, Susanne *4*
Subond, Valerie
  See Grayland, Valerie (Merle Spanner)
Sudbery, Rodie 1943- *42*
Suen, Anastasia 1956(?)- *157*

Sufrin, Mark 1925- *76*
Sugarman, Joan G. 1917- *64*
Sugarman, Tracy 1921- *37*
Sugita, Yutaka 1930- *36*
Suhl, Yuri (Menachem) 1908-1986 .... *8*
  Obituary *50*
  See also CLR *2*
  See also SAAS *1*
Suhr, Joanne *129*
Suid, Murray 1942- *27*
Sullivan, Edward T. *206*
Sullivan, George (Edward) 1927- *147*
  Earlier sketches in SATA *4, 89*
Sullivan, Jacqueline Levering *203*
Sullivan, Jody
  See Rake, Jody
Sullivan, Kathryn A. 1954- *141*
Sullivan, Mary Ann 1954- *63*
Sullivan, Mary W(ilson) 1907- *13*
Sullivan, Pat
  See Messmer, Otto
Sullivan, Paul 1939- *106*
Sullivan, Sarah G. 1953- *179*
Sullivan, Silky
  See Makowski, Silvia Ann
Sullivan, Sue
  See Sullivan, Susan E.
Sullivan, Susan E. 1962- *123*
Sullivan, Thomas Joseph, Jr. 1947- *16*
Sullivan, Tom
  See Sullivan, Thomas Joseph, Jr.
Sully, Tom 1959- *104*
Sumichrast, Jozef 1948- *29*
Sumiko
  See Davies, Sumiko
Summerforest, Ivy B.
  See Kirkup, James
Summers, Barbara 1944- *182*
Summers, James L(evingston) 1910-1973 .... *57*
  Brief entry *28*
Summertree, Katonah
  See Windsor, Patricia
Sun, Chyng Feng 1959- *90*
Sunderlin, Sylvia (S.) 1911-1997 .... *28*
  Obituary *99*
Sung, Betty Lee *26*
Supeene, Shelagh Lynne 1952- *153*
Supplee, Suzanne *204*
Supraner, Robyn 1930- *101*
  Earlier sketch in SATA *20*
Supree, Burt(on) 1941-1992 .... *73*
Surface, Mary Hall 1958- *126*
Surge, Frank 1931- *13*
Susac, Andrew 1929- *5*
Susi, Geraldine Lee 1942- *98*
Sussman, Cornelia Silver 1914-1999 .... *59*
Sussman, Irving 1908-1996 .... *59*
Sussman, Susan 1942- *48*
Sutcliff, Rosemary 1920-1992 .... *78*
  Obituary *73*
  Earlier sketches in SATA *6, 44*
  See also CLR *138*
Sutcliffe, Jane 1957- *138*
Sutherland, Colleen 1944- *79*
Sutherland, Efua (Theodora Morgue)
  1924-1996 .... *25*
Sutherland, Jon 1958- *167*
Sutherland, Jonathan D.
  See Sutherland, Jon
Sutherland, Jonathan David
  See Sutherland, Jon
Sutherland, Margaret 1941- *15*
Sutherland, Zena Bailey 1915-2002 .... *37*
  Obituary *137*
Suttles, Shirley (Smith) 1922- *21*
Sutton, Ann (Livesay) 1923- *31*
Sutton, Eve(lyn Mary) 1906-1992 .... *26*
Sutton, Felix 1910(?)-1973 .... *31*
Sutton, Jane 1950- *52*
  Brief entry *43*
Sutton, Larry M(atthew) 1931- *29*

Sutton, Margaret Beebe 1903-2001 .... *1*
  Obituary *131*
Sutton, Myron Daniel 1925- *31*
Sutton, Roger 1956- *93*
Suzanne, Jamie
  See Hawes, Louise
  and Lantz, Francess L(in)
  and Singleton, Linda Joy
  and Zach, Cheryl (Byrd)
Suzuki, David 1936- *138*
Suzuki, David Takayoshi
  See Suzuki, David
Svendsen, Mark 1962- *181*
  Earlier sketch in SATA *120*
Svendsen, Mark Nestor
  See Svendsen, Mark
Svenson, Andrew E(dward) 1910-1975 .... *2*
  Obituary *26*
Swaab, Neil 1978- *191*
Swaim, Jessica 1950- *202*
Swain, Carol 1962- *172*
Swain, Gwenyth 1961- *134*
  Earlier sketch in SATA *84*
Swain, Ruth
  See Swain, Ruth Freeman
Swain, Ruth Freeman 1951- *161*
  Earlier sketch in SATA *119*
Swain, Su Zan (Noguchi) 1916- *21*
Swallow, Pamela Curtis *178*
Swamp, Jake 1941- *98*
Swan, Susan 1944- *108*
  Earlier sketch in SATA *22*
Swann, Brian (Stanley Frank) 1940- *116*
Swann, E. L.
  See Lasky, Kathryn
Swann, Ruth Rice 1920- *84*
Swanson, Diane 1944- *203*
Swanson, Helen M(cKendry) 1919- *94*
Swanson, June 1931- *76*
Swanson, Wayne 1942- *167*
Swarthout, Glendon (Fred) 1918-1992 .... *26*
Swarthout, Kathryn 1919- *7*
Swayne, Sam(uel F.) 1907- *53*
Swayne, Zoa (Lourana) 1905- *53*
Sweat, Lynn 1934- *168*
  Earlier sketch in SATA *57*
Swede, George 1940- *67*
Sweeney, James B(artholomew) 1910-1999 . *21*
Sweeney, Joyce 1955- *167*
  Earlier sketches in SATA *65, 68, 108*
Sweeney, Joyce Kay
  See Sweeney, Joyce
Sweeney, Karen O'Connor
  See O'Connor, Karen
Sweeney, Matthew (Gerard) 1952- *156*
Sweet, Melissa 1956- *172*
Sweet, Sarah C.
  See Jewett, Sarah Orne
Sweetland, Nancy A(nn) 1934- *48*
Swenson, Allan A(rmstrong) 1933- *21*
Swenson, May 1919-1989 .... *15*
Swentzell, Rina 1939- *79*
Swiatkowska, Gabi 1971(?)- *180*
Swift, Bryan
  See Knott, William C(ecil, Jr.)
Swift, David
  See Kaufmann, John
Swift, Hildegarde Hoyt 1890(?)-1977
  Obituary *20*
Swift, Jonathan 1667-1745 .... *19*
  See also CLR *53*
Swift, Merlin
  See Leeming, Joseph
Swiger, Elinor Porter 1927- *8*
Swinburne, Laurence (Joseph) 1924- *9*
Swinburne, Stephen R. 1952- *188*
  Earlier sketch in SATA *150*
Swinburne, Steve
  See Swinburne, Stephen R.

Author Index

Swindells, Robert (Edward) 1939- 150
  Brief entry 34
  Earlier sketches in SATA 50, 80
  See also SAAS 14
Swinford, Betty (June Wells) 1927- 58
Swinford, Bob
  See Swinford, Betty (June Wells)
Swithen, John
  See King, Stephen
Switzer, Ellen 1923- 48
Swope, Sam 156
Swope, Samuel
  See Swope, Sam
Sybesma, Jetske
  See Ironside, Jetske
Sydney, Frank
  See Warwick, Alan R(oss)
Sydor, Colleen 1960- 207
Sykes, Julie 1963- 202
Sylvada, Peter 1964- 202
Sylvester, Natalie G(abry) 1922- 22
Syme, (Neville) Ronald 1913-1992 87
  Earlier sketch in SATA 2
Symes, R. F. 77
Symes, Ruth Louise 1962- 179
Symons, (Dorothy) Geraldine 1909- 33
Symons, Stuart
  See Stanley, George Edward
Symynkywicz, Jeffrey B. 1954- 87
Symynkywicz, Jeffrey Bruce
  See Symynkywicz, Jeffrey B.
Synge, (Phyllis) Ursula 1930- 9
Sypher, Lucy Johnston 1907- 7
Szasz, Suzanne (Shorr) 1915-1997 13
  Obituary 99
Szekeres, Cyndy 1933- 157
  Autobiography Feature 157
  Earlier sketches in SATA 5, 60, 131
  See also SAAS 13
Szekessy, Tanja 98
Szpura, Beata 1961- 93
Szudek, Agnes S(usan) P(hilomena) 57
  Brief entry 49
Szulc, Tad 1926-2001 26
Szydlow, Jarl
  See Szydlowski, Mary Vigliante
Szydlowski, Mary Vigliante 1946- 94
Szymanski, Lois 1957- 91

T

Taback, Simms 1932- 170
  Brief entry 36
  Earlier sketches in SATA 40, 104
  See also CLR 100
Taber, Gladys (Bagg) 1899-1980
  Obituary 22
Tabor, Nancy Maria Grande 1949- 161
  Earlier sketch in SATA 89
Tabrah, Ruth Milander 1921- 14
Tackach, James 1953- 123
Tackach, James M.
  See Tackach, James
Tadgell, Nicole 1969- 177
Tafuri, Nancy 1946- 192
  Autobiography Feature 192
  Earlier sketches in SATA 39, 75, 130
  See also CLR 74
  See also SAAS 14
Tagg, Christine Elizabeth 1962- 138
Tagliaferro, Linda 173
Taha, Karen T(erry) 1942- 156
  Earlier sketch in SATA 71
Tai, Sharon O. 1963- 153
Tait, Douglas 1944- 12
Takabayashi, Mari 1960- 156
  Earlier sketch in SATA 115
Takahashi, Rumiko 1957- 163
Takakjian, Portia 1930- 15

Takashima, Misako
  See Misako Rocks!
Takashima, Shizuye 1928- 13
Takayama, Sandi 1962- 106
Takeda, Pete(r M.) 1964- 148
Tal, Eve 1947- 176
Talbert, Marc (Alan) 1953- 154
  Autobiography Feature 154
  Earlier sketches in SATA 68, 99
Talbot, Charlene Joy 1928- 10
Talbot, Toby 1928- 14
Talbott, Hudson 1949- 131
  Earlier sketch in SATA 84
Taliaferro, Dorothy L.
  See Martin, Del
Talifero, Gerald 1950- 75
Talker, T.
  See Rands, William Brighty
Tallarico, Tony 1933- 116
Tallcott, Emogene 10
Tallec, Olivier 1970- 197
Tallis, Robyn
  See Smith, Sherwood
Tallon, Robert 1939- 43
  Brief entry 28
Talmadge, Marian 14
Tamaki, Jillian 1980- 201
Tamar, Erika 1934- 150
  Earlier sketches in SATA 62, 101
Tamarin, Alfred H. 1913-1980 13
Tamburine, Jean 1930- 12
Tames, Richard (Lawrence) 1946- 102
  Earlier sketch in SATA 67
Tamminga, Frederick W(illiam) 1934- 66
Tammuz, Benjamin 1919-1989
  Obituary 63
Tan, Amy 1952- 75
Tan, Amy Ruth
  See Tan, Amy
Tan, Shaun 1974- 198
Tanaka, Beatrice 1932- 76
Tanaka, Shelley 136
Tang, Charles 1948- 81
Tang, Greg 172
Tang, You-Shan 1946- 53
Tania B.
  See Blixen, Karen
Tankard, Jeremy 1973- 191
Tannen, Mary 1943- 37
Tannenbaum, Beulah Goldstein 1916- 3
Tannenbaum, D(onald) Leb 1948- 42
Tanner, Jane 1946- 74
Tanner, Louise S(tickney) 1922-2000 9
Tanobe, Miyuki 1937- 23
Tanselle, Eve 1933- 125
Tapio, Pat Decker
  See Kines, Pat Decker
Tapp, Kathy Kennedy 1949- 88
  Brief entry 50
Tarbescu, Edith 1939- 107
Tarkington, (Newton) Booth 1869-1946 17
Tarpley, Natasha A(nastasia) 1971- 147
Tarr, Judith 1955- 149
  Earlier sketch in SATA 64
Tarry, Ellen 1906- 16
  See also CLR 26
  See also SAAS 16
Tarshis, Jerome 1936- 9
Tarshis, Lauren 187
Tarsky, Sue 1946- 41
Taschek, Karen 1956- 185
Tashjian, Janet 1956- 151
  Earlier sketch in SATA 102
Tashjian, Virginia A. 1921-2008 3
Tasker, James 1908- 9
Tate, Don(ald E.) 159
Tate, Eleanora E. 1948- 191
  Earlier sketches in SATA 38, 94
  See also CLR 37
Tate, Eleanora Elaine
  See Tate, Eleanora E.

Tate, Ellalice
  See Hibbert, Eleanor Alice Burford
Tate, Joan 1922- 86
  Earlier sketch in SATA 9
  See also SAAS 20
Tate, Mary Anne
  See Hale, Arlene
Tate, Nikki 134
Tate, Richard
  See Masters, Anthony (Richard)
Tate, Suzanne 1930- 91
Tatham, Betty 142
Tatham, Campbell
  See Elting, Mary
Tatham, Julie
  See Tatham, Julie Campbell
Tatham, Julie Campbell 1908-1999 80
Tavares, Matt 198
  Earlier sketch in SATA 159
Tavares, Victor 1971- 176
Taves, Isabella 1915- 27
Taylor, Alastair 1959- 130
Taylor, Andrew 1951- 70
Taylor, Andrew John Robert
  See Taylor, Andrew
Taylor, Ann 1782-1866 41
  Brief entry 35
Taylor, Audilee Boyd 1931- 59
Taylor, Barbara J. 1927- 10
Taylor, Ben
  See Strachan, Ian
Taylor, Brooke 205
Taylor, Carl 1937- 14
Taylor, Cheryl Munro 1957- 96
Taylor, Cora (Lorraine) 1936- 103
  Earlier sketch in SATA 64
  See also CLR 63
Taylor, Dave 1948- 78
Taylor, David
  See Taylor, Dave
Taylor, David 1900-1965 10
Taylor, Debbie A. 1955- 169
Taylor, Eleanor 1969- 206
Taylor, Elizabeth 1912-1975 13
Taylor, Florance Walton 9
Taylor, Florence M(arian Tompkins)
  1892-1983 9
Taylor, Gage 1942-2000 87
Taylor, Geoff 1946- 204
Taylor, G.P. 1958(?)- 156
Taylor, Graham Peter
  See Taylor, G.P.
Taylor, Herb(ert Norman, Jr.) 1942-1987 22
  Obituary 54
Taylor, J. David
  See Taylor, Dave
Taylor, Jane 1783-1824 41
  Brief entry 35
Taylor, Jerry D(uncan) 1938- 47
Taylor, John Robert
  See Taylor, Andrew
Taylor, Judy
  See Hough, Judy Taylor
Taylor, Kenneth N. 1917-2005 26
Taylor, Kenneth Nathaniel
  See Taylor, Kenneth N.
Taylor, Kim 180
Taylor, L(ester) B(arbour), Jr. 1932- 27
Taylor, Lois Dwight Cole
  See Cole, Lois Dwight
Taylor, Louise Todd 1939- 47
Taylor, Margaret 1950- 106
Taylor, Mark 1927- 32
  Brief entry 28
Taylor, Mildred D. 1943- 135
  See also CLR 144
  See also SAAS 5
Taylor, Mildred Delois
  See Taylor, Mildred D.
Taylor, Paula (Wright) 1942- 48
  Brief entry 33

Taylor, Robert Lewis 1912-1998 .... *10*
Taylor, Sean 1965- *192*
Taylor, Sydney (Brenner) 1904(?)-1978 .... *28*
    Obituary *26*
    Earlier sketch in SATA *1*
Taylor, Theodore 1921-2006 .... *128*
    Obituary *177*
    Earlier sketches in SATA *5, 54, 83*
    See also CLR *30*
    See also SAAS *4*
Taylor, William 1938- *164*
    Earlier sketches in SATA *78, 113*
    See also CLR *63*
Tazewell, Charles 1900-1972 .... *74*
Tchana, Katrin
    See Tchana, Katrin Hyman
Tchana, Katrin H.
    See Tchana, Katrin Hyman
Tchana, Katrin Hyman 1963- *177*
    Earlier sketch in SATA *125*
Tchekhov, Anton
    See Chekhov, Anton
Tchen, Richard *120*
Tchudi, Stephen N. 1942- *55*
Teague, Bob
    See Teague, Robert
Teague, Mark 1963- *205*
    Earlier sketches in SATA *68, 99, 170*
Teague, Mark Christopher
    See Teague, Mark
Teague, Robert 1929- *32*
    Brief entry *31*
Teal, Val 1902-1997 .... *10*
    Obituary *114*
Teal, Valentine M.
    See Teal, Val
Teale, Edwin Way 1899-1980 .... *7*
    Obituary *25*
Teasdale, Sara 1884-1933 .... *32*
Tebbel, John (William) 1912-2004 .... *26*
Teckentrup, Britta 1969- *200*
Teensma, Lynne Bertrand
    See Bertrand, Lynne
Tee-Van, Helen Damrosch 1893-1976 .... *10*
    Obituary *27*
Tegner, Bruce 1928- *62*
Teitelbaum, Michael 1953- *116*
    Earlier sketch in SATA *59*
Tejima
    See Tejima, Keizaburo
Tejima, Keizaburo 1931- *139*
    See also CLR *20*
Telander, Todd (G.) 1967- *88*
Teleki, Geza 1943- *45*
Telemaque, Eleanor Wong 1934- *43*
Telescope, Tom
    See Newbery, John
Tellis, Annabel 1967- *191*
Temkin, Sara Anne Schlossberg 1913-1996 . *26*
Temko, Florence *13*
Tempest, Margaret Mary 1892-1982
    Obituary *33*
Templar, Maurice
    See Groom, Arthur William
Temple, Arthur
    See Northcott, (William) Cecil
Temple, Charles 1947- *79*
Temple, Frances (Nolting) 1945-1995 .... *85*
Temple, Herbert 1919- *45*
Temple, Paul
    See McConnell, James Douglas Rutherford
Temple, William F(rederick) 1914-1989 .... *107*
Tenggren, Gustaf 1896-1970 .... *18*
    Obituary *26*
Tennant, Kylie
    See Rodd, Kylie Tennant
Tennant, Veronica 1947- *36*
Tenneshaw, S.M.
    See Beaumont, Charles
    and Garrett, Randall
    and Silverberg, Robert

Tenniel, John 1820-1914 .... *74*
    Brief entry *27*
    See also CLR *146*
Tepper, Sheri S. 1929- *113*
Terada, Alice M. 1928- *90*
Terban, Marvin 1940- *54*
    Brief entry *45*
Teresi, Judith M.
    See Goldberger, Judith M.
ter Haar, Jaap 1922- *6*
    See also CLR *15*
Terhune, Albert Payson 1872-1942 .... *15*
Terkel, Susan N(eiburg) 1948- *103*
    Earlier sketch in SATA *59*
Terlouw, Jan (Cornelis) 1931- *30*
Terrell, John Upton 1900-1988
    Obituary *60*
Terrill, Beth *198*
Terrill, Elizabeth
    See Terrill, Beth
Terris, Susan 1937- *77*
    Earlier sketch in SATA *3*
Terry, Luther L(eonidas) 1911-1985 .... *11*
    Obituary *42*
Terry, Margaret
    See Dunnahoo, Terry Janson
Terry, Walter 1913-1982 .... *14*
Terry, Will 1966- *205*
Terzian, James P. 1915- *14*
Tessendorf, K(enneth) C(harles) 1925-2003 . *75*
    Obituary *142*
Tessler, Manya *200*
Tessler, Stephanie Gordon
    See Gordon, Stephanie Jacob
Tester, Sylvia Root 1939- *64*
    Brief entry *37*
Tether, (Cynthia) Graham 1950- *46*
    Brief entry *36*
Tetzner, Lisa 1894-1963 .... *169*
Thach, James Otis 1969- *195*
Thacher, Mary McGrath 1933- *9*
Thackeray, William Makepeace 1811-1863 .. *23*
Thaler, Michael C.
    See Thaler, Mike
Thaler, Mike 1936- *93*
    Brief entry *47*
    Earlier sketch in SATA *56*
Thaler, Shmuel 1958- *126*
    Earlier sketch in SATA *72*
Thamer, Katie 1955- *42*
Thane, Elswyth 1900-1984(?) *32*
Tharp, Louise (Marshall) Hall 1898-1992 ...... *3*
    Obituary *129*
Tharp, Tim 1957- *189*
Thayer, Ernest Lawrence 1863-1940 .... *60*
Thayer, Jane
    See Woolley, Catherine
Thayer, Marjorie 1908-1992 .... *74*
    Brief entry *37*
Thayer, Peter
    See Wyler, Rose
Thelwell, Norman 1923-2004 .... *14*
Themerson, Stefan 1910-1988 .... *65*
Thermes, Jennifer 1966- *155*
Theroux, Paul 1941- *109*
    Earlier sketch in SATA *44*
Theroux, Paul Edward
    See Theroux, Paul
Thesman, Jean *124*
    Earlier sketch in SATA *74*
The Tjong-Khing
    See Khing, T.T.
Thieda, Shirley Ann 1943- *13*
Thiele, Colin 1920-2006 .... *125*
    Earlier sketches in SATA *14, 72*
    See also CLR *27*
    See also SAAS *2*
Thiele, Colin Milton
    See Thiele, Colin
Thiesing, Lisa 1958- *159*
    Earlier sketch in SATA *95*

Thimmesh, Catherine *189*
Thiry, Joan (Marie) 1926- *45*
Thistlethwaite, Miles 1945- *12*
Thollander, Earl 1922- *22*
Thomas, Abigail 1941- *112*
Thomas, Andrea
    See Hill, Margaret (Ohler)
Thomas, Art(hur Lawrence) 1952- *48*
    Brief entry *38*
Thomas, Carroll
    See Ratliff, Thomas M.
    and Shmurak, Carole B.
Thomas, Dylan 1914-1953 .... *60*
Thomas, Dylan Marlais
    See Thomas, Dylan
Thomas, Egbert S.
    See Ellis, Edward S.
Thomas, Estelle Webb 1899-1982 .... *26*
Thomas, Frances 1943- *171*
    Earlier sketch in SATA *92*
Thomas, H. C.
    See Keating, Lawrence A.
Thomas, Ianthe 1951- *139*
    Brief entry *42*
    See also CLR *8*
Thomas, J. F.
    See Fleming, Thomas
Thomas, Jan 1958- *197*
Thomas, Jane Resh 1936- *171*
    Earlier sketches in SATA *38, 90*
Thomas, Jerry D. 1959- *91*
Thomas, Joan Gale
    See Robinson, Joan (Mary) G(ale Thomas)
Thomas, Joyce Carol 1938- *137*
    Autobiography Feature *137*
    Earlier sketches in SATA *40, 78, 123*
    See also CLR *19*
    See also SAAS *7*
Thomas, Lee
    See Floren, Lee
    and Pendleton, Thomas
Thomas, Lowell Jackson, Jr. 1923- *15*
Thomas, Margaret
    See Thomas, Peggy
Thomas, Meredith 1963- *119*
Thomas, Michael
    See Wilks, Michael Thomas
Thomas, Middy 1931- *191*
Thomas, Patricia 1934- *199*
    Earlier sketch in SATA *51*
Thomas, Peggy *174*
Thomas, Rob 1965- *97*
Thomas, Scott 1959- *147*
Thomas, Velma Maia 1955- *171*
Thomas, Vernon (Arthur) 1934- *56*
Thomas, Victoria
    See DeWeese, Thomas Eugene
    and Kugi, Constance Todd
Thomasma, Kenneth R. 1930- *90*
Thomassie, Tynia 1959- *92*
Thompson, Brenda 1935- *34*
Thompson, Carol 1951- *189*
    Earlier sketch in SATA *85*
Thompson, China
    See Lewis, Mary
Thompson, Colin 1942- *198*
    Earlier sketches in SATA *95, 163*
Thompson, David H(ugh) 1941- *17*
Thompson, Eileen
    See Panowski, Eileen Thompson
Thompson, George Selden 1929-1989 .... *73*
    Obituary *63*
    Earlier sketch in SATA *4*
    See also CLR *8*
Thompson, Harlan 1894-1987 .... *10*
    Obituary *53*
Thompson, Hilary 1943- *56*
    Brief entry *49*
Thompson, Joanna Maxwell Pullein
    See Pullein-Thompson, Joanna Maxwell

Thompson, Julian F(rancis) 1927- *155*
  Brief entry *40*
  Earlier sketches in SATA *55, 99*
  See also CLR 24
  See also SAAS *13*
Thompson, K(athryn Carolyn) Dyble
  1952- *82*
Thompson, Kate 1956- *204*
Thompson, Kay 1912(?)-1998 .... *16*
  See also CLR 22
Thompson, Lauren 1962- *200*
  Earlier sketches in SATA *132, 174*
Thompson, Lauren Stevens
  See Thompson, Lauren
Thompson, Megan Lloyd
  See Lloyd, Megan
Thompson, Richard 1951- *184*
Thompson, Ruth Plumly 1891-1976 .... *66*
Thompson, Sharon 1952- *119*
Thompson, Sharon Elaine
  See Thompson, Sharon
Thompson, Stith 1885-1976 .... *57*
  Obituary *20*
Thompson, Vivian L(aubach) 1911- *3*
Thomson, Bill 1963- *187*
Thomson, Celia
  See Lynn, Tracy
Thomson, David (Robert Alexander)
  1914-1988 .... *40*
  Obituary *55*
Thomson, Melissa 1979- *205*
Thomson, Pat 1939- *122*
  Earlier sketch in SATA *77*
Thomson, Peggy 1922- *31*
Thomson, Sarah L. *178*
Thon, Melanie Rae 1957- *132*
Thong, Roseanne *174*
Thorburn, John
  See Goldsmith, John Herman Thorburn
Thorn, John 1947- *59*
Thorndyke, Helen Louise
  See Benson, Mildred
Thorne, Ian
  See May, Julian
Thorne, Jean Wright
  See May, Julian
Thornhill, Jan 1955- *148*
  Earlier sketch in SATA *77*
Thornton, Hall
  See Silverberg, Robert
Thornton, W. B.
  See Burgess, Thornton Waldo
Thornton, Yvonne S(hirley) 1947- *96*
Thorpe, E(ustace) G(eorge) 1916- *21*
Thorpe, J. K.
  See Nathanson, Laura Walther
Thorvall, Kerstin 1925- *13*
Thorvall-Falk, Kerstin
  See Thorvall, Kerstin
Thrasher, Crystal (Faye) 1921- *27*
Threadgall, Colin 1941- *77*
Three Little Pigs
  See Lantz, Francess L(in)
Thum, Gladys 1920- *26*
Thum, Marcella *28*
  Earlier sketch in SATA *3*
Thundercloud, Katherine
  See Witt, Shirley Hill
Thurber, James 1894-1961 .... *13*
Thurber, James Grover
  See Thurber, James
Thurlo, Aimee *161*
Thurlo, David *161*
Thurman, Judith 1946- *33*
Thurman, Mark (Gordon Ian) 1948- *63*
Thwaite, Ann (Barbara Harrop) 1932- *14*
Tibbetts, Peggy *127*
Tibbles, Jean-Paul 1958- *115*
Tibo, Gilles 1951- *107*
  Earlier sketch in SATA *67*
Tiburzi, Bonnie 1948- *65*

Ticheburn, Cheviot
  See Ainsworth, William Harrison
Tichenor, Tom 1923-1992 .... *14*
Tichnor, Richard 1959- *90*
Tichy, William 1924- *31*
Tickle, Jack
  See Chapman, Jane
Tiegreen, Alan F. 1935- *94*
  Brief entry *36*
Tierney, Frank M. 1930- *54*
Tierney, Tom 1928- *113*
Tiffault, Benette W. 1955- *77*
Tiller, Ruth L. 1949- *83*
Tilley, Debbie *190*
Tilly, Nancy 1935- *62*
Tilton, Madonna Elaine 1929- *41*
Tilton, Rafael
  See Tilton, Madonna Elaine
Timberlake, Amy *156*
Timberlake, Carolyn
  See Dresang, Eliza (Carolyn Timberlake)
Timmers, Leo 1970- *190*
Timmins, William F(rederick) *10*
Tinbergen, Niko(laas) 1907-1988
  Obituary *60*
Tincknell, Cathy *194*
Tiner, John Hudson 1944- *32*
Tingle, Dolli (?)-
  See Brackett, Dolli Tingle
Tingle, Rebecca *174*
Tingum, Janice 1958- *91*
Tinkelman, Murray 1933- *12*
Tinkham, Kelly A. *188*
Tinkle, (Julien) Lon 1906-1980 .... *36*
Tinling, Marion (Rose) 1904- *140*
Tipene, Tim 1972- *141*
Tippett, James S(terling) 1885-1958 .... *66*
Tirone Smith, Mary-Ann 1944- *143*
Titlebaum, Ellen *195*
Titler, Dale M(ilton) 1926- *35*
  Brief entry *28*
Titmarsh, Michael Angelo
  See Thackeray, William Makepeace
Titus, Eve 1922- *2*
Tjia, Sherwin 1975- *204*
Tjong Khing, The 1933- *76*
Tobias, Katherine
  See Gottfried, Theodore Mark
Tobias, Tobi 1938- *82*
  Earlier sketch in SATA *5*
  See also CLR 4
Todd, Anne Ophelia
  See Dowden, Anne Ophelia Todd
Todd, Barbara 1961- *173*
Todd, Barbara K(eith) 1917- *10*
Todd, Chuck *195*
Todd, H(erbert) E(atton) 1908-1988 .... *84*
  Earlier sketch in SATA *11*
Todd, Loreto 1942- *30*
Todd, Peter
  See Hamilton, Charles (Harold St. John)
Toews, Miriam 1964- *165*
Tofel, Richard J. 1957- *140*
Toft, Kim Michelle 1960- *170*
Tokunbo, Dimitrea *187*
Tolan, Stephanie S. 1942- *142*
  Earlier sketches in SATA *38, 78*
Toland, John (Willard) 1912-2004 .... *38*
Tolbert, Steve 1944- *143*
Toledo, Francisco 1940- *198*
Toledo, Natalia 1967- *197*
Tolkien, J. R. R. 1892-1973 .... *100*
  Obituary *24*
  Earlier sketches in SATA *2, 32*
  See also CLR 56
Tolkien, John Ronald Reuel
  See Tolkien, J. R. R.
Toll, Emily
  See Cannon, Eileen E(mily)
Toll, Nelly S. 1935- *78*

Tolland, W. R.
  See Heitzmann, William Ray
Tolles, Martha 1921- *76*
  Earlier sketch in SATA *8*
Tolliver, Ruby C(hangos) 1922- *110*
  Brief entry *41*
  Earlier sketch in SATA *55*
Tolmie, Kenneth Donald 1941- *15*
Tolstoi, Lev
  See Tolstoy, Leo
Tolstoy, Leo 1828-1910 .... *26*
Tolstoy, Count Leo
  See Tolstoy, Leo
Tolstoy, Leo Nikolaevich
  See Tolstoy, Leo
Tomalin, Ruth *29*
Tomaselli, Rosa
  See Pausacker, Jenny
Tomecek, Steve *172*
Tomes, Margot (Ladd) 1917-1991 .... *70*
  Brief entry *27*
  Obituary *69*
  Earlier sketch in SATA *36*
Tomey, Ingrid 1943- *77*
Tomfool
  See Farjeon, Eleanor
Tomic, Tomislav 1977- *202*
Tomkins, Jasper
  See Batey, Tom
Tomline, F. Latour
  See Gilbert, W(illiam) S(chwenck)
Tomlinson, Heather *192*
Tomlinson, Jill 1931-1976 .... *3*
  Obituary *24*
Tomlinson, Reginald R(obert) 1885-1979(?)
  Obituary *27*
Tomlinson, Theresa 1946- *165*
  Earlier sketch in SATA *103*
  See also CLR 60
Tommaso, Rich 1970(?)- *200*
Tompert, Ann 1918- *139*
  Earlier sketches in SATA *14, 89*
Tompkins, Troy
  See Cle, Troy
Toner, Raymond John 1908-1986 .... *10*
Tong, Gary S. 1942- *66*
Tong, Paul *188*
Took, Belladonna
  See Chapman, Vera (Ivy May)
Tooke, Louise Mathews 1950- *38*
Tooke, Susan *173*
Toonder, Martin
  See Groom, Arthur William
Toothaker, Roy Eugene 1928- *18*
Tooze, Ruth (Anderson) 1892-1972 .... *4*
Topek, Susan Remick 1955- *78*
Topping, Audrey R(onning) 1928- *14*
Tor, Regina
  See Shekerjian, Regina Tor
Torbert, Floyd James 1922- *22*
Torgersen, Don Arthur 1934- *55*
  Brief entry *41*
Torley, Luke
  See Blish, James
Torrecilla, Pablo 1967- *206*
Torres, Andres Segovia
  See Segovia, Andres
Torres, Daniel 1958- *102*
Torres, John A. 1965- *163*
  Earlier sketch in SATA *94*
Torres, John Albert
  See Torres, John A.
Torres, Laura 1967- *146*
  Earlier sketch in SATA *87*
Torres, Leyla 1960- *155*
Torrey, Rich
  See Torrey, Richard
Torrey, Richard *189*
Torrie, Malcolm
  See Mitchell, Gladys (Maude Winifred)
Toten, Teresa 1955- *99*

Totham, Mary
  See Breinburg, Petronella
Touponce, William F. 1948- *114*
Tournier, Michel 1924- *23*
Tournier, Michel Edouard
  See Tournier, Michel
Towle, Wendy 1963- *79*
Towne, Mary
  See Spelman, Mary
Townley, Rod
  See Townley, Roderick
Townley, Roderick 1942- *177*
Townsend, Brad W. 1962- *91*
Townsend, John Rowe 1922- *132*
  Autobiography Feature *132*
  Earlier sketches in SATA *4, 68*
  See also CLR *2*
  See also SAAS *2*
Townsend, Michael 1981- *194*
Townsend, Sue
  See Townsend, Susan Lilian
Townsend, Susan Lilian 1946- *93*
  Brief entry *48*
  Earlier sketch in SATA *55*
Townsend, Thomas L. 1944- *59*
Townsend, Tom
  See Townsend, Thomas L.
Townsend, Wendy 1962- *201*
Townson, Hazel *134*
Toye, William Eldred 1926- *8*
Traherne, Michael
  See Watkins-Pitchford, Denys James
Trahey, Jane 1923-2000 .... *36*
  Obituary *120*
Trapani, Iza 1954- *116*
  Earlier sketch in SATA *80*
Trapp, Maria Augusta von
  See von Trapp, Maria Augusta
Travers, P(amela) L(yndon) 1899-1996 ...... *100*
  Obituary *90*
  Earlier sketches in SATA *4, 54*
  See also CLR *93*
  See also SAAS *2*
Travis, Lucille *133*
  Earlier sketch in SATA *88*
Treadgold, Mary 1910- *49*
Trease, (Robert) Geoffrey 1909-1998 .... *60*
  Obituary *101*
  Earlier sketch in SATA *2*
  See also CLR *42*
  See also SAAS *6*
Treat, Lawrence 1903-1998 .... *59*
Tredez, Alain 1926- *17*
Tredez, Denise 1930- *50*
Treece, Henry 1912-1966 .... *2*
  See also CLR *2*
Tregarthen, Enys
  See Sloggett, Nellie
Tregaskis, Richard 1916-1973 .... *3*
  Obituary *26*
Treherne, Katie Thamer 1955- *76*
Trell, Max 1900-1996 .... *14*
  Obituary *108*
Tremain, Ruthven 1922- *17*
Trembath, Don 1963- *168*
  Earlier sketch in SATA *96*
Tremens, Del
  See MacDonald, Amy
Trent, Robbie 1894-1988 .... *26*
Trent, Timothy
  See Malmberg, Carl
Treseder, Terry Walton 1956- *68*
Tresilian, (Cecil) Stuart 1891-(?) *40*
Tresselt, Alvin 1916-2000 .... *7*
  See also CLR *30*
Trevino, Elizabeth B(orton) de 1904- *29*
  Earlier sketch in SATA *1*
  See also SAAS *5*
Trevor, Elleston 1920-1995 .... *28*
Trevor, Frances
  See Teasdale, Sara

Trevor, Glen
  See Hilton, James
Trevor, (Lucy) Meriol 1919-2000 .... *113*
  Obituary *122*
  Earlier sketch in SATA *10*
Trewellard, J.M. *195*
Trewellard, Juliet
  See Trewellard, J.M.
Trez, Alain
  See Tredez, Alain
Trez, Denise
  See Tredez, Denise
Trezise, Percy 1923-
  See CLR *41*
Trezise, Percy James
  See Trezise, Percy
Triggs, Tony D. 1946- *70*
Trimble, Marshall I(ra) 1939- *93*
Trimby, Elisa 1948- *47*
  Brief entry *40*
Tring, A. Stephen
  See Meynell, Laurence Walter
Tripp, Eleanor B(aldwin) 1936- *4*
Tripp, Janet 1942- *108*
Tripp, Jenny *188*
Tripp, John
  See Moore, John Travers
Tripp, Nathaniel 1944- *101*
Tripp, Paul 1916-2002 .... *8*
  Obituary *139*
Tripp, Valerie 1951- *168*
  Earlier sketch in SATA *78*
Tripp, Wallace (Whitney) 1940- *31*
Trivelpiece, Laurel 1926- *56*
  Brief entry *46*
Trivett, Daphne Harwood 1940- *22*
Trivizas, Eugene 1946- *84*
Trnka, Jiri 1912-1969 .... *43*
  Brief entry *32*
Trollope, Anthony 1815-1882 .... *22*
Trost, Lucille W(ood) 1938- *149*
  Earlier sketch in SATA *12*
Trott, Betty 1933- *91*
Trotter, Deborah W. *184*
Trotter, Grace V(iolet) 1900-1991 .... *10*
Trottier, Maxine 1950- *175*
  Earlier sketch in SATA *131*
Troughton, Joanna (Margaret) 1947- *37*
Trout, Kilgore
  See Farmer, Philip Jose
Trout, Richard E. *123*
Trudeau, Garretson Beekman
  See Trudeau, G.B.
Trudeau, Garry
  See Trudeau, G.B.
Trudeau, Garry B.
  See Trudeau, G.B.
Trudeau, G.B. 1948- *168*
  Earlier sketch in SATA *35*
Trueit, Trudi
  See Trueit, Trudi Strain
Trueit, Trudi Strain 1963- *179*
Trueman, Matthew *183*
Trueman, Terry 1947- *178*
  Earlier sketch in SATA *132*
Truesdell, Judy
  See Mecca, Judy Truesdell
Truesdell, Sue
  See Truesdell, Susan G.
Truesdell, Susan G. *108*
  Brief entry *45*
Trumbauer, Lisa (Trutkoff) 1963- *149*
Truss, Jan 1925- *35*
Truss, Lynne 1955(?)- *194*
Tryon, Leslie *194*
  Earlier sketch in SATA *139*
Tubb, Jonathan N. 1951- *78*
Tubby, I. M.
  See Kraus, (Herman) Robert
Tucker, Caroline
  See Nolan, Jeannette Covert

Tudor, Edward
  See Browne, Anthony
Tudor, Tasha 1915-2008 .... *160*
  Obituary *205*
  Earlier sketches in SATA *20, 69*
  See also CLR *13*
Tuerk, Hanne 1951- *71*
Tugeau, Jeremy *199*
Tulloch, Richard 1949- *180*
  Earlier sketch in SATA *76*
Tulloch, Richard George
  See Tulloch, Richard
Tulloch, Shirley *169*
Tully, John (Kimberley) 1923- *14*
Tumanov, Vladimir A. 1961- *138*
Tung, Angela 1972- *109*
Tunis, Edwin (Burdett) 1897-1973 .... *28*
  Obituary *24*
  Earlier sketch in SATA *1*
  See also CLR *2*
Tunis, John R(oberts) 1889-1975 .... *37*
  Brief entry *30*
Tunnell, Michael
  See Tunnell, Michael O.
Tunnell, Michael O. 1950- *157*
  Earlier sketch in SATA *103*
Tunnell, Michael O'Grady
  See Tunnell, Michael O.
Tunnicliffe, C(harles) F(rederick)
  1901-1979 .... *62*
Turck, Mary C. 1950- *144*
Turk, Hanne
  See Tuerk, Hanne
Turk, Ruth 1917- *82*
Turkle, Brinton 1915- *79*
  Earlier sketch in SATA *2*
Turlington, Bayly 1919-1977 .... *5*
  Obituary *52*
Turnbull, Agnes Sligh 1888-1982 .... *14*
Turnbull, Ann 1943- *160*
  Earlier sketch in SATA *18*
Turnbull, Ann Christine
  See Turnbull, Ann
Turner, Alice K. 1940- *10*
Turner, Ann 1945- *188*
  Autobiography Feature *188*
  Earlier sketches in SATA *14, 77, 113, 178*
Turner, Ann Warren
  See Turner, Ann
Turner, Bonnie 1932- *75*
Turner, Elizabeth 1774-1846
  See YABC *2*
Turner, Glennette Tilley 1933- *183*
  Earlier sketch in SATA *71*
Turner, Josie
  See Crawford, Phyllis
Turner, Megan Whalen 1965- *174*
  Earlier sketch in SATA *94*
Turner, Philip (William) 1925- *83*
  Earlier sketch in SATA *11*
  See also CLR *89*
  See also SAAS *6*
Turner, Robyn 1947- *77*
Turner, Sheila R.
  See Seed, Sheila Turner
Turngren, Annette 1902(?)-1980
  Obituary *23*
Turngren, Ellen (?)-1964 .... *3*
Turska, Krystyna (Zofia) 1933- *31*
  Brief entry *27*
Turteltaub, H.N.
  See Turtledove, Harry
Turtledove, Harry 1949- *166*
  Earlier sketch in SATA *116*
Turtledove, Harry Norman
  See Turtledove, Harry
Tusa, Tricia 1960- *207*
  Earlier sketches in SATA *72, 111*
Tusiani, Joseph 1924- *45*

Twain, Mark 1835-1910 .... *100*
  See also YABC 2
  See also CLR 66
Tweit, Susan J 1956- *94*
Tweit, Susan Joan
  See Tweit, Susan J
Tweton, D. Jerome 1933- *48*
Twinem, Neecy 1958- *92*
Twohill, Maggie
  See Angell, Judie
Tworkov, Jack 1900-1982 .... *47*
  Obituary *31*
Tyche
  See Papademetriou, Lisa
Tyers, Jenny 1969- *89*
Tyers, Kathy 1952- *82*
Tyler, Anne 1941- *173*
  Earlier sketches in SATA *7, 90*
Tyler, Linda
  See Tyler, Linda W(agner)
Tyler, Linda W(agner) 1952- *65*
Tyler, Vicki 1952- *64*
Tyne, Joel
  See Schembri, Jim
Tyrrell, Frances 1959- *107*

U

Ubell, Earl 1926-2007 .... *4*
  Obituary *182*
Uchida, Yoshiko 1921-1992 .... *53*
  Obituary *72*
  Earlier sketch in SATA *1*
  See also CLR 56
  See also SAAS 1
Udall, Jan Beaney 1938- *10*
Uden, (Bernard Gilbert) Grant 1910- *26*
Uderzo, Albert 1927-
  See CLR 37
Udovic, David 1950- *189*
Udry, Janice May 1928- *152*
  Earlier sketch in SATA *4*
Uegaki, Chieri 1969- *153*
Ueno, Noriko
  See Nakae, Noriko
Ugliano, Natascia *196*
Uhlberg, Myron *174*
Uhlig, Richard 1970- *195*
Uhlig, Susan 1955- *129*
Ulam, S(tanislaw) M(arcin) 1909-1984 .... *51*
Ullman, James Ramsey 1907-1971 .... *7*
Ulm, Robert 1934-1977 .... *17*
Ulmer, Louise 1943- *53*
Ulmer, Wendy K. 1950- *201*
Ulrich, Maureen 1958- *206*
Ulyatt, Kenneth 1920- *14*
Umansky, Kaye 1946- *188*
  Earlier sketch in SATA *158*
Unada
  See Gliewe, Unada (Grace)
Uncle Carter
  See Boucher, (Clarence) Carter
Uncle Eric
  See Maybury, Richard J.
Uncle Gus
  See Rey, H. A.
Uncle Mac
  See McCulloch, Derek (Ivor Breashur)
Uncle Ray
  See Coffman, Ramon Peyton
Uncle Shelby
  See Silverstein, Shel
Underhill, Alice Mertie (Waterman)
  1900-1971 .... *10*
Underhill, Liz 1948- *53*
  Brief entry *49*
Underwood, Deborah 1962- *206*
Unger, Harlow G. 1931- *75*
Unger, Jim 1937- *67*

Ungerer, (Jean) Thomas 1931- *106*
  Earlier sketches in SATA *5, 33*
  See also CLR 77
Ungerer, Tomi 1931-
  See Ungerer, (Jean) Thomas
Unkelbach, Kurt 1913-1992 .... *4*
Unnerstad, Edith (Totterman) 1900-1982 .... *3*
  See also CLR 36
Unobagha, Uzo *139*
Unrau, Ruth 1922- *9*
Unstead, R(obert) J(ohn) 1915-1988 .... *12*
  Obituary *56*
Unsworth, Walt(er) 1928- *4*
Untermeyer, Bryna Ivens 1909-1985 .... *61*
Untermeyer, Louis 1885-1977 .... *37*
  Obituary *26*
  Earlier sketch in SATA *2*
Unwin, David S(torr) 1918- *14*
Unwin, Nora S(picer) 1907-1982 .... *3*
  Obituary *49*
Unzner, Christa 1958- *141*
  Earlier sketch in SATA *80*
Unzner-Fischer, Christa
  See Unzner, Christa
Updale, Eleanor 1953- *175*
Updyke, Rosemary K. 1924- *103*
Upitis, Alvis *109*
Urban, Helle (Denise) 1957- *149*
Urban, Linda *199*
Urbanovic, Jackie *189*
Urbigkit, Cat 1965- *196*
Ure, Jean 1943- *192*
  Autobiography Feature *192*
  Earlier sketches in SATA *48, 78, 129*
  See also CLR 34
  See also SAAS 14
U'Ren, Andrea 1968- *142*
Uris, Leon 1924-2003 .... *49*
  Obituary *146*
Uris, Leon Marcus
  See Uris, Leon
Ursu, Anne *177*
Ury, Allen B. 1954- *98*
Uschan, Michael V. 1948- *129*
Usher, Margo Scegge
  See McHargue, Georgess
Uslan, Michael E. 1951- *169*
Uston, Ken(neth Senzo) 1935-1987 .... *65*
Uttley, Alice Jane 1884-1976 .... *88*
  Obituary *26*
  Earlier sketch in SATA *3*
Uttley, Alison
  See Uttley, Alice Jane
Utz, Lois (Marie) 1932-1986 .... *5*
  Obituary *50*

V

Vaeth, J. Gordon 1921- *17*
Vaeth, Joseph Gordon
  See Vaeth, J. Gordon
Vagin, Vladimir (Vasilevich) 1937- *142*
Vail, Rachel 1966- *201*
  Earlier sketches in SATA *94, 163*
Vainio, Pirkko 1957- *123*
  Earlier sketch in SATA *76*
Valen, Nanine 1950- *21*
Valencak, Hannelore
  See Mayer, Hannelore Valencak
Valens, Amy 1946- *70*
Valens, E(vans) G(ladstone), Jr. 1920-1992 ... *1*
Valentine, Johnny *72*
Valerio, Geraldo 1970- *180*
Valgardson, W. D. 1939- *151*
  Earlier sketch in SATA *101*
Valgardson, William Dempsey
  See Valgardson, W. D.
Valleau, Emily 1925- *51*
Van Abbe, Salaman 1883-1955 .... *18*

Van Allsburg, Chris 1949- *156*
  Earlier sketches in SATA *37, 53, 105*
  See also CLR 113
Van Anrooy, Francine 1924- *2*
Van Anrooy, Frans
  See Van Anrooy, Francine
Vanasse, Deb 1957- *170*
Van Buren, David *203*
Vance, Cynthia *207*
Vance, Eleanor Graham 1908-1985 .... *11*
Vance, Gerald
  See Garrett, Randall
  and Silverberg, Robert
Vance, Marguerite 1889-1965 .... *29*
Vance-Abrams, Cynthia
  See Vance, Cynthia
VanCleave, Janice 1942- *116*
  Autobiography Feature *123*
  Earlier sketch in SATA *75*
Vandenburg, Mary Lou 1943- *17*
Vander Boom, Mae M. *14*
Vander-Els, Betty 1936- *63*
van der Heide, Iris 1970- *183*
van der Linde, Laurel 1952- *78*
van der Meer, Ron 1945- *98*
van de Ruit, John 1975- *199*
Van der Veer, Judy 1912-1982 .... *4*
  Obituary *33*
Vanderwerff, Corrine 1939- *117*
Vander Zee, Ruth *199*
  Earlier sketch in SATA *159*
Vande Velde, Vivian 1951- *141*
  Earlier sketches in SATA *62, 95*
  See also CLR 145
Vandivert, Rita (Andre) 1905-1986 .... *21*
Van Draanen, Wendelin *207*
  Earlier sketch in SATA *122*
Van Dusen, Chris *173*
Van Duyn, Janet 1910- *18*
Van Dyne, Edith
  See Baum, L. Frank
  and Sampson, Emma (Keats) Speed
  and van Zantwijk, Rudolf (Alexander
  Marinus)
Vane, Mitch
  See Vane, Mitchelle
Vane, Mitchelle *176*
van Frankenhuyzen, Gijsbert 1951- *132*
Van Genechten, Guido 1957- *165*
van Haeringen, Annemarie *193*
Van Hook, Beverly H. 1941- *99*
Van Horn, William 1939- *43*
van Hout, Mies 1962- *178*
Van Iterson, S(iny) R(ose) *26*
Van Kampen, Vlasta 1943- *163*
  Earlier sketch in SATA *54*
Van Laan, Nancy 1939- *105*
van Lawick-Goodall, Jane
  See Goodall, Jane
Van Leeuwen, Jean 1937- *141*
  Autobiography Feature *141*
  Earlier sketches in SATA *6, 82, 132*
  See also SAAS 8
van Lhin, Erik
  See del Rey, Lester
van Lieshout, Maria *201*
Van Loon, Hendrik Willem 1882-1944 .... *18*
van Ommen, Sylvia 1978- *186*
VanOosting, James 1951- *170*
Van Orden, M(erton) D(ick) 1921- *4*
Van Patter, Bruce *183*
Van Reek, Wouter *204*
Van Rensselaer, Alexander (Taylor Mason)
  1892-1962 .... *14*
Van Riper, Guernsey, Jr. 1909-1995 .... *3*
van Rossum, Heleen 1962- *174*
Van Rynbach, Iris 1952- *102*
Vansant, Rhonda Joy Edwards 1950- *92*
Van Steenwyk, Elizabeth (Ann) 1928- *89*
  Earlier sketch in SATA *34*

Van Stockum, Hilda 1908-2006 5
  Obituary 179
van Straaten, Harmen 1961- 195
Van Tuyl, Barbara 1940- 11
van Vogt, A(lfred) E(lton) 1912-2000 14
  Obituary 124
Van Wassenhove, Sue 1951- 202
Van Woerkom, Dorothy (O'Brien)
  1924-1996 21
Van Wormer, Joe
  See Van Wormer, Joseph Edward
Van Wormer, Joseph Edward 1913-1998 35
Van Wright, Cornelius 173
Van Zwienen, Ilse Charlotte Koehn
  1929-1991 34
  Brief entry 28
  Obituary 67
Van Zyle, Jon 1942- 176
  Earlier sketch in SATA 84
Varela, Barry 180
Varga, Judy
  See Stang, Judit
Varley, Dimitry V. 1906-1984 10
Varley, Susan 1961- 134
  Earlier sketch in SATA 63
Varon, Sara 195
Vasileva, Tatiana
  See Wassiljewa, Tatjana
Vasiliev, Valery 1949- 80
Vasilieva, Tatiana
  See Wassiljewa, Tatjana
Vasiliu, Mircea 1920- 2
Vass, George 1927- 57
  Brief entry 31
Vaughan, Carter A.
  See Gerson, Noel Bertram
Vaughan, Harold Cecil 1923- 14
Vaughan, Marcia (K.) 1951- 159
  Earlier sketches in SATA 60, 95
Vaughan, Richard 1947- 87
Vaughan, Sam(uel) 1928- 14
Vaughn, Ruth 1935- 14
Vaught, Susan 1965- 195
Vaupel, Robin 198
Vautier, Ghislaine 1932- 53
Vavra, Robert James 1935- 8
Vecsey, George Spencer 1939- 9
Vedral, Joyce L(auretta) 1943- 65
Vega, Denise 174
Vega, Denise B.
  See Vega, Denise
Veglahn, Nancy (Crary) 1937- 5
Vejjajiva, Jane 1963- 189
Velasquez, Eric 192
Velasquez, Gloria 1949- 113
Velasquez, Gloria 1949-
  See Velasquez, Gloria
Velthuijs, Max 1923-2005 110
  Obituary 160
  Earlier sketch in SATA 53
Venable, Alan (Hudson) 1944- 8
Venezia, Mike 1945- 150
Ventura, Anthony
  See Pellowski, Michael (Joseph)
Ventura, Piero (Luigi) 1937- 61
  Brief entry 43
  See also CLR 16
Vequin, Capini
  See Quinn, Elisabeth
Verba, Joan Marie 1953- 78
Verboven, Agnes 1951- 103
verDorn, Bethea (Stewart) 1952- 76
Vere, Ed 197
Verissimo, Erico (Lopes) 1905-1975 113
Verne, Jules 1828-1905 21
  See also CLR 88
Verne, Jules Gabriel
  See Verne, Jules
Verner, Gerald 1897(?)-1980
  Obituary 25

Verney, John 1913-1993 14
  Obituary 75
Verniero, Joan C. 1949- 181
Vernon, (Elda) Louise A(nderson) 1914- 14
Vernon, Rosemary
  See Smith, Susan Vernon
Vernon, Ursula 204
Vernor, D.
  See Casewit, Curtis W(erner)
Verr, Harry Coe
  See Kunhardt, Edith
Verral, Charles Spain 1904-1990 11
  Obituary 65
Verrillo, Erica 1953- 199
Verrillo, Erica F.
  See Verrillo, Erica
Verrone, Robert J. 1935(?)-1984
  Obituary 39
Versace, Marie Teresa Rios 1917- 2
Vertreace, Martha M(odena) 1945- 78
Vesey, A(manda) 1939- 62
Vesey, Mark (David) 1958- 123
Vesey, Paul
  See Allen, Samuel W(ashington)
Vestergaard, Hope 178
Vestly, Anne-Cath(arina) 1920- 14
  See also CLR 99
Vevers, (Henry) Gwynne 1916-1988 45
  Obituary 57
Viator, Vacuus
  See Hughes, Thomas
Vicar, Henry
  See Felsen, Henry Gregor
Vick, Helen Hughes 1950- 88
Vicker, Angus
  See Felsen, Henry Gregor
Vickers, Sheena 1960- 94
Vickery, Kate
  See Kennedy, T.A.
Victor, Edward 1914- 3
Victor, Joan Berg 1942- 30
Vidrine, Beverly Barras 1938- 188
  Earlier sketch in SATA 103
Viereck, Ellen K. 1928- 14
Viereck, Phillip 1925- 3
Viertel, Janet 1915- 10
Vigliante, Mary
  See Szydlowski, Mary Vigliante
Vigna, Judith 1936- 102
  Earlier sketch in SATA 15
Viguers, Ruth Hill 1903-1971 6
Vila, Laura 207
Villareal, Ray 187
Villasenor, Edmund
  See Villasenor, Victor E.
Villasenor, Edmundo
  See Villasenor, Victor E.
Villasenor, Victor
  See Villasenor, Victor E.
Villasenor, Victor E. 1940- 171
Villasenor, Victor Edmundo
  See Villasenor, Victor E.
Villiard, Paul 1910-1974 51
  Obituary 20
Villiers, Alan (John) 1903-1982 10
Vilott, Rhondi
  See Salsitz, Rhondi Vilott
Vincent, Eric Douglas 1953- 40
Vincent, Erin 1969- 188
Vincent, Felix 1946- 41
Vincent, Gabrielle 1928-2000 121
  Earlier sketch in SATA 61
  See also CLR 13
Vincent, Mary Keith
  See St. John, Wylly Folk
Vincent, William R.
  See Heitzmann, William Ray
Vinegar, Tom
  See Gregg, Andrew K.
Vinest, Shaw
  See Longyear, Barry B(rookes)

Vinge, Joan (Carol) D(ennison) 1948- 113
  Earlier sketch in SATA 36
Vining, Elizabeth Gray 1902-1999 6
  Obituary 117
Vinson, Kathryn 1911-1995 21
Vinton, Iris 1906(?)-1988 24
  Obituary 55
Viola, Herman J(oseph) 1938- 126
Viorst, Judith 1931- 172
  Earlier sketches in SATA 7, 70, 123
  See also CLR 90
Vip
  See Partch, Virgil Franklin II
Vipont, Charles
  See Foulds, Elfrida Vipont
Vipont, Elfrida
  See Foulds, Elfrida Vipont
Viramontes, Helena Maria 1954-
  See CLR 285
Viscott, David S(teven) 1938-1996 65
Visser, W(illem) F(rederik) H(endrik)
  1900-1968 10
Vitale, Stefano 1958- 180
  Earlier sketch in SATA 114
Vivas, Julie 1947- 96
Vivelo, Jackie 1943- 63
Vivelo, Jacqueline J.
  See Vivelo, Jackie
Vivelo, Jacqueline Jean
  See Vivelo, Jackie
Vizzini, Ned 1981- 179
  Earlier sketch in SATA 125
Vlahos, Olivia 1924- 31
Vlasic, Bob
  See Hirsch, Phil
Voake, Charlotte 180
  Earlier sketch in SATA 114
Voake, Steve 1961- 178
Vo-Dinh, Mai 1933- 16
Vogel, Carole Garbuny 1951- 105
  Earlier sketch in SATA 70
Vogel, Ilse-Margret 1918- 14
Vogel, John H., Jr. 1950- 18
Vogt, Esther Loewen 1915-1999 14
Vogt, Gregory L. 94
Vogt, Marie Bollinger 1921- 45
Vohwinkel, Astrid 1969- 207
Voight, Virginia Frances 1909-1989 8
Voigt, Cynthia 1942- 160
  Brief entry 33
  Earlier sketches in SATA 48, 79, 116
  See also CLR 141
Voigt, Erna 1925- 35
Voigt-Rother, Erna
  See Voigt, Erna
Vojtech, Anna 1946- 108
  Earlier sketch in SATA 42
Vollstadt, Elizabeth Weiss 1942- 121
Volponi, Paul 175
Volting, Dr. R.E.
  See Lerangis, Peter
Von Ahnen, Katherine 1922- 93
von Buhler, Cynthia 185
Vondra, J. Gert
  See Vondra, Josef
Vondra, Josef 1941- 121
Vondra, Josef Gert
  See Vondra, Josef
Von Gunden, Kenneth 1946- 113
Von Hagen, Victor Wolfgang 1908-1985 29
von Klopp, Vahrah
  See Malvern, Gladys
von Schmidt, Eric 1931-2007 50
  Brief entry 36
  Obituary 181
von Storch, Anne B. 1910- 1
von Trapp, Maria Augusta 1905-1987 16
von Wodtke, Charlotte Buel Johnson
  1918-1982 46
von Ziegesar, Cecily 1970- 161

Vos, Ida 1931-2006 121
  Earlier sketch in SATA 69
  See also CLR 85
Vosburgh, Leonard (W.) 1912- 15
Votaw, Carol 1961- 201
Voyle, Mary
  See Manning, Rosemary
Vrettos, Adrienne Maria 187
Vriens, Jacques 1946- 151
Vugteveen, Verna Aardema
  See Aardema, Verna
Vulture, Elizabeth T.
  See Gilbert, Suzie
Vuong, Lynette Dyer 1938- 110
  Earlier sketch in SATA 60

W

Waas, Uli
  See Waas-Pommer, Ulrike
Waas-Pommer, Ulrike 1949- 85
Waber, Bernard 1924- 155
  Brief entry 40
  Earlier sketches in SATA 47, 95
  See also CLR 55
Wachtel, Shirley Russak 1951- 88
Wachter, Oralee (Roberts) 1935- 61
  Brief entry 51
Waddell, Evelyn Margaret 1918- 10
Waddell, Martin 1941- 129
  Autobiography Feature 129
  Earlier sketches in SATA 43, 81, 127
  See also CLR 31
  See also SAAS 15
Waddy, Lawrence (Heber) 1914- 91
Wade, Mary Dodson 1930- 151
  Earlier sketch in SATA 79
Wade, Suzanne
  See Kirby, Susan E.
Wade, Theodore E., Jr. 1936- 37
Wademan, Peter John 1946- 122
Wademan, Spike
  See Wademan, Peter John
Wadsworth, Ginger 1945- 157
  Earlier sketch in SATA 103
Wagenheim, Kal 1935- 21
Wagner, Michele R. 1975- 157
Wagner, Sharon B. 1936- 4
Wagoner, David (Russell) 1926- 14
Wahl, Jan (Boyer) 1933- 132
  Earlier sketches in SATA 2, 34, 73
  See also SAAS 3
Wahl, Mats 1945- 186
Waide, Jan 1952- 29
Wainscott, John Milton 1910-1981 53
Wainwright, Richard M. 1935- 91
Wainwright, Ruth
  See Symes, Ruth Louise
Wait, Lea 1946- 137
Waite, Judy 174
Waite, Judy Bernard
  See Bernard, Patricia
Waite, Michael
  See Waite, Michael P.
Waite, Michael P. 1960- 101
Waite, P(eter) B(usby) 1922- 64
Waites, Joan C. 187
Waitley, Douglas 1927- 30
Wakefield, Jean L.
  See Laird, Jean E(louise)
Wakin, Daniel (Joseph) 1961- 84
Wakin, Edward 1927- 37
Wakiyama, Hanako 1966- 192
Walck, Henry Z. 1908(?)-1984
  Obituary 40
Walden, Amelia Elizabeth 3
Walden, Mark 188
Waldherr, Kris 1963- 76
Waldman, Bruce 1949- 15

Waldman, Neil 1947- 203
  Earlier sketches in SATA 51, 94, 142
Waldrep, Richard 198
Waldron, Ann Wood 1924- 16
Waldron, Kathleen Cook 176
Wales, Dirk 1931- 205
Walgren, Judy 1963- 118
Walker, Addison
  See Walker, (Addison) Mort
Walker, Alice 1944- 31
Walker, Alice Malsenior
  See Walker, Alice
Walker, Barbara (Jeanne) K(erlin) 1921- 80
  Earlier sketch in SATA 4
Walker, Barbara M(uhs) 1928- 57
Walker, (James) Braz(elton) 1934-1983 45
Walker, David 1965- 197
Walker, David G(ordon) 1926- 60
Walker, David Harry 1911-1992 8
  Obituary 71
Walker, Diana 1925- 9
Walker, Diane Marie Catherine
  See Walker, Kate
Walker, Dick
  See Pellowski, Michael (Joseph)
Walker, Frank 1931-2000 36
Walker, Holly Beth
  See Bond, Gladys Baker
Walker, Kate 1950- 165
  Earlier sketch in SATA 82
Walker, Kathrine Sorley
  See Sorley Walker, Kathrine
Walker, Lou Ann 1952- 66
  Brief entry 53
Walker, Louise Jean 1891-1976
  Obituary 35
Walker, Mary Alexander 1927- 61
Walker, Mildred
  See Schemm, Mildred Walker
Walker, (Addison) Mort 1923- 8
Walker, Pamela 1948- 142
  Earlier sketch in SATA 24
Walker, Paul Robert 1953- 154
Walker, Robert W. 1948- 66
Walker, Sally M(acArt) 1954- 135
Walker, Stephen J. 1951- 12
Walker-Blondell, Becky 1951- 89
Wallace, Barbara Brooks 1922- 136
  Earlier sketches in SATA 4, 78
  See also SAAS 17
Wallace, Beverly Dobrin 1921- 19
Wallace, Bill 1947- 169
  Brief entry 47
  Earlier sketches in SATA 53, 101
Wallace, Daisy
  See Cuyler, Margery
Wallace, Ian 1950- 141
  Earlier sketches in SATA 53, 56
  See also CLR 37
Wallace, John 1966- 155
  Earlier sketch in SATA 105
Wallace, John A(dam) 1915-2004 3
  Obituary 155
Wallace, Karen 1951- 188
  Earlier sketches in SATA 83, 139
Wallace, Nancy Elizabeth 1948- 186
  Earlier sketch in SATA 141
Wallace, Nigel
  See Hamilton, Charles (Harold St. John)
Wallace, Paula S. 153
Wallace, Rich 1957- 196
  Earlier sketches in SATA 117, 158
Wallace, Robert 1932-1999 47
  Brief entry 37
Wallace, Ruby Ann 1923(?)- 77
Wallace, William Keith
  See Wallace, Bill
Wallace-Brodeur, Ruth 1941- 169
  Brief entry 41
  Earlier sketches in SATA 51, 88
Wallenta, Adam 1974- 123

Waller, Leslie 1923-2007 20
Walley, Byron
  See Card, Orson Scott
Wallis, Diz 1949- 77
Wallis, G. McDonald
  See Campbell, Hope
Wallner, Alexandra 1946- 156
  Brief entry 41
  Earlier sketches in SATA 51, 98
Wallner, John C. 1945- 133
  Earlier sketches in SATA 10, 51
Wallower, Lucille 11
Walrod, Amy 1973(?)- 182
Walsh, Ann 1942- 176
  Earlier sketch in SATA 62
Walsh, Ellen Stoll 1942- 194
  Earlier sketches in SATA 49, 99, 147
Walsh, George Johnston 1889-1981 53
Walsh, Gillian Paton
  See Paton Walsh, Jill
Walsh, Jill Paton
  See Paton Walsh, Jill
Walsh, Joanna 1970- 182
Walsh, Lawrence 1942- 170
Walsh, Marissa 1972- 195
Walsh, Mary Caswell 1949- 118
Walsh, Mitzy
  See Walsh, Marissa
Walsh, Suella 170
Walsh, V. L.
  See Walsh, Vivian
Walsh, Vivian 1960- 120
Walsh Shepherd, Donna 1948- 78
Walter, Frances V. 1923- 71
Walter, Mildred Pitts 1922- 133
  Brief entry 45
  Earlier sketch in SATA 69
  See also CLR 61
  See also SAAS 12
Walter, Villiam Christian
  See Andersen, Hans Christian
Walter, Virginia
  See Walter, Virginia A.
Walter, Virginia A. 134
Walters, Audrey 1929- 18
Walters, Celeste 1938- 126
Walters, Eric 1957- 205
  Earlier sketches in SATA 99, 155
Walters, Eric Robert
  See Walters, Eric
Walters, Helen B. (?)-1987
  Obituary 50
Walters, Hugh
  See Hughes, Walter (Llewellyn)
Walther, Thomas A. 1950- 31
Walther, Tom
  See Walther, Thomas A.
Waltner, Elma 1912-1987 40
Waltner, Willard H. 1909- 40
Walton, Darwin McBeth 1926- 119
Walton, Fiona L. M. 1959- 89
Walton, Richard J. 1928- 4
Walton, Rick 1957- 204
  Earlier sketches in SATA 101, 151
Waltrip, Lela (Kingston) 1904-1995 9
Waltrip, Mildred 1911- 37
Waltrip, Rufus (Charles) 1898-1988 9
Walworth, Nancy Zinsser 1917- 14
Wangerin, Walter, Jr. 1944- 98
  Brief entry 37
  Earlier sketch in SATA 45
Waniek, Marilyn Nelson 1946-
  See Nelson, Marilyn
Wannamaker, Bruce
  See Moncure, Jane Belk
Warbler, J. M.
  See Cocagnac, Augustin Maurice(-Jean)
Warburg, Sandol Stoddard
  See Stoddard, Sandol

Ward, E. D.
   See Gorey, Edward (St. John)
   and Lucas, E(dward) V(errall)
Ward, Ed
   See Stratemeyer, Edward L.
Ward, Helen 1962- 206
   Earlier sketches in SATA 72, 144
Ward, Jay 1920-1989
   Obituary 63
Ward, Jennifer 1963- 146
Ward, John (Stanton) 1917- 42
Ward, Jonas
   See Ard, William
   and Cox, William R(obert)
   and Garfield, Brian (Francis Wynne)
Ward, Lynd (Kendall) 1905-1985 36
   Obituary 42
   Earlier sketch in SATA 2
Ward, Martha (Eads) 5
Ward, Melanie
   See Curtis, Richard
   and Lynch, Marilyn
Ward, Nicholas John
   See Ward, Nick
Ward, Nick 1955- 190
Ward, Tom
   See Stratemeyer, Edward L.
Wardell, Dean
   See Prince, J(ack) H(arvey)
Wardlaw, Lee 1955- 115
   Earlier sketch in SATA 79
Ware, Cheryl 1963- 101
Ware, Chris 1967- 140
Ware, Leon (Vernon) 1909-1976 4
Wargin, Kathy-jo 1964- 145
Warhola, James 1955- 187
Warner, Frank A. 67
   Earlier sketch in SATA 1
Warner, Gertrude Chandler 1890-1979 9
   Obituary 73
Warner, J(ohn) F. 1929- 75
Warner, Lucille Schulberg 30
Warner, Matt
   See Fichter, George S.
Warner, Oliver (Martin Wilson) 1903-1976 . 29
Warner, Sally 1946- 131
Warner, Sunny (B.) 1931- 108
Warnes, Tim 1971- 166
   Earlier sketch in SATA 116
Warnes, Timothy
   See Warnes, Tim
Warnick, Elsa 1942- 113
Warren, Andrea 1946- 98
Warren, Betsy
   See Warren, Elizabeth Avery
Warren, Billy
   See Warren, William Stephen
Warren, Cathy 1951- 62
   Brief entry 46
Warren, Elizabeth
   See Supraner, Robyn
Warren, Elizabeth Avery 1916- 46
   Brief entry 38
Warren, Jackie M. 1953- 135
Warren, Joshua P(aul) 1976- 107
Warren, Joyce W(illiams) 1935- 18
Warren, Mary Phraner 1929- 10
Warren, Robert Penn 1905-1989 46
   Obituary 63
Warren, Scott S. 1957- 79
Warren, William Stephen 1882-1968 9
Warrick, Patricia Scott 1925- 35
Warriner, John 1907(?)-1987
   Obituary 53
Warsh
   See Warshaw, Jerry
Warshaw, Jerry 1929- 30
Warshaw, Mary 1931- 89
Warshofsky, Fred 1931- 24
Warshofsky, Isaac
   See Singer, Isaac Bashevis

Wartski, Maureen (Ann Crane) 1940- 50
   Brief entry 37
Warwick, Alan R(oss) 1900-1973 42
Wa-Sha-Quon-Asin
   See Belaney, Archibald Stansfeld
Wa-sha-quon-asin
   See Belaney, Archibald Stansfeld
Washburn, Bradford 1910-2007 38
   Obituary 181
Washburn, Henry Bradford, Jr.
   See Washburn, Bradford
Washburn, Jan(ice) 1926- 63
Washburn, Lucia 193
Washburne, Carolyn Kott 1944- 86
Washburne, Heluiz Chandler 1892-1970 10
   Obituary 26
Washington, Booker T. 1856-1915 28
Washington, Donna L. 1967- 159
   Earlier sketch in SATA 98
Wasserman, Robin 1978- 207
Wasserstein, Wendy 1950-2006 94
   Obituary 174
Wassiljewa, Tatjana 1928- 106
Watanabe, Shigeo 1928- 131
   Brief entry 32
   Earlier sketch in SATA 39
   See also CLR 8
Waters, John F(rederick) 1930- 4
Waters, Summer
   See Sykes, Julie
Waters, Tony 1958- 75
Waterton, Betty 1923- 99
   Brief entry 34
   Earlier sketch in SATA 37
Waterton, Betty Marie
   See Waterton, Betty
Watkins, Dawn L. 126
Watkins, Gloria Jean
   See hooks, bell
Watkins, Lois 1930- 88
Watkins, Peter 1934- 66
Watkins, Yoko Kawashima 1933- 93
Watkins-Pitchford, Denys James
   1905-1990 87
   Obituary 66
   Earlier sketch in SATA 6
   See also SAAS 4
Watling, James 1933- 117
   Earlier sketch in SATA 67
Watson, Aldren A(uld) 1917- 42
   Brief entry 36
Watson, Amy Zakrzewski 1965- 76
Watson, B. S.
   See Teitelbaum, Michael
Watson, Carol 1949- 78
Watson, C.G. 193
Watson, Clyde 1947- 68
   Earlier sketch in SATA 5
   See also CLR 3
Watson, Helen Orr 1892-1978
   Obituary 24
Watson, James 1936- 106
   Earlier sketch in SATA 10
Watson, Jane Werner 1915- 54
   Earlier sketch in SATA 3
Watson, Jesse Joshua 199
Watson, John H.
   See Farmer, Philip Jose
Watson, Mary 1953- 117
Watson, N. Cameron 1955- 81
Watson, Nancy Dingman 32
Watson, Pauline 1925- 14
Watson, Richard F.
   See Silverberg, Robert
Watson, Richard Jesse 1951- 62
Watson, Sally (Lou) 1924- 3
Watson, Wendy (McLeod) 1942- 142
   Earlier sketches in SATA 5, 74
Watson Taylor, Elizabeth 1915- 41
Watt, Melanie 1975- 193
   Earlier sketch in SATA 136

Watt, Thomas 1935- 4
Wattenberg, Jane 174
Watterson, Bill 1958- 66
Watt-Evans, Lawrence 1954- 121
Watts, (Anna) Bernadette 1942- 103
   Earlier sketch in SATA 4
Watts, Ephraim
   See Horne, Richard Henry Hengist
Watts, Franklin (Mowry) 1904-1978 46
   Obituary 21
Watts, Helen L. Hoke 1903-1990
   Obituary 65
Watts, Irene N(aemi) 1931- 111
   Earlier sketch in SATA 56
Watts, Isaac 1674-1748 52
Watts, James K(ennedy) M(offitt) 1955- 59
Watts, Jeri Hanel 1957- 170
Watts, Julia 1969- 103
Watts, Leander 1956- 146
Watts, Leslie Elizabeth 1961- 168
Watts, Mabel Pizzey 1906-1994 11
Watts, Nigel 1957-1999 121
Waugh, C. C. Roessel
   See Waugh, Carol-Lynn Rossel
   and Waugh, Charles G(ordon)
Waugh, Carol-Lynn Rossel 1947- 41
Waugh, Dorothy -1996 11
Waugh, Sylvia 1935- 169
Waugh, Virginia
   See Sorensen, Virginia
Wax, Wendy A. 1963- 163
   Earlier sketch in SATA 73
Wayland, April Halprin 1954- 143
   Earlier sketch in SATA 78
   See also SAAS 26
Wayland, Patrick
   See O'Connor, Richard
Wayne, (Anne) Jenifer 1917-1982 32
Wayne, Kyra Petrovskaya 1918- 8
Wayne, Richard
   See Decker, Duane
Wayshak, Deborah Noyes
   See Noyes, Deborah
Waystaff, Simon
   See Swift, Jonathan
Weales, Gerald (Clifford) 1925- 11
Weary, Ogdred
   See Gorey, Edward (St. John)
Weatherford, Carole Boston 1956- 181
   Earlier sketch in SATA 138
Weatherill, Cat 203
Weatherly, Lee 1967- 192
Weatherly, Myra 1926- 130
Weatherly, Myra S.
   See Weatherly, Myra
Weaver, Harriett E. 1908-1993 65
Weaver, John L. 1949- 42
Weaver, Robyn
   See Conley, Robyn
Weaver, Robyn M.
   See Conley, Robyn
Weaver, Tess 197
Weaver, Ward
   See Mason, F(rancis) van Wyck
Weaver, Will 1950- 161
   Earlier sketches in SATA 88, 109
Weaver, William Weller
   See Weaver, Will
Weaver-Gelzer, Charlotte 1950- 79
Webb, Christopher
   See Wibberley, Leonard
Webb, Jacqueline
   See Pearce, Margaret
Webb, Jacquelyn
   See Pearce, Margaret
   and Pearce, Margaret
Webb, Jean Francis (III) 1910-1991 35
Webb, Kaye 1914- 60
Webb, Lois Sinaiko 1922- 82
Webb, Margot 1934- 67
Webb, Sharon 1936- 41

Webb, Sophie 1958- *135*
Webber, Andrew Lloyd
    See Lloyd Webber, Andrew
Webber, Desiree Morrison 1956- *170*
Webber, Irma E(leanor Schmidt)
    1904-1995 .... *14*
Weber, Alfons 1921- *8*
Weber, Bruce 1942- *120*
    Earlier sketch in SATA *73*
Weber, Debora 1955- *58*
Weber, EdNah New Rider 1919(?)- *168*
Weber, Jill 1950- *127*
Weber, Judith E(ichler) 1938- *64*
Weber, Ken(neth J.) 1940- *90*
Weber, Lenora Mattingly 1895-1971 .... *2*
    Obituary *26*
Weber, Michael 1945- *87*
Weber, Sandra 1961- *158*
Weber, William J(ohn) 1927- *14*
Webster, Alice Jane Chandler 1876-1916 ..... *17*
Webster, David 1930- *11*
Webster, Frank V. *67*
    Earlier sketch in SATA *1*
Webster, Gary
    See Garrison, Webb B(lack)
Webster, James 1925-1981 .... *17*
    Obituary *27*
Webster, Jean
    See Webster, Alice Jane Chandler
Wechsler, Doug *189*
Wechsler, Herman J. 1904-1976
    Obituary *20*
Wechter, Nell (Carolyn) Wise 1913-1989 .. *127*
    Earlier sketch in SATA *60*
Weck, Thomas L. 1942- *62*
Wedd, Kate
    See Gregory, Philippa
Weddle, Ethel Harshbarger 1897-1996 .... *11*
Wedekind, Annie *204*
Weeks, Sarah *194*
    Earlier sketch in SATA *158*
Weems, David B(urnola) 1922- *80*
Wees, Frances Shelley 1902-1982 .... *58*
Weevers, Peter 1944- *59*
Wegen, Ronald 1946-1985 .... *99*
Wegman, William (George) 1943- *135*
    Earlier sketches in SATA *78, 129*
Wegner, Fritz 1924- *20*
Weidhorn, Manfred 1931- *60*
Weidt, Maryann N. 1944- *85*
Weigel, Jeff 1958- *170*
Weigelt, Udo 1960- *201*
    Earlier sketch in SATA *168*
Weihs, Erika 1917- *107*
    Earlier sketch in SATA *15*
Weik, Mary Hays 1898(?)-1979 .... *3*
    Obituary *23*
Weil, Ann Yezner 1908-1969 .... *9*
Weil, Lisl 1910- *7*
Weilerstein, Sadie Rose 1894-1993 .... *3*
    Obituary *75*
Weill, Cynthia 1959- *167*
Wein, Elizabeth E(ve) 1964- *151*
    Earlier sketch in SATA *82*
Weinberg, Larry
    See Weinberg, Lawrence (E.)
Weinberg, Lawrence (E.) *92*
    Brief entry *48*
Weinberger, Tanya 1939- *84*
Weiner, Sandra 1922- *14*
Weingarten, Violet (Brown) 1915-1976 .... *3*
    Obituary *27*
Weingartner, Charles 1922- *5*
Weinheimer, Beckie 1958- *186*
Weinstein, Ellen Slusky 1959- *200*
Weinstein, Nina 1951- *73*
Weinstock, Robert 1967- *204*
Weir, Bob 1947- *76*
Weir, Diana (R.) Loiewski 1958- *111*
Weir, Joan S(herman) 1928- *99*
Weir, LaVada *2*

Weir, Rosemary (Green) 1905-1994 .... *21*
Weir, Wendy 1949- *76*
Weis, Margaret 1948- *164*
    Earlier sketches in SATA *38, 92*
Weisberger, Bernard A(llen) 1922- *21*
Weisburd, Stefi 1957- *202*
Weiser, Marjorie P(hillis) K(atz) 1934- *33*
Weisgard, Leonard (Joseph) 1916-2000 .... *85*
    Obituary *122*
    Earlier sketches in SATA *2, 30*
    See also SAAS *19*
Weiss, Adelle 1920- *18*
Weiss, Ann E(dwards) 1943- *69*
    Earlier sketch in SATA *30*
    See also SAAS *13*
Weiss, Edna
    See Barth, Edna
Weiss, Ellen 1953- *44*
Weiss, Harvey 1922- *76*
    Earlier sketches in SATA *1, 27*
    See also CLR *4*
    See also SAAS *19*
Weiss, Jaqueline Shachter 1926- *65*
Weiss, Malcolm E. 1928- *3*
Weiss, Margaret Edith
    See Weis, Margaret
Weiss, Miriam
    See Schlein, Miriam
Weiss, Mitch 1951- *183*
    Earlier sketch in SATA *123*
Weiss, Nicki 1954- *86*
    Earlier sketch in SATA *33*
Weiss, Renee Karol 1923- *5*
Weissberger, Ela 1930- *181*
Weissberger, Ela Stein
    See Weissberger, Ela
Weissenborn, Hellmuth 1898-1982
    Obituary *31*
Weitzman, David L. 1936- *172*
    Earlier sketch in SATA *122*
Wekesser, Carol A. 1963- *76*
Welber, Robert *26*
Welch, Amanda (Jane) 1945- *75*
Welch, D'Alte Aldridge 1907-1970
    Obituary *27*
Welch, Holly *206*
Welch, Jean-Louise
    See Kempton, Jean Welch
Welch, Pauline
    See Bodenham, Hilda Morris
Welch, Ronald
    See Felton, Ronald Oliver
Welch, Sheila Kelly 1945- *130*
Welch, Willy 1952- *93*
Weldin, Frauke 1969- *188*
Welford, Sue 1942- *75*
Weller, George 1907-2002 .... *31*
    Obituary *140*
Weller, George Anthony
    See Weller, George
Welling, Peter J. 1947- *135*
Wellington, Monica 1957- *157*
    Earlier sketches in SATA *67, 99*
Wellman, Alice 1900-1984 .... *51*
    Brief entry *36*
Wellman, Manly Wade 1903-1986 .... *6*
    Obituary *47*
Wellman, Paul I. 1898-1966 .... *3*
Wellman, Paul Iselin
    See Wellman, Paul I.
Wellman, Sam(uel) 1939- *122*
Wells, H. G. 1866-1946 .... *20*
    See also CLR *133*
Wells, Helen
    See Campbell, Hope
Wells, Helen 1910-1986 .... *49*
    Earlier sketch in SATA *2*
Wells, Herbert George
    See Wells, H. G.
Wells, J. Wellington
    See de Camp, L. Sprague

Wells, June
    See Swinford, Betty (June Wells)
Wells, Robert
    See Welsch, Roger L(ee)
Wells, Robert E. *184*
Wells, Rosemary 1943- *207*
    Earlier sketches in SATA *18, 69, 114, 156*
    See also CLR *69*
    See also SAAS *1*
Wells, Susan (Mary) 1951- *78*
Wels, Byron G(erald) 1924-1993 .... *9*
Welsbacher, Anne 1955- *89*
Welsch, Roger L(ee) 1936- *82*
Welsh, David
    See Hills, C.A.R.
Welsh, Mary Flynn 1910(?)-1984
    Obituary *38*
Welsh, T.K. 1956- *184*
Weltner, Linda R(iverly) 1938- *38*
Welton, Jude 1955- *143*
    Earlier sketch in SATA *79*
Welty, S. F.
    See Welty, Susan F.
Welty, Susan F. 1905- *9*
Wemmlinger, Raymond *190*
Wendelin, Rudolph 1910-2000 .... *23*
Weninger, Brigitte 1960- *189*
Wentworth, Robert
    See Hamilton, Edmond
Werlin, Nancy 1961- *161*
    Earlier sketches in SATA *87, 119*
Werner, Elsa Jane
    See Watson, Jane Werner
Werner, Herma 1926- *47*
    Brief entry *41*
Werner, Jane
    See Watson, Jane Werner
Werner, K.
    See Casewit, Curtis W(erner)
Wersba, Barbara 1932- *58*
    Autobiography Feature *103*
    Earlier sketch in SATA *1*
    See also CLR *78*
    See also SAAS *2*
Werstein, Irving 1914(?)-1971 .... *14*
Werth, Kurt 1896-1983 .... *20*
Wesley, Alison
    See Barnes, Michael
Wesley, Kathryn
    See Rusch, Kristine Kathryn
Wesley, Mary (Aline) 1912-2002 .... *66*
Wesley, Valerie Wilson 1947- *168*
    Earlier sketch in SATA *106*
West, Andrew
    See Arthur, Robert, (Jr.)
West, Anna 1938- *40*
West, Barbara
    See Price, Olive
West, Betty 1921- *11*
West, Bruce 1951- *63*
West, C. P.
    See Wodehouse, P. G.
West, Dorothy
    See Benson, Mildred
West, Emily Govan 1919- *38*
West, Emmy
    See West, Emily Govan
West, James
    See Withers, Carl A.
West, Jerry
    See Svenson, Andrew E(dward)
West, (Mary) Jessamyn 1902-1984
    Obituary *37*
West, John
    See Arthur, Robert, (Jr.)
West, Owen
    See Koontz, Dean
West, Ward
    See Borland, Harold Glen

Westall, Robert (Atkinson) 1929-1993 .... *69*
  Obituary *75*
  Earlier sketch in SATA *23*
  See also CLR *13*
  See also SAAS *2*
Westaway, Jane 1948- *121*
Westcott, Nadine Bernard 1949- *130*
Westera, Marleen 1962- *187*
Westerberg, Christine 1950- *29*
Westerduin, Anne 1945- *105*
Westerfeld, Scott 1963- *161*
Westervelt, Virginia Veeder 1914-2005 .... *10*
Westheimer, David 1917-2005 .... *14*
  Obituary *170*
Westheimer, David Kaplan
  See Westheimer, David
Westmacott, Mary
  See Christie, Agatha
Westman, Barbara *70*
Westman, Paul (Wendell) 1956- *39*
Westmoreland, William C. 1914-2005 .... *63*
Westmoreland, William Childs
  See Westmoreland, William C.
Weston, Allen
  See Hogarth, Grace (Weston Allen)
  and Norton, Andre
Weston, Carol 1956- *135*
Weston, Carrie *190*
Weston, John (Harrison) 1932- *21*
Weston, Martha 1947- *119*
  Earlier sketch in SATA *53*
Westphal, Arnold Carl 1897- *57*
Westrup, Hugh *102*
Westwood, Jennifer 1940-2008 .... *10*
  Obituary *192*
Wexler, Jerome (LeRoy) 1923- *14*
Weyland, Jack 1940- *81*
Weyn, Suzanne 1955- *164*
  Earlier sketches in SATA *63, 101*
Weyr, Garret
  See Freymann-Weyr, (Rhoda) Garret
  (Michaela)
Wezyk, Joanna 1966- *82*
Whaley, Joyce Irene 1923- *61*
Whalin, W. Terry 1953- *93*
Wharf, Michael
  See Weller, George
Wharmby, Margot *63*
Wharton, Edith 1862-1937
  See CLR *136*
Wharton, Edith Newbold Jones
  See Wharton, Edith
Whatley, Bruce 1954- *177*
Wheatley, Arabelle 1921- *16*
Wheatley, Nadia 1949- *147*
Wheeler, Cindy 1955- *49*
  Brief entry *40*
Wheeler, Deborah 1947- *83*
Wheeler, Janet D. *1*
Wheeler, Jill C. 1964- *136*
  Earlier sketch in SATA *86*
Wheeler, Jody 1952- *148*
  Earlier sketch in SATA *84*
Wheeler, Lisa 1963- *200*
  Earlier sketch in SATA *162*
Wheeler, Opal 1898- *23*
Whelan, Elizabeth M(urphy) 1943- *14*
Whelan, Gloria 1923- *178*
  Earlier sketches in SATA *85, 128*
  See also CLR *90*
Whelan, Gloria Ann
  See Whelan, Gloria
Whipple, A(ddison) B(eecher) C(olvin)
  1918- *64*
Whipple, Cal
  See Whipple, A(ddison) B(eecher) C(olvin)
Whisp, Kennilworthy
  See Rowling, J. K.
Whistler, Reginald John 1905-1944 .... *30*
Whistler, Rex
  See Whistler, Reginald John

Whitaker, Zai *183*
Whitcher, Susan (Godsil) 1952- *96*
Whitcomb, Jon 1906-1988 .... *10*
  Obituary *56*
Whitcomb, Laura 1958- *171*
White, Anne Terry 1896-1980 .... *2*
White, Bessie (Felstiner) 1892(?)-1986
  Obituary *50*
White, Carolyn 1948- *130*
White, Dale
  See Place, Marian T(empleton)
White, Dori 1919- *10*
White, E. B. 1899-1985 .... *100*
  Obituary *44*
  Earlier sketches in SATA *2, 29*
  See also CLR *107*
White, Eliza Orne 1856-1947
  See YABC *2*
White, Elwyn Brooks
  See White, E. B.
White, Florence M(eiman) 1910- *14*
White, Laurence B(arton), Jr. 1935- *10*
White, Lee *176*
White, Martin 1943- *51*
White, Nancy 1942- *126*
White, Ramy Allison *67*
  Earlier sketch in SATA *1*
White, Robb 1909-1990 .... *83*
  Earlier sketch in SATA *1*
  See also CLR *3*
  See also SAAS *1*
White, Ruth C. 1942- *186*
  Autobiography Feature *186*
  Earlier sketches in SATA *39, 117, 165*
White, T(erence) H(anbury) 1906-1964 .... *12*
  See also CLR *139*
White, Tekla N. 1934- *115*
White, Timothy (Thomas Anthony)
  1952-2002 .... *60*
White, Tom 1923- *148*
White, William, Jr. 1934- *16*
Whitehead, Don(ald) F. 1908-1981 .... *4*
Whitehead, Jenny 1964- *191*
Whitehead, Kathy 1957- *176*
Whitehouse, Arch
  See Whitehouse, Arthur George Joseph
Whitehouse, Arthur George Joseph
  1895-1979 .... *14*
  Obituary *23*
Whitehouse, Elizabeth S(cott) 1893-1968 .... *35*
Whitehouse, Jeanne
  See Peterson, Jeanne Whitehouse
Whitelaw, Nancy 1933- *166*
  Earlier sketch in SATA *76*
Whitesel, Cheryl Aylward *162*
Whiting, Sue 1960- *205*
Whiting, Susan Allana
  See Whiting, Sue
Whitinger, R. D.
  See Place, Marian T(empleton)
Whitley, Mary Ann
  See Sebrey, Mary Ann
Whitley, Peggy 1938- *140*
Whitlock, Pamela 1921(?)-1982
  Obituary *31*
Whitlock, Ralph 1914-1995 .... *35*
Whitman, Alice
  See Marker, Sherry
Whitman, Sylvia (Choate) 1961- *135*
  Earlier sketch in SATA *85*
Whitman, Walt 1819-1892 .... *20*
Whitman, Walter
  See Whitman, Walt
Whitmore, Arvella 1922- *125*
Whitmore, Benette 1955- *203*
Whitney, Alex(andra) 1922- *14*
Whitney, David C(harles) 1921- *48*
  Brief entry *29*
Whitney, Kim Ablon *162*

Whitney, Phyllis A. 1903-2008 .... *30*
  Obituary *189*
  Earlier sketch in SATA *1*
  See also CLR *59*
Whitney, Phyllis Ayame
  See Whitney, Phyllis A.
Whitney, Phyllis Ayame
  See Whitney, Phyllis A.
Whitney, Sharon 1937- *63*
Whitney, Thomas P. 1917-2007 .... *25*
  Obituary *189*
Whitney, Thomas Porter
  See Whitney, Thomas P.
Whittington, Mary K(athrine) 1941- *75*
Whitworth, John 1945- *123*
Whybrow, Ian *202*
  Earlier sketch in SATA *132*
Whyte, Mal(colm Kenneth, Jr.) 1933- *62*
Whyte, Mary 1953- *148*
  Earlier sketch in SATA *94*
Whyte, Ron 1942(?)-1989
  Obituary *63*
Whytock, Cherry *177*
Wiater, Stanley 1953- *84*
Wibbelsman, Charles J(oseph) 1945- *59*
Wibberley, Leonard 1915-1983 .... *45*
  Obituary *36*
  Earlier sketch in SATA *2*
  See also CLR *3*
Wibberley, Leonard Patrick O'Connor
  See Wibberley, Leonard
Wiberg, Harald (Albin) 1908- *93*
  Brief entry *40*
Wick, Walter 1953- *148*
Wickberg, Susan
  See Rottman, S.L.
Wickens, Elaine *86*
Wicker, Ireene 1905(?)-1987
  Obituary *55*
Wickstrom, Sylvie 1960- *169*
Wickstrom, Thor 1960- *200*
Widdemer, Mabel Cleland 1902-1964 .... *5*
Widener, Terry 1950- *105*
Widerberg, Siv 1931- *10*
Wiebe, Rudy 1934- *156*
Wiebe, Rudy Henry
  See Wiebe, Rudy
Wieler, Diana (Jean) 1961- *109*
Wiener, Lori 1956- *84*
Wier, Ester (Alberti) 1910-2000 .... *3*
Wiese, Kurt 1887-1974 .... *36*
  Obituary *24*
  Earlier sketch in SATA *3*
  See also CLR *86*
Wiesel, Elie 1928- *56*
Wiesel, Eliezer
  See Wiesel, Elie
Wiesner, David 1956- *181*
  Earlier sketches in SATA *72, 117, 139*
  See also CLR *84*
Wiesner, Portia
  See Takakjian, Portia
Wiesner, William 1899-1984 .... *5*
Wiggers, Raymond 1952- *82*
Wiggin, Eric E. 1939- *167*
  Earlier sketch in SATA *88*
Wiggin, Eric Ellsworth 1939-
  See Wiggin, Eric E.
Wiggin (Riggs), Kate Douglas (Smith)
  1856-1923
  See YABC *1*
  See also CLR *52*
Wiggins, VeraLee (Chesnut) 1928-1995 .... *89*
Wight, James Alfred 1916-1995 .... *135*
  Brief entry *44*
  Earlier sketch in SATA *86*
  See also CLR *80*
Wignell, Edel 1936- *69*
Wijnberg, Ellen *85*
Wikland, Ilon 1930- *93*
  Brief entry *32*

Wikler, Madeline 1943- *114*
Wilber, Donald N(ewton) 1907-1997 .... *35*
Wilbur, C. Keith 1923- *27*
Wilbur, Frances 1921- *107*
Wilbur, Helen L. 1948- *204*
Wilbur, Richard 1921- *108*
  Earlier sketch in SATA *9*
Wilbur, Richard Purdy
  See Wilbur, Richard
Wilburn, Kathy 1948- *68*
Wilcox, Charlotte 1948- *72*
Wilcox, Leah 1975(?)- *207*
Wilcox, R(uth) Turner 1888-1970 .... *36*
Wilcox, Roger
  See Collins, Paul
Wild, Jocelyn 1941- *46*
Wild, Kate 1954- *192*
Wild, Margaret 1948- *197*
  Earlier sketch in SATA *151*
Wild, Robin (Evans) 1936- *46*
Wild, Robyn 1947- *117*
Wilde, D. Gunther
  See Hurwood, Bernhardt J.
Wilde, Oscar 1854(?)-1900 .... *24*
  See also CLR *114*
Wilde, Oscar Fingal O'Flahertie Willis
  See Wilde, Oscar
Wilder, Buck
  See Smith, Tim(othy R.)
Wilder, Laura Elizabeth Ingalls
  See Wilder, Laura Ingalls
Wilder, Laura Ingalls 1867-1957 .... *100*
  Earlier sketches in SATA *15, 29*
  See also CLR *111*
Wildsmith, Brian 1930- *124*
  Earlier sketches in SATA *16, 69*
  See also CLR *52*
  See also SAAS *5*
Wiles, Deborah *171*
Wilhelm, Doug 1952- *190*
Wilhelm, Hans 1945- *196*
  Autobiography Feature *196*
  Earlier sketches in SATA *58, 135*
  See also CLR *46*
  See also SAAS *21*
Wilkie, Katharine E(lliott) 1904-1980 .... *31*
Wilkin, Eloise 1904-1987 .... *49*
  Obituary *54*
Wilkins, Frances 1923- *14*
Wilkins, Kim *147*
Wilkins, Marilyn (Ruth) 1926- *30*
Wilkins, Marne
  See Wilkins, Marilyn (Ruth)
Wilkins, Mary Huiskamp 1926- *2*
  See also CLR *42*
Wilkins, Mary Huiskamp Calhoun
  See Wilkins, Mary Huiskamp
Wilkins, Rose *180*
Wilkinson, (Thomas) Barry 1923- *50*
  Brief entry *32*
Wilkinson, Beth 1925- *80*
Wilkinson, Brenda 1946- *91*
  Earlier sketch in SATA *14*
  See also CLR *20*
Wilkinson, (John) Burke 1913-2000 .... *4*
Wilkinson, Sylvia 1940- *56*
  Brief entry *39*
Wilkon, Jozef 1930- *133*
  Earlier sketches in SATA *31, 71*
Wilkowski, Sue *193*
Wilks, Michael Thomas 1947- *44*
Wilks, Mike
  See Wilks, Michael Thomas
Will
  See Lipkind, William
Willard, Barbara (Mary) 1909-1994 .... *74*
  Earlier sketch in SATA *17*
  See also CLR *2*
  See also SAAS *5*
Willard, Mildred Wilds 1911-1978 .... *14*

Willard, Nancy 1936- *191*
  Brief entry *30*
  Earlier sketches in SATA *37, 71, 127*
  See also CLR *5*
Willcox, Isobel 1907-1996 .... *42*
Willems, Mo *180*
  Earlier sketch in SATA *154*
  See also CLR *114*
Willett, Edward 1959- *115*
Willett, Edward C.
  See Willett, Edward
Willey, Bee *184*
Willey, Margaret 1950- *86*
Willey, Robert
  See Ley, Willy
Willhoite, Michael A. 1946- *71*
William, Kate
  See Armstrong, Jennifer
Williams, Arlene *171*
Williams, Barbara 1925- *107*
  Earlier sketch in SATA *11*
  See also CLR *48*
  See also SAAS *16*
Williams, Barbara 1937- *62*
Williams, Beryl
  See Epstein, Beryl
Williams, Brian (Peter) 1943- *54*
Williams, Carol Lynch 1959- *110*
Williams, Charles
  See Collier, James Lincoln
Williams, Clyde C. 1881-1974 .... *8*
  Obituary *27*
Williams, Coe
  See Harrison, C(hester) William
Williams, Colleen Madonna Flood 1963- .. *156*
Williams, Cynthia G. 1958- *123*
Williams, Dar 1974- *168*
Williams, Donna Reilly 1945- *83*
Williams, Dorothy
  See Williams, Marcia
Williams, Dorothy Snowden
  See Williams, Dar
Williams, Eric (Ernest) 1911-1983 .... *14*
  Obituary *38*
Williams, Ferelith Eccles
  See Eccles Williams, Ferelith
Williams, Frances B.
  See Browin, Frances Williams
Williams, Garth (Montgomery) 1912-1996 .. *66*
  Obituary *90*
  Earlier sketch in SATA *18*
  See also CLR *57*
  See also SAAS *7*
Williams, Guy R(ichard) 1920- *11*
Williams, Hawley
  See Heyliger, William
Williams, Helen 1948- *77*
Williams, J. R.
  See Williams, Jeanne
Williams, J. Walker
  See Wodehouse, P. G.
Williams, Jay 1914-1978 .... *41*
  Obituary *24*
  Earlier sketch in SATA *3*
  See also CLR *8*
Williams, Jeanne 1930- *5*
Williams, Jenny 1939- *60*
Williams, Karen Lynn 1952- *99*
  Earlier sketch in SATA *66*
Williams, Kit 1946(?)- *44*
  See also CLR *4*
Williams, Laura E. *180*
Williams, Laura Ellen
  See Williams, Laura E.
Williams, L.E.
  See Williams, Laura Ellen
Williams, Leslie 1941- *42*
Williams, Linda 1948- *59*
Williams, Louise Bonino 1904(?)-1984
  Obituary *39*

Williams, Lynn
  See Hale, Arlene
Williams, Marcia 1945- *159*
  Earlier sketches in SATA *71, 97*
Williams, Marcia Dorothy
  See Williams, Marcia
Williams, Margery
  See Bianco, Margery Williams
Williams, Mark
  See Arthur, Robert, (Jr.)
Williams, Mark London 1959- *140*
Williams, Maureen 1951- *12*
Williams, Michael
  See St. John, Wylly Folk
Williams, Patrick J.
  See Griffin, W.E.B.
Williams, Pete
  See Faulknor, Cliff(ord Vernon)
Williams, S. P.
  See Hart, Virginia
Williams, Sam *177*
  Earlier sketch in SATA *124*
Williams, Selma R(uth) 1925- *14*
Williams, Sherley Anne 1944-1999 .... *78*
  Obituary *116*
Williams, Sheron 1955- *77*
Williams, Shirley
  See Williams, Sherley Anne
Williams, Slim
  See Williams, Clyde C.
Williams, Sophy 1965- *135*
Williams, Susan
  See Beckhorn, Susan Williams
Williams, Suzanne
  See Williams, Suzanne Morgan
Williams, Suzanne 1953- *202*
  Earlier sketch in SATA *71*
Williams, Suzanne M.
  See Williams, Suzanne Morgan
Williams, Suzanne Morgan 1949- *207*
Williams, Ursula Moray
  See Moray Williams, Ursula
Williams, Vera B(aker) 1927- *102*
  Brief entry *33*
  Earlier sketch in SATA *53*
  See also CLR *9*
Williams-Andriani, Renee 1963- *98*
Williams-Ellis, (Mary) Amabel (Nassau
  Strachey) 1894-1984 .... *29*
  Obituary *41*
Williams-Garcia, Rita 1957- *160*
  Earlier sketch in SATA *98*
  See also CLR *36*
Williamson, Gwyneth 1965- *109*
Williamson, Henry (William) 1895-1977 ..... *37*
  Obituary *30*
Williamson, Joanne S(mall) 1926- *122*
  Earlier sketch in SATA *3*
Williamson, Melanie *196*
Willis, Charles
  See Clarke, Arthur C.
Willis, Connie 1945- *110*
  See also CLR *66*
Willis, Jeanne 1959- *195*
  Earlier sketches in SATA *61, 123*
Willis, Jeanne Mary
  See Willis, Jeanne
Willis, Meredith Sue 1946- *101*
Willis, Nancy Carol 1952- *139*
  Earlier sketch in SATA *93*
Willis, Paul J. 1955- *113*
Willms, Russ *95*
Willoughby, Lee Davis
  See Avallone, Michael (Angelo, Jr.)
  and Brandner, Gary (Phil)
  and Deming, Richard
  and DeAndrea, William L(ouis)
  and Laymon, Richard (Carl)
  and Streib, Dan(iel Thomas)
  and Toombs, John
  and Webb, Jean Francis (III)

Willson, Robina Beckles
  See Beckles Willson, Robina
Wilma, Dana
  See Faralla, Dana
Wilsdorf, Anne 1954- 191
Wilson, April 80
Wilson, Barbara Ker
  See Ker Wilson, Barbara
Wilson, Beth P(ierre) 8
Wilson, Budge 1927- 55
  Brief entry 51
Wilson, Carletta 1951- 81
Wilson, Carter 1941- 6
Wilson, Charles Morrow 1905-1977 30
Wilson, Christopher B. 1910(?)-1985
  Obituary 46
Wilson, Darryl B(abe) 1939- 90
Wilson, Diane Lee 172
Wilson, Dirk
  See Pohl, Frederik
Wilson, Dorothy Clarke 1904-2003 16
Wilson, Edward A(rthur) 1886-1970 38
Wilson, Ellen (Janet Cameron) (?)-1976 9
  Obituary 26
Wilson, Eric (H.) 1940- 34
  Brief entry 32
Wilson, Erica 51
Wilson, Forrest 1918- 27
Wilson, Gahan 1930- 35
  Brief entry 27
Wilson, Gina 1943- 85
  Brief entry 34
  Earlier sketch in SATA 36
Wilson, (Leslie) Granville 1912- 14
Wilson, Hazel (Hutchins) 1898-1992 3
  Obituary 73
Wilson, J(erry) M. 1964- 121
Wilson, Jacqueline 1945- 199
  Brief entry 52
  Earlier sketches in SATA 61, 102, 153
Wilson, John 1922- 22
Wilson, John 1951- 182
Wilson, John Alexander
  See Wilson, John
Wilson, Johnniece Marshall 1944- 75
Wilson, Jonathan 1950- 181
Wilson, Joyce M. 84
  Earlier sketch in SATA 21
  See also SAAS 24
Wilson, Karma 174
Wilson, Leslie 1952- 166
Wilson, Linda Miller 1936- 116
Wilson, Lionel 1924-2003 33
  Brief entry 31
  Obituary 144
Wilson, Marjorie
  See Wilson, Budge
Wilson, Martin 1973- 205
Wilson, Maurice (Charles John) 1914- 46
Wilson, Nancy Hope 1947- 138
  Earlier sketch in SATA 81
Wilson, Nathan D.
  See Wilson, N.D.
Wilson, N.D. 1978- 194
Wilson, Nick
  See Ellis, Edward S.
Wilson, Phil 1948- 181
Wilson, Ron(ald William) 1941- 38
Wilson, Sarah 1934- 142
  Earlier sketch in SATA 50
Wilson, Tom 1931- 33
  Brief entry 30
Wilson, Troy 1970- 169
Wilson, Walt(er N.) 1939- 14
Wilson-Max, Ken 1965- 170
  Earlier sketch in SATA 93
Wilton, Elizabeth 1937- 14
Wilton, Hal
  See Pepper, Frank S.
Wilwerding, Walter Joseph 1891-1966 9

Wimmer, Mike 1961- 194
  Earlier sketch in SATA 70
Winborn, Marsha (Lynn) 1947- 75
Winch, John 1944- 165
  Earlier sketch in SATA 117
Winchester, James H(ugh) 1917-1985 30
  Obituary 45
Winchester, Stanley
  See Youd, Samuel
Windawi, Thura al- 1983(?)- 165
Winders, Gertrude Hecker -1987 3
Windham, Basil
  See Wodehouse, P. G.
Windham, Kathryn T(ucker) 1918- 14
Windham, Sophie 184
Windling, Terri 1958- 151
Windrow, Martin
  See Windrow, Martin Clive
Windrow, Martin C.
  See Windrow, Martin Clive
Windrow, Martin Clive 1944- 68
Windsor, Claire
  See Hamerstrom, Frances
Windsor, Linda 1950- 124
Windsor, Patricia 1938- 78
  Earlier sketch in SATA 30
  See also SAAS 19
Wineman-Marcus, Irene 1952- 81
Winer, Yvonne 1934- 120
Winerip, Michael 175
Winfield, Arthur M.
  See Stratemeyer, Edward L.
Winfield, Edna
  See Stratemeyer, Edward L.
Winfield, Julia
  See Armstrong, Jennifer
Wing, Natasha 1960- 200
  Earlier sketch in SATA 82
Wingerter, Linda S. 1973(?)- 207
Winick, Judd 1970- 124
Winks, Robin William 1930-2003 61
Winn, Alison
  See Wharmby, Margot
Winn, Chris 1952- 42
Winn, Janet Bruce 1928- 43
Winn, Marie 1936(?)- 38
Winnick, Karen B(eth) B(inkoff) 1946- 51
Winn-Lederer, Ilene 198
Winslow, Barbara 1947- 91
Winstead, Rosie 180
Winston, Clara 1921-1983 54
  Obituary 39
Winston, Richard 1917-1979 54
Winston, Sherri 1964(?)- 201
Winter, Janet 1926- 126
Winter, Jeanette 1939- 184
  Earlier sketch in SATA 151
Winter, Jonah 1962- 179
Winter, Milo (Kendall) 1888-1956 21
Winter, Paula Cecelia 1929- 48
Winter, R. R.
  See Winterbotham, R(ussell) R(obert)
Winter, Susan 182
Winterbotham, R(ussell) R(obert)
  1904-1971 10
Winterbotham, Russ
  See Winterbotham, R(ussell) R(obert)
Winterfeld, Henry 1901-1990 55
Winters, J. C.
  See Cross, Gilbert B.
Winters, Jon
  See Cross, Gilbert B.
Winters, Katherine 1936- 153
  Earlier sketch in SATA 103
Winters, Kay
  See Winters, Katherine
Winters, Nina 1944- 62
Winters, Paul A. 1965- 106
Winterson, Jeanette 1959- 190
Winterton, Gayle
  See Adams, William Taylor

Winthrop, Elizabeth 1948- 164
  Autobiography Feature 116
  Earlier sketches in SATA 8, 76
  See also CLR 89
Winton, Ian (Kenneth) 1960- 76
Winton, Tim 1960- 98
Wintz-Litty, Julie
  See Litty, Julie
Wirt, Ann
  See Benson, Mildred
Wirt, Mildred A.
  See Benson, Mildred
Wirtenberg, Patricia Z. 1932-2007 10
Wirtenberg, Patricia Zarrella
  See Wirtenberg, Patricia Z.
Wirth, Beverly 1938- 63
Wirths, Claudine (Turner) G(ibson)
  1926-2000 104
  Earlier sketch in SATA 64
Wise, Bill 1958- 191
Wise, Lenny
  See Wise, Leonard
Wise, Leonard 1940- 167
Wise, Leonard A.
  See Wise, Leonard
Wise, Leonard Allan
  See Wise, Leonard
Wise, William 1923- 163
  Earlier sketch in SATA 4
Wise, Winifred E. 2
Wiseman, Ann (Sayre) 1926- 31
Wiseman, B(ernard) 1922-1995 4
Wiseman, David 1916- 43
  Brief entry 40
Wishinsky, Frieda 1948- 166
  Earlier sketches in SATA 70, 112
Wisler, G(ary) Clifton 1950- 103
  Brief entry 46
  Earlier sketch in SATA 58
Wismer, Donald (Richard) 1946- 59
Wisner, Bill
  See Wisner, William L.
Wisner, William L. 1914(?)-1983 42
Wisnewski, David 1953-2002
  See Wisniewski, David
Wisniewski, David 1953-2002 95
  Obituary 139
  See also CLR 51
Wister, Owen 1860-1938 62
Witham, (Phillip) Ross 1917- 37
Withers, Carl A. 1900-1970 14
Withers, Pam 1956- 182
Withrow, Sarah 1966- 199
  Earlier sketch in SATA 124
Witt, Dick 1948- 80
Witt, Shirley Hill 1934- 17
Wittanen, Etolin 1907- 55
Wittels, Harriet Joan 1938- 31
Wittig, Susan
  See Albert, Susan Wittig
Wittlinger, Ellen 1948- 189
  Autobiography Feature 128
  Earlier sketches in SATA 83, 122
Wittman, Sally (Anne Christensen) 1941- 30
Witty, Paul 1898-1976 50
  Obituary 30
Wodehouse, P. G. 1881-1975 22
Wodehouse, Pelham Grenville
  See Wodehouse, P. G.
Wodge, Dreary
  See Gorey, Edward (St. John)
Woelfle, Gretchen 1945- 145
Wohlberg, Meg 1905-1990 41
  Obituary 66
Wohlrabe, Raymond A. 1900-1977 4
Wohnoutka, Mike 195

Wojciechowska, Maia (Teresa) 1927-2002 ... 83
  Autobiography Feature 104
  Obituary 134
  Earlier sketches in SATA 1, 28
  See also CLR 1
  See also SAAS 1
Wojciechowski, Susan 126
  Earlier sketch in SATA 78
Wojnarowski, Adrian 1970- 190
Wolcott, Patty 1929- 14
Wold, Allen L. 1943- 64
Wold, Jo Anne 1938- 30
Woldin, Beth Weiner 1955- 34
Wolf, Allan 1963- 192
Wolf, Bernard 1930- 102
  Brief entry 37
Wolf, Erica (Van Varick) 1978- 156
Wolf, Gita 1956- 101
Wolf, Janet 1957- 78
Wolf, J.M.
  See Wolf, Joan M.
Wolf, Joan M. 1966- 193
Wolf, Sallie 1950- 205
  Earlier sketch in SATA 80
Wolfe, Art 1952- 76
Wolfe, Burton H. 1932- 5
Wolfe, Gene 1931- 165
  Earlier sketch in SATA 118
Wolfe, Gene Rodman
  See Wolfe, Gene
Wolfe, Gillian 199
Wolfe, Louis 1905-1985 8
  Obituary 133
Wolfe, Rinna (Evelyn) 1925- 38
Wolfenden, George
  See Beardmore, George
Wolfer, Dianne 1961- 167
  Autobiography Feature 117
  Earlier sketch in SATA 104
Wolff, Alexander (Nikolaus) 1957- 137
  Earlier sketch in SATA 63
Wolff, Ashley 1956- 203
  Earlier sketches in SATA 50, 81, 155
Wolff, Diane 1945- 27
Wolff, Ferida 1946- 164
  Earlier sketch in SATA 79
Wolff, Jennifer Ashley
  See Wolff, Ashley
Wolff, Nancy 202
Wolff, Robert Jay 1905-1977 10
Wolff, Sonia
  See Levitin, Sonia
Wolff, Virginia Euwer 1937- 137
  Earlier sketch in SATA 78
  See also CLR 62
Wolfman, Judy 1933- 138
Wolfson, Evelyn 1937- 62
Wolitzer, Hilma 1930- 31
Wolkoff, Judie (Edwards) 93
  Brief entry 37
Wolkstein, Diane 1942- 138
  Earlier sketches in SATA 7, 82
Wollheim, Donald A(llen) 1914-1990
  Obituary 69
Wolny, P.
  See Janeczko, Paul B(ryan)
Wolters, Richard A. 1920-1993 35
Wondriska, William 1931- 6
Wong, Jade Snow 1922-2006 112
  Obituary 175
Wong, Janet S. 1962- 148
  Earlier sketch in SATA 98
  See also CLR 94
Woo, Howie 1974- 207
Wood, Anne (Savage) 1937- 64
Wood, Audrey 198
  Brief entry 44
  Earlier sketches in SATA 50, 81, 139
  See also CLR 26
Wood, Catherine
  See Etchison, Birdie L(ee)

Wood, David 1944- 87
Wood, Don 1945- 50
  Brief entry 44
  See also CLR 26
Wood, Douglas 1951- 180
  Earlier sketches in SATA 81, 132
Wood, Douglas Eric
  See Wood, Douglas
Wood, Edgar A(llardyce) 1907-1998 14
Wood, Esther
  See Brady, Esther Wood
Wood, Frances Elizabeth 34
Wood, Frances M. 1951- 97
Wood, James Playsted 1905- 1
Wood, Jenny 1955- 88
Wood, John Norris 1930- 85
Wood, June Rae 1946- 120
  Earlier sketch in SATA 79
  See also CLR 82
Wood, Kerry
  See Wood, Edgar A(llardyce)
Wood, Kim Marie 134
Wood, Laura N.
  See Roper, Laura (Newbold) Wood
Wood, Linda C(arol) 1945- 59
Wood, Marcia 1956- 80
Wood, Marcia Mae
  See Wood, Marcia
Wood, Nancy
  See Wood, Nancy C.
Wood, Nancy C. 1936- 178
  Earlier sketch in SATA 6
Wood, Nuria
  See Nobisso, Josephine
Wood, Owen 1929- 64
Wood, Phyllis Anderson 1923- 33
  Brief entry 30
Wood, Richard 1949- 110
Wood, Tim(othy William Russell) 1946- 88
Wood, Wallace 1927-1981
  Obituary 33
Woodard, Carol 1929- 14
Woodburn, John Henry 1914- 11
Woodbury, David Oakes 1896-1981 62
Woodford, Peggy 1937- 25
Woodhouse, Barbara (Blackburn)
  1910-1988 63
Woodhull, Ann Love 194
Wooding, Chris 1977- 166
Wooding, Sharon
  See Wooding, Sharon L(ouise)
Wooding, Sharon L(ouise) 1943- 66
Woodman, Allen 1954- 76
Woodrich, Mary Neville 1915- 2
Woodruff, Elvira 1951- 162
  Earlier sketches in SATA 70, 106
Woodruff, Joan Leslie 1953- 104
Woodruff, Liza 1971(?)- 182
Woodruff, Marian
  See Goudge, Eileen
Woodruff, Noah 1977- 86
Woods, George A(llan) 1926-1988 30
  Obituary 57
Woods, Geraldine 1948- 111
  Brief entry 42
  Earlier sketch in SATA 56
Woods, Harold 1945- 56
  Brief entry 42
Woods, Lawrence
  See Lowndes, Robert A(ugustine) W(ard)
Woods, Margaret 1921- 2
Woods, Nat
  See Stratemeyer, Edward L.
Woods, Titania
  See Weatherly, Lee
Woodson, Jack
  See Woodson, John Waddie Jr.
Woodson, Jacqueline 1964- 189
  Earlier sketches in SATA 94, 139
  See also CLR 49

Woodson, Jacqueline Amanda
  See Woodson, Jacqueline
Woodson, John Waddie Jr. 1913- 10
Woodtor, Dee
  See Woodtor, Delores Parmer
Woodtor, Dee Parmer 1945(?)-2002
  See Woodtor, Delores Parmer
Woodtor, Delores Parmer 1945-2002 93
Wood-Trost, Lucille
  See Trost, Lucille W(ood)
Woodward, (Landon) Cleveland 1900-1986 . 10
  Obituary 48
Woodworth, Chris 1957- 168
Woodworth, Viki 1952- 127
Woody, Regina Jones 1894-1983 3
Woodyadd, Charlotte
  See Hough, Charlotte
Woog, Adam 1953- 125
  Earlier sketch in SATA 84
Wooldridge, Connie Nordhielm 1950- 143
  Earlier sketch in SATA 92
Wooldridge, Frosty 1947- 140
Wooldridge, Rhoda 1906-1988 22
Wooley, Susan Frelick 1945- 113
Woolf, Paula 1950- 104
Woolfe, Angela 1976- 169
Woolley, Catherine 1904-2005 3
  Obituary 166
Woolman, Steven 1969-2004 163
  Earlier sketch in SATA 90
Woolsey, Janette 1904-1989 3
  Obituary 131
Worcester, Donald E(mmet) 1915- 18
Word, Reagan 1944- 103
Work, Virginia 1946- 57
  Brief entry 45
Worline, Bonnie Bess 1914- 14
Wormell, Christopher 1955- 154
  Earlier sketch in SATA 103
Wormell, Mary 1959- 96
Wormser, Richard 1933- 106
  Autobiography Feature 118
  See also SAAS 26
Wormser, Sophie 1897-1979 22
Worth, Richard 1945- 59
  Brief entry 46
Worth, Valerie 1933-1994 81
  Earlier sketches in SATA 8, 70
  See also CLR 21
Worthington, Leonie 1956- 200
Wortis, Avi
  See Avi
Wortis, Edward Irving
  See Avi
Wosmek, Frances 1917- 29
Woychuk, Denis 1953- 71
Wrede, Patricia C(ollins) 1953- 146
  Earlier sketch in SATA 67
Wriggins, Sally Hovey 1922- 17
Wright, Alexandra 1979- 103
Wright, Betty Ren 1927- 109
  Brief entry 48
  Earlier sketch in SATA 63
Wright, Cliff 1963- 168
  Earlier sketch in SATA 76
Wright, Courtni
  See Wright, Courtni C(rump)
Wright, Courtni C(rump) 1950- 84
Wright, Courtni Crump
  See Wright, Courtni C(rump)
Wright, Dare 1914(?)-2001 21
  Obituary 124
Wright, David K. 1943- 112
  Earlier sketch in SATA 73
Wright, Elinor
  See Lyon, Elinor
Wright, Enid Meadowcroft (LaMonte)
  1898-1966 3
Wright, Esmond 1915-2003 10
Wright, Frances Fitzpatrick 1897-1982 10

Wright, J. B.
  See Barkan, Joanne
Wright, Judith 1915-2000 .... *14*
  Obituary *121*
Wright, Judith Arundell
  See Wright, Judith
Wright, Katrina
  See Gater, Dilys
Wright, Kenneth
  See del Rey, Lester
Wright, Kit 1944- *87*
Wright, Leslie B(ailey) 1959- *91*
Wright, Michael 1954- *198*
Wright, Nancy Means *38*
Wright, R(obert) H(amilton) 1906- *6*
Wright, Rachel *134*
Wright, Susan Kimmel 1950- *97*
Wrightfrierson
  See Wright-Frierson, Virginia (Marguerite)
Wright-Frierson, Virginia (Marguerite)
  1949- *110*
  Earlier sketch in SATA *58*
Wrightson, (Alice) Patricia 1921- *112*
  Earlier sketches in SATA *8, 66*
  See also CLR *14*
  See also SAAS *4*
Wroble, Lisa A. 1963- *134*
Wrongo, I.B.
  See Katz, Alan
Wronker, Lili
  See Wronker, Lili Cassel
Wronker, Lili Cassel 1924- *10*
Wryde, Dogear
  See Gorey, Edward (St. John)
Wu, Elizabeth
  See Wu, Liz
Wu, Liz *184*
Wu, Norbert 1961- *155*
  Earlier sketch in SATA *101*
Wulf, Linda Press *205*
Wulffson, Don 1943- *155*
  Earlier sketches in SATA *32, 88*
Wulffson, Don L.
  See Wulffson, Don
Wummer, Amy 1955- *201*
Wunderli, Stephen 1958- *79*
Wunsch, Josephine (McLean) 1914- *64*
Wuorio, Eva-Lis 1918- *34*
  Brief entry *28*
Wurts, Janny 1953- *98*
Wyatt, B. D.
  See Robinson, Spider
Wyatt, David 1968- *185*
Wyatt, Jane
  See Bradbury, Bianca (Ryley)
Wyatt, Melissa 1963- *177*
Wyeth, Betsy James 1921- *41*
Wyeth, N(ewell) C(onvers) 1882-1945 .... *17*
  See also CLR *106*
Wyler, Rose 1909-2000 .... *18*
  Obituary *121*
Wylie, Betty Jane *48*
Wylie, Laura
  See Matthews, Patricia
Wylie, Laurie
  See Matthews, Patricia
Wyllie, Stephen *86*
Wyman, Andrea *75*
Wyman, Carolyn 1956- *83*
Wymer, Norman (George) 1911- *25*
Wynard, Talbot
  See Hamilton, Charles (Harold St. John)
Wyndham, John
  See Harris, John (Wyndham Parkes Lucas)
  Beynon
Wyndham, Lee
  See Hyndman, Jane Andrews Lee
Wyndham, Robert
  See Hyndman, Robert Utley

Wynne-Jones, Tim 1948- *186*
  Autobiography Feature *136*
  Earlier sketches in SATA *67, 96, 136*
  See also CLR *58*
Wynne-Jones, Timothy
  See Wynne-Jones, Tim
Wynter, Edward (John) 1914- *14*
Wynyard, Talbot
  See Hamilton, Charles (Harold St. John)
Wyss, Johann David Von 1743-1818 .... *29*
  Brief entry *27*
  See also CLR *92*
Wyss, Thelma Hatch 1934- *202*
  Earlier sketches in SATA *10, 140*

                        X

Xavier, Father
  See Hurwood, Bernhardt J.
Xuan, YongSheng 1952- *116*
  Autobiography Feature *119*

                        Y

Yaccarino, Dan *192*
  Earlier sketch in SATA *141*
Yadin, (Rav-Aloof) Yigael 1917-1984 .... *55*
Yaffe, Alan
  See Yorinks, Arthur
Yagher, Kevin 1962- *143*
Yakovetic, (Joseph Sandy) 1952- *59*
Yakovetic, Joe
  See Yakovetic, (Joseph Sandy)
Yamada, Utako 1963- *188*
Yamaguchi, Marianne (Illenberger) 1936- *7*
Yamaka, Sara 1978- *92*
Yamanaka, Lois-Ann 1961- *166*
Yamasaki, Katie *206*
Yancey, Diane 1951- *138*
  Earlier sketch in SATA *81*
Yancey, Richard *193*
Yancey, Rick
  See Yancey, Richard
Yang, Belle 1960- *170*
Yang, James 1960- *190*
Yang, Jay 1941- *12*
Yang, Mingyi 1943- *72*
Yarbrough, Camille 1938- *79*
  See also CLR *29*
Yarbrough, Ira 1910(?)-1983
  Obituary *35*
Yaroslava
  See Mills, Yaroslava Surmach
Yarrow, Peter 1938- *195*
Yashima, Taro
  See Iwamatsu, Jun Atsushi
Yates, Elizabeth 1905-2001 .... *68*
  Obituary *128*
  Earlier sketch in SATA *4*
  See also SAAS *6*
Yates, Janelle K(aye) 1957- *77*
Yates, John 1939- *74*
Yates, Philip 1958- *149*
  Earlier sketch in SATA *92*
Yates, Raymond F(rancis) 1895-1966 .... *31*
Yaukey, Grace S(ydenstricker) 1899-1994 ... *80*
  Earlier sketch in SATA *5*
Yazzie, Johnson 1946- *205*
Ye, Ting-xing 1952- *106*
Yeahpau, Thomas M. 1975- *187*
Yeakley, Marjory Hall 1908- *21*
Yeatman, Linda 1938- *42*
Yee, Brenda Shannon *133*
Yee, Lisa 1959- *160*
Yee, Paul (R.) 1956- *143*
  Earlier sketches in SATA *67, 96*
  See also CLR *44*
Yee, Tammy *206*

Yee, Wong Herbert 1953- *172*
  Earlier sketches in SATA *78, 115*
Yeh, Chun-Chan 1914- *79*
Ye Junjian
  See Yeh, Chun-Chan
Yelchin, Eugene 1956- *196*
Yenawine, Philip 1942- *85*
Yensid, Retlaw
  See Disney, Walt(er Elias)
Yeo, Wilma (Lethem) 1918-1994 .... *81*
  Earlier sketch in SATA *24*
Yeoman, John 1934- *80*
  Earlier sketch in SATA *28*
  See also CLR *46*
Yep, Kathleen S. *203*
Yep, Laurence 1948- *176*
  Earlier sketches in SATA *7, 69, 123*
  See also CLR *132*
Yep, Laurence Michael
  See Yep, Laurence
Yepsen, Roger B(ennet), Jr. 1947- *59*
Yerian, Cameron John *21*
Yerian, Margaret A. *21*
Yerxa, Leo 1947- *181*
Yetska
  See Ironside, Jetske
Yezerski, Thomas F. 1969- *190*
Yin *194*
Ylvisaker, Anne 1965(?)- *172*
Yoder, Carolyn P. 1953- *149*
Yoder, Carolyn Patricia
  See Yoder, Carolyn P.
Yoder, Dorothy Meenen 1921- *96*
Yoder, Dot
  See Yoder, Dorothy Meenen
Yoder, Walter D. 1933- *88*
Yolen, Jane 1939- *194*
  Autobiography Feature *111*
  Earlier sketches in SATA *4, 40, 75, 112, 158*
  See also CLR *149*
  See also SAAS *1*
Yolen, Jane Hyatt
  See Yolen, Jane
Yonezu, Yusuke *196*
Yonge, Charlotte 1823-1901 .... *17*
Yonge, Charlotte Mary
  See Yonge, Charlotte
Yoo, Paula 1969(?)- *174*
Yoo, Taeeun *191*
Yoon, Salina 1972- *204*
Yorinks, Adrienne 1956- *171*
Yorinks, Arthur 1953- *200*
  Earlier sketches in SATA *33, 49, 85, 144*
  See also CLR *20*
York, Alison
  See Nicole, Christopher (Robin)
York, Andrew
  See Nicole, Christopher (Robin)
York, Carol Beach 1928- *77*
  Earlier sketch in SATA *6*
York, Rebecca
  See Buckholtz, Eileen (Garber)
  and Glick, Ruth (Burtnick)
York, Simon
  See Heinlein, Robert A.
Yoshida, Toshi 1911- *77*
Yoshikawa, Sachiko *181*
Yost, Edna 1889-1971
  Obituary *26*
Youd, C. S.
  See Youd, Samuel
Youd, Samuel 1922- *135*
  Brief entry *30*
  Earlier sketch in SATA *47*
  See also CLR *2*
  See also SAAS *6*
Young, Amy L. *185*
Young, Anne Mortimer
  See Mortimer, Anne

Young, Bob
    See Young, Robert W(illiam)
    and Young, James Robert
Young, Carol 1945- 102
Young, Catherine
    See Olds, Helen Diehl
Young, Clarence
    See Stratemeyer, Edward L.
Young, Collier
    See Bloch, Robert (Albert)
Young, Dan 1952- 126
Young, Dianne 1959- 88
Young, Dorothea Bennett 1924- 31
Young, Ed 1931- 173
    Earlier sketches in SATA 10, 74, 122
    See also CLR 27
Young, Ed Tse-chun
    See Young, Ed
Young, Edward
    See Reinfeld, Fred
Young, Elaine L.
    See Schulte, Elaine L(ouise)
Young, James
    See Graham, Ian
Young, Jan
    See Young, Janet Randall
Young, Janet 1957- 188
Young, Janet Randall 1919-1994 3
Young, Janet Ruth
    See Young, Janet
Young, Jeff C. 1948- 132
Young, John
    See Macintosh, Brownie
Young, Judy 1956- 207
    Earlier sketch in SATA 155
Young, Judy (Elaine) Dockrey 1949- 72
Young, Karen Romano 1959- 168
    Earlier sketch in SATA 116
Young, Ken 1956- 86
Young, Lois Horton 1911-1981 26
Young, Louisa 161
Young, Louise B. 1919- 64
Young, Margaret B. 1922-2009 2
Young, Margaret Buckner
    See Young, Margaret B.
Young, Mary 1940- 89
Young, Miriam 1913-1974 7
Young, Noela 1930- 89
Young, (Rodney Lee) Patrick (Jr.) 1937- 22
Young, Percy M(arshall) 1912-2004 31
    Obituary 154
Young, Richard Alan 1946- 72
Young, Robert W(illiam) 1916-1969 3
Young, Ross B. 1955- 150
Young, Ruth 1946- 67
Young, Sara
    See Pennypacker, Sara
Young, Scott A. 1918-2005 5
Young, Scott Alexander
    See Young, Scott A.
Young, Selina 1971-2006 201
Young, Vivien
    See Gater, Dilys
Younger, Barbara 1954- 108
Youngs, Betty 1934-1985 53
    Obituary 42
Younkin, Paula 1942- 77
Yount, Lisa (Ann) 1944- 124
    Earlier sketch in SATA 74
Yourgrau, Barry 179
Yuditskaya, Tatyana 1964- 75
Yumoto, Kazumi 1959- 153

Z

Zach, Cheryl (Byrd) 1947- 98
    Brief entry 51
    Earlier sketch in SATA 58
    See also SAAS 24

Zacharias, Gary L. 1946- 153
Zaffo, George J. (?)-1984 42
Zagarenski, Pamela 1969(?)- 183
Zagwyn, Deborah Turney 1953- 138
    Earlier sketch in SATA 78
Zahares, Wade 193
Zahn, Timothy 1951- 156
    Earlier sketch in SATA 91
Zaid, Barry 1938- 51
Zaidenberg, Arthur 1908(?)-1990 34
    Obituary 66
Zalben, Jane Breskin 1950- 170
    Earlier sketches in SATA 7, 79, 120
    See also CLR 84
Zallinger, Jean (Day) 1918- 115
    Earlier sketches in SATA 14, 80
Zallinger, Peter Franz 1943- 49
Zambreno, Mary Frances 1954- 140
    Earlier sketch in SATA 75
Zanderbergen, George
    See May, Julian
Zappa, Ahmet 1974- 180
Zappa, Ahmet Emuukha Rodan
    See Zappa, Ahmet
Zappler, Lisbeth 1930- 10
Zarchy, Harry 1912-1987 34
Zarin, Cynthia 1959- 192
    Earlier sketch in SATA 108
Zaring, Jane (Thomas) 1936- 40
Zarins, Joyce Audy
    See dos Santos, Joyce Audy
Zaslavsky, Claudia 1917- 36
Zaugg, Sandra L. 1938- 118
Zaugg, Sandy
    See Zaugg, Sandra L.
Zaunders, Bo 1939- 137
Zawadzki, Marek 1958- 97
Zebra, A.
    See Scoltock, Jack
Zebrowski, George 1945- 67
Zebrowski, George T.
    See Zebrowski, George
Zecca, Katherine 207
Zeck, Gerald Anthony 1939- 40
Zeck, Gerry
    See Zeck, Gerald Anthony
Zed, Dr.
    See Penrose, Gordon
Zei, Alki 1925- 24
    See also CLR 6
Zeier, Joan T(heresa) 1931- 81
Zeinert, Karen 1942-2002 137
    Earlier sketch in SATA 79
Zeises, Lara M. 1976- 184
    Earlier sketch in SATA 145
Zelazny, Roger 1937-1995 57
    Brief entry 39
Zelazny, Roger Joseph
    See Zelazny, Roger
Zeldis, Malcah 1931- 146
    Earlier sketch in SATA 86
Zelinsky, Paul O. 1953- 154
    Brief entry 33
    Earlier sketches in SATA 49, 102
    See also CLR 55
Zellan, Audrey Penn
    See Penn, Audrey
Zemach, Harve
    See Fischtrom, Harvey
Zemach, Kaethe 1958- 149
    Brief entry 39
    Earlier sketch in SATA 49
Zemach, Margot 1931-1989 70
    Obituary 59
    Earlier sketch in SATA 21
Zemach-Bersin, Kaethe
    See Zemach, Kaethe
Zeman, Ludmila 1947- 153
Zepeda, Gwendolyn 1971- 206
Zephaniah, Benjamin 1958- 189
    Earlier sketches in SATA 86, 140

Zephaniah, Benjamin Obadiah Iqbal
    See Zephaniah, Benjamin
Zephaniah, Benjamin Pbadiah Iqubal
    See Zephaniah, Benjamin
Zephaniah, Benjamin Pbadiah Iqubal
    See Zephaniah, Benjamin
Zerman, Melvyn Bernard 1930- 46
Zettner, Pat 1940- 70
Zevin, Gabrielle 176
Zhang, Christopher Zhong-Yuan 1954- 91
Zhang, Song Nan 1942- 170
    Earlier sketch in SATA 85
Ziefert, Harriet 1941- 205
    Earlier sketches in SATA 101, 154
Ziegler, Jack (Denmore) 1942- 60
Ziemienski, Dennis (Theodore) 1947- 10
Ziliox, Marc
    See Fichter, George S.
Zillah
    See Macdonald, Zillah K(atherine)
Zim, Herbert S(pencer) 1909-1994 30
    Obituary 85
    Earlier sketch in SATA 1
    See also CLR 2
    See also SAAS 2
Zim, Sonia Bleeker 1909-1971 2
    Obituary 26
Zima, Gordon 1920- 90
Zimelman, Nathan 1921- 65
    Brief entry 37
Zimmer, Dirk 1943- 147
    Earlier sketch in SATA 65
Zimmer, Tracie Vaughn 169
Zimmerman, Andrea 1950- 192
    Earlier sketch in SATA 123
Zimmerman, Andrea Griffing
    See Zimmerman, Andrea
Zimmerman, H. Werner 1951- 101
Zimmerman, Heinz Werner
    See Zimmerman, H. Werner
Zimmerman, Naoma 1914-2004 10
Zimmermann, Arnold E. 1909- 58
Zimmett, Debbie
    See Becker, Deborah Zimmett
Zimmy
    See Stratemeyer, Edward L.
Zimnik, Reiner 1930- 36
    See also CLR 3
Zindel, Bonnie 1943- 34
Zindel, Lizabeth 187
Zindel, Paul 1936-2003 102
    Obituary 142
    Earlier sketches in SATA 16, 58
    See also CLR 85
Ziner, Feenie
    See Ziner, Florence
Ziner, Florence 1921- 5
Zingara, Professor
    See Leeming, Joseph
Zinger, Yitskhok
    See Singer, Isaac Bashevis
Zion, Eugene 1913-1975 18
Zion, Gene
    See Zion, Eugene
Zoehfeld, Kathleen Weidner 1954- 193
Zohorsky, Janet R. 1958- 148
Zolkower, Edie Stoltz 171
Zolkowski, Cathy (A.) 1969- 121
Zollars, Jaime 191
Zolotow, Charlotte 1915- 138
    Earlier sketches in SATA 1, 35, 78
    See also CLR 77
Zolotow, Charlotte Gertrude Shapiro
    See Zolotow, Charlotte
Zolotow, Ellen
    See Dragonwagon, Crescent
Zonderman, Jon 1957- 92
Zonia, Dhimitri 1921- 20
Zonta, Pat 1951- 143
Zubrowski, Bernard 1939- 90
    Earlier sketch in SATA 35

Zubrowski, Bernie
    See Zubrowski, Bernard
Zucker, Miriam S.
    See Reichert, Miriam Zucker
Zuckerman, Linda 190
Zudeck, Darryl 1961- 61
Zug, Mark 204
Zupa, G. Anthony
    See Zeck, Gerald Anthony

Zupancic, Lilijana Praprotnik
    See Prap, Lila
Zurbo, Matt(hew) 1967- 98
Zurhorst, Charles (Stewart, Jr.) 1913-1989 .. 12
Zurlo, Tony 1941- 145
Zuromskis, Diane
    See Stanley, Diane
Zuromskis, Diane Stanley
    See Stanley, Diane

Zusak, Markus 1975- 149
Zwahlen, Diana 1947- 88
Zweifel, Frances W. 1931- 14
Zwerger, Lisbeth 1954- 194
    Earlier sketches in SATA *66, 130*
    See also CLR *46*
    See also SAAS *13*
Zwinger, Ann (H.) 1925- 46
Zymet, Cathy Alter 1965- 121